Robert Williams

Lexicon Cornu-Britannicum

A dictionary of the ancient Celtic language of Cornwall

Robert Williams

Lexicon Cornu-Britannicum
A dictionary of the ancient Celtic language of Cornwall

ISBN/EAN: 9783337219383

Printed in Europe, USA, Canada, Australia, Japan

Cover: Foto ©Paul-Georg Meister /pixelio.de

More available books at **www.hansebooks.com**

Lexicon Cornu-Britannicum:

A

DICTIONARY OF THE ANCIENT CELTIC LANGUAGE

OF

CORNWALL,

IN WHICH THE WORDS ARE ELUCIDATED BY

Copious Examples from the Cornish Works now remaining;

With Translations in English.

THE SYNONYMS ARE ALSO GIVEN IN THE COGNATE DIALECTS

OF

WELSH, ARMORIC, IRISH, GAELIC, AND MANX;

SHEWING AT ONE VIEW THE CONNEXION BETWEEN THEM.

BY

THE REV. ROBERT WILLIAMS, M.A.

Ch. Ch. Oxford. P.C. of Llangadwaladr, and Rhydycroesau, Denbighshire.

LLANDOVERY, RODERIC. LONDON, TRUBNER & Co.

MDCCCLXV.

Some Observations on the Rev. R. Williams' Preface to his "Lexicon Cornu-Britannicum."

The Rev. ROBERT WILLIAMS, author of the learned *Lexicon Cornu-Britannicum*, just published at Llandovery, states in his preface that PRYCE's *Cornish Vocabulary*, printed in 1770, was so full of errors that he (Mr. WILLIAMS) soon felt satisfied that the author was entirely ignorant of the Cornish language, and had no acquaintance whatever with the Welsh. Mr. WILLIAMS adds, " The discovery of the original manuscript, now in the possession of PRINCE LOUIS-LUCIEN BONAPARTE, shows the work to have been compiled in 1730, by TONKIN or GWAVAS, and disingenuously published by PRYCE as his own."

As I placed on evidence, for the first time, in a letter published in *The Cambrian Journal* for 1861, the plagiarism of PRYCE, and described the volume as the joint production of TONKIN and GWAVAS, it seems proper to propose the substitution of the following sentence for that cited above:—
" The discovery of the original manuscript, made by PRINCE LOUIS-LUCIEN BONAPARTE, has enabled him to show that the work was compiled in 1730 by TONKIN and GWAVAS, and disingenuously published by PRYCE as his own."

Such being the fact, it follows that if the work displays an ignorance of Cornish and Welsh, such ignorance is to be ascribed to the original authors, and not to PRYCE, who was only the transcriber of their manuscript. I admit that neither of these two Cornish gentlemen had any pretensions to a knowledge of Welsh, but for the Cornish of the 18th century, I am satisfied that they were the very best authorities of their time, and ought not to be despised by Welsh linguists, over whom they had certainly the immense advantage of a practical knowledge of their mother-tongue, although they may have been inferior in general linguistic attainments.

I conclude these observations with the following letter from GWAVAS to TONKIN, from which it will appear that Cornish men then considered themselves as much entitled to judge of what was really Cornish, as Welshmen now do to determine what is good Welsh.

L. L. B.

London, May 1865.

From the inedited Correspondence prefixed to the Manuscript Cornish Vocabulary of Tonkin and Gwavas.

SIR,

I have, what you mention, in ye Cornish Language, with severall other varietys, but have not time to transcribe them fair. Mr. GEORGE BOLLASE (being near me) will endeavour to have it done, in all its parts, throughout, who shall have it of me for that purpose, and what you write for to be sent you speedily will lye on his dispatch.

As to ye translation of Mr. LHUYD's preface, it is difficult to performe by any here without ye help of a learned Welsh Man, being nearer to it, than ye moderne Cornish in use here.

I remaine,
    Sir,
        Your most humble Servant,
            WM. GWAVAS.

Penzance, 25th Jan. 1732.
   To
     Thomas Tonkin, Esq.,
       at *Pol Gorran*, near
         Grandpont,
           Cornwall.

PREFACE.

THE oject of the Editor in the compilation of this work was to collect and explain all the emains of the ancient British language of Cornwall, and by comparing the words with the ynonyms in the cognate dialects to supply an acknowledged want in Celtic literature. The ources for the supply of material are very few, and may be briefly enumerated. The earned philologist Edward Llwyd, in his Archæologia Britannica, (fol. Oxford, 1709;) first ublished a Grammar of the Cornish language, as spoken in his time, being then in a state f corruption and decay. He also gave a promise of a Cornish Vocabulary, which he did ot live to accomplish. In 1769, Dr. Borlase published a Cornish-English Vocabulary, in is Antiquities of Cornwall, which is chiefly derived from Llwyd. The next work published as the Vocabulary by Dr. Pryce, in 1790, 4to. This is so full of errors that the Editor oon felt satisfied that Pryce was entirely ignorant of the Cornish Language, and had no acuaintance whatever with the Welsh. The discovery of the original manuscript, now in he possession of Prince Louis Lucien Bonaparte, shews the work to have been compiled in 730, by Tonkin or Gwavas, and disingenuously published by Pryce as his own. These rinted works relate to late Cornish, but more important documents existed, which would urnish examples of the language, when spoken in a state of purity, and which it was esirable should be properly elucidated. The earliest is a Vocabulary of Latin words with Cornish explanations, preserved in the Cottonian Library, in the British Museum, and there ntitled "Vocabularium Wallicum," (Bibl. Cot. Vespas. A. 14.) This was first noticed by lwyd in the Cornish Preface to the Archæologia, (p. 222,) and proved by him to be not Velsh but Cornish. It has been printed in the same order as it is written, and elucidated y Zeuss, in his Grammatica Celtica, (2 vols. 8vo. Leipsic, 1853.) It has since been printed lphabetically by Mr. Norris in his "Cornish Drama," with additional illustrations from the ognate dialects. This Vocabulary is of great philological importance. The manuscript was vritten in the thirteenth century, and may have been a copy of an older original, even of he ninth century, as it closely agrees with the Welsh of that age, and it contains important roofs than the Welsh then more closely approximated to the Cornish than in later ages. The next important document is a Poem, entitled Mount Calvary; a manuscript of the ifteenth century; it contains 259 stanzas of 8 lines each in heptasyllabic metre with alternate rhymes. The subject of this Poem is the Trial and Crucifixion of Christ. There are our copies of this manuscript, the oldest being in the British Museum, and the other three ppear to be copies taken from it. Two of them are in the Bodleian Library, and in these translation by John Keigwyn is written on the opposite page. This Poem was published y Mr. Davies Gilbert, in 1826. The typographical errors are so numerous, that Zeuss bserves that it does not seem to have been corrected after leaving the hands of the compositor, and eight errors in every stanza are below the average. The Editor had carefully ollated the manuscript in the British Museum, with the intention of adding a corrected opy as an appendix to this Dictionary, but the necessity no longer remains, as an excellent dition has lately been printed for the Philological Society under the care of a most able Celtic Scholar, Mr. Whitley Stokes, of Lincoln's Inn, (8vo. 1862.) The text now given is ery accurate, and the numerous errors in the translation have been rectified. The only ther work accessible was a Drama, called "The Creation of the World with Noah's Flood," vhich was written, as stated upon the manuscript containing it, on the 12th of August, 611, by William Jordan. Of this Drama the oldest manuscript is in the Bodleian Library, nd there is another in the British Museum, with a translation by John Keigwyn, in 1693. This was also printed by Mr. Davies Gilbert, in 1827, and is equally remarkable for its typoraphical errors. A new and corrected edition, by Mr. Whitley Stokes, was printed for the Philological Society in 1864. This Drama, being of much later date, shews the Cornish anguage to have become greatly corrupted, and it is full of English words. The above nentioned works comprised all the accessible material for the Dictionary when the Editor drew out the plan some thirty years ago. Llwyd had mentioned that there were three Dramas preserved in the Bodleian Library, of which he gave the first lines, and the Editor, finding that his Dictionary would be a meagre performance without obtaining a copy of them, in vain endeavoured to meet with a transcriber to supply him. Several commenced, but after a short attempt they gave up the task in despair. This circumstance has delayed the Dictionary for many years, and it would never have been completed, but for the publication of these Dramas in 1859. They turn out to be of much greater importance than could have been supposed; they are of greater amount than all the other remains of the Cornish language taken together, and are most invaluable specimens of it when spoken in great purity. The three are of the same antiquity as the Poem of Mount Calvary. The series represents Scriptural subjects from the Creation to the Death of Pilate, the first being entitled Ordinale de Origine Mundi. 2, Passio Domini Nostri Ihesu Christi. 3, Ordinale de Resurrectione Domini; and they are of the same kind as the old Mysteries, or Miracle-plays, so common in the middle ages. They were published by the University of Oxford, in 2 vols. 8vo. being most ably edited by Mr. Edwin Norris, who has added a literal translation on the opposite page. He has also added a Sketch of Cornish Grammar, and the early Cornish Vocabulary, with a valuable appendix. By the appearance of these volumes the Editor's difficulties were overcome, and he hastened to complete his cherished work. The whole of the Dramas and other documents are now incorporated in the Dictionary, and copious examples are given for the illustration of the words.

To complete the subject the Editor intends publishing in due time a copious Grammar of the Cornish, compared with the cognate dialects, and an essay on the characteristics of the six Celtic Languages, together with alphabetical tables of words, common to two or more of them. A list of words will also be given of words borrowed from Latin by the Welsh during the stay of the Romans in Britain, which will be found much more extensive than is generally imagined. The whole it is presumed will be found of service, in arriving at the history of the population of the British Isles.

ABBREVIATIONS EXPLAINED.

a.	Active.	neg.	Negative.
adj.	Adjective.	num.	Number.
adv.	Adverb.	obs.	Observe.
æol.	Æolic dialect of the Greek.	opt.	Optative.
Ang. Sax.	Anglo Saxon.	part.	Participle.
Arm.	Armoric or Breton.	pass.	Passive.
art.	Article.	pers.	Person.
Card.	Cardinal.	pl.	Plural.
C. Corn.	Cornish.	pluperf.	Pluperfect.
comp.	Compounded.	poss.	Possessive.
comp.	Comparative.	prep.	Preposition.
conj.	Conjunction.	pres.	Present.
D. Du.	Dutch.	pret.	Preterite.
dim.	Diminutive.	priv.	Privative.
Eng.	English.	pron.	Pronoun.
f.	Feminine.	qd. v.	quod vide, which see.
Gael.	Gaelic.	rel.	Relative.
Gaul.	Gaulish.	s.	Substantive.
Gr.	Greek.	Sansc.	Sanscrit.
ibid.	ibidem, in the same place.	sing.	Singular.
i. e.	Id est, that is.	subj.	Subjunctive.
id. qd.	Idem quod, the same as.	superl.	Superlative.
imp.	Imperative.	Teut.	Teutonic.
imperf.	Imperfect.	v.	Verb.
ind.	Indicative.	Voc.	Vocabulary.
inf.	Infinitive.	W.	Welsh.
intens.	Intensive.	†	Old and obsolete forms.
interj.	Interjection.	‡	Late and corrupted forms.
Ir.	Irish.	ë	Not silent.
irr.	Irregular.	C.W.	Creation of the World.
Lat.	Latin.	M.C.	Mount Calvary.
m.	Masculine.	O.M.	Origo Mundi.
med.	Medieval.	P.C.	Passio Christi.
n.	Neuter.	R.D.	Resurrectio Domini.

GERLYVYR CERNEWEC.

A

A, THE first letter of the Cornish alphabet, had the same sound as in Welsh and Armoric. When short as in the English words *bar, can, dart;* and when long as in *father, hard, warm.* In this work the long vowels are distinguished by a circumflex.

A, an auxiliary particle used in most tenses before the verb. It softens the initial of the following word, but the rule is not always followed in Cornish. *Mi a wôr*, I know. *Mi a dhanvon*, I will send. *Y a colmas y dhefrech*, they bound his arms. M.C. 76. *Mi a wort*, I will stay. M.C. 49. *Ef a wodhya*, he knew. M.C. 54. It is similarly used in Welsh, Armoric, Irish, and Gaelic In Welsh, as *pa bêth bynag a wnêl*, whatever he shall do; *mi a welais dhŷn*, I saw a man. In Armoric, *Doue a zo mâd*, God is good; *Ho choar a garann*, I love your sister. In Irish, *a deir me*, I say; *A dubhairt se*, he said; *An ait as a tiocfadh*, the place from which he shall come. Gaelic, *Nuair a thuirt e rium*, when he said to me. When thus employed the relative is often understood, as in Cornish, *Mi a wôr a wheleuch why*, I know (whom) ye seek. R.D. 781. *Yw gwir dhym a leveryth*, is it true (that which) thou tellest me? P.C. 1941. So also in Welsh, as *y dŷn a welais*, the man (whom) I saw. In Gaelic, *An duine a bhuail mi*, the man (whom) I struck.

A, conj. If. *A pe yn della ve, neffré ne vean fethys*, if it were so, I should never have been taken. M.C. 73. *A pe, ow thús dhewy ny'm delyrsens yn delma*, if it were, my people to you would not have delivered me thus. M.C. 102. *A menné gchwel gyvyans*, if he would call for forgiveness. P.C. 1816. *A nynsosé pryeryn*, if thou wert not a stranger. R.D. 261. It strictly hardens the following initial as *a callen (gallen) dôs*, if I could come. C.W. 44. Welsh *o*.

A, poss. pron. His, her, its, their. *A dhillas*, his clothes. *Yn a snow*, in his mouth. Lhwyd, 231. This is a late form of *y*, qd v.

A, poss. pron. My. †*A breihow*, my arms. ‡*Dho a bredar vi*, my brother. Lhwyd. 255. ‡*Et a phoccat*, in my pocket. 253. A late form of *ow*, qd. v.

A, prep. From, out of, of, by, with, to, for, *on*. *A pûp squythens y sawyé*, from all weariness cure him. P.C.

A

477. *Gyllys a lema*, gone from hence. C.W. 140 *A dhorn Dew y feela gwrŷs*, by the hand of God that thou wert made. C.W. 24 *Wy a bŷs a lenn golon*, ye shall pray with faithful heart. M.C. 1. *Mear a beyn*, much of pain. 54. M.C. *Curyn a spern*, crown of thorns. R.D. 2554. *Re hyrchys dhywhy a dhôs*, he hath commanded you to come. P.C. 1648. *Ysedheuch a termyn ver*, sit ye for a short time. R.D. 1312. *A hŷs*, at length. O.M 2759. *A barth*, on the side. Welsh *â*, with ; *o, of*, from. Armoric *a, of*, as *Eunn aval leun a zour*, (Welsh, *aval llawn o dhwr*,) an apple full of water. Irish, *a*, in, out of, from. Gaelic, *a*, in, to, out of. Latin, *a*, from.

A, the sign of the present participle, which is formed by placing it before the infinitive mood, as *cusga*, to sleep, *a cusga*, sleeping : *môs*, to go, *a môs*, going. It also changes the initials, when sonants into surds, thus,— *Ma'n dhavas a prrea (brivia,)* the sheep bleats. Lhwyd, 230. *A* is a late form, *ow* being always used in the Ordinalia. In Irish and Gaelic, *a* is used, as *a dusgadh*, awakening. In Welsh *yn*, as *yn cysgu*, sleeping ; *yn canu*, singing. In Armoric, *ô*, as *ô cana*, singing. Compare also the English forms, *I was a walking*. *A hunting Chloe went. They go a begging to a bankrupt's door.*

A, a particle, used before adjectives to form them into adverbs, when the initial assumes the soft sound, as *desympys*, immediate, *a dhesympys*, immediately. *Yn is* similarly used, as *lowen*, joyful, *yn lowen*, joyfully. In Welsh *yn* only is thus used, as *llawen, yn llawen*; *disymmwth, yn dhinymmwth.* In Irish *go*, as *maith*, good ; *go maith*, well. In Gaelic *gu*, as *maith, gu maith.* In Manx, *dy*, as *mie*, good ; *dy mie*, well. Compare also the English words, *along, abroad, anew*.

A, adv. Used as the sign of the vocative case, as *A venen*, O woman. *A dâs*, O father. *A gowethé*, O companions. P.C. 1883. It softens the following initial, and the same rule is followed in the other Celtic languages, as Welsh, *O dhŷn*, O man. *O dâd*, O father. Armoric *Ha, ai.* Irish, *A dhuine*, O man. Gaelic, *A ghrian*, O sun. Manx, *Y*, or *O voddee*, O dog.

A, interrogative, used in asking a question. *A na wylta*, dost thou not see ? M.C. 120. *A ny wodhas*, knowest thou not ? M.C 144. *A glewsynych why cowethé*, did you hear comrades ? O.M. 2727. So also in Welsh, *A wydhost ti*, dost thou know ? *A glywsoch chwi*, did ye hear ? Armoric, *ha*; *Ha choui a ielô*, will ye go ? Irish, *A bhfuil se ann*, is he there ? Gaelic, *A bheil Dia ann*, is there a God ?

A, adverb. Part. forming an absolute sentence. *A Grist ow cothaff mernans, anken y a wodhevys*, Christ suffering death, they endured trouble. M.C. 211. So also in Welsh, *A'r Cymry yn cysgu, rhuthrodh y gelyn am eu penau*, the Cymry being asleep, the enemy fell upon them.

A, conj. And. More commonly written *Ha*, which see.

A, v. n. He will go. 3rd pers. s. fut. of irr. v. *môs*. *Mi â genes*, I will go with thee. P.C. 461. *Nyns â dên vyth dhe'n tŷr sans*, not any man shall go to the holy land. O.M. 1878. So also in Welsh, *Nid â dyn vyth i'r tir sanctaidh*. *Ev a â gyda thydi*, he will go with thee.

ABAL, adj. Full. *Crist, arluth merci abal*, Christ, Lord of mercy full. *Pryce*.

ABAN, adv. Above, up, upright. Compounded of *a*, on, and *ban*, high. As the *a* softens the initial, *avan* is more correct. *Map Dew an nêf aban*, Son of God of heaven above. P.C. 3080. (Welsh, *i cyny*.) *Yn ban* is another form.

ABAN, adv. Since, insomuch, when. *Aban na vynta crety*, since thou wilt not believe. O M. 241. *Bythqueth aban nêf genys*, ever since I was born. O.M. 1731. *Aban yw e yn della*, since it is so. R.D. 1874. This is compounded of *a*, from, and *ban*, a mutation of *pan*, when. Welsh, *o ban*, *er pan*, since. Armoric, *aba*.

ABARH, adv. On the side, or part. This is a late form of *abarth*, as spoken in Llwyd's time. ‡ *Gwras cona abarh an ni*, do sup with us. *Archæologia Brit.* 252. Though the more correct form *abarth* only occurs in all the Dramas, in the earliest document of the Language, the Cornish Vocabulary, *abarh* is found, as *Eviter abarh mam*, an uncle on the side of the mother. *Modereb abarh tat*, an aunt on the side of the father.

ABARTH, adv. On the part, or side; in the name of. *Abarth dichow ythesé*, on the right side there was. M.C. 198. *Abarth an lâs veneges*, in the name of the blessed Father. O.M. 1792. *Mars yw abarth Dew an nêf*, if he be on the part of the God of heaven. R.D. 2103. Compounded of *a*, on, and *barth*, a mut. of *parth*, part or side. Welsh, *o barth*. Armoric, *a barz, e-barz*.

ABAT, s. m. An abbot. Cornish Vocabulary, *Abbas*. Welsh, *abud*. Armoric, *abad*. From the Latin, *abbate*. Irish, *ab*. Gaelic, *ab*.

ABELL, adv. Afar off. *Pedyr a holyas abell*, Peter followed afar off. M.C. 77. *Prest abell dheworth an gwir*, very far off from the truth. M.C. 203. *Y fy an deves abell*, the sheep will flee far. P.C. 894. Compounded of *a*, from, and *bell*, a mutation of *pell*. Welsh, *o bell*.

ABEM, s. m. A kiss. *Pryce's Vocabulary*.

ABER, s. m. A confluence of waters; the junction of rivers; the fall of a less river into a greater, or into the sea. In the Cornish Vocabulary, it is translated "Gurges," a gulf or whirlpool, and in Welsh besides its primitive meaning, it signifies a port or harbour. Welsh *aber*, in old Welsh *aper*, and more correctly *atber*. being derived from *at*, to, and *beru*, to follow. Armoric, *aber*. The form more peculiar to the Erse dialects is *inbhear*. Scot. *inver*. Aber enters into the composition of numerous names of places, originally inhabited by the Cymry, as *Aberconwy, Abergele, Aberystwyth, &c.*, in Wales; *Aberdeen, Aberdour, Aberfeldy, Aberbrothic, &c.*, in Scotland. Note also *Hâvre*, in France.

ABER, s. m. A servant, an assistant. *My bel aber, dûs dhymmo ketoth an gêr, râg colenwel vôdh ow brŷs*, my fair servant, come to me as soon as the word to fulfil the wish of my mind. O.M. 2271.

ABER, prep. In, within. An abbreviated form of *aberth*. *Dh'y worré aber an bêdh*, to place him within the grave. R.D. 2108.

ABERTH, prep. In, within, on, upon. *Rag y vôs war bronteryon mester brâs aberth an wlâs*, because he was a great master over the priests within the kingdom. M.C. 89. *Pan o dampnys aberth an crows may ferwé*, when he was condemned on the cross that he should die. M.C. 151. *Crês Dew aberth an chymma*, the peace of God within this house. P.C. 667, 705. *Aberth yn bêdh*, within the tomb. R.D. 311, 514. *Aberth an pow*, in the land. R.D. 609.

ABERVEDH, adv. In, within, on, upon. *Dûn abervedh desympys*, let us come in immediately. O.M. 1062. *Dreuch an profus abervedh*, bring the prophet in. P.C. 1465. *Abervedh yn crows cregy*, on the cross to hang. M.C. 146. *Whêth mŷr arté abervedh*, yet look again within. O.M. 789. Written also *aperfeth*. It is compounded of *a*, in, and *bervedh*, a mutation of Welsh *pervedh*, the centre, or inward part.

ABESTELY, s. m. Apostles. The plural of *abostol*. *Pan esé yn mŷsc y abestely*, when he was in the midst of his apostles. M.C. 26. *Du a sonas an bara dhe rag y abestely*, God blessed the bread in the presence of his apostles. M.C. 44. Another plural is *abesteleth*, as *Lemmyn, a Abesteleth, lavarav dhruch newodhow*, now, O Apostles, I speak to ye new. R.D. 893. *Ty a alsé sûr crygy dhe'n Abesteleth*, thou mightest surely believe the apostles. R.D. 1469.

ABLE, adv. Whence. Compounded of *a*, from, *ba*, a mutation of *pa*, what, and *le*, a place. *Orth Crist ef a wovynnys, te dhen, ablé ota gy*, of Christ be asked, thou man, whence art thou ? M.C. 144. Welsh, *o ble*, i. e. *o ba le*.

ABOSTOL, s. m. An apostle. Plural, *abosteleth, abestely*, qd. v. This word is borrowed from the Latin *apostolus*, and is adopted by all the Celtic Languages. Welsh, *apostol*, plural, *apostolion* and *ebestyl*. Armoric, *apostol*, plural, *abostoled, ebestel*. Irish, *absdal*. Gaelic, *absdol*. Manx, *ostyl*.

ABRANS, s. m. Eyebrow. Cornish Vocabulary *supercilium*. Welsh, *amrant*, eyelid, eyelash. Armoric, *abrant*. Irish, *abhradh, abhraid*. Gaelic, *abhradh*. Manx. *firroogh*. Sansc. *bhrûs*. Greek, ὀφρύς. Latin, *frons*.

ACH, s. f. Offspring, progeny. Cornish Vocabulary, *soboles*. Stock, or kindred, *Llwyd*. 155. Plural, *achow*, (v *aho*.) Welsh, *ach*.

ACHESON, s. m. Accusation, fault, guilt. *Me ny wour bonas kefys yn dên-ma bŷth acheson*, I know not that there was found in this man any guilt. M.C. 141. *Pilat a vynnas screfé a veunas Crist acheson*, Pilate would write of the life of Christ an accusation. M.C. 187. *Na allons caffus acheson*, let them not be able to find cause. O.M. 1835. This is probably a plural form of a singular *achos*. Welsh, *achos*, plural *achosion*. Irish, *cas, cos, cuis*. Gaelic, *cas, cuis*. Latin, *causa, casus*.

AD, comp. pron. Of. or concerning thee ; of thy. Compounded of *a*, and the characteristic of the 2nd pers. pronoun. The *a* is sometimes the aux. particle ; and sometimes the preposition. *My a'd peys*, I pray thee. O.M. 375. *Ha me a'd wra Arluth brâs*, and I will make of thee a great lord. M.C. 16. *Preder a'd enef*, think of thy soul. O.M. 479. *Yn amendys a'd pehosow*, in atonement of thy sins. O.M. 2259. *Dên fûr a'd cuvullyow*, a wise man of thy counsels. O.M. 2611. *A'th* is similarly used in Cornish. So also in Welsh, *mi a'th wnâv*, I will make thee. *Mi a'th welais*, I saw thee.

ADAL, adv. Although. *Pryce*.

ADEN, s. f. The leaf of a book. Cornish Vocabulary, *folium*. If not a wrong reading of *delen* in the MS. it may be used metaphorically from the Welsh, *aden*, a wing.

ADLA, s. m. A knave, an outlaw; from which latter word it is formed. *A dhew adla*, O two knaves. O.M. 1409. *Teweuch râk méth dew adla*, be silent for shame, two knaves. R.D. 1405. *Me a geim scon lovan dha worth conna-brêch an adla*, I will forthwith bind a good rope around the wrist of the knave. P.C. 2762.

ADOF, s m. Recollection. *I'n oys me yw yn urma, tri cans, tri ugans, ha whôth pymp mwy, pan és dhym adof, yn gêdh hydhew*, in age I am in this hour, three hundred, three score, and yet five more, when I call it to mind, on this very day. C.W. 152. *Pan és dhym adof*, lit. when there is to me recollection. *Adof* is compounded of *ad* re, and *cof* memory, and ought correctly to be written *adgof*, as in Welsh, *adgov*.

ADOR, prep. From, out of. *Pryce*.

ADOTH, s. m. A vow. *Gans brás adoth êth yn dhe chy*, with a great vow went into the house. *Pryce*.

ADRE, adv. Homewards. *Lhwyd*, 248. See *dre*. Welsh, *adrev, adre*. Armoric, *adrè*.

ADRES, adv. Across, abroad. *Adres pow sûr palmoryon y a fŷdh mûr gouyggyon, hag a lever dhe tûs gow*, about the country palmers surely are great story tellers, and tell people lies. R.D. 1477. Compounded of *a* on; and *dres*, a mutation of *tres*, across. Welsh, *ar draws*.

ADRIFF, adv. Purposely, on purpose, to the end that. *Ny gowsyn yn tewolgow adryff tûs y'm cavas*, I spake not in the dark, on purpose that men might find me. M.C. 79.

ADRO, adv. about, around. *Laye es yn pow adró*, the law is in the country about. M.C. 121. *My a's gor adró dhodho*, I will put it round it. O.M. 2101, 2500. *Yn crŷs an drê, adró dhe'n templa*, in the middle of the town, about the temple. O.M. *Adró dhum bryangen*, around my throat. P.C. 1527. *Dhyneortheuch mennaf mones adró yn pow*, from you I will go about in the country. R.D. 1135. *Adró* is sometimes divided, and *dhe. dre* or *der* inserted between, as *ow doon an pren a dhe dró*, carrying the tree about. O.M. 2820. *Hag a'th whyp war an wolok, may whylly gurychon ha môk dhe dhewlagas a dre dró*, and whip thee on thy face, that thou mayest see sparks and smoke round about thy eyes. P.C. 2102. *Golsowch a der drû orthaf ve, myns es omma*, hearken round about unto me, all that are here. C.W. 104. *Gwins adró*, a whirlwind. In later Cornish occur the phrases ‡ *an heves adro y gein*, the shirt on his back : ‡ *An lydrow adro'z garro*, the stockings on your legs : ‡ *An esgisow adro'z treis*, the shoes on your feet : ‡ *An manac adro'z dorn*, the glove on your hand. *Lhwyd*, 250. Compounded of *a* on, and *dro* a mutation of *tro*. Welsh, *ar dro*. Armoric, *tro*.

ADRUS, adv. Across. *Tresters dredho ty a pyn adrus, rag na vo deyees*, beams through it thou shalt nail, that it may not be opened. O.M. 964. Compounded of *a* on, and *drus*, a mutation of *trus*, across. It is the same as *adres*.

ADHAN, comp. prep. From under. *Lhwyd*, 249.

ADHELHAR, comp. prep. After, behind. This is a corrupt form of the Armoric *a dilerch*, and occurs only in late Cornish, as ‡ *adhelhar dhyn remenat*, behind the rest. *Lhwyd*, 123, 249.

ADHEWORTH, comp. prep. From by, from. *Lhwyd*, 249. Welsh, *odhiwrth*. Armoric. *diwar*. Irish, *ua*. Gaelic, *ua*. Manx, *veih*.

ADHORT, comp. prep. From by, from. ‡*Adhort an drê*, from the town. *Lhwyd*, 249. This is only a more recent form of *adheworth*.

ADHYRAGOF, pron. prep. Before me. *My re welas ym hunrus adhyragof el dyblans*. I have seen in my dream before me a bright angel. O.M. 1955. Compounded of *a*, and *dyragof*, qd. v.

ADHYRAGON, pron. prep. Before us. *A lés ol y wolyow adhyragon pan guylsyn*, all his wounds disclosed when we saw before us. R.D. 1332. *An arluth adhyragon torth vara ef a torras*, the Lord before us a loaf of bread he broke. R.D. 1490. Compounded of *a*, and *dyragon*, qd. v.

ADHYRAGOS, pron. prep. Before thee. *Me a's doro pûr anwhek adhyragos*, I will bring them very roughly before thee. P.C. 2333. Compounded of *a*, and *dyragos*, qd. v.

ADHYRAGOUCH, pron. prep. Before ye. *Adhyragouch me a pŷs*, before you I pray. P.C. 1414. *Ysedheuch a termyn ver, adhyrageuch me a ter torth a vara*, sit ye for a short time, before you will break a loaf of bread. R.D. 1313. Compounded of *a*, and *dyragouch*, qd. v.

ADZHAF, subs. I am. Written also *adzhav*, by *Lhwyd*. This is the most recent and corrupt form of *ythof*, or *ossof*, 1st pers. sing. pres. tense, of the verb substantive *bôs*. Welsh, *ydwyv*.

ADZHAN, v. irr. I know, perceive, recognize, or am acquainted with. ‡*My ty adzhan*, I know thee. This and *azwen*, are late corruptions of *anwon*, qd. v.

ADZHYI, adv. Within. *Lhwyd*, 249. A late corruption of *yn chy*, in the house.

AERAN, s. m. Plums, prunes. This is a plural aggregate. Welsh, *aeron, eirin*. Armoric, *irin*. Irish, †*airune*.

AF, v. subs. I am. 1st pers. pres. of *bôs*. Welsh, *wyv*. More commonly written *óf*, qd. v.

AF, v. n. I shall go. 1 pers. f. s. fut. of irr. v. *môs*. *Neffré dhe drê nyns âf*, ever to the town I will not go. R.D. 811. *Ple tôf na ple yth âf, ny won*, where I shall come, or where I shall go, I know not. R.D. 1665. *Dhe'n kêth plâs-na dhyuch yth âf*, to that same place to you I will go. R.D. 2400. Welsh, *âv*.

AFFO, v. a. He may pardon. A mutation of *gaffo*, 3 pers. s. subj. of *gafé*, qd. v. *Mersy war Dew agan tûs may uffo an pechasow*, mercy of God our Father that he may pardon our sins. O.M. 1666.

AFLYDHYS, adj. Unfortunate, miserable, wretched. *Del leveryth a vŷdh gwrys dhe'n plosek gwás aflydhys*, as thou sayest, it shall be done to the foul wretched fellow. P.C. 451. Welsh, *avlwydh*, misfortune, whence *avlwydhog*, unfortunate.

AFLYDHYGYON, adj. Wretches. *Powesouch aflydhygyon rág marow yw an voron*, rest ye, wretches, for dead is the maid. O.M. 2745. This is a corruption of *aflydhyayon*, the plural of *aflydhys*.

AG, conj. And. More frequently written *hag*, qd. v.

AGA, pron. poss. Their. *Nyns yw aga Dew pleysys genes gy*, their God is not pleased with thee. O.M. 1562. *Dhe wethyl aga mynnas yn della ef a vynné*, to do their purpose, so he would have it. M.C. 70. It aspirates the following initial. *Gansé y an hombronkyas, yn prŷs hanter nôs, bŷs yn aga fryns Annas*, with them they him led, at the time of midnight, even to their prince Annas. M.C. 76. *Avel olow aga threys*, like the prints of their feet. O.M. 760. *Aga hynwyn*, their names. O.M. 35. *Aga hán*, their song. O.M. 310. *Aga sona ny a wra*, bless them we will. O.M. 143. *May hyllyf aga hedhes*, that I may reach them. O.M. 202. Welsh, *eu*. Gaelic, *aca*.

AGAN, pron. poss. Our. *Gwyn agan bŷs*, happy our lot. O.M. 411. (W. *gwyn ein byd*.) *Lemyn ef yw agan gwâs*, now he is our fellow. O.M. 910. *Agan gorhyl a wartha yans glaw ef a vŷdh cudhys* our ark, from above, with rain it will be covered. O.M. 1063. *An re-ma yw oberys del vynsyn agan honan*, these are wrought as we ourselves would wish. O.M. 16. *Gans y gŷg agan perna gwyn agan bŷs*, with his flesh to redeem us, happy our lot. M.C. 4. *Hen o dhodho calys feyn, agan péch ny ow prené*, this was to him grevious pain, atoning for our sin. M.C. 196. *Lemyn agan sona gwra*, now do bless us. O.M. 1721. *An kéth máp ol agan grúk*, the same son (who) made us. R.D. 1975. Welsh, *ein, (eidho-ni.)* Gaelic, *again*. Manx, *ain*. Compounded of *aig*, with, and *sinn*, us.

AGARY, s. m. An enemy. *Dhe Cesar êv agary*, to Cæsar is an enemy. *Pryce's Vocabulary*. Compounded of *a*, neg, and *cary*, to love.

AGAS, pron. poss. Your. Written indiscriminately also *ages, agis, agos, agys*. *Mésk ow pobel ny vynnaf na fella agos godhuf*, among my people I will not any longer endure you. O.M. 1595. *An tás an néf a danvon dhcuch agos whans*, the Father of Heaven will send you your desire. O.M. 1806. *Gwir yw agas cows*, true is your speech. P.C. 1345. *Olouch rag agis flechys ha ragouch agos honon*, weep ye for your children and yourselves. M.C. 169. *My agas pŷs*, I pray you. O.M. 2346. Welsh, *eich*. Armoric, *och, hô*. Manx, *eu*.

AGE, v. a. To leave. A mutation of *gagé*, a corrupt form of *gasé*, qd. v. *Anodho dycheth vye y wokyneth na agé ha'y muscochneth*, of him it were a pity his folly not to leave, and his madness. P.C. 1989.

AGENSOW, adv. A while since, lately. *A wylsta ken yn torma ys del egé agensow*, dost thou see more now than what there was just now. O.M. 796. *Agensow my a'n gwelas*, lately I saw him. R.D. 911. Written also *agynsow*.

AGERY, v. a. To open. Part. *agerys;* preterite *agores*, qd. v. More generally written *egery*, qd. v. Welsh, *agori, egori*. Armoric, *egori*.

AGES, conj. Than. *Me a'n dreha arté kyns pen trydydh teké ages kyns y van*, I will build it again, before the end of three days, fairer than it stood before. P.C. 347. *Gwel yw un dén dhe verwel ages ol an bobyl lél dhe vôs kyllys*, better it is that one man die than all the faithful people to be lost. P.C. 447. *Ythesé gynef moy ages mŷl vŷl enef;* there are with me more than a million souls. R.D. 141. Written also *agis*. *Gweth agis cronek*, worse than a toad. M.C. 47. *Moy agis gavel tredden*, more than the hold of three men. M.C. 237. *Ys* is another mode of expressing *than*, of which *agis* is an amplified form.

AGESOS, comp. pron. Than thou. *Arluth, kepar del wrusys púp tra, nag ûs ken Dew agesos*, Lord, like as thou hast made every thing, there is not another God than thou. R.D. 2477. Compounded of *ages* and *ti*.

AGESOUCH, comp. pron. Than ye. *A pe vódh Dew yn della, ken agesouch venytha ny zensen*, if the will of God were so, otherwise than you ever we do not consider. O.M. 2357. *Yn certan gonesugy ken agesouch why ny's ty, rág sotel ouch yn púp creft*, certainly, workmen, others than ye shall not cover it, for subtle ye are in every craft: O.M. 2190. Compounded of *ages*, and *chwi*.

AGESSO, comp. pron. Than he. *Ken Arluth agesso ef ny'n gordhyaf bŷs venary*, other Lord than him I will not worship for ever. O.M. 1789. Compounded of *ages* and *o*.

AGOLAN, s. f. A whetstone, a hone. *Llwyd*, 16. Welsh, *agalen, calen*, and *hogalen*, from *hogi* to whet. Armoric, *igolen*.

AGORES, v. a. He opened: *An scryptor dhyn agores púr wŷr a dhalleth, Moyses ha lyes profus aral*, the scripture he opened to us truly from the beginning, Moses and many other prophets. R.D. 1483. This is the preterito of *agery*, qd. v. Welsh, *agores, agorodh*.

AGOS, adj. Near. *En agos*, near, *Llwyd*, 248. More frequently written *ogas*, qd. v. Welsh, *agos*. Armoric, *egos*. Irish, *agus*, † *acus* + *ocus, fogus*. Gaelic, *fogus*. Manx, *aggys, faggys*.

AGY, adv. Within. *Agy dhe'n yet gor dhe ben*, within the gate put thy head. O.M. 743. *Aves hag agy yn ta gans pék bedhens stanchurys*, without and within, well with pitch let it be staunched. O.M. 953. *Y tús ûs trygyn agy dheth wlâs*, his people which are dwelling within thy country. O.M. 1483. *My a fystyn agy*, I will hasten within. O.M. 2319. *Agy dhe eviché an geydh*, within the evening of the day. R.D. 275. Compounded of *a* in, and *chy* a house. Welsh, *yn ty*. Armoric, *c-ti*.

AGYNSOW, adv. A while since, lately. *Jhesu dasserchys a'n bédh, me a'n gwelas agynsow*, Jesus is risen from the grave, I saw him lately. R.D. 896. Written also *agensow*.

AH, interj. Ah, alas. Welsh, *A!*

AHANAF, pron. prep. From me, on me. *Ahanaf kymer mercy*, on me have mercy. P.C. 306. *Yn gylwys máp Dew yn próf, ahanaf may pertho côf pan deffé dh'y wlascor éf*, I called him the Son of God, in proof that he would keep remembrance of me when he should come to his kingdom. R.D. 272. *Arluth pan dyffys dhet pow predery ahanaff gwra*, Lord, when thou comest to thy country, do think of me. M.C. 193. Welsh, *ohonov*. Armoric, *ahanoff*. Compounded of *ahan* and *mi*.

AHANAN, pron. prep. From us ; of us. *Ty re'n ladhes, hag ef ahanan mar gér*, thou hast killed him, and he so beloved of us. O.M. 612. *My a's dyllo ahanan, ny dhue arté my a greys*, I will send it from us, it will not come again I believe. O.M. 1101. *Euch alemma ahanan*, go hence from us. P.C. 151. It is also used adverbially, like Arm. *ahanen*, to signify *hence* only. *Awos Dew dún ahanan dh'y gerhas dhe dré*, for God's sake let us come away to bring it to the town. O.M. 2564. *Sevyn yn ban, dún ahanan scon alemma*, let us stand up, and go away soon from hence. P.C. 1029. Compounded of *ahan* and *ni*. Welsh, *ohonom, ohonam.* Armoric, *achanomp.*

AHANAS, pron. prep. From thee, of thee. *Marth ahanas a'n geses*, he wonders at thee. O.M. 1484. *Yma marth dhym ahanas*, there is to me wonder at thee. P.C. 2415. *Ahanas marth yn gené*, I have wonder of thee. R.D. 2505. Written also *ahancs; Dhyso ef a veyth besy, hag ahanes a dheffo*, to thee it shall be indeed, and that which shall come out of thee. O.M. 406. Compounded of *ahan* and *ti*. Welsh, *ohonot*. Armoric, *achanol*.

AHANE, pron. prep. From me, of me. Used for *ahanaf*, metri causâ. *Arluth Cryst me ath pyssé a prydcry ahané pan vysé yn dhe wlascor*, Lord Christ, I would pray thee to think of me, when thou shalt be in thy kingdom. P.C. 2907.

AHANOUCH, pron. prep. From ye, of ye. *Onan ahanouch haneth rum gwerthas dhom yskerens*, one of you this night has sold me to my enemies. P.C. 736. *Ahanouch neb yn mochya*, he who is greatest of you. P.C. 792. *Kyn leverry gwyrf dén fyth ahanouch ny vyn cregy*, though I speak truly, any man of you will not believe. P.C. 1482. *Yma dhymmo gorgys brás ahanouch yn pûr deffry*, there is to me a great distrust of you in pure earnest. R.D. 1500. Compounded of *ahan* and *chwi*. Welsh, *ohonoch,* †*ohonawch.* Armoric, *achanoch.*

AHAS, adj. Hateful, detestable, dreadful. *Oté cowes púr ahas*, see a shower very dreadful. O.M. 1081. *A Pedar ty a'n nahas rák bés y peyn mar ahas*, O Peter thou deniedst him, because his pain was so dreadful. R.D. 1352. *An laddron an dyalas dre lyes torment ahas*, the thieves mocked him, by many hateful torments. R.D. 1427. *Ma'n geffo peyn mar ahas*, that he may have such dreadful pain. R.D. 2049. Compounded of *a* intens. and *câs*, hatred. Welsh, *achas*.

AHO, s. m. Pedigrees. *Pryce.* More correctly *ahow*, i.e. *achow*, plnr. of *ach*.

AHOZON, s. m. Occasion, opportunity. *Pryce.* Plural *ahozonow*, from the English *occasion.*

AHUCH, adv. Above. *My a set ahuch an gwrydh yn creys an ebren avan*, I place them over the trees in the midst of the sky above. O.M. 37. Compounded of *a* on, and *uch* high.

AHUEL, s. m. A key. A late form of *alwedh*. qd. v.

AI, comp. pron. *Mi ai didhiwys dhodho*, I promised it to him. Lluyd, 242. (Welsh, *mi ai adhewais idho.*) *Ev ai dýg dhym*, he brought it to me. Lluyd, ibid. *Mi ai gwerha*, I will sell it. Lluyd, 246. Though agreeing with the Welsh, this form is only found in late Cornish. The more classical being *a'n* and *a's*.

AIDHLEN, s. f. A fir tree. Written in the Cornish Vocabulary, *aidlen*, abies. This word is doubtful in reading, and of uncertain derivation. The Welsh is *fawydhen*, of which it is possibly a corruption.

AIL, s. m. An angel. This is the form in the Cornish Vocabulary, *angelus.* In later writings *él*, which see.

AIROS, s. m. The poop or stern of a ship. Cornish Vocabulary, *puppis.* Armoric, *aros.* Irish, †*eross.*

ALEMMA, adv. Hence, from this place. *Yn més alemma ty á*, out of this place thou shalt go. O.M. 83. *Fystyn alemma duwhans*, hasten thou hence quickly. O.M. 169. *Dún alemma*, let us come hence. O.M. 446. *My a vyn môs alemma*, I will go hence. 1003. *Alemma bys gorfen býs*, henceforth to the end of the world. P.C. 1704. Compounded of *a* from, *le* a place, *ma* here.

ALENA, adv. Thence, from that place. *Ha ny ow tôs alena*, and we coming from thence. O.M. 714. *Kyns ys dones alena*, before coming from thence. O.M. 791. *Ty a wra gorré an tús alena*, thou shalt bring the people thence. O.M. 1428. Compounded of *a* from, *le* place, *na* there.

ALES, adv. Abroad, *An dour a uger alés*, the water will open widely. O.M. 1666. Compounded of *a* on, and *lés* breadth. Welsh, *ar lê'd*.

ALLA, v. n. He will be able. A mutation of *galla*, 3 pers. s. fut. of *gally*. qd. v. *My a wra y ascusié mar ver del alla dén výth*, I will excuse him as soon as any man can. P.C. 2212. *Rak mar cláf yw ow dulé, my alla handle toul výth*, for my hands are so sore, I cannot handle any tool. P.C. 2678. *Mara keller y vythé a chy, na alla yntré dhe'n darasow*, if he can be kept from the house, that he may not enter the doors. P.C. 3059.

ALLAF, v. n. I shall be able. A mutation of *gallaf*, 1 pers. s. fut. of *gally*. qd. v. *Dal bf, ny allaf gweles*, I am blind, I cannot see. O.M. 2007. *Ny allaf pella trega*, I cannot longer stay. O.M. 2190. *Pandra allaf dhe wruthyl*, what can I do. O.M. 194. *My ny allaf gúl kenter dhyychy*, I cannot make a nail for you. P.C. 2676.

ALLAN, v. n. I may be able. A mutation of *gallan*, 1 pers. s. subj. of *gally*, qd. v. *Ow dywluef colm ha'm garrow gans louan fast colmennow na allan sevel a'm sáf*, my hands bind and my legs with a rope fast knots, that I may not stand up. O.M. 1348.

ALLAS, v. n. He was able. A mutation of *gallas*, 3 pers. s. pret. of *gally*, qd. v. *Rak ny allas dén yn beys anodho gúl defnyth vás*, for no man in the world has been able to make a good use of it. P.C. 2547. *Ef a allas dyôngel sawyé bewnens tús erel*, he could indeed save the life of other men. P.C. 2873.

ALLO, v. n. He may be able. A mutation of *gallo*, 3 pers. s. subj. of *gally*. (Welsh, *allo, gallo*.) *Predcrys fettyl gorfenné*, thinking how it can end. O.M. 228. *Pûp dén ôl degyns ganso y pýth, an méns a allo*, let every man take with him his things, all that he can. O.M. 1592. *Kelmeuch warbarth y dhywvrech na allo dyank*, bind ye his arms together that he may not escape. P.C. 1180.

ALLONS, v. n. They may be able. A mutation of *gallons*, 3 pers. pl. subj. of *gally*. (Welsh, *allont, gallont*.) *May rollo dour dhe evé dhedhé y, na allons cafus kén dhe dhyscrysy*, that he may give water to drink to them, that they may not find cause to disbelieve. M.C. 1826. *Gwreuch y pûr fast ma na allons yn pryveth y laddra a'n bédh*, make ye them very fast, that they may not privily steal him out of the tomb. R.D. 34.

ALLOS, s. m. Power. A mutation of *gallos*, qd. v. *Dew a allos*, God of power. R.D. 331. *Rak luen ôs a huneldcr hag a hallus kekeffrys*, for thou art full of greatness, and of power likewise. R.D. 425. *Ef yw arluth a allos, hag a prynas gans y wós pobel an beys*, He is the Lord of power, and he has purchased with his blood the people of the world. R.D. 1183.

ALLOSTI, comp. v. Art thou able. ‡ *Pan na hwêl allosti guîl*, what work canst thou do. *Llwyd*, 251. This form is only found in late Cornish. It is compounded of *allos*, a mutation of *gallos*, 3 pers. pret of *gally*, and the pron. *ti*. The characteristic of the 2 pers. s. pret. *st* may be contained in it.

ALLOYS, s. m. Power. A mutation of *galloys*. *Mear o an pryn dar ken vâb Duw, meâr y alloys*, much was the pain inflicted on the son of God, much his power. M.C. 135.

ALLYF, v. n. I may be able. A mutation of *gallyf*, 1 pers. s. snbj. of *gally*, qd. v. *Mars ôs Dew a nêf golow, dysqua lemman marthusow may allyf vy y welvs*, if thou art the God of bright heaven, show now miracles that I may see them. P.C. 83. Welsh, *gallwyv, a allwyv*.

ALS, s. f. A cliff, an ascent, the seashore. Cornish Vocabulary, *litus*. Welsh, *allt*, †*alt*, a cliff, a hill. Irish, *aill*. Gaelic, *all*. Manx. *alt*. Sanscrit, *alitas*, increased; from *al* to fill. Latin *altus*.

ALSE, v. n. He had been able. A mutation of *galsé*, 3 pers. s. plup. of *gally*. *Tekkê alter yn nêp pow ny alsé dên aspyé*, a fairer alter in any country, a man could not see. O.M. 1178. *Ef a alsé bôs yn ta, hanter dên ha hanter Dew*, he might have been well, half man and half God. P.C. 1740. *An pren yw terrys da, ny alsé vŷth bones gwell*, the tree is well cut, it could never be better. P.C. 2560. Welsh, *gallasai, allasai, all'sai, all'sé*.

ALSEN, v. n. I had been able. A mutation of *galsen*, 1 pers. s. plup. of *gally*. *Laka mester ny alsen y dhyerbyn*, a worse master I should not be able to meet. P.C. 2276. Welsh, *gallaswn, allaswn, all'swn*.

ALSENS, v. n. They had been able. A mutation of *galsens*, 3 pers. pl. plup. of *gally*. *Y a alsens*, they might. *Llwyd*, 247. Welsh, *gallasent, allasent, all'sent*.

ALSEST, v. n. Thou hadst been able. A mutation of *galsest*, 2 pers. pl. plup. of *gally*. *Ti a alsest*, thou mightest. *Llwyd*, 247. An amplified form of this occurs in *alsesta*. *A'n guelesta adhyragos, a alsesta y aswonfos?* If thou shouldst see him, couldest thou know him. R.D. 862.

ALTER, s. f. An altar. *Yn onour Dew gurên un alter têk ha da*, in the honour of God, let us make an altar fair and good. O.M. 1170. *Tekkê alter yn nêp pow ny alsé dên aspyé*, a fairer altar in any country a man could not see. O.M. 1177. *Bûch offrynné my a vyn wharê war an alter-na*, a cow I will offer forthwith upon that altar. O.M. 1146. This is written in the Cornish Vocabulary, *altor*. Welsh, *allor*. Armoric, *altor, aoter*. Irish, *altoir*. Gaelic, *altoir*. Manx. *altar*. All from the Latin *altare*.

ALTROU, s. m. A stepfather. So defined in the Cornish Vocabulary, *victricus*. In later Cornish *aultra* meant a godfather, *Llwyd*, 159, which agrees with Welsh *alltraw*. In the British dialects the etymology is not obvious, but in Irish *altrannus* signifies *nursing*. Athair *altrannus*, a foster-father. Irish, *altra*, foster-father. Gaelic, *altrach*.

ALTRUAN, s. f. A stepmother. Cornish Vocabulary *noverca*. In later Cornish *altruan* meant a godmother. *Llwyd*, 159. So Welsh, *elldrewen*.

ALWEDH, s. m. A key. Written also *alwhedh*; pl. *alwedhow, alwhedhow, alwheow*. *Yn dan naw alwedh gureuch y pûr fast*, under nine keys make you them very fast. R.D. 31. *Naw alwedh agas pryson*, the nine keys of your prison. R.D. 89. *Ro dhym dhe alwhedhow*, give me thy keys. R.D. 84. *Yn mês duech why, hep terry chy, ha hep alwhedh*, come ye out, without breaking house, and without a key. R.D. 334. *Ottê omma alwedhow*, see here the keys. R.D. 631. *A nyngesé alwheow warbarth yn ages guŷth why?* were not the keys together in your keeping. R.D. 650. Welsh, *allwedh*. Armoric, *alchouez, alhues*.

AM, pron. poss. My, mine. *Yn nêf y fethaff tregis an barth dychow gans am câr*, in heaven I shall dwell, on the right side with my father. M.C. 93. *A Dhew gorwyth am ené*, O God, keep my soul. O.M. 1356. Welsh, *ym*, as *yn ym ty*, in my house. Gaelic, *am*, as *ann am thigh*.

AM, prep. pron. With my, of my. *A dâs, ty re dhrôs dhymmo ascorn a'm kŷk ha corf*, O father, thou hast brought to me bone of my flesh and body. O.M. 112. *Guûn ef re gollas an plas a'm luf dhychyow a worussen*, clean he has lost the place, which with my right hand I had made. O.M. 921. *Out warnas harlot pen cok scon yn mês quyk a'm golok*, out upon thee, rogue, blockhead, immediately ont of my sight. O.M. 1530. *Gordhyans dhe'n tâs, arluth nef, a'm luen golon my a bŷs*, worship to the father, Lord of heaven, of my full heart I pray. O.M. 2088. *A'm leff dychow pan worussen*, with my right hand when I had made. C.W. 160. Compounded of a of, and *am*. Welsh, *â'm*.

AM, (a and me,) *Govyn orto mar a'm bŷdh*, ask him if there will be to me. O.M. 693. *Dew a'm danfonas dhyso dhe wofyn*, God has sent me to thee to ask. O.M. 1480. *Yn wêdh dewdhek warnugans a virhas my a'm be*, likewise thirty two daughters I have. C.W. 144. *An kynsa benfys a'm been*, the first benefice I have. O.M. 2613. *Te a'm gwêl ve devethys*, thou seest me come. C.W. 141. *Am* with the verb substantive is frequently used to denote possession. *Marth a'm bues a'th lavarow*, wonder is to me of thy words. P.C. 2392. *Mûr varth a'm bus dyogel*, a great wonder is surely come to me. O.M. 371. *Own a'm bus vy*, fear is on me. O.M. 1452. *Ha'n maystri brâs ôl a'm bo*, and all the great power that was mine. P.C. 148. So also in Welsh, *goody y parch a'm buai*, after the respect I experienced. *Llywarch Hên*, 78. *Brodyr a'm bwyad a dhûg Duw rhagov*, brethren I have had whom God hath taken from me. *Ll. Hên* 96. *Brodyr a'm bwyad innau*, brothers also I have had. *Ll. Hên*, 100. *Pedwar pwn broder a'm buant*, four brothers of a fruitful stock to me there were. *Ll. Hên*, 103. *Aur mal a'm bu*, the pure gold was my recompense. See also *bus, nymbus*.

AM, s. m. A kiss. *Pryce's Vocabulary*.

AMAN, adv. Up, upwards. ‡ *Dho dcreual aman*, to raise up. *Llwyd*, 69. ‡ *Sâv aman, kcbmer dha li, ha ker dha'n hâl*, get up, take thy breakfast, and go to the moor. *Pryce*. This is late Cornish, and incorrectly used for *avan*.

AMBOS, s. m. A contract, covenant, promise. Pl. *ambosow*. *My a wra dhys ambos da*, I will make a good promise to thee. O.M. 1232. *Yn dan ambos ytheses*, under agreement thou wert. P.C. 2259. *Ambosow orth tryher gureys annedhê nynses laha*, promises made by the mighty, of them there is not law. O.M. 1235. *Lell ôs ha trêsi, ha stedfast y'th ambosow*, faithful thou art and trusty, and steadfast in thy agreements. P.C. 949. Welsh, *ammod*.

AMBOSE, v. a. To promise. Pret. *ambosas*. *Ha gynef y tanfonas, y te dheuch, pare veuch wár, kepar ha del ambosas*, and by me he sent, that he would come to you, as ye may be aware like as he promised. R.D. 915. Welsh, *amrnodi*.

AME, v. a. To kiss. Written also *ama, amma, ammé*. Pret. *amas*. Governing the dative. *Enef Judas ny allas dós y mês mar y annow, rag y annow a amas dhe Jhesus*, the soul of Judas could not come out from his mouth, for his mouth kissed Jesus. M.C. 106. *Am lemyn dhe'n gwellynny a barth an tás veneges, hag y a wra eredy a púp cleves dhys jehes*, kiss now the rods on the part of the blessed father, and they will cause surely from every disease to thee a cure. O.M. 1794. *Me a ra dhe Christ amé may hallouch y aswonvos*, I will kiss Jesus, that you may know him. M.C. 63. *My a vyn dyso amma*, I will kiss thee. O.M. 2191. *Me a vyn dheth treys ammé*, I will kiss thy feet. P.C. 480. *Dhym ny dhogouth ammé dheth pen*, it becomes me not to kiss thy head. R.D. 872.

AMENEN, s. m. Butter. This and *emenin*, are the old forms preserved in the Cornish Vocabulary. In late Cornish *amman*. Welsh, *ymenyn*, †*emmenin*. Armoric, *aman, amanen*. Irish, *im*. Gaelic, *im*. Manx. *eeym*.

AMES, adv. Without, out of doors, in the field. See *vés*, and *més*.

AMOUNT, v. irreg. It concerns. *Pandra amount dhyn gonys*, what avails it to cultivate. O.M. 1223. *Ny amount man*, it avails nothing. O.M. 2791. This is a foreign word borrowed from the English.

AMPYDGNYAN, s. m. The brains. *Raytha te a výdh ledhys, a fals lader casndow squattiys yw dhe ampydgnyan*, for this thou shalt be slain, thou false foul thief, struck out are thy brains. C.W. 124. This is a corruption of *empynyon*.

AMSER, s. m. Time. It occurs in the Cornish Vocabulary, corruptly written *anser*. Welsh, *amser*. Armoric, *amzer*. Irish, *aimsir*, †*aimser*. Gaelic, *aimsir*. Manx. *emshir*. Sanscrit, *amasa*.

AMSEVY, v. a. To raise up, to excite. *En marrek-na amsevys ol yn ban y gowethé, ha dhedhé a leverys a Jesus falell vye*, that soldier stirred up all his companions, and to them said of Jesus how it was. M.C. 245. Compounded of *am*, id. qd., *em* and *om*, reflective particle, and *sevel*, to raise.

AN, definite article. The. When the substantive is feminine the initial assumes the secondary or soft sound. *Dén* a man, *an dén* the man. *Tre*, f. a town, *an dre*, the town. *Tra*, f. a thing, *an dra*, the thing. *Del ve helheys war an býs avel carow*, so was hunted on the world like a deer. M.C. 2. *Cusil an tás*, the counsel of the father. O.M. 188. Written also *en*, qd. v. In Welsh *yr*, and *y*, are now used but anciently *ir*. In Armoric, *ann* before vowels, and words beginning with *d, n, t*. Before other consonants *ar* is used, and *al* before *l*. The Irish use *an, na*. Old Irish *in, inna, na*. Gaelic, *an, na*. Manx. *y, yn*.

AN, (a prep. *an* art.) From the, out of the, on the. *A'n uchelder may 'thesé dhe'n býs pan deyskynnas*, from the height that he was to the world when he descended. M.C. 4. *Hag a'n grows, del o prýs, corf Jesus a gemeras*, and from the cross, as it was time, the body of Jesus they took. M.C. 230. *A'n nêf y fe danvenys dheworth an tás eleth dy*, from heaven there were sent from the father angels to him. M.C. 18. *Ty a saw a'n trôs dhe'n pen*, thou shalt be healed from the foot to the head. O.M. 1762. *A'n lôst kemer dhedhy yn ban*, by the tail take it up. O.M. 1454. *A'n barth clêdh néb o cregis*, on the left side, he that was hanged. M.C. 191. *Ladh e, ladh e, mernens an grows desympys*, kill him, kill him, the death of the cross immediately. M.C. 142.

AN, (a aux. 'n him.) Him, it, them. *Nep a'n gordhyé, gwyn y veys*, who worships him, happy his lot. O.M. 1938. *Hay dhyscyplys a'n sewyas*, and his disciples followed him. M.C. 52. *Why a'n clewas*, ye have heard him. M.C. 95. *A dorras an aval têk, hag a'n dug dhym*, who plucked the fair apple, and brought it to me. O.M. 268. *Ny a'n kyrch dhys*, we will bring him to thee. O.M. 548. *Me a'n gor*, I will put him. O.M. 1289. *Kemmys a'n gwrello*, as many as do them. O.M. 605. *Me a'n te dhys*, I swear it to thee. O.M. 2124.

AN, pron. poss. Our. *An bewnans ny regollas*, we have lost our life. M.C. 246. *Nans ôn lafuryys ganso, hag an yssuyly púr squyth*, now we are oppressed with it, and our limbs are very weary. O.M. 2824. *An Tás ny és yn nêf*, our Father which is in heaven. Pryce. The more common form is *agan*. Welsh, *ein*.

AN, (a aux., an our.) Us. *Rag ef o tebel edhen, néb a glewsys ow cané, hag a'n doro dhe anken*, for he was an evil bird, whom thou didst hear singing, and will bring us to sorrow. O.M. 225. (So also in Welsh, *ag a'n dygo i angen*.) *Cúth gweles y dheweth, fe namna'n dallas*, a grief to see his end it was, it almost blinded us. R.D. 42.

ANAF, s. m.. An evet, or newt. Cornish Vocabulary, *stellio*. Armoric, *anv*, a blind worm.

ANAL, s. f. The breath. *Ber anal*, short breath. Welsh, *anal, anadl*. Armoric, *anal*. Irish, *anal*. Gaelic, *anail*. Manx. *ennal*. Sanscrit, *anila*, from *an* to breathe.

ANCAR, s. m. An anchorite, or hermit. Cornish Vocabulary, *anachorita*. From the Latin.

ANCAR, s. m. An anchor. Cornish Vocabulary, *anchora*. Welsh, *angor*, and *heor*. Armoric, *heor*. Irish, *angcaire, anncoire*, †*ingor*. Gaelic, *acair*. Manx. *aker*.

ANCEN, s. m. Grief, sorrow, trouble, pain. *Hag a'n doro dhe anken*, and will bring us to sorrow. O.M. 225. *Dhe vôs denladh yw anken*, to be a mankiller is grievous. O.M. 2335. *Mara quelyn dhys anken*, if we see grief to him. P.C. 733. *Ma an glows dre ow colon râk galarow hag anken*, there is a pang through my heart for sorrow and grief. P.C. 1148. *Ty a fýth cowal anken*, thou shalt have full pain. P.C. 2530. *Nyn sparyaf awos anken*, I will not spare it because of trouble. P.C. 2566. *Anken ha tristys*, grief and sorrow. R.D. 204. *Whŷs hag anken*, sweat and sorrow. R.D. 245. Welsh, *angen*. Armoric, *ancen*. Irish, *gann, eigean*. †Gaelic, *eigin*, †*gann*.

ANCENEC, s. m. An elegy, a penitential hymn. *Ow conselar whêk yth pesaf, dýsk dhymmo un ankenek râg ow fehas*, my sweet adviser, I pray thee, teach me a penitential hymn for my sins. O.M. 2256. From *anken*, grief.

ANCENSY, s. m. Vexation, trouble. *Púr ankensy gans dornow dhodho war an scovornow reuch boxescow trewysy*, very vexation, with fists to him on the ears give sad blows. P.C. 1360. Written also *ankynsy*. *Mear ankynsy dhe Christ may fe crehyllys oll y gorf hay esely*, much vexation to Christ, that was crushed all his body and limbs. M.C. 184.

ANCEVY, v. a. To forget. Part. *ancevys*. *Gans y ny vŷdh ankevys an murder bŷs venary*, by them will not be forgotten the murder for ever. C.W. 98. *Gans pêb me yw ankevys, nyn aswon, na mc. rc adues*, by every one I am forgotten, I neither know them, nor they me. C.W. 108. *Pûp tra oll yn bŷs-ma screphys y ma yn ryma, doul na vôns y ankevys*, every thing all in this world is written in these, lest they should be forgotten. C.W. 158. Compounded of *an* neg. and *côf* memory. Welsh, *anghovio*, to forget.

ANCLEDHY, v. n. To bury, inter. Imp. *ancladh*. Part. *anclydhys, anclydhyys, ancledhys*. *Ancledhyas* is also used for the infin. *May hallo bôs ancledhys yn bêdh mên*, that he may be buried in a stone tomb. P.C. 3115. *Hag yn bêdh mên ancladh e, y cafus aban vynnyth*, and in a stone tomb bury him, since thou wilt have him. P.C. 3131. *Jhesu a fue ancledhys*, Jesus who was buried. R.D. 1. Written also *ancledhyes*. *Me a wrûk y ancledhyes*, I did bury him. R.D. 439. *Wogé y vôs gurŷs marow, tûs yn bêdh a'n ancledhyas*, after he was put to death, people buried him in a tomb. O.M. 1269. *Droga galar ew dhymmo y ancledhyas mar uskys*, worst sorrow it is to me, his being buried so immediately. O.M. 869. *Encledhyes* is another form, qd. v. Welsh, *anghladhu*, to bury.

ANCLEDIIYAS, s. m. A burial, a funeral. Written also *anclydhyas*. *An keth oyncment a scollyas warnaf râk ow anclydhyas*, that same ointment she poured on me for my burial. P.C. 548.

ANCOW, s. m. Death. Also sorrow, or grief. *Na moy scony ny vynnas, rag own caffos y ancow*, no more would he not shun, for fear of finding his death. M.C. 174. *Mar dha yw genef a vrŷs mervoci kyns dôs drôk ancow*, as well it is in my opinion to die before evil sorrow comes. O.M. 1230. *Awos godhevel ancow ny nahas hy lavarow*, though suffering death, she retracted not her words. O.M. 2760. *Râk y-ma yn ow enef trystys fast bŷs yn ancow*, for there is in my soul great sadness even unto death. P.C. 1023. *Pâr oges yw dhe ancow*, very near is thy death. P.C. 2660. *Why a's bydh ages ancow*, you shall have your death. R.D. 612. Welsh, *angau*, †*anghou*, †*ancou*. Armoric, *ancou, ankeu*. Irish, *eug, gus*. Gaelic, *aog, eug*. Sanscrit, *ghus*, to kill.

ANCREDOUR, s. m. A pirate, or robber on the sea. This word occurs in the Cornish Vocabulary, *ancredvur môr*, pirata. It must be the Welsh *anrheithiwr*, a spoiler or robber, from *anrhaith*, pillage. Cf. also Irish, *ancride*, wrong.

ANCRES, s. m. Disquiet, grief. *Wogé bôs yn lowené ty dhe dôs, drôk yw gyné, dhe vûr encres*, after being in joy, I am sorry that thou shouldst come to great disquiet. R.D. 208. Compounded of *an* neg. and *crés* quiet.

ANDELLA, adv. So, thus. *Andella re bo*, so be it. Written also *yn della*, which see.

ANDYLLAS, v. a. To forgive. Pryce. Properly, *a'n dyllas*. *Gwrên grassé dh'agen maker, agan lavyr yn bysma ny a'n dyllas, ha moy*, let us give thanks to our maker, our labour in this world that he remit to us and more. C.W. 94. See *Dylly*.

ANEDHE, prep. Of them, from them. Written also *anethé, annethé*. *Hag anedhé na wra vry*, and of them that he made not account. M.C. 26. *Y wrég dhe re ancdhé môs dhe'n dré*, he caused some of them to go to the town. M.C. 27. *Anedhé ty a wylfyth tŷr gwedhen tevys wharé*, from them thou wilt see three trees grow presently. O.M. 627. *Haga flechys vynytha a dheffo anedhé y*, and their children afterwards who should come from them. O.M. 2835. *Na'n Edhewon ny wodhyé an prennyer py fêns keffis dhe wuthyll crows anedhé*, nor did the Jews know the sticks where they could be found to make a cross thereof. M.C. 151. Welsh, *ohonynt*, †*onadunt*. Armoric, *anezo*.

ANEDHY, prep. pron. Of, or from her, or it. Written also *anethy, annethy*. *May rollo brês anedhy*, that he might give judgment of her. M.C. 32. *Gwerthens y hugh dhe brenné anedhy dhodho cledhé*, let him sell his cloak to buy with it for him a sword. P.C. 923. *Ef a wrûk ow husullyé frut annedhy may torren*, ho did advise me that I should gather fruit from it. O.M. 218. *Me a ysten an scoran, cymmar an frût annedhy*, I will reach the bough, take the fruit from it. C.W. 50. Welsh, *ohoni*, †*ohonei*. Armoric, *anezi, anezy*.

ANETII, adv. To-night. *Saw lytygyns cresouch why an corf-na dhe dhasserchy kyns yw aneth*, but nevertheless believe ye, that body to rise again before it is to night. R.D. 1302. More correctly *haneth*, qd. v.

ANFUGY, s. m. Correction, punishment, harm, mischief. *Y a's tevyt anfugy*, punishment shall come upon them. O.M. 2328. *Dûs yn râk dheth anfugy*, come forth to thy punishment. P.C. 1472. *Scon ty a fŷdh anfugy*, soon thou shalt have punishment. P.C. 2044. *Pûr vrâs a anfugy, mara gwrês ow dyskyvera*, very great harm (will be to thee) if thou wilt discover me. C.W. 42. Written also *enfugy*, qd. v.

ANFUGYK, adj. Hypocritical, mischievous. *My a gl bôs cuthygyk ow bones mar anfugyk drcys pûp dên ôl ûs yn beys*, I may be ashamed being so wicked above all men that are in the world. P.C. 1424. Another form of *anfusyg*, (q for s.)

ANFUR, adj. Imprudent, unwise. Cornish Vocabulary, *imprudens*. Compounded of *an* neg., and *fûr* wise. Welsh, *anfur*.

ANFUS, s. m. Wickedness, punishment. *Dûn ganso er y anfus, dhe Pilat agan Justis*, let us come with him for his wickedness to Pilate our Justice. P.C. 1501. *Es bŷdh deydh brues mûr a anfues, nêb a'n gwerthas*, he shall have on the day of judgment much punishment, who sold him. P.C. 2940. *Arluth, yn trok a horn crîf, yn dour tyber ef a sêf er y anfeus*, Lord, in a box of strong iron, in the water of Tiber he shall stay for his wickedness. R.D. 2137. Welsh, *anvoes*, wickedness; *anfawd*, misfortune.

ANFUSYK, adj. Wicked, hypocritical. Thomas, *ty yw dyscrygyk, pûr wŷr, ha mûr anfusyk*, thou art unbelieving, and very wicked. R.D. 1520. Plur. *anfusygyon*. *A treytors, anfesugyon, euch abervedh lemmyn scon*, O traitors, hypocrites, go in now immediately. R.D. 95.

ANGHESPAR, adj. Unequal, unlike. Lluyd, 55. Welsh, *anghymhar*. See *Cespar*.

ANHEDHY, v. a. To inhabit, to dwell in. Part. *anhedhys*. *Awot omma onan do ragon ordenys parys, lemyn agan soné gura kyns ys bones anhedhys*, behold here a good one (tent) intended for us ready; now bless us before it is inhabited. O.M. 1722. From *annedh*, a habitation. Welsh, *annedhu*. Armoric, *annexa*.

ANIACH, adj. Infirm, unhealthy, unwell. Cornish Vocabulary, *infirmus*. Compounded of *an*, neg., and *iach*, healthy. W. *aviach*.

ANNEDH, s. f. A habitation, house, dwelling. *Crês Dew aberth yn annedh, ha'm benneth ragas bo whêth*, the peace of God be in the house, and my blessing also be upon you. P.C. 705. W. *annedh*. Arm. *annez*, which now means the furniture of a house.

ANNES, adj. Wearied, ill at ease. *Lavar annes ow vôs vy a'm bewnens, my dh'y bysy a leverel gwyronedh*, say, being wearied of my life, that I pray him to say the truth. O.M. 700. I consider this word to be the same as the Armoric *anez*, id. qd. *diez*, uneasy.

ANNETHE, prep. pron. Of them. See *Anedhe*.

ANNEYLY, v. n. To go apart, to retire. *Pryce's* Vocabulary.

ANNEZ, s. m. A cold. *Llwyd*, 28. A corruption of *anwos*, qd. v.

ANODHO, prep. pron. Of or from him, or it. (*Anodho, Llwyd*, 244.) Written also *annotho*. *Anodho mar 'thês predcr, worth y wythyes govynné*, of him if there is to thee a care, ask him of his keeper. O.M. 608. *Anodho ef grêns del vyn, pan gleufo y launrow*, with him let him do as he will, when he hears his words. P.C. 371. *An bara-ma kymereuch, hag anodho ol dybreuch*, this bread take, and of it all eat. P.C. 763. *Kymereuch, eveuch an gwŷn, rág ny evaf bŷs dêdh fŷn geneuch anpodho na moy*, take, drink the wine, for I will not drink till the last day with you of it any more. P.C. 725. *Lavar dhymmo pandra yw ôl an gwyryonedh pan geusyth mûr annodho*, tell me, what all is the truth, since thou speakest much of it. P.C. 2030. W. *ohono*, †*ohonaw*. Arm. *anezeff, aneshann*.

ANOTHANS, prep. pron. Of them. This form occurs in the later Drama by Jordan, *anedhé* only being found in the Ordinalia, it must not however be considered a corruption, but a colloquial form of great antiquity, as it agrees with the Welsh *ohonynt*, †*onadunt*. *Awos henna ny wrdf vry, na anothans y bŷth voye me ny seltyaf gwail gala*, of that I will not make account, nor (of) them will I value the stalk of a straw. C.W. 98. *Ny sparyaf anothans y, malbew onyn a vo têg*, I do not spare of them in any wise one that is handsome. C.W. 106. *Hag a vyn gans ow sethow ladha part anothans y*, and I will with mine arrows kill some of them. C.W. 108.

ANOW, s. m. The mouth. A mut. of *ganow*. *An try sprus yn y anow, my a's gor, hep falladow*, the three grains into his mouth, I will put them without fail. O.M. 870. *Yn y anow bos gorrys*, in his mouth be put. O.M. 876. *Dhe cnef plos casadow ny vyn dôs dre dhe anow*, thy soul, dirty villain, will not come through thy mouth. P.C. 1535. W. *cnau*, *genau*; yn ei *enau*, in his mouth.

ANOW, s. m. A name, appellation. *Dên vŷth ny gl leverel war anow ôll mŷns peynys a'n gevé kyns ys y vonas marrow*, no man can tell by name all the pains he had before that he was dead. M.C. 59. *Kepar del ve dhe'n Justis dûn leveryn war anow*, as it was to the Justice let us come and tell by name. M.C. 247. In the other Dramas it is written *hanow*, qd. v. W. *cnw* and *henw*. Arm. *hanô*. Ir. *ainm, ainm*. Gael. *ainm*. Manx, *ennym*. Sanscrit, *naman*. Gr. ὄνομα. Lat. *nomen*. Pers. *nam*. Mœso-Gothic, *namo*.

ANTELL, s. m. A hazarding, venture a bold attempt,

danger. *Ha satnns gans y antell, hay scherewneth, Crist, y demtyé pan prederys*, and Satan with his bold attempt and his pride, Christ, to tempt him when he thought. M.C. 19. *Na hombrenc ny en antel, mês gwŷth ny dheworth drôk*, lead us not into temptation, but deliver us from evil. *Pryce*. W. *antur*.

ANTERHUCH, s. m. A flitch of bacon. *Llwyd*, 5. Literally half a hog, being compounded of *anter*, for *hanter*, half, and *huch* a hog. So Welsh, *hannercb*, from *hanner* half, and *hôb* a pig.

ANTROMET, s. m. The sex. It only occurs in the Cornish Vocabulary, and its etymology is unknown. It is probably corrupt.

ANTYMAN, adv. On this side. Compounded of *an* on, *ty* or *tu* side, and *man*, or *ma* here.

ANVAB, adj. Childless, barren. *Llwyd*, 154. Compounded of *an* neg. and *mâb* a son. W. *anvab*.

ANVABAT, s. m. Sterility, barrenness. Cornish Vocabulary, *sterilitas*. From *anvab*.

ANVODH, s. m. A displeasure, a displeasing, a disliking. *Ef a dhûk an grows gansé, pûr wŷr henno a y anvodh; ny wrêns y na hên seyle, lymmyn sawyé aga bôdh*, he carried the cross with them; very truly that was against his will, they gave no other reason but followed their will. M.C. 175. Compounded of *an* neg. and *bôdh* the will. W. *anvodh*.

ANUAN, s. f. An anvil. Written *anwan* by *Llwyd*, 15, 69. W. *eingion*, *einion*, †*eingon*, †*ennian*. Arm. *annean*. Ir. *inneoin*, †*indein*. Gael. *inuenn, innein*. Manx, *ingan*.

ANUEIN, adj. Weak. Cornish Vocabulary, *invalidus*. Compounded of *an* neg. and *guein*. W. *gwain*, lively. Arm. *gwên*; or W. *en* intens. and *gwan*, weak; like Gael. *anfhann*, (*an* intens, and *fann* weak.)

ANUESEC, adj. Particular. *En anuesek* in particular. *Pryce*. W. *enwedig, yn enwedig*.

ANWIIEC, adj. Unsweet, unpleasant, rough. *Cachaf ybcn pûr anwhek*, I will seize the other very sharp. O.M. 2816. *Me a's doro pûr anwhek adhyragos*, I will bring them very roughly before thee. P.C. 2332. *My a gl bôs morethek, gwelas ow mâp mor anwhek dychtys del yw*, I may be mournful, seeing my son so roughly treated as he is. P.C. 3188. Compounded of *an* neg., and *whêk* sweet.

ANWOS, s. m. A cold, a chill. *Rag fout gwêsc ha goscutter namna vyrwyn rág anwos*, for want of clothes and shelter I am almost dying from cold. O.M. 362. *Rag, rum fey, rûk ewen anwos ny glewaf yender dhum troys*, for by my faith, from very chilliness, I do not feel the cold to my feet. P.C. 222. W. *anwyd*. Arm. *anoued*.

ANYDHA, prep. pron. Of or from them, thence. *Llwyd*, 244, 248, writes *annydha*. id. qd. *anedhé*. qd. v.

ANYSYA, v. n. To preserve, secure. *An bêdh me re anysyas, warnodho y ma mên brâs dros ol an mŷn*, I have secured the tomb, upon it there is a great stone, above all the stones. R.D. 390.

AO, adj. Ripe, mature. W. *haw*. Arm. *aô, haô*.

AOR, s. f. The earth. An abbreviated form of *daor*, as *an daor, an naor, an 'aor*. See *Dour*.

APELEH, adv. Whence, from what place. *Llwyd*, 258. (*A* from, *pa* what, *le* place.)

APERFETH, adj. Within. Another form of *abervedh*. qd. v.

APERT, adj. Open, unconcealed, perfect. *Pûr apert hag yn golow y leverys ow dyskas*, very open and in light

I spake my doctrine. M.C. 79. *An bedhow yn lower le apert a ve egerys*, the graves in many places abroad were opened. M.C. 210. *Den apert ha mear y rôs, golow cleyr ow tewenê*, a Man perfect and much his grace, a light clear shining. M.C. 243. *Apert vythqueth y tyskys ow dyskes dhe'n Yedhewon*, openly I ever taught my doctrine to the Jews. P.C. 1252. From the Latin *apertus*.

APOSTOL, s. m. An apostle. This is the form given in the Cornish Vocabulary, and is also used in Welsh. The *p* should strictly have been softened into *b*, that is *abostol*, from which the plurals *abestely, abesteleth*, are formed; which see.

AR, prep. Upon, on. More commonly written *war*, qd. v. W. *ar*. Arm. *ar* and *war*.

AR, s. f. Slaughter, battle. Written also *hár*. Lhuyd, 45. W. *aer, hár,* †*air,* †*hair*. Ir. *aer,* †*ar,* †*ur*. Gael. *ar,* †*iur*. Gr. ἄρης. Cantabrian, *hara*. Dan. *ar*, a wound.

ARADAR, s. m. A plough. Cornish Vocabulary, *aratrum*. *Dên aradar*, a ploughman. Written also *ardar; dorn ardar*, the plough-tail or handle. Lhuyd, 155. ‡ *Gora an ohan en arder*, put the oxen in the plough. Pryce. W. *aradr, arad*. Arm. *arar*. Lat. *aratrum*.

ARADERUUR, s. m. A ploughman. *Araderuur* arator, Cornish Vocabulary. Compounded of *aradar*, a plough, and *gour*, a man. W. *aradwr*. Arm. *arer*. Gael. *arndair, aoirain, arear*. Manx, *erroo*.

ARADOW, s. m. Commandments. *An dek aradow*, the ten commandments. Pryce. This is an abbreviated form of *arhadow*, plur. of *arhad*.

ARAG, adv. Forward, in front, before. *Dûs arág*, come forth. *Kemer dhe welen a-rag an debel bobyl*, take thy rod in presence of the wicked people. O.M. 1843. *Aspy ahas ha glu a-rag hag a denewen*, watch continually and listen, forwards and sideways. O.M. 2063. *(A on, rag* before.)

ARALL, adj. Other, another. Plur. *erell*. *Taw, gans Christ me a'd welas, gurêc arall a leverys*, be silent, with Christ I thee saw, another woman said. M.C. 84. *Dhe'n leyff arall pan dolhyans war an grows rág y fasté*, to the other hand when they came on the cross to fasten it. M.C. 180. *En Edhewon beteggyns gûl toll arall ny vynné*, the Jews nevertheless make another hole would not. M.C. 180. *An barth arall*, on the other side. M.C. 198. *Pan dethens y bŷs an bêdh, yth êth on marrek dh'y ben hag arall dh'y dreys*, when they came to the grave, there went one soldier to his head, and another to his feet. M.C. 242. *War nga dewlyn ythe perag Christ re erell*, on their knees there went before Christ some others. M.C. 195. W. *arall*, pl. *eraill*. Arm. *arall*. Ir. *aroile,* †*araill*.

ARAS, v. a. To plough, to till. *Dho aras tir*, to plough land. *Aras an kensa an ton*, plough first the lay. Pryce. W. *aru*. Arm. *arat* and *ara*. Ir. *ar*. Gael. *ar*. Gr. ἀρόω. Lat. *aro*. Goth. *aria*. Lith. *aru*. Russ. *oria*. Sanscrit *arv*, to break or cleave. Teut. *aeren*. Etrurian *arfer* and *ar*. Old English, *ear*. Egyptian, *er* or *ert*, ploughing.

ARBEDNEC, adj. Usual, customary. Pryce. This is a later form of *arbennec*. W. *arbennig*. Ir. †*airchinnech*.

ARCH, s. f. A chest or coffer. Pl. *archow*. qd. v. W. *arch*. Arm. *arch*. Ir. *arg*. Gael. *airc*. Manx, *arg*. Lat. *arca*. Sanscrit *ark*, to enclose.

ARCHA, v. a. To command, charge, enjoin. 2 pers. s. Imp. *arch*; 3 pers. s. fut. *yrch*, or *erch;* part. and pret. *erchys*, and *yrchys*, commanded. *Me a yrch, me a hyrch*, I will command. *Serafyn, dhe Adam ke, hag arch dhodho growedhé dre ow gorhemmynadow*, Seraph to Adam go, and enjoin him to lie down, by my commands. O.M. 635. *Mars ôs máp Dew awartha, dysempys arch a lavar dhe'n cals meyn-ma bôs bara*, if thou art the son of God above, forthwith command and say to these stones that they become bread. P.C. 61. *Yn êr-na dhe'n mynydhyow why a erch warnouch codhé*, in that hour to the mountains ye shall call on yon to fall. M.C. 170. *Dhys y'th archaf, a dyreyth, gûs Adam dheth agery*, I command thee, O earth, allow Adam to open thee. O.M. 381. W. *arch*, command thou, *erchi,* †*erchim*, to command.

ARCHAD, s. m. A command, commandment. Pl. *archadow*. The aspirate was softened into *arhad* and *arhas;* pl. *arhadow*, and *aradow*. *Arludh cûf dhe archadow y wruthyl rês ew dhymmo*, dear Lord, thy injunctions need is to me to do them. O.M. 996. *A dûs benyges del ôs, dhe aradow me a wra*, O Father, blessed as thou art, thy commands I will do. O.M. 1034. *Me â gencs yn lowen ha'm dyscyblyon kettep pen dheth arhadow*, I will go with thee joyfully, and my disciples every head at thy commands. P.C. 463. *Y a ruge a dhesympys ol war lyrch y arhadow*, they did immediately all after his commands. M.C. 247. W. *arch*, a command, a request. Ir. *iarraigh, artha,* †*ortha*. Gael. *iarr*. Manx, *aghin*. Sanscrit *artha*, a prayer, from *arth* to ask.

ARCHAIL, s. m. An archangel. Cornish Vocabulary, *archangelus*. Compounded of *arch*, chief, and *ail*, an angel.

ARCHANS, s. m. Silver. *A lena yn hombronkyas uchel war ben un menedh, ha dhodho y tysquedhas ow hag archans, gwêls, ha gwêdh*, from thence he led him high on the top of a mountain, and to him he shewed gold and silver, grass and trees. M.C. 16. *Ena Judas, pan wclas Christ an bewnans na sawyê, an archans a gemeras, rag corf Jesus dhe ryssevê, ef a's tewlas dre sor brâs dhe'n Edhewon yntredhê*, then Judas, when he saw Christ his life should not save, the silver he took, (which) for the body of Christ he received, he cast it with great wrath to the Jews among them. M.C. 103. This is also the form preserved in the Cornish Vocabulary. It is also written *arhans*, or *arrans*, the *h* taking the place of the guttural. *Avel arhans*, like silver. O.M. 771. *My a vyn vôs garlont gureys a arhans adré dhedhé*, I will that a garland be made of silver around it. O.M. 2097. *Awos cost arhans nag our gurcuch y tenné mês a'n dour*, for the cost of silver and gold drag him out of the water. R.D. 2231. W. *ariant, arian,* †*argant*. Arm. *archant,* †*argant*. Ir. *airgid*. Gael. *airgiod*. Manx. *argid*. All from the Lat. *argentum*, and that from the Greek ἀργεννὸς candidus, from the root ἀργὸς white; ἄργυρος silver. Sanscrit, *rajalan, rajan*, or *ranj* to shine.

ARCHESCOP, s. m. An archbishop. Cornish Vocabulary, *archiepiscopus*. W. *archesgob*. Arm. *archescop*. Ir. *ardcaspog,* †*ardepscop*. Gael. *ardcasbuig*. Manx. *ardaspick*. Lat. *archiepiscopus*.

ARCHOW, s. m. A treasury. *En arhans me a gymer, hag a's gwŷth kettep dyner râk an termyn; ny goth aga bos gorrys yn archow rak bos prennys ganse mernans dyn brynyn*, the money I will take, and keep it every penny for the time; they ought not to be put into the treasury because that there was bought with them the death of a noble man. P.C. 1541. *Archow* must be the plural of *arch*. W. *arch*, a chest or coffer.

ARD, adj. High, lofty. *Pryce*. W. *hardh*. Ir. †*ard*. Gael. *ard*. Manx,*ard*. Lat. *arduus*. Gr. ἀρδην. Sanscrit, *ardh* to rise.

ARDAC, s. m. A choking, strangling. *Ol dheth vódh ow arludh kér, dynythys ôn hep danger bŷs dŷs omma hep ardak*, all to thy wish, dear Lord, come we are without delay, to thee here without demur. P.C. 1870. From *ar* on, and *taga* to choke.

ARDAR, s. m. A plough. This is a late form of *aradar*, qd. v. *Dén ardar*, a ploughman. *Llwyd*, 43.

AREDY, adv. Immediately, forthwith. *Me a vyn un dén formya rag colenwel aredy an le may toth anetha*, I will form a man to fill up immediately the place that he went from. C.W. 26. Written also *credy* and *yredy*. qd. v.

ARETH, s. f. A speech, oration. *Heyl volaneth volaneth, uthyk múr yw dhe areth leman worth agan gylwel*, hail, high priest, high priest, very loud is thy speech now calling to us. P.C. 954. W. *araeth*. Ir. *araid, oraid*. Gael. *oraid*. à Lat. *oratio*.

ARFETH, s. m. Wages, hire. *Pryce. Ow arfeth byth na whyla, ahanas gy un demma my ny sensaf yn torma*, my hire I have never seen, of thee one halfpenny I do not hold at this time. P.C. 2262. As W. *arvaeth* means a purpose, or design, the above will bear the following interpretation, "My attention do thou never seek, I do not value thee a halfpenny at this time."

ARGILA, v. n. To recoil. *Llwyd*, 245. W. *argilio*. Arm. *argila*. From *ar* on, and *cil* a retreat.

ARGRAPHY, v. a. To print, impress. *Dho argraphy. Pryce*. Part. *argraphys*. W. *argraphu*. Gr. γράφω.

ARGRAPHYS, s. m. An impression. *Pryce*. W. *argraphiad*.

ARHAD, s. m. A command. Pl. *arhadow, aradow*; a later form of *archad*. qd. v.

ARJIO, s. m. A goad, a prick. *Llwyd*, 154. This may be a corruption of *garthon*. qd. v. W. *ierthi*.

ARLOTTES, s. m. A lordship, manor, jurisdiction. *Lewreuch dhymno whar mars yw dén a Galylé, hag a gallos Erodes, me a wra súr y dhanfon dhe'n turont Erod yn scon mars yw e a'y arlottes*, tell me directly, if he is a man of Galilee, and of the dominion of Herod, I will surely send him to the tyrant soon, if he is of his jurisdiction. P.C. 1604. From *arloth*, a lord. W. *arlwydhineth*.

ARLUDHES, s. f. A lady. This is occasionally written *arlodhes, arluthes*; and in the Cornish Vocabulary *arludes*. *Arlodhes kér, me a wra agas nygys fystyné*, dear lady, I will hasten your errand. P.C. 1965. *Ow arlodhes gyné agas pygys na wrellouch cammen ladhé an profus*, my lady by me prayed you, that ye do not unjustly slay the prophet. P.C. 2194. *Ty a vŷdh rewardys hag arludhes a vŷdh gurys war múr a tŷr*, thou shalt be rewarded, and shalt be made lady over much land. R.D. 1701. W. *arglwydhes, arlwydhes*.

ARLUIDH, s. m. A lord, a ruler. This is variously written *arludh*, or *arluth*, and sometimes *arloth*; in the Cornish Vocabulary, *arluit*. Pl. *arludhi*, *Llwyd*, 128, and *arlydhy*, or *arlythy*. *An tás Dew Arluth a-van re'm gorré dhe gorwieth*, the Father God, Lord above, may he put me to rest. O.M. 857. *Dhe volungeth yn púp le Arluth whel my a wra*, thy will in every place, O high Lord, I will do. O.M. 1166. *Arloth Dew an néf, an tás*, Lord God of Heaven, the Father. O.M. 105. ‡ *Padar an Arluydh*, the Lord's prayer. *Pryce*. *Pa na vynné gorthyby a dhyrak an arlythy*, when he would not answer before the lords. P.C. 1821. *Arlythy caradowyon, dreuch dhym ow máp, cúf colon*, dear lords, bring to me my son, wise of heart. P.C. 3163. *Gylwys o why, pen arlythy, gortheuch an bédh*, ye are called, chief lords, honour the tomb. R.D. 325. W. *arglwydh*, and *arlwydh*. The etymology is not very obvious, but perhaps it is compounded of *arch* chief, (Ir. *arg* noble, *airech* first,) and *llywydh* a ruler. Ir. *iarfhlath*, †*ardlath* (*ardflath*.) Gael. *iarfhlath*.

ARMAS, v. a. He cried. A mut. of *garmas*, 3 pers. s. preterite of *garma*. qd. v. *Arludh Du, y a armas, pu a gi henna bonas*, Lord God, they cried out, who can that be. M.C. 42.

ARMOR, s. m. A surge, or wave of the sea. *Llwyd*, 176. W. *arvor*, the sea-side, maritime. Arm. *armor*; and *arvor*. From *ar* upon, and *mór* sea; hence the name of Armorica.

ARNA, adv. Until. ‡ *Ty a dhebbar yn dha wherys dheth vara púr wyr nefra, arna veys arta troyles an kéth doer, kyns a vorugaf*, thou shalt eat in thy sweat thy bread in very truth for ever, until thou art again turned to the same earth, when first I made thee. C.W. 70. This is a late form of *erna*. qd. v.

ARROW, s. m. Legs. A mut. of *garrow*, pl. of *gar*, qd. v. *Josep dhe Gryst a cwnnas y arrow, hay dhefrech whék, yn vanner del yn whas, hag a's ystynnas par dék*, Joseph to Christ disposed of his legs, and arms sweet, in the manner as they used, and extended them very fairly. M.C. 232.

ARSE, v. a. He had commanded. An abbreviated form of *archsé*, 3 pers. s. pluperf. of *archa*, qd. v. *War lyrch Christ enef dhe ry púb onan ol dhe gelé, Jovan y vam a sensy Marya, Christ dd arsé*, after that Christ his soul yielded every one to one another, John for his mother accounted Mary, as Christ had commanded. M.C. 199.

ARTE, adv. Once more, again. *Te a gi sevell arté*, thou mayest rise again. M.C. 22. *Christ a wovynnys arté orth an Edhewon woky*, Christ asked again of the churlish Jews. M.C. 69. *Ila'n bewnans pan yn kylly, dhe'n dór ty a dreyl arté*, and the life when thou losest it, to the earth thou shalt turn again. O.M. 54. It is written as often *arta*. *Ena Christ a's gasas, hag éth arta dhe besy*, there Christ left them, and went again to pray. M.C. 56. *Cayphas arta a geways, yn hanow Dew te lavar*, Caiaphas again said, in the name of God do thou speak. M.C. 93. W. *etto, etwa*.

ARTII, adj. High, lofty. The same word as *ard*, qd. v.

ARTHELATH, s. m. Lordship. *A'n tressa degree a wolas, me a wra try order moy; Arthelath, order púr vrás deuch a-rág omma dhe vee*, of the third degree below I will make three orders more, Lordship, an order very great, come forth here to me. C.W. 6. If not a corruption of W. *arlwydhiaeth*, it may be connected with W. *ardhelwad* an averment, or *ardhyled* incumbency. Cf. also W. *ardalaeth*, a marquisate.

ARUROU, adv. Now and then, sometimes. *Llwyd*, 72. Compounded of *ar* on, and *urow*, pl. of *úr* an hour.

ARV, s. f. A weapon, dart. Pl. *arvow*, arms, armour. *Jesus a gewsys arté, why a dhêth dhym yn arvow, gans boelers ha cledhyow*, Jesus said again, you came to me in arms, with bucklers and swords. M.C. 74. *An princis esa yn pow gans Judas a dhanvonas tûs ven gweskis yn arvow*, the princes that were in the country with Judas sent trusty men, clad in armour. M.C. 64. *Why re dhueth dhym gans arvow, gans fustow ha cledhydhyow, ye have come to me with arms, with staves and swords. P.C. 1171. *Arvow lour dhynny yma, ha gwesyon stout yn torma*, arms enough to us there are, and stout fellows at this time. P.C. 614. W. *arv*, pl. *arvau*, †*arm*. Arm. *armel*. Ir. *arm, armail*. Gael. *arm*. à Lat. *arma*.

ARVETH, v. a. To plau, design, to plot against. *Arludh, ny a dhy wharré, rak ny yllyn yn nêp tre trygé dres nôs, del ûs an Yedhewon whêth pûp ûr worth agan arveth hag ow koddros*, Lord, we will go to it directly, for we cannot in any town dwell over night, as the Jews are still always plotting against us, and annoying us. R.D. 2497. W. *arvaethu*.

ARVEZ, adj. Ripe, mellow. *Llwyd*. W. *adhvrd*. Ir. *abaidh*. Gael. *abiuch*. Manx. *appee*. Gr. ώραιος.

ARVIS, adj. Early, in the morning. *Llwyd*, 87.

AS, pron. poss. Your. An abbreviated form of *agas*. *Rag as lafur why a's bedh Behethlan ha Bosaneth*, for your labour ye shall have Bohellan and Bosaneth. O.M. 2766. *Az*, is similary used in Armoric. *Rêd eo rei kelen d'az mipien*, it is necessary to give instruction to thy children.

AS, pron. pers. Him, her, it, you, them. This is compounded of the auxiliary particle *a*, and *'s*, which is used when the personal pronoun is the object of a verb, in which case it precedes it. The *s* denotes three different persons. *Ila'n wolok a's kemeras mar dyn may clamderas hy arté*, and the sight took her so sharp that she fainted again. M.C. 171. *My a's henow Vyrago*, I name her Virago. O.M. 114. *An Tâs Dew gorthvys re bo, a's ordnys dhym rag ow li's*, the Father God be worshipped who has appointed her to me for my advantage. O.M. 116. *My a's dyllo ahanan*, I will send it from us. O.M. 1101. *My a's gweres pup huny, mar mynnyuch perfyth cresy*, I will cure you, every one, if you will believe perfectly. O.M. 207. *Mar a's ladtre dheworto*, if he steal it from him. O.M. 2232. *Rag mar a's gwel, ef a wra môs dhe cudhé*, for if he sees you, he will go to hide. P.C. 1003. *An try sprus yn y anow my a's gor hep falladow*, the three grains in his mouth I will place without fail. O.M. 870. *Pyro ytho a's hembronk dhy*, who then will lead them to it. O.M. 1874. *As for agas* is also in frequent use with the verb substantive to denote possession. *Mar ny fystyn pûp huny why a's bydh drôg vommennow*, unless every one hastens, ye shall have bad blows. O.M. 2324. *An tekter a's bedheuch why*, the enjoyment you will have. P.C. 33. *Pahan cheyson a's bues why erbyn Jhesu*, what accusation have ye against Jesus. P.C. 1971. *Kên dhe olé why a's bydh*, cause to weep ye shall have. P.C. 2644. *Why a's bydh ages uncow*, ye shall have your death. R.D. 612. *As* was formerly used in Welsh in the same manner, as †*Gwedi as caffo ef en llegredic*, when he shall have found her polluted. *Welsh Laws*. †*Yr nas gwelsei eiryoet*, although he had never seen her. *Mabinogion*,

ij. 277. †*Ti a allut dywedut pei as mynhut*, thou couldst have said, if thou hadst wished it. j. 249.

AS, comp. pron. (If-it.) *Arludh, lemmyn a's dysken, dyragouch nôth y fyen*, Lord, now if I take it off, before you naked I should be. R.D. 1941. In this case *as* is compounded of *a* if, and *'s*, it.

AS, a. He will leave. A mutation of *gás*, 3 pers. s. fut. of *gasé*, qd. v. *War paradys my a'th ás*, over paradise I leave thee. O.M. 65. *Râg sythyn wosé hemma dew ugens dydh my a ás glaw dhe godhé awartha*, for a week after this, forty days I will allow rain to fall from above. O.M. 1027. *Me a adhyow dhum tâs, yn confort dhyuch my a ás an Spyrys Sans*, I go to the right of my Father, in comfort to you I will leave the Holy Ghost. R.D. 2371.

ASAS, v. a. He left. A mutation of *gasas*, pret. of *gasé*, qd. v. *Nagonan cf ny asas hep uré a'y esely*, not one he left, without perfuming of his limbs. M.C. 235.

ASCALL, s. m. A wing. Pl. *asgelli, escelly*. *Rum fay, lemmyn a'n caffen, er an ascal y'n tovlsem yn ercys an tân*, by my faith, now if I caught him, by the wing I would cast him into the midst of the fire. R.D. 290. ‡ *Kenefra edhau geu ascall worlêr e kenda*, every bird with a wing after its kind. M.C. 94. W. *asgell*, pl. *esgyll*. Arm. *ascal*, pl. *escel*, aud *ascellou*. In the three British languages *asgell* means a *wing*, but *Pryce* also gives it the meaning of *armpit*, (see *cesal*,) which alone is held by the Erse dialects, as Ir. *asgal*. Gael. *asgall*. Lat. *axilla*. Gr. μ-ασχαλ-η, Fr. *aisselle*. Germ. *achsel*. A bat was called in Cornish *asgelli grohen*, lit. wings of skin, so also in Arm. *askel-grochen*, and the bat is now called in Devonshire *a leather-wing*. So also in Irish, *ialtog leathair*.

ASCALLEN, s. f. A thistle. Pl. *ascall*. *Llwyd*, 46. Cornish Vocabulary, *askellen* cardus. W. *ysgallen*, pl. *ysgall*. Arm. *ascolen*, pl. *ascol*. Dr. Owen Pughe derives this word from W. *call*, that which is knotty, or of irregular growth, whence *callavedyr*, rough stalks of plants; *called*, stalks of thistles. Legonidec erroneously derives *ascol*, from *as*, for *axen*, an ass, and *caol* cabbage, or nerb in general.

ASCEN, v. a. To ascend, to go up. *A Jhesu, mychtern a nêf, ty re glewas agan lêf yr ascen dhys*, O Jesus, king of heaven, thou hast heard our voice ascending to thee. R.D. 175. This is borrowed from the Latin *ascendo*. So also W. *esgyn*. Ir. *ascnaim, easgnaim*. Gael. *ascnadh*.

ASCOR, s. f. Offspring. *Pryce's Voc*. W. *cegor*.

ASCORN, s. m. A bone. Pl. *cscarn, yscurn*, qd. v. *A dâs, ty re dhrôs dhymmo ascorn am kyk, ha corf, o par may fo ow howethes*, O Father thou hast brought to me bone of my flesh and body, it was meet that she should be my companion. O.M. 112. *Pan fue purpur war skuych kychys dhe vês gan dyw dhorn, worto y glynes hardlych ran an kyc bys yn ascorn*, when the purple was on a sudden snatched away with hands, to it stuck closely a piece of the flesh even to the bone. R.D. 2598. *Ascorn an hein*, the backbone. *Llwyd*, 53. W. *asgwrn*, †*ascurn*, pl. *esgyrn*. Arm. *askourn*, and *askorn*, pl. *eskêrn*. Sansc. *asthi*.

ASE, v. a. To leave. A mutation of *gasé*, qd. v. *Bythquyth re bue ûs geneuch war pask my dhe nsé dheuch un prysner, ha'y dhelyffre*, there has always been a custom with you, on the passover, that I should leave to you a prisoner, and liberate him. P.C. 2035.

ASEDH, s. f. A seat, a habitation. *Golyouch ha pesouch ow thås, may hallouch môs dh'y asedh; ha na vedhouch temptyys dygnas gans gow ha gans schereweneth,* watch ye and pray my Father, that ye may go to his habitation; be not tempted to aggrieve with a lie and wickedness. M.C. 52. (The verbal forms are *csedhé*, and *ysedhé*, qd. v. W. *eistedh*, †*estid*, sedile. Oxf. Gloss.)

ASEDHVA, s. f. A sitting place, a seat. *Own a gachyas an Justis pan glewas cows yn della, råg hena a dhesympys y trylyas dh'y asedhva,* fear seized the justice when he heard a speech of that sort, therefore he turned immediately to his seat. M.C. 143. Compounded of *asedh* a seat, and *ma* a place. W. *eistedhva*.

ASELY, s. m. Limbs. This is the plural form of *asel*, which is written in the Cornish Vocabulary *esel*, qd. v. *Corff Jesus hay aswly y dhe denna mar velen, neb a wynné a ylly nevera oll y yseren,* the body of Jesus, and his limbs they drew so brutally, who wished might count all his bones. M.C. 183.

ASEN, s. f. A rib. Pl. *asow*. It is written *asen* in the Cornish Vocabulary, and by *Lhwyd* and *Keigwyn*, as vulgarly pronounced in their days, *asan*. *Adam, cúsk dha ge lemyn, ahanas tenaf asan, me a vyn a'th tenewan,* Adam sleep thou now, from thee I will draw a rib, I will from thy side. C.W. 30. *Dha henna yma gureiety benyn, yw henwys Eva, gwryes ay asan y fe hy,* to him there is a wife, a woman, is named Eve, fashioned from his rib was she. C.W. 34. *Yn corf Jesus caradow en gew lym a bechyé, pur ewn yn dan an asow, dre an golon may'th csé,* into the body of Jesus beloved the sharp spear he thrust very right under the ribs, through the heart that it went. M.C. 218. *Scon a onan a'th asow my a wra dhyso parow,* forthwith with one of thy ribs, I will make to thee an equal. O.M. 99. W. *asen*, pl. *asenau*, and *asau*. Ir. *asna*. Gael. *aisinn*, *aisne*. Manx. *asney*.

ASEN, s. m. An ass. *Asen guill*, a wild ass. Cornish Vocabulary, *onager*. *Ens Dew a'm dyscyblyon dhe'n castel ûs a ragon, ena why a gýf asen hag ebel yn un golmen,* let two of my disciples go to the village which is before us, there ye will find an ass and foal in a halter. P.C. 176. *My a genes yn lowen hag a dhoro an asen genen, ham ebel keffrys,* I will go with thee gladly, and bring the ass with us, and the foal likewise. P.C. 192. *Oût an asen omma,* behold the ass here. P.C. 200. W. *asyn*, †*assen*, m; *asen*, f. Arm. *azen*. Ir. *asal*. Gael. *asal*. Manx. *essyl*. Anglo-Sax. *asal*. Germ. *esel*. Belg. *esel*. Dan. *aesel*. Croat. *ossal*. Dal. *oszal*. Pol. *osiel*. Boh. *ossel*, *wossel*. Lus. *woscl*. Goth. *asilus*. O. H. G. *esil*. Lith. *asilas*. Gr. ὄνος for ὄσνος. Lat. *asinus*. It. *asino*. Sp. *asno*. Fr. †*asne*.

ASENS, v. subs. They are. A reduplicate form of *ens*. 3 pers. pl. pres. of *bôd*.

ASGORNEC, adj. Bony. *Llwyd*, 110. From *ascorn*, or *asgorn* a bone. W. *asgyrnog*. Arm. *ascournee*.

ASO, v. subs. Ye are. An abbreviated form of *asouch*, a reduplicate form of *ouch*, 2 pers. pl. pres. of *bôs*. *A Dhu aso why bybin, ow ladhé gwyryon hep kén,* O God ye are wretches, killing the innocent without cause. P.C. 2624. *A anfesugyon, cuch, abercedh, lemmyn scon, a Dhew aso why gocky,* O hypocrites, go in now immediately, O God, ye are fools. R.D. 87.

ASPER, adj. Bold. *Ty inwedh my a'd pŷs may fy asper, avel marrek fyn yrcys,* thou also, I pray thee to be bold, like a horseman well armed. O.M. 2203.

ASPYE, v. a. To spy, look out, watch, examine. Imp. *aspy*, look thou; *aspyouch*, look ye. *Hag yn nôs oll aspyé, ha gwythé tam na guskens,* and by night all to look out, and guard that they slept not a jot. M.C. 241. *Aspy yn ta pûp echen,* examine well every particular. O.M. 747. *Hy a wra aspyé mars ûs dôr sêch yn nêp pow,* she will look if there be dry land in any country. O.M. 1115. *Ha why aspyeuch yn ow cossow pren dhe gýst,* and do ye seek in my forests a tree for a beam. O.M. 2558. *Ens pûp dhe tré hag aspyouch yn pup le mar cews dén výth er ow fyn,* let all go to the town, and see ye in every place if any man speak against me. R.D. 1918. *Cowyth, growedh an ngl tu hag aspy ahas, ha glu,* comrade, lie on one side, and look out continually and listen. O.M. 2062. W. *yspio*. Arm. *spia*. Ir. †*spioth*. Gael. *spioth*. Manx. *speeik*. Sans. *spasa*, a spy; from *pas*, to spy.

ASSAF, v. a. I will leave. A mutation of *gassaf*, 1 pers. s. fut. of *gasé*, qd. v. *Popel Ysral ny assaf nas gorren y dhy whýl créf,* the people of Israel I will not allow that I put them not to hard work. O.M. 1489.

ASSE, v. a. He may leave. A mutation of *gassé*, 3 pers. s. subj. of *gasé*. *Jhesu assé yllyn ny lemmyn kymeras mûr joy,* may Jesus permit that we may now receive great joy. R.D. 1201.

ASSEVYE, v. subs. It would be. A reduplicate form of *vye*. *Ow arludh kêr caradow, mychtern ôs war ol an býs, assevyé plygadow genef gruthyl bôdh dhe vrýs,* my dear beloved Lord, king thou art over all the world, it would be a pleasure to me, to do the will of thy mind. O.M. 2115.

ASSO, adv. Then, though. *Arludh, assyw warthusek, pan dhueth dh'agan myras, ha leverel dhynny crês, asso fast ytho dyges agon daras,* Lord it is wonderful, when thou, comest to look at us, and to speak peace to us, though fast our door was shut. R.D. 1181.

ASSO, v. subs. He was. A reduplicate form of *o*, 3 pers. s. pret. of *bôs*. *Asso mûr tyn ow passyon, pan êth dreyn yn empynnyon, a pûp parth dre an grogen,* very sharp was my suffering, when the thorns went into the brain, on all parts through the skull. P.C. 2556.

ASSOGE, v. subs. Thou art. A reduplicate form of *ogé*, qd. v. 2 pers. s. pres. of *bôs*. *Taw, assogé gocky,* be silent, thou art foolish. R.D. 2897. *A asogé mus ha goky,* thou art mad and foolish. R.D. 971. *Hessogé (ha assogé) goky, mar asos fûr ty a tew,* and thou art foolish, if thou art wise thou wilt be silent. R.D. 983.

ASSOMA, v. subs. I am. A reduplicate form of *oma*, 1 pers. s. pres. of *bôs*. *A Dew kêr assoma squyth, prynnyer derow ow trehy,* O dear God, I am weary, cutting oak sticks. O.M. 684, 1009.

ASSON, v. subs. We are. A reduplicate form of *ôn*, 1 pers. pl. pres. of *bôs*. *Asson whansek ôl dhe pysy, lettrys ha lêk, war Dhu mersy,* we are desirous all to pray, lettered and lay, to God for mercy. P.C. 37.

ASSOS, v. subs. Thou art. A reduplicate form of *ôs*, 2 pers. s. pres. of *bôs*. *A venen assos goky,* O woman thou art foolish. O.M. 173. *A Urry assos gentyl,* O Uriah thou art excellent. O.M. 2153. *Mar asos fûr ty a tew,* if thou art wise thou wilt be silent. R.D. 981. *Warlerch Cryst mar asos trést, lemmyn pûr lowenek fest bôs ty a ýl,* after Christ if thou art grieved, now very joyful indeed thou mayest be. R.D. 1417. W. *yduyt*.

ASSOSA, v. subs. Thou art. A reduplicate form of *osa*, 2 pers. s. pres. of *bôs*. *A Thomas assosa fôl*, O Thomas thou art foolish. R.D. 953. W. *ydwyt ti*.

ASSOTA, v. subs. Thou art. The same as *assosa*, of which it is an earlier form. *Asota gokky, an woran rc gocsys gow, na preder kên*, thou art foolish, the girl has told a lie, do not think otherwise. R.D. 1043. W. *ydwyt ti*.

ASSYW, v. subs. He is. A reduplicate form of *yw*, 3 pers. s. pres. of *bôs*. *Assyw whêk an hûn myttyn*, sweet is the morning sleep. O.M. 2074. *Mar asyw dhynny eun hŷs*, if it is to us a just length. O.M. 2563. *Du asyw emskemwnys*, black is he accursed. P.C. 3091. *Assyw varthusek*, it is wonderful. R.D. 1177. *Asyw joy gynef godhfos*, it is a joy with me to know. R.D. 2608. W. *ydyw*.

ASTEL, s. f. A board, a plank. A stage of boards in a mine is still called *astull*. W. *asdell*. Ir. *sdiall*, †*astal*. Gael. *sdiall*.

ASTEL, v. a. To attempt, endeavour, begin. *An mychtcrn a worhemmyn may fôns y ganso myttyn, omma dhe wûl an temple a rûk y dâs dhe-astel*, the king commands that they be with him in the morning, here to build the temple which his father attempted. O.M. 2426. *Dûn alemma cowethé, y weles me a garsé owth astel ymdhrehevel*, let us go hence comrades, I should like to see him endeavouring to raise himself. R.D. 395. W. *ystelio*.

ASUGY, v. subs. He is. A reduplicate form of *ugy*, qd v. *Rak mar asugy yn wlâs, me a vyn môs dhe vyras ow honan*, for if he is in the country, I will go to see myself. R.D. 1368. *Mar asugy yn bys-na pûr wŷr dhe'n mernans ef â*, if he is in this world, very truly to death he shall go. R.D. 1758.

ASWON, v. a. To know, recognize, be acquainted with. Pretor. *aswonys*. *Yn pûr wŷr Dew a aswon volungeth ol dhe colon*, very truly God knows all the wish of thy heart. C.M. 1375. *A pŷth yw an keth Dew-na, y aswon ny wrâf*, what is that same God, I will not acknowledge him. O.M. 1488. *Pedyr arta a gowsas bytheueth me nyn aswonys*, Peter again said, I never knew him. M.C. 84. *Kettel tersys an bara, aswonys Cryst a gara*, as thou breakest the bread, I knew Christ whom I loved, R.D. 1319. *Rag ganso y ma mur a'y tus dhodho haval na aswonyn an profus*, for with him there are many of his people like to him so that we cannot know the prophet. P.C. 970. W. *adwaen*, †*atwen*. Arm. †*ezneo*. Ir. *aithnim* †*adciam*. Gael. *aithnich*. Manx. *enncy*. Sans. *âtman*, the soul.

ASWONVOS, v. a. To know, recognize, be acquainted with. *Me a ra dhe Christ amé may hallouch y aswonvos;* I will kiss Christ that you may know him. M.C. 63. *Lavar cowyth del os, fatel yllyn aswonvos en harlot yn mysk y tus*, say good fellow as thou art, how we may know the knave among his people. P.C. 966. *Nas ervys na nyn aswonfys yn fas*, I have not served nor have I known him indeed. P.C. 1412. *Why a wra y aswonvos*, ye will acknowledge it. P.C. 1495. *A alsesto y aswonfos*, couldst thou know him? R.D. 862. This is compounded of *aswon*, and *bôs*. W. *adnabod*, †*amgnaubot*, in Oxf. Gloss. Arm. *anaout*. Sansc. *anabhûti*.

ATAL, s. m. Refuse, waste. *Adam, a ôl dhe drevas an degves ran dhymmo gâs whêth in atal dhe kesky*, Adam, of all thy tillage leave the tenth part to me, still to remain waste. O.M.427. W. *adhail*, refuse. Vid. Davies's Welsh Dictionary. 1632.) By this name, vulgo, *attle*, the tinners call the deads or castaways, raised out of the mines. *Atal Sarazin*, the offcasts of the Saracens, old works supposed to have been wrought by them. (Keigwyn, quoted by Pryce, in his Cornish-English Vocabulary.)

ATH, com. pron. *(a* aux. and *ty*, thine.) *A Dâs Dew Arludh huhel, my a'th wordh gans ôl ow nel*, O Father God, high Lord, I worship thee with all my strength. O.M. 510. *My a'th wheres orth y dhôn*, I will help thee to bring him. O.M. 893. *Yn hanow Dew, ty môr glân, me a'th wŷsk gans ow gwelan*, in the name of God, thou fair sea, I strike thee with my rod. O.M. 1676. *Dheth bobil, ha'n epscobow kekuffrys, a'th drôs bŷs dhymmo omma*, thy people, and the bishops also, have brought thee even to me here. P.C. 2006. *A'd* is similarly used in Cornish; and *a'th* in Welsh, as *mi a'th welais*, I saw thee. In Arm. *az*, as *me az gwel*, I see thee.

ATH, comp. pron. *(a* prep. and *ty* thine.) Of thy, from thy. *Scon a onan a'th asow my a wra dhyso parow*, forthwith, from one of thy ribs, I will make to thee an equal. O.M. 99. *Noe my a worhemmyn dhys, ke yn mês a'th gorhel scon*, Noah I command thee, go out of thy ark immediately. O.M. 1158. *Er-dhe-byn eousaf cowal, marth a'm bues a'th lavarow*, I speak against thee entirely; wonder is to me of thy words. P.C. 2392. *My ny wodhyen a'th vernans, na vŷth moy a'th dhaserchyans, pan y'th whylsyn devethys*, I knew not of thy death, nor ever of thy resurrection, when I saw thee come. R.D. 2545. W. *o'th*, as *un o'th asau*, one of thy ribs.

ATH, pron. adj. Thy, thine. *O me, dha vôs ledhys en ath dowlé ena lemyn*, O me, to be killed in thy hands here now. C.W. 120. W. *yth*, used after vowels, as *bûm gyda 'th dâd*, I have been with thy father.

ATHYRAGOF, prep. pron. Before me. See *adhyragof*.

ATTAMYE, v. a. To redeem. *Ha war an pren fruit degis may fe, dhagan sawyé, may têth fruit may sên kellys râg Adam dhe attamyé*, and on the tree a fruit borne that he might be, to save us, that he became a fruit where we were lost for Adam to redeem. M.C. 153. The first part *ad* is the Cornish particle equivalent to *re*, and *tamye* seems formed from *deem*, in *redeem*.

ATTEBRES, a compound of *a*, if, and *tebres*, thou atest. *Attebres ty ha'th worty a'n wedhen ha'y avalow y fyeuch yn surredy yn ûrna avel dewow*, if thou atest, thou and thy husband, of the tree and its fruits, ye would be of a surety, in that hour like Gods. O.M. 175.

ATTOCK, s. m. A shock, or sheaf of corn. Pryce. Ir. *aday*. Gael. *adag*.

ATTOMA, adv. See here, behold. Compounded of *att* for *atte*, behold, and *omma* here. *Attoma hagar vyadge, may hallaf kyny ellas*, lo here is a foul voyage, that I may sing alas. C.W. 66. *Attoma tayr spruzan dryes mês a Baradis dhe why*, behold here three kernels brought out of Paradise for you. C.W. 140. It is also written *attomma*. *Adam, attomma dyllas, hâg Eva, dh'ages quetha*, Adam, here are clothes, and Eve, to cover you. C.W.72. *Meyr, attoma tair spruzan, a dheth mês an aval-ma*, see here are three kernels (that) came out of this apple. C.W. 134.

AUCH, adv. Above, over, on high. *Colom whêk, glâs hy lagas, ke nŷg a-uch lues vow*, sweet blue-eyed dove, go

AVAS 15 AVY

fly over much country. O.M. 1136. Compounded of *a* on and *uch* high.

AULTRA, s. m. A godfather. A late form of *altrou*, qd. v.

AULTRUAN, s.f. A godmother. A late form of *altruan*, qd.v.

AUR, s. m. Gold. More frequently written *our*, qd. v. W. *aur*.

AV, v. n. I will go. 1 pers. s. fut. of *môs*. Though this form is given by Lhuyd, 247, it is always written in the Ordinalia *af*; it was pronounced probably as in W. *av*.

AVA, v. a. To forgive. A mutation of *gava*, qd. v. *Moy ew ow felusow es tell ew dha mercy, Dew, dhym ava*, more are my sins than so is thy mercy, God, to forgive me. C.W. 86.

AVAIN, s. m. An image. *Imago vel agalma*, Cornish Vocabulary, where only it is found. It is regularly formed from the Lat. *imagine*, by the mutation of *m* into *v*, and *g* into *gh*, which is mute, and disappears. Ir. *imhaigh*. Gael. *iomhaigh*.

AVAL, s. m. An apple. It also signifies all manner of tree fruit of a similar kind, as *pomum* was used by the Romans. *Aval saban*, a pine cone. Pl. *avalow*. *An ioul dhe Adam kewsis a'n aval te kemer tam*, the devil to Adam said, of the apple take thou a bit. M.C. 6. *Honna yw ôl dhe vlamye, a dorras an aval têk*, she is all to blame, who plucked the fair apple. O.M. 267. *Kemmer tyyr sprús a'n aval, a dybrys Adam dhe dâs*, take three kernels of the apple which Adam thy father ate. O.M. 823. *Pan dorrasa an aval, an arludh a fue scrrys*, when he had plucked the apple, the Lord was angry. O.M. 879. *Attebres ty ha'th worty a'n wedhen ha'y avalow*, if thou didst eat, thou and thy husband, of the tree and its fruits. O.M. 176. W. *aval*. Arm. *aval*. Ir. *abhall*, *ubhall*. Gael. *abhal*, *ubhal*. Manx. *ooyl*. Lat. *malum*. O. Germ. *effel*. M. Germ. *apfel*. Lith. *apfal*. Serv. *iablo*. Styria and Corinthia, *iablan*. Bohem. *gablon*. Isl. *eple*. Runic *eple*. Little Tartary *apel*.

AVALLEN, s. f. An apple tree. Cornish Vocabulary, *malus*. *Nans avallen*, the valley of appletrees: *nomen loci*. W. *avallen* †*aballen*. Arm. *avalen*. Cf. nom. loci in Gaul, *Aballone*.

AVAN, adv. Up, above, on high. Compounded of *a* on, and *ban* high. *Aga hymwyn y a vŷdh an houl ha'n lôr ha'n steryan, my a set ahuch an gwedh yn creys an ebron avan*, their names shall be the sun, and the moon, and the stars; I place them over the trees in the midst of the sky above. O.M. 38. *An Tás Dew, Arludh avan, rêm gorrê dhe gosoleth*, the Father God, Lord above, may he put me to rest. O.M. 857. Written also less correctly *aban*.

AVAR, adv. Early. *Yn kêth dŷdh-na, par avar, ha'n houl nowydh drehevys, Maré a dhêth dhe'n vêdh leverys*, in that very day, very early, and the sun newly risen, Mary came to the grave mentioned. M.C. 252. *Kemys drûk ûs ow codhé, ha dewedhes hag avar*, so much evil is falling both late and early. O.M. 629. *An gwary yw dywydhys, ha deuch avar avorow, my agas pŷs*, the play is ended, and come ye early tomorrow, I pray you. P.C. 3230. This is compounded of *a* in, and *bar*. W. *bore*, morning, (*yn vore*, early.) Or *mar*, Arm. *mare*, season.

AVAS, v. a. He forgave. A mutation of *gavas*, preter. of *gava*, qd. v. *Eddrec mear a'n kemeras rag an ober re wresté, Jesus dhodho n avas pan welas y edregê*, sorrow much seized him for the work he wrought, Jesus forgave him, when he saw his sorrows. M.C. 220.

AVEL, adv. Like to, similar, as. *Del ve helheys war an beys avel carow*, so was hunted on the world like a deer. M.C. 2. *Y fyeuch yn surredy yn ûr-na avel dewow*, ye would be of a surety in that hour like gods. O.M. 178. *My a'd pŷs may fy asper avel marrek fŷn yrvys*, I pray thee to be bold, like a horseman well armed. O.M. 2204. *Bŷth nyns yw ragos, dhe arludh avel ôs gy*, never is it for thee, for a lord as thou art. R.D. 1931. *Kyn fo mur pôs avel mên*, though it be so heavy as stone. R.D. 2274. *An eledh omma yw gwyn, avel an houl pan dhywhyn*, the angels here are white, like the sun when it shines.' R.D. 2533. This the is same word as W. *mal*, *val*, *vel*. Arm. *ma*, *evel*. Ir. *mar*, *amhail*, †*amal*. See also *Haval*.

AVERTU, adv. On either side. *Lavar lemyn pa'n drôk vo yn avertu a dhysquydhysta dhynny, pan wrela mar coynt fara*, tell now what evil is there on either side, which thou shewest us, when thou actest so rudely. P.C. 338.

AVES, adv. Without, out, abroad. *Raghenna fystyn ke gura gorhel a blankos playmyys; hag agy yn-ta gans pêk bedhens stanchurys*, therefore hasten, go, make a ship of planed plaoks; without and within, let it bo well staunched with pitch. O.M. 953. *Oll monas y a vynê bŷs yn Mount a Galvary, avés dhen drê ytheé menedh uchel yredy*, all would go even to the Mount of Calvary, without the town it was a mountain high indeed. M.C. 162. Compounded of *a* in, and *vês*, a mutation of *mês*, qd. v. W. *ymaes*, *i-vaes*. Arm. *e-meaz*. Ir. *a-magh*. Gael. *muigh*, *a-muigh*. Manx. *chew-mooie*.

AVLAVAR, adj. Speechless, dumb, mute. Written in Cornish Vocabulary, *aflavar*, *mutus*, *mab aflavar*, infans, a child that does not speak. ibid. Compounded of *an* neg. which changes into *av* or *af*, before *l*, and *lavar* speech. W. *avlavar*. Arm. *dilavar*. Ir. *amhlabhar*, †*amlabar*.

AVLETHYS, adj. Facetious, witty. Pryce. *Cooth yw ēv hag avlethys, pan na ylla omweras*, complaisant he is and witty, when I could not prevent him. C.W. 84. It must be connected etymologically with *aflythys*, qd. v.

AVON, s. f. A river. Written in Cornish Vocabulary *auon*, *amnis*. W. *avon*, †*amon*. Arm. *avon*. Ir. *abhan*, *amhan*. Gael. *abhuinn*, *amhainn*. Manx. *awin*. Sansc. *apnas*, liquid, from *ab* to go, or move. (W. *au*.) Lat. *amnis*. Swed. *aen*, *au*. Germ. *am*. Eng. †*afene*.

AVOROW, adv. Tomorrow. *Me a wra dhe worhemmyn, hag a warn dhe vysterdens avorow dhys moy teffens yn ketep pen*, I will do thy command, and will warn the architects, that they come to thee tomorrow, every one of them. O.M. 2417. *Ow kelwel dhe vysterdens dhys a dhe avorow pûr dyogel*, calling to thy architects that they come to thee tomorrow, very surely. O.M. 2432. *Gwetyeuch bones avorow ow conys yn crŷs an drê*, take care to be tomorrow working in the middle of the town. O.M. 2300. *Kyns avorow hanter dêdh*, before tomorrow mid-day. P.C. 722. *Ha deuch avar avorow*, and come ye early tomorrow. P.C. 3240. W. *yvory*, †*avoru*.

AVY, s. m. The liver, ill-will, spite, enmity. Cornish Vocabulary, *avi*, jecur. *Pan welas an Edhewon bôs Christ ow cuthyl mestry, ow caré edhomogyon, hag anedhé na wre vry, rag henna an vusgogyon orto a borthas avy*, when the Jews saw that Christ was doing his mastery; loving the beggars, and of them made no account, for that cause the fools against him bore malice. M.C. 26.

Ytho bedhyth mylyges, púr wýr drys ôl an bestes, a gerdho war an nôr veu, ha nefré y fýdh avey yntré dhe lynneth dhesy, ha lynneth benen púp preys, now bo thou accursed, very truly above all the beasts which walk on the face of the earth; and ever shall there be enmity between thy offspring, and the offspring of woman always. O.M. 314. W. *avu, nu.* Arm. *avu, au, eu.* Ir. *aodh, ao,* †*oa,* †*oo.* Gael. *adha, atha.* Manx. *aane.*

AWAN, s. m. A river, torrent, landflood. *Llwyd,* 22. *Ternewan an awan,* bank of a river. *ibid.* A late form of *aron,* qd. v.

AWARTHA, adv. Above. *Dhyso gy y levaraf, mars ôs mâp Dew awartha, dysempys arch ha lavar dhew cals meyn-ma bôs bara,* to thee I say, if thou be the Son of God above, forthwith command, and say to these hard stones to become bread. P.C. 60. *An meyn esa awartha hy a'n gwelas dreherys,* the stones that were above she saw them raised. M.C. 253. *(a* on, and *warthav.* W. *warthav, gwarthav,* the top or summit.)

AWATTA, interj. Behold, lo. *Awatta, ef a gowsas, agis migtern ple mevé, ol warbarth y a'n nachas, hag a yrchys y ladhé,* behold, he said, your king where he is, altogether they denied him, and charged him to kill him. M.C. 147. This is also written *awetta,* and *awettê. Heil volaneth, a wetta ny devedhys warbarth ha'n kensa galow,* hail, priest, behold us come together with the first call. P.C. 2050. *Awette vy dheuch dyvythys,* see me come to you. R.D. 1612. It is a contracted form of *a-wel-di,* dost thou see, behold thou. W. *a weli di.* Manx, †*awatta,* ho brave !

AWAYL, s. m. A tragedy. *Puppenak ma fo redys an awayl-ma tavethlys hy a vydh púr wyr neffre,* wherever may be read this tragedy, much talked of she shall be, very truly, ever. P.C. 550. *Reys yw vôs gwŷr an awayl,* used is that the tragedy be true. P.C. 924.

AWEDH, adv. In like manner, also. *Llwyd,* 249. id. qd. *yn wêdh.*—W. *un wêdh, gwêdh,* a manner, or fashion.

AWEL, s. f. A breeze, wind, weather. Written in Cornish Vocabulary *auhel,* aura: *an auhel,* procella. *Awel vâs, têg awel,* good weather, a calm; *hagar awel,* bad weather, a storm. *Llwyd,* 84, 161. *Bôs sêch ha têg an awel, dhe Dew y côth dhyn grassé,* that the weather is dry and fair, it is incumbent on us to thank God. O.M. 1147. *A dhesempys gwreuch tán da, rák yeyn fest yw an awel,* make immediately a good fire, for very cold is the weather. P.C. 1209. W. *awel.* Arm. *awel,* †*awel.* Gael. *aile.* Gr. *ἀελλα.* Lat. *æolus.*

AWEYL, adv. In the sight of, openly. *Aweyl ôl dhe'n arlythy, me a's pe yn surredy dhyso wharé,* in the sight of all the Lords I will pay it surely to thee forthwith. P.C. 1558. *Hag yn wêdh why dew ha dew a pregoth yn aweyl grew yn ol an beys,* and also you, two and two, preach openly in all the world. R.D. 2464. *Aweyl dheuch yth yskennaf a dhesempys yn púr wŷr yn ban dhe'n nef,* in your sight I shall ascend immediately, very truly, up to heaven. R.D. 2482. Arm. *a-wêl.* The radical form is *gwêl,* a view, qd. v.

AWHER, s. m. Sorrow. *Ow mam whêk ha'm kerengé, me re dhúth dhêth confortyé, nak na vy gy yn awher,* my sweet mother and my love, I am come to comfort thee, that thou be not in sorrow. R.D 474. *Na gows un gêr, navyth navyth yn awher, ny sevys nês,* do not speak a word, never never unhappily, he has not risen again. R.D. 1020. See *Wher.*

AWHESYTH, adj. Tender. *Dhe'n tâs Dew yn múr enor war y alter my a voor grugyer têk hag awhesyth,* to the Father God in great honour, upon his altar I will put a partridge fair and tender. O.M. 1203.

AWOS, adv. Because of, on account of, for, notwithstanding, for fear of. *Awos bôs clâf y dhewlé, toche vŷth gonys ef na ŷll,* because his hands are sore, he cannot work ever a stroke. M.C 158. *Awos an Tas Dew an nêf, gura y worhemmynnadow,* because of the Father God of heaven, do his commands. O.M. 480. *Ty a drŷg nefré, awos ol dhe wŷr dhegé, yn tewolgow brâs,* thou shalt dwell ever, notwithstanding all thy true tithe, in great darkness. O.M. 557. *Awos me dhe gows dhedhe,* notwithstanding that I spake to them. O.M. 1437. *Ny vynnyth dhe pobel Dew gasé crês dhyn yn nêp tu, awos tryga yn pow-ma,* thou wilt not to the people of God allow peace to us on any side, for the purpose of dwelling in this country. O.M. 1599. *Awos Dew dún ahanan,* for God's sake, let us come away. O M. 2564. *Awos own bones ledhys,* for fear of being killed. P.C. 886. This is the same word as W. *achos, o achos.*

AWOT, interj. Lo ! behold ! *Awot omma onan da ragon ordenys parys,* behold here a good one, intended for us ready. O.M. 1719. This is an abbreviated form of *awatta.*

AYR, s. m. Air, sky. Written by *Llwyd,* 41, *awyr.* Cornish Vocabulary, *auuit,* aer, (cf. W. *chwyth,* a gale, and Arm. *aezen,* a gentle breeze.) *Hag a lever y vones mâp Dew, neb a dhue dh'agan brugy yn ayr dêth brús púl huny,* and says that he is the Son of God, who will come to judge us in the sky at the judgment day, every one. P.C. 1669. *Yta an puskas, edhen yn ayr, hu bestas, kekeffrys yn tŷr ha môr,* behold the fishes, birds in air, and beasts, both in land and sea. C.W. 30. W. *awyr, (wy-r.)* Arm. *ear, er.* Ir. *aidheoir,* †*aer.* Gael. *athar.* Manx. *aer.* Gr. *ἀηρ, αιθηρ.* Lat. *aer, aether, aura.* Sansc. *aghira,* from *ag* to go.)

AYUH, adv. Above, over. *Llwyd,* 249. *Ayuh y ben,* over his head. id. qd. *auch,* qd. v.

B.

B, has the same sound in the Celtic languages as in English. It is both a radical or primary consonant, and a secondary. When radical it changes into *v,* as *bara,* bread ; *y vara,* his bread. W. *bara, ei vara.* Arm. *bara, he vara.* In common with Armoric, the Cornish also changes the sonant *b* into the surd form *p,* as *bewé* to live, *ow pewé,* living ; *be* he was, *a pe,* if he were. Arm. *breûr,* a brother, *hô preûr,* your brother; *bioch,* a cow, *pemp pioch,* five cows. This mutation does not occur in Welsh initials, but is found in other positions, as *gwypo,* he may know, from *gwybod; cyfelyb* like, *cyfelypach,* more like. The nasal mutation of *b* into *m* is only known to the Welsh, Irish, and Manx dialects ; thus, W. *bara,* bread, *vy mara,* my bread. Ir. *brón,* sorrow, *ar mrón,* our sorrow. Manx. *bea,* life, *nyn mea,* our life. (Cf. also Gael. *bean,* a woman, gen. *mna* of a woman.) In the Erse dialects the mutation is the same, for though written *bh,* it is pronounced as *v.* Thus Irish and Gaelic *brathair*, a brother, *a bhrathair*, his brother. In Manx, *v* is used as in Welsh, thus, *braar*, a brother, *e vraar*, his brother. When secondary *b* is a mutation of *p*, as *pen*, a head, *y ben*, his head. So also in Welsh, as *pen*, *ei ben*. And Armoric, as *penn*, *he benn*. Irish, *pian*, pain, *ar bian*, our pain; *peacaighe*, *muna beacaighe se*, if he does not sin. Manx, *padjer*, a prayer, *nyn badjer*, our prayer; *pian* pain, *nyn bian*, our pain.

BA, pron. adj. Which, what. A mutation of *pa*. *Llwyd*, 134. *Ba dhen*, what man? The light sound being used in asking a question.

BAAL, s. m A spade, or shovel. This word, more correctly written *bál*, is a mutation of *pál*, qd. v. *Adam, cummyns scon a fydh, hŷs dhe baal luen dhe drehy*, Adam, permission forthwith shall be, to cut full the length of thy spade. O.M. 380.

BABAN, s. m. A babe, a child. W. *baban*. This is a mutation of *maban*, diminutive of *máb*, a son; but used primarily in Cornish and Welsh, as is the case in other instances. Ir. *babun*. Gael. *bab*. Manx, *bab, baban*. Eng. *babe*.

BACHE, v. a. To deceive, lay snares. *Luen tregereth me a pŷs, del ús Yethewon pŷp prŷs omma worth agan baché*, abundant mercy I pray, as the Jews are always here laying snares for us. R.D. 1150. W. *bachu*, from *bách*, a hook.

BAD, adj. Foolish, stupid, insane. *Euch whyleuch dhymmo Pilat, godhfedheuch ma na veuch bád, lús óch a brŷs*, go seek Pilate for me, see that ye be not foolish, ye are men of account. R.D. 1774. *Whét, cerchouch dhymmo Pilat, yn y gever del fuef bád, y fúf tollys*, again bring Pilate to me, in respect of him as I was foolish, I was deceived. R.D. 1886. This word is not extant in this sense in Welsh, but is preserved in the Armoric, *bad*, stupidity.

BADNA, s. m. A drop. A late corruption of *banna*, qd. v.

BADUS, s. m. A lunatic. Cornish Vocabulary, *lunaticus*.

BAEDH, s. m. A boar, a male pig. This is written in the Cornish Vocabulary *bahet*, aper, vel vorres. W. *baedh*. This word is preserved only in Cornish and Welsh. *Houch-tourch*, (W. *hwch-twrch*,) being the term used in Armoric, and in Irish and Gaelic, *torc*. (W. *twrch*.) Sansc. *bahusú*, a sow; *varáhas*, a boar.

BAGAS, s. m. A bush, a cluster. *Bagas eithin*, a furze bush. *Pryce*. This is the same word as *bagat*, with a later termination.

BAGAT, s. m. A multitude, an assembly, council, consultation. *Llwyd*, 50. W. *bagad*. Arm. *bagat*. Gael. *bagaid*.

BAH, s. m. A hook, a hinge. Pl. *bahow. Bahow an darras*, the hinges of the door. *Llwyd*, 46. The final *h* here represents the earlier guttural *ch*, as in Welsh, *bách*. Arm. *bách*. Ir. *bacan*, †*bacc*. Gaelic, *bacan*.

BAIOL, s. m. Elecampane. Cornish Vocabulary, *enula*. Unknown to the other dialects.

BAL, s. f. A plague, or pestilence, *an val*, the plague. *Llwyd*, 119. Cornish Vocabulary, *pestis*. Welsh, *ball, y vall*, eruption, plague. (Irish, *ballach*, freckled; from *ball*, a spot. Gael. *ballach*, id.) Aug. Sax. *bealu*. Eng. †*bale*.

BAL, s. m. A spade, or shovel. *Cafes moy dhys aban rês, try heys dhe bál kemery*, since it is necessary for thee to have more, take three lengths of thy spade. O.M. 392. This is a mutation of *pál*, qd. v. A parcel of Tinworks in Cornwall is now called a *Bal*, and *Bal du*, black mine, is the name of a village.

BALAS, v. a. To dig, to delve. *Adam ké yn més a'n wlds, troha ken pow dhe vewé, ty dhe honyn dhe balas, dhe wrêk genes dhe nedhé*, Adam go out of the country, towards another land to live; thou thyself to dig, thy wife with thee to spin. O.M. 345. *Môs dhe balas my a vyn rág susten vewnans dhyn*, I will go to dig to sustain life to us. O.M. 681. *Balas* is a mutation of *palas*, qd. v.

BALLIAR, s. m. A hogshead, tun, barrel. *Llwyd*, 55. W. *baril*. Arm. *barazik*. Gael. *baraill*. Manx, *barrel*. Fr. *baril*. Eng. *barrel*.

BALY s. m. Satin. *Hedhouch cercot a baly, dhodho me a vyn y ry, rôg éf dhym dhe lafuryé*, reach a surcoat of satin, to him I will give it, for he did deceive me. P.C. 1784. A mutation of *paly*, qd. v.

BAN, s. m. That which is high, a height, mountain, summit. It is also used as an adjective. *Gans henna a'n Edhewon onan yn ban a sevys*, thereupon one of the Jews stood up. M.C. 81. *Ena pan sevys yn ban hy a gewsys del ylly*, there when she stood up she spake as she could. M.C. 166. *Ow guarak a fydh scityys yn ban yn creys an ebren*, my bow shall be set up in the midst of the sky. O.M. 1245. W. *ban*. It enters into the names of many mountains in Wales. *Banuchdeni* in Breconshire. *Tal y-van* in Glamorganshire, and Arvon. Ir. *beann*. Gael. *beann*. Manx, *beinn*. Gr. βοῦνος. Sanscrit, *pinda*. Germ. *bann*, *pinn*. Latin, *pinnæ, pinnacula*.

BAN, adv. When. A mutation of *pan*. *Ny strechyaff pell a ban nag és a wodhfé dheuch purys a's gurellé gwell*, I will not tarry long, insomuch that there is not ready for you one that knows to do them better. M.C. 158.

BAN, s. m. A drop. *Llwyd*, 154. An abbreviated form of *banna*, qd. v.

BANAL, s. m. Broom. This is a late form. In the Cornish Vocabulary it is written *banathel* genista. It enters into the names of many places in Cornwall, as *Bannel, Bunathlek, Bennathlick, Bennalack*. W. *banadyl, banal*. Arm. *banal, balan*. Gael. *bealaidh*. Fr. *balai*.

BANC, s. m. A blow. *Pryce*. This is the same word as *bynk*, qd. v.

BANCAN, s. m. A bank, a dyke, a dam. W. *banc, bonc*. Gael. *bank*. Eng. bank. It. *banca*.

BANEN, s. f. A woman, female. *Llwyd*, 95. More frequently written *benen*, qd. v.

BANER, s. m. A banner, or ensign. *My a'd pŷs dóg manerlich ow baner, del vynny bôs rewardyys*, I pray thee, carry valiantly my banner, as thou wishest to be rewarded. O.M. 2200. *Dyspleytys yw y vaner, ha kelmys worth an grows pren*, displayed is his banner, and bound to the cross tree. P.C. 3044. *Ganso crows worth y baner wharré ef a dhyspleytyas*, with him a cross on his banner soon he displayed. R.D. 527. *Ganso del fethas yw eds worth crows baner*, by him thus the cause is gained through the banner of the cross. R.D. 580. W. *baner, baniar*. Arm. *bannier*. Fr. *banniera*. It. *bandiera*. Span. *bandera*. Germ. *fahne, panier*. Dutch, *vaan, vaandel*. If a Celtic term, the root must be *ban*, high; but if foreign, cf. Goth. *fana*, cloth. Sax. *fana*. Lat. *pannus*. Ir. *fuan*, id.

BANEU, s. f. A sow. Cornish Vocabulary, *sus*. W. *banw*, m. a barrow pig, *banwes*, f. a barrow sow. Arm, *banô*, *banv.* f. Ir. *banabh, banbh.* Gaelic, *bainbh.* Manx, *bainniu*, a pig.

BANNA, s. m. A jot, the smallest portion of any thing, a drop of liquid. *Gans quêth y ben y quedhens, gwelas banna na ylly,* with a cloth his head they covered, so that he could not see a jot. M.C. 96. *Dal o, ny wely banna, ef reben dén a brŷs,* he was blind, he saw not a glimpse, he was a man of account. M.C. 217. It is written also indiscriminately *banné. Ny wylys gansé banné,* I have not seen a drop with them. P.C. 398. (This is the same idiom as the French *ne voir goutte*.) *Ny gôsk un banné,* he does not sleep a bit. P.C. 1078. *Ny clew banné,* he does not hear a bit. P.C. 2321. Arm. *banne,† bannech.* Ir. *bain.* Gael. *bainne.* Manx, *bine.*

BANNETH, s. f. A blessing. Pl. *bannethow. Ow banneth,* my blessing. *Dhe vanneth,* thy blessing. *Dhe vanneth dhym mûr a blêk, ha banneth ow mam inwêdh,* thy blessing to me is most delightful, and the blessing of my mother likewise. O.M. 455. *Ny lettys saw un lam, ow cafus bunneth ow mam, ha banneth ow thás kefrys,* I stopped only a space, getting the blessing of my mother, and the blessing of my father likewise. O.M. 471. *Ow banneth dheuchwy,* my blessing on yc. O.M. 911. *Banneth an Tás ragas bo,* the blessing of the father be upon thee. O.M. 1723. *Ow banneth dhyuch why kyfrys; ry dhym agns bannethow,* my blessing on you also; give me your blessings. O.M. 464. Written also *benneth,* and *bannath.* W. *bendith.* Arm. *bennaz, †bennoez.* Ir. *beannacht.* Gael. *beannachd.* Manx, *bannacht.* These are all derived from the Lat. *benedictio.*

BANNOLAN, s. f. A broom, a besom. *Llwyd,* 240. This is the singular form of the plural aggregate *banal.* W. *banadlen.* Arm. *banalen.*

BAR, s. m. The top or summit, a branch. *Bar an pen,* the crown of the head. *Llwyd,* 172. *Bargus,* the top of the wood, in Gwennap. *Rôsbargus,* in Gorrau. It enters into the names of several mountains in Wales, as *Brym Barlwm,* the bare-topped hill, in Glamorgan. *Mynydh Berwyn,* the white-topped mountain in Merioneth. W. *bar.* Arm. *bar.* Ir. *barr.* Gael. *barr.* Manx, *baare.*

BAR, s. m. A board. *Llwyd,* 44. An abbreviated form of *barf,* qd. v.

BARA, v. a. To bolt, or bar. *Me a bar daras an yet, na gercho alemma chet,* I will bar the door of the gate, that he may not carry a friend hence. P.C. 3049. W. *bario,* to bar, from *bar, †barr,* a bolt or bar. Arm. *barren.* Ir. *barra.* Manx, *barrey.*

BARA, s. m. Bread. *Bara can, bara gwyn,* white bread. *Bara gwaneth,* wheaten bread. *Bara haiz,* barley bread. *Bara kerh,* oaten bread. *Mars ôs mâb Du, a'n vrynma, gura bara dhys,* if thou art the son of God, of these stones make bread for thee. M.C. 11. *Arch ha lavar dhe'n cals meyn-ma, bôs bara,* command and say to these hard stones to become bread. P.C. 62. *Hep ken ys bara,* without other than bread. P.C. 65. *An barama kynereuch dheuch yn kettep pen,* this bread take to you every head. P.C. 761. *Mars euch lemyn mes a drê, nefré ny dhebraf vara,* if you go now from home, never will I eat bread. O.M. 2166. W. *bara.* Arm. *bara.* Ir. *aran, †bairgen.* Gael. *aran.* Manx, *arran.* Gr. βορά. Cf. also Heb. בר, *bara,* corn, food. Basque, *bar.*

Goth. *bari.* Old Sax. *bere.* Scotch, *bear,* barley. Isl. *burt.* Germ. *brot.* Belg. *broot.* Eng. *bread.*

BARDH, s. m. A bard, poet, player, mimic, buffoon. In Corn. Voc. written *barth,* mimus vel scurra. *Barth hirgorn,* Corn. Voc. *tubicen,* a trumpeter a player on the long horn. W. *bardh.* Arm. *barz.* Irish, *bard.* Gaelic, *bard.* Manx, *bardogh.* Gr. βάρδος. Lat. *bardus.*

BAREN, s. f. A branch, or bough of a tree. Pl. *barennow.* The root is *bar. Ha hy warbarth dyruskys, kefrys ben ha barennow,* and it was altogether without bark, both the stem and the boughs. O.M. 788. *Hŷr gans mûr a scorennow, hag yn creys hy varennow un flôch maylys gan lystcn,* tall with many boughs, and in the middle of its branches a child swathed with napkins. O.M. 838. W. *baren.*

BARF, s. f. A beard. Written in Cornish Vocabulary, *barf, barcf.* W. *barv, †baryf.* Arm. *barf, barv.* Lat. *barba.* Ir. *bearbh,* and Gael. *bearr,* to shave.

BARFUS, s. m. A cod-fish. Pl. *barfusy. Y rôf hynwyn dhe'n puskes, syllyes, lencsow, ha barfusy,* I give names to the fishes, congers, ling, and cod. O.M. 136. Another form is *barvas.* qd. v.

BARGES, s. m. A kite, or puttock. *Llwyd,* 241. Written also *bargos. Hôs, payon, colom, grugyer, bargos, bryny, ha'n er, moy dredhof a vydh hynveys,* duck, peacock, pigeon, partridge, kite, crows, and the eagle, further by me are named. O.M. 133. W. *barcud.* Arm. *barced, barged.*

BARH, prep. On the side of, on. This is another form of *barth,* qd. v. It occurs in the earliest Cornish document, the Cornish Vocabulary, as *Euiter a barh mam,* an uncle on the mother's side. *Modereb a barh mam,* aunt on the mother's side. *Modereb a barh tat,* aunt on the father's side. *Barh* was also the form in the latest Cornish, as *dix barh a ni,* come with us; *ew barh a ni,* go with us. *Llwyd,* 252.

BARLYS, s. m. Barley. ‡ *Da chardge ge a vŷdh war kerch, barlys, ha gwaneth, dha wethyl dega leal,* thy charge shall be over oats, barley, wheat, to make true tithe. C.W. 78. This seems to be a pure Welsh term, and derivable from *bara,* bread, and *llys,* a plant. Cf. also Ang. Sax. *bere.* Lat. *far.* Gr. πυρός. But the common name of barley in Welsh, is *haidh,* in Cornish *haidh.* qd. v.

BARNE, v. a. To judge. *Dhe barné.* W. *barnu.* Arm. *barna.*

BARNER, s. m. A judge. W: *barnwr.* Arm. *barner,* and *barnoar.* Ir. †*barn.* Pryce gives also the form *barnyz,* a judge. W. *barnydh.*

BARRI, v. a. To part, or divide. Another form of *barhy,* a mutation of *parhy.* qd. v.

BARTH, s. f. A side, a part. This is a mutation of *parth,* qd. v. *Yn nêf y fedhaf tregis an barth dychow gans am cdr,* in heaven I shall dwell on the right side with my father. M.O. 93. *A barth an Tás pebouch wharé,* in the name of the Father, pipe ye immediately. O.M. 2845. *Pepenag vo a'n barth wŷr,* whoever is of the true side. P.C. 2025. *Pyw a'n gwyskys an barth clédh,* who struck him on the left side. P.C. 1380. *A barth dyow dhe'n tás,* on the right side of the father. P.C. 1467. *Y ma ef a dhyow barth,* he is on the right side. R.D. 928. *Me re clewas tús ow cows mûr a barth brás,* I have heard people speaking in great part. R.D. 1232. *Bôs tra an par-na gwelys yn dhymmo en mûr a barth,* that a thing like that should be seen is to me of much value. R.D. 1725.

BARTHESEC, adj. Wonderful. *Arluth créf ha gollosek, hag yn battyl barthesek*, Lord, strong and powerful, and in battle wonderful. R.D. 100. Written also *barthesec*, an irregular mutation of *marthusck*, id. qd. *marthys*, qd. v.

BARVAS, s. m. A cod-fish. *Pen barvas*, a cod's head. This is the same word as *barfus*, and derived from *barf*, or *barv*, a beard. *Barvog*, and *barvogyn*, are names given to fish in Welsh from the same root, viz., to the finfish, and barbel.

BAS, adj. Shallow. *Bâs-dhour*, a ford. *Llwyd*, 169. Lit. shallow water, (W. *bâs-dhwr*.) W. *bâs*. Arm. *baz*. Fr. *bas*, low. It. *basso*. Sp. *baxo*. Eng. *base*.

BASCED, s. f. A basket. *Basced dorn*, a hand basket. *Llwyd*, 51. W. *basged*, *basgod*, *†bascawt*, from *basq*, plaiting of splinters, basket-work. Ir. *basceid*. Gael. *bascaid*. Manx, *baskaid*. Fr. †*bascod*. Lat. *bascauda*. *Barbara de Pictis venit bascauda Britannis.* Martial.

BASNET, s. m: Shame, disgrace. This word is thus given only in *Pryce*, probably incorrectly. It occurs for a helmet in R.D. 2581. *Yn le basnet war ow fen euryn a spern lym a glew*, instead of a helmet on my head a crown of thorns sharp and stiff.

BASSE, v. n. To fall, lower, abate. Part. *basseys*. *Gallas an glaw dhe vée gulan, ha'n dour, my a greys, basseys*, the rain is clean gone away, and the water, I believe, abated. O.M. 1098. *Nans yw an lyfow basseys; pan us gweydh ow tesché, yn més whéth dylleuch tryssé*, now the floods are abated; when the trees are drying, send outside yet a third. O.M. 1127. *Bassé* is also written *bashé*. *Ro dhodhans aga henwyn, y a dhéth gorhemmyn, saw na bashé*, give to them their names, they will come to thy command, rise, do not fall. C.W. 30. W. *basu*, from the root *bâs* shallow.

BASTARDH, s. m. A bastard. *Llwyd*, 100. W. *bastardh*. Arm. *bastard*. Ir. *basdard*. Gael. *basdard*. Fr. *bâtard*, †*bastard*. Span. and Port. *bastardo*. Dutch, *bastaard*. The Welsh alone furnishes the etymology, *bâs* low or base, and *tardh* issue.

BAT, s. m. A dormouse. *Pryce*. W. *bathawr*.

BATH, s. m. A coin, money. Cornish Vocabulary, *bat, numisma*. W. *bâth*. *Th* being a secondary letter, the original root was *bat*, and is preserved in the mediæval Latin *battare, battere, battire*. (See Du Cange.) Fr. *battre*, to beat, to coin. Cf. also Arm. *baz*, a stick. W. *pastwn* ; and Arm. *bazata*, to beat.

BATHOR, s. m. A banker, an exchanger of money, a coiner. Cornish Vocabulary, *trapezeta, vel nummularius. Guas bathor fur*, sollers. Id. *Fur* alone means *sollers*, *guas* being a servant. W. *bathwr*, derived from *bâth* a coin.

BATTYS, s. pl. Staves. *Gueytyeuch bôs tús parys gans battys ha clydhydhyow*, take care that the men be ready with staves and swords. P.C. 269. This is the plural of *bat*, borrowed from the English.

BAW, s. m. A foot. a paw. A mutation of *paw*. qd. v. *Kymercuch er an dhyw baw, ha gorreuch ef yn dôr down*, take ye (him) by the two feet, and put bim in deep ground. R.D. 2078.

BAY, s. m. A kiss. Pl. *bayow*. *Llwyd*, 110. *Bythqueth bay dhym ny ryssys, ha homma vgth ny sestyas*, never a kiss to me didst thou give, and she has never ceased. P.C. 522. *Jesus a genosys par dêk, Judas, ow ry te a vyn, dre dhe vay a reyth mar whêk dhe nêb am tormont mar dyn*, Jesus spake very mildly, Judas, thou wilt give me, by the kiss thou gavest so sweet, to those who will torment me so sharply, M.C. 66. Cf. Lat. *basium*. Fr. *baiser*.

BAYE, v. a. To kiss. *Keityl y'n geffo a'n bay*, when he finds him, he shall kiss him. P.C. 986. *Kensa bledhan byzla ha bayé*, the first year hug and kiss. *Pryce's Vocabulary*. Lat. *basio*. Fr. *baiser*.

BE, v. subs. He was. 3 pers. s. pret. of *bós*. It changes in construction to *ve, fe*, and *pe*. qd. v. *Warnedhy pren ve teulys, oll an pows pyn a'n gyffê*, on it a lot was cast, all the coat who should have it. M.C. 190. *Deg'is na ve*, was not taken. M.C. 23. *Ty a ve*, thou wast. C.W. 18. *An prennyer a ve kerhys, en grows soon dythqtis may fe*, the sticks were fetched, that the cross might he formed immediately. M.C. 153. It is also written *bue*. qd. v. W. *bu*.

BE, v. subs. He may be. 3 pers. s. subj. of *bós*. *Try hês ow fál mar a'm be*, three lengths of my spade if there should be to me. O.M. 396. *Hog a pe yn della ve nefre ne vean fethys*, and if it were so I should never be taken. M.C. 73. W. *bai*. Arm. *be*.

BE, s. m. A burden, a load. *Y ma gené un bé da, gorra hag eys kemyskys*, I have a good load, hay and corn mixed. O.M. 1057. *Bé cunys*, a load of fuel. The final guttural is here lost, having first been changed into *h*. W. *baich*. Arm. *bench*.

BEA, v. subs. He would be. 3 pers. s. subj. of *bós*. In construction it changes into *vea*. *Yn úrna mestry vgth te ny vea*, then power thou shouldst not have. M.C. 145. *Mage fúr te a vea avel Dew ûs avartha*, as wise thou wouldst be, like God that is on high. C.W. 44. *Henna vea hager dra*, that would be an ugly thing. *ibid*. *Pûr lowen me a vea*, very glad I should be. *ibid*. 186.

BEAN, v. subs. I should be. 1 pers. s. subj. of *bós*. In construction *vean*. *Ny vean fethys*, I should not be taken. M.C. 73.

BEAN, adj. Little, small. *Bêan ha brâs*, small and great. C.W. 10, 180. This is another form of *bian*, or *bihan*. See *Bechan*.

BEARN, s. m. Sorrow, regret, concern. *Me a guntell dreyn ha spern, ha glôs, dhe lesky hep bearn*, I will gather briars and thorns, and dried cowdung, to burn without regret. C.W. 80. This a later form of *bern*. qd. v.

BEASE, v. subs. He had been. 3 pers. s. preterplup. of *bós*. *Llwyd*, 245. W. *buasai*.

BEASEH, v. subs. Ye had been. 2 pers. pl. preterplup. of *bós*. *Llwyd*, 245. W. *buasech*.

BEASEN, v. subs. We had been. 1 pers. pl. preterplup. of *bós*. *Llwyd*, 245. W. *buasem*.

BEASENS, v. subs. They had been. 3 pers. pl. preterplup of *bós*. *Llwyd*, 245. W. *buasent*.

BEASES, v. subs. Thou hadst been. 2 pers. s. preterplup. of *bós*. *Llwyd*, 245. W. *buasit*.

BECH, s. m. sin. A mutation of *pêch*. qd. v. *A'n ladhas múr yw y bêch*, who killed him, great is his sin. P.C. 3162.

BECHAN, adj. Little, small. *Dhewortê un lam bechan yth êth, pery may hallé dh'y dâs*, from them a little space he went, that he might pray to his father. M.C. 53. *Nyng-yw ow faynys bechan ús lemyn war ow sensy*, my pains are not small, that are now holding me. M.C. 166. Written also *bichan, bihan, byhan, bian, byan*, and in the Cornish Vocabulary, *bochan*, parvus. W. *bychan*, †*bichan*, and in Flintshire *biwchan*, m. *bechan*. f. Arm. *bichan, bihan, bian*. The root is W. *bách*, little. Ir. *beag*, †*bec*, †*becc*, and *beagan*, †*becan*. Gael. *beag* and *beagan*. Manx, *beg* and *beggan*. Old Fr. *bechan*, and in Franche Comté, *pechon*.

BECHAS, v. a. He sinned. A mutation of *pechas*, 3 pers. s. preterite of *pechy*, qd. v. *My re bechas*, I have sinned. O.M. 1862.

BECHYE, v. a. To thrust. *Yn corf Jesus caradow an gew lym cf a bechyé*, into the body of Jesus beloved, the spear sharp he thrust. M.C. 218. This is not a Celtic word, being, I think, a mutation of *pechye*, which is the English word to *pitch*.

BEDEROW, s. m. Beads. A mutation of *pederow*, pl. of *pader*, qd. v. *Pub tedh oll neb a vynné leverel pymthek pater, a lên golon rág gordhyé pascon agan Ariudh kér; yn blydhen y a vye ha bederow kenever, hag a owleow esé yn corf Jesus worth never*, every day whoever will say fifteen paters, with faithful heart, to honour the passion of our dear Lord, in a year there would be as many beads as there were marks in the body of Jesus, according to number. M.C. 228.

BEDEWEN, s. f. A birch tree. Lluyd, 241. In the Cornish Vocabulary it is interpreted *populus*, the poplar, or aspen tree. In late Cornish, *bezo* and *bedho*. In all the Celtic languages it means the *birch*. Old Gaulish *betulla*. "Gallica hæc arbor mirabili candore atque tenuitate." Pliny, 16, 18. W. *bedw*;—*bedwen*, a single birchtree. Arm. *bezo*;—*bezven*. Ir. *beithe, bethe*. Gael. *beithe*.

BEDGETII, s. m. A face. ‡*Ha 'thera an noar heb roath, ha gwág, ha vêdh an tewider war bedgeth an downdor; ha speres Dew rig gwayath war bedgeth an dowrow*, and the earth was without form, and void, and darkness was on the face of the deep; and the spirit of God moved on the face of the waters. Keigwyn, 189. This word occurs only in late Cornish.

BEDIDHIA, v. a. To baptize. Lluyd, 13; who gives the late corrupt pronunciation as *bedzhidhia*. Another form was *bysydha*, qd. v. This is one of the few words from the ancient language preserved in Cornwall at the present day. See *Polwhele's Vocabulary*. W. *bedydhio*. Arm. *badeza*. Ir. *baisdeadh*. Gael. *baisteadh*. Manx, *bashtey*. All borrowed from the Lat. *baptizo*.

BEDIDHIANS, s. m. A baptism, christening. Lluyd, 44.

BEDNATH, s. f. A blessing. This is a late and corrupt form of *bennath*, or *banneth*, qd. v. ‡*En metten pan a why sevel, why rez cawse dha 'gus tâs, ha 'gus damma wor agus pednhowlin,—Bednath Dew, ha an bednath war a vee, me pidge dhu Dew*, in the morning when you rise, you must say to your father and your mother on your knees,—The blessing of God, and the blessing upon me, I pray to God. Pryce.

BEDH, s. m. A grave. Pl. *bedhow, bedhyow*. *Pan dethens y bŷs an bêdh, yth êth on marrek dh'y ben, hag arall dh'y dreys ynwêdh*, when they came to the grave, one soldier went to his head, and another to his feet also. M.C. 242. *Try dêdh wogé môs yn bêdh*, three days after going into the grave. P.C. 1746. *Aberth an bêdh*, within the grave. R.D 311. *Bêdh a vên*, tomb of stone. R.D. 2. *Agy dhe'n bêdh mên*, within the tomb of stone. R.D. 389. In construction it changes into *vêdh*, as *yn y vêdh*, in his grave. *Ha'n bedhow owth egery, me a's gwél, war ow ené*, and the graves opening, I see them, on my soul. P.C. 2999. W. *bêdh*. Arm. *bez*.

BEDH, v. subs. Be thou. 2 pers. s. imp. of *bôd*. Written also *bez*. Lluyd, 245. W. *bydh*, †*bedh*. Arm. *bez*.

BEDH, v. subs. He shall or will be. 3 pers. s. fut. of *bôd*. *Mar a'm bêdh*, if there will be to me. O.M. 2015. *Why a vêdh*, ye shall be. O.M. 2390. *Why a's bêdh*, ye shall have. O.M. 2766. Written also *bydh*. qd. v.

BEDHAF, v. subs. I shall or will be. 1 pers. s. fut. of *bôs*. *Rôf dhys ow thour, vedhaf dhe wour*, I give thee my tower, I will be thy husband. O.M. 2111. Written also *bydhaf*. qd. v. W. *bydhav* and *bedhav*.

BEDHAN, v. subs. I should be. 1 pers. s. subj. of *bôs*. In construction the initial *b* changes into *v*, which after *y* is again hardened into *f*. *An serpent a'n temptyas dhe wruthyl henna, hag y promyssyas dhe vee, y fedhan dhe well neffra*, the serpent tempted me to do this, and promised to me, that I should be the better for ever. C.W. 64. *Der henna me a dhowtyas, gans pêb y fedhan ledhys*, for this I doubted, by every one that I should be slain. *ibid*, 118. Other forms are *bedhon* and *bein*. Lluyd, 245. W. *bydhwn*.

BEDHE, v. subs. He would be. 3 pers. s. subj. of *bôs*. *Dysquedhyens war lyrch an bêdh bedhé mygtern yn dewedh*, a shewing after the grave he would be king at last. M.C. 236. In construction it changes into *vedhe* and *fedhe*. qd. v.

BEDHENS, v. subs. Let them be. 3 pers. pl. imp. of *bôs*. *Y lavaraf, nêf ha tyr, bedhens formyys orth bêdh ow brŷs*, I say, Heaven and Earth, let them be formed by my judgment. O.M. 8. *Bedhens kyrhys masons plenté*, let there be brought masons plenty. O.M. 2262. Written also *bedhans*. *Adam attoma dyllas, hag Eva, dh' ages quedha, fystenowch bedhans gweskes*, Adam, here are clothes, and Eve, to cover you, make haste, let them be worn. C.W. 72. *Gor sprusan yn y anow, ha'n dhew arall kekeffrys, bedhans gorrys yn y dhew fricg*, put one kernel in his mouth, and the two others likewise, let them be put in his two nostrils. *ibid*, 134. *Bedhens* is very frequently used for the 3rd. person singular, *bedhes*. *Kymer dhymmo ve kunys, gans lowan bedhens strothys, ha war dhe keyn doga cf*, take for me fuel, with a rope let it be bound, and on thy back carry it. O.M. 1297. *Yn pren crows bedhens gorrys, ha treys ha dyulef kelmys, ha gwenys dre un golon*, on the cross tree let him be put, and feet and hands bound, and pierced through the heart. P.C 2374. W. *bydhant*.† *bint*.

BEDHES, v. subs. Let him be. 3 pers. s. imp. of *bôs*. Lluyd, 245. W. *bydhed*.

BEDHON, v. subs. Let us be. 1 pers. pl. imp. of *bôs*. Lluyd, 245. It is also of the future tense. W. *bydhwn*.

BEDHOUCII, v. subs. Be ye. 2 pers. pl. imp. of *bôs*. In construction it changes into *vedhouch*, and *pethough*. *Ha bedhouch wâr colonow*, and be ye of cautious hearts. P.C. 879. *Cowetha, bedhouch parys, an dhewullow pûb onyn, e ma Adam tremenys*, companions, be ye ready, ye devils every one, Adam is dead. C.W. 146. *Na vedhouch dyscomfortys*, be ye not discomforted. M.C. 255. *Yn ûr-na, mar a pedhouch repentys, an kêth plâg a wra voydya*, in that hour, if ye will repent, this same plague

BEGEL 21 BELL

shall be made void. C.W. 170. In later Cornish the guttural *ch*, was changed into *h*. ‡ *Bedhouch wâr na bo ledhys mâb dên genn why neb pryce*, be ye ware that a son of man be not killed by you at any time. *ibid*, 182. *Bedhoh lên a hâs*, be ye full of seed. *ibid*, 191. (W. *bydheuch*.) It is also written *bedhcuch* and *bydheuch. Bedheuch why fur*, be ye careful. R.D. 2276. See *Bydheuch.*

BEDHY, v. a. To drown. Part. *bedhys. Why a wêl agy dha space, der lyvyow a dhower an brassa oll an bys a vgdh bedhys*, ye shall see within a space, by floods of the greatest water all the world shall be drowned. C.W. 168. *Ogas an norr yn cudhys der an glaw ës a wartha; te benyn, abervath dês, ow der bedhy a vynia*, the earth is near covered by the rain from above; thou woman come in, wouldst thou by it be drowned. *ibid*, 176. *Rag Dew a vyn, agen Tâs, danvon lyno a dhower, pur leal, dha vedhy an bys*, for God will, our Father, send a deluge of water, very faithfully to drown the world. *ibid*, 171. Written also *budhy*. W. *bodhi*. Arm. *beuzi*. Ir. *baidheadh*, †*bathaig*. Gael. *bath*. Manx, *baih.*

BEDHY, v. n. To bury. Part. *bedhys*. From *bedh*, a grave. *Me a vyn may foes uskys bedhys yn corf hag ena, bydh parys yn termyn-ma*, I will that thou be forthwith buried in body and soul, be thou ready this instant. C.W. 154.

BEDHYN, v. subs. We shall be. 1 pers. pl. fnt. of *bôs*. In construction *vedhyn*. qd. v.

BEDRYTH, v. subs. Thou shalt be. 2 pers. s. fut. of *bôs*. In construction *vedhyth*. *Yn lowen dhys kemer e, rag nechys by ny bedhyth*, gladly take him to thee, for thou shalt never be denied. P.C. 3130. *Hedrê vo yn dhe hervydh, fythys nefré ny vedhyth gans tebeles war an beys*, as long as it is in thy power, thou shalt never be overcome by evil men in the world. O.M. 1465. It is written equally common *bydhyth*. qd. v.

BEEN, v. subs. We should be. 1 pers. pl. subj. of *bôs*. *Yrverys ew ru'm leute sol-a-thyth dhe avonsyê an kynsé benfys a'm been*, it has been intended, on my truth, for a long time to advance thee to the first benefice we may have. O.M. 2613. In construction *feen*. qd. v. Written also *bein* and *bên.*

BEF, v. subs. I should be. 1 pers. s. subj. of *bôs*. In construction *vêf*. qd. v.

BEFER, s. m. A beaver. Cornish Vocabulary, *fiber*. This word is unknown to Welsh and Armoric, though it is supposed to have existed in ancient Gaulish, from a comparison of the name *Bibrax*, a town of the Ædui, mentioned by Cæsar, with *befer = beber, biber*. The beaver is called by the Welsh, *llostlydan*, i. e. broad-tail, *adhanc* and *avanc*; and by the Armoric Bretons, *avank*. Gael. †*leas-leathann*. Germ. *biber*. Ang. Sax. *beofor*. Eng. *beaver*. Fr. *bievre*. Scand. *bifr*. Slav. *lober*. Lith. *bebrus*. Lat. *fiber.*

BEGEL, s. m. The navel. Lluyd, 17. ‡ *Flo vye gennes en mis Merh, ni trehes e begel en mis East, E a rôs towl dho proanter Powl, mis du ken Nadelik*, a child was born in the month of March, We cut his navel in the month of August, and he gave a fall to the parson of Paul, the black month before the Nativity. Cornish Riddle, in Pryce's Vocabulary. Welsh, *bogel*, from *bog* a swelling or rising up. Arm. *begel*. Ir. *boilsgean*. Gael. *buillsgean*. Manx, *imleig*. Cf. Lat. *umbilicus.*

BEGEL, s. m. A herdsman, a shepherd. *Rag an termyn re devé may fydh an begel kyllys, ha cheehys yntre dewle, ha'n deves dhe vês fyys*, for the time has come that the shepherd will be lost, and taken between hands, and the sheep fled away. M.C. 48. Written also *bugel*. qd. v.

BEGY, v. n. To bray. W. *beichio*. Arm. *begia*. Ir. *beiceadh*. Gael. *beucaidh*. Sansc. *vach.*

BEGYAS, v. a. He ceased. A mutation of *pegyas*, preterite of *pegya*. qd. v. *Yn della hy a begyas bys hanter dydh, yrody, yn er-na Christ a vynnns leverel, Ely, Ely*, so it ceased till midday, surely, in that hour Christ would say, Eli, Eli. M.C. 201.

BEHAN, adj. Little, small. Another form of *bechan*, *h* being substituted for the guttural *ch*. Compar. *behannah*, less, which was corrupted in late Cornish to *behadnah, behatnah.* ‡ *Ha Dew wrüs dew golow bras; an brossah golow dha roulia dêdh, ha an behatnah golow dha roulia an nôr, e wrûs an sterres a weth*, and God made two great lights, the greater light to rule the day, and the lesser light to rule the night, he made the stars also. Keigwyn, 190.

BEHAS, v. a. He sinned. A mutation of *pehas*, preterite of *pché*. qd. v. *Och! tru! tru! my re behus, ha re dorras an dyfen*, Oh, woe, woe, I have sinned, and have broken the prohibition. O.M. 249.

BEHE, v. n. To sin. A mutation of *pehê*. qd. v. *Rag henna my a's temptyas dhe behê may fe ellas aga hân kepar ha my*, for that I tempted them to sin, so that "alas" may be their song like as mine. O.M. 300.

BEIN, v. subs. I would be. 1 pers. s. subj. of *bôs*. Lluyd, 245. This is a contracted form of *bedhan*. Another form is *byen*, qd. v. W. *bawn.*

BEIS, v. subs. Thou wouldst be. 2 pers. s. subj. of *bôs*. Lluyd, 245. Id. qd. v. *byes.*

BEISDER, s. f. A window. Lluyd, 12. *Der an veisder*, through the window. Lluyd, 240. Written also *besidar*, Pryce. The Cornish had also *fenester* and *prenest*, qd. v. W. *fenestyr*. Arm. *prenestr*, †*fenestr*, *fanast*. Ir. †*seinistir*. All from the Lat. *fenestra.*

BEL, adj. Fair. Pryce. *Messyger, my bel aber, dûs dhymmo ketuth an gêr, rag colenwel vôdh ow brûs*, messenger, my fair servant, come to me soon as the word, to fulfil the wish of my mind. O.M. 2271. This is not a Celtic word, but is probably formed from the French fem. *belle.*

BELENDER, s. m. A miller. From *belin*, a mill. Lluyd, 240. W. *melinydh*. Arm. *meliner, miliner*. Ir. *muilleoir*. Gael. *muilnear*. Manx, *beihllinder.*

BELER, s. m. Water-cress. Cornish Vocabulary, *carista*, vel *kerso*. W. *berwr, berw, berwy*. Arm. *beler*. Ir. *biolar*, †*birur*. Gael. *biolar, biorar*. Manx, *burley.*

BELIN, s. f. A mill. Lluyd, 92. This is a later form of *melin*, qd. v. by the substitution of *b* for its cognate *m*, of which there are frequent examples.

BELL, adj. Far, distant. A mutation of *pell*, qd. v. *Pe festé mar bell, ny gothé dhys bones hel ow mones dhe'n sacrefys*, where hast thou been so long? thou oughtest not to be slow, going to the sacrifice. O.M. 467. *Pan vo gwyskys an bugel, y fy an deves a bell, hag ol an flok a dhybarth*, when the shepherd is smitten, the sheep will flee far, and all the flock will separate. P.C. 694. So Welsh *mor bell*, 'so far; *o bell*, from far.

BELYNY, s. m. Shame, disgrace, reproach, villainy, malice, abuse. In construction *velyny*. It is also written *belynny*, and *bylynny*. *Mes mara keverys yn ta, han gwirionedh y synsys, prag om gwrysketh yn delma, nyng-yw mernas belyny*, but if I have spoken well, and the truth held fast, why dost thou strike me thus, it is not but abuse. M.C. 82. *Yn delma heb velyny orto Jesus a gowsas*, in this manner, without railing, to him Jesus spake. M.C. 80. *Ena mur a vylyny Pedyr dhe Gryst a welas*, there mue' abuse Peter to Christ saw. M.C. 83. This word may be derived either from the English *villainy*, from *villain*; Lat. *villanus*; Fr. *vilain*; or it may be a mutation of the W. *milain*, that which is of the nature of a brute, from *mil*, a brute.

BEN, s. m. A stem, or base; the trunk or butt end. *Adrô dhedhy rusken nyns esê, a'n blŷn dhe'n bên, nôth yw ol hy scorennow*, about it there was no bark, from the point to the stem, bare are all its boughs. O.M. 779. *Ha hy warbarth dyruskys, kefrys bên ha barennow*, and it (was) altogether without bark, both the stem and the boughs. O.M. 788. W. *bôn*. Arm. *bonu, bun*. Ir. *bon, bun*. Gael. *bonn*. Manx, *boyn, bun*. Sansc. *budhna*. Lat. *fundus*.

BEN, s. m. A head. A mutation of *pen*, qd. v. *Agy dhe'n yet gor dhe ben*, within the gate put thy head. O.M. 743. *War ben ow dewlyn*, upon my knees. O.M. 1196. *Brâs ha crom y ben goles*, large and rounded its lower end. O.M. 2444. *Tackeueh c a huyh y ben*, tack it above his head. P.C. 2793.

BEN, v. subs. We may be. 1 pers. pl. subj. of *bôs*. *Me a'th pŷs. Arluth a râs, a dhanfon dhynny cannas, may bên nepith answonfus fatel yw dhys*, I pray thee, Lord of grace, to send a messenger to us, that something we may be knowing how it is with thee. R.D. 789. In construction *ven, fen*, qd. v. It is also written *been, beyn, feyn*.

BENARY, adv. Continually, for ever, hourly. In construction *venary*, qd. v. *Ha'n stêr ynwedh kekeffrys, rag guyl golow benary*, and the stars too likewise, to yield light for ever. C.W. 8. *Mar gwrêth henna honorys ty a vŷdh bŷs venary*, if thou doest that, honoured thou shalt be for ever. ibid. 38. Written also *lynary*. As *boynedh*, W. *bownydh*, is compounded of *bob* every, and *dydh* a day; so *benary* must be formed from *bob*, and *ur* (W. *awr*) an hour.

BENAW, s. f. A female. Written also *benow*, qd. v.

BENC, s. f. A bench. Llwyd, 23, 145. W. *mainc*. Arm. *menk*. Gael. *being*. Manx, *beck, benk*.

BENEGES, part. Blessed. Written also indiscriminately *benegas, benyges, bynyges*, being the participle of *benigin*. *Benegas yw nêb a garé Du drís pûb tra ûs yn bŷs*, blessed is he that loves God above every thing that is in the world. M.C. 24. *Yn hanow Du yntrethow benegas yw nêb a dhe*, in the name of God among you blessed is he who comes. M.C. 30. *Beneges re bo an Tâs, a vynnas dysquedhes dhyn gwelynny a gemmys râs*, blessed be the Father, who willed to shew us rods of so much grace. O.M. 1745. *Benyges nefré re bo*, blessed ever be he. O.M. 819. *Bynygos re by pûb tŷdh*, blessed be thou every day. O.M. 831. *Benigas bêdh do hanow*, hallowed be thy name. *Pryce*.

BENEN, s. f. A woman, female. Pl. *benenes*. It is also written *bennen* and *benyn*. Cornish Vocabulary, *sponsa; benen rid, femina*, an unmarried woman, one that is at liberty. *Bennen vat*, matrona, lit. a good woman,— Scottish, *gudewife*. *Drefen ow bones benen*, though I am a woman. O.M. 181. *Dew an Tâs re sorras drewyth benen*, God the Father a wretched woman hath angered. O.M. 256. *Keffrys gorryth ha benen, flocholeth, an gwary yw dué lymmyn*, men and women likewise, children, the play is now ended. O.M. 2837. *Dredho ef prynnys bydheuch oll ow tûs gour ha benen*, through him ye are redeemed, all my people, male and female. P.C. 768. *Rag colé orth un venen, gulân ef re gollas an plâs*, for listening to a woman he has clean lost the place. O.M. 919. *Ha dhyso qy yth esê benenes lour*, and to thee there were wives enough. O.M. 2247. *Mur a dûs ha benenes a Jerusalem yn dre erbyn Cryst râg y welas y êth ha râg y wordhyé*, many men and women from Jerusalem in the town towards Christ for him to see they went, and to worship him. M.C. 29. W. *bun* and *ben, benen, benyw*. Ir. *bainion, bean, ben*, †*ban*. Gael. *bainnion, bean*. Manx, *ben, y ven*. Gr. βάνα, γυνή. Lat. *venus*. Sansc. *vanitâ*. The Armoric term is *gwamm*,— Fr. *femme*. Lat. *femina*. Sansc. *vâmâ*.

BENES, s. f. A blessing. This is another form of *benneth*. *Benes vôs dheueh, powesouch lymmyn un cors, me agas pŷs*, a blessing be on you, rest now a while, I pray you. P.C. 2145. From this was formed in late Cornish, the term *bene-tu-gana*, fare well, fare thou well; from *benes* a blessing, *tu* for *ti*, thee, and *gan* with. *Pryce*.

BENEWES, s. m. An awl, a cobbler's awl. Llwyd, 157. W. *menawyd, benawyd*. Arm. *menaoued*. Ir. *meanadh*. Gael. *minidh*. Manx, *mennee*.

BENIGIA, v. a. To bless, to hallow. Llwyd, 44. Part. *benigas*, written also indiscriminately *beniges, benyges, bynyges*. See *beneges*. *Rak y tue dydhyow may fenygouch an tarrow nas tevé vythqueth fleles*, for the days shall come, that ye will bless the wombs that have never borne children. P.C. 3646. W. *bendigo, bendithio*. Arm. *benniga*. Ir. *beannaigh*. Gael. *beannaich*. Manx, *bannee*. All from the Lat. *benedico*.

BENNAG, adv. Soever. A mutation of *pennag*, which is also written *pynag*, qd. v. It answers to *cunque* in Latin, and as in English is joined to nouns, pronouns, and adverbs. *Pa bennag*, whatsoever. *Pa le bennag*, wheresoever: *pandra bennac*, whatever thing. *Piwa bennac*, whosoever. Llwyd, 244. W. *pynnag. pa bynnag, pa le bynnag*. Arm. *bennag, piou bennag*, whosoever.

BENNATH, s. f. A blessing. Written also *benneth*, and *banneth*. *Ow bennath y'th chy re bo*, my blessing be on thy house. P.C. 1803. *Ow benneth dhys vynytha*, my blessing to thee for ever. P.C. 2567. *Gosloweuch oll a tûs vâs, bennath Jhesu luen a râs dheueh keffrys gôr ha benen*, hear all, O good people, the blessing of Jesus, full of grace, upon you male and female also. P.C. 3218. *Dhe kekemmys na'm gwello, hag yn perfyth a'n cresso, or lên benneth me a pŷs*, to as many as shall not see me, and shall perfectly believe it, my full blessing I pray. P.C. 1556. *Ow bennath genoch re bo*, my blessing be upon you. R.D. 1579. See *Banneth*.

BENOW, s. f. A female. *A lûb eehen a kunda, gorow ha benow ynwedh, aga gora ty a wra yn dhe gorhel aberuedh*, of every sort and kind, male and female likewise, them thou shalt place in thy ark within. O.M. 990. *A pûp bêst kemmyr wharé gorow ha benow defry*, oll a'n edhyn ow nygé guet copel may kenery, of all beasts take forth—

with males and females really, of all the birds flying be careful to take a couple. O.M. 1022. *Drewhy dhym orth copploc, cattell, edhyn kekeffrys, dew ha dew, benow ha gorrow,* bring to me by couples, cattle, fowls also, two and two, female and male. C.W. 174. It is also written *benaw.* W. *benyw.* See *Benen.*

BENS, v. subs. They should be. 3 pers. pl. subj. of *bós.* A contracted form of *bedhens.* Llwyd, 245. In construction *véns. Me a'n ty dhys, renothas, kyn na véns neffre golhys, ty nys golhyth yn nép cas,* I swear it to thee, by my father, though they be never washed, thou shalt not wash them in any case. P.D. 852. W. *baent.*

BENYTHA, adv. Ever. *Na heb múr lavur defry benytha nys tevyth flóch,* nor without great labour indeed shall ever children be to her. O.M. 300. In construction it changes regularly into *venytha,* qd. v. *Moy ys Dew ny a vye, býs venytha na sorren,* greater than God we should be, nor be troubled for ever. O.M. 220.

BEPPRES, adv. Always, at all times. Compounded of *peb, every,* and *prés* time; the initial being made light when used absolutely. W. *bob-pryd.* Arm. *bepred.*

BER, s. m. A spit, lance, spear. Cornish Vocabulary *veru; kiguer,* fuscinula; a flesh-spit. ‡ *Ha pa ryg dós dhe'n geyen, cnna e welas an ost an chy, ha dén coth o c, a gwan, a trailia an bér,* and when he was come into the kitchen, there he saw the boast of the house, and an old man he was, and feeble, turning the spit. Llwyd, 252. W. *bér.* Arm. *bér.* Ir. *bior, bear, †bir.* Gael. *bior.* Manx, *bher.* Lat. *veru.* Sansc. *hvr.* Arab. *habar,* a lance. Span. *ber,* a point.

BER, adj. Short, diminutive, brief. Cornish Vocabulary *brevis.* In construction it changes into *ver,* qd. v. *Me a'th kelm fast a ver termyn,* I will bind thee fast in a short time. O.M. 1302. *Mar ny fyn dre y rasow ow gweres a termyn ver,* if he will not, through his graces, help me in a short time. R.D. 706. W. *byr,* m. *ber,* f. Arm. *berr.* Ir. *†bear, gear, †gair.* Gael. *bearr, gearr.*

BERA, adv. Within. *En bera,* within. Llwyd, 248. This is a contracted form of *barh a.*

BERANAL, s. m. Asthma, shortness of breath. Llwyd, 50. Compounded of *ber* short, and *anal* breath. W. *beranadl.* Arm. *berranal, berralan.*

BERHEN, s. m. An owner, possessor. A mutation of *perhen,* qd. v. *An harlot foul y berhen, awos kemmys drók a wrén, a'n beys ny fyn tremené,* the knave, foul his owner, notwithstanding so much harm as we do, will not pass from the world. P.C. 2112.

BERN, s. m. A heap, a rick of hay, a stack of corn. Cornish Vocabulary, *acervus.* W. *bera,* a rick; *bryn,* a hill. Arm. *bern,* a heap.

BERN, s. m. Concern, sorrow, grief, regret. *Ellas, ellas, och tru tru, yn ow colon assyw bern, pan welaf ow máp Jhesu adro dhy pen curyn spern,* alas! alas! oh! sad! sad! in my heart is sorrow, when I see my son Jesus, about his head a crown of thorns. P.C. 2932. *Lavar dhymmo vy pyw ós, rág omma awos dhe vós, genef vy ly nynsyw bern,* tell me who thou art, for because of thy being here, with me there is never concern. R.D. 264. *Gorreuch ef yn schath dhe'n môr, hy frenné býth nyns yw bern, an schath a'n dék dhe yfern,* take him in a boat to the sea, to buy it is never a matter of concern, the boat shall carry him to hell. R.D. 2234. *Me a guntell dreyn ha spern, ha glós, dha lesky heb bern,* I will gather briars and thorns, and dry cowdung, to burn without regret. C.W. 80. *Bern,* in construction *vern,* is used in Cornish and Armoric as a verb. *Ny vern tra vyth assaye,* it is not worth while to try. O.M. 2477. See *vern.* Arm. *ny vern kéd,* it is of no consequence. It may possibly be a contracted form of W. *berthyn, a berthyn.* See Llwyd, 197.

BERNA, v. a. To buy, purchase. A mutation of *perna,* qd. v. *Dew dhén Christ a dhanvonas dhe berna boys ha dewas, an kéth re-na a spedyas, ha'n soper a ve parys,* two men Christ sent to buy meat and drink, those very same did speed, and the supper was ready. M.C. 42.

BERNIGAN, s. f. A limpet. Llwyd, 114. This is incorrectly for *brenigen.* See *Brenuic.*

BERRI, s. m. Fatness, grossness. Cornish Vocabulary, *pinguedo.* From *bor,* fat.

BERRIC, adj. Fat, gross. *Pronter berric,* a gorbellied priest. *Pryce.*

BERTYL, s. m. Bartholomew. *A Bertyl asogé mús ha goky dres oll an dús py ytho fól,* O Bartholomew, thou art mad and stupid beyond all the men who are fools. R.D. 971.

BERTH, adv. Within. This is an abbreviated form of *aberth. An fér a fue dallethys dre tús vás berth an tempel,* the market was begun by good men within the temple. P.C. 2410. *A Maria, del won dhe bós berth an bysma, onan a'y wós,* O Mary, as I know thee to be within this world, one of his blood. R.D. 800.

BERTHHUAN, s. f. A screech owl. Cornish Vocabulary, *parrax.* This may be derived from *berth,* fair; or *berth,* the feminine form of *perth,* a bush. The screech owl is generally called by the Welsh *dalluan wen,* or *aderyn y corph,* and in Armoric, *caouan, couchan.*

BERTHY, v. a. To bear, carry, take. A mutation of *perthy,* qd. v. *A dás doul na bertheuch why, wharé my a vyn mones,* O father, have no fear, forthwith I will go. O.M. 729. *My a'n musur lour yn ta, na bertheuch own a henna,* I will measure it well enough, do not have fear of that. O.M. 2508. *Yn bys-ma rág dhe wreans, ty a berth gossythyans, ken na broder,* in this world for thy deed, thou shalt bear punishment, though thou art a brother. C.W. 82. *Na berth dovt y fýth gwyskes,* do not doubt that he will be struck. C.W. 12.

BES, s. m. A finger. Pl. *bessi,* and *bysias.* The Cornish Vocabulary has *bes,* and *bis,* digitus; and *bessi,* digiti. *Bés brás,* the thumb. Llwyd, 123. *Bés crés,* (Arm. *bez creis*) the middle finger. W. *bys, †bis;* pl. *bysedh.* Arm. *biz, bez;* pl. *biziad* and *†bisiai.* Old Irish, *bos,* hand. Gael. *bas,* palm of the hand.

BES, s. m. The world. *Yn médh Pilat, marth an bés, kymmys drók a wodhevyth; ha te reson výth a dres eragas-fyn, na gowsyth,* says Pilate, wonder of the world, so much evil thou endurest, and speakest no reason against them. M.C. 120. *Ha guréns an gy kymer gallus dres an puscas an môr, ha dres an edhen an elvarn, ha dres an miliow, ha dres oll an bés,* and let them have dominion over the fish of the sea, and over the fowls of the air, and over the cattle, and over all the earth. *Keigwyn,* 192. It is more frequently written *býs,* qd. v.

BES, v. sub. Thou shouldst be. 2 pers. s. subj. of *bós.* In construction *vés, fes,* and *pés,* qd. v. It is also used as the aorist. *Te a wodhyé dhe honan pe dre gen re'vés gwarnys*, thou knewest thyself what by some thou wert warned. M.C. 101.

BES, conj. But. This is a later form of *mês*. ‡ *An lavar gôth ew lavar gwir, ne vedn nevera dôs vâs a tavas re hir; bes dên heb tavas a gollas e dir*, the old saying is a true saying; never will good come from a tongue too long; but a man without a tongue lost his land. *Cornish Proverb*. Pryce.

BES, adv. Even to, though. *Hay qureydhow dh'an doer ysal, bes yn effarn ow hedhas*, and its roots to the earth below, even to hell reaching. C.W. 138. This is also written *bys*, qd. v.

BESADOW, s. m. Prayers. A mutation of *pesadow*, pl. of *pesad*. *Pan o y besadow guris, dhe'n dowdhek y leverys, coscwuch lemyn mars ew poys, powessouch*, when his prayers were ended, to the twelve he said, sleep now, if ye be heavy, rest ye. M.C. 61.

BESAW, s. m. A ring. *Besaw our*, a ring of gold. Llwyd, 242. A latter form of *bisow*, qd. v.

BESE, v. subs. Ye should be. 2 pers. pl. subj. of *bôs*. This is a later and corrupted form of *beseh, bedhech*. Llwyd, 245. So 3 pers. *besens*, for *bedhens*.

BESGA, adv. Ever, at any time. Llwyd, 176. A late corruption of *bysgweth*, qd. v.

BESGAN, s. m. A thimble, a finger stall. Llwyd, 54. W. *byswain*, comp. of *bys*, a finger, and *gwain*, a sheath. Arm. *besken*, derived by Legonidec from *bes*, a finger, and *kenn*, skin, leather. This word is still in use in Cornwall. "*Biscan*, a finger glove of leather, used by the harvest women, particularly in support of a wounded finger." *Polwhele's Vocabulary*.

BESIDAR, s. m. A window. Pryce. Another form of *beisder*, qd. v.

BESL, s. m. A muscle, shell fish. *Beslen* is also used for a single one. Llwyd, 241. This is a later form of *mesclen*, qd. v.

BEST, s. m. A beast, an animal. Pl. *bestes*. *March yw bêst hep parow dhe vâp dên rôg ymiveres*, a horse is a beast without equals for the son of man to help himself. O.M. 124. *Un sarf yn gwedhen y ma, bêst uthek hep falladow*, there is a serpent in the tree, an ugly beast without fail. O.M. 789. *A bûb echen bêst yn wlas gor genes dew annedhe*, of every sort of beast in the land, put two of them with thee. O.M. 977. *Yn pympes dydh me a vyn may fo formyys dre ow nel bestes, puskes, hag edhyn*, on the fifth day I will that be made by my power beasts, fishes, and birds. O.M. 42. *Ytho bedhyth mylyges pûr wŷr dyos oll an bestes a gerdho war nôr veis*, uow thou shalt be accursed very truly above all the beasts which walk on the earth of the world. O.M. 312. This is not a Celtic word, but like Irish, *biast*, and Gaelic *biast*. Old Fr. †*beste*, is derived from the Latin *bestia*. English *beast*. The Celtic equivalent is *mil*, which is also preserved in Cornish. See *Mil*.

BESTE, v. subs. Thou hast been. 2 pers. s. pret. of *bôs*. In constructiou *vestê*, as *te a vestê*. Llwyd, 243.

BESTYL, s. m. The gall. This is written *bistel* in the Cornish Vocabulary, and *bystel*, and *bystyl* in the Ordinalia. *Gans an Edhewon drôk dhewas a ve dythgtis, tebel lycour, eysyll bestyl kemeskis*, by the Jews bad drink was brought, wicked liquor, hyssop and gall mixed. M.C. 202. The later forms were *besl, bezl*. See *Bistel*.

BESY, v. a. To pray. A mutation of *pesy*, qd. v. *My a lever, ow broder, ny a vyn môs dhe besy*, I say, my brother, we will go to pray. O.M. 1820. *An lader a'n barth dychow a besys yn ketelma*, the thief on the right side prayed in this manner. M.C. 193. *Christ a besys yn delma yn luas le*, Christ prayed in this manner in many a place. M.C. 204.

BESYN, adv. Even to. This a late form, compounded of *bes* even to, and *yn* the. *Tenny yn ban besyn peyll*, draw it up to the knot. C.W. 112. In one MS. this is written *bys an*. *Lead ve guyke besyn dhodha*, lead me quickly to it. *ibid.* 114. *Me a wêl wedhan, ha'y thop pur uchel yn ban, besyn nêv ma ow tevy*, I see a tree, and its top very high above, even to heaven it is growing. *ibid.* 132.

BET, prep. Up to, as far as. *Bet an urma*, hitherto, thus far, to this time. Llwyd, 24. Arm. *bete, bete urema*. W. †*bet*, †*behet*, †*behit*. It is of frequent occurrence in the *Liber Landavensis*, and is a contracted form of *pe hit*, or *pa hyd*, which are the forms which occur in the Mabinogion. †*Bet nant ireilin; bet gebenni; bet rit ir main; bet tal ir brinn; behet tal ir fos; behet hirmain*; Lib. Land. *Pyhyt bynnac y bych yma*, as long as thou shalt be here. *Pahyt bynnac y kerdei velly*, as long as it proceeded so. *Hyt y bu dy glot ympedryvol byt bellaf*, as far as thy glory was extended, even to the greatest distance. Mabinogion, ij. 204. quoted by Zeuss. 655. *Bes* and *bys* are later forms of *bet*.

BETEGYNS, adv. Nevertheless. *Gans quêdh y ben y quedhens, gwelas banna na ylly, dhe Jesus Christ betegyns ow kuthyl di ôk ha belyny*, with a cloth his head they covered, see a jot he could not, to Jesus Christ nevertheless doing hurt and abuse. M.C. 96. *Y a wiskis Christ gans gwyn, avel fôl y an scornyê, hag a'n gweskas fest yn lyn, betegyns gêr ny gewsy*, they clad Christ with white; like a fool they him scorned, and struck him in sharp measure, nevertheless a word he spake not. M.C. 114. It is also written *bytegyns* and *bytygyns*.

BETH, adv. Ever, at all. Joined to a substantive it signifies *any*, as *traveth*, any thing. *Tra vêth oll a rolla lcas, ny guvaf' omma nêb tew*, any thing at all that will give enough, I shall not find here on any side. C.W. 76. With a negative it signifies *none*. *Ni or dên vêth, no inau at all knows*. †*Nag es triwath vêth dho vi*, I do not at all pity. Llwyd, 274. In the Ordinalia it is always written as in Welsh, *byth*, qd. v.

BETH, v. subs. He shall be. 3 pers. s. fut. of *bôs*. More correctly written *bêdh*, qd. v.

BEUCH, s. f. A cow. *Yth henwaf beuch, ha tarow, oll an caitel debarow aga henwyn kemerans*, I will name them cow, and bull; all the cattle feeding, their names let them take. C.W. 30. In the Cornish Vocabulary and the Ordinalia it is written *buch*, qd v. In the last age of the Cornish the guttural was softened into *h*, as *bcuh*, and finally omitted altogether. ‡ *Es leath luck gen veu*, is there milk enough with the cow; i. e. has the cow milk enough ? Pryce, 234. W. *bu, buwch*, †*bou*, †*buch*. The Welsh plural *buchod*, now in common use, is formed from the old term *buch*. Arm. *bu, buoch*, †*bioch*, †*buch*. Ir. *bo*; pl. †*bobes*. Gael. *bo*. Manx, *bua, booa*. Gr. βοῦν. Lat. *bos, vacca*.

DEUCII, v. subs. Ye should be. 2 pers. pl. subj. of *bos*. Llwyd, 245.

BEUZI, v. a. To immerge, drown. This is a later form of *bedhy*, or *budhy*, qd. v.

BEVA, v. subs. Be he. 3 pers. s. subj. of *bós*. *Púb ér te dhên gwora levoté, beva dên yonk lo dên cóth*, continually do thou loyalty to man, be he a young man or an old man. M.C. 175. *Púb ér te dhên gwra levoté, beva dên yonk bo dên cóth, orthaff mar mynnyth oolé, neffré gans an fals na sóth*, continually do thou loyalty to man, be he a young man or an old man, if thou wouldst listen to me, never flatter with the false. M.C. 175.

BEW, v. a. To possess. A mutation of *pew*, qd. v. *Noe dre dhe dhadder brás, ty o bew ow grath neffré*, Noah, for thy great goodness, thou shalt ever possess my favour. O.M. 974. *Yssé yn dhe see, a bewé dhe tás Daveth*, sit in the seat which thy father David possessed. O.M. 2392. *Lemmyn dyskudh ha lavar, pyw an pren a bew hep mar pous Jhesu an Nazaré*, now shew and say, which is the lot that shall obtain the coat of Jesus of Nazareth. P.C. 2853. *Ro dhym cusyl dysempys may bew vy crés*, give me counsel immediately, that I may obtain peace. R.D. 2224.

BEW, adj. Alive, living, quick, active. It changes in construction into *vew*, qd. v. *Oll del vynny, arluth kér, my a wra yn púp tyller hedré veyn bew yn bys-ma*, all as thou wishest, dear Lord, I will do in every place, as long as we are living in this world. P.C. 115. *Me a wra prest hep ynny hedré veyf bew yn bys-na*, I will do ever without denial, so long as I am living in this world. P.C. 1020. *Mara vedhuf bew vledhen, my a'n takyth dhyuch*, if I shall be alive a year, I will pay it to you. O.M. 2387. Written also *biu*, and *lyw*, qd. v. W. *byw*, †*biu*. Arm. *beó*. Ir. *beo,*†*biu*. Gael. *bco*. Manx, *bio*. Sansc. *báva*, existence. Gr. βίος.

BEW, s. m. Life, the living principle. *Yn pryson môs ny treynyn agan bew, kyn kentrynmyn ol agan kijc*, to go to prison we torment not our lives, though we should pierce all our flesh. R.D. 74. *An houl ny golsé y lyw, awos mâp dên dhe verwel, na corf dasserhy dhe vew*, the sun would not have lost its colour because of a son of man to die, nor a body rise again to life. R.D. 3085. Written in the Cornish Vocabulary *biu*, qd. v. W. *byw*, subs. Gr. βίος.

BEW, v. n. To live, exist. In construction it changes into *vew*, and *pew*, qd. v. It was also written *bewé* and *bewa*. *Yn bys-ma rák dry ascor ty a vew bys may fy loys*, in this world to bring offspring, thou shalt live till thou be grey. O.M. 72. *Ny a wohyth yn dhy vody sperys, may hylly bewé*, we breathe into thy body a spirit, that thou mayest live. O.M. 62. *Múr a wokyneth yw mones dhe lesky peyth a ĝl dén orto bewé*, a great folly it is to go to burn a thing which a man can live upon. O.M. 475. *Púp oll a gár bewé*, every one loves to live. R.D. 600. *Ny ĝl an corf-na bewé, na sevel yn ban arté*, that body cannot live, nor rise up again. R.D. 1121. *Oll an beys a rós dhedhé, may hallons ynno bewa*, all the world he gave to them, that they might in it live. O.M. 2832. *Ny rynnaf gnsé onan vyth-ol dhe bewé*, I will not leave any one of them to live. O.M. 1697. *Kynyver dén ús yn velds-na tra yn bỳs ow pewé*, as many men as are in the land, or thing in the world living. O.M. 1030. W. *byw*. Arm. *beva, da veva*.

BEWENS, v. n. Let them live. 3rd pers. pl. imp. of *bewé*. *Dhedhé me a worhemmyn, encressyens ha bewens pell*, to them I command, let them increase and live long. O.M. 48.

BEWNANS, s. m. Life, existence. It changes in construction into *vewnans*, qd. v. *Ha'n bewnans pan y'n kylly, dhe'n dór ty a dreyl arté*, and the life when thou losest it, to the earth thou shalt turn again. O.M. 63. *Rág hŷr lowr ew ow bewnans, kymmer dyso ow enef*, for long enough is my life, take my soul to thee. O.M. 848. *Dynythys yw ow thermyn a'm bewnans yn bys-ma*, arrived is the term of my life in this world. O.M. 1886. *Spyrys a vewnans*, the spirit of life. O.M. 1090. *An wedhan a vewnans*, the tree of life. C.W. 131. In latest Cornish it was written *bewnas*. W. *bywyd, buchedh*. Arm. *buez*. Ir. *beadhas, beatha, bioth*, †*beothu*. Gael. *beath*. Manx, *bea, biuid*. Gr. βίοτος, βιοτή. Lat. *vita*.

BEYDH, s. m. A grave. Another form of *bédh*, qd. v. *Ha mar ny wrer y wythé, y dhyskyblon a'n lader yn més an beydh*, and if it is not guarded, his disciples will steal him out of the tomb. R.D. 343.

BEYF, v. subs. I may be. 1 pers. s. subj. of *bós*. In construction *veyf* and *fyf*, qd. v.

BEYN, s. f. Pain. A mutation of *peyn*, qd. v. *Gwytheuch why y, ma na vôns remuvys dhe gen tyller, war beyn tenné ha cregy*, watch ye them, that they be not removed to another place, on pain of drawing and hanging. O.M. 2064.

BEYN, v. subs. We should be. 1 pers. pl. subj. of *bós*. *Ha saw ny gynes ymcédh, na'n beyn mar hager dhywedh no mar garow*, and save us with thee also, that we may not have so cruel an end, nor so sharp. P.C. 2895. Another form of *byen*.

BEYS, s. m. The world. *Yn penweré gurreys perfyth dhe'n beys ol golowys glân*, on the fourth be made perfect to the world all bright lights. O.M. 34. *Bŷs gorfen beys*, to the end of the world. O.M. 584. Another form of *bỳs*, qd. v.

BEYS, v. a. He will pray. Another form of *bỳs*, a mutation of *pŷs*, qd. v. *Banneth dhe vam kekyfrys nefre dhyso, my a beys*, the blessing of thy mother likewise be ever on thee, I pray. O.M. 461.

BEZO, s. m. A little hoop, a small wheel. Llwyd, 109. This is a late form of *bisow*, qd. v.

BIAIL, s. f. An axe, hatchet, bill. Pryce. *Boell* is another form, qd. v. W. *bwyell*, from *pwyo*, to smite, or strike. Arm. *bouchal*. Ir. †*biail*. Gael. †*biail*. Germ. *biel*. Eng. *bill*.

BIAN, adj. Little, small. *Dén bian*, a little man. *Marh bian*, a colt, i. e. a little horse. Llwyd, 57. This is a later form of *biohan;* the guttural *ch* being first changed into *h*, and finally omitted. See *Bechan*.

BIBAN, s. f. A pipe. A mutation of *piban*, qd. v. *as an biban*, the pipe. Llwyd, 231.

BIDN, s. m. The head. This is a late corruption of *byn*, a mutation of *pyn*, used in the formation of the preposition *war byn*, against. ‡ *Ha ryney vedn dirra bidn mor ha gwens*, and they will last against sea and wind. Pryce. ‡ *Ha gava do ny agan cabmow, pokara ny gava an gy leb es camma warbidn ny*, and forgive us our trespasses, as we forgive them that trespass against us. *ibid*.

BIDNETHEIN, s. m. A hawk. Cornish Vocabulary *accipiter*. This word should perhaps be read *bid*, *an edhyn*, i. e. *bid*, the bird. *Bid* must be connected with W. *bod*, a buzzard. Lat. *buteo*.

BIDHEN, s. m. A meadow. Llwyd, 33. This is not a Celtic word, being unknown to the Welsh and Armoric, and is formed from the English *mead*, by the change of the initial into its cognate *b*. So Gael. *miadan*.

BIDHY, v. a. To drown. Part. *bidhis*. *Lhwyd*, 250. Another form of *budhy*, qd. v.

BIDHYZI, v. a. To dip, baptize. *Pryce*. A late form of *bedidhia*, qd. v.

BIGAL, s. m. A shepherd. *Lhwyd*, 114. The same as *bugel*, qd. v.

BIGEL, s. m. The navel. The same as *begel*. qd. v.

BIHAN, adj. Little, small. *Lhwyd*, 113. A later form of *bichan*. See *bian*, and *bechan*.

BINDORN, s. m. A hall. Cornish Vocabulary, *refectorium*, where only it is found. Supposed to be corrupted in the MS. and to be read *buidorn*, from *buid* meat. See *Norris's Cornish Drama*, ij. 327.

BIS, v. subs. Let him be. 3 pers. s. imp. of *bôs*. *Lhwyd*, 245. W. *bid*. It is also used as the 3 pers. of the fut. ‡ *Bis reis dhodho*, he will be obliged, i. e. there will be need to him. *Lhwyd*, 247. In this case it is a late form of *bydh*.

BIS, s. m. A finger. This form as well as *bes*, is given in the Cornish Vocabulary, which also furnishes *bis truit*, allax, the toe; literally, the finger of the foot, as in W. *bys trocd*. Arm. *biz-troad*. For the Celtic synonyms see *Bês*.

BISGWETH, adv. Ever, continually This word, written also *bisgweth*, is a later form of *bythgweth*, qd. v. *Rag gans tu yw an michtcrueth, ha'n crêvder, ha'n worryans, rag bisgweth ha bisgweth*, for thine is the kingdom, and the power, and the glory, for ever and ever. *Pryce's Vocabulary.*

BISOU, s. f. A ring. This is the form preserved in the Cornish Vocabulary; in later Cornish it was written *besaw*. W. *byson*, from *bŷs*, a finger. Arm. *bizou*.

BISTEL, s. m. The gall. This is the form preserved in the Cornish Vocabulary, *fel*. In the Ordinalia it is generally written *bystel*, *bystyl*, and *bestel*. *Ottensé gynef purys, bystel eysyl kymyskys, wassel, mars us seches crâs*, behold them with me ready, gall and hyssop mixed, wassail, if there is great thirst. P.C. 2977. *Dywes a yrhys dedhé, dhym rosons bystyl wherow, bŷth ny fynnys y evê*, drink I asked of them, to me they gave bitter gall, never would I drink it. R.D. 2601. W. *bustyl*. Arm. *bestl*.

BIT, s. m. The world. *En bit*, Cornish Vocabulary, *mundus*, the world. *En* being the definite article. This is the old orthography of W. *bŷd*, and Cornish *bŷs*, qd. v.

BITH, adv. Ever. More generally written *byth*, qd. v., as in Welsh.

BITHGUETH, adv. Ever. *Ni wêl bithgweth*, he will never see. *Lhwyd*, 248. The same as *bythgueth*, qd. v.

BIU, s. m. Life. This the old orthography preserved in the Cornish Vocabulary, where also we have *biu en lagat*, pupilla, the pupil of the eye, lit. the life of the eye. The orthography followed in the Ordinalia is *bew*, qd. v.

BIUH, s. f. A cow. This is the late form of *buch*. ‡ *Ma'n viuh gen leauh*, the cow is in calf. *Lhwyd*, 230. ‡ *Ma hueh biuh dhodho*, he has six cows. *ibid.* 224.

BLANSE, v. a. To plant. A mutation of *plansé*, qd. v. *Môs dhe blansé my a yn dôr an dŷr gwelen-ma*, I will go to plant these three rods in the ground. O.M. 1887. *Môs dhe blansé my a vyn en gwcel yn nep plath têk hag ylyn*, I will go to plant the rods in some fair and pleasant place. O.M. 2060.

BLEC, v. n. He will please. A mutation of *plêk*, qd. v. *Dhe vanneth dhym mûr a blêk, ha banneth ow mam ynwedh*, thy blessing is most delightful to me, and the blessing of my mother likewise. O.M. 415. *Dhe whcyl yn ta dhym a blêk, dew vody dha ouch yn gwyr*, thy work delights me well, two good bodies ye are truly. O.M. 2460. *Yn ûr-na mar a gcwsys fulsury, ha na blêk genas henna ha fals, te dôk dustunny*, in that hour, if I have spoken falsehood, and that is not pleasing to thee and false, do thou bear witness. M.C. 82.

BLEC, s. m. A fold, turn, course. A mutation of *plec*, qd. v. *Ha pup ûr chatel Abel, y a sowyn mŷl blêk gwel, Abel a'n pren rag henna*, and always the cattle of Abel, they thrive a thousand times better, Abel shall pay for that. O.M. 523.

BLEDHEN, s. f. A year. In the Cornish Vocabulary, it is written *blidhen*, and in the Ordinalia *bledhen*, *bledhyn*, *blydhen*, pl. *bledhynnow*. By *Lhwyd*, it is written *bledhan*, which is the late form given by *Jordan* also, the plural being corrupted in late Cornish into *bledhydnyow*, *bledhednyow*. *May haller goves dhe wŷr ha gweles yn bledhen hŷr, py gymmys hŷs may taffô*, that it may be known truly, and seen in a year long, to how great a length it may grow. O.M. 2103. *Rây y fue kyns ŷ vôs gurys dew ugens blydhen ha whê*, for there were, before it was done, forty years and six. P.C. 351. *Y a vŷth y vody na potré bys vynary, kyn fe yn bêdh mŷl vlydhen*, they will preserve his body, that it never decays, though it be in the grave a thousand years. P.C. 3201. *Nans yw lemmyn tremenes nêp dew cans a vledhynnow*, now there are gone by some two hundred years. O.M. 657. W. *blwydh*, *blwydhyn*. Arm. *bloaz*, *blizen*, †*blizien*. Ir. *bliaghain*, †*bliadan*. Gael. *bliadna*. Manx, *blein*.

BLEDZHIAN, s. m. A flower. This form as well as *bledzhan*, given by *Lhwyd*, 240, are late corruptions of *blodon*, qd. v. W. *blodeuyn*.

BLEGADOW, s. m. Wishes. A mutation of *plegadow*, qd. v. *En Edhewon yntredhé a whelas dustunneow rag prynê Christ ha syndyé, ny gewsys dhe blegadow*, the Jews between them sought witnesses to punish Christ and keep him fast, they spake not to (their) wishes. M.C. 90.

BLEGYOW, s. m. Blossoms, flowers. This word is a corruption of a plural, answering to the Welsh *blodau*, the *g* having the same sound as in English *regent*, which is a frequent corruption of *d* in Cornish. The singular is *blodon*, which was also corrupted into *bledzhan*, *bledzhian*, = *blegyan*, or *blejyan*. *Diu-syl blegyow*, Palm Sunday, which is also called in Welsh, *Dyw sul y blodau*, Sunday of the blossoms, and in Arm. *Disul-blouniou*. *Dewsulblegyow, pan esé yn mŷsk y abestcly, y wrûg dhe re anedhê môs dhe'n drê, ha degylmy an asen, ha dry gansé*, Palm Sunday, when he was among his apostles, he caused some of them to go to the town, and to untie the ass, and bring it with them. M.C. 27.

BLEIDH, s. m. A wolf. Cornish Vocabulary, *bleit*, lupus. The same authority explains *Linx*, by *commisc bleit hahchi*, for which a more recent hand has substituted *kynmysk bleid a chi*, which is pure Welsh. It means the mixture of a wolf and dog. W. *blaidh*, †*bleid*. Arm. *bleiz*, †*bled*. Ir. †*bled*, *faol*. Gael. *faol*.

BLENYDNYOW, s. m. Years. This is a late corruption of *bledhynyow*, but there is a similar form in the Welsh *blynydhoedd*. *Bês vŷdh mar vrâs, nangew termyn tremenys a vlenydhyow moy es naw cans*, though it be so great, not is the time passed over of years more than nine hundred. C.W. 138.

BLES, s. m. Flour, meal. *Blês fin*, fine flour. *Lhwyd*, 123. This is a later form of *blot*, qd. v.

BLEW, s. m. Hair. Written in Cornish Vocabulary *bleu*. *Bleu yn pen*, capillus, hair of the head ; *bleu en lagat*, palpebræ, eye-lash. *Blew melyn*, yellow hair ; *blew glâs*, gray hairs. *Yma daggrow ow clybyé dhe dreys, råk own karengé, saw me a's vêch gans ow blew*, there are tears wetting thy feet, for true love, but I will dry them with my hair. P.C. 484. *Homma gans daggrow keffrys ré's holhas, gans y blew y fôns syhys*, this one with tears also hath washed them, with her hair they were dried. P.C. 521. *Why a'm gwêl overdevys ythoma warbarth gans blêw*, you see me overgrown that I am altogether with hair. C.W. 110. W. *blew*, †*bleu*. Arm. *bleô*. Cf. also Ir. †*clumh*. Gael. *cluimh*. Manx, *clooie*. Lat. *pluma*. W. *pluv*. Eng. *flue*, *fluff*. Sansc. *pal*, to grow. Observe in Welsh, *blew* means hair in general, but the hair of the head is called *gwallt*, which is preserved in the old Cornish *gols*, and Ir. *falt*, Gael. *follt*, Manx, *folt*. But a single hair of the head is called in Welsh *blewyn*. The long hair of the tails and manes of animals is called *rhawn*, in Welsh, and in Cornish *rên*, qd. v.

BLEWAC, adj. Hairy, full of hair, shaggy. *Lhwyd*, 120. *Blewac, coynt yw, ha hager, ny won pana vêst ylla bôs*, hairy, rough it is, and ugly, I know not what beast it is. C.W. 114. W. *blewog*. Arm. *bleouec, blevec*.

BLEWEN, s. f. A hair, a single hair. *Blew* is the plural aggregate, from which the singular *blewen* is formed, and from *blewen* again, the plural *blewennow*. (Compare Welsh *gwlân*, wool, sing. *gwlanen*, flannel, pl. *gwlaneni*.) *Del wascaf y peydrennow, may fo gôs y clewennow, ha' y corf oll kyns ys hothy*, as I strike behind, that his hairs may be bloody, and all his body, before leaving off. P.C. 2095. W. *blewyn*. Arm. *bleven*.

BLIDHEN, s. f. A year. This is the older form preserved in the Cornish Vocabulary. See *Bledhan*.

BLODON, s. m. A flower, a blossom. Cornish Vocabulary, *flos*. W. *blodon, blodyn, bloden, blawd*, and †*blot*, pl. *blodeu*, whence s. *blodeuyn*. Arm. *bleun*. Ir. *bladh, blaidhin*. Gael. *blath, blaithin*. Manx, *blaa*. N. H. Ger. *blüte*. Germ. *bluthe*. Lat. *flos*. Sansc. *phul*, to flourish.

BLODH, s. m. A year. *Me a servyas pell an beys, aban vena kyns formys, naw cans blôdh of, me a gryes, ha dêk varnegans*, I have served long the world, since I was first formed, I am nine hundred years, I believe, and thirty. C.W. 142. This form answers to the Welsh *blwydh*. Arm. *bloaz*

BLONEC, s. m. Fat, lard, grease. Cornish Vocabulary, *adeps*. W. *bloneg*. Arm. *blonec*. Ir. *blunag*, †*blonac*. Gael. *blonag*. Manx, *blennick*.

BLONOGATH, s. m. The will. *Ow blonogath yw henna ; may toccans omma pûr splan frutes, dhom bôdh rág maga*, my will is this ; that they bear here very bright fruits, to feed the appetite. C.W. 8. *Arluth, benegas reby, orth ow gwarnya yn della ; dheth vlonogath pûr dheffry rebo collewcys neffra*, Lord, blessed be thou, to warn me in this manner ; thy will very truly be fulfilled for ever. *ibid.* 96. *Gordhys rebo Dew an Tâs, dha vlonogath rebo gwrỳs*, worshipped be God the Father, thy will be done. *ibid.* 154. *Parys ôv, Arluth Brentyn, dha vlonogath lavar dhaf*, ready I am, Lord King, thy will speak to me. *ibid.* 162. This is a later form of *bolungeth*, qd. v.

BLOT, s. m. Flour, meal. Cornish Vocabulary, *farina*. This is the older form of the word, which was changed in recent times into *blês*. W. *blawd*, †*blot*. Arm. *bleud, bled*. Gael. *bleith*, to grind. Fr. *bled, blé*, corn.

BLU, s. m. A parish. A mutation of *plû*, qd. v. *H'a nyns yw ef a parth Dew, bysy vye oll an blû rag y wythé, dh'y worré aber yn bêdh*, and if he not on the side of God, hard would it be for all the parish to keep him, to lay him in the grave. R.D. 2106.

BLUTHYE, v. a. To wound. *Peder, Androw, ha Jowan; yn mêdh Christ, deuch holyouch ve, bỳs yn menedh, ha me gwan, trystys ûs worth ow bluthyé*, Peter, Andrew, and John, said Christ, come follow me, even to the mountain, and I being weak, sadness is me wounding. M.C. 53.

BLYGYE, v. a. To bend, to bow down, to pray. A mutation of *plygye*, qd. v. *Ha y grás dheuchwy re wrontjo, nefré dhe blegyé dhodho, yn dalleth hag yn dyweth*, and his grace may he grant to you, ever to bow down before him, at the beginning and at the end. O.M. 1727.

BLYN, s. m. The point. *Warnedhy yma gwedhen whel gans lues scoren ; saw nôth oll ġns hep dylyow, hag adrô dhedhy rusken nyns esé a'n blġn dhe'n bên, nôth yw oll hy scorennow*, in it there is a tree high with many boughs ; but they are all bare, without leaves, and around it, bark there was not from the top to the stem, all its boughs are bare. O.M. 779. I consider *bên* to be the same word as W. *bôn*.

BLYTHEN, s. f. A year. *Sġth cans blythen*, seven hundred years. R.D. 2494. This is to be read *blydhen*. See *Bledhen*.

BLYVEN, s. f. A feather, a pen. *An blyven-ma*, this pen. *Lhwyd*, 244. A mutation of *plyven*, qd. v.

BO, v. subs. He may be. 3 pers. s. subj. of *bôs*. In construction it changes into *vo*, and *fo*. *Amen, yn della re bo*, Amen, so be it. O.M. 462. *Banneth an Tâs r'agas bo*, the blessing of the Father be yours. O.M. 1723. *Beneges re bo an Tâs*, blessed be the Father. O.M. 1745. *Rak lowené ny 'gen bo yn le may fuen*, for joy may not be ours in the place where we have been. R.D. 168. *Ragas bo crês*, peace be to you. R.D. 1285. *Agan guryans ua'm bo meth*, let not our work be a shame to me. R.D. 1878. *Yn mêdh Pedyr, dhym na ês troys na leyf na vo golhys*, says Peter, to me omit not foot or hand, that it be not washed. M.C. 46. *Y' êth, ha Jesus gansé bỳs yn Pilat o Justis, anodho brês may rollé, dre y vrês may fo ledhys*, they went, and Jesus with them, even to Pilate who was justice, of him judgment that he might give, by his judgment that he might be killed. M.C. 98. W. *bo*.

BO, conj. Either, or. *Benegas yw nêb a garé Du dris pub tra ûs yn bỳs, hag a wodheffo yn wharé dhodho kymmys ûs ordnys, bo clevas bo peth kescar bo dre preson presonys, oll en da ha drôk kepare, dhe Jesus bodhens grassys*, blessed is he that loves God above every thing that is in the world, and beareth patiently as much as is decreed to him, be it sickness, or poverty, or by prison imprisoned, all the good and evil alike, to Jesus be thanks. M.C. 24. *Pub êr te dhên gurê lowté, bew dên yonk bo dên côth*, always to man do loyalty whether he be a young man or an old man. M.C. 175. *Me a grỳs ynno y sêf, mars yw a barth Dew a nêf, bo ken deaul yw*, I believe he will stay in it, if he be on the part of the God of heaven, or else he is a devil. R.D.

2104. This word as well as its mutation *po*, which is similarly used, is evidently an adaptation of the verb *bo*, be it; exactly the same as *soit* in French.

BOBA, s. m. A blockhead, a booby. *Nyns yw iemyn un boba, kyng-ys y vôs alemma, yn gwyn ef a fydh gwyskys*, he is not now a booby, before that he goes hence, iu white he shall be clad. P.C. 1778. *Tewel avel un bobbu a wrûk, pan fue acussys*, hold his tongue like an idiot he did, when he was accused. P.C. 2385. *Marth a'm bues a'th lavarow, dhe gewsel mar dal gans an bobba casadow*, wonder is to me of thy words, to speak so blindly with the hateful idiot. P.C. 2394. This word is borrowed from the English. The word *boba* is in common use in Wales, but with a very different meaning, and applied to elderly females, answering exactly to *gammer*, in English. It is borrowed from the child's Vocabulary, being its pronunciation of *modryb*, an aunt.

BOBYL, s. f. A people. A mutation of *pobyl*, qd. v. *Mar ny wrêth, hep falladow, mûr an bobyl a verow, ha henna dyeth vye*, if thou dost not, without fail, many of the people will die, and that would be a pity. O.M. 1803. *A Dâs Dew, y'th wolowys, clew galow an bobyl-ma*, O Father God, in thy lights, hear the call of this people. O.M. 1832. *Gwell yw un dên dhe verwel ages oll an bobyl lêl dhe vôs keyllys*, better it that one man should die than all the faithful people to be lost. P.C. 447.

BOCH, s. f. The cheek. *En vôch*, Cornish Vocabulary, *facies*. The later form was *bôh*, qd. v. W. *bôch*. Arm. *boch*. Lat. *bucca*. Sansc. *mukhas*.

BOCH, s. m. A buck, he-goat. Cornish Vocabulary, *caper* vel *hyrcus*. W. *bwch*. Arm. *bouch*. Ir. *boc*, and *bocc*. Gael. *boc*. Manx, *bock*. Swed. and Germ. *bock*. Belg. *bocke*. Ang. Sax. *bucca*. Eng. *buck*. Fr. *buc*. It. *becco*. Sansc. *bucca*, (*buk*, to cry.)

BOCHAN, adj. Little. This form is preserved in the Cornish Vocabulary, and approaches nearly the Welsh *bychan*. which in parts of Flintshire is pronounced *bwchan*. Seo *Bcchan*.

BOCHES, s. m. A little, a small matter. *Och, me re bue bochès coynt, hag ê̂th yn râk re a poynt pûr wêr, pan wrêk dhe Pylat lâdh Cryst*, Oh, I have been little cunning, and went forward too much point blank truly, when I made Pilate kill Christ. P.C. 3031. The guttural was sometimes displaced for *h*, and written *bohes*, qd. v. (W. *bychod*.) The oldest form must have been *bochod*, whence *bochodoc*.

BOCHESOG, adj. Poor. Another later form of *bochodog*. Pl. *bochesogyon*. *Ef a galse bôs gwyrthys a try cans dyner ha moy, ha re-na galscr dhe rey dhe vochesogyon yn beys*, it might have been sold for three hundred pence and more, and those might have been given to the poor in the world. P.C. 538. Other forms are *bohosugion*, and by contraction *bohosogyon, bosogyon*. W. *bychydog*, pl. *bychydogion*. Ir. †*bocht, bochlan*. Gael. *bochd*. Manx, *bocht*. Cf. Sansc. *bhiks*, to beg.

BOCHODOC, adj. Poor. This is the oldest form preserved in the Cornish Vocabulary, and derived from *bochod*,— W. *bychod*, which is represented by *boches*.

BOD, s. m. A dwelling, house. It enters into the names of several parishes and villages in Cornwall, as *Bodmin, Bodwen, Bodrugan*, &c. The *d* is frequently changed into *s*, as *Bosanketh, Boskerras*, and often omitted, as *Bohurtha, Bokelly*. In Wales also it is of common occurrence in the names of mansions, as *Bodidha, Bodysgallen, Bodidris*, and also of parishes as *Bodedern*, and *Bodwrog*, in Anglesey; *Botwnog*, in Arvon. Teut. *bod*. Old Swed. *buda*, a village. Swed. *boo*, a dwelling. Old Sax. *boed*. Eng. *abode*. Germ. *bude*. Pol. *bauda, budo*. Goth. *bouden*. a temple. Sansc. *abad*.

BODREDHES, s. m. Bruises, sores. *Vythqueth na ve bom a won, a rollo whaf mar gales, del y's brewaf yn dan gên; kekyfrys kyc ha crohen, del vêdh luen a bodredhes*, never was a stroke that I know of, that could give a blow so hard, as I will strike her under the chin; flesh and skin also, that it shall be full of sores. O.M. 2714. This is a mutation of *potredhes*, the plural of *potredh*. qd. v.

BODH, s. m. The will, good pleasure. *Dhe parathys scon yth âf, râg gruthyl ôl bôdh dhe vrys*, to Paradise soon I shall go, to do all the will of thy judgment. O.M. 340. *Dhynny ny travyth ny grêf, aban yw y vôdh ef y lesky hep falladow*, to us there is nothing grievous, since it is his will to burn it without fail. O.M. 463. *Dêns pan vo bôdh gansé y, aga bôs a vydh parys*, let them come when they will, their food will be ready. P.C. 604. *Râg miyternes yw yn nêf, dhe vôs gordhys hy yw gyw; eleth dherygdhy a sêf, leas myl y bôdh a syw*, for queen she is in heaven, to be worshipped she is worthy; angels before her shall stand, many thousands her will shall follow. M.C. 226. W. *bôdh*.

BODHAR, adj. Deaf. *Dhe dên bodhar na glew vêth, mychtern kêr dre grâs an Tâs, au gwcel gwevres mar a'm vêdh, dhe Dew dhu voy y whon grâs*, to a deaf man that heareth nothing, dear king, by the grace of the Father, if the rods shall be help to me, I give the more thanks to God. O.M. 2013. *Yn pow may 'th esé, ef a sawyé an glevyon, dall na bodhar ny asé nag owlanas nugonon*, in the country that he was, he healed the sick; blind, nor deaf, he left not, nor lame none. M.C. 25. This was at last corrupted into *bythac*. W. *bydhar*. Arm. *bouzar*. Ir. *bodhur*. Gael. *bodhar*. Manx, *bouyr*. Sansc. *badhira*, (*badh*, to bind.) Eng. *bother*.

BOELL, s. f. An axe, a hatchet. *Gans ow borll nowydh lemmys me a squat pûb pcis tymber, hag a pleyn oll an planckes, hag a svil pûb plankyn sure*, with mine axe newly sharpened, I will hew every piece of timber, and will plane all the planks, and will set every plank sure. C.W. 166. This is another form of *Bimil*. qd. v.

BOEN, s. m. Beef. Written also *bowen*. Pryce. Lat. *bovina*.

BOES, v. subs. Let him be. 3 pers. s. imp. of *bôs*. Lhwyd, 245. W. *boed*.

BOH, s. f. The cheek. In construction *vôh*. Pl. *bohow*. ‡*Dho rei stîran wur an vôh*, to give a slap on the cheek. Lhwyd, 117. This is a later form of *Bôch*. qd. v.

BOHES, s. m. A little, a small matter. *A arluth perfeth, bohes ew henna dhynny, mŷns a defynno an gcydh, my ha'm gwrek a wra dybry*, O Lord perfect, that is a small matter for us, all that comes in one day my wife and I will eat. O.M. 384. This is a later form of *boches*, qd. v.

BOHOSOG, adj. Poor. Pl. *bohosogyon*. *Why a gŷf bohosugyon pûp ûr warnoch ow carmé; pan vynnoch agas honon, why a gŷl gûl da dhedhé*, you have the poor always on you calling; when ye will yourselves, you may do good to them. P.C. 543. *Why a gŷf bohosogyon*. M.C. 37. *Lyes torn do yn bys-ma re wrûk dhe vohosugyon, many a* good turn in this world he hath done to the poor. P.C. 3108. This is a later form of *Bochodoc*, qd. v.

BOL, s. m. The belly, paunch. *Ridh y couth dhymmo bones ow hobersen, a fue gures tevy dar bol*, red it behoves my habergeon to be for me, which was made to spread round my belly. R.D. 2537. W. *bol, bola*. Ir. *bolg*, †*bolc*. Gael. *bolg*. Manx, *bolg*. In Welsh and Erse, it also means a bag. "Bulgas Galli sacculos scorteos vocant." Festus. Gr. βολγός, a hide. Æol. βολγός. Lat. *bulga*. Goth. *bulga*. Belg. *balg*. Ang. Sax. *belge*. Eng. *bilge*.

BOL, s.m. A pit, a hole. A mutation of *pol*, qd. v. *Y codhas war bol y hŷll*, she fell on the nape of her neck. M.C.165.

BOL, s. m. Clay. *A dâs, del whythres, a bol hag a brys formyys, bydh dynny north ha gweres, rag warnas. prest ny a bŷs*, O Father, as we are thy work, made of clay and soil, be to us strength and help, for on thee ever we pray. O.M. 1070. W. *môl*, concrete.

BOLENEGETH, s. m. The will. *Llwyd*, 240. It is generally written in the Ordinalia *Bolungeth*, qd. v.

BOLLA, s. m. A drinking cup, a bowl. *Llwyd*, 114. Ir. *bolla*. Gael. *bôl*.

BOLUNGETH, s. m. The will. *Bolungeth Dew yw hemma, bones gorrys an spus-ma, pan dremenna a'n bŷs-ma, yn y anow*, the will of God is this, that these kernels be put, when he passes away from this world, in his mouth. O.M. 873. *Dhe volungeth yn pûp le, Arluth whel, my a wra*, thy will in every place, O high Lord, I will do. O.M. 1165. *Ow bolungeth mar mynnyth y collenwel hep let vŷdh, dhe vâp Ysac a geryth, y offrynné reys yw dhys war venedh a dhysquedhaf dhyso gy, del lavaraf*, my will if thou wilt fulfil it without any hesitation, thy son Isaac, whom thou lovest, it is necessary for thee to offer him on the mountain which I shall shew to thee, as I say. O.M. 1277. Formed from the Latin *voluntate*, by the common change of the first *t* into *s*, and then into *g* soft. The Welsh equivalent is *ewyllys*. Arm. *ioul*. Sansc. *val, vli*, to wish.

BOM, s. m. A blow, a smith's sledge hammer. Pl. *bomyon, bommyn*. *Ty a fŷdh wharé drog lam, dhe escarn ol, ketep tam, gans ow bom a fŷdh brewys*, thou shalt soon have a bad chance, thy bones all, every bit, with my blow shall be bruised. O.M. 2744. *Rág my a vŷdh an kynsa, bom yn vyag a rollo*, for I will be the first that will give a blow on the journey. O.M. 2163. *Awos agas fas ha tros, ny wra bom y vorfené*, notwithstanding your bragging and noise, a blow will not finish him. P.C. 2111. *Ow bommyn yw marthys glew*, my blows are wondrous light. P.C. 2088. *Gwask war an min, bommyn dreys keyn*, strike on the edge, blows over the back. P.C. 2729. W. *pwmp*.

BOME, comp. v. There may be to me, I may have. *Ro dhym an grâs, may bomé vu, ha gwêl a'th fâs*, give me the grace, that I may have a view and sight of thy face. R.D. 842.

BONDHAT, s. m. A round, or circle. *Llwyd*, 153.

BONES, v. subs. To be. This is an enlarged form of *bôs*, qd. v., and is generally written *bonus* in M.C. *Nyns yw da bones un dên y honan heb cowyth py cowethas*, it is not good that any man should be by himself without a male or female companion. O.M. 94. *Pa'n dra gi henna bones, lavar dhymmo vy wharré*, what thing can that be ? tell me directly. O.M. 157. *Drefen ow bones bonen, ty a gî dhym daryvas*, though I am a woman, thou mayest make it known to me. O.M. 161. *Lemyn agan soné gwra, kyns ys bones anhedhys*, now bless us before it is inhabited. O.M. 1722. *Me a grŷs bones an gwâs ow kûl maystri brâs*, I believe that the fellow is making great violence. P.C. 358. *Pyw a yltu gy bones*, who canst thou be. R.D. 2511. *Rag bonas agan pêch mar vear*, because our sin was so great. M.C. 8. *Ol warbarth y a armas, gweff yw dhe vonas ledhys*, altogether they cried out, he is worthy to be killed. M.C. 95. *Me ny won bonas kefys yn dên-ma bŷth acheson may rŷs y vonas ledhys*, I know not that there is found in this man any guilt that it is necessary that he should be killed. M.C. 141.

BONS, v. subs. They should be. 3 pers. pl. subj. of *bôs*. In construction it changes into *vôns*, and *fôns*. *Rŷs yw porrys dhe onon meruel rag pobyl an wlâs, pobyl Jesus y honon na vôns tregis gans Satnas*, very necessary it is that one should die for the people of the country, that the people of Jesus themselves should not be dwelling with Satan. M.C. 89. *Ha'n dhew-na bŷs pan vôns squyth, war Christ y fôns ow cronkyé*, and those two until they were weary, Christ were beating. M.C. 132. *Py le vŷdh an gwoel plynsys, may fôns mocha omourys, ha'n gwella may wrôns tevy*, where shall these rods be planted, that they may be most honoured, and may grow best. O.M. 2033. See *vôns*, and *fôns*. W. *bônt*. *Bôns* also occurs as the 3 pers. pl. of the preterite, answering to W. *buant*. *Ow treys homma gans dagrow re's holhas, gans y blew y fôns syhys*, my feet this one with tears hath washed, with her hair they were dried. P.C. 521.

BONY, s. m. An axe, a hatchet. *Yntré dew gwrên y trehy, rák cafus três pren dedhy, ha y fastie gans ebyl pren ; otté genef vy bony, me a'n trech wharré gynsy, ny'n sparyaf awos anken*, in two let us cut it, to have a cross piece for it, and fasten it with pegs of wood ; behold I have an axe, I will cut it soon with it, I will not spare it because of trouble. P.C. 2564. Possibly a mutation of *pony*, which would be connected with Welsh *pwynjad*, any pointed tool.

BOOL, s. f. An axe, hatchet. "*Oo* in Cornish is pronounced as in English, or as *û* long, for *bool* is to be read *bûl*." *Llwyd*, 228. It is the same word as *boell*, or *biail*. *Heedh ow bool dhymmo touth ta, ow thardar, ha'm mortholow*, reach me my axe quickly, my auger, and my hammers. O.M. 1001.

BOR, adj. Fat. Cornish Vocabulary, *pinguis*. This word is unknown to the Welsh and Armoric, but the Irish and Gaelic have *barr*, fat, suet.

BORD, s. f. A board, a table. *Llwyd*, 88. W. *bord, bwrdh*. Arm. *bourz*. Ir. *bord*. Gael. *bord*.

BORE, s. m. The morning. The existence of this word in the Cornish language is proved by the compound *boreqweth*, but the word in common use was *metin*, qd. v. W. *boré*. Arm. *beuré*. Ir. †*buarach*. Gr. πρωί. Sansc. *prac, (pur*, to move, advance.)

BOREGWETH, s. m. The morning time, morning. *Llwyd*, 249. Compounded of *boré*, morning, and *gwêth*, a time ; so Welsh *boregwaith*.

BORELES, s. m. The herb comfrey. Cornish Vocabulary, *consolda*. "Consolida in the dictionaries is variously rendered, but always with reference to some herb with a thickening or strengthening quality. *Pryce* translates *boreles*, 'the herb comfrey, the incrassating herb,' taking it from *bor*, without doubt. Zenss refers to *bore*, morning, but this is hardly so plausible." Norris's Cornish Drama, ij. 330. See *Lês*, a plant.

BORTH, v. a. Bear thou. This is a mutation of *porth*, 2 pers. s. imp. of *porthy*, qd. v. *Frût an wedhen a skyans, dybbry bŷth na borth danger*, the fruit of the tree of knowledge, never make delay to eat. O.M. 168. *My a lever dhys, Urry, na borth dout ahanaf vy, rág ny fŷdh kên dhe perthy*, I tell thee, Uriah, bear no doubt of me, for there is no reason to bear it. O.M. 2206.

BOS, v. subs. To be, to exist. In construction it changes into *vôs*. *Saw an wedhen dhym yma hy bôs sychys marthys vrâs*, but the tree it is to me a great wonder that it is dry. O.M. 756. *Bôs sêeh ha têk an awel, dhe Dew y côth dhyn grassé*, that the weather is dry and fair it is incumbent on us to thank God. O.M. 1147. *Yma câs brâs wharfethys ha codhys war dhe pobrl, ny yllons bôs nyfyrys*, great misfortunes have occurred and fallen on thy people, they cannot be numbered. O.M. 1544. *Gwell yw y vôs ef marow, ys bôs an popel kellys, ha dampnys dhe tewolgow*, it is better that he should be dead, than that the people should be lost and condemned to darkness. P.C. 2464. W. *bôd*, + *bot*. Arm. *bout*. Ir. *beith*. Gael. *bi*. Manx, *be*. Sansc. *bhu*.

BOS, s. m. Meat, food. *Pup mâner bôs yn bys-ma ûs dhe dybry may teleth, râg dên ha bêst magata, yn dhe lester ty a fŷdh*, all manner of food in this world, which ought to be eaten, for man and beast as well, in thy vessel thou shalt have. O.M. 993. *Arluth me a'th peys a dhybry gynef un prŷs, dre dhe vôdh, ha'th dyskyblon, rag yma bôs paruys dhyso ha dhedhê kefrys*, Lord I pray thee to eat with me a meal, by thy will, and thy disciples, for there is food prepared for them and for them likewise. P.C. 458. This is a contracted form of *boys*, qd. v.

BOS, s. m. A dwelling, a house. *Govy er bôs dywoolow*, woe is me for the abode of devils. R.D. 301. This is a later form of *bôd*, qd. v

BOS, s. m. A bush. *A dhysempys whyleschê mar as ethê dho cudhê yn nêp bôs, tewl, py yn sorn*, immediately seek ye, if he be gone to hide in some bush, hole, or in a corner. R.D. 539. This is formed from the English *bush*.

BOSA, v. subs. To be. This is a poetic form of *bôs*. *Me a leverys dhywhy ow bosa henna deffry*, I have told you that I am he really. P.C. 1120.

BOSAF, v. subs. I am. This is an anomalous form, found only in late Cornish, being the infinitive mood, with a personal ending attached. *Splanna es an howl devery, why a gill warbarth gwelas, ow bosaf pûb preys*, more resplendent than the sun shining, ye may together see that I am at all times. C.W. 10.

BOSCA, s. m. A cottage, hut. *Pryce*. This is a late word.

BOSIAS, s. m. Fingers. This is given by *Lhwyd*, 243, as a late plural of *bês*.

BOSNOS, s. m. A bush of thorns. *Yma marth dhym a un dra an pŷth lemmyn a welaf, an bosnos dywy a wra, saw nyns ugy ow lesky*, there is a wonder to me of one thing which now I see ; the bush is on fire, but is not burning. O.M. 1397.

BOSSE, v. a. He could lean. *Rag gwan spyrys, hag ef yn ten, caman na ylly guythê, warnans na bossé y ben, rag an arlant a usyê, mar possé an neyll tenewen rag y scodh hy a'n grevye, ha whâth gwêth a wre an pren war dhellareh mar an gorré*, through weak spirit, and straitened, so that he could not any way keep, nor lean his head on them, for the garland he wore, if he leaned on the side, for his shoulder it him grieved, and yet worse did the wood backward if he laid it. M.C. 205. A mutation of *possé*, qd. v.

BOST, s. m. A boast, bragging, or boasting. *Pan dethens y bŷs an bêdh, yth êth on marree dhy ben, hag arall dhy dreys a-wêdh, yrvys fast bys yn dhewen, hag a dhychow, hag a glêdh, onon pûb tenewen, bôst y wrêns tyn, yn gwythens worth y ehen*, when they came to the grave, there went one soldier to the head, and another to his feet also, armed quite to the jaws, and on the right side and on the left, one each side, boast they made great, that they could keep him against his effort. M.C. 242. *Corf yn bêdh a worscuch why, a wre bôst a dhusserchy dhe pen try deydh*, the body ye have put in the tomb, he boasted it would rise again at the end of three days. R.D. 44. W. *bôst*. Gael. *bost*.

BOSTA, v. subs. Thou art. *Rág y bosta melegas, hag yn golon re othys*, because thou art a wicked one, and in thy heart too proud. C.W. 24. *Gâs re dha entra agye, rag ty ny vedhys dowtyes, drefan y bosta mar dek*, let me enter into thee, for thou wilt not be mistrusted because thou art so fair. *ibid*. 40. This word is a combination of *bôs*, inf. to be, and *te*, thou.

BOSTYE, v. a. To boast, brag. Pret. *bostyas*. *Ef ny wra lemyn bostyé*, he will not boast now. P.C. 385. *Me a'n clewas ow tyffen na vo reys, awos hechen, trubit vŷth dhe Syr Cesar, hag ow bostyé y bôs ef Gryst gwŷr un vâp Dew a nêf*, I heard him forbidding that there be given, for any consideration, any tribute to the Lord Cæsar, boasting that he is Christ, the true only son of the God of heaven. P.C. 1576. *Lyes gwŷth y wrûk bostyé*, many times he boasted. P.C. 2439. *Grveyteuch oll er agas fŷdh, pan y bostyas, dhe pen try deydh, y lasserchy dhe cewnans*, all take care on your faith, since he boasted, at the end of three days, he would rise again to life. R.D. 374. W. *bostio*. Cf. Germ. *pausten*, to blow, swell, bonnec. Russ. *chvastayu*, to boast. Lat. *fastus*.

BOTH, s. m. The will. See *Bôdh*.

BOTHOC, s. m. A hut, a cottage. *Pryce*. This is a diminutive of *bôth*, a hut or booth. W. *bwth*, *bythyn*. Arm. *bothon*. Ir. *both*, *bothan*. Gael. *both*. Manx, *bwaane*. Sansc. *vâti*, a house. Hebr. *beth*. Arab. *beith*. Pers. *tat*, *abad*.

BOUDI, s. m. A cowhouse, a fold for cattle, or sheep. (*Boudzhi deves*, a sheep fold. *Lhwyd*, 110.) This is the same as the Welsh *beudy*, or *boydy*, which is the modern form of the word + *bowi*, from the old form *bou*, a cow, and *ti*, or *ty*, a house.

BOUNDER, s. f. Feeding ground, a pasture. Cornish Vocabulary, *pascua*. Pryce translates it, a common, a lane. *Bounder tre*, a village. *Lhwyd*, 173. *Chy Vounder*, the house in the lane, in St. Agnes. *Vounder vor*, is the name of a lane in Penzance, and *pedn y vounder*, the head of the lane, near the Logan Stone.

BOURN, s. m. A heap, a hill. This is also written *burn*, and is found in the names of places, as *Burnwhal*, in St. Burian. It is the same as *Bern*, qd. v.

BOWES, v. n. He will rest. A mutation of *powes*, 3 pers. s. fut. of *powesy*, qd. v. *Hen yw dydh a bowesva dhe pup dén a vo sylwys, yn dysrpydhyens a henna, ny a bowes desempys,* this is a day of rest to every man that may be saved, in declaration of that we will rest forthwith. O.M. 148.

BOWESAS, v. n. He rested. A mutation of *powesas*, 3 pers. s. preterite of *powesy*, qd. v. *Cosel my re bowesas, assyne whek an hûn myttyn,* I have rested softly, sweet is the morning sleep. O.M. 2073.

BOWESVA, s. f. A resting place, rest. *Hen yw dydh a bowesva, dhe pup dén a vo sylwys,* this is a day of rest, to every man that may be saved. O.M. 148. A mutation of *Powesva,* qd. v.

BOWIN, s. m. Beef. *Lhwyd,* 33. This is also written *bowen,* and *boen,* and is derived from the Latin, *bovina*.

BOWNAS, s. m. A living, life, livelihood. *Lhwyd,* 251. A late form of *bewnans,* qd. v.

BOWS s. f. A coat. A mutation of *pows,* qd. v. *Honna yw y bows nessa,* that is his nearest garment. R.D. 1867. *Cafas an bows-na hep gury, ûs y'th kerchyn, me a vyn,* take that robe without seam, which is about thee, I will. R.D. 1921. *Arluth why yw a dhy gre an bows, ha my dhygwysk e,* Lord, to your liking is the robe, and that I should take it off? R.D. 1924.

BOX, s. m. The box tree. Pl. *byxyn*. Cornish Vocabulary, *byxus,* whence is derived also the English *box*. *Palm ha bayys, byxyn erbys gynef yma,* palm and bays, herbs of box there are with me. P.C. 261. W. *boccys,* pronounced *box*. Arm. *beux.* Ir. *bucsa*.

BOXSES, s. m. A blow with the fist, a box. Pl. *boxsesow*. *Pur ankensy guns dornow dhodho war an scovornow reuch boxsesow trewysy,* very painful with fists to him on the ears give sad blows. P.C. 1362. *Ty a sydh boxsesow tyn war an dywcen,* thou shalt have sharp blows on the chops. P.C. 1368. From the English *box*.

BOYNA, adv. Unless. *Cool ge dhym mar mynta bôs exaltys, po ken venary why a vŷdh avel flehys, boyna assentys,* hearken to me, if thou wilt be exalted, otherwise for ever you will be like children, unless you assent. C.W. 48.

BOYNEDH, adv. Daily, every day. *Lhwyd,* 249. This is a mutation of *poynedh,* and used as the Welsh *beunydh*. The component parts are *pôb,* every, and *dédh,* a day.

BOYS, s. m. Meat, food. *Dew dhên Christ a dhanvonas dhe berna boys ha dewas, an keth re-na a spedyas, ha'n soper a ve parys,* two men Christ sent to buy meat and drink, those very same did speed, and the supper was prepared. M.C. 42. *My re dhysyryas fest mêr dybry genoch why haneth boys pask kyns ow bôs marow,* I have desired very greatly to eat with you this night the paschal food before I am dead. P.C. 720. It is also written *bôs*. The oldest form was *buit,* qd. v. W. *bwyd*.

BOYS, adj. Heavy, weighty. A mutation of *Poys*, qd. v.

BOZZORES, v. a. To sing after others. *Lhwyd,* 157.

BRAF, adj. More. *Pryce*. W. *praf,* large, ample. Arm. *braõ*.

BRAG, s. m. Malt. Cornish Vocabulary, *bratium*. *Bŷs may codhé hy dhe'n dôr, ha y brewy mar venys avel skyl brág,* until that she fall upon the earth, and bruise her as small as malt dust. O.M. 2720. ‡*Why el eva cor gwella, mars ees dhyuh brág,* you may drink best beer if you have malt. *Pryce's Voc.* W. *brág*. Arm. †*brag,* (*bragezi,* to sprout.) Ir. *braich*. Gael. *braich.* Manx, *bragh*. The old Gauls, according to Pliny, prepared a sort of fine grain, of which they made beer, and this grain they called *brace.*—"Genus farris quod illi vocant bracem."

BRAGOT, s. m. Sweet drink. It was a liquor made of the wort of ale, and mead fermented together, called by the English, *bragget*. It is still made in some parts of Wales, and within my recollection it was usual for the inhabitants of Aberconwy to attend the one annual afternoon service in Gyffin church on Easter Sunday, and then go to drink *bragawd,* which was made for that special occasion, in the village. Lhwyd writes the word also *bracat,* but in the Cornish Vocabulary it is *bregaud,* qd. v. W. *bragawd,* †*bracaut*.

BRAM, s. m. A fart. Pl. *bremmyn*. P.C. 2104. *A y vestry ny re'n bram,* of his power I value not a puff. O.M. 2739. *Me a grŷa ny dâl vŷdh bram,* I think it will not be of the least value. P.C. 3078. W. *bram*. Arm. *bramm*. Ir. *bram*. Gael. *braim*. Manx, *breim*. Gr. βρόμος, a noise, βρέμω, to make a noise. Ang. Sax. *breman*. Germ. *brummen*.

BRAMME, v. a. To fart. Pret. *brammas,* in construction *vrammas*. *Rák pur own me re vrammas,* for very fear I exploded. R.D. 2091. *Y fyys yn un vrammé,* thou fleest in a tremor. R.D. 2094. W. *brammu*. Arm. *bramma*.

BRAN, s. f. A crow. Pl. *bryny*. *Brân vrás,* a raven, i.e. a great crow, called also *marchvrân*. *Brân drê,* a town crow. *Gallas an glaw dhe vés gwlân, ha'n dour my a grés basseys ; da yw yn més dyllo brân, mars ès dôr sech war an beys,* the rain is clean gone away, and the water, I believe, abated ; it is well to send out a crow, if it be dry ground over the world. O. M. 1099. *Docs ny vynnas an vrân vrás, neb carryn hy a gafas,* the raven would not return, some carrion she has found. C.W. 178. *Hôs, payon, colom, gruyger, bargos, bryny, ha'n er, moy dredhof a vŷdh hynwys,* duck, peacock, pigeon, partridge, kite, crows, and the eagle further by me are named. O.M. 133. W. *brân,* pl. *brain*. Arm. *brân,* pl. *brini*. Ir. *bran*. Gael. *bran*. Slav. *vran, wran*.

BRANGIAN, s. m. The throat, or gullet. This word, written by Lhwyd, 64, *brandzhian,* is a corruption of *briangen,* and this is a later form than that preserved in the Cornish Vocabulary, *briansen,* qd. v.

BRAS, adj. Great, gross, big, large, coarse. *Noe, dre dhe dhadder brás, ty a bew ow grâth nefré,* Noah, for thy great goodness, thou shalt ever possess my favour. O.M. 973. *Rag lŷf brás my a dhoro, a gudho oll an nôr boys,* for I will bring a great flood, that will hide all the land of the world. O.M. 982. *Lavaraf dheuch, a dús vás, kekyfrys byan ha brás, lemmyn gureuch oll ow sywé,* I say to you, O good people, as well little and great, now do ye all follow me. O.M. 1673. *Rág caffos ran vrás a'n pencôn, mar a callé,* to have a great share of the pay, if he could. M.C. 38. *Pen brás,* a jolt head. C.W. 96. *Logosan vrás,* a rat, i.e. a great mouse. *Benen vrás,* a big woman. *Dên brás,* a great man. *Menedh brás,* a great mountain. Lhwyd. It is also used adverbially, as *Del yw ef gallosek brás,* as he is very powerful. O.M. 1494. *Dhe colon yw cales brás,* thy heart is very hard. O.M. 1525. Comp. *brassh*.

Super. *brassa.* W. *brâs.* Arm. *brâs.* Ir. †*breas.* Gael. †*breas.*

BRASDER, s. m. Greatness, largeness, bigness, pride. *Râg henna an vuscogyon orto a borthas avy, dre vrasder brâs yn golon y dhugtyons y dhestrewy,* for that reason, the fools to him bore spite, through great pride in the heart they thought to destroy him. M.C. 26. W. *brasder.* Arm. *brasder.*

BRASLAVAR, adj. Grandiloquent. *Dén braslavar,* a grandiloquent man. *Lhuyd,* 84. Comp. of *brâs,* great, and *lavar,* speech.

BRASOBERYS, adj. Magnificent. *Lhuyd,* 84. Compounded of *brâs,* great, and *ober,* work.

BRASSA, adj. Greatest. The superlative of *brâs.* *Nêb a vo yn mochya gre, a vŷdh an brassa henwys,* he who is in the highest degree shall be called the greatest. P.C. 778. *Pechadores es hwb gow, an brassa egé yn pow,* thou art a sinner without a lie, the greatest that was in the country. R.D. 1095. Written also *brasa,* and *brassé. Ahanouch neb yw mochya, ha'n brasa gallos dodho,* he who is the greatest of you, and has the greatest power. P.C. 793. *Pyw an brassé dên senges,* who is esteemed the greatest man. P.C. 773. W. *brasav.* Arm. *brasa.*

BRASSAH, adj. Greater. The comparative of *brâs.* *Ha Dew wrûs dew golow brâs, an brassah rag an dêdh, ha an behannah rag an nôs, êv a wrûs an sterres yn wêdh,* and God made two great lights, the greater for the day, and the less for the night, he made the stars also. M.C. p. 94. The comparative was distinguished, as in Welsh and Armoric, by the final guttural, *ch.* This was softened into *h,* and in the Ordinalia, omitted altogether. W. *brasoch.* Arm *brasoch.*

BRATHCY, s. m. A mastiff, or hound. Literally a biting, or savage, dog, being compounded of W. *brathu,* to bite, and *ki,* a dog. Pl. *brathken. Me a'th weres orth y dhôn dhe yffarn kepar hag ôn, war gcyn lowarn py brathky,* I will help thee to bring him to hell like as we are, on the back of a fox or mastiff. O.M. 895. *Ty vŷl brathky,* thou vile hound. P.C. 2087. *Pan dothyans bŷs yn tyller, may 'thesé Christ ow pesy, lowenny dhys, ow vester, yn mêdh Judas, an brathky,* when they came to the place where Christ was praying, Joy to thee, my master, said Judas the mastive dog. M.C. 65. *Avel brathken aga dens orto y a dheskerny,* like mastive dogs their teeth on him they did grin. M.C. 96. Pryce gives a corrupted form of this word in *brakgye,* which is translated *a badger,* or *gray,* probably in connection with *broch.* It is found also in the Ordinalia, in a doubtful place, *Na brakgye rag ef a sur,* no mastiff surely he goes forth. R.D. 2018.

BRAUD, s. m. A brother. Cornish Vocabulary, *frater.* This is the oldest form, agreeing exactly with the W. *brawd.* The common form was *broder,* qd. v. W. *brawd,* †*braut,* pl. *brodyr.* Arm. *breûr, brêr,* pl. *bredeur, breder,* †*breuder.* Ir. *braithair,* †*brathir.* Gael. *braithair.* Manx, *braar.* Goth, *brôthar.* Sansc. *brâtâ, brâtar.* Gr. φρήτηρ. Lat. *frater.*

BRE, s. f. A mountain, a hill. Of frequent occurrence in the names of places in Cornwall, as *Bray,* in St. Just, and Llogan. *Goonvra,* the hill downs, in St. Agnes. *Carn brea.* So also in Wales, as *Moelvré, Pembré.* W. *bré.* Old Ir. †*bri.* Gael. *braigh.* Sansc. *vâra.*

BRECH, s. f. The arm. Cornish Vocabulary, *brachium.* Instead of a plural, the Celtic dual is here as in other instances generally made use of, *dywvrech,* (*dyw,* feminine.) *Pyw a dhysquedhes dhyso dhe vôs noeth corf, trôs, ha brêch,* who disclosed to thee that thy body, feet, and arms are naked? O.M. 262. *Ty losel, foul y perhen, ystyn dhe vrêch war an pren,* thou knave, foul his owner, stretch out thy arm on the wood. O.M. 2753. *Me a gelm scon lovan dha worth conna brêch an adla, ha why tynnewch agas try,* I will forthwith bind a good rope around the wrist (neck of the arm) of the knave, and you pull, you three. P.C. 2762. *Crêf yw gwrydhow an spedhes, may 'thyw ow dyw-vrêch terrys,* strong are the roots of the briars, so that my arms are broken. O.M. 688. See *Dywvrech.* W. *braich,* †*breich,* dual, *dwyvraich,* plur. *breichiau.* Arm. *breach, brêch,* dual, *divrêch.* Ir. †*brac, raigh.* Gael. †*brae.* Manx, *ri, roih.* Gr. βραχ-ίων. Lat. *brachium.*

BRECHOI, s. m. A sleeve. Cornish Vocabulary, *manica.* From *brêch,* the arm. By the time of Lhuyd, it had been corrupted into *brehal,* and *brohal.* W. *brcichell.*

BREDAR, s. m. A brother. A later form of *broder,* qd. v. *Govynna worth e vredar,* ask his brother. *Lhuyd,* 242.

BREDER, s. m. Brothers, brethren. The plural of *broder,* qd. v. *Par del y'th prynnys yn kêr, ha fasta gy dhe vreder yn luen grygyans,* like as I redeemed thee dearly, strengthen also thy brethren in full belief. R.D. 1163. See *Braud,* and *Broder.*

BREDER, s. m. Shortness, briefness. *Festyn leman me a'th pys may fo dychtys e vreder,* hasten now, I pray thee, that it may be dressed speedily. P.C. 276. *Breder* is for *berder,* being derived from *ber* short. W. *byrder.*

BREDER, s. m. Thought. A mutation of *preder,* qd. v. *Ha Pylut dhe war breder a leverys dhe Jesus,* and Pilate after thinking said to Jesus. M.C. 129.

BREDERETII, s. m. Brothers, brethren. One of the plurals of *broder,* qd. v. *An Tas Dew roy dhym bôs gwyw dhe vôs lên servyey dhys, ha'm bredyredh ynwedh,* God the Father grant us to be worthy to be faithful servants to thee, and my brethren also. P.C. 714. This is also written *bruderedh.* P.C. 1430.

BREDERYS, adj. Studious, thoughtful, diligent. A mutation of *prederys,* qd. v. *Gwrée brederys,* a diligent wife. *Lhuyd,* 243.

BREDERYS, v. a. Thought. A mutation of *predery,* preterite of *predery.* Written also *predyrys. My re bredyrys gûl prat râg y wythé erbyn hâf,* I have thought of doing a thing to keep it against summer. O.M. 487.

BREDION, v. a. To boil. Cornish Vocabulary, *coctio.* This was finally corrupted into *bridzhan,* to boil, *bridzhias,* boiled. W. *brydian,* to boil, from *brwd,* hot.

BREF, v. a. He will prove. A mutation of *prêf,* 3 pers. s. fut. of *prevy,* qd. v. *Rák dhe gows a brêf neffré dhe vôs dên a Galilé,* for thy speech proves ever that thou art a man of Galilee. P.C. 1408. *Me a brêf bôs gow henna,* I will prove that that is false. P.C. 1729. *Me ny wodhyan gwyll dodha, kemys gyrryow tek a'm brêf,* I knew not what do to it, so many fair words it told me. C.W. 74.

BREFSYS, v. a. Thou hast proved. A mutation of *prefsys,* 2 pers. s. preterite of *prevy. Yn boys awos godhaf crôk, ny brefsys anken na drôk, Dew! gwyn dhe vys,* notwithstanding suffering hanging, thou hast not felt grief nor evil. O God I happy thy lot. R.D. 278.

BREFYAS, v. a. Proved. A mutation of *prevyas*, preterite of *prevy*. *Ef a brefyas lower gow dhys*, he told thee many lies. C.W. 00.

BREGAUD, s. m. Sweet drink, bragget. Cornish Vocabulary, *idromellum vel mulsum*. This is the older form of *bragot*, qd. v. W. *bracawd*, †*bracaul*. In Bailey's Dictionary, *bragget* is explained to be "a drink made of honey and spice." Ancient Receipts for making bragget are given in Wright's Dictionary of Obsolete and Provincial English, 1857.

BREGEWTHY, v. a. To preach. A mutation of *pregewthy*, qd. v. *Taw, an él a bregewthys a'n vedhen hag a'y veriu, a'y früt a wrello dybry, y fedhé kepar ha dew*, be silent, the angel preached, of the tree and its virtue, of its fruit he who would eat would be like a god. O.M. 229.

BREH, s. f. The arm. This is a later form of *brêch*, qd. v. Pl. *breihow*. Lhwyd, 244. ‡ *E ryg hedhas rág e vrêh*, he stretched forth his arm *ibid*, 250. *Dibreh*, the arms.

BREILU, s. m. A rose. Cornish Vocabulary, *rosa*. Though Dr. Owen Pughe gives *breilie*, and *breila*, as the synonyms in Welsh, I am doubtful of these being really found in Welsh. Dr. Davies quotes as his authority the *Liber Landavensis*, but I believe the word with some others, *côth* for instance, must have been transferred from a copy of the Cornish Vocabulary, which was attached to a copy of the Liber Landavensis.

BREITHIL, s. m. A mackerel. Cornish Vocabulary, *mugilus vel mugil*. This is an old form of *brithel*, qd. v.

BREMAN, adv. Now, at this time, at present. Lhwyd, 66. Perhaps from *an-pred-ma*. Arm. *brema, bremann, a-vrema*.

BREMMYN, s. m. Puffs. Pl. of *bram*, qd. v. *Ty a wor gwell bremmyn brás dyllo*, thou knowest better to make a smell. P.C. 2104.

BREN, s. m. A tree. A mutation of *pren*, qd. v. *Fie bren*, Cornish Vocabulary, *ficus*. *Dew tckka bren rág styllyow*, bring the fairest tree for rafters. O.M. 2441.

BREN, v. a. He will buy. A mutation of *pren*, 3 pers. s. fut. of *prenna*, qd. v. *Ef a bren Adam, dhe dâs, gans y gŷk ha'y wôs kefrys, pan vo termyn denythys, ha'th vam, hag ol an dûs vâs*, he will redeem Adam, thy father, with his flesh and blood also, when the time is come, and thy mother, and all the good people. O.M. 811.

BRENNAS, v. a. Bought. A mutation of *prennas*, 3 pers. s. preterite of *prenna*, qd. v. *Prag ythela cr-y-pyn, rák Cryst, a brennas yn tyn, omma a'th drós*, why goest thou against him, for Christ, who painfully redeemed, hath brought thee here. R.D. 242.

BRENNE, v. a. To buy. A mutation of *prenné*, or *prenna*, qd. v. *Ha nêp na'n geffo na ngl gwerthens y hugk dhe brenné anedhy dhodho cledhé*, and he who has not one, let him sell his cloak to buy with it for him a sword. P.C. 922.

BRENNIAT, s. m. He that sits in the prow of a ship to guide the same, a boatswain. Cornish Vocabulary, *proreta*. The steersman, gubernator, sits at the stern. In Irish *braine*, †*bruine*, is the fore part or beginning; the prow of a ship; and in Gaelic, †*brain*; whence the obsolete †*braine*, †*braineach*, the captain of a ship, nauclerus. The root is *brent*. W. *braint*, prerogative.

BRENNIC, s. m. Limpets. Lhwyd, 114. This is an aggregate plural, from which was formed the singular *brennigen*. Lhwyd, 241. The corrupted form *bernigan* was also in use in his time. W. *brennig*. sing. *brennigen*. Arm. *brennic, brinnic*, sing *brennigen*. Gael. *bairneach*. Manx, *barnagh*. Cf. also English *barnacle, bernicle*. It is regularly formed from *bron*, a breast, which it resembles in form.

BRENTYN, adj. Privileged, sovereign, noble, excellent. *Parys ôr, Arluth Brentyn, dha volonogath lavar dhaf*, ready I am, sovereign Lord, thy will speak to me. C.W. 162. Written also *bryntyn*, qd. v. The root is *brent*. W. *braint*, prerogative, whence W. *brennhin*, a king.

BRES, s. m. Judgment, understanding. In construction *vrês. Y eth, ha Jesus gansé bŷs yn Pilat o Justis, anodho brês may rollé, dre y vrês may fo ledhys*, they went, and Jesus with them, even to Pilate (who) was Justice, of him judgment that he might give, by his judgment that he might be killed. M.C. 98. *May fo crowsys ow brês yn*, my judgment is that he be crucified. P.C. 2504. *An brês*, the understanding. Lhwyd, 88. *Der tacklow minnis ew brês tûs gonvethes, avel an tacklow brás*, by small things are the minds of men discovered, as well as by great matters. Pryce. Written also *breus, brcys, brûs*, and *brŷs*. See Breus.

BRESEC, s. m. A judge. Pryce. From *brês*, judgment.

BRESEL, s. m. War, contest, strife, dispute, argument. *Bresell cref a ve sordyis, en growz pyw ellé dhy dón, dre vear stryff y fe juggiys ys degy Christ y honon*, great dispute was raised, the cross who could carry it, through much strife it was judged, that Christ should carry it himself. M.C. 160. *Ternoys y sordyas bresell gans an Edhewon goky, lavarow tyn hag uchel fest yn fol y a gewsys*, over night there was a strife among the churlish Jews, speeches sharp and high very foolishly they spake. M.C. 238. It is also written *bresul*, and *bresyl*. *Pyth a cusyl a rêth dhym orth am vresyl*, what counsel givest thou me in my dispute. O.M. 1814. *Hag a wra dhyn drôk bresul*, and he will do us au evil war. P.C. 1918. W. †*bresel*. Though now obsolete in Welsh, it is preserved in the proper names, *Cenbresel, Conbresel, Combresel*, and *Cilbresel*. See Liber Landavensis, quoted by Zeuss, 156. Arm. †*bresel*. ibid.

BRESELER, adj. Warlike, valiant. Lhwyd, 86.

BREST, s. m. Brass, copper. Lhwyd, 100. This is a mutation of *prest*. W. *prés*. Ir. *prais*. Gael. *prais*. Manx, *prash*. Ang. Sax. *bræs*.

BRETHIL, s. m. A mackerel. Lhwyd, 243. Written also *brethal*, other forms of *brithel*, qd. v.

BRETHON, s. m. Britons. Lhwyd, 242. W. *brython*. Arm. *breton*. Ir. *breathnach*. Gael. *breatannach*. Manx, *bretnagh*.

BRETHONEC, adj. British, the British or Welsh language. *Brethonec Cembrian*, Welsh British. Pryce. W. *brythonaeg*. Arm. *brezonec*. Manx, *bretnish*, the British, or Welsh language.

BREUS, s. m. Judgment. *Hag a le-na bynytha ny dhue yn ban, bŷs yn dédh breus*, and from that place he will never come up, till the day of judgment. R.D. 2140. Written also *breuth, breys, brûs, brês*, and *brŷs*. W. *brawd*, †*braut, brŷd*. Arm. *breûd*. Ir. *breath, breth*, †*bruth*, †*brat*, †*brel*. Gael. *breth*. Gaulish, *brátu*.

BREUTH, s. m. Judgment. *Me a grys a lavassen scon war ow breuth y'n ladhen*, I think we might venture at once in my judgment to kill him. R.D. 1836. id. qd. *breus.*

BREW, adj. Broken, bruised. Pl. *brewyon.* In construction *vrew. Vytheth powes my ny'm bŷdh, mar vrew ew ow yssyly,* there is never rest to me, so bruised are my limbs. O.M. 1012. *Me an cnouk ef er y wew, otté mellow y geyn brew,* I will beat him on his lips, see the joints of his back broken. P.C. 2060. *A gweresouch, laddron, gallas an porthow brewyon, hag ol mŷns o,* Oh! help! thieves! gone are the gates to pieces, and all that there was. R.D. 126. *Cryst o brew y czyly, ha war y gorf mŷl woly,* Christ was bruised as to his limbs, and on his body a thousand wounds. R.D. 998.

BREW, s. m. A bruise, a wound. Pl. *brewyon. Me a vyn môs dhe uré ow arluth treys ha dewlé, a púp sguythens y sawyé, hag ylyé y vrewyon,* I will go to anoint my Lord's feet and hands, from all weariness cure him, and anoint his bruises. P.C. 478. W. *briw.* Ir. *briochd.* Gael. *brinch.* Manx, *broo.*

BREWY, v. a. To bruise, to break in pieces. Part. *brewys. Vythqueth na ve bom a won a rollo whaf mar gales, del y's brewaf yn dan gén,* never was a stroke, I know, that could give a blow so hard, as I will strike her under the chin. O.M. 2712. *Bŷs may codhé hy dhe'n dôr, ha y brewy mar venys avel skyl brág,* until she fall upon the earth, and bruise her as small as malt dust. O.M. 2719. *Dhe escarn oll kctep tam gans ow bom a fŷdh brewys,* thy bones all, every bit, with my blows shall be broken. P.C. 2744. *Yn ûr-na y fŷdh clewys, del ony gansé brewys,* in that hour it will be heard, as we are wounded by them. R.D. 573. W. *briwo.* Arm. *breva.* Ir. *bris.* Gael. *bruth.* Manx, *brish.*

BREWYONEN, s. f. A fragment, a piece, a crumb. Cornish Vocabulary, *mica.* Pl. *brewyon. Me a'n kcrch dheuch hep hokyé, mar lrvesyn y knoukyé oll dhe brewyon, y wrên dhodho hep mar,* I will bring him to you without delay, if I might venture to knock him all to pieces, I would do it without doubt. R.D. 1893. W. *briwionyn,* pl. *briwion.* Arm. *brienen,* pl. *brien.* Ir. *brughach.* Gael. *bruan, bruanach.*

BREYS, s. m. The mind, understanding, judgment. *Giwréns Dew y vôdh ha' y vynnas, py-penag vo yn y vreys,* let God do his will and his pleasure, whatever be in his mind. O.M. 1154. This is another form of *brès,* qd. v.

BREYSI, v. a. To judge. Another form of *brusy,* qd. v.

BRIANSEN, s. f. The throat. Cornish Vocabulary, *guttur.* The *s* indicates an older form *brianten,* the Welsh being *breuant. Briansen* became again corrupted into *briangen,* which is the form preserved in the Ordinalia. *Me a vyn setyé colm re may fastyo an colm wcharré adro dhum bryangen,* I will put a running noose, that the knot may fasten soon about my throat. P.C. 1527. See also *vryongen. Brangian* is another later corruption. W. *breuant.* Arm. *brennid.* Ir. *braighe,* †*brage.*

BRIDIAN, v. a. To boil. Id. qd. *bredion,* qd. v. Sounded in *Llwyd's* time *bridzhian,* to boil; *bridzhias,* boiled. *Llwyd,* 51.

BRILLI, s. m. Mackerel. A contracted form of *brithelli,* pl. of *brithel,* qd. v.

BRITH, adj. Streaked, motley, variegated, parti-coloured, pied or speckled, variegated with black and white. *Llwyd,* 169. W. *brith.* Arm. *briz.* Ir. *brit.* Gael. *briot.*

BRITHEL, s. m. A mackerel. Pl. *brithelli,* and by contraction, *brilli. Pryce.* In the Cornish Vocabulary it is written *brcithil.* It is derived from *brith,* variegated. For the same reason a trout is called in Welsh *brithyll,* and a mackerel, in Armoric, *brezel.* A trout, in Irish and Gaelic, is *brcac,* which means speckled, and is the same word as W. *brych,* f. *brech.* In Manx, *brack* is the name given to trout and mackerel.

BRIVIA, v. a. To bleat. ‡ *Ma'n dhavas a privia,* the sheep is bleating. *Llwyd,* 230. W. *brevu.* Ir. *buireadh.* Gael. *buireadh.* Sansc. *bhar, bhran.* Gr. φρέω. Lat *fremo.*

BRO, s. f. A country, region, land, territory, coast. In construction *vro; an vro,* the country. *Rag hena Pylat a rôs dhen varogyon aga ro, may leverrans ha dolos y' pub tyller dris an vro,* therefore Pilate gave to the villains their gift, that they should say and publish in every place through the country. M.C. 250. W. *bro.* Arm. *bro.* The Bretons of Armorica frequently use it in the names of countries, as *Bro-chall,* France, lit. the land of the Gauls. *Bro-zaoz,* England, lit. the land of the Saxons. It is evident that the original form of *bro,* in the British dialects, was *brog,* as may be seen from the Erse forms, (Ir. *bruach,* Gael. *brunch,* Manx, *broogh,)* and the classic term *allobroges;* but the regular mutation of the final *g* into its secondary form *gh,* which has no sound, led to its disappearance. It may also be the prior element in the proper names *Brochan,* or *Brychan,* and *Brochmael.*

BROCH, s. m. A badger. Cornish Vocabulary, *taxo vel melus. Benen a welté dhe floch mŷl wŷth dyghtys ages bróch gan nép mylgy,* woman, dost thou see thy son a thousand times worse treated than a badger by some greyhounds. P.C. 2926. W. *broch.* Arm. *broch.* Ir. *broc.* Gael. *broc.* Manx, *broc. Brock* is the term used in the North of England and in Scotland. There is a family in Lancashire of the name of Brockholes, who bear a badger for their crest.

BRODER, s. m. A brother. Pl. *breder, bredereth,* qd. v. This form as well as *braud,* is given in the Cornish Vocabulary. *Broder* is also written *bruder,* and by Keigwyn, *brodar. Ow broder, pur lowenck my ô genes dhe'n menedh,* my brother, very gladly I will go with thee to the mountain. O.M. 449. *Ow broder whêk, dún dhe dré, yma un posygyon brâs war ow colon ow codhé,* my sweet brother, let us come home, there is a great heaviness falling on my heart. O.M. 525. *Lavar ple ma dhe vroder,* say where is thy brother. O.M. 572. *Rág dha wreans, ty a berth gossythyans, ken na brodar,* for thy deed, thou shalt suffer punishment, though thou art a brother. C.W. 82. For the synonyms, see *Braud.*

BRODIT, s. m. A judge, a peer, a lord lieutenant. The Cornish Vocabulary, by *judex,* gives the first meaning, deriving it from *brod,* i. e. W. *brawd,* judgment. *Llwyd,* 144, in giving it as equivalent to *satrapa,* a lord lieutenant, evidently derived it from *bro,* a country, making it equivalent to the W. *ardalydh.* The *d* however proves that the meaning given in the Cornish Vocabulary is the correct one.

BROHAL, s. m. A sleeve. *Llwyd,* 85. This is the late corrupted form of *brechol,* qd. v.

BROHALEC, adj. Sleeved, having sleeves. *Llwyd,* 85. From *brohal.*

BRON, s. f. A round protuberance, a breast, a pap, the slope of a hill. Pl. *bronnow. Govy vyth, pan vêf genys, a dor ow mam dynythys, na vythqueth pan denys bron,* woe is me that I was ever born, or from my mother's womb brought, or ever sucked the breast. O.M. 1755. *Ketep mâb bron,* every sou of the breast. P.C. 802. *Ha kekyffrys an bronnow, na dhenes flehesygyow, gwyn aga beys er bones,* and also the breasts, that children have not sucked, happy their fate shall be. P.C. 2648. *Bron,* like the names of other parts of the body, enters into the composition of many names of places, as *Bronschan,* the dry round hill, and *Lambron,* or *Lambourn,* the round hill inclosure in St. Peran in Sabulo. It is thus in very frequent use in Wales, as *Bronheulog, Bronlledraith, Tynyvron,* &c. W. bron. Arm. bronn. Ir. *bruinde,* †*bronn.* Gael. *bruinne.* †*bronn.*

BRONNEN, s. f. A rush. *Del lcvaraf pen bronnen, râk ny alsé ymquen del ol degys,* as I say, rush-head, for he could not move himself, as all was brought. R.D. 2096. This is the same word as *brunnen,* qd. v.

BRONTERYON, s. m. Priests. *Rêg y vôs war bronteryon mester brâs aberth an wlâs,* for he was over priests a great master within the country. M.C. 69. This is a mutation of *pronteryon,* pl. of *pronier,* qd. v.

BROS, s. m. A sting, the point of a sharp instrument. Cornish Vocabulary, *aculeus.* W. *brwyd.* Arm. *broud.* Ir. *brad, brod.* Gael. *brod.* Manx, *brod.*

BROS, s. m. A portage, or broth. *Evé, ythesé gynef moy ages mỹl vỹl enef yn brôs pûr dêk,* drink, there were with me more than a million of souls in a pottage very fair. R.D. 142. W. *bryws.* Arm. *brouet.* Manx, *broaish.*

BROSTER, s. m. Greatness, majesty. This is a late corruption of *braster,* qd. v. *Lemyn yn second jorna, gworâf broster a dhesympys yn ybron, es awartha,* now in the second day, I will make majesty immediately, in the sky, that is above. C.W. 8.

BROSY, v. a. To destroy. *Yn medh Pylat, worth an myns an pêch, penas rŷs yw ry, me ny gaffa moy's kyns reson gans gwŷr dh'y vrony,* says Pilate, on the whole of the offence, it is necessary to give judgment, I find not, more than before, reason, with truth, to destroy him. M.C. 117. It may be *vrusy* to judge, but cf. W. *divrodi,* à *di-brody.*

BROU, s. f. A mill, a hand-mill. Cornish Vocabulary, *mola.* W. *breuan,* à hand-mill, from *brau,* brittle. Arm. *brcô, breou.* Ir. *bro,* †*bron,* †*broon* Gael. *bra.* Manx, *braain.*

BROWIAN, s. m. Crumbs. *Llwyd,* 90. The same word as *brewyon.* See *Brewyonen.*

BROWSIAN, s. m. Crumbs. *Llwyd,* 90. The same word as W. *briwsion,* pl. of *briwys,* a crumb, a fragment.

BRUDER, s. m. A brother. Pl. *brudereth. Dûn yn kerth, ow bruder whêk, me a gews dhodho mir dêk na sconyer pendra wreny,* let us come along, my sweet brother, I will speak to him very fair, so as not to be refused, whatever we do. P.C. 188. *My ny fedhaf râk medh dôs yn mýsk ow brudereth, awos cows gêr vŷth gansé,* I shall not for shame come among my brethren to speak over a word with them. P.C. 1430. *Bruder* is only another form of *broder,* qd. v.

BRUDIAS, part. Boiled. This word, written by *Llwyd,* 81, as pronounced in his time, *brudzhias,* is the same as W. *brydias,* pret. of *brydian,* to boil. See *Bredion.*

BRUES, s. m. Judgment. *Dydh brues y wrêch ysedhé, oll an bys-ma râk juggé,* the day of judgment you shall sit to judge all this world. P.C. 814. *Geseuch vy dhe worthyby kyns ry brues dhe vôs dysenŷs,* allow me to reply, before giving sentence to be put to death. P.C. 2494. This is the same word as *brûs, brŷs,* or *brês,* qd. v.

BRUGY, v. a. To judge, to pass sentence. Part. *brugys. An prysners kettep onan, drewhy yn râk dyssempys,* may *hallons bones brugys,* the prisoners every one bring forward immediately, that they may be judged. P.C. 2234. *Ke, ty mylyyes, ena yn dour dhe woles ty ê, ha genes mollath pup plu drefen fals brugy mâp Deu,* go, thou cursed, there in the water to the bottom thou shalt go; and with thee the curse of every parish, because of thy false sentencing the Son of God. P.C. 2199. This is another form of *brusy,* by the corruption of the *s* into *g* soft, or *j.*

BRUHA, s. m. Victuals. Cornish Vocabulary, *victus.* This is probably a corrupted form of the W. *brwchan,* pottage. Ir. *brochan.* Gael. *brochan.* Gr. βρωκω, sorbeo.

BRUINIC, adj. Abounding in rushes. *Pryce.* From *bruin,* id. qd. W. *brwyn.* See *Brunnen.*

BRUIT, adj. Spotted of various colours. Cornish Vocabulary, *varius.* This is an old orthography of *brith,* qd. v.

BRUNNEN, s. f. A rush, a reed. Cornish Vocabulary, *juncus,* vel *scirpus.* This word is written *bronnen,* R.D. 2096, and the pl. would be *bruin,* whence *bruinic,* and the sing. more correctly *bruinen.* W. *brwynen,* pl. *brwyn.* Arm. *broenen,* pl. *broenn.* Ir. *brôn.* Gael. *bròn.*

BRUS, s. m. Judgment. *Why a wra y anconvos dêdh brûs hag a'n kŷf ys prôf,* you will acknowledge it on the day of judgment, and have it in proof. P.C. 1496. *Dûn ganso, er y anfus, dhe Pylat agan iustys, may hallo enfus y vrûs, ha kyns dôs Sabot ledhys,* let us come with him, for his wickedness, to Pilate our magistrate, that he may have his judgment, and be put to death before Sabbath comes. P.C. 1503. It is the same word as *brŷs,* or *brês,* qd. v.

BRUSY, v. a. To judge, to pass sentence. From *brûs. Ha leverouch bôs gevys oll ow sor, bedhens lowen, ha'm gallys y vôs grontis dhodho, dhe vrusy an dên,* and say, that all my wrath is forgiven, let him be merry, and my power that it is granted to him, to judge the man. M.C. 113.

BRY, s. m. Account, value, worth, price. *Pan dra ny vyn Dew gŷl vry ahanaf, na sowyny an peyth a wrchaf ny wra,* why will not God make account of me, nor will not thrive the thing which I do. O.M. 519. *Ken fe y golon terrys, a henna my ny wraf vry,* though his heart be broken, of that I will not make account. P.O. 2244. W. *bri.* Ir. †*brìg.* Gael. *brìgh.* Manx, *brec.* Sans. *baras,* excellent, (fr. *bark,* to excel.) Gr. βρι-, βριαν, βριθω.

BRY, s. m. Mould, or earth ; soil, clay. *Mâb dên a bry yn perfyth, me a vyn y vôs formyys,* the son of man from earth perfectly, I will that he be formed. O.M. 55. *Ny a'd wra ty dhên a bry,* we make thee, man, of earth. O.M. 59. This is a mutation of *pry,* qd. v.

BRYBOR, s. m. A hypocrite. *Pryce. An fals brybor,* the false hypocrite. P.C. 375. *Dûn warbarth dhy examnyé, an vyl brybor,* let us come to examine him, the vile hypocrite. P.C. 1452. *An brybor,* the hypocrite. P.C. 1710. The only obvious etymology is the English *briber.*

BRYES, s. m. and f. A spouse, husband, or wife. *Prâg y whrusté sy tullé dhe bryes hep kên,* why didst thou deceive thy husband without mercy. O.M. 278. *Râg ty dhe gola worly, ha tullé dhe brycs lên,* because thou hast harkened to her, and deceived thy faithful spouse. O.M. 294. A mutation of *prycs,* qd. v.

BRYGE, s. m. Judgment. *Ny wodhoch pendra gewseuch, na pandra a bryge wreuch,* ye know not what ye say, nor what judgment ye make. P.C. 444. Id. qd *brŷs.*

BRYN, s. m. *A hill, a mountain. *Pryce.* W. *bryn.*

BRYNNIAN, s. m. Oats cleared of the husks; groats, oatmeal. This is a pl. aggregate. It was lastly corrupted into *brydnian.* W. *rhynnion.*

BRYNTYN, adj. Privileged, royal, noble, excellent. *Oll tús ow chy, deuch genef vy, bryntyn ha kêth,* all men of my house, come with me, nobles and commons. O.M. 1962. *Ke, gorhemmyn may tyffons umma myttyn, dhe wûl fôs u ryyn bryntyn, hag a lŷm yn creys an dré,* go command that they come here in the morning to make a wall of noble stones, and of lime, in the midst of the town. O.M. 2281. *Ny gôth agn bôs gorrys yn archow, râg bôs prennys gansé mernans dên bryntyn,* they ought not to be put into the treasury, because there has been bought with them the death of a noble man. P.C. 1542. The same word as *brentyn,* qd. v.

BRYONGEN, s. f. The throat. In construction *vryongen. Kychouch ef yn vryongen, ha dalynnouch mur cales, ma na allo pertheges yn dyspyt oll dh'y echen,* catch him in the throat, and hold him very hard, that he cannot endure it, in spite of all his efforts. R.D. 1007. This is a later form of *briansen,* qd. v.

BRYNY, s. m. Crows. This is the plural of *brân,* qd. v. *Hôs, payon, colom, grugyer, bargos, bryny, ha'n er, moy dredhof a vŷdh hynwys,* duck, peacock, pigeon, partridge, kite, crows, and the eagle, further by me are named. O.M. 133.

BRYS, s. m. Judgment, mind, advice, counsel. *Y lavaraf, nêf ha tŷr bedhens formyys orth ow brŷs,* I say, Heaven and Earth, let them be created by my judgment. O.M. 8. *Râg governyé ow bewnans, y na loer orth bôdh ow brŷs,* to govern my life, there is much according to the will of my mind. O.M. 90. *Râg colenwel bôdh dhe vrŷs, nyns ûs parow dhys yn beys,* to fulfil the desire of thy mind there are not equals to thee in the world. O.M. 434. This is the same word as *brés,* qd. v. W. *brŷd.*

BRYS, s. m. The womb, the matrix. *Creator a brys benen,* creature from the womb of woman. R.D. 19. *Nêp na grŷs y bôs sylwyas, goef genys y vonas a brŷs benen,* who does not believe that he is a Saviour, woe to him, that he was born from the womb of woman. R.D. 2420. W. *bru.* Ir. *bru.* Gael. *bru.* Manx, *brey, brein.*

BRYS, s. m. Price, value, worth. A mutation of *prys,* qd. v. *Mŷr lowené oll an bŷs, trevow a brŷs, castilly brâs hag uchel,* see the joy of all the world, houses of price, castles large and high. P.C. 132. *Sevys, gallas dhe gen le, dên apert ha mear y brŷs,* he is risen and gone to another place, a man perfect and much his worth. M.C. 255.

BUB, adj. Every, all. A mutation of *pûb,* qd. v. *Pan dethens y bŷs an bêdh, yth-eth on marrek dhy ben, hag a dychow hag a gledh onon a bûb tenewen,* when they came even to the grave, there went one soldier to the head, and on the right side and on the left, one on each side. M.C. 242. Written also *bûp.*

BUCCA, s. m. A hobgoblin, bugbear, scare-crow. *Me a'n syns gwêth es bucca, ny won py 'theth dha wandra,* I hold him worse than a hobgoblin, I know. not where he is gone to wander. C.W. 86. *Blewac, coynt yw, ha hager, ny won pana vêst ylla bôs, yth falsé orth y savour y bôsa nêb bucca nôs,* hairy, rough it is, and ugly, I know not what beast it is; it seems by its savour that it is some hobgoblin of the night. *ibid.* 114. W. *bwg, bwgan.* Ir. *puca, bogain.* Gael. *bogan.* Manx, *buggane.*

BUCH, s. f. △ cow. Cornish Vocabulary, *vacca vel juccula. Ythanwaf bûch ha tarow, ha march yw bêst hep parow dhe vâb dên râg ymweres,* I name cow and bull, and horse (that) is a beast without equals for the son of man to help himself. O.M. 123. *Buch offrynné my a vyn wharé war an alter-na,* I will offer a cow forthwith upon that altar. O.M. 1185. W. *by, buwch,* †*bou,* †*buch.* The Welsh plural *buchod,* now in common use, is formed from the old form *buch.* Arm. *bu, buoch,* †*bioch,* †*buch.* Ir. *bo ;* pl. †*bobes.* Gael. *bo.* Manx, *bua, booa.* Gr. βοῦς. Lat. *bos, vacca.*

BUCHAR, s. m. Bucked milk, sour milk. *Pryce.*

BUDIN, s. f. A meadow. Cornish Vocabulary, *pratum.* This is written by *Pryce bidhin, vidn, vethan, vythyn,* and, by *Lluyd* in his Cornish Preface, *bidin,* and in p. 127, *bydhin.* See *Bidhen.*

BUDHY, v. a. To drown, to be drowned. 3 pers. s. fut. *budh.* Part. *budhys. Dûn oll dhe'n gorhyl tôth da, gans lŷf na wrellen budhy,* let us all come to the ark quickly, that we be not drowned by the flood. O.M. 1048. *Gwythys ŷns agy dhe clos, nys bûdh dour neffre,* they are kept within the enclosure, water will never drown them. O.M. 1692. *Ellas ! govy ! budhys ôn ny, ny wren scapyé,* alas ! woe is me! drowned we are, we shall not escape. O.M. 1705. *Codhys warnan an môr brâs, ny a vŷdh cowal vudhys,* fallen on us is the great sea, we shall be quite drowned. O.M. 1701. *Gorhel vŷth ny tremené an for-na na fe budhys,* a ship never passed that way, that was not drowned. R.D. 2324. Written also *bedhy,* qd. v.

BUE, v. subs. He was. 3 pers. s. preterite of *bôs,* qd. v. With the perfect sense *has been,* it has the preterperfect particle *re,* preceding. In construction it changes into *vue,* or *vye,* and *fue. Pan dorrasa an aval, an arluth a fue serrys,* when he plucked the apple, the Lord, was angry. O.M. 880. *Ow arluth kêr, my re bue yn cyté fast ow kelwel,* my dear lord, I have been in the city urgently calling. O.M. 2429. *Na fyllys, a arluth da, na fout bythqueth nygen bue,* it was not wanting, O good Lord, there never was default to us. P.C. 916 *Dhys lowené, my re bue war ow ené, owth emlodh may 'then pur squyth,* joy to thee ! I have been, on my soul, wrestling till I was very much tired. P.C. 2508. *En deskyens del vye, ha dhodho a leverys,* they taught him how it was, and to him said. M.C. 248. Another form of *buc* is *be,* qd. v. W. *bu, vu.*

BUEF, v. subs. I was. 3 pers. s. pret. of *bôs.* It is written also *buf.* In construction it changes into *fuef,* qd. v.

BUEN, v. subs. We were. 1 pers. pl. preterite of *bôs.* In construction it changes into *vuen,* or *fuen,* qd. v. *My ha'm gwerek, râg gûl foly, helhys warbarth a fuen ny yn mês scon a paradys,* I and my wife, for doing folly, driven together we were quickly out of Paradise. O.M. 710. W. *buom.*

BUES, v. impers. There is. It is in frequent use with the

characteristic of the personal pronouns preceding, to denote possession. *Pahan cheyson a's bues erbyn Jhesu*, what accusation have you against Jesus. P.C. 1970. *Na'm bues gvlâs ynno deffry*, my kingdom is not in it really. P.C. 2014. *Gallos a'm bues dhe'th crowsye*, power is to me to crucify thee. P.C. 2154. *Marth a'm bues a'th lavarow*, wonder is to me (I wonder) from thy words. P.C. 2392. *Ny'm bues own vyth annodho*, there is not to me any fear of him. R.D. 385. Written also *bûs*.

BUGEL, s. m. A herdsman, a shepherd. Cornish Vocabulary, *pastor*. *Pan vo gwyskys an bugel, y fy an deves a bell, hag oll an flok a dhybarth*, when the shepherd is smitten, the sheep will flee far, and all the flock will separate. P.C. 893. Written indiscriminately *begel, bigel, bygel*. W. *bugail, bygel*. Arm. *bugel*. Ir. *buchail*, †*bochaill*. Gael. *buchaill*. Manx, *boehil*. Gr. βουκόλος.

BUIT, s. m. Meat, food. Cornish Vocabulary, *cibus* vel *esca*. This is the oldest form, which had changed into *boys*, at the time of the Ordinalia, qd. v. W. *bwyd*, †*buit*. Arm. *boued*. Ir. *biadh*, †*biad: buadh, cuadh*. Gael. *biadh, cuid*. Manx, *bee*. Sanse. *bhuj*, and *kid*, to eat. Gr. βίοτος.

BUL, s. f. An axe, or hatchet. *Lhwyd*, 228. This was pronounced *bool*, qd. v.

BULHORN, s. m. A snail. *Lhwyd*, 48. This word is unknown to the other dialects.

BUM, s. f. A blow. *An sêth yw rag leverys a's gwyskys tyn, gans mear angus; war y holon may cronnys dre nerth an bum fyntyyn woys*, the arrow (that) is above mentioned struck her sharply, with much anguish; in her heart, so that there stagnated, by the force of the blow, a fountain of blood. M.C. 224. Written also *bom*, qd. v.

BUP, adj. Every, all. A mutation of *pûb* or *pûp*, qd. v. *War bûp frût, losow, ha hâs, a vo ynny hy tevys*, over all fruit herbs, and seed, that are grown in it. O.M. 77.

BUR, adj. Very. A mutation of *pûr*, qd. v. *A bûr fals dyscryggynyon, tebel agas mancrow*, O very false disbelievers, evil (are) your ways. O.M. 1655.

BURM, s. m. Barm, yeast. W. *burym*. Gael. *beirm*. Germ. *berm*. Ang. Sax. *beorm*. Dan. *baermes*.

BUS, v. impers. There is. The same as *bues*, qd. v. *Ny'm bus byrê na fella*, living is no longer for me. R.D. 2210. It seems to be formed by borrowing a letter cognate with the characteristic of the pronoun preceding, and putting it before *ûs*, there is. *Nymb-us*. *A's bues* is however an exception.

BUS, s. m. Meat, food. This is the latest form of *bôs*, or *boys*, qd. v. ‡*Lian bûz*, a table cloth. *Prês bûz*, a repast, or meal of food. *Lhwyd*. It is written by Keigwyn, *boos*. *Pûb maner boos yn bŷs-ma ês dhu dlybbry*, every sort of food in this world that is to eat. 164.

BUS, s. m. The will. *Levercuch dhynny an kên agos bûs dhe wûl genen*, tell us the cause your will is to do with us. R.D. 2154. This is a corruption of *bodh*, qd. v.

BUSL, s. m. Dung, cow dung. ‡*Buzl verh*, horse dung. *Lhwyd*, 242. W. *bincal*. Arm. *beuzel*. Ir. *bualtrach*. Gael. *bualtrach*.

BUTT, s. m. A beehive, a dung cart. This is one of the few old Cornish words still in use in Devonshire and Cornwall. W. *bwt*, a dung cart; a sort of basket to place in the stream to catch fish.

BY, v. s. Be thou. 2 pers. s. imp. of *bôs*. *Kepar del ôs luen a râs, venytha gordhyys re by*, as thou art full of grace, for ever be thou worshipped. O.M. 107. *Mylleges nefrê re by*, cursed ever be thou. O.M. 580. An abbreviated form of *bŷdh*.

BY, v. subs. Thou mayest be. 2 pers. s. subj. of *bôs*. In construction it changes into *vy*, and *fy*, qd. v.

BY, adv. Ever. *Râg nechys by ny bydhyth*, for denied thou shalt never be. P.C. 3130. *By na porth dout*, never fear. R.D. 381. *By ny gewsy ken ys wŷr*, thou never sayest other than truth. R.D. 1195. *Kynyver peyn ûs yn beys, dhodho by ny vye re*, whatever pain is in the world, for him would never be too much. R.D. 2056. An abbreviated form of *byth*.

BYAN, adj. Little, small. The same as *byhan*, qd. v. *Lavaraf dheuch a tûs vâs, kekyfrys byan ha brâs*, I say to you, O good men, little and great also. O.M. 1673. *Brâs ha byan deuch yn râg ketep onan*, great and small, come forth every one. O.M. 2683. *Reys yw dhys gynê pols byan lafurye*, need is to thee with us a little while to labour. P.C. 3004.

BYDH, v. subs. Be thou. 2 pers. s. imp. of *bôs*. *Bŷdh dynny nerth ha gweres, râg warnas prest ny a'bŷs*, be to us strength and help, for to thee ever we pray. O.M. 1071. *Bŷdh lemmyn a confort da, pan yw bôdh Dew yn della*, be now of good comfort, when the will of God is so. O.M. 1341. *Del levaraf an gwŷr dhys, lemyn bŷdh fûr*, as I tell the truth to you, now be prudent. O.M. 1639. W. *bŷdh*.

BYDH, v. subs. He shall, or will be. 3 pers. s. fut. of *bôs*. In construction *vŷdh*, and *fŷdh*. *Pyw a gl henna bones, ahanan ny vŷdh onon*, who can that be, he will not be one of us. P.C. 772. *Tra ny vŷdh yn pow adro na wodhfo dhe dharryvas*, there will not be a thing in the country round which he will not know how to discover. O.M. 188. It is used impersonally with all persons. *Te a vŷdh yn keth golow yn paradis genama*, thou shalt be in the same day in Paradise with me. M.C. 193. In the same manner as the present *bues*, *bŷdh* is used with the possessive pronoun preceding, to denote possession. *Gowyn orto mar a'm bŷdh oyl a vercy yn dywedh*, ask him if there will be to me oil of mercy at the last. O.M. 693. *Why a's bŷdh drôg vommennow*, ye shall have evil blows. O.M. 2324. *Gobar da why agas bŷdh*, a good reward ye shall have. R.D. 376. *Ny'm bŷdh gweres*, there will be no help to me. R.D. 2221. This idiom was formerly common in Welsh also. See Llywarch Hên, 102. *Chwiorydh a'm bu didhan*, sisters I had who made me happy. *Chwiorydh a'm bu hevyd*, sisters to me there were besides. So also in Armoric, *Nem boe quet dram fez*, there was not (money) to me, by my faith. *Buhez Nonn*, 158. *Gant goas,—da ober nem boe quet en bet man na nem bezo muy bizuiquen*, with boys I had nothing to do in this world, nor will I have ever more. *ibid*. 50. And again in Ancient Irish, *Nimbia fochricc darhesi mo precepte*, there will not be to me, i.e. I shall not have a reward for my doctrine. *Zeuss*, 617. In Gaelic also, as *aig am bi i*, but he who has her. W. *bŷdh*.

BYDHAF, v. subs. I shall or will be. 1 pers. s. of *bôs*. *Wharrê dhedhy yn scon me ê, bydhof bysy war an dra*, anon to her soon I will go, I will be diligent on the business. P.C. 1932. Written also *bedhaf*, qd. v. W. *bydhav*.

BYDHENS, v. subs. They shall or will be. 3 pers. pl. fut. of *bôs*. It is written also *bedhens*, and *bydhons*. It is also tho 3 pers. pl. of the imperative, which in Cornish is frequently used for the singular. *Ahanouch neb yn mochya, ha'n brasa gallos dodho, bydhens kepar an lyha*, he who is the greatest of you, and has the greatest power, let him be like the least. P.C. 794. W. *bydhant*.

BYDHEUCH, v. subs. Ye shall, or will be. The future is often used for the present. *Dredho ef prynnys bydhcuch, oll ow tûs, gour ha benen*, through it ye are redeemed, all my people, male and female. P.C. 767. *Syre Arluth bydheuch attes*, Sire Lord, be you at ease. R.D. 1679. Written also *bedheuch*, or *bedhouch*, qd. v. W. *bydhwch*.

BYDHONS, v. subs. They shall, or will be. 3 pers. pl. fut. of *bôs*. *Pur wîr y fydhons dampnys dhe tân yfarn, droka le*, very truly, they shall be condemned to the fire of hell, worst place. P.C. 3094.

BYDHYTH, v. subs. Thou shalt, or wilt be. 2 pers. s. fut. of *bôs*. *Gynen bydhyth yn dowses, râk na yllyn dhe weles, cuth ny 'gen gâs*, with us thou shalt be in the Godhead, because we shall not be able to see thee, sorrow leaves us not. R.D. 2454. *Boken ny fydhyth sylwys*, otherwise thou shalt not be saved. O.M. 1510. Written also *bedhyth*, qd. v.

BYE, v. subs. He would be. 3 pers. s. subj. of *bôs*. In construction *vye*, and *fye*. It is used with all the persons. *Moy es Dew ny a vye*, greater than God we should be. O.M. 219. *Y fye medh hedré veyf byw*, it would be a shame as long as I live. P.C. 846. W. *bai*.

BYEN, v. subs. I should be. 1 pers. s. subj. of *bôs*. *Mar cedhfo an casadow, dystouch y fyen ledhys*, if the villain knew, immediately I should be killed. O.M. 2120. W. *bawn*.

BYES, v. subs. Thou wouldst be. 2 pers. s. subj. of *bôs*. *Gwyw vyes dhe gafus crôk, me a'n te re'a geydh hydhew*, thou wert deserving of getting a hanging, I swear it to thee by this day. P.C. 2683. W. *bait*.

BYEUCH, v. subs. Ye would be. 2 pers. pl. subj. of *bôs*. *Attebrys ty ha'th worty a'n wedhen ha'y avalow, y fyeuch yn ûr-na avel dewow*, if thou didst eat, and thy husband, of the tree and its fruits, ye would be in that hour like Gods. O.M. 177.

BYF, v. subs. I may be. 1 pers. s. subj. of *bôs*. In construction *vŷf*. *Pa'n drok-kuleth a wrusta, gorthyp vy na vŷf tollys*, what evil deed hast thou done? answer me, that I be not deceived. P.C. 2008. Written also *brŷf*, qd. v. W. *buyv*. Arm. *benn*.

BYGEL, s. m. A shepherd. *Lhwyd*, 114. Another form of *bugel*, qd. v.

BYGYDHYS, part. Baptized. *Kemmys a'n crys, hag a vo fêl vygydhys, sylwel a wraf*, as many as believe it, and shall be faithfully baptized, I will save. R.D. 1143. A later form of *bysydhys*, qd. v.

BYHAN, adj. Little, small. This form prevailed, after substituting *h*, for the original guttural *ch*. *My ha'm gwrêk, hu'm flôch byhan, bysy vŷdh dhe sostené*, me and my wife, and my little child, it will be hard to support. O.M. 397. *Mâb Dew o nêb a weisys, avel flôch byhan maylys*, the son of God it was whom thou sawest, like a little child swathed. O.M. 810. *Reys yw dhyso lafurrya un pols byhan alemma*, it is necessary for thee to labour a little while hence. O.M. 1269. See *Bechan*.

BYLEN, s. m. A villain, a wicked one. Used also adjectively. *Oll ny a pŷs, yowynk ha hên, may fên gwythys râk an bylen*, we all pray, young and old, that we may be preserved from the evil one. P.C. 41. *A Dhu aso why bylen*, O God ye are wretches. P.C. 2624. *Saw scrîf ynno an bylen dhe leverel y tôs ef mychtern*, but write on it that the villain said he was a king. P.C. 2798. Most probably from the English *villain*.

BYLYNY, s. m. Villainy, wickedness. *En Edhewon skyntyll kêth resteffo mear vylyny*, those same learned Jews, much villainy had they. M.C. 216. See *Belyny*.

BYMA, comp. verb. Be to me. *Herwedh dhe grath, na'm byma peyn yn gorfen*, according to thy grace, let not there be to me punishment to the end. O.M. 2254. Compounded of *by*, and *ma* for *me*, me.

BYN, s. m. The head. This is a mutation of *pyn*, for *pen*, and used in the phrases *er dhe byn*, against thee; *er y byn*, against him. *Mollath dên, gour ha gwrêk, a dhe poran erdhebyn*, the curse of man, husband and wife, will come for this cause against thee. M.C. 66. *Offens vythol er dhe byn*, whatever offence against thee. O.M. 1330. *Ena Pilat pan welas kymmys cowsys er y byn*, then Pilate when he saw so much spoken against him. M.C. 100. *Er y byn mennaf mones, me a garsé y weles*, to meet him I will go, I would wish to see him. P.C. 232. See *Erbyn*.

BYNARY, adv. For ever. *Hag a'th carvyth bynary*. and will love thee for ever. P.C. 2872. See *Benary*.

BYNC, s. m. A blow, a stroke. *Lhwyd*, 67. W. *ysponc*.

BYNCIAR, s. m. A cooper. *Lhwyd*, *bynkiar*, 174.

BYNEN, s. f. A woman. Pl. *bynenes*. Another form of *benen*, qd. v.

BYNEIt, adv. Never. *Frut da byner re dhocco, na glasé bŷs gorfen beys*, may it never produce good fruit, nor grow green even to the end of the world. O.M. 583. *Saw vyner re dhewhylly genes me a vyna pysy*, but always that thou mayest return I will pray with thee. O.M. 2196. It is the same word as *benary*, qd. v.

BYNOLAN, s. f. A broom, or besom. *Lhwyd*, 146. Written also *banolan*, or *bannolan*, qd. v.

BYNYGAF, v. a. I bless. 1 pers. s. pres. ind. of *bynigia*, or *benigia*, qd. v. *Dre ow mâp, pŷth yw ow cher, pûp ûr oll y'n bynygaf*, through my son, what is my state? at all times I bless him. P.C. 2596.

BYNYGES, part. Blessed. *Bynyges re bo an prŷs*, may fe gwrîs an gorholeth, blessed be the time, that the agreement was made. O.M. 674. It is variously written *bynoges*, *bynygys*, and *beneges*, qd. v.

BYNYTHA, adv. Ever. *Oll an tekter a wylys, ny fl taves dên yn bŷs y leverel bynytha*, all the beauty that I saw, the tongue of no man in the world can tell it ever. O.M. 766. *My a cyrch an gwâs wharré bynytha rag growedhé genen ny yn tewolgow*, I will bring the fellow soon, ever to lie with us in darkness. O.M. 888. *Gans lŷf ny wrdŷf bynytha ladhé an dûs gwyls na dôf*, by flood I will not ever destroy mankind wild nor tame. O.M. 1253. *Hag a le-na bynytha ny dhue yn ban bŷs yn dêdh breus*, he will never come up, till the day of judgment. R.D. 2139. In construction it changes into *vynytha*, qd. v.

BYPPRYS, adj. Always. *Pryce*. Written also *beppres*, and *buprys*. Compounded of *bûb*, a mutation of *pûb*, every, and *prŷs*, time.

BYPUR, adv. Hourly, continually. *Llwyd*, 249. Compounded of *byp*, a mutation of *pûp*, every, and *ûr*, hour.

BYRLA, v. a. To embrace. *Llwyd*, 42.

BYRLUAN, s. m. The morning star. *Llwyd*, 171. *Byrlûan*. In Armoric, *gourleuen;* the words are evidently connected, but the etymology is uncertain. The last syllable may be *louen*, cheerful.

BYS, s. m. The world, the universe. Written also *bés*, and in the Cornish Vocabulary, *bit*, qd. v. *Ha pan vryllyf tremené a'n bŷs, ru'm gorré dhy wlâs*, and when I shall pass away from the world, may he place me in his land. O.M. 532. *Dre y vernans yredy oll an bŷs a fydh sylwys*, through his death clearly all the world will be saved. O.M. 818. *Kyn fynnyf war an bŷs-ma wulel dyal*, if I ever should wish upon this world to cast a deluge. O.M. 1249. In construction it changes into *vŷs*, qd. v. *Dhe nôr vŷs ythaf arté*, to the earth world I will go again. R.D. 200. *Bŷs* has the sense of world—condition in the following idiom, which is also common to Welsh; qu. d. The world shines upon us. *Pub ûr ol obereth da, gwyn bŷs kymmys a'n gwrello*, always good works, happy they. as many as do them. O.M. 605. *Gwyn ow bŷs* (W. *gwyn vy mŷd*) *cafus cummyas*, happy my lot to have permission. O.M. 750. *Gwyn dhe vŷs* (W. *gwyn dy vŷd*) happy thy lot. R.D. 279. *Gwyn y vŷs* (W. *gwyn ei vyd*) *pan ve genys*, happy his lot when he was born. O.M. 1476. *Gwyn agan bŷs* (W. *gwyn ein bŷd*,) happy our lot. M.C. 4. The adjective *gwyntydedig*, happy, also occurs in Welsh, and *gwyntvidik*, in Armoric. W. *byd*, †*bit*, †*byt*. Arm. *béd*, †*bet*. Ir. *bioth*, *bith*, †*búd*, †*budh*. Gael. †*budh*.

BYS, s. m. A finger. Pl. *bysias*. *Llwyd*, 54. Written also *bés*, and *bis*, qd. v.

BYS, v. a. He will pray. *War an Tás Dew ny a bŷs, y gráth dhyn may lanvonno*, to the father God we pray that he send his grace to us. O.M. 668. *Dew an néf me a bŷs d'agan gweres*, the God of heaven, I pray to help us. O.M. 732. This is a mutation of *pŷs*, future of *pysy*, qd. v.

BYS, adv. Ever. This is a later form of *býth*. *Yntré me ha lynneth dén bŷs venytha ef a vrys*, between me and the race of man, for ever it shall be. O.M. 1242. *Ny wréth dhymo chy bŷs venary*, thou shalt never make me a house. O.M. 2334. *Awos henna ny wráf vry, na anodhans y bŷs voy me ny settyaf gwail gala*, of that I will make no account, nor of them ever more will I care a straw. C.W. 98.

BYS, prep. As far as, even to, to, until, till. *Y'th whŷs lavur dhe dhybry ty a wra bŷs y'th worfen*, in thy sweat, labour to eat thou shalt, even to thy end. O.M. 274. *Na glasé bŷs gorfen beys*, nor flourish to the end of the world. O.M. 584. *Dún alemma desempys bŷs an menedh*, let us go hence immediately unto the mountain. O.M. 1303. *Râg ny evaf bŷs dédh fŷn, genouch annodho na moy, bŷs may 'th yllyf yn ow gwlâs*, for I will not drink till the last day, with you of it any more; until that I enter into my kingdom. O.M. 724. W. *med*, *bet*, †*beheit*. *Bet* is a contracted form of *peheit*, which may be resolved into *pa*, what, and *hyd*, length. *Bet* is of constant occurrence in the *Liber Landavensis*: but it is not in use now in Welsh; *med*, which is a mutation of it, being used in South Wales, and *hŷd*, the radical form, in North Wales. Arm. *bed*, †*bet*, †*bis*.

BYSMER, s. m. Contumely. *Dyeth vye dhe dén mâs bós gwrŷs mar vêr a vysmer*, it were a pity to a good man so much contumely to be made. P.C. 2968. This is not a Celtic term, being the Anglo Saxon *bismer*.

BYSNE, s. m. A loathing. *Me a'n knouk fest dybyte ma'n geffo pûp ol lysné ow myres worth y vody*, I will beat him hard without pity, that all may have shuddering, looking at his body. P.C. 2092.

BYSQUETH, adj. Ever. *Llwyd*, 231. A later form of *bythqueth*, qd. v.

BYSTERDEN, s. m. An architect. *My a wra dhe worhemmyn, hag a warn dhe vysterdens, avorow dhys may teffens yn kelep pen*, I will do thy command, and will warn the architects, that they come to thee to-morrow, every one. O.M. 2416. *Ow arluth kér, my re buc fest ow kelwel dhe vysterdens dhys a dhe avorow pûr dyogel*, my dear Lord, I have been urgently calling the architects to come to thee to-morrow very surely. O.M. 2431. Derived in Pryce's Vocabulary, from *beisdar*, a window, and *dén*, a man. *Vysterden* may however be a mutation of *mysterden*, and compounded of *myster*, a master, and *dén*, a man, and the first meaning would be a superintendent.

BYSY, adj. Diligent, important, weighty, grievous. *Pur vysy a veydh dhedhé*, very grievous it will be for them. O.M. 335. *Aspy yn ta pûp echen, whythyr pup tra ol bysy*, examine well every particular, search out every thing diligently. O.M. 748. *Bysy yu dheuch bones wûr, coynt mûr yw an gwâs hep mar*, it is important for you to be cautious; the fellow is very sharp. without doubt. P.C. 999. *H'a nyns yu ef a parth Dew bysy vye ol an blu rôk y wythé, dh'y worré aber yn bédh*, and if he is not on the side of God, it would be important for all the parish to keep him, to place him within the grave. R.D. 2106. This word in the first sense is the same as the English *busy*, but in the latter, it would be a mutation of *pysy*, id. qd. W. *pwysig*, Arm. *poezus*, weighty; the root being *pwys*, weight.

BYSY, v. a. To pray. *Lavar, an-nes ow vos vy a'm bewnens, my dhy bysy a leverel gwyronedh*, say, being wearied of my life, that I pray him to tell the truth. O.M. 701. A mutation of *pysy*, qd. v.

BYSYDHYA, v. a. To baptize. Part. *bysydhyys*. *Pynv penag a lén grysso, yn wédh bysydhyys a vo, a vydh sylwys*, whoever may faithfully believe, and be also baptized, he shall be saved. R.D. 2467. This is another form of *bedidhia*, qd. v.

BYTEGYNS, adv. Nevertheless, notwithstanding. *Saw bytegyns pan y'th welaf, bûs hep hyreth my ny allaf*, but, nevertheless when I see thee, be without regret I cannot. P.C. 3175. *Bytegyns reys yu cryggy*, nevertheless it is necessary to believe. R.D. 1016. Written indiscriminately *betegyns*, and *bytygyns*.

BYTH, adv. Ever, for ever, always. *Yn della bŷth ny vennaf*, I never will do so. O.M. 486. *Na bŷth moy ef ny gaffus prág may fe rŷs y dampnyé*, nor evermore he found not why there should be need to condemn him. M.C. 116. *Ny ŷl dén vŷth amontyé mŷns a gollas yn chyffar*, not any man can reckon all that he lost in the bargain. M.C. 40. *Daver vyth wy ny dheesyuch dhe worré trenyth ynno*, convenience none ye brought not, to put anything in it. M.C. 50. *Byth* was often changed into *bys*, qd. v. W. *býth.* Arm. *bi, bis.* Ir. *bioth, †bith, †bid.* Gael. *bith.*

BYTHAC, adj. Deaf. *Llwyd,* 13. A late corruption of *bodhar*, qd. v.

BYTHOL, adj. Constant, continual, everlasting. *Mar pethaf kelmys lemmyn, offens vythol er dhe byn, pan clewyf vy a'n tán lyn, parhap y werussen fyé,* if I be not bound now, an everlasting offence against thee, when I should feel the fire smart, perhaps I should flee. O.M. 1350. *Nynges dên vythol yn býs dha wythyll an kéth-na,* there is no man in the world to commit that same. C.W. 90. W. *bythol.*

BYTHQUETH, adv. Ever. *Pedyr arta a gowsas, bythqueth me ny'n aswonys,* Peter again said, I never knew him. M.C. 84. *Ny welys lekké bythqueth aban véf genys,* I have not seen a fairer, over since I was born. O.M. 1731. *Gans y blew y fúns syhys, bythqueth bay dhym ny rysays,* with her hair they were dried, never a kiss to me didst thou give. P.C. 522. *Omma aberth yn pen wlás, le na fue denses bythqueth,* here within at the head of the country, where mankind never was. R.D. 2532. Composed of *byth,* ever, and *queth,* a mutation of *gweth,* a time, or turn. It was frequently changed into *bysqueth,* qd. v.

BYTYGYNS, adv. Nevertheless. *Saw betygyns cresouch why an corf-na dhe dhasserchy kyns yw aneth,* but nevertheless believe that body to rise again before it is tonight. R.D. 1301. Written also *betegyns,* and *bytegyns.*

BYUH, s. f. A cow. *Llwyd,* 168. This is a late form of *binch,* or *buch,* qd. v.

BYVE, v. subs. I shall be. *Byve* is a contracted form of *bydh,* the future sing. of *bós,* and the pronoun *ve. Genoch na'm byré trygé,* with you I shall not stay. P.C.264.

BYW, adj. Alive. *Ow máp coroneuch, h'agas mychtern of synscuch, hedré vyuch byw yn bys-ma,* crown ye my son, and for your king hold him, while you are alive in this world. O.M. 2349. *Dhym y fye mêdh, hedré veuf byw,* it would be a shame to me as long as I may be alive. P.C. 847. *Cryst a fue lydhys garow, y vôs byw my ny gresaf,* Christ was cruelly slain, his being alive I will not believe. R.D. 904. Written also *bew,* qd. v.

BYWFY, v. a. To possess, to be owner of. *Mylleges nefré re by, hag oll an tŷr a bywfy yw mylleges y'th ober,* cursed ever be thou, and all the earth thou possessest is cursed in thy deed. O.M. 581. This is the second person fut. of a verb, which would be *bywfos,* compounded of *byw,* or *bew,* to possess; and the verb *bós,* and equivalent to the W. *piewod.* "*Piewo y vuwch, aed yn ei llosgwrn,* he that owns the cow, let him go at her tail." *Welsh Adage.*

C.

This letter in all the Celtic languages has exactly the sound of the English *k,* or that of *c* before *o* and *u,* or a consonant, and to express this sound *c* is used in the Ordinalia before consonants, and *k* before the vowels. In Cornish, C is both a primary and secondary letter; when primary it changes in construction into *g* and *ch,* which is generally represented by *h,* as *colon,* a heart;

y golon, his heart; *y holon,* her heart. In Welsh it changes in the same way, as *calon, ci golon,* his heart; *ei chalon,* her heart. In Welsh only it has a further mutation into the nasal letter *ngh,* as *vy nghalon,* my heart. In Armoric it changes also into *g,* and *ch,* as *caloun, hé galoun,* his heart; *hé chaloun,* her heart. In Irish and Gaelic, *c* also changes into *g* and *ch,* as *cail,* loss; *ar gail,* our loss; *mo chail,* my loss: *ceann,* a head; *mo cheann,* my head: *cailin,* a maid; *do'n gailin,* to the maid. In Manx, into *g,* and *ch,* as *carrey,* a friend; *nyn garrey,* our friend; *e charrey,* his friend. When secondary, *c,* in Cornish, is a mutation of *g,* as *gallaf,* I shall be able; *mar a collaf,* if I shall be able. So also in Armoric, *galvo,* will call; *me a'z calvo,* I will call you. This mutation is unknown to Welsh initials.

CABEL, s. m. Cavil, detraction, calumny; an examination, a trial. *My a'th cusyl lep cabel, mar mynnyth hy dystrewy, orden dhe'th iûs hy cnoukye gans meyn, na hedhens nefré er na varwa eredy,* I counsel thee without a trial, if thou wishest to destroy her, order thy people to beat her stones, nor ever stop until she be dead quite. O.M. 2673. W. *cabyl.*

CABLY, v. a. To cavil, calumniate, try, or examine. Part. *cablys. Corf Jesus rág comfortyé gures par sur o yredy, Judas Scaryoth a's cablé, ha gans incar a falsury,* the body of Jesus to comfort, made very sure it was already, Judas Iscariot calumniated her, and with much falsehood. M.C. 35. *Conciens da na syns ladhé dên nag yw cablys, ny glowys drôk nag onan ef dhe wûl bythqueth yn beys,* it is not good conscience to kill a man who is not tried; no one has heard any evil that he has done in the world. P.C. 2434. W. *cablu.* Arm. *cablux,* blameable.

CAC, s. m. Ordure, excrement, dung. W. *cách.* Arm. *cách.* Ir. *cac.* Gael. *cac.* Manx, *cuch.* Sansc. *cakan.* Gr. *κακκή.* Lith. *szcku.* Du. *kak.* Span. & Port. *caca.*

CACA, v. a. To void, or evacuate ordure, to go to stool. W. *cachu.* Arm. *cacha.* Ir. *cac.* Gael. *cac.* Manx, *keck.* Lat. *caco.*

CACAN, s. f. A cake. Pl. *caces. Llwyd,* 121. This is from the English, the Welsh term being *teisen.*

CAD, s. f. Battle, war. The later form of this word was *cás,* qd. v. W. *cád, †cat.* Arm. *cad.* Ir. *cath.* Gael. *cath.* Manx, *caggey.* Basque, *cuda.* Old Gaulish, *catu.* Sansc. *cath,* to hurt, or wound. It enters into the composition of many names among the Ancient Britons, or Welsh, as *Cadvarch, Cadvrawd, Cadwaladr,* &c. Compare also W. *Cadvor,* anciently written *Catmor,* with the Gaulish *Catumaros,* and the old German name *Hadumar.* The same root is also evident in the classic names, *Cauriges, Cataslogi,* &c.

CADAR, s. f. A chair. W. *cader.* Arm. *cador.* Ir. *cathaoir, cathair.* Gael. *cathair.* Manx, *cathair.* All from the Latin *cathedra.* "The word *cader* is still used in Cornwall, for a small frame of wood, on which the fisherman keeps his line." *Polwhele's Vocabulary.*

CADARN, adj. Strong, stout, valiant. *Pryce's Vocab.* From *cád,* battle. W. *cadarn.* Arm. *cadarn.* Ir. *†cadranta.* Gael. *†cadranta.* Basque, *cadarn.*

CADLYS, s. m. A camp, or intrenchment. This word, compounded of *cád,* battle, and *llys,* a court, is preserved in the name *Gadles,* a place in Gluvias parish. W. *cadlys.*

CADWUR, s. m. A warrior, soldier, a champion. Cornish Vocabulary, *miles* vel *adletha*. Compounded of *câd*, battle, and *gûr*, a man. W. *cadwr*.

CAEL, v. a. To find, get, have, or obtain. Inf. *dho gael*, to have. *Llwyd*, 72. The inflected tenses are derived from *cafos*, qd. v. W. *cael*.

CAER, s. f. A town, city, a fortified place, a castle. It is often contracted into *câr*, as *Caresk*, Exeter. This word enters into the names of a host of places, once inhabited by the *Cymry*, as *Carbean, Carcarick, Cardew, Carhallock*, &c., in Cornwall. *Caernarvon, Caerdiff, Caermarthen*, &c., in Wales. *Cahir, Carbury, Carlow*, in Ireland. *Caerlaveroch*, in North Britain. As *Caer* is the exact equivalent of *Castrum*, it has been derived by writers not well versed in the laws of philology from the Latin, but it is impossible that such should be the case, as the *st* would not have been elided in the process. Compare the W. *cebystr*, from the L. *capistrum*. W. *distrywio*, from the L. *destruo*. W. *estron*, from L. *extraneus*. W. *fenestr*, from L. *fenestra*. As *castrum* is not reducible to any Latin roots, the probability is that it is derived from the Celtic *Caer*, which is regularly formed from the W. *cae*, an inclosure, a fence. The suffix *r* must be a portion of a predicate, such as *er*, intensive. That *Caer* was not borrowed by the Welsh from *castrum*, is further proved by its occurrence in the proper names of *Caeraesi* mentioned by Cæsar, and *Caeracales* by Tacitus. W. *caer*, †*cair*. Arm. *cear, ker*, †*cear*. Ir. *cathair*, †*cathir*, (pronounced *cair*.) Gael. *cathair*. Pers. *car*. Phenic. *kartha*. Pun. *karta, cartha, cirtha*. Syr. *karac*, an enclosure, *kerac*, a fortress. Chald. & Syr. *kartha*, a town. Arab. *carac*, a fortress. Basq. *caria*. Chin. *cara*, dwell. Jap. *kar*, a horse. Troj. *cair*. Scyth. *car*. Hindoo, *gurh*, a citadel, or fort.

CAER, adj. Fair, beautiful. *Pryce*. W. *cadr*. Arm. *caer*, †*caezr*. Sansc. *câru*.

CAETH, adj. Captive. *Gûr caeth*, a prisoner. *Llwyd*, 85. Written in the Cornish Vocabulary, *caid*, qd. v. W. *caeth*. Arm. †*kez*, †*keaz*. Though Llwyd derives this word from the L. *captus*, it is regularly derivable from the W. *cae*, shut up, or bound. The *th* is a later form of *d*, which denotes a sufferer, and is the characteristic of the passive participle, as *cauwyd*.

CAFAF, v. a. I shall have. 1 pers. s. fut. of *cafos*. *Dalhen mar cafaf ynno, pûr wûr ny scap, kyn fynno, na'n geffo clout*, if I shall have hold in him, very truly he shall not escape, though he may wish, so that he gets not a beating. R.D. 382. *Mar ny's cafaf scon dhum dues, ty a fŷdh drôk*, if I shall not find them soon come to me, thou shalt have harm. R.D. 847. W. *cafav*.

CAFAN, v. a. We shall find. 1 pers. pl. fut. of *cafos*. *An re-na a worthebys Jesus yns an caffan ny*, those answered, Jesus it is that we would find. M.C. 67. *Mars mara pedha degis gans y dîls, nan caffan ny, yn ûrna bŷdh leverys ef dhe sevell dre vestry*, but if he be carried away by his people, that we shall not find him, in that hour it will be said that he rose through his power. M.C. 240. Written also *cefyn*.

CAFAS, v. a. He had. 3 pers. s. pret. of *cafos*. *Christ a gafas goekorion yn templys aberth yn dre*, Christ found traders in the temples within the town. M.C. 30. *Judas êth a dhesympys a nryl tu dhe omgregy, cafas daffar pûr parrys, lovan crûf râg y synsy*, Judas went immediately on the one side to hang himself, he found convenience very ready, a rope strong to hold him. M.C. 105. *Me re'n cafas ow treylyé agan tüs yn lyes le*, I have found him turning our people in many places. P.C. 1570. Written also *cafes*, as *hy re gyfes*, she has found. O.M. 1143. W. *cavodh, caves*.

CAFAT, s. m. A vessel. Cornish Vocabulary, *vas*. W. *cafad*, from *caf*, what grasps, or holds.

CAFEL, v. a. To find, or have. *Llwyd*, 250. The common form is *cafos*. W. *cafuel*.

CAFEN, v. a. I may have. 1 pers. s. subj. of *cafos*. *Ru'm fay, lemmyn a'n caffen, er an ascal y'n toulsen yn creys an tân*, by my faith, now if I could catch him, I would cast him in the midst of the fire. R.D. 289. *Ple ma haneth a wor dên vyth may caffen wheth cryst lên a teryth*, where is there to-night any man who knows where I may yet find Christ full of sorrow. R.D. 850. W. *cafwyv*.

CAFONS, v. a. They may have. 3 pers. pl. subj. of *cafos*. *Whâth kentrow dhedhé nyngo, Jesus yn crows rag synsy, y hwalsons oll a-dro, mar caffons gôff yredy*, yet nails to them there were not, Jesus on the cross to hold, they searched all about, if they could find a smith ready. M.C. 154. Written also *cefons*, qd. v.

CAFOR, s. m. A locust, a caterpillar. Cornish Vocabulary, *brucus*. This is unknown to the other dialects, and is not Celtic, being the Ang. Sax. *ceafor*. Eng. *chafer*. Germ. *käfer*. D. *kever*, a beetle.

CAFOS, v. a. To have, find, obtain. Written indiscriminately *cafes*, and *cafus*. Part. *cefys*. 3 pers. s. fut. *cyff*. *Lemen rag caffos ran vrâs a'n pencon mara callé*, but to have a large share of the pay if he could. M.C. 38. *Yn oll an bŷs ny ylly dên cafos kymmys anfueth*, in all the world a man could not find so much misery. M.C. 225. *Rag dhym yma govgnek cafes dhe geus tregereth*, for my request is, to have thee to speak love. O.M. 454. *Ny lettys san un lam, ow cafus banneth ow mam*, I stopped only a space, receiving the blessing of my mother. O.M. 471. *Pŷth ow an odhom dynny cafus lafur an par-na*, what is the need for us to have such labour as that. O.M. 968.

CAFSONS, v. a. They have found. 3 pers. pl. pret. of *cafos*. *Pan y'n cafsons yntrethé ol warbarth y a yheys, te Pylat ladh e, ladh e, mernans am grows desympys*, when they found him, among them altogether they cried, then Pilate, kill him, kill him, the death of the cross immediately. M.C. 149.

CAHENRYD, s. m. A landflood, a torrent. This word is only found in the Cornish Vocabulary, where it is written *chahen rit, torrens*. Its etymology is obscure, and the only word approximate is the Arm. *gwaz-red*, or *gwech-rid, gwech* being a stream, and *rid*, flowing.

CAIAUC, s. m. A volume, a book. *Pryce*. W. *caewg*, what closes up.

CAID, s. m. A slave, or bondman. Cornish Vocabulary, *servus*. This is the old orthography of *caeth*, qd. v. *Caid prinid*, emptius, a bought slave. *ibid*.

CAILLAR, s. m. Dirt, mire. *Pryce*.

CAIRDER, s. m. Beauty, comeliness. *Llwyd*, 152. From *cair*, i.e. *caer*, comely, and *der*, the suffix of derivative substantives. In the Cornish Vocabulary, it is written *carder*, and wrongly translated *speciosus* vel *decorus*.

CAITES, s. f. A bondwoman, a servant maid. Cornish Vocabulary, *ancilla*, vel *abra*, vel *serva*. W. *cacthes*. Arm. *keazes*.

CAI, s. m. The penis. W. *cal*. Arm. *cal*. Sansc. *cal*, (penetrare.) Gr. καυλός.

CAL, adj. Cunning, sly. Cornish Vocabulary, *astutus*. W. *call*. Gael. *callaidh*.

CALA, s. m. Straw. *Cala gueli*, stramentum, Cornish Vocabulary, a straw bed, or mattress. *Moran cala*, a strawberry. Llwyd, 44. *Otté omma skyber dêk, ha cala lour war hy luer*, behold here a fair room, and straw enough on its floor. P.C. 680. W. *cala, calav*. Arm. *côlô*. Ir. *colbh*. Gael. *calbh, colbh*. Lat. *calamus*. Sansc. *cala*, a lance, (à rad. cal, to penetrate.)

CALAN, s. m. The Calends, or first day of the month. *Deu halan gûav*. All Saints' day, q.d. the Calends of winter, Llwyd, 45. We use *Calan* similarly in Wales, as *Dydh Calan*, New Year's day ; *Calan Mai*, the first day of May ; *Calan gauav*, the first of November. So also in Britanny, as *Cala' Meurs*, the first of March ; *Calamae*, the first of May. W. *calan*. Arm. *cala*. Ir. *callain*. Gael. *calluinn*. All from the Latin *calendæ*.

CALANEDH, s. f. Carnage, murder, manslaughter. W. *celanedh*, from *celan*, a dead body. Ir. *colan*, †*colinn*. Gael. *calain*, flesh.

CALASSA, adj. Hardest. This is a later form of *calessa*, the superlative of *cales*, qd. v. After changing the original *ch* into *h*, at the end, there was no difference in sound between the comparative and superlative, nor even in orthography. *Me a wra dhen horsen cam bós calassa presonys*, I will cause the crooked whoreson to be more hardly imprisoned. C.W. 148. By the time of Llwyd, 243, it had been further corrupted into *calatsha*.

CALATTER, s. m. Hardness. Llwyd, 240. A later form of *caletter*, qd. v.

CALCH, s. m. Lime. Llwyd, 45. W. *calch*. Ir. *calc*. Gael. *cailc*. Manx, *kelk*. Lat. *calx*. Swed. *kalk*. Germ. *calk*. Du. *kalk*. Eng. *chalk*.

CALES, adj. Hard, difficult. Written also indiscriminately *calas*, and *calys*. Comp. *culessah*, sup. *calessa*. *Y a vẏdh gwithys calas hedré vyns y yn ow gwlās*, they shall be kept hard, as long as they are in my kingdom. O.M. 1502. *Vythqueth na vi bom a won a rollo whaf mar gales*, never was a stroke, that I know of, that could give a blow so hard. O.M. 2711. *Yma omma dew cledhé parys gans ow cowethé, cales ha scherp kekeffrys*, here are two swords ready with my companions, hard and sharp also. P.C. 927. *Dalynnouch múr cales ma na allo pertheges*, hold ye very hard, so that he cannot endure it. P.C. 1008. *An beys yw cales kylden*, the world is a hard lodging. R.D. 244. *Calas ran cf a whylas*, a hard portion he has sought. R.D. 2260. *Hen o dhodho calys fryn, ngan péch ny ow prené*, this was to him grievous pain, our sins atoning for. M.C. 196. W. *caled*, †*calet*, †*calut*. Arm. *caled*. Ir. *cala*, †*caladh*. Gael. †*caladh*. Gr. χαλεπός.

CALETTER, s. m. Hardness, difficulty. *Ny vynnyth clewas Dew kêr, lemyn môs dhe'n caletter ; dhe colon yw cales brās*, thou wilt not hear the dear God, but go to hardness ; thy heart is very hard. O.M. 1524. Derived from *caled*, the original form of *cales*, hard, qd. v.

CALLAF, v. n. I shall be able. A mutation of *gallaf*, 1 pers. s. fut. of *gally*. *My a dhe n yet desempys, may callaf gweles ken ta*, I will go the gate immediately, that I may see further good. O.M. 794. *My a vyn môs dhy temptyé, mar a callaf y tenné dhe wuel glotny war nep tu*, I will go to tempt him, if I can draw him to do gluttony on any side. P.C. 52. *Lemyn dús alena, dhe dhylyfryé me a wra, mar a callaf yredy*, now come away, I will deliver thee, if I can, really. P.C. 2153. *Mar y callaf y wythé, pur wŷr ledhys bŷth ny vŷdh*, if I can preserve him, very truly, he shall never be slain. P.C. 2209.

CALLAMINGI, s. m. Tranquillity, stillness, quietness. Llwyd, 166.

CALLE, v. n. He might be able. A mutation of *galle*, 3 pers. s. subj. of *gally*. *Mar callé bós yn della*, if it can be so. P.C. 1034. *Arluth mar callé wharfos gynen ty dhe vynnes bós omma pup úr*, Lord if it could be, with us that thou wouldest be here always. R.D. 2430.

CALLEN, v. n. I might be able. A mutation of *gallen*, 1 pers. s. subj. of *gally*. *Assevyé plygadow genef gruthyl bodh dhe wŷs, a callen hep kelladow*, it would be a pleasure with me, to do the will of thy mind if I can without losses. O.M. 2177. *Me a geneweh yn lowen, mar callen guthyl hehen*, I will go with you gladly, if I can make any effort. P.C. 3007. *Lemmyn a'n caffen, er an ascal y'n toulsen yn creys an tán*, now if I should catch him, by the arm I would cast him in the midst of the fire. R.D. 289.

CALLEUCH, v. n. Ye might be able. A mutation of *galleuch*, 3 pers. s. subj. of *gally*. *Why a dhyndhylsé onor, mar callewch dry dhe cen crygyans*, you would deserve honour, if ye could bring to another belief. P.C. 1903.

CALLO, v. n. He could. A mutation of *gallo*, 3 pers. s. subj. of *gally*. *Ganso mar callo clewas whelth nowydh a vo coyntis, mar callo trylyé dhe hês lavar Christ pan vo cleuys*, with him if he might hear a new story that was recounted, if he might turn at length the word of Christ when it was heard. M.C. 109.

CALONEO, adj. Hearty, valiant, stout, courageous. Llwyd, 84. Derived from *calon*, the heart, which is generally written in Cornish, *colon*, qd. v. W. *calonog*. Arm. *caloneo*.

CALS, adj. Hard. A contracted form of *cales*. *Ha dhodho y tysquedhas cals meyn ha leverys, mars os máb Du, leun a rás, an meyn-ma giera bara dhys*, and to him he shewed hard stones, and said, if thou art the son of God full of grace, these stones make bread for thee. M.C. 11. *Mars os máp Dew awartha, dysempys arch ha lavar dhe'n cals meyn-ma bós bara*, if thou be the son of God above, forthwith command and say to these hard stones to become bread. P.C. 62. This word is still in use among the Cornish miners to signify their castaways, or *killas*.

CALTOR, s. m. A kettle. Cornish Vocabulary, *cacabus*. W. *callawr*, †*callaur*. Arm. *kaoter*. From the Latin, *caldarium*.

CALYS, adj. Hard, grievous. This is another form of *cales*, qd. v. In Llwyd's time it had been corrupted into *calish*, or *callish*. 28, 54.

CAM, s. m. Wrong, injury, a crime, trespass. Pl. *cammow*. *Rag ef gans cam a gerch dhyworthyn Adam hag Eva ha lyes smat*, for he with wrong will fetch from us Adam and Eve, and many friends. P.C. 3034. *Ha falslych yn iuggyas gans cam pur brâs*, and falsely sentenced him with very great wrong. R.D. 2264. *Gava dhyn agan cammow*, forgive us our trespasses. *Pryce's Vocabulary*.

CAM, adj. Crooked, wry, distorted, squint-eyed, perverse, wrong, wicked. It changes in construction into *gam*, and *ham* for *cham*. *Ty re gam wrûk credy, ha re'n drôs dhe vûr enken*, thou hast done evil verily, and hast brought him to much sorrow. O.M. 281. *May whrussons cam dremené y vyllyk an prŷs*, that they committed the evil transgression, they will curse the time. O.M. 336. *Ny vyn an vyl harlot cam awos an lŷs dyiccdhé*, the vile evil knave will not end for the world. P.C. 2014. *Ow ham wŷth bras, gâf dhym a lâs*, my great evil deed forgive me, O Father. P.C. 3029. *Cam* is also used as a substantive. *Settyouch dalhennow yn cam a lever y vôs mâp Dew*, set ye hands on the rogue who says that he is the son of God. P.C. 1126. *Ma stryf yntré an dhew cam*, there is a strife between the two rogues. P.C. 2248. *Why kelmoch an dew gam yn dyw crows kyns bôs prŷs bôs*, ye bind the two rogues on two crosses before it be meal time. P.C. 2783. *Cam* is given in the Cornish Vocabulary, as the translation of the Lat. *strabo*, squint-eyed, which meaning is still preserved in Welsh, and the other dialects. Sir David Gam, the famous opponent of Owen Glyndwrdu, was so called from this peculiarity. W. *cam*, †*camm*. Arm. *camm*. Ir. *cam*, †*camm*. Gael. *cam*. Manx, *cam*. Gaulish, *cambo*. Germ. *cam*. Old Eng. *kam*. Lith. *kumpas*. Lat. *camus, camurus*. Sansc. *kamar*, to be crooked. Gr. κάμπτω, κάμπτω, to bend, καμάρα, an arch. Pers. *cumu*, bending. Chald. *kamar*, to make a vaulted roof. Obs. that a final *b* has been absorbed in its cognate *m*, as is evident from the proper names *Cambodunum, Moricambe*, which latter name is still preserved in Morecambe Bay, in Lancashire, being compounded of *môr*, the sea, and *camb = camm*, curved. It is singular that in late Cornish the *mm* was resolved into *bm*, as *cabm*, pl. *cabmow*, for *camm, cammow*.

CAM, s. m. A step, or stride; a pace in going. *Hembrynkeuch an harlot gwâs, ha gans ow whyp me a'n cheus, ma kerdho garow y cam*, bring the knave fellow, and with my whip I will drive him, that he go at a rough pace. P.C. 1197. W. *cam*. Arm. *camm, cammed*. Ir. *ceim*. Gael. *ceum*. Manx, *kcm*.

CAMAN, conj. So that, that, so, as. *Y beyn o niar créf ha lyn caman na ylly bewe*, his pain was so strong and sharp that he could not live. M.C. 204. Written also *camen*, and *cammen*. *Camen Pilat pan welas na ylly Christ delyffre*, so Pilate when he saw that he could not deliver Christ. M.C. 150. *Ellas dhe vôs môr wokky cammen na vynnyth crygy pen vycterneth*, alas that thou art so foolish, that thou wilt not believe the head sovereignty. R.D. 990.

CAMDYBIANS, s. m. Suspicion, evil thought. Compounded of *cam*, wrong, and *tybyans*, opinion.

CAMDHAVAS, s. m. A rainbow. Llwyd, 73. ‡*Camdhavas en mettyn, glaw bôs etten*, a rainbow in the morning, rain is in it. *Cornish Proverb. Pryce*. Compounded of *cam*, curved, and *davas*, for *tavas*, a tongue.

CAMGARREC, adj. Bandy-legged. *Pryce*. Compounded of *cam*, curved, and *garr*, the shank.

CAMHINSIC, adj. Injurious, unjust. Cornish Vocabulary, *injuriosus, injustus*. Compounded of *cam*, wrong, and *hins*, a way, id. qd. W. *hynt*.

CAMLAGADEC, adj. Squint-eyed. Corrupted in Llwyd's time into *cabnlagadzhac*, 155. Compounded of *cam*, wry, and *lagad*, eye.

CAMMA, v. a. To bend, curve, make crooked; to trespass. *Hag y'thens dhe ben dewlyn, hag y keusens dhe scornyé, hag a gamma aga meyn pûb onon râg y eynyé*, and they went on their knees, and they spake to scorn him, and they made wry their mouths every one to extol him. M.C. 137. *Gava dhynny agan cammow, kepar ha gavan ny neb ês camma erbyn ny*. forgive us our trespasses, as we forgive them that trespass against us. *Pryce*. W. *cammu*. Arm. *camma*.

CAMMEN, s. f. A way, a path. *Drôk yu gyné na venta cammen trylé yn maner têk*, I am sorry that thou wilt not turn thy way in a fair manner. P.C. 1293. *Ow arlothes gyné agas pysys na wrellouch cammen ladhé an profus a Nazaré*, my lady by me prayed you that ye do not in any way kill the prophet of Nazareth. P.C. 2196. *Me a vynsv y wythe, ha ny yllyn cammen vŷth, pûp oll esé ow cryé y ladhé awos travyth*, I would have preserved him, and I was not able any way; all were crying to kill him notwithstanding every thing. P.C. 3126. *Dên na gresso dyougel an kêth dên-na dhe selwel cammen vŷth na ǵl wharfos*, the man who does not believe really, that same man to save not any way can exist. R.D. 2480. *My ny won pyw e cammen*, I know not who he is at all, or in any way. R.D. 2493. W. *caman*, pl. †*cemmein*. *Oxford Glosses*. Med. Lat. *caminus*. Fr. *chemin*.

CAMNIVET, s. f. A rainbow. Cornish Vocabulary, *yris vel arcus*. Compounded of *cam*, a curve, and *nivet*, celestial, tho adjective formed from *név*, heaven, qd. v. In Armoric it is called *gwarek-ar-glaô*, and also *caneveden*, which is compounded of the same elements. The Welsh names are *envys, bwa gwelaw, pont wlaw*.

CAMPIER, s. m. A champion. *Pryce*. Written by Llwyd, 44, *campur*. W. *campiwr*, (from *camp*, a game, the prize obtained at the games, the place where games are celebrated. Lat. *campus*.) Ir. †*caimper*. Gael. †*caimfear*. Germ. *kämpfer*. Dan. *kæmper*.

CAMS, s. f. A surplice. Cornish Vocabulary, *alba*. Another form of the same word is *hevis*, qd. v. W. *cams, camse, hevys*. Arm. *camps, hiviz*. Ir. †*caimmse*. Gael. †*caimis*. Lat. *camisia*. Ital. *camicia*. Fr. *chemise*. Arab. *kemys*. Germ. *hemd*.

CAMSGUDHEC, adj. Crooked-shouldered. Llwyd, 63, ‡*cabmsgudhac*. Compounded of *cam*, crooked, and *sgudhec*, the adjective derived from *sgodh*, or †*scuid*, the shoulder.

CAMWUL, v. a. To do wrong. *A arluth kêr, my a wra mar a kyllyn yn della; ny dhe gamwul y won gwŷr*, O dear Lord, I will do if I can so; that we do wrong I know truly. P.C. 1065. Compounded of *cam*, wrong, and *gûl*, to do.

CAN, s. f. pl. *canow*. In construction it changes into *gân*, and *hân* for *chân*. *Menestrouthy ha cân whêk*, minstrels, and a sweet song. O.M. 770. *Râg henna, me a's lemptyas dhe behé*, may *fe ellas aga hân kepar ha my*, for this I tempted them to sin, that "alas" may be their song as well as I. O.M. 310. *Gorrys dhe néf gans cân*, placed in heaven with a song. O.M. 6402.

CANNAS 44 CAR

Me a vyn gwethyl canow, I will make songs. C.W. 180. W. *cân*. Arm. *cân*. Ir. *caint*. Gael. *cainnt*.

CAN, v. irr. We shall have. 1 pers. pl. fut. of the irr. v. *cafos*. *Ni a gân*. Llwyd, 247. W. *cawn*.

CAN, adj. White. *Bara can*, panis albus, Cornish Vocabulary. W. *can*. Arm. *cann*. Ir. *can*. Gael. *cain*. Lat. *canus, candidus*. Sansc. *kan*, to shine.

CAN, num. adj. Hundred. *Hayl Cayfas syr epscob stout, dêk can quyth dhys lowené*, hail, Caiaphas, bold sir bishop, ten hundred times joy to thee. P.C. 574. This is an abbreviated form of *cans*, qd. v. *Can* is similarly used in Welsh for *cant*, as *can mil*, a hundred thousand. *Can* is also used as a substantive in Cornish. *Nêb esé aberth yn bêdh, gans can ha mûr a eleth, dhe vewnans y tassorchas*, he that was within the tomb, with a hundred and more of angels to life has risen. R.D. 515.

CANAS, s. m. A song. Pl. *canasow. Y a vŷdh ryal ha splan, canasow dhe'm danvenys*, they shall be royal and resplendent, songs unto me sending. C.W. 4. W. *caniad*.

CANCER, s. m. A crab fish. Cornish Vocabulary, *cancher*, cancer. Pl. *cancres*, and *concras*. Llwyd, 243. W. *cranc*, pl. *crancod*. Arm. *caner*, and *crank*, pl. *cranked*. Manx, *grangan*. Lat. *cancer*. Gr. καρκίνος. Sansc. *karkas, karkatas*.

CANE, v. a. To sing, to sing a song, to sing as birds, to crow. 2 pers. s. imp. *cân*, sing thou. 1 pers. s. fut. *canaf*. 3 pers. s. fut. *cân*. Part. *kenys*. *Un el ow talleth cané, a uchaf war an wedhen*, an angel beginning to sing above me on the tree. O.M. 215. *Râg ef o tebel edhen, nêb a glewsys ow cané*, for he was an evil bird, whom thou didst hear singing. O.M. 224. *Servys dhe Dew dhe gané, y sacra seon my a venn*, to sing the service to God, consecrate him forthwith I will. O.M. 2603. *An maystri brâs oll a'm bo, my re'n collas dredho, may canaf trew*, all the great power that was mine, I have lost through him, that I may sing "alas!" P.C. 150. *Peb ol war pen y dew glyn a gân yn gordhyans dodho*, every one upon his knees will sing in worship to him. P.C. 248. *Ow tywedh na ganno tru*, at last that he may not sing "alas!" P.C. 1810. *Kyns ys bos cullyek kenys*, before the cock has crowed. P.C. 903. *Kenouch why faborden brâs, ha my a cân trebyl fyn*, sing ye a great bass, and I will sing a fine treble. R.D. 2359. In Keigwyn and Llwyd's time, it was written *cana*. *Fir ow cuna*, singing wisely. C.W. 56. *Ddo gana*, to sing. Llwyd, 230. W. *canu*. Arm. *cana*. Ir. *can*. Gael. *can*. Lat. *cano*. Sansc. *kan*, to utter a sound.

CANGUER, s. m. A hundred men. *Pen canguer*, Cornish Vocabulary, *centurio*. The captain of a hundred men, a centurion. Compounded of *can*, hundred, and *guer*, the plur. of *gour*, a man. W. *canwr*.

CANNA, s. m. A flagon, or can. Cornish Vocabulary, *lagena*. From the English.

CANNAS, s. m. A messenger, apostle. Pl. *cannasow*. *Ow cannas whêk*, my sweet messenger. P.C. 1041. *Danfon dhe Pilat cannas*, send a messenger to Pilate. P.C. 1936. *Me a vyn danvon ow cannas râg y warnyé*, I will send my messenger to warn him. P.C. 1955. *Me a'th pŷs a dhanfon dhynny cannas*, I pray thee to send to us a messenger. R.D. 768. *Cregyans an Cannasow*, the Creed of the Apostles. Pryce. W. *cennad*. Arm. *cannad*. Ir. *cead*. Gael. *cead*. Manx, *kied*.

CANORES, s. f. A female singer, a songstress, a singing woman. Cornish Vocabulary, *cantrix*. From *canor*, id. qd. W. *canvor*, a singer, with the feminine addition. The equivalent terms used in Welsh are *canwraig*, and *cantores*. Arm. *caneres*.

CANQUYTH, adv. A hundred times. *Dek canquyth dhys lowené*, ten hundred times joy to thee. P.C. 574. Llwyd, 248, has another form, *canswyth*. Compounded of *can*, or *cans*, a hundred, and *gwyth*, a time. W. *canwaith*.

CANS, num. adj., and subs. m. A hundred. *Nans yw lemmyn tremenes nêp dew cans a vledhynnow*, now there are gone by some two hundred years. O.M. 657. *Try hans kevelyn da, an lester a vŷdh a hŷs; ha hanter cans kevelyn yn wedh ty a wra y lês*, three hundred cubits good the ship shall be in length; and half a hundred cubits also thou shalt make its width. O.M. 955. *Moy ys cans vyl*, more than a hundred thousand. O.M. 1614. *Cans puns*, a hundred pounds. P.C. 3144. *Sŷth cans blydhen*, seven hundred years. R.D. 2494. W. *cant*. Arm. *cant* Ir. *ccad*, †*cét*. Gael. *ciad*. Manx, *keead*. Sansc. *cata*. Gr. ἑκατόν. Lat. *centum*. Gothic and O. H. German, *hunda, hunta*.

CANS, prep. By, with. Cornish Vocabulary, *Greg cans gur*, uxor, a wife; lit. woman with a man. This is the original form, which changes regularly into *gans*, qd. v. W. *can, gan*, †*cant*. Arm. *gant*.

CANS, v. a. They shall have. 3 pers. pl. fut. of irr. v. *cafos*. *Y a gâns*. Llwyd, 247. W. *cânt*.

CANTLY, s. m. A lamp. Llwyd, 81. From *cantal*, a candle.

CANTUIL, s. f. A candle. Cornish Vocabulary, *candela*. The late forms were *cantl*, and *cantal*, pl. *cyntulu*. W. *canwyll*. Arm. *cantol*. Ir. *cainneal, coinnill*. Gael. *coinneal*. Manx, *cainle*. All from the Latin *candela*.

CANTULBREN, s. m. A candlestick. Cornish Vocabulary, *candelabrum*. Compounded of *cantuil*, a candle, and *pren*, a stick. W. *canwyllbren, canwyllyr*. Arm. *cantoler*. Ir. *caindloir*. Gael. *coinnlcir*. Manx, *cainleyr*.

CANVAS, v. a. To find. ‡*Dho canvas fowt*, to find fault. Llwyd, 60. W. *canvod*.

CAOL, s. m. Cabbage. Llwyd, 45. Written in Cornish Vocabulary, *caul*, qd. v.

CAPA, s. m. A cap. Cornish Vocabulary, *cappa*. Plur. *capies*, and *cappios*. Llwyd, 243. W. *cap, capan*. Arm. *cab, cabel*. Ir. *ccap*. Gael. *ceap*. Manx, *ccap*. The original *caps* and *cabins* of the Celts were of the same shape, being circular at the base, and forming a cone, whence the agreement in the appellations, a cabin being called in Welsh, *cab, caban*. Arm. †*caban*. Ir. *caban*. Gael. †*caban*. Manx, *cabbane*. Cf. also the *capanna*, a cottage, of Isidore, the Span. *cabanna*, Fr. *cabane*, Eng. *cabin*, and *Capellatium*, the old Gaulish name of the Limes Transrhenanus of Ammianus.

CAR, s. m. A friend, ally, a dear neighbour, a kinsman, a cousin; also a father, which in Armoric is the most common meaning. Cornish Vocabulary, *amicus*. *Câr ogos*, affinis vel consanguineus. Plur. *kerans*. Llwyd, 50. *Yn nêf y fedhaf tregis an barth dychow gans am câr*, in heaven I shall dwell on the right side with my father. M.C. 93. *Me ny allaf convethas y bosta ge ow hendas, na câr vŷth dhym yn teffry*, I cannot discover that thou art my grandsire, nor any relation to me in reality. C.W. 116. W. *car*, pl. *ceraint*. Arm. *câr*, pl. *cerent*. Ir. *cara*. Gael. *cara*. Manx, *carrey*. Sansc. *craiyas*, dear. Gr. χαριεις. Lat. *carus*.

CAR, v. a. Will love. 3 pers. s. fut. of the verb *caré*. *My a'd câr mûr*, I love thee much. O.M. 2154. *Mur me a'n câr*, much I love him. R.D. 1802. *Me a'th câr*, I love thee. R.D. 1812. *Saw nep a'n gwello a'n câr yn y colon*, but whoever sees him will love him in his heart. R.D. 1895. *Dew na sijns ny'n câr*, God or saints love him not. R.D. 2114. *I'up oll a gâr bevé*, every one loves to live. P.C. 600. W. *câr, a gâr*. Arm. *câr, a gâr*.

CAR, conj. Like as, as. Llwyd, 134. It mostly occurs in the composite form *pocâr*, qd. v.

CARA, conj. Like as, so as, as, as it were. Llwyd, 150. It is the same word as *câr*, and is generally joined to *po*. See *Pocara*.

CARA, v. a. To correct, to chastise. *Yn egis mijsk pan esen, lays Du dheuch ow tysky, gallus nyng-esé kemmen dhom cara na dhom sensy*, when I was amongst you, teaching the laws of God, there was not power at all to chastise me, nor to sleze me. M.C. 75. W. *ccrydhu*, from *cerydh*, †*cared*, nequitiæ. From Lat. *correctio*. Ir. *cairv, cairiyim*.

CARADOW, adj. Beloved, loving, dear. Pl. *caradowyon*. *An tâs an nef caradow*, the Father of heaven beloved. O.M. 670. *A dâs colon caradow*, O father, dear heart. O.M. 721. *A dâs whêk oll caradow*, O sweet father, all beloved. O.M. 1346. *Arlythy caradowyon, dreuch dhym ow mâp cûf colon*, dear lords, bring to me my son, wise of heart. P.C. 3163. *Me a'n gordh omma del reys, râg y bôs mar garadow*, I will worship him here as is necessary, because he is so loving. Keigwyn, 40. W. *caradwy*.

CARCATH, s. f. A thornback, ray, or skate. Compounded of *car*, abbreviation of *carrec*, and *câth*, a cat. It is called in W. *câth vôr*. Arm. *kaz-vôr*. Written by Llwyd, *karcath*, 156.

CARDER, s. m. Beauty. Llwyd, 152. The Cornish Vocabulary which furnishes this word translates it *speciosus* vel *decorus*, but erroneously, as *der* is the suffix of derivative substantives. The root is *caer*, beautiful, qd. v.

CARDOWYON, adj. Friends. Llwyd, 242. *Tormentours cardowyon, hep whethé corn, na gûl son, keruch ihesu dhynny ny*, executioners, dear fellows, without blowing horn, or making a noise, bring Jesus to us. P.C. 1357. This is a contraction of *caradowyon*, the plural of *caradow*, qd. v.

CARE, v. a. To love. 1 pers. s. fut. *caraf*. 3 pers. s. fut. *câr, a gâr*. Part. *kerys, kerrys, kyrys*. *An Tâs Dew re bo gordhyys, eyneys mûr ôn dh'y garé*, the Father God he worshipped, we are much bound to love him. O.M. 1126. *An keth dên-ma dhe caré*, this same man to love. P.C. 511. *Pan welas an Edhewon bôs Christ ow cuthyl meystry, ow caré adhomygyon, hag anedhé na were vry*, when the Jews saw that Christ was doing mastery, loving the needy, and of them made no account. M.C. 26. *If a gara Christ gwelas*, to love Christ. M.C. 109. *Y welas ef ny gara na bôs yn y gowethas*, he loved not to see him, nor to be in his company. M.C. 110. *Del y'th caraf mûr pûp prŷs*, as I love thee much always. P.C. 710. *Synt Jovyn whêk re'n carro*, sweet saint Jove love him. P.C. 1847. *Hag a'th carvyth bynary*, and will love thee for ever. P.C. 2872. *Y weles me a garsé*, I would have liked to see him. R.D. 435. *Gwelas ow mâp y carsen*, I should have liked to have seen my son. R.D. 442. *Neb a geryn an moycha*, whom I love the most. C.W. 88. *Mar a'm kerouch*, if ye love me. *ibid.* 182. See also *Cyrry, cyrreuch, cyrys*. In Keigwyn and Llwyd's time, the infinitive was written *cara*. W. *caru*. Arm. *carout*. Ir. *caram*, †*cairim*, *gradhaigh*. Gael. *gradhaigh*. Manx, *graih*.

CARENSE, s. f. Love, friendship. More frequently written *cerense*, qd. v. *Po kelly an garensa*, or lose the love. C.W. 62. It was corrupted into *carengé*, or *carenga*, by substituting *g* soft, sounded as *j* in English, for *s*. *Râg dha garenga lemyn*, for thy love now. C.W. 28. *Adam whêk, ow harenga*, sweet Adam, my love. *ibid.* 56.

CARESK, s. f. Exeter. Llwyd, 252. Compounded of *Câr*, for *Caer*, a city, and *Esk*, the name of the river. W. *Caeriysg*.

CARG, s. m. A load, burden, charge, cargo. Pryce. W. *carg*. Arm. *carg*.

CARHAR, s. m. A jail, or prison. Llwyd, 46. W. *carchar*. Ir. *carcar, carcair*. Gael. *carcar*. Lat. *carcer*. Gr. καρκάρ-ον. Germ. *kircher*.

CARIA, v. a. To bear, or carry. ‡ *Cariah an stuff stena dha an stumpes*, carry the tin stuff to the stamping mill. ‡ *Cariah an stean dha an fôg*, carry the tin to the blowing-house. Pryce. W. *cario*. Arm. *carren*. Manx, *car*. The root is the W. *car*, a wain, or dray. Fr. *charrier*. Span. *acarrear*. Dan. *kiôrer*. Sw. *kiora*. Germ. *karren*.

CARIOS, s. m. A cart, or carriage. *Me a fyn, re dhu am rôs, dhe gemeres gans carios, hug yn pryson dhe teulel*, I will, by him that made me, take thee with a cart, and throw thee into prison. P.C. 2266. *Carios* is probably the plural of *car*. W. *car*, †*carr*, Oxford Glosses. Arm. *carr*. Ir. *carr*. Gael. *carr*. Manx, *cayr*. Lat. *carrus*; in Cæsar, *Gallorum currus*. Sansc. *car*, to move, or advance.

CARME, v. a. To cry out. *Why a gŷf bohosugyon pup ur warnoch ow carmé*, ye will have the poor always crying out to you. P.C. 544. A mutation of *garmé*, qd. v.

CARN, s. m. A rock, a rocky place, a high rock, a shelf in the sea, a heap of stones; the hilt, or handle of an instrument, as *carn colhan*, the hilt of a knife, Llwyd, 86. Also the hoof, as *ewincarn*, qd. v. Pl. *carnow*. *Lemmyn hertheuch hy yn vês, me a glew un hager noyes, yn carn yn môr er y byn*, now push her out, I hear an ugly noise on a rock in the sea meeting him. R.D. 2297. *Dhe un carn y fue tewlys*, to a rock he was cast. R.D. 2333. *Tân ha môk ha pocvan brâs yn carna* (= *carn-na*) *neffre y sêf*, fire and smoke and great sickness in that rock shall ever remain. R.D. 2432. ‡ *Mi rig gwelas an carnow idsha an idhen môr kil y ge neitho*, I saw the rocks where the sea birds make their nests. Llwyd, 245. W. *carn*, a rock, haft, hoof. Arm. *carn*, rock, hoof. Ir. *carn*. Gael. *carn*. Manx, *carn*. In the Erse dialects it means a rock only.

CAROL, s. m. A choir, a concert. Cornish Vocabulary, *chorus*. In Welsh, *carol* means a song, or panegyrical poem; *caroli*, to sing carols; and *côr*, a circle, the choir of a church, whence *coroli*, to move in a circle, to dance. Arm. *coroll*, a dance; *corolli*, to move in cadence, to dance. Gael. *caruill*, to sing. Manx, *carval*, a carol.

CAROW, s. m. A deer, stag, or hart. *Ythanwaf buch ha tarow, ha march yw bêst hep parow dhe vâp dên râg ymweres, gaver ywyges carow, daves war ve lavarow hy hanow da kemeres*, I name cow, and bull, and horse which is a beast without equals for the son of man to help himself; goat, steer, stag, sheep, according to my words, let her take her good name. O.M. 126. *Suel a vynno bôs sylwys, golsowens ow lavarow, a Jesus del ve helheys war an bŷs avel carow*, whoever wishes to be saved, let him hearken to my words, of Jesus, how he was hunted in the world like a deer. M.C. 2. W. *carw*. Arm. *carô, carv*. Ir. *cairfhiadh*, †*searbos*. Gael. *cairfhiadh*. As the Welsh does not give us any radical meaning, it is evident that the Britons must have borrowed the term from the Lat. *cervus*, which again was derived from the Gr. κεραὸς, horned, the root being κέρας, a horn, one of the chief characteristics of a stag. Of. Sansc. *carngin*, a horned beast. The Celtic term for a stag was the W. *hŷdh*; Arm. *heiz*; Ir. *fiadh*; Gael. *fiadh*; Manx, *feeaih*. In the Irish and Gaelic *cairfhiadh*, the two names are combined. With the above compare also the Lat. *hœdus*, a kid; and Sansc. *aidhakas*, a ram, from *aidh*, to grow.

CARRA, v. a. He may love. 3 pers. s. subj. of *caré*. *Kyn yn carra vyth mar veur, awos y ladhé ny'm duer*, though he may love him ever so much, for killing him, I have no concern. R.D. 1897. This should properly be written *carro*, qd. v.

CARRAG, s. f. A stone, a rock. *An garrac*, the stone. Llwyd, 241. Pl. *carrygy*. *Pyth yw an gordhyans dhe Dew, bôs leskys dhe glow lusew war an carrygy degé*, what is the worship to God, that the tithe should be burnt to coal ashes on the stones? O.M. 478. W. *carreg*, †*carrec*. Arm. *carrec*. Ir. *carraic*. Gael. *carraig, carragh*. Manx, *carric*. Gr. χάραξ.

CARRO, v. a. He may love. 3 pers. s. opt. of *caré*. *Synt Jovyn whêk re'n carro, ha dres pup ol re'n gortho, kepar del ylly yn ta*, may sweet saint Jove love him, and honour him above every one, like as he can well. P.C. 1847. *Benneth sewys, synt Jovyn whêk re'th caro*, a blessing follow thee, may sweet saint Jove love thee. P.C. 3016. W. *caro*.

CARSE, v. a. He had loved, or would have loved. 3 pers. s. plup. of *caré*. *Ny garsé pellé bevé*, he would not wish to live longer. O.M. 738. *Me a garsé y weles*, I would wish to see him. P.C. 233. *Cows ganso me a garsé*, I should have liked to speak with him. R.D. 744. W. *carasai*, and hy contraction *carsai, a garsai*.

CARSEN, v. a. I had loved, or would have loved. 1 pers. s. plup. of *caré*. *Dhe vôdh mar pe genes, gwelus ow mâp y carsen*, thy will if it be with thee, I would like to see my son. R.D. 442. *Y carsen gwelas an fuu anodho, y vôdh mar pe*, I would wish to see the form of him, if it he his will. R.D. 469. *Clew mar a'th dûr dhys daryvas del garsen mûr*, hear, if it concerns thee, as I would desire much to declare to thee. R.D. 846. W. *caraswn*, and contractedly *carswn, a garswn*.

CARSESTA, v. a. Thou hadst loved, or wouldst have loved. 2 pers. s. plup. of *caré*. *A garsesta bynené, mar mynnyth, war ow ené, me a gerch onan dêk dhys*, wouldst thou love women? If thou wishest, on my soul, I will fetch a fair one for thee. P.C. 2638. *Carsesta* is compounded of *carses*, the second person, and the pronoun *te*, thou.

CARVYTH, v. a. He will love. 3 pers. s. fut. of *caré*. *Vynytha dalasias, ef a'th carvyth me a grŷs*, for ever, in requital, he will love thee I believe. P.C. 1846. *Me a'n carvyth y'm colon, alemma bŷs gorfen beys*, I will love him in my heart henceforth to the end of the world. P.C. 1703. *Hag yn ûr-na martesen dheth lavarow y cresen, hag a'th carvyth bynary*, and in that hour perhaps I would believe thy words, and will love thee for ever. P.C. 2872.

CAS, s. f. A battle, conflict. *An Princis esa yn pow gans Judas a dhanvonas tûs ven gweskis yn arvow kepare ha delens dhe'n gâs*, the Princes (that) were in the country with Judas sent men trusty, clad in armour like as they go to the battle. M.C. 64. *Me yw mychtern re wruk câs ol rag dry Adam ha'y hâs a tebel scuth; mychtern of a lowene, ha'n victory eth gyné yn arvow rudh*, I am the king that did battle all to bring Adam and his seed from evil plight; the king I am of joy, and the victory went with me in arms red. R.D. 2517. The earliest form was *cdd*, qd. v.

CAS, s. m. Hatred, enmity, trouble, anguish, misfortune. *Yn Egip whyrfys yw câs, ow popel vy grevyys brâs gans Pharow, yw mylyges, ymons dhymo ow cryé*, in Egypt trouble has arisen, my people, greatly aggrieved by Pharaoh, who is accursed, are to me crying. O.M. 1415. *Yma câs brâs wharfethys ha codhys war dhe pobel*, a great misfortune has occurred, and fallen on thy people. O.M. 1542. *Mûr a gâs vye gené trehy henna*, much trouble it would be to me to cut that. O.M. 2501. *Ha nep na'n grûk war nêp tro yn peynys trygens yno, hep ioy prest may's teffo câs*, and whoever has not done it on any occasion, in pains let him dwell there, without joy always, that he may obtain anguish. R.D. 160. W. *câs*. Arm. *câs*. Ir. †*cais*. Gael. †*cais*, (*câs*, misfortune.) Sansc. *hath*. Gr. κότος; χόω, to hate. Fr. *hair*. Goth. *hata*. Aug. Sax. *hasse*. Eng. *hate*.

CASADOW, adj. Hateful, odious, detestable, villainous, worthless, rotten. Often used as a substantive. *Fystyn duwhans gweres vy, ow tôn a' plos casadow*, hasten quickly to help me, bringing the odious villain. O.M. 892. *Mar cothfo an casadow, dystouch y fyen ledhys*, if the villain knew, immediately I should be killed. O.M. 2199. *Euch tynneuch an gasâdow, usy ow cul fals dewow, yn mês agan temple ny*, go drag the detestable (woman), who is making false gods out of our temple. O.M. 2691. *Yn della, a gasadow, y gorthebyth epscobow*, thus, O detestable one, dost thou reply to bishops? P.C. 1265. *Gans an bobba casadow*, with the odious idiot. P.C. 2394. *Del lavaré war anow war an pren glays mar a te, yn pren seych ha casadow yn er-na fatel ve*, as they say by mouth; on the green wood if it come, in wood dry and rotten, in that hour how shall it be? M.C. 170. W. *casadwy*.

CASAL, s. f. The armpit. Written by Llwyd, 44, *cazal*. W. *cesail*. Arm. *cazel*. Ir. *asgal, oscul*. Gael. *achlais*. Manx, *achlish*. Lat. *axilla*. See *Ascal*.

CASE, v. a. To hate, detest. *Râk ef yw drôk wâs, war ow fay, me a'n câs, a'n plôs fleryys*, for he is a wicked fellow, on my faith I hate him much, the stinking villain. R.D. 1889. W. *casâu*. Arm. *casaat*.

CASEC, s. f. A mare. Cornish Vocabulary, *cassec*, equa. Keigwyn and Llwyd write it *casac*, which was the pronunciation of their time, and so it is pronounced vulgarly in many parts of Wales at present. Pl. *cassigy*. *Y'thenwaf beuch ha tarow, oll an cattel debarow, aga henwyn kemerans; march, hu casac, ha asan, ky, ha câth, logosan, deffrans chan serpents,* I will name them cow and bull, all the cattle feeding, let them take their names; horse and mare, and ass, dog, and cat, mouse, different kinds of serpents. C.W. 32. *Casac dhal,* a blind mare. Llwyd, 243. *Casec coid,* the green woodpecker. (Arm. *cazek coad.* W. *caseg wanwyn, caseg y drychin.*) W. *caseg.* Arm. *cazek.*

CAST, s. m. A trick. *Ty vavo, lemyn syng-e fast, râk ef a wor lyes cast, râk dhe tollé,* thou boy, now hold him fast, for he knows many tricks to deceive thee. P.C. 1884. *Gureuch y pur fast, ma na allons yn priceth y laddra yn mês an bêdh, dre nêp fals cast,* make them very fast, that they may not be able privily to steal him out of the tomb, by some false trick. R.D. 36. W. *cast.* Ir. *gastog.* Gael. *gasdag.*

CASTEL, s. m. A castle, fort, fortress; also a village. Pl. *castilly. My a vyn gruthyl castel, ha drehevel dhym ostel, ynno jammes rag tregé,* I will make a castle, and build for myself a mansion, in it ever to dwell. O.M. 1709. *Myr lowené ol an bŷs, trevow a brŷs, castilly brâs hag huchel,* behold the joy of all the world, towns of price, castles large and high. P.C. 131. *Ens dew am dyscyblyon dhen castel ûs a ragon,* let two of my disciples go to the village that is before us. P.C. 174. *Stout avos castel Maudlen, mar querth me a ter dhe pen dhys awartha,* though thou be as strong as Castle Maudlen, if thou dost I will break thy head for thee from above. R.D. 920. *Ny iuggyn mones nep pel, lemmyn bŷs yn un castel henwys Emmaus,* we do not think to go any distance, but as far as a village called Emmaus. R.D. 1205. W. *castell.* Arm. *castel.* Ir. *caiseal.* Gael. *caisteal.* Manx, *coshtal.* All from the Lat. *castellum.*

CATH, s. f. A cat. Written in the Cornish Vocabulary, according to the old orthography, *cat*, cattus vel murilegus. *Aga henwyn kemerans, march ha casac, ky, ha câth, logosan,* let them take their names, horse and mare, dog, and cat, mouse. C.W. 32. *Oll dha lavyr myn dîl câth,* all thy labour is not worth a cat. ibid. 166. *Bram an gâth,* the wind of a cat. ibid. 172. *Gurenth,* a he-cat. *Coidgath,* a wild cat, or cat of the woods. Pryce. W. *câth.* Arm. *caz.* Ir *cat.* Gael. *cat.* Manx, *cayt.* Gr. κάττος, κάττης, κάτα. Lat. *catus, cattus, catta.* Fr. *chat.* It. *gatta.* Span. *gato.* Isl. *katt.* Swed. *katt.* Da. *kat.* Ang. Sax. *cat.* Germ. *katze.* Sansc. *câvas,* a young animal, from *ovi*, to grow, propagate.

CAUCH, s. m. Ordure, manure, dung. *Cawch.* Llwyd, 154. The same word as *cac*, qd. v.

CAUCHWAS, s. m. A filthy fellow, a base fellow, a coward. *Ty an gwysk avel cauch-was*, thou strikest him like a coward. F.C. 2103. *Ty a whŷth avel cauch gwâs, whyth war gam, ny dryk grychonen yn fôk,* thou blowest like a coward, blow athwart, there remains not a spark in the forge. P.C. 2715. Compounded of *cauch*, dung, and *gwas*, a fellow. *Câch* is similarly used to denote baseness in the W. compound *cachgi*, a coward, from *câch*, and *ci*, a dog.

CAUGEON, s. m. A filthy fellow. Used also as an adjective. *Henna me a wra, râk ny won yn beys gwell toul dhyn dhe wruthyl dhen caugeon,* that I will do, for I know not a better trick in the world for us to do to the dirty fellow. P.C. 2921. *Ha my caugeon lawethan, merwel a wrên ny ow cul tân yn dan an chek,* and my dirty fiends, we will die making a fire under the kettle. R.D. 137. *Ple 'thesos caugyon, ha'th couyth,* where art thou, dirty fellow, and thy comrade. R.D. 644. From *cauch.*

CAUL, s. m. Cabbage, colewort, any kind of pottago in which there is cabbage, or any sort of potherbs. Cornish Vocabulary, *caula* vel *magdulans*, olera. It is written by Llwyd, *cwol, caul, cowl.* W. *cawl.* Arm. *caol, col.* Ir. *cál.* Gael. *câl.* Manx, *kail.* Gr. καυλὸς. Lat. *caulis.* Lith. *kolas.* Fr. *chou.* Germ. *kohl.* Belg. *koole.* Swedo. *kol.* Aug. Sax. *caul.* Eng. *cole, kail.*

CAUR, s. m. A giant. It is preserved in the composite *caurmarch,* qd. v. In Welsh, it bears the meaning of a mighty man morally as well as physically, a hero, or great chief. W. *cawr.* Ir. *cirb*, a warrior; *curadh*, a champion; †*gur*, valiant. Gael. *còrr*, very great; *curaidh*, a champion, from *cur*, power. Manx, *foawr*, a giant. Sansc. *sûra*, a hero, from *sûr*, to be strong.

CAURMARCH, s. m. A camel. Cornish Vocabulary, *camelus.* Compounded of *caur*, gigantic, and *march*, a horse. So also in W. *caurvarch.*

CAUS, s. m. Cheese. Cornish Vocabulary, *caseus*, where also it is written *cos.* The latest form was *cês*, qd. v. W. *caws.* Arm. *caous.* Ir. *cais.* Gael. *cuise.* Manx, *caashey.* Lat. *caseus.*

CAV. v. a. He will have. 3 pers. s. fut. of *cavas*, or *cavel*, qd. v. *Mar menta gwelas an ost an chy, ki da'n gegen, hag enna ti a'n câv,* if thou wilt see the host of the house, go into the kitchen, and there thou wilt find him. Llwyd, 252.

CAVANSCIS, s. m. An excuse, an escape. *Gans mear a Justice yn wlas, ef a ve veyl rebukis, cavanskis ef a whelas, rag own y vonas ledhys,* by many a justice in the country, he was vilely rebuked, escape he sought for, for fear that he should be slain. M.C. 156.

CAVANSCUSE, v. a. To make excuse. *Ny dâl dhys cavanscusé, dre dhe wrêk y vôs terrys, rag orty ty dhe gole, mŷl vâp mam a ueydh damneys,* it will not do for thee to make excuse through thy wife that it was broken, because thou didst hearken to her, a thousand mother's sons shall be damned. O.M. 321.

CAVAS, v. a. To have. Written also *cavos*, being another form of *cawas*, or *cafos*, qd. v. *Ni allaf cuvos powes*, I cannot find rest. C.W. 110. It is also given by Llwyd, 247, as the preterite, answering to the W. *caves.* Thus *me a gavas*, I had; *ev a gavas*, he had; *y a gavas*, they had.

CAVEL, v. a. To have, or find. *Dho gavel*, to find. This is the same word as *cafel,* qd. v. W. *cafuel.*

CAVOW, s. m. Grief, sorrow. *Râg cavow sevell a'm sâf, war doer lemyn omhelaf, ow holan ter dew gallas*, for sorrow I stand upright, on the ground now I will throw myself, my heart is parted in two. C.W. 88. *Ildg henna sâf, ha gâs cavow dha wandra, me ne brederaf gwell for,* therefore stand up, and leave sorrow to wander, I know no better way. ibid. 90. *Kemmys ew gamy murnys aga holan ew terrys râg cafow, medhaf y dy,* so much is it bewailed by them, their hearts are broken for grief, I say to thee. ibid. 98. *Cavow* is the same as

CEAN 48 CEFONS

the Old Armoric *caffou,* (solicitudines,) preserved in Buhez Nonn, 200. and is connected with the W. *cawdh,* Arm. *keuz, ké;* Ir. †*caodh;* Gael *caoidh;* Sansc. *kôd,* to be overwhelmed with sorrow.

CAWAL, s. m. A hamper, a basket. *Cawal groanan,* a beehive. Lluyd, 42. *Cauwal,* or *cowal,* is still in common use in Cornwall, for a pannier, or fishwoman's basket. W. *cawell.* Arm. *cavel.* Ir. *cliabh,* †*cliab.* Gael. *cliubh.*

CAWAS, v. a. To have, or find. *Me a yll bôs lowenheys, kyns es bôs dewedh an bŷs, cawas an oyl a vercy,* I may be made glad, before it is the end of the world, to have the oil of mercy. C.W. 70. *Kemmys yw an mollathow, dout yw dhym cawas trigva,* so many are the curses, there is doubt to me to find a dwelling. C.W. 88. *Reys yw porrys lavyrrya, ha gones an bŷs omma, dha gawas dheny susten,* needs is that we should labour, and till the ground here, to procure for us sustenance. C.W. 60. It is also written *cawys.* *Ny whyla dhym na moy cows, me a vyn cawys an pows, kyn fy mar pyth,* seek not any more talking to me, I will have the coat, though it ever be so. R.D. 1957. *Cawas* is only another form of *cavas, cavel,* and *cafos,* qd. v.

CAWS, v. a. To speak, or talk. Lluyd, 245. Generally written *cows,* qd. v.

CAWSYS, part. Spoken. *Hena Pilat pan welas kymmys cawsys er y byn,* then Pilate when he saw so much spoken against him. M.C. 100. Generally written *cewsys,* qd. v.

CAWYS, adj. Dirty. *Cawys pows,* a dirty gown. *Pryce.*

CE, v. n. Go thou. Used as the imperative of the irregular verb *mones,* to go. *Ke, growel war an dôr gulan, ha côsk,* go, lie down on the earth clean, and sleep. O.M. 96. *Ke yn mês an wlds, troha ken pow dhe vewé,* go out of the country, towards another land to live. O.M. 343. *Ke yn râk, del ym kyrry,* go before, as thou lovest me. O.M. 537. *Ke yn kerth,* go away. O.M. 725. *Ke wêth tressé treveth dh'y,* go yet the third time to it. O.M. 799. *Ke yn ban war an cunys,* go up upon the wood. O.M. 1333. *Ke* is also written *ki,* Llwyd, 247, which sound is also found in the Ordinalia. *Kee kymmer myns a vynny a'n beis oll adro,* go take all that thou wilt of the world all around. O.M. 403. Arm. *ké.*

CE, s. m. A hedge, fence; inclosure, field. Pl. *ceow.* *Cê linec,* a field of flax. *Y fensan y vôs cudhys yn nêb tall kê,* I would he were hid in some hole of the hedge. C.W. 82. ‡*Na dallé dees perna kinnis war an saw, na môs cuntell an dreis dro dan keow,* men ought not to buy fuel by the load, nor go to gather the brambles about the hedges. *Pryce.* In construction it changes into *gé,* as *golvan gé,* a hedge sparrow. The root is W. *cau,* to inclose. W. *cae,* †*cai.* Arm. *kae, ke.* Ir. *fe,* †*cae,* †*ce.* Gael. *faich.* Manx, *faaie.* Cf. O. H. Germ. *hag,* N. H. G. *gehege,* Fr. *haie,* Eng. *hedge.*

CE, conj. Though, although. An abbreviated form of *ken.* *Me a vyn môs dha gudha, ce ythew gryff,* I will go to hide, though it is grievous. C.W. 112. *Whath 'ke thyns y mar venys, me a dhôg ran war ow heyn,* since they are so small, I will carry a portion of my back. *Ibid.* 100.

CEAN, s. m. A supper. Written also *côn,* qd. v. W. *ciniaw,* a dinner, *cwynos,* supper. Arm. *coan.*

CEANY, v. a. To sup. *Pryce.* The same word as *cona,* qd. v.

CEAR, adj. Dear. Another form of *cêr,* qd. v.

CEAS, v. a. To shut up, inclose. Lluyd, 104. W. *cau.* Arm. *casa.*

CEBER, s. m. The matrix. Cornish Vocabulary, *vulva.* This word is the W. *cwybyr,* a covering, honeycomb. Compare also W. *cwthyr,* the vagina; and the Old Irish *cacbh,* the liver; Old Bohemian *kepp,* (vulva;) and Old German *chepis, chebis, chebisa, kebisn,* a concubine. *Keb* remains in several German words, such as *kebsche, kebsfrau,* &c.

CEBER, s. f. A rafter, beam. Cornish Vocabulary, *tignum.* W. *ceber,* pl. *cebyr,* †*cibrion, Oxford Gloss.* Arm. *kebr.* Gael. *cabar.* Fr. *chevron.*

CEBMER, v. a. Take thou. ‡*Cebmer wyth,* take care. Lluyd, 251. A late corruption of *cemer,* qd. v.

CEBMYS, adj. So much. ‡*Kebmys pehas es yn beys,* so much sin is in the world. C.W. 156. A late corruption of *cemmys,* qd. v.

CECEFFRYS, adv. Likewise, also, as well. *Yma ow cûl sacryfys, ha'y pobel ef kekeffrys, dhen kêth dew-na gans mûr tros,* he is making a sacrifice, and his people also, to that same God, with a loud noise. O.M. 1557. *Yma omma dew clodhé, parys gans ow cowethé, cales ha scherp kekeffrys,* there are here two swords, ready with my companions, hard and sharp also. P.C. 927. It is also written *kekyfrys.* *Lavaraf dheuch a tûs vûs kekyfrys byan ha brâs, lemmyn gwereuch oll ow syweé,* I say to you, O good men, little and great also, now do ye all follow me. O.M. 1673. Compounded of *ce,* id. qd. *cev,* qd. v., and *ceffrys.*

CECEMMYS, adj. As much as, as many as. *Gostryth dhymo y a vŷdh, kekemmys us ynné gureys,* obedient to me they shall be, as much as is in them made. O.M. 84. *Ha kekemmys na'n cresso, goef termyn a dheffo devones a brys bencn,* and whoever would not believe it, woe to him the time that he came nurtured from the womb of woman. R.D. 1348. *Dhe kekemmys na'n gwello, hag yn perfyth a'n cresso, ow len benneth me a pys,* to as many as shall not see me, and shall perfectly believe it, my full blessing I pray. R.D. 1554. Compounded of *ce,* id. qd. *cev,* qd. v., and *cemmys.*

CEDVA, s. f. A synod, or convention. Lluyd, 51. Written in Cornish Vocabulary, *chetwa,* conventus vel conventio. W. *cydva.* Compounded of *ced,* id. qd. W. *cyd,* together, and *ma,* a place.

CEFALS, s. m. A joint, or limb. Cornish Vocabulary, *chefals,* artus. W. *cyvall,* being joined together; *cyvaillt,* a friend. *Cymmal,* a joint, compounded of *cym,* or *cyd,* together, and *mal,* a limb, which is now obsolete in Welsh, but is preserved in the C. *mell;* Arm. *mell;* Ir. *ball;* Gael. *ball.* Compare also the Ir. †*alt,* a limb, †*comallte,* a companion.

CEFER, v. pass. Is found. 3 pers. of the pres. and fut. tense passive of *cafos.* *Saw levereuch cowethé, py kefer pren dh'y crowsyé,* but say, companions, where shall be found wood to crucify him. P.C. 2535. Written also *kefyr.* *Ple kefyr dyw grows aral râk an dew ladar hep fal, levereuch dhym cowethé,* where shall be found two other crosses for the two thieves without fail, tell me comrades. P.C. 2576. W. *cefir.*

CEFONS, v. a. They may find. 3 pers. pl. subj. of *cafos.*

CEGIN 49 CELES

Danvon tûs dh'y axpye, mar a'n kefens yn ncp chy, ha'n kelmyns treys ha dulé, ha'n hembrynkys bÿs dhynny, send men to look for him, if they should find him in any house, let them bind him feet and hands, and bring him to us. P.C. 582. W. *cafoni.*

CEFOUCH, v. a. Ye shall find. 2 pers. pl. fut. of *cofos. Rag mar ny'n cefouch, a plygth why a'n pren,* for if ye do not find him, a plight ye shall catch it. R.D. 620. W. *cafoch.*

CEFRYS, adv. Likewise, also, as well. *Ottè an yuskes, ydhyn an néf, ha'n bestes kefrys yn tyr hag yn môr,* behold the fishes, the birds of heaven, and the beasts, as well on land as in sea. O.M. 110. *Ow cafus banneth ow mam ha banneth ow thâs kefrys,* receiving the blessing of my mother, and the blessing of my father likewise. O.M. 472. Written also *cyffrys,* and *cyfreys.* W. *cyfred,* compounded of *cyn,* together, and *rhêd,* a running.

CEFUIDOC, adj. Almighty. Cornish Vocabulary, *omnipotens.* W. *cycoethog,* adj., from *cyvoeth,* power. Ir. †*cumachtach,* †*cumachtig,* powerful; *comhachd,* †*cumacht,* †*cumacct,* power. Gael. *cumachd,* power.

CEFYN, v. a. We shall have, or find. 1 pers. pl. fut. of *cofos. Saw levereuch dhym defry pren dhe gyst ple kefyn ny, a vo compes avel sheft,* but tell me seriously, wood for the beam where shall we find, which may be straight like a shaft. O.M. 2493. *Fystynyn fast alemma, del gorhemynys deffry, mar kefyn dên a'u par-na, ny a'n syw bÿs yn y chy,* let us hasten quickly, as commanded indeed; if we shall find a man of that sort, we will follow him even to his house. P.C. 647. W. *cafem.*

CEFYON, adj. Dear, beloved. Pl. of *cuf,* qd. v. *Godheveuch omma lavur, ha gollyouch gynef, ow kefyon kér colonow,* endure ye here labour, and watch with me my dearly beloved hearts. P.C. 1026.

CEFYS, part. Found. Part. pass. of *cafos. Mars éth corf Dew y honan, py le y fÿdh e ceffys,* if the body of God himself is gone, where shall it be found. R.D. 702. *Ollefé lemmyn keffys, dûs dhum arluth dyssempys,* behold him now taken; come to my lord immediately. R.D. 1701. *Lavarsons y heb pyté agon traytour yw kefys,* they said without pity, our traitor is found. M.C. 98. In Keigwyn's time it was generally written and pronounced *cevys,* qd. v.

CEFYTH, v. a. Thou shalt have. 2 pers. s. fut. of *cofos. Tyr sêch yn guel nag yn pras, mar kefyth yn gwyr hep gow, ynno guoet in-in whelas bôs dheth ly, ha dheth kynyow,* dry land in field, or in meadow, if thou shalt find truly without deceit, in it take good care to seek food for thy breakfast, and for thy dinner. O.M. 1138. Written later *cevyth,* qd. v.

CEGAS, s. m. Hemlock. *Lluyd,* 47. W. *cegid.* Arm. *cegit.* Lat. *cicuta.*

CEGEL, s. m. A distaff. *Gans kegel a dhesempys nedhé dyllas my a wra,* with a distaff immediately I will spin clothes. O.M. 415. Written also *cigel,* qd. v.

CEGIN, s. f. A kitchen. Cornish Vocabulary, *keghin,* coquina. *Ema Adam tremenys, dûn dhe hedhas dha'n gegon,* Adam is dead, let us come to fetch him to the kitchen. O.M. 146. *Mar menta gwelas an ost on chy, ki da'n gegen, ha enna ti a'n câv,* if thou wishest to see the host of the house, go into the kitchen, and there thou shalt find him. *Lluyd,* 252. Though *cegin* might be formed from *côg,* by the regular change of *o* into *é*; the final *n* shews that it is borrowed from the Latin *coquina.* So also W. *cegin.* Arm. *kegin.* Ir. †*cucann.*

CEHAFAL, adj. Equal, like, similar. *A buh sort a levcrow, egwall unna ew gorrys, pekar ythew an sortow, gorrys unna der devyes, in deffrans ha kehaval,* of every sort of books, equally in them are put, as are the sorts put in them by pairs, in proportion and equal. C.W. 160. Compounded of *ce,* id. qd. *ccv,* qd. v., and *haval,* like. W. *cyhaval, cyval.* Ir. *cosmail.*

CEHEDZHE, s. m. A reaching, or stretching of the body. *Lluyd,* 112. W. *cyhyda.*

CEI, s. m. A dog. *Lluyd,* 241. A later form of *ci,* qd. v.

CEIN, s. m. The back, the ridge of a hill. Cornish Vocabulary, *chein,* dorsum. In construction it changes into *gein,* and *kein* for *chein. My a'th wheres worth y dhon dhe yffarn, kepar hag on, war geyn lowarn py brathky,* I will help thee to bring him to hell, like as we are, on the back of a fox, or a mastiff. O.M. 895. *Kymer dhymmo ve kunys, gans lovan bedhens strothys, ha war dhe keyn doga ef,* take firewood for me, with a rope let it be bound, and on thy back carry it. O.M. 1298. *Pùp dên ol degyns ganso y pyth, an mêns a allo war aga keyn fardellow,* let every man bear with him his things, all that he can, burdens on their back. O.M. 1593. *Pyw henna a dhue dhe'n tre, war keyn asen hag ebel,* who is that that is come to the town, on the back of an ass and foal. P.C. *Ha'gan flehys kekeffrys; whath kethyns y mar venys, nie a dhôg ran war ow heyn uskes lemyn,* and our children likewise; yet since they be so small, I will carry a portion on my back immediately now. C.W. 100. W. *cevn,* †*cecin,* Lib. Land. Arm. *cevn, cein.* Fr. and Eng. *chine.*

CEINAC, s. m. A shad fish. *Lluyd,* 240.

CEIRCH, s. m. Oats. Cornish Vocabulary, *avena. Bara ceirch,* panis avena, oaten bread. Written also *cerch. Dda churdgè a vÿdh war kerch, barlys, ha gwaneth, dha wethyl an dega leal,* thy charge shall be over oats, barley, wheat, to make true tithe. C.W. 78. The latest form was *cerh.* W. *cuirch, cerch.* Arm. *cerch.* Ir. *coirec,* (†*cerchae,* arundo.) Gael. *coirce.* Manx, *corkey.* Obs. in Wales, *ceirch* is the form used colloquially in Anglesey; *cerch* in Arvon and Denbighshire; and *cyrch* about Oswestry, in Eastern Powys.

CEISWAS, s. m. A keeper. *Pryce.* W. *cridwad.*

CELE, s. m. A companion, a fellow, one of two. *Hay yll leff a ve tachin ord an grows fast may 'th esé, hay yll troys a ve gorris poran war ben y gelé worth an grows y fôns ladhys gans kenter gwyskys dredhé,* and the one hand was nailed on the cross, so that it was fast, and one foot was put right over its fellow; on the cross they were laid, with a nail struck through them. M.C. 179. W. *gilydd,* †*cilid.* Arm. (*cila*) *e gile,* †*eguile.* Ir. *ceile, da chrile,* †*cele.* Gael. *a cheilley.* Manx, *cheilley.* Sanso. *kil,* to bind.

CELEGEL, s. m. A chalice. Cornish Vocabulary, *calix.* Derived from the Lat. *calice,* with a British termination.

CELES, v. a. To hide, conceal. Part. *celys. A váp, ny dal keles man, an pyth a dhue gwrîs veydh,* O son, it will not avail to conceal anything, the thing which is coming will be seen. O.M. 853. *Adam ny fl vôs kelys, an pyth a dhue yn dywedh, yma floch genaf genys, dre vôdh an tâs, Dew in wordh,* Adam, it cannot be concealed, the thing will come at last, there is a child born to me, by the will of the father, God also. O.M. 670. W. *celu*. Ir. *ceil*. Gael. *ceil*. Manx, *keil*. Lat. *celo, culo*. Sansc. *cal*, to cover ; *hul*, to cover. Gr. ελείω, κολύω. Goth. *hulia*. Germ. *hülle, hehle*. Lith. *kaliu*.

CELIN, s. m. Holly. Cornish Vocabulary, *ulcia*. W. *celyn*. Arm. *kelen*. Ir. *cuileann*. Gael. *cuileann*. Manx, *hollyn*.

CELINEN, s. f. A holly tree. *Llwyd*, 241. W. *celynen*. Arm. *kelennen*.

CELIOC, s. m. A cock. Cornish Vocabulary, *chelioc*, *gallus*. Written in the Ordinalia, *colyek*, and *kullyek*. *Yn medh Christ, yn nôs haneth kyns ys bôs colyek clewys, te a'm nâch torgweth*, says Christ, in this night, before that a cock be heard, thou wilt deny me thrice. M.C. 49. *Gans henna ef a clewas en colyek scon ow cané*, thereupon he heard the cock immediately crow. M.C. 86. *Kyns ys bôs kullyek kenys, ter gwŷth y wrêch ow naché*, before that the cock hath crowed, three times thou wilt deny me. P.C. 903. W. *ceiliog*. Arm. *cilec, cilok*. Ir. *caileach*. Gael. *coilcach*. Manx, *kellach*. Sansc. *kalas*. sonorous, fr. *kal*, to resound.

CELIOC-GUIT, s. m. A gander. Cornish Vocabulary, *anser*. Compounded of *celioc*, a cock, and *guit*, a goose. W. *ceiliog gwydh*. This term is unknown to Armoric, *kilok gwez* meaning a pheasant, or heath-cock, from *guez*, id. qd. W. *gwŷdh*, wild.

CELIOC-REDEN, s. m. A grasshopper. Cornish Vocabulary, *locusta*. Compounded of *celioc*, a cock, and *reden*, fern. Literally " the cock of the fern." So Welsh *ceiliog rhedyn*, and Arm. *kilek-raden*.

CELIONEN, s. f. A fly. Cornish Vocabulary, *musca*. W. *cylionen*, pl. *cylion*. Arm. *kelienen*, pl. *kelien*. Ir. *cuil, cuileog*, †*cuilenn*, †*culenn*. Gael. *cuil, cuileag*. Manx, *carchuillag*. Lat. *culex*.

CELLAD, s. f. Loss, damage, hazard. Pl. *celladow*. *Assevyé plygadow genef gruthyl bôdh dhe wŷs, a callen hep celladow, ha dout ow vôs hellyrchys*, it would be agreeable to me to do the will of thy mind, if I could without losses, and fear of my being persecuted. O.M. 2117. Derived from *celli*, to lose. W. *colled*. Arm. *collad*. Ir. *cuilleadh*. Gael. *calldach*.

CELLER, v. pass. It is possible. A mutation of *geller*, 3 pers. s. pres. and fut. passive of *gally*. *Fleisebuc whêk, whŷth dhe corn, ha galwy dre a pup sorn an dhewolow, mara keller y wythé a chy, na alla yntré dhe'n darasow*, sweet Beelzebub, blow thy horn, and call home from every corner the devils, if it be possible to keep him from the house, that he may not enter the doors. P.C. 3058. W. *gellir*.

CELLESTER, s. f. A pebble, or small stone. So interpreted in Pryce's Vocabulary, but it must originally have meant a flintstone, being the Welsh *callestyr*. Arm. *calastr*. Gr. χάλιξ. Lat. *silex*.

CELLI, s. f. A grove. Cornish Vocabulary, *nemus*. Pl. *kelliow*. *Bo' kelly*, the house of the grove, in St. Kew. *Pen gelly*, the head of the grove, in Breage. The more common form is *killi*. W. *celli, y gelli*. Ir. *coill*, †*caill*. Gael. *coille*. Manx, *keil*. Gr. ὕλα. Lat. *sylva*. Sansc. *guhila*, (*guh*, to hide.)

CELLILLIC, s. m. A penknife. Cornish Vocabulary, *ortavus*. The diminutive of *collel*, a knife, qd. v.

CELLY, v. s. To lose. Part. *kellys*. 3 pers. s. fut. *ceyl, a geyl*, qd. v. *Pilat a yrchys dhedhé, war beyn kelly an bewnans, monas dhe'n corf dh'y wethé, na'n kemerré y yskerans*, Pilate charged them, on pain of losing their life, to go to the body to keep it, that his enemies should not take it away. M.C. 241. *Gwell ync y vôs ef marow, ys bôs an popel kellys, ha dampnys dhe tewolgow*, it is better that he should be dead, than that the people be lost, and condemned to darkness. P.C. 2465. *Dyswrys a vŷdh ol iudy, ha kellys an lacha ny*, undone will be all Judea, and lost our law. R.D. 11. This is another form of *colli*, qd v.

CELLYN, v. aux. We shall be able. A mutation of *gellyn*, 1 pers. pl. fut. of *gally*. *In lowen gynouch my a, mar a kellyn dheuch gûl da, na scvel yn le tyller, yn le may fynny a-wŷth*, joyfully with yon I will go, if we can do good to you, nor stay in any place, to the place that, thou mayest wish moreover. P.C. 1836. W. *gallwn*.

CELMY, v. a. To bind, fasten, knot, tie. 3 pers. s. fut. *kelm*. Part. *kelmys, kylmys*. *Me a'th kelm fast a ver termyn*. I will bind thee fast in a short time. O.M. 1361. *Otté an ascn omma, ha'n ebel kelmys yma gynsy*, behold the ass here, and the foal is tied with her. P.C. 201. *Danvon tûs dh'y asnye, mar a'n kefons yn nêp chy, ka'n kelmyns treys ha dulé*, send men to look for him, if they find him in any house, and let them bind him feet and hands. P.C. 583. *Kelmeuch warbarth y dhywvrech, na allo dyank*, bind together his arms, that he may not escape. P.C. 1179. *Me a'n kelm*, I will bind him. P.C. 1889. *Worth an pôst y gelmy fast why a wra*, to the stake you shall bind him fast. P.C. 2039. *Ty a vŷdh kelmys*, thou shalt be bound. P.C. 2071. *Kelmouch fast gans lovonow ef yn pren crocs*, bind fast with ropes him on the cross tree. P.C. 2520. *Celmy* is another form of *colma*, qd. v., and is also written *cylmy*. W. *cylymu*. Arm. *coubnu, clomein*.

CELWEL, v. a. To call. A mutation of *gelwel*, qd. v. *Otté voys mernans Abel dhe vroder prest ow kelwel a'n dôr warnaf pup teller*, behold that the death of Abel thy brother is always calling from the ground on me every where. O.M. 578. *My re bue fost ow kelwel*, I have been urgently calling. O.M. 2430. *Yma ow kelwel Eli*, he is calling Elias. P.C. 2959.

CELYNNEC, s. f. A holly grove, or place where holly trees grow. *Pryce*. From *kelyn*, or *celin*, qd. v. W. *celynneg*. Arm. *celennek*.

CEMBRION, s. m. Welshmen, the Welsh. *Llwyd*, 242, *Cembrion*. *Cymry* is the name by which the Welsh people have always designated themselves. It is of uncertain derivation, but in all probability identical with the Gr. κιμμέριοι. Zenss derives the word from *cym*, or *cyd*, together, and *bro*, a country, i.e. a compatriot; being opposed to *allobroges*, persons of another country. This however is no more certain than Dr. Owen Pughe's analysis, into *cyn*, first, and *bro*, a country; signifying aborigines. It is worthy of notice that in Irish, *Breathnach* is used only for a Welshman, and *Breattain* for Wales. *Graig na mbreathnach, sliabh na mbreathnach*, are places in Ireland, so called because formerly inhabited by Welshmen. So also in Manx, *Bretnagh* means exclusively a Welshman; *Bretyn*, Wales; and *Bretnish*, the Welsh language.

CEMEAS, s. m. Leave, permission. *Erbyn bonas henna guris nanso prŷs gwesper yn wlds, yn er-na yn wedh*

CEMYNNY 51 CEN

kemeas dhe Joseph y a rontyas, by the time that that was done, it was now time of even-service in the country, in that hour leave to Joseph they granted. M.C. 231. Written also *cummyas*, qd. v.

CEMERES, v. a. To take, accept, receive. 3·pers. s. pret. *kemeras*. 2 pers. s. imp. *kemer*. *Daves war ve lavarow hy hanow da kemeres*, sheep from my words, her good name let her receive. O.M. 128. *Kemmer clodhé, fystyn trocha paradhys*, take thou a sword, hasten towards Paradise. O.M. 331. *Kemer tyyr spus an aval*, take three kernels of the apple. O.M. 823. *Hy cemeres me a wra, ogy dhe'n gorhyl*, I will receive her within the ark. O.M. 1123. *Wosé cows ha lafuryé, an vuner a vye da kemeres croust hag cvé, ha powes wosé henna*, after talk and labouring, the custom would be good, to take food and drink, and rest after that. O.M. 1901. *Ow môs war tu a'n temple, me a grîfs y kemersé wéth an vîl kyngys marwel*, going towards the temple, I believe the vile man would take it yet, before that he dies. P.C. 323. *Reys yw dhych dry gweres, gynef vy dh'y gemeres yn nôs prywth*, need is to you to bring help with me, to take him at night privately. P.C. 597. *Ytho why kemereuch e, ha herwydh agas laha gwrech y iuggys dhe'n mernans, mar coth henna*, now take ye him, and according to your law do ye judge him to death, if that is right. P.C. 1977. *Dôk an grows war dhe geyn, kemerry (= kemer hy) a dhysempys*, bear the cross on thy back, take it immediately. P.C. 2620. *Yntre Du ha pehadur acord del ve kemerys*, between God and sinner how accord was taken. M.C. 8. *Ha'n wolok a's hemeras mar dyn may clumderas hy arté*, and the sight took her so sharp that she fainted again. M.C. 171. *Dyskys fatel dons dhow hemeres*, taught how they shall come to take me. M.C. 61. *Why a dhéth dho'm kemers*, ye came to take me. M.C. 74. *Aga henwyn kemerans*, their names let them take. C.W. 30. Written equally common *cymeres*. Compounded of *cyd*, together, and *bery*, to carry. W. *cymmeryd*. Arm. *cemeret*.

CEMESCYS, n. s. A mixture. *Dour ha goys yn kemeskis wcys Christ ieu dhe gerensé*, water and blood in a mixture sweat did Christ for thy sake. M.C. 58. *A'n golon ytheth strék brás, dour ha goys yn kemeskys*, from the heart there came a great stream, water and blood in a mixture. M.C. 219. See *Cemyscy*. W. *cymmysgiad*.

CEMMYS, adj. So much, so great, so many. Frequently written *kemys*, and *kymmys*. *Kemys druk ûs ow codhé*, so much evil is falling. O.M. 628. *Rag dhe ladhé den mar qura, ef a'n gevyth seyth kemmys*, for if a man do kill thee, he shall get it seven times as much. O.M. 599. *Pâp ûr oll oberet da, gwyn bys kymnys a'n gwrello*, always good works, happy as many as do them. O.M. 605. *Râg kemmys hy dhom caré*, for so much she loved me. P.C. 530. *Bôdh dhe vâp yw yn della, râk selwel kemnys yw da*, the will of thy son is so, for to save as many as are good. P.C. 2953. Compounded of *cym*, together, and *myns*, all. W. *cymmaint*, †*cemeint*. Arm. *cement*. Ir. *cuibheis*, †*cemeit*. Gael. *cuibheas*.

CEMYNNY, v. a. To bequeath, leave by will. *Yssé yn dhe see yn wéth, a bewé dhe lâs Daveth, râg ef a'n kemynnys dhys*, sit in thy seat also, which the father David possessed, for he has left it to thee. O.M. 2394. *A lâs yntré dhe dhulé my a gemmyn ow spyrys*, O Father, between thy hands I commit my spirit. P.C. 2986. Frequently written *cymmyny*. W. *cymmynu*. Arm. *cemenna*. Manx, *chymnee*. Though agreeing with Latin *commendo*, the W. *cymmynu* is regularly compounded of *cy*, with, and *mynnu*, to will, from *myn*, = Lat. *mens*, the will or mind.

CEMYSCY, v. a. To mingle, mix. Part. *kemyskys*, which is also written *cymyscys*. *Yma gené un bé da, gorra hag eys kemyskys*, there is with me a good load, hay and corn mixed. O.M. 1058. *Drôk dhewas, cysyll bestyl kemyskis*, bad drink, vinegar and gall mixed. M.C. 202. W. *cymmysgu*, from *cyd*, with, and *myscu*, to mix. Arm. *cemmesci*. Ir. *comhmeasg*, †*cummasc*, †*cumasg*. Gael. *coimeasg*. Lat. *commisceo*.

CEN, s. m. Anguish, vexation, grief, pity ; a cause, lawsuit, complaint. Cornish Vocabulary, *chen*, causa. *Ty r'um tullas hep kên*, thou hast deceived me without pity. O.M. 252. *Yma kên dhym dhe olé daggrow gois in gwyr hep mar*, there is cause to me to weep tears of blood truly without doubt. O.M. 630. *Na allons cafus kên dhe dhyscrysy*, that they may not find cause to disbelieve. O.M. 1826. *Râg ny fýdh kên dhe perthy*, for there will be no complaint to bear it. O.M. 2208. *My ny welaf kên yn bys muy fe a'n kéth dên-ma gwyw dre reson dhe vôs ledhys*, I see no cause in the world that this man is worthy through reason to be slain. P.C. 1589. *Mychtern an Yedhewon, ymwyth lemman râg an kên*, King of the Jews, preserve thyself now from the torture. P.C. 2144. *Ha buxow lcas heb kên, ha tumnasow kekyffrys*, and buffets many without pity, and heats alike. M.C. 138. W. *cwyn*, whence *cwyno*, to complain. Arm. *keina*. Ir. *caoine*. Gael. *caoin*. Manx, *keayn*. Obs. The long *o* is often represented in Welsh by *wy*, as may be seen by comparing the W. *trwy*, through, with C. *tre, dre*; W. *cwybyr*, C. *ceber*; W. *cwyr*, wax, with Latin *cêra*; W. *eglwys*, Lat. *ecclêsia*; W. *cwynos*, Lat. *cœna*; W. *pluyv*, Lat. *plêbe*; W. *canwyll*, Lat. *candêla*.

CEN, s. m. The hide or skin of an animal; the peel or skin of any thing. *Tynnouch oll gans mûr a grîfs, may fo drcyn an guryn cys yn empynnyon, dre an cen*, pull ye all with much of force, that the thorns of the crown may penetrate to the brains, through the skin. P.C. 2138. *Me a's ten gans oll ow nerth may 'th entré an spikys serth dre an cen yn y grogen, ha scullyé y ympynnyon*, I will pull it with all my strength, that the stiff spines may enter through the skin into his skull, and scatter his brains. P.C. 2141. W. *cenn*, †*ceen* in Oxf. Gloss. *ysgen*. Arm. *cenn, ceon*, scant. Ir. *sgann*. Gael. *sgann, coinneach*. Manx, *keynnach*. Sansc. *c'anna*, a cover, svan, to clothe.

CEN, adj. Other, different. *A wylsta ken yn tor-ma ys del egé agensow*, dost thou see more now than as there was just now. O.M. 795. *Why a dhyndylsé onor, mar callcuch dry dhe cen crygyans*, ye would deserve honour, if ye can bring to another belief. P.C. 1994. *Gwyr a leversys dhym a'th ganow dhe honan, py gans ken re yw dyscys*, the truth thou hast spoken to me of thy own mouth, or by other persons that are instructed. P.C. 2002. *Na fors kyn na dhrehedho, ken tol ny vydh gwrys ragdho*, no matter though it does not reach, another hole shall not be made for him. P.C. 2759. *Ef a'th saw, hep ken yly*, he will heal thee, without other remedy. R.D. 1695. *Yn ken lyw, ny's gwylys whêth,* in other form, I have not yet seen them. R.D. 2534. Used also adverbially. *Screfys yw, ha ken me nyn lavarsen,* it is written, and otherwise I would not have said it. M.C. 183. *Mars yw a barth Dew an nêf, bo ken deaul yw,* if he be on the side of the God of heaven, or else he is a devil. R.D. 2104.

CEN, conj. Though, although, if, unless. *Me a vyn dheth treys ammê, dre dhe vôdh, ken nay ôf gwyw,* I will kiss thy feet, through thy will, though I am not worthy. P.C. 481. *Ow thås, ken fóva serrys, pan glow an nowedhys,* my father, though he may be angry, when he hears the news. O.W. 82. *Whâth ken 'thosa ow hendas, dha aswon me ny wodhynn,* yet although thou art my grandfather, I knew not how to recognize thee. *ibid.* 120. *Ow grantya dhymo sylwans wosé henna, ken 'thew pell,* granting to me salvation hereafter, though it is long distant. *ibid.* 140. *Ken teffo y ges golok, dhodho ny yllouch gûl drôk,* if he should come into your sight, to him ye cannot do harm. R.D. 1861. *Yn ûr-na mestry vŷth te ny vea warnaf ve, drôk vyth na du, ken onan thys na'n rolla,* in that hour power thou wouldst never have over me, evil nor good, unless one should give it thee. M.C. 145. Written also *cyn,* qd. v. W. *cyd.* Arm. *ken.*

CEN, adv. First, before, before that. ‡ *Bes mar menta rei dem arta, me a desca dis cen point a skinns,* but if thou wilt give them to me again, I will teach thee first a point of wit. ‡ *Bedhes gwenkys dhiveth, ken gweskal onweth râk henna yw an gwella point a skinns oll,* be twice struck, before striking once, for that is the best point of wit of all. *Llwyd,* 251. This is the later form of *cyn,* qd. v.

CENCIA, v. a. To contend, strive. *Llwyd,* 80, *Dho kennkia.* Gael. *caonnag.*

CENCRAS, s. m. Crabs, crabfishes. *Llwyd,* 213. One of the plurals of *cancr,* qd. v.

CENDE, s. m. Kind, nature. *Me a brêf bôs gow henna, râk dew ha dên yw dew dra, pur contraryys yn kendê,* I will prove that to be false, for God and man are two things very contrary in nature. P.C. 1731. Derived from the English.

CENDEL, s. m. Fine linen. *Aga malye my a vyn, yn cendel hag yn owlyn,* I will wrap them in fine linen and in silk. O.M. 1752. Written also *cendal,* and pronounced as in English, *sendal. Llwyd. Joseph whêk, recewv e dhys, hag yn cendal ylân maylye,* sweet Joseph, receive him to thee, and in clean fine linen wrap him. P.C. 3166. *Oud cendal glôn a lês, parys rág y enrledhyes,* behold clean linen spread, ready for burying him. P.C. 3160.

CENDONER, s. m. A debtor. *Kyns y un teller yn beys dew kendoner yth egê, dhe un dettor; me a grŷs an nŷl dhodho a dellé pymp cans dyner monyys, ha hanter cans y gylé,* formerly in a part of the world there were two debtors to one creditor; I believe the one to him owed five hundred pence of money, and half a hundred the other. P.C. 502. Derived from *cendon,* id. qd. *cyndon,* qd. v.

CENEFRA, adj. So many, every. ‡ *Ha Dew rig gwres an puskas brâs, ha kenefra tra bew es a gwayah, neb rig an dowrow dry râg pur vear warlêr go has, ha kenefra edhan eskelly warler go has, ha Dew welas tro va dâ,* and God created great whales, and every living creature that moveth, which the waters brought forth abundantly, after their kind, and every winged fowl after his kind, and God saw that it was good. (*Keigwyn,* p. 191.) This is a late corruption of *ceniver,* qd. v.

CENEWAL, v. a. To dine. *Llwyd,* 127; who also writes it *kynewal,* p. 245. W. *ciniawa.* It is the same word as *cona,* qd. v.

CENIAT, s. m. A singer. Written in the Cornish Vocabulary *cheniat,* cantor, and *keniat,* in *Keniat combricam, liticen.* It is derived from *cané,* to sing, and the termination *at,* which is the earliest form, denotes the agent, as in Welsh and Armoric; but in mediæval Cornish the termination was changed into *as,* as in *gwythyas,* a keeper; *sylwyas,* a saviour. W. *ceiniad.* Arm. *kiniad.*

CENIN, s. m. A leek, chive, shalot. *Cenin ewinoc,* algium, garlic. *Cornish Vocabulary.* The literal meaning of *cenin ewinoc* is leeks with claws, or clawed. It is written by Llwyd *cinin.* W. *cenin,* †*cennin.* Arm. *cinen. Cenin ewinog* is also the name of garlic in Wales.

CENIVER, adj. So many, every, every one. *A vernans Christ pan welsé kenyver tra marthusy,* of the death of Christ when he had seen so many marvellous things. M.C. *Yn blydhen y a vye, ha bederow keniver hag a owlwow esé yn corf Jesus worth never,* in a year they would be, and beads so many as there were marks in the body of Jesus in number. M.C. 228. Written indifferently *cnifer, cenyver, cenever,* and also *cyniver,* qd. v.

CENOUCH, v. n. Sing ye. 2 pers. pl. imp. of *cané. Kenouch why faborden brâs, ha me a cân trebyl fyn,* sing ye a great bass, and I will sing a fine treble. R.D. 2359. W. *cenwch.* Arm. †*canouch.*

CENS, adv. Before, formerly, rather. *Kens nôs eyf ten gwyn pymeth, ha dhe scufé ytheth yn ow nygys,* before going, drink a draught of spiced wine, and thou more nimbly wilt go in my errand. O.M. 2294. *Kepar hag ef ôn crowsys, ha dre vyr vreus iuggys râk agan drôk ober kens,* like as he, we are crucified, and by true judgment sentenced for our evil deed before. P.C. 2002. *Nep yw ioy ow colon, ha'm melder kepar ha kens,* who art the joy of my heart, and my sweetness as formerly. R.D. 467. In construction *cens* is mutable into *gens* and *hens.* ‡ *Po ti ha de wrêg an moiha lian warbarh, nenne greuh lerhi an desan, ha na hens,* when thou and thy wife are most merry together, then break the cake, and not before. *Llwyd,* 251. The aspirate form is required after *na, na hens.* So also in Welsh, *na chynt.* Written also *cyns,* qd. v. W. *cynt,* †*cent.* Arm. *kent.* Ir. *ceid.* Gael. *ceud.*

CENS, prep. With. Another form of *cans. Kens dha gledhé,* with thy sword. *Llwyd,* 230.

CENSA, adj. The first, chief. *Bedhens nêp a ddeppro kensa, kepar ha nêp a servyo,* let him be who eats first, as he who serves. P.C. 795. *A wetta ny develhys warbarth ha'n kensa galow,* seest thou us come together with the first call. P.C. 2051. *Galsen yn ta, dhe'n kensu fu,* I could well, at the first view. R.D. 863. *Crnsa* is the superlative of the irregular comparative *cens.* Written also *cynsa,* qd. v. W. *cyntav,* †*centav,* †*cintam.* Arm. *cenla,* †*centaf.* Ir. *ceadna,* †*cetne, ceud,* †*cita.* Gael. *ceud.* Maux, *chied.*

CENSEMMYN, adv. Before now. *Llwyd,* 249. A corrupt contraction of *cens,* before, and *lemmyn,* now.

CENSENNA, adv. Before that, ere that. *Llwyd*, 249. Compounded of *cens*, before, and *henna*, that.

CENTER, s. f. A nail, a spike. Pl. *centrow*. *Doro kenter, ha me a ink y luef gledh*, bring me a nail, and I will fasten his left hand. P.C. 2748. *Hag onan, gwyskyns kenter scon ynny*, and one, let him drive a nail in it at once. P.C. 2766. *Treys ha dewlef a pup tu fast lackyes gans kentrow hern*, feet and hands on every side fast fixed with iron nails. P.C. 2938. *Yw sow oll dhe wolyow, a wrûk an gu ha'n kentrow*, are all thy wounds healed, which the spear and nails made? R.D. 491. ‡ *Gwisgo un genter ma ed eskas vi*, knock this nail in my shoe. *Llwyd*, 230. W. *cethyr*. Arm. *kentr*, a spur. Ir. †*cinteir*. Gr. κέντρον.

CENTREVEC, s. m. A neighbour, one of the same town. *Den a'n geffé cans davas ha'y centrevek saw onan, mar a's ladtré dheworto, pa'n pýn a gotho dhodho*, a man may possess a hundred sheep, and his neighbour only one; if he steal it from him, what punishment is due to him? O.M. 2231. Written also *contrevec*, qd. v. Compounded of *cen*, with, and *trev*, a town. W. *cyd-drevawg*. Arm. †*contrevek*. But the common term in Welsh for a neighbour is *cynmydog*, one of the same *cwmmud*, or wapentake; being a division of the *Cantred*, or hundred: and in Armoric, *amezek*.

CENTREVNY, v. a. To breed maggots, to rot. *Yn prison môs ny ircymyn agan bew, kyn kentrevynyn oll agan kýc*, going to prison, we will not torment our lives, though we may rot our flesh. R.D. 74. From *contron*, qd. v. W. *cyndhroni*.

CENTROW, s. m. Nails. The plural of *center*, qd. v.

CENTRE, v. a. To nail, to fasten with nails. *Tynneuch kettep pen, y vellow kettep onan dyscavylsys gns, lemmyn kentr'y worth an pren*, pull ye every one, his joints, every one, are strained, now nail it to the wood. P.C. 2772. From *center*, a nail.

CENTHEW, comp. v. Although he is. *Whath kenthew ow hendas pur drôk dên accomplys*, yet although my grandsire is accounted a very bad man. C.W. 106. *Kenthew* is a contraction of *cen*, although, and *ythew*, is.

CENZHOHA, s. m. The morning. ‡ *En kenzhoha*, in the morning. *Llwyd*, 249. This is a corrupt word of late occurrence. The root is *cens*, first.

CENYS, part. Sung. *Peder, me a levar dhys, kyns ys bôs kullyek kenys, ter gwyth y wrêch ow naché*, Peter, I say to thee, before that the cock has crowed, three times thou wilt deny me. P.C. 903. The participle pass. of *cané*, qd. v.

CEPAR, adv. Equally, in the same manner, alike, like to, as. It is generally followed by *del*, or *ha*. *Avel plow aga threys, nych gns oll kepar ha leys*, like the prints of their feet, they are all dry, like herbs. O.M. 761. *Kepar del fuwé drummas*, like as he was a just man. O.M. 864. *Kepur hag ôn, like as we are*. O.M. 894. *Kepar ha my, ef gordhyruch*, like me, honour ye him. O.M. 2350. *Kepar del fue dhyn yrhys*, as it was enjoined to us. O.M. 2375. *Kepar ha del loverys*, just as I said. P.C. 2690. *Kepar hâg ef, ôn crowxys*, like as he, we are crucified. P.C. 2900. *Dew ha dên kepar del ôf*, God and man, like as I am. R.D. 2385. Compounded of *ce*, id. qd. *ced*, *ecv*, with, and *par*, equal. W. *cymhar*, is derived from the same roots. So also the Irish *comparaid*, †*copar*. Gael. *coimhcart*.

CER, adj. Dear, beloved, dearly beloved. In construction *gêr*. Superlative, *kerra*. *Dres dyfen ow arluth kêr*, against the prohibition of our dear Lord. O.M. 172. *Râg dhe offryn kêr*, because of thy dear offering. O.M. 567. *Hag ef ahunan mar gêr*, and he so dearly beloved of us. O.M. 612. *A dûs kêr*, O dear Father. O.M. 835. *Yn gordhyans dhe tâs Dew kêr*, in worship to the dear God the Father. O.M. 1200. *A mester kêr caradow*, O dear beloved master. P.C. 73. W. *câr, caredig*. Arm. *cêr*. Lat. *charus*. Fr. *cher*.

CER, v. n. Go thou. ‡ *Sav aman, kemer dha li, ha ker dha'n hâl, môr-teed a metten travyth ne dâl*, get up, take thy breakfast, and go to the moor, the seatide of the morning is nothing worth. Cornish Proverb. *Pryce*. This is an abbreviated form of *cerdh*, 2 pers. s. imp. of *cerdhes*, to go, qd. v.

CER, adv. Away. ‡ *Dho kemeras kerr*, to take away. *Llwyd*, 44. ‡ *Dho punnya kerr*, to run away. *ibid*. 61. ‡ *Ke yn ker, benyn vâs*, go away, good woman. C.W. 52. ‡ *Omskemynes del otta, quick yn ker ke alemma*, accursed as thou art, quickly go away from hence. *ibid*. 88. This is a late abbreviation of *cerdh*, qd. v.

CERCOT, s. f. A surcoat, a surplice. *Hedhouch cercot a baly, dhodho me a vyn y ry*, reach ye a surcoat of satin, to him I will give it. P.C 1784. *Me a'n kelm, hag a cach an cercol vrâs dhe vês, ûs adro dhodho*, I will bind him, and snatch the large surcoat away, that is about him. P.C. 2074. From the English *surcoat*.

CERCH, v. a. He will fetch. 3 pers. s. fut. of *cerchy*, and also 2 pers. s. imp. *Kerch dhys ow ené gans êl*, bring to thee my soul by an angel. P.C. 429. *Ow maplyen kerch Annas*, my clerk fetch Annas. P.C. 553. *Kerch a'n fenten dhym dour*, fetch from the well for me water. P.C. 650. *Me a gerch dour dhys wharré*, I will fetch water for thee soon. P.C. 655. *Me a'n kerch dheuch*, I will fetch him to you. R.D. 1801.

CERCH, s. m. A road, journey. *Dûn yn kerch*, let us come away. P.C. 2289. *Ke yn kerch dyrehans*, go thy way quickly. R.D. 116. *Hag an bêdh yn kerch gyllys dhe'n nef deffry*, and from the grave forth gone to heaven really. R.D. 809. W. *cyrch*.

CERCH, s. m. Oats. *Kerch, barlys, ha gwaneth*, oats, barley, and wheat. C.W. 78. Written also *ceirch*, qd. v.

CERCHEN, adj. Surrounding, about. *Dyeth fest rye, y vôs yn kerchen unp gâl*, great pity it would be, that it should be about the son of evil. P.C. 2131. Written also *kerchyn*. *Lemmyn jevody, cafus an bows-na hep gwry, ûs y'th kerchyn, me a tyn*, now, I tell you, I will have that coat without seam, that is about thee. R.D. 1922. *Gynef nyns yw medh, awos guyské an queth a fue yn kerchyn Ihesu*, with me there is no shame, because of wearing the cloth that was about Jesus. R.D. 1937. W. *cyrchyn*. Ir. †*cerceun*. Lat. *circinus*, a pair of compasses.

CERCHES, v. a. To fetch, carry, bring. 3 pers. s. fut. and 2 pers. s. imp. *kerch*. Part. pass. *kerchys*. *Me a pŷs ragouch ow thâs, may fench sylwys, hag oll kerchys dodho dh'y wlâs*, and I will pray my father for you, that ye may be saved, and all brought to him to his country. P.C. 29. *Cerch a'n fenten dhym dour clêr*, fetch clear water for me from the well. P.C. 650. *Me a gerch dour dhys wharré, ottê ow fycher gyné yn ow dorn râk y gerches*, I will fetch water for thee soon,

CERENSE 54 CERNOW

behold my pitcher with me in my hand to fetch it. P.C. 655. *Kerchyn Longys, an gwâs dall,* let us fetch Longius, the blind fellow. P.C. 2918. *Whet kerchouch dhymmo Pilat,* again, fetch Pilate to me. R.D. 1885. *Re'n kercho an dewolow,* may the devils fetch him. R.D. 2277. *Deuch gynef dhe kerchas corf Pilat,* come with me to fetch the body of Pilate. R.D. 2309. W. *cyrchu,* †*circhu.* Arm. *cerchout.* Lat. *circo, circare.* It. *cercare.* Fr. *chercher.* Eng. *search.* Sansc. *char,* to go.

CERDEN, s. f. The quicken tree, or mountain ash. *Lhwyd,* 109. W. *cerdhin.* Arm. *kerzin.* Ir. *caorthain.* Gael. *caorthunn.* Manx, *ceirn.*

CERDYN, s. m. Cords. *Yn scorgiys prenyer esé yn devlé an dew edhow, hag yn fast kelnys dhedhé kerdyn, gwethyn yn mesk cronow, may fôns hyblyth dhe gronkyé, hug a râg gwrÿs colmenow, gans pûp colmen may 'th elté, pan wyskens, yn mês an crow,* in the scourges there were rods in the hands of the two Jews, and fast bound to them cords, weaved among thongs, that they might be pliant, to beat him, and before (at the ends) knots made, with every knot that the blood might come, when they struck him. M.C. 131. It is the plural of *cord,* qd. v.

CERDH, s. f. A road, journey. Written in Cornish Vocabulary *kerd,* Iter. *Ke yn kerdh, ow nâp,* go thy way, my son. O.M. 725. *Dûn yn kerdh, ow bruder whêk,* let us come away, my sweet brother. P.C. 188. *Me effi-redh a'th pÿs, awos an tâs hynygeys ro dhym ow kerdh dre dhe râs,* I maimed pray thee, for the sake of the blessed father, give to me my. walking by thy grace. P.C. 401. W. *cerdh,* †*kerd.* Arm. *kerz.*

CERDHES, v. a. To go, walk, proceed. *Galsof ysel na allaf kerdhes yn fâs,* I am become low, so that I cannot walk well. O.M. 374. *An dour a uger a lês, may hylly yn ta kerdhes, ty ha'th pobel oll drydhy,* the water will open widely, that thou mayest walk well, thou and all thy people through it. O.M. 1677. *Yma Moyses pell gyllys yn môr, del hewel dhymmo, a râg dyrchans ow kerdhes, an dour ow fysky a lês pûp oll a dhyragdho,* Moses is far gone into the sea, as it seems to me, walking quickly forward, striking the water wide before him. O.M. 1684. *Euch yn drê, hag ordeneuch bôs pask dhynny, kerdheuch nay fova purys wharré,* go into the town, and order the pasohal food for us, go that it may be ready soon. P.C. 619. *An antecryst, yn lyes plu, a treyl pobyl dhyworth Dew ya pûp le may kerdho ef,* the antichrist, in many a parish, will turn people from God in every place that he may go to. R.D. 249. Preterite *cyrdhys,* qd. v. W. *cerdhed.* Arm. *cerzed.* Ir. *corruigh.* Gael. *caraich.* Sansc. *car, kharb, khôr, svart.*

CERENGE, s. m. Love, affection. *Râg kerengé orthys, my ny gemeré neffré trom dyal war oll an veys,* for love to thee, I will never take heavy vengeance on all the world. O.M. 1207. *Yma dagyrow ow clybbyé dhe dreys, râk ewn kerengé,* tears are wetting thy feet, for true love. P.C. 483. *Lemmyn gura, ow karengé, kepar yn beys del vynny,* do now, my love, as in the world thou wouldst. R.D. 453. It is a later form of *cerense.*

CERENSE, s. m. Love, affection. *En kêth oynement a scollyas warnaf, rák ow anclydhyas, hy a'n grûk dre kerensé,* the same ointment she poured on me, for my burial, she did it through love. P.C. 549. *Jesus Christ mear gerensé dhe vâb dên a dhyswedhas,* Jesus Christ much love to mankind shewed. M.C. 5. *Tachys fast gans kerensé,* fastened close with love. M.C. 223. It is the same word as *carensé,* qd. v., and derived from the verb *caré,* to love. W. *carennydh,* †*carennyd,* †*carentid.* Arm. *karentiez.* Ir. *cairdeas.* Gael. *cairdeas.* Manx, *caardys.* Cf. also the ancient Gaulic names, *Curantonus, Carentomagus.*

CERENYS, part. Crowned. *Dûn dhe gerhus Salamon, ha gorym ef yn y drôn avel mychtern yn y se,* may hallo vôs *kerenys,* let us come to fetch Solomon, and let us place him on his throne, like a king in his seat, that he may be crowned. O.M. 2374. *Râg dewesys ôs mychtern dhyn, ha kerenys a ver dermyn ty a vÿdh,* for chosen thou art a king to us, and crowned in a short time thou shalt be. O.M. 2381. It is the same word as *cerunys,* the part. pass. of *ceruné,* qd. v.

CEREOR, s. m. A shoemaker, a cordwainer. Cornish Vocabulary, *sutor.* W. *crÿdh.* Arm. *kerê, kereour.* Ir. *caireamhan,* †*cairem.* Gael. †*caireamhan.* Manx, *greasce.* I consider the W. *crÿdh* to be a contracted form of *carreiydh,* from *carrai,* a thong, = Lat. *corrigium,* with the usual suffix *ydh,* to denote the agent.

CERH, s. m. Oats. *Lhwyd,* 26, *kerh.* This is the latest form of *cerch,* or *ceirch,* qd. v. *Bara kerh,* oaten bread.

CERHES, v. a. To fetch, bring, carry. *Awos Dew, dûn ahanan dh'y gerhas dhe drê, may hallo bôs musurys,* for God's sake, let us come away to fetch it home, that it may be measured. O.M. 2565. *Cardowyon, hep whethé corn, na gûl sôn, keruch (kerheuch) Jhesu dhynny ny,* my dear fellows, without blowing horn, or making a noise, bring Jesus to us. P.C. 1359. *Dynolow yffarn a squerdyas corf Judas oll dhe dharnow, hag uncdho a gerhas y enef dhe dewolgow,* the devils of hell tore the body of Judas all to pieces, and from him carried his soul to darkness. M.C. 106. *An prennyer a ve kerhys, en grows scon dythgtis may fe,* the pieces of wood were brought, the cross that it might immediately be formed. M.C. 153. This is another form of *cerches,* qd. v., the guttural *ch* being softened into *h.*

CERHIDII, s. m. A heron. In Cornish Vocabulary written *cherhit,* ardea. Pryce furnishes the later form *kerhes.* W. *crychydh, crehyr, cryhyr, creyr, crÿr, creyr glâs.* Arm. *cercheiz.* Ir. *corr, corr ghlais.* Gael. *corr, curra, corra-ghlas.* Manx, *coayr.*

CERHYN, adj. Surrounding, about. *Dhe dhyskyblion yn serrys mâr, ha'n Yedhewon gans nerth pûp ûr ygé kerhyn,* thy disciples are very sad, and the Jews with violence are continually surrounding them. R.D. 886. This is another form of *cerchen,* qd. v., the guttural being softened into *h.*

CERNA, v. a. To tremble. *Dho kerna,* to tremble. *Lhwyd,* 166. A late corruption of *crenna,* qd. v.

CERNEWEC, adj. Cornish. Written by Pryce, *Kernuak.* ‡*Metten da dha why; elo why clapier Kernuak,* good morning to you; can you speak Cornish?

CERNIAS, s. m. A horn blower, a trumpeter, a piper. *Lhwyd,* 241. This is a later form of *cerniat,* which is written in the Cornish Vocabulary, *cherniat,* cornicen. Derived from *corn,* a horn, the *o* being regularly changed into *e,* as is also the case in Welsh, though now written *y.* W. *corn, cyrniad,* †*cerniat.*

CERNIC, adj. Rocky. From *carn,* a rock. Hence *Kernick,* nom. loc. in St. Stephen's.

CERNOW, s. m. Cornwall. *Me a whÿth avel gwâs dâ ;*

nyns-ûs dén vŷth yn pow-ma a whytho gwell; ny won góf yn ol Kernow a whytho gans mygenow bŷth well, I will blow like a good fellow; there is never a man in this country, who can blow better; I know not a smith in all Cornwall, who can blow with bellows any better. P.C. 2712. ‡*Stean San Agnes an gwella stean en Kernow*, the tin of St. Agnes (is) the best tin in Cornwall. Pryce. W. *Cernyw*. The root of the word is *Corn*, a horn; from the shape of the country running like a horn into the sea. One of the four cantons of Britanny is also called *Kerneô*, in French *Cornouaille*.

CEROIN. s. f. A tub, pipe, or tun. Cornish Vocabulary, *keroin*, cupa. W. *cerwyn*.

CERRA. adj. Dearest, most beloved. The superlative of *cér*, qd. v. *Ow cleth, sevauch yn ban, euch alemma ahanan, dhe servya ow máp kerra*, my angels, stand up, go hence from us to serve my most dear son. P.C. 153.

CERRAS, v. n. To go, to walk. ‡*Dda Adam kerras pur gryyf me a vyn, dhe sallugyé, ha'n aval y presentya*, to Adam I will walk very strongly, to salute him, and present to him the apple. C.W. 54. A late corruption of *cerdhes*, qd. v.

CERRY, v. a. Thou shalt love. 2 pers. s. fut. of *caré*, to love; often used as the present tense. *Lavar dhymmo dywngel, del ym kerry, me a'd peys*, speak to me clearly, as thou lovest me, I pray thee. O.M. 1370. *Gor ost genes yrrys da dhe omladh, del y'm kerry*, take with thee a host, well armed, to fight, as thou lovest me. O.M. 2142. Written also *cyrry*, qd. v.

CERRYS, part. Carried. Part. pass. of *caria*, to carry, qd. v. ‡*I'an deffa oyle a vercy, te a výdh kerrys the'n joye, dhe'n nêf uchel a uchan*, when the oil of mercy shall come, thou shalt be carried to joy, to the high heaven above. C.W. 150.

CERT, s. f. A cart. *Holyns ôf, me a fue yn kert a tán, dhe'n kêth plas-ma kymerys*, Elijah I am, I was in a cart of fire, to this same place being brought. R.D. 236. W. *cart, cert*. Ir. *cairt*. Gael. *cairt*. Manx, *cart*.

CERUNE, v. a. To crown. *Ha rág why dhum keruné, my a re dhwch Boswené*, and because ye have crowned me, I will give you Boswene. O.M. 293. Written also *curuny*, qd. v.

CERYN, v. a. We love, or shall love. 1 pers. pl. fut. of *caré*, to love; often used as the present. *Neb a geryn an moycha*, whom we love the most. C.W. 88.

CERYS, part. Loved. Part. pass. of *caré*, to love, qd. v. *Dhe gryggy Thomas a dhue, rág gans ow arluth y fue kyns lemmyn marthys kerys*, to believe Thomas will come, for by our lord he was before now greatly loved. R.D. 1221.

CES, adj. Joint, common, united. *Dhyuch lavaráf, ow dyskyblyon, pysouch toyth da oll kes-colon Dew dreys pûp tra*, to you I say, my disciples, pray ye forthwith, all with one heart, God above all things. P.C. 2. *Whêth ow cufyon dyfunouch, ha kes colon oll pesouch na gyllouch yn temptacion*, again, my dear (companions) awake, and with one heart all pray, that ye enter not into temptation. P.C. 1076. *Ddodho Jesus dhy dhampnyé Pylat býs pan danvonas, yn ur-na kes-kow-dhé y a ve*, to him Jesus to condemn until he sent to Pilate, in that hour united companions they became. M.C. 110. It is also written *cys*, qd. v. W. *cŷd*, †*ced*, (*cyd-yalon*.) Arm. *ked*.

CES, s. m. Cheese. This is a late form of *cœus*, qd. v., and is the pronunciation in use in the times of Keigwyn and Llwyd. ‡*Es kês? ês po neg ês? ma 'n-ês kês, drô kês; po ney és kês, drô peth ês*, is there cheese? is there, or is there not? if there is cheese. bring cheese; if there be not cheese, bring what there is. Pryce's *Vocabulary*.

CESADOW, adj. Hateful, odious, detestable. *Ty wás cesadow, ygor scon an darasow ha kêth an prysnes yn mês*, thou odious fellow, open immediately the doors, and bring the prisoners out. R.D. 631. Another form of *casadow*, qd. v.

CESAN, s. f. A sod, or turf. *Llwyd*, 45. Pl. *cesow*. ‡*Whelas tees dha trehé kesow*, look for people to cut turves. Pryce's *Vocabulary*.

CESCAR, v. a. To separate, disperse, wander. *Yn mês a'm ioy ha'm whekter, rês ew keskar dre terros, rág fout gwesc ha goscotter, namna vyrwyn rág antvos*, away from my joy and my delight, I must wander through lands, for want of clothes and shelter, I am almost perishing for cold. O.M.360. *Gwifr a gowsaf vy, ha me a'n prêf kyn keskar*, I speak true, and I will prove it before separating. R.D. 910. Compare this sentence with the following: *Me a'n prêf ywŷr a gowsaf, kyns ys dybarth*, I will prove that I speak truly, before separating. R.D. 925. In the following sentence, *peth kescar* means the condition of a vagrant, whence that of a beggar, or poverty. *Benegas ynu nêb a garé Du dris pûp tra ûs yn bŷs; hag a wodheffo yn wharé dhodho kymmys ûs ordnys; bo clevas bo peth kescar, bo dre prison presonys, oll en da ha'n drôk kepuré, dhe Jesus bedhens grassys*, blessed is he that loves God above every thing that is in the world, and endureth patiently as much as is ordained to him; be it sickness or poverty, or by prison imprisoned, all the good and evil alike, to Jesus he thanks. M.C. 24. W. *cydysgaru, gwasgaru*.

CESCER, adj. Affectionate, loving. *Oll eleth nêf, golsowouch dha ve lemyn; cresouch ow bôsaf prince crêf, hag yn-wedh dhe why cescer, bian ha brás*, all angels of heaven, hearken to me now; believe ye that I am a strong prince, and also to you affectionate, small and great. C.W. 10. Compounded of *ces*, together, and *cêr*, dear. W. *cydgar*.

CESCY, v. n. To be at rest, to lie quiet, to sleep. *Adam, a oll dhe drevas, an degves ran dhymmo gás, whêth yn atal dhe kesky*, Adam, of all thy tillage, leave the tenth part to me, still to remain waste. O.M. 427. Another form of *cuscé*, qd. v.

CESENYANS, s. m. Agreement, concord, consent. Pryce. W. *cydsyniant*, from *cyd*, together, & *syniant*, sentiment.

CESER, s. m. Hail. Cornish Vocabulary, *grando*. Written by Keigwyn and Llwyd, *kezzar*, and *kezer*. ‡*Ema a kil kezzar*, it is hailing, lit. it is making hail. *Llwyd*, 250. ‡*Yein kuer, taredrrow, ha golowas, er, ren, gwens, ha clehe, ha kezer*, cold weather, thunder, and lightning, snow, frost, wind, and ice, and hail. Pryce's *Vocab*. W. *cesair*. Arm. *casarch*, †*caserch*. Ir. †*casair*, a shower.

CESOLETH, s. m. Tranquillity, rest, peace. *Ysedheuch yn kesoleth, rák scon why a fŷdh servys*, sit down in quietness, for you shall soon be served. P.C. 715. Written by Llwyd, *cysolath*, qd. v.

CESON, s. m. An accusation. More generally written *ceyson*, qd. v.

CESOW, s. m. Turves, sods. The plural of *cesan*, qd. v.
CESPAR, s. c. A spouse, a married person. Cornish Vocabulary, *conjux*. Compounded of *ces*, together, and *par*, a mate. From the same roots are the W. *cymhar*, a partner. Arm. *kever*, *kenver*, comparison. Ir. *comharaid*, † *copar*. Gael. *coimheart*. Lat. *compar*.
CESSONYIS, s. m. A consonant. *Pryce*. W. *cydseiniad*, fr. *cyd*, together, and *seiniad*, a sounding.
CESTEL, s. m. Castles. One of the plurals of *castel*, qd. v.
CESULYE, v. a. To consult. *Me'a gesul*, I advise. P.C. 1543. Generally *cusulye*, qd. v.
CESVOWA, v. a. To live with. ‡ *Råg henna yn chast gwren ny kesvowa*, *ha carnall joye yn bys-ma ny a vyn warbarth nacha*, wherefore chastely let us live together, and carnal joy in this world we will altogether deny. C.W. 90. Comp. of *ces*, together, and *bewa*, to live. W. *cydvyw*.
CET, a prefix in composition. It denotes co-operation, conjunction, and equality, and has the power of the Latin and English prefixes, *co*, *com*, *con*. It is the older form of *ces*, and was also written *ced*, and is now written in Welsh *cyd*, but anciently, † *cet*, † *ced*, † *cyt*; and in Ancient Gaulish, *cata*, *catu*, as may be seen in the proper names *Catamantelides*, *Catalauni*, *Catmelus*. The prefix *con*, in *contrevak*, &c., has the same power. Arm. *ked*. Ir. *con*, *co*, *coss*. Gael. *con*, *co*. It is the same word as C. *cans*; W. *cant*, with; and the primitive form is preserved in the W. composites, *canhymdaith*, a companion; *canlyn*, to follow. Lat. *con*. Gr. σὺν. Sansc. *sam*.
CETEL, adv. In the manner that, as, as soon as, when. Written also indiscriminately, *kettel*, and *kettyl*. *Råg dhym yma tokyn da, råk y gafus, kettyl y'n geffo a'n bay*, for there is to me a good token to take him, as soon as he finds him, he shall kiss him. P.C. 985. *Kettel tersys an bara, aswonys Cryst a qara, mar dha del reys*, as thou didst break the bread, I knew Christ whom I love, so well as there is need. R.D. 1318. *Wharré y gen lowennas, kettel dhueth er agan pyn*, soon he gladdened us, when he came to meet us. R.D. 1329. Compounded of *ceth*, the same, and *del*, manner.
CETELLA, adv. In such a manner, in that way, so, likewise. *Yn pûr ny defry nép a rolla yn ketella, mernans yn gwyw dhy vody*, very positively, whoever has acted in that way, death is due to his body. O.M. 2241. *Y'n ketella ty re wrúk*, in that way thou hast acted. O.M. 2243. *Honna yw cusyl da, yn ketella me a wra*, that is good advice, so I will do. P.C. 1454. *Yn ur-na dhe'n menydhyow why a erch warnouch codhé, yn ketella an nansow uy a býs ragas cudhé*, in that hour ye shall call to the mountains to fall on you, likewise the cliffs ye shall pray you to hide. M.C. 170.
CETELMA, adv. In this manner, thus. *Mes y dhensys o mar feyn púb or a'n trylya dhedha may 'th éth war ben y dhewleyn, ha pesy yn ketelma*, but his manhood was so delicate every hour that he turned himself to it, that he went on his knees, and prayed in this manner. M.C. 54. *An lader a'n barth dychow a besys yn ketelma, Arluth pan dyffy dhet pow, predery ahanaf gwra*, the thief on the right side prayed in this manner, Lord, when thou shalt come to thy country, do thou think of me. M.C. 193. Compounded of *cetel*, and *ma*, here.
CETEP, adj. Every. *Cresseuch, coullenweuch an brys, avel kyns, ketep måp bron*, increase, fill the earth, as before, every son of the breast. O.M. 1162. *Oyeth my, glewsyuch dhym oll masons an dré ketep pol*, hear ye, listen to me all masons of the town, every head. O.M. 2298. *Ha dhym y a worthebys, y fedhons myttyn parys ketep onan*, and to me they have answered, that they will be in the morning ready every one. O.M. 2608. *Deuch yn råg ketep onan*, come forward every one. O.M. 2683. *Dhe esgarn oll ketep tam gans ow bom a fydh brewys*, thy bones all, every bit, with my blows shall be broken. O.M. 2744. *Me â genes yn lowen, ha'm dyscyblyon ketlep pen dhe'th arhadow*, I will go with thee joyfully, and my disciples, every head, at thy commands. P.C. 462. *Godhvedhouch ketoponon*, know ye every one. M.C. 141. The same term occurs in Armoric, see *guitibunan*, in Dubez Noun, 58, 94.
CETGORRA, v. a. To compare, to collate. *Dhe getgora*. *Pryce*. Compounded of *cet*, and *gorra*, to place.
CETORVA, s. f. The groin. *Llwyd*, 70. W. *cedorva*, from *cedor*, † *caitoir*, Oxf. Gloss., and *ma*, a place. Arm. *cezour*, *caezour*. Ir. *caethair*.
CETTERMYN, adv. Likewise. *Pryce*. Compounded of *cet*, together, and *termyn*, time.
CETTOTH, adv. As soon as. *Dús dhymmo ketoth ha'n gér*, *råg colenvel bódh ow brýs*, come to me as soon as the word, to fulfil the wish of my mind. O.M. 2272. *May tanfunno dhyuch yn scon, kettuth ha'n gér*, that he send to you forthwith, as soon as the word. R.D. 1598. *Hedheuch dhymmo ow kledhé, råk may hyllyf y ladhé, kettoth ha'n gér*, reach me my sword, for that I may kill him as soon as the word. R.D. 1970. Comp. of *cet*, together, and *tóth*, haste.
CETVA, s. f. A convention, an assembly. Cornish Vocabulary, *chetua*, *conventus vel conventio*. Comp. of *cet*, together, and *ma*, a place, whence the proper meaning is the place of meeting. The meeting itself is also the meaning of the W. *cydva*.
CETH, adj. The same. *Ng dyf gwéls na flour yn býs yn kéth fordh-na, may kyrdhys*, neither grass nor flower in the world grows in that same road, that I went. O.M. 713. *Gwren un alter têk ha da, may hyllyn sacryfyé dhodho war an kéth honna*, let us make an altar fair and good, that we may sacrifice to him upon that same. O.M. 1172. *Nyns ê dén vgth vynytha a'n keth re-na dhe'n tyr sans*, no man shall go ever of those same to the holy land. O.M. 1879. *Laha Moyses dhym yma, hag yn oll an kéth henna nyns ûs y hanow scryffys*, I have the law of Moses, and in all that same, his name is not written. O.M. 1645. *Py ngl o mochn sengys an kéth dén-ma dhe caré*, which one was most bound this same man to love. P.C. 511. W. *cyd*.
CETH, adv. Since, whilst, as long as. *Whåth keth fyns y mar venys, me a dhóg raw war ow heyn uskes lemyn*, yet since they are so small, I will carry some on my back immediately now. C.W. 100. W. *cyd*.
CETH, s. m. The common people. *Oll tûs ow chy, deuch genef vy, bryntyn ha kéth*, all men of my house, come with me, nobles and commons. O.M. 1962. *Oyeth yn wêdh sy glewsyuch bryntyn ha kéth, an mychtern a worhemmyn*. hear likewise ye, listen nobles and commons, the king commands. O.M. 2420. *Néb o tús kéth dhe Pylat a lavarys*, some that were common people to Pilate said. M.C. 115.

CETHEL, s. f. A knife. Cornish Vocabulary, *cultellus, cultellum.* See also *collel.* W. *cythell, cyllell.* Arm. *contel.* Lat. *cultellus.*

CEV, a prefix in composition. It denotes conjunction, and equality, and agrees in meaning with *cet*, and the following are examples where it occurs, *kepar*, equally; *kekeffrys*, also; *cefals*, a joint; *cemar*, a spouse; *cevelyn*, a cubit, &c. Written also *com, cov, co,* as in *colenwel, coulenwel.* W. *cyv, cy, cym, cyn;* formerly written †*cum*, †*cem*, †*cav*, †*cev*, †*cim*, †*com.* Arm. *ken*, †*cem*, †*com.* Ir. *comh*, †*com*, †*co.* Gael. *comh, coimh.* Lat. *com, con.*

CEVARDHIU, s. m. December. Lit. *mis kevardhiu* means the month following the black month, November. Arm. *keverdu, kerdu, kerzu.* The Welsh name is *rhageyr.*

CEVARVOS, v. a. To recover. *Pryce.* W. *cyvarvod.*

CEVARWOUDH, v. a. Direct thou. *Ow cannas whêk, dhe'n boys touth, lowenna tecka godhfy, Ihesu ow mûp kevarvoudh, ugy warnaf ow pygy,* my sweet messenger, to the world quick, the fairest joy thou knowest, Jesus my son direct thou, who is on me praying. P.C 1043. I take this to be the W. *cyvarwydh,* 2 pers. s. imp. of *cyvarwydho*, to direct or guide.

CEVE, v. a. He did have. 3 pers. s. imp. of *cafus*, qd. v. *Lavar dhym, del y'm kerry, pan vernans a'n gevê cf*, tell me, as thou lovest me, what death did he meet with ? O.M. 2219. See *Gevê*.

CEVELEP, adj. Like, similar. *Pryce.* The more frequent form is *hevelep*, qd. v. W. *cyfelyb.* Arm. *hevelep.*

CEVELYN, s. f. A cubit, the length from the elbow to the point of the middle finger, half a yard. *Tryhans kevelyn da an lester a vydh a hys. ha hanter cans kevelyn yn wêdh ty a vora y lês,* three hundred cubits good the vessel shall be in length, and half a hundred cubits thou shalt make its breadth. O.M. 955. *Ny yl an gyst yn y blâs, re hŷr ew a gevelyn,* the beam will not go into its place, too long it is by a cubit. O.M. 2529. *Lemyn re got ew a gevelyn,* now it is too short by a cubit. O.M. 2541. Compounded of *cev*, and *elyn*, or *elin*, the elbow, qd. v. W. *cynelin.* Arm. *cefelyn.*

CEVIL, s. m. A horse. The word is preserved in the names of places, as *Nankevil*, *Penkevil*. W. *cefyl.* Ir. *capall*, a mare, a horse. Gael. *copull*, a mare. Manx. *cabbyl.* Gr. *καβαλλης*, a work-horse. Lat. *caballus*, a horse. It. *cavallo.* Fr. *cheval*; *cavale*, a mare. Pol. *kobela.* Both. *kobyla.* Hung. *kabalalo.*

CEVER, s. m. A relative position. *Whet kerchouch dhymmo Pilat, yn y gever y fyf tollys,* again bring ye to me Pilate, in relation to him I was deceived. R.D. 1886. W. *oyver.* Arm. *cover.* Ir. *comhair, comhar.* Gael. *comhair.*

CEVEREI, s. m. A kid, or young goat. *Keverel* is a family name in St. Martin's by Loo, and a *cheverel*, or *keverel*, a kid, is borne by them on their arms. *Pryce.* The word is not derived from the Cornish *gaver*, a goat, but rather from the French *chevreau,* †*cheverel.* The Cornish and Welsh term for a kid is *mynnan*, qd. v.

CEVERYS, adv. Likewise, also. ‡*Arluth nef, ha'n byes keverys,* Lord of heaven, and earth likewise. C.W. 70. A late form of *cefrys,* qd. v.

CEVYS, part. Found. ‡*Mes an for a vydh kevys yn vanerma der ow oberow,* but the way will be found in this manner by my works. C.W. 126. ‡*Pan deffa an termyn a pymp mil ha pymp cans vledhan, an oyle a vercy yn nena o vydh kevys,* when shall come the period of five thousand and five hundred years, the oil of mercy then will be found. C.W. 138. A later form of *cefys*, qd. v.

CEVYTH, v. a. Thou shalt find. 3 pers. s. fut. of *cafus*, qd. v. *Pŵr wŷr ef a'n gevyth gu pan dyffo yn ow goloc,* very truly he shall have woe, when he comes into my sight. P.C. 963. *Byth nyn gevyth fout a ioy nêp a yl gwelas dhe fas,* never shall he have lack of joy, whoever can see thy face. P.C. 1501. Written equally common *cefyth.*

CEWAR, s. f. Weather, a storm, tempest. *Lhuyd,* 128. *Cewar lêb*, wet weather. *id.* 243. It is written by Pryce, *kuer.* ‡*Yein kuer, tarednow, ha golowas, er, reu, gwens, ha clehé, ha kezer,* cold weather, thunder, and lightning, snow, frost, wind, and ice, and hail. I think this word must be a corruption of the W. *garwedh*, roughness, from *garw*, (C. *garow*,) rough; so *tywydh garw*, severe weather.

CEWS, s. m. Speech, discourse. *Cafes dhe gews tregereth*, to obtain thy word of love. O.M. 454. Written also *cows*, qd. v.

CEWSEL, v. a. To speak, say, tell, relate. Pret. and part. pass. *cewsys.* 3 pers. s. fut. *cews. Pyw ôs a gews mar huhel*, who art thou, that speakest so lofty ? O.M. 1368. *Rŷs ew dhym kewsel defry orth ow gwrêk kyns môs a drê,* I must speak really to my wife before going from home. O.M. 2171. *Mara kewsys fulsury, a henna dôk dustuny, mes mara kewsys yn lêl, prâg y wreth ow boxuny, nyns yw lemmyn vyleny awos gwyr yonedh kewsel,* if I have spoken falsehood, of that bear witness, but if I have spoken honestly, why dost thou strike me ? there is not now villainy because of speaking truth. P.C. 1271. *Kewseuch lemmen, gwyckoryon, del ouch syneys giocryon, pendra gewsys an dên-ma,* say yo now, traders, as ye are esteemed true, what did this man say ? P.C. 1304. *Mar kews ken es gwyryonedh, ef a'n pren kyns trennen,* if be spoke other than truth, he shall catch it before passing. P.C. 1468. *A benen, pendra kewsyth,* O woman, what sayest thou ? R.D. 1688. *Kewsyns dên myns a vynno,* let a man say all that he will. R.D. 2448. *Hag y thêns dhe ben dewlyn, hag y kewsens dhe scornye,* and they went to their knees, and they spake to scorn him. M.C. 137. *Ena Pilat a gewsys yn delma,* there Pilate spake in this manner. M.C. 141. It is also written *cowsa*, qd. v. W. *comm,* a discourse, whence *commio, ymgommio*, to discourse. Arm. *comz, comps,* a discourse; *comza, compsa,* to discourse. Ir. *comhradh.* Gael. *comhradh.* The Cornish form approaches nearer the French *causer.*

CEYL, v. a. He will lose. 3 pers. s. fut. of *celly*, qd. v. In construction it changes into *geyl*, qd. v.

CEYSON, s. m. An accusation, cause, reason. ‡*Pa han keyson,* what charge, or accusation ? *Lhuyd*, 240. It is also written *ceson* or *cheson*, the *ch* before *e* having the power of *k*. *Na allons caffus cheson dhe wruthyl crothval na sôn warnas,* let them not be able to find cause to make a complaint, nor a sound against thee. O.M. 1835. *Levereuch dhym pahan cheyson a's bues why erbyn Ihesu. pan vynnouch y dhystrewy,* tell ye me, what accusation have ye against Jesus, when ye wish to destroy him. P.C. 1970. *Me re wrûk scrifé agas cheson dh'y ladhé,* I have written your accusation to put him to death. P.C. 2792. *Hep guthyl na moy cheyson*, without suffering any more trouble. R.D. 460. This is an abbreviated form of *acheson*, qd. v.

CI, s. m. A dog. Cornish Vocabulary, *ki*, canis. Pl. *kên, kuen. Sâf yn ban, del y'm kerry, râk nans yw Pilat serryt, ow krye, kepar ha ky*, stand up, as thou lovest me, for now Pilate is angered, crying out like a dog. P.C. 2242. *Ty a vŷdh mernans cales, yn ta ty a'n dyndylas, gwêth ôs ys ky*, thou shalt have a hard death, well thou hast deserved it, thou art worse than a dog. R.D. 2026. ‡ *Aga henwyn kemerans, march ha casak, hag asan, ky, ha câth, logosan*, let them take their names, horse and mare, and ass, dog, and cat, mouse. O.W. 32. In the Cornish Vocabulary, a *Linz* is called *commisc bleit hah chi*, for which a more recent hand has substituted *kymmysk bleid a chi*, the literal meaning being, "mixture of wolf and dog." This sentence furnishes us with a proof of *c* being changed into the aspirate *ch* after *a*, and; which is the rule in Welsh. *Ci hir, milgi*, a greyhound. W. *ci*, pl. *cwn*. Arm. *ki*, pl. *koun*. Ir. and Gael. *cu*, pl. *coin*. Manx, *coo*. Gr. κύων, κύνες. Lat. *canis*. Germ. *hund*. Sansc. *svan, s'un*.

CIBMIAS, s. m. Leave. ‡ *Cibmias têg ev a kymeras*, fair leave he took. Llwyd, 251. This is a late corruption of *cummyas*, qd. v.

CIDNIADH, s. m. Autumn. Llwyd, 40. Who also gives *cidniaz*, as a modern form, 13. Both being corruptions of *cyniaf*, qd. v.

CIDNIO, s. m. Dinner. Llwyd, 10. A modern corruption of *ciniow*, qd. v.

CIDHA, v. a. To hide. Llwyd, 50. More frequently written *cudha*, qd. v.

CIG, s. m. Flesh, flesh meat. Written in Cornish Vocabulary *kig, chic*, caro. *Na'm buef dhe wruthyl genes, yn kŷk hag yn kues hep won*, that I have not had to do with thee in flesh nor in blood, without falsehood. O.M. 659. *Ef a bren Adam dhe dâs, gans y gŷk ha wôs kefrys*, he will redeem Adam thy father, with his flesh and blood too. O.M. 812. *Parys fest yw an spyrys, ha'n kŷc yw marthys grevyys gans cleves ha govegyon*, very ready is the spirit, and the flesh is wondrous afflicted with sickness and sorrows. P.C. 1061. *Kewsyns dên mŷns a vynno, ow kŷc ha'm gôs bŷdh ynno, ha ken ny dhothyê dhe'n nêf*, let a man say all that he will, my flesh and my blood shall be in him, and else he will not go to heaven. R.D. 2449. W. *cig*, †*cic*. Arm. *kig*, †*cic*. Ir. †*cuach*, †*cich*.

CIGEL, s. m. A distaff. Cornish Vocabulary, *kigel*, colus. *Eva, kymmer dhe gygel, râg nedhê dhynny dyllas, ha my â gans oll ow nel, yn dôr dhe dhallath palas*, Eve, take thy distaff to spin clothes for us, and I will go with all my strength, to begin to dig in the ground. O.M. 367. Written also *kegel. Gans kegel a dhesempys nedhê dyllas me a vra*, with a distaff immediately I will spin clothes. O.M. 415. W. *cogel*. Arm. *kegel, kigel*. Ir. *ciogal, coigeal*. Gael. *cuigeal*. Manx, *quiggal*. Germ. *kunckel*. O. High German, *cuncla*. As the word is not derivable from a Celtic root, it is evident that all these, like the French *quenouille*, It. *conocchia*, are adopted from the Latin *conucula*, for *colucula*, from *colus*.

CIGLIU, adj. Flesh-coloured. Llwyd, 63. Compounded of *cig*, flesh, and *liw*, colour. W. *cigliw*. Arm. *kigliou*.

CIGVER, s. m. A flesh-fork. Cornish Vocabulary, *kig-uer*, ficinula. Compounded of *cig*, flesh, and *bêr*, a spit. The equivalent in Welsh is *cigwain*, a flesh-fork, compounded of *cig*, flesh, and *gwanu*, to pierce.

CIL, s. f. A recess, a back, the nape of the neck. Cornish Vocabulary, *chil*, cervix. *Och, tru, tru, skyndyys ôf gans cronek du, ha whethys gans y venym, ow coskê yn haus yn hâl, lyskys ôf a'n kŷl dhe'n tal*, Oh, sad, sad, spit on I am by a black frog, and blown by his venom, sleeping down in the moor, burned I am from the nape to the forehead. O.M. 1781. *Pol kîl*, the hinder part of the head. Llwyd, 104. *Heb cows gêr y clamderys, y codhas war bol y hŷll*, without saying a word she fainted, she fell on her back. M.C. 165. W. *cil*. Arm. *kil*. Ir. †*cul*. Gael. *cul*. Manx, *cooyl*.

CIL, v. a. To make. A mutation of *gil*, qd. v. ‡ *Ema a kil err*, it snows. ‡ *Ema a kil cessar*, it hails. Llwyd, 250.

CILLI, s. f. A grove. Pl. *killiow*. It is the same word as *celli*, qd. v. It enters into the names of many places in Cornwall, as *Killaworgy, Killegorgan, Killigannoon, Killigrew*, &c.

CILYGAN, s. f. The sheath-fish. Pl. *kilygys*. Pryce.

CINAC, s. m. A worm. Pl. *kinougas*. Pryce.

CINBYC, s. m. A wether goat. Llwyd, 65.

CINEDEL, s. f. A generation. Written in Cornish Vocabulary, *kinethel*, generatio. This is read by Llwyd, 4, *kinedhel*. On the margin of the MS. is written *kinedyl*, which is more correct. W. *cenedl, ccnedyl, cenel*, †*cenetel*, †*cenilol*, †*cenetl*. Ir. *cineal*, †*cenel*, †*ceneel*. Gael. *cincal*.

CININ, s. m. A leek, chive, shalot. Llwyd, 15. Another form of *cenin*, qd. v.

CINNIS, s. m. Fuel. Llwyd, 19. ‡ *Na dallê dees perna kinnis war an saw, na môs cuntle an dris dro dan keaw*, men ought not to buy fuel by the load, nor go to gather the brambles about the hedges. Pryce's Vocabulary. Another form of *cunys*, qd. v.

CINS, adv. Before. ‡ *Kins es dewath an bŷs*, before the end of the world. C.W. 68. Another form of *cyns*, qd. v.

CIO, s. f. A snipe. Llwyd, 146. W. *giach*. Arm. *kioch, eur gioch*.

CISTINEN, s. f. A chestnut. Llwyd, 5. W. *castan, castanen*. Arm. *kistin, kistinen*. From the Lat. *castanea*.

CITHA, v. a. To hide. Llwyd, 47. More frequently written *cudha*, qd. v.

CLABITTER, s. m. A bittern. The only apparent derivation is from the English *clawbiter*. The proper name of the bird is in W. *aderyn y bwn*, or *aderyn y bwmp*, and *bwmp y gors*, (bwmp, a hollow sound.) Arm. *bongors*. Ir. *bunnan*. Gael. *bunnan*.

CLADHVA, s. f. A burying place. *Me a gesul bôs gansê prennys da gwon yn nêp le râg an cladhva Crystunyon*, I advise that there be with them bought a good field in some place, for the burial of Christians. P.C. 1545. W. *cladhva*, from *cladhu*, to bury, and *ma*, a place.

CLAF, adj. Sick, disordered, sore. Pl. *clefyon, clevyon. Ow colon yw marthys clâf*, my heart is wondrous sick. O.M. 1337. *Ow colon reseth yn clâf*, my heart is gone sick. P.C. 1027. *Gallas ow colon pûr clâf dre pryderow*, gone is my heart very sick through cares. P.C. 2610. *My ny allaf gŷl kenter dhywhy bythyth râk mar clâf yw ow dulê*, I cannot make any nails for you, for my hands are so sore. P.C. 2677. *Pûp echon clefyon*, all sorts of sick persons. P.C. 3109. *Ellas ow colon yw cláf*, alas! my heart is sick. R.D. 724. *Rák hyreth galsof púr cláf*, through regret I am become very sick. R.D. 775. It is written *claf*, æger vel ægrotus, in the Cornish Vocabulary, but by Llwyd and Keigwyn, *cláv*, pl. *clevion*. *Dens cláv*, toothache, I.l. 105. *Dén cláv*, a sick man, pl. *dynion clevion*, 243. ‡ *Yma ow gwyl ow holan cláv*, it maketh my heart sick. C.W. 86. W. *cláv*, pl. *cleivion*. Arm. *clanv*, + *claff*. Ir. *clamh*, s orbutic. Gael. *clamh*, id. Sansc. *kliv*, to be feeble.

CLAFOREC, adj. Leprous. Cornish Vocabulary, *claforec*, leprosus. From a substantive, *clafor*, leprosy, in Welsh *clavar*, whence the verbs *clavru*, *clauriaw*, to become leprous. Arm. *lovr*, + *loffr*, leprous; *lovrentez*, *lorncz*, + *lofrnez*, leprosy; *lovri*, *lôri*. to be leprous; *lovrez*, a hospital for lepers. Legonidec derives the name of the Louvre in Paris from this word. Ir. *lubhra*, + *lubra*, leprosy. Gael. *luibhre*. Manx, *lourey*. Gr. λέπρα. Lat. *lepra*.

CLAMDER, s. m. A faint; a fainting fit. *Ellas, dre cueth, yn clamder, dhe'n dôr prág na ymwhclaf*, alas! through grief, in a fan t to the ground why do I not throw myself? P.C. 2593.

CLAMDERE, v. a. To faint away, to swoon. Part. pass. *clamderys*. *Mar tué moy nystevyth man, rag nown y wróns clamderé*, if more come, it will not be enough, they will faint with hunger. O.M. 400. *Rák ewen anwous ny glewaf yender dhum troys, ythesaf ow clamderé*, for very chilliness I do not feel the cold to my feet, I am fainting. P.C. 1224. *Heb cows gêr y clamderys*, without speaking a word she fainted. M.C. 163. *Ha'n woloc a's kemeras mar dyn, may clamderas hy arté*, and the sight her took so sharp, that she fainted again. M.C. 171.

CLAP, s. m. Prating. *Sens dhe clap, na fydh bysy, rák ny fynnaf dhys crygy*, hold thy prating, be not busy, for I will not believe thee. R.D. 1113. W. *clep*. Du. *klappen*. Germ. *klappen*. Ang. Sax. *cleopian*. Eng. *clap*, + *yclepe*. Scarcely a Celtic word.

CLAPIER, v. a. To speak. ‡ *Metten dah dha why*; *clo why clapier Kernuak*, good morning to you, can you speak Cornish? *Pryce's Vocab*.

CLECHIC, s. m. A little bell. Cornish Vocabulary, *tintinnabulum*. This is the diminutive of *clôch*, a bell; with the regular mutation of *o* into *e*, as was formerly the case in Welsh, but now into *y*. Thus the Welsh form would be *clôch, clychig*, + *clechic*. Arm. *klochik*.

CLECHTI, s. m. A belfry. Cornish Vocabulary, *cloccarium* vel *lucar*. Compounded of *clôch*, a bell, and *ti*, a house. W. *clochdy*.

CLEDH, s. m. A dyke, ditch, or trench; also a fence. Pl. *cledhiow*. ‡ *Do en dowla en klédh*, to cast him into a ditch. Llwyd, 244. ‡ *Merouch pymava towlys, yn clêdh, dhe vonas pedrys*, see where he is cast into the ditch, to be rotten. C.W. 82. W. *clawdh*, + *claud*, + *clad*. Arm. *klevz*. Ir. *cladh*. Gael. *cladh*. Manx, *cleigh, cleiy*.

CLEDH, adj. The left; the north, in the same way as *dehow* signifies the right side and the south. *Pyno a'n gwyskys an barth clédh*, who struck him on the left side. P.C. 1380. *Ha mear a bobyl gansé, a dhychow, hag a glédh*, and many people with him on the right, and on the left. M.C. 97. *An barth clêdh neb o cregis dywedh o*,

ha lader púr, on the left side he who was hanged shameless was, and a very thief. M.C. 191. ‡ *Po rês deberra an bês, tidn heerath a sew; po rês dal an vor, na oren pan a tu, dhuyran, houlzethas, po glédh, po dihow*, when thou comest into the world, sharp sorrow followeth; when thou beginnest the way, it is not known which side, east, west, or north, or south. *Pryce*. *Dorn-kledh*, left-handed. Llwyd, 145. W. *clêdh, gogledh*. Arm. *clciz*. Ir. *clith*, + *cli*, + *cle*. Gael. *clith*. Goth. *hlei*. Sansc. *kri*. Cf. also Gr. λαιός, Lat. *lævus*, Sansc. *laicas*.

CLEDHE, s. m. A sword. Pl. *cledhyow*, and irr. *cledhydhyow* and *clydhydhow*, qd. v. *Mar pue drôk a oberys, trôch y hy gans dhe glcdhé*, if she was evil of works, kill her with thy sword. O.M. 292. *Tán ha cledhé, yma gené lemmyn parys*, fire and sword, they are with me ready. O.M. 1305. *Gans ow cledhé dhe ladhé soon my a vyn*, with my sword soon I will kill thee. O.M. 1363. *Yma omma dew cledhé parys gans ow cowethé, cales ha scherp kekeffrys*, there are here two swords ready with my companions, hard and sharp also. P.C. 925. *Why a dhêth dhym yn arvow, gans boclers ha cledhydhyow*, ye came to me in arms, with bucklers and swords. M.C. 74. In Keigwyn and Llwyd's time, it was pronounced *cledha*, and this is the vulgar pronunciation in many parts of Wales. *Cledha bian*, a small sword, or dagger. Llwyd, 63. W. *cledhyv*, + *cledif*. Arm. *clezef, clezé*. Ir. *cloidheamh*, + *claideb*. Gael. *claidheamh*. Manx, *clive*. Lat. *gladius*.

CLEDHEC, adj. Lefthanded. Llwyd, 145. From *cledh*, the left.

CLEGAR, s. m. A rock, cliff, precipice. It is preserved in the names of places; *West Clicker, Low Clicker, Cligga, Cleghar*. W. *clegyr*.

CLEM, s. m. Defence. *Me a lever dhys, rák clem, dyswé dhynny Nychydem, ha Ioseph Baramathya*, I say to you, for defence, shew to us Nicodemus, and Joseph of Arimathea. R.D. 625.

CLEVES, s. m. A disease, malady, sickness. In the Cornish Vocabulary it is written *clevet*, morbus, of which *cleves* is a later form. *Y a ura eredy a pûp cleves dhys jehes*, they will surely make from every disease to thee a cure. O.M. 1794. *Dhodho yma cleves brás, ny gûf medhek a'n sawya*, to him there is a great malady, he finds not a leech that can cure him. R.D. 1647. *Ha mar soon del y'n gwylly, ef a'th saw, hep ken yly, oll a'th cleves yn tyen*, and as soon as thou shalt see him, he will heal thee, without other remedy, of all thy disease entirely. R.D. 1696. *Yn mêdh an gôff, clevas brás ês om dewleff devedhys*, says the smith, great disease has happened to my hands. M.C. 156. Llwyd, 80, 156, supplies the following: *Clevas y mantedh*, the stone in the kidneys; *clevas an mytern*, the king's evil: this is also called in Welsh *clwyv y brenhin*, and in Armoric, *drôk ar roué*. The root of *cleves* is *claf*, qd. v. W. *clevyd*. Arm. *clenved, clioued*, + *cleffet*, + *clevet*.

CLEVET, s. m. The hearing. Llwyd, 18. W. *clywed*. Arm. *cleved*. Ir. *clu*.

CLEVYON, adj. The sick. This is the plural of *claf*; qd. v, and is generally used as a substantive. *Aban ethe dhe'n teller bôs clevyon dredho sawyys*, when they went to the place, that the sick were healed by it. O.M. 2796. *Iyes torn da yn bys-ma re wrúk dhe vohosugyon, sawyé pûp echen clefyon, a vewhé yn bewnans da*; many a good turn in this world he hath done to the poor, healing all sorts of sick persons, that live in good life. P.C. 3109. *Dynion clevion*, sick men. Llwyd, 243.

CLEWAS, v. a. To hear, to perceive, to feel, to smell. 3 pers. s. fut. and 2 pers. s. imp. *clew*. part. pass. *clewys*. *My pan esen ow quandre, clewys a'n ugl tenewen un el ow tulleth cane, a uchaf war an wedhen*, when I was walking about, I heard on one side au angel beginning to sing above me ou a tree. O.M. 214. *Pan clewfyf vy an tân tyn, parhap y wrussen fyé*, when I should feel the sharp fire, perhaps I should flee. O.M. 1351. *A Dhew on nef, clew ngan lef*, O God of heaveu, hear our voice. O.M. 1389. *Arluth ny vynnons crysy, na clewas ow vogv a vy*, Lord, they will not believe, nor hear my voice. O.M. 1436. *An re-ma ow gweli a râs, rag ny glewsyuch yn neja plâs sawor an par-ma vythqueth*, these are rods of grace, for ye have not smelt in any place savour like this ever. O.M. 1990. *Gordhyans dhe tâs Dew an nêf, lemyn clewas agan lef*, worship to the Father God of heaven, now he has heard our voice. O.M. 2097. *Ow arluth whêk ol, lâdh e, ken of a wra ow shyndye, mar clewvyth agan gwary*. my all sweet Lord kill him, otherwise he will injure me, if he shall hear of our sport. O.M. 2134. *Ple eleusta yelwel Dew Cryst. gans dên yn bys-ma genys*, where hast thou heard God called Christ, by a man in this world born? O.M. 2642. *Me a'n clewes ow tyffen*, I heard him forbidding. P.C. 1573. *Me a dhêk dustyny y'n clewys ow leverel*, I will bear witness, I heard him saying. P.C. 1314. *Pepenag vo a'n harth wôr, a clewfyth ow voys yn tyr*, whoever is of the true side, shall hear my voice in the land. P.C. 2026. *Me a whyth gans mûr a grys, kynyver dyaul ûs yn bays yn in may cleufo*, I will blow with much force, that as many a devil as is in the world may hear well. P.C. 3063. *Lavur Du maga del wra nêb a vynno y glewas*, word of God how it will feed whoever may be willing to hear it. M.C. 12. *Orto of y a sedhas, may clewo lêff Jesu whêk*, by him they sat, that they might hear the voice of sweet Jesus. M.C. 77. *Ha dew a dhûk dystunny y'n clewsons yn leverel*, and two bore witness (that) they heard him say. M.C. 91. *Ha whâth may, ivy a glewyth a dormont Christ del whorfê*, and yet more ye shall hear of the torment of Christ how it happened. M.C. 132. This word in the Cornish, Welsh, and Armoric, is not confined to the signification of hearing only, but it may be defined to conceive from the impulse of any of the senses except the sight. In Welsh, we say, *clywed blâs*, to taste ; *clywed arogl*, to smell ; *clyiced llais*, to hear a voice ; *clywed dolur*, to feel a pain. In Armoric it signifies to hear, to smell, to perceive. W. *clywed*. Arm. *clevout*. Ir. *cluin*. Gael. *cluim*. Manx, *clum*. Gr. κλύω. Sansc. *sr'u*.

CLEYR, adj. Bright, clear. *Dên apert ha mear y rûs, golow cleyr ow tewynnyé*, a man perfect, and much his grace, a light clear shining. M.C. 243. *Deuth war avorow, my agas pys, dhe welas fetel sevys Cryst nês an bêth, clêr ha wâr*, come ye early to-morrow, I pray you, to see how Christ rose out of the tomb, bright and gentle. P.C. 3242. W. *claer*, *disglaer*, *eghvr*. Arm. *sklear*, *sklêr*. Ir. †*glauir*. Lat. *clarus*.

CLIHI, s. f. Ice. Written by Llwyd, 33. *glihi*. ‡*Yrin huer, tared nno, ha golowas, er, rew, gwens, ha clehê, ha hezer*, cold weather, thunder, and lightning snow, frost,

wind, and ice, and hail. *Pryce's Vocab.* Arm. *sklas* From Lat. *glacies*.

CLIN, s. m. The knee. Cornish Vocabulary, *elin*, genu, *penclin*. genu. The more common form is *glin*, qd. v., which is common to the other dialects, but this form is also found in the Ordinalia. *Oll an re-nn ty a fyth, ow gordhyê mara mennyth war pen dhe dhew glyn ysel*, all these thou shalt have, if thou wilt worship me low on thy knees. P.C. 136. *Glyn*, here is a mutation of *clyn*, or *clin*, the initial being regularly softened after *dew* preceding.

CLOCH, s. m. A bell. Cornish Vocabulary, *cloch*, *clocca* ; *clochmuer*, campana, a great bell, (*cloch* and *muer* great.) W. *cloch*. Ir. *clog*. Gael. *clog*. Manx. *clagg*. Germ. *glocke*. Fr. *cloche*. From Med. Lat. *clocca*.

CLOCHPREDNIER, s. m. A prison. ‡ *Enna an dzhei a vea kemerys, ha dha an clochprednier dzhyi a ve lediyz*, then they were taken, and to the prison they were led. *Llwyd*, 252.

CLOF, adj. Lame. Cornish Vocabulary, *claudus*. W. *clôf*.

CLOG, s. m. A steep rock. *Pryce*. W. *clog*, *clogwyn*. Ir. *cloch*. Gael. *clogh*. Manx, *clagh*, *cloch*.

CLOH, s. m. A bell. Llwyd, 45. This is a late form of *cloch*, qd. v.

CLOIREC, s. m. A clerk, or clergyman. Cornish Vocab. *clericus*. Arm. *cloarec*. Ir. *cleireach*. From the Latin.

CLOMIAR, s. m. A dove-cot, pigeon-house. Llwyd, 49. From the Latin *columbarium*.

CLOPPEC, adj. Lame, crippled. Llwyd, 48. A late form of *clof*, qd. v.

CLOR, s. m. Glory, beauty, renown. *Adam sâf yn ban yn clôr, ha treyl dhe gyk ha dhe woys*, Adam, stand up in glory, and turn to flesh and blood. O.M. 85. If correctly rendered, *clor* must be borrowed from the Latin, but probably the meaning is different. *Gordhyans* is the Cornish term for glory, qd. v., and *gogoniant* the Welsh. But the Arm. has *gloar*. Ir. *gloir*. Gael. *gloir*.

CLOS, s. m. Glory, happiness, praise. *Pan fy a'n bys tremenys, gans Crist y fythyth tryggys agy dh'y clôs*, when thou shalt be passed from the world, with Christ thou shalt be dwelling in his glory. P.C. 3234. *Yn parudys deuch dhum clôs, dh agas prennê me a rôs gôs ow holon*, in paradise come ye to my glory, to purchase you I gave the blood of my heart. R.D. 164. *An corf a whyleuch deffry, ganso yth cuch yredy yn y clôs*, the body (that) you seek really, with it ye shall go into his glory. R.D. 1290. W. *clôd*, † *clot*. Ir. † *clodh*, † *clu*. ♫ Gael. *cliu*. Slav. *slowo*, *slawa*. Gr. κλυτόν. Lat. *in-clytus*, *laude*. Sansc. *clagha*, (*cal* to proclaim.) Cf. also the Gaulish name *Clotomârus*,=W. *clodvawr*, (clot-mawr;) O. H. Germ. *Hlodomâr*.

CLOWANS, s. m. The hearing, an echo. *Pryce*. From *clowas*, to hear.

CLOWAS, v. a. To hear. *Dho glowas*. Llwyd, 44. *Ty a glow ken newodhow*, thou shalt hear other news. C.W. 84. *Ha me ow gwandra, me a glowas owarthu, war an wedhan, un êl whêk fir ow cana*, and as I was walking, I heard from above, on the tree, a sweet angel wisely singing. C.W. 56. *Drôg polat o, nêb a glowses ow cana*, a bad pullet he was, which thou heardest singing. C.W. 36. *Dheth voys, Arluth. a glowuf*, thy voice, Lord, I hear. C.W. 84. *Worth aha glowas yn torma*, by hearing thee at this time. *Ibid.* 88. *Clow qe ow lef*, hear thou my voice. C.W. 104. This is the late form of *clewes*, qd. v. W. *clywed*.

CLUIT, s. f. A hurdle, a wattle, crate, a wattled gate. Cornish Vocabulary, *cluit*, clita. W. *clwyd*, †*cluit*. Arm. *cloued*, *clud*. Ir. *cliath*, †*cliab*. *Ath cliath*, the ford of hurdles. the old name of Dublin. Gael. *cliath*. Manx, *clea*. Med. Lat. *cleta*. Provençal *cleda*. Fr. *claie*. *Cluid duinron*, Cornish Vocabulary, *pectus*; lit. the wattles or basket of the breast. So W. *dwyd y dhwyvron*, and *cliath* in Gaelic has the same meaning.

CLUN. s. f. The hip, haunch. Cornish Vocabulary, *clunis*. *Penclun*, clunis; *duiqlun*, renes. (In Welsh *clun* also means the thigh, therefore *penclun* would be the hip.) *Pós ve teulseuch agas clún, rûg me a'n gwelas dufun, dreses of a tremenas*, heavily have ye thrown down your haunches, for I saw him wide-awake, by me he passed. R.D. 533. W. *clun*. Arm. *klun*. Ir. †*kluan*. Lat. *clunis*. Eng. *loin*. Sansc. *s'róni*.

CLUNK, v. a. To swallow. This word is now in common use in Cornwall, and is derived from a Celtic term,=W. *llyncu*, †*lunca*. Arm. *lonca*. Ir. *slugadh*. Gael, *sluig*. Manx, *lhuggey*.

CLUT, s. m. A clout. *Clut lestri*, a dish-clout. *Llwyd*, 116. W. *clut*. Gael. *clút*. Manx, *clooid*. Eng. *clout*.

CLUYAN, s. m. A disease, sickness. ‡*Gwelliglwyrn*, a bed sickness. *Pryce*. *Cluyan* is derived from *cluy*,= W. *clwyo*, a disease.

CLYBYE. v. a. To wet, or moisten. *Yma daggrow ow klybbyé dhe dreys, rák ewn kerengé. saw me a's sêch gans ow blew*, tears are wetting thy feet for true love, but I will dry them with my hair. P.C. 182. This is a regular mutation of *glybyé*, qd. v., the initial being hardened after *ow*.

CLYDHYDHOW, s. m. Swords. *Gweytyeuch bôs tús parys gans battys ha clydhydhow*, take ye care that men be ready with staves and swords. P.C. 608. *Why re dhweth dhyn, gans arvow, gans fustow ha clydhydhow, kepar ha pan veue vy an puré lader yn pow*, ye have come to me with arms, with staves and swords, as if I were the veriest thief in the land. P.C. 1172. This is an irregular plural of *cledhé*, qd. v.

CLYMIAR, s. m. A dove cot. *Llwyd*, 49. Who also writes it *klymmiar*, 33. See *Clomiar*.

CNEU, s. m. A fleece. *Cnéu glán*, a fleece of wool. *Llwyd*, 170. W. *cnu*. Arm. *cneô*.

CNOUCYE, v. a. To beat, knock, strike. *Orden dhe'th tus hy knoukyé gans mrryn, na hedhens nefré er na varwa eredy*, order thy people to beat her with stones, nor let them ever stop until she be dead quite. O.M. 2676. *Gans myyn gureuch hy knoukyé er na wrello tremenć*, with stones do ye beat her until she be dead. O.M. 2694. *Lemyn ol byan ha brás, knoukyouch ef del dyndylus may cosso y lyniwennow*, now all, little and big, strike him as he deserves, that his sides may itch. P.C. 2064. *My a'n knouk ef er y wew*, I will strike him on his lips. P.C. 2085. *Mar dhues own bones knoukyé*, if thou hast fear of being beaten. P.C. 2245. *Powes lemyn, lovel wâs, ha knouk an horn*, stop now, idle fellow, and strike the iron. P.C. 2719. The late form as given by Llwyd, 251, was *cnakia*. W. *cnociaw*. Ir. *cnag*. Gael. *cnag*.

CNYFAN, s. f. A nut. *Gwedhan knyfan*, a hazel tree. *Llwyd*. 51. Written also *kynyfan*, or *kynyphan*; *kyny*

phan frenc, a wall nut, lit. a French nut. *Llwyd*, 74. (W. *cneuen frengig*. Arm. *craouen Galek*. Ir. *Gallchnu, cnu fhrancach*. Gael. *cno-fhrancach*.) W. *cneuen*. Arm. *cnaouen, craouen*. Ir. *cnu, cro*. Gael. *cnu, cro*. Manx. *cro*.

CO, s. m. The memory, remembrance. ‡*Ma co dhn vi*, I remember,'lit. there is remembrance to me. *Llwyd*, 138. This is an abbreviated form of *cov*, or *cof*, qd. v.

COAT, s. m. Wood, timber, a wood, a forest. *Llwyd*, 79. Another form of *coid*, qd. v.

COBER, s m. Copper. Cornish Vocabulary, *gueidvur cober*, ærarius, a coppersmith. W. *cobyr, (erydh.)* Arm. *kouevr*. Ir. *copar*. Gael. *copar*. Lat. *cuprum*. Fr. *cuivre*. Eng. *copper*.

COC, s. m. A boat. Plnr. *kuku, (coocoo.)* *Llwyd*, 53. W. *cwch*. Ir. *cuach*, †*coca*. Gael. *cuuch*.

COC, adj. Empty, vain, foolish. *Out warnas harlot pen cok scon ym mes a'm golok*, out upon thee, rogue, blockhead, immediately out of my sight. O.M. 1629. *Fystyneuch a dhew pen côk*, make haste, O ye two blockheads. P.C. 2328. *Na sparyé kyn wrello són, eu yw pen cók*, spare not though he make a noise, he is a blockhead. R.D. 2017. The oldest form was *cuic*, qd. v. W. *coeg*, whence *coegio* to make void, to deceive. Eng. to *cog*, i.e. to lie, falsify. "To cog the dice." *Dryden*. Arm. *goak, gogca*, to deceive.

COCH, adj. Red. *My a dhybarth ynterthoch hag a uma dheuch pennow couch*, I will divide between you, and will make for you red (bloody) heads. P.C. 2326. W. *cóch*. Ir. †*cuicc*, red,†*cocuir*, murex. Gr. κοκκος. Lat *coccus*.

CODDROS, v. a. To hinder, disturb, annoy. *Del ûs an yedhevron whêth púp ûr worth agan arveth, hag ow koddros*, as the Jews are still armed against us, and annoying us. R.D. 2480. *Coddros* is a regular mutation after *ow*, of *goddros*, id. qd. W. *godori*, to hinder, or *godrisio*, to be oppressive.

CODNA, s. f. The neck. ‡ *Codna tál*, the forehead. *Llwyd*, 61. ‡ *Codna brêh*, the wrist, i.e. the neck of the arm, id. 46. ‡ *Ter i kodna*, about her neck, id. 230. This is a late form of *conna*, qd. v.

CODNAGWYN, s. f. A weasel, a whitethroat. *Llwyd*. 13. Compounded of *codna*, the neck, and *gwyn*, white. In Welsh, this animal is similarly called *bronwen*, i.e. whitebreast. Another very expressive Welsh name is *guenci*, from *gwenc*, voracity.

CODNAHWILAN, s. f. A lapwing. *Llwyd*, 241. W. *cornchwiglen*.

CODHA, v. a. To fall, to happen. Written also *codhé*. *Yma un posygayon brás war ow holon ow codhé*, there is a great heaviness falling on my heart. O.M. 427. *Yma cás brás wharfedhys ha codhys war dhe pobel*, a great misfortune has occurred and befallen thy people. O.M. 1543. *Me a re lemyn strokyas vrâs, bys may codhé hy dle'n dór*, I will give now great strokes, until she fall on the earth. O.M. 2718. *Mûr dhe voy ef re pechas, ha drôk warnodho a gódh*, much the more he hath sinned, and evil will fall upon him. P.C. 2192. *Mar tue venians vyth ragdho, warnan ny ef re godho, ha war oll agan flechas*, if any vengeance should come for him, upon us may it fall, and upon all our children. P.C. 2502. *Rág gwander ef re codhas*, for weakness he has fallen. P.C. 2618. *Yn ur-na whreuch pyiadow, may codhdho an mynydhyow warnouch*, in that hour ye shall make prayers, that the mountains may fall upon ye. P.C. 2652. *Arluth dremas, mar codhas mŷr Cryst ow sylwyas, ple ma dhe wŷr*, good lord, if thou hast happened to see Christ my Saviour, where is he truly ? R.D. 855. *Râg gwander y a godhas*, for weakness they fell. M.C. 68. *Y'na hy a ve gesys dhe godha*, there it was left to fall. M.C. 184. W. *cwydho*, †*cuido*. Arm. *coueza*, †*coeza*. Ir. *cudaim, tuit*. Gael. *tuit*. Manx, *tuitt*. Sansc. *cad*. Lat. *cedo*.

CODHAF, v. a. To bear, to suffer. *Govy vŷdh oll ow pewé ow codhaf lues galar*, unhappy will be all living, suffering much sorrow. O.M. 633. *Dower, ha lêr, ha tân, ha gwyns, houl ha loar, ha steyr kyffris, a Grist ow codhaff mernans, anken y a wodhevys*. Water and earth, and fire, and wind, sun and moon and stars also, from Christ suffering death trouble knew. M.C. 211. A regular mutation after *ow*, of *godhaf*, or *godhef*, qd. v.

CODHEVEL, v. a. To bear, to suffer. *Henn o payn a vear byte esé Crist ow codhevel*, this was pain of much pity (that) Christ was enduring. M.C. 134. A mutation of *godhevel*, qd. v.

CODHFEN, v. a. I should know. *Arluth ny vyen lowen, mar fûr torment a codhfen y bones dhys*, I should not have been joyful, if I had known that such fierce torment was to thee. R.D. 2542. A mutation of *godhfen*, 1 pers. pl. pluperf. of *godhfos*, qd. v.

CODHFO, v. a. He should know. *Mar codhfo an cawadow, dystouch y fyen ledhys*, if the villain knew, immediately I should be killed. O.M. 2119. A mutation of *godhfo*, 3 pers. s. subj. of *godhfos*, qd. v.

CODHFONS, v. a. They should know. *A lâs'whêk, gáf dhedhé y, râg ny wodhons yn leffry py nŷl a wróns drôk py da, hag a codhfons yredy, ny wrussens ow dystrewy*, O sweet Father, forgive them, for they knew not really whether they did good or evil, and if they knew in truth, they would not destroy me. P.C. 2776. A mutation of *godhfons*, 3 pers. pl. subj. of *godhfos*, qd. v.

CODHOUCH, v. a. Ye know. *Levereuch dhymmo wharre mar codhouch, ple ma kentrow yn pren crows râg y fastye*, tell me directly if ye know where there are nails for fastening him on the cross tree. P.C. 2665. A mutation of *godhouch*, 2 pers. pl. pres of *godhfos*, qd. v.

COER, s. m. A court, a choir. W. *côr*. Arm. *côr*. Ir. *cora*. Gael. *coradh*. Gr. χορὸς. Lat. *chorus*.

COF, s. m Remembrance, recollection, memory. *My a vyr scon orth honna, hag a'n acord a vŷdh côf*, I will immediately look at that, and of the covenant there shall be remembrance. O.M. 1252. *Arluth porth côf yn deydh dywedh a'm enef vy*, Lord bear remembrance on the last day of my soul. O.M. 1272. *Gwyn y vŷs pan ve gynys, a allo gûl dhys servys, a'y côf nỳ'n gâs*, happy he when he was born, that is able to do thee service, out of his recollection he will not leave him. O.M. 1478. *Pertheuch côf oll a'n tokyn a leverys kyns lemyn dhywy why, a gowethé*, all ye bear remembrance of the token which I told before now to you, O companions. P.C. 1081. ‡ *Ema có dho vi*, I remember, lit. there is memory to me. Llwyd, 128. This idiom obtains also in Welsh, *y mae genyv góv*. W. *côv*, †*cob*. Arm. *coun*. Ir. *cuimhne*. Gael. *cuimhne*. Manx, *cooinaght*.

COFOR, s. m. A chest, a coffer. *Cofor brâs*, a great chest. Llwyd, 43, 48. W. *cofswr*, from *côf*, a hollow trunk. Arm. *cufer*. Ir. *cofra*. Gael. *cobhan*. Manx, *coir*.

COFUA, v. a. Shall remember. *Eveuch lemyn oll an gwŷn, râg hemma yw ow gós fŷn, hag a vŷdh ragouch skullys yn dewyllyens pechusow, why a'm cofua vy hep gow, pysouch may fevé evys*, drink ye now all the wine, for this is my perfect blood, and it shall be shed for you, in atonement of sins, ye shall remember me, without falsehood, pray ye that it be drunk. P.C. 827. This must be the 3 pers. s. fut. of the verb, of which we have no other example, unless *cove*, in C.W. 162, is the late form. Pryce gives the verb *covio*, to remember, but that is literally the W. *covio*. Arm. *kouna*. Ir. *cuimhnighim*. Gael. *cuimhnich*.

COG, s. m. A cook. Cornish Vocabulary, *cocus*. ‡ *Tshi côg*, a cook shop. Llwyd, 123. W. *côg*, †*coc*. Arm. *cok*. Ir. *coca*. Gael. *coca*. Manx, *coagyrey*. Lat. *coquus*. Sansc. *kvath, pac*, to cook. Gr. πέπτω.

COG, s. f. A cuckoo. *An gôg*, the cuckoo. Llwyd, 52. W. *côg, y gôg*. Arm. *coucoug*. Ir. *cuach*. Gael. *cuach, cubhag*. Manx, *civag, cooag*. Gr. κόκκυξ. Lat. *cuculus*. Russ. *kokuszka*. Sansc. *kaukilas*, from *kuc*, to cry.

COICLINHAT, s. m. The herb archangel. Cornish Vocabulary, *archangelica*. It is doubtful in the MS. whether it is to be read *coiclinhat*, or *coidlinhat*. If the former it is compounded of *coic*, or *cuic*, the old form of *côc*, which see above, the same as W. *coeg*, vain, and the herb may be the same as the W. *llinhad y coed*. See Norris's Cornish Drama, ij. 341.

COID, s. m. Wood, timber, trees, a wood, a forest. *Koidgath*, a wild cat. Llwyd, 241. This word was variously written *coit, coat, cuit*, and in later times *côs, coys, cûz*. It enters into the names of many places in Cornwall, as *Penquite*, (W. *pen cocd*,) the head of the wood. *Colquite, Cois pen haile, Cosgarne*, &c. W. *coed*, †*coet*, †*coil*. Sansc. *kâstu*.

COIFINEL, s. m. Wild thyme. Cornish Vocabulary, *serpillum*. Probably a contraction of *coid-finel*, wood fennel.

COILEN, s. m. A quill. Pryce. From the English.

COIR, s. m. Wax. Cornish Vocabulary, *cera*. It is written *côr*, as the late form, by Llwyd, 18. W. *cŵyr*, (*wy=ê*.) Arm. *coer*. Ir. *ceir*. Gael. *ceire*. Manx, *kere*. Gr. κηρός. Lat. *cera*.

COL, s. m. Any projecting body, or pointed hill, a peak, a promontory. It enters into the names of many places in Cornwall. It also meant the awn, or beard of corn, as in Welsh and other Celtic dialects. The plural form *colow*, is given by Llwyd, who writes it *culu*, or *culhu*, qd. v. W. *col*. Ir. *colg*. Gael. *colg*. Manx, *caulg*.

COLA, v. a. To hearken, to listen. Written also *colé*. 2 pers. s. imp. *côl*. *A out warnas drôk venen, worto pan urvssys colc, râg ef o tebel edhen, neb a glewsys ow cané*, Oh ! out upon thee, wicked woman, when thou listenedst to him, for he was an evil bird whom thou didst hear singing. O.M. 222. *Rag cola worth un venes, gulan ef re gollas an plâs*, for listening to a woman, he has quite lost the place. O.M. 419. *Ellas ryth pan ruk colé mar hogul worth ow eskar*, Alas ! when I ever listened so readily to my enemy. O.M. 626. *Râg ty dhe gola worty, ha tollé dhe bryes lên*, because thou hast hearkened to her, and deceived thy faithful spouse. O.M. 293. ‡*Me a levar dhys, ha cool orthaf*, I will tell thee, and listen thou to me. C.W. 44. ‡ *Cool gethym, mentha gesky ?*

hearken to me, would I flout thee? C.W. 48. This word seems to be formed from *clewes*.

COLAN, s. m. A coal. Pl. *coles*, Llwyd, 243. *Colan bew*, a live coal, 131. *Colan marow*, a firebrand quenched, 164. *Colan leskis*, a burning firebrand, 165. This word is from the Eng., the Celtic term being *glow*, qd. v.

COLANNAC, adj. Hearty, courageous, valiant. Llwyd, 43. From *colan*, or *colon*, qd. v.

COLENWEL, v. a. To fulfil, till up, fill. Part. *colenwys*. Written also *collenwel*, and *covlenwel*. *Cresseuch collenweuch kefrys an nôr veys a dûs arté*, increase ye, fill also the land of the world with men again. O.M. 1211. *Fystyné gûra, ha dûs dhynmo wharré, râk collenwel bôdh ow breys*, do thou hasten, and come to me immediately, to fulfil the wish of my mind. O.M. 1267. *Dhe egipt yth âf uskys râk colenwel bôdh dhe vrŷs*, to Egypt I will go immediately to fulfil the will of thy mind. O.M. 1474. *Yn lyfryow scryfys yma, bós collenwys lowené a ganow an flechys da, ha'n munys ow tené*, in books it is written, that joy is fulfilled out of the mouths of good children, and little ones suckling. P.C. 436. Compounded of *com* or *cov*, id. qd. *cev*, qd. v., and *lenwel* to fill. W. *cyvlawni*. Ir. *comhlionadh*, †*comalnad*. Gael. *coimhlion*. Manx, *cooilleen*.

COLL, s. m. Loss, damage. *Lemyn me agis pŷs a'baynys Christ predery, ha na vo gesys dhe goll an lahys a rŭg dhynny*, now I beseech you all of Christ's pains to think, and that there be not left 'to loss the laws that he made for us. M.C. 182. W. *coll*. Arm. *coll*. Ir. *caill, coll*. Gael. *call*. Manx, *coayl*.

COLLAN, s. A knife. It changes regularly in construction into *gollan*, and *hollan*. *Worth henna whéth a wyth yn beys na allo dén vŷth gŭl hager vernans dhynmo; rag ow colon ow honan gans ow hollan me a wán*, against that I will ow'guard, so that never a man in the world may do a cruel death to me; for my own heart with my knife I will pierce. R.D. 2043. *Pylat yw marow, dre payn ha dre galarow, y honan yth ymwanas; gans y gollan narthys soon yth emwyksys yn golon*, Pilate is dead, through pain and through sorrows, himself he stabbed; with his knife wondrous soon he struck himself in the heart. R.D. 2066. It is the same word as *collel*, qd. v.

COLLEL, s. f. A knife. Cornish Vocabulary, *cultellus*. *Collel gravio*, scalprum *vel* scalbellum. W. *cyllell*, from the Latin *cultellus*. Arm. *contel*. Gael. *golaidh*.

COLLET, s. f. Loss, damage. Cornish Vocabulary, *jactura*. W. *colled*. Arm. *collat*. Ir. *cailleadh*. Gael. *calldhch*.

COLLI, v. a. To lose, to spill. *Dho golli*, Llwyd, 117. 3 pers. s. fut. *cyll*, part. *kyllys*, (*kolhys*, Llwyd, 248.) *Rag cola worth un venen, gulan ef re gollas an plûs*, for listening to a woman, he has quite lost his place. O.M. 450. *Ha'n maystri brâs oll a'm bo, my re'n collas dredho may canaf trew*, and all the great power that was mine, I have lost it through him, that I may sing "alas!" P.C. 149. *An houl ydyw re gollas*, the sun its brightness has lost. P.C. 2902. *Dre ow fech ty a'm collus*, through my sin thou didst lose me. R.D. 164. *Y rané dhe vohosogyon yn bŷs gwell vye ys y scotyé*, it were better to share it to the poor in the world than to spill it. M.C. 36. *Po ow harenga ty a gyll*, or my love thou shalt lose. C.W. 60. *Nangew mear. a. for pur wŷr a ban gylsen an tŷr*, it is now much way very truly, since we lost the land, *ibid*. 178. *Colli* is another form of *celly*, qd. v. W. *colli*. Ir. *caill*. Gael. *caill*. Manx, *caill*.

COLLOWY, v. n. To shine. ‡*Me cw landhorn néf avel tân ow collowy, moy splanna es an Drengys*, I am the lantern of heaven, like fire shining, more resplendent than the Trinity. C.W. 10. A regular mutation of *gollowy*, or *golowa*, qd. v.

COLOIN, s. m. A whelp, a puppy, or young dog. Cornish Vocabulary, *catulus*. W. *colwyn*, from *col*, fœtus. Arm. *colen*. Ir. *coilean*, †*cuilen*. Gael. *cuilean*. Manx, *quallian*. Scotch, *collie*.

COLM, s. m. A knot, a tie; a bond. *Me a vyn setyé colm re, may fastyo an colm wharré adro dhum bryangen, a dhyscempys dhum tagé*, I will put a running noose, that the knot may fasten soon around my throat, immediately to choke me. P.C. 1525. *Na vynnyn, saw Barabas ny a pŷs, ugy yn colm yn pryson*, we will not, but Barabbas we pray for, that is in bond in prison. P.C. 2042. W. *cwlwm*. Arm. *coulm*.

COLMA, v. a. To bind, to tie. 2 pers. s. imp. *colm*. *A tûs whêk oll caradow, ow dywluef colm ha'm garrow, gans lovan fast colmennow, na allan sevel a'm sâf*, O sweet father, all beloved, tie my hands and my legs with a rope, fast knots, that I may not stand upright. O.M. 1346. *Yn urna y a colmas y dhefrech fast gans cronow, eu goys yn més may tardhas, del fustnens an colmennow*, in that hour they bound his arms fast with thongs, the blood out that it burst, so they fastened the knots. M.C. 76. *War post fast a'n colmas, unwyth na ylly ptygé*, on a post fast they bound him, so that he could not once beud. M.C. 130. *Enef Christ dhe yffarn éth, hag a dorras an porthow dre y nerth brâs, hay sleyveth, ena golmas dewolow*, the soul of Christ to hell went, and broke the gates, by his great strength and skill, there he bound devils. M.C. 212. *Celmy* is another form of *colma*, qd. v. W. *cylymu*. Arm. *coulma*, *clouicin*.

COLMEN, s. f. A knot, or tie, bond, halter. Pl. *colmennow*. *A tûs whêk oll caradow, ow dywluef colm ha'm garrow gans lovan fast colmennow, na allan sevel a'm sâf*, O sweet father, all beloved, tie my hands and my legs with a rope, fast knots, that I may not stand upright. O.M. 1347. *Ena why a gŷf asen, hag ebel yn un golmen, drew y dhynmo vy wharré*, there you will find an ass, and a foal in a halter, bring them to me presently. P.C. 177. *Kelmys yw whâth pûr fast yn y gulmenow*, he is bound yet fast in his bonds. M.C. 212. From *colma*.

COLMUR, s. m. A binder. Pl. *colmurion*. ‡*Whelas megowozian, dha medge an iz; whelus colmurian dha kelmé an iz*, look reapers, to reap the coru; look binders, to bind the corn. Pryce's *Vocab*. Compounded of *colm*, a knot, and *gûr*, a man. W. *cylymwr*.

COLOM, s. f. A dove, a pigeon. Cornish Vocabulary, *columba*. *An golow glâs hy lagas, yn més gwra hy delyfré, lellé edhen ren ow thâs, leverel ny won ple fe*, the dove, with blue eyes, do liberate her abroad; a more faithful bird, by my Father, I cannot say where there is. O.M. 1109. *Colom whêk, glas hy lagas, ke nŷg a-uch lues pow, tŷr sêch yn guel nag yn prâs war kefyth yn ywŷr hep-gow*, sweet blue-eyed dove, go fly over much country, dry land in field or in meadow if truly thou find without deceit. O.M. 1135. W. *colomen*. Arm. *coulm colm*. Ir. *colom, colm*, †*colum*. Gael. *columan, colman*. Manx, *calmane*. All from the Latin *columba*.

COLON, s. f. The heart. Cornish Vocabulary, *cor*. Pl. *colonow*. In construction it changes into *golon*, and *holon*. *A váp whêk, ythof cuthys, marthys claf*, O sweet son, I am grieved, my heart is wondrous sick. O.M. 1337. *Dhe colon yw cales brás*, thy heart is very hard. O.M. 1325. *Gans nader ythof gwranheys, hag oll warbarth vynymmeys, a fyne trois dhe'n golon*, by an adder I am stung, and altogether poisoned from the end of the foot to the heart. O.M. 1758. *Ha bedhouch wár colonow*, and be ye of cautious hearts. P.C. 879. *Gollyouch gynef, ow kefyon kêr colonow*, watch with me my dearly beloved hearts. P.C. 1026. *Y'ma dhys colon galas*, thou hast a hard heart. R.D. 1523. *Ow holon yn tre myll darn, marth yw genê na squardy*, my heart into three thousand pieces, it is a wonder to me that it hath not broken. M.C. 166. *Ha'y holon whêk a rannê, me a lever, rag trystans*, and her sweet heart would have broken, I say, for sorrow. M.C. 222. W. *calon*. Arm. *calon*.

COLON, s. m. A gut, entrail, bowel. Plural, *coloneiou*. Pryce. W. *coludh*, pl. *coludhion*. Ir. *caolain, cadhla*. Gael. *caolan*. Manx, *chiolg, collane*. Gr. χολὰς, κῶλον. Lat. *colon*.

COLTER, s. m. The coulter of a plough. Cornish Vocabulary, *culter*. W. *cwllyr*, †*cultir*. Arm. *coultr*. Ir. *coltar*. Gael. *collar*. Manx, *coltar*. All from the Latin *culter*.

COLWIDHEN, s. f. A hazel tree. Cornish Vocabulary, *colwiden*, corillus. Compounded of *coll*, hazel, and *gwidhen*, a tree. W. *collwydhen, collen, coll*. Arm. *kelvezen, keloueen*. Ir. *coll*. Gael. *calltuinn*. Manx. *coll*. Cf. also Anc. Gaulish, *cosl*, in the proper name *Coslum*, now *Kusel*, = Germ. *hasal*: and Slav. *shesl*. a rod, (of hazel?) whence the names of places *Scheslà*, and *Scheslitz*. (Zeuss. 1116.)

COLYAS, v. a. To watch. *Arluth agan dew lagas yw marthys cláf ow colyas, golyas o agan dysyr*, Lord, our eyes are wondrous tired watching, watching was our desire. P.C. 1057. A regular mutation after *ow*, of *golyas*, qd. v.

COLYEC, s. m. A cock. *Y'n nôs haueth kyns ys bôs colyck clewys, te a'm nâch tergwyth*, this night before the cock is heard, thou wilt deny me thrice. M.C. 49. *Gans henna ef a clewas en colyek scon ow canê*, with that he heard the cock immediately crow. M.C. 16. This is another form of *celioc*, qd. v.

COLYTH, v. a. Thou wilt listen. 2 pers. s. fut. of *colê*, qd. v. *Mar a colyth, ty a tew gans dhe whetllow*, if thou wilt listen, thou wilt be silent with thy tales. R.D. 1388.

COMBRYNSY, s. m. Rightness, exactness. *An combrynsy war dhe ben, mar lêl y synsys dhe lyn, kyns ys trehy war an pren, re got o a gevelyn*, the exactness on thy head, so true thou holdest thy line before cutting on the tree, too short it was by a cubit. O.M. 2517. *Drehefyn ef yn ban lemyn, re got ew a gevelyn da yn gwyr, an combrynsy yw henma*, let us raise it upright now, it is too short a good cubit in truth, the exact measure is this. O.M. 2542. W. *cywraint*, accurate.

COMER, s. m. Pride. Pryce.

COMMENA, v. a. To commend. ‡*Ha rág henna, gwraf commena dhe leal Drengys ow eneff*, and therefore I do commend to the faithful Trinity my soul. C.W. 146. Another form of *cemynny*, qd. v.

COMMISC, s. m. A mixture. Cornish Vocab. *commisc bleit ha chi*, lynx. Written also *cymmysk*. See *Cemysgy*.

W. *cymmysg*. Arm. *cemmesc*. Ir. *cumaisg, comhmvasg*, †*cummasc*. Gael. *coimeasg*, †*cumusg*.

COMOLEC, adj. Cloudy, dark. Lhuyd, 162. W. *cymylog*. Arm. *commoulec*. The substantive is in W. *cwmwl*, a cloud, a collection of clouds. Arm. *coumnoul, commoul*. From Lat. *cumulus*, a heap.

COMPOS, adj. Straight, even, right. *Dew teka bren rág styllyow, ha compes y denwennow, brás ha crom y ben goles*, lo, the fairest tree for rafters, and straight its sides, large and rounded its lower end. O.M. 2442. It is written indiscriminately *compes*, and *compys*. *Cowyth profuyn an styllyow, mars êns compes dhe'n fosow, may haller aga ladhyê gans owrbles*, comrades, let us try the rafters, if they are straight to the walls, that they may be laid with joists. O.M. 2472. *Rág ef a'm hembroncas pûr compys býs yn losel*, for he conducted me very straight to the rogue. P.C. 1206. This is the same word as the W. *cymmheys*, even, of even weight. Compounded of *cyd*, equally, and *poys*, weight. *Compos* therefore is compounded of *com*, id. qd. *cev*, equally, and *poys*, heavy. Arm. *compez, compoez*.

COMPOSSE, adj. Straighter. *Ny gaffen compossé pren yn nep le, na rág an plas-ma výth well*, we shall not get a straighter tree in any place, nor for this place any better. O.M. 2577. The comparative of *compos*.

COMPOSTER, s. m. Form, order, fitness. ‡*Ha dhera an noar heb composter, ha heb kencfratra; ha tulder war bedgeth an downder; ha speres Dew reeg gwnyath war bedgeth an dowron*, and the earth was without form, and without any thing, and darkness (was) on the face of the deep, and the Spirit of God moved on the face of the waters. M.C. p. 93. W. *cymmhwysder*.

CON, s. f. A supper. Lhuyd, 48, *côn*. This is the contracted form of *coyn*, qd. v.

CONA, v. a. To sup. ‡*Na huât, mêdh an dzhei, gurâz cona abarhan ni*, not yet, quoth they, do sup with us. Lhuyd, 282.

CONERIOC, adj. Rabid, mad, frantic. Cornish Vocabulary, *rabidus*, vel *amens*, vel *demens*. Derived from a substantive *connar*, = W. *cyndhar, cyndharedh*. Arm. *kounnar*, hydrophobia. The word in Welsh is compounded of *cwn*, dogs, which in composition changes regularly into *cyn*, as *cynos*, little dogs, *cynydh*, a hunter with dogs, and *dar*, a tumult. W. adj. *cyndheiriog*; *ci cyndheiriog*, †*konderawc*, a mad dog.

CONFETHYS, part. Discovered, convicted. ‡*Ow voice oll yta changys avel mayteth yn tevery, me ne vedhaf confethys om bôs ynaf falsury*, my voice is all changed like to a maiden in earnest, I shall not be discovered that there is in me any falsehood. C.W. 40. Written also *convethys*, qd. v.

CONNA, s. m. The neck. Cornish Vocabulary, *collum*. *Ow arluth, my a der erak ow conna, mars euch lemyn nês a drê, nefrê my dhebraf vara*, my lord, I will shortly break my neck, if you go now away from home, never will I taste bread. O.M. 2184. *Dhe conna a grêg*, thy neck be hanged. P.C. 2813. *Cona brêch*, the wrist, lit. the neck of the arm. *Me a gelm scon lovan dha worth conna brêch an adla ha why iynneuch agas try, býs may hedho hy dhe'n tol*, I will forthwith bind a good rope around the wrist of the knave, and do you draw, you three, until it reaches to the hole. P.C. 2762. (The wrist is called in Manx, *mwannal laue*, i. e. neck of the band.) The latest form of this word was *codna*, qd. v It differs much from the equivalents in the sister dialects, which are in W. *gwdhwv, gwdhwg*. Arm. *gouzouc*. The nearest form is the Gael. *coinne*, a meeting, joining. W. *cyduno*.

CONNES, part. Supped. The part. pass. of *cona*, qd. v. ‡ *Ex connez dhiuh*, have you supped ? Lluyd, 242.

CONS, s. f. The vagina. W. *cont*. Ir. *coint, coinne*. Gael. *coint*, †*coinne*, a woman. Lat *cunnos*. Gr. γυνή. Runic, *quinde*, a wife. Da. *quinde*, a woman. Eng. *quean*. Chaucer, *queint*.

CONTREVÁ, v. a. To dwell together. *Lluyd*, 49. Compounded of *con*, id. qd. *ced*, together with, and *treva*, to dwell, from *trêv*, a dwelling place. W. *cyd-drevu*.

CONTREVAC, s. m. One living in the same community, a neighbour. Pl. *contrevagion*, or *contrevogion*. ‡ *Na raz linh gow erbyn dhe contrevak*, do thou not swear falsely against thy neighbour. Pryce. ‡ *Na ra chee gawas whans warlyrch chy de contrevak, na ra gawas whans warlyrch gwrêg de contrevak*, do thou not entertain a desire of the house of thy neighbour, do thou not entertain a desire of the wife of thy neighbour. Pryce. ‡ *Owna Dew, parth an mnteyrn, ha cara'gos contrevogion*, fear God, honour the king, and love your neighbours. Pryce. From *contreva*. This is a later form of *centrevec*, qd. v. W. *cyddrevawg*. Arm. †*contrevek*.

CONTREWEYTYS, part. Overcome. *Gwell yw dhyn dôn, me a grŷs, râk doul bôs contrewcytys, púp y cledhé*, it is better for us to bring, I believe for fear of being overcome, every one his sword. P.C. 2299.

CONTRONEN, s. f. A bug. Cornish Vocabulary, *cimex*. The plural would be *contron*. It is evidently the same word as the W. *cyndhron*, maggots; sing. *cyndhronyn*. Arm. *contron*, sing. *contronen*.

CONVEDHAS, v. a. To understand, discover, find out. Part. pass. *convedhys*. *Serra, ny won convedhas ages dewhan yn néb for*, Sir, I do not understand your sorrow in any manner. C.W. 90. ‡ *Me ny allaf convedhas, y bosta ge ow hendas, na nôr vŷth dhym yn teffry*, I cannot discover that thou art my grandsire, nor any relation to me in reality. C.W. 116. ‡ *Hena ythew convedhys, der an diskans es dhym reis gans an Tâs ès a uchan*, that is understood, by the science that is to me given by the Father, that is on high. C.W. 156. ‡ *Der tacklow minniz ew bréz tees gonvedhes, avel a'n taclow broaz*, by small things are the minds of men discovered, as well as by great matters. Pryce. W. *eanvod*.

CONYS, v. a. To work, to labour. *Gwetyeuch bones avorow ow conys yn crŷs an drê, war beyn cregy ha tenné*, take ye care to be to-morrow working in the middle of the town, on pain of hanging and drawing. O.M. 2300. *Arluth whêk, yma ow conys dhyuwhy chyf gwythoryon oll an gwlâs, a wodher dhe dysmegy*, sweet lord, there are working for you all the chief workmen of the land, who can be mentioned. O.M. 2330. This is a regular mutation after the participial particle *ow* of *gonys*, qd. v.

COOL, v. a. Listen thou, hearken. 2 pers. imp. of *cola*. *Me a lever dhys, eva, ha cool orthav ow chân*, I will tell thee, Eve, and listen thou to my song. C.W. 44. ‡ *Cool gethym, men dha gesky*, hearken to me, would I flout thee. C.W. 48.

COOTH, adj. Familiar, complaisant. ‡ *Henna vea real dra, ha maga fûr acomplys, bôs cooth dha Dhew neartha,*

ha yn pûb poynt equal gensn, that would be a royal thing, and as wise accounted, to be familiar with God above, and in every point equal with him. C.W. 44. ‡ *Cooth ew êv hag avlethys, pan na ylla omveras, y vaw ny vennaf bôs*, he is complaisant and witty, when I could not prevent him, his boy I would not be. C.W. 84. This word may be the W. *cooth*, ardent, but more probably *couth*, as in Eng. *uncouth*.

COP, s. m. The top, or summit, a tuft. This term is found in the W. *cob, cop*. Ang. Sax. *cop, copp*. Du. *kop*. Germ. *kopf*, the head or top of a thing. Fr. *coupeau*. Gr. κύβη. Lat. *caput*. In English, *cob-castle*, or *cop-castle*, means a castle on a hill. I have found no authority for it in Cornish, in this sense, and it occurs only in P.C. 931.

COP, s. f. A cloak, coat, cope. *Heyl syr epscop, esos y'th côp owth ysedhé*, hail, sir bishop, thou art in thy cope sitting. P.C. 931. W. *côb*. Ang. Sax. *cœppe*. D. *kap*. Dan. *kappe, kaabe*. Sw. *kappa*. Fr. *capa*. Sp. *capa*. It. *cappa*. Port. *capa*.

COR, s. m. A dwarf. Cornish Vocabulary, *nanus*. W. *corr*. Arm. *corr, corric, corrigan*. Ir. *gor*, short, *corrigan*, a sprite. Gael. *gearr, goirid*. Lat. *curtus*. Sansc. *kartas*, from *kart*, to cut.

COR, s. m. Manner, sort, way, nook, corner. *Ytho dre henna ythyw, dhe vôs mychtern war nep cor, pan leverta dhyso gy bones gwlascor*, then by that it is, that thou art a king in some sort, when thou sayest that there is to thee a kingdom. P.C. 2016. *Yn chy Dew ny gôth marchas termyn vŷth oll war nêp cor*, in the house of God there ought not to be a market at any time, on any account. P.C. 2420. *Me a wŷsk, ha henna gans mûr a râch, may dhys tenno a well cor*, I will strike, and that with much care that it be drawn out for thee in the best way. P.C. 2723. *Pendra wrâf orth en ioul, mar ny gaffaf toul war nêp cor, ef a lâdh gans fleyryngy ol ow glascor*, what shall I do, if I find not for the devil a hole in some corner, he will kill with the smell all my kingdom. R.D. 2133. W. *cwr*. Ir. *curr*, †*coor*, †*corr*. Gael. *curr*.

COR, s. m. Wax. Llwyd, 18, *côr*. A contracted form of *coir*, qd. v.

COR, s. m. Ale, beer. ‡ *Why el eva cor gwella, mars ees dhys brôg*, you may drink best beer, if you have malt. *Pryce's Vocabulary*. The late form of *coref*, qd. v.

COR, v. n. He knows. *Me a vyn y examyne, y dhrehevel mar a kôr*, I will examine him, if he knows how to build it. P.C. 390. A mutation of *gôr*, qd. v.

CORD, s. m. A cord. Pl. *cerdyn*. *An scorgys prenyer ese yn dewlé an dew edhow ; hag yn fast kelmys dhedhé kerdyn gwedhyn yn mêsk cronow*, the scourges of sticks were in the hands of the two Jews, and fast bound to them cords weaved among thongs. M.C. 131. W. *cord*. Ir. *corda*. Gael. *cord*. Gr. χορδὴ. Lat. *chorda*.

CORDEN, s. f. A string. The string of a musical instrument. Cornish Vocabulary, *fidis*. The diminutive of *cord*. W. *corden*. Arm. *korden*.

CORDIIYAF, v. a. I shall worship. *Pysk ragof ny wra skusy, mar cordhyaf Dew yn perfyth* a fish from me shall not escape, if I worship God perfectly. O.M. 140. A regular mutation after *mar* of *gordhyaf*, 1 pers. s. fut. of *gordhyé*, qd. v.

CORDHYE v. a. To worship. *Maglys cans vŷl, y a dredhanger, ugy Dew kér ow cordhye*, more than a hundred thousand, they shall pass without delay, who are worshipping the dear God. O.M. 1616. A regular mutation after *ow* of *gordhyé*, qd. v.

COREF, s. m. Ale, beer. Cornish Vocabulary *cervisia vel celea*, where it is also written *coruf*. W. *curyv, cwrw*. Ir. *coirm, cuirm*. Gael. †*coirm*. Gr. κοῦρμι σκευαζόμενον ἐκ τῆς κριθῆς, (Potionis genus ex hordeo, interdum et ex tritico, Iberis occidentalibus et Britannicis usitatum.) Dioscor. Laer. 2, 110, κορμα, Athen. 4, 13. *Curmen*, in Ducange, from a Latin-Greek Glossary, and Ulpian.

CORF, s. m. The body, a body, the human body. Pl. *corfow*. In construction it changes into *gorf* and *horf*, for *chorf*. *A dâs mâp ha spyrys sans, gordhyans dhe'th corf whêk pûp prŷs*, O Father, Son, and Holy Ghost, worship to thy sweet body always. O.M. 86. *A dâs a nêf dhe gorf kêr gordhys re bo*, O Father of Heaven, be thy dear body worshipped. O.M. 408. *Dûn goryn y gorf yn vêdh*, let us go and put his body in the grave. O.M. 2367. *Bŷth ny wrûk ef leverel, corf hag enef y eyvy*, never did he say body and soul that they would rise. P.C. 1753. *An corf êth hydhew yn pry*, the body went to day into the earth. R.D. 21. *Agan corfow nôth gallas, gans deyl agan cudhê gwren*, our bodies are become naked, let us cover ourselves with leaves. O.M. 254. *Ow horf a ve yw henna ragouch wy*, this is my body for you. M.C. 44. W. *corph, corf*. Arm. *corf*. Ir. *corp*. Gael. *corp*. Manx, *corp*. Basque, *corputza*. Lat. *corpus*. Fr. *corps*. Sp. *cuerpo*. It. *corpo*. Da. *krop*. Sansc. *garbhas*, embryon, from *garh*, to enclose.

CORHLAN, s. f. A churchyard, a burial place. Llwyd, 149. Probably for *corphlan*, being compounded of *corph*, or *corf*, a body, and *lan*, an enclosure. W. *corphlan, cordhlan*.

CORLAN, s. f. A sheep fold, a sheep cote. It is found in the names of places, as *Boscorla* in St. Austle, and St. Kevern. W. *corlan*. It is compounded of *cor*, a sheep, and *llan*, an enclosure. *Cor* is now obsolete in the British dialects as a simple term for sheep, *davad* being the name employed. It is preserved however in the W. compounds, *corlan*, a sheep fold, and *corgi*, a sheep dog. In the Erse dialects it is the common name of a sheep. Ir. *caor*, †*cair*. Gael. *caora*. Manx, *keyrrey*. Sansc. *kurarl*.

CORN, s. m. What projects out, a horn, a horn to blow in, a trumpet, a corner. Pl. *cernow*. *Ystyn dhym dhe dhorn, tan henna dheworthef vy, dyson hep whethe dhe gorn dysempys gwra y dhybry*, extend to me thy hand, take that from me, quietly without blowing thy horn, immediately do thou eat it. O.M. 207. *Cardowyon, hep whethe corn na gul sôn, kemuch Jhesu dhynny ny*, my dear fellows, without blowing a horn or making a noise, bring Jesus to us. P.C. 1358. *Tewleuch ef yn trôk a hôrn, yn dour tyber yn nep corn may fo budhys*, cast ye it, in a box of iron, into the river Tiber in some corner, that it may be drowned. R.D. 2163. *Ot en corf yn trôk gorrys, degeuch e a dhesympys dhe corn an dour*, behold the body placed in the box; carry it immediately to the corner of the water. R.D. 2185. W. *corn*. Arm. *corn*. Ir. †*corn*. Gael. †*corn*. Manx, *cayrn*. Lat. *cornu*. Sp. *cuerno*. Fr. *corne*. Sansc. *carnis*. Heb. *kern, karn*. Syr. *karen, karn*. Eth. *karan, karn*. Gr. κάρνον τὴν σάλπιγγα, Γαλαταs, Hesych. 2, 151, on account of the curve. It is the root of the names *Cornubia, Carniu, Kernyw, Kernow, Cornwall*, in Britain, and *Cornouaille*, in Britanny.

CORNAT, s. f. A corner. Llwyd, 13. W. *cornel*.

CORNEL, s. f. An angle, a corner. Llwyd, 43, who writes it *cornal*. W. *cornel*. Arm. *corn*. Ir. *cearna, coirneul*. Gael. *cearn*. Manx, *corneil*.

CORNIWILLEN, s. f. A lapwing. This word is now in common use in Cornwall. W. *cornchwiglen*. It has also other names in Welsh, *corn y wich*, and *cornicell*. Arm. *cornigel*.

COROLLI, v. a. To dance. Pryce. W. *coroli*, to dance, or move in a circle. The root is *cór*, a circle, thence *corawl*, circling. Arm. *corolli*.

CORONE, v. a. To crown. *Arlythy, my agas pŷs, Salmon ow mâp coroneuch, h'agas mychtern ef synseuch, hedrê vyuch byw yn bys-ma*, Lords, I pray you, crown ye Solomon my son, and for your king hold him, while ye are alive in this world. O.M. 2347. From *coron*, or *curun*, a crown, qd. v.

CORRE, v. a, To place, or put. *Ny vern tra vŷth assaye, h'ow gwcreseuch cowethê ow corré tumbyr yn ban, may haller aga lathye*, it is not of the least consequence to try, and help me, comrades, putting the timber up, that they may be adjusted. O.M. 2479. A regular mutation after *ow*, of *gorré*, qd. v.

CORS, s. m. A while. *Benes vôs dheuch, powesouch lymmyn un cors, mc agas pŷs, hag euch dhe drê dhe coské*, blessing to you, rest now a while I pray you, and go home to sleep. P.C. 2146. W. *cors*.

CORS, s. f. A moor, a bog, a fen. It enters into the names of places in Cornwall, as in Wales. Thus *Pencorse*, the head of the moor, in St. Enoder. *Pengersic* in Breage. W. *cors*. Arm. *cors*. Ir. *currach*, †*curchas*. Manx, *curragh*. Lat. *carex*.

CORSEN, s. f. A reed, a bog plant. Cornish Vocabulary, *calamus*. W. *corsen*. Arm. *corsen*. Ir. †*curchuslach*.

CORTES, v. a. To stay, or tarry. *Ny a dreha ragon chy pols dhe wonys, rag ny a yl gûl scovva, ow cortes vôs goskesys*, we will raise for us a house, a while to labour, for we may make a tent, waiting to be sheltered. O.M. 1717. A regular mutation after *ow* of *gortes*, qd. v.

CORWEDHA, v. n. To lie down. ‡*A corwedha*, lying down. Llwyd, 648. A mutation after the adverbial particle *a*, id. qd. *ow*, of *gorwedha*, qd. v.

COS, s. m. A wood, a forest. Pl. *cosow*, or *cossow*. *Ny wodhen râg ponvotter py 'th een yn gweal py yn côs, ow holon gwâk dyvoller ru'm kymmer hag awel bôs*, I know not for trouble, whether I am in a field or in a wood, a vain appetite has seized my heart, and a desire of food. O.M. 364. *Yn oll dhe gosow nyns ûs gyst vythol, hep wow, vôs dhe dra vŷth ragdho*, in all thy woods, there is not a beam, without falsehood, good for any thing for it. O.M. 2495. *Why aspyeuch yn ow cossow pren dhe gŷst hep toll na gûl*, seek ye in my forests a tree for a beam without hole or fault. O.M. 2558. This is a later form of *coid*, qd. v.

COS, s. m. Cheese. Cornish Vocabulary, *caseus*, where it is also written *caus*, qd. v.

COSCASA, v. a. To shade, defend, shelter. Part. pass. *coskesys*. *Ny a dreha ragon chy, pols dhe wonys, rag ny a yl gûl scovva, ow cortes vôs goskesys*, we will raise a house for us, a while to labour, for we may make a tent, waiting to be sheltered. O.M. 1718. Written by Llwyd, 248, *kosgara, kosgezys.* W. *cysgodi, gwascodi.* Arm. *gwasked̃.* The substantive is *cuscys,* a shelter, qd. v.

COSCE, v. n. To sleep. *Ke, growel war an dôr gulan, ha côsk, bŷth na saf yn ban,* go, lie down on the earth clean, and sleep thou, nor ever stand up. O.M. 97. *Rŷs yw dhym porrys coské, possygyon yn pen yma,* it is necessary for me to sleep, drowsiness is in my head. O.M. 1905. *Ow cufyon leman coskeuch, hag olwarbarth powesouch,* my dear (companions) now sleep, and rest ye all together. P.C. 1003. *Euch dhe dré dhe coské,* go ye home to sleep. P.C. 2148. *Coskyn ny gans dyalva, kyn dasvewo ny'n drecha dhywar y geyn,* let us sleep with security, though he should revive, he will not raise it from off his back. R.D. 402. *Me re goskes pós,* I have slept heavily. R.D. 511. *Koscouch lemyn mars ew prys, powesouch, wy yw grevys,* sleep ye now, as it is time, rest yourselves, ye are grieved. M.C. 61. W. *cysgu, †cescu.* Arm. *cousga.* Ir. *ceisgim.* Gael. *coisg.* Lat. *quiesco.* Sansc. *ci.*

COSE, v. n. To itch. *Me a gelm fust an loscl, may hallo pûp oll dhe wêl dodho ef ry strekesow; lemyn oll byan ha brâs, knoukyouch ef del dyndylas may cosso y tymwennow,* I will bind the villain fast, that all may be able to see to give him strokes; now all, little and great, strike him as he has deserved, that his sides may itch. P.C. 2084. W. *cosi.*

COSEL, adj. Soft, quiet, slow, sluggish. *Cosel my re bowesas, assyno whék an hún myttyn,* I have rested quietly, sweet is the morning sleep. O.M. 2074. It is written by Llwyd, 120, *kozal,* as the late form.

COSGOR, s. m. A retinue, a guard, clients, dependents, a tribe, a family, servants, children, boys, lads. Cornish Vocabulary, *den cosgor, cliens vel clientulus.* It is written by Llwyd, 243, as pronounced in his time, *kosgar.* ‡ *Gen kosgar,* our boys, 245. W. *cosgordh, gosgordh.* Arm. *cozgor.* Ir. *cosgar.* Gael. *coisridh.*

COSOLETH, s. m. Quiet, rest. *Ef a'n gefyth yn dywedh an ioy na dhyfyk nefré, yn ow gwlas, ha cosoleth,* he shall obtain in the end the joy that will never fail, in my land, and rest. O.M. 518. *An ths Dew Arluth a-van ré'm gorre dhe gosoleth,* the Father God, Lord above, may he put me to rest. O.M. 858. *Bannath an ths ragas bo, hag ef prest ragas gwythy venytha yn cosoleth,* the blessing of the Father be on you, and may it always preserve you for ever at rest. O.M. 1725. From the adj. *cosel,* quiet.

COSOWA, v. n. To ease, lighten, lessen. *Dho cosowa,* Llwyd, 78.

COSSO, v. a. He may itch. 3 pers. s. subj. of *cosé,* qd. v.

COSSYLYA, v. a. To counsel, advise. ‡ *Drôk polat o, neb a glowses ow cana, ha a'th cossylyes dhe derry an avalna,* a bad pullet he was, whom thou heardest singing, and counselled thee to break off that apple. C.W. 56.

CYSSYTHY, v. a. To punish. Pryce. W. *cystudhio, cystwyo.* Arm. *castiza.* Manx, *custhee.* Lat. *castigo.*

COSSYTHYANS, s. m. Punishment. *Yn bys-ma, râg dha wreans ty a berth gossythyans, ken na brodar,* in this world, for thy deed, thou shalt bear punishment, though thon art a brother. C.W. 82. W. *cystudhiant, cystwyacth.*

COST, s. f. Charge, expense, cost. *Awos côst arhans nag our, goreuch y tenné mês an dour, gorreuch ef yn schath dhe'n môr,* notwithstanding the cost of silver and gold, draw him out of the water, place him in a boat to the sea. R.D. 2231. W. *cost.* Arm. *coust.* Ir. *cosdas.* Gael. *cosd.* Manx, *cost.*

COSTAN, s. f. A buckler, shield, target. Llwyd, 48.

COT, adj. Short, sudden, hasty, quick. Comp. *cottah, cotta,* shorter. *Mar gura, godhvedhys mar pŷth, yn scon dysureys ef a vŷdh, ha dhe'n mernans cot gorrys,* if he does, if it shall be discovered, soon destroyed he shall be, and to death quickly put. O.M. 1522. *My a'n mesur lour yn ta, na vo hyrre esumsyn, na vŷth cotta war nép cor,* I will measure it well enough, that it be not longer, I undertake, nor shorter in any way. O.M. 2512. *Yn bysma na tryst na moy, cot yw dhe dhydhyow dhe gy, nahen na grŷs,* in this world trust thou no more, short are thy days to thee, believe not otherwise. R.D. 2037. Written also *cut,* qd. v. W. *cot, cota, cwt, cwta.* Ir. *cutach.* Gael. *cutâch.*

COTA, s. m. A coat. Llwyd, 33. W. *côd,* a wrapper. Ir. *cota.* Fr. *cotte.* It. *cotta.*

COTELLE, s. m. A wood, a forest, a plantation of wood. Pryce. Comp. of *coid,* wood, and *le,* a place. W. *coedle.*

COTH, adj. Old, ancient. Cornish Vocabulary, *senex.* Comp. *cothah,* superl. *cotha.* *A êl, me a levar dhys, ow thâs ew côth, ha sguytheys, ny garsé pellé bewé,* O angel, I tell thee, my father is old, and weary, he would not wish to live longer. O.M. 737. *Hemma yw an côth wâs gôf,* this is the old smith fellow. P.C. 1695. *Pub ér te dhén gwra lewté, beva dên yonk bo dên côth, orthaff mar mynnyth colé, neffré gans an fals na soth,* continually, do thou right to man, be he a young man or old man, if thou wilt hearken to me, with the false do not follow. M.C. 175. *Nyng es dén vyth ol yn bŷs, mês te, ha'w mab cotha Cayn,* there is never a man in the world, but thou and my eldest son Cain. C.W. 90. *An lavar gôth ew lavar gwir,* the old saying is a true saying. *Pryce's Vocab.* Arm. *koz.* Dr. Davies quotes the Liber Landavensis, as authority for *côth* being a Welsh word, but I believe erroneously, as I have not yet found it in any Welsh document. His mistake must have arisen from a copy of the Cornish Vocabulary being attached to a MS. copy of the Liber Landavensis.

COTH, v. imp. It behoveth, it is incumbent, it is due. A mutation of *gôth,* qd. v. *Bôs sêch ha têk an awel, dhe Dew y côth dhyn grassé,* that the weather is dry and fair, it is incumbent on us to thank God. O.M. 1148. *Y côth dhyn oll y wordhyé, kefrys yn tŷr, hag yn môr,* it behoves us all to honour him, as well on land as in sea. P.C. 391. *Kyn na gowso, dre laha y côth dodho drôk dywedhé,* though he may not speak, by law there is due to him an evil ending. P.C. 1827. *Herwydh agas laha gwrêch y juggyé dhe'n mernans, mar côth henna,* according to your law judge ye him to death, if that is due. P.C. 1980.

COTHFO, v. imp. It should behove. A mutation of *gothfo.* 3 pers. s. subj. of *gôth.* *Euch ganso kettep pen, my ny gaffaf yno kên, may cothfo dhym y ladhé,* go with him every head, I do not find in him a cause, that it should behove me to kill him. P.C. 1798.

COTHMAN, s. m. A companion, a friend. *A gothman da, prâk y wreta dhymmo ammé,* O good friend, why dost thou kiss me. P.C. 1106. *Mar a'n dyllyfryth, hep mar, nyns ôs cothman dhe Cesar yno agan arluth mychtern,* if thou wilt liberate him, doubtless, thou art not a friend to Cesar, (that) is our lord king. P.C. 2220. *Dhodho ef nyns ôs cothman, del hevel dhymmo yn wŷr,* to him thou art not a friend, as it seems to me in truth. P.C. 2431. ‡*Ow hothman, na gymmar marith, ty an ool, ha lyas mŷl,* my friend take not wonder, thou shalt weep, and many thousands. C.W. 168. W. *rydymmaith, cymdaith, cyvaeth, cyveithydh.* Ir. *comhthach,* †*coinnthocht.*

COTHYS, s. m. Grief, sorrow. *Yma dhymmo mûr duon ha cothys war ow colon, ny won vythol pendra wraf,* there is to me much grief, and sorrow on my heart, I know not at all what I shall do. R.D. 1765. Id. qd. *cuth,* qd. v.

COUL, s. m. Broth, porridge. *Dûs yn mês, vynytha ny cfyth coul, marrow cowal ty a vŷdh,* come out, thou shalt never drink broth, thou shalt be quite dead. O.M. 2701. *Mar ny'n gorraf, an mŷl dyaul re dorro mellow y gŷn, vynytha na cfhŷ coul,* if I take him not, may a thousand devils break the joints of his back, so that he may never drink broth. P.C. 1620. Another form of *caul,* qd. v.

COUTH, v. imp. It behoveth. *Rûdh y couth dhymmo bones,* red it behoves me to be. R.D. 2535. The same word as *côth,* qd. v.

COV, a prefix in composition, denoting equality, and cooperation, and written also *cev,* qd. v. It answers to *cyv* in Welsh; Corn. *covlenwel,* to fulfil, is in Welsh *cyvlawni.* The final *v* is a mutation of *m,* which shows the relationship to the Latin *com,* which form is also preserved in Old Irish, as *comalnad,* to fulfil. Lat. *compleo.* In modern Irish, the final *m* has changed into the secondary form *mh,* which is pronounced as it is written in Welsh, *v.* Compare Ir. *comhlionadh.* Gael. *coimhlion.* Manx, *cooilleen.*

COV, s. m. The memory, remembrance. *Noy mâb Lamec gylwys ôv, arluth brâs, oll perthow côv, ythof omma yn bys-ma,* Noah the son of Lamech called I am, a great lord, bear ye all remembrance, I am in this world. C.W. 162. *Perûh côv dhe gwithê sans an dŷdh Sabboth,* remember to keep holy the Sabbath day. *Pryce.* In the Ordinalia, it is more generally written *côf,* qd. v. W. *côv.*

COVAITH, s. m. Riches, wealth. *Pryce.* W. *cyvoeth.* Ir. *comhachd,* †*cumacct.* Gael. *cumhachd.*

COVAITHAK, adj. Rich, wealthy. *Pryce.* The oldest form in Cornish was *cefuidoc,* qd. v. W. *cyvoethog.* Ir. *cumachtach,* †*cumachtig.*

COVATH, s. m. Remembrance, recollection. *Dhe vâp Ysac a gcruyth, y offrynné reys yw dhys, war vencdh a dhysquedhaf dhyso gy, del lavaraf, u'n covath byth ny hassnf, mar qureth dhym an sacryfys,* thy son Isaac (whom) thou lovest, it is necessary for thee to offer him upon a mountain (that) I shall shew thee, as I say, I will never leave thee from remembrance, if thou wilt make to me the sacrifice. O.M. 1283. *Na parth a wher, Dew a'th weres, ef Dew a râs a'n covath ny hâs,* do not complain, God will help thee, he is a God of grace, he will not leave thee from remembrance. O.M. 1358. W. *coviad.*

COVENEC, adj. Remembered. *Yma govenec dhym,* it is in remembrance to me, i.e. I remember. Llwyd, 242. It appears more correct to derive *govenec* from *govyn,* to ask. See *Govenec.*

COVIO, v. a. To remember, recollect, call to mind. *Pryce. Saw gura un dra a'n gooys,* but do thou remember one thing. O.M. 76. W. *covio.* See *Cofua.*

COVLENWEL, v. a. To fulfil, to fill. Llwyd, 228. In the Ordinalia it is generally written, *coullenwel. Yn pympes dŷdh me a vyn, uury fo formyys dre ow nel, bestes, puskes, hag edhyn, tŷr ha môr dhe goullenwel,* on the fifth day I will that there be made by my power, beasts, fishes, and birds, earth and sea to fill. O.M. 44. *Gorhemmyn Dew dres pûp tra rês ŷw y vôs coullenwys,* the command of God, above all things, need is that it be fulfilled. O.M. 655. *Cresseuch, coullenveuch an beys, avel kyns, ketep mâp pron,* increase, fill the earth, as before, every son of the breast. O.M. 1162. Comp. of the prefix *cov,* and *lenwel,* to fill. W. *cyvlawni.* Ir. *comhlionadh,* †*comalnad.* Manx, *cooilleen.* Lat. *compleo.*

COVYNNAF, v. a. I shall ask. *Kyn loverryf gwŷr, dên ahanouch ny vyn crygy, mar a cofynnaf trafyth ny wodhouch ow gorthyby,* though I speak truly, not any man of you will believe, if I ask any thing, ye know not how to answer me. P.C. 1483. A regular mutation after *mara* of *govynnaf,* 1 pers. s. fut. of *govynné,* qd. v.

COVYS, adj. Mindful, remembering. Llwyd, 88. From *côv,* remembrance. W. *covus.*

COWAL, adj. Full, complete, entire, perfect. Often used adverbially, fully, quite. *Codhys warnan an môr brâs, ny a vŷdh cowal vudhys,* fallen on us (is) the great sea, we shall be quite drowned. O.M. 1701. *Marrow cowal ty a vŷdh,* quite dead then shalt be. O.M. 2702. *A pur voren plos, myrch gâl, ty a verow sur cowal,* O very dirty jade, daughter of evil; thou shalt die quite surely. O.M. 2737. *Ila tewleuch e, dral ha dral, yn Bessedé pûr gowal,* and cast ye it, piece by piece, in Bethsaida very completely. O.M. 2783. *Er dhe pyn cowsaf cowal,* against thee, I speak entirely. P.C. 2391. *Ty a fŷdh cowal anken,* thou shalt have full pain. P.C. 2530. Written also *coul,* qd. v. W. *cwbyl.*

COWAS, v. a. To have, obtain, procure. *Dho gowas,* Llwyd, 125. ‡ *Gwrêns gowas poher drês an puskas en môr, ha dres an edhen en ebarn,* and let them have power over the fish of the sea, and over the birds of the air. M.C. p. 94. ‡ *Hy oar gwile padn dah gen hy glawn, ha et hy olkas, hy delveath gowas tân,* she knows to make good cloth with her wool, and on her hearth, she ought to have fire. *Pryce's Vocab.* This is a late form of *cafos,* qd. v.

COWAT, s. f. A shower. Cornish Vocabulary, *couat,* nimbus. This is the oldest form of *cowes,* qd. v. W. *cawod,* ‡*cauat.* Arm. *caouad.* Ir. *ceatha, caoth, cith, coth.* Gael. *cith.*

COWEIDLIVER, s. m. A manual, hand-book. Cornish Vocabulary, *manuale.* Read by Llwyd, 36, *cowaithliver.* This word appears to me to be compounded of the W. *cywaith, cowaith,* †*coweil,* co-operating, auxiliary, what is at hand to help, and C. *liver,* a book.

COWERAS, s. m. Perfection, the fulfilment of a promise, accomplishment. *Henna o poynt a falsury dedhewys heb coweras,* that was a point of falsehood, promised without fulfilment. M.C. 83. W. *cyveiriad.*

COWES, s. f. A shower. *Yma ow tegens ywe hager gowes, war ow fêdh; ota cowes pur ahas, ny's pyrth dên, mara peys pel,* here there is coming a shower very dreadful, man cannot bear it, if it drops long. O.M. 1083. A later form of *cowat,* qd. v.

COWETH, s. m. A companion, fellow, mate, comrade. Pl. *cowethê.* It is written equally often *coweyth. Nyms yw da bones un dêny honon hep cowyth py cowethes,* it is not well that a man should be by himself without a

COWL 69 COYNT

male or female companion. O.M. 95. *Cowyth, growedh an ngl tu*, comrade, lie on one side. O.M. 2061. *H'ow gweresewh, cowethé, ow corré tumbyr yn ban*, and help me, comrades, putting the timber up. O.M. 2478. *A glewsyuch why, cowethé*, did ye hear, comrades ? O.M. 2727. *Dún alemma cowythé*, let us come hence, comrades. P.C. 107. *Ty hag oll dhe gowethé*, thou and all thy companions. P.C. 1580. W. *cyweithydh*, from *cywaith*, co-operation, comp. of *cy*, id. qd. *cyv*, together, and *gwaith*, work.

COWETHAS, s. f. Company, society. *Dhe Herodes ythesa pûr wgr worth Pilat sor brâs, y welas ef ny gara, na bós yn y gowethas*, to Herod there was very truly against Pilate a great grudge, he loved not to see him, nor to be in his company. M.C. 110. *Ha Christ yn crês, leun a ras, leun y golon a voreth, gans laddron y cowethas, del yw scryfys-a'y dhewedh*, and Christ in the midst, full of grace, full his heart of sorrow, with thieves his companions, so it is written of his end. M.C. 166. W. *cyweithas.*

COWETHE, s. f. Company, society. *Camm Pilat pan welas na ylly Christ delyffré, ma na'n geffo ef sor brâs dheworth oll an gowethé*, so Pilate when he saw that he could not deliver Christ, so that he should not meet with great discontent from all the society. M.C. 150. *Ytho levereuch waré, kepar del ouch fûr syngys, yn mŷsk oll an gowethé, pyw henna, my agas pys*, now say presently, like as you are accounted wise, among all the company, who is it I pray you. P.C. 783. W. *cyweithi.*

COWETHES, s. f. A female companion, a help-mate. *Nyns yw da bones un dên y honan, heb cowyth py cowethes, ke growedh war an dor gwlan, ha côsk, bŷth na sâf yn ban, erna fo cowethes gwrés*, it is not good that a man should be by himself, without a male or female companion; go, lie down, and sleep; never stand up until a help-mate be made. O.M. 95. *Dues, ow howethes Eva, groweth yn gwyly a hŷs*, come, my companion Eve, lie in the bed at length. O.M. 652.

COWETHYANS, s. m. Communion, fellowship. *Me a credy yn Speris sans, an egles sans dres an bês, an cowethyans an sansow, an dewhyllyans pehasow, an dedhoryans an corf, ha bewnans heb dywedh*, I believe in the Holy Ghost, the holy church throughout the world, the communion of saints, the forgiveness of sins, the resurrection of the body, and the life without end. *Pryce's Vocabulary*. W. *cyweithiani.*

COWETHYS, part. Acquainted. *Gans Judas del o tewlys, drey Jesus sur del vynné, gans Christ ytho cowethys, bŷth nyng ens y cowethé*, by Judas so it was designed, bring Jesus surely he would, with Christ he was acquainted, never were they companions. M.C. 41. This is strictly the participle of a verb, *cywethé*, id. qd. W. *cyweithio*, to co-operate.

COWG, adj. Empty, vain. ‡ *Y lesky ny vanaf ve, an eys na'n frutes deffry; taw, Abel, dhymo pedn cowga*, burn I will not the corn nor the fruits really, be silent, Abel, for me dolt head. C.W. 80. In the MS. in the British Museum, this word is written *cooge*. It is a later form of *côc*, qd. v.

COWL, s. m. Broth. See *Coul.*

COWL, adv. Fully, quite. *Arluth ytho pyw a wra cowl drehevel oll dhe chy.—Salamon, dhe vâp kerra a'n cowl dreha eredy*, Lord, now who shall fully build all thy house? Solomon, thy son most dear shall build it verily.

O.M. 2340. *An temple may fe cowl wreys*, that the temple may be fully made. O.M. 2412 *Ha pan vo hy cowl devys, hy a vŷdh pûb êr parys*, and when it is full grown, it will be every hour ready. C.W. 134. This is a contracted form of *cowal*, qd. v.

COWLENWEL, v. a. To fulfil. *Pur wyr leskys ef a vŷdh, rûg coulenwel lôdh dhe vrŷs*, very truly it shall be burnt, to fulfil the desire of thy mind. O.M. 434. *Lemyn na fo oll ow bôdh cowlynwys dhymmo lemyn*, but be not all my will fulfilled to me now. P.C. 1038. This is another form of *cowlenwel*, qd. v.

COWMS, s. m. Discourse, talk. *Llwyd.* 48. An older form of *cows*. W. *comm.* Arm. *comps.*

COWS, s. m. Speech, discourse. *Ma ow wolon ow ranné, pan glewaf cows an par-na*, my heart is parting when I hear talk of that kind. O.M. 2182. *Ty a gl y atendyé bós gwgr ow cows kettep gêr*, thou mayest attend to it, that my speech is true every word. R.D. 478. *Dre dhe gows ythew previs*, by thy speech it is proved. M.C. 85. *Dh'y gows ny worthebys*, to his speech he answered not. M.C. 144. A later form of *cowms*, qd. v.

COWS, v. n. To speak, say, tell. *Prâg na dheuté nês râg cows orthyf*, why dost thou not come nearer to speak with me. O.M. 150. *Mars ellen hep cows orty*, if I should go without speaking to her. O.M. 2173. *Kyn na gowso dre laha y côth dotho drôk dywedh*, though he may not speak, by law there is due to him an evil end. P.C. 1826. *Ma na gaffo gorthyp vŷth, er agan pyn dhe cows gêr*, that he may not find an answer, against us to say a word. P.C. 1840. *Ny allaf gwelas an fu anodho ef yn nep tu, cows ganso me a garsé*, I cannot see the form of him in any side, I would have liked to speak with him. R.D. 744. *Arluth, gwgr a leversouch, y gowsys yntrethé*, Lord, truth you said, they spake among them. M.C. 50. *Pandra gowsow dhym lemyn*, what say ye to me now. C.W. 12. *Yn cutt termyn agas negys cowsow*, in a short time your errand tell me. C.W. 44. *Cewsel*, is another form of this word, qd. v.

COWSES, s. m. A speech, discourse. Pl. *cowsesow*. The singular is generally written *cowsys*. *Ha whâth an Jowl a dewlys towl ken maner mar callé, dre nêp fordh a govaytis, gudhil dh'y gowsys trylé*, and yet the devil desired a way some other manner if he could, through some way of covetousness, make him to his speech turn. M.C. 15. *Christ a worthebys y gowsys ef a wodhyé*, Christ answered his speech he knew. M.C. 30. *Lyes bysys, na dreylé y gowsesow, awos own bones ledhys*, many a time I have prayed, that he turn not his speeches, for fear of being killed. P.C. 885.

COYN, s. f. A supper. *Crist worth an goyn a warnyas, dre onan bós treson gurjis, Arluth Du y a armas, pu a gl henna bonas*, Christ at the supper gavo notice, by one that treason was made, Lord God, they cried out, who can that one be. M.C. 42. In Llwyd's time, it was contracted into *côn*, qd. v. W. *cwynos.* Arm. *coan.* Ir. *cuid*, † *sene*. Lat. *cæna*. Gr. κοινὴ.

COYNT, adj. Rough, rude, sharp, cunning. *Pan wreta mar coynt fara, ow scollyé agan gwara, ha'n fêr orth y dhystrewy*, when thou actest so rudely, scattering our wares, and destroying the fair. P.C. 340. *Coynt mûr yw an gudâ, hep mar, hag a awon lyes wrynch*, the fellow is very sharp, without doubt, and he knows many a trick. P.C. 1000. *Ottê ha coynt o an gudâ*, zee how cunning the fellow was. P.C. 1819. *My re bue boches coynt,* I have been little cunning. P.C. 3031. *Par del oma quicker coynt,* as I am a rough dealer. C.W 84. *Blewak coynt yu, ha hager, ny wôn pana vêst ylla bôs,* hairy, rough it is, and ugly, I know not what beast it can be. C.W. 114.

COYNTIS, s. m. Cunning, artifice. *Ha satnas gans y antell, hay scherewneth hay goyntis, Crist mab an Arluth uchell y demptyé pan prederis,* and Satan with his danger and his wickedness and his cunning, when he thought to tempt Christ, the Son of the High Lord. M.C. 19. *Pylat a vynssé gwythé beronans Jesus dre goyntis,* Pilate would preserve the life of Christ through cunning. M.C. 125.

COYS, s. m. A wood, forest. *Warbarth oll gweel Behethlen, ha coys Penryn, yn tyen, my n's re lemyn dheuch why,* together all the field of Bohellan, and the wood of Penryn, entirely, I give them now to you. O.M. 2589. This is a later form of *coyd,* or *coid,* qd. v.

COYTH, adj. Old, ancient. *Galsof coyth ha marthys gnoan, dyvythys ew ou dewedh,* I am become old and wondrous weak, my end is arrived. O.M. 85. This is another form of *côth,* qd. v.

CRA, conj. If, although. Llwyd, 150.

CRA, v. a. He will do. A mutation of *gra,* for *gwra,* 3 pers. s. fut. of *gwrey,* qd. v.

CRABALIAS, s. m. Worms creeping like crabs. *Pryce.*

CRAC, s. m. A clap. *Ellas na dhelleys dhy lesky un luhusen, ha crack taran,* Alas! that I did not send forth a thunderbolt to burn him, and a clap of thunder. R.D. 294. W. *crêch,* a shriek.

CRAC, adv. Shortly. *My a der crak ow conna, mars euch mês adré, nefré ny dhebraf vara,* I will break shortly my neck, if you will go from home, never will I eat bread. O.M. 2184. *Mar remufé y pen crak me a torsé, kyn cousé vŷth mar huhel,* if he moved, his head shortly I would break, though he should talk ever so high. R.D. 397. W. *crig,* a crack. Arm. *crak,* short.

CRAF, adj. Covetous. Cornish Vocabulary, *avarus.* W. *crâf.* Arm. *cráf.*

CRAMPEDHAN, s. f. A pancake, a fritter. Pl. *crampedh.* Llwyd, 75. It was also written *crampodhan,* and *crampessan.* W. *crammcyth, crempogen,* pl. *crempog.* Arm. *crampoezen,* pl. *crampocz, crampoesch.*

CRAMYAS, v. a. To creep. ‡*Ha Dew wrûs bestas an 'oar warlêr 'go hâs, ha 'n ludnu warlêr 'go hâs, ha cenefratra ês a cramyas war an 'oar, warlêr go hâs, ha Dew a welas tro va da,* and God made the beasts of the earth after their seed, and the cattle after their seed, and every thing that creepeth on the earth after their seed; and God saw that it was good. M.C. p. 94.

CRANAG, s. m. A frog. Pl. ‡*cranougas. Cranac melyn,* a yellow frog; *cranag diu,* a black frog or toad. *Pryce.* Llwyd derives this word from the Latin *rana,* but erroneously, as it is only a corruption of *croinec,* qd. v.

CRANAGAS, adj. Crawling like a frog. *Pryce.*

CREADOR, s. m. A creator. Cornish Vocabulary, *creator.* Borrowed from the Latin, as is also W. *creawdwr.* Arm. *crouer.* Ir. *cruthaightheoir.* Gael. *cruithfhear.* Manx, *fer-croo.*

CREATER, s. m. A creature. *Pan o Jesus Christ dampnys aberth an crows may farsé, hacra mernans vŷth ordnys dhe creater ny vye,* when Jesus Christ was condemned on the cross that he should die, a more horrid death was never ordained for a creature. M.C. 151. *Ty creator bynyges fattel dhuthié gy dhe'n crês, na fues gynen yn yfarn,* thou blessed creature how camest thou to peace? thou wast not with us in hell. R.D. 259. Written in the Cornish Vocabulary, *croadur.* W. *creadur.* Arm. *crouadur.* Ir. *creatur.* Gael. *creutair.* All from the Latin *creatura.*

CRED, s. f. Belief, faith. This early form is only found in the name of a parish, *San Créd,* or *Creed,* Holy Faith. See the corrupted form *crês.* W. *créd, credhyu.* Arm. *créd, creden.* Ir. *cre,* †*credem,* †*cretem.* Gael. *creud,* †*cre.* Manx, *crea.*

CREDY, v. a. To believe. ‡*Me a gredy yn Dew an Tâs ollgalluster, gwrêar an nef, hag an 'oar,* I believe in God the Father Almighty, maker of heaven and earth. C.W. p. 200. The more common form in the Ordinalia, is *cresy,* by the corrupt change of *d,* into *s,* and then into *g,* as *cregy,* which sound prevailed at the last, being written by Keigwyn and Llwyd, *credgy, credzhi.* W. *credu.* Arm. *credi.* Ir. *creid.* Gael. *creid.* Manx, *creid.* Lat. *credo.*

CREDGYANS, s. m. The Creed, or Belief. ‡*Credgyans an Abesteleth,* the Apostles' Creed. *Pryce's Vocabulary.* Written by Llwyd, *credzhans,* 132. Id. qd. *cregyans,* qd. v.

CREEG, s. f. A heap, mound, hillock; a barrow. Pl. *cregow.* This word is a later form of *crue,* qd. v., and is preserved in the names of many places in Cornwall, as *Creegebroaz, Creegcarrow, Creeglaze, Creegvose,* and the plural form in *Creggo,* and *Cregoe.*

CREF, adj. Strong, mighty, vigorous, hardy. *Dre vôdh an Tâs caradow, yma gorhyl créf ordnys,* by the will of the beloved Father, there is a strong ship ordained. O.M. 1040. *Popel Ysral ny assaf, nas gorren y dhy whyl créf,* the people of Israel, I will not leave, that I put them not to their hard work. O.M. 1490. *Mychtern Israel, Arluth créf,* king of Israel, mighty Lord. P.C. 276. *Oll tus a'n beys, créf ha gwan,* all men in the world, strong and weak. P.C. 1334. *Arluth créf ha gallosck,* Lord, strong and powerful. R.D. 108. *Yn créf brâs me re pechas,* very grossly I have sinned. R.D. 1569. *Ena yn wêdh y torras an veyn o créf ha calys,* there also broke the stones (that) were strong and hard. M.C. 209. Written also *crŷf,* qd. v. In the Cornish Vocabulary, it is written *crŷf,* and by Llwyd, *crev,* qd. v. W. *crŷv, crŷ,* m. *crêv, crê,* f. Arm. *cre, cren.* Ir. *crodha.* Gael. *crodha.* Manx, *crevidey.* Sansc. *krudh,* to be in a passion.

CREFNYE, adj. Greedy, grasping. In construction it changes into *grefnye,* qd. v. W. *crafnin.*

CREFT, s. f. An art, or craft. Cornish Vocabulary, *ars. Gonewgy ken agesouch why ny's ty, râg sotel ouch yn pûp créft,* workmen others than ye shall not cover it, for subtle-ye are in every art. O.M. 2491. W. *crêft.* From the English.

CREFTOR, s. m. An artificer, craftsman. Cornish Vocabulary, *artifex.* W. *creftwr.*

CREG, adj. Hanging. ‡*Ma agen ost nei destries nahuer, ha nei dôl crég ragta,* our host was murdered last night, and we must needs be hanged for it. Llwyd, 252. W. *crôg.*

CREGY, v. a. To hang, suspend, to be hanging, to be hanged. Part. pass. *cregys. Gwytheuch why y, ma na*

CREIA 71 CRESY

vôns remuvys dhe gen tyller, war beyn tenné ha cregy, watch ye them, that they be not removed to another place, on pain of drawing and hanging. O.M. 2046. *My a'n bŷdh râk ow wage ha ty a grêk,* I will have it for my wage, and thou shalt be hanged. P.C. 1188. *Me a lever dheuch, gwell yw cregy Baraban, ha dyllyfré an profos,* I tell you, it is better to hang Barabbas, and liberate the prophet. P.C. 2366. *Oll an dus-ma a lever, dhe vôs cregis te yw gyw,* all these men say to be hanged thou art deserving. M.C. 129. *Ha'n Edhewon a grogas lader dhe Christ a barth cledh, hag a dhychow lader brâs cregy a russons yn wedh,* and the Jews hanged a thief to Christ on the left side, and on the right a great thief they did hang. M.C. 186. *Rag genen cregis neb ês, dên glân yw a bêch, ynno ef dyfout nyng-es, agan cregy ny yw mall,* for with us he that is hanged, is a man clear of sin, our hanging is not wrong, there is no fault in him. M.C. 192. *Cregy* is the same word as *crogy*, qd. v., which was generally used in the preterite tense, as *crogas, a grogas*.

CREGY, v. a. To believe. *An gwyryonedh kyn clewyth, awos tra vŷth ny'n cregyth; marth yw henna,* though thou hearest the truth, for any thing thou dost not believe it, that is a wonder. R.D. 1385. *Ef a provas lower gow dheis, ha genas ymons cregys,* he told thee abundant lies, and by thee they are believed. C.W. 60. *Ny allaf cregy henna,* I cannot believe that. C.W. 116. *Râg henna dheth cregy me ny vannaf moy es ky,* therefore I will not believe thee more than a dog. C.W. 173. This word is a corruption of *cresy*, qd. v., the *g* being sounded soft, as *j* in English.

CREGYANS, s. m. Belief, faith, creed. *An deppro gans cregyans da, gober têk ef a'n gevyth,* that eateth with good faith, he shall receive a fair reward. M.C. 44. *Rág y dhe vynnas gordhyé fals duwow erbyn cregyans,* for they worshipped false gods against belief. O.M. 1832. ‡*Mar tregow why yn gregyans-na, moreth why a's bŷdh ragdha,* if ye abide in that faith, sorrow ye shall have for it. C.W. 14. *Cregyans an Canason Christ,* the Creed of Christ's Apostles. *Pryce's Vocabulary.* Derived from *cregy*, to believe, the *g* being sounded soft, as *j* in English.

CREHAN, s. m. A skin. ‡*Sgelli grehan*, a bat, lit. leather wing. *Llwyd*, 173. This is a late corruption of *crohen*, qd. v.

CREHEN, s. m. Skins. The plural of *crohen*, qd. v.

CREHYLLY, v. a. To crush, squeeze, rattle, shatter. *Ena hy a ve gesys dhe godha mar ankyusy, dhe Christ may fé crehyllys oll y gorf ha'y esely,* there it was left to fall so grievously, that to Christ were shattered all his body and limbs. M.C. 184. *Marthys ycyn yw an gwyns, ma 'thew crehyllys ow dŷns,* wondrous cold is the wind, that my teeth are chattering. P.C. 1218. *Hemma yw iag an pla; y gorf yw crehyllys da ganso,* this is a cure of the plague; his body is shattered well by it. P.C. 2818.

CREI, s. m. A call, a cry. ‡*Ha an dzhyi a dalladhas dha uil krei; ha genz an krei a ryg an vartshants guêl, Dzhuan a greiaz avet, leddarn, leddarn,* and they began to cry; and with the cry that the merchants made, John cried out too, thieves, thieves! *Llwyd*, 252. This is the latest orthography of *cry*, or *cri*, qd. v.

CREIA, v. a. To call, cry, name. Pret. and pt. pass. *creies.*

‡*En termen ez passiez tera trigas en St. Levan, dên ha bennen en teller creiez Tshei an hur,* in time past there were dwelling in St. Levan, a man and woman in a place called Chy an hur, (the Ram's house.) *Llwyd*, 252. The late form of *cria*, qd. v.

CREIS, s. m. A shirt, a smock. Cornish Vocabulary, *camisia*. It is written by Llwyd, 45, *crŷs*. W. *crŷs.* Arm. *crês.*

CREN, adj. Round, circular. *Llwyd*, 141. W. *crwn*, †*cron*, m. *cron*, f. Arm. *crenn*. Ir. *cruin*, †*cruind*, †*crund*. Gael. *cruin*. Manx, *cruin*. Sansc. *krunch*, curved.

CRENNE, v. n. To tremble, quake. *Serpount yw hy, euth hy gwelas, own a'm bus vy, crenné a wraf,* it is a serpent, horrid to see it, I am afraid, I do tremble. O.M. 1453. *Yma an dôr ow crenné, sevel un vŷth ny yllyn,* the earth is trembling, I am not able to stand once. P.C. 2995. *Lemmyn worth agan gelwel, rak own desefsen merwel me a crennus,* now calling for us, from fear I would have desired to die, I trembled. R.D. 1712. *Hag ef râg own ow crenné,* and he for fear trembling. M.C. 53. *Tresse gwŷth hag ef yn cren' y pesys Du,* the third time he trembling prayed to God. M.C. 57. W. *crynnu*. Arm. *crena*. Ir. *croithnuigh*. Gael. *croithnaich*. Manx, *creanagh*. Sansc. *hri*, to be moved, or troubled. Gr. κηριόω. Lat. *horreo*.

CRES, s. f. Belief, faith. *A Judé, gâs dhe grês, y golon squyrdys a lês me a welas,* O Judah, leave thou thy belief; his heart torn in pieces I saw. R.D. 1031. Llwyd, 230, writes it *krez*. See the older form *créd*.

CRES, s. m. The middle, the centre, the midst, the heart. *Yn crês an chy rês vye cafus gyst crêf, na vo gwan,* in the midst of the house, it would be necessary to have a strong beam, that it be not weak. O.M. 2481. *Me a'n kelm yn crês an wast may pysso ef gefyens war pen y dhewlyn,* I will bind him in the middle of the waist, that he may pray for pardon on his knees. P.C. 1889. *Yth egen yn crês Almayn, orth un prys-ly, yn pûr wŷr, pan fûf gylwys,* I was in the middle of Germany, at a breakfast meal, when I was called. R.D. 2148. *Bês cres*, the middle finger. *Llwyd*, 172. Written also *creys*, qd. v. W. *craidh, crai*. Arm. *creiz*. Ir. *crioidhe*, †*cride*. Gael. *cridhe*. Manx, *cree*. Gr. κέαρ, καρδία. Lat. *cor*. Sansc. *hard*, from *hri*, to be moved. Goth. *hairto*. Lith. *ssirdis*. Aug. Sax. *heort*. Eng. *heart*. Germ. *herz*. Du. *hart*. Sw. *hierta*. Dan. *hierte*.

CRES, s. m. Peace, tranquillity, quiet. *Ny vynnyth dhe pobel Dew gasé crês dhyn yn neyi tu, awos tryya yn powma,* thou wilt not to the people of God allow peace to us on any side, for to dwell in this land. O.M. 1598. *Aban yw mychtern Faro budhys, ha'y ost oll ganso, ny a'm bŷdh crês dhe wewé,* since king Pharaoh is drowned, and all his host with him, we shall have peace to live. O.M. 1714. *Crês Dew aberth yn chymma,* the peace of God within this house! P.C. 667. *Crês Dew aberth yn annedh,* the peace of God be in the house! P.C. 705. *Crês oll dhynhy why,* peace to you all. R.D. 1361.

CRESY, v. a. To believe; to have faith in. 2 pérs. s. imp., and 3 pers. s. f. *crês, crŷs a grŷs,* or *creys, a greys*. *Dhysso ny vrnnaf cresy, na dheth fykyl lavarow,* I will not believe thee, nor thy vain words. O.M. 233. *An sarf re rûk ow thollé, dh'y falsury y cresys, pythweth re rûg ow syndyé,* the serpent did deceive me, her falsehood I believed, ever she hath injured me. O.M. 268. *Vyth ny'n cresons ef neffre,* they will never believe it. O.M. 1440. *Mar vynnyth cresy, nag ûs Dew lemyn onan, a gotho ynno cresy,* if thou wilt believe that there is not a God but one, in whom it is incumbent to believe. O.M. 1765. *Hag yn ur-na martesen, dhe'th lavarow y cresen, hag a'th carvyth bynary,* and in that hour perhaps, I might believe thy words, and love thee for ever. P.C. 2871. *My Cryst dhe sevel a'n bedh, cresseuch yn ta; râk kemmys a'n crys, hag a vo lêl vygydhys, sylwel a wraf,* that I Christ have risen from the grave, believe ye well; for as many as believe it, and shall be faithfully baptized, I will save. R.D. 1141. *Saiw bytygyns cresouch whỹ an corf-na dhe dhasserchy kyns yw ancth,* but nevertheless believe ye, that body to rise again before it is night. R.D. 1300. *Ha kekemmys na'n cresso goef termyn a dheffo devones a brys benen,* and whoever will not believe it, unhappy the time that he came nurtured from the womb of woman. R.D. 1348. *My ny gresaf dheso whâth,* I will not believe thee yet. C.W. 172. *Marya, me a grys, pur ylwys, an gweresas,* Mary, I believe, being called helped him. M.C. 230. *Hag a výdh dhynny neffré, mar a cresyn, ha bôs vâs,* and will be to us ever, if we will believe and be good. M.C. 258. ‡ *Crês dhebm,* believe me. *Rág fraga na gresyth dhym lavarow,* why dost thou not believe my words. Llwyd, 242. Though this is the more general form in the Ordinalia, it is later than *credy,* qd. v., by the corruption of the *d*; the *s* was again corrupted into *g,* whence *cregy,* and *crygy,* qd. v.

CREV, adj. Strong, mighty, hardy. Llwyd, 61, gives as the late form *krêv.* In the Ordinalia it is always written *crêf,* qd. v.

CREVAN, s. f. A crust; the scab of a sore. Llwyd, 52. W. *crawen, craven.* Arm. *creűen, creűn.* Ir. *carra, carruidhe.* Gael. *carr, criomhan.* Manx, *cron.*

CREVDER, s. m. Strength, vigour, power, security; a stay or ground. Llwyd, 60, 141, 240. *Rág gans te yw michterneth, an crêvder, há'n worryans, rág bisqueth ha bisqueth,* for thine is the kingdom, the power, and the glory, for ever and ever. Pryce's *Vocabulary.* ‡ *Gwra, O mateyrn, an tacklow ma gen an gwella crêvder el bôs predyrys an marthugyon a go termyn, ha'n tacklow a ven gwaynia clôs dhees rág nevra,* do, O King, these things which with the best strength may be thought the wonders of their time, and the things will gain glory to thee, for ever. *ibid.* W. *cryuder.* Arm. *crevder.*

CREYS, s. m. Strength, vigour, force, vehemency. *Cowethé, hedheuch kynys, ha me a whýth gans mûr greys, may tewê an tân wharré,* comrades, reach ye fuel, and I will blow with much force, that the fire may kindle soon. P.C. 1220. *Drou' e dhymmo dhe tackyé a uch y pen gans mûr greys,* bring it to me to fasten above his head with much strength. P.C. 2808. W. *craid.*

CREYS, s. m. The middle, centre; the midst, the heart. *Ow gwarrak a vŷdh setlyys yn ban yn creys an ebren,* my bow shall be set up in the midst of the sky. O.M. 1245. *Dhe wûl fôs a vyyn bryntyn, yn creys an drê,* to make a wall of noble stones, in the centre of the town. O.M. 2282. Another form of *crês,* qd. v.

CREYS, s. m. Peace, tranquillity, quiet. *Tru! y disky aban reys, alemma rág ny'm bŷdh creys, gon dhe wyr lour,* alas! since it is necessary to take it off, henceforth there will be no peace for me; I know true enough. R.D. 1860. Another form of *cres,* qd. v.

CREYS, v. a. Believe thou, he will believe. 2 pers. s. imp., and 3 pers. s. fut. of *cresy,* qd. v. *Nyns-us dên orth ow servyé, lên ha gwyryon, me a greys,* there is not a man serving me, trusty and true, I believe. O.M. 930. *Mar kỹf tŷr sŷch, me a greys, dynny ny dhewhel arté,* if it shall find dry ground, I believe, that it will return to us again. O.M. 1131. *Nep na grys ny fŷdh sylwys, na gans Dew ny vŷdh tryggys, ha râk henna, me a'th pỹs, creys a termyn,* whoever believes not shall not be saved, nor with God shall he dwell, and therefore I pray thee, believe in time. R.D. 1112. Written also *crês,* and *crŷs.*

CRI, s. m. A call, cry, clamour, noise. *Orth Pylat oll y setsans, ha warnodho a rûg cry,* on Pilate all pressed, and on him made a cry. M.C. 117. *War ty ha'y vam a'n pewo, y ben a vynnas synsy, hay enef êth anodho, gans garm eyn, hag uchel gry,* on the side his mother was, his head he would hold, and his soul went from him with cold cry and loud noise. M.C. 207. *Ha'n enef del dascorsé ertyn noter gans un cry,* and his soul how he yielded it against nature with a cry. M.C. 208. *A pur harloth, ple fûch why, pûr uth o clewas an cry genef orth agas gylwel,* O very rascals, where have you been, very horrid it was to hear the cry by me in calling you. R.D. 2244. W. *cri.* Arm. *cri.* Sansc. *kûr,* to resound.

CRIA, v. a. To call, cry, cry out. ‡ *Ha Dew a grias an golow dydh, ha an tewlder ev a grias nôs, ha gurihùher ha metten o an kensa jorna,* and God called the light day, and the darkness he called night, and the evening and the morning were the first day. M.C. p. 93. Llwyd gives also as modern forms, *kriha,* to call, 43, and *crio,* to cry or weep, 75. But in the Ordinalia it is generally written *cryé,* qd. v. W. *crio.* Arm. *cria.*

CRIB, s. f. A comb; a ridge, the crest or summit of any thing. Llwyd, 115. *Crîb an tŷ,* the ridge of the house, 53. (W. *crib y ty.*) "Hence the rocks called *Crebs* in many places, for that they appear like the comb of a cock at low water." Pryce. W. *crib,* † *crip.* Arm. *crib.* Ir. *cior,* † *cir.* Gael. *cior.* Manx, *kere.*

CRIBA, v. a. To comb. *Dho criba an pen,* to comb the head. Llwyd, 49. The infinitive was also written *cribas.* ‡ *Dho cribas.* Llwyd, 119. W. *cribaw.* Arm. *criba.*

CRIBAN, s. f. A comb; a crest, a tuft or plume. *Criban kuliog,* a cock's comb. Llwyd, 13. *Criban mêl,* a honey comb, 59. A bird's crest. 240. W. *crib, urbell,* a bird's comb, or crest; *crib y gwenyn,* honey comb. Arm. *cribell, criben.*

CRIBIA, v. a. To card wool. Llwyd, 245.

CRIF, adj. Strong. Cornish Vocabulary, *fortis.* See *Cref.*

CRISTYON, s. m. A Christian. Pl. *Cristenyon, Crustonnion, Crystunyon. Dyswedhouch bôs pryns wmper, râk dyswyl an Cristenyon,* shew yourself to be a prince without equal to destroy the Christians. P.C. 979. *Ragon y fynnes merwel ha môs yn bedh, ha sevel, râk dry pûp Crystyon dhe'n nef* for us he would die, and go to the tomb, and rise, to bring every Christian to heaven. P.C. 970. *Me a gesul bôs ganse prennys da gwon yn nép le, rág an cladhva Crystunyon,* I advise that there be with them bought a good field in some place, for the burial place of Christians. P.C. 1545. *Na'n ladavo an Crysten-*

you, gwytheuch war pcyn, that the Christians steal him not, guard ye under penalty. R.D. 365. W. *Cristion,* pl. *Cristianogion.* Arm. *Cristen,* pl. *Cristenien.*

CRIV, adj. Rude, raw, green or newly made, unripe. *Llwyd,* 52. W. *cri.* Arm. *criz.* Lat. *crudus.*

CROADUR, s. m. A creature. Cornish Vocabulary, *creatura.* See *Creater.*

CROBMAN, s. m. A reaping-hook. *Llwyd,* 9. A late corruption of *Cromman,* qd. v.

CROC, s. f. A hanging, a suspension. *A vyl gadlyng, dues yn rág, wor tywedh woheth a'th tág,* O vile vagabond, come forth, at last hanging will choak thee yet. P.C. 1818. *A vyl losel, re'th fo crók,* O vile rogue, hanging be to thee. P.C. 2097. *Gwyna vyes dhe gafus crók,* thou wert deserving to get a hanging. P.C. 2683. *Yn beys awos godhaf crók, ny brefiys anken na drok,* notwithstanding suffering hanging in the world, thou hast not felt grief nor evil. R.D. 277. W. *crôg.* Arm. *croug.* Ir. *croch.* Gael. *croich.* Manx, *criy.* Lat. *cruce.*

CROC, adj. Hanging, suspended, overhanging. *Powes lemmyn, losel wûs, ka knouk an hórn tys ha tas, mar ny wréth,-ty a fydh crók,* stop now, idle fellow, and strike the iron tick-a-tack, if thou dost not, thou shalt be hanged. P.C. 2720. W. *crôg.*

CROCCAN, s. f. A springe, or springle. *Pryce.* W. *croglath.*

CROCHEN, s. m. A skin. *Nyns-us warnedhé crochen, nag yw tróch ha dyruskys,* there is no skin upon them, that is not broken and peeled. P.C. 2686. *Y a wyth y vody na poré bys vynary kyns fe yn bédh mŷl vlydhen, na'y grochen unwŷth terry,* they will preserve his body that it do not ever decay, though it be in the grave a thousand years, nor shall his skin be once broken. P.C. 3202. *Heys oll ow crochen scorgyys,* all the length of my skin scourged. R.D. 2538. By the substitution of *h* for the guttural, the word became *crohen,* which again was softened into *croen.* This however was not a late form, as it is *croin* in the Cornish Vocabulary. W. *croen.* Arm. *crochen.* Ir. *croicion,* †*crocenn.* Gael. *croicionn.* Manx, *crackan.* Sansc. *kartis, ciran,* from *ciri,* to cut.

CRODAR, s. m. A sieve, a riddle. *Llwyd,* 52. This is a late form of *croider,* qd. v.

CRODDRE, v. a. To sift, riddle, winnow. *Bedhouch war colonow, rák Satnas yro yrvyrys, avel ys y'nothlennow dh' agas kroddré, me a grŷs,* be of cautious hearts, for Satan is desirous, like corn in winnowing sheets to sift you, I believe. P.C. 682. From *eroder,* a sieve.

CROEN, s. m. A skin. Cornish Vocabulary. *Croen luan,* a louse's skin. *Pryce.* See *Crochen.*

CROFFOLAS, s. m. Lamentation. *Del lwaraf vy dhywhy, ef a emblodh ragon ny; gesouch dhe wús croffolas,* as I say to you, he will fight for us; leave off lamentation. O.M. 1662.

CROG, s. f. A hanging. *Cróg ro'm bo, er an dhewen,* may hanging be to me, on the gills. O.M. 2651. This is the same word as *croc,* qd. v.

CROGEN, s. f. A shell. Cornish Vocabulary, *concha.* Pl. *cregyn.* In Cornish it also means the skull. *Me a's ten gans oll ow nerth, may 'th entré an spikys serth dre an cen yn y grogen,* I will pull it with all my strength, that the stiff spines may enter through the skin into his skull. P.C. 2141. *Asso mur tyn ow passyon, pan éth*

L

dreyn yn empynnyon, a púp parth dre an grogen, very sharp was my suffering, when the thorns went into the brain, on all parts through the skull. R.D. 2558. It is written by Llwyd, 240, *crogan.* W. *cragen,* provincially *crogan, crogen,* pl. *cregyn,* a shell. Arm. *crogen,* pl. *creg-'in,* a shell. *Crogen an penn,* the skull.

CROGI, v. a. To hang, to suspend, to be hanged. This is the same word as *cregy,* which is formed from *crôg,* by the regular mutation of *o* into *e.* The preterite is generally *crogas. Ha'n Edhewon a grogas lader dhe Christ a barth, cledh, hag a dhychow lader brás cregy a russons yn-wedh,* and the Jews hung a thief to Christ on the left side, and on the right a great thief they also did hang. M.C. 186. W. *crogi.* Arm. *cregi, crouga.* Ir. *croch.* Gael. *croch.* Manx, *croch.*

CROHEN, s. m. Pl. *crehen. A vyne gwarthé y ben war y gorf, bys yn y droys, squardiys oll o y grohen, hag ef cudh-ys yn y woys,* from the top of his head on his body to his feet, torn was all his skin, and he covered with his blood. M.C. 135. *Del y's brewaf yn dan gên, kekyfrys kýc ha crohen, del védh luen a bodredhes,* as I will strike her under the chin ; likewise flesh and skin, that it shall be full of sores. O.M. 2713. *Gans crehen an bestas-na me a wra dyllas dhyma, par del wrûg ow hendasow,* with the skins of those beasts, I will make clothes for me, so as my ancestors did. C.W. 108. Keigwyn and Llwyd write the word *crohan.* It is the same as *crochen,* qd. v.

CROIDER, s. m. A sieve, or riddle. Cornish Vocabulary, *cribrum* vel *cribellum.* Written by Llwyd, *crodar.* In Welsh a sieve is now *gogor,* but it formerly existed in the Old Welsh, †*cruitr,* pala, a winnowing shovel; quoted by Stokes, "Irish Glosses," 162. Arm. *crouzer, crouer, croer.* Ir. *criathar, creathar.* Gael. *criathair.* Manx, *creear.* The root is W. *crydu,* to shake ; *crŷd,* †*criot, crihot;* crydian, †*cretian,* a shaking. Arm. *cridien.* Ir. *crathadh.* Gael. *crathadh.* Manx, *craa.* Gr. κραδάω.

CROIN, s. m. The skin. Cornish Vocabulary, *pellis.* This is another form of *crochen,* qd. v.

CROINOG, s. m. A toad. Cornish Vocabulary, *rubeta.* Derived from *croin,* a skin. In the Ordinalia, it is written, *cronec,* qd. v.

CROIS, s. m. A cross. Cornish Vocabulary, *crux* vel *staurus.* In the Ordinalia the common form is *crows,* qd. v. W. *croes.* Arm. *croez.* Ir. *crois.* Gael. *crois.* Manx, *crosh.* Lat. *cruce.* Eng. *'rood.*

CROM, adj. Bending; bowed, or bent; crooked; convex ; rounded. *Dew tekka bren rag styllyow, ha compos y denweunoc, brás ha crom y ben goles,* lo, the fairest wood for rafters, and straight its sides, large and rounded its lower end. O.M. 2443. Llwyd, 53, gives *crum* as another form. W. *crwm,* m., *crom,* f. Arm. *crounim.* Ir. *crom, crum,* †*cruim.* Gael. *crom.* Manx, *croym.* Dan. *krum.* Flem. *krom.* Germ. *krumb.* Eng. *crump.*

CROMMAN, s. m. A reaping hook, a sickle. In Llwyd's time it was corrupted into *crobman.* From *crom,* crooked. W. *crymman,* †*ereman.* Ir. *cruman, corran.* Gael. *cromag.* Manx, *corran.*

CRON, s. m. A thong, a lash of skin. Pl. *cronow. Yn ur-na y a colmas y dhefrech fast gans cronow, en guys yn més may tardhas, del fastsens an colmenow,* in that hour they bound his arms fast with thongs, that the blood burst ones so they fastened the knots. M.C. 76. *In scorgiys par'mer esé yn dewlé an dew Edhow, hag yn fast* *kelmys dhedhé, kerdyn gwethyn yn mesk cronow*, in the scourges of rods that were in the hands of the two Jews, and fast bound to them, cords weaved among thongs. M.C. 131. *Crôn* is a contracted form of *croen*, qd. v.

CRONCYE, v. a. To beat, strike, knock, thump, bang. *Hag yn fast kelmys dhedhé kerdyn gwethyn yn mesk cronow may fôns hyblyth dhe gronkye*, and fast bound to them cords woven among thongs, that they might be pliant to beat. M.C. 131. *Ha'n Edhewon bys pan vôns squyth war Christ y fôns ow cronkyé*, and the Jews until they were weary on Christ were beating. M.C. 132. *An keth gwâs-na gans skorgys ha whyppys da gwrêch y cronkyé, tor ha keyn*, this same fellow with scourges and good whips, do ye smite him, belly and back. P.C. 2057.

CRONEC, s. m. A frog. *Cronec du*, a toad, lit. a black frog. *Och, tru, tru, shyndyys of gans cronek du, ha whetlys gans y venym*, Oh, sad, sad, I am hurt by a toad, and blowu by his venom. O.M. 1778. *Saw kyn fens y mortholek, dhe wêth vydhons dhe'n cronek, ha garow yn y dhulé*, but though they be hammered, they shall be for worse to the toad, and rough in his hands. P.C. 2732. *An joul ynno redrecsé, may 'tho gwêth agis cronek*, the devil in him dwelt, that he was worse than a toad. M.C. 47. This is another form of *croinoc*, qd. v. This word is peculiar to Cornish. A frog in Welsh is *llyffant*, and a toad, *llyffant du*, being derived by Llwyd from the Latin *lymphatica*.

CRONNY, v. n. To stagnate; to collect together. *An sêth yw rag leverys a's gwykis tyn, gans mear angus, war y holon, may cronnys, dre nerth an bum, fynten woys*, the arrow, is before spoken, struck her sharply with much anguish, on her heart so that stagnated, by force of the blow, a fountain of blood. M.C. 224. W. *cronni*. Arm. *creuenna*. The root is W. *crawn*, a collection. Arm. *creûn*.

CROPPYE, v. n. To enter into; to penetrate. *An arlont y dhe denné war y benn gan kymmys nell, ma têth an dreyn ha croppyé dhe'n empynyon dre an tell*, the garland they drew on his head with so much strength, that the thorns went and penetrated to the brains through the holes. M.C. 134. As there is no synonym in the other dialects, it is probably a borrowed word from the English *grope*.

CROTHAC, adj. Frothy, trifling. ‡*Taw, dhe'th cregy, hemma yw gwell defry, te fool crothak*, be silent, be hanged to thee, this is better truly, thou frothy fool. C.W. 80. W. *crothawg*, swelling out.

CROTHVAL, s. m. A complaint. *Na allons caffus cheson dhe wruthyl crothval na son warnas, a das veneges*, let them not be able to find cause to make a complaint, nor a sound against thee, O blessed Father. O.M. 1837.

CROW, s. m. Gore, blood, death. *Dhom kemeres, dhom syndyé, dhom peynyé bys yn crow*, to take me, to hurt me, to torture me even to death. M.C. 74. *Hag a râg guris colmennow, gans pûb colmen may'th ellé, pan wyekens, yn mês an crow*, and forward were made knots, with every knot that might come, when they struck, out the blood. M.C. 131. W. *crau*. Ir. †*cro*. Gael. †*cru*. Slav. *krovje*. Pol. Bohem. *krew*. Lat. *cruor*. Sansc. *kravya*, flesh.

CROW, s. m. A hovel, hut, sty. *Crow môh*, a pigsty. *Idwnd*, 158. At the present day in Cornwall a pigsty is called a pig's crow. W. *craw*. Arm. *craou*. Ir. *cro*. Gael. *cro*. Manx, *croe*.

CROWD, s. m. A fiddle, or violin. *Whethouch menstrels, ha tabours, trey-hans harpes ha trompours, cythol, crowd, fylh, a sautry*, blow ye minstrels, and tabours; three hundred harps and trumpets; dulcimer, fiddle, viol, and psaltery. O.M. 1997. A fiddle is still called a *crowd* in Cornwall. W. *cruith*, †*crot*. Gael. *cruit*. Lat. *chrotta, Britanna*, in Venant. Fortun. The Ancient British *crwth* differed from the modern fiddle, inasmuch as it had six strings. A specimen is of very rare occurrence at the present day, and to be found only in the collection of the curious, but a beautiful engraving of it is given in Jones's "Welsh Bards."

CROWDER, s. m. A fiddler. W. *crythor*.

CROWEDHE, v. n. To lie down. *Dall, na bodhar, ny asé, nag omlanas nag onan, na clâf vŷth ow crowedhé, mar pesy a leun golon*, blind, nor deaf, he left not, uncured, not one, nor any sick lying down, if he prayed with a full heart. M.C. 25. *Otté ve ow crowedhé, my re urûg y vusuré rag an kêth wheit-ma dewyth*, behold it lying down, I have measured it for this same work twice. O.M. 2567. A regular mutation after *ow* of *growedhé*, qd. v.

CROWS, s. f. A cross. *May fo rŷs, un deydh a due, guthyl crows annedhé y*, that it is necessary, a day will come, to make a cross out of them. O.M. 1952. *Gorr e dhe'n mernans, gorr e yn pren crows a dhysempys*, put him to death, put him on the cross tree forthwith. P.C. 2162. *Kynyr y, ty plos lorden, syns war dhe geyn an grows pren*, take it thou dirty lurdane, hold the cross tree on thy back. P.C. 2586. *En grows whêth nynj o parys, na'n Edhewon ny wodhyé an prennyer py fêns keffis dhe wuthyll crows anedhé*, the cross yet was not ready, and the Jews knew not the timbers where they should be found, to make a cross out of them. M.C. 151. The older form was *crois*, qd. v.

CROWSE, v. a. To crucify. Written also *crowsyé*. Part. pass. *crowsys*. *Hag anedhé crows y wrêr, râg crowsé Cryst, ow mâp kêr*, and of them a cross shall be made, to crucify Christ, my dear son. O.M. 1936. *Ottensé, kemereuch e, ha crowsyouch ef, a ver spys*, behold him, take ye him and crucify him, in a short time. P.C. 2166. *Gallos a'm bues dhe'th crowsyé, ha gullos dhe'th tyllyfré, an ngl a vynnaf yn beys*, I have power to crucify thee, and power to deliver thee, which ever of the two I please in the world. P.C. 2186. *Ytho why a vyn porrys bôs agas mychtern crowsys*, then ye wish absolutely your king to be crucified. P.C. 2360. *Ytho dre pûp reson da, ny gôth dhodho bôs crowsys*, theu, by reason good, it does not behove him to be crucified. P.C. 2390. *Syr justis, dyllyrf dhynny Baraban, ha crows Jhesu*, Sir Magistrate, deliver to us Barabbas, and crucify thou Jesus. P.C. 2486. Derived from *crows*, a cross. The corresponding word in Welsh is *croesi*, to cross, to put cross-wise, to make the mark of a cross; to tbwart: but not to crucify, which is admirably rendered by *croeshoelio*, compounded of *croes*, a cross, and *hoelio*, to nail. Arm. *croaza*, to cross.

CROWST, s. m. A luncheon. *Wosé cows ha lafuryé an vaner a vye da, kemeres crowst, hag evé, ha powes wosé henna*, after talk and labouring, the custom would be good, to take food and drink, and rest after that. O.M. 1901. Written by Llwyd, 89, *crûst*. Probably from the English, a *crust*, or Lat. *crusta*, which seems to be connected with W. *crest*, a crust, from *crês*, hardened by heat.

CRUC, s. m. A hillock, a mound, a barrow. Corn. Voc. *collis*. *Gwrytench oll er agas fÿdh, gobur dn why agas bŷdh, gôn Dansotha, ha cruk heyth*, all take care on your faith, a good reward ye shall have, the plain of Dansotha, and Barrow Heath. R.D. 377. It is preserved in the names of many places. See *Crecg*. Llwyd, 94, writes it *crŷc*. W. *crug*, †*cruc*. Arm. *crèch*, *crugel*. Ir. *crunch*. Gael. *cruach*. Manx, *creagh*.

CRUGE, v. a To do, or make. *Mester genouch ym gylwyr-hag arluth, hennu yw gwŷr, ytho mar krugé golhy agas treys, hag a seché, golhens pùp treys y gylê ahanouch, kepar ha my*, master by you I am called and Lord, that is true ; now if I wash your feet, and dry them, let all wash the feet of each other of you, like as I. P.C. 875. A mutation of *gruge*, qd. v.

CRUM, adj. Crooked, bent, curved. *Llwyd*, 53. Another form of *crom*, qd. v.

CRUPPYA, v. n. To creep. ‡*Ha te privf a wra cruppya, ha slrynkya war doar a heys; ynter y hays hy ha tec, me a wra envy neffra*, and thou worm, shalt creep, and slide on the ground along ; between her seed and thine I will put envy for ever. C.W. 66. ‡*Me a vyn dallath cruppya, ha slynkya war doer a heys*, I will begin to creep, and slide upon the ground along. C.W. 68. W. *crepian, cropian*.

CRUST, s. m. A luncheon. *Llwyd*, 80. The same as *crowst*, qd. v.

CRUSTE, v. a. Thou didst make. *Lavar dhym, awos travyth, mara crusté leverel ken fe an temple dyswrŷs, kyn pen try dŷdh y wrussys gwell ys kyns y dhrehevel*, tell me above any thing, if thou didst say, though the temple should be destroyed, before the end of three days thou wouldst raise it better than before. P.C. 1758. A mutation of *grusté*, componnded of *grust*, the 2 pers. pret. of *gwrey*, and *te*, thou.

CRY, s. m. A call, a cry. This is the orthography in the Ordinalia of *cri*, qd. v.

CRYE, v. a. To call, cry, to cry out. *Ow popel vy grevyys brâs, gans Pharow yw mylyges, ymons dhymo ow cryê, râg an lafur us dhedhê*, my people greatly aggrieved by Pharaoh, (that) is accursed, are to me crying, for the labour that is upon them. O.M. 1418. *Rak nans yw Pilat serrys, ow cryé kepar ha ky*, for now is Pilate angered, crying out like a dog. P.C. 2242. *Cryeuch fust gans mûr a grys*, cry ye aloud with much vehemence. P.C. 2477. *Me a grycs warnodho, rûk paynys pan nan gffo tyller dh'y pen*, I cried unto him, for pains when he found not a place for his head. R.D. 268. *Me re bue pechadores, a pechas marthys yn frâs, war Ihesu me a cryas ow trespes dhymmo gafê*, I have been a sinner (that) hath sinned wondrous much, on Jesus I cried, that he would forgive me my trespass. R.D. 1090. Written also *crya*, and *cria*, qd. v.

CRYF, adj. Strong, mighty, vigorous. *Judas êth a dhesympys a neyl tu dhe omgregy, cafas daffar pûr parrys, Iowan cryff râg y synsy*, Judas went immediately on the one side to hang himself, he found convenience very ready, a strong rope to hold him. M.C. 105. This is the same as *crêf*, qd. v.

CRYGY, v. a. To believe, to have faith in. *Kyn leverryf gwŷr, dên fŷth ahanouch wy vyn crygy*, though I speak truly, not any man of you will believe. P.C. 1482. *Mars ogé mâp Dew a râs, dyswé dhym nêp meystry brâs, may hyllyn dyso crygy*, if thou art the son of the God of grace, shew me some great power, that we may in thee believe. P.C. 1771. *Neffré of dhe dhasserchy, me ny vynnaf y grygy, bew hedré vên*, that be ever rose again, I will not believe it, as long as I may be alive. R.D. 1047. *Yma marth dhym ahanas, bôs dhe golon mar cales na'n crygyth ef*, there is to me wonder of thee, that thy heart is so hard, that thou wilt not believe. R.D. 1088. This is another form of *crysy*, qd. v., *g* soft, sounded as *j* in English, being a corruption of *s*.

CRYGYANS, s. m. Belief, faith, credence. *Me re'n cusullyes mĝl wÿth, saw ny vyn, awos travyth, gagé y tebel crygyans*, I have advised him a thousand times, but he will not, for any thing, leave his evil belief. P.C. 1813. *Dh'agas fastyé yn crygyans, dheuch confort a Spyrys Sans a dhanfonaf*, to strengthen you in belief, to you the comfort of the Holy Ghost I will send. R.D. 1174. *Y grygyans pûp oll gwythes, puppenag ol a wharfo*, his belief let every one keep, whatever may happen. R.D. 1537.

CRYHIAS, v. n. To neigh like a horse. ‡*Cryhiaz*, a *cryhiaz*, neighing. *Llwyd*, 245, 248. W. *gweryru*, †*guirgiriam*, I neigh. Oxf. Gloss. Arm. *gourisial*.

CRYLLIAS, adj. Curled. *Llwyd*, 52. From the old English *crull*. "With locks crull." Chaucer.

CRYS, s. m. A shirt, a shift, chemise. *Llwyd*, 45. Written in Cornish Vocabulary, *creis*. W. *crŷs*. Arm. *crés*.

CRYS, s. m. The middle, the centre, the midst, or heart of any thing. *Gwetyeuch bones avorow, ow conys yn crŷs an drê, war beyn cregy ha tennê*, take care to be to-morrow, working in the middle of the town, on pain of hanging and drawing. O.M. 2300. *Ny a'n tréch del levereth, hen yw an crŷs, dre pûp mark oll yn bys-ma*, we will cut it as thon sayest, this is the middle, by every mark in this world. O.M. 2534. Written also *crês*, and *creys*, qd. v.

CRYS, v. a. He will believe. 3 pers. s. fnt. and 2 pers. s. imp. of *crysy*, qd. v. *Me a vôr gwŷr, crys yn crŷs, y vôs yn ban dasserchys yn gedh hydhew*, I know truly, and I believe it, that he is risen up in this day. R.D. 727. *Ihesu Cryst dhe dhasserchy, un deydh ûs ow tôs, goy kemmys na'n crŷs*, that Jesus Christ is risen again, a day is coming, miserable as many as believe it not. R.D. 1188. *My a grŷs yn pyrfet aga vôs gwcel a vûr râs*, I will believe perfectly that they are rods of great grace. O.M. 2011. *Cot yw dhe dhydhyow dhe gy, nahen na grŷs*, short are thy days, think not otherwise. R.D. 2038.

CRYS, v. a. To shake, to quake. *An houl ny golsé y lyw, awon mâp dên dhe verwel, na corf dasserhy dhe vew, na dôr grŷs, yn tyougel*, the sun would not have lost its colour, because of a son of man to die, nor a body rise again to life, nor the earth quake, really. P.C. 3086. W. *crydu, cryd, crydian*. Arm. *cridien*. Ir. *crith*. Gael. *crith*. Manx, *craa*.

CRYSSAT, s. m. A hawk, a kestrel. *Llwyd*, 41.

CRYSY, v. a. To believe, to have faith in. *Arluth ny vynnous crysy*, Lord, they will not believe. O.M. 1435. *Reys yw dhŷs ynno crysy*, need it is for thee to believe in him. O.M. 1508. *Mar a gureva yn della, crysy dhodho ny a wra, y vos profus lymyges*, if he will do so, we will believe in him, that he is a blessed prophet. P.C.

2883. *Crŷs dhym, kyn ôf tôs*, believe thou me, though I am gray. R.D. 965. This is the same word as *cresy*, qd. v.

CRYWEDHE, s. f. A bed. *Llwyd*, 77. A corruption of *growedhé*, from *gorwedhé*, to lie down. W. *gorwedhva*.

CUAS, s. f. A shower. *Llwyd*, 28. This is the same word as *cowes*, qd. v.

CUBMA, s. n. To fall, to fall down, to be slain. *Llwyd*, 104. Though this example is a corruption, it shows the existence of a purer form, *cumma*. W. *cwympo*.

CUDIN, s. m. Hair, a lock of hair. Corn. Voc. coma. Pl. *cudinow; kydynow*. Llwyd, 49. W. *cudyn*. Arm. *cuden*. Ir. *ciabh*. Gael. *ciabh, cas*. Manx, *kiog, casag*. Sansc. *kacha*.

CUDON, s. f. A wood-pigeon. Cornish Vocabulary, *palumba*. W. *cudhan*, from *cûdh*, a covert. Arm. *cudon*. Ir. †*ciadcholum*. Gael. *caidhean*.

CUDHE, v. a. To hide, or conceal; to cover. *Bedhens ebron dreys pûp tra, rak cudhé mŷns ûs formyys*, let there be a sky above every thing, to cover all that is created. O.M. 22. *Agan corfono nôth gallas, gans deyl agan cudhé gwrén*, our bodies are become naked, with leaves let us cover ourselves. O.M. 254. *Kepar del fuvé dremmas, yn dôr my a vyn palas tol, may fo ynno cudhys*, like as he was a just man, in the earth I will dig a hole, that ho may be covered in it. O.M. 866. *Agan gorhyl a wartha, gans glaw ef a vydh cudhys*, our ark, from above, with rain it will be covered. O.M. 1064. *Mûr yu ow fyenasow, ythof cudhys*, great are my anxieties, I am overwhelmed. R.D. 2032. *Han y, worth y dormontyé, y cudhens y ben gans gueth*, and they when tormenting him, covered his head with a cloth. M.C. 97. *Râg lŷf brâs my a dhoro, a gudho oll an nôr beys*, for I will bring a great flood, that shall cover all the land of the world. O.M. 982. *Ha dew gwêth dothans gwra doen, dh'aga hudha pôb season, aga noatha na vo gwellys*, and two garments to them do thou bear, to cover them at all seasons, their nakedness that it be not seen. C.W. 70. Llwyd, 50, writes it *cidha*, which shews that the u had the same sound in Cornish as in Welsh. W. *cudhio*. Arm. *cuza*. Gael. *comhdaid*. Manx, *coodee*. Sansc. *kud*.

CUDHYGYC, adj. One that conceals himself, bashful, ashamed. *Me a ûl bôs cudhygyk, ow bones mar anfugyk dres pûp dén ol ûs yn beys*, I may be ashamed, being so wicked, beyond all men that are in the world. P.C. 1423. *Ty yw dyscrygyk pur wŷr, ha mûr anfusyk, ty a ûl bôs cudhygyk na grŷs y vôs dasserchys*, thou art unbelieving very truly, and very wicked; thou mayest be ashamed, that thou wilt not believe that he has risen. R.D. 1721. W. *cudhiedig*.

CUBF, adj. Dear, kindly. *In medh Christ an cueff calon, pûr wûjr te re leverys, te a wodhyé dhe honon ye dre gen re vês gwarnys*, says Christ, the kindly heart, very truly thou hast said; didst thou know it of thyself, or by some others wast thou warned? M.C. 101. Written also *cûf*, qd. v.

CUEIA, conj. If, although. *Llwyd*, 150.

CUEN, s. m. Dogs. *Lemmyn pocvan ha lesky, ow fleryé, ow mowsegy kepar ha kuen*, but disease and burning, smelling, stinking like dogs. R.D. 172. One of the plurals of *ci*, qd. v.

CUER, s. m. Hemp. Llwyd, 46, *cûer*. W. *cywarch*. Arm. *couarch*. Gael. *corcach*.

CUER, s. m. A court. *A' nef whel un tas mêr re'th ordené, ty ha'th wrêk, pan vy marow, yn y cuer*, of high heaven the great Father, may he ordain thee and thy wife, when ye die, into his court. P.C. 686. Written also *cûr*, qd. v.

CUER, s. m. Weather. ‡*Yein kuer, tarednow, ha golowas, er, reu, gwenz, ha clehé, ha kezer*, cold weather, thunder, and lightning, snow, frost, wind, and ice, nd hail. *Pryce*. Written also *cewar*, qd. v.

CUES, s. m. Blood. *Nans yw lemmyn tremenes, nêp dew cans a vledhynnow na'm buef dhe wruthyl genes, yn kŷk nag yn kues, hep wow*, now there are gone some two hundred years, that I have not had to do with thee, in flesh nor in blood, without falsehood. O.M. 659. *Es bŷdh deydh brues mûr a anfus, y kŷk ha'y kues, nêp a'n gwerthas*, he shall have on the day of judgment much harm, his flesh and his blood, who hath sold him. P.C. 2941. This word appears to be a modification of *Goys*, qd. v.

CUETH, s. m. Sorrow, grief. *Ellas dre cueth yn clamder, dhe'n dôr prâg na ymwhelaf*, alas! through grief, in a faint, to the ground why do I not cast myself? P.C. 2593. *A vâb dhe gueth ru'm ladhas*, Oh son, thy suffering hath killed me. P.C. 2008. *Kueth ûs y'm colon, eyhan, mars êth corf Dew y honan, pe le y fŷdh e ceffys*, sorrow is in my heart, alas! if the body of God himself is gone, where will it be found? R.D. 700. *A vynyn ryth, py le ytheth, rag cueth pygyyth, garmé a wrêth*, O woeful woman, where goest thou? for grief thou prayest, cry out thou dost. R.D. 852. Written also *cûth*, qd. v. †W. *chwith*. *Y mae yn chwith genyv weled*, I am sorry to see, is a common Welsh phrase.

CUF, adj. Dear, amiable, beloved, loving. Pl. *cufyon, cefyon*. *A dâs cûf g'th wolowys*, O dear Father in thy lights. O.M. 285. *A dâs cûf ker, my a vora, Arluth nêf roy dhym gûl da yn pûp ober a wrellyn*, O Father, dearly beloved, I will do, Lord of heaven, grant to me to do well in every work that I do. O.M. 443. *Arluth cûf, dhe archadow, y wruthyl rês ew dhymmo*, O dear Lord, thy injunctions, need is to me to do them. O.M. 997. *Ow Arluth ker cûf colon, pyw ytho a's hembronk dh'y*, my dear Lord of loving heart, who then will lead them to it. O.M. 1873. *Whêth, ow cufyon, dyfunouch, ha cês colon ol pesouch na gyllouch yn templacion*, again, my dear (companions) awake ye, and with one heart all pray, that ye enter not into temptation. P.C. 1075. *Ow cufyon leman coskeuch, hag ol warbarth powceseuch*, my dear (friends) now sleep ye, and rest altogether. P.C. 1093. W. *cu*. Arm. *cuff*. Ir. *caomh*, †*coim*. Gael. *caomh*.

CUGOL, s. m. A monk's hood, a cowl. Corn. Voc. *cucullus*. W. *cwcwll, cowyll*. Arm. *cougoul*. Ir. †*cocall*. Eng. cowl. From the Celtic the word passed into the Latin. "*Gallia Santonico vestit te bardo-cucullo, Circopithecorum penula nuper erat.*" *Martial*.

CUHUDHAS, s. m. A judgment. *Pryce*. W. *cyhudhed*.

CUHUDHE, v. a. To accuse; impeach; indict. *Cuhudhas* is another form. *Eva, ny allaf medhes, rag own ty dhom cuhudhé*, Eve, I cannot speak, for fear thou shouldst accuse me. O.M. 160. *Awos travyth ny wrussen venytha dhe guhudhas*, because of any thing I would not ever accuse thee. O.M. 164. *Dhe'n tyller Cryst re dethyé, ha'n Edhewon o dygnas, ythrsê an venyn gansé, parys êns dh'y huhudhas*, to the place came Christ, and the Jews (that) were opposed, the woman was with them; they were ready to accuse her. M.C. 33. *Pe ma, yn medh Christ dhydhy, nêb a vyn dhe guhudha,* where is, says Christ to her, he who will accuse thee. M.C. 34. *Múr a dús o cuntyllys er y byn dh'y guhudhas,* much people were gathered together against him to accuse him. M.C. 88. W. *cyhudho.* Ir. *casaoid,* an accusation; *casaoidim,* to accuse. Gael. *casaid; casaidich.* Manx, *casid, casseydach.*

CUHUDHUDIOC, s. m. An accuser. Corn. Vocab. *accusator.* It would have been more correct, as Zeuss has observed, 396, to have been written *cuhudhadioc,* from the substantive *cuhuthat,* the old form of *cuhudhas.* W. *cyhudhed.*

CUIC, adj. Blind of one eye. Corn. Voc. *luscus* vel *monoptalmus.* W. *coeg,* vain, empty; *coegdhall,* purblind. Lat. *cæcus,* blind.

CUILCEN, s. f. A frog. Written by Llwyd, *kwilken,* and in the Cornish Vocabulary, *gwilscin,* qd. v.

CUILLIOC, s. m. A soothsayer. Cor. Voc. *augur.* W. *coiliog,* from *coel,* an omen. "*Etncoilhaam* is an ancient Welsh Gloss on the word *aspicio,* quasi *avispicio,* where the writer obviously understood *etn,* to be *edn.*" Zeuss. 1079.

CUILLIOGES, s. f. A female diviner. Corn. Voc. *phitonissa.* Dr. Owen Pughe has wrongly introduced these two words into the Welsh Dictionary. His authority being only the Cornish Vocabulary, attached to a copy of the Liber Landavensis.

CUIT, s. m. A wood, or forest. Corn. Voc. *silva.* Another form of *coid,* qd. v.

CUITHA, v. a. To keep, to preserve. Llwyd, 53. *Dho cwitha.* A mutation of *gwythé,* qd. v.

CUITHIAS, s. m. A guardian. Llwyd, 240. A mutation of *gwythias,* qd. v. Pl. ‡*kuithizi.* Llwyd, 242.

CUL, v. a. To make, to do. *Yma ow cúl sacryfys, ha'y pobel ef kekeffrys, dhe'n kéth Dew-na, gans mŭr tros,* he is making a sacrifice, and his people likewise, to that same God, with a loud noise. O.M. 1556. *Euch tynneuch an gasadow, usy ow cúl fals dewow, yn mês agan temple ny,* go ye, drag the hateful woman, who is making false Gods, out of our temple. O.M. 2692. *Govy ragos, mar tebel dychtys dhe vôs, ha ty ow cúl kemmys da,* woe is me for thee, to be so evil entreated, and thou doing so much good. P.C. 2635. A regular mutation of *gúl,* qd. v.

CUL, adj. Narrow; strait, or confined; slender, lank, lean. Corn. Voc. *macer* vel *macilentus.* W. *cûl.* Ir. *caol,* †*coil.* Gael. *caol.* Manx, *keyl.* In Armoric *cûl* has quite the contrary meaning, being *plump* or *fat.*

CULETH, s. m. An act, or deed. *Lavar mars ôf vy Yedhow, dhe bobil hép falladow, ha'n spicobow kekyffrys, a'th drôs bỹs dhymmo omma, pa'n drok kuleth a wrusta?* say if I am a Jew! thy people, without falsehood, and the bishops likewise, have brought thee even to me here; what evil deed hast thou done? P.C. 2007. *Culeth* is a mutation of *guleth,* from *gúl,* to do. It is only found in conjunction with *drôk,* and generally written *Drocoleth,* qd. v.

CULHU, s. m. Chaff, beards of corn. Llwyd, 13, 43. This word is a late corruption of *colow,* the plural of *col,* qd. v.

CULIN, s. m. Chaff, corn-straw, Corn. Vocab. *palea,* which also gives as a synonym, *usion,* qd. v. *Culin* must be another plural of *col,* as in Welsh, *colion.*

CULLYEC, s. m. A cock, the male of birds. *Peder, m^e a lever dhys, kyns ys bôs kullyck kenys, ter'gwyth y wréch ow naché,* Peter, I tell thee, before that the cock hath crowed, three times thou shalt deny me. P.C. 903. Another form of *celioc,* qd. v. Llwyd writes as the pronunciation of his time, *kuliog, kuliak, kulliag. Kuliag gini,* a guinea hen; *kiliagaws,* a drake, 88, 241. *Kulliages.* Pryce. *Kulliag godho,* a gander.

CULSTE, v. a. Thou couldst. *Mar culsté,* if thou couldst. Llwyd, 247. A mutation of *gulsté,* for *gálsté.* 2 pers. s. subj. of *gally,* to be able.

CULURIONEIN, s. f. The bowel. Corn. Voc. *viscus.* Pryce's Vocabulary gives as a plural *colonein,* both evidently corruptions, if not mis-printed. Llwyd, 175, writes *kylyrion,* as a plural, evidently considering the singular to be *culurionen.* W. *coludh,* sing. *coludhen.* Ir. *caolain, cadhla.* Gael. *caolan.* Manx, *collane, chiolg.* Gr. χολάς, χολάδος, κώλον. Lat. *colon.*

CUM, s. m. A valley, or dingle; more correctly, a valley opening downwards, from a narrow point, which in Wales is called *Blaen y cwm.* It is preserved in many places in Cornwall and Devon, as *Coom, Coome, Coombe.* Arm. *coum,* in *coumbant.* Ir. *cumar.* Gael. †*cumar.*

CUMMYAS, s. m. Leave, license, permission. Written also indiscriminately *cummyes,* and *cummeas. Eva war an beys meystry, luen gummyas yma dhymmo,* Eve, power over the world, full permission there is to me. O.M. 410. *Gwyn agan beys, ow fryes, bôs granntyes dhynny cummyas,* happy our lot, my spouse, that leave is granted to us. O.M. 412. *Fest yn lowen me a wra, gwyn ow bỹs kafus cummyas,* very joyfully I will do it, I am glad to have permission. O.M. 750. *Ro dhym cummeas me a'th pỹs,* give me leave I pray thee. P.C. 3112. *Us dhyso cummyas an corf kêr dhe ancledhyas,* is there permission to thee to bury the dear body? P.C. 3139.

CUNDA, s. m. Nature, kind. *A arluth kêr, me a'n kymer yn ban wharré, an welen-ma yn hy kunda treylys arté,* O dear Lord, I will take it up immediately, this rod into its natural form is turned again. O.M. 1469. *Rôg henna warbyn cunda ytho, dhys môs y ladha,* therefore against nature it was, for thee to go to kill him. C.W. 94. *A bub echan a kunda, gorow ha benow yn wedh,* of every sort of species, male and female also. O.M. 989. ‡*A bub echan a kunda, gorow ha benow yn wedh.* C.W. 164. From the English *kind.*

CUNDURU, s. m. A door post. Llwyd, 124. This is a modern term, and a corrupt one, being possibly compounded of *cyn,* chief, and *duru* for *dorow,* plural of *dôr,* a door.

CUNTELL, s. m. A gathering together; a collection. Written also *contell.* ‡*Ha Dew a grias an tir séh an 'oar, ha'n contell warbarth an dowrow ev a grias môr, ha Dew a welas tro va da,* and God called the dry land earth, and the gathering together of the waters he called sea, and God saw that it was good. M.C. p. 93. W. *cynnull,* comp. of *cyd,* together, and *dull,* form. Arm. *cutul.*

CUNTELL, v. a. To gather together, to collect. Part. pass. *cuntellys,* written also *cuntullys, cuntyllys,* and *contellyos. Me a guntell dreyn ha spern, ha glôs, dh'y lesky heb lern,* I will gather briars and thorns, and dry cowdung, to burn without regret. C.W. 80. *Cuntell warbarth ow fegans, my a vyn môs púr uskys,* gather together my necessaries, I will go very hastily. C.W. 94. *Mûr a dûs o cuntullys er y byn dh'y guhudhas,* much folk were gathered against him to accuse him. M.C. 88. *Ha Dew leveras gwrêns an dowrow yn dan an nêf bôs cuntellys warbarth dha un teller, ha gwerêns an tir sêh disquedhas; ha an tellna etho,* and God said, let the waters under the heaven be gathered together to one place, and let the dry land appear, and it was so. C.W. p. 190. W. *cynnull.* Arm. *cutul,* †*cuntil.* Ir. *comhdhail, connall.* Gael. *coimh-thionnil.*

CUNTELLET, s. f. A congregation. Cornish Vocabulary, *congregatio* vel *concio.* W. *cynnulliad,* †*cuntellet,* †*cuntullet.* Lux. Glosses, Zeuss, 873.

CUNTELLYANS, s. m. A gathering together, a collection. ‡ *Hu Dew a grias an tîr sêh an noar, contellyans warbarh an dowrow e crias môr; ha Dew a welas tro va da,* and God called the dry land the earth, the gathering together of the waters he called sea; and God saw that it was good. C.W. p. 190.

CUNYS, s. m. Fuel; firewood. *Otté omma vê kunys, ha fast of gynef kelmys,* behold here a load of firewood, and fast it is bound by me. O.M. 1299. *Ke yn ban war an kunys, hag ena gorwedh a heys,* go thou up upon the fuel, and there lie down at length. O.M. 1333. *Cowethé, hedhcuch kunys, ha me a whŷth gans mûr greys,* may *tewé an tân wharré,* comrades, fetch ye firewood, and I will blow with much force, that the fire may kindle soon. P.C. 1219. *Otté lour kunys gyné, whythyns lemmyn yûp frêth,* behold fuel plenty with me, let all blow now rigorously. P.C. 1241. W. *cynnud,* from *cynneu,* to kindle. Arm. *ceünëud, cened.* Ir. *connadh.* Gael. *connadh.*

CUR, s. m. The coast, or border of a country; the utmost part or end of a thing. Llwyd, 108. *Gwasg war an mŷn, bommyn dreys keyn, mar pêdh c ycyn, ny dhuc dhr gur,* strike thou on the edge, blows over the back, if it be cold, it will not come to the end. P.C. 2730. W. *cwr.* Arm. *cer.* Ir. *curr, corr,* †*coor.* Gael. †*curr.*

CUR, s. m. A court. *Out warnas, harlot, pen côk, soon yn mês a'm golok, na trŷk y'm cûr,* out upon thee, rogue, blockhead, immediately out of my sight, stay not in my court. O.M. 1531. *A Dhew an nêf, clew agan lêf, gwyth ny y'th cûr,* O God of heaven, hear our voice, keep us in thy court. O.M. 1620. *Kyn y'n carra vyth mar veur, awos y lauhê ny'm duer, neffré ny gân ef yn cûr, gans y ganow,* though he may love him ever so much, for killing him, I have no concern, he shall never sing in the court with his mouth. R.D. 1899. Fr. *cour.*

CURUN, s. f. A crown, a diadem. Corn. Voc. *curun rwy, corona regis,* a king's crown. In the Ordinalia it is written *curyn. Y curyn a fŷdh sythyys avel mychtern war y pen, lynnouch oll gans mûr a grŷs, may fo dreyn an guryn cys yn empynyon dre an cen,* his crown shall be set, like a king upon his head: drag ye all with much of force, that the thorns of the crown may be together in the brains through the skin. P.C. 2138. *Namna fue ow colon trôch, pan wylys gorré an gu yn golon dre'n tencwen, ha'n guryn spern war y pen,* my heart was almost broken, when I saw the lance put into the heart through the side, and the crown of thorns on his head. R.D. 1247. W. *coron.* Arm. *curun.* Ir. *coroin.* Gael. *coron.* Manx, *crown.* From Lat. *corona.* Gr. κορώνη. As neither the Greek nor Latin preserves the root, it may be the W. *côr,* a circle.

CURUNE, v. a. To crown, to put on a crown. Part. pass *curunys. Gans spern gwerêch y curené, râk an harlot dhe fucié y vôs mychtern Yedhewon,* with thorns do ye crown him, for the knave pretended that he was king of the Jews. P.C. 2064. *Aban na fyn dewedhé, me a vyn y curuné avel mychtern Yedhewon,* since he will not end, I will crown him as king of the Jews. P.C. 2116. *A fo nowydh curunys, mychtern Yedhewon, heil dhys, râk dhe sallugy ny vern,* that is newly crowned king of the Jews, hail to thee, for to salute thee, there is no concern. P.C. 2124. *I'an welas y mâb dygtis gans an Edhewon mar veyll, ha'y vôs gans spern curunys,* when she saw her son treated by the Jews so vilely, and that he was crowned with thorns. M.C. 165. W. *coroni.* Arm. *curunni.* Lat. *corono.*

CUS, s. m. A wood, a forest. Written also *cûz* and *cooz.* ‡ *En cûz-na,* in that wood. Llwyd, 244. ‡ *Na ra henz moaz dan cooz, do kuntle go booz,* they should not go to the wood to gather their meat. Pryce. This is the latest form of *coid,* qd. v.

CUSAL, adj. Serene, quiet. Written by Llwyd, 149, *kuzal;* and by Pryce also, *cusnl. Cusal hn iêg sirra whêg môs pell,* soft and fair, sweet sir, goes far. This is a later form of *cosel,* qd. v.

CUSC, s. m. Sleep; a state of quietude. Llwyd, 152, *kûsg.* W. *cwsg.* Arm. *cousc.*

CUSCE, v. n. To be at rest; to sleep. *Râg my a vyn pols cuské venytha kyns ys dybry, squyth ôf dre vêr lafuryé, powes my a vyn defry,* I will sleep a little ever before eating; tired I am through much labouring, I will rest really. O.M. 2047. *Hag yn nôs oll aspyé, ha gwythé tam na guskens,* and in the night all to look about, and to take care that they slept not a jot. M.C. 241. *En varogyon a guskas myttyn ha'n gŷdh ow tardhé,* the soldiers slept in the morning, the day breaking. M.C. 243. This is another form of *coscé,* qd. v. Llwyd, 55, 245, gives *cusga* and *cysga* as recent forms.

CUSCADUR, s. m. A sleeper. *Cuscadur desimpit, letargus,* Corn. Voc. *Desimpit* is the old form of *desympys,* immediate. *Cuscadur desimpit,* therefore, is one that falls asleep immediately. W. *cysgadur.* Arm. *cousker.*

CUSCTI, s. m. A sleeping room. Corn. Voc. *dormitorium.* Comp. of *cusc,* sleep, and *ti,* a house.

CUSSIN, s. m. A kiss. Corn. Voc. *osculum.* Llwyd, 110, *kysyn.* W. *cusan,* from *cuso,* to kiss. Sansc. *kus.* Cf. also Gr. κυνέω, κύσαι.

CUSUL, s. f. Counsel, advice. Corn. Voc. *consilium.* Pl. *cusullyow.* In construction it changes regularly into *gusul,* and *husul. A'y frût hy nêp a dheppro a woryth cusyl an tâs,* of its fruit whoever eats, will know the counsel of the Father. O.M. 187. *Conseler gentyl y'th pysaf a ry dhymmo cusyl dha,* gentle counsellor, I pray thee to give me good advice. O.M. 1567. *Hon yw cusyl fyn,* this is fine advice. O.M. 2267. *Oll warlerch dhe gussullyow lys venytha my a wra,* every thing after thy counsels ever in future I will do. O.M. 2269. *Dên fûr a'd cusullyow,* a prudent man of thy counsels. O.M. 2681. *Ow mâp lyen, kerch Annas, may hyllyf clewas pyth yw an gusyl wella,* my clerk, fetch Annas, that I may hear what is the best counsel. P.C. 555. *Ha dre aga husyl oll war y ben a ve gorris,* and by their counsel all on his head was put. M.C. 133. *Ow husyl mar gwrêth naha,* my counsel if thou wilt deny. C.W. 50. W. *cysesyl,*

CWETH 79 CYLBAH

†*cusil.* Arm. *cuzul.* Ir. *constal.* All from the Latin *consilium.*

CUSULIODER, s. m. A counsellor. Corn. Voc. *consiliarius;* where only it occurs. Derived from *cusul.* The equivalent in Welsh would be *cyssyliadur.*

CUSULYE, v. a. To counsel, advise. *Ha bys dhodho whaŕe a, dhe'n bys, râg y cusyllyé,* and will soon go even to him, to the world, to advise him. O.M. 643. *Me a'th cusyl hep cabel,* I counsel thee without cavil. O.M. 2673. *A dhûs dhodho bys yn trê, dre dhe vôdh dh'y cussyllyé,* to come to him into the town, by thy will to advise him. P.C. 567. *Cussyllyouch menouch a gasé y wokyneth,* advise ye frequently that he leave his folly. P.C. 1807. *Me re'n cussulyes myl wyth,* saw ny vyn awos travyth gagé *y tebel crygvans,* I have advised him a thousand times, but he will not for any thing leave his evil belief. P.C. 1811. *Me a'th cusulsé ordyné tûs dhe wythé bédh an treytor yw marow,* I would advise thee to order men to guard the grave of the traitor that is dead. R.D. 335. *Y cussylyaf leverel dús nerth warnan,* ha'y dhôn dhe vês, I advise saying that a force came upon us, and bore him away. R.D. 569. *Hag ef éth dh'y gusulyé may fe ledhys,* and he went to advise him that he should be killed. M.C. 119. W. *cyssyliuw.* Arm. *kuzulia.*

CUT, adj. Short, brief. *An môr brâs yn cut termyn adro dhom tŷr a vŷdh dreys râg y wetha pûr elyn,* the great sea in a short time about my land shall be brought, to keep it very clean. C.W. 8. *Yn cutt termyn ages neges cowsow,* in a short time your errand tell ye me. C.W. 44. This is another form of *cot,* qd. v.

CUTH, s. m. Sorrow, grief. *Nyns yw marth cûth ken y'm bo, ow toon an pren a dhe dro, ha'n agan bydh gobyr vyth,* it is no wonder if sorrow be in me, carrying the tree about, and not any wages will be for us. O.M. 2819. *Cûth gweles y dhewedh fe, namna'n dallas,* a grief to see his end it was, it almost blinded us. R.D. 41. *Itak an torment u'n gefé y'n colon yns neffré; cûth-ma na'm gâs,* for the torment which he had is always in my heart; this sorrow does not leave me. R.D. 696. *Mars ns cûth war dhe colon,* if there is sorrow on thy heart. R.D. 2156. *Râk na yllyn dhe weles, cûth ny gen gâs,* for if we may not see thee, sorrow leaves us not. R.D. 2456. This is a contracted form of *cueth,* qd. v.

CUTH, s. f. A pod, or husk. The first meaning is, a wrapper, a bag, or pouch. Pl. *cuthow.* Llwyd writes it *cûth,* pl. *cûthu.* ‡*Câthu fâv,* bean pods. ‡*Cûthû pés,* pease cods, 150. W. *côd.* Arm. *cos.* Ang. Sax. *codd.* Eng. *cod.* Fr. *cosse, ecosse.* Sansc. *kudis,* from *kud,* (W. *cudh.*) to cover, or contain.

CUTHYL, v. a. To do, or make. *Why gwycoryon cueth yn mês, ythesouch ow kuthyl ges a Dhu, hag e sans eglos,* ye traders go out, ye are making a jest of God, and his holy church. P.O. 332. A mutation of *guthyl,* qd. v.

CUTHYS, adj. Grieved, sorrowful. *A vâp whêk, ythof cuthys, ow colon yw marthys clâf,* O sweet son, I am grieved, my heart is wondrous sick. O.M. 1336. *Gallas cf dhe ken tyreth, ha ganso mûr a cleth; ellas lemmyn râk moreth ythof cuthys,* gone he is to another land, and with him many angels; alas! now for grief I am sorrowful. R.D. 766. From *cûth,* sorrow.

CWETH, s.m. A cloth, a garment. Generally written *queth,* pl. *quethow,* qd. v. *Drefen ow bôs noeth hep queth, ragos yth yth dhe gudhé,* because I am naked without a cloth,

I went to hide from thee. O.M. 259. *Yn wedhen me a welas yn ban whel worth scorch flôch byan nowydh gynys, hag ef yn quethow maylys,* in a tree I saw high up on a branch, a little child newly born, and he in clothes was swathed. R.D. 807. *Drefen ow bôs nooth heb gweth, ragas yth eth dha gudha yn tellru-ma,* because I was naked without a cloth, from thee I went to hide in this place. C.W. 64. *Hellouch Adam gans cledha dân, ha'y wrêg mês a Baradys, ha dew gweth dothans gwera doen th'aga hudha pub season, aga nootha na vo gwelys,* chase Adam with a sword of fire, and his wife from Paradise, and two garments to them do thou bear; to cover them at all seasons, that their nakedness may not be seen. C.W. 70. This is the same word as the W. *cûdh,* what covers, whence *cudhio,* and C. *cudhé,* to cover.

CWILCEN, s. f. A frog. Llwyd, 240, *kwilken.* It is written in the Cornish Vocabulary, *guilscin,* qd. v.

CY, conj. So, as. *Ky mal, ky vel,* as, so. ‡*Ky gwêr vel an gwels,* as green as grass. Llwyd, 248. W. *cyn.*

CYC, s. m. Flesh. See *Cig.*

CYDHA, v. n. To fall. *An hwêl a cydhas scent,* the work fell short. Llwyd, 251. Another form of *codhé,* qd. v.

CYDHMAN, s. m. A mate or companion. Llwyd, 151. Another form of *cothman,* qd. v.

CYF, v. a. He shall have, or find. *My a's dyllo ahanan, ny dhue arté, me a greys, mar kyf carynnyas, warnedhé y trŷg pûp preys,* I will send it from us, it will not come again, I believe, if it shall find carrion, it will always stay upon it. O.M. 1103. *Ena why a gyf asen,* there ye will find an ass. P.C. 176. *Why a wra y aswonvos dêdh brûs, hag a'n kyf yn brôf,* ye will acknowledge it on the day of judgment, and have it in proof. P.C. 1496. 3 pers. s. fut. of *cafos.* W. *caif.*

CYFFE, v. a. He should have. *Y bows ef o mar dêk guris, y ny vynsans y ranné, warnedhy pren be tewbys, oll an bows pync a'n gyffé,* his coat was so fairly made, they were not willing to divide it, on it a lot was cast, who should have all the coat. M.C. 190. 3 person s. subj. of *cafos.* W. *caffai.*

CYFFRYS, adv. Likewise, also. *Saw te ha me cyffrys, agan bewnans may fên sûr,* save thee and me alike, of our life that we may be sure. M.C. 191. Another form of *cefrys,* qd. v.

CYFFYF, v. a. I shall find. *Drewh e dhymmo, ma'n gwyllyf, marow vydh pan y'n kyffyf a dhesempya,* bring ye him to me, that I may see him, he shall die, when I shall have found him, immediately. R.D. 1776. 1 pers. s. subj. of *cafos,* qd. v. W. *caffwyv.*

CYFFYN, v. a. We shall find. *Yn ketella sy a vyn; branchys olyf pan kyffyn, me a set a dhyragtho,* in this way we will; branches of olive when we shall find, I will set before him. P.C. 244. *Homma yw cusyl da, my a vyn yûl yn della, py le penag y's kyffyn,* this is good advice, I will do so, wherever we shall find it. P.C. 1551. 1 pers. pl. subj. of *cafos,* qd. v. W. *caffwn.*

CYGEL, s. m. A distaff. See *Cigel.*

CYHYDHA, v. a. To accuse. *Dho gyhydha,* Llwyd, 41. Another form of *cuhudha,* qd. v.

CYL, s. f. A recess. See *Cil.*

CYLBAH, s. m. The bottom, the behind. ‡*Râg errya war ow fyn me a'th wŷsk may thomelly dheth kylbah,* for striving against me, I will strike thee that thou fall to thy bottom. C.W. 82.

CYLLYTH 80 CYMMYS

CYLDEN, s. m. A lodging, an inn. *An beys yw cales kylden, yn lafur, whŷs, hag anken, ha deydh ha nôs*, the world is a hard lodging, in labour, sweat, and sorrow, both day and night. R.D. 244.

CYLDENE, v. a. To draw backward, to let down. *Whyp an tŷn, kymer an pen, er an treys me an kylden aberth yn beydh*, Breechwhip, take thou the head, by the feet I will let him down within the grave. R.D. 2052. W. *cildynu.*

CYLEDNAC, adj. Sincere, downright, entire. Llwyd, 150. A late form of *colenec*, or *colanec*, qd. v.

CYLIGI, s. m. A cockle. Llwyd, 241. This is the same word as *cilygan*, qd. v.

CYLL, v. n. He will be able. *Ha dhum arluth fystynyn, mar a kŷll bones yocheys, ty a fŷdh dhe lyfreson*, and to my lord let us hasten, if he can be healed, thou shalt have thy liberty. R.D. 1675. *Del yw screfys, prest yma adro dhymny ganso try, mara kŷll dheworth an da, dhe wethyl drôk, agan dry*, as it is written, ready there are about us with him three, if he can from the good bring us to do wrong. M.C. 21. A mutation of *gŷll*, 3 pers. s. fut. *gally*, qd. v.

CYLL, v. a. He will lose. *Aban na vynta cresy, ty a kyll ow herensé*, since thou wilt not believe, thou shalt lose my love. O.M. 242. 3 pers. s. fut. of *colli*, qd. v. W. *cyll.*

CYLLE, v. n. He should be able. *Rák mara kyllé entré agy dhe'n yet, ef a wra dhymny drôk tro*, for if he should be able to enter within the gate, he will do us an ill turn. P.C. 3064. A mutation of *gyllé*, 3 pers. s. subj. of *gally*, qd. v.

CYLLER, v. n. It is possible. *Ellas! ny won py tyller bŷth moy py le y trygaf; eychan rág y fynner, mara kyller, gans baynys mêr ow dyswul glân*, alas! I know not in what place, ever more where I shall dwell; alas! for it is wished, if it could be with great pains to destroy me quite. P.C. 2600. A mutation of *gyllcr*, (W. *gellir*,) 3 pers. s. pres. pass. of *gally*, qd. v.

CYLLY, v. a. Thou shalt lose. *Ny a whŷth yn dhe vody sperys may hylly bewé, ha'n bevnans pan y'n kylly dhe'n dôr ty a dreyl arté*, we breathe in thy body a spirit that thou mayest live, and the life when thou shalt lose it to the earth thou shalt turn again. O.M. 63. 2 pers. s. fut. of *colli*. W. *colli.*

CYLLYN, v. a. We shall be able. *A arluth kêr, my a wra, mar a kyllyn yn della, ny dhe gamwul y won gwŷr*, O dear Lord, I will do, if we shall be able so, that we have done wrong, I know truly. P.C. 1064. *Mar a kyllyn y gafus, vynytha na dheppro bous, me a'n kelm avel pusorn*, if we shall be able to find him, may he never eat food, I will tie him like a bundle. R.D. 540. A mutation of *gyllyn*, (W. *gallwn*,) 1 pers. pl. fut. of *gally*, qd. v.

CYLLYS, part. Lost. *Ellas vŷth, pan yw kyllys Abel whêk, ow map kerra*, alas ever, when is lost sweet Abel, my dearest son. O.M. 614. *Máp dên my re wruk prenné, gans gôs ow colon, na fe nêp a wrussyn ny kyllys*, mankind I have redeemed with the blood of my heart, that there may not be any, that we have made, lost. R.D. 2624. Part. pass. of *colli.*

CYLLYTH, v. a. Thou wilt be able. *A benen, pendra kewsyth, lavar dhym mar a kyllyth yn nep point ow lawenhé*, O woman, what sayest thou? tell me if thou canst in any point gladden me. R.D. 1689. A mutation of *gyllyth*, 2 pers. s. fut. of *gally*, qd. v.

CYLLYTH, v. a. Thou shalt lose. *Ahanas marth yw gyné, mar a kyllyth dhe ené, nyns ôs dén fûr*, of thee a wonder is to me; if thou losest thy soul, thou art not a wise man. R.D. 1409. 2 pers. s. fut. of *colli*, qd. v.

CYLMY, v. a. To bind. Part. *cylmys*. *Kyn ve dhe dhyuvrech mar brâs, my a's kylm warbarth, avel lader pûr*, though thy arms be so large, I will bind them together, like a very thief. P.C. 1190. *Me a gylm an nŷl wharré, otté ow lovan, rák y gylmy*, I will bind the one soon; behold my rope with me to bind him. P.C. 2787. *Me a welas flôch byan nowydh gynys, hag ef yn quethow maylys, ha kylmys fast gans lystyn*, I saw a little child newly born, and him in cloths swathed, and bound fast with napkins. O.M. 808. Written also *celmy*, qd. v.

CYLOBMAN, s. f. A pigeon, a dove. ‡ *Cylobman cuz*, a wood-pigeon. Llwyd, 241. This is a late form, and a corruption of *colommen*, which is also the Welsh term. In the Ordinalia we only find *colom*, qd. v.

CYLYRION, s. m. Entrails, the bowels. Llwyd, 175, who evidently considers the singular to be *culurionen*, qd. v.

CYLYWI, v. n. To lighten. ‡ *Patl yzhi a cylywi ha trenna*, how it lightens and thunders. Llwyd, 248. This is a mutation of *gylywi*, in which late form *golowa* is to be understood, qd. v.

CYMERES, v. a. To take; take hold of, to seize. *Adam ottensy umma, ry hanow dhedhy hy gwra, dhe'th pár rák hy kymmeres*, Adam, behold her here, do thou give her a name, for thy equal to take her. O.M. 104. *Ke kymmer mŷns a vynny a'n beys oll adro*, go take thou all thou wilt of the world all around. O.M. 403. *Kymmer dyso ow enef*, take thou to thee my soul. O.M. 849. *Kyn fen marow yn tor-ma, an mernans me a'n kymmer*, if I die at this time, the death I will take it. O.M. 1332. *Oll dh'y vôdh a's kemerens, aban vynné yn della*, all to his will let him take them, since he wills it so. P.C. 210. *Kymereuch, eveuch an gwŷn*, take ye, drink ye the wine. P.C. 723. *Me a's pew, kymerens pêp ran a'y tu, degens dhe dré*, I have it, let every one take a share on his side, let him take it home. P.C. 2859. *An barama kymereuch dheuch lemman yn kettep pen*, this bread take ye to you now, every head. P.C. 761. *Ro dhym cumneas, me a'th pŷs, a kymeres corf Ihesu*, give me leave, I pray thee, to take the body of Jesus. P.C. 3113. *Me a fue yn cert a tân dhe'n kêth plas-ma kemerys*, I was, in a chariot of fire, brought to this same place. R.D. 237. Written also *cemercs*, qd. v.

CYMMYAS, s. m. Leave, permission. *War bûp frût, losow, ha hâs, a vo yanny hy tevys, saw an frût ny vŷdh kynmyas, yw pren a skeyens hynwys*, over all fruit, herbs, and seed, which are in it grown, but of the fruit there is not permission, that is named the tree of knowledge. O.M. 79. Written also *cwmmyas*, qd. v.

CYMMYNY, v. a. To commend, entrust, bequeath. *A dâs yntré dhe dhewlé, me a gymmyn ow ené, gwŷth e rág tarofvan*, O Father into thy hands I commend my soul, preserve it from terrors. O.M. 2303. Another form of *cemynny*, qd. v.

CYMMYS, adv. So much, so great, so many. *Ny allaf gweles yn fâs, kynmys daggrow re olys*, I cannot see well, so many tears I have shed. P.C. 2608. *Why a pŷs an runyow dh'agas gorhery, kymmys vŷdh an ponveter,* ye shall pray the hills to hide you, so great will be the trouble. P.C. 2656. *Henna Pylat pan welas, kymmys cowsys er y byn,* when Pilate saw that, so much spoken against him. M.C. 100. *Gans re a gymmys colon en loven a ve lennys,* by some with so much heart the rope was pulled. M.C. 181. *Râg ny wodhons py gymmys y môns y ow peché,* for they know not how much they are sinning. M.C. 185. This is another form of *cemmys,* qd. v. The last corrupted form was *cybmys.*

CYMMYSC, s. m. A mixture. *Cymmysc bleid a chi,* a mixture of wolf and dog. Liux. Corn. Voc. Another form of *commisc,* qd. v. W. *cymmysg.*

CYMMYSCY, v. a. To mix, mingle. Part. pass. *cymmyscys. Ottensé gynef parys, bystel eysel kymyskys, mars ûs seches brâs,* behold them with me ready, gall (and) vinegar mixed, if there is great thirst. P.C. 2977. The more frequent form in the Ordinalia is *cemyscy,* qd. v.

CYMPES, adj. Right, even, straight. ‡ *Ev a dhelledzhaz an termen mal dha va prèv erra e wrêg guitha kympes et i gever,* he delayed the time, that he might prove whether his wife had kept right in relation to him. Lluyd, 253. This is a late form of *compos,* qd. v.

CYN, conj. Though, if. *Arluth, dhe vôdh a vŷdh gwerys, moy kyn fennas dhe gafys, pûr wyr leskys ef a vŷdh,* Lord, thy will shall be done, more if thou wish to take, very truly it shall be burnt. O.M. 432. *Dre sor kyn fêns y terrys,* in anger though they may be broken. O.M. 1237. *Me a'n gwŷth kyn tassorcho,* I will keep him, though he should rise again. R.D. 379. *Coskyn ny gans dyaha, kyn dasvewo, ny'n drecha dhywar y geyn,* let us sleep with security, though he should revive, he will not raise it from off his back. R.D. 403. *Ny scap kyn fo vŷdh mar fûr, na'n gesso drôk,* he will not escape though he be ever so cunning, that he shall not get harm. R.D. 2019. This is the same word as *cen,* qd. v. W. *cyd.* Arm. *ken.*

CYN, adv. First, before, before that. *A dâs kêr ol caradow, ow paynys a vŷdh garow, kyn vôs leskys dhe lusow,* O father dear, all beloved, my pains will be cruel, before being burnt to ashes. O.M. 1355. *Kyn pen vis,* before the end of a month. Lluyd, 230. W. *cyn.*

CYN, s. m. The back. *Ota saw bôs war ow kŷn, Jafet degyns saw arral,* behold a load of food on my back, let Japhet bring another load. O.M. 1053. *Pûr wŷr, me a henrosas, ha war ow kŷn a'n clewas yn mês a'n bêdh ow sevel,* very truly, I dreamed, and on my back I heard him rising out of the tomb. R.D. 518. A contracted form of *ceyn,* or *cein,* qd. v.

CYNAC, s. m. A worm. Tinea capitis, Lluyd, 164. The same word as *cinac.*

CYNDAN, s. m. Debt. *Dha bôs en cyndan,* to be in debt. Lluyd, 53. ‡ *Ny vedn e nevra dos vês a gyndan,* he will never get out of debt, 230. *Cendoner,* a debtor, qd. v.

CYNGYS, adv. Before that, before. *Dûn dh'y gerhes, cowethé, rag may hyllyn y sellyé yn grows kyngys dôs sabot,* let us come to fetch it, companions, that we may put him on a cross before Sabbath comes. P.C. 2557. *Me a pys an tâs a nêf, re dhanfono vengeans crêf warnouch kyngys dybry,* I pray the Father of heaven, that he may send heavy vengeance on ye all before eating. P.C. 2632. *Gynef hydhow ty a vŷdh, râk dhe fry, yn Parades kyngys hanter docha geydh,* with me to day thou shall be for thy faith, in Paradise, before mid-day arrives, P.C.

2912. *Cyngys* is another form of *cyns-ys,* the *s* being softened into *g* soft, or English *j*.

CYNIAF, s. m. Autumn, harvest time. Corn. Vocab. *autumpnus.* Lluyd, 4, reads the old form *kyniav,* and he gives *cidniadh,* and *cidniaz,* as recent forms. W. *cynauav,* comp. of *cyn,* before, and *gauav,* winter.

CYNIHAS, s. m. A neighing. Lluyd, 65. Who also writes it *kynihias,* 33. *Cryhias,* is another term, qd. v. Cf. the Lat. *hinnio.* Eng. *to neigh, to whinny.* The Welsh term is *gweryru.* †*guirgirio.* Arm. *gouririal.* Ir. *sithreach.* Gael. *sitir, sitrich.*

CYNIN, s. f. A rabbit, a coney. Lluyd, 53. W. *cwning.* Arm. *council, conifl.* Ir. *cuinin.* Gael. *coinean.* Manx, *conning.* Fr. †*conin.* Dan. *canin.* Du. *conyn.* Lat. *cuniculus.*

CYNINGEN, s. f. A rabbit. Pryce. W. *cwningen.*

CYNIVER, adj. So many, as many as, every, every one. *Cynyver dên ûs yn wlâs, na tra yn bŷs ow pewé, saw unsol ty ha'th flehas, gans lŷf y wrêf dhe ladhé,* as many men as are in the land, or thing in the world living, save only thee and thy children, with a flood I will destroy. O.M. 1029. *Kynyver bêst ûs yn tŷr, ydhyn ha puskes kefreys,* as many beasts as are on the earth, birds and fishes also. O.M. 1215. *Kynyver peyn ûs yn bys, dhodho by ny vyé ré,* as much pain as is in the world, for him would never be too much. R.D. 2055. It is variously written *cynyfer, conifer, cenyver,* and *ceniver,* qd. v. W. *cynniver,* comp. of *cyd,* even, and *niver,* a number.

CYNIVIAS, v. a. To shear, to clip. Lluyd, 164. W. *cneiviuw.* Arm. *crevia.*

CYNS, adv. Before, before hand, rather. *Eva kyns del vy serrys, my a wra oll del vynny,* Eve, rather than thou shalt be angry, I will do all as thou wishest. O.M. 245. *Ma'm gasso kyns ys myrwel ynno bôs dhym dhe welas,* that it allow me before dying to see food for myself in it. O.M. 377. *My a'd pŷs ow sona gwra kyns ys môs,* I pray thee, do thou bless me before going. O.M. 724. *An lŷf wôth gwrêns ymdenné, dh'y teller kyns êns arté,* let the fierce flood withdraw, to its former place let it go again. O.M. 1093. *Mar a'th caffaf, y'th ladhaf kyns y's vythyn a'm dew lucf,* if I find thee, I will kill thee before morning with my hands. O.M. 1533. *Lemyn agan soné gwra kyns ys bones anhedhys,* now bless us before that it is inhabited. O.M. 1722. *Kyns y un teller yn beys, dew kendoner yth egé,* once in a part of the world, there were two debtors. P.C. 501. *Kyns pen sythyn,* before the end of a week. R.D. 30. *Y vyrys y wolyow, aga gwelas y trueth, dhe'n bŷs kyns êns ylyow,* I looked on his wounds, it was pitiful to behold them, to the world rather they are healings. R.D. 900. It is written also *cens,* qd. v. W. *cynt,* †*cent.* Arm. *cent.* Ir. *ceud,* †*cét.* Gael. *ceud.*

CYNSA, adj. First, chief. *Rag ythevel dhym bôs da, yn kynsa dŷdh môns ûs gwrŷs,* for it appears to me to be good, on the first day all that is made. O.M. 20. *Râg my a vŷdh an kynsa, bon a rollo, hag a perfo ow meystry,* for I will be the first, that will give a blow, and perform my duty. O.M. 2163. *Yrverys ew sola-thyth dhe avonsyé an kynsé benfys a'm been,* it has becu thought of a long time to advance thee to the first benefices I may have. O.M. 2613. *Ellas na varwen yn wêdh, na fe kynsé ow dywedh ys dywedh ow mâp yn beys,* alas! that I die not also, that my end was not sooner than the end of my son in the world. P.C. 2947. W. *cyntav*, †*centav*, †*cintam*. Arm. *centa*, †*centaf*. Ir. *ceudna*, *ceud*, †*céine*, †*cita*. Gael. *céud*. Manx, *chied*.

CYNTIL, v. a. To gather, to collect. *Llwyd*, 77. Another form of *cuntell*, qd. v.

CYNTREVAC, s. m. A neighbour. *Llwyd*, 173. Pl. *cyntrevagion*. Another form of *contrevac*, qd. v.

CYNY, v. n. To mourn, to lament, to weep. *Attoma hagar vyadge, may hallaf kyny, ellas!* lo here is a horrid voyage, that I may mourn, alas! C.W. 68. (*Cyny* may also signify here *to sing*.) *Lemyn, Eva, ow fryes, henna ytho dhe folly gy ; râg henna paynes pûr vrâs yma ornes ragon ny, may hellyn kyny dreiha,* now, Eve, my wife, this was thy folly ; therefore pains very great are ordained for us, that we may lament for it. C.W. 74. W. *cwyno*. Arm. *keina*. Ir. *caoine*, †*cóine*. Gael. *caoin*. Manx, *keayn*. Goth. *qvainon*. O. Norse, *qveina*. Eng. *whine*.

CYNYFAN, s. f. A nut. *Cynyfan frenc*, a walnut. *Llwyd*, 74. Written also *cnyfan*, qd: v.

CYNYOW, s. m. A dinner. *Tyr séch yn gwêl, nag yn prâs, mar kefyth yn gwêr hep gow, ynno gweet in-ta whelas bôs dheth ly ha dheth kynyow*, dry land in field, or in meadow, if thou shalt find truly without a lie, in it take good care to seek food for thy breakfast, and for thy dinner. O.M. 1140. W. *ciniaw*. Arm. *coan*. Ir. *cuid*. Gael. *coinne*. Lat. *cæna*. Gr. *χοίνη*.

CYR, adj. Dear, beloved. *Llwyd*, 54. Another form of *cêr*, qd. v.

CYRCHES, v. a. To fetch, to carry, to bring. *Euch alemma pûr thoth brâs, del y'm kyrreuch, ages dew, ha kyrchouch dhe drê an gwâs, may hallo cané ellas, nefré yn lewolgow lew*, go ye hence with very great speed, as ye love me, you two, and bring home the youth, that he may sing "alas," ever in thick darkness. O.M. 544. *Agan arluth, ny a'n kyrch dhŷs hep danger*, our Lord, we will bring him to thee without delay. O.M. 548. *My a kyrch an gwâs wharré*, I will bring the fellow soon. O.M. 887. *Ow messyger, kyrch ow courser dhe varogeth*, my messenger, bring thou my courser to ride. O.M. 1959. This is the same word as *cerches*, qd. v.

CYRDHYS, v. m. He went. *Sew olow ow thryys lyskys, ny dŷf gwîls, na flour yn bŷs, yn keth fordh-na may kyrdhys*, follow thou the prints of my feet burnt, no grass, nor flower in the world grows in that same road, where I went. O.M. 713. 3 pers. s. preterite of *cerdhes*, qd. v.

CYRHES, v. a. To fetch, to carry, to bring. Part. pass. *cyrhys*. *Bys dhyn umnia yn un lam ef a vydh kyrhys*, even to us here in a trice he shall be brought. O.M. 886. *Ha pesyn rag y enê, may fo Dew re'n kyrho dhodho dh'y wledh*, and let us pray for his soul, that God may carry him to him to his kingdom. O.M. 2370. *Dûn dhe gyrhas Salamon, ha goryn ef yn y dron*, let us to fetch Solomon, and let us place him in his throne. O.M. 2371. *Pûp Crystyon oll yn wêdh a vynno pyggy gufyans, y's kyrhâf gans ow eleth*, and every Christian also, that will pray for pardon, I will bring them with my angels. R.D. 1577. This is another form of *cyrches*, tho aspirate *bei* ftened into *h*.

CYRIA, n. A pimple, or speckle. Llwyd, 78, *kyriak*.

CYRREUCH, v. a. Ye shall love. *Euch alemma pûr thoth brâs, del y'm kyrreuch, agas dew, ha kyrchouch dhe drê an gwâs*, go ye hence with great speed, as ye love me, ye two, and bring home the youth. O.M. 543. 2 pers. pl. fut. of *caré*, qd. v.

CYRRY, v. a. Thou shalt love. *Ke yn râk, del y'm kyrry*, go thou before, as thou lovest me. O.M. 537. *Dûs yn râk, del y'm kyrry*, come thou forth, as thou lovest me. O.M. 2403. *Drôk handlé, del om kyry, pan gyffy dalhen ynno*, handle him roughly, as thou lovest me, when thou gettest hold in him. P.C. 991. *Lavar dhym, del y'm kyrry*, tell me as thou lovest me. P.C. 1289. 2 pers. s. fut. of *caré*, qd. v.

CYRTAS, v. n. To tarry behind, to remain. *Llwyd*, 138. Part. pass. *cyrtas*, delayed, 248. This is a later form of *gortas*, or *gortos*, qd. v.

CYRYN, s. f. A crown. ‡*Tan gyryn*, to the crown. *Llwyd*, 249. Another form of *curun*, qd. v.

CYRYS, part. Loved, beloved. *Porth côf, lavar comfort yn ta, dhymmo Pedar mûr yw kyrys*, bear thou in memory to seek comfort well, by me Peter is much beloved. R.D. 892. Part. pass. of *care*, qd. v.

CYS, adj. United, joint or common, joined together. *Tynnouch ol gans mûr a grŷs, may fo dreyn an guryn cŷs yn empynnyon dre an cen*, pull ye all with much force, that the thorns of the crown may be together in the brain through the skull. P.C. 2137. Written also *ces*, qd. v.

CYSOLATH, s. m. Peace, rest, peaceableness, tranquillity, concord. *Llwyd*, 240. Who also writes it *cyzaleth*, 243. It is the same word as *cesoleth*, qd. v.

CYSOLATHA, v. a. To make friends, to reconcile. *Dho kyzalatha*, Llwyd, 50.

CYSSYL, s. f. Counsel. Pl. *cyssylyow*, and corruptly *cysylgow*. Llwyd, 242. See *Cusul*.

CYSSYLIER, s. m. A counsellor. *Llwyd*, 240.

CYSYN, s. m. A kiss. *Llwyd*, 110. This is the same word as *cussin*, qd. v.

CYTIORCH, s. m. A wild buck. Corn. Voc. *capreolus*. Comp. of *coyt*, wood, and *yorch*, a roe.

CYVEDHA, adj. So drunken. *Llwyd*, 125. Compounded of *cy*, so, and *medha*, drunken.

CYVELAC, s. m. A wood-cock. *Llwyd*, 62, 156. W. *cyfylog*, from *gylv*, a bill. Arm. *cyfelec, cyvelcc*. Lat. *scolopax*. The latter term has no meaning in Latin or Greek, and must have been derived from the Celtic, as Llwyd has well observed. *Ysgyvlog* means the Bill Bird, from *ysgwlv*, a bill, its most distinguishing value. For the same reason it is called *Becasse*, by the French, and *Schnepff*, by the Germans. So again the Welsh call a Curlew, *gylvinhir*, the Long Bill.

CYVELYN, s. m. A cubit. Written also *cevelyn*, qd. v.

CYVETHIDOG, adj. Able, potent, powerful. *Llwyd*, 125. This is the same word as *covuithac*, derived from *covaith*, wealth, qd. v. W. *cyvocthog*. Ir. †*cumachtach*, †*cumachtig*.

CYVUR, s. m. A piece of land. This is the Welsh *cyvar*, compounded of *cyv*, together, and *âr*, a ploughing, and its first meaning is, ploughing in concert, a day's ploughing, hence an acre. "In the four parishes of Redruth, Gwennap, Kenwyn, and St. Agnes, where, at a point, the four western Hundreds of Cornwall meet or unite, is a barren heathy spot denominated *Kynur ankou ;* where all self murderers belonging to those parishes are deposited by virtue of the coroner's warrant, a custom immemorial, whence the spot takes its name." *Polwhele's Cornish Glossary.*

CYWEDH, s. m. A companion, a colleague. *Llwyd*, 49. See *Coweth*.

CYWEDHIAD, s. m. A colleague. *Llwyd*, 49.

CYWERAS, s. m. Help, succour. *Llwyd*, 44. Incorrectly for *gweres*, qd. v.

CH.

This is both an immutable radical, and a secondary letter. In the first case it is invariably followed by *w*, or its representative, in the three British dialects. Thus W. *chwerw*, bitter; *chwi*, ye. C. *chuero*, *chwy*. Arm. *chouero*, *choui*. In Cornish it was afterwards softened into *h*, in the initials of words, and this is the rule in the Ordinalia, so *chwerow* became *hwerow*; *chwy*, *why*; *chwans*, *whans*, &c. The guttural was however often preserved in the middle of words, as *archow*, chests, *cerchen*, about, *cerchys*, fetched; but more generally at the end, as *collenweuch*, fill ye, *coskeuch*, sleep ye, *dywvrech*, the arms, &c. When secondary, *ch* is the aspirate mutation of *c*, in all the Celtic languages. Thus W. *calon*, a heart, *ei chalon*, her heart. Arm. *calon*, *hé chalon*. C. *colon*, *y holon*. W. *cyhudhaw*, to accuse, *i'w chyhudhaw*, to accuse her. C. *cuhudhas*, *dhy huhudhas*. Ir. *cri*, a heart, *a chri*, his heart. Gael. *cridhe*, *a chridhe*. Manx, *cree*, *e chree*.

The proper sound of *ch* in all Celtic languages is guttural, like the χ of the Greeks, *x* in Spanish, and *ch* in German. There are a few foreign words in Cornish, where *ch* has the sound of *ch* in the English word *church*.

CHALLA, s. m. The jaw-bone. Written also *chal*. *Venytha na souyny, lan hemma war an challa*, that thou mayest never thrive, take this on the jaw-bone. O.M. 640. *Ef an gevyth war an chal, dèn vythol na dhoutyans peg*, he shall catch it on the jaw, let not any man doubt a bit. P.C. 1181. This is borrowed from the English *jole* or *jowl*.

CHEC, s. m. A kettle. *Ha my caugeon lawethan, merwel a wrên ow cûl tân yn dan an chek*, and my dirty fiends, we will die making a fire under the kettle. R.D. 139.

CHET, s. m. A companion, a fellow. Pl. *chettys*. *Tyorryon yn ketep chet, tyeuch an temple hep let, na dheffo glaw dhe'n styllyow, tilera*, every fellow, cover ye the temple without stopping, that the rain may not come to the rafters. O.M. 2486. *Me a bar daras an yet, na gercho alemma chet*, I will bar the door that he may not carry a friend hence. P.C. 3050. *Sytleuch gystys worth an yet; agas dyweodh ketteb chet hertheuch worty hy yn wêdh*, put ye beams against the gate; your shoulders, every fellow, thrust ye against it also. P.C. 3068. *Rôg mar tue dh'agan porthow, ef a ter an darasow, hag a dhylyrf an chettys*, for if he comes to our door-ways, he will break the doors, and liberate the company. P.C. 3042. "*Chet* is, I think, allied to the Welsh *cyd*, and is frequently used in the Dramas for 'a companion.' But the *ch*, almost exclusively limited in the Dramas to English words, and the pl. *chettys*, seem to shew that the Celtic origin was forgotten. Perhaps it was connected, in the opinion of the writer, with *chat*, gossip." Norris's Cornish Drama, ij. 339.

CHI, s. m. A dog. This is a regular mutation of *ci*, and is preserved in the Cornish Vocabulary, where *Linx* is translated *commisc bleid ha chi*, literally 'a mixture of wolf and dog.' W. *cymmysg blaidh a chi*.

CHOARION, s. m. Sports, pastimes, or plays. *Llwyd*, 82. This is the plural of *choary*. W. *chwareu*. Arm. *choari*. Ir. *egeara*, a player.

CHUERO, adj. Bitter, cruel, hardhearted. *Pryce*. The common form was *wherow*, qd. v. W. *chwerw*, prov. *hwerw*. Arm. *chouerô*. Ir. *searbh*, †*serb*. Gael. *searbh*. Manx, *sharroo*.

CHUI, pron. Ye, or you. *Llwyd*, 244. Generally written *why*, qd. v. W. *chwi*. Arm. *choui*, †*hui*, †*huy*. Ir. *sibh*, †*si*, †*sib*. Gael. *sibh*. Manx, *shiu*. Lat. *vos*, litoris transpositis. Gr. σφῶι. Sansc. *vas*, *vas*.

CHUYVYAN, v. a. To escape, to flee. W. *chwiviaw*. "From hence the family of *Vyvyan* is supposed to take its name, for fleeing on a white horse from Lioness, when it was overflown; that person being at that time governor thereof; in memory whereof this family gives a lion for its arms, and a white horse, ready caparisoned, for the crest." *Pryce's Archæologia Cornu-Britannica*.

CHY, s. m. A house, a dwelling. *Ny won vyth pe 'th ûf lemyn; nymbus gwêsc, guskys, na chy*, I know not where I shall go now; there is not for me clothes, shelter, nor house. O.M. 356. *Oll tûs ow chy, deuch genef vy*, all men of my house, come ye with me. O.M. 1961. *Arluth, ytho pyw a wra coul drehevel oll dhe chy*, Lord, now who shall fully build thy house. O.M. 2340. *Yn crês an chy res vye kafus gysl crêf, na vo gwan*, in the middle of the house, it would be necessary to have a strong beam, that it be not weak. O.M. 2481. *Aban dhuthé y'th chy*, since I came to thy house. P.C. 517. *Aban duthé yn chy dhys*, since I came into the house to thee. P.C. 524. *Pepenagol may 'th ello, yn kêth chy-na euch ganso*, wherever that he may enter, into that same house go ye with him. P.C. 631. *Levereuch dhe gour an chy*, say to the man of the house. P.C. 633. *Ny an syw bŷs yn y chy*, we will follow him even to his house. P.C. 648. We have here a solitary instance in a Cornish word of the corruption of the proper sound of *t* into that of the English *ch*, as in *church*. It never occurs in Welsh or Armoric, but in the Erse languages it is the common sound of *t*, before *e*, and *i*. Thus *tân*, fire, in Welsh, Cornish, and Armoric, though written *teine* in Irish and Gaelic, is pronounced as it is phonetically written in Manx, *chenney*. So also W. C. Arm. *tês*, heat; Ir. and Gael. *teas*. Manx, *chias*. W. C. *teyrn*, a king. Ir. Gael. *tighearna*. Manx, *chiarn*. W. C. Arm. *tir*, land; Ir. Gael. *tir*. Manx, *cheer*.

CHYMMA, s. m. This house. *Crês Dew aberth an chymma*, the peace of God within this house. P.C. 667. This word is compounded of *chy*, a house, and *omma*, here. It is written also *chemma*. *Cryst, yw pen gôr ha benen, yn chemma y fue gynen pûr wŷr hydhyw*, Christ, (who) is head of man and woman, in this house was with us very truly to-day. R.D. 1397.

D.

This letter is both radical and secondary. When radical it changes in construction into *dh*, which has the sound of *th*, in the English words, *this*, *than*; as *dên*, a man, *dew dhên*, two men. W. *dŷn; dau dhŷn*. In Armoric, *dh* is now represented by *z*, but the proper sound is preserved at the present day in some parts of Britanny. *Dên, daou zên*. Ir. *duine, da dhuine*. Gael. *duine, da dhuine*. Manx, *dooinney, daa ghooinney*. The Welsh has a further nasal mutation into *n*, as *vy nŷn*, my man; this is unknown to Cornish and Armoric, but it prevails in the Irish. Again in Cornish and Armoric, *d* changes into *t*, as *dôs*, to come, *ow tôs*, coming. Arm. *dont, ô tont*. This mutation occurs also in Welsh, but not in initials. Cf. *creto*, 3 pers. s. subj. of *credu*. Gato *(na utto)* from *gadu*. Caled, hard; *caletach*, harder; *caletav*, hardest. When secondary, *d* is the soft sound of *t*, in the Cornish, Welsh, Armoric, and Irish languages. Thus *tâs*, a father, *y dâs*, his father. W. *tâd, ei dâd*. Arm. *tâd, hé dâd*. Ir. *tart*, thirst, *ar dart, (ttart,)* our thirst.

DA, s. m. A good. Cor. Voc. *bonum*. *Del yw scrifys, prest yma adro dhynny ganso try, mar a kŷll dheworth an da dhe wethyll drôk agan dry*, as it is written, ready there are about us with him three, if he can bring us from the good to do wrong. M.C. 21. *Oll en da ha'n drôk kepar, dhe Jesus bedhens grassys*, all the good and hurt alike, to Jesus be thanks. M.C. 24. *Pan vynnouch agis honon, uy a ŷll gŷll da dhedhê*, when ye will yourselves, ye can do good to them. M.C. 37.

DA, adj. Good. In construction it changes into *dha*, and *ta. Nyns yw da bones un dên y honan hep cowyth py cowethes*, it is not good that a man should be alone without a male or female companion. O.M. 93. *Pûp ûr oll obereth da, gwyn bŷs kymmys a'n gwrello*, always good works, happy as many as do them. O.M. 604. *Ny a dhynyth un flôch da*, we shall produce a good child. O.M. 604. *Gynef yma fardhel pûr dha war ow kryn*, I have a burden good on my back. O.M. 1617. *Ken na fe da genes, gŷl dhe servys ty a wra*, though it may not be good with thee, i.e. though thou mayest not like it, thou shalt do thy service. P.C. 2260. (This is the Welsh idiom, *y mae yn dha genyv*, I like, or am pleased.) *Mar dha del reys*, as well it behoveth. R.D. 1320. *Gans colan dha*, with good heart. Lhwyd, 230. *Aspy yn ta pûp echen*, examine well every particular. O.M. 747. *Degê oll agan edhyn, bestes yn wêdh mnga ta*, tithe of all our birds, beasts also as well. O.M. 1182. W. *da*. Arm. *da*. Ir. *deagh*, †*dagh*, †*dag*. Gael. *deagh*. Literis transpositis, Gr. 'αγαθός. Goth. *gôd*.

DA, s. m. A fallow deer. Cor. Voc. *dama vel damula*. W. *danas*. Arm. *dam, demm*. Ir. *damh*. Gael. *damh*. Lat. *dama*. Fr. *daim*.

DA, pr. poss. Thy. *Da ynan*, thyself. Lhwyd, 167. *Er dha byn*, against thee. *ibid*. 249. ‡ *Scon a wonyn dha asow me a wra dhedha parow*, immediately of one of thy ribs I will make to thee an equal. C.W. 30. ‡ *Mester da, der dha gymmyas*, good master, by your leave. C.W. 112. This is the latest form; in the Ordinalia it is always written *de, dhe*, qd. v.

DA, prep. To, unto. In construction *dha*. *Reys yw purrys lavyrrya, ha gones an bŷs omma, dha gawas dheny susten*, needs we must by force labour, and till the ground here, to have to us sustenance. C.W. 80. This is a later form of *de, dhe*, qd. v.

DADER, s. m. Goodness, excellence. *Noé dre dhe dhadder brâs ty a bew ow grath nefré*, Noah for thy great goodness, thou shalt have my favour ever. O.M. 973. *Bythqueth me ny wrûk foly, leman prest dader dhywhy*, never have I done folly, but always good to you. P.C. 1296. *Govy y vones ledhys, kemmys dader prest a wre; y dhadder yw drôk tylys pan y'n ladhsons dybyté*, woe is me that he is killed! so much good he always did; his goodness is ill requited, when they killed him without pity. P.C. 3096. This is the abstract substantive of *da*, good. W. *daioni*.

DADLOYER, s. m. A speaker, orator. Pryce. Cor. Voc. *datheluwr*, concionator. W. *dadleuwr*, from *dadyl, dadl*, †*datl*, concio. Ir. †*dâl*, curia, forum.

DADLYNCY, v. a. To swallow. Pryce. Comp. of the prefix *dad*, afterward *das*, qd. v., and *lyncy*, or *lency*, to swallow.

DADN, prep. Below, under, beneath. ‡ *Ha Dew urâz an ebbarn, ha dheberhaz an dowrow era en dadn en ebbarn, dhort an dowrow era euh an ebbarn; ha an dellna etho*, and God made the firmament, and divided the waters that were under the firmament from the waters that were above the firmament, and it was so. C.W. p. 189. This is a late corruption of *dan*, qd. v.

DADNO, pron. prep. Under him. Lhwyd, 231. A late corruption of *dano*, qd. v.

DAFFAR, s. m. Convenience, opportunity. *Judas êth a dhesympys a neyl tu dhe omgregy; cafas daffar par parrys, lovan crŷf rag y synsy*, Judas went immediately on one side to hang himself; he found convenience very ready, a rope strong to hold him. M.C. 105. The plural is *daver*, qd. v. W. *daffur*, a recompense.

DAFOLE, v. a. To deform, to deride, to mock. *Ha why yn wêdh cowethe, pûp ûr gwreuch y dhyspytyé, ha daffolé fast an gwôs*, and ye also, comrades, do ye continually worry him, and mock the fellow much. P.C. 1438. *Yw saw oll dhe wolyow, a wylys vy dhe squerdyé ? a wrûk an gu ha'n kentrow dhe kŷc precius dafolé*, are all thy wounds healed, which I saw tearing thee, which the spear and the nails made, deforming thy precious flesh ? R.D. 492. W. *dyvalu*.

DAGER, s. m. A tear. Pl. *dagrow, daggrow*. *Fest yn tyn hy a wolê, dhe wherthyn nys teva whans, ha'y dagrow a dheveré a'y dew lagas pûr dhewhans*, very sharply she wept, to laugh, she had not a desire, and the tears dropped from her eyes very copiously. M.C. 222. *Yn ur-na râg pur dhwan daggrow tyn goraf dyveré*, in that time, for very sorrow, bitter tears I shall shed. O.M. 402. *Yma kên dhym dhe olé daggrow goys yn guyr hep mar*, there is cause to me to weep tears of blood really without doubt. O.M. 631. W. *dagr, dagyr, deigyr*, †*dacr*. Arm. †*daer*, pl. *dacrou*. Ir. *dear, deur*, †*dêr*. Gael. *deur*. Manx, *jeir*. Gr. δάκρυ. Lat. *lacryma*. Goth. *lagr*. Ang. Sax. *tear*. Germ. *zahre*. Sansc. *aṣra*.

DAGREN, s. m. A small drop, a tear. Pl. *dagrennow*. *A'n goys-na dagrennow try dre y dew lagasyth êth, nyng-o comfort na yly a wrello y holon hueth*, of that blood three drops through her eyes went, there was not com-

fort nor remedy that would raise her heart. M.C. 225.
W. *deigryn.* Gael. *devran.*

DAL, v. imp. It behoveth. *Mark Dew warnaf ew settys, te an gwêl yn corn ow thâl, gans dên pan vo convethys, worthaf ve ny dâl bôs mellyes a ûs nêb tra,* the mark of God on me is set, thou seest it in the horn of my forehead; with me ought not any thing whatever be meddled. C.W. 118. ‡ *Mêdh Juan, me dal gwellas an oet a chy,* saith John, I must see the host of the house. ‡ *Ha rag na erra dên na flôh en chy bez an vartshants, an dzhei dâl krêg ragta,* and because there was neither man nor boy in the house but the merchants, they should surely be hanged for it. *Lluyd,* 252. *E dâl,* it ought, 108. *Why dâl,* ye ought, 247. W. *dylu, dŷl.*

DAL, v. a. To pay, to be worth. A mutation of *tâl,* 3 pers. s. fut. of *taly,* qd. v. *Dew a dâl dheuch oll henna,* God shall pay to you all that. O.M. 1198. *Dew a dâl dheuh,* God shall reward you. *Lluyd,* 242. *Ow box mennaf dhe terry, a dâl mûr a voné da,* my box I will break, which is worth much good money. P.C. 486. *Ny dâl dhodho y naché,* it will not do for him to deny it. P.C. 1280. (W. *ni thâl idho ei nagu.*) *Ni dâl dhys scornyê gynê,* it will not do for thee to strive with me. R.D. 105. *Dhynny gweres ny dâl man,* nothing avails to help us. R.D. 131.

DALASIAS, s. m. Requital. *Mychtern Erod re dhanfonas Jhesu dhys, hag yn gwyn ef re'n gwyscas; vynyitha dalasias ef a'th carvyth, me a grŷs,* King Herod has sent Jesus to thee, and in white he has clothed him; for ever in requital, he will love thee, I believe. P.C. 1845. This word is probably corrupted, but evidently derived from *taly,* to requite.

DALHEN, s. m. A holding, a taking hold of, a seizing, a capture. Pl. *dalhennow. Henna yw ef, syttyouch dalhen ynno,* that is he, lay ye hold on him. P.C. 976. *Drôk handlé, del om kyry, pan guffy dalhen ynno,* handle him roughly, as thou lovest me, when thou shalt lay hold on him. P.C. 992. *Syttyouch dalhennow yn cam, a lever y vôs ef mab Dew,* lay ye hold upon the rogue, who says that he is the son of God. P.C. 1126. *Dalhen mar ca'af ynno, pûr wŷr, ny scap kyn fynno, na'n geffo clout,* if I shall lay hold on him, very truly he shall not escape, that he shall not have a blow. R.D. 382. Arm. *dalch.* W. *daliad.*

DALHENNE, v. a. To lay hold of, to seize. 3 pers. s. fut. *dalhen. Me an dalhen fest yn tyn, ha gans ow dornow a'n guryn no sowenno,* I will seize him very tight, and with my hands make him that he thrive not. P.C. 1131. *Arluth lavar dyssempys dhynny, mars yio bôdh dhe vreys, ha bolenegoth an tâs, my dhe wyskel gans cledhé neb ûs worth dhe dalhenné,* Lord, say immediately, if it is the will of thy judgment, and the wish of the Father, that I should strike with the sword him that is laying hold of thee. P.C. 1141. *Tewlyn grabel warnodho scherp, ha dalgenné ynno, bŷth na schapyé,* let us cast a grappling-iron on him sharp, and lay hold on him, that he may never escape. R.D. 2269.

DALONS, v. a. They will be worth. A mutation of *talons,* 3 pers. pl. fut. of *taly,* qd. v. *Dhe levarow, kyns gns stout, ny dalons man,* thy words, though they are stout, are not worth a mite. R.D. 1437.

DALVYTH, v. a. He will pay. It will be worth. A mutation of *talvyth,* 3 pers. s. fut. of *taly,* qd. v. *Råg yma ef deffry ow toen oll agan maystry, me a grŷs ny dalvyth bram,* for he is bearing away all our power, I think it will not be worth a crumb. P.C. 3078. *Yn y golon fast regeth mûr a gerensé worthys, hag ef a dalvyth dhys whêth, y honoré del wrussys,* into his heart there hath gone much love towards thee, and he will requite thee yet, as thou hast honoured him. M.C. 115.

DALL, adj. Blind. Corn. Voc. *dal, cecus. Te yw dall, rag genen cregis nêb es, dên glân yw a bêch,* thou art blind, for he that is hanged with us is a man clear of sin. M.C. 192. *Dall ên, ny welyn yn fâs ow bôs mar veyl ow pevé,* blind I was, I saw not well, that I was living so vile. M.C. 220. *Awos an Tâs fysienym, rag own namnag of pûr dhal,* because of the Father, let us hasten; for fear I am almost quite blind. O.M. 1056. *Dal ôf, ny allaf gweles,* I am blind, I cannot see. O.M. 2007. *Na gowsé moy ye march dal,* that he speak not more than a blind horse. P.C. 1658. *Kerchyn an gwâs dal,* let us fetch the blind fellow. P.C. 2916. *Râk dal ôf, ny welaf man,* for I am blind, I see not at all. P.C. 3104. W. *dall.* Arm. *dall.* Ir. *dall.* Gael. *dall.* Manx, *doal.*

DALLA, v. a. To blind, to make blind. *A's wrussouch cam tremené, cûth gweles y dhywedh fe, namna'n dallas,* ye did to him an evil transgressiou, a grief to see his end it was, it almost blinded us. R.D. 42. *Namn'agan dallas golow, pan dhueth an gwâs,* light almost blinded us, when the fellow came. R.D. 302. W. *dullu.* Arm. *dalla.* Ir. *dall.* Gael. *dall.*

DALLATHFAS, s. m. A beginning, or commencement. *Yn wêdh devodhec warnugans a virhas my a'm be a dhallathfas an lys-ma,* likewise two and thirty of daughters I have from the beginning of this world. C.W. 144. *En dallathvas Dew a wras nev ha'n 'oar,* in the beginning God made heaven and earth. C.W. p. 189.

DALLATHFAS, v. a. To begin, to commence. ‡ *Nangew ogas ha bledhan aban dallathfas an lyw,* it is now near a year since the flood began. C.W. 178. The following are the late corrupted forms, *a dhalladhas, hei a dhalasvas,* she began. *Lluyd,* 252.

DALLETH, s. m. A beginning or commencement. *Ha'y grâs dheuchwhy re wronntyo, nefré dhe blyggyé dhodho, yn dalleth hag yn dywedh,* and his grace may he grant to you, ever to bow down to him, at the beginning and at the end. O.M. 1728. *Del ôs dalleth a pûp tra, y reyth kusyl,* as thou art the beginning of all things, thou givest counsel. P.C. 471. *Yn della mar a whyrfeth, mŷl wêth a vŷdh an dywedh, ha hackré es an dalleth,* if it shall happen so, a thousand times worse will be the end and more odious than the beginning. R.D. 350. *An scryptor dhyn agores pûr wŷr a dhalleth,* the Scripture he opened to us very truly from the beginning. R.D. 1484. *En dallath Dew a wrâs nev ha'n 'oar,* in the beginning God created the heaven and the earth. M.C. p. 93.

DALLETHY, v. a. To begin, to commence. Written also *dalleth,* and *dallath.* Part. *dallathys,* or *dallethys. Hedhyw yw an whefes dŷdh aban dalletheys gonys,* this day is the sixth day since I began to work. O.M. 50. *Ha my â gans oll ow nel yn dôr dhe dhallath palas,* and I will go with all my strength to begin to dig in the ground. O.M. 370. *Yma ow treylé deffry oll an wlascor a Iudi, ow talleth yn Galilé,* he is turning really all the land of Judea, beginning in Galilee. P.C. 1595. *Dalleth cowyth, me a'th pŷs,* begin thou comrade, I pray thee. P.C. 2382. *An fêr a fue dallethys dre tûs vâs berth yn tempel*, the market was begun by good men within the temple. P.C. 2709. *Dûs omma scon dhe whethé, ha me a dhalleth aga gûl y*, come here directly to blow, and I will begin presently to make them. P.C. 2701. *Pyw a dhalleth? dallathans nêp a fynno, râk coské reys yw dhymmo*, who will begin? let him begin that will, for need is to me to sleep. R.D. 412. W. *dal*, to begin. *O'r awr y delisai*, from the hour he began.

DALYNNOUCH, v. a. Hold ye. *Más yw dhe cusyl deffry, mar scon dhodho delymmy, kychouch ef yn vryongen, ha dalynnouch mûr cales, ma na allo pertheges yn dyspyt oll dh'y echen*, good is thy counsel really, as soon as thou kissest him, catch him in the throat, and hold him very hard, that he cannot escape in spite of all his efforts. P.C. 1008. This would have been more correctly written *dalhennouch*, being the 2 pers. pl. imp. of *dalhenné*, qd. v.

DAMA, s. f. A dame, a mother. *Me ny wraf vry a henna, me a levar dhys, dama*, I will not make account of that, I tell thee, mother. C.W. 92. ‡ *En metten pan a why sevel, why rez cows dha guz damma wor aguz pedn dowlin,—Bednath Deew, ha an bednath war a vee, me a pidge dhu Deew*, in the morning when you rise, you must say to your father and your mother upon your knees,—The blessing of God, and a blessing upon me, I pray to God. Pryce. ‡ *Dama wyn*, a grandmother. Lhwyd, 44. Literally, a white mother. *Mam wen*, in Welsh, means a step-mother, and *mam gu*, and *nain*, a grandmother. *Dama* occurs only in late Cornish, and is borrowed from the English, or French.

DAN, s. m. Fire. A mutation of *tân*, qd. v. ‡ *Mehal, yskynyow, Eal splan, hellouch Adam gans cledha dân, ha'y wrêg mês a Baradys*, Michael, descend, angel bright, chase Adam with a sword of fire, and his wife, out of Paradise. C.W. 70. *A dân*, of fire. Lhwyd. 231.

DAN, prep. Under, beneath. This is properly a mutation of *tan*, qd. v., but it generally is used as if it were the primary form, an irregularity of which there are also examples in Welsh. In Cornish *dan* is generally preceded by *yn*. *Del y's brewaf yn dan gên*, as I will strike her under the chin. O.M. 2712. *My a vyn ordené yn scon tûs dh'y denné ef bys d'y, yn dan dryys may fo pottyys*, I will at once order men to drag it to that place, under feet that it may be placed. O.M. 2807. *Dyswedh y a dhan dhe glôk*, shew thou them from under thy cloak. P.C. 2682. *Yn dan naw alwedh gwreûch y pûr fast*, under nine keys make ye them very fast. R.D. 31. *Yn dan dôr un tuch ny sef*, under ground he will not stay a moment. R.D. 2112. W. *tan*, *dan*. Arm. *didan*, *indan*.

DANFENYS, part. Sent. *Map Dew o dhyn danfenys*, the Son of God was sent to us. P.C. 3104. This is only another form of *danvenys*, part. of *danvon*, qd. v.

DANIN, v. a. To send. Lhwyd, 245. ‡ *Rag danyn dheuh*, to send to yon. Lhwyd, 242. This is a late corruption of *danvon*, qd. v.

DANO, pr. prep. Under him, or it. Lhwyd, 231. *Yma gynef flowrys têk, yn onor dhum arluth whêk aga skulyé yn danno*, I have fair flowers, in honour to my sweet Lord, (I will) scatter them under him. P.C. 260. Comp. of *dan*, under, and *o*, he, or it. W. *dano*.

DANS, s. m. A tooth. Corn. Voc. *dens*; pl. *dannet*, *dentes*. Another plural preserved by Llwyd, 243, was *deins*, agreeing with the old Welsh, *deint*, as found in Taliesin's poems. This is the form preserved in the Ordinalia; though written *dŷns*, it was sounded as *deins*, exactly as the English word *dines*. *Pan varwo, gorr'y hep fal yntré y dhŷns ha'y davas*, when he dies put them without fail between his teeth and his tongue. O.M. 826. *Avel brathken aga dŷns orto y a dhiskerny*, like mastiff dogs their teeth on him they gnashed. M.C. 96. In Lhwyd's time, the plural was written *dens*. *Dans rag*, a fore tooth, (W. *rhagdhant*.) *Dens rŷg*, fore teeth. *Dens dhelhar*, jaw teeth, or grinders. Llwyd, 13, 27, 54. *Dans* is a later form of *dant*. W. *dant*, pl. *dannedh*, †*deint*. Arm. *dant*, pl. *dent*. Ir. *dead*. Gael. *deud*. Manx, †*jeid*. Lat. *dens*. Gr. οδόντα. Goth. *tunthus*. Lith. *dantis*. Sansc. *dat*, *danta*.

DANTA, v. a. To bite. Lhwyd, 245. W. *deintio*. Arm. *danta*.

DANVA, s. f. A hiding place, concealment. Pryce.

DANVON, v. a. To send. It is written indiscriminately *danfon*. Part. pass. *danvenys*. *Ow mâp my a dhanvon*, my son I will send. O.M. 690. *Y gras re dhanvonno dhyn*, his grace may he send to us. O.M. 1187. *Dew a'm dhanvonas dhyso*, God has sent me to thee. O.M. 1480. *Pan danfensys dhe cannas*, when thou hast sent thy messenger. O.M. 1670. *Danfon jeches dhymmo vy a'm clevas*, send health to me from my disease. O.M. 2630. *Leverouch dhe gour an chy, agas mester dhe dhanvon*, say ye to the man of the house, your master to send. P.C. 634. *Gwrys da vye, dhodho y vôs danvenys*, well done it would be, his being sent to him. P.C. 1609. *Me a'th pŷs a dhanfon dhynny cannas*, I pray thee to send a messenger to us. R.D. 768. *Dheuch comfort a Spyrys Sans a dhanfonaf*, to you the comfort of the Holy Ghost I will send. R.D. 1176. *Danvenouch why dhe Pyladt*, send ye to Pilate. R.D. 1594. *Pŷs e dhym ma'n danfunno*, pray thou him that he send him to me. R.D. 1620. *An Tâs Dew dré'n Spyrys Sans dhe'n beys danvonas sylwyans*, God the Father, through the Holy Ghost, to the world has sent salvation. R.D. 2611. *A'n nef y fe danvenys êl dhodho*, from heaven there was sent an angel to him. M.C. 58. *Rag henna y tanvonas Christ dhodho cf*, for that he sent Christ to him. M.C. 108. W. *danvon*.

DANVONAD, s. m. A mission, a message, a command, or injunction. Pl. *danvonadow*. *Dûn alemma, cowethé; me a'n doro dheuch dhe dré, Arluth, dhe'th danvonadow*, let us come hence, comrades; I will bring him to you home, Lord, according to thy injunctions. P.C. 998. W. *danvoniad*, pl. *danvoniadau*.

DAON,; adj. The first. The only authority is Pryce, and an evident corruption.

DAOR, s. f. The earth, the ground. A late form of *doar*, qd. v. ‡ *Dho dowla'n daór*, to throw on the ground. Lhwyd, 154. ‡ *Gûdh dhaór*, a mole, 180.

DAORN, s. m. A hand, a fist. A late form of *dorn*, qd. v.

DAOS, v. a. To go. ‡ *Daoz meas*, to go abroad. Lhwyd, 129. ‡ *Daoz war dhelhar*, to come back, to return, 137. A late form of *dôs*, qd. v.

DAR, s. m. An oak. Corn. Voc. *quercus vel jllex*. Pl. *derow*, qd. v. It is preserved in the names of many places in Cornwall, as *Pendarves*, the head of the oak field. *Pendar*, oak head. *Darless*, oak green. *Treluddero*, gray oak town, in Newlyn. W. *dâr*, pl. *deri*;

and *derw*, whence *derwen*, a single tree. Arm. *dero, derv, derf.* Ir. *dair, darach, duir, derg, darog.* Gael. *darach.* Goth. *triu.* Ang. Sax. *treov, trjv.* Eng. *tree.* Gr. δρῦς, ἔαρν. Δαρούεργον, a town in Britain. Sansc. *daru.*

DAR, s. m. Sadness, sorrow, doubt. These are the meanings given in Pryce's Vocabulary, but the true signification is very obscure. The following are the sentences in which it occurs. *Dar marow yw Syr Urry,* alas (1) Sir Uriah is dead. O.M. 2217. *Bys may codhé hy dhe'n dôr ha'y brewy gwyls yn dar clor, mar venys avel skyl brâg,* until she fall upon the earth, and break her, (?) in fierce pain, as small as malt dust. O.M. 1719. *Dar desevos a wreuch why, na allaf ow thás pygy,* do ye raise a doubt (?) that I cannot pray to my Father? P.C. 1161. *Nagues ioy y ges colon, lemyn dar nep marthegyon us wharfethys,* there is not joy in your heart through (?) some wonders that have occurred. R.D. 1259. *Ow habersen a fue gures, levy dar bol,* my habergeon was made,(?) to spread round my body. R.D. 2537. *Mûr o an payn dar ken dhe vôb Du,* much was the pain beyond other to God's son. M.C. 135. In Welsh, *dar* means a noise.

DAR. A prefix in composition. It implies before, upon, or about to be. The most analogous to it is *pre* in English. Thus *darbary,* to prepare.

DARADOR, s. m. A doorkeeper. Corn. Voc. *hostiarius.* Derived from *darat,* a door. W. *drysor.* Ir. *doirseoir.* Gael. *dorsir.* Manx, *darreyder.*

DARALLA, s. m. A tale, a relating. ‡ *Ha an della ma divedh me daralla dodhans,* and so is the end of my tale of them. Lluyd, 253.

DARAS, s. m. A door. Pl. *darusow. Fystynyuch trôh an daras,* hasten ye through the door. O.M. 349. *Ygor an daras,* open thou the door. P.C. 1985. *Rág mar tue dh'agan porthow, ef a ter an darasow, hag a dhylyrf an cheltys,* for if he comes to our doorways, he will break the door, and liberate the company. P.C. 3041. *Ygor dhe dharasow,* open thy doors. R.D. 81. *Na war dharas ny dhue dhynny,* nor through doors he comes not to us. R.D. 329. *Býs yn daras y chy,* even to the door of his house. R.D. 1631. Lluyd writes the word *darras, dacerys,* the fore-door, 13. (W. *rhugdhor.*) *Bahow an darras,* the hinges of the door, 45. *Dorras dhelhar,* the back door, 124. *Daras* is a later form of *darat,* qd. v. W. *dôr, drws.* Arm. *dôr.* Ir. *dorus, duras.* Gael. *dorus.* Manx, *dorrys.* Gr. θύρα. Lat. *fores.* Sansc. *dvár.* Goth. *daur.* Lith. *durrys.* Slav. *dver.* Eng. *door.*

DARAT, s. m. A door. Corn. Voc. *hostium.* This is the old form of *daras.*

DARBARY, v. a. To prepare, make ready, provide. 2 pers. s. imp. *darbar. Ty vaow, darbar lym ha pry, meyn whegl, elodyys, ha genow, ha me a fystyn agy, ow trehevel an fosow,* thou boy, prepare lime and clay, building stones, trucks, and wedges; and I will hasten within, erecting the walls. O.M. 2713. Comp. of the prefix *dar,* and *pary,* ld. qd. Lat. *paro,* to prepare. W. *darparu.* Arm. *darbari.*

DARN, s. m. A fragment, a piece. Pl. *darnow. Ow holon yntré mýl darn marth yw gené na squardy,* my heart into a thousand pieces it is a wonder to me that it is not broken. M.C. 166. *Dyncolow yffarn a squerdyns corf Judas oll dhe dharnow,* the devils of hell broke the body of Judas all to pieces. M.C. 106. W. *darn.* Arm. *darn.* Hence the English *darn,* to piece, or mend. Sansc. *darana.*

DARYVAS, v. a. To declare, to make known, to tell, to shew. *Drefen ow lones benen, ty a gl dhym daryvas.* because I am a woman, thou mayest make it known to me. O.M. 162. *Gwýr dhym ty a dharyvas, an varchvran-na dh'y whelé,* truth thou hast told me, to look for that raven. O.M. 1105. *Ygor an daras, rák me a vyn daryvas worth Ihesu whêth, anodho dycheth vyé, y wokyneth na ugé, ha'y muscochneth,* open thou the door, for I will show to Jesus yet, for him it would be a pity, his folly not to leave, and his madness. P.C. 1986. *Uferelh fôl yw na'm gás, lemmyn môs dhe dharyvas tra na wra lês,* foolish vanity it is that he does not leave it, but to go to assert a thing that will not benefit. R.D. 951.

DARYVAS, s. m. A declaration, an information. *Yma dhymmo, cowyth da, mur a ioy yn torma, a'th daryvas* there is to me, good friend, much joy from thy information. R.D. 1301. *Ioy yw gynef dhe clewas, mar têk yw dhe dheryvas ; dredhos ythof lowenhýs,* it is a joy to me to hear, so fair is thy declaration ; through thee I am made glad. R.D. 2607. *Sêth, ow mâb, dês omma, ha golsow ow daryvas,* Seth, my son, come here, and listen to my declaration. C.W. 124.

DAS, a prefix in composition. This is a later form of *dad,* of which we have an example in *dadlyncy.* It has the force of *re* in Latin, as *dasvewé,* to revive ; *dasserchy,* to rise again ; *dasprenna,* to redeem. W. *dad,* †*dat,* comp. of *do-at.* Old Irish, *do-aith, taith.* Arm. *das.*

DAS, s. m. A father. A mutation of *tás,* qd. v. *A dás kér,* O dear father. O.M. 696. *Ef a bren Adam, dhe dás,* he will redeem Adam, thy father. O.M. 811. *A dês Dew yn uchelder,* O Father God on high. O.M. 937.

DASARGRAPHA, v. a. To re-print. Pryce. Comp. of prefix *das,* and *argraphy,* to print.

DASCEMERAS, v. a. To recover. Pryce. Comp. of prefix *das,* and *cemeras,* to take.

DASCEVIAN, v. a. To find. Pryce. Comp. of prefix *das,* and *cafos,* to have.

DASCOR, v. a. To deliver, yield up, resign. Part. pass. *dascerys. An êl dhym a leverys, pan vu tryddydh tremenys, ty a dhascor dhe enef,* the angel told me, when three days are passed, thon shalt give up thy soul. O.M. 846. *Rák henna an gwella ús dascor mýns mond yw pýs,* therefore the best is to deliver up all the money (that) is paid. P.C. 1508. *Nans o marow, ha daskcrys y spyrys,* now he was dead, and his spirit yielded. P.C. 3122. *I beyn o mar créff ha tyn, caman na ylly bewé, heb dascor, y eneff gwyn,* his pain was so strong and sharp that he could not live any way without yielding, his pure soul. M.C. 204. *Ila'n enef del dascorsé erbyn nater gans un cry,* and bei he yielded the soul against nature with a cry. M.C. 208. Comp. of pref. *das,* and *goré,* to place. Arm. *duscor.*

DASPRENA, v. a. To redeem. Lluyd, 249. More frequently written *dysprena,* qd. v. W. *dadbrynu.* Arm. *dasprena.*

DASSERCHY, v. n. To rise again. Part. pass. *dasserchys.* 3 pers. s. pret. *dassorchas,* as if from *dassorchy. Ef a tasserch dyougel lyes prýs wogé merwel,* he will rise indeed many times after dying. P.C. 1754. *Corf yn bêdh a worseuch why, a wre bôst a dhasserchy dhe'pen try deydh,* the body ye have put in the tomb, he boasted at the end of three days. R.D. 358. *Pan bostyas dhe pen try deydh y tasserchy dhe vewnans*, when he boasted, at the end of three days he would rise again to life. R.D. 375. *Me a'n gwŷth kyn tassorcha*, I will keep him though he should rise again. R.D. 379. *Ef re dhassorchas hydhyw yn mês a'n bêdh, râk na wrello dasserchy, nefré ny gen byen ny ioy hep dhywedh*, he has risen to-day out of the grave; for if he should not rise again, never should we have joy without end. R.D. 1026. *An keth corf-na gordhewyth ny dhasorchas*, that same body very certainly has not risen. R.D. 1036. *Aban oma dasserchys, dew hugens deydh dyvythys bŷdh, pan fo nôs*, since I am risen, forty days will be ended when it is night. R.D. 2436. Comp. of pref. *dad*, and *serchy*, id. qd. Lat. *surgo*. Arm. *dazorchi*. Ir. *oiseirche, eirche*, †*esseirge*, †*seirge*. Gael. *eirich*.

DASSERCHYANS, s. m. Resurrection. *My ny wodhyen a'th vernans, ny vŷth moy a'th dasserchyans, pan y'th whylsyn dewedhys*, I knew not of thy death, nor any more of thy resurrection, when I saw thee ended. R.D. 2545. *A tûs vâs, why re welas a dhasserchyans Cryst del fue*, O good people, ye have seen of the resurrection of Christ how it was. R.D. 2632.

DASSERHY, v. n. To rise again. *An houl ny golsé y lyw, awos mâp dên dhe verwel, na gorf dasserhy dhe vew*, the sun would not lose its colour, because a son of man to die, nor a body rise again to life. P.C. 3085. *Ha cows ef dhe dhasserhy*, and say that he has risen again to life. R.D. 24. *Corf Cryst dasserhys marsyw, môs dhe vyras*, if the body of Christ be risen, go to see. R.D. 692. *Del yw leverys dhymny, lemmyn ef re dhassorhas*, as it is told to us, now he has risen again. R.D. 1272. Another form of *dasserchy*, the aspirate being softened into *h*.

DASVEWE, v. n. To revive, to come to life again. *Meneuch fest y wrûk bostyé, an tregé deydh dasvewé, kyn fé ledhys mar garow*, very often he did boast the third day to revive, though he were killed so cruelly. R.D. 339. *Ydhyskyblon yn pryvé a'n lader yn mês a'n beydh, hag a lever yn pûp le y vôs dasvewys arté*, his disciples privily will steal him out of the tomb, and will say in every place, that he has revived again. R.D. 345. *Coskyn ny gans dynha, kyn dasvewo ny'n drecha dhywar y geyn*, let us sleep with security; though he rise, he will not lift it from off his back. R.D. 403. *Dên a vo marow ny dhasvew nês*, a man that is dead does not live again. R.D. 949.

DATHELUUR, s. m. A speaker, orator. Corn. Voc. *concionator*. See *Dadloyer*.

DAVA, v. a. To feel, or handle. *Corta, gâs vy dhe dava, áresym gwelas mar nebas*, hold, let me feel it, since I see so little. C.W. 116. The word occurs again in a doubtful passage. P.C. 1002. *Scolkyouch dh'y an dan dava, rag mar a's gwêl, ef a wra môs dhe kudhé war un plynch*, lurk after him, (?) under silence, for if he sees you, he will go to hide at a start. The sense would allow a connection with *tewel*, to be silent.

DAVAS, s. f. A sheep. Pl. *deves*. *Gaver, yweges, lurow, daves, war ve lavarow, hy hanow da kemeres*, goat, steer, sheep, according to my words, let them take their good name. O.M. 127. *Dên an geffé cans davas, ha'y centrevak saw onan, mar a's ladré dheworto, pa'n pŷn a godho dhodho*, a man may have a hundred sheep, and his neighbour only one; if he steal it from him, what punishment is due to him? O.M. 2230. *Pan vo gwyskys an bugel, y fy an deves a bel, hag oll an flok a dhybarth*, when the shepherd is smitten, the sheep will flee far, and all the flock separate. P.C. 894. *Râg an termyn re devé may fŷdh an begel kyllys, ha chechys yntré dewlé ha'n deves dhe vês fŷs*, for the time is come, that the shepherd will be lost, and caught between hands, and the sheep driven out to flight. M.C. 48. Llwyd gives the following examples; ‡*davas tanow*, a lean sheep; ‡*davas dhiu*, a black sheep; ‡*boudzhe devas*, a sheep fold; ‡*lodon davas*, a wether sheep, 172. ‡ *Trei cans lodon davaz*, three hundred sheep, 244. We find another late plural, *devedgyow*, in C.W. 78. Written in Corn. Voc. *davut*. W. *davad*, pl. *devaid*. Arm. *davad, danvad*, pl. *devcd, denved*. In the three British dialects only does this word mean a sheep; in the Irish and Gaelic, *damh*, is an ox. The root seems to be *dov*, †*dom*, tame. Sansc. *dam*.

DAVAS, s. m. A tongue. A mutation of *tavas*, qd. v. *Kemer tyyr spûs an aval, a dybrys Adam dhe dâs; pan varwo gorr 'y, hep fal, yntré y dhŷns hay davas*, take three kernels of the apple, which Adam thy father ate; when he dies put them, without fail, between his teeth and his tongue. O.M. 826. *Dên heb davas a gollas e dir*, a man without a tongue lost his land. Llwyd, 251.

DAVAT, s. f. A sheep. Corn. Voc. *ovis*. This is the old form of *davas*.

DAVER, s. m. A convenience, a scrip, pouch, a budget. *In mêdh Christ a ban rûg dheuch ernoyth fernoyth ów holyé, daver vŷth wy ny dhecsyuch dhe worré trevyth ynné*, saith Christ, when I cause you naked unclad me to follow, conveniences ever ye carried not to put any thing in them. M.C. 50. This is the plural form of *daffar*, qd. v.

DAW, v. n. He will come. Llwyd, 247, gives this as the 3 pers. s. fut. of *dôs*, but it is literally the Welsh form, and is not to be found in the Ordinalia.

DAYL, v. imp. It behoveth. *Mûr a dûs a leverys, ny dayl dhys lam y naché*, many men said, it avails thee nothing to deny him. M.C. 85. Another form of *dêl*, qd. v.

DE, adj. Yesterday. ‡*De genzhete*, the day before yesterday. Llwyd, 249. A late form of *doy*, qd. v.

DE, s. m. A day. An abbreviated form of *dêdh*, qd. v. *Drôk na yl dên vŷth dhe wûl dhe weyth, na dhe Sûl*, no man is able to do harm to thee, neither work day nor Sunday. R.D. 1833. It was always used in the names of the days of the week, which were all borrowed from the Romans. *De Sûl*, Sunday; *De Lun*, Monday; *De Merh*, Tuesday; *De Marhar*, Wednesday; *Dr Jeu*, Thursday; *De Gwenar*, Friday; *De Sadurn*, Saturday. So also in Armoric, *di* is used for *deix*, as *Disûl, Dilûn, Dimeurs, Dimercher, Diziou, Digwener, Disadorn*. In Welsh again, though never written, the *dydh* is generally contracted in conversation into *dy*, or *di*: thus *Disûl, Dillûn, Dimawrth, Dimercher, Dydh Iau*, (here the final is preserved before the vowel, as occurs in Armoric,) *Digwener, Disadwrn*.

DE, pr. poss. Thy, thine. This is strictly the secondary form of *te*, but it was always used as the primary form, and in construction changed into *dhe*. *Dhe lêf Arluth a glewaf*, thy voice, Lord, I hear. O.M. 587. *Pandra yw dhe nygys*, what is thy errand? O.M. 733. *Me a wra 'dhe arhadow*, I will do thy commands. O.M. 1134. *An* re-na a ġll dhe dhysky, yn della y re dhyskas, those may teach thee, as they have learned. M.C. 80. *Hag oll rag dhe gerensé*, and all for thy sake. O.M. 139. ‡*Na ra chee gwoas whans warlyrch chy de contrevak, na ra gawns chwans warlyrch gwrég de contrevak*, do thou not entertain a desire of the house of thy neighbour, nor do thou entertain a desire of the wife of thy neighbour. *Pryce*. Written also *dy*, qd. v. W. *ty, dy*. Arm. *ta, da*. Ir. *do*. Gael. *do*. Manx, *dty*. Gr. τεον, σὸν. Lat. *tuus*.

DE, v. n. He will come. 3 pers. s. fut. of *dós*, qd. v. *Yn hanow Du yntredhon benegas yno néb a dhe*, in the name of God amongst us blessed is he that comes. M.C. 30. *Ow thermyn a dhe yn scon, genouch mc num bȳdh tregé*, my time will come immediately, with you I shall not stay. M.C. 37. *Râk ow thorment a dhe scon, genoch na'm byvé trygé*, for my suffering will come soon, that with you I shall not stay. P.C. 541. *Ha gynef y tanfonas y te dheuch, pare veuch wâr, kepar ha del amboesas*, and by me be sent that he will come to you, as ye are aware, like as he promised. R.D. 915. W. *daw*. Arm. *deù*.

DE, v. a. He will swear. A mutation of *te*, 3 pers. s. fut. of *toi*, qd. v. *Rag henna dhys my a de gordhyé Iovyn veneges*, therefore I swear to thee to worship Jove the blessed. O.M. 1811.

DE, prep. To, unto. It changes in construction into *dhe*, and softens the initial following. *Jesus Christ mûr gerensé dhe vâb dén a dhyswedhas*, Jesus Christ much love to mankind shewed. M.C. 5. *Dybbry boys ef ny vynnas, lymmyn pûp ẽr 'ol olé, dhodho bȳs pan danvonas Christ y to dhe Galylé*, eat meat he would not, but every hour weep, until when Christ sent to him that he would come to Galilee. M.C. 87. *Adam, ke yn mês a'n wlâs, troha ken pow dhe vevé, ty dhe honan dhe balas, dhe wrêk genes dhe nedhé*, Adam, go thou out of the country, towards another land to live; thou thyself to dig, thy wife with thee to spin. O.M. 344. *Dre ow thrȳs y tûth un emat, gans kentrow d'aga gorré*. through my feet a fellow came, with nails to put them. R.D. 2588. This word was also written *do, dho*, and *du*. W. †*di*, †*do*. Arm. *da*. Ir. *do*, †*du*. Gael. *do*. Manx, *da*. Slav. *do*. Germ. *du*. In Welsh *di* is now obsolete, is being used instead, but it constantly occurs in the earliest documents; †*hin map di iob* (mod. *yn vâb i Iou*) a son of Jove: †*di litas (i·lydaw)* to Latium: *di aperthou (i aberthau)* to gifts: and with the article *dir arpedticion ceintiru (i'r arbededigion gevndyrw)* to the wretched cousins. Oxford Glosses, quoted in Zeuss's Grammatica Celtica. It is also of constant occurrence in the Liber Landavensis. "*Aper Cafrui in guy ar i hit diuinid bet penn ar cuieir hadrech dindirn dir alt diuinid di drec dindirn. o drec dindirn diguairet di guy. maliduc guy ar i hit bet nper catfrut*." 217. The older form *do*, is also found in composition, in the Luxemburg and Oxford Glosses, quoted by Zeuss, 627, as †*doguomisuram*, I measure; †*doguohintiliat*, a walker, &c.

DE, prep. From, of. In construction it changes into *dhe*. It is used only with *worth*, and *rag*, and their derivatives, as *deworth, dheworth*, from by, from ; *dheworto*, from him, &c. *Dhe rag*, from before, before ; *dherygthy*, before her. It is also written *dy*, qd. v. W. †*di*. Arm *di*. Ir. *di*.

DEALL, s. m. A deluge. *Ow bôdh ythew yn della, gweyll deall war oll an bȳs, may fȳdh pup tra consumys*, my will is thus, to make a deluge over all the world, that every thing shall be consumed. C.W. 168. Written also *dyal*, qd. v.

DEAN, s. m. A man. *Determys ove dha un dra, dha wythyll un dean omma, a dhôr, dhom servia*, determined I am to one thing, to make a man here on earth, to serve me. C.W. 18. A late form of *dén*, qd. v.

DEANC, v. a. To escape. *En varogyon pan glewas Pylat ow cows yn della, mûr a ioy a's kemeras y, dhe dheank yn della*, the soldiers, when they heard Pilate speaking thus, much joy took possession of them, to escape so. M.C. 251. Written also *dyanc*, qd. v. W. *dianc*. Arm. *dianca*.

DEAU, num. adj. Two. ‡*Deau mark*, two horses. *Llwyd*, 244. A late form of *dew*, qd. v.

DEAWL, s. m. A devil. Pl. *dewolow, dywolow, devolugy*, qd. v. *Ty sathnas deawl mylygys*, thou Satan, devil accursed. P.C. 137. *War ow fay, hemma yw deawl ymskemunys*, on my faith, this is a devil accursed. R.D. 2088. *Ef yw deawl créf*, he is a strong devil. R.D. 2111. *Me a'n nabow dyougel ytho fe deawl kyns merwel*, I know it certainly, that he was a devil, before dying. R.D. 2121. In the Cornish Vocabulary, the form is *diavol*, qd. v. It is also written *diawl*, where see the synonyms.

DEBARN, s. m. The itch. *Llwyd*, 145.

DEBEL, adj. Wicked, evil. A mutation of *tebel*, qd. v., pl. *tebeles. A debel vemyn, hep râs, ty rum tullas hep kén*, O wicked graceless woman, thou hast deceived me without pity. O.M. 251. *A sôn an debel bobel*, at the noise of the wicked people. O.M. 1815. *May wñello an debeles ow gweres menouch dhedhé*, that the wicked may see my frequent help to them. O.M. 1849.

DEBERHY, v. a. To divide, to separate. ‡*Ha Dew rig deberrhee an golow dhurt an twolder*, and God did divide the light from the darkness. ‡*Ha gréns e deberrhé an dowrow dhurt an dowrow*, and let it divide the waters from the waters. ‡*Ha dew wrûs an ebbarn ha dheberhas an dowrow*, and God made the sky, and divided the waters. ‡ *Gwrêns enna bôs golow der an ebbarn nêv, dha deberhé an dȳdh dhort an nôs*, let there be light in the sky, to divide the day from the darkness. C.W. p. 189. This is a corruption of *deberthy*, written also *dybarthy*, qd. v. W. *dybarthu*.

DEBERTH, s. m. A division, a separation. *Pryce*. Written also *dybarth*, qd. v.

DEBERTHVA, s. f. A division, separation, distinction. *Me a vyn bôs golow gwryes, hag ynwêdh bôs deberthva inter an gȳdh ha'n nôs*, I will that light be made, and likewise that there be a distinction between the day, and the night. C.W. 8. Comp. of *dyberth*, and *ma*, a place.

DEBONER, adj. Lowly, humble, meek. *Lavar gwȳr dhymmo un gẽr, marsola mâb dén ha Du ; Cryst a genys dyboner, te a leverys del yu*, tell true to me one word, if thou art the son of God ; Christ spake lowly, thou hast said as it is. M.C. 129. *Te ra degé colon deboner trog dhy tâs, ha dh y mam*, thou shalt bear a humble heart towards thy father, and thy mother. *Pryce*. From the French *debonnaire*, qd. v.

DEBR, s. m. A saddle. Another form of *diber*, qd. v. '*⁺ Debr dour*, a hat; lit. "sella pluralis," which some use, seems a later invented word.' *Llwyd*, 62.

DEBRY, v. a. To eat. *Attebres* (a tebres,) *ty ha'th worty, a'n wedhen ha'y avalow, y fyeuch yn úr-na avel dewow*, if thou didst eat, thou and thy husband, of the tree and its fruits, ye would be iu that hour like gods. O.M. 175. *Hag ynwëdh gwra dhe'th worty, may tebro ef annodho*, and also make to thy husband, that he may eat of it. O.M. 200. *Pyw a symsow why mochya, nép a serf, py a dheber? A nyns yw nép a dheppro?* whom think ye the greatest, the one who serves, or who eats? Is it not he that eats? P.C. 799. *Ny dhebbraf bòs, bones marow an profos a alsé ow yaché*, I will not eat food, because the prophet is dead, who could cure me. R.D. 1685. It is written as often *dybry*, or *dibri*, qd. v.

DEC, num. adj. Ten. *Y'n uhelder my a vyn dèk warnugans y vôs gures*, in height I wish it to be made thirty (cubits.) O.M. 960. *Hayl Cayfas syr cpscob stout, dèk can quỳth dhys lovené*, hail, Caiaphas, bold sir bishop, ten hundred times joy to thee. P.C. 574. *Dèk warnugans a moné, me ny vennaf cafus le, yn gwyryoneth*, thirty of money, I will not take less, in truth. P.C. 593. *Yma goon vràs dhymmo vy, me a's gwerth dheuch yredy, a dhèk warnugans sterlyn*, I have a large down, I will sell it to you now, for thirty sterling. P.C. 1554. By Keigwyn, and Llwyd, it was written *dég. Déqwarnygans.* C.W. 164. ‡*Padzhar igans a dég*, ninety. *Llwyd*, 100. W. *dég*, †*dec*. Arm. *dég*, †*doc*. Ir. *deich, deag*, †*deae*, †*dece*, †*dce*. Gael. *deich, deug*. Manx, *jeih*. Gr. δέκα. Lat. *decem*. Chald. *deka*. Pers. *dch*. Slav. *desiat*. Goth. *taihun*. Sansc. *dasan*.

DEK, adj. Fair, comely. *Gódh dèk scon my a offryn dhe Dew war ben ow dewlyn, hag a's gor war y alter*, a fair goose forthwith I will offer to God on my knees, and place it on his altar. O.M. 1195. *Ha dhedhé prest gorhemmyn gruthyl wheyl dèk ha prive*, and command them quickly, to do fair and secure work. O.M. 2440. *My a gews dhodho nûr dèk*, I will speak to him very fair. P.C. 189. *Me a gerch onan dèk dhys*, I will fetch a fair one for thee. P.C. 2840. A mutation of *tèk*, qd. v.

DEK, v. a. He will bring. 3 pers. s. fut. of *degy*. Written also *dég*, qd. v. *Ha me a dhèk dustyny, y'n clewys ow leverel, treydydh woxi y terry y wrefs y dhrehevel*, and I bear witness, I heard him saying, three days after destroying it, that he would re-build it. P.C. 1313.

DEDH, s. m. A day. Pl. *dedhyou*. *Kyns avorow hanter dédh*, before to-morrow mid-day. P.C. 722. *Why a wra y ascunvos dédh brús, hag a'n kỳf yn próf*, ye will acknowledge it on the day of judgment, and have it in proof. P.C. 1496. *Gans dhe golon y wordhyé gwra, dédh ha nós*, with thy heart do thou worship him, day and night. P.C. 3231. *An trygé dédh yw hydhew, dhyworthyf aban ethé*, the third day it is to day, since he went from me. R.D. 465. *An dedhyow a vỳdh gwelys, hag a dhe ynirethon, may fỳdh torrow benegis bythqueth na allas e dhôn*, the days shall be seen, and shall come among us, that the wombs shall be blessed that could never bear. M.C. 169. Written as commonly *dýdh*, qd. v.

DEDHE, pron. prep. To them. *Dewes a yrhys dedhé, dhym rosons byntyl wherow*, drink I required of them, they gave me bitter gall. R.D. 2600. In construction it changes into *dhedhé*. *May rollo yn nép teller dour, dhe evé dhedhé y*, that he may give in some place, water to them to drink. O.M. 1824. W. *idhynt, idhynt hwy*. Arm. *dezó*. Ir. *dóibh*, †*doib*. Manx, *daue*.

DEDHEWY, v. a. To promise. *Henna o poynt a falsury dedhewys heb koweras*, this was a point of falsehood promised without fulfilment. M.C. 83. Written also *dedhycy*, and *dydhywy*, qd. v.

DEDHORY, v. n. To rise again. *En varogyon a guskas myttyn, ha'n gỳdh ow tardhé, ha Jherus a dhedhoras, hag éth yn le may fynné*, the soldiers slept in the morning, while the day was breaking, and Jesus rose up, and went whither he would. M.C. 243. *An tressa dýdh ef a dhedhoras dort an marow*, the third day he rose again from the dead. *Pryce*. W. *dydhwyre*.

DEDHORYANS, s. m. A rising again, resurrection. *Cowethyans an sansow, dewhyllyans pehasow, dedhoryans an corf, ha bewnans heb dyweedh*, the communion of saints, forgiveness of sins, resurrection of the body, and life without end. *Pryce*.

DEDHY, pron. prep. To her. *Ol y fechas guldn dedhy hy y feydh gefys, ràg kemmys hy dhom caré*, all her sin clean to her is forgiven, for so much she loved me. P.C. 529. In construction it changes iuto *dhedhy*. *Kyns mós alemma, ry whaf dedhy my a wra gans myyn grow yn bràs garow*, before going hence, give a blow to her I will with gravel stones very sharply. O.M. 2755. W. *idhi*. Arm. *dezi*. Ir. *di*.

DEDHYWY, v. a. To promise. *Hen ew an ocl a verry o dedhywys dyso sy, dheworth an Tàs Dew an néf*, this is the oil of mercy which was promised to thee by the Father God of Heaven. O.M. 842. *Ow máp whèk, my a vynsé a luen golon dhe pygy a dhós dhym ha fystyné del dhedhywys dhymmo vy*, my sweet son, I would wish with full heart to pray thee, to come to me and hasten, as thou promisedst to me. R.D. 450. *Dhe'n bèdh pan y ges gorrys, dhymmo why a dhedhywys, na'n laddro dèn*, to the grave when I set you, ye promised that man should not steal him. R.D. 624. Written also *dydhywy*, qd. v. W. *adhaw*.

DEES, s. m. Men, people. Another form of *dus*, qd. v.

DEF, v. n. He will grow. A mutation of *tef*. 3 pers. s. fut. of *tevy*, qd. v. *Bohes yw henna dhynny, mỳns a dèf ynno, un grydh my ha'm gwrèk a wra dybry*, little is that for us, all that will grow in it, in one day, I and my wife will eat. O.M. 365.

DEF, s. m. A captain. *Ha why Annas, ow dèf kêr, dyswodhouch bòs pryns somper ràk dyswyl an Cristenyon*, and yon, Annas, my dear captain, shew yourself to be a prince without equal to destroy the Christians. P.C. 797. Written also *duf*.

DEFALEBY, v. a. To disfigure, to deform. l'art. pass. *defalebys*. *Defalebys ós ha cam, overdevys oll gans henna ytbos gans blew*, deformed thou art and crooked overgrown all with that thou art with hair. C.W. 116. *Dha aswon me ny wodhyan, drefan bós defalebys*. *Defalebys óv pùr vear, hag overdevys gans blew*, to recognize thee I knew not, because thou art deformed. Deformed I am very much, and overgrown with hair. C.W. 120. Compounded of *de*, neg. prefix, and *hyvelep*, form, likeness.

DEFEN, s. m. A forbidding, a prohibition. *Aban goistè worty hy, ha gruthyl dres ow defen, mylygé a wrnf defry an nór y'th whythres hogen*, because thou hearkenedst to her, and actedst beyond my prohibition, I will assuredly curse the earth in thy evil deed. O.M. 270. *Gulán ef re gollas an plás, a'm lúf dhyrhyow a wrussen, pan wrugé dres ow defen,* clean he has lost the place, (that) I had made with my right hand, when he acted against my prohibition. O.M. 922. Written also *dyfen*, qd. v., and by Keigwyn, *deffan*.

DEFENA, v. a. To awake. See *Dyfuny*. *Y tefenas un marrek,* there awoke a soldier. M.C. 244.

DEFENNAD, s. m. A prohibition. Pl. *defennadow*. *Rag néb a'n grûk ny a bry, a rôs dhyn defennadow, frût na wrellen dhe dhybry a'n wedhen,* for ho who made us of clay gave us prohibition, that we should not eat the fruit of the tree. O.M. 238.

DEFFNNY, v. a. To forbid, to prohibit. Written also *defen*. Part. pass. *defennys*. *Eva prâg y whrusté sy tullé dhe bryes hep kên, an avel worth y derry woaé my dhys dh'y dhefen,* Eve, why didst thou deceive thy husband without pity, by plucking the apple after I had forbidden it to thee. O.M. 280. *Adam dres pub hunyth me a'n cûr, po Dew deffan,* Adam, above every thing, I love, or God forbid. C.W. 50. *Mar pe hemma terrys, mês a'n wedhan defennys, ragdha me a vŷdh grevys,* if this should be broken from the forbidden tree, for this I shall be grieved. C.W. 56. *Rag terry an kéth frutes a wrûg defenna dheworthys, spern y tég dhys ha spedhes,* for breaking that same fruit, which I did forbid from thee, thorns it shall bear for thee, and briars. C.W. 70. *Peva! Abel yw ledhys! Dew defan y vôs gwyr !* What, Abel is killed! God forbid it should be true. C.W. 90. Written also *dyfen*, qd. v.

DEFFE, v. n. He should come. 3 pers. s. imp. subj. of irr. v. *dôs*. *Yn gyhcys máp Dew yn prôf ahanaf may portho côf, pan deffé dh'y wlascor ef,* I called him the Son of God, in proof that he would bear remembrance of me, when he came to his kingdom. R.D 273.

DEFFO, v. n. He shall come. 3 pers. s. 2 fut. of irr. v. *dôs*. *Kee kymmer mêns a vynny, Adam a'n beis oll adro, dhyso ef veydh besy, hag ahanes a dheffo,* go, take as much as thou wilt Adam of the world all around, it shall be indeed for thee, and what shall come out of thee. O.M. 406. *Ha kekemmys na'n cresso, goef termyn a dheffo, devones a brys benen,* and as many as will not believe it, woe to him the time that he came, coming from the womb of woman. R.D. 1349. *Arluth ple yth én alemma dhyn dhe gymeres tryafa na dheffo dén vŷth gynen,* Lord, where shall we go from hence, for us to take a dwelling, that not any man may come with us. R.D. 2393.

DEFFRYTH, adj. Deformed. *Lemyn deffryth ôv, ha gwôg, pûr vegr drys oll an'dencs an bŷs,* now deformed I am, and hungry, very truly, beyond all the men of the world. C.W. 86. This is probably the same as the W. *difruyth*, feeble.

DEFFYN, v. n. Wo shall come. 1 pers. pl. fut. of *dôs*. *Pandra wrên, agan penwar, a rák Pilat pan dheffyn ny yn teffry,* what shall we do, we four, before Pilate, when we come, seriously. R.D. 565. *A Ihesu, luen a vercy, ahunan gwra prydyry, dhe'th wlascor pan deffyn ny, olew agan lêf, O Jesus,* full of mercy, do think of us, to thy kingdom when we shall come, hear our voice. R.D. 773.

DEFNYDH, s. m. Use, substance, matter. *War Cedron ow crowedhé yma pren da, ha hen yw emskemunys, rák ny allas dén yn beys anodho gûl defnydh vâs,* on Kedron there is lying a good tree, and this is accursed; for no man in the world has been able to make a good use of it. P.C. 2548. W. *devnydh*. Arm. *danvez*, †*danues*. Ir. *damhna*.

DEFRAN, s. m. The bosom. *Yn top an wedhan dêk, ythesé un virgyn whêk, hay flôch pûr semely maylyes yn y defran,* in the top of the tree there was a sweet virgin, and her child very seemly swathed in her bosom. C.W. 138. Another form of *duivron*, qd. v.

DEFRECH, s. m. The arms, the two arms. *Yn ur-na y a colmas y dhefrech fast gans cronow,* in that hour they bound his arms fast with thongs. M.C. 76. *Josêp dhe Gryst a vynnas y arrow ha'y dheffrech whêk, yn vanner del yn whâs, hay a's ystynnas pûr dêk,* Joseph to Christ made-white his legs and arms in the manner as they used, and extended them very fairly. M.C. 232. Written also *dwyvrech*, qd. v.

DEFRY, adj. Without trifling; earnest, serious, real, true; quick, soon. *Fenten bryght avel arhans, ha pedyr streyth vrâs defry, ow resek a dywrorty,* a fountain bright like silver, and four streams, large indeed, flowing from it. O.M. 772. *A pûp bêst kemmyr wharé, gorow ha benow defry,* of every best take forthwith a male and and female, really. O.M. 1022. *Henna my a grêys a luen golon, pûr dheffry,* that I believe with full heart, very earnestly. O.M. 1264. *Rag henna ymden yn scon a dhyworto cf deffry,* therefore, withdraw thou immediately from him, in earnest. O.M. 1378. *Ty a dhedhy a dhysempys yn teffry rák y cusyllyé,* thou shalt go to her, really, immediately soon to counsel her. P.C. 1929. It was written at a later period *devry*. W. *divriw*. Arm. *devri*. Ir. *dibhirceach*. Gael. *dibheareach*.

DEFYDH, v. a. To quench, to extinguish. Written also *dufydh*, qd. v.

DEFYTH, s. m. A wilderness, a desert. *Ke yn vês, ymskemenys, yn defyth yn tewolgow, dhe vestry a vŷdh leyhys neffré war an enevow,* go thou away, accursed, into the desert, into darkness; thy power shall be diminished over over the souls. P.C. 142. *Ha'm hendas Cayn whath yw bew, yn defyth yn mŷsk bestes yma ef prest ow pewa,* and my grandsire Cain is yet alive, in the desert among beasts he is now living. C.W. 109. Another form of *difeid*, qd. v.

DEG, num. adj. Ten. *Degwarnygans,* thirty; lit. ten upon twenty. C.W. 164. Thus written in Keigwyn, and Llwyd's time, but in the Ordinalia, *dec,* qd. v.

DEG, v. a. He will bear. 3 pers. s. fut. of *degy*. *Ha rag henna desempys ny a'th dêg, bŷs gorfen vŷs yn ponow dhe worowedhé,* and therefore forthwith we will carry thee, till the end of the world in pains to lie. O.M. 903. *Me a'th dêg,* I will bring thee. Lhwyd, 331. Written also *dec,* qd. v. W. *dwg*.

DEGE, s. m. The tenth, tithe. *Hag oll agas gwyr dhegé, dhodho gweteyeuch offrynné, ha'y lesky, del yrchys ef,* and all your true tithe, to him take yo care to offer, and burn it, as he hath enjoined. O.M. 440. *Ytho prâg na lewes rf kafus y dhegé hep grêf, hag aban vyn y lesky,* now, why didst thou not leave him to have his tenth without complaint, and burn it since he will. O.M. 497. *Tan resyf dheworthyf ve ow degé, ha'm offryn gulán,* take, receive from me my tithe, and my offering pure. O.M. 504. *Degé oll agan edhyn, bestes yr. wêdh maga la, warnydhy my a offryn yn gordhyans dhe'n tâs gwella*, tithe of all our birds, beasts also as well, upon it I will offer, in worship to the best Father. O.M. 1181. W. *degwm*, †*decum*, from the Latin *decumæ*. Arm. *deog*. Ir. *deachmhadh, dechmadh*. Gael. *deachamh*. Manx, *jaghee*.

DEGENOW, part. Departed. *Ellas my ny wodhyen man, bones mâp Dew y honan dagenow yn mês a'n néf*, alas! I knew not at all, that the son of man had departed out of heaven. R.D. 2561. This word is of doubtful derivation, but I am inclined to connect it with *descené*, to descend.

DEGES, part. Shut, enclosed. *Tresters dredho ly a pyn adrus rág na vo degees*, beams through it thou shalt nail across, that it may not be shut. O.M. 964. *Ihesu Cryst, mâp Dew an néf a dhueth yn chy, ha'n darasow oll deges; whêt y lavar a fue, crês oll dhywhy*, Jesus Christ, Son of heaven came into the house, and the doors were all shut; yet his speech was, "Peace to you all." R.D. 1360. *Tarosfan a dhue deffry war tûs vâs, pan vôns yn chy, h'aga darasow degeys*, phantoms come indeed upon good people, when they are in the house, and all their doors shut. R.D. 1452. *Deges* is the participle of *degy*, qd. v., and is written also *dyges*.

DEGHES, v. a. Brought. *Aban nagus ken maner, an arhans kettep dyner me a's deghes war an luer*, since there is not another way, the silver, every penny, I have brought upon the floor. P.C. 1514. *Deghes* is the preterite of *dega* or *degy*, and the *h* was inserted to shew that the *g* was to be hard.

DEGL, s. m. A festival, holiday. *Llwyd*, 59. ‡*Degl Stûl*, Epiphany, 57. This is a contraction of *dêdh*, a day, and *goil*, a holiday, qd. v.

DEGLENE, v. a. To unloose, to give away. *Gwrẏs da vye cafus tán, râg marthys yeyn yw an gwyns; yma ow trẏs ha'm dulé dhyworthef ow teglené, ma 'thew krehyllys ow dẏns*, it would be well done to have a fire, for wondrous cold is the wind; my feet and hands are loosening, so that my teeth are chattering. P.C. 1217. *Mar ethuk yw dhe weles, may tyglyn an tybeles, pan y'n gwellons, ketep pen*, so awful is it to see, that the devils will wince, when they see it, every head. P.C. 3047. Comp. of neg. pref. *de*, and *gleny*, to adhere.

DEGOTH, v. imp. It behoveth, it becometh. *Arluth dhe vôdh my a wra, del degoth dhym yn pûp le*, Lord, I will do thy will, as it becomes me in every place. O.M. 641. *Euch growedheuch, ow arluth, may haller agas cudhé gans dylles rych del degoth dhe vychtern a dynyté*, go, lie down, my lord, that you may be covered with rich clothes, as it becomes a king of dignity. O.M. 1925. *Nêp na'n gordhyo del dhegouth, nyns yw dén fûr, del greaaf*, he that does not worship him as he ought, is not a wise man, as I believe. P.C. 215. Comp. of *de*, id. qd. *dy*, intens. prefix, and *góth*, it behoveth.

DEGVES, num. adj. Tenth. *Adam, a oll dhe dreves an degves ran dhymmo gâs, whêth in atal dhe kesky*, Adam, of all thy sheaves, the tenth leave thou to me, still to remain waste. O.M. 426. Comp. of *deg*, ten, and *mes*, for †*med*, a measure. W. *degved*. Arm. *degved*. Ir. *deachmhadh*. Gael. *deachamh*. Manx, *jeigoo*.

DEGWYTH, adv. Ten times. *Llwyd*, 248. Comp. of *deg*, ten, and *gwyth*, a time. W. *degwaith, dengwaith*.

DEGY, v. a. To shut up, to inclose. *A'n bêdh pan dhueth ha lammé, y fyys yn un vramné, own kemerys, del leveraf pen bronnen, râk ny alsé yngwen del oll degys*, from the grave when he came and leaped, thou fleddest in a tremor, seized by fear, as I say, rush head, for he could not move himself as he was entirely shut up. R.D. 2098. The participle was also written *deges*, qd. v. It seems to be compounded of intens. prefix *de*, and *ced*, W. *cau*, to shut.

DEGY, v. a. To bear, carry, bring, produce. *Otté omma prynner genef dhe wûl tân, degys a drê*, behold here wood with me to make a fire, brought from home. O.M. 1315. *Pûp dén oll degens ganso y pŷth, an mêns a allo, war aga keyn fardellow*, let every man carry with him his things, as much as he can, burdens on their back. O.M. 1593. *Degeuch an pren a dhyhons war dhour Cedron may fo pons*, carry ye the tree quickly over the waters of Cedron, that it may be a bridge. O.M. 2810. *Na dhegouch sor yn colon*, do not ye bear anger in heart. P.C. 539. *Me a vyn degy udro, ha dhe worré gy dhe'n fo a dhesempys*, I will carry round, and put thee to flight immediately. P.C. 2313. *Kymerens pûp ran a'y lu, degens dhe drê*, let every one take a share on his side, let him take it home. P.C. 2860. *Daver vyth wy ny dheccxyuch dhe worré trevyth ynné*, conveniences ye never brought to put any thing in them. M.C. 50. Another form of this word is *doga*, qd. v. W. *dygu, dyged*, †*docu*. Arm. *douga*. Ir. *tug*, †*tuc*. Gael. *iog, tug*. Manx, *dug*. Gr. τεύχω, τέχομαι. Lat. *duco*. Fr. *duis*. Goth. *tiuha*. Germ. *ziehe*. Eng. *tug*. Sansc. *duh, tak*.

DEGYLMY, v. a. To untie. *Dewsull blegyow pan esé yn mysc y abestely, y wrêk dhe re aneuhe môs dhe'n drê, ha degylmy an asen, ha dry gansé, ha ieverel yrody mur teffa tûs, ha gwethé, bós dhe Dhu dhe wûl gynẏy*, Palm Sunday, when he was in the midst of his apostles, he caused some of them to go to the town, and untie the she-ass and bring (her) with them, and to say readily, if men should come and keep (her) that it was for God to do with her. M.C. 27. Comp. of neg. prefix *de*, and *cylmy*, to bind.

DEHEN, s. m. Cream of milk. *Pryce*. Arm. *dienn*.

DEHESY, v. a. To strike. *War, gâs vy dhe dhehesy, gans morben, bom trewysy, dhe'n vyl hora war an tâl*, mind, let me strike, with mallet, a terrible blow to the vile strumpet on the forehead. O.M. 2703. Arm. *darchaoui*.

DEHOU, s. m. The right, the south. This word is variously written, *dyhow, dyow*, and also in the Ordinalia, *dychou*, qd. v. W. *deheu*, †*dehou*. Arm. *dehou*.

DEHOULES, s. f. Southernwood. Corn. Voc. *aprotanum*. Comp. of *dehou*, south, and *les*, a herb. W. *deheulys*.

DEIL, s. m. Leaves. This is a plural aggregate; for the singular, *delen* is the term, which had another plural, *delyow, dylyow*. *Agan corfow nôth gallas, gans deyl agan cudhé gwrên*, our bodies are become naked, with leaves let us cover us. O.M. 254. ‡*Gweithu ny gans deel glâs*, let us cover with green leaves. C.W. 62. W. pl. *dail*, s. *deilen, dalen*. Arm. s. *delien*, pl. *deliou*. Ir. *duille, duilleog, duilein, duillen*. Gael. *duille, duilleag*. Manx, *duillag*. Anc. Gaulish, *dula*. Sansc. *dala*.

DEISCYN, v. a. To descend. *Llwyd*, 44. Written also *dyeskenné*, qd. v.

DEL, s. m. A semblance, form, or manner. *Yn del-ma*, in this manner, thus. *Yn della (del-na)* In that manner, so. *Yn ketel-ma, (keth-del-ma)* in this same manner, thus. *Yn ketella (keth-del-na)* in that same manner, so. *Fatel (pa del,* W. *pa dhelw)* In which manner, as. *An ioul dhe Gryst a genesys yn del-ma rag y demptyé*, the devil to Christ said in this manner to tempt him. M.C. 14. *Yn del-ma heb velyny orto Jesus a gowsas*, in this manner, without rudeness, Jesus to him spake. M.C. 80. *Yn della re bo*, so be it. O.M. 462. *Pan vyn an Tás yn della, reys yw y wruthyl porrys*, when willeth the Father so, very necessary it is to do it. O.M. 648. *Bódh dhe vàp yw yn della*, the will of thy son is so. P.C. 2952. *Prag na výdh Adam yn keth della tremowntys*, why shall not Adam be in the like manner tormented ? C.W. 148. ‡*Pandra gowsow dhym lemyn, del nag oma polat brás*, what say you to me now, as I am not a great pullet. C.W. 12. ‡*Ha an dellna etho*, and it was so. C.W. p. 190. W. *delw, dull.* Ir. *dealbh*, †*delb.* Gael. *dealbh.* Manx, *jalloo.*

DEL, adv. So, as, like as, than. *Ny a vyn formyé an bys, par del ón try hag onan*, we will create the world, like as we are three and one. O.M. 12. *Arloth Dew, a'n nef an Tás, kepar del os luen a rás, venytha gordhyys re by*, Lord, God, the Father of heaven, as thou art full of grace, for ever be thou worshipped. O.M. 106. *Kyns del vy serrys, my a wra oll del vynny*, rather than thou shouldst be angry, I will do all as as thou wishest. O.M. 245. *A wylsta ken yn torma ys del egé agensow*, dost thou see more now than as there was just now ? O.M. 796. *Gor ost genes yrvys da, dhe omladh, del y'm kerry*, take a host with thee well armed, to fight as thou lovest me. O.M. 2142. *Dhynamo vy mar ny gresouch, ottengy a wél oll dheuch, kepar ha del levorys*, if ye will not believe me, behold them in the sight of you all, just as I have said. P.C. 2690. *Ha mar scon del y'n gwylly, ef a'th saw hep ken yly oll a'th cleves yn tyen*, and as soon as thou seest it, it will heal thee, without other remedy, of all thy malady entirely. R.D. 1694. *Gweeskis yn arvow, kepare ha del êns dhen gás*, clad in arms just as if they were going to battle. M.C. 64. *Ef a doys a dhesempys maga town ty del wodhyé*, he sware immediately as deep an oath as he knew. M.C. 85.

DELC, s. m. A leaf. Llwyd, 13. Pl. *delciow.* ‡*Delciow gwér*, green leaves. Llwyd, 61, 243. ‡*Rag delciow sevi gura musi lég*, for strawberry leaves make maidens fair. Pryce. This is a late corruption of *deil.* Llwyd gives another late singular, ‡*tair delkian*, three leaves, 243.

DELC, s. m. A necklace. Corn. Voc. *monile.* This word is no where else to be found, and has no synonyms in the other dialects. The nearest forms are Ir. *dealg,* †*delg*, a thorn, skewer, or bodkin. Gael. *dealg.*

DELE, s. f. The yard of a ship. Corn. Voc. *antempna.* Arm. *delez, delé.*

DELEN, s. f. The leaf of a tree. Corn. Voc. *folium.* Pl. *delyow*, and *dylyow*, qd. v. See also *Deil.* W. *dalen, deilen.* Arm. *delien.* In modern Welsh, *dalen*, pl. *dalenau*, is the leaf of a book, and *deilen*, pl. *dail*, the leaf of a tree.

DELHAR, adv. Back, behind. ‡*Dens delhar*, the back teeth, or grinders. ‡*A dhelhar*, behind. ‡*War dhelhar*, backwards, behind. Llwyd, 140. ‡*Dws war dhelhar*, to go back, to return, 137. This is a late form of *dellarch*, qd. v.

DELLA, adv. In that manner, so. *Synays ve dre govaytis, yn della yw leas huny*, hurt he was by covetousness, so is many a one. M.C. 62. *Own a gachyas an Justis, pan glewas cows yn della*, fear seized the Justice, when he heard such a speech. M.C. 143. Comp. of *del*, manner, and *na*, there. See *Del.*

DELLARCH, adv. Back, behind, backward. *Mar possé an neyll kenewen, rág y scódh hy a'n grevyé, ha whálh goëth a wre an pren, war dhellarch mar an gorré*, if he leaned on one side, for his shoulder it him grieved, and yet worse did the wood, behind if he laid it. M.C. 205. Comp. of *di*, and *lerch*, a footstep, whence *war lerch*, behind. Arm. *dilereh.*

DELLE, v. a. To let out, discharge. *Me a greys an harlot a dhellos bram*, I believe the fellow has let out a puff. O.M. 1200. *Ellas na dhelleys a'm gwen dhy lesky un luhesen, ha erak turan*, alas, that I did not send forth to burn him a lightning and a clap of thunder. R.D. 292. Written also *dyllo*, qd. v.

DELLO, comp. v. So he was. *Un venyn da a welas dello Jesus dystryppyys, pytel múr a's kemeras rag y vôs mar veyll dyglys*, a good woman saw how Jesus was stript, great pity took her because he was so vilely treated. M.C. 177. Comp. of *del*, as, and *o*, was.

DELLY, v. a. To bore a hole. A mutation of *telly*, qd. v. *Y delly scon my a wra, rag ebyl parys yma, dh'aga fastyé dyowgel*, I will soon bore it, for the pegs are ready, to fasten them truly. P.C. 2570. *Dew droys Jesus caradow ha'y dew leyff y a delly*, the feet of Jesus beloved and his hands they bored. M.C. 159.

DELMA, adv. In this manner, thus. *An ioul dhe Grist a gewsys yn delma, rag y demptyé*, the devil to Christ spoke in this manner, to tempt him. M.C. 14. Comp. of *del*, manner, and *ma*, here. See *Del.*

DELNA, adv. In that manner, so. *Ha an delna ytho*, and so it was. C.W. p. 192. Comp. of *del*, manner, and *na*, there. It was euphouized into *della*, qd. v. See also *Del.*

DELVETH, v. n. She ought. ‡*Hye oare gwile padn dah gen tye glawme, ha et eye ollaz, hye delveath gowas tane*, she knows to make good cloth with her wool, and on her hearth she ought to have fire. Pryce. This is the 3 pers. s. fut. of *dely.*

DELY, v. a. To owe, to deserve. Llwyd, 247, gives the following inflexions of it; *delev, delon*, or *mi a dhelon*, I ought ; *delix*, or *ti a dheli*, thou oughtest ; *delé* or *ev a dhylé*, he ought. *Mai dhyllyn*, that I ought or should. *Kyns y un teller yn beys, dew kendoner yth egé dhe un dettor ; me a grýs, an ngl dhodho a dhellé pymp cans dyner monyys, ha hanter cans y gylé*, once in a part of the world there were two debtors to one creditor ; I believe the one owed to him five hundred pence of money, and half a hundred the other. P.C. 504. Written also *dylly*, qd. v. W. *dylai*, †*dyly*, †*dele. Ny dele mab uchelwr vod yn pen teulu ; sef achaus nas dele*, a freeholder ought not to be the president of the household, for this reason, that he ought not. *Welsh Laws.*

DELYMMY, v. a. To touch. This word thus explained in Pryce's Vocabulary is a blunder. It must be read as two words, being *del*, as, and *ymmy*, thou shalt kiss, qd. v.

DELYOW, s. m. *Púp gwedhen tefyns a'y sáf, ow tôn hy frut ha'y delyow, ha'n losowys erbyn háf, degyns hás yn erberow*, let every tree grow from its stem, bearing its fruit and its leaves, and let the plants against summer produce seed in gardens. O.M. 30. One of the plurals of *delen*, qd. v.

DELYRSENS, v. a. They would have delivered. *Yn medh Jesus, nyng-ugy ow michternes yn bys-ma, hag a pe, ow thûs dhewy nym delyrsens yn delma*, says Jesus, my kingdom is not in this world, and if it were, my men to you would not have delivered me in this manner. M.C. 102. 3 pers. pl. pluperfect subj. of *delyfré*. a word borrowed from the English. *An golom glas hy lagas yn mês gwra hy delyfré*, the dove with blue eyes, do thou liberate her outside. O.M. 1110.

DEM, pron. prep. To me. *Drefen un wyth dhe henvel, lydhys ôf pûr dhyogel; gâf dhem ow fêch, me a'd pŷs*, because I named thee once, I am killed very certainly; forgive me my sins, I pray thee. O.M. 2726. ‡*Bez nar menta rei dem arla, me a deska dis kên point a shians*, but if thou wilt give them to me again, I will teach thee another point of wit. Llwyd, 251. Another form of *dym*, qd. v.

DEMIDHY, v. a. To espouse, to marry. Part. pass. *demidhys.* ‡*Ketmer with na rey ostia en tshei lebma vo dem koth dewidhys dhe benen iyngk*, take care that thou do not lodge in a house where an old man is married to a young woman. Llwyd, 251. W. *dywedhio*, fr. *dy*, intens. prefix, and *gwêdh*, a yoke. Arm. *demezri*. Ir. †*dimhadh*, a dowry.

DEMIG, s. m. A small piece, a particle. A mutation of *temig*, or *temmig*, qd. v., pl. *temigow*. *En demigow*, in pieces, piecemeal. Llwyd, 113.

DEMMA, s. m. A halfpenny. *Ow arfeth byth ny whyla, ahanas yy un demma my ny sensuf yn torma*, my hire I never see, of thee one half-penny I do not hold at this time. P.C. 2263. W. *dimai*. From the Lat. *dimidium*.

DEN, s. m. A man. Llwyd, 243, gives *dynion* as the plural, but this is exactly the Welsh plural, and I can find no other authority for this form. In late Cornish *denes*, and *dens* occur, but in the Ordinalia *tus* is always used for the plural, as *gens* in French is employed for the plural of *homme*. *Mâp dén a bry yn perfyth me a vyn y vôs formyys*, the son of man of clay perfectly I will that he be formed. O.M. 55. *My a'd wra ty dhên a bry*, we make thee, man, of clay. O.M. 59. *Dew dhên a gefyth ena*, two men thou shalt find there. O.M. 333. *Dén vyth na'th ladho*, that no man kill thee. O.M. 603. *Kynyver dén ûs yn wlâs*, as many men as are in the land. O.M. 1029. *Ryprden ol ynno*, every man in it. O.M. 1043. *Drôk dhên. ôs kepar del vês*, a wicked man thou art, as thou hast been. M.C. 192. *Dén iune*, a young man, a youth; *dén huel*, a workman; *dén brâs lavar*, a great talker, a vaunter; *dén môr*, a mariner; *dén Dew*, a godly man; *dén côth*, an old man; *dén brâs*, a great man; *dén clâv*, a sick man; pl. *dynion clevion*, Llwyd, 242. *Dén cosgor*, a client; *den unchui*, a stranger; *don maur*, a great man, or grandee. Corn. Voc. *Lemyn deffryth ôv, ha gwâg, pûr wŷr. dres oll denes yn bŷs*, now deformed I am, and hungry, very truly beyond all men in the world. C.W. 86. *Na mear a dern da ny wraf, mês pûp car oll ow pela an dens wan mar a callaf*, nor will I more do a good turn, but always driving away the weak men if I can, C.W. 104. W. *dyn*, †*den* Arm. *dén*. Ir. *duine*. Gael. *duine*. Manx, *dooinney*. Sansc. *g'ana*.

DEN, comp. prep. To the Compounded of *de*, to, and *an*, the. In construction it changes into *dhen*. *Ef o Christ a dhêth dhen leur, mab Dwhu dén yw kyffrys*, he was Christ that came to the earth, the son of God and man he is likewise. M.C. 8. *Y wrêg dhe rê anedhé môs dhe'n dré ha degytmy an asen*, he caused some of them to go to the town, and untie the ass. M.C. 27. *Ha'n bewnans pan y'n kylly, dhe'n dôr ty a dreyl arté*, and the life when thou losest it, to the earth thou shalt turn again. O.M. 64.

DEN, pron. prep. To us. *Judas fals a leverys, trehans dynar a voné; nabox oll bedhens gwerthys, ha vôs den râg y ranné*, false Judas said, three hundred pence of money I let the box all be sold, and be to us to share it. M.C. 36. Comp. of *de*, to, and *yn*, us. Written also *dyn*, qd. v.

DENA, v. a. To suck, to draw, to absorb. to withdraw. Llwyd, 158. It was also written *dené*, and *deny*. *Me a vyn môs dhe vyras. hag a wodhfyth, kyns denas a dhyworto, oll an câs*, I will go to see, and shall know, before withdrawing from it, all the case. O.M. 1400. *Govy vŷth pan vêf genys, a dor ow mam dynythys, na vythqueth pan denys brou*, sad, that ever I was born, out of my mother's womb brought, or ever sucked the breast. O.M. 1755. *Râg y tue dydhyow, may fenygouch an torrow, nas tevé vythqueth flehes, ha kekyffrys an bronnow na dhencs flehesyggow*, for the days will come, that ye will bless the wombs that have never borne children, and also the breasts that little children have not sucked. P.C. 2649. *Gans y vam y fye guris, hag ef gensy ow tené*, by his mother it was made, and he with her sucking. M.C. 161. W. *dyvnu*. Arm. *dena*. Ir. *dinim*, *dighin*, *dín*. Gael. *dith*.

DENATAR, adj. Unnatural. *Lemmyn gorquyth y garé, ha gweyth denatar na vy*, now be thou careful to love him, and take care that thou be not unnatural. M.C. 139. Comp. of *de*, negative, and *natar* from the English.

DENDEL, v. a. To earn, get, deserve. ‡*Me a vedn moz da huillaz huêl da ûl; ha huei el dendel'gys bounas ybma*, I will go to look for work to do, and you may get your living here. Llwyd, 231. ‡*Na ra hens moaz dan coos, do kuntle go booz, buz gen nebas lavirians, eye venja dendle go boox ha dillaz*. they should not go to the wood to gather their meat but with little labour they would get their meat and clothes. Pryce. A late form of *dyndyly*, qd. v.

DENETHY, v. n. To give birth to, to produce Part. pass. *denethys*, born, which is also written indiscriminately *denythys*, and *dynythys*, qd. v. *Ty a vŷdh náb denethys a dhe corf, henna a vŷdh hayal dhys, ny yll dén bôs havalla, ha genef y fŷdh kerrys*, thou shalt have a son born of thy body, he shall be like to thee no man can be more like, and by me he shall be laved C.W. 96. *Flehys a'm bes denethys a Eva ow freus mer dewdhek warnigans genys a vybbyan, hei or wab Cayn hag Abel*, children to me are born of Eve my will many, twelve and twenty born of sons, without my sons Cain and Abel. C.W. 144. *Denethys a n gwerehas Vary*, born of the Virgin Mary. C.W. p. 200.

DENETHYANS. s. m. A generation. Written also *denythyans*, qd. v.

DENEWEN, s. m. A side. A mutation of *tenewen*, qd. v. *Cowyth, growedh an nŷl tu, hag aspy ahas, ha glu, a rôg hag a denewen*, comrade, lie on one side, and look out continually, and listen, forwards and sideways. O.M. 2063.

DENEWOIT, s. m. A steer. Corn. Voc. *juvencus.* W. *diniawed.*

DENEWY, v. a. To pour, shed, or effuse. *Ow box mennaf dhe terry, a dál múr a voné da, war dhe pen y dhencry, ha war dhe treys magata,* my box I will break, which is worth much good money, upon thy head I will pour it, and on thy feet likewise. P.C. 487. W. *dynëu, dyneuo.*

DENLADH, s. m. Homicide, murder, manslaughter. *Onon esa yn preson, Barabas yth o gylwys, presonys o ef dre dreyson, ha rág denladh kekyffris,* there was one in prison, Barabbas, he was called. imprisoned he was for treason, and for homicide also. M.C. 124. Comp. of *dén,* a man, and *ládh,* slaughter. W. *dynladhiad.*

DENS, s. m. Teeth. The plural of *dans,* qd. v. ‡*Gora an dens harrow dha an gov, dha lebma,* put the harrow tines to the smith to sharpen. *Pryce. Dens-clav,* toothache. *Llwyd,* 105. Written also *dyns,* qd. v.

DENS, s. m. Men. One of the late plurals of *den,* qd. v.

DENS, v. n. Let them come. 3 pers. pl. imp. of *dós,* qd. v. *Otté an tán ow tewy, déns pan vo bódh gansé y, aga bós a vÿdh parys,* behold the fire burning; let them come when the will is with them, their food shall be ready. P.C. 694. W. *deuant.*

DENSES, s. m. Manhood, humanity, men. *Pyw a ylta gy bones, pan yw mar rúdh dhe dhillas yn gulascor néf; rák me a wôr lour, denses, marnes dre an luen duses, omma ny séf,* who canst thou be, when thy clothing is so red, in the kingdom of heaven? for I know certainly that men, unless through the full Godhead, remain not here. R.D. 2514. *Prág yth yw rúdh dhe dhyllas, omma aberth yn pen wlás, le na fue denses bytheuth?* why are thy garments red, here within the head country, where humanity never was. R.D. 2531. *Arluth kér, bynyges ós; asyw ioy gynef godhfos, an denses dhe dhôs dhe'n nef,* dear Lord, blessed thou art; it is a joy with me to know that the manhood hath come to heaven. R.D. 2609. Written also *densys. Deuguans dÿdh ow penys y speynas y gÿk ha'y woys, ha wotewedh rag denays eff a'n gevé excell boys,* forty days in doing penance he wasted his flesh and his blood, and at last through (his) manhood he had a desire for food. M.C. 10. W. *dyndawd, dyndod.*

DENSETH, s. m. Humanity. *Dre y holon yth éth séth; y máb syndis pan welsé, moreth an séth ha pylet; natureth o ha denseth,* through her heart there went an arrow, her son hurt when she saw; sorrow was the arrow and pity; natural affection and humanity. M.C. 223. Another form of *denses.*

DENSHOC, adj. Toothed. Corn. Voc. *denshoc dour,* lucens, a lucy fish, a hake, (dentatus aquæ.) *Denshoc* would have been more correctly written *densoc,* from *dens,* teeth. W. *deintiawg, deintiog.* Arm. *dantek.* Ir. †*daintech.*

DENUNCHUT, s. m. A stranger. Corn. Voc. *advena;* where only it is found. Comp. of *dén,* a man; and *unchut,* an unknown term, and most probably corrupted.

DENWENNOW, s. m. Sides. *Deu teka bren rág styllyow, ha compos y denwennow, brás ha crom y ben goles,* lo, the fairest trees for rafters, and straight its sides, large and rounded its lower end. O.M. 2442. A mutation of *tenwennow,* which is a contracted form of *tenewennow,* the plural of *tenewen,* qd. v.

DENYTHY, v. m. To give birth to, to produce. Part. pass. *denythys,* and written also *denethys,* and *dynythys,* qd. v. *Arluth, hen yw re-nebes, mar qurén flóch vÿth denythy,* Lord, this is too little, if we shall ever produce a child. O.M. 390.

DENYTHYANS, s. m. A generation. *Rág me an Arluth dhy Dew, yw Dew a sor, ha vyn towlé pehasow an tasow war an flehes, bÿs an tressa ha'n peswerra denythyans,* for I the Lord thy God, am a jealous God, and will visit the sins of the fathers upon the children, unto the third and fourth generation. *Pryce.*

DEPPRO, v. a. He may eat. 3 pers. a. subj. of *debbry,* qd. v. *Mara kyllyn y gafus, vynytha na dheppro bous, me an kelm avel pusorn,* if I can find him, that he may never eat meat, I will tie him like a bundle. R.D. 541.

DER, prep. Through, by. This is a late form of *dre,* qd. v., and was always used in Keigwyn and Llwyd's time. *Praga na wrela prefery, y festa formyys devery, der y wreans ëv omma,* why dost thou not consider that thou wast formed surely by his workmanship here? C.W. 16. *Der henna ythof grevys, y wellas ëv exaltys, ha me dres dha yseldar,* by that I am grieved, to see him exalted, and myself brought to lowness. C.W. 34. *Kellys der mernans ow flôch,* lost through the death of my child. C.W. 90. *Der an veisder,* through the window; *der an toll,* through the hole. *Llwyd,* 249, 252.

DER, adj. Back. *Rág ow keusel y dhe der, aban éth e dhe'n teller bós elevyon dretho sawyys,* for they are come back, saying, since it went to the place, that the sick are healed by it. O.M. 2794. *May dhe der, worth dhe vlamyé, ha henna marthys yn frás, a'n temple ty dh'y dennë, ha bós dhodho kymys rás,* they are coming back blaming thee, and that is very wonderful, from the temple that thou drewest it, and there being to it so much virtue. O.M. 2797. *Henna ytho gworÿs pár dha; pyma Abel? cows henna, der nag en e devethys,* that was done very well; where is Abel? tell that, that he is not come back. C.W. 86. Cf. Arm. *diadré.* Fr. *derricre.*

DER, v. a. He will break. A mutation of *ter,* 3 pers. s. fut. of *terry,* qd. v. *Ow Arluth, me a der crak ow conna, mars cuch lemyn mês a dré, nefré ny dhebraf vara,* my lord, I will break shortly my neck, if you go away from home, never will I eat bread. O.M. 2184.

DER, v. n. It concerneth. *Otté omma skyber dék, ha cala war hy luer, pynak vo leitrys py lék a weles an chy, ny'm dér,* behold here a fair room, and straw enough on its floor, whether he be lettered or lay, that hath seen the house, it concerns me not. P.C. 682. Written also *dur,* qd. v.

DERA, v. n. I do. This word occurs only in the Cornish, and is used as an auxiliary with the infinitive mood, as ‡*dera vi laviria,* I do labour. *Llwyd,* 246. ‡*Dera mi tón,* I carry, 247. He seems to consider it as compounded of the intens. prefix *de,* and *ra,* for *wraf,* I do. It was also written *gera* and *thera.*

DERAFFA, s. m. A rising again, a resurrection. ‡*An dehilians a'n pehazow, an deraffa arta an corf, ha an bewnans heb dywadh,* the forgiveness of sins, the rising again of the body, and the life without end. *Pryce.* This is a late word formed from *derevel,* to raise.

DERAGLA, v. a. To chide, to brawl. *Llwyd*, 74.

DERAGON, pron. prep. Before ns. *Dyskynnouch ketep mâp. pron, oté an gwél dheragon glás ow levy*, alight ye, every son of the breast, behold the rods before us growing green. O.M. 1984. Another form of *dyragon*, qd. v.

DERAY, s. m. A deed, an exploit. *Marow yno, ef a vynsé gúl deray, hag a rôs strokosow tyn*, he is dead, he wished to do a deed, and he gave sharp strokes. O.M. 2224. *Ef re wrûk mûn a dheray; dre gôth y wrûk leverel, kyn fe dysurgys an temple, yn tri dýdh yn drehnfsé bythqueth whel na fe ee gwell*, he hath made much tumult; through pride he did say, though the temple were destroyed, in three days he would re-build it, that never yet it was better. P.C. 380. This is not a Celtic word. Mr. Norris suggests the Anglo-Saxon *dere*, an assault, or damage.

DEREVAL, v. a. To raise up, to build, to lift up, to rise. *Dho derecal aman*, to lift up, to incite. *Llwyd*, 68. *Neb ef dheravas dhe ocumans dryth an Sperys Sans*, whom he raised to life through the Holy Ghost. *Pryce*. ‡ *An tridga dýdh of daravas arta dort an marow*, the third day he rose again from the dead. *ibid*. ‡ *Buz mor mennow direval war bidn an pow yein, why dalvcya gowas an brossa mine*, but if you will build up against the country cold you must have the biggest stones. *ibid*. This a later form of *drehcvel*, qd. v.

DEREVAS, v. a. To declare, to publish. Written also *deryfas*. *Táys ha mâb ha'n Speris Sans vy a býs a leun golon, re wronte dheuch grás ha skyans dhe dherevas par levarow, may fo dhe Dhu dhe wordhyans, ha sylvans dhe'n enevow*, Father, Son, and Holy Ghost ye shall pray with faithful heart, that be may grant to you grace and desire to hear his passion, and to me grace and knowledge to declare by words, that there be to God the glory and salvation to the souls. M.C. 1. *Yn le may 'th ên yn trevow yn splan me a's derevas*, in the place that I was in towns openly I published them. M.C. 79. *Confortys yw ow colon, pan clewys ow teryfas bones leyhýs dhe pascyon a fue tyn garow ha brâs*, my heart is comforted, when I have heard (thee) declaring thy passion to be alleviated, which was very cruel and great. R.D. 504. Qu. W. *dyrivo*, to enumerate.

DERHI, v. a. To break. *Llwyd*, 251. A mutation of *terhy*, qd. v.

DERMYN, s. m. Time, season. A mutation of *termyn*, qd. v. *Ty a výdh puneys pûr tyn râg dhe dhrôg a ver dermyn gans Arluth wéf awartha*, thou shalt be punished very severely, for thy evil, in a short time, by the Lord of heaven above. O.M. 1601. *Râg dewesys ôs mychtern dhyn, ha kerenys a ver dermyn ty a výdh*, for chosen thou art a king to us, and crowned in a short time thon shalt be. O.M. 2381. *Ha dhe welas an passyon a Jhesus hep gorholeth, a wodhevys Cryst ragon, a-vorow deuch a dermyn hag ens pûp drê*, and to see the passion of Jesus without delay, which Christ suffered for us, to-morrow come ye in time, and let all go home. O.M. 2843.

DEROW, s. m. Oak, oak trees, an oak tree. *Derw* is the aggregate substantive, but it may also be considered as the plural of *dâr*, qd. v. *Ef assoma squyth, prynnyer derow ow trehy, vytheth powes my ny'm bŷdh, mar vrew ew ow yssyly*, Oh, dear God, I am weary cutting oak sticks; there is never rest to me, so bruised are my limbs. O.M. 1010. W. *derw*. Arm. *deró*. Ir. *darach, darog*. Gael. *darach*.

DERRES, pron. prep. By or through your. *Llwyd*, 244. A contracted form of *der ages*.

DERRIC, s. m. A grave digger, a sexton. *Prycc*. From *dor*, earth.

DERRUS, s. m. Land, territory, country. A mutation of *terrus*, qd. v. *Mal yw genen dhe gafus dhe vôs, lemyn dhe derrus, ha dhe peyn kepar ha ny*, our will is to take thee, to go now to (our) country, and to torment like us. O.M. 554.

DERRY, v. a. To break. A mutation of *terry*, qd. v. *Eva prâg y whrusté sy tullé dhe bryes hep kên, an avel worth y derry, wosé my dhys dli'y dhefen*, Eva, why didst thou deceive thy husband, without mercy, by plucking the apple after I had forbidden it to thee. O.M 279. *An sarf re rûk ow thollé; mar derré hy leverys, kepar ha dew y fedhé*, the serpent hath deceived me; if I plucked it, she said like a god I should be. O.M. 289.

DERTHEN, s. f. A fever. Llwyd, 87, gives *lês derthen*, feverfew. The only authority is the Cornish Vocabulary, where it is read by Zeuss and Norris, *lesdeith*. I think Llwyd's reading preferable, as I believe *derthen* to be the regular mutation after *lês*. fem., of *terthen*. W. *tyrton, y dyrton*, both adaptations of the Latin *tertiana*.

DERYGTHY, pron. prep. Before her. In construction *dherygthy*. *Rag mygternas yw yn nêf, dhe vôs gordhijs hy yw gyw; eleth dherygthy a séff; leas mýll y bôdh a syw*, for queen she is in heaven, to be worshipped she is worthy; angels before her shall stand, many thousands her will shall follow. M.C. 226. Comp. of *derag*, id. qd. *dyrag*, before, and *hy*, her. Written also *dyraghy*.

DES, v. n. Come thou. 2 pers. s. imp. of *dôs*, qd. v. *Ré dhe Gryst a levery, aberth an grows pan csé, mars ogé Christ mâb Davy, des a'n grows heb pystegé*, some to Christ said, upon the cross when he was, if thou art Christ, the son of David, come from the cross without sorcery. M.C. 197. *Ow servant, des mês omma, ha'w gwarac dro hy genas*, my servant, come ont here, and my bow bring it with thee. C.W. 108. Written also *dus*, qd. v.

DES, v. n. Come. Participle of *dôs*. *Heyl Sir Cayfas, epscop stout, may des Ihesu an gods proud, re wrûk re maystry yn drê*, hail, Sir Caiaphas, stout bishop! here is come Jesus, the proud fellow, he has done too much violence in town. P.C. 362.

DES, v. n. He came. 3 pers. s. pret. of *dôs*. *Ti a dhês*, thou camest. *Llwyd*, 247.

DES, pron. prep. To thee. ‡ *Whey dydhiow ehce ura wheel, ha wra mêns ês dez do geil*, six days shalt thou labour, and do all that thou hast to do. *Pryce*. A late form of *dys*, qd. v.

DESAN, s. f. A cake. ‡ *Ha an dzhei a wyns an naw pens en dezan*, and they put the nine pounds in the cake. *Llwyd*, 251. A mutation of *tesan*, qd. v.

DESCA, v. a. To teach, tell, inform; to learn. *Dûn ny dhe desca in scon d'agan epscop, del yw gwreys*, let us go to declare immediately to our bishop how it is done. O.M. 2749. *Dûn dhe desca dhe Cesar scon, agan dew*, let us come to tell to Cæsar, at once, we two. R.D. 2115. It is written also *descy*, and *dyscy*, qd. v. *A Jerusalem dhynny ef a dhueth a Galydé, lays nowydh ow tesky, lene ganso ow trylé*, to Jerusalem to us be came from Galilee, new laws teaching, many with him turning. M.C. 107. *En deskyens del vyé, ha dhodho a leverys,* they taught him how it was, and to him said. M.C. 248.

DESCADER, s. m. A teacher, a doctor. ‡*Deskadzher,* Pryce.

DESCANS, s. m. Skill, cunning, knowledge, skilfulness. *Llwyd,* 118.

DESCAS, s. m. A teaching, doctrine. *Mester kêr, re by gordhys, del góth gans tûs oll an bŷs, rág dhe dhescas yw pûr dha,* dear Master, he thou worshipped, as it behoveth, by all men of the world, for thy doctrine is very good. P.C. 121. *Mester lynyges re by, rák dhe dhescos têk dynny yw parys yn pûp termyn,* Master, blessed be thou, for thy fair doctrine to us is ready at all times. P.C. 818. Written also *desces. Me a vyn y examné ha'y dús ha'y deskes tcharré,* I will examine him and his men, and his doctrine soon. P.C. 1211. See also *dysces.*

DESCIANS, adj. Without knowledge, foolish. *Llwyd,* 156. Comp. of *de,* neg., and *scians,* knowledge.

DESCRIRYA, v. a. To forsake. *Yn erna Christ a vynnas leverel Ely, Ely, dhescrirya yw a gonesas Arluth prag y hysta vy,* in that time Christ would say, Ely, Ely, forsaken it is (that) he said why hast thou me. M.C. 201.

DESCRISSA, v. a. To distrust. *Llwyd,* 249. Another form of *dyscryssy,* qd. v.

DESCYDHYANS, s. m. A demonstration. *Pryce.* From *descydhé,* id. qd. *dyscudhé,* to shew, qd. v.

DESCYN, v. a. To descend, to come down. Part. *descennys.* Written also *deiscyn,* and *dyeskenné,* qd. v.

DESEF, v. a. To desire, to wish. *Adam plós a dhesefsé warnan conquerryé neffré; lemyn ef yw agan gwas,* the foul Adam would desire over us to be a conqueror always; now he is our servant. O.M. 908. *Hy a dhesefsé scorné gans an epscop,* ha'y dollé dhe wordhyé dewow nowcydh, she would wish to strive with the bishop, and delude him to worship new gods. O.M. 2730. *Desefsen dodho ry what, dhynny ef a wrûk an pral, hag a fyes dhyworthyn,* we wished to give him a blow; to us he did the trick and fled from us. R.D. 604. *Lemmyn worth agan gelwel, rák own desefsen mervel, me a crennas,* now calling us for fear I would have desired to die, I trembled. R.D. 1772. W. *deisyu.* Ir. †*deothas.*

DESEMPYS, adj. Sudden, immediate. *Hen yw dŷdh a bowesva dhe pûp dén a vo sylwys; yn dysquydhyens a henna, ny a bows desempys,* this is a day of rest to every man that may be saved; in declaration of that we will rest forthwith. O.M. 148. *Dew dhén a gefyth ena, gor y yn mês desempys,* thou wilt find two men there, put them out immediately. O.M. 334. Though the adjective is constantly used for the adverb, the adverbial particle *a* ought strictly to precede. *Am dhedhé a dhesempys yn hanow an tás an néf,* kiss them immediately in the name of the Father of heaven. O.M. 1769. The word is written indiscriminately *desympys, dysempys,* and *dysympys.* W. *disymmwth.*

DESETHY, v. a. To stir up, to excite. Part. pass. *desethys.* Pryce. *Onon gans an kêth welen yn leuff Christ a ve gorris, a'n gwyskys lasche war an pen, bum pûr gewar desthys,* one with the same rod in the hand of Christ (that) was put, struck him a lash on the head, a blow very accurately struck. M.C. 138. W. *dysuthu.*

DESEVY, v. a. To throw down. *Ihesu Crist múr gerensé dhe váb dén a dhyswedhas, a'n uchelder may thesé dhe'n bŷs pan deyskynnas, peñadoryon rag perna o desevys dre Satnas,* Jesus Christ shewed much love to the son of man, when he descended to the world from the height that he was, to redeem sinners (that) were thrown down by Satan. M.C. 5. Comp. of *de,* neg., and *sevy,* id. qd. W. *sevyd,* to stand.

DESGA, v. a. To learn. *Llwyd,* 55. Id. qd. *desca,* qd. v.

DESGIBL, s. m. A scholar, a disciple. *Llwyd,* 55. See *Dyscybel.*

DESIMPIT, adj. Sudden, immediate. Corn. Voc. *cuscadur desimpit,* letargus *vel* letargicus, a lethargic man, one who sleeps immediately. *Hun desempit,* letargia, lethargy, immediate sleep. This is the old form of *desempys,* qd. v.

DESMOS, s. f. A rite, or custom. *Llwyd,* 284. W. *dedhv, dedhvod,* †*dedhmod.* Ir. *deachdach.* Gael. *deachdach.* Gr. θεσμὸς.

DESMYGY, v. a. To declare, to tell, to make known. *Pûp cowyth oll prydyrys, martesen vŷdh yn y orŷs desmygy pren vás ple fo,* let every comrade consider, perhaps it will be in his mind to tell where there is a good tree. P.C. 2542. Written also *dysmegy,* qd. v.

DESO, pron. prep. To thee. *Lavarsons y heb pyté, agan traytour yw kefys, reys yw dheso y dhamnyé dhe'n mernans a dhesympys,* they said without pity, our traitor is found, necessity is for thee to condemn him to death immediately. M.C. 98. *Na ve bós fals an dén-ma nyn drosen ny bys deso,* were not this man false, we should not have brought him to thee. M.C. 99. An enlarged form of *des,* qd. v.

DESONS, v. n. They came. 3 pers. pl. pret. of *dós,* qd. v. *Lavar dhymmo vy yn scon, ple re-seth dhe dhyscyblon, prág na dhesons y yn chy,* tell me now immediately, where are gone thy disciples, why have they not come into the house? P.C. 1247. The same word as *dethons.*

DESTREWY, v. a. To destroy, ruin, kill. *Rag henna an vuscogyon orto a borthas avy, dre vraster brás yn golon y dhugiyons y dhestrewy,* for that reason the fools to him bore spite, through great pride in heart they bethought to destroy him. M.C. 26. Written also *dystrewy,* qd. v.

DESTRIA, v. a. To destroy, ruin, kill. This is the late form of *destrewy,* as used in the time of Jordan and Llwyd. *May fŷdh an bŷs destryes, der levyow a dhower pûr vrás,* that the world shall be destroyed by floods of water very great. C.W. 156. *Destrea an bys-ma,* to destroy this world. C.W. 182. *Dho destria an dén cóth,* to kill the old man. ‡*Ma agen ost destriez neheur,* our host was killed last night. *Llwyd,* 252.

DESYMPYS, adj. Immediate. *Del yrchys Jesus dhedhé y a rúg a dhesympys,* as Jesus commanded them, they did immediately. M.C. 28, id. qd. *desempys,* qd. v.

DET, s. m. A day. This is the old orthography, preserved in the Cornish Vocabulary, of *dêdh,* qd. v.

DETH, v. m. He came. 3 pers. s. pret. of irr. v. *dos.* In construction it changes into *dhêth,* and *têth. Ef o Christ a dhêth dhe'n leur, máb Du ha dén yw kyffris,* he was Christ (that) came to the earth, the Son of God and man he is likewise. M.C. 8. *Cryst kymmys payn y'n gevé, angus tyn ha galarow, ma têth an goys ha dropyé war y fás, an caradow,* Christ so much pain had, anguish sharp, and pangs, that the blood came, and dropped on his face, the beloved. M.C. 59. *Jesus a gewsys arté, why a dhêth dhym yn'arvow,* Jesus said again, ye have come to me in arms. M.C. 74. *Pan déth leyff Christ war en toll dre an nerth may tensons hy*, when came the band of Christ on the hole by the strength that they drew it. M.C. 182. W. *daeth*.

DETH, pron. prep. To thy. *A Dás Dew y'th wolowys, gronni dhe'th wythres, nep pcyth a oel a vercy*, O Father God, in thy lights, grant to thy workmanship, some portion of the oil of mercy. O.M. 326. *Ynno gweet yn-ta whelas bôs dhe'th ly ha dhe'th kynyow*, in it take good care to seek food for thy breakfast and thy dinner. O.M. 1140. Comp. of *de*, to, and *yth*, thy. W. *i'th*.

DETHENS, v. n. They came. 3 pers. pl. pret. of irr. v. *dôs. Pan dethens y bŷs yn bêdh, yth êth on marrek dh'y ben, hag arall dh'y dreys*, when they came to the grave, there went one soldier to his head, and another to his feet. M.C. 242. W. *daethant*.

DETHEWY, v. a. To promise. Part. pass. *dethewys*. *Hag ef rag oun ny ylly gans Jesus kewscl gêr vâs, hena o poynt a falsury dethewys heb koweras*, and he for fear could not with Jesus speak a good word, that was a point of falsehood promised without fulfilment. M.C. 83. Written also *didhyuy*, qd. v. W. *adhaw*.

DETHONS, v. n. They came. 3 pers. pl. pret. of *dôs*. *Dhe joy y tethons gynef, kemmys a wrûk bôdh ow thâs*, to joy they are come with me, as many as have done the will of my Father. R.D. 2577. Id. qd. *dethens*.

DETHORY, v. n. To rise again. See *Dedhory*.

DETHY, pron. prep. To her, or it. See *Dedhy*.

DETHYE, v. n. He had come. 3 pers. s. pluperf. of irr. v. *dôs*. *Dhen tyller Crist re dethyé, ha'n Edhewon o dygnas, yth esé ha'n venyn gansé, parys ens dh'y huhudhas*, to the place Christ had come, and the Jews were opposing, and the woman was with them, they were ready to accuse her. M.C. 33. W. *daethai*.

DEUCH, v. n. Come ye. 2 pers. pl. imp. of irr. v. *dôs*. *Oll tûs ow chy, deuch gencf vy, brymtyn ha kêth*, all men of my house, come ye with me, nobles and commons. O.M. 1691. *Deuch yn râg kctep onan lemyn yn ow othommow*, come forth every one now in my necessities. O.M. 2683. *Deuch holyouch vy bŷs yn menedh*, come, follow ye me ever to the mountain. M.C. 53. In late times the final aspirate was softened into *h*, and then lost, as *deuh, deu'*. W. *drwwch, dowch*.

DEUCH, pron. prep. To ye or you. *Re wronte dheuch grás ha whans dhe wolsowas y bascorn*, to grant you grace and desire to hear his passion. M.C. 1. *My a wôlch scon ow dulé, a wél dheuch kettep onan*, I will wash immediately my hands, in the sight of you every one. P.C. 2500. *Ha'y vennath dheuch pûp huny*, and his blessing on you every one. R.D. 2643. This was also written *dyuch, deych, dŷch*, and finally softened into *deuh, dheuh, dheu*. ‡ *Dew a dâl dheuh*, God shall reward you. Lhwyd, 242. W. *iwch*. Arm. *deach, †dich*. Ir. *dhaoibh, dhibh, †duib, †duibsi*. Gael. *dhuibh*. Manx, *diu*.

DEUN, v. n. Let us come. 1 pers. pl. imp. of *dôs*. *Meer, meer, a'n gwella, Eva, yma ef ow tous omma, rag mêth deun ny alemma, dhe gudhé yn tellar clôs*, look, look, dost thou see him, Eve, he is coming here ; for shame let us go hence, to hide in some close place. C.W. 62. Written also *dûn*, qd. v.

DEVAR, s. m. Duty. ‡ *Ny a vidn gwyll in della, del ew devar, dheny ha theth wordhya rag nefra, par dell ew agen deuty*, we will do so, as it is becoming to us, and thee worship for ever, as it is our duty. C.W. 182. This is not a Celtic word, being the French *devoir*.

DEVE, v. n. He came. 3 pers. s. pret. of *devos*, qd. v. Written also *defé*. *Rág an termyn re devé, may fŷdh an begel kyllys*, for the time is come, that the shepherd will be lost. M.C. 48. *Lemmyn devé ken termyn, ow thás rom gronntyas dhe wy*, now is come another time, my father hath granted me to you. N.C. 75. *A tûs benyges y'th sé, lemmyn dhys my re devé gans deusys yn mês a'n beys*, O Father, blessed on thy throne, now I am come to thee with the manhood out of the world. R.D. 2620. *An grows y a rúg gorré war scôdh Jesus dh'y dôn dhy, Ihesus Crist may leffé oll an gref ha'n belyny*, the cross they did put on Jesus to carry it thither, to Jesus Christ that might come all the grief and the shame. M.C. 162.

DEVEDHYS, part. Come, arrived. Part. pass. of *devos*, qd. v. *Ow arluth lowené dhys, ow olte vy devedhys arté dhe dré*, my lord joy to thee, behold me come again home. O.M. 2212. *Lemyn my a wôr dhe wôfr, bôs ow thermyn devedhys*, now I know truly, that my term is arrived. O.M. 2344. *Neungo devedhys an prŷs may'tho ogas dh'y dheweedh*, the time was not come, that he was near his end. M.C. 200. *Devedhys* is the participle of a verb, the Welsh equivalent of which is *dyvod*, and of which *dôs* is a contracted form.

DEVELO, adj. Weak, impotent, infirm. Lhwyd, 53.

DEVERGI, s. m. An otter. Lhwyd, 241. Written also *dourgi*, and *dofergi*, qd. v.

DEVERY, v. n. To drop, to trickle down. *Ha dhe'n doar an goys ha'n lyn annodho dell deveras*, and to the earth the blood and the humour how it dropped. M.C. 221. *Fest yn tyn y a wolé, dhe wherthyn nysteva whans ; ha'y dagrow a dhevcré a'y dew lagas pûr dhewhans*, very grievously she wept, to laugh she found not desire ; and her tears dropped from her eyes very fast. M.C. 222. *Mam Jesus Crist a ammé corf y mab par drewssy, ha'y dagrow a dheveré anodho pan predery*, the mother of Jesus Christ kissed the body of her son very dolefully, and the tears dropped when she thought of him. M.C. 231. Written also *dyvery*, qd. v.

DEVES, s. m. Sheep. The plural of *davas*, qd. v. *Pan vo gwyskys an bugel, y fy an deves a bell*, when the shepherd is smitten the sheep will flee far. P.C. 894.

DEVETH, adj. Shameless, unabashed. *Hag a dhychow, hag a glêdh, onon a bub tenewen, bôst a wréns tyn ha doveth, y'n gwythans worth y ehen*, and on the right, and on the left, one on each side, boast they made strong and shameless, that they would keep him against his effort. M.C. 242. Written also *diveth*, qd. v.

DEVIDGYOW, s. m. Sheep. ‡ *War an bestas, ha'n olian, ha'n devidgyow oll yn gweall*, over the beasts, and the oxen, and all the sheep in the field. C.W. 78. This is a late plural of *davas*.

DEVIDHYS, part. Choked. Pryce.

DEVINA, v. a. To awake. Pret. *devinas*. Pryce. See *Dyfuny*.

DEVONES, v. n. To come. *Tûs ûs dhym ow tevones yro gans ow thraytor dyskis*, people are coming to me, by my betrayer taught. M.C. 61. *Ow tevones wy a'n gwylvyth heb neb mar*, ye shall see me coming without any doubt. M.C. 93. *Ha kekemys na'n cresso, goef termyn a dheffo devones a brŷs benen*, and as many as shall not believe,

DEW 99 DEWEN

woe to him the time that he came coming from the womb of woman. R.D. 1350. *Fystynyn fast dh'agan pow, rák devones dewolow dhe'n teroge, y môns ow cryê huthyk*, let us hasten quick to our country, for devils are coming to the land; they are crying horridly. R.D. 2302. This is an enlarged form of *devos*, as *mones* of *môs*.

DEVOS, v. n. To come. *Arluth ow tcvos a Spayn, yth egen yn crês Almayn, orth un prys-ly yn púr wŷr, pan fúf gylwys*, Lord, coming from Spain, I was in the middle of Germany, at a breakfast meal, very truly when I was called. R.D. 2147. This is the original form, of which *dós* is a contraction. (W. *dyvod.*) The participle is *devedhys*, qd. v.

DEVRA, s. f. The bosom. *Hag in top an keth wedhan, me a wêl un mayteth whêg ow sedha, hag yn y devra flóch têg*, and in the top of the same tree, I see a virgin sitting, and in her bosom a beautiful child. C.W. 132. A late form of *duivron*, qd. v.

DEVRAC, adj. Watery. *Tir devrak*, watery ground, a bog, marsh, or fen. *Llwyd*, 112. Derived from *dever*, id. qd. *dour*, qd. v. W. *dyvrog*. Arm. *dourek*.

DEVRY, adj. Without trifling, serious, earnest. *Yn pur dhevry*, very earnestly. *Henna yw ow thowl devery*, that is my design seriously. C.W. 10. Another form of *defry*, qd. v.

DEVYS, part. Grown. *Ha pan vo hy cowl devys, hy a vŷdh púb êr parys dha dhôn an oyl a vercy*, and when it is full grown, it will always be ready to bear the oil of mercy. C.W. 134. A mutation of *tevys*, qd. v.

DEVYTH, s. m. A wilderness, a desert. C.W. 94. A later form of *defyth*, qd. v.

DEW, s. m. God. Pl. *dewow, dewyow*. *Y fyeuch yn úrna avel dewow*, ye would be in that hour like gods. O.M. 178. *Y won dhe wŷr Dew an tûs re sorras drewyth benen*, I know truly, God the Father, a sorry woman hath angered. O.M. 255. *A Dhew a nêf*, O God of heaven. O.M. 1607. *Hag a wordh dewow tebel*, and will worship evil gods. O.M. 1818. *Plema an offryn, a dâs, a vŷdh leskys dhe Dhew rás, rag y wordhyé*, where is the offering, O father, which shall be burnt to the God of grace, to worship him. O.M. 1317. *Te ny'n vŷdh dhys Dewyow eraill mês me*, thou shalt have none other Gods but me. Pryce. Written also *Du*, and in the Cornish Vocabulary, *Duy*. W. *duw*, *dai*, † *diu*, † *diwu*. Arm. *doue*, † *doe*. Ir. *dia*, † *de*. Gael. *dia*. Manx, *jee*. Gaul. *devos*. Gr. θεὸs. Lat. *deus*. Lith. *dicvas*. O.N. *tivi*. Sansc. *daivas*, from *div*, to shine.

DEW, num. adj. Two. *Dew dhên a gefyth ena*, two men thou shalt find there. O.M. 333. *Nep dew cans vledhynnow*, some two hundred years. O.M. 657. *Agan dew lagas yw marthys clâf ow colyas*, our (two) eyes are wondrous tired watching. P.C. 1066. *A dhew harlot*, O ye two knaves. P.C. 2322. *Dew* is used with nouns masculine, and *dui*, qd. v., with feminines. The same rule holds good in W. *dau*, † *dou*, with·nouns masculine, and *duy*, with feminine. Arm. *daou*, † *dou*. Ir. *da, do*, † *dau*, † *de*. Gael. *da*. Manx, *daa*. Lith. *dwi*. Goth. *twai*. Gr. δύο. Lat. *duo*. Sansc. *dvâu*, from *dau*, to separate, or divide.

DEW, s. f. Two, a pair, a couple. Pl. *dewyes*. *Gor an dhew-ma yn pryson, pan fôns fast, ro dhym, hep sôn, dhe alwedhow*, put thou this pair in prison; when they are fast, give me without noise thy keys. R.D. 82. *Deuch agas dew scon yn râk*, como ye forth at once ye two. P.C. 1867. ‡ *A búb sort a lverow egual unna ew gorrys, pekûr ythew an sortow, gorrys unna dór dewyes in dífrans ha kehaval*, of every sort of books equally in them are put, as are the sorts put in them by pairs, in proportion and equality. C.W. 160. W. *dau*, pl. *deuoedh*.

DEWCH, v. n. Ye shall come. 2 pers. pl. fut. of *dós*. *Nefra ny dhewch a-lena*, never shall ye come from thence. C.W. 134. Written also *deuch*. W. *deuwch*.

DEWDHEC, num. adj. Twelve. *Oll dhe'n bestes ús omma a gêf bôs lour dewdhec mŷs*, all the beasts (that) are here shall find food enough twelve months. O.M. 1060. *Dewysys ouch dewdhec lêl*, ye are chosen twelve faithful. P.C. 223. *Flehys a'm bês denethys, a Eva ow frêas mear, dewdhec warnigans genys a vybbyon, heb ow mab Cayn hag Abel*, children to me are born, of Eve, my wife many, two and thirty (12+20) born of sons without Cain and Abel. C.W. 144. Comp. of *dew*, two, and *dêc*, ten. W. *deudheg*, † *deudeg*, † *doudec*. Arm. *douzec*. Ir. *dadheag*. Gael. *dadheug*. Manx, *daa-jeig*. Gr. δώδεκα. Lat. *duodecim*. Sansc. *dvâdas'an*.

DEWEDH, s. m. End, conclusion. *Gans laddren y tewedhas, del yw screfys a'y dhewedh*, with thieves he ended, as it is written of his end. M.C. 186. *Neungo devedhys an prŷs may 'tho agas dh'y dhewedh*, the time was not come that he was near his end. M.C. 200. *Dysquedhyens warlyrch anken bedhê mygtern yn dewedh*, a proof after sorrow that he was a king at last. M.C. 236. Written also *diwedh*, or *dywedh*, qd. v.

DEWEDHE, v. a. To end, finish, accomplish. Written also *dewedhy*. Part. pass. *dewedhys*. *A Dew kêr, assoma sowyth, wyn veys a quellen un wŷth an termyn dhe dhewedhê*, O dear God, I am weary, happy if I should once see the time to end. O.M. 686. *Aban na fyn dewedhé, me a vyn y curuné, avel mychtern Yedhewon*, since he will not end, I will crown him, as king of the Jews. P.C. 2115. *Râg mar urâs yw dalethys, neffra ny vŷdh dewedhys*, for so large is it begun, it will never be ended. C.W. 174. W. *diwedhu*.

DEWEDHES, s. m. The evening. *Kemys drûk ús ow codhé, ha dewedhes hag avar, yma kên dhym dhe olé daggrow gois in gwyr hep mar*, so much evil is falling, oboth late and early; there is cause to me to weep tears of blood, without doubt. O.M.629. *Tryk gynen a gowyth kêr, rag namnyg yw gorthuer ha dewedhes*, stay with us, O dear comrade, for it is almost dark and late. R.D. 1305. W. *diwedydh*, from *diwedh*, end, and *dydh*, day.

DEWELLENS, s. m. Remission, forgiveness, atonement. *Yn dewellens pechadow gûl alter da vye, ha dhodho ngan lodhnow warnedhy sacryfyé*, in atonement of sins, to make an altar would be good, and to him our bullocks upon it to sacrifice. O.M. 1173. One of the various forms of *dewhyllyans*, qd. v.

DEWEN, s. m. The gills. *Ha buxow leas heb kên, ha tummaeow kekyffrys, dhe Gryst adro dhe dhewen gans nerth brâs a ve sytyys*, and buffets without pity, and thumps alike, to Christ about the cheeks with great strength were laid. M.C. 138. *Pan dethens y bŷs yn bêdh yth êth en marrek dh'y ben, hag arall dhy dreys yn wêdh, yrvys fast bŷs yn dhewen*, when they came to the tomb, one soldier went to his head, and another to his feet also, armed quite to the chaps. M.C. 242. Written also *dywen*, qd. v.

DEWES, s. m. Drink, beer. Written also *dewas*, and *dywes*. *Dewes mar nystovyth, y a dreyl fyth, hag a wordh dewow tebel*, for if drink be not found, they will turn, and worship evil gods. O.M. 1816. *Rag gwell dewes vytheth vyn nyns a yn agas ganow*, for better drink of wine will never go into your mouth. O.M. 1912. *An dewes yw da ha clêr*, the drink is good and clear. O.M. 1948. *Otta dywes dhys omma, prag na wrela y effe*, behold a drink for thee here ; why dost thou not drink it ? P.C. 2980. *Dew dhên Crist a dhanvonas dhe berna boys ha dewas*, two men Christ sent to buy meat and drink. M.C. 42. *Gans Edhewon drôk dhewas a ve dythgtis*, by the Jews bad drink was brought. M.C. 202. *Dewas côth*, stale beer; *dewas creev*, strong beer. *Pryce*. This is a late form of *diol*, qd. v.

DEWESY, v. a. To choose, to elect, to select. Part. pass. *dewesys*. *En gydh o devow hablys may fennê. Jesus sopyê, gans an rê yn y servys war an bŷs re dhewessê*, the day was the Thursday of preparation that Jesus would sup with those people in his service in the world the had chosen. M.C. 41. *Lowenè dhys Salamon, dùs genen ny dhe trôn dhe dâs David; rag dewesys ôs mychtern dhyn ha kerenys a ver dermyn ty a vŷdh*, hail to thee, Solomon, come with us to the throne of thy father David; for chosen thou art a king to us, and crowned in a short time thou shalt be. O.M. 2380. Written also *diwys*, and *dyneys*, qd. v. W. *dewis*. Arm. *diwis*. Ir. *tocha*, *toa*, †*togu*. Gael. *tagh*, *tughadh*.

DEWETH, adv. Twice. Lluyd, 232. Comp. of *dew*, two, and *gwêth*, a time. Written also *dewyth*, qd. v. W. *dwywaith*.

DEWHAN, s. m. Sorrow, grief, vexation. *Gwyn ow bŷs, bôs dhym fethys lavyr ha dewhan an bŷs, pell me ren scwyas omma*, happy my lot that the labour and sorrow of the world are vanquished for me, too long they have followed me here. C.W. 146. Written also *duwon*, and *duwhan*, qd. v.

DEWHANHE, v. n. To be grieved, to be sorrowful. *Pandra whêr dha why, yn delma bonas serrys ? yn ow holan pur dhefry ythoma pûr dewhanhees, orth dhe welas en stalema*, what doth ail you, in this manner to be troubled ? in my heart very seriously I am much grieved, at seeing thee in this state. C.W. 88. Written also *duwhenê*, qd. v.

DEWHANS, adv. Eagerly, hastily, quickly, directly, copiously. *Ha'y dagrow a dheverê a'y dew lagas pûr dhewhans*, and her tears dropped from her eyes very copiously. M.C. 222. *Cuntell warbarth ow fegans, me a môs pûr uskys, ha wosê hemma downs, pell yn devyth dha wandra*, gather together my necessaries, I will go very soon, and afterwards speedily, far in the desert to wander. C.W. 94. Written also *duwhans* and *dynohans*, qd. v.

DEWHELES, v. n. To return, to come back. *Gwra dhe nyggys eredy, kyns dewheles, my a'd pŷs*, do thy errand surely, before returning, I pray thee. O.M. 728. *Ow mebyon my agy peys, yn mês whêth dylleuch tryssê ; mar kyf tŷr sŷch, my a greys, dynny ny dhewel artê*, my sons I pray you, send outside a third; if it will find dry ground, I believe it will not come back again. O.M. 1132. *Saw vynerrê dhewhylly genes my a wra pysy*, but always that thou wilt return, with thee I will pray. O.M. 2196. W. *dychwelyd*.

DEWHYLLYANS, s. m. Remission, forgiveness, atonement. *Yn dewhillyans pehasow gwrêthyl altar me a vyn*, in atonement for sins, I will erect an altar. C.W. 180. *Cowethyans an sansow, dewhyllyans pehasow, dedhoryans an corf, ha'n bewnans heb dywedh*, the communion of saints, forgiveness of sins, resurrection of the body, and the life without end. *Pryce*. It is found written also *dewellens*, and *dewyllyens*, qd. v. Derived from *dewheles*.

DEWLAGAS, s. m. The two eyes, the eyes. This is the Celtic dual and always used when speaking of the eyes of one person. *Yn dyspyt dh'y dhewlagas my a wŷth an gweel a rôs*, in spite of his eyes, I will keep the rods of grace O.M. 2058. *Kepar del osê sylwyas, me a'th pŷs a suwyê ow dew-lagas, byth queth whel tebel na môs ny wylys ganse bannê* like as thou art a Saviour, I pray thee to cure my eyes; never yet, bad or good, have I seen a drop with them. P.C. 396. *My a'th wor bŷs yn Cayphas yn dgspyt dhe'th dew-lagas*, I will bring thee even to Caiaphas, in spite of thy eyes. P.C. 1193.

DEWLE, s. m. The two hands, the hands. *A dâs yntrê dhe dhewle my a gymmyn ow enef*, O Father, into thy hands I commend my soul. O.M. 2362. *Me a vyn môs dhe urê ow arluth treys ha dewlê gans onement kêr*, I will go to anoint my Lord's feet and hands with precious ointment. P.C. 475. *Gew a ve yn y dewlê gans an Edhewon gorris*, a spear was in his hands by the Jews placed. O.M. 217. This is an abbreviated form of *dewlef*, the final *f* or *v* often disappearing in Cornish, as is also the case in Welsh. Thus *trê* is used for *trev*, and the W. *dwylaw* is a corruption of *dwylof*.

DEWLEF, s. m. The two hands, the hands. *Y dhewleff Pylat a wolhas, hag a leverys dhedhê*, his hands Pilate washed, and said to them. M.C. 149. *Yn mêdh an gôff clewas brês ês om dewleff dewedhys*, says the smith, a great sickness is come on my hands. M.C. 156. This is a later and less correct form of *duilof*, qd. v., where the distinction of gender is preserved. See also *Dywlef*.

DEWLIN s. m. The two knees, the knees. Comp. of *dew*, two, and *glin*, the knee. *Gôdh dêk scon my a offryn dhe Dew war ben ow dewlyn*, a fair goose forthwith I will offer to God upon my knees. O.M. 1196. *Me a'n kelm yn krês an wast, may pysso ef gefyens war pen y dhewlyn*, I will bind him in the middle of the waist, that he may pray for pardon on his knees. P.C. 1891. *Arluth dhym gâf del y'th pysaf, war ben dewlyn, an pŷth a worên*, Lord, forgive me, I pray thee on my knees, what I did. P.C. 3020. *War aga dewlyn yth êpe rag Christ rê erell*, on their knees there went some others that were before Christ. M O 195. W. *deulin*. Arm. *daoulin*.

DEWLSEUCH, v. a. Ye threw. A mutation of *tewlseuch*, 2 pers. pl. pret. of *tewly*, qd. v. *Pôs re dewlseuch agas clûn, rag me a'n gwelas dufun. dresof ef a tremenas*, heavily have ye thrown down your haunches, for I saw him wide awake, he passed by me. R.D. 523.

DEWLUGY, s. m. Devils. One of the plurals of *Jewal*, qd.w. *Yn beydh pan y'n gorsyn ny wharrê y tueth dewlugy, warnan codhas. haq a'n lewl ef sêon un ban, ha'n dôr warnodho a ran. euth y clewns*, in the grave when we put him, presently there came devils, they fell upon us, and throw him forthwith, upwards, and divide the earth over him; it was horrible to hear them. R.D. 2124. *Y'ma ganso dewlugy; tân an joul mûr dhy lysky, na dheffo na moy yn pow,* devils are with him, the fire of the great devil to burn him, that he may come no more into the country. R.D. 2174.

DEWNANS, s. m. Devonshire. W. *Dyvnaint;* from *down,* deep, and *nant,* pl. *naint,* a ravine.

DEWN, v. n. Let us come. 1 pers. pl. imp. of *dós. Yma Cayn adla marow; dewn dhe hedhas dhe benow, ha'n pagya Lamec ganso,* the villain Cain is dead; let us come to fetch him away to pains, and the homicide Lamech with him. C.W. 124. Written also *deun,* and contractedly *dûn.* W. *dewch, down.*

DEWNOS, s. m. Witchery, craft, subtlety. *Yowynk ha lows, kyn fo tullys dre y deunos, mercy gylwys, scon y gallos a vydh lehys,* young and grey, though they may be deceived by his witchery, let them call for mercy, soon his power will be lessened. P.C. 20. W. *dewiniad.*

DEWOLGOW, s. f. Darkness. A mutation of *tewolgow,* qd. v. *Gwrên yn ker dhe hellyé ef dhe effarn dhe dewolgow,* let us drive him away to hell, to darkness. C.W. 24.

DEWOLOW, s. m. Devils, fiends. One of the plurals of *deawl,* qd. v. *Ha dewolow hep nyver pûp ûr orthys ow scrynkyé,* and devils without number always grinning at thee. O.M. 569. *Why pryncys an dewolow, scon egereuch an porthow,* ye princes of the devils, immediately open the gates. R.D. 97.

DEWON, s. m. Grief, sorrow. *Ow arluth kêr, Salamon, awos lavur na dewon nefré ny fallaf dheuchwhy,* my dear Lord Solomon, because of labour nor sorrow, I will never fail you. O.M. 2405. *Bythweth my nyn beys moy dewan,* never yet is to me more sorrow. C.W. 106. Id. qd. *dewhan.*

DEWORTO, pron. prep. From him, or it. *(Deworth-o.) Dên a'n geffé cans davas, ha'y kentrevek saw onan; mar a's ladré dheworto, pan pŷn a godho,* a man may possess a hundred sheep, and his neighbour only one; if ho steal it from him, what punishment is due to him? O.M. 2232. Written also *dyworto,* qd. v.

DEWORTH, prep. From by, from. *(De-worth.) Nep ma'n ressys dhe wethé, dheworth henna govynné; py ûr fûf vy y wythes,* he to whom thou gavest him to keep, ask that of him; what time was I his keeper? O.M. 575. *Hen ew an oel a versy a dedhywys dyso sy dheworth an Tás Dew an néf,* this is the oil of mercy, that was promised to thee by the Father God of heaven. O.M. 843. Written also *dyworth,* qd. v.

DEWORTHYF, pron. prep. From me. *(Deworth-my.) My ny allaf dhe nahé lemyn pûp tra ol gronntyé dheworthyf a wovynny,* I cannot deny thee, now every thing to grant from me what thou askest. O.M. 2131. Written also *deworthef. Na wreuch why, war ow ené, dheworthef vy vynytha,* do not you go, on my soul, from me ever. O.M. 2180. It is the same as *dyworthyf,* qd. v.

DEWORTHYN, pron. prep. From us. *(Deworth-ny.) Mar tuc nêp grous ha laddré en gwed dheworthyn pryvé, mêth vŷdh ol d'agen chen,* if any one will come and steal the rods from us privily, all shame it will be to our class. O.M. 2065. *Me a lever an cûs dhys; y a gl bones kechys gans tûs war fordh dheworthyn,* I tell the case to thee; they may be seized by people on the road from us. P.C. 2294. *Rág mar a tuefé yn chy, ef a's gor dheworthyn ny yn kettep pol,* for if he comes to the house, he will take them from us, every one. P.C. 3053. Writ ten also *dyworthyn,* qd. v.

DEWORTHYS, pron. prep. From thee. *(Deworth-ty.) Saf ena, na nês na dhûs na ella, râg ny fynnaf; dheworthys dŷsk dhe skyggyow dhe vês, sevel war tŷr veneges a wrêth,* stand thou there, not nearer, and come no further, for I will not; from thee take off thy shoes, stand on blessed ground thou dost. O.M. 1405. Written also *dyworthys,* qd. v.

DEWSCOL, adv. All abroad. *Hag a genosy pûr debell worth Ihesus rag y angré; a wotta omma nêb yll tempel Du dewscoll squardyé, ha dh'y vôdh y dhrehevel,* and they said very foully to Jesus, to anger him; seest thou here one that can the temple of God all abroad tear, and to his will raise it. M.C. 195. Qu. W. *dwgwall,* perfectly, without defect. Read by Mr. Stokes *dowstoll.*

DEWSUL, s. m. Sunday. *Dewsul blegyow pan esé yn mysk y abestely, y wrêg dhe ré anedhé môs dhe'n drê, ha degymmy an asen, ha dry gansé,* Palm Sunday when he was among his apostles, he caused some of them to go to the town, and untie the ass and bring it with them. M.C. 27. The names of all the days of the week were borrowed by the Ancient Britons from the Romans; thus *Dewsul* is the Lat. *dies solis.* W. *dywsul.* Arm. *disûl.* Old Irish, †*dia sul.* The term is unknown to the modern Irish, who use *dia-domhna,* dies dominica. Gael. *di-domhnuich.* Manx, *jedoonee.*

DEWSYS, s. m. Godhead, divinity. *Onan yw an Tás a neff, arall Crist y un vaaw eff, a vŷdh a wyrchas genys, ha'n Sperys Sans yw tressa, try hag onan ow trega yn un dewsys, me a grŷs,* one is the Father of heaven, another Christ his one son, who shall be born of a virgin, and the Holy Ghost is the third; three and one dwelling in one Godhead, I believe. O.M. 2660. *Pyw henna gans dewsys mâs, re dhueth mar uskys dhe'n wlâs, gwyskys yn rûdh,* who is that with Godhead good, that hath come so swiftly to heaven, clothed in red? R.D. 2487. *Marth dhym a'n dewsys yma, mar yskys del dhueth omma, êl bŷth ny neys,* wonder to me if this is the Godhead! so swiftly as he came here, an angel never flies. R.D. 2504. W. *duwdawd, duwdod.* Ir. *deacht.* Gael. *diadhachd.*

DEWUGENS, num. adj. Two score, forty. *Rag sythyn wosé henma, dewugens dŷdh my a âs glaw dhe godhé awartha,* for a week after this, forty days I will allow rain to fall from above. O.M. 1027. *Dewugens nôs dhym dewydhys a wêl dhe vôs,* forty nights to me completed appear to be. P.C. 45. *Rág y fué kyns y vôs gurŷs dew-ugens blydhen ha whê,* for there were before it was done forty years and six. P.C. 351. W. *deugain,* †*douceint.* Arm. *daou-ugent.* Ir. *da-fhichead.* Gael. *da-fhichead.* Manx, *daeed.*

DEWVRECH, s. m. The two arms, the arms. Written also *defrech,* and *dywvrech,* qd. v.

DEWYLLYENS, s. m. Remission, forgiveness, atonement. *Evouch lemyn oll an gwŷn rag henna yw ow gôs fŷn, hag a vŷdh ragouch skullys yn dewyllyens pechasow,* drink ye now all the wine, for this is my perfect blood, and it shall be shed for you in atonement of sins. P.C. 826. Another form of *dewhyllyans,* qd. v.

DEWYTH, adv. Twice. *Ottevé ow crowedhé; my re wrûk y vusuré rag an kêth wheil-ma dewyth,* behold it lying; I have measured it for this same work twice. O.M. 2569. Comp. of *dew*, two, and *gwyth*, a time. *Dywyth* is a more correct form, qd. v. W. *dwywaith*.

DEÝDH, s. m. A day. *Arluth, porth côf yn deydh dywedh a'n enef vy,* Lord, bear remembrance in the last day of my soul. O.M. 1272. *Yn mêsk flechys Israel dysky laha Dew huhel a wra dhedhé, deydh ha nôs,* among the children of Israel teaching the law of the high God he is, day and night. O.M. 1555. *Un deydh a dhue yredy, ma'n taluedhaf ol dhynchy, kemmys enor dhym yw gorŷs,* a day will come surely, that I will repay it all to you, as much honour as to me is done. P.C. 268. Another form of *dêdh*, or *dŷdh*, qd. v., shewing the elongation of the vowel.

DEYM, pron. prep. To me. (*De-my.*) *Preder my dhe'th whûl a dôr, haval dheym a'n pen dhe'n troys,* think that I have wrought thee of earth, like to me from the head to the foot. O.M. 68. Another form of *dym*, qd. v.

DEYN, pron. prep. (*De-ny.*) *Lowené dhys, te yw dheyn mychtern, rŷs yw dhe wordhyé,* joy to thee, thou art to us a king, used is to honour thee. M.C. 137. Another form of *dyn*, qd. v.

DEYOW, s. m. Thursday. *An gŷdh o deyow hablys may fenné Jesus sopyé, gans an rê yn y servys war an bŷs re dhewessé,* the day was the Thursday of preparation, that Jesus would sup with those people in his service, in the world he had chosen. M.C. 41. Written also *duyow*, qd. v. This word is borrowed from the Latin *dies Jovis.* So also W. *dydh Iau*. Arm. *diziou.* It is unknown to the Erse dialects, which use—Ir. *diardaoine;* Gael. *dìrdaoine;* Manx, *jerdein:* from *Thor*, the Teutonic Jupiter.

DEYS, pron. prep. To thee. (*De-ty.*) *Adam yn dywedh an beys, me a wronnt oel mercy dheys, ha dhe Eva dhe wregŷs,* Adam, in the world, I will grant the oil of mercy to thee, and to Eve thy wife. O.M. 329. *Y wordhyé y teleth dheys, mar uskys pan glew dhe lêf,* to worship him is incumbent on thee, so quickly when he hears thy voice. O.M. 1775. Another form of *dys*, qd. v.

DI, pron. pers. Thou, thee. A mutation of *ti*, qd. v.

DI, num. adj. Two. An abbreviated form of *dew*, used in composition, as *dibrêh*, the arms; *discodh*, the shoulders.

DI, a privative prefix, used in composition, when it softens the initial following, as *dibeh*, sinless; *dibenna*, to behead. It is thus used in Welsh, Armoric, Irish, and Gaelic. *Di* is sometimes intensive, as it is also in Welsh, where it is written *dy*.

DIAGON, s. m. A deacon. Corn. Voc. *diaconus vel levita.* From the Latin *diaconus*. Gr. διάκονος. W. *diagon*. Arm. *diagon*.

DIAHE, s. m. Safety, security. Pryce. Written also *dyaha*, qd. v.

DIAL, s. m. Revenge, vengeance, punishment. *Noe rág kerengé orthys my ny gemeré neffré trom dyal war oll an veys, na dre dhyal pûp ladhé,* Noah for love to thee, I will never take vengeance on all the world, nor destroy all by flood. O.M. 1209. *Pan wo oll dhyn lafurryys, agan wheyl a vŷdh mothow, dre trom dyhal war an veys, ty a wra pûp oll marow,* when all is laboured by us, our work will be failing, by heavy vengeance on the world, thou wilt make all dead. O.M. 1228. *Pilat u'n ladhas, hep fâl, warnotho telywch dyal,* Pilate killed him, without fail, take ye retribution of him. R.D. 1753. W. *dial*. Ir. *dioghail*. Gael. *dioghail, diol*.

DIAL, s. m. A deluge, a flood. Written indiscriminately *diel*, and *dyal*. *Pûp huny gans pêch mar ûr ew flerys, na allaf sparié na moy hep gûl dyel a ver speys war pûp oll marnas ty,* everyone with such great sin is fetid, that I cannot spare any longer without bringing a flood over all except thee. O.M. 947. *Na dre dhyal pûp ladhé,* nor destroy all by flood. O.M. 1210. *Honna a vydh tokyn da an acord us gurreys hep fâl, kyn fynnyf war an bys-ma tewlel vengeans na dyal,* that will be a good sign of the agreement which is made without fail, if ever I should wish upon this world to cast vengeance or flood. O.M. 1250. W. *diluw, dyliv*, comp. of *dy*, intens. particle, and *lliv*, a flood. Arm. *dilus*. Ir. *dìle, tuile*. Gael. *tuil*. Manx, *twoilley*. Lat. *diluvium*.

DIALHWEDH, s. m. A key. Corn. Voc. *dialhwet*, clavis. Comp. of *di*, intens. prefix, and *alhwedh*, or *alwedh*, qd. v.

DIALWHEDHE, v. a. To unlock, to open. From *dialwhedh*, or *dialhwedh*, a key. *A creys dhe'n nêp a'n gwelas yn few, aban dassorchas y fue gynen: mûr festi y gen lowenhas; dodho ny dhyalwhedhas, gour ha benen,* Oh! I believe those that saw him alive, since he rose again, that he was with us: very much he gladdened us; to him we unlocked, man and woman. R.D. 1445.

DIAVOL, s. m. A devil. This is the old form preserved in the Cornish Vocabulary. See *Sach diavol*. Other forms are *diawl*, and *deawl*, qd. v.

DIAWL, s. m. A devil, a fiend. Written also *deawl*, qd. v. The plural is written in various ways; *dewolow, dywolow*, and *dewlugy*, qd. v. *Mar ny'n gorraf, an mŷl dyawl re dorrow mellow y gŷn, vynytha na effo cowl,* if I do not put him, may a thousand devils break the joints of his back, so that he may never drink broth. P.C. 1618. *Me a whŷth gans mûr a grŷs, 'kynyver dyawl ûs yn beys yn ta may clewfo,* I will blow with much force, every devil that is in the world, that he may hear well. P.C. 3062. *Dhynny gweres ny dâl man, mŷl vŷl dyawl a vye gwan er y ŷyn ef,* nothing avails to help us, a million devils would be weak against him. R.D. 132. Lluyd, 62, *diawl*. *Di* before a vowel had often the sound of *j* in Cornish, of which there are traces in colloquial Welsh, and it is the rule in the Erse dialects. Thus *diavol* was sounded and written also *jawl*, or *jowl*, qd. v. This sound is expressed by Llwyd, 54, 55, *dzhiawl.* W. *diavol, diawl*. Arm. *diaoul*. Ir. *diabhal*, (pronounced *diowl*.) Gael. *diabhol*. All from the Lat. *diabolus*. Gr. διάβολος.

DIBARH, adj. Consisting of two parts, bipartite. ‡ *Nenna thera vor dhibarh, ha an varishants a vendzha arla dho Dzhuan môs dre barh an dzhei,* there, there was a road dividing into two, and the merchants would have John to go home with them. Lluyd, 253. Comp. of *di*, two, and *parh*, for *parth*, a part. W. *deubarth*.

DIBBLANS, adj. Proportionable, distinct. *Me a lavar dhys dibblans, henna lell ythew henwys, ew an Wedhan a Vewnans,* I will tell thee distinctly, this, that is truly called, is the Tree of Life. C.W. 134. *Yn wedh dewdhec warnugans a virhas yn pur dhibblans me a'm be,* likewise thirty-two of daughters very proportionably I have. C.W. 144. Written also *dyblans*, qd. v.

DIBEH, adj. Without sin, sinless, guiltless. Lluyd, 249,

dibêh. Comp. of *di*, negative prefix, and *pên*, a late form of *péch*, sin. W. *dibech.*

DIBENNA, v. a. To behead, decapitate. Llwyd, 104. Comp. of *di*, neg. pref., and *pen*, a head. W. *dibennu.* Arm. *dibenna.* Ir. *dicheann.* Gael. *dicheann.*

DIBER, s. m. A saddle. Corn. Voc. *sella.* W. *dibyr, dibr.* Arm. *dibr.*

DIBERI, v. a. To eat. This is the form preserved in the Cornish Vocab. (see *Cloch diberi,*) and is the earliest and most correct. It is a compounded word, and agrees with W. *dybori*, to browse. A contracted form is only found in the Ordinalia, and is variously written *debry, dibry, dibbry, dybry, dybbry:* and by Llwyd, 172, *dibri. Mar a tyooryth a henna yw hynwys pren a skyens,* if thou wilt eat of that, which is named the tree of knowledge. O.M. 81. *A'y frut dybry ny'm bês whans,* of its fruit to eat I have not a desire. O.M. 171. *Attebres, ty ha'th worty, a'n wedhen ha'y avalow,* if thou atest, thou and thy husband, of the tree and its fruits. O.M. 175. *A'y frût hy nép a dheppro a wovyth cusyl a'n Tás,* of its fruit, whoever eats, will know the counsel of the Father. O.M. 187. *Hag inwedh gwra dhe'th worty may tebro ef annodho,* and also cause to thy husband, that he may eat of it. O.M. 200. *Desempys gwra y dhybry,* immediately do thou eat it. O.M. 208. *An bara-ma kymereuch, hag anodho oll dybreuch,* this bread take ye, and of it all eat. P.C. 763. *Pyw a synsow why mocha? nép a serf, py a dheber,* whom think ye greatest? him who serves, or who eats. P.C. 799. *Ny dhebbraf bôs, bones marow an profus,* I will not eat food, because that the prophet is dead. R.D. 1685. W. †*dibri,* †*dipri.* Arm. *dibri. Dibri* has been long lost to the Welsh Vocabulary, but is restored by Zeuss, 1098, from the Luxemburg Glosses.

DIBREH, s. m. The two arms, arms. Llwyd, 242. A later form of *dywvrech,* qd. v.

DICREFT, adj. Dull, sluggish. Corn. Voc. *iners.* Comp. of *di,* neg. pref., and *creft,* a craft. W. *digreft.*

DIDHYWY, v. a. To promise. *An oyl a versy o dhydhyneys dhymmo vy gans an Tás a'y dregereth,* the oil of mercy that was promised to me by the Father of his pity. O.M. 704. *Lavereuch dh'y dhyskyblon, par del dydhynys dhedhê, ef a dhue dhe Galilê,* say ye to his disciples, like as he promised to them, he will go to Galilee. R.D. 796. *Mi a'i didhiwys dhodho,* I have promised it to him. Llwyd, 242. W. *adhaw.*

DIEL, s. m. A deluge. See *Dial.*

DIERBYN, v. a. To meet. See *Dyerbyn.*

DIESGIS, adj. Without shoes, unshod. Llwyd, 55. W. *diesgid.*

DIEW, num. adj. *An diew,* the two, both. Llwyd, 178. Id. qd. *dow,* qd. v.

DIFEID, adj. Rough, wild, unquiet. Corn. Voc. *mor difeid,* pelagus, the sea; more correctly, the unquiet sea. The same word as *diveyth,* or *dyveyth,* a wilderness, qd. v. W. *difaith; mor difaith,* a rough sea.

DIFFENNOR, s. m. An excuser, a defendant. Corn. Voc. *excusator.* W. *difynwr.* Arm. *difenner.* W. *difynnu,* to defend, from Lat. *defendo.*

DIFRETH, adj. Feeble, miserable, wretched. Written also *dyfreth,* and *dyffryth. Lemyn dyfreth óf ha gwâg, púr wŷr dres oll tús a'n beys,* now feeble I am and empty, very truly above all men in the world. O.M. 593.

Lemyn dyffryth óv ha gwâg. C.W. 86. W. *difrwyth,* comp. of *di,* neg., and *frwyth,* (Lat. *fructus,*) vigour.

DIFUN, adj. Sleepless, awake. *El a'n leverys dedhy haneth ha hy yn gwyly púr dhyfun, mŷns re gewsys,* an angel said it to her this night, and she in bed quite awake; he said the whole. P.C. 2204. W. *dihun,* comp. of *di,* neg., and *hûn,* sleep.

DIFUNE, v. a. To awake. *Whêth ow cufyon dyfunouch, ha kês colon oll pesouch na gyllouch yn temptacion,* again my dear (companions) awake, and with one heart all pray, that ye enter not into temptation. P.C. 1077. *Pan o púr holerch an gŷdh y tefenas un marrek, del dêth a'n nêf war y fyth ef a welas golow têk,* when it was far on in the day there awoke a soldier, as it came from heaven on his face he beheld a fair light. M.C. 244. W. *dihuno.*

DIFYDHY, v. a. To extinguish, to quench. Written also *defydhy,* and *dufydhy. Dew an nêf dre dhe vertu dufydh nerth an flam ha'n tân,* God of heaven through thy virtue, extinguish the power of the flame and the fire. O.M. 2637. W. *difodhi,* from *difawdh,* comp. of *di,* neg., and *fawdh,* faw, brightness. = Gr. φάος.

DIFYGY, v. a. To fail, to decay. *Rág bós Abel gwyr dhegê, ef a'n gevyth yn diwedh an joy na dhyfyk nefrê yn ow gwlás ha cosoleth,* because Abel's tithe is true, he shall find in the end unfailing joy ever, in my land and rest. O.M. 517. *Ha maga fuer drók deffry mones hepcor an joy byth na dhyfyk,* and as it would be bad indeed to go to reject the joy that never fails. R.D. 1434. W. *difygio,* from the Lat. *deficio.*

DIGWISCA, v. a. To undress, unrobe, strip off. *Arluth, why yw a dhy gre an bows, ha my dhygwysk e, yn sur ragouch hy ny wra,* Lord, to your liking is the robe, and that I should take it off? surely for you it will not do. R.D. 1924. Comp. of *di,* neg., and *gwisca,* to dress. W. *diwisgaw.*

DIGWYDHA, v. n. To fall, to happen. Llwyd, 104. W. *dygwyddaw.* Arm. *digwezout.* Ir. †*tecmang.* Manx, *taghyr.*

DIHOG, s. m. A great grandfather. Corn. Voc. *proavus.* This word is doubtful, and may be read *dinvog.* It is unknown to all the other dialects. See Norris's Cornish Drama, ij. 352.

DILECHA, v. n. To depart. Llwyd, 55. W. *dileu.* Arm. *dilechi.*

DILLA, v. a. To deceive. Llwyd, 58. This is a mutation of *tilia,* id. qd. *tollê,* qd. v.

DILLADAS, s. m. Apparel, clothing. Llwyd, 173, *dilladzhas.* W. *dilladiad.*

DILLAS, s. m. Clothes, apparel. *Ma ow dyllas ow lesvy, dheworth pren Cryst,* my clothes are burning from the wood of Christ. O.M. 2633. *Me a vyn lemmyn ranné yntrethon oll y dhyllas,* I will now divide between us all his clothes. P.C. 2842. *Prag yth yw ridh dhe dhyllas, omma aberth yn pen wlds, le na fue denses byth queth,* why are thy garments red, here within the head country, where humanity never was? R.D. 2529. This is a later form of *dillad,* or *dillat.* W. *dillad,* †*dillat.* Arm. *dilad.* Ir. †*dillait.* In modern Irish *diallnú* is a saddle. So also Gael. *diallaid, diollaid.* Manx, *jcel.*

DILLASY, v. a. To clothe. Llwyd, *dho dilladzhi,* 173. W. *dilladu.*

DILLAT, s. m. Clothes. *Dillat gueli,* bed clothes. Corn. Voc. This is the oldest form of *dillad,* or *dillas.*

DIMEDHA, v. a. To espouse, to marry. *Llwyd*, 18. Written also *demidhy*, qd. v.

DIN, s. f. A heap, a mount, a hill, a fortified hill, a fortress. This enters into the names of numerous places inhabited by the Cymry or Celts,—as *Dunmear*, in Bodmin; *Dunvedh*, in St. Breock; *Denzell*, in Mawgan. *Dinbren*, in Denbighshire; *Dinorwig*, in Arvon; *Tinsvlwy*, and *Tindaethwy*, in Môn. Hence also the Latin terminations,—*dinium*, *dinum*, and *dunum*, in the names of so many towns in Ancient Gaul. According to Clitophon, Δοῦνον καλοῦσι τὸν ἐξέχοντα. W. *din*. Arm. *tun*. Ir. *dinn*, *duan*, †*dun*. Gael. *dinn*. The word is to be found in many other languages. See Armstrong's Gaelic Dictionary.

DINAIR, s. m. A penny. Corn. Voc. *nummus*. In the Ordinalia it is written indiscriminately, *dinar*, *diner*, *dynar*, *dyner*, *dynnar*. *An ngl dhodho a dellé pymp cans dyner monyys*, the one owed to him five hundred pence of money. P.C. 505. *Ef a galué bôs gwyrthys a try cans dyner ha moy*, it might have been sold for three hundred pence and more. P.C. 536. *En arhans me a gymer, hag a's gwyth kettep dyner*, the money I will take, and keep it every penny. P.C. 1539. *Trehans dynar a voné en box oll bedhens gwerthys, ha vôs den rag y ranné*, for three hundred pence of money let the box all be sold, and be to us to share it. M.C. 36. *Hanter diner*, a halfpenny. *Llwyd*, 103. *Hwêh dinar*, sixpence. 148. Arm. *diner*, †*dinair*. From the Latin *denarius*. It is unknown to the Welsh, who use a pure Celtic term, *ceiniog*, from *cain*, bright, or *can*, white. So Arm. *gwennek*, from *gwenn*, white. Ir. †*cionog*. Gael. †*cionag*.

DINAS, s. f. A fortress, a fortified town, a city. W. *dinas*. It enters into the names of places in Cornwall, and Wales; as *Dinas*, in Padstow, and St. Anthony. *Pendennis Castle*, in Falmouth. *Bryn Dinas*, *Dinas Cordhin*, *Dinas Mawdhwy*. *Dinas Emrys*, in Wales. Ir. *Dinas*, near Killarney.

DINERCHY, v. a. To greet, to salute. *Pryce*. Written also *dynerchy*, qd. v.

DIOC, adj. Slothful, sluggish, idle. Corn. Voc. *piger*. W. *diog*, †*diwc*. Arm. *diek*.

DIOGEL, adj. Unexposed, secure, safe, certain. Corn. Voc. *securus*. In the Ordinalia it is often used adverbially, with or without the adverbial particle preceding. It is also written *dyougel*. *Ow fryes lel, rÿs yw gruthyl dyogel vôdh agan arluth*, my faithful wife, it is necessary to do immediately the will of our lord. O.M. 2189. *My re bue fust ow kelwel dhe vystêrndens dhys a dhe avorow pîr dyogel*, I have been urgently calling to the architects to come to thee to-morrow very surely. O.M. 2432. *Saw me warlerch drehevel a's dyerbyn dyougel yn Galilé ol warbarth*, but I after rising will meet them certainly in Galilee altogether. P.C. 897. *Rág ebyl parys yma, dh'aga fastyd dyougel*, for the pegs are ready, to fasten them truly. P.C. 2572. *En dhiougel, en dhiûgel*, certainly, most assuredly. *Llwyd*, 248. W. *diogel*, comp. of *di*, neg., *go*, partly, *celu*, to conceal. Arm. †*dipugucl*.

DIOT, s. f. Drink, beverage. Corn. Voc. *potus*. This is the oldest form of *dewes*, qd. v. W. *diawd*, *diod*, †*diot*. Ir. *dioch*, *deoch*, *daif*. Gael. *dioch*. Manx, *jouch*. Sansc. *d'â*, to drink.

DIOTHENES, s. m. Hurt, loss, damage. Corn. Voc. *dispendium* vel *dampnum*. This is a doubtful word, and evidently corrupt. *Zeuss* suggests *diormes*, id. qd. W. *dyormes*, vexation, trouble. Norris *diotheves*, id. qd. W. *dyodhevus*, from *dyodhev*, to suffer.

DIOU, v. n. Come ye. ‡ *Diou gennan nei*, come with us. *Llwyd*, 252. A late form of *deuch*, qd. v.

DIOWL, s. m. A devil. *Ty dyowl gwra ow gorthyby, prâg y tolsté sy hep kên*, thou devil, do thou answer me, why didst thou deceive her without pity. O.M. 301. Another form of *diawl*, qd. v.

DIOWLES, s. f. A she devil, a hag. *Llwyd*, 62, writes it *dzhoules*. W. *diawles*. Arm. *diaoulez*.

DIP, v. a. He will think. *Taw, sedhé, vyn ty Phelip, râk pûr wîr ty a gam dip warnodho ef*, be silent, sit, wilt thou Philip, for very truly thou thinkest wrongly respecting him. R.D. 996. A mutation of *tip*. 3 pers. s. fut. of *tibias*, qd. v.

DIPEH, adj. Without sin, sinless. ‡*Na ra chee kymeres hanow an Arluth de Dhew heb otham, rag an Arluth na vyn sensy e dipêh, nêb es kemeras e hanow en gwâg*, do thou not take the name of the Lord thy God without necessity, for the Lord will not hold him guiltless, that taketh his name in vain. *Pryce*. More correctly written *dibêh*, being compounded of *di*, neg., and *pêh*, the late form of *pêch*, sin. W. *dibêch*.

DIRAG, adv. Before, in presence of. *Pryce*. Written also *dyrag*, qd. v.

DIS, a prefix in composition. It has sometimes a negative power, answering to *dis*, *un*, and *im*, in English, as *diswrey*, to undo; *discrysy*, to disbelieve. Sometimes it denotes continuation or the iteration of an action, as *dys*, in Welsh; thus *dislyn-y*, to swallow; *disprenna*, to redeem. It is written also *dys* and *des*. W. *dis*, *dys*. Arm. *dis*, *diz*. Ir. †*do-aih*, †*taith*, †*tath*, †*taid*.

DIS, s. f. People. ‡ *An diz*, the people. *Llwyd*, 241. Id. qd. *dus*, qd. v.

DIS, v. n. Come thou. ‡*Diz barha nei*, come with us. *Llwyd*, 152. Another form of *dus*, qd. v.

DISCANS, s. m. A teaching, doctrine. *A dûs kêr, mear rôs dhe why ha'ges diskans*, O dear father, much thanks to you and your doctrine. C.W. 142. *Hennu ythero convethys, der an diskans es dhymmo reys gans an Tâs es a uchan*, this is understood by the doctrine that is given to me by the Father that is on high. C.W. 156. From *discy*, id. qd. *dyscy*.

DISCAVYLSY, v. a. To stretch out. *Pryce*. Written also *dyscavylsy*, qd. v.

DISCEBEL, s. m. A disciple. Corn. Voc. *dicipulus*. Other late forms are *disgibl*, and *desgibl*. Pl. *dyscyblon*, *dyscyblyon*. *Arluth, me a'th peys a dhybry gynef un prÿs dre dhe oêdh ha'th dyskyblon*, Lord, I pray thee, to eat with me a meal, by thy will, and thy disciples. P.C. 457. *Me á genes yn lowen ha'm dyscyblyon, ketep pen, dho'th arhedow*, I will go with thee joyfully, and my disciples every head, at thy commands. P.C. 462. W. *disgybl*, pl. *disgyblion*. Arm. *diskibl*. From the Latin *disipulus*.

DISCERNY, v. a. To grin, to shew the teeth, to gnash. *Avel bruthken aga dÿns orto y a dheskerny, er-aga-fyn betegyns Crist un gêr ny lavery*, like hounds their teeth upon him they gnashed, against them, nevertheless, Christ a word would not speak. M.C. 96. W. *dysgyrnu*, *ysgyrnygu*. Arm. *scrina*, *grigonsa*. Fr. *grincer*.

DISCIANS, s. m. Madness. Llwyd, 71, gives this as a noun substantive, but it is properly an adjective, as he has it, p. 156, being a later form of *discient.*

DISCIENT, adj. Without sense or judgment, witless, insane, foolish. Corn. Voc. *diskient,* insipiens. Comp. of *di,* neg., and *scient,* knowledge, from the Lat. *scientia.* Arm. *diskient.*

DISCLIEN, s. f. A smoother. Corn. Voc. *plano.* "The word comes between *quaternio* and *diploma,* and must therefore refer to books; perhaps a folder, or some tool for smoothing paper or parchment." Norris's Cornish Drama, ij. 353. *Dysgloen* in Welsh is a splinter, or chip.

DISCODH, s. m. The two shoulders, the shoulders. *Llwyd,* 242. Another form of *dyscscodh,* qd. v.

DISCORUUNAIT, s. m. Madness. Corn. Voc. *rabies.* " Unknown elsewhere, and uncertain ; perhaps connected with the Armoric *kurun,* thunder, making *thunderstruck,* as in *follerguské,* qd. v." Zeuss's Celtica Grammatica.

DISCRUGYER, s. m. An unbeliever. *Pryce.* From *discrugy,* a later form of *dyscrygy.*

DISCRYGYC, adj. Unbelieving. *Pryce.* Written also *dyscrygyc,* qd. v.

DISCUDHE, v. a. To uncover, to discover, to shew. *Me a vyn y dhyscudhé, hag yn spyt dhodho tru é war y fás ha'y dew lagas,* I will uncover him, and in spite to him spit on his face and eyes. P.C. 1393. *Lenmyn dyscudh, ha lavar pyw an pren a bew hep mar pows Ihesu an Nazaré,* now shew and say, which is the die that shall have without doubt the coat of Jesus of Nazareth. P.C. 2852. It is the same word as *discwedha,* and *dysquedhas,* qd. v. W. *dadgudhio.*

DISCY, v. a. To strip, undress. *Pryce.* Written also *dyscy,* qd. v.

DISCY, v. a. To learn, to teach. *Pryce.* Written also *dyecy,* qd. v.

DISCWEDHA, v. a. To uncover, to discover, to shew. *Llwyd,* 70, 249. ‡ *E vester a disgwedhas dhodho,* his master shewed him. 251. See *Dysquedhas.*

DISCWEDHYANS, s. m. A discovery, demonstration, revelation. *Llwyd,* 240. Written also *dysquedhyens,* qd. v.

DISCYNNA, v. n. To descend, to come down. Written also *dyyscynné. Gans aga garm hag olva Ihesus Crist a ve mevys, may fynnas diyskynna yn gwerhas ha bós genys,* with their cry and lamentation Jesus Christ was moved, that he would descend into a virgin, and be born. M.C. 4. *Ihesu Crist múr gerensé dhe váb dén a dhyswedhas, a'n uchelder may 'thesé dhe'n bŷs pan deyskynnas,* Jesus Christ much love to mankind shewed, from the height that he was, to the world when he descended. M.C. 5. *Mars és máb Du a vár brŷs dyyskyn ha dhe'n dór ke,* if thou art the Son of God of great value, descend and to the ground go. M.C. 14 ; P.C. 100. *Dyskynnouch kelep máp bron, olé an gwél dheragon, gíds ow tevy,* alight ye, every son of the breast, see the rods before us, growing green. O.M. 1983. *Lemyn púp dyyskynnes, saw kyns ys yn tour mones, leverruch dhyn,* now let every one alight, but before going to the palace, speak to me. O.M. 2020. W. *disgyn, disgynu.* Arm. *diskenn, diskenni.* From the Latin *descendo.*

DISCYS, adj. Learned, lettered. Llwyd, 80, *diskys.* W. *dysgedig.*

DISEWYTHY, v. a. To dry up. Part. pass. *disewythys.* Pryce.

DISIL, v. n. To undo, ruin, destroy. *Llwyd,* 249. Comp. of *dis,* neg., and *gil,* to do.

DISLAIAN, adj. Disloyal, unfaithful. Corn. Voc. *infidelis.* Comp. of *dis,* neg., and *laian,* loyal, from *laha,* law.

DISLER, adv. Behind. *Llwyd,* 248. It is another form of *delhar,* qd. v.

DISLIU, adj. Deformed, discoloured. Corn. Voc. *deformis, discolor.* Comp. of *dis,* neg., and *liw,* form, colour. W. *disliw.* Arm. *disliv.*

DISLONCA, v. a. To swallow. Llwyd, 245, *dislonka* Comp. of *dis,* iter. prefix, and *lonca,* to swallow. W *dyslyncu.*

DISMIGO, v. a. To suspect, to mistrust. *Llwyd,* 159. See *Dysmegy.*

DISPRENNA, v. a. To redeem. *Pryce.* Written also *dysprenna,* qd. v.

DISPRESY, v. a. To esteem of no value, to despise, to misprize. Part. pass. *dispresys. Del ve helheys war an bŷs avel carow, ragon menouch rebekis, ha dyspresijs yn harow,* how he was hunted, on the world like a deer, for us he was often reproached, and despised cruelly. M.C. 2. *Pernys aberth yn bys-ma, dyspresys haneth o vŷdh,* bought within this world, despised this night it shall be. M.C. 44. *Moy péch o pan dyspresyas ys del o pan y's gwerthé,* more sin it was when he despised him than so it was when he sold him. M.C. 104. Comp. of *dis,* neg., and *prís,* the Eng. *price.* W. *dibrisio.* Arm. *disprizout.*

DISPRYNNIAR, s. m. A redeemer. *Pryce.* Written also *dysprynias,* qd. v.

DISTAIN, s. m. An excuse. *Pryce.* . *Rég an lays dhynny és a vyn y dampnis porres, yn medhens, y fordh nyng és may hallo bós distain guris,* for the laws to us are, by which she must be condemned ; say they, there is not a way that an excuse can be made. M.C. 32. This word is read by Mr. Stokes, *deflam.*

DISWREY, v. a. To undo, ruin, destroy. Part. pass. *diswreys, diwerŷs. Grussons cuwyll nag o vás, rág may fo Jesus diwerŷs,* they took counsel that was not good, that Jesus should be destroyed. M.C. 31. *Yn scon dywereys ef a vŷdh, ha dhe'n mernans col gorrys,* soon destroyed he shall be, and to death quickly put. O.M. 1521. *An temple ef a dhyswra, yn trydydh ef a'n drecha gwell ages kyns múr yn próf,* the temple he will destroy ; in three days he will raise it, better much than before in proof. P.C. 1696. Comp. of *dis,* neg., and *gorey,* to do.

DISWRUG, v. a. He destroyed. Used irregularly as the preterite to *diswrey,* and *discul.* Comp. of *dis,* neg., and *gurúg,* or *grúc,* qd. v. *Ty re dhyswrug credy hevelep dhom face vy,* thou hast destroyed verily the likeness of my face. O.M. 2336. *Ef re dhyswrug an marhas,* he has destroyed the market. P.C. 376. *Rák an harlot a dhyswruk an kéth máp oll agan grúk,* for the villain hath destroyed the same Son who made us all. R.D. 1974.

DISWRUTHYL, v. a. To undo, to ruin, to destroy. *Da vyé kyns dós sabout, dyncruthyl an fals profus,* it would be well before Sabbath comes, to destroy the false prophet. P.C. 562. Comp. of *dis,* neg., and *gruthyl,* to do, qd. v.

DIEWUL, v. a. To undo, to ruin, to destroy, to spoil. *Ow ku' maystri brâs, dyswel an fér ef a vyn,* making great violence, he wishes to spoil the fair. P.C. 360. *Rág y fyr ner, mar a kyller gans paynys mêr ow dyswul glân,* for it is wished, if it is possible, to destroy me quite. P.C. 2602. *Ef a galsê púp tra y dhyswul arté moy ys na fe,* he might have destroyed every thing again more than it was. R.D. 978. *Dyswul lyes corf a wra,* it will destroy many bodies. R.D. 2216. Comp. of *dis,* neg., and *gúl,* to do.

DIU, adj. Black, dark, sable, gloomy. This is Llwyd's orthography of *du,* qd. v. *Dên diu,* a black man. *Mis diu,* the black month, November. 100. *Mola dhiu,* a black bird, 89. *Spernan diu,* a black thorn, 131. *Davas dhiu,* a black sheep, 243.

DIW, num. adj. Two. Llwyd, 242. Another form of *dew,* qd. v.

DIVESGERGAM, adj. Bowlegged. Comp. of *diw,* two, *esger,* the leg, and *cam,* crooked. Crooked as to his two legs. Llwyd, 5.

DIVETH, adj. Shameless, impudent. *An barth cleydh nêb o cregis dyveth o ha lader púr,* on the left side he that was hauged was shameless, and a thorough thief. M.C. 191. Written also *deveth.* Comp. of *di,* neg., and *meth,* shame. Arm. *divéz.*

DIVRES, s. m. An exile. Corn. Voc. *exul.* Comp. of *di,* neg., and *bro,* a country. W. *divro.* Arm. *divro, divroet.*

DIVULEUUIT, s. m. Crown of the head. Corn. Voc. *vertex.* W. *llewydh,* a radiating point, with the prefix, *divu = di-guo,* anc. Ir. *do-fo;* modern Welsh, *dyo.* Zeuss, 1101.

DIWEDH, s. m. An end, bound, goal, limit. *Ny gíl vós kelys, an pŷth a dhue yn dywedh,* it cannot be concealed, the thing will come at last. O.M. 671. *Y grás dheuchwhy re wronntyo, nefré dhe blygyê dhodho, yn dalleth hag yn dywedh,* his grace may be grant to you, ever to bow to him, at the beginning, and at the end. O.M. 1728. *Ellas na varwen yn wêdh, na fe kynsê ow dywedh ys dywedh ow máp yn beys,* alas! that I died not also, that my end was not sooner than the end of my Sou in the world. P.C. 2947. *Mĝî with a vŷdh an dywedh,* a thousand (times) worse will be the end. R.D. 348. *Vyngens re'n geffo, ha drôk dywedh,* vengeance take him, and a bad end. R.D. 2086. *War an diwedh,* finally, at length, at last. Llwyd, 54. Written also *dewedh,* qd. v. W. *aiwedh.* Arm. *divez.* Ir. *deire, diaigh, †dead, †diad, †degaid, tiudh.* Gael. *deireadh.*

DIWEDHA, adj. Late, utmost. Llwyd, 175. W. *diwedhav.* Arm. *diveza.*

DIWEDHAS, adj. Late. Pryce. Arm. *divezad.*

DIWEDHE, v. a. To end, finish, accomplish. *Tý o fŷdh cowal drôk lam; ny vyn an harlot cam, uwos an bŷs, dywedhé,* thou shalt have a fully bad leap; the perverse knave will not end, for the world. P.C. 2915. *Joy dhe púp ús yn bys-ma yn bewnans gulan dywedhé,* joy to every one that is in this world, in pure life to end. P.C. 3216. *Aban oma dasserchys, dew hugens deydh dywydhys bŷdh pan fo nôs,* since I am risen, forty days will be, when it is night. R.D. 2437. W. *diwedhu.* Arm. *diveza.*

DIWEDHVA, s. f. An ending place, end, conclusion. *Bys may 'th yllyf yn ow gwlás, ha why gynef gans ow tás hep dywedhva prest yn ioy,* until that I enter into my kingdom, and you with me, with my Father, without end, ever in joy. P.C. 728. *Ego sum Alpha et Omega, heb dallath na diwedhva,* I am Alpha and Omega, without beginning or end. C.W. 1. Comp. of *diwedh,* end, and *ma,* a place.

DIWENNYS, part. Descended, come down. Pryce. A corruption of *diskynnys.*

DIWES, s. f. Drink, beverage. *Wogê ow da oberow, dynves a yrhys dedhé; dhym rosons bustyl wherow, bŷth ny fynnys y evé,* after my good works, drink I asked of them; they gave to me bitter gall, never would I drink it. R.D. 2600. Another form of *dewes,* and *diot,* qd. v.

DIWLA, s. m. The two hands, the hands. Llwyd, 242. A late form of *dewlef* or *duilof,* qd. v.

DIWORTO, pron. prep. From him. Llwyd, 244. See *Dyeorto.*

DIWY, v. a. To kindle, set on fire. Pryce. Written also *dywy,* qd. v.

DO, prep. To. In construction *dho. Ro do uy hidhow agan púb dŷdh bara,* give to us to day our daily bread. Pryce. *Ha disquedhes truath do milliow neb ês a cara ve, ha gwytha ow gurhemynadow,* and shew mercy unto thousands of them that love me, and keep my commandments. *ibid. Ma tesan rages dho dhôn drê, dho do wrêg,* here is a cake for thee to take home to thy wife. Llwyd, 242. In the earlier Ordinalia, *de, dhe,* are the forms used, and in Jordan's "Creation of the World," *da, dha.* See *De.* In Old Welsh *di* was the form, and *do,* in composition, of which Zeuss gives copious examples, but in modern W. *i.* Arm. *da, †di, †do.* Ir. *do.* Gael. *do.* Manx, *dy.*

DO, pron. poss. Thy, thine. In construction *dho. Agan Tás neb es en nêv, beniges bedh do hanow,* our Father which art in heaven, hallowed be thy name. *Rág an mychierneth ew chee do hannan,* for the kingdom is thine. Pryce. The common forms in the Ordinalia are *de, dhe,* and *dy, dhy.* See *De, Dy.*

DOAR, s. m. The earth, soil, laud, ground. When preceded by the article, *an doar,* from a greater ease in pronouncing became *an noar,* aud *an 'oar.* The same change has occurred in Armoric, to the word *dôr,* a door, where for *ann dôr,* are substituted *ann nôr,* or *ann ôr. Un Edhow a brederys, hag a leverys dhedhé, bonas pren yn doar lewlys, a-us yn houl na vyé,* a Jew bethought, and said to them, that there was a piece of wood on the ground thrown, above in the sun that had not been. M.C. 152. *Ha dhe'n doar an goys ha'n lŷn annodho del deveras,* and to the ground the blood and humour from him so dropped. M.C. 921. *En dallath Dew a wrás nêv ha noar; ha thera an noar heb roath, ha gwág,* in the beginning God created heaven and earth; and the earth was without form and void. C.W. p. 189. *En dallath Dew wrás nêv ha an oar.* M.C. p. 93. Written also. *doer,* and contractedly *dôr,* qd. v. W. *daear, dayar, †dair.* Arm. *douar, †doar.* Ir. *uir.* Gael. *uir, †daor.* Manx, *ooir.* Sausc. *dhara.*

DOC, v. a. Bear thou. 2 pers. s. imp. of *doga,* qd. v. *Mara kewsys falsury, a henna dôk dustuny,* if I have spoken falsehood, of that bear witness. P.C. 1271. *Dôk an grows war dhe geyn,* bear thou the cross on thy back. P.C. 2617. Written also *dôg.*

DOCHAGEYDH, s. m. The afternoon, evening. *Púr wŷr a lavaraf dhys, gynef hydhow ty a vŷdh rág dhe fey yn par-*

DOF 107 DOLLE

adys, kyngys hanter dochageydh, very truly I say to thee, with me this day thou shalt be, for thy faith in Paradise, before half the evening. P.C. 2912. Llwyd gives *dohadzhedh,* 5; *dyhodzhydh,* 10; *dyhodzhedh,* 248; as late sounds of this word. It is the same as W. *dywedydh,* i. e. *diwedh dydh,* the end of the day.

DODLOS, s. m. Service, office. *Pryce.* A doubtful and probably corrupted word.

DODHANS, pron. prep. To them, relating to them. *Ha dew queth dodhans gwra doen dh'aga hudha, aga nootha na vo gwelys,* and two garments do thou bear to them, to cover them, that their nakedness be not seen. C.W. 70. *Dout sor Dew nyng-esé dhodhans nena, me a wôr gwŷr,* the fear of God's anger was not on them then, I know truly. C.W. 176. *Ha an della ma diwedh me daralla dodhans,* and so is the end of my tale about them. Llwyd, 253. This is another form of *dedhé,* qd. v. W. *idhynt.*

DODHO, pron. prep. To him, or it. In construction *dhodho.* *Mûr fest y gen lowenhas, dodho ny dhyalwhedhas, gour ha benen,* very much he gladdened us, to him we unlocked, man and woman. R.D. 1445. *Mûr a foly ew dhodho, an keth frût-na mar a'n gâs,* it is a great folly in him, if he leaves that same fruit. O.M. 191. *Saw un pren gans garlontow a arhans adro dhodho,* but one tree with garlands of silver about it. O.M. 2500. *Ha kymmys a dheseryas dhodho eff a ve grontis,* and as much as he desired to him was granted. M.C. 9. Comp. of *do, to,* and *o, him, dh* being inserted. W. *idho.* Arm. *dezaf.* Ir. *do,* †*dosom.* Gael. *da, dha.* Manx, *da.* Goth. *thamm.*

DOEN, v. a. To bear, to bring, to produce, to carry. *An tryssa dŷdh me a wra dhe'n gwŷdh sevel yn ban, ha doen dellyow îck ha da,* the third day I will make the trees to stand upright, and bear leaves fair and good. C.W. 8. *Ha dew queth dodhans gwra doen,* and two garments to them do thou bear. C.W. 70. *Môr vŷth nyng-esé deffry dhe doen yn ker,* there was not any sea, to bear it away. C.W. 176. Written also *doyn,* and by contraction *dôn,* qd. v. W. *dwyn.* Arm. *dougen,* †*doen.* Ir. †*denom.*

DOENS, v. n. Let them come. Llwyd, 247. Id. qd. *dêns,* qd. v.

DOER, s. f. Earth, the earth. Corn. Voc. *terra. Trevedic doer,* incola, lit. an inhabitant of the land. *ibid. Ha'n bewnans pan a'n kelly, dhe'n doer ty a dreyl aria,* and the life when thou losest it, to the earth thou shalt turn again. C.W. 28. *Pellys on a Paradice dhu'n noer veys er agan gew,* driven out we are from Paradise to the earth of the world for our woe. C.W. 78. *War doer lemyn umhelaf,* on the ground I will cast myself. C.W. 88. *Henna o gwan ober gwrŷs, may ma Dew hä'n noer keffrys, warnas pûb êr ow 'rya,* that was a foul act committed, so that God and the earth likewise are on thee every hour crying. C.W. 72. Written also *doar,* and by contraction *dôr,* qd. v.

DOES, v. n. Let him come. Llwyd, 247. 3 pers. s. imp. of *dôs,* qd. v.

DOF, s. m. A son-in-law. Corn. Voc. *gener.* W. *daw, dawv,* †*dauu.* Arm. *daf, deuf, dof.* Sansc. *daivar,* a brother-in-law.

DOF, adj. Tame, gentle. *Gans lyf ny wrâf bynytha ladhé an dûs gwŷls na dôf,* with flood I will not ever destroy mankind, wild or tame. O.M 1254. Written also *dôv,* qd. v. W. *dôv,* †*dom.* Arm. *don.*

DOF, v. n. I will come. 1 pers. s. fut. of irr. v. *dôs,* qd. v. *Venytha ny dhôf a'n plen erna'n prenné an gwas-na,* never will I come from that place, until I take that fellow. O.M. 2151.

DOFERGI, s. m. An otter. Corn. Voc. *doferghi,* lutrius. Comp. of *dofer,* an old form of *dour,* water, and *ci,* a dog. Written also *devergi,* and *dourgi.* W. *dyvrgi, dourgi.* Arm. *dourgi, ki-dour.* Ir. *dobhar-chu.* Gael. *dobhar-chu.*

DOFYS, part. Chosen. *Pryce. Adam, me a lavar dhys, dha vâb Seth ew dofys genef prest dhom servya ve,* Adam, I tell thee, thy son Seth is chosen by me ready to serve me. C.W. 102. This is a wrong reading of *dewesys,* which is the orthography in the British Museum MS.

DOGA, v. n. To bear, bring, produce, carry. 2 pers. s. imp. *dôc, dôg, doga.* 3 pers. s. fut. *dôc, dôg.* 3 pers. s. pret. *dûc,* a *dhûc. Gansé y a dhûk golow, nos o, ny welons yn fôs,* with them they carried a light, it was night, they saw not well. M.C. 64. *Ha na blêk genas henna ha fals, te dôk dustuny,* and (if) that does not please thee, and false, do thou bear witness. M.C. 82. *Pan o an kentrow lemmys, hy a's dûk dhe'n Edhewon,* when the nails were sharpened, she brought them to the Jews. M.C. 160. *Kymer dhymmo ve kunys; gans lovan bedhens strothys, ha war dhe keyn doga ef,* take thou firewood for me ; with a rope let it be bound, and on thy back carry it. O.M. 1298. *Dôg alena tŷr gwelen,* bring thence three rods. O.M. 1945. *An joul re'n dogo dh'y plath,* the devil carry him to his place. R.D. 2189. *Ow blonogath yw henna, may toccans omma pûr splan frutes,* my will is this, that they produce here very bright fruits. C.W. 8. *Frût da bynnar re dhocca,* good fruit may it never bear ! C.W. 84. *Whâth keth ŷns y mar venys, me a dhôg ran war ow heyn uskes lemyn,* yet since they are so small, I will carry some on my back, immediately now. C.W. 100. Written also *deggy,* qd. v. W. *dygyd, dygu,* (imp. *dwg,* pret. *dug.*) †*doan.* Arm. *douga.* Ir. *tug,* †*tuc.* Gael. *tog.* Manx, *dug.* Sansc. *tak, duh.* Gr. θεχω, δεχομαι. Lat. *duco.* Goth. *tiuha.* Germ. *ziehe.* Eng. *tug.*

DOGOTH, v. n. It behoveth, it becometh. *Ny dogoth dhynny ladhé dên vŷth ol yn nôr bŷs-ma,* it behoveth us not to kill any man at all in the earth of this world. P.C. 1081. *A kêr Arluth, êth yn grows pren, dhym ny dhogowth ammé dhe'th pen,* O dear Lord, that wentest on the cross tree, to me it becometh not to kiss thy head. R.D. 872. Written also *degoth,* qd. v.

DOL, s. f. A valley, a dale, a mead through which a river flows. It is preserved in the names of places, in Cornwall, as *Dollywhiddens, Godolphin, &c.,* and is of very frequent occurrence in Wales, as *Blarnydhôl, Dolgarrog, Dolwydhelen, &c.* W. *dôl.* Arm. *dôl.* Ir. *dail.* Gael. *duil.* Manx, *dayll.* Germ. *dal, thal.* Dan. Swed. Du. *dal.* Eng. *dale.* Goth. *dal, dallei.* Runic, Dal. Isl. *doele.*

DOL, s. m. A share, part, one eighth, a dole. *Pryce.* This is not Celtic, being borrowed from the English.

DOLL, s. m. A hole. A mutation of *toll,* qd. v. *Worth an lês y a dollas dew doll yn grows heb kên,* on the breadth they holed two holes in the cross without pity. M.C. 178.

DOLLAS, v. a. He bored a hole. A mutation of *tollas,* preterito of *tolly,* qd. v.

DOLLE, v. a. To deceive, to delude. *Hy a dhesefsé scorné gans an epscop ha'y dollé dhe wordhyé dewow nowydh,* she would wish to strive with the bishop, and delude him to worship new gods. O.M. 2732. A mutation of *tollé*, qd. v.

DOLOS, v. a. To proclaim, to publish. *Rág henna Pylat a rós dhe'n varogyon aga ro, may lavarsans ha dolos y púp tyller dris an vro, dhe vôs tûs yrvys yn nos warnedhé kymmys adro, nag ens y hardh dhe wortos lemmen oll monas dhe'n fo*, therefore Pilate gave to the soldiers their gift, that they should say and proclaim in every place through the country, that armed men in the night were upon them, so many about, they were not bold to stay, but that all fled away. M.C. 250. Cf. W. *dolevain*, to shout.

DOLVA, s. f. A breach, a separation. This word furnished by Pryce, as existing in the names *Pednolva*, the head of the breach, in Paul, must be a mutation of *tolva*, and comp. of *toll*, a hole, and *ma*, a place.

DOM, pron. prep. To my. (*Do-my*.) *My a vyn alemma môs dhom gwrêk, ha'm flehes totus*, I will go hence to my wife, and children, in haste. O.M. 1036. *Ty re dhysworug eredy hevelep dhom face vy*, thou hast destroyed verily the likeness to my face. O.M. 2337. *Ol y fechas gulan dedhy hy y feydh gyfys, rag kemmys hy dhom caré*, all her sin clean to her shall be forgiven, for so much she loved me. P.C. 530. Written also *dum*, qd. v.

DON, v. a. To bear, to bring, to carry. A contracted form of *doen*, qd. v. It changes in construction into *dhôn*, and *tôn*. *Rág mar ny wrêth, my a vyn y dhôn genef arté dré*, for if thou wilt not, I will take it home with me again. O.M. 508. *Me a vyn aga threhy, ha'ga dôn genef yn chy*, I will cut them, and carry them with me into the house. O.M. 1737. *Pan veuch agey dhe'n cyté why a dhyerbyn wharré dén ow tôn pycher dour glân*, when ye shall be within the city, ye will meet soon a man carrying a pitcher of clean water. P.C. 629. *Lemyn dreheveuch an gist, yn gorjs crous, war duscodh Cryst dh'y dôn dhe dré*, now raise ye the beam, is made a cross, upon the shoulders of Christ to carry it to the town. P.C. 2584.

DONES, v. n. To come, to arrive. *Whêth mŷr arté abervedh, hag oll ken ty a wel'yth kyns ys dones a lena*, look yet again within, and all else thou shalt see before that thou come from it. O.M. 792. This is an enlarged form of *dós*, which does not exist in Welsh, but it does in Armoric, *donet*.

DONS, v. n. They shall come. 3 pers. pl. fut. of *dós*. *Tús ús dhym ow tevones yw gans ow thraytor dyskis, fatel dôns dhow hemeres, ha del vedhaf hombronkis*, men are coming to me by my traitor taught, how they shall come to take me, and how I shall be led. M.C. 61. *Ha múr a bobyll gansé, a dhychow hag a glêdh, dhe Gryst y tôns dh'y syndyé ha dhe dry dhe'n dôr gans mêth*, and many people with them, on the right, and on the left, to Christ they come to hold him, and to bring to the ground with shame. M.C. 97. Llwyd, 247. W. *deuant*, *dônt*.

DOR, s. f. Earth, the earth, ground, land. A contracted form of *doar*, qd. v. Written in the Corn. Voc. *doer*. *Ha'n bewnans pan y'n kylly, dhe'n dôr ty a dreyl arté*, and the life when thou shalt lose it, to the earth thou shalt turn again. O.M. 64. *Ke growedh war un dôr*, go lie down on the ground. O.M. 370. *Ha my d, gans oll ow nel, yn dôr dhe dhallath palas*, and I will go, with all my strength, to begin to dig in the ground. O.M. 370. *Ha hy a wra aspyé mars ûs dôr séch yn nép pow*, and she will look about, if there is dry land in any place. O.M.

1116. *Yma an dôr ow krenné*, the earth is trembling. P.C. 2935.

DOR, s. f. A belly. *Govy vŷth pan vêf genys, a dor ow mam dynythys, na vythqueth pan denys bron*, sad that ever I was born, out of my mother's womb brought, or ever when I sucked the breast. O.M. 1754. A mutation of *tor*, qd. v.

DORGRYS, s. m. An earthquake. *An houl ny golsé y lyw, awos máp dén dhe verwel, na corf dasserhy dhe veo, na dôr-grys yn tyougel*, the sun would not have lost its colour, because of a son of man to die. nor a body rise again to life, nor an earthquake really. P.C. 3036. Comp. of *dôr*, earth, and *crŷs*, id. qd. W. *crŷd*, a quaking. It is also written incorrectly *dorgis*. *Newngo devethys an prŷs, may 'tho ogas dh'y dhewedh, yn er-na y fe dorgis, ha dris oll an bŷs ef éth*, now the time was come that he was near to his end, in that hour there was an earthquake, and over all the world it went. M.C. 200. *Nango hanter dŷdh yn wlâs po moy del yma scryfis, dorgis eva, ha luchas, ha'n twolgow kekyffris*, it was now mid-day in the country, or more as it is written, there was an earthquake, and lightning, and darkness likewise. M.C. 209. W. *daeargryd*, *daeargryn*. Arm. *kren-douar*.

DORN, s. m. A fist, a hand, a handle, a hilt. Pl. *dornow*. *Adam ystyn dhym dhe dhorn; tan henna dheworthef vy*, Adam, reach me thy hand; take that from me. O.M. 205. *A'n lôst kymmer dhedhy yn ban; y'th tarn hep gêr sens dhe honan, dhys lavaraf*, by the tail take it up; in thy hand without a word, hold it thyself, I tell thee. O.M. 1455. *Otté ow fycher gyné yn ow dorn râk y gerchas*, behold my pitcher with me in my hand, to fetch it. P.C. 647. *Me a'n dalhén fest yn tyn, ha gans ow dornow a'n guryn na sowenno*, I will hold him very tightly, and with my hands make him that he thrive not. P.C. 1133. *Pur ankensy gans dornow dhodho war scovornow reuch boxsusow trewysy*, very painful with fists to him on the ears give ye sad blows. P.C. 1360. *Rén dhodho boxsusow gans dornow ha gwelnyny war an scovornow bysy*, let us give him blows with fists and rods on the ears diligently. P.C. 1390. *Pan fue an purpur war skwych kychys dhe vês gans dyn dhorn*, when the purple on a sudden was snatched away with hands. R.D. 2596. The following are from Llwyd: *Dorn dehow*, the right hand; *basced dorn*, a hand basket, 51; *dorn gledh*, *dorn glikin*, left handed, 150; *dorn ardar*, a plough tail, 155. *An manac adro's dorn*, the glove on your hand, 250. W. *dwrn*. Arm. *dourn*. Ir. *dorn*, *durn*. Gael. *dorn*. Manx, *doarn*, *durn*.

DOROY, v. a. To bring. 3 pers. s. fut., and 2 pers. s. imp. *doro*. *Rag ef o tebel edhen, neb a glevesys ow cané, hag a'n doro dhe anken*, for he was an evil bird, whom thou didst hear singing, and will bring us to sorrow. O.M. 225. *Botler fystyn hep lettyé, doro dhym an gwŷn gwella*, butler hasten without stopping, bring me the best wine. O.M. 1904. *My â gynes yn lowen, hag a dhoro asen an genen ha'n ebel keffrys*, I will go with thee gladly, and will bring the ass with us, and the foal likewise. P.C. 192. *Doro kenter*, bring a nail. P.C. 2746. *Doro dhe luef yn woly, gwynys may fuef dre an golon*, put thy hand into the wound, where I was pierced through the heart. R.D. 1539. ‡ *Dowoy an golow dhonna, médh Dzhuan, nenna hei a dhoroas an golow*, come hither with the light, quoth John; then she brought the light. Llwyd, 253. *Doroy*

DOTHE 109 DOVA

is comp. of *do*, id. qd. *dy*, intens. prefix, and *roy*, to give. *Dry* is a contracted form, qd. v. W. *dyroi*.

DORRAF, v. a. I will break. A mutation of *torraf*, 1 pers. s. fut. of *torry*, qd. v. *My ny dorraf bys vycken an acord ûs lemyn gwreys*, I will not break for ever the agreement that is now made. O.M. 1239. W. *mi ni dorraw bŷth*.

DORRAS, v. a. He broke. A mutation of *torras*, 3 pers. s. pret. of *torry*, qd. v. *Och, tru, tru, my re behas, ha re dorras an dyfen*, Oh, woe, woe, I have sinned, and broken the prohibition. O.M. 250. *Honna yw oll dhe vlamyé a dorras an aval têk*, that one is all to blame, that plucked the fair apple. O.M. 265. *Y vôs mâp Dew da y zyw, pan dorras queth an tempel*, that he was the Son of God it follows, when the cloth of the temple tore. P.C. 3088.

DORRASA, v. a. He had broken. A mutation of *torrasa*, 3 pers. s. pluperf. of *torry*, qd. v. *An Tâs an nêf a'n grûk ef dhodho haval; pan dorrasa an aval, an Arluth a fue serrys*, the Father of heaven made him like to himself; when he plucked the apple, the Lord was angry. O.M. 879.

DORRO, v. a. He may break. A mutation of *torro*, 3 pers. s. subj. of *torry*, qd. v. *Me a'n gor dhodho, mar ny'n gorraf, an mŷl dyawl re dorro mellow y gŷn*, I will take him to him, if I do not take him, may a thousand devils break the joints of his back. P.C. 1619.

DORT, prep. From. *Ha na dêg ny en antail, bûs gwithn ny dort drôg*, and lead us not into temptation, but keep us from evil. *Pryce. An tresa dydh ef a dheravas arta dort an marrow*, the third day he rose again from the dead. *ibid. Dho gwitha dhort*, to keep from. *Llwyd*, 71. *Dhort gudra an devas ha'n gowr*, from milking the sheep and the goats. 240. *Dort* is another form of *deworth*, or *dyworth*, and is compounded of *do*, from, and *ort*, by.

DOS, v. m. To come. It changes in construction into *dhôs*, and *tôs*. For the various tenses, see the Grammar. *Ha ny ow tôs alena*, and we coming from that place. O.M. 714. *Mar dha yw genef a vrŷs merwel kyns dôs drôk ancow*, so well it is, in my opinion, to die before the evil sorrow comes. O.M. 1930. *Ro dhymmo grâth a dhôs dhe'th plâth gans dhe eleth*, give me grace to come to thy place, with thy angels. P.C. 291. *Ha a'th pys a dhôs dhodho bŷs yn tré*, and prays thee to come to him into the town. P.C. 566. *Dhe'n Edhewon, pan dothyé, y leverys, hag y ow tôs*, to the Jews when he came, he said, and they coming. M.C. 63. *Eneff Judas ny allas dôs yn mês war y anow*, the soul of Judas could not come out by his mouth. M.C. 106. W. *dywod*, and poet. *dôd*. Arm. *donet, dond*. Ir. *deanam, tigh*. Gael. *tainig*. Sansc. *dhi, dhiv*, to come ; *tag, tig*, to go.

DOTH, s. m. Haste, despatch. A mutation of *tôth*, qd. v. *En debell wrêk casadow gans mûr a dôth êth yn chy, war hast dhe wethyll kentrow, may fêns crêff ha trewesy*, the wicked wife detestable with much hurry, went into the house, in haste to make nails, that they might be strong and painful. M.C. 169.

DOTHE, v. n. He would come. 3 pers. s. subj. of *dôs*. *A losowys ol an bŷs, mar whêk smyllyng, my a grŷs, ny dhothé bŷs venary*, from all the herbs of the world, such sweet smelling, I believe, would never come. O.M. 1744. W. *daethai*.

DOTHYANS, v. n. They had come. 3 pers. pl. pluperf. of irr. v. *dôs. Pan dothyans bŷs yn tyller may 'thesé Crist ow pesy*, when they had come to the place, where Christ was praying. M.C. 63. *Pan dothyans dh'y, yntrethé pows Jesus a ve dyskys*, when they had come there, among them the coat of Jesus was taken off. M.C. 176.

DOTHYE, v. n. He had come. 3 pers. s. pluperf. of irr. v. *dôs. Dhe'n Edhewon, pan dothyé, y leverys, hag y ow tôs*, to the Jews when he had come, he said, and they coming. M.C. 63. *Kevsyns dên mŷns a vynno, ow kyc ha'm gôs bŷdh ynno, ha ken ny dhothyé dh'e'n nêf*, let a man say all he will, my flesh and my blood shall he in him, and else he would not go to heaven. R.D. 2450.

DOTHYNS, pron. prep. To them. ‡*Ha Dew rig go benigas an gy, ha Dew lavaras dothyns*, and God did bless them, and God said to them. C.W. p. 192. ‡*Na ra chee plegy a'n dôr dothyans, na ge worry*, do thou not bow down to them, nor worship them. *Pryce*. This is to be read *dodhyns*, and is the same as *dodhans*, another form of *dedhé*.

DOUR, s. m. Water. Corn. Voc. *aqua vel amnis*; where it is also written *douer*, and *dofer*. Pl. *dowrow*. Obs. that the singular had the sound of the W. *dŵr*, while the plural is formed from *dower*, or *dowr*, exactly as the Welsh for the plural always use *dyvroedh*, from *dwvyr*, or *dwvr. Dower* is another form found in the Ordinalia, qd. v. *A'n golon yth êth strêt brâs, dowr ha goys yn kemeskys*, from the heart there went a great stream, water and blood mingled. M.C. 219. *Dour, may fêns y dysehys, a vewnans ry dedhi gwra*, that they may be refreshed, the water of life do thou give them. O.M. 1833. *Nyns ûs pons war dhour Cedron*, there is no bridge over the water of Cedron. O.M. 2604. *Dên ow tôn pycher dour glân*, a man carrying a pitcher of clean water. P.C. 629. *Ha Speres Dew rig gwayath war bedgeth an dowrow*, and the Spirit of God moved on the face of the waters. C.W. p. 189. W. *dwr, dwvr, dwvyr*, †*dubr*. Corn. *dour, dowr, dower*, †*dûr*, †*douer*, †*dofer*. Arm. *dour*. Ir. *dur, dobhar*. Gael. *dur, dobhar*. Manx, *docur*. Basque, *ura*. Gr. ὕδωρ. Sansc. *var, vari*. water; *dabhra*, ocean. From *dúr* comes *durum*, the Latin termination and beginning of so many names of towns situated on the seaside, or near rivers ; and by transposition of letters, *dubr*, or *duber*, became *watar*, in German, and *woda*, in Slavonic.

DOUR, s. m. Care, concern, anxiety. *Esé dour, ha ponvos brâs, wharré y gen lowenhas, kettel dhueth er agan pyn*, there was concern and great trouble ; soon he gladdened us, when he came to meet us. R.D. 1327. This is variously written *der, dûr, duer*, qd. v. W. *dawr*.

DOURGI, s. m. An otter. *Llwyd*, 241. Written also *dofergi*, qd. v.

DOURIA, v. a. To water, to irrigate. *Llwyd*, 83. Written also *dourhi*, 141. W. *dyvru*. Arm. *doura*.

DOV, v. n. I will come. *Mi dhôv*. Llwyd, 247. 1 pers. s. fut. of *dôs*.

DOV, adj. Tame. Written also *dôf*, qd. v. W. *dôv, dom*. Arm. *don*. Sansc. *dam*, to tame.

DOVA, v. a. To make tame, to tame, to subdue. *Llwyd*, 55. W. *dovi*, †*domi*. Arm. *donva*. Sansc. *dam*. Gr. δέμω, δαμάω. Lat. *domo*. Fr. *dompte*. Goth. *damia*. Germ. *zähme*. Eng. *tame*.

DOWDHEC, num. adj. Twelve. *Pan o y besadow guris, dhe'n dowdhek y leverys*, when his prayers were ended, to the twelve he said. M.C. 61. *Dowdhec legyon yn un ro vye an nêf danvenys*, twelve legions in one gift would be from heaven sent. M.C. 72. Written also *dewdhec*, qd. v.

DOWDHEGVES, num. adj. Twelfth. Written also *dowdhegvas*. Pryce.

DOWEDHYANS, s. m. End, the close, termination. *Yn dowedhyans a hena me a bowes desempys*, in the latter end of that I will rest immediately. C.W. 32. From *dowedh*, id. qd. *dewedh*, an end.

DOWER, s. m. Water. *Dower ha lêr, ha tân, ha gwyns, houl, ha lour, ha steyr keffrys*, water and earth, and fire, and wind, and sun, and moon, and stars likewise. M.C. 211. Written also *dour*, qd. v.

DOWH, v. n. Ye will come. 2 pers. pl. fut. of *dôs*. Llwyd, 247. A late form of *deuch*. W. *dowch*.

DOWL, s. m. A fall. A mutation of *towl*, qd. v. *Gallas genef hager dowl, dhe pytt effarn mês an nef*, I have had a cruel fall to the pit of hell out of heaven. C.W. 32.

DOWLA, v. a. To throw, to cast. A mutation of *towla*, qd. v. *Do e dowla en clêdh*, to cast him into a ditch. Llwyd, 244.

DOWN, adj. Deep, profound, low. *Paynys a'd wra morethiek yn yffarn down pûb termyn*, pains shall make thee miserable in hell deep at all times. M.C. 66. *Ef a doys a dhesympys maga town ty del wodhye*, he swore immediately as deep an oath as he knew. M.C. 85. *Yn dôr my a vyn palas toll, may fo ynno cudhys, ha'y wûl hŷr ha doun ragdho*, in the earth I will dig a hole that he may be covered in it, and make it long and deep for him. O.M. 867. *Down y'm kŷc may 'tho tellys lyes mŷl toll*, so that deep in my flesh were pierced many thousand holes. R.D. 2539. W. *dwvn*. Arm. *doun*, †*don*. Ir. *doimhin*, †*domun*. Gael. *domhain*. Manx, *dowin*; y *diunid*, the profound. Gr. δυνω, to go down. Eng. *down*.

DOWN, v. n. We will come. 1 pers. pl. fut. of *dôs*. Llwyd, 247. Another form of *dún*. W. *down*.

DOWNDER, s. m. Deepness, depth, profundity, a gulf, a bottomless pit. *Ha 'thera an noar hep composter ha gwâg, ha bulder war bedgeth an downder, ha Speres Dew rig gwayath war bedgeth an dowrow*, and the earth was without form and void, and darkness on the face of the deep; and the Spirit of God did move on the face of the waters. C.W. p. 189; M.C. p. 93. W. *dyvnder*. Arm. *dounder*.

DOWSES, s. m. Godhead, divinity. *Pan ylly gy ahanan dhe'n nef, dhe'n Tâs, gynen bydhyth yn dowses; râk na yllyn dhe weles, cûth ny gen gâs*, when thou goest from us to heaven, to the Father, thou wilt be with us in Godhead; because we are not able to see thee, sorrow leaves us not. R.D. 2455. This is another form of *dewsys*, qd. v.

DOY, adj. Yesterday. Corn. Voc. *heri*. The latest form was *de*, qd. v. W. *doe*. Arm. *deach, dech*. Ir. *ne, ane; nae, anae*; †*indhe*. Gael. *de, an de*. Manx, *jea*. Gr. χθὲς. Lat. *heri*. Fr. *hier*. Sansc. *hyas*, from *hi*, to leave. Cf. also χθεσινὸν. Lat. *hesternus*. Goth. *gistra*. Germ. *gestern*. Eng. *yester*.

DOYN, v. a. To bring, to bear, to carry. *An Edhewon a geusys, doyn dhyn dustuny a wra, mychtern y fyn bôs synsys ha mester brâs yn bys-ma*, the Jews said, he will bear witness to us, that he will be accounted a king, and a great master in this world. M.C. 111. Another form of *doen*, qd. v.

DOYS, v. a. He swore. A mutation of *toys*, qd. v. *Ef a doys a dhesympys maga town ty del wodhye, gans Christ na vye tregis, na bythqueth ef na'n quelsê*, he swore immediately as deep an oath as he knew, with Christ that he had not been living, nor ever had seen him. M.C. 85.

DOYS, v. n. To come. *I vam whêk Marya wyn pûb ûr fystené a wre, may hallê doys war-y-byn, y mâb kemmys a garê*, his dear mother, blessed Mary, every hour made haste, that she might come to meet him, her son she loved so much. M.C. 171. Another form of *dôs*, qd. v.

DRA, s. f. A thing. A mutation of *tra*, qd. v. *Lavar dysempys dymmo an dra ûs war dhe vreys*, speak at once to me the thing which is on thy mind. P.C. 499. *Dew ha dên yw dew dra*, God and man are two things. P.C. 1730. *An dra-na na gl bôs gwŷr*, that thing that cannot be true. R.D. 1400. *A ny wodhouch why un dra*, do ye not know one thing? R.D. 2445.

DRAEN, s. m. A thorn, a prickle. Corn. Voc. *drain*, spina, pl. *drein*, sentes. By Llwyd, the singular is written *drên*. *Hag ynno fest luhas toll gans an dreyn a ve tellys*, and in it very many holes by the prickles were holed. M.C. 133. *Asso mur tyn ow passyon, pan êth dreyn yn empynnyon a pûp parth dre a' gragen*, very sharp was my suffering, when tho thorns went into the brain, on all parts through the skull. R.D. 2557. W. *draen*, pl. *drain*. Arm. *draen, drean*, pl. *drein*. Ir. *draighean, draighen, droighin*, †*draigen*. Gael. *droighionn*, (pron. *droiun*.) Manx, *drine*. Sansc. *drunaka*. Goth. *thaurn*. Germ. *thorn*. Du. *doren*. Du. *doren, doernen*. Ang. Sax. *thyrn*. Eng. *thorn*.

DRAENEN, s. f. A bramble, a brier, a thornbush. Llwyd, 148. W. *draenen*.

DRAGUN, s. m. A dragon. Llwyd, 55. Another term is *druic*, qd. v. W. *dragon, draig*, †*dreic*. Arm. *dragon*. Ir. *dragun, drcagan, draig, drig*. Gael. *drag, dreug*. Lat. *draco, dracone*. Eng. *dragon*.

DRAITH, s. m. A sandy beach. Pryce. A mutation of *traith*, qd. v.

DRAL, s. m. A piece, a fragment, a part. *Dûs alena ty Gebal, gor an pren yn mês gans mal, ha'th wereses Amalek, ha icwleuch e dral ha dral yn Bessedê pur gowal*, come away from there, thou Gebal, place the tree outside with a will, and let Amalek help thee; and cast ye it, piece by piece, into Bethsaida very completely. O.M. 2782. W. *dryll*. Arm. *dral*.

DRE, s. f. A town. A mutation of *trê*, qd. v. *Masons an drê ketep pol, guetyeuch bones avorow ow conys yn erŷs an drê*, masons of the city, every head, take ye care to be to-morrow working in the midst of the city. O.M. 2298. *An gwâs prout re wrûk re maystry yn drê*, the proud fellow has done too much violence in town. P.C. 363. *Oll monas y a vynnê bŷs yn Mont a Gulvary, a vês dhe'n drê ythesê*, all would go even to Mount Calvary, outside the town it was. M.C. 162. *Dre* is often used with or without a preposition to express *home*, at home, homewards. *Ow mâp py'theth dhe vroder, prâg na dhêth e genes drê*, my son, where is thy brother gone, why is he not come with thee home? O.M. 607. *Ow arluth lowenê dhys, ow olê vy devthys artê dhe drê*, my lord, hail to thee! behold me come again home. O.M. 2213.

Ellas výth pan dhueyth a dré, alas, that I ever came from home. R.D. 1661.

DRE, prep. Through, by. *Rág púp tra oll a fydh da, dre weres agan Dew ny*, for all things will be good, by the help of our God. O.M. 535. *Dre vôdh an Tâs caradow*, by the will of the Father beloved. O.M. 1039. *Hy a'n grûk dre kerensé*, she did it through love. P.C. 549. *Yn golon, dre'n tenewen, dhe restyé syngys ow gú ; dre ow thrŷs y tûth un smai, gans kentrow d'aga gorré ; y fue ow manegow plat spygys brás dre ow dywlé*, in heart, through the side, I felt my spear thrust, through my feet a fellow came with nails to put them ; and my smooth gloves were great spikes through my hands. R.D. 2585. *Dre* is a mutation of *tre*, but it only occurs in the secondary form. *Der* is another form, qd. v. W. *trwy, drwy,* †*tre*, †*troi*, †*trui*. Arm. *dre*. Ir. *tre*, †*tri, dar*. Gael. *tre, troimh, trid*. Manx, *trooid*. Sansc. *tiritas*. Goth. *thairu*. Aug. Sax. *thurh*. Eng. *through*.

DRE, conj. While, whilst. *Ha dre vôn bew, on súr a ura penys ; nymbes joy a dra yn býs*, and whilst we are alive, he will surely punish ns; there is no joy to me of any thing in the world. C.W. 90. It occurs more frequently in the compound form *hedré*, qd. v. *Dre* is a mutation of *tre*, id. qd. *try*, qd. v. W. *tra*. Arm. *andra, endra*. Ir. *traih*. Gael. *traih*.

DREAFSE, v. a. He would raise. *Hag ef dhyn re leverys, kyn fe an temple dysurŷs yn tri dŷdh y'n dreafsé*, and he hath said to ns, although the temple were destroyed, in three days he would re-build it. P.C. 366. This is an incorrect form of *drehefsé*, 3 pers. s. plup. and subj. of *drehevel*, qd. v.

DREATH, s. m. A sandy shore, a sand. *Dréath leuky*, a quicksand. Llwyd, 160. A mutation of *treath*, id. qd. *traith*, qd. v.

DRECHA, v. a. He will raise. 3 pers. s. fut. of *drehevel*, qd. v. *An temple ef a dhysurra, yn trydydh ef a'n drecha gwill ages kyns múr yn próf*, the temple he will destroy ; in three days he will build it, better much than before in proof. P.C. 1697. *Coskyn ny gans dyaha ; kyn dasvewo ny'n drecha dhywar y geyn*, let us sleep with security ; though he should revive, he will not lift it from off his back. R.D. 403. This form was also softened into *dreha*. (See *Drehevel*.) W. *dyrcha*.

DREDH, prep. By, through. Llwyd, 117.

DREDHE, pron. prep. By or through them. *Aban yw an pren tellys, bedhens an ebyl gorrys dredhé rag aga lacié*, since the wood is bored, let the pegs be put through them, to fasten them. P.C. 2575. *Hag yll troys a ve gorris poran war ben y gelé, worth an grows, y fôns laithijs gans kenter gwyskis dredhé*, and the one foot was put straight over the other, on the cross they were laid, with a nail struck through them. M.C. 179. (*Dre-dh-y*.) W. *trwydhynt, drwydhynt*. Arm. *drezhô*. Ir. *triotha*, †*tritu*, †*treu*, †*treo*, †*trempu*, †*treoimpa*. Gael. *trompa*.

DREDHO, pron. prep. By or through him, or it. *Yn plath may môns y u céf, dredho cf pan ŷns plynnys*, in the place that they are they shall stand, through him when they are planted. O.M. 2002. *Dredho ef prynnys bydheuch, oll ow tûs, gour ha benen*, by it ye shall be redeemed, all my people male and female. P.C. 767. (*Dre-dh-o*.) W. *trwydho, drwydho*, †*trwydo*, †*trio*, †*truio*. Arm. *drezhan*, †*dreizef*. Ir. *trid, tridsenn*, †*triit* †*triisom*, †*triitsom*. Gael. *troimhe*. Manx, *trooidsyn*.

DREDHOF, pron. prep. By or through me. *Bargos, bryny, ha'n êr, moy dredhof a vŷdh hynwys*, kite, crows, and the eagle further by me shall be named. O.M. 134. *Ha'n býs yhew increasys dredhof ve hag ow flechys, heb niver dhe vôs comptys*, and the world is increased by me and my children, without number to be counted. C.W. 144. (*Dre-dh-my*.) W. *trwydhov, drwydhov*. Ir. *triom*, †*truim*. Gael. *tromham*.

DREDHON, pron. prep. By or through us. (*Dre-dh-ni*.) W. *trwydhom, drwydhom*. Ir. *trinn*, †*triunni*. Gael. *tromhainn*.

DREDHOS, pron. prep. By or through thee. *Hep towl púr wŷr me a grys dredhos y fydhyn sylwys*, without a doubt very truly I believe through thee we shall be saved. P.C. 287. *Dredhos dhe gy y fŷdh oll ny yn gwŷr sawys*, through thee we shall all be saved truly. P.C. 295. *Ioy yw gynef dhe clewas, mar tèk yw dhe dheryvas, dredhos ythof lowenhys*, joy is with me to hear, so fair is thy declaration, through thee I am gladdened. R.D. 2618. (*Dre-dh-ty*.) W. *trwydhot, drwydhot*. Ir. *triot*. Gael. *tromhad*.

DREDHOUCH, pron. prep. By or through you. *Pilat a gowsys arté, dredhouch why bedhens ledhys, rag ynno me ny gaffé scyle vâs may so dampnys*, Pilate said again, by you let him be killed, for in him I have not found good grounds that he should be condemned. M.C. 142. W. *trwydhoch, drwydhoch*. Ir. *tribh*, †*triib*. Gael. *tromhaibh*.

DREDHY, pron. prep. By or through her. *Rag an grows ytho ordnys, ha'n Hudhewon ny wodhyé, hag an aval devethys dredhy Adam may pechsé*, for the cross it was ordained, and the Jews knew it not, and the apple came by it that Adam had sinned by. M.C. 152. Written also *drydhy*, qd. v. (*Dre-dh-hy*.) W. *trwydhi, drwydhi*, †*irwydi*. Arm. †*dreizi*. Ir. *tridhe, triithi*, †*tree*. Gael. *troimpe*.

DREFEN, prep. Because, because of. *Drefen ow bones benen, ty a gîl dhym daryvas, awos travyth ny wrussen venytha dhe guhudhas*, because I am a woman, thou mayest declare it to me ; because of any thing, I would not ever accuse thee. O.M. 161. *Drefen ow bôs noeth hep queth, ragos yth-yth dhe gudhé*, because I am naked without a cloth, I went to hide from thee. O.M. 259. *Drefen luen ty dhum servyé, ow crês a fêdh venary*, because thou servest me fully, my peace shall be with thee for ever. O.M. 1019. *Drefen un wŷth dhe henwel, lydhys ef pûr dhyogel*, because of once naming thee, I am killed very certainly. O.M. 2724. Written also *drevan*. Arm. *dre-ma*.

DREGE, v. a. To stay, wait for, remain, sustain. *Ha'n bedhow owth egery me a's gwél, war ow ené ; mar str*c*hyn omma na moy, ny agan bŷdh y dregé*, and tho graves opening, I saw them on my soul ; if we stay here any more, we shall not bo able to sustain it. P.C. 3001. A mutation of *tregé*, qd. v.

DREGERETH, s. m. Compassion, pity, mercy. *An oyl a versy, o dydhynwys dhymmo vy gans an Tás a'y dregereth pan wêf chaeys gans an êl*, the oil of mercy, (that) was promised to me by the Father, of his compassion, when I was driven by the angel. O.M. 705. A mutation of *tregereth*, qd. v.

DREHEDHY, v. a. To reach, to attain to. *Na fors kyn na dhrehedho, ken toll ny vŷdh gurŷs rugdho ; ny a's len may fôns lour hŷr,* no matter though it may not reach, another hole shall not be made for it; we will stretch it, that it may be long enough. P.C. 2758. Comp. of prefix *dre,* thoroughly, and *heslhy,* to reach.

DREHEVEL, v. a. To elevate, to raise up, to erect, to rise. Part. *drehevys.* 3 pers. s. fut. *drcha,* and *drccha,* qd. v., from the earlier form *drechevel. My a vyn grutthyl castel, ha drehevel dhym ostel ynno rag tregé,* I will make a village, and build for myself a mansion, in it to live. O.M. 1710. *Moyses whêk, ny a dreha ragon chy pols dhe wonys,* sweet Moses, we will raise for us a house, a while to labour. O.M. 1715. *My a fystyn agy, ow trehevel an fosow,* I will hasten within, erecting the walls. O.M. 2320. *Ha pen créf warnedhé y gwreuch drehevel,* and a strong top upon them do ye erect, O.M. 2452. *Drehevyn ef yn bm,* let us raise it up. O.M. 2539. *Drc góth y wrûk leverel, kyn fe dysurys an temple yn tri dýdh y n drchufsé, bythqueth whet na fe gwell,* through pride he did say, though the temple were destroyed, in three days he would re-build it, that never yet was better. P.C. 383. *Kyn pen try dýdh y wrussys gwell ys kyns y drehevel,* before the end of three days thou wouldst raise it better than before. P.C. 1761. *Lemyn drcheveuch an gist,* now lift ye the beam. P.C. 2582. *Drehefouch an grows yn bun,* lift ye the cross up. P.O. 2812. *Sûr lour of vy annodho, dén marow na dhrchavo, bfs drydh fyn,* sure enough I am of him; that a dead man will not rise, till the last day. R.D. 415. *A fystynyn ny yn fen, rag drehevys yw an mên dhyworth an bêdh,* Oh ! let us hasten diligently, for the stone is raised from the tomb. R.D. 716. W. *dyrchavad.* Ir. *driuchadh, circhim, dicreach.* Gael. *cirich, dirich.* Manx, *trog, troggal.*

DREHY, v. a. To cut. A mutation of *trehy,* qd. v. *Adam cummyas scon a fýdh hŷs dhe baal luen dhe drchy,* Adam, permission shall be forthwith, to cut full the length of thy spade. O.M. 380. *An gwél a rás dhyworth an lûr gwróf dhe drehy,* the rods from the ground I will them. O.M. 1988. *Euch dh'y drchy kep lcttyé,* go yo to cut it without stopping. O.M. 2505.

DREIN, s. m. Thorns, prickles. Corn. Voc. *scntes.* It is the plural of *draen,* qd. v.

DREIS, s. m. Brambles, briars. Corn. Voc. *vepres.* This is a plural aggregate, from which was formed the sing. *dreisen,* written by Llwyd, 141, *dreisan,* a raspberry bush. W. *dyrysi,* sing. *dyrysien,* †*dryssien.* Arm. *drez, dreiz,* sing. *drezen, dreiven.* Gael. *dreas, dris.* Ir. *dris,* †*driss.* Manx, *dress.* The root is W. *dyrysu,* to be entangled, or twisted together.

DREM, s. m. A complaint, lamentation. *Myrches a Jerusalem na olowch na na wreuch drem warnaf vy, nag onan ofth ; saw warnouch agas honan, ha war 'gas flches vyan, kén dhe olé why a's býdh,* daughters of Jerusalem, weep not, no, nor make lamentation on me, not any one; but on yc yourselves, and on your little children, cause to weep ye shall have. P.C. 2640.

DREMAS, s. m. One exceedingly good, a good man, a just man, a husband. *Dremas yw ef leun a rás, nêb re werthys, yn mêrth e,* he is a just man, full of grace, whom I have sold, says he. M.C. 103. *Kepar del fuvé dremmas, yn dôr my a vyn palas toll, may fo ynno cudhys,* like as he was a just man, in the earth I will dig a hole, that he may be covered in it. O.M. 864. *Ha mara gureth, renothas, me a syns dhe vôs dremas, hag a'th werdh bŷs vynary,* and if thou wilt, by my father, I will hold thee to be a good man, and worship thee for ever. P.C. 1773. *Arluth dremas, mar codhus myr Cryst, ow sylwyas,* good lord, if thou hast happened to see Christ, my Saviour. R.D. 855. Comp. of the prefix *dre,* thoroughly, and *mâs,* good.

DREMENE, v. a. To pass over, to transgress, to depart, to die. A mutation of *tremené,* qd. v. *Ganso drys nôs yth olyas yn y servis nêb o lên,* with him by night there watched in his service one (that) was faithful in his service. M.C. 237. *May whrussons cam dremené, sur y ryllyk an prŷs,* that they did evil transgressions, surely they will curse the time. O.M. 337. *Bolungeth Dew yn hemma, bones gorrys an spûs-ma, pan dremenna o'n bysma, yu y anow,* the will of God is this, that these kernels be put, when he passes from this world, in his mouth. O.M. 875.

DREMMA, s. f. This town. *My a rea dhyuch an dremma, hag el Chennary an Clôs,* I will give you these places, and all Chennary of the Close. O.M. 2771. *Drcmma* is a mutation of *tremma,* compounded of *tre,* a town, and *omma,* here; and it may be of *tra,* a thing, and *omma.*

DREN, s. m. A thorn. Llwyd, 148, 153. *Drén* is a contracted form of *draen,* qd. v.

DRENGES, s. f. Trinity. Written also *drengys.* It is another form of *drenses ; g* soft, sounded as *j,* being substituted for *s. Ihcsu máp rás, agan sylwyas, dues gweres ny, ha Drengys, Tás, a wrûk pûp giolas, ha dén a pry,* Jesus, Son of grace, our Saviour, come help us; and Trinity, Father, who hath made every country, and man of earth. R.D. 309. *Me ew lantorn néf, avel tán ow collowy, moy splanna es an Drenges, henna degoch why destunny,* I am the lantern of heaven, like to fire shining, more resplendent than the Trinity, of that bear ye witness. C.W. 10. Written by Llwyd, *drenzhes,* 243.

DRENIC, adj. Abounding in thorns, thorny. It is preserved in the name of a place, *Drinnik Town,* in South Petherwin. W. *dreiniog.* Arm. *dreinek.*

DRENS, v. a. Let them bring. 3 pers. pl. imp. of *dry,* qd. v. It is also used after a singular nominative. *Ef a gíff yn Araby, yn Mount Tabor gwelynny a plansas Moyses ; a's drêns dhe Jerusalem,* he will find in Arabia, in Mount Tabor, rods which Moses planted; let him bring them to Jerusalem. O.M. 1933.

DRENSES, s. f. Trinity. *Máp dén hep kên ys bara, byth nyn ieves oll bewnes, leman yn levarow da a dhue dhyworth Drenses,* son of man, without other bread, never found all life, but in good words that come from the Trinity. P.C. 68. This is another form of *drindas,* a mutation of *trindas,* qd. v.

DRES, prep. Beyond, over, above, against, across. *Yn trevyth y nyng ens gyw dhe wethyl dres y vynnas,* in any thing they were not fit to do beyond his will. M.C. 68. *A'y frût dybry ny'm bûs whans, dres dyfen ow Arluth kêr,* of its fruit to eat I have not a desire, against the prohibition of our dear Lord. O.M. 172. *Arluth del bs drcs pûp tra, dhe worhemmyn a vŷdh gwreys,* Lord, as thou art above every thing, thy command shall be done. O.M. 1255. *Del osé pryns, ha fûr dres dhe cowethé,* as thou art prince, and wise beyond thy companions. P.C. 1927. *Nynsouch lemmyn gowygyon, ow môs dres pow flattiuryon, ow leverel an nedhow,* are ye not now liars, going across the country, telling the news ? R.D. 1511.

Written also *dris, drys, dreis,* and *dreys.* W. *tros, dros.* Arm. *drcist.* Ir. *tairis.* Gael. *thairis.*

DRES, part. Brought. Part. and pret. of *drey.* *Otté an Ihesu gyné drés býs dhyso yn kelmys,* behold Jesus with me is brought to thee bonnd. P.C. 1569. *Te reson výth a drés er aga fyn,* thou hast brought no reason against them. M.C. 120.

DRES, adj. Bold, audacious. *Agan cregy ny yw mall, rág ny rebé laddron drés,* our hanging is not wrong, for we have been bold thieves. M.C. 193. Written also *drews,* qd. v. W. *drúd.*

DRESOF, pron. prep. Over me, by me. (*Dres-my.*) *Pós re teulneuch agas clún; rág me a'n guelas dufun, dresof ef a tremenas,* heavily ye have thrown down your baunches; for I saw him wide awake, he passed by me. R.D. 525.

DRESTO, pron. prep. Over him, or it. (*Dres-o.*) *Nynsus Arluth dresto ef, na ngl yn nôr, nag yn néf, Dew hep parow,* there is not a Lord over him, nor one on earth, or in heaven, God without equals. R.D. 1746. *Neffré yn dour hedré vo, ny dhue dresto na varwo, gour, gwrék, na bést,* ever in water while he is, no one goes over it that does not die, man, woman, or beast. R.D. 2226. W. *trosto, drosto,* †*drosdaro,* †*trusso,* †*trostau,* †*trosdau.*

DREUCH, v. a. Bring ye. 2 pers. pl. imp. of *drey.* *Dreuch býs omma dhum tyller an harlot gwás,* bring ye even here to my place the knave fellow. P.C. 980. *Dreuch an profus aberedh,* bring ye the prophet in. P.C. 1465. *Dreuch dhym ow máp cúf colon,* bring ye to me my son, dear of heart. P.C. 3164. The final aspirate was often softened into *h,* or omitted altogether. *Drew hy yn més,* bring them out. R.D. 318. *Drewh e dhymmo ma'n gwyllyf,* bring them to me that I may see him. R.D. 1776.

DREVAL, v. a. To lift up, to erect. Llwyd, 164. A late form of *drehevel,* qd. v.

DREVAN, prep. Because of. Another form of *drefen,* qd. v.

DREVAS, s. m. Tillage. *Adam, a oll dhe drevas, an degves ran dhymmo gás, whéth in atal dhe kesky,* Adam, of all thy tillage, leave thou the tenth part to me still to remain waste. O.M. 425. A mutation of *trevas.*

DREWESY, adj. Mournful, doleful, sad. A mutation of *trewesy,* qd. v. *Mam Ihesus Crist a ammé corf y máb púr drewesy,* the mother of Jesus Christ kissed the body of her son very dolefully. M.C. 231.

DREWS, adj. Bold, froward. *Dew lader drews o dampnys a ve dydhgtis gans Ihesu, ganso ef may féns cregis, onon dhodho a búb tu,* two froward robbers, (that) were condemned, were prepared with Jesus, that they might be hanged with him, one on each side of him. M.C. 163. W. *drúd.* Ir. *druth.* Gaul. *drutos.*

DREWYTH, adj. Wretched, lamentable. A mutation of *trewyth,* qd. v. *Y won dhe wýr Dew an Tás re worras drevyth benen,* I know truly, God the Father a wretched woman has angered. O.M. 256.

DREY, v. a. To bring. *Dho drei,* Llwyd, 247. Written also *dry,* qd. v. 3 pers. s. pret. *dreys, drôs, drés, dris.* *Gans Judas del o tewlys, drey Jesus sur del vynné,* with Judas so it was arranged that he would surely bring Jesus. M.C. 41. *Na ve bôs fals an dén-ma, nyn drossen ny býs deso,* were not this man false, we should not have brought him to thee. M.C. 99. *Cayphas a'n droys arté dhe Pylat o pen Justis,* Caiaphas brought him again to Pilate, (that) was chief Justice. M.C. 119. *Ha te reson výth a drés er aga fyn, na gewsyth,* and thou hast brought no reason against them, nor speakest. M.C. 120. *A Dâs, ty re dhrôs dhymmo,* O Father, thou hast brought to me. O.M. 111. *Pan yllyn ny ynirethon drey dour a'n meen flynt garow,* when we can between us bring water from the rough flint stone. O.M. 1860. *A's drêns dhe Jerusalem,* let him take them to Jerusalem. O.M. 1933. *Dreuch an profus abervedh,* bring ye the prophet in. P.C. 1465. *A'n dour y fue drehevys, ha dreys arté dhe'n tŷr mûr,* from the water he was raised, and brought again to the great land. R.D. 2328. *Me a'n drossa dhe baynes,* I will bring him to pains. O.W. 36. *Drewhy (drewh-why) dhym orth copplow,* bring ye to me by conples. C.W. 174. *Drey* is a contracted form of *dyrey,* and compounded of the prefix *dy,* and *rey,* to give. W. *dyroi.*

DREYL, v. a. He will turn. A mutation of *treyl,* 3 pers. s. fut. of *treylé,* qd. v. *Ha'n bewnans pan y'n kylly, dhe'n dôr ty a dreyl arté,* and the life when thou losest it, to the earth thou shalt turn again. O.M. 64. *Rág dewes mar nystewyth, y a dreyl fýth, hag a wordh dewow tebel,* for if a beverage be not found, they will ever turn, and worship evil gods. O.M. 1817. *Saw rák Peder caradow, lyes gwýth me re bysys, na dreyl e y gowsesow, awos own bones ledhys,* but for Peter the beloved, many times I have prayed, that ho turn not his speeches, for fear of being killed. P.C. 885.

DREYLE, v. a. He turned. A mutation of *treylé,* 3 pers. s. imp. of *treylé,* qd. v. *Why re dhrôs dhym an dén-ma kepar ha pan dreylé ef en dús dhyworth Dew an néf,* ye have brought this man to me, as though he turned the people from the God of heaven. P.C. 1853.

DREYN, s. m. Thorns. See *Drein.*

DREYNYN, v. a. To torment. *Yn pryson môs ny dreynyn agan bew, kyn kentreynnyn oll agan kýc,* going to prison we will not torment our lives, though our flesh may rot. R.D. 73. This word is a mutation of *treynyn,* 1 pers. pl. fut. of *treynyé,* qd. v.

DREYS, s. m. Feet. A mutation of *treys,* qd. v. *Yma daggrow ow klybyé dhe dreys, rák ewn kerengé, saw me a's sêch gans ow blew,* tears are wetting thy feet, for true love, but I will dry them with my hair. P.C. 483. *Y dreys ha'y dulé, yn ten gans kentrow worth an plynken bedhens tackys,* his feet and his hands, firmly, with nails to the planks, let them be fastened. P.C. 2516.

DREYS, part. Brought. *Gwyryoneth a reys bôs dreys abervedh yn mater-ma,* need is that truth be brought within this affair. P.C. 2447. Part. of *drey,* qd. v.

DREYS, prep. Over, above, beyond. *Bedhens ebron dreys púp tra, rák kudhé myns ûs formyys,* let a sky be above every thing, to cover all that is formed. O.M. 21. *Bommyn dreys kryn,* blows over the back. P.C. 2729. Another form of *dres,* qd. v.

DRI, num. adj. Three. A mutation of *tri,* qd. v. *E vester a dhrôs on dri pens,* his master brought the three pounds. Llwyd, 251.

DRIG, v. n. He will remain. 3 pers. s. fnt. of *triga,* qd. v. *Lemmyn omma ty a drŷk, býs pan pottro oll dhe gýk, iugqys may fey,* now here thou shalt stay, until when all thy flesh may rot, when thou art sentenced. R.D. 2021. *Ny drŷk grychonen yn fôk,* there remains not a spark in the forge. P.C. 2717.

DRIGAS, v. a. He stayed, or remained. A mutation of *trigas*, 3 pers. s. preterite of *triga*, qd. v. *Yn creys me re ysedhas, avel servont ow servyé, ha why gynef re drygas yn templacyon yn pùp le*, in the midst I have sat, like a servant serving, and ye have dwelt with me in temptation every where. P.C. 805.

DRIGVA, s. f. A dwelling place. A mutation of *trigva*, qd. v. *Effarn yw y drigva*, hell is its dwelling place. C.W. 122.

DRINDAS, s. f. Trinity. *Llwyd*, 166. *An drindas*, the Trinity. A mutation of *trindas*, qd. v.

DRIS, prep. Above, over, beyond. *Ha'n strokosow trewesy war y gorf dris pùb manner*, and the sad stripes on his body above every measure. M.C. 173. *Ganso drys nôs yth olyas yn y servis nêb o lên*, with him through the night there watched in his service one that was faithful. M.C. 237. *May lavarsans yn pùb tyller dris an vro*, that they should say in every place through the country. M.C. 250. One of the various forms of *dres*, qd. v.

DRISLEMMAL, v. a. To leap over. Comp. of *dris*, over, and *lemmel*, to leap. In late times it was corrupted into *dris-lebmal*. Pryce.

DRO, v. a. Bring thou. 2 pers. s. imp. of *drey*. *Dro ve dhymmo dysempys, ha my a ra y dybry*, bring it to me immediately, and I will eat it. O.M. 247. *Dôg alena tŷr gwelen, ha dro y genes dhe drê*, take thou thence three rods, and bring them with thee home. O.M. 1947. *Dro hy dhymmo war ow scoudh*, bring it to me on my shoulder. P.C. 2624.

DRO, adv. About, thereabout, on all sides. *Llwyd*, 127, 176. *Lays es yn pow a dro*, the laws are in the country about. M.C. 121. (See *Adro*.) *Nyns yw marth, cùth ken y'm bo, ow toon an pren a dhe dro*, it is no wonder, if sorrow be in me, carrying the tree about. O.M. 2820. ‡ *Rag hedda vedn bôz cowses dro dan pow*, for that will be spoken about the country. Pryce. *Dro* is a mutation of *tro*, qd. v.

DROAGA, v. a. To hurt. *Llwyd*, 75. A late form of *droga*, qd. v.

DROC, s. m. Evil, wickedness, harm, injury, wrong. Written also *drôg*, as in the Cornish Vocabulary, *droy, malum*. *Mara kyll dheworth an da dhe wethyll drôk agan dry*, if he can from the good bring us to do evil. M.C. 21. *Ef ny ylly dre dhewsys godhaff na nyll drôk na da*, he could not by godhead suffer either evil or good. M.C. 60. *Dên vŷth drôg dhys ny wra*, no man shall do thee harm. O.M. 1462. *Me a wra dhys mûr a dhrôk*, I will do thee much evil. P.C. 2098.

DROC, adj. Bad, evil, wicked, hurtful, mischievous. Written also *drog*. *A out warnes, drôk venen, worto pan wrussys colé*, Oh, out upon thee wicked woman, when thou didst listen to him. O.M. 221. *Drôg yw genef gruthyl dên*, I am sorry to have made man. O.M. 417. (This idiom is the common form in Welsh, *drwg yw genyv, y mae yn drwy genyv*.) *Mar dha yw genef a vrŷs, merwel kyns dôs drôk ancow*, so well it is in my opinion, to die before the coming of evil sorrow. O.M. 1230. *Ty a fÿdh wharé drôg lam*, thou shalt soon have a bad chance. O.M. 2742. *Dre wŷr vreus iuggys râk agan drôk ober kens*, by true judgment sentenced for our evil work before. P.C. 2902. *Ty dhe dôs drôk yw gyné dhe vûr ancres*, I am sorry that thou shouldest have come to great disquiet. R.D. 207. W. *drwg*. Arm. *droug*, †*drouc*. Ir.

droch, †*drog*. Gael. *droch*. Manx, *drogh*. Sansc. *druh*, to seek to hurt.

DROCA, adj. Worst. Written also *droga*. *Droga galar ew dhymmo y ancledhyas mar uskys*, the worst grief is to me, the burying him so immediately. O.M. 868. *Droka ober o henna, ladhé mâp Dew y honan*, the worst deed was that, to kill the Son of God himself. P.C. 3081. *Pûr wŷr y fydhons dampnys dhe tân ufarn, droka le*, very truly they will be condemned to the fire of hell, the worst place. P.C. 3094. W. *drycav*. Besides the regular comparison, *droc, drocah, droca*, the Cornish had also the irregular comparative *gwéth*, and superlative, *gwetha*. So in Welsh, *drwg, drycach, drycav*, and *gwaeth, gwaethav*; and in Arm. *droug, gwaz, gwasa*.

DROCOLETH, s. m. An evil deed, ill doing, injury, damage. *Mar a mynnê amendyé, gwell vye y dhylyfryê hep drocoleth dhyworthyn*, if he would amend it would be better to liberate him without injury from us. P.C. 1864. *Pa'n drok-kuleth a wrusta? gorthyp vy na vyf tollys*, what evil deed hast thou done? answer me that I be not deceived. P.C. 2008. *Mars ôs mâp Dew a vêr brys, ymsaw scon a dhroceleth*, if thou art the Son of God, of great price, save thyself soon from ill usage. P.C. 2866. Comp. of *droc*, evil, and *culeth*, a deed, from *cul*, to do.

DROGA, v. a. To do harm, to hurt, to injure. Written by Llwyd, *droaga*. W. *drygu*.

DROGBREDERYS, adj. Evil-minded, malicious, envious. *Llwyd*, 84. Comp. of *drôg*, and *prederys*, minded, qd. v.

DROGBRES, s. m. Ill will, spite, grudge. *Llwyd*, 84. Comp. of *drôg*, and *brés*, mind. W. *dryguryd*.

DROGDAVASEC, adj. Ill-tongued, foul-mouthed, backbiting, reviling. *Llwyd*, 84. Comp. of *drôg*, and *tavasec*, tongued. W. *drwg-davod, tavod-drwg*.

DROGGER, s. m. Ill report, infamy, reproach. Corn. Voc. *drocger*, infamia. Comp. of *dróc*, or *drôg*, and *gêr*, a word. W. *drygair*.

DROGGERIIT, adj. Infamous, reproachful. Corn. Voc. *drocgeriit*, infamis. From *drogger*, with an adjectival termination, as in *Geriù da*, qd. v.

DROGGRAS, s. m. Revenge, requital. *Agan harluth Lucifer, ny a'n kyrch dhys hep danger, pûr lowenek, yn drog-gras dh'y dâs Adam, venytha na'n geffo tam a wolow têk*, our lord Lucifer, we will bring him to thee without delay very joyfully; in requital to his father Adam, that he may never have a bit of fair light. O.M. 550. Comp. of *drôg*, and *grás*, a return of favour.

DROGOBER, s. m. An evil deed, a crime. *Llwyd*, 58. *Kepar hag ef ùn crowsys, ha dre wŷr vreus juggys râk agan drôk-ober kens*, like as he we are crucified, and by true judgment sentenced for our evil deed before. P.C. 2902. Comp. of *drôg*, and *ober*, a work. Arm. *drougober*.

DROGOBEROR, s. m. A worker of evil, a malefactor. *Llwyd*, 88. Corn. Voc. *drochoberor*, maleficus.

DROGSAWARN, s. m. A bad smell, a stink. *Llwyd*, 69. Comp. of *drôg*, and *sawarn*, a smell, qd. v.

DRON, s. f. A throne. A mutation of *tron*. qd. v. *Din dhe gyrhas Salamon, ha goryn ef yn y dron, avel mychtern yn y sê*, let us come to fetch Solomon, and let us put him in his throne, like a king in his seat. O.M. 237.

DROS, v. a. He brought. 3 pers. s. preterite of *drey*. *A Dâs ty re dhrôs dhymmo ascorn a'm kŷk, (ha'm) corf*, O

Father, thou hast brought to me bone of my flesh and body. O.M. 111. *Ty re gam wrûk eredy, ha re'n drôs dhe vûr anken*, thou hast done evil verily, and hast brought him to much sorrow. O.M. 282. *Why re dhrôs dhym an dén-ma*, ye have brought to me this man. P.C. 1852.

DROSSA, v. a. He will bring. 3 pers. s. 2 fut. of *drey*. *Saw mar callaf der dhavys gwyl dhe Adam dhym cola, me a'n drossa dhe baynes na dhefo dhe'n néf nevera*, but if I can by device make this Adam to listen to me, I will bring him to pains, that he shall never come to heaven. C.W. 36.

DROSSEN, v. a. We had brought. 1 pers. pl. preterpl. and subj. of *drey*. *Yn médh Pilat pan a dra a ynnyouch wy warnodho? Na ve bôs fals an dén-ma ny'n drossen ny bŷs deso*, Pilate says, what do ye charge against him? Were not this man false, wê would not have brought him ever to thee. M.C. 99. *Tebel dén ef mar ny fe, ny ny'n drosen dhyso gy*, if he were not a wicked man, we would not have brought him to thee. P.C. 1976.

DROU, v. a. Bring ye. An abbreviated form of *drouch*, 2 pers. pl. imp. of *drey*. *Pur lowen, re'n Arluth Dew, ha lowenné a pe bew, drou' e yntré ow dyworech*, very gladly, by the Lord God, and more gladly if he were alive; bring him to my arms. P.C. 159.

DRUIC, s. f. A dragon. Corn. Voc. *draco*. W. *draig*, †*dreic*; dragon. Arm. *dragon*. Ir. *draig, drig; dragun, dreagan*. Gael. *drag, dreug*. Lat. *draco*. Gr. δράκων; δέρκω, to see.

DRUS, adv. Across, athwart. Written also *drues*. *Cafes moy dhya aban rês, try heys dhe bâl kemery; a drûs musury trylles, ha gwet na wra falsury*, to have more since there is need to thee, three lengths of thy spade thou shalt take; athwart thou shalt measure three breadths, and take thou care that thou doest no deceit. O.M. 393. *A Iowan na gows a drues, râk ahanas marth a'm bues, ty dhe leverel folneth*, O John speak not absurdly, for I am surprised at thee, to be speaking folly. R.D. 961. *Ty Pilat dhum arluth dues, kyn whrylly nfth cows a drues dhynny lemmyn, gennen ny ty d*, thou Pilate come to my lord, though thou shouldst ever speak against it, with us thou shalt go. R.D. 1792. W. *traws, draws*, †*trus*. Arm. *treuz*. Ir. *trasd*. Gael. *trasd*. Lat. *trans*. Sansc. *tar*, to cross.

DRUS, s. m. A foot. A mutation of *trûs*, a late form of *troys*. *A druz*, on foot. Llwyd, 115.

DRUTH, s. f. A harlot. W. *trythyll, drythyll*. Ir. *druth, druis*, †*drus*, †*tudracht*. Gael. *druiseal*.

DRUYTH, part. Brought. Part. pass. of *drey*; written also *drúth*. *Dhe Arluth néf ythouch druyth, dûn alemma dhe'n môr ruyth, tûs, venenes, ha flehys*, to the Lord of heaven ye are brought, let us go hence to the Red Sea; men, women, and children. O.M. 1621. *Mur ioy ûs er y byn ef; pûr dha yth heuel yn néf y bones druth*, great joy is meeting him; very good it seems in heaven that he is brought.' R.D. 2492.

DRY, v. s. To bring. Another form of *drey*, qd. v. *Mar a kyll dhewurth an da dhe wethyll drôk agan dry*, if he can from the good to do evil us bring. M.C. 21. *Y wrêg dhe rê anedhé môs dhe'n drê, ha degylmy an asen ha dry gansé*, he caused some of them to go to the town, and untie the ass, and bring (her) with them. M.C. 27. *Honna yw y bones nessa, ha whêth gwreuch y dhry omma*

arté dhywhy, ha dyscow y dheworto, that is his nearest garment, and do ye yet bring him here again to you, and strip it from him. R.D. 1870.

DRYDH, prep. Through, or by. *Me a credy yn Dew an Tâs olgallusec, gwrêar an név, ha'n 'oar; hag yn Jesus Christ y mâb y honou, nêb ef dheravas dhe veunans drydh an Speris Sans*, I believe in God the Father Almighty, maker of heaven and earth; and in Jesus Christ his own Son, whom he raised to life through the Holy Ghost. Pryce. This is also written *drédh*; and is the form of *dre*, before a vowel.

DRYDHY, pron. prep. Through or by her, or it. (*Drydhhy*.) *Dew a erchys dhys Moyses dhe welen y kemeres, ha gwyskel an môr gynsy, an dour a uger a lês, may hylly yn la kerdhes, ty ha'th pobel oll drydhy*, God has commanded thee, Moses, thy rod to take, and strike the sea with it; the water will pen wide, that thon wilt be able well to go, thou and all thy people through it. O.M. 1668. Written also *dredhy*, qd. v. W. *trwydhi, drwydhi*, †*trwydi*. Arm. *dreizi*. Ir. *trithe, trithi*, †*trée*. Gael. *troimpe*.

DRYLLYN, v. a. We will bring back. A mutation of *trylyn*, 1 pers. pl. fut. of *trylê*, qd. v. *Dhe Pilat na'n dryllyn ny*, to Pilate that we bring him not back. R.D. 648.

DRYNSYS, s. f. Trinity. A mutation of *trynsys*, which is variously written *drindas, drynses, drynges*. *Yn gwŷrder an tŷr gwelen yw dysquydhyans ha token an try person yn Drynsys*, in truth, the three rods are a declaration and token of the three persons in the Trinity. O.M. 1734. *Rdg an tyyr gwelen defry a ve gans Davyd plynsys, hag a iunnyas dhe onan, yn token da an try person yn Drynsys*, for the three rods really were by David planted, and he joined (them) into one as a good type of three persons in the Trinity. O.M. 2650. See *Trindas*.

DRYNYA, v. a. To grieve. *Geneuch why môs ny drynyaf; dhum arluth loven yth af, Tyber Cesar*, to go with you I shall not grieve; to my lord gladly I will go, Tiberius Cesar. R.D. 1797. This is a mutation of *trynya*, which is also written *treynyé*, qd. v.

DRYS, prep. Over, above, beyond. *Ytho bedhyth mylyges pûr wŷr drys oll a bestes a gerdho war an nôr veis*, now thou shalt be accursed, very truly above all the beasts, that walk on the earth of the world. O.M. 312. *Ellas gweles an termyn, ow Arluth pan wrûk serry, pan rûk drys y worhemmyn*, alas to see the time, when I made my Lord angry, when I acted against his command. O.M. 353. *Yma Dew whâth ow pewé, neb ew Arluth drys pûp tra*, there is a God yet living, who is Lord above all things. O.M. 623. Written also *dres*, qd. v.

DU, s. m. God, a god, a divinity. Pl. *duow*. *Wy a bŷs a leun golon,—may fo dhe Dhu dhe wordhyans, ha sylwans dhe'n encvow*, ye shall pray with faithful heart,— that there be to God the glory, and salvation to the souls. M.C. 1. *A'n aval te kemer tam, avel Du y fedhyth gwyrys*, of the apple take thou a bit, like a god thou wilt be made. M.C. 6. *Mês pan vôns dyschys gulân, y a dynach aga duow myleges*, but when they are quite refreshed, they will reject their cursed gods. O.M. 1840. This is another form of *dew*, qd. v.

DU, adj. Black, sable, dark, gloomy. Corn. Voc. *duw, niger*. Pl. *duon*. *Och, tru, tru; shyndyys ôf gans cronek du, ha whethys gans y venym*, Oh, sad, sad, hurt I am by a black toad, and blown by his venom. O.M. 1778. *Du asyw emskemunys nêp re ordenes y ladhe*, black accursed is he, who decreed to kill him. P.C. 3091. *Púr hardh dûn dhodho wharré, gorryn ef yn bêdh arté; du yw y lyw*, very boldly let us go to him soon, let us put him into the grave again; black is his hue. R.D. 2101. In late Cornish it was written also *diu. Davaz dhiu*, a black sheep; *hor' diu*, a black ram; *hyrrox dyon*, black rams. Llwyd, 243. W. *du*. Arm. *du*. Ir. *dubh*, †*dub*. Gael. *dubh*. Manx, *doo*.

DU, s. m. A day. An abbreviated form of *dýdh*, qd. v. *Du Yow*, Thursday. *Du Pasc*, Easter day. *Thomas ythos púr woky, drefen na fynnyth crygy, an arluth dhe dhasserchy du pask vytiyn*, Thomas, thou art very stupid, because thou wilt not believe the Lord to have risen Easter day morning. R.D. 1108.

DU, s. m. A side. A mutation of *tu*, qd. v. *A y du*, on his side.

DU, num. adj. Two. Another form of *dew*, qd. v., and chiefly used in composites, as *duscoudh*, the shoulders; *dugans*, forty.

DUADH, s. m. End, termination. Llwyd, 251. Another form of *diwedh*, qd. v.

DUAN, s. m. Grief, sorrow. *Yn úr-na, rág púr dhuan, daggrow tyn gwráf dyveré*, in that time, for very sorrow, bitter tears I shall shed. O.M. 401. *Mar a quellan drók dhum flechys, na duan, ow colon a výdh terrys*, if I see evil to my children, or sorrow, my heart will be broken. P.C. 1945. Another form of *duwhan*, qd. v.

DUBM, adj. Warm. A mutation of *tubm*, as *mar tubm*, so warm. Llwyd, 231.

DUC, v. a. He brought. 3 pers. s. preterite of *doga*, or *degy*, qd. v. Written also *duc. Ef a dhúk an grous gansé, púr wýr henn o n'y anvodh*, he bore the cross with them, very truly this was against his will. M.C. 175. *Honna a dorras an aval têk, hag a'n dúg dhym dhe dastyé*, she plucked the fair apple, and brought it to me to taste. O.M. 268. *Dasserchy ef a wrúk, ha múr a paynys re dhúk war y corf kêr*, rise he did, and many pains he bore on his dear body. R.D. 1280. *Rág dry Adam a yfarn, me a dhúk curyn a spern, nép try our adro dhum pen*, to take Adam out of hell, I wore a crown of thorns some three hours around my head. R.D. 2554. W. *dúg*, †*duc, a dhúg*.

DUCHAN, s. f. Grief, sorrow, lamentation. *Ny amount gwythell duchan lemyn ragdha*, it avails not to make lamentation now for it. C.W. 124. British Museum MS. The more common forms are *dewhan, duwhan, duan, dwon, duwon*. See *Duwhan*.

DUE, v. m. He will come. 3 pers. s. fut. of *dós*. In construction it changes into *dhue*, and *tue. An pyth a dhue yn dywedh*, the thing will come at last. O.M. 671. *Pan vo gurex my a dhue dhys*, when it is done I will come to thee. O.M. 988. *War agan keyn ef a dhue*, on our back it will come. O.M. 2570. *Bynyges yw néb a dhue yn hanow Dew*, blessed is he who comes in the name of God. P.C. 274. *Ha kemmys a'n gordhyo ef, gans múr ioy y tue dhe'n néf dre y dhadder oberys*, and as many as worship him, with great joy shall come to heaven, by his goodness wrought. R.D. 1223. W. *daw, a dhaw*. Arm. *deú*.

DUE, part. Ended. *Rýs yw dymmo lafuryé dhe un vatel yredy, suw dystoch hy a výdh dué*, I must labour at a battle certainly, but very soon it will be ended. O.M. 2178. *An gwary yw dué lymmyn*, the play is now ended. 2830. *Mar ny výdh an whethlow dué yn ages mýsk, nép onon me a wýsk*, if the tales be not ended amongst you, some one I shall strike. R.D. 1400. *Ha mýl dén ef u wrúk dué yn dour-na rák uth hag own*, and a thousand men he caused to be finished in that water, for horror and fright. R.D. 2331. An anomalous form from *diwedhé*, qd. v.

DUECH, v. n. Come ye. *Tormentores duech dhym scon*, executioners, come to me forthwith. R.D. 2240. *Ow dewolow duech gynef warparth oll me agas peys*, my devils come with me together all I pray you. R.D. 2307. This is the same word as *deuch*, qd. v.

DUELLO, v. a. To let out, to discharge. *Ellas, dhynny ny dâl man duello lukes na taran dh'y lesky ef*, alas, it avails us not a bit to discharge lightning nor thunder to burn him. R.D. 296. It is the same word as *dellé*, and *dyllo*, qd. v.

DUER, v. n. It concerneth. *Kyn y'n carra výdh mar veur, awos y ladhé ny'm duer*, though he may love him ever so much, for killing him, there is no concern to me. R.D. 1898. Id. qd. *dêr*, and *dúr*, qd. v.

DUES, v. n. Come thou. 2 pers. s. imp. of *dós. Dues ow howethes Eva*, come thon, my companion Eve. O.M. 652. *Dues nés hag ysé gené*, come thou nearer, and sit with me. P.C. 576. *A vyl gadlyng, dues yn rág*, O vile vagabond, come forth. P.C. 1817. *Ihesu mâp rás, agan sylwyas, dues gweres ny*, Jesus, Son of grace, our Saviour, come help us. R.D. 308. Written as frequently *dús*, qd. v. Arm. *deuz*.

DUES, v. n. Thou camest. 2 pers. s. preterito of *dós. Kepar yn beys ha dues, dhe'n néf grusses yskenné*, as thou camest into the world, to heaven thou wouldest ascend. O.M. 155. Arm. *deuez*.

DUES, part. Come. *Mar ny's cafaf scon dhum dues, ly a fýdh drók oremus*, if I do not find them soon come to me, thou shalt have an evil oremus. R.D. 647. *Gúl ges ahanaf a wrêth, marth yw gynef na dhues mêth ow kewsel gow*, thou dost make a jest of me; it is a wonder to me, that shames comes not speaking lies. R.D. 1391. Written also *des*. Arm. *deúet, dcút*.

DUES, s. f. A goddess. Pryce. W. *duwies*. Arm. *douéez*, †*dues*.

DUETH, s. f. He came. 3 pers. s. preterite of *dós. Rák whêth býth ny dhueth deydh brues*, for yet the day of judgment has not come. R.D. 234. *Namn 'agan dallas golow, pan dhueth an gwâs*, light almost blinded us, when the fellow came. R.D. 303. *Pyw a dhueth a'n beys yn rúdh*, who is it that has come from the earth in red. R.D. 2499. Written also *dúth*, qd. v. W. *daeth*.

DUETH, v. n. Thou shalt come. 2 pers. s. fut. of *dós. Arluth assyw varthusek, pan dhueth, Ihesu gallosek, dh'agan myras, ha leverel dhynny crês, asso fast ytho dyges agan dorras*, Lord it is wonderful, when thou comest, Jesus powerful, to see us, and speak peace to us, though fast our door was shut. R.D. 1178. *Ty gcyler, dús yn rák, ha mar ny dhueth, me a'ith têk, hag a ver spys*, thou gaoler, come forth, and if thou wilt not come, I will strangle thee, and in a short time. R.D. 199. Written also *dúth*, qd. v. Arm. *deúez*.

DUETH, v. n. I came. 1 pers. s. preterite of *dós. Ellas výth pan dhucyth a drê, an keth corf-na byw a pe, ow arluth a vye saw*, alas over when I came from home! if that same body were alive, my lord would be cured. R.D. 1661. Written also *duyth*, qd. v. Arm. *deúis*.

DUM 117 DUS

DUF, s. m. A captain. *Fystyn ow dûf whêk a vy, gweyt an harlot na scapyo,* hasten my sweet captain of me; take care that the knave escape not. P.C. 989. Written also *def,* qd. v.

DUFE, v. n. He will come. Comp. of *duf,* id. qd. *dyf,* 3 pers. s. fut. of *dôs,* and pronoun *fe,* he. *Mar tufé ha datherchy mûr a dûs a wra crygy ynno,* if he will come and rise, much people will believe in him. R.D. 7.

DUFUN, adj. Sleepless, awake, wide awake. *Pôs re tewlseuch agas clûn, rág me a'n gwelas dufun, dresof ef a tremenas,* heavily have ye thrown down your haunches, for I saw him wide awake, he passed over me. R.D. 424. This is a less correct form of *difun,* qd. v.

DUFYDHY, v. a. To quench, to extinguish. *Ow Arluth kêr, Cryst Ihesu, Dew an nêf, dre dhe vertu, dufydh nerth an flam ha'n tán,* my dear Lord, Christ Jesus, God of heaven, through thy virtue, assuage the power of the flame and fire. O.M. 2637. W. *difodhi,* comp. of *di,* neg., and *fawdh,* splendour.

DUG, v. n. He brought. 3 pers. s. preterite of *doga,* or *degy,* qd. v. *Honna a dorras an avaliêk, hag a'n dûg dhym dhe dastyé,* she plucked the fair apple, and brought it to me to taste. O.M. 268. More frequently written *duc,* qd. v.

DUGANS, num. adj. Two score, forty. *Llwyd,* 133. *Dîg ha dugans,* ten and two score, fifty. *Pryce.* This is a late form of *dewigans,* qd. v.

DUGTYE, v. a. To prepare, to provide. *Râg henna an vuscogyon orto a borthas avy, dre vraster brâs yn golon y dhuglyons y dhestrewy,* for that reason the fools against him bore spite, through great pride in the heart they prepared to destroy him. M.C. 26. It is the same word as *dychtyé,* qd. v.

DUI, num. adj. Used with substantives feminine, as *dew* was with masculines. The same rule obtains in Welsh and Armoric. It is also written *diw* or *dyw,* qd. v. W. *dwy,* †*dui.* Arm. *diou.* Sansc. *dwê.*

DUIGLÛN, s. m. The reins. Corn. Voc. *renes.* Comp. of *dui,* two, and *clun,* the haunch, qd. v.

DUILOF, s. m. The hands. This is the Celtic dual. *Lien duilof,* mantergium *vêl* mantilo, a towel, a hand cloth. Corn. Voc. Comp. of *dui,* two, and *lof,* a hand, qd. v. In the Ordinalia the word is generally written *dewlof, dynolef,* and *dywluef,* qd. v. W. *dwylaw,* †*duilof.*

DUIVRON, s. m. The breasts. *Cluil duivron,* pectus, the breast. Corn. Voc. Another instance of the Celtic dual. Comp. of *dui,* two, and *bron,* a breast. W. *dwyvron.*

DULE, s. m. The hands. An abbreviated form of *dywlef,* or *duilof.* *Ha'n kelmyns treys ha dulé, ha'n hembrynkys bŷs dhymny,* let them bind him feet and hands, and bring him to us. P.C. 583. *Yma ow trŷs ha'm dulé dhyworthef ow teglené,* my feet and hands are loosening from me. P.C. 1216. *Dhe wêth vydhons dhe'n cronek, ha garow yn y dhulé,* they shall be worse for the toad, and rough in his hands. P.C. 2733. Llwyd writes this word *dula, gravar dula,* a hand-barrow. 46. ‡*Tre dha dhula,* betwixt thy hands. 230.

DUM, pron. prep. To my. (*Do-my.*) *A venen, assos goky, na grezyth dhum lavarow,* O woman, thou art foolish, that thou wilt not believe my words. O.M. 174. *Adam pandra wrêth, prâg na dhêth dhum wolcummé,* Adam what art thou doing, why camest thou not to welcome me. O.M. 258. *Er na gyllyf dhe'n nêf dhum Tás, may tewhyllyf arté dhum gwlás, dhe gows worthys,* until I go to heaven to my Father, that I may return again to my country to speak to thee. R.D. 878.

DUN, s. f. A hill. Written also *dîn,* qd. v. This form is preserved in the names of places; as *Dun mear,* the great hill, in Bodmin; *Dun vedh,* the hill of the grave, in St. Breock.

DUN, v. n. Let us come. 1 pers. pl. imp. of *dôs.* *Abel whêk dûn alemma,* sweet Abel, let us come hence. O.M. 446. *Ow broder whêk, dûn dhe dré,* my sweet brother, let us come home. O.M. 525. *Dûn ol dhe'n gorhyl, toth da, gans lŷf na wrellen budhy,* let us come all to the ark quickly, that we may not be drowned by the flood. O.M. 1047. *Dûn ganzo er y anfus, dhe Pylat agan iustys,* let us come with him, for his wickedness, to Pilate our justice. P.C. 1501. This is the common Welsh idiom for *let us bring.* W. *deuwn, down.* Arm. *deuomp.*

DUON, s. m. Grief, sorrow. *Dre pûr anger ha duon, me a woor lour nêp onon me a wŷsk,* for very anger and vexation, I know very well, some one I shall strike. R.D. 1402. *Duon agas lavarow, ha hyreth bôs Cryst marow, pûr wŷr a gî ow gwethé,* grief of your words, and regret that Christ is dead, very truly may destroy me. R.D. 1414. *Yma dhymmo mûr duon, ha cothys wàr ow colon,* there is much grief and sorrow on my heart. R.D. 1764. This is variously written *duan, duwhan,* and *duwon.* See *Duwhan.*

DUR, s. m. Water. Corn. Voc. *aquam.* Written also *dour,* qd. v.

DUR, v. n. It concerns. *Cryst ow sylwyas, clew mar a'th dûr, dhys daryvas del garsen mûr,* Christ my saviour, hear if it concerns thee, disclose to thee as I would much desire. R.D. 843. *Kyn whryllŷ flattré mar mûr ahanas tra vŷth ny'm dûr, kyn 'thos bysy,* though thou dost chatter so much, any thing from thee concerns me not, though thou be busy. R.D. 1059. Written also *dêr,* and *duer.* W. *dawr.* (*Ni'm dawr, ni'm dawr i,* it concerns me not; *ni'th dawr,* it concerns thee not; and fut. *ni'm dorbi.* *Er gwaith Arderydh ni'm dorbi,* for the action of Arderydh, I shall not be concerned. *Merdhyn.*) Arm. †*deur.* (*Nem deur,* I am unwilling; *nos deur,* ye are unwilling.)

DURDALA, s. m. Thanks. ‡*Fatla ello why giel ? po fatla gan a why ?* how do you do, or how is it with you. ‡*Dah, durdala dha why,* well, thanks to you. This is a late and corrupt term of uncertain origin, and is given by Pryce.

DURGY, s. m. A small turf hedge. *Pryce.* The primary meaning was probably a water dyke, being compounded of *dûr,* water, and *ge,* a fence.

DURN, s. m. A hand. *Llwyd,* 3. Generally written *dorn,* qd. v. In Cornish and Armoric, it generally means a hand, while in Welsh, Irish, Gaelic, and Manx, it is applied to a fist.

DUS, v. n. Come thou. 2 pers. s. imp. of *dôs.* *Eva, dús nês, kemer y,* Eve, come nearer, take it. O.M. 179. *Abram, fystyné gwra, ha dús dhymmo wharré,* Abraham, hasten do thou, and come to me soon. O.M. 1266. *Moyses, sûf ena, na nês, na dhús na fella,* Moses, stand there, not nearer come not, no further. O.M. 1404. *Dôs genen ny,* come thou with us. O.M. 2378. *Dús yn mês,* come thou out. O.M. 2700. Written also *dues,* qd. v.

DUS, s. f. A people, people. A mutation of *tús,* qd. v. *Ha'th vam, hag oll an dús vás,* and thy mother, and all the good people. O.M. 814. *Cresseuch, collemweuch kefrys an nôr veys, a dûs, arté,* increase ye, fill likewise the earth of the world, O men, again. O.M. 1212. *Gans lyf ny wráf bynytha ladhé an dûs gwyls na dôf,* by flood I will not ever destroy mankind wild nor tame. O.M. 1245.

DUSCODH, s. m. The shoulders. This is a Celtic dual, being compounded of *du,* two, and *scodh,* shoulder. Written also *duscoudh. Lemyn drehveuch an gist, yw gwrys crows, war duscoudh Cryst dh'y dôn dhe dré,* now lift ye up the beam, that is made a cross, on the shoulders of Christ, to carry it to town. P.C. 2582. *Pyw a dhueth a'n beys yn rûdh, avel gôs, pen ha duscoudh, garrow ha treys,* who is it that came from the earth in red, like blood, head, and shoulders, legs, and feet. R.D. 2500.

DUSES, s. m. Godhead, divinity. *Râk me a wôr lour, denses, marnes dre an luen duses, omma ny séf,* for I know full well, that men, unless through full Godhead, remain not here. R.D. 2515. This is another form of *dewsys,* qd. v.

DUSHOC, adj. Tufted, spiked. *Les dushoc,* betonica, betony. Corn. Voc. *Les dushoc,* is literally the tufted plant, which is characteristic of it. *Dushoc* is a mutation of *tushoc,* id. qd. v. *W. twysog,* from *twys,* a tuft.

DUSTUN, s. m. A witness. A mutation of *tustun,* qd. v. Pl. *dustuneow, dustenyow, dustynyow. En Edhewon yntrethé a whelas dustuneow,* the Jews between them sought for witnesses. M.C. 90. *Mŷns a wrûk me a'n avow, hag a gŷf dustynyow, ty dhe gows erbyn laha,* all I did I confess it, and have witnesses that thou speakest against the law. P.C. 1302. *Travyth ny wrêth gorthyby erbyn dustenyow lêl,* dost thou not reply any thing against trusty witnesses? P.C. 1318. *Pyth yw an ethom gortos, na cafus dustynyow, aban wrêth y aswonvos,* what is the need to stay, or find witnesses, since thou dost acknowledge it? P.C. 1498.

DUSTUNE, v. a. To bear witness, to witness, to testify. A mutation of *tustuné,* qd. v. It is written also *dustynyé. Hag êth porau dhe'n cyté, gan luas y flîns gwelys, en gwŷr dhe dhustunyé, bôs Mâb Du neb o ledhys,* and went straight to the city, by many they were seen, the truth to witness that it was the Son of God who was killed. M.C. 210. *Nynsus ethom nag onan dhywhy a dustynyé, pan clewseuch gows an gewan,* there is no need of any one to testify to you, when ye have heard him speak the lies. P.C. 1338. *Sûr Maria Jacobé, ha Maria Salomé, dhym dustyny,* surely Mary, (mother of) James, and Mary Salome will witness to me. R.D. 1075.

DUSTUNY, s. m. A witnessing, witness, testimony. A mutation of *tustuny,* qd. v. It is written also *dustyny. Ha dew a dhûk dustuny y'n clewsons ow leverel,* and two bore witness they heard him say. M.C. 91. *Mara kewsys falsury, ha henna dôk dustuny,* if I have spoken falschood, of that bear thou witness. P.C. 1272. *Ha me a dhêk dustyny, y'n clewys ow leverel,* and I bear witness, I have heard him saying. P.C. 1313.

DUTH, v. n. He came. 3 pers. s. preterite of *dôs. Dhym dhe ammé ty re dûth sûr, râg ow gwerthé, dhe'n traylors pûr,* to kiss me thou hast surely come, to sell me to very traitors. P.C. 1107. *Ty creator bynyges, fattel dhuthté gy dhe'n crês,* thou blessed creature, how camest thou to peace? R.D. 200. *Me re dhûth dhe'th confortyé, nak na ty gy yn a whêr,* I am come to comfort thee, that thou be not in sorrow. R.D. 473. *Me re dhûth dh'agas myres,* I am come to see you. R.D. 1536. *Dre ow thrŷs y tûth un smat gans kentrow d'aga gorré,* through my feet a fellow came with nails to put them. R.D. 2587. Written also *dueth,* qd. v. W. *daeth.*

DUTH, v. n. Thou shalt come. 2 pers. s. fut. of *dôs. Cryst clew ow léf, lavar an ûr may tûth a'n néf arté dhe'n lûr, dhe cows worthyn,* Christ hear my voice, say the hour that thou wilt come from heaven again to the earth to speak to us. R.D. 862. Written also *dueth,* qd. v.

DUTHE, v. n. I came. 1 pers. s. subj. of *dôs. Whet aban dhuthé y'th chy, golhy ow treys ny hyrsys,* yet since I came into thy house, to wash my feet thou hast not offered. P.C. 517. *Ha homma vŷth ny sestyas, aban duthé yn chy dhys, pûp ûr oll ammé dhum treys,* and this woman has never ceased, since I came into thy house continually to kiss my feet. P.C. 524.

DUTHEUCH, v. n. Ye came. 2 pers. pl. preterite of *dôs. Creator a brys benen, yn yfarn na feuch gynen; fatel dhutheuch why omma,* creatures from the womb of woman, in hell ye were not with us; how came ye here? R.D. 193. W. *daethoch.*

DUTHYS, v. n. Thou camest. 2 pers. s. pret. of *dôs. Ha fattel duthys yn ban, dre dhe gallos dhe honan, ha war dhe corf mar drôk scuth,* and how camest thou up, through thy own power, and on thy body such evil plight? R.D. 2568. W. *daethost*

DUW, adj. Black. Corn. Voc. *niger.* Id. qd. *du,* qd. v.

DUWEDHVA, s. f. An end, termination. *Heb dallath na duwedhva,* without beginning or ending. C.W. 3. Id. qd. *diwedhva,* qd. v.

DUWENHE, v. a. To vex, to grieve, to afflict. *Ow bôs serrys nyns yw marth, ages bones ol warbarth porrys worth ow duwenhé,* my being angry is no wonder, all of you together being willed to grieve me. R.D. 1413. Written also *dewhanhé,* qd. v. From *duwon,* sorrow. W. *duchanu.*

DUWHAN, s. f. Grief, sorrow, vexation, lamentation. *Ny amount gwythell duwhan lemyn ragdha,* it avails not to make lamentation now for it. C.W. 124. This word is variously written *duchan, dewhan, duwon, duan, dwon. Gwyn bŷs vones dhym fethys lafur ha duwon an bŷs,* happy that for me is vanquished, the labour and sorrow of the world. O.M. 851. *Duwon yn y gorf a'n meck, ny vŷdh hutyk y golon,* sorrow in his body chokes him, nor is his heart glad. O.M. 2817. *Ken ben vŷth mar mûr duwon,* though there be ever so much grief. R.D. 1530. W. *duchan, dychan.*

DUWHANS, adj. Eagerly, hastily, fast, quickly, directly. *Fystyn alenma duwhans, worthyf na gows na moy gêr,* hasten thou hence quickly; to me speak not another word. O.M. 169. *Del y'm kyrry, fystyn duwhans gweres vy, ow tôn a plos casadow,* as thou lovest me, hasten quickly to help me, bringing the foul villain. O.M. 891. Written also *dewhans,* and *dywhans,* qd. v.

DUY, s. m. God. Corn. Voc. *deus.* Written more frequently *Dew,* and *Du,* qd. v.

DUYOW, s. m. Thursday. *Dies Jovis. Ke alemma, servont kêr, kerch a'n fenten dhym dour clêr dhe dhychyé bôs dhynny ny erbyn soper, kepar del yw an vaner duyow hamlos,* go hence, dear servant, fetch from the fountain for me clear water, to prepare food for us for supper, like as is the custom on Thursday of the preparation. P.C. 654. Written also *deyow,* qd. v.

DUYRAN, s. m. The east. ‡ *Po rez deberra an bez, tidn heerath a sew; po rez dal an vor, na oren pan a tu, duyran, houl zethas, gogleth, po dihow,* when thou comest into the world, length of sorrow follows; when thou beginnest the way, 'tis not known, which side, east or west, to the north, or south. Pryce. W. *dwyrain*. Ir. *soir, oir*. Gael. *ear*. The Armoric equivalent is *sevelheol*, or *sav-heol*, sunrising.

DUYTH, v. n. I came. 1 pers. s. preterite of *dós*. *Mychtern óf war wlds ha týr, yn henna y fŭf genys, rák henna dhe'n býs y tuyth*, a king I am over the land and earth; in that I was born, for that I came to the world. P.C. 2022. Written also *ducyth*, qd. v.

DY, pron. prep. To him, or it. Comp. of *do, to,* and *e*, him. *Dhe Ihesu may fóns parys dh'y gomfortyé, yredy, a'n neff y fe danvenys dheworth an Tás eleth dy,* to Jesus that they might be ready to comfort him surely, from heaven there were sent from the Father angels to him. M.C. 18. *Ihesus Crist a wovynnys worth an bobyl a dhéth dy,* Jesus Christ asked of the people that came to him. M.C. 67. *A vés dhe'n dré yth esé menedh uchel yredy, an grows y a rûg gorré war scódh Jesus dli'y dón dhy,* without the town, there was a high hill indeed, the cross they did put on the shoulder of Jesus to carry it there, (to it.) M.C. 162. *I éth yn un fystené dhe'n tyller ganso o ordnys, pan dothyans dhy, yntreuhé pous Ihesus a ve dyskys,* they went in a hurry to the place by him (that) was ordained, when they came there, among them Jesus's coat was taken off. M.C. 176. *A dás kér dhe'th worhemmyn, my á dhy a dhysempys,* O father dear, at thy command, I will go to him immediately. O.M. 697.

DY, prep. From, of. In Cornish it is only found compounded with *worth*, and its derivatives, as *dyworth*, from by, from. Written also *de*, qd. v. In old Welsh it is also found in its simple form, as *hin map di iob*, the son of Jupiter. *Oxford Glosses.* It is now in common use in the compounds *o dhnerth*, and its derivatives. W. *di*. Arm. *di*. Ir. *di*.

DY, a prefix in composition. Its power is privative, and answers to *less* in English, as *dybyté*, pitiless. *Y dhadder yw drók tylys, pan y'n ladhsons dybyté*, his goodness is ill rewarded, when they have killed him without pity. P.C. 3098. Sometimes it has an intensive power, as in *dybarth*, a division. It is also written *di*, qd. v. W. *di*.

DYAC, s. m. A husbandman, a farmer. A mutation of *tyac*, qd. v. *Ythom brovas gwan dyack, may 'thof poynlyes dha bayn brás, dha pyl efarn,* I am proved a weak husbandman, that I am appointed to great pain, to the pit of hell. C.W. 68.

DYAG, prep. Towards. A mutation of *tyag*, or *tuag*, qd. v.

DYAHA, s. m. Safety, security. *Coskyn ny gans dyaha kyn dasvewo ny'n drecha dhynoar y geyn,* let us sleep with security; though he should revive, he will not lift it from off his back. R.D. 402. Comp. of *dy*, intens., and *aha*, id. qd. W. *rehw*, *echwydh*, rest.

DYAL, s. m. Revenge. *Pilat a'n ladhas hep fal ; warnodho telynech dyal, rák ef o Crist an mychtern néf,* Pilate killed him undoubtedly; upon him inflict ye vengeance, for he was Christ, the king of Heaven. R.D. 1753. Written also *dial*, qd. v.

DYAL, s. m. A deluge. *Noe rag kerengé orthys, my ny gemere neffré trom dyal war oll an veys, na dre dhyal púp ladhé,* Noah, for love to thee, I will never take vengeance on all the world, nor destroy every one by a flood. O.M. 1209. Written also *dial*, qd. v.

DYALE, v. a. To mock, to deride. *An laddron a'n dyalns dre lyes torment ahas, ha dre mír a galarow,* the thieves mocked him, by many torments unceasing, all my many sorrows. R.D. 1426. *Arluth, ot ommé an gwás, del gleseuch, a dhyallas an profus,* lord, behold here the fellow, as you have heard, who mocked the prophet. R.D. 1804. *Out warnas ly harlot wás, Ihesu ly a dhyallas, ow arluth kér*, out upon thee, thou rascal fellow, thou hast mocked Jesus, my dear Lord. R.D. 1966.

DYALWHEDHE, v. a. To open, to unlock. *Dodho ny dhyalwchedhas*, to him we opened. R.D. 1445. Id. qd. *dialwhedhé*, qd. v.

DYANC, v. a. To escape. Part. *dyencys*. *A traytor brás, máp gal, dhe gafus gynen yw mal ; kelmeuch warbarth y dhyuvroch, na allo dyanc,* O great traitor, son of evil, it is our desire to take thee; bind yo his arms together, that he may not escape. P.C. 1180. *Mars yw dyenkys, ellas ! rák me a wél an mén brás war glan an bédh fest huhel,* if he is escaped, alas ! for I see the large stone on the side of the grave very high. R.D. 520. Written also *deanc*, qd. v. W. *dianc*. Arm. *dianca*.

DYANTEL, adj. Hazardous, dangerous. *An tebell él a vynnas yn ken manner y demptyé ; war penakyll y'n goras dyantell dhe esedhé, a uch eglos ték yn wlds as ysedhva yth esa,* the wicked angel would in another manner tempt him ; on a pinnacle he put him hazardous to sit, above a fair church in the country the sitting place was. M.C. 13. *Huhel ythos ysedhys, ha dyantel rom lauté ; yn lyvyr yma scryfys bós eleth worth dhe wythé, rdg onn dhe vós dessesys dhe trós worth mén,* high thou art seated, and dangerously, by my truth ; in a book it is written, that there are angels guarding thee, for fear that thy foot be hurt against a stone. P.C. 94. Comp. of *dy*, intens., and *antell*, id. qd. W. *antur*, hazard.

DYBARTH, s. m. A division, a separation. *Yn tressé dýdh dybarth gwraf yntré an mór ha'n tyryow, hag yn týr gorhemmennaf may tefo gweydh ha losow,* on the third day I will make a separation between the sea and the lands, and I will command in the land that trees and herbs shall grow. O.M. 25. *Awos own my ny tauvaf ; me a'n préf gwyr a gowsaf kyns ys dybarth,* because of fear I will not be silent ; I will prove it true that I say, before separating. R.D. 925. *Dús nés dhym, del y'm kerry, rák keusel moy yn teffry worthys gy kyngys dybarth,* come nearer to me, as thou lovest me, for speaking more indeed to thee before separating. R.D. 1729. Comp. of *dy*, intens., and *parth*, a part. W. *dybarth*.

DYBARTHY, v. a. To divide, to separate. *Pan vo gwyskys an bugel, y fy an deves a bell, hag oll an flok a dhybarth,* when the shepherd is smitten, the sheep will flee far, and all the flock will separate. P.C. 895. *Yma dhcuch múr a dhylyt a ymknouké ; my a dhybarth ynterthoch, hag a wra dheuch pennow couch,* there is to you much delight to beat each other, I will divide between you, and will make to you bloody heads. P.C. 2325. W. *dybarthu*.

DYBLANS, adj. Proportionable, distinct, bright. *A Dás, Máp, ha Spyrys Sans, gordhyans dhe'th corf whék púp prýs ; ow formyé ték ha dyblans ly rum grúk púr havel dhys,* O Father, Son, and Holy Ghost, worship to thy sweet body always; me creating fair and bright, thou hast made me very like to thee. O.M. 87. *My re weles y'm hunrus a-dhyragof êl dyblans*, I have seen in my dream before me a bright angel. O.M. 1955. *I rôf henwyn dha'n puskas, dhe wyan, pengarnes, selyas, me a's recken oll dyblans*, I will give names to the fishes, to broams, gurnards, congers, I will reckon them distinct. C.W. 32. *An êl a ornas dhe wy, gorré sprusan y'th ganow, ha'n dhew arall pûr dhyblans yn dha dhew freig*, the angel commanded to you, to put one kernel in thy mouth, and the two others very distinctly in thy nostrils. C.W. 140.

DYBBRY, v. a. To eat. *Frût an wedhen a skyans dybbry, byth na borth danger*, the fruit of the tree of knowledge eat thou, never make a difficulty. O.M. 168. *Ef a rûk agan dyfen aval na wrellen dybbry, na môs oges dhe'n wedhen*, he did forbid us that we should not eat the apple, nor go near the tree. O.M. 183. *A'y frût a wrella dybry, y fedhé kepar ha dew*, of its fruit he that would eat would be like a god. O.M. 231. *Dro ve dhymmo dyaempys, ha my a ra y dybry*, bring it to me immediately, and I will eat it. O.M. 248. *Ellas, pan dhybrys an tam*, alas, when I ate the morsel. O.M. 762. *Arluth me a'th peys a dhybry gynef un prÿs*, Lord, I pray thee to eat with me a meal. P.C. 456. *Ow tybbry gynef yma n'm tallyour yn kêth bôs-ma*, he is eating with me of my plate in this same food. P.C. 745. The same word as *diberi*, qd. v.

DYCH, pron. prep. To or for you. (*Dy-chui.*) *Me a vyn lemyn ranné yntrethon oll y dhyllas, ha my a's ran dÿch wharré, hep fout vyth ol, renothas*, I will now divide between us all his clothes, and I will soon divide them for you, without any fault, by my father. P.C. 2843. Another form of *deuch*, qd. v.

DYCHETH, s. m. Pity. *Anodho dycheth vye, y wokymeth na agé, ha'y muscochneth*, of him it were a pity, his folly not to leave, and his madness. P.C. 1938. By the softening and rejection of the guttural, it was also written *dyeth*, qd. v.

DYCHLOS, adj. Without happiness. *Aban omma towles dychlos, hag a Paradys hellys, me a vyn dallath palas*, since I am thrown out of happiness, and from Paradise driven, I will begin to delve. C.W. 76. Comp. of *dy*, neg., and *clôs*, happiness.

DYCHOW, adj. Right. *Ha mûr a bobyll gansé, a dhychow hag a glêdh*, and much people with them, on the right and on the left. M.C. 97. *Hag yn y lêff dhychow yn wêdh gwelen wyn a ve gorris*, and in his right hand a white rod was put. M.C. 136. *An Edhewon a grogas lader dhe Gryst an barth clêdh, hag a dhychow lader brâs cregy a russons yn wêdh*, and the Jews hung a thief to Christ on the left side, and on the right a great thief they did hang likewise. M.C. 186. *An lader a'n barth dychow a besys yn ketelma*, the thief on the right side prayed in this manner. M.C. 193. The aspirate was sometimes softened into *h*, as *dyhow*, or omitted altogether, as *dyow*. W. *dehau, dcheu, +dchou*. Arm. *dehou*. Ir. *deise, deas, +des, +dess*. Gael. *deise*. Manx, *jiass*. Sansc. *daksa*. Gr. δεξιά. Lat. *dexter*. That the guttural existed in early Celtic, as in Cornish, seems evident from the term *Dexsiva, Dexsivin* (dea.) See Zeuss, 55. 147.

DYCHTYE, v. a. To prepare, to procure, to treat to use. Written indiscriminately *dychye, dychthye, dydhgtye, dyg-thye, dygtye. I vam whegol a weles del evons worth y dhygtyé*, his mother dear saw how they were treating him. M.C. 164. *Pan welas y mâb dygtys gans an Edhewon mar veyl*, when she saw her son used by the Jews so vilely. M.C. 165. *Dre vraster brâs yn golon y dhugtyons y dhestrewy*, through great pride in the heart they bethought to destroy him. M.C. 26. *Ha hager fest a'n dygtyas*, and very foully they used him. M.C. 130. *Ha me a'n dygth yredy*, and I will provide it at once. P.C. 624. *Gweytheuch dygtyé bôs ynny, lour dh'agan soper ragon*, take ye care to prepare food in it, enough for our supper before us. P.C. 639. *Kerch a'n fenten dhym dour clêr dhe dhychyé bôs dhynny ny erbyn soper*, fetch thou clear water for me from the fountain, to prepare food for us for supper. P.C. 651. *Fystyn lemnn may fo dychtys a vreder*, hasten now, that it may be prepared speedily. P.C. 692. *Mgl wyth dychtys ages brôch gan nêp mylgy*, a thousand times worse treated, than a badger by some honud. P.C. 2926. This word is borrowed from the old English *dight*. Ang. Sax. *dihtan*, to prepare.

DYDH, s. m. A day. Pl. *dydhyow, dydhow. Râg bones oll têk ha da, yn whed-dydh mÿns yw formyys, aga sona ny a wra; may fe scythves dydh hynwys, hen yw dÿdh a bowesva*, for that all is fair and good, in six days all that is created, bless them we will; that it be called the seventh day, this is a day of rest. O.M. 142. *Dÿdh brues y wrêch ysedhé oll, an bÿs-ma râk juggé*, the day of judgment ye shall sit, all this world to judge. P.C. 814. *Râg y tue dydhyow may fenygouch an torrow nas levé vythqueth fiches*, for the days shall come, that ye will bless the wombs that have never borne children. P.C. 2645. *Drôk dên a fue bythqueth, a wôll drôk ny'n gefé mêth yn y dhydhow*, bad man he was ever, to do evil he had no shame in his days. R.D. 1784. *Cot yw dhe dhydhyow dhe gy, nahen na grÿs*, short are thy days to thee, believe thou not otherwise. R.D. 2037. *Dÿdh goil*, a holiday. *Hanter dydh*, mid-day. *Dydh Pasch*, Easter day. M.C. 124. Written also *dedh*, qd. v. W. *dÿdh, dyw, +did, +diu, +dieu*. Arm. *dez, dvez, +dez*. Ir. *dia, die, de*. Gael. *de, di, dia*. Manx, *jc*. Lat. *dies*. Sansc. *dyu, divas*, from *div*, to shine.

DYDHANE, v. a. To amuse, to make glad, to gladden, to comfort. *Un dra a won, a'n godhfos, a russé dhe dhydhané; beys vymytha y whorthes râg ioy ha rag lowené*; one thing I know, if thou knowest it, would amuse thee; for ever thou wouldst laugh for joy and mirth. O.M. 152. *Ioy del Gl ow dydhané, ny ny lywyn ow cané*, as joy may gladden me, we will not cease from singing. R.D. 2526. W. *dydhanu; dydhamiad*, consolation. Ir. *didnad*.

DYE, v. a. To swear. A mutation of *tye*, qd. v. *Me a levar, heb y dye; genef Dew a wrig serry, ha'y volleth yn pûr dheffry dhym a rôs*, I will tell, without swearing it, with me God was angry, and his curse in very earnest to me did give. C.W. 118.

DYEL, s. m. A flood, a deluge. *Na allaf sparié na moy hep gûl dyel a vêr speys war pêp oll marnas ty*. I cannot spare any longer without bringing a flood of great duration over all except thee. O.M. 947. Another form of *dyal*, or *dîal*, qd. v.

DYEN, adj. Whole, entire, perfect. *Na blamyouch ny, a nyngesé aiwheow warbarth yn ages gweyth why, ha dyen an darasow*, do not blame us, were not the keys in your keeping, and the doors whole? R.D. 651. *Gwÿr a gew-*

DYFEN 121 DYFLAS

syth, ievody ; hem yw marth hep falladow, râk an darasow deffry, dyen oll ŷns, ha'n fosow, truth thou sayest, I tell you ; this is a miracle without fail, for the doors indeed are all whole, and the walls. R.D. 656. *Crist a settyas yn tyen an scovern arté dhe dré,* Christ fastened whole the ear again close home. M.C. 71.

DYENOYS, part. Escaped. *Mars yw dyenkys, ellas,* if he is escaped, alas! R.D. 520. Part. pass. of dyanc, qd. v.

DYENE, v. n. To be void of soul, to be breathless, to pant, to faint. *Uskys na yllyn ponyé, del esof ow tyené, ha whŷs pûp godh ol ha lyth,* I could not run immediately, as I am out of breath, and sweat all the neck and face. P.C. 2511. Comp. of dy, neg., and ené, soul. W. *dien.*

DYERBYN, v. a. To receive, to come against, to meet. Written also *dyerbyné. Pan veuch agey dhe'n cyté, why a dhyerbyn wharré dén ow tôn pycher dour glân,* when ye are within the city, ye will meet soon a man carrying a pitcher of clean water. P.C. 628. *Saw me war lerch drehevel, a's dyerbyn dyougel yn Galilé ol warbarth,* but I, after rising, will meet you certainly in Galilee altogether. P.C. 897. *Alemma bŷs yn Tryger, lacka mester ny alsen y dhyerbyn,* from hence to Treguer, a worse master I should not be able to meet. P.C. 2276. *Y a fystena yn fen arté dh'y dyerbyné,* they hastened at once again to meet him. M.C. 167. *Un dén a's dyerbynnas, Symon o a'y ewn hanow; y leverys dhodho, gwâs, te a dhík an grows heb wow,* a man met them, Simon he was by his right name; they said to him, fellow, thou shalt bear the cross without a lie. M.C. 174. Comp. of dy, intens., and *erbyn,* against. W. *dyerbyn, dyerbynu.* Arm. *diarben.*

DYESOYNNE, v. n. To descend, to come down. Written also *dyescenné. Me a vyn dyeskenné, ha môs yn tumpil waré, dhe weles oll an fèr-na,* I will dismount, and go into the temple at once, to see all that fair. P.C. 313. *Maras osé mâp Dew mûr, dyeskyn a'n vŷnk dhe'n lûr, ha dynoé ran a'th veystry,* if thou be Son of the great God, descend from the post to the ground, and shew a portion of thy power. P.C. 2868. *Mars yw mychtern Israel, leveryn oll dhodho heil, hag a'n grows dyeskennes,* if he is king of Israel, we will all say hail to him, and let him come down from the cross. P.C. 2881. The form given by Llwyd, 54, is *deiscyn.* W. *discyn, discynu.* Arm. *diskenn.* From the Latin *descendo.*

DYETH, s. m. Pity. *Mar ny wréf, hep falladow, mûr a'n bobyl a verow, ha henna dyeth vyé,* if thon dost not, without fail, many of the people will die, and that would be a pity. O.M. 1804. *Maga gwyn avel an gurys, dyeth vyé bones reys quêth a'n par-ma dhe iaudyn,* as white as the glass, it were a pity that should be given a cloth of this sort to the obstinate man. P.C. 1791. *Dyeth mûr yw dhym skuerdyé, na terry powes an piûs wâs,* it is a great pity for me to tear, or rend the coat of the dirty fellow. P.C. 2845. Another form of *dycheth,* qd. v.

DYF, v. n. He will grow. 3 pers. s. fut. of *tyvy,* qd. v. *Sew olow ow thryys lyskys, ny dŷf gwels na flour yn bŷs yn kéth forah-na may kyrdhys,* follow thou the prints of my feet burnt; neither grass nor flower in the world will grow in that same road that I walked. O.M. 713.

DYFEN, s. m. A forbidding, a prohibition. *A'y frût dybry ny'm bes whans dres dyfen ow Arluth kér,* of its fruit to eat I have no wish against the prohibition of my dear Lord. O.M. 172. *Och, tru, tru, my re behas, ha re dorras an dyfen,* Oh, woe, woe, I have sinned, and have broken the prohibition. O.M. 250. *Prâg y tolsté sy hep kén, worth hy thempté dhe dyrry an frût erbyn ow dyfen,* why didst thou deceive her pitilessly, by tempting her to break off the fruit against my prohibition? O.M. 304.

DYFEN, v. a. To forbid, to prohibit. Part. pass. *dyfynnys. Néb a'm grûk vy ha'm gorty, ef a rûk agan dyfen aval na wrellen dybbry, na môs oges dhe'n wedhen,* he that made me and my husband, he did forbid us, that we should not eat the apple, nor go near to the tree. O.M. 182. *Lavar dhymmo, ty venen, an frût ple rusays tyrry? mara pe a'n kéth echen o dyfynnys orthyn ny,* tell me, thou woman, where didst thou break off the fruit? was it of that sort, which was forbidden to us? O.M. 212. *Me a'n clewas ow tyffen, na vo reys, awos hechen, trubit vŷth dhe syr Cesar,* I heard him forbidding that there be given, for any consideration, any tribute to Cæsar. P.C. 1575. Written also *defen,* and *defenny,* qd. v. W. *difyn, difynu, difwyn.* Arm. *difenn, difenni.* From the Latin *defendo.*

DYFF, v. n. He will come. 3 pers. s. fut. of irr. v. *dôs. Obereth dremns a dyff, yn èr-na rych ef a vŷdh,* full of works the just man shall come, in that hour rich he shall be. M.C. 259. *Dyff,* or *deyff,* is often used in North Wales in common conversation, for *daw,* and it is an older form, preserving the characteristic of the pronoun. In the same manner *dwylof* is an older form than *dwylaw,* hands. *Dyvi* is also an old Welsh form.

DYFFO, v. n. He shall have come. 3 pers. s. 2 fut. of *dôs. Euch alemma dhe gerhas an gwâs muscok ; pûr wŷr ef a'n gevyth gu, pan dyffo yn ow goloc,* go ye hence to fetch the crazed fellow ; very truly he shall have woe, when he shall have come into my sight. P.C. 964. This form is also found in Welsh; as, *Pan dhyffont i'r gâd nid ymwadant,* when they shall have come to the battle, they will not deny themselves. *Golydhan.*

DYFFRES, v. a. To relieve, protect, defend. *Râg gwander ef re codhas, rês yw dhyso y dhyffras, kemerry a dhysempys,* for weakness he has fallen; need is tot hee to relieve him, take it immediately. P.C. 2619. *Me a's dék fest yn lowen rag y dhyffres a anken ; dro hy dhymmo war ow scoudh,* I will bear it very joyfully, to relieve him from pain ; bring it to me on my shoulder. P.C. 2622. *Reys yw dhe onan golyas, war y torn pûp y dhyffras y gowyth, pyw a dhalleth,* need is that one should watch, in his turn every one relieving his companion, who will begin? R.D. 410. W. *difred.*

DYFFRY, adv. Truly, indeed. *In ny wrêth dyffry dodho abervedh yn crows cregy,* wilt thou not cause him indeed on cross to hang? M.C. 146. Generally written *defry,* qd. v.

DYFFY, v. a. Thou shalt have come. 2 pers. s. 2 fut. of *dôs. An lader a'n barth dychow a besys yn ketelma ; Arluth pan dyffy dhet pow, predery ahanaff gura,* the thief on the right side prayed in this manner ; Lord when thou shalt have come to thy country, do think of me. M.C. 193.

DYFLAS, adj. Shameful, disgraceful. *Tru, govy, ellas, ellas, me dhe nachê mar dhyfflas, ow arluth nép a'm curé,* Oh, woe is me, alas, alas, I to deny so shamefully my Lord who loved me. P.C. 1418. *Och, govy, ellas, ellas, gwelas ow mâp mar dyflas gans tebel wesyon dychtys,* Oh,

R

woe is me, alas, alas, to see my son so shamefully by wicked fellows used. P.C. 2604. W. *divlas*, from *di*, neg., and *blds*, taste. Arm. *divlaz*.

DYFLASE, v. a. To disgust, to displease, to grow tired of a thing. *Ha kyn fôns y ol sclandrys, nefré awos bôs ledhys, my wrâf dhe dhyflasé*, and though they all be offended, ever for fear of being killed, I will not displease thee. P.C. 901. W. *divlasu*. Arm. *divlaza*.

DYFRETH, adj. Wretched, miserable. Written also *difreth*, qd. v.

DYFUN, adj. Sleepless, awake. Id. qd. *difun*, qd. v.

DYFUNY, v. a. To waken, to awake. See *Difuny*.

DYFYGY, v. n. To fail. Id. qd. *difygy*, qd. v.

DYFYNNYS, part. Forbidden. Part. pass. of *dyfen*, qd. v.

DYG, v. a. He brought. *Ev ai dyg dhym*, he brought it to me. Llwyd, 242. More frequently written *duc*, qd. v.

DYGAVELSYS, part. Stript naked. Pryce. See *Dyscavylsy*.

DYGES, part. Barred, shut, closed. *Arluth assyw varthusek, pan dhueth, Ihesu gallosek, dh'agan myras, ha leverel dhynny crês, asso fast ytho dyges agan daras*, Lord, it is wonderful, when thou comest, Jesus powerful, to look at us, and to speak peace to us, though fast was shut our door. R.D. 1181. *A abestleleth, dhyuch crês; lemmyn an daras dyges fast warnouch why sûr kyn o, me re dhûth dh'agas myres*, O apostles, peace unto you, now though the door was shut fast upon you, I have come to see you. R.D. 1534. Written also *deges*, qd. v.

DYGNAS, v. a. To oppose, to trouble, to molest, to aggrieve. *Dhe'n tyller Crist re dethyé, ha'n Edhewon o dygnas*, to the place Christ came, and the Jews were opposing. M.C. 33. *Golyouch ha pesouch ow thás may hallouch môs dh'y aseth, na vedhouch temtijs dygnas gans gow ha gans scherewneth*, watch ye and pray my father that ye may go to his seat; that ye be not tempted to molest with falsehood and wickedness. M.C. 52. *Ow nesaé yma an preys, may fydh niáp Dew ynno reys dhe'n fals l'edhewon dygnas*, drawing near is the time, that the Son of God shall be given in it to the false Jews to be afflicted. P.C. 1098. W. *dygnu*. Ir. *dingim*. Gael. *dinn*. Scot. *ding*.

DYGWYSCA, v. a. To undress, to strip. See *Diguisca*.

DYHODZHYDH, s. m. The afternoon. Llwyd, 10. ‡ *Dyhodzhedh*, 249. A late and corrupt form of *dochageydh*, qd. v.

DYHOGEL, adj. Secure, safe, certain. *Na nyl oges nag yn pell, ny's gwelaf ow trenygé: hy re gafes dyhogel dôr dysechys yn nép le*, neither near nor far, I see her not flying over; she has certainly found the ground dried in some place. O.M. 1143. Written also *diogel*, qd. v. Kelgwin gives it the meaning of reverend. *Ny won, Arluth dyhogall, henna te a wôr yn ta, my nyngof warden dhodho*, I know not, reverend Lord, that thou knowest well, I am not his keeper. 84. *Cayn ha Abell, te a wôr ornys yns dhe Vownt Tabor, dhe weyl offren dehogall*, Cain and Abel, thou knowest, ordered are to Mount Tabor, to make a reverend offering. 90. In both instances it probably means *certainly*.

DYHONS, adj. Soon, quick. *Degeuch an pren a dhyhons war dhour Cedron may fo pons*, carry ye the tree quickly, over the water of Cedron that it may be a bridge. O.M. 2810. *A dhydhons for a dhyhuans*, for the sake of the metre. Written by Llwyd, 249, *dyhuanz*, as a late form. It is the same word as *dywhans*, qd. v.

DYHOW, adj. Right. Llwyd, 54, who also writes *dyhyow, am lev dhyhyow*, with my right hand. 244. It is also written *dyow*, qd. v., and is another form of *dychow*.

DYL, v. a. He will bore. A mutation of *tyl*, 3 pers. s. fut. of *tolla*, qd. v. *My a dyl tol râk hybeen*, I will bore a hole for the other. P.C. 2749.

DYLARG, adv. Behind. *War tu dylarg daras yn ty a wra yw port hynwes*, on the hinder part a door in it thou shalt make, that is called a port. O.M. 961. Id. qd. *dellarch*, qd. v.

DYLIES, part. Avenged. Llwyd, 175, 248, *dyliez*. The verb *dylié*, would be another form of *diala*, from *dial*, vengeance.

DYLLA, s. m. A sending out, a letting out. ‡ *Dilla gudzh*, phlebotomy, a letting out of blood. Llwyd, 120. Written also *dyllo*, qd. v.

DYLLAS, s. m. Clothes, raiment, apparel. See *Dillas*.

DYLLO, v. a. To send forth, to emit, to let out, to liberate. *Bedhens ebron dreys pûp tra, râk kudhé mŷns ús furmyys, râk synsy glaw a waritha, dhe'n nôr veys may fe dyllys*, let there be a sky above every thing, to cover all that is created, to keep the rain above, that it may be sent forth on the earth of the world. O.M. 24. *Da yw dyllo brân, mars ês dôr sêch war an beys*, it is good to send out a crow, if there is dry ground in the world. O.M. 1099. *My a's dyllo ahanan, ny dhue arié, my a greys; mar kyf carynnys, warnedhé y trŷg pûp preys*, I will send it from us, it will not come again, I believe; if it shall find carrion, upon them it will stay at all times. O.M. 1101. *Ow mebyon, my a gy peys, yn mês whêth dylleuch tryssé, mar kyf tŷr sŷch, my a greys dynny ny dhewhel arté*, my sons, I pray you, send outside yet a third; if it shall find dry ground, I believe it will not return to us again. O.M. 1130. *Belsebuc ha lawethan, dylleuch luhes ha taran quyt a'n losco*, Beelzebub and fiends, send forth lightning and thunder, that it burn him quite. R.D. 129. W. *dyllwng*. Arm. *dilocha*. Ir. *diolg*, †*dilugud*, †*dilgion*, †*dilgiad*.

DYLLY, v. a. To deserve, to owe. *Y beynys o crêf ha brâs warnodho heb y dylly, reson o râg oll an wlâs ef a wodhyé y verwy*, his pains were strong and great on him without deserving them, the reason was, for all the world he knew that he should die. M.C. 56. *Colon dên a yll crakyé a vynha prest predery an paynys brâs a'n gevé, ha'n dyspyth heb y dylly*, the heart of man may break, that will but consider the great pains he had, and the spite without. deserving them. M.C. 139. The same word as *dely*, qd. v. W. *dylu*. Arm. *dleout*. Ir. †*dil*, †*diliu*, †*dlig*, *tuill*. Gael. *dligh*. Manx, *toill*.

DYLYOW, s. m. Leaves. *Warnedhy yma gwedhen, whel gans lues scoren, saw nôth oll yns hep dylyow*, in it there is a tree, high with many a bough; but they are all bare, without leaves. O.M. 777. One of the plurals of *delen*, qd. v.

DYM, pron. prep. To me. (*Do-my*.) *Arluth, leverel dym gwra, mars ôf vy an kêth henna, na vo dên aral svlandrys*, Lord, do tell me, if I am that same, that another man may not be accused. P.C. 741. *Ihesus a gewsys arté, why a dhêth dhym yn arvow*, Jesus said again, ye have come to me in arms. M.C. 74. W. *i mi, i'm*. Arm. *d'in*, †*dif*, †*diff*. Ir. *damh*, †*domsa*. Gael. *dhom, dhomh*. Manx, *hym*. Lat. *mihi*. Gr. ἐμοί.

DYMMO, pron. prep. To me. An enlarged form of *dym*. *Bersabé ow whêk e vy, rŷs yw dymmo lafuryé dhe un vatel yredy*, Bathsheba, my sweet of me, need is to me to labour at a battle certainly. O.M. 2176. *Pandra ýll henna bones, lavar dhymmo vy wharré*, what thing can that be ? tell me directly. O.M. 158.

DYMMYN, s. m. Pieces, fragments. A mutation of *tymmyn*, pl. of *tam*, qd. v. *Ny won výth pe'th áf lemyn, nymbus gwese, guskys, na chy ; ow holan oll dhe dymmyn rág moreth a wra terry*, I know not where I shall go now, I have not raiment, shelter, nor house ; my heart all to pieces for grief will break. O.M. 357. *Saw un marrek a'n ladhas, ha dhe'n dôr scon a'n goras, hag a'n hakyas dhe dymmyn*, but a soldier killed him, and soon drove him to the earth, and hacked him to pieces. O.M. 2228.

DYN, pron. prep. To us. *(Do-ny.) Arluth kér, fattel výdh dyn, mars éth arté dhyworthyn*, dear Lord, how will it be to us, if thou wilt go again from us ? R.D. 2361. *Osé Máb Du leun a râs, lemyn gwyr lavar dhyn*, art thou the Son of God, full of grace, now truth tell to us. M.C. 100. The simple pronoun is often added, and sometimes repeated. *Bydh dynny nerth ha gweres*, be thou to us strength and help. O.M. 1071. *Ef dhe sevel a'n bédh mên, ha'y vôs datherys, y gows ny dâl dhynny ny*, that he has risen from the tomb of stone, and is ascended, it behoves us not to say. R.D. 568. W. *i ni, i'n, †ynni*. Arm. *deomp*. Ir. *duinn, dhuinn, †duun, †dun, †duunni, †dunni*. Gael. *dinn, dhuinn, dhuinne*. Manx, *dooin*.

DYN, a prefix in composition. It answers to the conjugate prefix *dn* in Welsh ; thus C. *dinerchy*, W. *annerchy*, to salute. Llwyd, 249. Comp. of *dy*, and *yn*.

DYNACHE, v. a. To deny, to reject, to retract. *Mês pan vôns dyschys gulân, y a dynach aga duow myleges*, but when they are quite refreshed, they will reject their cursed gods. O.M. 1839. *Rág máp an pla agan temptyé pûr feyl a wra prest yn pûp le dhe gúl drôk tra, ha dynaché oberow da*, for the son of evil us tempt very craftily will, always in every place to do evil things, and to reject good works. P.C. 13. *Gow a lever an iaudyn ; ef a'n pren, mar ny dhynach y whethlow*, the wilful man tells a lie ; he shall pay for it, if he will not retract his tales. P.C. 369. *Y vôs vf re leverys ; lyes trefeth y'n clewys, ma na ýll y dhynaché*, that he is he has said ; 'many times I heard him, so that he cannot retract it. P.C. 1725. *Mar ny fyn dynaché y gow*, if he will not retract his lie. P.C. 2061. Comp. of *dy*, *iutens*., and *naché*, to deny. Arm. *dinacha*.

DYNAS, adj. Obstinate, unyielding. *Wharé yn mês y trylyas, ha'y golon namna dorré, rag y Arluth, leun a râs, mar dhynas ef dh'y naché*, anon out he turned, and his heart almost broke, for his Lord, full of grace, so obstinately that he should deny. M.C. 87. This is a doubtful word, and until a better explanation is suggested, I derive it from *tyn*, tight.

DYNDYLY, v. a. To deserve, to owe. *Ef re dhyndyles yn ta godhaf mernens yn bys-ma, mara pedhé lél iuggys*, he has deserved well to suffer death in this world, if he be fairly judged. P.C. 1342. *Ef a'n pren, yn ta del y'n dyndylas*, he shall pay for it, well as he has deserved it. P.C. 1347. *Yn ta cf re'n dyndylas*, well he has deserved it. P.C. 1402. *Why a dhyndylsé onor, mar calleuch dry an Ihesu dhe cen crygyans*, ye would deserve honour, if ye can bring Jesus to another belief. P.C. 1992. *Yn ban tynnyn ef a'n dour, ha dyndylyn agan*

DYNDYLY 123 DYNYTHY

our, a cowethé, up let us draw him, and let us deserve our gold, O comrades. R.D. 2266. *Ny dhyndylas lowené, lemmyn yn tân lôs cudhys*, he has not deserved bliss, but to be covered in fire. R.D. 2325. Componnded of *dyn*, *(dy-yn,)* prefix, and *dyly*, or *dylly*, to deserve.

DYNER, s. m. A penny. *An ngl dhodho a dellé pymp cans dyner monyys, ha hanter cans y gylé*, the one owed to him five hundred pence of money, and half a hundred the other. P.C. 505. Another form of *dinair*, qd. v.

DYNERCHY, v. a. To greet, to salute. *Syr Cayfus gynef a'th dynyrchys, hag a'th pýs a dhôs dhodho býs yn tré dre dhe vôdh dh'y cusullyé worth Ihesu pandra výdh gwreys*, Sir Caiaphas by me hath greeted thee, and prays thee to come to him into the town, by thy will to advise him what shall be done regarding Jesus. P.C. 565. Its later form was *dynerhy*. Llwyd, 249. Comp. of *dyn*, prefix, and *erchy*, to command, from *arch*, an injunction. W. *annerchu*.

DYNION, s. m. Men. Plural of *dén*, qd. v. *Dén cláv*, a sick man ; *dynion clevion*, sick men. Llwyd, 243. W. *dýn cláv*, pl. *dynion clevion*.

DYNNARCH, s. m. A greeting, a salutation. *Ow arlothes gyné dre dhynnarch agas pysgys na wrcllouch cammen ladhé an profus a Nazaré*, my lady by me through greeting prayed you, that you do not unjustly slay the prophet of Nazareth. P.C. 2195. Comp. of prefix, *dyn*, and *arch*, a request, an injunction. W. *annerch*.

DYNNY, pron. prep. To us. An enlarged form of *dyn*, qd. v. *Pyth ew an othom dynny cafus lafur a'n par:na*, what is the need to us to have labour of that kind ? O.M. 967. *Dalleth dhynny ny cané*, begin to sing to us. R.D. 2354. W. *i nyni*. Ir. *†duunni, †dunni*. Gael. *dhuinne*.

DYNS, s. m. Teeth. One of the plurals of *dans*, qd. v. *Kemer tyyr spûs an aval, a dybrys Adam dhe dâs, pan varwo, gorr'y hep fal yntré y dhýns ha'y davas*, take thou three kernels of the apple, that Adam thy father ate ; when he dies, put them without fail between his teeth and his tongue. O.M. 826. *Yma ow trýs ha'm dulé dhyworthef ow teglené, ma 'thew krehyllys ow dýns*, my feet and hands are loosening from me, so that my teeth are chattering. P.C. 1218.

DYNWA, v. a. Will produce. 3 pers. s. fut. of *doen*, or *doyn*, qd. v. *Ty a wra wogé hemma gorré an tûs a lena, býs yn tyreth a dhynwa lanwes leyth ha mêl kefrys*, thou shalt after this bring the people thence to a land that produces fulness of milk and honey also. O.M. 1429.

DYNYRCHYS, v. a. Greeted. 3 pers. s. preterite of *dynerchy*, qd. v.

DYNYTHY, v. a. To bear, to bring forth, to produce, to beget. *Ef a wra dynythy un máp da hep falladow*, he shall beget a good son without fail. O.M. 639. *Dre gráth an Arluth gwella, ny a dhynyth un flôch da, dhyn a servyo*, by the grace of the best Lord, we shall produce a good child, that may serve us. M.C. 664. *Govy výth pan véf genys, a dor ow mam dynythys, na vythqueth pan denys bron*, woe is me that I ever was born, out of my mother's womb brought, or ever sucked the breast. O.M. 1754. *Máp Dew pûr, ha dên keffrys, a vachteth gulân dynythys, ha henna mûr varth vyé*, Son of very God, and man also, of a pure virgin born ; and that would be a great wonder. P.C. 1727.

DYNYTHYS, part. Come. *A Seth osa dynythys agy dhe yet paradys, lavar dhym pa'n dra wylsta*, O Seth, thou art come within the gate of Paradise; tell me what thou sawest. O.M. 763. *Galsof coyth ha marthys gwan, dynythys ew ou deweydh*, I am become old and wondrous weak, my end is arrived. O.M. 856. *Dynythys yw, hag yma yn hy myyn branch olyf gláś*, she is come, and there is in her beak a branch of green olive. O.M. 1121. *Dynythys ôf dhe'th volungeth*, I am come to thy will. O.M. 1271. *Dynythys ôn hep danger*, we are come without delay. P.C. 1869. Part. pass. of *dones*, qd. v.

DYON, adj. Black. The plural of *du*, qd. v. ‡*Hyrrox dyon*, black rams. Llwyd, 243. W. *duon, hyrdhod duon*.

DYOW, adj. Right. *Wogé hemma why a wêl mâp Dew ow ysedhé a barth dyow dyougel dhe'n Tás Dew yn lowené*, after this ye shall see the Son of God sitting on the right side truly of God the Father in bliss. P.C. 1487. *Gans an Tás Dew yma ef a dhyow barth*, with God the Father he is on the right side. R.D. 928. *Ysedhé del reys dhymmo yn néf a dhyow dhum Tás*, to sit as necd is to me, in heaven at the right of my Father. R.D. 1562. *Dyow* is the same as *dychow*, qd. v., formed by first softening the guttural *ch* into *h*, and then omitting it.

DYOWGEL, adj. Certain, sure, safe. *Yn triddydh dyowgel ef a wra y trehevel*, in three days certainly he will build it up. P.C. 352. Another form of *diogel*, qd. v.

DYP, v. a. Will think. A mutation of *typ*, 3 pers. s. fut. of *tybyé*, qd. v. *Rág me a dŷp bôs hemma an kêth mâp êth alemma, yw mychiern a lowené*, for I think that this is the same son that went hence, that is the king of joy. R.D. 2508.

DYRAG, prep. Before, in presence of. *Otté ha coynt o an gwâs, pa na vynné gorthyby a dhyrâk an arlythy dhe resons an doctors brás*, behold how cunning the fellow was! when he would not answer, before the lords, the arguments of the great doctors. P.C. 1821. *Dyrâg*, Llwyd, 51. Comp. of *dy*, id. qd. *de*, from, qd. v., and *rac*, before. Arm. *dirak*.

DYRAGOF, pron. prep. Before me. (*Dyrag-my.*) *My re weles y'm hunrus a dhyragof êl dyblans*, I saw in my dream before me a bright angel. O.M. 1955. *Yn hanow an Tás huhel, ke abervedh yn castel a dhyragof, ny a'th pŷs*, in the name of the Father high, go within into the village before me, I pray thee. P.C. 196.

DYRAGON, pron. prep. Before us. (*Dyrag-ny.*) *A lés oll y wolyow a dhyragon pan gwylsyn*, all his wounds disclosed when we saw before us. R.D. 1332. *An Arluth dhyragon torth vara ef a torras*, the Lord before us a loaf of bread he broke. R.D. 1490.

DYRAGOS, pron. prep. Before thee. (*Dyrag-ty.*) *A'n gweleste a dhyragos, alsesta y aswonfos*, if thou shouldst see him before thee, wouldst thou be able to know him? R.D. 861. *Hydhew a tryckes yn trê, dhyragos ty a'n gwrisé byw yn poynt da*, to day, if thou hadst stayed at home, before thee thou wouldest have seen him living in good condition. R.D. 1382.

DYRAGOUCH, pron. prep. Before you. (*Dyrag-chui.*) Written also *dyragoch*. *Otté dheuch mychtern Ihesu, a dhyragouch ow sevel*, behold for you king Jesus before you standing. P.C. 2365. *Me a grŷs pan y'u gwyllouch dhyragoch why, dhodho ny ylleuch gûl drôk, hedré ve y gys golok*, I believe, when you see him before you, you will

not be able to do him harm, while he is in your sight. R.D. 1913. *Arluth, lemmyn a's dysken, dyragouch nôth y fyen*, Lord, if I take it off now, before you naked I should be. R.D. 1942.

DYRAGTHO, pron. prep. Before him, or it. (*Dyrag-o.*) *A rág dynchans ow kerdhes, an dour ow fysky a lês pŷp úr ol a dhyragtho*, forth quickly going, the water striking wide, continually before him. O.M. 1684. *Me a vyn yn della dysky ow dyllas gwella, ha tywlel a dhyragtho*, I will so take off my best clothes, and cast before him. P.C. 257.

DYREYTH, s. m. Land, earth. A mutation of *tyreyth*, id. qd. *tyreth*, qd. v. *Adam, cummyas scon a fŷdh, hŷs dhe baal luen dhe drehy: dhys yth archaf a dyreyth, gás Adam dhe'th egery*, Adam, permission shall be forthwith, to cut the full length of thy spade; I command thee, O earth, allow Adam to open thee. O.M. 381.

DYRRY, v. a. To break, to break off, to pluck. A mutation of *tyrry*, qd. v. *A meys of ow predyry, pandra altaf dhe wruthyl, an aval orth y dyrry, rág owu genes bones gŷl*, I am outside (puzzled) thinking, what I may do, as to plucking the apple, for fear of there being deceit with thee. O.M. 195. *Prâg y tolsté sy hep kên*, worth hy themptés dhe dyrry an frút erbyn ow dyfen, why didst thou deceive her pitilessly, by tempting her to pluck the fruit against my prohibition? O.M. 303.

DYRUSKY, v. a. To strip off the bark, to decorticate. *Ha'y branchys yn van tyvys bŷs yn néf uhel golow; ha hy warbarth dyruskys, kefrys bên ha barennow*, and its branches growing up even to heaven high in light; and it was unbarked altogether, both the trunk, and the boughs. O.M. 785. *My a's dyswé yn lowen: nŷns ûs warnethé crochen, nag yw trôch, ha dyruskys*, I will shew them willingly; there is no skin upon them that is not broken and peeled. P.C. 2687. Comp. of *dy*, or *di*, privative, and *rusk*, bark. W. *dirisgo*. Arm. *diruska*.

DYRYVAS, v. a. To declare, to relate, to make known, to shew. *Abram, scon goslow lemyn orth ow lavarow a fynnaf dyryvas dhys*, Abraham, immediately hearken now to my words, that I will declare to thee. O.M. 1367. *Yma dhymmo, cowyth da, múr a ioy yn torma a'th tyryvas*, there is to me good comrade, much of joy at this time from thy declaration. R.D. 1308. *Judas êth yn y negis, en iowl yw e'n hombronky; dhe'n Edhewon dyrryvys del o y fynnas synsy*, Judas went on his errand, the devil it was that guided him; to the Jews he shewed how it was that he wished to seize. M.C. 62. Written also *daryvas*, qd. v.

DYS, pron. prep. To thee. (*Do-ty.*) *Messyger, ow baneth dys, my a vyn a dhysempys marogeth waré bŷs ty*, messenger, my blessing to thee, I will immediately ride presently even to it. O.M. 1969. *Oll dhe'th vôdh, ow arluth kêr, dynythys ôn hep danger bŷs dys omma hep ardak*, all to thy will, dear Lord, come we are without delay, even to thee here without demur. P.C. 1870. W. *ti, it*, †*itti*, †*ytti*, †*iit*. Arm. *d'id*, †*dit*. Ir. *duit*, †*deit*, †*dit*. Gael. *dhuit*. Manx, *hood*. Lat. *tibi*. Gr. *τοί, σοί*.

DYS, v. n. Come thou. *Dŷs yn rág*, come forward. Llwyd, 250. The same as *dús*, qd. v.

DYSCAS, s. f. A teaching, doctrine. Written also *dyskes*. *Púr apert hag yn golow y leveris ow dyskas*, very openly and in light I spake my doctrine. M.C. 79. *Dên yw* dhe pûp dhe weles; saw y ober ha'y dhyskes pûp ol a wra tremené, he is a man for all to see; without his work and his teaching every one will die. P.C. 57. *Dysvé dhym nêp reson d'th tyskes omma dyson, may hyllyn gynes dysky*, shew thou to me some reason of thy teaching here quietly, that we may teach with thee. P.C. 1249. *Apert vythqueth y tyskys ow dyskes dhe'n Yedhewon*, openly always I have taught my doctrine to the Jews. P.C. 1252. W. *dysgad*.

DYSCAVYLSY, v. a. To stretch out, to strain. Part. *dyscavylrys. Y vellow, kettep onan, dyscavylsys gns, lemmyn kentr'y worth an pren*, his joints, every one, are strained, now nail it to the wood. P.C. 2771. *Ellas bones dhe treys squerdys, oll dhe yscarn dyscavylsys, tell y'th dywluef*, alas, that thy feet should be torn, all thy bones stretched; holes in thy hands. P.C. 3173. *Myres y gorf del yw squerchys, yscarn Mâp Dew dygavelsys, ha Dew warbarth*, to see the body how it is torn, the bones of the Son of God strained, and a God at the same time. P.C. 3179.

DYSCRYGYANS, s. m. Unbelief. *Galsos lemmyn pûr woky, rák na fynnyth dhyn crygy; galeos mûr yn dyscrygyans*, thou art become now quite foolish, for thou wilt not believe us; thou art gone much in unbelief. R.D. 1516. Comp. of *dys*, privative, and *crygyans*, belief, qd. v.

DYSCRYOYC, adj. Unbelieving. Pl. *dyscrygygyon*, and contractedly *dysgrygyon. Thomas, na vgâh dyscrygyk, pys gans colon dywysyk war Cryst an nêf*, Thomas, be thou not unbelieving; pray with undoubting heart to Christ of heaven. R.D. 1369. *Ty yw dyscrygyk pûr vêr, ha mûr anfusyk*, thou art unbelieving very truly, and very mischievous. R.D. 1519. *A bûr fals dyscrygygyon, tebel agas manerow, na gresouch a lucn golon, bôs an Tâs Dew hep parow*, O very false unbelievers, evil are your ways; that ye will not believe with full heart, that God the Father is without equals. O.M. 1855. *Râg na worsys ow honow, a rôg an fiehysygow a Israel dyscryggyon, ny's goryth dhe'n tgr*, because thou honourest not my name, before the children of Israel unbelievers, thou shalt not bring them to the land. O.M. 1869.

DYSCRYSY, v. a. To believe, to distrust. *Na dhyscrysouch Dew a nêf, rág ef a glew agas lêf, gwreuch why trestyé yn y grâs*, do not ye distrust the God of heaven, for he will hear your voice; do ye trust in his grace. O.M. 1667. *May rollo yn nêp teller dour dhe evé dhedhé y, na allons kafus kên dhe dhyscryzy*, that he may give in some place water to drink to them, that they may not find cause to disbelieve. O.M. 1826. *Dasserchys yw; yn sûr re re dhyscryseys, râk Maria a gewsys worto hydhyw*, he is risen; surely too much thou hast disbelieved, for Mary has spoken to him to day. R.D. 1040. Comp. of *dys*, privative, and *crysy*, to believe, qd. v.

DYSCUDHE, v. a. To uncover, to disclose, to shew. *Yn hanow an Tâs whel, an gorhel gwrên dyscudhé*, in the name of the Father high, the ark let us uncover. O.M. 1146. More frequently written *dysquedhas*, qd. v.

DYSCY, v. a. To teach, to instruct, to learn. *Tús ús dhym ow tevones yw gans ow thraylor dyskis*, men that are coming to me are by my traitor taught. M.C. 61. *Bys yn Ihesus caradow y êth, del dyskas Judas*, even to Jesus the beloved they went, as Judas taught. M.C. 64. *In agis mysk pan êsen lays Du dheuch ow tysky*, among you

when I was the laws of God to you teaching. M.C. 75. *An ré-na a gll dhe dhysky yn della y re dhyskas*, those may teach thee in the same manner as they learnt. M.C. 80. *Gor gwra del dyscaf dhyso, but do, as I instruct thee. O.M. 987. *Ow conselar whêk y'th pesaf, dysk dhymmo un ankenek rág ow fehas*, my sweet adviser, I pray thee, teach me a penitential hymn for my sin. O.M. 2256. *A mester whêk, gordhys re by, pan wrêth mar têk agan dysky*, O sweet master, be thou worshipped, when thou dost so sweetly teach us. P.C. 36. *Me a dhÿsk dheuch tokyn da*, I will shew you a good token. P.C. 971. *Pan dyskys yn eglusyow, ny wrûg dên fyth ow sensy*, when I taught in the churches, no man did seize me. P.C. 1175. *Apert vythqueth y tyskys ow dyskes dhe'n Yedhewon*, openly always I taught my doctrine to the Jews. P.C. 1251. *Y êth yn un fystené dhe Pylat aga Iustis, e'n dyskyens del vyê, ha dhodho a leverys*, they went in a hurry to Pilate their Justice; him they taught how it was, and to him said. M.C. 248. W. *dysgu*. Arm. *deski, diski*. Ir. *teagasc, †coag, †cosc*. Gael. *teagaisg*. Sansc. *dic*. Gr. δείκω, δεικνύω, (δαίξις.) Lat. *disco, dico, doceo*. Goth. *teiha*. Germ. *zeige*. Eng. *teach*.

DYSCY, v. a. To throw off, or put aside; to strip, to undress. 2 pers. s. imp., and 3 pers. s. fut. *dysc. My a vyn yn della dysky ow dyllas gwella, ha tywtel a dhyragtho*, I will in this manner take off my best clothes, and cast before him. P.C. 256. *Dyskyn y vantel wharré, rág yn y dyllas arté an harlot a vgâh gwyskys*, let us take off his mantle soon, for in his clothes again the knave shall be dressed. P.C. 2531. *Honna yw y bows nessa, ha whêth gwreuch y dhry omma-arté dhynchy, ha dyscow y dheworto*, that is the nearest garment, and do ye yet bring him here again to you, and strip it from him. R.D. 1870. *Arluth lemmyn a's dysken, dyragouch nôth y fyen*, Lord, now if I take it off, before you naked I should be. R.D. 1941. *Râk hedré vyuch ow pleghyé dhywhy bÿth ny's dÿsk neffré*, for as long as you are yielding, he will never take it off for you. R.D. 1951. *Dÿsk an quêth a dhysempys*, take off the cloth immediately. R.D. 1953. *Pan dothyans dh'y, yntrethé pows Jesus a ve dyskys*, when they came there, among them the coat of Jesus was taken off. M.C. 176. W. *dyosg, diwisgo*. Arm. *diuskein, diwiska*.

DYSCYANS, s. m. Learning. Llwyd, 240.
DYSCYBEL, s. m. A disciple. See *Discybel*.
DYSEHY, v. a. To quench thirst, to refresh. Part. *dysehys. A Dâs Drw y'th wolowys, clew galow an bobyl-ma; dowr, may fêns y dysehys, a vewnans ry dedhé gwra*, O Father God in thy lights, hear the call of this people; that they may be refreshed, the water of life do thou give to them. O.M. 1833. *Més pan vôns dysehys guilán, y a dynach aga duow myleges*, but when they are quite refreshed, they will reject their cursed gods. O.M. 1838. Comp. of *dy*, neg., and *sehy*, to dry. W. *disychedu*.

DYSEMPYS, adj. Sudden, immediate. *Dyson hep whethé dhe gorn, dysempzys gwra y dhybry*, quietly without blowing thy horn, eat it immediately. O.M. 208. *A dds ker, dhe'th worhemmyn my â dh'y a dhysempys*, O father dear, at thy command, I will go to him immediately. O.M. 697. The same word as *desempys*, qd. v.

DYSMEGY, v. a. To utter, to speak, tell, declare. Written also *dysmygy. Yma ow conys dhywwhy chyff gwythoryon ol an gulas a wodher dhe dysmegy*, there are working for you all the chief workmen in the land (that) can be mentioned. O.M. 2332. *Yn ûr-na ef dysmegys py ganssé y fue gwyskys*, at that time let him declare by whom he was struck. P.C. 1372. *Gwyskys lemmyn nêp cowyth may hallo ef dysmygy pyw a'n gwyskys*, let some comrade now strike that he may declare who struck him. P.C. 1378. *Dysmyg lemmyn ty gwâs smat, pyw a rôs dhyso an wat*, declare now, thou brave fellow, who gave to thee the blow. P.C. 1382. *Kyn na vynno dysmcgy, dûn yn râk gans an gwary*, though he will not tell, let us go forward with the play. P.C. 1387. Written also *desmygy*, qd. v. W *dysmegu*.

DYSO, pron. prep. To thee. An enlarged form of *dys*. *Hen yw an oel a versy o dedhywys dyso sy dheworth an Tâs Dew an nêf*, this is the oil of mercy (that) was promised to thee by the Father God of heaven. O.M. 842. *Hŷr lour ew ow bewnans, kymmer dyso ow enef*, long enough is my life, take to thee my soul. O.M. 849. *Ow banneth dhyso Gryffyn*, my blessing on thee Gryffyn. O.M. 2433. *Dûs gené pols dhe wandré, ha dyso my a lever yntrethon tacklow pryvé*, come to walk with me a while, and I will tell thee between ourselves private things. O.M. 935. *Dysmyg lemmyn ty gwâs smat pyw a rôs dhyso an wat*, tell now, thou brave fellow, who gave to thee the blqw. P.C. 1384. Written also *deso*. Old Irish †*duitso*, †*detsiu*, †*detso*, †*deitsiu*.

DYSON, adj. Without noise, silent, quiet. *Adam, ystyn dhym dhe dhorn; tan henna dheworthef vy, dyson hep whethé dhe gorn, dyscmpys gura y dhybry*, Adam, reach me thy haud; take that from me, quietly without blowing thy horn, eat it immediately. O.M. 207. *Dyswé dhym nêp reson a'th tyske's omma, dyson, may hyllyn gynes dysky*, shew to me some reason of thy teaching here, quietly, that we may teach with thee. P.C. 1249. Comp. of *dy*, neg., and *sôn*, a sound. W. *disun*, *dison*.

DYSPLEVYAS, v. a. To display. *Geseuch y dhe dhysplevyas, heilyouch an mychtern brâs a dhysempys*, leave them to display, and salute the great king immediately. P.C. 2632. This must be borrowed from the English. We have another form in *dyspleytyé*. *Ow arluth kêr, Lucifer, dyspleytys yw y vaner, ha kelmys worth an grows pren*, my dear lord Lucifer, displayed is his banner, and bound to the cross tree. P.C. 3044. *Ganso crows worth y buner wharré ef a dhyspleytyas*, with him a cross on his banner soon he displayed. R.D. 528.

DYSPRENE, v. a. To redeem. *A's drens dhe Jerusalem, râg y fêdh mâp yn Bethlem genys a dhyspreen an bŷs*, let him take them to Jerusalem, for there will be a son in Bethlehem born (that) will redeem the world. O.M. 1935. *Ow Arluth Cryst, dr'y verey, a woruk ow dysprenné vy mês a yfarn yn teffry gans y kŷc ha'y voôs keffrys*, my Lord Christ, by his mercy, did redeem me out of hell, really with his flesh and his blood also. R.D. 216. Comp. of *dys*, id. qd. *das*, prefix iter., and *prena*, to buy. Written also *dasprenna*. W. *dadbrynu*. Arm. *dasprena*.

DYSPRYNNYAS, s. m. A redeemer. *Ha venytha me a grŷs dhe vôs a werches genys, Mâb Dew agan dysprynnyas*, and hereafter I will believe that thou art of a virgin born, Son of God, our Redeemer. P.C. 404. *Del ôs formyns dhe'n nêf ha'n lûr, ha dysprynnyas dhynny pûp ûr, Cryst, ow sylwyas, clew mar a'th dûr, dhys daryvas del garsen mûr*, as thou art Creator of heaven and earth, and a Redeemer to us always, Christ my Saviour, hear if it concerns thee, disclose to thee as I would much desire. R.D. 844.

DYSPYTYE, v. a. To spite, to insult, to worry. *Ha why yn wêdh cowethé, pûp ur gwreuch y dhyspytyé, ha duffolé fast an gwâs*, and do ye also, comrades, continually worry him, and mock the fellow much. P.C. 1397.

DYSPYTH, s. m. Spite, despite, insult. *Colon dên a yll crakyé a vynna prest predery an peynys brâs a'n gevé ha'n despyth, heb y dylly*, the heart of man may break, that will but consider the great pains he had, and the spite, without deserving them. M.C. 139. Fr. *depit*, †*despit*. Lat. *despectus*.

DYSQUEDHAS, v. a. To uncover, to open, to make known, to declare, to shew. 2 pers. s. imp. *dysqué*. *Ha tûs vyan, ha tûs vrâs, ny wrûk Dew dhym dysquedhas, vŷth ny'n cresons ef neffré*, and people small, and people great (will say,) God has not declared to me; they will never believe it. O.M. 1439. *Beneges re bo an Tâs, a vynnas dysquedhes dhyn gwelynny a gemmys râs*, blessed be the Father, who would shew to us rods of so much grace. O.M. 1746. *Dysqué dhym a'd kerensé*, shew me of thy love. O.M. 2106. *Lavar lemyn pan drôk vo yn a-ver-tu a dhysquydhysta dhynny*, tell me now, what evil is there on any side, that thou shewest to us. P.C. 339. *Dysqué dhodho kerengé*, shew thou love to him. P.C. 3229. *Pyw a dhysquedhas dhysod ha vôs nôth*, who has discovered to thee that thou art naked. C.W. 64. *Mêr a râs dhe why, Eal Dew, ow tysquedhas dhym pûp tra*, much thanks to you, Angel of God, in shewing to me every thing. C.W. 136. This word is variously written *dascudhé*, *dyscudhé*, *disquedha*, *dyswedha*. Comp. of *das*, or *dys*, neg. prefix, and *cudhé*, to cover. W. *dadgudhio*.

DYSQUYDHYANS, s. m. A declaration, a shewing, a discovering. *Hen yw dŷdh a bowesva dhe pûp dên a vo sylwys, yn dysquydhyens a henna ny a bowes desempsys*, this is a day of rest to every man that may be saved, in declaration of that we will rest forthwith. O.M. 147. *Yn gwyrder, an thyr gwelen yw dysquydhyans ha token an try person yn drynsys*, in truth, the three rods are a declaration and token of the three persons in the Trinity. O.M. 1733. *Dysquedhyens war lyrch anken bedhé migtern yn dewedh*, a shewing after sorrow that he was a king at last. M.C. 236.

DYSTOUCH, adv. Immediately, directly, very soon. *Ny a yll yn nôs hancth fest dystouch bonas kellys*, we may this night very soon be lost. M.C. 239. *Mar codhfo an casadow, dystouch y fyen ledhys*, if the villain knew, immediately I should be killed. O.M. 2120. *Rŷs yn dymmo lafuryé dhe un vatel yredy, saw dystoch hy a vŷdh dué*, used is to me to labour at a battle surely, but very soon it will be ended. O.M. 2178. *A dystouch mar ty a dhêg a neyl pen dhe dour Cedron*, if immediately thou wilt carry one end to the water of Cedron. O.M. 2814. *My a vyn môs alemma pûr dhystouch dh'y*, I will go hence very directly to him. R.D. 1239. *Rum leauté, dûn a dhystouch*, by my truth, let us come immediately. R.D. 1243.

DYSTREWY, v. a. To destroy, to ruin, to overthrow. *Mar mynnyth hy dystrewy, orden dhe'th tûs hy hnoukyé gans meyn*, if thou wilt put her to death, order thy people to beat her with stones. O.M. 2675. *Pan wreta mar coynt fara, ow scollyé agan gwara, ha'n fêr orth y tystrywy*, when thou actest so rudely, scattering our wares, and destroying the fair. P.C. 342. *Leverewch dhym paham cheyson a's bues why erbyn Ihesu Nazaré, pan vynnouch y dhystrewy*, tell me what accusation have ye against Jesus of Nazareth, when ye wish to destroy him. P.C. 1972. *Drcdho y fue dystrewys*, by him it was destroyed. P.C. 2413. *Hag a codhfons yredy, ny wrussens ow dystrewy*, and if they knew truly, they would not destroy me. P.C. 2777. W. *dystrywio*. Both from the Latin *destruo*.

DYSWEDHY, v. a. To uncover, to open, to discover, to shew. 2 pers. s. imp., and 3 pers. s. fut. *dyswé*, an abbreviation of *dyswedh*. *Ihesus Crist múr gerensé dhe váb dén a dhyswedhas*, Jesus Christ much love to man shewed. M.C. 5. *Hag ef a dyswé dhychy un skyber efan yn scon*, and he will shew to you a large room soon. P.C. 637. *Deuch gynef, me a dyswé chy dh'agas mester wharré*, come ye with me, I will shew (you) a house for your master presently. P.C. 673. *Ha why Annas, ow def kér, dyswedhouch bós pryns somper rák dyswyl an Cristenyon*, and you, Annas, my dear captain, shew yourself to be a prince without equal to destroy the Christians. P.C. 978. *Pan syfsys hydhew myttyn, yach éns aga ieyw; dyswedh y a dhan dhe glok*, when thou gottest up to day in the morning, sound were their sinews; shew them from under thy cloak. P.C. 2682. *Dyeskyn a n vŷnk dhe'n lúr, ha dyswé ran a'th veystry*, descend from the post to the ground, and shew a portion of thy power. P.C. 2869. *Dyswé dhynny Nychodem, ha Joseph Baramathya, ha ny a dhyswé yn wédh an corf a sytscuch yn bédh yw Ihesu máp Maria*, shew thou to us Nicodemus, and Joseph of Arimathœa, and we will shew also the body you put in the tomb, is Jesus, the son of Mary. R.D. 626. Another form of *dysquedhas*.

DYSWREY, v. a. To undo, to spoil, to destroy. *Mar qura, godhvedhys mar pŷdh, yn scon dyswreys ef a vŷdh, ha dhe'n mernans col gorrys*, if he does, if it be discovered, soon destroyed he shall be, and to death quickly put. O.M. 1521. *Ty re dhyswrúg eredy hevelcp dhom face vy*, thou hast destroyed verily the likeness to my face. O.M. 2336. *Ke gorhemmyn dhe'n cyté, may teffons omma wharré, war beyn aga bós dyswrŷs*, go command the city, that they come here soon, on pain of their being destroyed. O.M. 2409. *Ef re dhyswrug an marhas*, he has destroyed the market. P.C. 376. *An temple ef a dhyswra, yn trydydh ef a'n drecha gwell ages kyns*, the temple he will destroy, in three days he will restore it better than before. P.C. 1696. Comp. of *dys*, neg. prefix, and *gwrey*, to do. W. *dadwneud*.

DYSWRUTHYL, v. a. To undo, to spoil, to destroy. *Da vyé kyns dós Sabout dyswruthyl an fals profus*, it would be good before Sabbath comes, to destroy the false prophet. P.C. 562. Comp. of *dys*, neg. prefix, and *gruthyl*, to do.

DYSWUL, v. a. To undo, to spoil, to destroy. *Me a grŷx bones an gwâs ow kúl maystri brás, dyswel an fér ef a vyn*, I believe that the fellow is making great violence, he will destroy the fair. P.C. 360. *Dyswedhouch bós pryns somper rák dyswyl an Cristenyon*, shew yourself to be a prince without equal to destroy the Christians. P.C. 979. *Rág y fynner, mara kyller, gans paynys mér ow dyswul glán*, for it is wished, if it could be, with great sorrows to destroy me quite. P.C. 2602. *Hen yw gwŷr, ef a galsé púp tra y dhyswul urté, moy ys na fé*, this is true, he might have destroyed every thing again, more than it was. R.D. 978. Comp. of *dys*, neg. prefix, and *gúl*, to do.

DYSWYTHYL, v. a. To undo, to spoil, to destroy. *Me â dhodho yn lowen, del yw e ow nyre da, rák dyswythyl an bylen, mar kews erbyn a laha*, I will go to him joyfully, as he is my good sire, to dispatch the villain, if he speaks against the law. P.C. 571. Comp. of *dys*, neg. prefix, and *guthyl*, to do.

DYSYMPYS, adj. Sudden, immediate. *Omma ny wreuch why trygé, euch yn més a dhysympys; why a gryl of lowené, a rŷs dhyuch yn paradhys*, here ye will not remain, go out immediately; ye will lose my joy, which I gave to you in Paradise. O.M. 318. *Dún ganso a dysympys, ha poynyn gans múr a grŷs, ha yn dour goryn an pren*, let us come with it immediately, and let us run with great strength, and into the water let us put the tree. O.M. 2788. This word is variously written *desempys, desympys, dysempys*. W. *disymmwth*.

DYTHGTHTYA, v. a. To prepare, to provide, to fashion, to dispose. *Rag henna dhe bôb dythgthtya fordh a rúg dhe vós sylwys*, therefore for every one he provided a way to be saved. M.C. 7. *Crist a settyas yn tyen an scovern arté dhe drê, hag a'n dythgthtyas púr lowen maga ték del rebye*, Christ fastened whole the ear again close home, and fastened it very gladly as fair as it had been. M.C. 71. *Yntrethé avel tús fól garloni spern a ve dythgthtys*, among them, like foolish men, a garland of thorns was framed. M.C. 133. *Nag onon ef ny asas heb uré a'y esely, yn delma ef a'n dythgtyas may eyn o y wely*, not one he left without anointing of his limbs, in this manner he disposed him that healthy was his bed. M.C. 235. Another form of *dychtyé*, qd. v.

DYTHYWYS, part. Promised. See *Didhywy*.

DYUCH, pron. prep. To ye. (*Do-chui*.) *Ha rág why dhum keruné, my a re dhyuch Bosvene, Lostuthyel, ha Lanerchy*, and because ye have crowned me, I will give you Bosvene, Lostwithiel, and Lanerchy. O.M. 2399. *A abesteleth dhyuch crés*, O apostles, peace unto you. R.D. 1533. This word is variously written *deych*, and *deuch*, qd. v. *Dyuwhy* is an enlarged form. *Arluth whék, yma ow conys dhyuwhy chyf gwythoryon ol an gwlâs a vodher dhe dysmegy*, sweet lord, there are working for you, all the chief workmen of the land that can be mentioned. O.M. 2330.

DYVERE, v. a. To drop, to trickle, to shed. *Mar tue moy nys lewyth man, rág nown y wrons clamderé, yn úr-na rág púr dhwan daggrow tyn gwrûf dyveré*, if more come, it will not be enough, for hunger they will faint, at that time, for very sorrow, bitter tears I shall shed. O.M. 402. Written also *devery*, qd. v. W. *dyveru*. Comp. of *dy*, prefix intens., and *meru*, to drop. Arm. *divera*.

DYVEAS, adj. Abroad, outside. ‡ *Dho towla dyveas*, to throw out. Llwyd, 51. Comp. of *dy*, to, and *meas*, id. qd. *més*, a field.

DYVETH, adj. Shameless. See *Diveth*.

DYVEYTH, s. m. A wilderness. *Ke dhe vés, omscumunys, dhe dhyveyth véth yn tewolgow*, go thou away, accursed, to a wilderness ever into darkness. M.C. 17. Another form of *difeid*, qd. v.

DYVOTTER, v. pass. Is become. *Ny wodhen rág ponvotter, pŷ'th een yn gweel py yn cós; ow holon gwák dyvotter, rum lymmer hag awel bós*, I know not from trouble whether we shall go into a field or wood; my heart is become empty and a desire of food has seized me. O.M. 365. This is a very doubtful word, and I can suggest nothing better than making it a passive impersonal from W. *dyvod*, to come.

DYVYTHYS, part. Come, arrived. *Râg dhe vones dyvythys yn hanow Dew bynyggys, me a grŷs dhe vôs deffry*, for that thou art come in the name of the blessed God, I believe thou art really. P.C. 280. *Máp Dew ôs, ha dên yn weydh, yn y hanow dyvythys*, Son of God thou art, and man likewise, in his name come. P.C. 426. Written also *devedhys*, qd. v. It must be formed from W. *dyvod*, to come.

DYW, s. m. God. *Bytegyns reys yw cryggy Ihesu Cryst dhe dhasserchy, del yw gwŷr Dhyw*, nevertheless need is to believe that Jesus Christ has risen again, as he is true God. R.D. 1018. More frequently written *Du*, and *Dew*, qd. v.

DYW, s. f. Two, a pair, a couple. *Otté pynsor da parys; me a's ten a dhysempys, an dhyw yn mês a'y dhywlé, hag a'y dhew trôs kekyffrys*, behold a good pincer ready; I will draw them immediately, the two out of his hands, and from his feet also. P.C. 3153. It refers to the nails in the preceding sentence, *kenter* being feminine. So Welsh *dwy, y dhwy*.

DYW, adj. Two. Used with substantives feminine, as *dew* is with masculines. *Oll y pobel ymôns y orth y syué pûp huny, ha'n môr a pûp tu dhedhé ow sevel avel dyw fôs*, all his people, they are following him every one; and the sea on every side to them standing like two walls. O.M. 1690. *Ple gefyr dyw grows arall râk an dew ladar, levereuch dhym, cowethé*, where shall be found two other crosses for the two thieves? tell me, comrades. P.C. 2576. *Ha why kelmoch an dew gam yn dyw crows kyns bôs prŷs bôs*, and bind ye the two rogues on two crosses, before it is time for food. P.C. 2754. Written in the Cornish Vocabulary, *dui*, qd. v. W. *divy*, †*dui*. Arm. *diou*. Sansc. *dvê*.

DYWEDH, s. m. An end, or termination. See *Diwedh*, and its derivatives.

DYWEN, s. m. The gills. *Wel y met harlot iowdyn, ty a fŷdh boxsesow tyn war an dywen*, well met, obstinate knave, thou shalt have sharp blows on the gills. P.C. 1368. Comp. of *dyw*, two, and *gên*, chin. Written also *dewen*. W. *dwyen*. Arm. *diu guen*.

DYWENYS, part. Descending. *Ha war voles, pan vyrys, my a welas hy gwrydhyow bŷs yn yffarn dywenys yn mŷsk mûr a tewolgow*, and at the bottom, when I looked, I saw its roots even to hell descending, in the midst of great darkness. O.M. 784. If not formed from *dyscynys*, it may be derived from *down*, deep.

DYWES, s. f. Drink. See *Diwes*.

DYWETH, s. m. An end. *Râk an porthow hep dyweth a vŷdh ygerys yn wêdh may'th ello abervedh an mychtern a lowené*, for the everlasting gates shall be opened also, that may enter in the king of joy. R.D. 101. See *Diwedh*.

DYWETHA, adj. Last, utmost. Lluyd, 175. Written also *diwedha*. W. *diwedhav, diwaetha*. Arm. *divera*.

DYWETHAS, adv. Late. Lluyd, 149. W. *diwedhar*. Arm. *divezud*.

DYWHANS, adv. Eagerly, quickly, fast. *A rác dywhans ow kerdhes*, forth quickly walking. O.M. 1684. *Gwercs dywhans, my a'd pŷs, ow fysadow dres pûp tra*, help quickly, I pray thee, my prayers above every thing. O.M. 1829. *Judas ny gôsk un banné, lymmyn dywans fystyné dhum ry dhe'n fals Yedhewon*, Judas does not sleep a bit, but quickly hastens to give me to the false Jews. P.C. 1079. *Fystyn dywhans gous en gêr a dhesempys*, hasten thou swiftly with the word immediately. P.C. 1642. Written also *dewhans*, and *duwhans*. Comp. of *dy*, prefix intens., and *whans*, a desire, eagerness. W. *dychwant*.

DYWHY, pron. prep. To you. (*Do-chuy*.) *Del levaraf vy dhywhy, vf a emblodh ragon ny*, as I say to you, he will fight for us. O.M. 1660. *Râg ow querthé Crist dhywhy, me re beches marthys mûr*, for selling Christ to you, I have sinned wondrous greatly. P.C. 1517. *Me a lever dhywhy why, ol warbarth dôn dustuny bôs Cryst a'n bêdh dasserchys*, I say to you, all together to bear witness that Christ is risen from the tomb. R.D. 1225. Written also *dywy*. *Perthewch côf ol an tokyn a leverys kyns lemyn dhywny why, a gowethé*, bear ye all remembrance of the token, which I told before now to you, O companions. P.C. 1083.

DYWHYNY, v. n. To shine. *An eledh omma yw gwyn, avel an houl pan dhywhyn, yn ken lyw ny's gwylys whêth*, the angels here are white, like the sun when it shines; in other form I have not seen them. R.D. 2533. W. *dynrynu*, from *dy*, intens. prefix, and *gwyn*, white, bright.

DYWLE, s. f. The two hands, the hands. *Un profus bynygys yn grows, ha dhyw vrêch a lês, squerdys y treys ha'y dhywlé*, a blessed prophet on a cross, and his two arms extended, torn his feet and hands. R.D. 1266. *Doro dhe luef yn woly, gwynys may fuef dre an golon; hag yn treys hag yn dhywlé*, put thy hand into the wound where I was pierced through the heart; and in my feet and hands. R.D. 1542. *Y fue ow manegow plat, spyggys brâs dre ow dywlé*, and my smooth gloves were great spikes through my hands. R.D. 2590. This is an abbreviated form of *dywlef*.

DYWLEF, s. f. The two hands, the hands. Written also *dywluif*. *A tâs whêk ol caradow, ow dynoluef colm ha'm garrow*, O sweet father, all beloved, bind my hands, and my legs. O.M. 1340. *Yn pren crows bedhens gorrys, ha treys ha dywlef kelmys, ha gwenys dre an golon, on the cross tree let him be put, and feet and hands bound, and pierced through the heart. P.C. 2375. *Treys ha dywlef a pûp tu fast tackyes gans kentrow hern*, feet and hands fast fixed with iron nails. P.C. 2937. Another form of *duilof*, qd. v. W. *dwylaw*, †*duilof*.

DYWOLOW, s. m. Devils, fiends. One of the plurals of *diawl*, qd. v. *Dywolow yfarn a squerdyas corf Judas ol dhe dharnow*, the devils of hell tore the body of Jesus all to pieces. M.C. 106. *My a grŷs y fŷdh agan ewsfow dre lewnrow Dew mygys, ha fethys an dywolow*, I believe that our souls shall be fed by the words of God, and the devils overcome. P.C. 77.

DYWORTO, pron. prep. From him, or it. (*Dyworth-o*.) *Dyworto ma'm boma grâs, môs dhe blansé my a vyn en gweel gans reonté urâs*, from him if have grace, I will go to plant the rods with great care. O.M. 2077. *Lemman lorch nêp a'n geffo, gorrens y scryp dyworto*, now he who has a staff, let him put his scrip from him. P.C. 920. *Arluth why a herch dhodho, an queth dysky dhyworto, hep na moy gêr*, Lord, do you command him, to take the cloth from him without any further word.

R.D. 1948. W. *odhiwrtho* Arm. *dioutaff.* Ir. *uadh*, †*uad*, †*ood*, *uadhasan.* Manx, *veihsyn.*

DYWORTY, pron. prep. From her, or it. *(Dyworth-hy.)* *Fenten bryght avel arhans, ha pedyr streyth vrâs defry ow resek a dyworty, worté myres may'th o whans,* a fountain bright like silver, and four great streams indeed flowing from it, that there was a desire to look at them. O.M. 773. W. *odhiwrthi.* Arm. *diouty.* Ir. *uaithe, uaithi.*

DYWORTH, prep. From by, from. *(Dy-worth.) Gwyn agan beys, ow fryes, bôs granntyes dhynny cummyes dywort an tâs Dew gwella, dhe bales, ha dhe wonys.* happy our lot, my husband, that there is leave granted to us from the best Father, God, to dig, and to cultivate. O.M. 413. *An gwêl a rûs dhyworth an lûr gwrâf dhe drehy,* the rods of grace from the ground I will cut. O.M. 1987. *Gallos varnaf ny fyes, na fe y vôs grantys dhys dyworth uhella Arloth,* power over me there would not be, were it not that it was granted from the most high Lord. P.C. 2189. Written also *deworth*, qd. v. W. *odhiwrth.* Arm. †*diouz.* Ir. *ua.* Gael. *uu.* Manx, *veih.*

DYWORTHE, pron. prep. From them. *(Dyworth-y.) Gwelynny a gymmys râs; dhyworthé ma gan bo grâs, aga malyé me a vyn yn cendel hag yn ourlyn,* rods of so much grace; from them that ours may be the grace, I will wrap them in fine linen, and in silk. O.M. 1749. W. *odhiwrthynt*, †*ywrthynt*. Ir. *uatha,* †*uaidib.*

DYWORTHYF, pron. prep. From me. *(Dyworth-my.) Mar callé bôs yn della, gorré an kêth mernans-ma dhyworthyf, na vûf ledhys,* if it can be so, put this same death from me, that I be not slain. P.O. 1036. *Fystyn dywhans gans cn gêr a dhesempys, ha rewardys ty a vgdh a dhyworthyf vy, rum fydh, kyns pen vfs,* hasten swiftly with the word immediately; and rewarded thou shalt be, on my faith, before the end of a month. P.C. 1645. Written also *dyworthef. Yma ow trŷs ha'm dulé dhyworthef ow teglené,* my feet and hands are loosening from me. P.C. 1217. W. *odhiwrthyv.* Ir. *uaim*, †*uaimse.*

DYWORTHYN, pron. prep. From us. *(Dyworth-ny.) Mar a mynné amendyé, gwell vye y dhylyfryé kep drocoleth dhyworthyn,* if he would amend, it would be better to liberate him without ill deed from us. P.C. 1564. *Arluth kêr, fattel vfdh dyn, mars cth arté dhyworthyn?* dear Lord, how will it be to us, if thou wilt go again from us? R.D. 2362. W. *odhiwrthym.* Ir. *uainn*, †*huanni*, †*uain,* †*uanni.*

DYWORTHYS, pron. prep. From thee. *(Dyworth-ty.) Godhfos gwŷr ol yredy, my a vyn môs dhyworthys,* knowing the truth all plainly, I will go from thee. O.M. 822. *My a's pren dhyworthys, otté an moné parys dhyso dhe pé,* I will buy it from thee; see the money ready to pay thee. P.C. 1555. W. *odhiwrthyt.* Ir. *uait*, †*uaitsiu.*

DYWSCODH, s. f. The two shoulders, the shoulders. *Sytleuch gystys worth an yet, agas dywscodh kettep chet, hertheuch worty hy yn wêdh,* put beams against the gate, your shoulders, every fellow, thrust ye against it also. P.C. 3068. See *Dyw*, and *Scôdh.*

DYWVRECH, s. f. The two arms, the arms. *Krêf yw gwerydhyow an spedhes, may 'thyw ow dyuvrech ierrys worté menouch yn quethé,* strong are the roots of the briars, that my arms are broken, working much at them. O.M. 688. *Kyn fe dhe dhywvrech mar brâs, my a's kylm warbarth avel lader pûr,* though thy arms be so large, I will bind them together like a very thief. P.C. 1189.

Drou' e yntré ow dywvrech, bring him into my arms P.C. 3159. W. *dwyuraich.*

DYWY, v. a. To kindle, to set on fire, to burn. Written also *dewy. Yma marth dhym a ur. dra. an pyth lemmyn a wela; an bosnos dynoy a wra, saw nynsugy ow lesky,* there is to me a wonder of one thing, what I now see; the bush is on fire, but is not burning. O.M. 1397. *Otté an tân ow tewy,* behold the fire burning. P.C. 693. *Cowethé hedheuch cunys, ha me a whfth gans mûr greys, may tewé an tân wharré,* comrades, fetch firewood, and I will blow with much force, that the fire may kindle soon. P.C. 1221. W. *deivio.* Arm. *devi.* Ir. *dagh,* †*doigh, doith.* Gael. *doth, dath.* Manx, *daah.* Sansc. *dah.*

DYWY', pron. prep. To ye. *(De, dhe to,—why, yc.) Pertheuch côf ol a'n tokyn a leverys kyns lemyn dhywy why, a gowethé,* bear ye all remembrance of the (token) I told before now to you, O companions. P.C. 1083. *Honna yw y bows nessa, ha whêth greuch y dhry omma arté dhywhy,* that is his nearest garment, and do you yet bring him here again to you. R.D. 1869.

DYWYDHYS, part. Ended, finished. *Yn nêf agas enefow neffré a trŷg hep ponow yn joy na vfdh dywydhys,* in heaven your souls ever shall dwell without pains in joy (that) shall not be ended. P.C. 9. *Ens pop ol war tuhé dré, an gwary yw dywydhys, ha deuch avar avorow,* let all go towards home, the play is ended; and come ye early to-morrow. P.C. 3238. *Aban oma dasserchys, dew hugens deydh dywoydhys bfdh pan fo nôs,* since I am risen, forty days ended will be when it is night. R.D. 2437. Part. of *diwedhé*, qd. v.

DYWYS, v. a. To choose, to select. Part. pass. *dywysys. Ma' gas bo lowyné nef, pân vyrwyf, dh'agas enef, dywysys ouch dewdhek lel,* that yonrs may be the joy of heaven when I die, to your souls, ye are chosen faithful twelve. P.C. 228. *Ny gewsyth, rák ny wodhns bôs grontys dhym gallos brâs hydhew may hallaf dywys,* thou speakest not, for thou didst not know, that great power is granted to me, this day that I may choose. P.C. 2182. *Benet sewys, syre Longys, synt Iovyn whêk re'th caro; henna yw pfth a dhywys,* a blessing follow thee, Sir Longius, sweet saint Jove love thee; that is what I choose. P.C. 3017. Written also *dewesy*, qd. v.

DYWYSYC, adj. Desirous, earnest, devout. *Thomas, na vydh dyncrygyk, pfs gans colon dywysyk war Cryst an nêf,* Thomas, be not unbelieving; pray with devout heart on Christ of heaven. R.D. 1370. W. *dyhewydus. Gwedhiau dyhewydus,* devout prayers.

DYWYTH, adv. Twice. *Moyses, kemer dhe welen, ha ty ha'th vroder Aren, a rôg an debel bobnl, gwask gynsy dywyth an mên,* Moses, take thy rod, and thou and thy brother Aaron, in presence of the wicked people, strike with it twice the stone. O.M. 1844. *Aban rês an brûs unwyth, ny fynnaf y ry dywyth,* since I have given the judgment once, I will not give it twice. P.C. 2496. Comp. of *dyw*, two, and *gwŷth,* a time. W. *dwywaith.*

DZHARN, s. m. A garden, an orchard. Lhoyd, 33, 66. This is more immediately derived from the *Fr. jardin.* W. *gardh*, †*garth*, an inclosure, a garden; whence *garthan,* a camp; *buarth*, a cow-yard; *lluarth*, a camp. Arm. *garz.* Ir. *gardha,* †*gart.* Gael. *garadh, gard.* Manx, *garey.* Gr. χόρτος. Lat. *hortus.* Goth. *gard.* Slav. *grad.* Eug. *yard.* Sansc. *garhan,* fr. *garh,* to enclose.

DZHEDH, s. m. A day. This orthography is used by

Llwyd to denote the sound of the word in his time. It is a corruption of *dédh*, qd. v. ‡*Rag an dzhédh*, for the day, or the whole day. ‡*Rag dout na vedho na mui gythefflaz dhyu' rag an dzhedhma*, lest there be no more offered to you this day. Llwyd, 250.

DZHEI, pers. pron. They. ‡ *Ena dzhei a varginiaz rag trei penz an vledhan guber*, so they bargained for three pounds the year wages. Llwyd, 247. It is also written by him *dzhyi*, as *An dzhyi a gánz*, they shall have. 247. It is a late form of *y*, qd. v.

DZHIAWL, s. m. A devil. Llwyd, 55. See *Jiawl*.

DZHOWLES, s. f. A female fiend, a she devil, a fury, a hag. Pryce. A late form of *diowles*, qd. v.

DZHYI, v. adv. In, within. Llwyd, 249. An abbreviated form of *adzhyi*, qd. v.

DZHYRNA, s. m. A day. ‡*Cynifar dzhyrna*, day by day, daily. Llwyd, 135. ‡*An dzhyrna-ma war seithan*, this day seven-night. 249. This is derived from the Fr. *journee*, a word still used in the English *journeyman*. The Welsh equivalent *diurnod* seems to be derived from the Latin *diurnus*, or *diuturnus*.

DH.

THIS is a secondary letter, and is the soft mutation of *d*, as *davas*, a sheep; *an dhavas*, the sheep. W. *davad*, *y dhavad*. C. *deanc*, *dhe dheanc*, to escape. W. *dianc*, *dhianc*. It is written in Armoric *z*, and so pronounced generally, but the proper sound is still preserved in parts of Britanny. Thus C. *debry*, *dhe dhebry*, is in Arm. *dibri*, *da zibri*. C. *dewdhec*, and W. *deunhcg* (*daudeg*,) twelve; in Arm. *daouzek*. The proper sound of *dh* is preserved in its purity in Welsh, and it is that of *th*, in the English words, *this*, *that*, *those*. The same mutation obtains in Irish and Gaelic, thus—Ir. *dadheag*; Gael. *dadheug*, twelve. The orthography is preserved, but the sound is corrupted into those of *gh*, *y*, *ee*, *vo*. The Manx again write phonetically, whence *gaa-yeig*, twelve; *dooinney*, a man; *e ghooinney*, his man. All Cornish words beginning with *dh*, as *dhe*, to; *dhedhy*, to her; *dhodho*, to him, &c., must be sought for under the primary initial, as *de*, *dedhy*, *dodho*, &c. The Cornish *dh* is generally written *th* in the MSS.

E.

THIS letter has only two sounds, in Cornish, Welsh, Armoric, and Manx—the long and short. When long it has the sound of *a*, in the English words, *lane*, *cane*; thus C. *dén*, a man; *név*, heaven, were sounded as the Eng. words, *dane*, *nave*. The long *é* is distinguished in this work by a circumflex. *E* short, was pronounced as in the English words, *fen*, *hen*, *pen*. In Cornish, *e* is constantly confounded with *y*, as in *dédh*, *dýdh*, a day; *dehow*, *dyhow*, the right, &c. In Welsh again, where *y* is now written, in early manuscripts, *e* is generally found. *E* is commutable with *o*, as *corn*, a horn; *cerniad*, a horn blower. So also in Welsh, as *corn*, pl. *cyrn*; *cyrniad*, †*cerniad*. And in Armoric, as *corn*, pl. *cern*, *cerniel*.

E, an auxiliary particle, used before verbs, in which case it is the same as *a*, similarly used. Not unfrequently it is joined to the verb, as *Dew ewyr* for *Dew e wyr*, God knoweth. It is also used alone with a verb, when it is the agent performing the action described without discrimination of persons, as *edal*, or *e dál*, it behoves.

E, pron. pers. He, him, it. *Agis negis pyth yw e ? pu yw néb a weleuch wy ?* your business, what is it? who is he that ye seek? M.C. 69. *Dremas yw ef, leun a rás, neb re wyrthys, yn medh e*, supremely good he is, full of grace, whom I have sold, says he. M.C. 103. *Ol warbarth y a ylwys, te Pylat, lâdh e, mernans an grows desympys*, altogether they cried, thou Pilate kill him, the death of the cross immediately. M C. 142. *Syr Justis, ládhe, ládh e, yn pren grows greuch y worré, del yw e gwyw dyougel*, Sir Justice, kill him, kill him, on the cross tree do you put him, as he is deserving truly. P.C. 2356. *Ha compys mar ny védh e, ny won pandra leveryn*, and if it be not straight, I know not what I may say. O.M. 2531. *Ilédh e dhe'n dôr*, reach it to the ground. O.M. 2521. Written also *ef, ev*. W. *ef, ev, e*, †*em*. Arm. *he*. Ir. *se, e*, †*he*. Gael. *se, e*. Manx. *eh*. Sansc. *i, idam, sva*. Gr. *ë*. Lat. *se*.

E, pron. poss. His, its. *Why gwycoryon, euch yn més, ythesouch ow kuthyl ges a Dhu, hag e sans eglos*, ye traders, go out; ye are making a jest of God, and his holy church. P.C. 333. *May fýdh torrow benegis bythqueth na allas e dhôn*, that the bellies shall be blessed, that could not bear it. M.C. 169. ‡*War e lêr*, after him. Llwyd, 124. ‡*E vredar*, his brother. 242. *E risc*, its bark. ‡*Et e üs céth*, in his old age. 244. ‡*E vréh*, his arm. 250. In the Ordinalia it is written *y*, qd. v. W. *ei*, †*e*, †*i*. Arm. *e. he*. Ir. *a*. Gael. *a*. Manx. *e*.

E, prep. In. *E méas*, without. Llwyd, 58. Lit. in the field. *E* is here the same as *y*, an abbreviation of *yn*, and the more common form is *yn més*, qd. v.

E, v. n. He went, was going. 3 pers. s. imp. of irr. v. *mós*. *War aga dewlyn yth e perag Christ ré erell, aga fen y a zickyé, hag a gewsy, pür debell*, on their knees there went before Christ some others, their head they shook, and spake very foully. M.C. 195. *Hag y ee dhe pen dewlyn, ha hager mowys a wre*, and they went on their knees, and made ugly mouths. M.C. 190. W. *ai*.

EAL, s. m. An angel. *An eal esa in wedhun, y cowsys gyrryow efan, ha me a'n creys*, the angel (that) was in the tree, spoke to me plain words, and I believe him. C.W. 60. More frequently written *él*, qd. v.

EAR, s. m. An hour. *Ha pan vo hy cowl devys, hy a vŷdh pûb ear parys dha dhôn an oyl a vercy*, and when it is full grown, it will always (every hour) be ready, to bear the oil of mercy. C.W. 134. The same as *ér*, qd. v.

EARTH, adj. High, lofty. It occurs in the names of places, as *Earth*, in St. Stephens, by Saltash; and *Earth*, on Carminow, in Mawgan. It is another form of *arth*, or *ard*, qd. v.

EAST, s. m. August. *Mis East*, the month of August. ‡*Fló vye gennes en mis Merh, ni trehes e bigel en mis East*; *e a rôs towl dho proanter Powl, mis du ken Nadelik*, a child was born in the month of March, we cut his navel in the month of August; and he gave a fall to the parson of Paul, the black month (November) before the Nativity. *Cornish Riddle*. Pryce. W. *awst*. Arm. *eost*. Ir. *ogost*. Fr. *aout*, †*aoust*. From the Lat. *augustus*.

EATH, card. num. Eight. *Eath degves*, eighteenth. *Pryce.* W. *wyth.* Arm. *eiz.* Ir. *ocht*, †*oct.* Gael. *ocht.* Manx, *hocht.* Gr. ὀκτώ. Lat. *octo.* Sansc. *ashtan.* In Welsh, *wyth* preceding requires the change of *b* into *m*, as *wyth mlynedh*, eight years. The same rule obtains in Irish, as *ocht m-bliadna*, the *b* being mute.

EATHAS, adj. Eighth. *Pryce.* Written by Llwyd, 105. *ethas.* W. *wythved.* Arm. *eizved.* Ir. *ochtmhadh.* Gael. *ochdamh.* Manx, *hochtoo.*

EBARN, s. m. The sky, the firmament. ‡*Ha Dew wrûs an ebbarn, ha dheberkus an dowrow era en dadn an ebbarn, dhort an dowrow era euch an ebbarn; ha an dellnn etho,* and God made the firmament, and divided the waters that were under the firmament, from the waters above the firmament; and it was so. C.W. p. 189; M.C. p. 93. A late form of *ebron*, qd. v.

EBBROW, adj. Hebrew. *Flechos Ebbrow, dûn yn un rew, scon hep lettyé, erbyn Ihesu, nêb yw gwŷr Dew, ow tôs dhe'n dré,* Hebrew children, let us come in a row, at once, without delaying, to meet Jesus, who is true God, coming to the town. P.C. 239. W. *evrei.* Arm. *hebré.* Ir. *eabhradhach.* Gael. *eabhruidheach, eabhrach.* Lat. *hebræus.*

EBIL, s. m. A peg, or pin. *Yntré dew guren y trohy, rák cufius trûs pren dedhy, ha'y fastyé gans ebyl pren,* in two let us cut it, for to get a cross piece of wood for it, and fasten it with pegs of wood. P.C. 2563. *Y delly scon me a vera, rák ebyl parys yma, dh'aga fustyé dyowgel,* I will soon bore it, for there are pegs ready, to fasten them truly. P.C. 2571. *Aban yw an pren tellys, bedhens an ebyl gorrys dredhé, rág aga lacié,* since the wood is bored, let the pegs be put through them, to fasten them. P.C. 2574. W. *ebill,* †*epill.* Arm. *ebil.*

EBOL, s. m. A colt, a foal. Corn. Voc. *pullus.* Written in the Ordinalia *ebel*, and more recently *ebal*, pl. *ebilli. Ens dew a'm dyscyblyon dhe'n castel us a ragon, a dhysempys, hep lettyé; ena why a gŷf asen, hag ebel yn un golmen, drew y dhymmo vy wharré,* let two of my disciples go to the village which is before us, forthwith, without delaying; there ye will find an ass and foal in a halter, bring them to me presently. P.C. 177. *My â gynes yn lowen, hag a dhoro an asen genen, ha'n ebel keffrys,* I will go with thee gladly, and will bring the ass with us, and the foal likewise. P.C. 193. *Ottè an asen omma, ha'n ebel kelmys yma gynsy,* behold the ass here, and the foal is tied with her. P.C. 201. *Rág ythostn drôk ebal,* for thou art a wicked colt. C.W. 174. *Trûs ebal,* the herb colt's foot. Llwyd, 168. In Welsh, *earn yr ebol,* lit. colt's hoof. W. *ebawl, ebol,* †*ebaul,* †*epaul.* Arm. *ebeûl.* The root of W. *ebol,* is *eb* = Old Irish †*ech,* id. qd. Lat. *equus.* Ir. *peall, feall,* a horse. Gr. πῶλoς. Lat. *pullus.* Sansc *pêlin,* a horse, from *pêl,* to go.

EBRAL, s. m. April. *Mís Ebral,* the month of April. Llwyd, 43. W. *ebrill.* Arm. *ebrel.* Ir. *aibrean.* Gael. †*aibreann.* From the Latin *aprilis.*

EBRON, s. f. The sky, the firmament. *Yn secund dŷdh y fynna gruthyl ebron, nêf hynwys,* on the second day I will make the sky called heaven. O.M. 18. *Ow gwarak a fŷdh settyys yn ban yn creys an ebren na allo bones terrys,* my bow shall be set up in the midst of the sky, that it may not be broken. O.M. 1245. Written also *ybron*, and *ybbern,* qd. v., and in Corn. Voc. *huibren.* W. *wybr,* *wybren.* Arm. *ebr,* †*coabr,* †*coabren.* (Ir. *spcir.* Gael. *speur.* Manx, *speyr.*) Sansc. *abhra, vâibhra.*

ECHEN, s. f. A tribe, family, kind, sort. *Lavar dhymmo, ty venen, an frût ple russys tyrry? mara pc a'n kêth echen, o dyfynnys orthyn ny,* tell me, thou woman, where didst thou break off the fruit? was it of that same sort, (that) was forbidden to us? O.M. 211. *Ha nŷr a pûp tenewen; aspy yn ta pûp echen, whythyr pûp tra ol bysy,* and look on every side; examine well every particular; search out every thing diligently. O.M. 747. *Kemer dhe wrêk ha'th flehus, h'aga gwragedh gor gansé; a bûb echen bêst yn wlâs, gor genes dew annedhé,* take thou thy wife and thy children, and put their wives with them; of every sort of beast in the land, put two of them with thee. O.M. 977. *Lyes torn da yn bŷs-ma re wrûk dhe vohosnggyon; sawyé pûp echen clefyon a vewhé yn bewnans da,* many a good turn in this world he hath done to the poor; he cured all sorts of sick persons, who lived in good life. P.C. 3109. Written also *eken, hechen, hehen,* qd. v. W. *echen,* from *ach,* a stem.

ECHEN, s. f. Effort, endeavour, rigour. *Mar scon dhodho del ymmy, kychouch ef yn vryongen, ha dalynnouch mûr cales, ma na allo perthe ges yn dyspyd ol dh'y echen,* as soon as thou kissest him, catch him in the throat, and hold ye very firmly, that he cannot escape in spite of all his effort. P.C. 1010. Written also *hechen, hehen,* qd. v. W. *egni.* Arm. *heg, hek.* Ir. *eigean,* ing, †*eene,* †*æene,* †*aithgne,* †*edgne.* Gael. *eigin.* Manx, *egin, eign,* †*eignee.* Sansc. *can,* to act. Gr. κονέω. Lat. *conor.*

ED, prep. In. This is a corruption of *en,* and is only met with in late Cornish. ‡*Gwigo an genter-ma ed eskaz vi,* knock this nail in my shoe. Llwyd, 230.

EDN, adj. Narrow, slender. Llwyd, 48. This must either be a corruption of W. *ing;* Arm. *enk;* Ir. †*ing;* Gael. *eigin;* or connected with W. *edwin,* decaying.

EDN, num. adj. One. A corrupt form of *un,* qd. v. ‡ *Edn degvas,* eleventh. *Pryce.*

EDNAC, card. num. Eleven. A late form of *unnek.* W. *unardheg.* Arm. *unnek.* Ir. *aon deag.* Gael. *aon deug.* Manx, *unnaneieig.* Gr. ἕνδεκα. Lat. *undecim.*

EDNAC, adj. Sole, alone. ‡*En ednak,* only. Llwyd, 56. A corruption of W. *unig,* id.

EDREC, s. m. Repentance, grief, sorrow. Pl. *edregé. Eddrek múr a'n kemeras, rák an ober re wressed; dh'y ben dowlyn y codhas, Arluth govyans, yn medh e, dall én, ny welyn yn fâs ow bôs mar veyl ow pewé; Ihesus dhodho a avas, pan welas y edregé,* great sorrow seized him, for the work he had done; to his knees he fell, Lord, forgiveness, says he; blind I was, I saw not well, that I was living so vilely; Jesus forgave him when he saw his sorrows. M.C. 220. *Codhys ôf yn edrek brûs,* fallen I am in great sorrow. P.C. 1440. *Govy ejth rák edregé, bôs mar hager ow gorfen,* woe is me for sorrows, that my end is so cruel. P.C. 1529. *Yma dhym edrek tyn, rák dhe naché gy lemmyn,* there is to me sharp repentance, for denying thee now. R.D. 1155. *Peder, geffyens ty a fŷdh, rák dhe eddrek yw perfyth, dré'n Spirys Sans,* Peter, pardon thou shalt have, for thy repentance is perfect, through the Holy Ghost. R.D. 1160. W. *edweirweh.* Arm. *asveh.* Ir. *aithreach,* †*aidrech,* †*aithirge.* Gael. *aithreachas.* Goth. *idreiga.*

EDHANOR, s. m. A fowler. Llwyd, 44. Arm. *eznelaer, eunelaer.* Ir. *eanadoir.* Gael. *eunadair.* Manx, *eeauleyder.*

EDHEN, s. f. A bird, a fowl. Pl. *edhyn*. *A out warnes, drók venen, worto pan wrussys colé, râg ef o tebel edhen, nêb a glewsys ow cané*, Oh, out upon thee, wicked woman, when thou didst listen to him ; for he was an evil bird, whom thou didst hear singing. O.M. 223. *Yn pympes dýdh me a vyn may fo formyys dre ow nel bestes, puskes, hag edhyn, týr ha môr dhe goullenwel*, on the fifth day I will that be made by my power beasts, fishes, and birds, land and sea to fill. O.M. 43. *Lemyn hanwaf goydh ha yâr, a sensaf edhyn hep pâr dhe vygyens dên vor an beys*, now I name goose and hen, (which) I esteem birds without equal, for food of man on the earth. O.M. 130. *A pûp best kemmyr wharé gorow ha benow defry ; ol an edhyn ow nygé quel copel may kemery*, of all beasts take thou forthwith a male and a female really ; of all the birds flying be careful that thou take a couple. O.M. 1023. *An golom glús hy lagas, yn mês gwrn hy delysfré ; lellé edhen, ren-ow-thas, leverel ny won plc fe*, the dove with blue eyes, do thou liberate outside ; a more faithful bird, by my father, I cannot say where there is. O.M. 1111. In the Cornish Vocabulary, it is written *hethen*. W. *eden*, pl. *ednod ;* †*etin,* †*etn,* pl. †*etinel,* †*atinel.* Arm. *czn, evn, ein, eun.* Ir. *eun, ean,* †*en.* Gael. *eun.* Manx, *eean*, pl. *ein.* Sansc. *áti.* Gr. δωνὸν.

EDHOW, s. m. A Jew. Pl. *Edhewon. Un Edhow a brederys, hag a leverys dhedhé, bonas pren yn doar tevolys a ws yn houl na vyé ; râg an grows yth o ordnys, ha'n Edhewon ny wodhyé*, a Jew bethought, and said to them, that there was a piece of wood in the ground cast above in the sun that had not been ; for the cross it was ordained, and the Jews knew it not. M.C. 152. *Un Edhow dhodho yn freth yn delma a leverys*, a Jew to him strongly in this manner said. M.C. 239. *Ha'n Edhewon a gewsys, pandr' ew henna dhynny ny*, and the Jews said, what is that to us. M.C. 105. Written also *Yedhow, Yudhow,* qd. v. W. *Iudhew,* pl. *Iudhewon ;* †*Idhew*. Arm. *Juzed.* Ir. *Uii,* (for *Uidh,*) *Juduighe,* †*Judide.* Gael. *Judhach.* Manx, *Ew.* Lat. *Judæus.* Gr. Ἰονδαῖος

EF, pron. suhs. He, him, it. *Nêb a'm grûk vy ha'm gorty, ef a rûk agan dyfen, aval na wrellen dybbry*, he who made me and my husband, he did forbid us that we should not eat the apple. O.M. 182. *Dhynny ny travyth ny grêf, aban yw y vôdh ef y lesky hep falladow*, to us there is nothing grievous, since it is his will to burn it without fail. O.M. 483. *Ytho prâg na lenes ef kafus y dhegé hep grêf, hag aban vyn y lesky*, now why not leave him to have his tithe, without complaint, and burn it, since he will. O.M. 496. *Kymmer dhymmo ve kunys, gans lovan bedhens strothys, ha war dhe keyn doga ef,* take for me a load of fuel ; with rope let it be bound, and on thy back carry it. O.M. 1298. *Otté omma ve kunys, ha fast ef gynef kelmys*, see here a load of fuel, and fast it is bound by me. O.M. 1300. Written also *e*, and in Llwyd's time *ev.* W. *ev, e*.

EFAN, adj. Large, plain. *Ef a dhyswé dhywhy un skyber efan yn scon ; gwcyteuch dygtyé bôs ynny lour dh'agan soper ragon*, he will shew (you) a large room soon ; take yo care to prepare food in it, enough for our supper before us. P.C. 638. *Deuch gynef, me a dhyswé chy dh'agas mester wharré, rak parusy y soper ; effan, may hýl pûp mâp bron, ef hag ol y dhyskyblon, cafus y ês hep danger*, come with me, I will shew you a house for your master presently, for preparing his supper : large, that every son of the breast may, he and his disciples, take his case without delay. P.C. 676. *An eal esa yn wedhen, y cowsys gyrryow efan, ha me a'n creys*, the angel (that) was in the tree, spoke to me plain words, and I believe him. C.W. 60. *An planats ês a wartha, ha'n stér yn wôdh maga ta, ow poyntya môns pûr efan*, the planets that are on high, and the stars also as well, are pointing all very evidently. C.W. 156. W. *ehang.*

EFER, s. m. The loins. *Pryce.* A doubtful word.

EFFARN, s. m. Hell. Pl. *effarnow. Ow ena ny won pyth â, dha effarn yw y drigva, ena tregeans goâv, ha hâv*, my soul I know where it shall go, to hell is its dwelling, there to inhabit winter and summer. C.W. 122. *Dún ny warbarth, a gowrethé, dha effarnow a lema, dhe'n payns a dhewr nefré*, let us come together, O comrades, to hell from hence, to the pains that shall endure for ever. C.W. 150. Written also *yffarn*, qd. v.

EFFO, v. n. He may drink. 3 pers. s. subj. of *evé. Me a'n gor dhodho ; mar ny'n gorraf, an mŷl dyaul re dorro mellow y gýn, vynytha na effo coul*, I will take him to him ; if I do not take him, may a thousand devils break the joints of his back, so that he may never drink broth. P.C. 1620.

EFFREDH, adj. Maimed, disabled, lame. *Ha me effredh a'th pŷs, awos an Tás bynygeys, ro dhym ow cerdh dre dhe rás*, and I, maimed, pray thee, because of the blessed Father, give to me my walking through thy grace. P.C. 399. *Evredhec* is another form, qd. v. W. *evrydh.*

EFFYE, v. a. To flee, to escape, to flee away. *Pryce.* From the Latin *effugio ;* in the same manner as *fyé,* the more common form, is from Lat. *fugio.*

EFIN, s. m. June. *Lhuyd*, 33. *Mis Efin*, the month of June. This may be derived from Lat. *Junius,* though the Welsh equivalent may be formed from *hevin,* estival, from *hâv*, summer. W. *mehevin.* Arm. *mezeven.* Ir. *mi meodhain.* Gael. *mios meadhoin.*

EGE, v. subs. He was. 3 pers. s. imperf. of *bôs. A wylsta kên yn tor-ma ys del egé agensow?* dost thou see more now than as it was just now ? O.M. 796. *Pechadores es hep gow; an brassa egé yn pow gans pûp ol ty o gylwys*, a sinner thou art without a lie ; the greatest that was in the country by every body thou wast called. R.D. 1095. This is a corruption of *esé,* qd. v., by the substitution of *g* soft.

EGEN, v. subs. I was. 1 pers. s. imp. of *bôs. Arluth, ow tevos a Spayn, yth egen yn crês Almayn, orth un prys-ly, yn pûr-wŷr, pan fûf gylwys*, Lord, coming from Spain, I was in the midst of Germany, at a breakfast meal, very truly, when I was called. R.D. 2148. A corruption of *esen*, qd. v.

EGERY, v. subs. To open. *Dhys yth archaf, a dyreyth, gâs Adam dhe'th egery*, I command thee, O earth, allow Adam to open thee. O.M. 382. *Syr arluth kêr, cûf colon, egerys yw an pryson*, Sir, dear lord, loving heart, opened is the prison. P.C. 1878. *Ha'n bedhow owth egery, me a's gwêl, war ow ené*, and the graves opening, I see them, on my soul. P.C. 2999. *Scon egereuch an porthow, py mar my wreuch, y fŷdh guow*, immediately open ye the gates, or if ye do..not, there will be woes. R.D. 98. *A nyns esé ynnon ny agan colon ow lesky, pan wrûk an lara terry, ha'n scryptor y egyry*, Ah, was not within us our heart burning ? when he did break the bread, and open the Scripture. R.D. 1325. Written also *ugery*. qd. v. The 2 pers. s. imp., and 3 pers. s. fut. is generally written *uger*, and *ygor*, qd. v. W. *egori*. Arm. *egori*.

EGLOS, s. f. A church. Corn. Voc. *ecclesia*. It is written indiscriminately *egles, eglis, cylys*; pl. *eglysyow, eglusyow*. *War penakyll y'n goras dynntell dhe esedhé, a uch eglos t̂k yn velâs an ysedhva ythesa*, on a pinnacle he put him, hazardous to sit; above a fair church in the country the seat was. M.C. 13. *Why guycoryon, ruch yn mès; ythesouch ow kuthyl ges a Dhu, hag e sans eglos*, ye traders, go out; ye are making a jest of God, and his holy church. P.C. 333. *Pan dyskys yn eglusyow, ny wrûg dên fŷth ow sensy*, when I taught in the churches, no man did seize me. P.C. 1175. W. *eglwys*, † *eccluis*. Arm. *iliz*. Ir. *eaglais*, † *eclais*, † *toelis*. Gael. *eaglais*. Manx, *agglish*. All from Lat. *ecclesia*.

EGR, s. m. A daisy. *Egr dew*, id. Llwyd, 44. ‡ *Egr dzharn*, a garden daisy. *Pryce*. In Welsh it is called *llygnd y dydh*, eye of the day.

EGRUATH, v. a. To roll, to wallow. *Dho egruath*. Ll. 177.

EHAL, s. m. An angel. Llwyd, 12. Writ. also *eal*, qd. v.

EHAL, s. m. All manner of cattle. Corn. Voc. *pecus vel jumentum*.

EHAZ, s. m. Health. ‡ *Ma 'gen ehaz nyi dhen*, we have our health. Llwyd, 242. ‡ *Tho ve loan guz gwellas an ehaz dah*, I am glad to see you in good health. *Pryce*. A late form of *iaches*, qd. v.

EBEN, s. f. Kind, sort. *Ihesus Christ a leverys, dhe Dhu ny gôth dhys temptyé, yn nêb ehan a servys lemmyn prêst y honoré*, Jesus Christ said, thy God it does not become thee to tempt, but in every kind of service to honour him. M.C. 15. *Ha spycis lean ehen of a worras yn y vedh*, and spices many sorts he put in his grave. M.C. 236. Another form of *echen*, qd. v.

EHEN, s. f. Effort. *Bôst a urêus lyn ha deveth, y n gwythens worth y chen*, boast they made, great and shameless, that they would keep him against his effort. M.C. 242. Another form of *echen*, qd. v.

EHIDIT, s. m. A lark. Corn. Voc. *alauda*. W. *ehedydh*, (high-flyer.) Arm. *echouedes*.

EHOC, s. m. A salmon. Corn. Voc. *isicius vel salmo*. W. *eurg, eog*, † *ehauc*. Arm. *eog*, † *eauc*. Ir. *eo*, † *iach*. Gael. *eo*, † *iach*. Lat. *esox*.

EHUAL, adj. High, lofty. Llwyd, 42. Id. qd. *huhel*, qd. v.

EI, v. n. Thou shalt go. Llwyd, 247. Ti *ei*. W. *ai ei*.

EIL, adj. Second, another. *Pryce*. It is also used to signify one of two. See *Eyl*. W. *ail*, † *cil*. † *ala*. Gael. *eile*. Manx, *elley*. Gr. ἄλλος. Lat. *alius, alter*.

EITAG, unm. adj. Eighteen. Llwyd, 105. A corrupt form of *cythek, (eyth*, eight,—*dêk*, ten.) Eighteen is expressed in W. by *tri-ar-bymtheg*, (3+15,) and *deunaw*, (2x9.) In Armoric, by *tri-chouech*, (3x6.) Ir. *ocht-deag*, † *ocht deac*. Gael. *ocht-deug*. Manx, *hoght-jeig*. Gr. ὀκτὼ καί δέκα. Lat. *octodecim*.

EITHIN, s. m. Gorse, furze. Corn. Voc. *eythinen*, rampus. *Eithin* is a plural aggregate; a single *eithinen*, a single plant. *Bagas eithin*, a bush of furze. Llwyd, 56. *Eithinan*, id. 240. W. *eithin, eithinen*. Ir. *attin, aiteann*, † *aithinne*, † *athinne*. Manx, *aautin*.

EL, s. m. An angel. Pl. *eledh*. *Clewys a'n nyl tenewen un êl ow talleth cané*, I heard on one side an angel beginning to sing. O.M. 215. *My re voles y'm hunrus adhyragof êl dyblans*, I have seen in my dream before me a bright angel. O.M. 1955. *Râk y wordhyê an eledh a fue danfenys dhodho*, to worship him the angels were sent to him. P C. 3209. *Me a fyn cafus gynef kekeffrys eledh ha syns*, I will take with me also angels and saints. R.D. 190. *A eledh splan*, with bright angels. Llwyd, 249. Written also *eal*, and *eyl*. W. *êl*, pl. *elod*. Arm. *eal, el*. This word has been derived from the Latin *angelus*, but I do not assent to this theory, as I know of no instance of *ng* in a Latin word entirely disappearing when adopted in Welsh. The Latin words, *evangelium, angelus, angulus, unguentum*, are in Welsh, *evengyl, angel, ongyl, ennaint*. The *ng* is also preserved in the Ir. *aingiol*, † *aingel*. Gael. *aingeal*. I therefore conclude that *el* is a genuine Celtic term, whence *ellyll*, a demon, goblin, from *el*, an angel, and *hyll*, horrid. The root is *elu*, to proceed, to move on. Ir. *aill*, † *laigh*. Gael. *aill*. Sansc. *il*, lay. Compare also Ang. Sax. *ælf*, a spirit, with Swedish *elf*, and Danish *ëv*, (whence *Elbe*,) a river; and *spirit* is from blowing, a flowing of air.

ELAR, s. f. A bier. Llwyd, 17, 59. *Geler* is another form, qd. v. W. *elawr, elor, gelor*. Arm. *laour*. Ir. *eleatrain*.

ELAW, s. f. An elm. Llwyd, 175. W. *llwyv, 'lwyvan*. Arm. *evlech, uloch*. Ir. *leamhan, sleamhan, ailm*. Gael. *leamhan*. Manx, *llieuan*. Lat. *ulmus*.

ELERCH, s. m. A swan. Corn. Voc. *olor vel cignus*. W. *alarch*, pl. *eleirch*.

ELESCER, s. f. The shank, shin bone. Corn. Voc. *elescher*, tibia. The first syllable is strange, but *esker* is the W. *esgair*, † *esceir*, whence *Sisillus esceir hir*, Sitayllt longshanks. Giraldus Itin. Cambr. 2, 2. Arm. *esker*. Ir. *eisgir*, † *aisgeir*. Gael. † *aisguir*.

ELESTREN, s. f. A sedge, a flag. Corn. Voc. *carex*. Pl. *elester*. *Strail elester*, matta, a mat of sedges. W. *elestr*, pl. *elestren*, s. Arm. *elestr*, pl. *elestren*, s. Ir. *eleastar*, *siolastar, feleastar*. Gael. *seilisdeir*.

ELGERT, s. f. The chin. Corn. Voc. *mentum*. W. *elgeth, aelgerth*. Arm. *elget*.

ELIN, s. m. An angle, an elbow. Corn. Voc. *ungulus, ulna*. *Bŷdh wâr yn ta a'th elyn, y tuché, a ver termyn, gans ow clethê me a ura*, be well aware of thy elbow, touch it in a short time I will with my sword. P.C. 2310. W. *elin*. Arm. *elin, ilin*. Ir. *uilleann*. Gael. *uilean*. Manx, *uillin*. Gr. ὠλένη. Lat. *ulna*. Germ. *ellen bogen*. Eng. *elbow*.

ELL, v. n. He will be able. ‡ *Ne el e ge dibre*, he cannot eat them. Llwyd, 244. ‡ *N' ell e clewes vŷth*, he cannot hear at all. 249. ‡ *Huei el dendel 'gyz bownas ybma*, you may earn your living here. 251. Another form of *yll*, qd. v.

ELLAM, v. n. I am able. ‡ *Ello why clapier Kernuak? Me ellam*, can you speak Cornish? I can. *Pryce*. Written by Llwyd, 124, *ellim*. *Ni ellim*, I cannot. This is a late form of *allaf*, a mutation of *gallaf*, 1 pers. s. pres. and fut. of *gally*, qd. v.

ELLA, v. n. Went. *Bythqueth.dên ny wodhevys payn ella dh'y golon nês*, never man endured pain that went nearer to his heart. M.C. 172. Id. qd. W. *elai*, 3 pers. s. imp. of *elu*, to go.

ELLAS, v. n. He went. ‡ *Galarowedges yn dan Pontius Pilat, gorris war an grows dhe murnans, marow, hag yn-*

ELYN 134 EMPINION

clydhys, dhyn iffarn ef a ellas, suffered under Pontius Pilate, put on the cross to death, dead, and buried, he went to hell. *Pryce.* 3 pers. s. pret. of W. *elu,* to go.

ELLE, v. n. He might go. *Goyl ha gnorn dhodho ordnys, may 'th ellé yn mês an wlds,* sail and mast (were) for him ordained, that he might go out of the country. R.D. 2332. Id. qd. W. *elai,* 3 pers. s. subj. of *elu.*

ELLE, v. n. He was able. *Bresell créff a ve sordiys, en grows pu ellé dh'y dôn; dre vůr stryff y fé juggiys, y's degy Christ y honon,* a great contention was raised, the cross who should bear it; through much strife it was judged that Christ should carry it himself. M.C. 160. A mutation of *gellé,* 3 pers. s. imp. of *gally.* W. *gallai, a allai.*

ELLEN, v. n. I went. *Reys eo dhym kewsel defry orth ow gwrêk kyns môs a dré; mars ellen hep cows orty, hy holon hy a torsé,* I must speak really, to my wife before going from home; if I should go without speaking to her, her heart would break. O.M. 2173. 1 pers. s. imp. of W. *elu.*

ELLO, v. n. He may go. *Byth nyn gewyth fout a ioy, nêp a yl gwelas dhe fas, pan ello ow corf yn pry, gwyth ry râk an iowl, drôk wâs,* never shall he have lack of joy, who can see thy face; when my body goes to the earth, preserve me from the devil, evil wight. R.D. 1564. *Y a dollas dew doll yn grows heb kên, may'th ello an kentrow brâs dre y dhewleff bŷs yn pen,* they bored two holes in the cross, without compassion, so that might pass the great nails through his hands up to the head. M.C. 178. W. *elo,* 3 pers. s. subj. of *elu.*

ELLOH, v. n. Ye are able. ‡*Hwi elloh,* ye can. *Llwyd,* 247. Another form of *ellouch,* a mutation of *gellouch.* 2 pers. pl. fut. of *gally.* W. *galluch, a alluch.*

ELLYS, v. n. I was able. *An trygé dêdh yw hydhew, dhyworthyf aban êth e, whet ny ellys yn nêp tu godhfos ganso faiel fe,* the third day is to-day, since he went from me, yet I could not on any side know how it was with him. R.D. 467. A mutation of *gellys,* 1 pers. s. pret. of *gally.* W. *gallais, a allais.*

ELOW, v. a. He will cry. *Moyses, me re bechas, hag a henna a elow merey war Dew agan Tâs, may affo an pechasow,* Moses, I have sinned, and for this I cry mercy on God our Father, that he may forgive my sins. O.M. 1864. A mutation of *gelow,* 3 pers. s. fut. of *gelwel.* W. *geilw, a eilw.*

ELS, s. m. A son-in-law, a step-son. Corn. Voc. *privignus. Els* is probably connected with *llys,* or *lles,* in the equivalent W. *llysvab.* Arm. *lesvab.* Ir. *leasmhac,* †*lesmac.* Gael. *leasmhac.* Manx, *linsvac.*

ELSES, s. f. A daughter-in-law, a step-daughter. Coru. Voc. which erroneously interprets it by *filiaster,* a step-son, as it is evidently the feminine of *els.* W. *llysverch.* Arm. *lesverch.* Gael. *leasinghean.* Manx, *Nasvinncen.*

ELSIH, v. n. Ye were able. ‡*Hwi a elsih,* ye might. *Llwyd,* 247. A late form of *elsich,* a mutation of *gelsich,* 2 pers. pl. pret. of *gally.* W. *gallasoch, gallsoch, a allsoch.*

ELSIN, v. n. We were able. *Ni a elsin,* we might. *Llwyd,* 247. A mutation of *gelsin,* 1 pers. pl. pret. of *gally.* W. *gallasom, gallsom, a allsom.*

ELYN, adj. Clean, fair. *An môr brâs yn cutt termyn adro dhom tŷr a bŷdh dreys, râg y wetha pûr elyn orth harlutry prêst pûb preys,* the great sea in a short time about my earth shall be brought, to keep it very clean from corruption at all times. C.W. 8. W. *ellain.* Ir. *aluin.* Gael. *aluinn.* Manx, *aalin.*

EM, a particle prefixed to verbs, which reflects the action on the agent. Thus *gwyska,* to strike; *emwyska,* to strike one's self. It changes the initial into the woft sound. It is also written in Cornish *om,* and *ym,* qd. v. It is also written in Cornish *om,* and *ym.* qd. v. Ir Gwasgu, ymwasgu. Arm. *em.* Ir. †*imm.* Sansc. *svayam,* self.

EMA, v imp. There is. More generally written *yma,* qd. v.

EMDHAL, v. a. To strive. *Llwyd,* 249. Written also *omdhal.* W. *ymdhal;* comp. of *ym,* refl. part., and *dal,* to hold.

EMENIN, s. m. Butter. Corn. Voc. *butirum;* where it is also written *amenen,* qd. v.

EMES, adv. Abroad, without doors, without. Comp. of *en,* in, and *mês,* a field, qd. v. *Yn mês,* and *a mês,* are other forms. W. *ymaes, ymaith,* †*y meith.* Arm. *emeax.* Ir. *a-magh.* Gael. *muigh, a-muigh.* Manx, *cheu-mooie.*

EMESC, prep. Among. *Llwyd,* 77. More frequently written *yn mysk,* qd. v.

EMLADHE, v. a. To kill one's self. *Bynyges re by, dhe'n harlot pan fynsys ry an hackré mernans yn beys; râk hacré mernans eys emladhé y honan ny goffé dên, me a grŷs,* blessed be thon, to the villain when thou wouldest give the cruellest death in the world, for a more cruel death than to kill himself, no mau may find, I believe. R.D. 2073. Comp. of *em,* refl. part., and *ladhé,* to kill.

EMLODH, v. a. To fight, to contend, to wrestle. *Del levaraf ry dhynchy, ef a emblodh ragon ny, yesouch dhe vês croffolas,* as I say to you, he will fight for us; leave off lamentations. O.M. 1601. *My re bue, scar ow ené, owth emlodh may'th ên pûr squyth, uskys na yllyn ponyé,* I have been, ou my soul, wrestling till I was very tired, that I could not run immediately. P.C. 2509. *Reys yw dhym agy dhe lyst emlodh worth an antecryst, hag ef dhum gruthyl marow,* need is to me in the lists to fight against the antichrist, and he to put me to death. R.D. 224. This is compounded from the same roots as *emladhé,* and is written by Llwyd, 249, *emladh, emladha,* as well as *emlodh, dho hemlodh.* 231. W. *ymladh.*

EMPERIZ, s. f. An empress. Corn. Voc. *imperatrix* vel *Augusta.*

EMPERUR, s. m. An emperor. Corn. Voc. *imperator,* vel *Cesar,* vol *Augustus.* It is written *emprour,* in O.M. 2053; R.D. 1668; and *emperour,* O.M. 2055; R.D. 1629. Derived from the English. The Welsh form is *ymheraudwr,* †*amheraudwr,* from the Latin *imperator.* Arm. *impalazr.* Ir. *impire.*

EMPINION, s. m. The brain. It is variously written *ympynnyon,* and in the Cornish Vocabulary, *impinion.* *Otlé spern grisyl gyné, ha dreyn lym, ha scharp ynné, a grup bŷs yn empynnyon,* behold I have sharp thorns, and prickles keen and sharp in them, (that) will pierce even to the brain. P.C. 2190. *Tynnouch ol gans nûr a grŷs, may fo dreyn an guryn eys yn empynnyon dre an cen,* drag yo all with much force, that the thorns of the crown may be together in the brain, through the skin. P.C. 2138. *Me a's ten gans ol ow nerth, may'th entré an spikys serth dre an cen yn y grogen, ha scullyé y ympynnyon,*

I will put it with all my strength, that the stiff spines may enter through the skin to his skull, and scatter his brains. P.C. 2140. *Asso mûr tyn ow passyon, pan éth dreyn yn empynnyon a pûp parth dre an grogen;* very sharp was my suffering, when the thorns went into the brain on all parts through the skull. R.D. 2557. *Empinnion* is a plural form, of which the singular would be *empen,* being compounded of *en,* in, and *pen,* the head. Hence also W. *ymenydh,* †*emennyd.* Arm. *empenn,* pl. *empennou.* Ir. *inchinn.* Gael. *eanchainn.* Manx, *iuchyn, enneeyn.* Cf. also Gr. ἐγ-κέφαλος.

EMSCUMUNYS, participle. Excommunicated, accursed. *Wharré an emscumunys yn trok horn a fŷdh tewlys yn tyber yn dour pûr down,* soon the accursed, in a trunk of iron, shall be cast into the Tiber, in water very deep. R.D. 2165. *An iowl re'n dogo dh'y plath; en corf emscumunys whâth ef yw pûr wŷr,* the devil carry him to his place! the body accursed yet it is very truly. R.D. 2190. *An corf yw emscumunys,* the body is accursed. R.D. 2222. Written also *ymscemunys,* qd. v.

EMWYSCA, v. a. To strike one's self. *Gans y gollan marthys scon yth emvyskys yn golon; hager vernans a whylas,* with his knife wondrous soon he smote himself in the heart; a cruel death he sought. R.D. 2067. Comp. of *em,* refl. part, and *gwysca,* to strike. W. *ymwasgu.* Ir. *umfasgaim.*

EN, a particle used in composition. It gives an intensive meaning, as *cledhys, encledhys,* buried.

EN, a particle, which placed before an adjective converts it into an adverb; as *lowenec,* joyful; *en lowenec,* joyfully. *Gwîr,* true; *en wîr,* truly. It is more generally written *yn,* qd. v. W. *yn,* †*en.*

EN, definite article. The. *En tebell 'él a vynnas y demptyé,* the wicked angel would tempt him. M.C. 13. *Oll en da ha'n drôk kepar,* all the good and evil alike. M.C. 24. *En Tâs a néf y'm gylwyr,* the Father of heaven I am called. O.M. 1. *En tregé deydh yw hydhew,* the third day is to-day. R.D. 691. *Yn dan en dôr,* under the ground. R.D. 2119. This is another form of *an,* qd. v.

EN, prep. In. *Rag migternas yw en néf, dhe vôs gordhyys hy yw gyu,* for queen she is in heaven, to be worshipped she is worthy. M.C. 226. Generally written *yn,* qd. v. W. *yn,* †*en.*

EN, comp. pron. *Y éth yn un fystené dhe Pylat, aga Justis; e'n dyskyens del vyé, ha dhodho a leverys,* they went in haste to Pilate, their Justice; him they taught how it was, and to him said. M.C. 248. This is more correctly written *an,* qd. v.

EN, v. subs. I was. 1 pers. s. imp. of *bós. My re'bue war ow ené, owth emlodh, may'th én pûr squyth,* I have been on my soul wrestling that I was very much tired. P.C. 2509. *Ow stone a fue crowes a pren, kyns én mychtern, dén, ha Dew,* my standing was a cross of wood, before I was a king, man, and God. R.D. 2580. *Dall én, ny welyn yn fâs ow bôs mar veyl ow pewé,* I was blind, I saw not well that I was living so vile. M.C. 290.

EN, v. irr. We shall go. 1 pers. pl. fut. of *môs. Ny wodhen, rág ponvotūr, py 'th én yn gweel py yn cós,* we know not, for trouble, whether we shall go into the field or wood. O.M. 364. *Hemma yw tewolgow brâs; fattel én ny war tu tré,* this is great darkness; how shall we go towards home. P.C. 2991. *Yma an dôr ow krenné, sevel unwyth ny yllyn; ny won fattel én dhe tré,* the earth is trembling, we cannot once stand; I know not how we shall go home. P.C. 2997. *Arluth, ple 'th én alemma,* Lord, where shall we go from hence. R.D. 2391. W. *awn.*

ENA, adv. In that place, there, therein, at that time, then. *Ena mûr a vylyny Pedyr dhe Gryst a welde,* there much abuse Peter to Christ saw. M.C. 83. *Ena Pylat a gewsys yn dcîma dhe'n Edhewon,* then Pilate spake in this manner to the Jews. M.C. 141. *Me a vyn môs dhe'n temple, ha Dew ena·y wordhyé,* I will go to the temple, and worship God there. O.M. 1260. Abbreviated into *na,* it is frequently joined to the substantives, when it has the force of the pronoun *that;* as *yn ur-na,* in that hour; *an den-na,* that man. *En re-na,* those, or more literally, *those there.* It is similarly used in Welsh, as *y dŷn yna,* that man; *y'rhai yna,* those there. See *Na.* W. *yna,* †*ena, yno.* Arm. *eno.* Ir. *ann,* †*and.* Gael. *ann.*

ENAGOS, adj. Near, nearly. *Llwyd,* 248. Comp. of *en,* adv. part., and *agos,* near. W. *yn agos.*

ENAP, s. m. The face, countenance. *Llwyd,* 58, 179. †*Ha Dew leveras, morro, e ma rez genna ve dha why keneffra lusu an toan hâz, leb ez war enap an ol noar, ha keneffra gwedhan, a es an hax an gwedhan a toan haz, dha why ta ra bôs rag boos,* and God said, behold, there are given by me to you every herb bearing seed, which is upon the face of all the earth, and every tree in the which is the fruit of a tree yielding seed, to you it shall be for meat. C.W. p. 192. This is a later form of *enep,* qd. v.

ENAP, prep. Against. *Llwyd,* 51. Lit. *in faciem,* = 1r. *an aghaidh.* 270. Written also *enep.* Arm. *enep.*

ENBERA, prep. Within, into. *Llwyd,* 248, 249.

ENCINEDEL, s. m. A giant. Llwyd, 93, thus reads *enchinethel,* Corn. Voc. *gigas.* Comp. of *en,* intens. particle, and *cinedel,* id. qd. W. *cenedl,* a sort, or species; a race, or nation.

ENCLEDHYES, v. a. To bury, to inter. *Josep Barumathia, whyla corf máb Maria dheworth Pylat an iustis; rág marow yn grows yma, y encledhyes vyé da, máp Dew o dhyn danfenys,* Joseph of Arimathæa, seek the body of the son of Mary, from Pilate the magistrate; for he is dead on the cross, it would be good to bury him, the son of God that was sent to us. P.C. 3103. *Drou' e yntré ow dyworech; otté cendal glân a lês, parys rág y encledhyes,* bring ye him into my arms; behold clean linen spread, ready for burying him. P.C. 3161. *Encledhys,* buried. *Llwyd,* 249. Written also *ancledhyes,* qd. v.

ENCOIS, s. m. Frankincense. Corn. Voc. *thus.* "The MS. may be read perhaps *entois,* from the Latin *thus,* which is *tuis* in Gaelic; *en* would be the article." Norris's Cornish Drama, ij. 358.

ENCOISLESTER, s. f. A censer. Corn. Voc. *thuribulum.* Comp. of *encois,* incense, and *lester,* a vessel. "With the change suggested in *cois,* we should have *toislester,* omitting the article; very near the old Irish word, †*tuislestar.*" Norris, *ibid.*

ENDHIOWGEL, adv. Certainly. *Llwyd,* 248. Comp. of *en,* adv. part., and adj. *diowgel,* qd. v.

ENE, s. m. The soul. *A Dhew, goruyth am ené,* O God, keep my soul. O.M. 1356. *Yn pûr wŷr, war ow ené,*

ENNIS 136 ENWETH

me a vyn aga nywé, very truly, on my soul, I will follow them. O.M. 1629. *Me a th pŷs, scryf ow ené, pan vyf marow, yn dhe rôl*, I pray thee write my soul, when I am dead, in thy roll. P.C. 421. An abbreviated form of *enef*, qd. v.

ENEDEREN, s. f. Entrail. Corn. Voc. *extum*. Zeuss, 149, furnishes us from the Oxford Glosses with the old Welsh word, *ingued*, entrail. Ir. *inne, innidhe*. Gr. ἔντερον.

ENEF, s. m. The soul. Corn. Voc. *anima*. Written by Llwyd, 43, *enev*. Pl. *enefow, enevow*. *Pan vo tryddydh tremenys, ty a dhascor dhe enef*, when three days are gone, thou shalt give up thy soul. O.M. 846. *Arluth, porth côf yn deydh dywedh a'm enef vy*, Lord bear thou remembrance, in the last day of my soul. O.M. 1273. *Yn nêf agas enefow neffré a trŷg hep ponow yn ioy na vŷdh dywydhys*, in heaven your souls ever shall dwell without pains in joy (that) shall not be ended. P.C. 7. *Dhe vestry a vŷdh leyhŷs neffré war an enevow*, thy power shall be diminished ever over the souls. P.C. 144. *A enefow ol warbarth, deuch gynef; ol why a wharth*, O souls, all together, come with me; all ye shall laugh. R.D. 155. *Christ a besys, ow eneff me a gymyn, Arluth, yntré dhe dheuvlé*, Christ prayed, my soul I commend, O Lord, into thy hands. M.C. 204. W. *en, enydh, enaid*, †*eneit*. Arm. *ené*, †*enef*, pl. *enow, enevou*. Ir. *anam*, †*anim*. Gael. *anam*. Manx, *annym*. Gr. ἄνεμος. Lat. *animus, anima*. Sansc. *anas, anilas*, breath, life, from *an*, to move, to live.

ENEP, s. m. A face, a countenance, a page of a book. Corn. Voc. *pagina*. Written in Llwyd's time, *enap*, qd. v. W. *gwyneb, wyneb*. Arm. *cnep*.

ENES, s. m. Shrovetide. Llwyd, 46, *enex*. W. *ynyd*, †*init*. Arm. *ened*. Ir. *inid*. Gael. †*inid*. Manx, *innid*. All from the Latin *initium*, the beginning (of Lent).

ENES, s. m. An island. Pl. *encsow, enesys*. Llwyd, 228, 243. Written also *enys*, qd. v.

ENEVAL, s. f. An animal. Pl. *enevalles*. *Cowethé, dhym lavercuch yn scon, prâg yth hembrenkych ow enevalles dhe vés*, comrades, tell me directly, why are you leading my animals away. P.C. 205. W. *anival, anivail*; pl. *aniveiliaid*. Arm. *aneval, eneval*; pl. *anevaled*. From the Latin *animal*. Ir. *ainmheach*. Gael. *ainmhich*.

ENEVALES, s. f. A female animal, a she beast. Llwyd, 241.

ENFUGY, s. m. Mischief. *Kyns es dôs a lena, dha Adam ha dha Efa, me a wra nêb enfugy*, before going hence, to Adam, and to Eve, I will do some mischief. C.W. 38. Written also *anfugy*, qd. v.

ENFUGYC, adj. Mischievous. Pryce. Written also *anfugy*, qd. v.

ENGORBOR, s. m. A patten, or altarplate. Corn. Voc. *patena*.

ENLIDAN, s. m. Plantain. Corn. Voc. *plantago*. (W. *llyriad, llydan y fordh*.) Arm. *hedledan, heledan*. The root is *ledan*, wide.

ENNA, adv. There, then. Llwyd, 71. Another form of *ena*, qd. v.

ENNIOU, s. m. A joining, a seam. Corn. Voc. *commissura*. Probably connected with W. *gwnio, wnio*, to sew, or stitch; whence *gwoniad*, a seam.

ENNIS, s. f. An island. Llwyd, 71. Another form of *enys*, qd. v.

ENO, adv. There, in that place. *Ha nêp na'n grûk war nêp tro, yn peynys trygens eno, hep ioy prêst may's leffo eas*, and he who has not done it on any occasion, in pains let him dwell there, without joy always that he may have anguish. R.D. 159. *An carna a ygoras, del o destnys dhodho ef; eno ny a'n recevas*, that rock opened, as it was destined for him; there we received him. R.D. 2339. W. *yno*. Arm. *eno*.

ENOGOS, adv. Near, nigh. Llwyd, 249. Written also *enagos*, qd. v.

ENRADN, adv. In part, partly. Pryce. This is a late corruption of *en ran*.

ENS, v. s. They are. 3 pers. pl. pres. of *bôs*. *Welcom êns, rê'n Arluth Dew*, they are welcome by the Lord God. P.C. 2353. *Y vyrys y wolyow; aga gwelas o trueth, dhe'n bŷs kyns êns ylyow*, I looked on his wounds, to see them was a pity; to the world rather they are healings. R.D. 900. Another form of *ŷns*, qd. v.

ENS, v. s. They were. 3 pers. pl. imp. of *bôs*. *Gans Christ ytho cowethys, byth nyng êns y cowethé*, with Christ he was acquainted, never were they companions. M.C. 41. *Tryugons moy gansé, ha pymthek pûr wŷr êns y*, three score more with them, and fifteen very true were they. M.C. 227. *Y eth yn un fystené, peswar marrek yrvys êns*, they went in a hurry, four soldiers armed they were. M.C 241. *Pûr gow a lover the vyn; pan seffsys hydhew myttyn yach êns aga ieyw*, a very lie thou wilt tell; when thou gottest up this morning, sound were their sinews. P.C. 2631. *Yach êns hydhew, nêp hûs ef re wrûk dhodho pûr dhyowgel*, they were sound to day; some jugglery he has done to him very certainly. P.C. 2694.

ENS, v. irr. Let them go. 3 pers. pl. imp. of *môs*. *Avorow deuch a dermyn, hag êns pûp dré*, to-morrow come ye in time, and let all go home. O.M. 2844. *Ens dew a'm dyscyblyon dhe'n castel ûs a ragon a dhysempys, hep lettyé*, let two of my disciples go to the village that is before us, forthwith without delaying. P.C. 175. *Lemmyn êns pûp war tu tré*, now let all go towards home. R.D. 2644. W. *ánt*. Arm. *aent, enni, eent*.

ENTRE, prep. Between, betwixt. Generally written *yntré*, qd. v.

ENTREDES, s. m. Swoon, lethargy. Corn. Voc. *cauma*.

ENVENOUCH, adv. Often. Pryce. Properly two words, *en*, adv. part., and *venouch*, a mutation of *menouch*, frequent.

ENVÔCH, s. m. The face. Corn. Voc. *facies*. This is to be read as two words, *en vôch*, *en* being the article, and *vôch*, a mutation of *bôch*, qd. v.

ENURMA, adv. At this hour, at this time, now. Llwyd, 249. Comp. of *en*, in, and *úr-ma*, this hour.

ENWEDEC, adj. Particular, in particular. Pryce, ‡*enuedzhek*. W. *enwedig*.

ENWEDH, adv. Also. Llwyd, 249. Generally written *ynwedh*, qd. v.

ENWEDHAN, s. f. An ash, an ash tree. Llwyd, 17. Pl. *enwydh*, or *enuydh*. W. *onwydh*. Comp. of *on*, ash, and *gwedyh*, trees. See Onnen.

ENWETH, adv. Once. ‡*Bedhes gwesgys dhiueth, ken gweskal cnueth, râg henna yw an gwella point a skians oll*, be twice struck, before striking once, for that is the best point of all wit. Llwyd, 251. A late form of *unweth*, qd. v.

ENYS, s. f. An island. *Llwyd*, 19. *My a's re lemyn dheuch why, hag ol guerdhour, un enys hag Arwennek, annedhé gwreuch dheuch chartour,* I will give them how to you, and all the water courses, the island and Arwinnick, make of them a charter to you. O.M. 2592. This word is variously written *enes, ennis, yncs, ynys, inee.* W. *ynys,* †*inis.* Arm. *enez.* Ir. *inis.* Gael. *innis,* †*ighe,* †*i.* Manx, *ellan.* Gr. *νῆσος.* Lat. *insula.*

EON, adj. Straight, right, just. *Pryce.* Generally written *ewn,* qd. v.

EPSCOP, s. m. A bishop. Pl. *epscobow, epscobon. Llwyd*, 243. *My a vyn lemyn ordné mab-lyen, ow sel pryvé, dhe vôs epscop yn temple,* I will now ordain a priest, my privy seal, to be bishop in the temple. O.M. 2001. *Dhe epscop guraf dhe sacré, kymmer dhe vytour wharé, ha bŷdh yn dhe servys lén,* to a bishop I will consecrate thee, take thy mitre forthwith, and be faithful in thy service. O.M. 2614. *Yn della, a gasadow, y gorthebyth epscobow?* thus, O detestable one, repliest thou to bishops? P.C. 1266. *Dhe bobil hep falladow, ha'n epscobow kekyffrys, a'th drôs bŷs dhymmo omma,* thy people, without fail, and the bishops also, have brought thee even to me here. P.C. 2005. The form preserved in the Cornish Vocab. is *escop,* and in Llwyd's time, *ispak.* W. *esgob,* †*escop,* vulg. *esbog,* pl. *esgobion,* †*escip,* †*escyp.* Arm. *escob.* Ir. *easbog,* †*epscop.* Gael. *easbuig.* Manx, *aspick.* All from the Lat. *episcopus.*

EPHAN, s. m. June. *Mis ephan,* the month of June. *Llwyd*, 74. *Gor-ephan,* July, qd. v. This is another form of *efen,* qd. v.

ER, s. m. An eagle. Corn. Voc. *aquila.* Late plural, *eriou. Pryce. Lemyn hanwaf goydh ha yâr, hôs, paynn, colom, grugyer, bargos, bryny, ha'n er, moy dredhof a vŷdh hynwys,* now I name goose and hen, duck, peacock, pigeon, partridge, kite, crows, and eagle, further by me shall be named. O.M. 133. W. *eryr.* Arm. *er, erer.* Ir. *iolar.* Gael. *iolair.* Manx, *urley.* Goth. *ara.* Old High German, *aro.*

ER, s. m. Snow. ‡*Enna a cil err,* it snows. *Llwyd*, 250. ‡ *Yein kuer, tarednow, ha golowas, er, reu, gwens, ha clehé, ha kezer,* cold weather, thunders, and lightning, snow, frost, wind, and ice, and hail. *Pryce.* This is a late form, the more ancient being *irch,* qd. v. W. *eira, eiry.* Arm. *erch.* Ir. *crog, oircog,* †*eirr,* †*oidhir.* Gael. †*oidhre.*

ER, s. f. An hour. *Why a gîff bohosogyon pûb êr warnouch ow carmé,* ye shall have the poor every hour on you calling. M.C. 37. *Yn êr-na dhe'n mynydhyow why a erch warnouch codhé,* in that hour to the mountains ye shall call on you to fall. M.C. 170. *Yn êr-na y fê dorgis, ha dris ol an bŷs ef éth,* in that hour there was an earthquake, and over all the world it went. M.C. 200. This is a various form of *ûr,* qd. v.

ER, adj. Fresh, juicy, full of sap, raw, green. *Llwyd*, 138, *êr.* W. *îr.* Ir. *ur.* Gael. *ur.* Manx, *'oor.*

ER, prep. For, for the sake of, by. *Dhe léf Arluth a glewaf, saw dhe face my ny welaf er ow geuw,* thy voice, Lord, I hear, but thy face I see not for my woes. O.M. 589. *Dûn ganso, er y unfus, dhe Pylat agan iustys,* let us come with him, for his wickedness, to Pilate our Justice. P.C. 1501. *Ha kekyffrys an bronnow na dhenes flehesygyow, gwyn agu beys er bones,* and also the breasts that children have not sucked, happy their fate for being. P.C. 2650. *Rum fay, lemmyn a'n affen er an ascal, y'n toulsen yn creys an tân,* by my faith, now if I should get hold of him by the wing, I would throw him in the midst of the fire. R.D. 290. *Arluth dremas, mar codhas mŷr Cryst ow sylwyas, ple ma dhe wŷr, er y whylas rôf dhys ow tŷr,* good Lord, if thou hast chanced to see Christ my Saviour, where is he truly? for seeing him I will give thee my land. R.D. 857. *Ty geyler scon ty ha'th vazo, kymereuch er an dhyso baw, ha gorrcuch ef yn dôr down,* thou gaoler, forthwith, thou and thy boy, take (him) by the two feet, and put him in deep ground. R.D. 2076. *Kymer an pen, er an treys me an kylden aberth yn beydh,* take thou the head, by the feet I will let him down, within the grave. R.D. 2082. W. *er,* †*yr.* Ir. *ar.* Gael. *air.* Manx, *er.*

ER, prep. On, upon. *Py hanow y fŷdh gylwys, lavar dhymmo er dhe fêdh,* what name shall he be called? tell me on thy faith. O.M. 677. *Crôg rom bo, er an dhewen,* may hanging be to me, on the gills. O.M. 2651. *My a'n knouk ef er y wew, otté mellow y geyn brew,* I will beat him on his lips, see the joints of his back broken. P.C. 2085. *Levcreuch er agas fŷdh dhymmo pa'n vernans a'm bŷdh,* tell ye on your faith to me what death I shall have. R.D. 2027. This is another form of *ar,* qd. v.

ERA, v. a. Was. 3 pers. s. imperf. of *bôs.* ‡*Ha Dew wrâs an ebbarn, ha dheberhas an dowrow era en dadn an ebbarn dhort an dowrow era euh an ebbarn; ha an dellna rtho,* and God made the sky, and divided the waters that were under the sky, from the waters that were above the sky, and so it was. C.W. p. 189. It is also written *erra.* ‡*Ha râg na erra dén na flok en tshei bez an vertshants, an dzhei dhal krêg ragta,* and for that there was neither man nor boy in the house, but the merchants, they ought to be hanged for it. *Llwyd*, 252. This form occurs only in late Cornish. See *Esa.*

ERAILL, adj. Others. *Te nyn vydh dhys Dewyow eraill més ve,* thou shalt have none other Gods but me. *Pryce.* This is the plural of *arall,* qd. v., and is more generally written *erell,* qd. v.

ERBER, s. m. A garden. Pl. *erberow. Ha'n losowys erbyn hâf degynis hâs yn erberow,* and let the plants against summer produce seed in gardens. O.M. 31. *Erber* is unknown to the other dialects, and must be derived from the Latin *herbarium.*

ERBYN, prep. Against. *Ha'n eneff del dascorsé erbyn natar gans un cry,* and the soul how he yielded it against nature with a cry. M.C. 208. *Prâg y tolsté sy hep kén, iworth hy thempylé dhe dyrry an frût erbyn ow dyfen,* why didst thou deceive her without pity, by tempting her to break off the fruit against my prohibition. O.M. 304. *My â dhodho yn lowen, rêik dyswythyl an bylen, mar kews erbyn a laha,* I will go to him joyfully to destroy the villain, if he speaks against the law. P.C. 572. *Erbyn* is compounded of *er,* upon, and *byn,* a mutation of *pyn,* id. qd. *pen,* a head. See *Pyn.* With pronouns it is separated, and the adjectival form inserted between, thus, *er ow fyn,* against me; *er dhe byn,* against thee; *er y byn,* against him; *er y fyn,* against her; *er agan pyn,* against us; *er agas pyn,* against you; *er aga fyn,* against them. *Aspyouch yn pûp le, mar kews dén vyth er ow fyn,* see ye in every place if any man speak against me. R.D. 1919. *Mollath dén, ha gour ha gwerêk a dhe poran er dhe byn,* the curse of man, and husband and wife, will come straight against thee. M.C. 66. *Er y byn mennaf mones,* *me a garsé y welcs*, to meet him I will go ; I would love to see him. P.C. 232. *Assyw an dén-na goky, mar myn er ngan pyn ny cows reson vŷth*, that man is a fool, if he will against us speak any reason. P.C. 1663. *Mar a lever dén vŷth er agas pyn why tra vŷth, waré gwréch y gorthyby*, if any man say against you any thing, soon do you answer him. P.C. 180. *Avel bruthken aga dýns orto y a dheskerny, er aga fyn betegyns Crist un gér ny levery*, like hounds their teeth on him they gnashed ; against them nevertheless Christ would not say a word. M.C. 96. In Welsh, *erbyn*, against, is never thus separated, though other compound prepositions follow the same rule, as for instance *gerbron*, before : thus, *ger vy mron*, before me ; *ger dy vron*, before thee ; *ger ei vron*, before him ; *ger ei bron*, before her ; *ger ein bron*, before us ; *ger cich bron*, before you ; *ger eu bron*, before them. The Manx furnishes an analogous form in the word *erskyn*, above ; comp. of *er*, upon, and *cione*, head : thus, *er my skyn*, above me ; *er dty skyn*, above thee ; *er e skyn*, above him ; *er nyn skyn*, above us, you, them. Again we find in Old Irish, *ar chenn*, before, lit. to the head, whence in front of, or against ; *ar mo chiunn*, before me ; *ar a chiunn*, before him ; *ar ar chiunn*, before us.

ERCH, v. a. He shall command, or ask. 3 pers. s. fut. of *archa*, qd. v. *Yn ér-na dhe'n mcnydhyow why a erch warnouch codhé, yn ketella an nansow wy a bŷs ragas cudhé*, in that hour the mountains ye shall bid on you to fall ; in the same manner the vallies ye shall pray you to hide. M.C. 170.

ERCHYS, v. a. Commanded, enjoined. Preterite of *archa*, qd. v. *Dew dhymmo vy a erchys may fydhé gy offrymmys dhodho ef war an alter*, God hath commanded me that thou be offered to him upon the altar. O.M. 1326. *Dew a erchys dhys Moyses dhe welen y kemeres, ha gwyskel an môr gynxy*, God has commanded thee, Moses, to take thy rod, and smite the sea with it. O.M 1663. *Gordhyans dhys ha lowené, dhe Dâs kêr a erchys gwella dhe cher*, glory to thee and joy, thy Father dear has enjoined (me) to better thy condition. P.C. 1050.

EREDY, adv. Surely, verily. *An aval worth y derry, wosé my dhys dh'y dhefen, ty re gum wrúk eredy*, by plucking the apple, after I had forbidden it to thee, thou hast done wrong verily. O.M. 231. *Gwra dhe nyggys credy kyns dewheles, my a'd pŷs*, do thy errand surely, before coming back, I pray thee. O.M. 727. *Salamon, dhe váb kerra, a'n coul dhreha eredy*, Solomon, thy son most dear, shall fully build it verily. O.M. 2342. Written also *yredy*, qd. v.

ERELL, adj. Others. *War aga dewlyn yth e perag Ihesus re erell, aga fen y a sackyé, hag a gewsy pûr debell*, on their knees there went before Christ some others ; their heads they shook, and spake very foully. M.C. 195. *En dhyw grows erel yn ban droheveuch kettep onan*, the two other crosses up raise ye every one. P.C. 2820. *Ef a allas dyougel, del glowys y leverel yn lyes le, savyé bewnens tús erel, lemmyn y honan ny gil ymsawyé*, he could indeed, as I heard him say in many places, save the life of other men, but himself he cannot save. P.C. 2876. Plural of *arall*, qd. v. W. *eraill*.

ERIEU, s. m. The temples of the head. Corn. Voc. *timpus*. It may be read *erleu*. W. *arlais*. Ir. †*are*.

ERNA, conj. Until, till. *Gans myyn gwreuch y knoukyé, na wrello tremené, venythu na wreuch hedhy*, with stones beat ye her until she does die ; never do ye stop. O.M. 2693. *Ny dhueth an prŷs erna gyllyf dhe'n nef dhum Tâs*, the time is not come, until I go to heaven to my Father. R.D. 878. *Vynytha erna whyllyn, a travyth ny gemeryn nép lowené*, ever until we see (thee,) from any thing we shall not receive any pleasure. R.D. 2364.

ERNOYTH, adj. Naked. *Yn medh Christ a ban rúg dheuch ernoyth fernoyth ow holyé, daver vŷth wy ny dhecsyuch dhe worré trévyth ynné*, says Christ, since I caused you naked unclad me to follow, conveniences ever ye carried not to put any thing in them. M.C. 50. Comp. of *er*, intensive, and *noyth*, naked.

ERRYA, v. a. To strive, to contend. *Rág errya war ow fyn, me a'th wysk harlot jaudyn. may thomelly dheth killban*, for striving against me, I will strike thee rogue, rascal, that thou fall backward. C.W. 62.

ERTECH, s. m. A heritage. O.M. 354. *Ellas gweles an termyn, ow arluth pan wrúk serry, pan rúk drys y worhemmyn, ow ertech grúk dhe gylly*, alas, to see the time when my lord was angry, when I acted against his command, I lost my heritage. O.M. 354. Borrowed from the English.

ERU, s. m. A field, an acre. Corn. Voc. *ager. Guuithial ereu*, agricola. *Erisy*, the dry acre, nom. loc. in Grade. W. *erw*. Arm. *eró, erf, erv*. Ir. *arbha*, †*arba*. Lat. *arvum*.

ERVYRE, v. a. To consider, to observe. *Rág y hyller ervyré ha'y welas yn suredy, y vos prest worth dhe velyé*, for it is possible to observe, and to see him certainly, that he is near meeting thee. M.C. 20. *Lemmyn ny a gil gwelas, hag ervyré fest yn ta, Christ dhe wodhaff ire dhensys múr a benans yn bŷs-ma*, now we may see, and consider very well, that Christ suffered through manhood much penance in this world. M.C. 60. Written also *yruyré*, qd. v.

ERVYS, adj. Armed. *Lavar lemyn mars yw prys danvon genes tús ervys dhe gerches an vŷl lusel*, say now if it is time to send armed men with thee to fetch the vile knave. P.C. 939. *Mŷl wéth a vŷdh an dyvvedh, hu hakcré es on dalleth, rák henna tús ervys freth gor dh'y wythé a lermyn*, a thousand (times) worse will be the end, and more odious than the beginning ; therefore men strongly armed place thou to guard him in time. R.D. 351. Written also *yrvys*, qd. v. It is strictly the participle pass. of *arva*, to arm.

ES, v. subs. Thou wast. 2 pers. s. imp. of *bós*. *Pechadores és hep gow, an brassa egé yn pow gans pûp ol ty o gylwys*, a sinner thou wast without a lie ; the greatest that was in the country by every body thou wast called. R.D. 1094.

ES, v. imp. There is. *Y hylwys en Edhewon, lays és yn pow adro*, the Jews cried out, there is law in the country about. M.C. 121. *Yn un fysteué me a'y gwra, aban naq és a wodhfé dheuch parys a'e gwrellé gwell*, in a hurry I will make them, since there is no one that knows for you ready to make them better. M.C. 158. *Dén glân yw a bech, hef fall, ynno ef dyfout nyng és*, a man clean he is of sin, without fail, in him default there is not. M.C. 192. *A'y frút dybry nymbes whans, dres dyfen ow arloth kêr*, of its fruit to eat there is not to me a desire, against the prohibition of my dear Lord. O.M. 171. ‡*Es connes dhiu'*, is there supper to you, i. e. have you supped. Lhwyd, 242. W. *oes*.

ES, v. irr. That is. *A na wylta ol myns es orth dhe olamyé yn soweth*, seest thou not all those that are blaming thee sadly ? M.C. 120. *Te yw dall, rág genen cregis neb és, den glán a bêch yne*, thou art blind, for he that is hanged with us, is a man clean of sin. M.C. 192. *Yn whêh djdh myns es formys, aga sona me a vera*, in six days all that are formed, bless them I will. C.W. 32. Written also *iis*, qd. v. W. *y sy*.

ES, conj. Than. *Ef a wrûk ow husullyé, frût annedhy may torren, moy es Dew ny a vyé*, he did advise me, that should I pluck off fruit from it, greater than God we should be. O.M. 219. *Mar kews ken es gwyryoneth, ef a'n pren kyns tremené*, if he will speak other than truth, he shall pay for it before dying. P.C. 1468. *Mgl wêth a vgdh an dyvedh, ha hakcré es an dalleth*, a thousand (times) worse will be the end, and more odious than the beginning. R.D. 350. *Ys, eys, ages*, are other forms of this word, qd. v. Like the prepositions, *es* and *ages* take suffixed pronouns, thus *esouch, agesouch*, than you.

ES, pron. adj. Your. *Lhuyd*, 244. An abbreviated form of *ages*, qd. v.

ESA, v. subs. He was. *Ha'n gwgn esa war en fuys, ef a rannas yntrethé*, and the wine (that) was on the table, he divided among them. M.C. 45. *Ha'n dús esa ol yn dré, ha pryncis yn pow yn wédh*, and the people (that) were in the town, and the princes in the country also. M.C. 97. In the Dramas it is written *esé*, qd. v.

ESAL, adj. Low. Comp. *esala*, lower. More frequently *isal*, qd. v.

ESCAR, s. m. An enemy. Pl. *yskerens*, qd. v. *Ellas vgth pan rûk colé mar hogul worth ow eskar, kemys drûk ús ow codhé ha dewethes hag avar*, alas, that I ever listened so readily to my enemy; so much evil is falling, both late and early. O.M. 627. *Gor ost gencs yrrys da, dhe omlath, del y'm kerry; un eskar brás dhym yma, war ow thyr ow gûl mestry*, take with thee a host well armed, to fight, as thou lovest me; a great enemy is to me, over my land doing violence. O.M. 2143. *Onan ahanouch haneth rum gwerthas dhom yskerens*, one of you to night has sold me to my enemies. P.C. 737. W. *esgar*. Ir. *eascara*. † *escara*, pl. † *escaraid*. Gael. *euscaraid*.

ESCARN, s. m. Bones. *Ty a fgdh wharé drôg lam, dhe escarn ol kenp lam gans ow bom a fgdh brewys*, thou shalt soon have a bad chance; thy bones all, every bit, with my blows shall be broken. O.M. 2743. The plural of *ascorn*, qd. v.

ESCELLY, s. m. Wings. ‡ *Ha Dew rig gweres an puskas brás, ha kenefra tra bew es a guayah, leb rig an dowrow dry rág pûr vour uarlér go hâs; ha kenefra edhan eskelly warlér go hâs; ha Dew welas tro va da*, and God made the great fishes, and every living thing that moveth, which the waters brought forth abundantly after their kind, and every winged fowl after his kind; and God saw that it was good. C.W. p. 191. The plural of *ascall*, qd. v.

ESCER, s. m. A giant. *Esker brás*, a great giant. *Pryce*.

ESCID, s. m. A shoe. Pl. *eskidieu*. Corn. Voc. *solulares*. In later times it was pronounced *eskis*, qd. v., and the plural *eskyggyow*. *Dheworthys dgsk dhe skyggyow dhe vés, sevel war tgr reneges a wréth*, from thee take off thy shoes quickly, stand on blessed ground thou dost. O.M. 1406. W. *esgid*, pl. *esgidiau*. Ir. ‡ *asa*.

ESCOP, s. m. A bishop. Corn. Voc. *episcopus*. *Ihesus a ve danvenys, ha dheworth an prins Annas, gans tûs ven a dhesympys bgs yn escop Cayphas*, Jesus was sent, and from the prince Annas, with strong men immediately, even to the bishop Caiaphas. M.C. 68. More generally written *epscop*, qd. v.

ESCOP, s. m. A snuffer pan. Corn. Voc. *lefiste*. See Norris's Note, "Cornish Drama," ij. 350.

ESCYNYA, v. a. To ascend. ‡ *An tridga djdh ef deravas arta dort an marrow, eskynyas do nêv, ha sedha war dorn dyhow an Tás Olgallusec*, the third day he rose again from the dead, and ascended to heaven, and sitteth on the right hand of God the Father Almighty. C.W. p. 203. Another form of *ascen*, qd. v. W. *esgynu*.

ESE, v. s. He was. 3 pers. s. imp. of *bós*. *Dewsull blegyow, pan esé yn mysc y abestely*, Palm Sunday, when he was in the midst of his apostles. M.C. 27. *Marow yw pûp tra esé spyrys a vevnans ynno*, dead is every thing that there was the spirit of life in it. O.M. 1090. *An prysners galsons yn wédh esé yn dan naw alwedh*, the prisoners are gone also, (that) were under nine keys. R.D. 661.

ESEDHE, v. n. To sit. *War penakyll y'n goras dyantell dhe esedha*, on a pinnacle he placed him hazardous to sit. M.C. 13. *An asen a ve kerchys warnedhy rág esedhé, dyllas pan a ve gorrys*, the ass was fetched, on it to sit, cloth clothes were placed. M.C. 28. Written also *ysedhé*, qd. v. W. *eistedhu*. Arm. *azeza*, † *asedha*. Ir. *suidh, eisidh, seis, deisidh*. Gael. *suidh*. Gr. ἕζω, ἕζω. Lat. *sedeo, sedo*. Goth. *sita, satia*. Sansc. *ás, sthas*.

ESEL, s. m. A limb, a member. Corn. Voc. *membrum*. Pl. *esely, esyly, ysyly*. *Ena hy a ve gesys dhe godha, may fe crehyllys oll y gorf ha'y esely*, there it was left to fall, so that was shattered his body and his limbs. M.C. 184. *Nag onan ef ny usas heb uré a'y escly*, not one he left not without anointing of his limbs. M.C. 235. *Crist o brew y esyly, ha war y gorf mgl woly*, Christ's limbs were bruised, and on his body a thousand wounds. R.D. 998. *Sawyys yw ow ysyly, ol a'n venym, ha'm cleves*, healed are my limbs, all of the poison and my disease. O.M. 1798. W. *esill*. Arm. *ezel, izel*, pl. *izili*. Ir. † *asil*.

ESEN, v. s. I was. 1 pers. s. imperf. of *bós*. *Yn agis mgsk pan esen, lays Du dhuuch ow tysky*, among you when I was, the laws of God to you teaching. M.C. 75. *My pan esen ow quandré, clewys a'n ngl tenewen un êl ow talleth cané, a uchaf war an wedhen*, I, when I was walking about, heard on one side an angel beginning to sing above me on the tree. O.M. 213.

ESEN, v. subs. We were. 1 pers. pl. imp. of *bós*. *Henna me a lever whîth, yth esen dre pûr hyreth war dhe lerch owth ymwéhé*, that I will say likewise, we were through real regret, after thee pining. R.D. 1169. *Arluth ple 'th én alemma, ha pygwn Dew gallosck; del esen agan unnek, ha na moy, gôr na benen*, Lord, where shall we go hence, and pray to mighty God? as we were eleven of us, and no more, man nor woman. R.D. 2395.

ESENS, v. subs. They were. 3 pers. pl. imperf. of *bós*. *Pylat éth yn més yn un lowarth, haq a worras Crist ganso ena orto rag kewsel; prest an Edhewon debell dhe Jesus esens adro*, Pilate went out into a garden, and put Christ with him there to him for to speak immediately; the wicked Jews to Jesus were round about. M.C. 140. Written also *esons*, qd. v.

ESES, v. subs. Thou wast. 2 pers. s. imp. of *bôs. Adam, ty a ve gothys, pan eses yn Paradys, avel harlot, ow lordyé*, Adam, thou wast proud, when thou wast in Paradise, like a rogue, lording it. O.M. 900. *Yn dan ambos yth eses, ha ken na fe da genes, gúl dhe servys ty a wra*, under a bargain thou wast, and though it be not good with thee, thou shalt do thy service. P.C. 2259.

ESGAR, s. m. A shank, a log. *Pryce.* W. *esgair*, † *esceir*. Arm. *esker*. Ir. † *aisgeir*. Gael. † *aisgeir*.

ESGARA, v. n. To leave, to forsake, to relinquish. *Llwyd*, 138. W. *esgaru*.

ESGIS, s. m. A shoe. Pl. *esgisow. Llwyd*, 28, 45. Written also *eskas*. ‡ *Gwisgo an genter-ma ed eskas vi*, knock this nail in my shoe. *Llwyd*, 230. ‡ *An esgisow adro 's treis*, the shoes on your feet. 250. *Diesgis*, shoeless. This is a later form of *escid*, qd. v. Pryce gives *eskitias* as a late plural.

ESIS, v. subs. It is. 3 pers. s. pres. of *bôs*, used impersonally with a verb of the infin. act. to express a passive signification. *Esis* is a reduplicate form, answering to the W. *ydys, ys*. ‡ *Ez eziz a kil hwêl ymma*, one is doing work here ; or, work is being done here. *Llwyd*, 246.

ESOF, v. subs. I am. A reduplicate form of *ôf*, 1 pers. s. pres. of *bôs*. *Uskys na yllyn ponyé, del esof ow tyené, ha whŷs pûp godh ol ha lyth*, I could not run immediately, as I am panting, and sweat all (my) neck and back. P.C. 2511. *Tormentors com hyder snel, namnag essof ow merwel, orth agas gortos*, executioners, come hither quick, I am almost dying, by waiting for you. R.D. 2145. W. *ydwyv*.

ESON, v. subs. We are. A reduplicate form of *ôn*, 1 pers. pl. pres. of *bôs*. *Kepar del eson yn wêdh keffrys yn kueth yn moreth ragdho, ny iuggyn mones nep pel lemmyn bŷs yn un castel henwys Emmaus*, as we are also both in grief (and) in sorrow for him, we do not think to go any distance, but as far as a village called Emmaus. R.D. 1998. *Asson* is another form.

ESONS, v. subs. They were. 3 pers. pl. imperf. of *bôs*. *Y vam whegol a welas del esons worth y dhygtyé, pyleth múr a's kemeras, y holon namna grakyé*, his mother dear saw how they were treating him : much pity seized her, her heart almost broke. M.C. 164. Written also *esens*, qd. v.

ESOS, v. subs. Thou art. A reduplicate form of *ôs*, 2 pers. s. pres. of *bôs*. *Heyl syr epscob, esos y'th cop owth ysedhé*, hail, sir bishop ! thou art in thy cope sitting. P.C. 931. *Ythos* is another form, qd. v. W. *ydwyt*.

ESOS, adv. Already. *Llwyd*, 249. W. *eisoes*.

ESOUCH, v. subs. Ye are. A reduplicate form of *ouch*, 2 pers. pl. pres. of *bôs*. *Why gwegcoryon, euch yn mês, yth esouch ow kuthyl ges a Dhu hag e sans eglos, yn ow thy a piyadow pan wreuch agas marhasow, ha fowys dhe laddron plos*, ye traders, go out, ye are making jest of God and his holy church, in my house of prayers when ye make your markets, and a den for foul thieves. P.C. 332. *Lemmyn ol crês yntrethouch, omma kepar del esouch worth ow gortos*, now all peace among you ! here like as ye are waiting for me. R.D. 2434.

ESOUCH, conj. pron. Than ye. *Lemmyn me a grŷs yn ta y fynnaf vy môs pella esouch haneth, saw bytygyns cresouch why an corf-na dhe dhasserchy kyns yw aneth*, now I believe well, I will go further than you to-night ; but nevertheless believe ye that body to rise again before it is to-night. R.D. 1299. Comp. of *es*, than, and *ouch*, the composite form of *chwi. Agesouch* is another form, qd. v.

ESOW, s. m. Corn. Plural of *ês*, which is generally written *eys*, or *ŷs*, qd. v. *Múr varth ambus dyogel, an beys dh'y terry na'm gâs rag esow ; galsof ysel na allaf kerdhes yn fâs*, great wonder is it to me surely, the earth to break it that it will not permit me for corn ; I am become low that I cannot walk well. O.M. 373.

ESTREN, s. f. An oyster. Corn. Voc. *ostrea* vel *ostreum*. Arm. *histr, histren*, † *ostren*. Ir. *ostrin*,

ESTREN, s. m. A stranger. *Pryce.* W. *estron*. From the Lat. *extraneus*.

ESUMSYN, v. a. To undertake. *Pryce. My a'n musur lour yn ta, na bertheuch own a henna, gans squyr compes ha scannt lŷn na vo hyrré esunsyn, na vŷth cotta war nep cor*, I will measure it well enough, do not ye have fear of that, with straight square and scant line, that it be not longer, I undertake, nor shorter in any way. O.M. 2511. A very doubtful word ; the English word *assumption* appears to be the nearest to it.

ET, prep. In. This is a late corruption of *en*. ‡ *Et e ûs côth*, in his old age. *Llwyd*, 21. ‡ *Et a phoccat*, in my pocket. 253. ‡ *Da va prêv erra e wrêg guita kympez et i gever*, to try whether his wife had kept alway in her duty. 253.

ETRE, prep. Between. *Llwyd*, 72. A late corruption of *entré*, or *yntré*, qd. v.

ETTA, pron. prep. In them. A late corruption of *ynné*. ‡ *Ha Dew laveras, gwerens an noar dry râg gwels, ha lusu toan hâs, ha'n gweedh toan lavallo warler go hendah leb go hâs etta go honnen war a doar ; ha an dellna etho*, and God said, let the earth bring forth grass, and herb yielding seed, and the trees yielding fruit after their kind, whose seed is in themselves on the earth ; and so it was. C.W. p. 190.

ETTANS, pron. prep. In them. ‡ *Rág en whêh dydhyow, an Arluih a wrûs nêf ha'n 'oar, an môr, ha mêns tra es ettans, ha powesas an seithvas dêdh*, for in six days the Lord made heaven, and earth, the sea, and all that in them is, and rested the seventh day. *Pryce.* This form occurs only in late Cornish, the *ns* however preserves the characteristic of the third pers. pronoun. So Welsh *yndhynt*, in them, from *yn*, and *hwynt*, while *etta*, and the classical form *ynné*, contain the Cornish *y*, or Welsh *hwy*.

ETTEN, pron. prep. † *Cabm-thavas en mettyn, glaw bôz etten*, a rainbow in the morning, sun is in it. *Cornish Proverb ; Pryce.* This form occurs only in late Cornish.

ETTOGE, v. s. Thou art. ‡ *Frank a leal ettogé*, frank and loyal art thou. *Earl of Godolphin's motto.* This is a corruption of *ythogé*, qd. v. of *ythosé*, qd. v.

ETH, v. n. He went. 3 pers. s. pret. of irr. v. *môs. Múr a dûs ha benenas a Ierusalem yn drê, erbyn Crist rág y welas y'th, ha rág y wordhyé*, many men and women from Jerusalem in the town, to meet Christ for to see him they went, and for to worship him. M.C. 29. *Iudas éth yn y negis, en ioul yw e'n hombronky*, Judas went on his errand, the devil it is (that) guided him. M.C. 62. *Och, my re bue boches coynt, hag éth yn râk re a poynt*, Oh, I have been little cunning, and went forward too much point blank. P.C. 3032. *An corf éth hydhew yn prŷ*, the body went to-day into the earth. R.D. 21. *Rág me a dýp bôs hemma an kêth môp êth alemma, yw mychtern a lowené,* for I think that this is the same son (that) went hence, (that) is the king of joy. R.D. 2509. W. *aeth.* Arm. *eaz.* Ir. †*eatha*, †*eil.* Sansc. *at, ath, ith,* to go.

ETH, v. n. Thou wilt go. 2 pers. s. fut. of irr. v. *môs. Kens môs, eyf ten gwŷn pymeth, ha dhe scafé yth êth yn ow nygys, my a grŷs,* before going, drink a draught of spiced wine, and thou more nimbly wilt go on my errand, I believe. O.M. 2205. *A vynyn ryth, py te yth êth ? râk kueth ŷygyth, garmé a wreth,* O woeful woman, where wilt thou go ? for grief thou prayest, cry out thou dost. R.D. 851. *Arluth kêr, fattel vŷdh dyn, mars êth arté dhyworthyn,* dear Lord, how will it be with us, if thou wilt go again from us. R.D. 2362.

ETH, s. m. A puff, blast, breath. *An rê-ma ew gwêl a râs, râg ny glewsŷuch yn nêp plâs sawor a'n par-ma vytlquëth ; yma Dew yn tyller-ma, my a wor lemyn yn ta, pan yw mar whêk aga êth,* these are rods of grace, for you have not smelt in any place savour like this ever ; God is in this place, I know it well, since their breath is so sweet. O.M. 1904. *Otté lour kunys gyné, whylhyns lemmyn pûp yn freth ; nêb na whytho grêns funnyé gans y lappa worth an eth,* see fuel enough with me, let all now blow vigorously ; he who does not blow, let him fan with his lap to the blast. P.C. 1244. This word seems to be connected with *whêth*. W. *eth, chwŷth.*

ETHAS, adj. Eighth. *Lluyd,* 105, 243. Written also *eathas,* qd. v.

ETHEUCH, v. n. Ye went. 2 pers. pl. preter. of irr. v. *môs. Yma tra varth wharvethys haneth ; an kêth gwêl-ma, yn dôr ynnôns ol gwrydhyys, ha'n thŷr dhe onan yw unŷys, aban etheuch a le-ma,* there is a wonderful thing happened to-night ; these same rods, in the earth they are all rooted, and the three are joined in one, since ye went from hence. O.M. 2086. W. *aethoch.*

ETHLAYS, adj. Cursed. *Ethlays, gwef pan vêv genys ; ow terry gormenadow Dew, pellys ôn a Paradys dhu'n noer veys er agan gew,* cursed, woe when I was born ; breaking the commandments of God, we are driven from Paradise to the earth world for our woe. C.W. 76. This may be formed from the Eng. *outlawed.*

ETHOM, s. m. Want, need, necessity. *Dhe'n Arluth ethom yma dhe wruthyl gans an rê-na,* to the Lord there is need to do with those. P.C. 182. *Pyth yw an ethom vyé an oynyment kêr y skullyé, ef a gutse bôs gwyrthys,* what is the need there was the precious ointment to spill, it might have been sold. P.C. 533. *Nêb a wo y gorf golhys, nyn jeves ethom golhy, saw y treys na vôns seohys, rag gullen yw ol yredy,* he whose body is washed hath need to wash only his feet, that they be not dried, for he is all clean surely. P.C. 803. *Yn agan ethom pûp tra pûp ür parys dhyn vedhé,* in our need every thing always would be ready for us. P.C. 917. W. *eisiau, esiw.* Arm. *ezom.* Ir. *easbha, easbadh.* Gael. *easbuidh.* Sansc. *esha.*

ETHOMOG, adj. Needy, necessitous. Pl. *ethomogyon. Pan welas an Edhewon bôs Crist ow cuthyl meystry, ow onré ethomogyon, hag anedhe na wre vry,* when the Jews saw that Christ was doing mastery, loving the poor, and that of them he made no account. M.C. 26.

ETHONS, v. n. They went. 3 pers. pl. preterite of irr. v. *môs. Pan ethons oll dhe wary, ancombrys y rebea, pema, y mêdh Crist dhydhy, nêb a vyn dhe guhudha,* when they went all out, not of one mind they were ; where is, says Christ to her, any one that will accuse thee. M.C. 34. W. *aethont.* Arm. *ezont.*

ETHUC, adj. Huge, great, awful, terrific, wonderful. *Dyspleytys yw y vaner, ha kelmys worth an growes pren ; mar ethuk yw dhe weles may tyglyn an tybeles, pan y'n gwellons, kettep pen,* displayed is his banner, and fastened to the cross tree ; so awful it is to see, that the devils will wince, when they see it, every head. P.C. 3046. ‡ *Ha me rig clowes an poble galarou, ta eth reas do chee ethic gwrîg da,* and I did hear the people complain, that there is to thee an awfully good wife. *Pryce.* It is variously written *ethec, cthyc, ithic, ythec, uthyc.* W. *uth, uthyr.* Arm. *euzic.* Ir. *uathmhar*, †*uath.* Gael. *uamharr.*

ETHYM, v. n. I went. 1 pers. s. preterite of irr. v. *môs. My a ethym, Lluyd, 247. W. aethum.*

ETHYS, v. n. Thou wentest. 2 pers. s. preterite of irr. v. *môs. Yn mêdh y wrêk, mûr a varth brâs yw henna dhym rum lewté, hedhow pan ethys yn mes cleves vŷth ny'th kemersé,* says his wife, much of great wonder is that to me indeed ; this day when thou wentest out, never a sickness had seized thee. M.C. 157. W. *aethost.*

EUCH, v. n. Go ye, ye shall go. 2 pers. pl. imp., and fut. of irr. v. *môs. Euch, yn fen dh'y dhyscyblon, ha leverouch wy dhedhé,* go ye at once to his disciples, and say ye to them. M.C. 256. *Euch, growedheuch, ow arluth, may haller agas cudhé gans dyllas,* go, lie down, my lord, that you may be covered with clothes. O.M. 1923. *Euch tynneuch an gasadow, usy ow cûl fals dewow, yn mês agan temple ny,* go ye, drag the wretched woman, who is making false gods, out of our temple. O.M. 2691. *Euch ganso yn kettep pen dhe'n iustis Pylat arté,* go ye with him every head to the magistrato Pilate again. P.C. 1796. *(To go with* is also the Welsh idiom for *to bring.) Euch dhe'n wovyn hep lettyé worth an gôf yn marches row,* go ye to ask, without delaying, of the smith in Market Row. P.C. 2667. *Mar scap yth euch dhe'n mernans,* if he escape, ye shall go to death. R.D. 378. *An corf a whyleuch deffry, ganso yth euch yredy yn y clos,* the body ye seek really, with it ye shall go indeed into his glory. R.D. 1289. W. *ewch.*

EUH, adv. Above, over. ‡ *Ha Dew wrûs an ebbarn, ha dhebherhas an dowrow, era en dadn an ebbarn, dhort an dowrow era euh an ebbarn ; ha andellna etho,* and God made the firmament, and divided the waters (that) were under the firmament, from the waters (that) were above the firmament ; and so it was. C.W. p. 189. A late form of *uch*, qd. v.

EUHEL, adj. High, lofty. Sup. *euhella,* supreme. ‡ *Chee dên krêv, leb es war tŷr, hidhew gwra, gen skians fŷr, ha'n Dew euhella vedn ry, pêth yw gwella-ol rag why,* thou strong man, who art on earth, this day act with wise knowledge, and God supreme will give the thing that is best for you. *Cornish Proverb. Pryce.* More generally written *huhel,* qd. v.

EUHELLE, v. a. To go up, to ascend. ‡ *An trŷga dŷdh ef deravas arta dort an marrow, ha euhellas do nêv, ha eedhas war dorn dyhow an Tâs ollgallosek,* the third day he rose again from the dead, and ascended to heaven, and sat upon the right hand of the Father Almighty. C.W. p. 203.

EUNOW, s. m. Lambs. *Pryce.* One of the plurals of *oan,* qd. v.

EURE, s. m. A goldsmith. Corn. Voc. *aurifex*. The root is *eur*, gold, the old form of *our*, and the termination *c* has the force of an appellative, as in *idné*, qd. v., answering to the Welsh *ai*: as in *gwestni*, a host; *blotai*, a meal-man; *cardotai*, a mendicant; *magai*, a nurse. W. *eurych*, a goldsmith.

EUS, v. n. Go ye. A late corruption of *euch*. ‡ *Eus barha nei*, go with us. *Llwyd*, 252.

EUS, v. subs. Is. *Dhyuch lavaraf, ow dyskyblyon, pyseuch toythda ol kes-colon Dew dreys pup tra, eus a huhon, dheych yn bys-ma y gráth danvon*, to you I say, my disciples, pray ye forthwith, all with one heart, God above all things, who is on high, to you in this world his grace to send. P.C. 3. *Euch, ow dew êl, dhum servons lêl, yn pryson eus*, go ye, my two angels, to my faithful servants, who are in prison. R.D. 316. Another form of *ús*, qd. v.

EUTH, adj. Fright, horror. *A Dhew a rás, serpont yw hy, euth hy gwelas, own a'mbus vy, crennd a wráf*, O God of grace, it is a serpent; it is a horror to see her, fear is upon me, I do tremble. O.M. 1452. *Yn beydh pan y'n gorsyn ny, wharré y tueth deulugy, warnan cothas, hag a'n teul ef scon yn ban, ha'n dôr warnodho a ran, euth y clewas*, when we put him in the grave: presently there came devils, they fell upon us; and they throw him forthwith upwards, and divide the earth over him; it was a horror to hear them. R.D. 2128. See *Uth*.

EV, pron. subs. He, him, it. A late form of *ef*, qd. v., and it was thus pronounced in Jordan and Llwyd's time. *Y festa formys devery, der y wreans êv omma*, thou wast formed surely, by his workmanship here. C.W. 16. *Der henna ythof grevys y wellas êv exaltys, ha me drês dha yselder*, at that I am grieved, to see him exalted, and me brought to lowness. C.W. 34. *Ev a vervcys*, he died. *Llwyd*, 230. *Ev ew dén da*, he is a good man. 246. *Ev ai dhyg dhym*, he brought it to me. 242. This is also the sound in modern Welsh.

EVALL, adj. Humble, lowly. *Cayn ythew ow máb cotha, ha Abel yw ow máb younka, flchys evall ha gentle*, Cain is my eldest son, and Abel is my youngest son, children humble and gentle. C.W. 78. *Me a wêl an eal yn yet ow sevell, splan dhe welas, me a vyn nós pûr evall en dhodho dh'y salugy*, I see the angel in the gate standing, bright to see, I will go very humbly to him to salute him. C.W. 128. A late form of *huvel*, qd. v.

EVE, v. a. To drink, to imbibe. Written also *efé*. 2 pers. s. imp. *eyf*; part. pass. *evys*. *Mara ós profus lêl, rýs yw dhyso dyogel ry dour dhyany dhe evé*, if thou art a faithful prophet, need is to thee certainly to give us water to drink. O.M. 1801. *Kens mós, cyf ten gwýn pymeth*, before going, drink thou a draught of spiced wine. O.M. 2294. *Wosé henna evyn pép ol adro dracht a wýn, rag comfortyé y golon*, after that let us drink every one all round a draught of wine, to comfort his heart. O.M. 2626. *Dûs yn mês, vynytha ny efyth coul, marrow cowal ty a fýdh*, come out, thou shalt never drink broth, thou shalt be quite dead. O.M. 2701. *Yn médh Christ, hemma yw goys, evouch why par cheryta*, says Christ, this is blood, drink ye through charity. M.C. 45. *Kymereuch, eveuch an gwýn, rág ny evaf bys dédh fýn genouch annodho na moy*, take ye, drink ye the wine, for I will not drink until the last day with you of it any more. P.C. 724. *Eveuch ol an gwýn*, drink ye all the wine.

P.C. 823. *Pysouch may fevé evys*, pray ye that it may be drunk. P.C. 828. *An mýl dyaul re dorro mellow y gýn, vynytha na effo coul*, may a thousand devils break the joints of his back, so that he may never drink broth. P.C. 1620. *Otta dywes dhys omma, prag na wreta y efé*, see a drink for thee here, why wilt thou not drink it. P.C. 2981. W. *yved; †iben*, I drank. Arm. *eva*. Ir. *ibh, †ib; †ibim*, I will drink. Gael. *ibh*. Manx, *ia*. Sansc. *pi*.

EVERETH, s. m. Vanity, frivolousness, idleness. *Peder, taw ha gás dhe flous, rák evereth yw dhe gows, ef dhe sevel*, Peter, be silent, and leave thy mockery, for idleness it is to say that he is risen. R.D. 936. Written also *ufereth*, qd. v. W. *overedh*.

EVREDHEC, adj. Maimed, disabled, lame. *Dhynmno evredhek yn weth, ro nerth dhe gerdhes yn fás, ha my a grýs yn pyrfeth aga vós guecl a vúr rós*, to me also the maimed, give thou strength to walk well, and I will agree perfectly that they are rods of great grace. O.M. 2009. Written also *effredh*, qd. v. W. *evrydh*.

EVY, pron. subs. Of me, mine. *Ke yn cerdh, ow máp evy, ha nefra ow bannat dhys*, go away, my son of me, and over my blessing to thee. O.M. 725. *Ow máp evi*. Llwyd, 245. *Evy* is used after a substantive preceded by *ow*, my, to add emphasis. The equivalent in Welsh is *vy máb i*.

EW, v. subs. He is. 3 pers. s. present of *bós*, to be. *Mûr a foly ew dhodho an kéth fruit-na mar a'n gás*, it is a great folly in him, if he leaves that same fruit. O.M. 191. *Yn mês a'm ioy ha'm whekter, rés ew keskyr dre terros, rag fout gwesc ha goscutter, namna vyrwyn rág anwos*, away from my joy and my delight, we must wander through lands, for want of clothes and shelter, we are well nigh perishing for cold. O.M. 360. *Ow thás ew cóth ha squythous, ny garsé pellé bewé*, my father is old and wearied, he would not wish to live longer. O.M. 737. Written indiscriminately *ew*, or *yw*, qd. v.

EWHAL, adj. High, lofty. *Llwyd*, 147. Another form of *huhel*, qd. v.

EWHE, s. m. Evening. *Dhym y leverys perfeyth, ugy dhe euhé an geydh, yn paradys ty a séf*, to me he said perfectly, within the evening of the day, in paradise thou shalt stand. R.D. 275. W. *echwydh*. Arm. *echoaz, anchoe, ache*. Ir. *oidhche, taidche, tasbuith*. Gael. *oidhche*. Manx, *oie*.

EWHELDER, s. m. Height. *Llwyd*, 240. A late form of *uchelder*, qd. v.

EWIC, s. m. A hind, a deer. Corn. Voc. *cuhie*, *cerva*; *loch euhic*, *hinnulus*, a hind-calf. *Ewig twyl*, a fallow deer. *Llwyd*, 53. W. *cwig, †cguic, †cuyc*. Ir. *agh*. Gael. *agh*. Sansc. *agha*, she-goat.

EWIDIT, s. m. A lark. Corn. Voc. *alauda*. Llwyd, 42, thus reads it, *ewidydh*. The reading of the Cornish Vocabulary is doubtful, whether *ewidit*, or *ehidit*. The former may be correct, being compounded of *ev*, id. qd. *uch*, high, and *héd*, flight. W. *uchedydh*. See *Ehidit*.

EWIN, s. m. The nail of the fingers or the toes. Corn. Voc. *euin*, *unguis*. Pl. *ewinas*. W. *ewin, †eguin*. Arm. *ivin, †yuyn*. Ir. *ionga, inga, †in*. Gael. *ionga, †in*. Manx, *ingin*. Gr. ὄνυξ. Lat. *unguis*. Sansc. *nakka*; from *nakk*, to pierce.

EWINCARN. s. m. A hoof of an animal. Corn. Voc.

ungula. Comp. of *ewin*, a nail, and *carn*, a hoof. W. *carn.*

EWINOC, adj. Having nails or claws. W. *cwinog.* Corn. Voc. *kenin euynoc*, garlic. See *Cenin.*

EWINREW, s. f. Numbness of the fingers or toes from cold. W. *ewinrew.* Arm. *ivinrev.* This word is still in use in Cornwall, under the form of *Gwenders;* "a disagreeable sensation in the fingers and toes, arising from violent cold. In some parts of Cornwall it is pronounced *wonders*." Polwhele. Comp. of *ewin*, and *rew*, frost.

EWITER, s. m. An uncle. Corn. Voc. *ewiter abard tat*, *patruus*, an uncle on the father's side; *ewiter abarh mam*, *avunculus*, an uncle on the mother's side. W. *ewythr.* Arm. *eontr.* Lat. *patruus.* Sansc. *pitarwyas.*

EWN, adj. Right, straight, just, meet, exact. *Seth a vŷdh y ewn hanow,* Seth shall be his right name. O.M. 678. *Yn ewn fordh dhy may'th yllyn, may fên hembrynkys, pesyn en Tâs Dew,* in the right way to it that we may go, that we may be led, let us pray the Father God. O.M. 1072. *Lemyn ythew ewn hŷs, ewnyn ef yn scon dh'y le,* now it is the right length, let us adjust it immediately to its place. O.M. 2525. *Râg ewen anwos, ny glewaf yender dhum troys,* for very chilliness, I do not feel the cold, to my feet. P.C. 1222. *Mar a'm ewn geryth, me a'th pŷs, dhymmo gâs crês,* if thou lovest me well, I pray thee, leave peace to me. R.D. 1449. W. *iawn*, *eunt.* Arm. *eun, eeun.* Ir. *eigean, ion.* Gael. *ion.*

EWNE, v. a. To make right, to rectify, to make straight, to adjust. *Harlyth my a'n trehy onnuu, hag ewnnê gans ol dhe nel,* I will cut it exactly here, and adjust thou it with all thy strength. O.M. 2516. *Ewnyn ef yn scon dh'y le,* let us adjust it immediately to its place. O.M. 2526. *An jawl re'th ewno dh'y glâs,* the devil adjust thee to his maw. O.M. 2526. *Lemmyn gorryn ef yn beydh, ewnyn an mên warnodho,* now let us put him in the tomb, let us adjust the stone over it. P.C. 3207. *Ewnê an mên me a wra;* a *wottensê ewnys da,* I will adjust the stone; behold it well adjusted. P.C. 3211. W. *iawni.* Arm. *euna.*

EWNHINSIC, adj. Just, upright. Corn. Voc. *ewnhinsic*, *justus.* Comp. of *ewn*, right, and *hins*, id. qd. W. *hynt*, a way. See *Camhinsic.*

EYCHAN, interj. Alas, woe, oh! *Ellas ny won py tyller, bŷth moy py le y trygaf; eychan, râg y fynner mar a kyller, gans paynys mêr ow dyswul glân,* alas, I know not (in) what place, ever more where I shall dwell: Oh woe! for it is wished, if it could be, to destroy me quite. P.C. 2599. *Eyhan* is another form, the aspirate being softened. W. *ochan.* Arm. *achân.* Ir. *och hone.* Gael. *ochoin.*

EYF, v. a. Drink thou. 2 pers. s. imp. of *evé*, qd. v. *Kens môs, eyf ten gwŷn pymeth ha dhe scafé yth êth yn ow nygys my a grŷs,* before going, drink thou a draught of spiced wine, and the more nimbly thou wilt go in my errand, I believe. O.M. 2294.

EYHAN, interj. Alas! woe, oh! *Kueth ûs y'm colon, eyhan! mars êth corf Dew y honan, py le y fŷdh e keffys,* sorrow is in my heart, alas! if the body of God himself is gone, where shall it be found? R.D. 700. Another form of *eychan*, qd. v.

EYL, pron. adj. One of two, the one, one or the other. *A'n golon yth êth strêt brâs dour ha goys yn kemeskys, ha ryp un gyw a resas dhe dhewelê nêb a'n gwyskis; y wholhas y dhewlagas gans y eyll leyf o goys, dre râs an goys y whelas Ihesus Crist del o dythgtis,* from the heart there went a stream great, water and blood mingled, and by the spear it ran to the hands of him that struck him; he washed his eyes with his one hand that was bloodied, by virtue of the blood he saw Jesus Christ how he was treated. M.C. 219. This is also written *yll*, qd. v. It has exactly the same meaning as *neyl*, qd. v. W. *aill*, other.

EYL, s. m. An angel. *Worth an pen y a welas dhe'n bêdh, yw leverys kens, un flôch yonk, gwyn y dhyllas, eyl o, ha y ny wodhyens,* at the head they saw of the grave, (that) is mentioned before, a young child, white his apparel, an angel it was, and they knew it not. M.C. 254. More generally written *êl*, qd. v.

EYN, adj. Icy, very cold, chilling. *War tu a y vam a'n pewo, y ben a vynnas synsy, ha'y enef êth anodho gans garm eyn hag uchel gry,* on the side of his mother that owned him, he would hold, and his soul went from him with a chilling wail and loud cry. M.C. 207. Another form of *iein*, qd. v.

EYR, s. f. An hour. *Rag henna y tanvonas Crist dhodho ef may'n dampnê; rûth veyr a dûs a'n sewyas, pûb eyr parys dh'y vlamyê,* therefore he sent Christ to him that he might condemn him; a great multitude of people followed him, every hour ready to accuse him. M.C. 108. Another form of *êr*, id. qd. *ûr*, qd. v.

EYRYSDER, s. m. Happiness. Though this word is given by Pryce, there is no authority for it in Cornish. It is evidently the Arm. *eurusded*, from *eurus*, happy; and this is the French *heureux.*

EYS, s. m. Corn. Pl. *esow. Y'ma genê un bê du, gorra hag eys kemyskys, ol dhe'n bestes ûs omma a gêf bôs lour dowdhek mŷs,* I have a good bundle of hay and corn mixed; all the beasts (that) are here shall find food enough twelve months. O.M. 1058. *An dour ha'n eys yw posnys, may'th êns mûr a dûs dyswreys, ha bestes y'th wlâs,* the water and the corn are poisoned, so that many of the people are destroyed, and beasts in thy land. O.M. 1559. Another form of *ŷs*, qd. v.

EYS, conj. Than. *Bynyges re dy, dhe'n harlot pan fynsys ry an hakerê mernans yn beys; râk hacrê mernans eys emladhê y honan, ny gaffê dên, my a grŷs,* blessed be thou, to the villain when thou wouldest give the most cruel death in the world; for a more cruel death than to kill himself, no man may find, I believe. R.D. 2073. Variously written *es*, and *ys*, qd. v.

EYSYE, v. a. To praise, to commend, to extol. *Iduyd, 77. Hag yth êns dhe ben dowlyn, hag y kewsens dhe scornyê, hag a gamma nga meyn, pûb onon râg y eysyê; lowenê dhys, te yw dheyn mychtern, rŷs yw dhe wordhyê,* and they went on their knees, and they spake to scorn (him,) and they made wry their mouths, every one to extol him; joy to thee, thou art to us a king, need is to worship thee. M.C. 137.

EYSEL, s. m. Vinegar. *Nyns yw Ely a gylwa; seches dhoîho yma, ef a'n gevê drôk wyras: ottensê gynef parys, bystel eysel kymyskys, wassel mars ûs seches brâs,* it is not Elias whom he calls; thirst to him there is, he has found it an evil relief; behold them with me ready, gall (and) vinegar mixed; wassail, if there is great thirst. P.C. 2077. *Gans an Edhewon, war hast drôk dhewas a ve dythgtis, tebell lycour, mûr y last, eysyll bestyll kemyskis*, by the Jews in haste bad drink was provided, bad liquor, great its nastiness, vinegar (and) gall mixed. M.C. 202.

EYTHINEN, s. f. Furze, gorse. Corn. Voc. *rhamnus*. See *Eithin*.

EZHOF, v. s. I am. Lluyd, 247. This is a reduplicate form of *of*. W. *ydwyv*.

F

This letter is a radical and immutable in Welsh and Armoric. In Cornish it is both a radical and a secondary. When radical in early Cornish it was also immutable. When secondary it is the aspirate mutation of *p*, as *pen*, a head, *ow fen*, my head; *aga fen*, their head. This is another form of *ph*, as written in Welsh, *pen, ei phen*; her head. In Armoric this mutation is also written *f*; as *penn*, *he fenn*, her head. In Cornish, *f* is also a regular mutation of *b*, and *m*, by hardening *v* after certain particles; thus *bydh*, will be; *ty a vydh*, thou shalt be; *y fydh ny*, we shall be. *Brás*, great; *yn frás*, greatly. *Más*, good; *yn fás*, well. In the Ordinalia *f* is often found after particles which always soften the initials, and the following sentence furnishes an instance of this confusion. *Nép na crȳs ny fȳdh sylwys, na gans Dew ny vȳdh trygys*, he that believes not shall not be saved, nor with God shall he dwell. R.D. 1109. In these cases *f* had the sound of *v*, as in modern Welsh. (See Lluyd, 227.) In the latest days of the existence of the language, *f* had a mutation like *b*, and *m*, into *v*. Lluyd, 241, gives as an instance *fordh*, a way; *an vordh*, the way. He also mentions another mutation of *f* into *h*, as *flóh*, a child; *a'n hlóh*, of the child; *dhe'n hlóh*, to the child. This is a regular mutation of *f*, in Irish, and Gaelic, but there is not a trace of it in the Ordinalia, or the other British dialects. In Irish, and Gaelic, *f* changes into *fh*, which however is sounded as *h*. *Fein*, self, *mi fhein*, myself. In Manx, *f* changes into *fh*, as in Irish; but having no sound it is not written; it also changes to *v*, as in late Cornish; thus—*faays*, advantage; *e oays*, his advantage, *nyn voays*, their advantage.

FABORDEN, s. m. The base in music. *Kenouch why faborden brús, ha me a cân trebyl fyn*, sing ye a great base, and I will sing a fine treble. R.D. 2359.

FACYE, v. a. To make a face, to pretend. *Ny remnaf pel ymbrcysé, rág nyns yw an vaner vás, dhe vow denvydh ny'm gorsé, kyn facyen mûr. renothas*, I will no longer judge, for the custom is not good, no man any more could place me, though we may pretend much. P.C. 1680. *Gans spern gwrech y curené, rák an harlot dhe facié y vós mychtern Yedhewon*. with thorns do ye crown him, for the knave pretended that he was king of the Jews. P.C. 2065.

FADIC, s. m. A fugitive. Corn. Voc. *profugus*. W. *fwediq* from *foi* Corn. *fyé*, to flee.

FAIDUS, adj. Beautiful. Cornish Vocab *formosus*. W. *gwedhus fuedhus*, luxuriant; *fawdhus*, radiant. Arm. *faezus, fezuz feazur*, surpassing.

FAL, s. m. A spade, a shovel. The aspirate mutation of *pál*, qd. v. *Arluth côf ol henna gulan, try hés ow fál mar a'm be, my ha'm gnorék, ha'm flóch byhan bysy vȳdh dhe sostené*, all wise Lord, that altogether, if I have three

lengths of my spade, me, and my wife, and my little child, it will be hard to support. O.M. 396.

FAL, s. m. A prince. *Pryce*.

FALHUN, s. m. A falcon. Corn. Voc. *falbun*, falco vel capum. W. *gwalch*. Arm. *falchan, falchun*.

FALL, s. m. A failing, deficiency, fail, fault. *Dèn glán yw a béch, heb fall, ynno ef dyfout myng es*, a man clean he is of sin, without doubt, default in him is not M.C. 192. *Pan varwo gorry hep fal, ynträ y dhȳns ha'y davas*, when he dies, put them, without fail between his teeth and his tongue. O.M. 825. W. *gwall*. Arm. *gwall, fall*.

FALLAF, v. a. I will fail. The asp. mutation of *pallaf*, 1 pers s. fut. of *pally*. *Ow arluth ker Salamon, awos lavur na dewon, nefré my fallaf dhewchwhy*, my dear lord Solomon, because of labour nor sorrow, I will never fail you. O.M. 2406. *Wharré dheithy yn scon me â; bydhaf bysy war an dra, hag yn teffry bȳth ny falla'*, ow *nygys ey spedyé a wra*, anon to her soon I will go; I shall be diligent on the business, and really I will never fail, my errand I will expedite. P.C. 1933. W. *pallav*, ni *phallav*.

FALLAS, s. m. Falseness, deceit, fraud, failing. Lluyd, 242. A later form of *fallad*, from which was formed the plural *falladow*. *Dhynny ny travyth ny gréf, aban yw y wódh ef y lesky hep falladow*, to us there is nothing grievous, since it is his will to burn it without deceit. O.M. 484. *Un sarf yn gwedhen yma bést uthek hep falladow*, there is a serpent in the tree, an ugly beast, without deceit. O.M. 798. W. *gwalliad*.

FALLE, v. n. To fail, to be deficient. *Kyn fullens ol, me a vêdh, yn mêdh Pedyr, y'th servis*, though all fail, I will be, says Peter, in thy service. M.C. 49. W. *gwallaw, pallu*. Arm. *fallaat*.

FALLIA, v. a. To cleave, to split, to rive. Lluyd, 59. ‡ *Dho falliu po feldzha*: from the English.

FALS, adj. False, deceitful, treacherous. *Na ve bás fals an dèn-ma, ny'n drossen ny bȳs deso*, were it not that this man is false, we should not have brought him to thee. M.C. 99. *My re gyrhas dhys dhe drè mâb Adam, a fals huder, may hallo genen tregé*, I have fetched home to thee the son of Adam, the false hypocrite, that he may dwell with us. O.M. 505. *Out warnouch, fals marregion, pȳth yw an whethlow, ha'n sôn a ylewaf aberth yn pow*, out upon ye, false soldiers, what are the tales, and the report that I hear in the land. R.D. 607. W. *fals*. Arm. *fals* Ir. *fallsa*. Gael. *fallsa*. Lat. *falsus*. Germ. *falsch, valsch*.

FALSE. v. imp. It seems. *Blewec, cuynt yw, ha hager; ny won pana vést ylla bús; yth falsé orth y savour y bosu nèb bucka nôs*, hairy, rough it is, and ugly, I know not what beast it is; it seems by its savour that it is some hobgoblin of the night. C.W. 114. *Me a welos wedhen moy, ha sarf yn bòn ynny, marow, seich, hy a falsa*, I saw one tree more, and a serpent on the top of it, dead, dry it appeared. C.W. 138.

FALSLYCH, adv. Falsely. *Trueth vyé dèn yw guldn falslych y bones dysnerȳs*, it were a pity that a man who is pure should be falsely destroyed. P.C. 2438. *Mûr vcnions ha calas ran ef a whylas, Jhesu Cryst mychtern a néf, ha falslych y'n iuggyas ef gans cam pûr vrâs*, great vengeance and a hard lot he sought, Jesus Christ the king of Heaven, and falsely hath sentenced him with very great wrong. R.D. 2263.

FALSURY, s. m. Falsehood. *Iudas Scharyoth a's cublé, ha gans mûr a falsury*, Judas Iscariot cavilled at her, and with much falsehood. M.C. 35. *Yn ûr-na mar a kewevys falsury, ha na blêk genas henna, ha fâls, te dôk dustuny*, in that hour if I spoke falsehood, and that does not please thee, and false, do thou bear witness. M.C. 82. *A Dâs kûf y'th wholowys, an sarf re rûk ow thollé, dh'y falsury y cresys*, O Father dear in thy lights, the serpent hath deceived me, her falsehood I believed. O.M. 287.

FARA, s. m. Regard, notice. *Lavar lemmyn, ty Ihesu, pa'n drôk vo yn a-wr-tu a dhysquydhysta dhynny, pan wrela nar coynt fara, ow scollyé agan guara, ha'n fêr orth y tystrycy*, tell now, thou Jesus, what evil is there on any side that thou hast shewn to us, when thou makest such sharp notice, scattering our wares, and destroying the fair. P.C. 340. *Me a vyn môs dhom scra dha weclas pana fara a wra ef a'n nowedhys*, I will go to my father, to see what regard he will make of the news. C.W. 86.

FARDEL, s. m. A load, a burden. Pl. *furdellow*. *Gynef ymn fardhel pûr dha war ow keyn*, I have a very good load on my back. O.M. 1617. *Pûp dên ol degyms ganso y pyth, an mêns a allo, war aga keyn fardellow*, let every man carry with him his things, all that he can, burdens on their back. O.M. 1593. This is not a Celtic term, being the old English *fardel*. Fr. *fardeau*. Sp. *fardel, fardo*. It. *furdello*.

FARIA, s. f. Mary. This is to be read *Varia*, a mutation of *Maria*. Re Faria, by St. Mary. *Pryce*.

FARWE, v. n. He may die. A mutation of *marwé*, 3 pers. s. subj. of *merwel*. *Me ha'm cowyth a dreha Dismas, ha why drehcveueh ybeyn, may farwé an dhew vylen*, I and my companion will raise Dismas, and do ye raise the other, that the two villains may die. P.C. 2826.

FAS, s. m. A boasting, a brag, bragging. *Fy dheueh, a vosteryon plos, awos agys fâs ha tros, ny wra bom y worlené*, fie on ye, dirty boasters, notwithstanding your bragging and noise, a blow will not quell him. P.C. 2110. Id. qd. *fos*.

FAS, adj. Good. Yn *fâs*, well. The asp. mutation of *mâs*. *Gansé y a dhûk golow, nôs o, ny welons yn fâs*, with them they took a light, it was night, they saw not well. M.C. 64. *Yn mêdh an gôff, clevas brâs ês om develff devethys, towyl vŷth ny alluf yn fâs ynué sensy dhe wonys*, says the smith, a great disease is come on my hands, I am not able in them to hold to work. M.C. 156. *Dhymmo evredhek yn wêdh, ro nerth dhe gerdhes yn fâs*, to me maimed also, give thou strength to walk well. O.M. 2010.

FASOW, adj. Weak. *Out, ellas! gallaf fasow, ythesnf yn tewolyow, ny allaf dôs anedha*, out, alas, I am gone weak, I am in darkness, I am not able to come from thence. C.W. 24.

FAST, adj. Fast, speedy, quick, strict. *Yn ûr-na y a colmas y dhefreeh fast gans cronow*, in that hour they bound his arms fast with thongs. M.C. 76. *Yn y golon fast regeth nuta a gerensé worthys*, into his heart fast there is gone much love towards thee. M.C. 115. *Yn spong orth gwelen fast dhe Grist hy a ve hedhys, gonys oll a wrêns yn fast rây nag o Crist attendyis*, in a sponge on a rod quickly to Christ it was reached, all worked in haste, because Christ was not attended. M.C. 202. *Dre vôdh an Tâs caradow, ymma yorhyl créf ordnys, ffystynnyn fast bys dhodho*, by the will of the Father beloved,

there is a strong ship ordained, let us hasten quickly to it. O.M. 1041. *Yreys fast bys yn dhewen*, armed quite to the jaws. M.C. 242. W. *fest*.

FASTE, v. a. To make fast, to fasten. Written also *fastyé*. *Dhe'n leyff arall pan dothyans worth an grows rag y fasté*, to the other hand when they came to the cross to fasten it. M.C. 180. *Ha'n grows a ve drehevys, ha Ihesus fusteys ynny*, and the cross was raised, and Jesus fastened on it. M.C. 184. *En goys yn môs may tardhas, del fastsens an colmennow*, the blood out so that it gushed, so they fastened the knots. M.C. 76. *Yntré dew gwrên y trehy, rûk eafus trûs pren dedhy, ha'y fastié gans ebyl pren*, in two let us cut it, for to got a cross piece to it, and fasten it with a peg of wood. P.C. 2563. *Ha fasta sy dhe vreder yn luen grygyans*, and strengthen thou thy brethren in full belief. R.D. 1164. *Dh'agas fastyé yn crygyans*, to strengthen you in belief. R.D. 1174. *Fasté dhe gy dhe vreder yn lêl grygyans*, strengthen thou thy brethren in trusty belief. R.D. 2368.

FATEL, adv. How, by what means, in what manner. *Tâs ûs dhym ow levones ym gans ow thraytor dyskis, fatel dôns dhow hemeres, ha del vedhaf hombronkis*, men are to me coming, (that) are by my traitor taught, how they shall come to take me, and how I shall be led. M.C. 61. *Yn ûr-na fatel vyé, a'm bevenans del gyo screfys*, in that hour how it would be, as it is written of my life. M.C. 73. *Lavar cowyth da del ôs, fattel yllyn awwonvos en harlot*, say good fellow as thou art, how we may know the knave. P.C. 966. *Me a vyn môs dhe vyras fattel ymo gans Ihesu kêr*, I will go to see how it is with Jesus dear. P.C. 2966. Variously written *fattel, fittel, fettyl*, and in late Cornish *fatl*. It is a mutation of *patel*, and compounded of *pa*, what, and *del*, form.

FATLA, adv. How. *Me a levar dhys fatla*, I will tell thee how. C.W. 38. This is a late form of *fatel*, and is a mutation of *patla*. Llwyd, 248.

FAV, s. m. Beans. A plural aggregate; *favan*, a single bean. *Cûthû fûv*, bean cods. *Llwyd*, 13, 150. W. *fa*, sing. *facn*. Arm. *fav, fû*, sing. *faven, fuen*. Ir. †*seib*. Lat. *faba*. Fr. *fêve*.

FAWT, s. m. A deficiency, a lack, or want. ‡*Ma fawt dho vi*, there is a want to me, i. e. I want. *Llwyd*, 59. ‡*Maga liaz try cz fawt dhiuh*, as many as you have occasion for. 232. This occurs only in recent Cornish, and is borrowed from the Eng. *fault*, in the old sense of a *defect*, as used by Shakspeare.

FAY, s. f. Faith. An abbreviated form of *fêdh*, qd. v. *My a wêl tyyr gwelen gay, ny welys tekké, rum fay, bythqueth aban vêf genys*, I see three gay rods, I have not seen fairer, on my faith, ever since I was born. O.M. 1730. *Dhe fay re wrûk dhe sawyé; ke yn crês, lwaraf dhys*, thy faith hath made thee whole; go in peace I say to thee. P.C. 531. *Agan arluth hep parow, me ny'n nachaf, war ow fay*, our Lord unequalled, I will not deny him, on my faith. P.C. 910.

FE, pron. s. He. Another form of *ef*, and used generally after the verb. *Otté-fe lemmyn keffys*, see him now taken. R.D. 1901. *Govynnowch orth an geiler kyns ol, pa'n pleyt y me fe*, ask of the gaoler before all, in what plight ho is. R.D. 2053. *Lavar ol an gwîr dhymmo fatel me fu (ma fu,)* tell thou all the truth to me how he is. R.D. 2062. *Me a'n nabow dyougel, yth o fe deaul kyns merwel, aberth yn nôr*, I know it certainly, he was a devil before dying, within the earth. R.D. 2121. It is also written *vc*. *Kyn ve dysxerys an temple, yn tri dÿdh y'n drehafsé bythqueth whet na fe ve gwell*, though the temple were destroyed, in three days he would raise it, that it never yet was better. P.C. 384. W. *vc*.

FE, v. s. He was. A mutation of *be*, 3 pers. s. preter. of *bôs*. *Reson prag y fe prynnys yw Ihesus Crist dhe ordna yn nêff y vonas tregys*, the reason why he was redeemed is that Jesus Christ ordained in heaven that he should dwell. M.C. 7. *A'n nêff y fe danvenys dheworth an Tâs cledh dy*, from heaven there were sent from the Father angels to him. M.C. 18. *Ha gevys may fe dhodho kyffrys y bêch ha'y fyltye, degis na ve dheworto gweläs nêff*, and that as well his sin and his filth were forgiven to him, nor was taken from him the kingdom of heaven. M.C. 23. *Bynyges re bo an prÿs, may fe gerÿs an gorholeth*, blessed be the time that the agreement was made. O.M. 675. *Gorhel vÿth ny tremené, an for-na na fe budhys*, a ship never passed that way, that was not drowned. R.D. 2324. See *Be, Ve*.

FE, v. subs. He may be. A mutation of *be*, 3 pers. sing. subj. of *bôs*. *Rág henna my a's temptyas dhe behé, may fe ellas aga hân kepar ha ny*, for that I tempted them to sin, that "alas" may be their song like as mine. O.M. 309. *Lafuryé a wra pûp prÿs, rák dry dên dhe vôs dampnys dhe ponow, na fe sylwys*, he will labour always to bring man to be condemned to pains, that he may not be saved. P.C. 17. *Yn dan ambos yth eses, ha ken na fe da genes, gûl dhe servys ty a wra*, under an agreement thou wast, and though it be not good with thee, thou shalt do thy service. P.C. 2260. Here *fe* must be read *ve*, after *na*.

FEA, v. a. He would sin. A mutation of *pea*, id. qd. *peha*, 3 pers. s. subj. of *pchy*. *Poken a whresnen fyllell, hag y fea pêch pûr vrâs*, otherwise I should work deceit, and should sin a very great sin. C.W. 44.

FECYL, v. a. To flatter. *Worth Ihesu ef a fcelé, kepar ha pan ve hegar, yn dewedh ny acordyé y golon gans y lavar*, Jesus he flattered, as when he was amiable, at the end his heart accorded not with his words. M.C. 40.

FECYLTHER, s. m. Flattery. *Lowené dhys, a vester, yn mêdh Judas, an brathky, dhodho y rûg fckylther, hag y amué trewesy*, joy to thee, O master, says Judas, the houud, to him he made flattery, and kissed him dolefully. M.C. 65.

FECH, s. m. Sin. A mutation of *pêch*, qd. v. *Ellas my a wor henna, bones ow fêch moy yn-ta es mercy Dew*, alas, I know that, that my sin is much greater than the mercy of God. O.M. 591. *Gâf dhem ow fêch, my a'd pÿs*, forgive me my sin, I pray thee. O.M. 2726. *Dre ow fêch ty a'm collas*, through my sin thou lostest me. R.D. 146.

FECHAS, s. m. Sin. A mutation of *pechas*, qd. v. *Ha rák henna warbarth ol y fechas gulân dedhy hy y feydh gufys*, and for that, together all her sin clean to her shall be forgiven. P.C. 528. So also W. *pechod, ci phechod*.

FEDN, s. m. A head. Pryce. A mutation of *pedn*, a late corruption of *pen*.

FEDH, s. f. Truth, belief. Pryce. *Py hanow y fÿdh gylwys, lavar dhymmo, er dhe fêdh*, what name shall he be called; tell me on thy faith. O.M. 677. *Yma ow legensycé hager gowes, war ow fêdh*, there is coming down a fierce shower, on my faith. O.M. 1080. *Hen yw an crÿs, tan ow fêdh, dre pûp merk ol yn bÿs-na*, this is the middle, under my faith, by every mark in the world. O.M. 2534. Written also *fÿdh*, qd. v.

FEDH, v. subs. He shall be. A mutation of *bêdh*, id. qd. *bÿdh*, 3 pers. s. fut. of *bôs*. *A's drêns dhe Ierusalem, rág y fêdh máp yn Bethlem genys, a dhyspreen an bÿs*, let them take them to Jerusalem, for there will be a son in Bethlehem born, (that) will redeem the world. O.M. 1934. *Dro y genes dhe Ierusalem yn fen, y fêdh othom annedhé dhe gundé mâb dên defry*, bring them with thee home to Jerusalem quite; there will be need of them to put to death the Son of man truly. O.M. 1949. Sometimes *fêdh* is found irregularly for *vêdh*, and so to be pronounced. *Ha kymmys yn bÿs ûs vâs, yn mêdh an ioul, te a fêdh*, and as much in the world as is good, says the devil, thou shalt have. M.C. 16.

FEDHAF, v. subs. I shall be. A mutation of *bedhaf*, 1 pers. s. fut. of *bôs*. *Gon gwyr y fedhaf marow*, I know truly I shall die. R.D. 2030. *Yn nêf y fedhuff tregis an barth dychow gans am câr*, in heaven I shall dwell on the right side with my father. M.C. 93. In the following, *fedhaf* must be read *vedhaf*, after *ny*. *My ny fedhaf rák mêth dôs yn mjsk ow brudereth*, I shall not for shame come among my brethren. P.C. 1420.

FEDHE, v. subs. He would be. The asp. mutation of *bedhé*, 3 pers. s. subj. of *bôs*. *Taw, an êl a bregewthy a'n werten hag u'y vertu; a'y frut a wrello dybry y fêdhé kepar ha dew*, peace! the angel preached of the tree, and of its virtue; that of its fruit he who should eat would be like a god. O.M. 232. *Na eláff vÿth, ow crowedhé, nar pesy a leun golon, wharé sawijs y fedhé, del vynna Crist y honon*, nor sick any lying, if he prayed with true heart, immediately he would be saved, as Christ himself wished. M.C. 25.

FEDHONS, v. subs. They shall be. The asp. mutation of *bedhons*, 3 pers. pl. fut. of *bôs*. *Ena tûs mara kaffuf, yn mês y fedhons gorrys*, there if I find people, out they shall be put. O.M. 342. *Y popel ny vÿdh sparyys, yssel y fedhons guythys*, his people shall not be spared, down they shall be kopt. O.M. 1515. *Ha dhym y a worthebys y fedhons myttyn parys, ketep onen*, and to me they answered, that they will be to-morrow ready, every one. O.M. 2307.

FEDHYTH, v. subs. Thou shalt be. The asp. mutation of *bedhyth*, 2 pers. s. fut. of *bôs*. *An ioul dhe Adam kewsys a'n aval te kemer tam, avel Du y fedhyth gwrÿs, pan y'n provas, nynjo mâs*, the devil to Adam said, of the apple take thou a bit, like God thou wilt be made, when he proved it, it was not good. M.C. 6.

FEEN, v. s. We may be. A mutation of *been*, 1 pers. pl. subj. of *bôs*. *Yn ewn fordh dhy may 'th yllyn, may feen hembrynkys, pesyn en Tâs Dew, luen a verey*, in the right road to it that we may go, that we may be led, let us pray the Father God, full of mercy. O.M. 1973.

FEER, adj. Prudent, wise. Pryce. More correctly written *fir*, qd. v.

FEETH, v. a. He will overcome. 3 pers. s. fut. of *fethy*, qd. v. *Dre grâth an nêf, agan Tâs ny a's feeth kyn fo mûr fel*, through the grace of heaven, our Father will overcome it, though it be so fierce. O.M. 1066.

FEGANS, s. m. Necessaries. A mutation of *pegans*, qd. v. *Cuntell warbarth ow fegans, me a vyn môs pûr uskys, ha wosé hemma dewhans, pell yn devyth dhe wandra*, gather together my necessaries; I will go very quickly, and henceforth speedily far in the desert to wander. C.W. 84.

FEHAS, s. m. Sin. A mutation of *pehas*, qd. v. *Ow conselar whêk y'th pesaf, dysk dhymmo un ankenek râg ow fehas*, my sweet adviser, I pray thee, teach me a penitential hymn for my sin. O.M. 2257.

FEL, adj. Subtle, cunning, wily. *Dên fel mûr yw, hag yngyn; gwcyt y werennyé prêst yn tyn, byth na seapyé*, a very cunning mau he is, and ingenious; take care to iron him very tightly, that he may never escape. P.C. 1886. W. *fel.* Ir. *feall*, trickery. Gael. *feall*, id.

FELDZIIA, v. a. To cleave, split, rive. *Llwyd*, 59.

FELEN, s. f. Wormwood. *Llwyd*, 41. A late form of *fuclin*, qd. v.

FELEN, adj. Brutal, cruel. *Erna'n preuny yn felen, ha nacha ol dhe gous gulân*, until thou catchest it cruelly, and clean recant all thy talk. O.M. 2653. A mutation of *melen*, qd. v.

FELLA, adv. Further. A mutation of *pella*, qd. v. *Sâf ena, na nês, na dhûs, na fella, râg my fynnaf*, stand thou there, nor nearer, come not, nor further, for I will not. O.M. 1404. *Mêsk ow pobel ny vynnaf na fella agas godhaf*, among my people I will not longer suffer you. O.M. 1595. *Ancow yw dynythys scon dhymmo vy, ny'm bûs lyneé na fella*, death is come soon to me, there is no longer living for me. R.D. 2210.

FELLET, adj. Corrupted. *Guin fellet*, Cornish Vocab. *acetum*, vinegar. *Fellet* is the participle passive of *fallé*, to fail, qd. v.

FELLORES, s. f. A female fiddler. Corn. Voc. *fidicina.* W. *flores ; fidor*, a fiddler, from the English.

FELLYON, adj. Foolish, silly. Plural of *fôl*, qd. v. *Ysouch gokky ha fellyon, ha teul yn agas colon, râk fout crygy*, ye are silly and foolish, and deceit is in your heart, for want of believing. R.D. 1273.

FEMA, v. subs. I was. *Ellas, pan fema gynys, ancow yw dynythys scon dhymmo vy*, alas, when I was born, death is come soon to me. R.D. 2207. To be read *vema*, a mutation of *bema*. This may be considered as compounded of *be*, was, and *ma*, for *my, I*; or it may be the regular Welsh form of *bum i*, 1 pers. s. preterite of *bôs*.

FEN, s. m. A head, an end. The aspirate mutation of *pen*, qd. v. *Yn le basnet war ow fen, curyn a spern lym ha glew*, instead of a helmet on my head, a crown of thorns sharp and stiff. R.D. 2581. *Aga fen y a saekyé, hag a gewsy pûr debell*, their heads they shook, and spake very foully. M.C. 195.

FEN, adj. Strong, strenuous, eager. *Y a fystena yn fen arté dh'y dyerbené*, they hastened eagerly to meet him. M.C. 167. *Dro y genes dhe drê dhe Ierusalem yn fen*, bring them with thee home to Jerusalem at once. O.M. 1948. *Yn fen kymmer a nyl pen*, firmly take thou the one end. O.M. 2767. *A fystynyn ny yn fen*, Oh, let us hasten eagerly. R.D. 715. *Hallyens pûp dên ol yn fen*, let every man haul strenuously. R.D. 2275. *Fen* is a mutation of *men*, qd. v., by the usual hardening after *yn*, of the soft mutation *ven*. So *mûs, vûs, yn fûs*.

FEN, v. subs. I should be. A mutation of *bên*, 1 pers. s. subj. of *bôs*. *Y volungeth mars ywa, y offendyé ny vynna kyn fên marow yn torma, an mernans me a'n kymi-*

mer, if it is his will, I will not offend him; though I should die at this time, the death I will take it. O.M. 1331. *Saw levercueh, concethé, py kefer pren dh'y crowsyé, my ny voon, kyn fên ledhys*, but say, comrades, where shall be found wood to crucify him? I know not, though I should be killed. P.C. 2536. *My ny'n grussen, kyn fên ledhys*, I would not have done it, though I should be killed. P.C. 3024.

FEN, v. subs. We should be. A mutation of *bên*, 1 pers. pl. subj. of *bôs*. *Ol ny a pys, may fên gwythys râk an bylen*, all we pray, that we may be preserved from the evil one. P.C. 41. *Yn dellu yth il codha, a his warnan yn torma, na fên hardh dh'aga gwythé*, so the people may fall on us at this time, that we may not be able to keep them. P.C. 2297. *Na gefyn, war ow ené, kyn fên neffré ow ponyé yn pâp toll worth y whylas*, we shall not find, upon my soul, though we be ever running in every hole seeking him. R.D. 550.

FENESTER, s. f. A window. Corn. Voc. *fenestra*. It is also called *prenest, besidar*, and *beisder*, qd. v. W. *fenestyr, fenestr*. Arm. *prencstr, prenest,* †*fenestr,* †*fanest*. Ir. †*scinistir*. All from the Lat. *fenestra*. It is also called in Ir. *fuindeog, fuinneog*. Gael. *uinneag*. Maux, *uinnug*. O. Norse, *vindauga*, (windeye.) Eng. *window*.

FENNAS, v. n. Thou wouldst. A mutation of *mennas*, 2 pers. s. imp. of *menny*. *Moy kyn fennas dhe gufys, pûr wgr, leskys cf a vydh, rûk cowlenwel bôdh dhe vrys*, more if thou wish to take, very truly, it shall be burnt, to fulfil the desire of thy mind. O.M. 432.

FENNE, v. n. He would. A mutation of *menné*, 3 pers. s. imp. of *menny*. *Ha dew a dhûk dustuny y'n clewsons ow levercl pûr wgr y fenné terry an tempel crêf, ha'y wuthel yn tressa dgdh*, and two bore witness, (that) they heard him say, very truly, (that) he would break the temple, and make it on the third day. M.C. 91.

FENOCHEL, s. m. Fennel. Corn. Voc. *feniculum*. In later Cornish, *funil*. Llwyd, 16. W. *fenigl*. Arm. *fanoul, fanuil*. Ir. *feneul*. Fr. *fenouil*. From the Lat. *feniculum*.

FENS, v. subs. They should be. A mutation of *bêns*, 3 pers. pl. subj. of *bôs*. *An Edhewon ny wodhyé an prennyer py fêns keffis dhe wuthyll crows anedhé*, the Jews knew not the timbers where they should be found to make a cross of them. M.C. 151. *En debell wrêk casadow gans mûr a dôth êth yn chy, war hast dhe wuthyll kentrow, may fêns crêff ha trewesy*, the wicked wife detestable with much hurry went into the house, in haste to make nails, that they might be strong and doleful. M.C. 159. *Saw kyn fêns y morthelok, dhe wêth vydhons dhe'n eronek, ha garow y yn dhulé*, but though they be hammered, they shall be worse for the toad, and rough in his hands. P.C. 2731.

FENSE, v. n. He would. A mutation of *mensé*, 3 pers. s. pluperf. of *menny*, qd. v. It is used generally as a subjunctive or conditional. *En Edhewon a govosys, henna yw dhyn bylyny ; bedheus dhe vês defendis y vonas mychtern dhynny, ha bedheus ena gorris y fensé bôs dre vestry*, the Jews said, this is to us a disgrace ; let it be put out that he was a king to us, and let there be put that he would be by force. M.C. 188.

FENSEN, v. n. I would. A mutation of *mensen*, 1 pers. s. pluperf. of *menny*, qd. v. *Yw gwgr dhyn a leveryth ; ny fensen awos travyth yn della bôs wharfethys*, is it true

FERYL 148 FETTOW

(that which) thou sayest to me? I would not for any thing so that it should happen. P.C. 1942. Here *fensen* must be read *vensen*, as in the following example also. *Hemma yw yeyn nawodhow, ow holan ythew terrys, fensan ow bosaf marow*, this is cold news, my heart is broken, would I were dead. C.W. 92.

FENTEN, s. f. A well, a fountain. Pl. *fentiniow*. *Fenten bryght avel arhans, ha pedyr streyth vûs defry ow resck a dywortty*, a fountain bright like silver, and four great streams truly, flowing from it. O.M. 771. *A dâs kêr, my a welas yn paradys fenten rûs, ha warnydhy un wedhen*, O father dear, I saw in Paradise the fountain of grace, and over it a tree. O.M. 836. *Mar ny gevyth medh py gwŷn, ke dhe fenten dhe evê*, if thou wilt not find mead or wine, go to a fountain to drink. O.M. 2436. Another form of *funten*, qd. v.

FENYGOUCH, v. a. Ye will bless. The aspirate mutation of *benygouch*, 2 pers. pl. fut. of *benygia*, or *benigia*, qd. v. *Râk y tue dydhyow, may fenygouch an torrow na's tevê vythqueth flehes*, for the days will come, that ye will bless the wombs that have never borne children. P.C. 2646.

FER, s. m. The leg. Corn. Voc. *erns*. The same authority gives *logoden fer*, sura, the calf of the leg. *Ber*, in construction *ver*, is another form. See *Ver*. In Welsh, *ber* is a leg, and *fêr*, the ankle. Gr. σφύρον. See *Logodenfer*.

FER, s. f. A fair, a mart. *Me a vyn dyskennê, ha môs yn tenpil warê dhe weles ol an fêr-na*, I will dismount, and go into the temple at once, to see all that fair. P.C. 315. *Pan wreta mar eoynt fara, ow scollyê agan gwara, ha'n fêr orth y tystryny*, when thou makest such sharp notice, scattering our wares, and destroying the fair. P.C. 342. *An fêr a fue dallethys dre tûs vûs berth yn tempel, dredho y fue dystrevys, yn môs y wrûg y teulel*, the market was begun by good men within the temple; by him it was destroyed, he did cast it out. P.C. 2400. W. *fair*. Arm. *foar*. Ir. *faidhir*. Gael. *faidhir*. Fr. *foire*. It. *fiera*. Span. *fira*. Lat. *feriæ*.

FERHAT, s. m. A thief. Corn. Voc. *fur*. There is nothing similar in the cognate dialects. Probably formed from the Latin, with the usual termination that denotes an agent.

FERNOYTH, adj. Unclad. *Yn medh Christ, a ban rûg dheuch ernoyth fernoyth ow holyê*, says Christ, since I caused you naked unclad to follow me. M.C. 50. This is a doubtful word, being written in one MS. *sernoth*.

FERROR, s. m. A blacksmith, a farrier. *Heil, ferror, lowenê dhys, ûs teyr spik vûs genes gurŷs*, hail, smith, joy to thee! Are there three great spikes with thee made? P.C. 2069. From the Lat. *ferrarius*.

FERWE, v. n. He may die. The asp. mutation of *merwê*, 3 pers. s. subj. of *merwel*, qd. v. *Pan o Ihesus Crist dampnys aberth yn crows may fervê, haccra vernans vŷth ordnys dhe creatur ny vyê*, when Jesus Christ was condemned on the cross that he should die; an uglier death was never decreed for a creature. M.C. 151. Id. qd. *farwê*.

FERYL, s. m. Peril, danger. The regular aspirate mutation of *peryl*, qd. v. *Torrê yn ow feryl vy, hag ynwêdh gwra dhe'th worty, may tebro ef annodho*, pluck it off at my risk, and also cause to thy husband that he may eat of it. O.M. 197.

FES, v. s. Thou mayest be. The asp. mut. of *bôs*, 2 pers. s. subj. of *bôs*. *Ha ganso kyn fês tewlys, te a ŷll sevell artê*, and with him though thou mayest be cast down, thou mayest stand again. M.C. 22. *A ny wodhas ow mestry, bôs dhynno may fês ledhys, bo delyffris dhe wary*, knowest thou not my power, that it is to me that thou mayest be killed, or delivered to liberty. M.C. 144.

FEST, adv. Quickly, fast, very. *Fest yn crêff me re beehas, Ihesus dhe vy ow querthê*, very strongly I have sinned, Jesus to you selling. M.C. 104. *Yth o squardijs adro ol, a'y ben y oys o scolijs, hag ynno fest luhas tol gans an dreyn a ve tellys*, all was torn about, from his head his blood was spilt, and in it quickly many a hole with the prickles was holed. M.C. 133. *Lavarow tyn hag uchel fest yn foll y a genesy*, speeches sharp and high very foolishly they spake. M.C. 238. *Fest yn tyn ef ruia sorras*, very grievously he has provoked me. O.M. 424. *My a wra fest yn lowen dhe nyggys*, I will do very joyfully thy errand. O.M. 719. *Fest pel my re'n servyas ef*, very long I have served him. O.M. 852. *A Tâs Dew, gallosek fest*, O Father, God, most powerful. P.C. 157. *A dhysempys gwercuch tân da, râk yeyn fest yw an awel*, immediately make ye a good fire, for very cold is the weather. P.C. 1209. W. *fest*.

FESTE, v. subs. Thou hast been. A mutation of *bestê*, 2 pers. s. pret. of *bôs*. *Abel, pe festê mar bel, ny gothê dhys bones hel, ow mones dhe'n sacrefys*, Abel, where hast thou been so long? thou oughtest not to be slow, going to the sacrifice. O.M. 467. More recently written *festa*. *Pragu na wreta predery, y festa formys devery, der y wreans ev onima*, why dost thou not consider, that thou wast formed surely by his workmanship here? C.W. 16. *Ty, prâg na bredersys, a dhorn Dew y festa gwrŷs*, why didst thou not consider, by the hand of God that thou wert made? C.W. 24.

FESTYNNA, v. a. To hasten, to make haste. 2 pers. s. imp. *festyn*. Written also *fysteny*, and *fystynny*, qd. v.

FET, v. subs. He shall or will be. This is to be read *vêdh*, a mutation of *bêdh*, id. qd. *bŷdh*, 3 pers. s. fut. of *bôs*. *Pûp maner bôs yn bŷs-ma ûs dhe dybry may telel, râg dên ha bêst maga ta, yn dhe lester ty a fet*, all manner of food in this world, that is incumbent to eat, for man and beast as well, in thy ship thou shalt have. O.M. 996. *Drefen luen ty dhum servyê, ow crês a fet venary*, because thou hast served me fully, my peace thou shalt have for ever. O.M. 1020.

FETEL, adj. How. Another form of *fatel*, qd. v., and indiscriminately written *fettel, fetyl, feityl*. *Lavar dhym, del y'm kerry, pan vernans a'n gevê ef, ha fetel vefê ledhys*, tell thou me, as thou lovest me, what (was) the death that he had, and how was he killed? O.M. 2220. *A tûs vûs, why re welas fetel formyas Dew an Tâs nêf ha nôr war lerch y vrŷs*, O good people, ye have seen how God the Father formed heaven and the earth after his judgment. O.M. 2826. *Fettel alhaf vy erygy corf Ihesu dhe dhasserchy, a wylys a vy marow*, how can I believe the body of Jesus to have risen, which I saw dead? R.D. 1423. *Prederys pêb a'y worfen; fettyl allo gorfenné*, let every one think of his end, how he may end it. O.M. 228.

FETTOW, v. imp. Said he. ‡*Pelen era why moaz, môz, fettow, teag*, whither are you going, fair maid, he said. Pryce. A late corruption of *medh e*.

FETH, s. m. The face, or countenance. *Tewolgow brâs a ve guris, an houl a gollas y fêth*, great darkness was made, and the sun lost his face. M.C. 200. *Y a welas war y fêth y vôs marow yredy*, they saw on his face, that he was dead already. M.C. 216. Written also *fŷth*. Borrowed from the English.

FETHE, v. a. To conquer, overcome, vanquish; to tire, fatigue; to fetch, take. *Gwyn bŷs vones dhym fethys lafur ha duwon an bŷs*, joyful that for me is vanquished the labour and sorrow of the world. O.M. 850. *Re fethas an fals ievan hydhew tergwyth*, he has overcome the false demon this day three times. P.C. 154. *Gweres, ty harlot iaudyn, ha dôk an grows war tha geyn, râk nans yw Ihesu fethys*, help, thou obstinate knave, and bear the cross on thy back, for Jesus is now fatigued. P.C. 2617. *Dhe'n beys ny â er-y-byn, hag yn y cows y'n fethyn, dre grath a vâp Dew an nêf*, to the world we will go against him, and in his talk we will vanquish him, through the grace of the Son of God of heaven. R.D. 251. *Y'th orden agan ladhé, râk na ŷl ngan fethé dre lavarow*, he will order us to be killed, for he cannot vanquish us by words. R.D. 254. *Mernans trystyns hag anger, me a wrûk aga fethé may 'th yw lemmyn da ow cher*, death, grief, and anguish, I have overcome them, that my state is now good. R.D. 500. *Par del o Dew luen a râs, ganso del fethas yw câs worth crows baner*, like as he was God full of grace, by him thus the cause is gained through the banner of the cross. R.D. 579. I take *fethy* to be another form of *gwethé*, from *gweêth*, worse. Arm. *faeza, feza*.

FEUCH, v. subs. Ye may be. A mutation of *beuch*, 2 pers. pl. subj. of *bôs*. *Dheych yn bŷs-ma y grâth dauvon, yn dywedh may feuch sylwys*, to you in this world to send his grace, in the end that ye may be saved. P.C. 5. *Me a pŷs ragouch ow thâs, may feuch sylwys dre y luen râs*, I will pray my Father for you, that ye may be saved through his full grace. P.C. 28. *Râg may feuch why sostoneys, euch dhe wonys guêl ha ton*, that he may be maintained, go ye to cultivate field and plain. O.M. 1163.

FEUCH, v. subs. Ye were. A mutation of *beuch*, 2 pers. pl. preter. of *bôs*. *Creator a brŷs benen, yn yfurn na feuch gynen, futel dhutheuch why omma*, creatures from the womb of woman, in hell ye were not with us; how came ye here? R.D. 192. Written also *fuch*.

FEVA, v. subs. I should be. The asp. mutation of *beva*. Another form of *béf*, 1 pers. s. subj. of *bôs*. *Kyn feva ledhys marow dre mûr peyn ha galarow, ny'th ty nahaf bynary*, though I should be killed dead, by great pain and sorrows, I will never deny thee. P.C. 905.

FEW, adj. Alive. A mutation of *bew*, qd. v. *A creys dhe'n nêp a'n greelas yn few, aban dassorchas y fué gynen*, Oh, believe thou those that saw him alive, since he rose again, he was with us. R.D. 1442.

FEY, s. m. Faith. *Rum fey, mûr a wokyneth yw mones dhe lesky peyth a ŷl dên orto bewé*, by my faith, a great folly it is to go to burn a thing which a man can live upon. O.M. 473. *Ef re trylyas lyes cans yn mês a'n fey*, he has turned many hundreds out of the faith. P.C. 1996. An abbreviated form of *fédh*, qd. v.

FEY, v. subs. Thou mayest be. A mutation of *bey*, id. qd. *by*, 2 pers. s. subj. of *bôs*. *Lemmyn omna ty a drŷk bŷs pan pottro ôl dhe gŷk, tuggys may fey, ty a vŷdh mernans calas*, now here thou shalt stay until when all thy flesh rots, that thou mayest be sentenced, thou shalt have a hard death. R.D. 2023.

FEYDH, s. f. Faith. Another form of *fédh*, or *fŷdh*. *My a'n te dhys, war ow feydh*, I swear it to thee, on my faith. P.C. 1469.

FEYDH, v. subs. He will be. A mutation of *beydh*, id. qd. *bŷdh*, 3 pers. s. fut. of *bôs*. *Ha râk henna warbarth ol y fethas gulân dedhy hy y feydh gufys*, and for that together all her sins clean to her shall be forgiven. P.C. 529. *Ow benneth dhyso pûp deydh, a henna crows da y feydh, pan yw c ymskemunys*, my blessing on thee every day, of that there will be a good cross, when it is accursed. P.C. 2550.

FEYF, v. subs. I may be. A mutation of *beyf*, 1 pers. s. subj. of *bôs*. *Arluth Ihesu, ro dhym an grûs par may feyf gwyw dhe gafos spâs gynes hydhew yn nêp plâs may boné vu, ha gwél a'th fâs*, Lord Jesus, give me the grace, that I may be worthy to find opportunity with thee to-day, in some place, that I may have a view, and sight of thy face. R.D. 840. See also *l'eyf*.

FEYL, adj. Crafty. *Râg mâp an pla agan temptyé yâr feyl a wra yn pûp le dhe gûl drôk tra*, for the son of evil very craftily will tempt us always in every place to do evil things. P.C. 11. W. *fel*.

FEYN, adj. Fine, keen. *Mâb Marya mûr a beyn a wodhevy yn ûr-na, râg ef a wodhya yn feyn, ha'n kŷg ny cynna henna; mês y dhensys o mar feyn pûp ûr a'n trylya dhedha, may 'th êth war ben y dhewlyn, ha pesy yn ketelma*, the Son of Mary much pain suffered at that time, for he knew keenly, and the flesh would not this; but his manhood was so fine every hour that he turned to it, that he went on his knees, and prayed in this manner. M.C. 54.

FEYN, v. subs. We may be. A mutation of *beyn*, 1 pers. pl. subj. of *bôs*. *Na hedhyn, râg yma war agan toul knoukyé fast bŷs nay feyn sqwyth*, we will not stop, for it is on our design to strike hard until we be weary. O.M. 2699.

FEYNTYS, s. m. A feint, fiction, deceit. *Lavar dhynny gwyryoneth, hep feyntys na falsury*, tell thou to us truth, without deceit or falsehood. P.C. 1478. From the English.

FICBREN, s. m. A fig-tree. Corn. Voc. *ficus*. Comp. of *fic*, from the Latin, and *pren*, a tree. So W. *figysbren*. Arm. *fiezen*.

FIGES, s. m. Figs. *Figes ledan*, broad figs, or figs properly so called. *Figes an houl*, figs of the sun, raisins. Pryce. The word is a plural aggregate, and borrowed from Latin *ficus*. So also W. *figys*. Arm. *fiez*. Ir. *figol*. Gael. *figis*. Manx, *fig*.

FILGETH, s. m. Soot. *Llwyd*, 21, who also writes it *filgedh*, 62. It is formed from the Latin *fuligo*. W. *hudhygl*. Arm. *huzil*.

FILII, s. f. A hook, sickle, scythe. *Llwyd*, 58, *filth*. *Voulz* was another corrupt form. Arm. *falch*. A Lat. *falx*.

FIN, s. m. An end, limit, boundary. *Gans nader ythof gwankys, hag ol warbarth vynyumcys a fyne trois dhe'n golon*, by a snake I am stung, and altogether poisoned from the end of my foot to the heart. O.M. 1758. W. *fin*. Gael. *finid*. Lat. *finis*. Fr. *fin*.

FIN, adj. Provident, wary, circumspect, careful. *Llwyd*, 131.

FINNEY, v. n. To proceed, to forward. *Pryce.* W. *fynu*, to produce; *fynnu*, to prosper. Arm. *finva*, to move.

FINWETH, s. m. An end. *Lucyfer kelmys yw whath pûr fast yn y golnennow, hag cf a drŷk heb fymoeth yn yffarn yn tewolgow*, Lucifer bound is very fast in his bonds, and he shall tarry without end in hell in darkness. M.C. 212. Comp. of *fin*, end, and *gwêdh*, form. Arm. *finuez*.

FIOL, s. f. A cup. Corn. Voc. *ciffus*. W. *fiol*. Arm. *fiol*. Gr. φιάλη. Lat. *phiala*. Fr. *fiole*. Eng. *phinl, vial*.

FIR, adj. Wise, sage, prudent, cunning, skilful. *Llwyd*, 248. *Fyrah*, wiser. This is the late orthography of *fûr*, qd. v.

FIRMAMENT, s. f. The firmament. Corn. Voc. *firmamentum*. In the margin *fyrvav*. Borrowed from the Latin. It is also used in Welsh, with the regular change of the mutable letters, *furvaven*. The native Welsh equivalent is *entrych*, or *entyrch*. Ir. *firmamint*.

FIRWY, v. n. To die. Written also *firwy*, qd. v.

FLAIR, s. m. A smell, a stink. Corn. Voc. *odor*. W. *flair*. Arm. *flear, flêr*. Fr. *flair*.

FLAM, s. f. A flame. Corn. Voc. *flamma*. *Ow Arluth kêr, Dew an nêf, dre dhe vertu dufydh nerth an flam ha'n tân*, my dear Lord, God of heaven, through thy virtue, assuage the power of the flame and fire. O.M. 2037. W. *flam*. Arm. *flamm*. Lat. *flamma*.

FLAMYA, v. a. To defame, to reproach. *Neb o mester ha Iustis worth Ihesus cf a gowsas, mŷns ûs omma cuntullys pûr apert y re't flamyas*, he that was master and Justice to Jesus spake, all that are here assembled, they have defamed thee very openly. M.C. 92.

FLATTOR, s. m. A chatterer. Pl. *flatturyon*. *Nyns ouch lemmyn gowygyon, ow môs dres pow, flatturyon, ow leverel an nedhow*, are ye not now liars, going through the country, chatterers, telling the news? R.D. 1511.

FLATTORES, s. f. A female chatterer. *Taw, flattores, na goes moy, ny fynnaf dhyso crygy, y vôs dhe'n nêf an corf a vrylys marow*, be silent, chattering woman, speak no more; I will not believe thee, that is gone to heaven the body I saw dead. R.D. 1067.

FLATTRYE, v. a. To chatter. Written also *flattré*. *Na wra flattryé, na gûl ges; doro an prysnes yn mês, bo ken syndys ny a vŷdh*, do not chatter, nor make mockery; bring the prisoners out, or we shall be punished. P.C. 2277. *Kyn whrylly flattré mar mûr, ahanas tra vŷth ny'm dûr, kyn 'thôs byŷy*, though thou dost chatter so much, anything from thee concerns me not, though thou be busy. R.D. 1058.

FLECHES, s. m. Children. Plural of *flôch*, qd. v. Written also *flrchys*. *Yn mêsk flechys Ysrael, dysky laha Dew huhel a wra dhedhé deydh ha nôs*, among the children of Israel, teach the law of God the High he does to them day and night. O.M. 1553. *Tûs, venenes, ha flrchys, ymóns omma dynythys*, men, women, and children, they are come here. O.M. 1611. *Fleches Ebbrow, dûn yn un rew, scon nep lettyé, erbyn Ihesu, nêb yw gwŷr Dew ow tôs dhe'n drê*, Hebrew children, let us come in a row, at once without delaying, to meet Jesus, who is true God, coming to the town. P.C. 239. *Mar tue venians vŷth ragdho, warnan ny cf re godho, ha war ol agan flechas*, if vengeance shall ever come for him, upon us may it fall, and upon all our children. P.C. 2503. *A, Adam, dhyso crês, yn wêdh dhe ol ow fleches, nŷns yw gwyryon*, O Adam, peace to thee, and to all my children, all who are innocent. R.D. 162.

FLECHET, s. m. Corn. Voc. *liberi*. The old plural of *flôch*, qd. v. In later times it was written *fleches, flechys, flrches*, qd. v.

FLEHES, s. m. Children. Plural of *flôh*, qd. v. *Noc ha'y wrêk, ha'y flehes kefrys*, Noah, and his wife, and his children also. O.M. 932. *Saw warnouch agas honan, ha war 'gas flehes vyan, kên dhe olé why a's bŷdh*, but on ye yourselves, and on your little children, cause to weep ye shall have. P.C. 2643. *Flehys mûr ha benenas, a wôr bôs ow feynys brâs, ragoff na wheleuch olé*, children many, and women, who know that my pains are great, for me seek not to weep. M.C. 108.

FLEHESSIG, s. m. A little child. *Llwyd*, 243. Plural *flehesyggow, flehysygow*. *Ha kekyffrys an bronnow na dhewes flehesyggow, gwyu aga beys er bones*, and likewise the breasts that children have not sucked, happy their fate shall be. P.C. 2649. *Râg na worsys ow hanow, ha râg an flehysygow a Israel dyscryggyon, ny's goryth dhe'n tŷr*, because thou knewest not my name, and because of the children of Israel, unbelievers, thou shalt not bring them to the land. O.M. 1868.

FLERYE, v. a. To make a bad smell, to stink. Written also *fleyryé*. *Neffré na wrello dybry, lemyn fleryé ha peddry, kepar ha seym py lyys haal*, that she may never eat, but stink and rot, like train-oil, or salt-marsh mud. O.M. 2707. *Lemmyn poevan a lesky, ow fleryé, ow mowsegy, kepar ha kueu*, but disease and burning, smelling, stinking, like as dogs. R.D. 171. *Hag y gûl dhys y greerthé dhe ancledhyas Cristenyon, na vôns yn mŷsk Yedhewon, ow fleyryé re*, and will sell it to thee to bury Christians, that they may not be among Jews, stinking too much. P.C. 1566.

FLERYS, adj. Fetid, stinking. *Noé, mar luen yw an beys lemyn a scherewynsy, may 'th ew dhewedh dynythys; ynno a gŷk pûp huny gans pêch mar er ow flerys, na allaf sparié na moy*, Noah, very full is the world now of wickedness, that the end is come, in it of flesh, every one with such great sin is fetid, that I cannot spare any longer. O.M. 945.

FLERYYS, s. m. A stinking fellow, a stinkard. *Me a wêjsk, mars êns garow, dhe voy scham dhe'n fleryys*, I will strike, if they are rough, the more shame to the stinkard. P.C. 2739. *Râk cf yw drôk wâs, war ow fay, mûr me a'n câs, an plôs fleryys*, for he is a bad fellow, on my faith, I hate him much, the dirty stinkard. R.D. 1800.

FLEYR, s. m. A bad smell, a stink. *Me a gesul bôs gansé prennys da gwôn yn nep le rag an cladhvn Crystunyon; ma na vôns y ow fleryé; aga fleyr a gl schyndyé ha ladhé mûr Yedhewon*, I advise that there be with them bought a good field in some place, for the burialplace of Christians, that they may not be stinking; their stink may injure and kill many Jews. P.C. 1547. Another form of *flair*, qd. v.

FLEYRYNGY, s. m. A stink, a stench. *Pendra wrâf orth en ioul, mar ny gaffaf toul war u'p cor; mars Cryst a weres deffry, ef a lâdh gans fleyryngy ol ow glascor*, what shall I do, if I find not for the devil a hole in some corner; unless Christ will help indeed, he will kill with the stench all my kingdom. R.D. 2133.

FLOCH, s. m. A child, a boy. Corn. Voc. *puer.* Pl. *flechet*, and later *flechos*. *Arluth hen yw re nebes, mar qurên flôch vŷth denythy*, Lord, this is too little, if we do ever a child produce. O.M. 330. *My ha'm gwrêk ha'm flôch byhan,* me and my wife and my little child. O.M. 397. *Ny a dhynyth un flôch da, dhyn a servyo,* we shall produce a good child, who may serve us. O.M. 664. *Benru, a welté dhe flôch,* woman, seest thou thy son? P.C. 2925. Arm. *flôch.* Gael. *fleasgach.* Lat. *filius.*

FLOCHOLETH, s. m. Children. *Y vennath dheuch yn tyen, keffrys gorryth ha benen, flocholeth, an gwary yw dué lemmyn,* his blessing to you wholly, men and women likewise, children, the play is now ended. O.M. 2638.

FLOH, s. m. A child, a boy. A late form of *flôch*, the guttural being lost. Pl. *flches*, qd. v., and *flchesow* is also given by Llwyd, 243. In his time it was changed in construction into *hlôh*, as *flôh*, a child; *a'n hlôh*, of the child; *gen hlôh*, with child; *an hlôh-na*, that child. 230, 242, 243.

FLOUS, s. m. Excuse, flattery, mockery. *Rum fay, gwŷr yw agas cous, ef a'n pren wythout flous, yn ta del y'n dyn-dylas,* by my faith, true is your speech, he shall pay, without excuse, well as he has deserved it. P.C. 1346. *Ha iesmas a barth aral, kycheuch ef, kerdheuch hep flous,* and Jusmas on the other side, hold ye him, go without excuse. P.C. 2524. *Peder, taw, ha gâs dhe flous, râk everth yw dhe gous ef dhe sevel,* Peter, be silent, and leave thy mockery, for idleness it is to say that he has risen. R.D. 935. Arm. *flôda,* to coax, to flatter.

FLURRAG, s. f. The prow of a ship, forecastle. Corn. Voc. *prora*. Dr. Owen Pughe has inserted *flureg*, in his Welsh Dictionary, on the authority of Dr. Davies, but as the latter gives the Liber Landavensis as his authority, it is evident that he is quoting from a copy of the Cornish Vocabulary, as I have noticed in other instances. *Flurrag* is evidently the Eng. *floor*, and Corn. *rag,* forward.

FLYRAN, s. f. A look. Llwyd, 149.

FO, s. m. A flight, retreat. *Nag êns y hardh dhe wortos, lemmen oll monas dhe'n fo,* they were not bold to stay, but all went to flight. M.C. 250. *Ny gafaf vy kên ynno, na blam dhe vones ledhys; y gasé dhe vôs dhe'n fo, nyns ûs gwel cusyl yn beys,* I find not cause in him, nor blame that he should be slain; to permit him to go away, there is not better advice in the world. P.C. 2159. *Me a vyn degy adro, ha dhe worré gy dhe'n fo a dhesempys,* I will bring around, and put him to flight, immediately. P.C. 2314. *Mgî vgî dynul a vyé gwan er-y-byn ef; yn nêp tol fyen dhe'n fo alemma,* a million devils would be weak against him; into some hole let us flee away hence. R.D. 134. W. *fo*, from the verb *foi*, to flee.

FO, v. subs. He may be. A mutation of *bo*, 3 pers. s. subj. of *bôs*. *Ke growedh war an dôr gulân, ha côsk, bŷth na sâf yn lan, erna fo cowethes gwrês,* go lie down on the earth clean, and sleep, nor ever stand up, until a help-mate be formed. O.M. 98. *A dâs, ty re dhrôs dhymmo ascorn a'm kŷk (ha'm) corf, par o may fo ow howethes,* O Father, thou hast brought to me bone of my flesh, and my body, it was meet that she should be my companion. O.M. 113. *Ow benneth prêst ty a fŷdh kefrys yn nôs hag yn geydh, ha mŷns ûs yn beys ry'th fo,* my blessing shall ever be on thee, equally by night and day, and all that is in the world be thine. O.M. 459. *An ngî torn y fŷdh re hŷr, tres wal re got yn gwŷr, ken fo mar lên musurys,* at one time it will be too long, at another too short in truth, though it be so carefully measured. O.M. 2550. Sometimes *fo* must be read *vo*, as, *ny a'n gura dhys wharré a dhyssempys hep lettyé pynag a fo,* we will do it for thee soon, immediately without stopping, whatever it might be. R.D. 2000. *Pan fo nôs,* when it is night. R.D. 2438.

FOC, s. f. A hearth, a fire-place, furnace. *Ty a whŷth avel cauch was, whŷth war gam, ny drŷk grychonen yn fôk,* thou blowest like a dirty fellow, blow athwart, there remains not a spark in the forge. P.C. 2717. *Bôs yn yfarn yw drôk fôk, ow lesky yn tân ha nôk, anken pûp prŷs,* to be in hell is an evil fire-place, burning in fire and smoke, sorrow always. R.D. 282. W. *foc.* Lat. *focus.*

FODIC, adj. Happy. Corn. Vocab. *felix.* W. *fodiawg, fodiog,* from subs. *fawd,* happiness, whence again the adj. *fawdus.* Lat. *fautus.*

FOG, s. f. A blowing house. ‡*Caria an stean dha an fôg,* carry the tin to the blowing house. *Pryce*. A later form of *fôc.*

FOL, adj. Foolish, silly, simple. Used both as an adjective and substantive. Pl. *fellyon,* qd. v. *Kayphas pûr wŷr a sorras, hag êth pûr fôl yn ûr-na,* Caiaphas very truly was angered, and went very foolish at that time. M.C. 94. *Yntrethé, avel tûs fôl, garlont spern a ve dythghthtys,* among them, like foolish men, a garland of thorns was framed. M.C. 133. *Un Edhow, avel pŷth fôll, a wyskis kenter ynhy,* a Jew like a foolish thing, struck a nail in it. M.C. 182. *Ufereth fôl yw na'n gâs,* foolish idleness it is not to leave it. R.D. 950. *A Thomas assosa fôl,* O Thomas thou art foolish. R.D. 953. W. *fôl.* Arm. *full.* Fr. *fou, folle.* Lat. *follis,* a wind-bag.

FOLIE, v. a. To play the fool, to brag. *Râg an harlot dhe folié,* for the villain did brag. *Pryce.* W. *foli.*

FOLLAT, s. m. A neckerchief, or neckcloth. *Pryce.* ‡*Ha genz hedna, an gwadngyrti genz e follat a destrias an dên kôth en gwili,* and with that the concubine with her cavalier destroyed the old man in bed. Llwyd, 252, so translates it.

FOLNETII, s. m. Folly, foolishness. *A Iowan, na gows a drues, râk ahanas marth a'm bues, ty dhe leverel folneth,* O John, speak not perversely, for I am surprised at thee, to be speaking foolishness. R.D. 961.

FOLTERGUSCE, adj. Frantic. Corn. Voc. *freneticus.* Compounded of *fulter*, id. qd. Arm. *foultr, foueltr, foeltr,* Fr. *foudre*, Lat. *fulgur, fulmen,* a thunderbolt, and *cuské,* to sleep. The literal meaning would be thunder-sleeping, or smitten by thunder.

FON, v. subs. I may be. A mutation of *bôn,* 1 pers. s. subj. of *bôs.* *Me a beys dhe wrear nessa, may fôn pûb er plegadow dhe voncs y servant ef, yn bŷs-ma, heb fallados, hu drevon bew,* I pray the Creator of heaven, that I may be desirous to be his servant in the world without deceit, and while I live. C.W. 132. An anomalous form of *bef, byf,* qd. v.

FONS, v. subs. They may be. A mutation of *bôns,* 3 pers. pl. subj. of *bôs.* *Dhe Ihesu may fôns parys dk'y gomfortyé yredy, a'n nêff y dannvenys dhworth an Tâs eledh dy,* to Jesus that they might be ready to comfort him surely, from heaven there were sent from the Father angels to him. M.C. 18. *Hag yn fast kelmys dhedhé kerdyn gwethyn yn mêsk cronow, may fŏns hyllyth dhe gronkyé*, and fast bound to them were cords weaved among thongs that they might be pliant to beat (him.) M.C. 131. *An mychtern a worhemmyn dhe ol an tyorryon way fŏns y ganso myttyn*, the king commands to all the tilers that they be with him in the morning. O.M. 2424. *Ha dhe dhulef cláf kyn fŏns, hep kentrow bŷth ny vedhons*, and though thy hands may be sore, they shall never be without nails. P.C. 2697. See *Bŏns*, *Vŏns*.

FONS, v. subs. They were. A mutation of *bŏns*, 3 pers. pl. preter. of *bós*. *Hn'n dhew-na, bŷs pan vŏns squyth, war Christ y fŏns ow cronkyé*, and those two, even until they were weary, on Christ they were beating. M.C. 132. *Hag yll troys a ve gorrys poran war ben y gelé, worth an groves y fŏns ladhyys, gans kenter gwyskis dredhé*, and the one foot was put straight over the other, on the cross they were laid, with a nail struck through them. M.C. 178. *Ow treys, homma gans daggrow re's lothas; gans y blew y fŏns syhys*, my feet she with tears has washed them; with her hair they were dried. P.C. 521. Written also *fêns, lêns*, qd. v.

FOR, s. f. A way, a road, a passage. Pl. *fúrú*. Llwyd, 45. *Ty a aswon an scryptor, ty dhe vennas sowthanas lemwyn yn mês a pŭp for*, thou knowest the Scripture, that thou shouldst wish Satan now out of every path. P.C. 2418. *Gorhel vŷth ny tremené an for-na na fe budhys*, a ship never passed that way, that was not drowned. R.D. 2324. An abbreviated form of *fordh*. W. *fôr*.

FORDH, s. f. A way, a road, a passage. Corn. Voc. *ford*. *Râg henna dhe bôb dydhythtya fordh a râg dhe vôs sylwys*, for that to every one a way he did form to be saved. M.C. 7. *War an fordh dyllas a lês a ve gorris dheragdho*, on the road garments abroad were placed before him. M.C. 29. *Lemman na veny ledhys nyng es fordh dhé onwethé*, now that we be not killed there is not a way to keep ourselves. M.C. 245. *Ny won na fordh dhum nygys*, I know not the way to my errand. O.M. 699. *Pandra yw dhe nygys, mar hŷr fordh dós may fynsys*, what is thy errand, that thou wouldst come so long a way? O.M. 734. *Y'n hanow Dew, ty môr glán, me a'th wŷsk gans ow gwelan, uger a lês fordh dhynny, may hyllyn wós dhe'n tyreth*, in the name of God, thou fair sea, I strike thee with my rod; open wide a path for us, that we may go to the land. O.M. 1677. Llwyd, 243, gives *fyrdhow*, as a plural; and in late Corn. *fordh* was changed in construction into *vordh*, as *ow vordh*, the way; '*gys fordh*, your way. Llwyd, 230. W. *fordh*. Ir. *furaimh*, a journey; *foras*, a road. In the Celtic dialects generally *ford* signifies a way by land, and in the Teutonic, one by water. The root is preserved in the Germ. *fahren*, to go.

FORH, s. f. A fork. Llwyd, 24. In late Cornish it changed in construction into *vorh*, as *an vorh*, the fork. *Vorh triverh*, a three-pronged fork. Llwyd, 166. *Forh arhans*, a silver fork. 242. The older form must have been *forch*. W. *furch*. Arm. *forch*. Ir. †*forc*. Gael. *fore*. Lat. *furca*. Germ. *vorcke*.

FORMYAS, s. m. A former, a creator. *Del ôs formyas dhe'n nêf ha'n lûr, ha dysprynnyas dhynny pŭp ŵr*, as thou art Creator of heaven, and earth, and a Redeemer to us always. R.D. 843. *Mychtern nêf re by gordhys, del ôs formyas nêf ha'n bys*, king of heaven, be thou worshipped! as thou art Creator of heaven and earth. R.D. 2524. From the verb *formyé*, with the termination denoting the agent.

FORMYE, v. a. To form, to fashion, to create, to make. Part. pass. *formyys, formys*. *Ny a vyn formyé an bŷs*, we will create the world. O.M. 11. *Ow formyé têk ha dyblans, ty rum grûk pûr havel dhys*, creating me fair and bright, thou hast made me very like to thee. O.M. 87. *Râk bones ôl têk ha du in wheddydh mŷns yw formyys, agn sona ny a wra*, for that all is fair and good, in six days all that is created, bless them we will. O.M. 143. *Ellas vŷth, pan yw kyllys Abel whêk, ow mâp kerra, na rythqueth pan vêf formys*, alas ever, when is lost sweet Abel, my dearest son, that I had ever been created! O.M. 616. *A ny vynta obeyé dhe Dhew a wruk dhe formyé, ha a formyas nêf ha'n veys*, wilt thou not obey the God who made thee, and made heaven and the world. O.M. 1506. W. *furvio*. Arm. †*furmi*. Ir. *fuirm*. Gael. *fuirm*. Lat. *formo*. For the substantive see *Furf*.

FORMYER, s. m. A former, maker, contriver, creator. *En Tâs a' nêf y'm gylwyr, formyer pŭp tra a vŷt gwerŷs*, the Father of Heaven I am called, Creator of every thing that is made. O.M. 2. W. *furvier*.

FORN, s. m. An oven, a furnace. Corn. Voc. *furnax vel clibanus*. *Gora an bara en forn*, put the bread in the oven. Pryce. In late Cornish it was changed in construction into *vorn*, as *eky vorn*, a bake house. Llwyd, 121. W. *fwrn*. Arm. *fôrn, fourn*. Ir. *sorn*. Gael. *sorn*. Manx, *surn*. Lat. *furnus*.

FORS, s. m. Aid, help, support, succour. *Nyns ûs fors awos henna; my a wôr whêth cusyl dha dhyn dhe wruthyl*, there is no help for that, I know yet a good plan for me to do. O.M. 2801. *Na fors kyn na dhrehedho, ken tol ny vŷdh gwerŷs ragdho; uy a's len may fŏns lowr hŷr*, no matter though it may not reach, another hole shall not be made for him; we will stretch them, that they may be long enough. P.C. 2758. W. *porth*. Arm. *porz*. Ir. *furtachd, beirt*. Gael. *furtachd, beart, beirt*. Sause. *bhar*, to support. (W. *beru*,) whence *bhartas*, supported. Gr. φέρτος. Lat. *partus*.

FOS, s. f. A ditch, a moat, a trench; an intrenchment, a wall. Pl. *fosow, fossow*. *Ol y pobel ymons y orth y synoé pŭp huny, ha'n môr a pŭp tu dhedhé ow sevel avel dyw fôs*, all his people they are following every one; and the sea on every side to them standing like two walls. O.M. 1690. *Dhe wûl fôs a vyyn bryntyn*, to make a wall of noble stones. O.M. 2281. *Ty vaow, darbar lym ha pry, meyn wheyl sloddyys ha genow; ha my a fystyn agy, ow trehevel an fosow*, thou boy, prepare lime and clay, building stones, trucks, and wedges; and I will hasten within, erecting the walls. O.M. 2320. *Fossow da gans lym ha pry, ha pen crêf warnedhé y gwercuh drehevel*, good walls with lime and clay, and a strong top upon them ye shall erect. O.M. 2450. W. *fôs*. Arm. *fôs*. Ir. *fos*. Gael. *fos*. All from the Latin *fossa*; à *fodio*, to dig.

FOS, s. m. A bragging. Pryce. A mutation of *bôs*, an abbreviated form of *bôst*.

FOULS, adj. False, deceitful, perfidious. Llwyd, 117. Id. qd. *fals*, qd. v.

FOVA, v. subs. He may be. A mutation of *bova*, comp. of *bo*, 3 pers. s. subj. of *bôs*, and *va* for *ve*, he. *Euch yn*

FRAUS* 153 FRINCAC

dré, *hag ordeneeh bôs pásk dhynny hep leityé, Peder hag Iowan, kerdhcuch, may fown parys wharré*, go ye into town, and order the paschal food for us without delaying; Peter and John proceed, that it may be ready soon. P.C. 620. *Scryffes yma dhym pûb tra a dhullathfas an bŷs-ma, may fova lêl recordys, a vŷns tra ês yna gwrŷs,* written it is for me every thing from the beginning of this world, that it may be truly recorded, of all things that are there done. C.W. 158.

FOW, s. f. A den, a cave, a lurking place of wild beasts. Pl. *fowis*. Llwyd, 243. *Why guycoryon, euch yn mês ; ythesouch ow kuthyl ges a Dhu hag e sans eglos, yn ow thy a piyndow pan wreuch agas marhusow, ha fowys dhe laddron plós,* ye traders, go out ; ye are making a jest of God and his holy church, in my house of prayers when ye make your markets, and dens for foul thieves. P.C. 336. W. *fau.* Ir. *fuathais.* Gael. *fuathais.* Lat. *fovea.*

FOWLS, s. f. A reaping hook, a sickle. Another form of *filh*, qd. v.

FOWS, s. f. A coat. *Y'th o ow fows ha'm brustplat purpur garow dhum strothé, dre an gôs a-râk Pilat worto an kîc a glené,* my coat and my breastplate were hard purple to wring me ; through the blood in the presence of Pilate the flesh stuck to it. R.D. 2591. The aspirate mutation of *pows*, qd. v.

FOWT, s. m. A fault, defect, want. *En golyas ha fowt dybbry a wodhevys Ihesus kêr,* the watching and want of eating Jesus dear endured. M.C. 173. *Rag eannas ôs hep danger, nyns ûs fowt ynnos gwelys,* for thou art a messenger without delay, there is not in thee a fault seen. O.M. 2293. ‡*Dho ennves fowt*, to find fault. Llwyd, 60. *Gorra fowt*, to lay the blame. 252. Borrowed from the English.

FOYS, s. f. A table. *Ha'n gwŷn esa war en foys, ef a rauns yntredhé,* and the wine (that) was on the table, he divided among them. M.C. 45. *Foys* is to be read *voys*, and is a mutation of *moys*, qd. v.

FRA, adv. Why, wherefore. An abbreviated form of *fraga*. *Rag fra*, why. Llwyd, 53. ‡*Ro why ran dh'ages drewas, po an voyadge ny dâl fra ; mês y bart ef a'n geffa,* give you a share to your husband, or the voyage is not worth the while ; but his part he shall have. C.W. 50.

FRAGA, adv. Why, wherefore. Llwyd, 53. *Rag fraga na gresyth dhum lavarow,* why wilt thou not believe my words ? 242. An irregular mutation of *praga*, qd. v., and occurs only in late Cornish.

FRANC, adj. Free, at liberty. ‡*Frank a leal etto ge,* free and loyal art thou. *Lord Godolphin's Motto.* W. *franc.* Arm. *franc.*

FRAS, adj. Great. *Mar te venions ha codhé, war ngan flehys yn frâs ha warnan bedhans neffré,* if vengeance will come and fall, upon our children heavily, and upon us let it be ever. M.C. 149. *Me re buc pechadores, a peehus marthys yn frâs,* I have been a sinner ; that has sinned wondrously much. R.D. 1098. The aspirate form, after the adverbial particle *yn*, of *vrás*, a mutation of *brás*, qd. v.

FRAUS, s. m. Fraud, deceit. *Kepar del eson yn wêdh keffrys yn kueth yn moreth raydho hep fraus, ny iuggyn mones nép pel, lemmyn bŷs yn un enstel hencvys Emmaus,* like as we were also both in grief (and) sorrow for him, without deceit, we do not think to go any distance, but so far as a village called Emmaus. R.D. 1293.

FRECH, s. m. Fruit. Corn. Voc. *fructus.* Arm. *frech.*

FREG, s. f. A wife, a woman. Corn. Voc. *freg gans gûr,* uxor, a wife, a married woman ; lit. a woman with a husband. This is another form of *greg*, or *gwreg*, qd. v. W. *gwraig.* Arm. *grég.* Ir. †*frâg*, †*gruag.* Gael. †*gruag.*

FRENC, adj. French. *Cynyphan Frenc,* a walnut. Llwyd, 74. *Poccys Frenc,* lues venerea. 82.

FRENNE, v. a. To buy. A mutation of *preuné*, qd. v. *Awos côst arhans nag our, greuch y tenné mês a'n dour, gorreuch ef yn schath dhe'n môr, hy frenné bŷth nyns yw bern,* notwithstanding the cost of silver or gold, drag ye him out of the water, place him in a boat by the sea, to buy it is never a great matter. R.D. 2234. Written also *frenna*. *Rag i frenna,* to buy it. Llwyd, 231.

FRETH, adj. Violent, fierce, strong, fervent, vigorous. *Lyvyreuch whet, pan 'theuch mar frêth, pyw a whyleuch,* say ye again, when ye are so violent, whom do ye seek. P.C. 1114. *Otté lour kunys gyné, whythyns lemmyn pûp yn frêth,* see fuel enough with me, let every one now blow vigorously. P.C. 1242. *Rŷs yw dheuch gynen lafuryé, râk an harlot a geus frêth, pûr wŷr ynno nyns ûs meth,* need is to you to labour with us, for the knave speaks boldly ; very truly in him there is not shame. P.C. 1833. *Râk henna tûs ervys frêth gor dh'y wythé a ternyn,* therefore men strongly armed, put to guard him in time. R.D. 351. W. *fraedh*, *frwys.* Arm. *freuz.*

FRETHY, v. a. To conquer, to overcome. Pryce.

FRIA, v. a. To fry. Llwyd, 61. W. *frio.* Arm. *frita.* Ir. *friochtalnim.* Gael. *frighig.* Lat. *frigo.*

FRIES, s. c. A spouse, a husband, or wife. A mutation of *pries*, qd. v. *Gwyn agan leys, ow fryes, bôs grauntyes dhynny cummyes dyvort an Tâs Dew gwella,* happy is our lot, my husband, that leave is granted to us from the best Father God. O.M. 411. *Bernabé, ow fryes lel, rŷs yw gruthyl dyogel vâth agan arluth sefryn,* Bathsheba, my faithful wife, it is necessary to do immediately the will of our sovereign Lord. O.M. 2187.

FRIG, s. f. A nostril. Pl. *frigow.* Llwyd, 97. Corn. Voc. *fruc*, naris, a nostril. *Frigow brâs,* that hath a great nose. Llwyd, 47. *Gor sprusan yn y anow ha'n dhew arall keheffrys, bedhens gorrys yn y dhyw frieg,* put a kernel in his mouth, and the two others likewise, let them be put in his two nostrils. C.W. 134. *Gora sprusan y'th ganow, ha'n dhew arall pûr dhybblans yn dhe dhew frieg,* put a kernel in thy mouth, and the two others very distinctly in thy two nostrils. C.W. 140. *Ha del ve dhym kyns ornys, an tair sprusan yw gorrys yn y anow ha'y fregow,* and as it was to me formerly commanded, the three kernels are put in his mouth and his nostrils. C.W. 150. W. *froen.* Arm. *fron,* (from *fri,* a nose.) Ir. *sron.* Gael. *sron.* Manx, *stroan,* a nostril. Gr. ῥίν, (with *i* long = χρίν, φρίν, as ῥῆξις = fractio, fractio.) ῥύγχος. The proper term for *a nose* in Cornish was *trein, tron,* qd. v.

FRINC, s. f. France. In late times it was changed in construction into *Vrinc.* W. *fraine.* Ir. *frainc.* Gael. *fraing, an fhraing (an raing.)* Manx, *rank.*

FRINC, s. m. A Frenchman. Pryce. *Nans Frink, Tre Frink,* the French Valley, and French town, in Gorran.

FRINCAC, s. f. The French language. In late times it

was changed in construction into *Vrinkak*, the French language. *Pryce.* W. *frengaeg.* Gael. *francais.* Manx, *frangish.*

FROS, s. m. Tide. *An frôs*, the tide. *Llwyd*, 42. A later form of *frot.*

FROT, s. m. A strait, a channel. Corn. Voc. *alveus.* W. *frwd*, †*frut*, a stream. Arm. *froud.* Ir. *sroth*, †*sruth.* Gael. *sruth.* Manx, *stroo.* Sansc. *srotas*, a river, from *sru*, to flow. Lat. *fretum.* Cf. the Gaulish name of a river in Ptolemy, Φρόντις, or Φρούδις. Cf. also the Gr. root ρυ (= W. *rhe*,) in ῥέω, ῥεύσω, ῥεῦμα, ῥυτόι. Lat. *ruo, rivus, rumis.* Lith. *srov-c, srav-a.* O. H. Germ. *stroum.* Eng. *stream.*

FROTH, s. m. Anger, wrath. ‡*Nenna dzhei a dorhaz an dezan, ha thera nau penz en dezan, ha an mona an dzhei a gavaz; ha'n bara dzhei a dhabraz ha na ve idn fröth na mikan na trauaran nór vêz*, then they broke the cake, and there were nine pounds in the cake, and the money they got, and the bread they ate; and there was no anger, nor strife, nor dispute between them. *Ll.* 253. W *froch.* Ir. *fraoch*, †*ferc.* Gael. *fraoch.* Manx, *ferg.*

FROW, s. m. A flux, or flowing. *Llwyd*, 60. W. *frau.*

FRUIT, s. m. Fruit. Corn. Voc. *fructus.* In the Ordinalia it is generally written *frût;* pl. *frutys. Pâp gwedhen lefyns a'y sâf, ow tôn hy frût ha'y delyow*, let every tree grow from its stem, bearing its fruit and its leaves. O.M. 30. *War bûp fint, losow, ha hâs, a vo ynny hy tevys, saw a'n frût ny fydh kynmyas yw pren a skeyens hynwys*, over every fruit, herbs, and seed, that are grown therein, but of the fruit there is no permission that is named the tree of knowledge. O.M. 77. *Henna lell yth ew henwys, ew an wedhan a vwwans, me a hêdh ran a frutys, hag a dhro part anodha*, this truly as it is called, is the Tree of Life; I will reach some of the fruit, and will bring part of it. C.W. 134. W. *frwyth.* Arm. *froues.* Ir. †*frith.* Gael. †*frith.* From the Lat. *fructus.*

FRUYN, s. f. A bridle. *Pryce.* W. *frwyn*, †*fruinn*, †*fruyn.* Arm. *fren.* Ir. †*srian.* Gael. *srian.* Maux, *srecan.* Lat. *frenum.*

FRY, s. m. A nose. *Pryce.* A late form of *frig*, qd. v

FU, s. m. A fetter, a shackle. *Heil doctors ha mestrygi, marregyon heil dhywhy, byan a brâs l olté Barabas ha Ihesu gans nûr a grŷs, Dismas, Iesmas yn un fu dheueh dyvythys*, hail doctors and masters, soldiers hail to you, little and great ! behold Barabbas and Jesus, with much force, Dysmas, Jesinas in one chain come to you. P.C. 2351. An abbreviated form of *fual.* Llwyd, 230, who gives as the secondary form *huul.* W. *hual*, †*fuul*, in Oxford Glosses. Arm. *hual.* Ir. *geibheal, geimhiol.* Gael. *geimheal.* Manx, *geul.* Lat. *fibula.*

FU, s. f. A form, shape, figure. *Ny allaf gwelas an fu anodho ef yn nêp tu; cows gunso me a garse, y volungeth mar a pe*, I cannot see the form of him in any side; I should like to have spoken to him, if it were his will. R.D. 741. *A'n gwelesta a dhyragos, a alsesta y aswonfos? Galsen yn ta dhe'n kensé fu mâp Muria, henwys Ihesu*, if thou shouldst see him before thee, couldst thou know him ? I could well the former shape of the Son of Mary, called Jesus. R.D. 863. An abbreviated form of *furf*, qd. v.

FUCH, v. subs. Ye have been. A mutation of *bûch*, 2 pers. pl. preter. of *bós. A pûr harloth, ple fûch why ? pûr ûth o clewas an cry genef orth agas gylwel*, O very rascals, where have ye been ? very terrible it was to hear the cry by me calling you. R.D. 2243. Written also *feurh*, qd. v.

FUE, v. s. He has been. A mutation of *bue*, 3 pers. s. preter. of *bós. Henna yw pûr scorn ha geys, râg y fue kyns y vôs gwerîs dew ugens blydhen ha whê*, that is a very sneer and jest, for there were before it was done forty years and six. P.C. 350. *Yn ûr-na ef dysmegys, py ganssé y fue gwyskys, senseueh ef yn agan mŷsk*, let him declare by whom he was struck; hold ye him in our midst. P.C. 1373. In the following examples *fue* must be read *vué. Pan dorrasa an aval, an Arluth a fue serrys*, when he had plucked the apple, the Lord was angered. O.M. 680. *May hallo vôs kerenys, kepar del fue dhyn yrhys gans y dâs kyns tremené*, that he may be crowned, like as it was to us enjoined by his father before departing. O.M. 2375. *Pan fue genouch aeusyys*, when he was accused by you. P.C. 1859. *Ny fue gotlhys sol-a-theth*, it has not been washed a long time. R.D. 1929. *Ty re fue fest lafur brâs*, thou hast had great labour. R.D. 2628.

FUE, v. a. To flee, to escape. *Pryce.* Generally written *fye*, qd. v.

FUEF, v. subs. I have been. A mutation of *buef*, 1 pers. s. preter. of *bós. A Thomas doro dhe luef yn woly gwynys may fuef, dre an golon*, O Thomas put thy hand in the wound where I was pierced through the heart. R.D. 1540. *A Dhew, yssé fuef goky, pana vynnan vy eryyy a'n bêdh y vôs dusserchys*, O God I was indeed a fool, when I would not believe, from the grave that he was risen. R.D. 1565. Written also *fûf.*

FUELEIN, s. f. Wormwood. Corn. Voc. *absinthium.* Arm. *vuelen, huelen, uehelen, † vihelen, † ivelen, † huzelen.*

FUEN, v. subs. We have been. A mutation of *buen*, 1 pers. pl. preter. of *bós. A Arluth mûr, grás re'th fo, rák lowené ny gen bo yn le may fuen*, O Lord, great thanks be to thee, for joy may not be ours in the place that we have been. R.D. 169. *Yw dhe henna y fuen ny, ow kerchas an gwâs dhywhy war uskys*, is it for that we were bringing the fellow to you so quickly ? R.D. 1823. In the following examples it is incorrectly written for *vuen. My ha'm gwrêk râg gûl foly helys warbarth a fuen ny yn nês seon a paradys*, I and my wife for doing folly driven together we were quickly out of Paradise. O.M. 709.

FUES, v. subs. Thou hast been. A mutation of *bues*, 2 pers. s. preter. of *bós. Hag a'th wor bŷs yn Cayphas yn dyspyt dhe'th dewlagas, rák un fues kyns tymmyn fûr*, and will bring thee even to Caiaphas, in spite of thy eyes, for thou hast not been wise hitherto. P.C. 1104. *Ty creator bynyges, fattel dhuthté gy dhe'n erês, na fues gynen yn yfurn*, thou blessed creature, how camest thou to peace ? thou wast not with us in hell. R.D. 261. In both these examples *fues* must be read *vues* after *na.*

FUF, v. subs. I have been. A mutation of *bûf*, 1 pers. s. preter. of *bós. Me a'th worthyp hep lettyé; ny fŷf dên dhodho bythqueth*, I will answer thee without delaying; I have never been a man to him. P.C. 1938. *Y'th egen yn crês Alınayn orth un prys-ly yn pûr wŷr pan fûf gylteys*, I was in the midst of Germany at a breakfast meal very truly when I was called. R.D. 2150.

FUGIO, v. a. To feign, to dissemble. *Pryce*, who also writes it *figio.* W. *fugio*, from *fûg*, a deception. Ir.

bog. Lat. *fucus*, a dye, a false appearance, a deception. Gr. φῦκος, alga.

FUNEN, s. f. A band, a ribband, a fillet. *Pryce.* Pl. *funiou*, from *fun*. W. *fûn, funnen*, pl. †*funiou*. Oxford Glosses. Arm. *fun*, pl. *funiou*. Lat. *funis*.

FUNIL, s. f. Fennel. *Pryce.* A late form of *fenochel*, qd. v.

FUNTEN, s. f. A fountain. Corn. Voc. *fons.* In the Ordinalia it is written *fenten*, qd. v. W. *fynnon, fynnawn*, †*finnaun.* Arm. *feuntcun*, †*fcuntcn*, from the Latin *fontana.* Ir. *fiowns*.

FUR, adj. Prudent, wise, careful, sage, clever, cunning. Corn. Voc. *prudens*. *Del levaraf an gwŷr dhys, lemyn bŷdh fûr*, as I tell the truth to thee, now be prudent. O.M. 1638. *Dên fûr a'd cusullyow*, a prudent man of thy counsels. O.M. 2681. *Nêp na'n gordhyo del dhegouth, nyns yw dên fûr, del gresa*, he that does not worship him as he ought, is not a wise man, as I think. P.C. 216. *Mar asos fûr, ty a tew*, if thou art wise, thou wilt be silent. R.D. 954. *Mar a kyllyth dhe enê, nŷns ôs dên fûr*, if thou wilt lose thy soul, thou art not a wise man. R.D. 1410. *Ny skap, kyn fo vŷth mar fûr, na'n geffo drôk*, he shall not escape, though he be ever so cunning, that he shall not have harm. R.D. 2019. *Bedheurh why fûr*, be ye careful. R.D. 2276. Comparative *furah, fyrah*, wiser. Superl. *fura*, wisest. In late Cornish it was often written *fir, fêer*. W. *fûr*. Arm. *fûr*.

FUR, adj. Much, great. A mutation of *mûr*, qd. v. *Arluth ny vyen lowen, mar fûr torment a codhfen y bones dhys*, Lord I should not have been glad, if I had knowu the great torment that was to thee. R.D. 2542. *Fûr* is here to be read *vûr*.

FURF, s. f. A form, a shape. Corn. Voc. *forma.* W. *furv.* Arm. †*furm.* Ir. *foirm.* Gael. *fuirm.* Lat. *forma.* Gr. μορφή.

FURNES, s. f. Prudence, wisdom. *Pryce.* Arm. *furnez.*

FURU, s. m. Ways. ‡ *Gwrcuh owna 'gys fûrû*, mend your ways. Llwyd, 250. Plural of *for*, qd. v.

FUS, v. subs. Thou hast been. A mutation of *lûs*, 2 pers. s. preter. of *bôs*. *Lavar dhymo vy yn seon, yw ty myghtern Yedhewon, kepar del fûs acusysys*, tell me directly, art thou the king of the Jews, like as thou hast been accused? P.C. 1990. *Fûs* is here to be read *vûs*.

FUST, s. f. A staff, a club, a flail. Pl. *fustow*. *Why re dhueth dhym gans arrow, gans fustow ha clydhyfhyow, kepar ha pan vreê vy au purê lader yn pow*, ye have come to me with arms, with staves and swords, as if I were the veriest thief in the country. P.C. 1172. In late Cornish it was changed in construction into *vâst*. *Fyst*, a flail, *an vyst*. Llwyd. W. *fûst*. Arm. *fûst*. Ir. *suist*. Gael. *suist*. Manx, *soost*. Lat. *fustis*. Qu. Eng. *fist*. The common Welsh term for threshing corn is *dyrnu*, from *dwrn*, a fist.

FUSTA, v. a. To beat, to thresh. Llwyd, 245, *fysta*. W. *fusta*. Arm. *fusta*.

FUVE, v. subs. He hath been. Comp. of *fu*, id. qd. *fue*, a mutation of *bué*, 3 pers. s. preter. of *bôs*, and *ve*, he. *Kepar del fuvé dremmas, yn dôr ny a vyn palas tol may fo ynno cudhys*, like as he was a just man, in the earth I will dig a hole, that he may be covered in it. O.M. 864. After *del* it must be read *vu-ve*.

FUW, s. f. A form, a shape. *Whet ny ellys yn nêp tu godhfos ganso fatel fe; y carsen gwelas an fuw anodho, y vôdh mar pe*, yet I could not on any side know how it was with him; I would have loved to see the form of him, if it were his will. R.D. 469. Another form of *fu*, qd. v.

FY, v. s. Thou shalt or mayst be. A mutation of *by*, 2 pers. s. fut. and subj. of *bôs*. *Yn bŷs·ma râk dry ascor ty a rew bŷs may fy loys*, in this world to bring offspring, thou shalt live till thou be gray. O.M. 72. *Ha ty in wêdh, botteler, my a'd pŷs may fy asper, avel marrek fyn yrvys*, and thou also, butler, I pray thee to be bold, like a horseman well armed. O.M. 2203. *Kyn fy mar proul, ty a'n pren*, though thou art so proud, thou shalt pay for it. O.M. 2669. *Pan fy a'n bŷs tremenys, gans Cryst y fydhyth tryggys agy dh'y clos*, when thou shalt be from the world passed, with Christ thou shalt be dwelling within his court. P.C. 3232. *Cryst clew ow lêf, pesaf y wêdh may fy gynef, orth ow dynecdh*, Christ hear my voice, I pray also that thou wilt be with me at any end. R.D. 838. After *kyn*, and *pan, fy* must be read *vy*.

FYDH, s. f. Faith, belief. *Y worthebys, ny vannaff uga guthyll, war ow fŷdh*, he answered, I will not make them, upon my faith. M.C. 373. *A Phelyp, lous ôs y'th fŷdh, ha ty gynef sollathyth, godhfydhy grygy yn fâs*, O Philip, thou art gray in thy faith, and thou with me a long time, shouldst know how to believe faithfully. R.D. 2370. Written also indiscriminately *fêdh*, qd. v. W. *fŷdh*. Arm. *feiz*, †*fez*. Lat. *fides*.

FYDH, v. subs. He shall or will be. A mutation of *bŷdh*, 3 pers. s. fut. of *bôs*. *Râg dre gledhê a vruehê, dre gledhê y fŷdh ledhys*, for by a sword he that lives, by a sword he shall be killed. M.C. 72. *Py hanow y fŷdh gylwys? lavar dhymmo, er dhe fêdh*, what name shall he be called? tell me on thy faith. O.M. 676. *Ow nessê yma an preys, may fŷdh nâp Dew yn no reys dhe'n fals Yedhewon dygnas*, drawing near is the time in which the Son of God shall be given to the false Jews to be afflicted. P.C. 1097. In the following and similar examples, *fydh* must be read *vŷdh*. (See Llwyd, 227.) *Cummyns scon a fŷdh, hŷs dhe baal luen dhe drehy*, permission shall be forthwith, to cut full the length of thy spade. O.M. 379. *Ow benneth prêst ty a fŷdh*, my blessing ever thou shalt have. O.M. 457. *Nêp na crŷs ny fŷdh sylwys, na gans Dew ny fŷdh tryggys*, he that believes not shall not be saved, nor with God shall he dwell. R.D. 1100.

FYDH, v. subs. Be thou. A mutation of *bŷdh*, 2 pers. s. imp. of *bôs*. *Sens dhe clap, na fŷdh bysy, râk ny fynnaf dhys crygy*, hold thy prate, be not busy, for I will not believe thee. R.D. 1113. Here *fŷdh* must be read *vŷdh*, after *na*.

FYDHE, v. subs. Thou shouldst be. A mutation of *bydhê*. 2 pers. s. subj. of *bôs*. *Me a lever, ow mâp, dhys, Dew dhymmo vy a erchys may fydhê gy offrynnys dhodho ef war an altcr*, I tell thee, my son, God hath commanded me that thou shouldst be offered to him upon the altar. O.M. 1327.

FYDHONS, v. subs. They shall be. A mutation of *bydhons*, 3 pers. pl. fut. of *bôs*. *Du asyw emskemunys, nêp re ordenes y ladhê, pûr wŷr y fydhons dampnys dhe tân yfarn droka le*, black is he accursed, who decreed to kill him; very truly they shall be condemned to the fire of hell, the worse place. P.C. 3093.

FYDHYE, v. a. To believe, to confide in, to trust. *Mar*

FYEN 156 FYN

myn Dew, rág an gwella del fydhyaf ef a vŷdh gurŷs, if God wills, for the best so I trust it shall be done. O.M. 651. *Reys yn dhys ynno crysy, ha luen fydhyé yn teffry, bo ken uy fydhyth sylwys*, need it is to thee in him to believe, and fully trust in earnest, else thou shalt not be saved. O.M. 1500. *Yn y Dhew y wrŷk fydhyé, lemmyn gworens y dhyllyffryé mar myn a dhrôk*, in his God he trusted, now let him deliver him from evil if he will. P.C. 2885. W. *fydhio, fydhiaw.*

FYDHYN, v. subs. We shall be. A mutation of *bydhyn*, 1 pers. pl. fut. of *bôs*. *Heb toul pûr wŷr me a grŷs, dredhos y fydhyn sylwys*, without a doubt very truly I believe, through thee we shall be saved. P.C. 287. *Nyns ês tryga na fella, del hevel, dhynny omma, ny fydhyn gcsys yn crês*, there is no staying any longer, as it seems, for us here, we shall not be left in peace. O.M. 1006. Here *fydhyn* must be read *vydhyn* after *ny*.

FYDHYTH, v. subs. Thou shalt or wilt be. A mutation of *bydhyth*, 2 pers. s. fut. of *bôs*. *Pan fy a'n bŷs tremenys, gans Cryst y fydhyth tryggys agy dh'y clôs*, when thou shalt be passed from the world, with Christ thou shalt be dwelling within his court. P.C. 3233. *Ha ty, corf brâs mylyges, dhe yfarn gans dhe enef gynen y fydhyth tynnes*, and thou, great cursed body, to hell with thy soul by us shalt be dragged. R.D. 2349. In the following example, *fydhyth* must be read *vydhyth* after *ny*. *Reys yw dhys ynno crysy, bo ken ny fydhyth sylwys*, need is to thee in him to believe, else thou wilt not be saved. O.M. 1510.

FYE, v. a. To flee, to run away, to retreat, to put to flight. Part. pass. *fyys*. *Rág an tcrmyn re devé may fŷdh an begel kyllys, ha chechys yntré dewlé, ha'n deves dhe vês fyys*, for the time hath come that the shepherd shall be lost, and caught between hands, and the sheep fled away. M.C. 48. *Thâ Christ dhe vês a fyas pêb aydu pûr worthek*, the men of Christ fled away, every one on his side, very sorrowful. M.C. 77. *Trussen an wlâs, fyan na veny kefys*, let us cross the country, let us flee that we may not be found. M.C. 246. *Pan vo gweyskys an bugel, y fy an deves a bel, hag ol an flok a dhybarth*, when the shepherd is smitten, the sheep will flee far, and all the flock will separate. P.C. 894. *Me a wra y tempré, byth na allo fe fyé*, I will tame him that never can he flee. P.C. 1893. *Ny wrêth whêth war ow ené guthyl dhymmo vy fyé*, thou wilt not yet on my soul make me flee. P.C. 2317. *Yn nêp tol fyen dhe'n fo alemma, bŷs may 'th cllo sâl â dhe'n nêf*, into some hole let us flee away hence, until they go as many as go to heaven. R.D. 134. *Dhynny ef a wrŷk an pral, hag a fyes dhyworthyn*, to us he did the deed, and fled from us. R.D. 606. *A'n bêdh pau dhueth ha lammé, y fyys yn un vrammé, own kemerys*, from the grave when he came and leapt, thou fleddest in a tremor, seized by fear. R.D. 2094. W. *foi ;* Lat. *fugio*. Gr. φεύγω.

FYE, v. subs. He would, or should be. A mutation of *byé*, 3 pers. s. subj. of *bôs*. *Arluth golhy mara quréth ow treys, dhym y fyé mêdh hedré veyf byw*, Lord, if thou wilt wash my feet, it would be a shame to me as long as I live. P.C. 845. *Marregyon, dheuch ny won blam, râk dhymmo y fyé, scham gûl drôk dhywchy*, soldiers, to you I know not blame, for to me it would be a shame to do harm to you. R.D. 658.

FYEN, v. subs. I would, or should be. A mutation of *byen*, 1 pers. s. subj. of *bôs*. *Mar codhfo an casadow, dystouch y fyen ledhys*, if the villain knew, immediately I should be killed. O.M. 2120. *Arluth, lemmyn a's dysken, dyragouch nôth y fyen*, Lord, now if I take it off, before you naked I should be. R.D. 1042.

FYENAS, s. m. Anxiety, trouble, perplexity. Pl. *fyenasow*. *Gyllys ôf yn prederow, mâr yw ow fyenasow*, lost I am in thoughts, great are my anxieties. R.D. 17. *Ow colon ynnof a ter pûr ewn dre fyenasow*, my heart in me will break very truly through troubles. R.D. 709. *Mâr yw ow fyenasow war y lerch ef*, great are my anxieties after him. R.D. 1071. *Mûr yw ow fyenasow, ythof cudhys*, great are my anxieties, I am overwhelmed. R.D. 2031.

FYES, v. s. Thou wouldst, or shouldst be. A mutation of *byes*, 2 pers. s. subj. of *bôs*. *Gallos warnaf ny fyes, na fe y vôs grantys dhys dyworth whella Arluth*, power over me thou wouldst not have had, were it not granted to thee from the most high Lord. P.C. 2187. *Fyes* must be read *vyes* after *ny*.

FYEUCH, v. subs. Ye would, or should be. A mutation of *bycuch*, 2 pers. pl. subj. of *bôs*. *Attebres, ty a'th worty, a'n wedhen ha'y avalow, y fyeuch yn ûr-na avel dewow*, if thou atest, thou and thy husband, of the tree and its fruits, ye would be in that hour like gods. O.M. 177.

FYLLEL, v. n. To fail, to be wanting. *Yn medhens, mar omercyth clâff, gorthewyth te a'n prenvyth, awos guthyll wheyll mar scâff yn ethom dhyn mar fyllyth*, say they, if thou feign thyself sick, most certainly thou shalt catch it, in respect of doing a work so light in need if thou wilt fail us. M.C. 155. *Yn mêdh gwrêk an yôff dhedhé, kentrow dhewry why ny fŷll, awos bôs clâf y dheurlé*, says the wife of the smith to them, nails to you shall not be wanting, because his hands are sore. M.C. 158. *Dhe'n leyff arall pan dothyans worth an growe rág y fiuté, y fylly moy ys treshrys dhe'n toll guris hy na hedhé*, to the other hand when they came, on the cross to fasten it, it failed more than a foot length, to the hole made that it reached not. M.C. 180. *Warlyrch henna dre vestry yn tressa dŷdh heb fyllell, dre nerth brâs y'n drehevy, bythquêth ef na vyé gwell*, after that by his power on the third day without failing by great strength that he would raise it, that it never was better. M.C. 91. *Y lewerys ef yn wêdh datherchy an tressa dêdh y vere pûr wŷr hep fyllel*, he said likewise, that rise on the third day he would very truly without failing. R.D. G. *Leverouch ow dyskyblon mar a fyllys dheuch travyth, pan wrugé ages dauven hep torch na scryp, nôs na dryth*, say ye, my disciples, If any thing was wanting to you, when I sent you without staff or scrip, night or day. P.C. 912. *Ny grysuf dhys ; ty a fŷl gûl dhym cryay*, I do not believe thee ; thou wilt fail to make me believe. R.D. 1056. *Nêp a wrello y pysy ny fŷl a grôs*, he that will pray to him shall not fail of favour. R.D. 1338. *Eva ty a fyllyas, ow cola orth an eal-na*, Eve, thou didst fail, hearkening to that angel. C.W. 56. W. *fuelu*, (*mallu, pallu*.) Arm. *falloui, fellel*. Irish, *failleadh*. Gael. *faillinn*. Manx, *failleil*. Sanse. *sphal*. Gr. σφάλλω. φηλέω, φηλόω. Lat. *fallo*. Fr. *faillir*. Eng. *fail, fall*.

FYN, adj. Fine, perfect. *Rum fy hon yw ensyl fyn*, on my faith, this is fine advice. O.M. 2041. *Ha ty yn wêdh, botteler, my a'd pŷs may fy asper avel marrek fŷn yrwys*, and thou also, butler, I pray thee that thou be bold, like a fine armed horseman. O.M. 2204. Probably borrowed from the English. W. *ffon*, ruddy. Gael. †*fin*. Germ. *fein*. Eng. *fine*.

FYN, s. m. A head. The regular aspirate mutation of *pyn, pen*. It is used after *ow* and *aga* in the separation of *erbyn*, against, qd. v. Thus *cr ow fyn*, against me ; *er aga fyn*, against them. *Ens pŭp dhe drê, hag aspyouch yn pŭp le, mar cews dèn vyth er ow fyn*, let every one go home, and see ye in every place if any man speak against me. R.D. 1919. *Mychtern ôf guyron ha crêf, er ow fyn travyth ny sêf*, a king I am true and strong, against me nothing will stand. R.D. 2573. *Avel brathken aga dyns orto y a dheskerny; er aga fyn beteggyns Crist un gêr ny levery*, like hounds their teeth on him they gnashed; against them nevertheless Christ a word would not speak. M.C. 96. *Marth a'm bes, kynmys drôk a wodhevyth, ha te vyth er aga fyn na gewsyth*, it is a marvel to me so much hurt thou endurest, and never speakest against them. M.C. 120.

FYN, adj. Last, final. *Kymereuch, eveuch an gwŷn, rág ny evaf bŷs dêdh fŷn genouch annodho na moy*, take ye, drink ye the wine, for I will not drink till the last day with you of it any more. P.C. 724. *Sûr lour ôf vy annodho, dèn marow na dhrehavo bŷs deydh fŷn*, sure enough I am of him, that a dead man will not rise until the last day. R.D. 416. The same word as *fin*, qd. v.

FYN, v. n. He will. A mutation of *myn*, 3 pers. s. fut. of *mynny*. *Mar ny fyn dynnché y gow, gans spern gurêch y curené*, if he will not retract his lies, with thorns do ye crown him. P.C. 2061. *Awos kemmys drôk a wrên, a'n beys ny fyn tremené*, in spite of as much harm as we do, from the world he will not pass. P.C. 2114. *Ty a fyn y gafos cf, del hevel dhymmo, ledhys*, thou wishest to have him slain, as it seems to me. P.C. 2455. *Fyn* must be read *vyn*, after *a* and *ny*.

FYNNAF, v. n. I will. A mutation of *mynnaf*, 1 pers. s. fut. of *mynny*. *Yn secund dŷdh y fynnaf gruthyl ebron nêf hynnys*, on the second day I will make the sky called heaven. O.M. 17. *Lemmyn me a grŷs yn la, y fynnaf vy môs pella esouch haneth*, now I believe well, that I will go further than you to-night. R.D. 1208. In the following examples, after *a* and *ny, fynnaf* must be read *vynnaf*. *Abram soon gosluno lemyn orth ow lavarow a fynnaf dyryvas dhys*, Abraham immediately hearken now to my words (that) I will declare unto thee. O.M. 1367. *A dhesempys lemmyn taw, dhys ny fynnaf bones muw*, immediately now, be silent, I will not be a servant to thee. P.C. 2281.

FYNNAS, v. n. He would. A mutation of *mynnas*, 3 pers. s. preter. of *mynny*. *Gans aga garm hag olva Ihesus Crist a ve mevgys, may fynnas dyyskynna yn gwerhas ha bôs genys*, with their cry and lamentation Jesus Christ was moved, that he would descend into a virgin, and be born. M.C. 4. *Wogé henna y fynnas Adam Eva dre y rás*, after that he would (create) Adam (and) Eve through his grace. O.M. 2828. *Ragon y fynnes merwel ha môs yn bêdh, ha sevel*, for us he would die, and go to the tomb and rise. R.D. 968.

FYNNER, v. pass. It is wished. A mutation of *mynner*, 3 pers. s. pres. pass. of *mynny*. *Ellas ny won py tyller bŷth moy py le y trygaf, cychan, rág y fynner, mara kyller gans pasynys mêr ow dyswul glân*, alas ! I know not (in) what place, ever more where I shall dwell, Oh ! woe ! for it is wished, if it could be, with great sorrows to destroy me quite. P.C. 2600.

FYNNO, v. n. He may wish. A mutation of *mynno*, 3 pers. s. subj. of *mynny*. *Cryst yw Arluth a vercy ; kenmys a fynno crygy, ha'y pygy cf, hep dout cf a vydh sylwys*, Christ is Lord of mercy; whoever will believe and pray to him, without doubt he shall be saved. R.D. 284. *Dalhen mar cafaf ynno, pûr wŷr ny scap, kyn fynno, na'n gcffo clout ;* if I shall have hold in him, very truly he will not escape, however he may wish, that he does not get a beating. R.D. 383. *Dallathans nêp a fynno, rák coské reys yw dhymmo*, let him begin who will, for need is to me to sleep. R.D. 411. In these examples *fynno* must be read *vynno*.

FYNNYS, v. n. I would. A mutation of *mynnys*, 1 pers. s. preter. of *mynny*. *Wogé ow da oberow, dynces a yrhys dedhé ; dhyn rosons bystyl wherow, bŷth ny fynnys y evé*, after my good works, drink I asked for to them ; to me they gave bitter gall, I would never drink it. R.D. 2002. *Fynnys* must here be read *vynnys* after *ny*.

FYNNYTH, v. n. Thou wilt. A mutation of *mynnyth*, 2 pers. s. fut. of *mynny*. *Thomas ythos pûr woky, drefen na fynnyth crygy an Arluth dhe dhasserchy du pask vyityn*, Thomas thou art very stupid, because thou wilt not believe the Lord to have risen Easter-day morning. R.D. 1106. *Galsos lemmyn pûr woky, rák na fynnyth dhyn crygy*, thou art become quite foolish, for thou wilt not believe us. R.D. 1514. In these examples *fynnyth* must be read *vynnyth* after *na*.

FYNSYS, v. n. Thou wouldst. A mutation of *mynsys*, 2 pers. s. preter. of *mynny*. *Pandra yw dhe nygys, mar hŷr fordh dôs may fynsys, lavar dymmo vy wharé*, what is thy errand, so long a way that thou wouldst come ? tell me directly. O.M. 734. *Bynyges re by, dhe'n harlot pan fynsys ry an hackré mernans yn beys*, blessed be thou, to the villain when thou wouldst give the cruelest death in the world. R.D. 2070. After *pan, fynsys* must be read *vynsys*.

FYNTEN, s. f. A fountain. *An sêth yw rág leveris a's gwyskis tyn gans mûr angus, war y holow may crunys dre nerth an bun fynten woys*, the arrow as aforesaid, struck her sharp with much anguish, in her heart that there stagnated by force of the blow a fountain of blood. M.C. 224. Another form of *fenten*, and *funten*, qd. v.

FYNWETH, s. m. An end. See *Finwedh*.

FYRWY, v. n. He would die. A mutation of *myrwy*, 3 pers. s. subj. of *merwel*. *Dhyn kyns cf a levcrys ol annodho del whyrys yn nôr bŷs-ma, rág an prenna y fyrwy, hag arté y tasserchy wogé henna*, to us before he told all how done by him, in the earth of this world, to redeem us that he would die, and again that he would rise up after that. R.D. 1192.

FYSADOW, s. m. Prayers. The regular aspirate mutation of *pysadow*, pl. of *pysad*, qd. v. *Gwercs dynchans, my a'd pŷs, ow fysadow dres pûp tra ; a Dâs Dew y'th wolowys, clew galow an bobyl-ma*, help quickly, I pray thee, my prayers above every thing ; O Father God in thy lights, hear the call of this people. O.M. 1830.

FYSCY, v. a. To strike. *Yma Moyses pel gyllys yn môr, del hevel dhynmo, a rág dynchans ow kerdhes, an dour ow fysky a lês, pûp ûr ol a dhyragdho*, Moses is far gone into the sea, as it seems to me ; forward quickly walking, the water striking wide every moment before him.

O.M. 1685. An anomalous mutation of *gwyscy*, qd. v.

FYSMANT, s. m. Countenance, visage. ‡ *Ty ny vedhys dowlycs, drefan y bosta mur dêk, ha gans Eva eregys, dhyth fysmant dhedhy a blêk*, thou wilt not be mistrusted, because thou art so fair, and by Eve believed, thy visage to her will please. C.W. 40. To be read *vysmant*.

FYST, s. f. A flail. In late Cornish it was changed in construction into *vgst*. Llwyd, 60. See *Fûst*.

FYSTYNE, v. a. To hasten, to make haste. Written indiscriminately *fystena, festena, festynna*. *Fystyn alemma dwhans, worthyf na gous na moy gêr*, hasten thou hence quickly ; speak not to me another word. O.M. 169. *Fystynynch troha'n daras, râg umma ny wrcuch trygé*, hasten ye towards the door, for here ye shall not stay. O.M. 349. *Awos an Tâs fystenyn, râg own namnag of pûr dhal*, because of the Father, let us hasten ; for fear I am almost blind. O.M. 1055. *Abram fystyné gwra, ha dûs dhymmo wharré*, Abraham hasten do, and come to me directly. O.M. 1265. *Lemyn pêp ol yskynnens, ha war tu trê fystenens, kefrys marrek ha squyer*, now let every one mount, and towards home let us hasten, knight and squire likewise. O.M. 2003. *Farwel, ow arluth gwella, râg my a vyn fystené*, farewell, my best lord, for I will make haste. O.M. 2290. *Mar ny fystyn pûp huny, why a's bydh drôg vommennow*, if every one makes not haste, ye shall have bad blows. O.M. 2323. *Fysteneuch fast alemma*, make ye haste quick hence. P.C. 1176. *Fystymyn dhodho wharré*, let us hasten to him forthwith. P.C. 3148. W. *festinio*. Lat. *festino*.

FYTH, adv. Ever. To be read *vyth*, a mutation of *byth*, qd. v. *Pan dyskys yn eglusyow, ny wrûg dên fyth ow sensy*, when I taught in the churches, no man ever did seize me. P.C. 1176. *Den fythol, nûrs dre pystry yn try deydh ny'n dhrehafsé*, never a man unless through sorcery, in three days would not raise it. P.C. 1765.

FYTHYS, part. Worsted, overcome, conquered. *Hedré vo yn dhe hercydh, fythys nefré ny vedhyth gans tebeles war an bcys*, as long as it may be in thy power, thou shalt never be worsted by evil ones in the world. O.M. 1466. *Govy vyth pan gth dhodho, pan of fythys dhyworto tergwyth hydhew*, woe is me when I went to him, when I am vanquished by him three times to-day. P.C. 146. An anomalous mutation of *gwythys*, part. of *gwythy*, to make worse; as *fysky* is of *gwyscy*.

FYVAR, s. m. An edge. Llwyd, 41. I think this is wrongly inserted as a Cornish word from the Irish *faobhar*. Gael. *faobhar*. Manx, *foyr*.

FYYN, v. subs. We may be. A mutation of *byyn*, 1 pers. pl. subj. of *bôs*. *Dhyso ny vennaf cresy, na dhe'th fykyl lavarow ; pysyn may fyyn servysy dh'agan Arluth hep parow*, I will not believe thee, nor thy vain words ; let us pray that we may be servants to our Lord without equals. O.M. 235.

G.

This letter is both primary and secondary in the six Celtic dialects. Its sound is the same as in the English words, *gain, get, give, go*. When radical or primary its commutation is formed in Cornish by omitting it altogether, as *gurée*, a wife ; *an wrêe*, the wife ; *gallos*, power ; *y allos*, his power. When however *g* was followed by *o* or *u*, then *w* was prefixed, as *goloc*, sight ; *an woloc*, the sight ; *gûl, dhe wûl*, to make. In certain cases, as after *y*, the Cornish after omitting the *g* aspirates the succeeding vowel :—thus, *gallouch, why a allouch*, ye will be able ; *may hallouch*, that ye may be able. The Cornish, as in Armoric, also changes *g* into *c*, as *gwerthé*, to sell ; *ow ewerthé*, selling. *Grugé, mar erugé*, if I do. In Welsh *g* is also omitted in its commutation, as *gwraig*, a wife ; *y wraig*, the wife ; *gallu*, power ; *ci allu*, his power. The Welsh has a further mutation into the nasal letter *ng*, as *vy ngallu*, my power ; and though not in initials, as in Cornish and Armoric, it also changes *g* into *e*, as *dyeco*, he may bring, from *dygu*, to bring ; and *gwacach*, more empty, from *gwâg*. In Armoric *g* changes into the aspirate *ch*, as *grêg*, a wife ; *ar ehrêg*, the wife ; and also into *c*, as *genou*, mouth ; *ho kenou*, your mouth. In Irish and Gaelic *g* changes into *gh*, as *lamh*, a hand ; *lamh gheal*, a white hand. This commutation agrees with the Welsh in a great measure, for *gh* at the end of words has no sound at all in Irish, and when an initial it is sounded as *y* in English. The first commutation of *g* in Welsh would be *gh* ; but as this letter has no sound, (which is also the case in English ; compare *sigh, bright, light, &c.,*) it was not written ; but there is a trace of the *g* sound also in Welsh, as in *argant, arghant, aryant*, silver, from Latin *argentum* ; *angen, anghen, anyan*, nature, from Lat. *ingenium*. In Manx *g* changes into the guttural *gh*, as *goo*, a report ; *e ghoo*, his report ; thus agreeing with the Armoric commutation.

When secondary in Cornish and the other dialects *g* is a mutation of *c*, as *cadar*, a chair ; *y gadar*, his chair. W. *cadair, vi gadair*. Arm. *cador, he gador*. Ir. *cail*, loss ; *ar gail*, our loss. Manx, *kirree*, sheep ; *ny girree*, of the sheep.

GAD, s. f. A hare. Llwyd, 5, gives this as a Cornish word. Arm. *gâd*. But the more common term was *scovarnog*, qd. v. W. *ysgyvarnog*.

GADLYNG, s. m. An idle fellow, a vagabond. *A vyl gadlyng, duws yn râg, wor tywcdh whet crôk a'th tâg*, O vile vagabond, come forth, at last hanging will choak thee yet. P.C. 1817. *A gadlyng, ty re wordhyns, war nêp tro, an fals losel*, O idle fellow, thou hast worshipped, on some occasion, the false knave. P.C. 2691.

GAEL, v. a. To find, to obtain. A mutation of *cael*, qd. v. *Dho gael*. Llwyd, 72.

GAFE, v. a. To forgive, to pardon. Written also *gave*. Part. pass. *gcfys, gyfys*. *Lythys of pûr dhyoyel, gâf dhem ow fêch, my a'd pys*, I am killed very certainly, forgive me my sin, I pray thee. O.M. 2726. *Y's garas dhedhé keffrys*, he forgave it to them both. P.C. 507. *Ol mêns trespas a wrugé, dhodho ef we a'n gafsé, a menné gelwel gyvyans*, all the evil he has done, to him I would forgive it, if he would call pardon. P.C. 1816. *War Ihesu me a cryas ow trespas dhymmo gafé*, on Jesus I cried to forgive me my trespass. R.D. 1100.

GAFFAF, v. a. I shall find. A mutation of *caffaf*, 1 pers. s. fut. of *cafos*, qd. v. *My ny gafaf ynno kên may eodhfo dhym y ludhé*, I do not find in him a cause that it should behove me to slay him. P.C. 1797. *Pendra wrâf, orth en ioul mar uy gaffaf toul war nêp cor*, what shall I do, if I find not for the devil a hole in some corner? R.D. 2130.

GAFFAS, v. a. He found. A mut. of *cafas*, 3 pers. s. pret. of *cafos*, qd. v. *Mós a wrên ny dhe'u castel Emaus gylwys, ha war furdh ny a gafas Ihesu yw Arluth a rās*, we were going to the village called Emmaus, and on the road we found Jesus (that) is Lord of grace. R.D. 1474. *Pan fue genouch acusyys, ef ny gafas fout yn bys, pan y'n danfonas ef dhyn*, when he was accused by you, he found no fault in the world, when he sent him to us. P.C. 1860.

GAFFE, v. a. He would have. A mutation of *caffé*, 3 pers. s. subj. of *cafos*, qd. v. *Rāk hacré mernans eys emladhé y honan, ny gaffé dên my a grŷs*, for a more cruel death than to kill himself, a man may not find, I believe. R.D. 2074.

GAFFEN, v. a. We would have. A mutation of *caffen*, 1 pers. pl. subj. of *cafos*, qd. v. *Ny gaffen war ow louté composse pren yn nép le, na râg an plâs-ma vŷth wel*, we may not get, upon my truth, a straighter tree in any place, nor for this place any better. O.M. 2579.

GAFFO, v. a. He may find. A mutation of *caffo*, 3 pers. s. subj. of *cafos*, qd. v. *Ma na gaffo gorthyp vŷth er-agan-pyn dhe cous gêr*, that he may not find any answer against us to say a word. P.C. 1839. Written also *geffo*, qd. v.

GAFUS, v. a. To get, to find. A mutation of *cafus*, or *cafos*, qd. v. *Rāg dhym yma tokyn da rāk y gafus*, for there is to me a good token to take him. P.C. 985. *Ty a fyn y gufos ef, del hevel dhymmo, ledhys*, thou wishest to have him slain, as it seems to me. P.C. 2455. *Mara kyllyn y gafus, vynytha na dheppro bous*, if I can find him, may he never eat food. R.D. 540.

GAGE, v. a. To leave. A corrupted form of *gasé*, qd. v. *Me re'n cusullyes mil wŷth, saw ny vyn awos travyth gagé y tebel crygyans*, I have advised him a thousand times, but he will not, for any thing, leave his evil belief. P.C.

GAHEN, s. f. Henbane. Coru. Voc. *simphoniaca*. Ir. *gafann*. Gael. *gafann*.

GAL, s. m. Rust, evil, wickedness; a wicked fellow. *A pûr voren plôs myrch gâl, ty a verow cowal*, O very jade, dirt, daughter of evil, thou shalt die quite. O.M. 2736. *A traytor brâs mâp gâl, dhe gafus gynen yw mal*, O great traitor, son of evil, it is our desire to take thee. P.C. 1177. *Kerchyn Longys an gwâs dal, gans guw dhe wané an gâl yn y golon*, let us fetch Longius, the blind fellow, to pierce the villain with a spear in his heart. P.C. 2917. W. *gâl*, an eruption, an enemy. Arm. *gal*, an eruption, the itch. Fr. *gale*. Ir. *gal*, warfare. Gael. *gall*, an enemy.

GALA, s. m. Straw. A mutation of *cala*, qd. v. *Awos henna ny wrâf vry, na anodhans y bŷs voy me ny settyaf gwail gala*, notwithstanding that I will not make account, nor of them any more I will not value the stalk of a straw. C.W. 98.

GALAR, s. m. Grief, sorrow, anguish, a pang, lamentation. Pl. *galarow*. *Gory vŷth ol ow pewé, ow codhaf lues galar*, unhappy me ever living, suffering much sorrow. O.M. 633. *Droyn galar ow dhymmo y ancledhyus mar uskys*, worst sorrow it is for me to bury him so immediately. O.M. 868. *Kyn feva ledhys marow, dre mûr peyn ha galarow, ny'th ty nahuf bynary*, though I be killed dead by great pain and sorrows, I will never deny thee. P.C. 906. *Us whêt dhe'th corf galarow na torment orth dhe greffyé*, are there yet pangs in thy body, or torment afflicting thee? R.D. 487. W. *galar*. Arm. *glachar*. Ir. *galar*. Gael. *galar*. Manx, *gallar*.

GALAROW, v. a. To weep for, to bewail, to lament. *Dho galarow*, Llwyd, 122. ‡ *Me rig clowas an poble galarow*, I did hear the people complaining. *Pryce*. *Galarowedges* was the preterite in late Cornish. ‡ *Hag en Jesus Christ, an Arluth ny, neb vye a humthan der an Sperys Sans, denethys a'n gwerches Vary, galarowedges dan Pontius Pilat, vye a crowsys, marow, hag ynclydhyys*, and in Jesus Christ, our Lord, who was conceived through the Holy Ghost, born of the Virgin Mary, suffered under Pontius Pilate, was crucified, dead, and buried. Pryce. W. *galaru*. Arm. *glachari*.

GALEC, adj. Gaulish, French. Llwyd, 5. The French language. W. *galeg*. Arm. *gallek*.

GALES, adj. Hard, difficult. A mutation of *cales*, qd. v. *My a's gwŷsk gans un blogon; vythqueth na ve bom a won a rollo whaf mar gales*, I will smite her with a bludgeon; never was a stroke I know that would give a blow so hard. O.M. 2711. *Yma dhys colon galus, na leys ty dhe eynnas*, thou hast a hard heart, that thou wouldst not lessen thy will. R.D. 1523.

GALLAS, v. n. Gone, is gone. *Awos henna nynsus vry, gallas hy gobyr gynsy ha, servyys yw del godhé*, with regard to that there is not concern, her reward is gone with her, and she is served as she ought. O.M. 2764. *Gory, ny won pendra wrâf, gallas ow colon pûr clâf dre pryderow*, woe is me, I know not what I shall do, gone is my heart very sick, through cares. P.C. 2610. *Gwerescuch, laddron, gallas an porthow brewyon*, help ye, thieves, gone are the gates to pieces. R.D. 120. *Agan corfow nôth gallas, gans deyl 'agan cudhé gwrên*, our bodies are become naked, with leaves let us cover them. O.M. 253. *Gallas ef dhe ken tyrch, ha ganso mûr a eledh*, gone is he to other lands, and many angels with him. This is the preterite of *gylly*, qd. v. W. *gallas*. *Gwae vy llaw, llam rym gallas*, woe my hand, the step that befel me. *Llywarch Hên*.

GALLOGEC, adj. Powerful, mighty. *Râg ty yw Dew gallogek, dhe pûp a vo othommek, warnos a pyssé mercy*, for thou art a mighty God to all who are needy, upon thee who may pray for mercy. R.D. 2370. A corrupted form of *gallosek*, *g* soft being substituted for *s*.

GALLOS, s. m. Power, might, authority. Written also *galloys*, and *gallus*. *War edhyn, bestes, pôp prŷs, gallos a fydh warnedhé*, over birds, beasts, always power shall be over them. O.M. 1214. *My a wra prest hep ynny ol dhum gallus vynytha*, I will do at once, without refusal, all in my power ever. O.M. 2149. *Scon y gallos a fŷdh lehŷs*, soon his power will be lessened. P.C. 21. *Awos of ow gallos*, notwithstanding all my power. P.C. 53. *Mars yw a Galilé, hag a gallos Erodes*, if he is of Galilee, and of the dominion of Herod. P.C. 1601. *Warnedhé kemer galloys*, over them have power. O.M. 70. *Ha hy a wolas kymmys gans mar vêr nerth ha galloys*, and she wept so much with so much strength and might. M.C. 224. W. *gallu*. Arm. *galloud*.

GALLOSEC, adj. Powerful, mighty, able. *Del yw ef gallosek brâs*, as he is very powerful. O.M. 1494. *Rāk lucn gallosek yw ef, hag yn pûp ober marthys*, for full

GALSEN 160 GAN

powerful is he, and in every work wonderful. O.M. 2089. *Arluth gallosek ha créf, worto an porthow ny séf*, Lord powerful and strong, against him the gates will not stand. R.D. 118. *Râk ty yu luen a vertu, ol gallosek*, for thou art full of virtue, all mighty. R.D. 752. W. *galluog*. Arm. *galloudek*.

GALLUIDOC, adj. Able, potent. Corn. Vocab. *potens*. This is the early form from the substantive *galluid*, of which *gallos* is the later form. Arm. *galloud*, power ; *galloudek*, powerful.

GALLY, v. n. To be able, may or can. *Râg henna môs alema, me a vyn qwell a gallaf*, therefore go from hence, I will as well as I can. C.W. 124. *Towyll vŷth ny allaf yn fâ synné sensy dhe wonys*, a tool never am I able in them to hold to work. M.C. 156. *Mar callé*, if he could. M.C. 15. *Mara kŷll dhevorth an du dhe wethyl drôk agan dry*, if he can from the good to do evil us bring. M.C. 21. *Why a ĝll ĝil da*, ye may do good. M.C. 37. *Pesouch ow thâs may hallouch môs dh'y asedh*, pray ye my Father that ye may go to his seat. M.C. 52. *May hallé pesy*, that he might pray. M.C. 53. *An rena a ĝll dhe dhysky*, those may teach thee. M.C. 80. *Gallas*, 3 pers. s. pret. *Eneff Judas ny allas dôs yn mês war y anow*, the soul of Judas could not come out by his mouth. M.C. 109. *Mar callo elevens*, if he could hear. M.C. 109. *Pan welas na ylly Crist delyffré*, when he saw that he could not deliver Christ. M.C. 150. *Manno allo*, that he may not be able. M.C. 19. *Ha na yllens y gwythé*, and they could not keep him. M.C 248. *Yth halsan rowlya*, that I could rule. C.W. 46. *May hellyn kyny*, that we may lament. C.W. 74. *May hallan tenna*, that I may shoot. C.W. 112. *Mara keller wythé a chy, na alla yntré dhe'n darasow*, if it is possible to keep him from the house that he may not enter the doors. P.C. 3058. See also *galsen*, I might. *Galsé*, he might. *Galser*, it was possible. W. *gallu*. Arm. *gallout*. Ir. *ala* ; *eolas*, ability. Gael. †*al*. Lat. *valco*. Sauso. *al*, *galb*.

GALOW, s. m. A call, an invitation. *A Dâs Dew, y'th wolowys, clew galow an bobyl-ma, dour, may féns y dysehys, a vewnans ry dedhé gwra*, O Father God in thy lights, hear the call of this people ; that they may be refreshed, the water of life do thou give to them. O.M. 1832. *A wetta ny devedhys warbarth ha'n kensa galow*, behold us come together with the first call. P.C. 2051. W. *galw*. Arm. *galv*. Ir. *glaodh*, *caol*. Gael. *glaodh*. Manx, *kiaull*, *yllee*. Sause. *klad*, *cal*, to proclaim. Gr. καλέω, κλαίω, κλάω.

GALSE, v. n. He might. 3 pers. s. plup. of *gally*. *Pyth yw an ethom vŷé an onyment kêr y skallyé ; ef a galsé bôs gwyrthys a try cans dyner ha moy*, what is the need to spill the precious ointment ? it might have been sold for three hundred pence and more. P.C. 535. *Hen yw gwÿr, ef a galsé pûp tra y dhyncul arté moy ys na fe*, this is true, he could destroy every thing again, more than it was. P.C. 977. W. *gallasai*, *gallsai*.

GALSE, v. n. Was gone. 3 pers. s. pluperf. of *gylly*, qd. v. *Rág porrys rýs o dhodho gasé y ben dhe gregy, râg galsé glân dheworto y woys, bewé ny ylly*, for very necessary it was for him to let his head to bang, for was gone clean from him his blood, that he could not live. M C. 207.

GALSEN, v. n. I might. 1 pers. s. plup. of *gally*. *A'n gwelesta a dhyragos, a alsesta y uswonfos ; galsen y ta, dhe'n kensé fu*, if thou shouldst see him before thee, couldst thou know him ? I could well, at the first view. R.D. 863. W. *gallaswn*, *gallswn*.

GALSER, v. n. It would have been possible. This is an impersonal passive tense of *gally*. *Ef a galsé bôs gwyrthys a try cans dyner ha moy, ha re-na galser dhe rey dhe vocheseqyon yn beys*, it might have been sold for three hundred pence and more ; and those might have been given to the poor in the world. P.C. 537.

GALSESTA, v. n. Thou mightest. An enlarged form of *galsest*, 2 pers. s. plup. of *gally*. (Llwyd, 247.) *A'n gwelesta a dhyragos, a alsesta y aswonfos*, if thou shouldst see him before thee, couldst thou know him ? R.D. 862. So also in Armoric. *Ni galsesde quet eguedou sarmon*, couldst thou not speak with us. *Buhez Nonn*, 74.

GALSOF, v. n. I am become, gone. 1 pers. s. pres. of irr. v. *gylly*, qd. v. *Mûr varth ambus dyogel an beys dh'y terry na'm gâs, râg csow galsof ysel, na allaf kerdhes yn fâs*, great wonder is to me surely ; the earth will not let me break it ; for corn I am become low, that I cannot walk well. O.M. 373. *Râk hyreth galsof pûr clâf, ny allnf syvel a'm saf*, for longing I am become very ill, and I cannot stand on my standing. R.D. 775.

GALSONS, v. n. They are gone. 3 pers. pl. preterite of irr. v. *gylly*. *An prysners galsons yn wêdh, csé yn dan naw alwedh, ny torsans chy*, the prisoners are gone also, (that) were under nine keys ; they have not broken house. R.D. 660.

GALWY, v. a. Call thou. 2 pers. s. imp. of *gelwel*, qd. v. *Belzebue whêk, wheyth dhe corn, ha galwy dré a pûp sorn an dhewolow, mara keller y wythé a chy, na alla yutré dhe'n darasow*, sweet Beelzebub, blow thy horn, and call home from every corner the devils ; if it is possible to keep him from the house, that he may not enter the doors. P.C. 3056. Llwyd, 249, gives *galŵ*, and *galwa*, as late forms.

GAM, s. m. A wrong, an injury, a wrong-doer. A mutation of *cam*, qd. v. *Ty a whŷth avel cauch gwâs, whŷth war gam*, thou blowest like a dirty fellow, blow athwart. P.C. 2716. *Gwâsk war gam, ha compys*, strike thou athwart, and straight. P.C. 2735.

GAM, adj. Crooked, wry, perverse, wicked. A mutation of *gam*, qd. v. *Râk ty dh'y gam worthyby, ty a vŷdh box trewysy*, for that thou answerest him wrongly, thou shalt have a hard blow. P.C. 126. *Râk pûr vŷr ty a gam dip warnodho ef*, for very truly thou thinkest wrongly respecting him. R.D. 996.

GAMMA, v. a. To make wry. A mutation of *camma*, qd. v.

GAMWUL, v. a. To do wrong. A mutation of *camwul*, qd. v.

GAN, prep. With, by. *Ol ny a pŷs, yowynk ha hên, war Dhu pûp prŷs mercy gan kên, may fên gwythys râk an bylen*, all we pray, young and old, to God always, mercy with pity, that we may be preserved from the evil one. P.C. 40. *A gan Cayn omskemynes ow mâb Abel yw ledhys, may 'thove genys dhe wâr bayn*, O by Cain the accursed, my son Abel is killed, that I am born to great sorrow. C.W. 90. *Gans* is another form, and the oldest authority *cans*, qd. v. It enters into composition with the pronouns, as *genef*, *gynef*, with me ; *genes*, *gynes*, with thee ; *ganso*, with him ; *gynsy*, with her ;

genen, gynen, with us ; *gencuch,* with you ; *gansé,* with them. W. *gan,* †*can.* Arm. *gan,* †*gant.*

GAN, pron. Our. An abbreviated form of *agan,* qd. v. Lhwyd, 231.

GAN, s. m. A song. A mutation of *cân,* qd. v. *Yn tân whyflyn of a séf, ha paynys neffré a pŷs, ha'y gân a rŷdh, ooh, goef, dhe'n bŷs-ma pan fue genys,* in hissing fire he shall stay, and tormented ever shall pray ; and his song shall be "O miserable me, when I was born to this world." R.D. 2313.

GAN, v. a. He shall sing. A mutation of *cân,* 3 pers. s. fut. of *cané,* qd. v. *My a gân an conternot,* I will sing the counter note. O.M. 561. *Me a dhystryp ow dyllas, hag a's sel y dan y trcys, hag a gân dh'agan sylwyas,* I will take off my clothes, and put them under his foot, and will sing to our Saviour. P.C. 252. *Neffré ny gân of yn cûr gans y ganow,* never shall he sing in the court with his mouth. R.D. 1899.

GAN, v. n. We shall have. A mutation of *cân,* 1 pers. pl. fut. of irr. v. *cavas. Ni a gân,* we shall have. Lhwyd, 247.

GANE, v. a. To sing. A mutation of *cané,* qd. v. *An lahé dhe venteyne, servys dhe Dew dhe gané, y sacra scon my a wra,* the law to maintain, to sing the service to God, consecrate him forthwith I will. O.M. 2603.

GANNO, v. a. He may sing. A mutation of *canno,* 3 pers. s. subj. of *cané. Cussyllyouch menouch Ihesu a gasé y wokyncth, ha treylé dhe skentuleth ow tywedh na ganno tra,* advise ye Jesus frequently, to leave his folly, and turn to wisdom, that he may not sing "sad" at last. P.C. 1810.

GANOW, s. m. The mouth. *Gwell dewes vytteth vŷn nyns â yn agas ganow,* any better drink of wine will not go into your mouth. O.M. 1913. *Yn lyfryow scrufys yma, bós collenwys lowené a ganow an flechys da, ha'n ré munys ow tené,* in books it is written that joy is fulfilled of the mouths of good children, and little ones sucking. P.C. 437. *Gwŷr a leversys dhym a'th ganow dhe honan,* truth hast thou spoken to me from thy own mouth. P.C. 2001. *Gans dhe ganow lavur dhymmo dhe hanow,* with thy mouth tell me thy name. R.D. 232. *Ny gân of yn cûr gans y ganow,* he will not sing in his court with his mouth. R.D. 1900. It changes in construction into *anow,* qd. v. *Yn y anow,* in his mouth. O.M. 870. *Gwarhas ganow,* the roof of the mouth, or palate. Lhwyd, 111. *Ganow* is more correctly written *genow,* qd. v.

GANS, prep. With, by. Another form of *gan,* qd. v. *Yn groves gans kentrow fustys,* on the cross with nails fastened. M.C. 2. *Why a dhéth dhym yn arvow, gans boclers ha. cledhydhyow,* ye came to me in arms, with bucklers and swords. M.C. 74. *Hag yuno fést luhas tol gans an dreyn a ve tellys,* and in it quickly many holes by the thorns were holed. M.C. 133. *Mars ny fedhé of gwythys, gans y tús y fŷdh leddrys,* if he should not be guarded, by his people he will be stolen. R.D. 354.

GANS, v. a. They shall have. A mutation of *câns,* 3 pers. pl. fut. of irr. verb *cavas.* ‡*An dzhyi a gâns,* they shall have. Lhwyd, 247.

GANSE, pron. prep. With them. (Gans-y.) *Gansé y a dhúk golow,* with them they brought light. M.C. 64. *Gansé y a'n hombronkyas,* with them they conducted him. M.C. 76. *Dhe'n Arluth dhe wûl yma, dre dhe vódh, gansé nebcs,* to the Lord to do there is, by thy will, something with them. P.C. 208. *Déns pan vo bódh gansé y, aga bós a vŷdh parys,* let them come when tho will is with them, their food shall be ready. P.C. 694. *Tan hemma, gor gansé y,* take this, put (it) with them. P.C. 28, 50. Written also *gansy.* W. *gandhynt, gandhynt hwy,* † *gantunt,* † *guntynt.* Arm. *gant-hô.*

GANSEN, v. a. I would have sung. A mutation of *cansen,* 1 pers. s. plup. of *cané. Râk na'n gwela dhym a nép tu, kueth a portha, ny gansen tru,* for that I will see him not on somo side to me, I feel sorrow ; I would not sing "alas." R.D. 866.

GANSO, pron. prep. With, or by him, or it. *(Gans-o.) Y doull ganso o lewlys,* his purpose by him was decreed. M.C. 7. *Henna ganso nynj-o poys,* that with him was not grievous. M.C. 10. *Ol y doul of o tewlys ganso yn néf râg tregé Ihesus ganso o kerys, ha nynj-o hard dh'y notyé,* all his purpose was decreed with him in heaven to dwell, Jesus by him was beloved, and it was not hard to note it. M.C. 214. *Dûn ganso dhe drê warnot dh'agan Arluth,* let us come with him home speedily to our Lord. O.M. 559. *Dûn ganso a dysympys,* let us come with it immediately. O.M. 2788. W. *gandho, gantho,* † *kanthau,* † *gantaw,* †*ganthav,* Arm. *gant-hau,* †*gantaff.*

GANSY, pron. prep. With or by them. *Kemmys ew gansy murnys, aga holan ew terrys râg cavow,* so much is it by them mourned, their hearts are broken by grief. C.W. 98. *Moy es un wrêg dhym yma, dhom pleasure râg gwyl gansy,* more than one wife there is to me, my pleasure for to do with them. C.W. 106. Another form of *gansé,* qd. v.

GAR, s. m. The shank, the leg. Pl. *garrow. Gans dour y wolhas aga garrow,* with water he washed their legs. M.C. 45. *Iosep dhe Gryst a vynnas y arrow ha'y dhe-ffrech whêk,* Joseph for Christ made white his legs and his sweet arms. M.C. 232. *Ow dywlof colm ha'm garrow gans lovan, fast colmennow,* my hands tie thou and my feet with a rope, fast knots. OM. 1346. *Pyw a dhueth a'n beys yn rûdh, avel gós, pen ha dusccudh, garrow, ha treys,* who is come from the world in red, like blood, head and shoulders, legs, and feet. R.D. 2501. ‡ *An lydrow adro'z garrow,* the stockings on your legs. Lhwyd, 250. W. *gar, garan.* Arm. *gar.* Ir. *cara.* Gael. *ceathramh ; caraich,* to move. Sanse. *carana,* the foot ; fr. *car,* to go.

GAR, v. a. He will love. A mutation of *câr,* 3 pers. s. fut. of *caré,* q. v. *Néb may fe mochya geffys a gâr mochyé yn pûp le,* he to whom most is forgiven will love most in every place. P.C. 514. *Mar a tallcth pertheges, ny y wra y wowheles, râk pûp ol a gâr bewé,* if he will begin to be angry, we will deceive him, for every one loves to live. R.D. 600.

GARADOW, adj. Beloved, loving, dear. A mutation of *caradow,* qd. v.

GARAF, v. a. I shall or will love. A mutation of *caraf,* 1 pers. s. fut. of *caré,* q. v. *Na wast na moy lavarow, râk yowegneth ny garaf,* waste thou not more words, for falsehood I do not love. R.D. 906. *My ny garaf strechê pel, na nýl dhe wŷth na dhe sul,* I do not like to stay long, neither work-day nor Sunday. R.D. 2249.

GARAN, s. f. A crane. Corn. Voc. *grus.* Derived from *gar,* the shank ; long legs being its distinguishing quality.

W. *garan*. Arm. *garan*. Gr. γέρανος. Lat. *grus*. One of the Welsh princes was called *Gwydhno Garanhir*, or Longshanks, which was also the well known nick-name of Edward I.

GARERA, v. a. To leave, quit, or forsake. *Dho garera*, Llwyd, 80. Written also *gara*. ‡ *Kemer wyth na rey gara an vor góth rág an vor newedh*, take thou care that thou leave not the old road for the new way. 251.

GARGAM, adj. Bandylegged. In late times it was corrupted into *gurgabm*. Llwyd, 169. Compounded of *gar*, a leg, and *cam*, crooked. W. *gargam*. Arm. *gargamm*.

GARGET, s. m. A garter. Pl. *gargettow*. Llwyd, 242.

GARLONT, s. f. A garland, a wreath. Pl. *garlontow*. *Yntredhé arel tús fól, garlont spern a ve dythythlys*, among them like foolish men, a garland of thorns was framed. M.C. 133. *Gans dén scyntyll a wodhyé me a glewas leverel, an arlont y dhe denné war y ben gans kymmys nell, ma léth an dreyn dhe'n empynnyou dre an tell*, by a man learned that knew, I heard say the garland that they drew on his head with so much force, that the spines went to the brains through the holes. M.C. 134. *Un pren gans garlontow a arhans adro dhodho*, a tree with garlands of silver about it. O.M. 2499. Borrowed from the English.

GARM, s. f. A cry, a shout, an outcry. *An dús vás a dheserya dhedhé gwlás néf o kyllys ; gans aga garm hag olva Ihesus Crist a ve meviys*, the good people desired for them the kingdom of heaven that was lost ; with their cry and lamentation Jesus Christ was moved. M.C. 4. *War tu a y vam a'n pewo, y ben a vynnas synsy, ha'y enef éth anodho gans garm cyn hag uchel gry*, on the side of his mother that owned him his head he would hold, and his soul went from him with a chilling cry, and a loud wail. M.C. 207. W. *garm*. Arm. *garm*. Ir. *gairm*. Gael. *gairm*. Lat. *carmen*. Gr. χόρμη.

GARME, v. a. To shout, to raise a shout, to cry aloud, to cry out. *W'y a gýff bohosogyon púb ér warnouch ow carmé*, ye shall have the poor always on you calling. M.C. 37. *Arluth Du, y a armas, pú a gl henna bonas*, Lord God, they cried out, who can that be. M.C. 42. *En Edhewon a armé treytour púr y vós keffys*, the Jews cried out that he was found a very traitor. M.C. 110. *A vynyn ryth, py le yth eth, rák kueth pygyth, garmé a wréth*, O woeful woman, where goest thou ? for grief thou prayest, cry out thou dost. R.D. 852. W. *garmio*. Arm. *garmi*. Ir. *gairim*. Gael *gairm*.

GAROW, adj. Rough, sharp, fierce, cruel, keen, severe. *Ow paymys a výdh garow, kyn vós leskys dhe tusow*, my pains will be cruel, before being burnt to ashes. O.M. 1354. *Pan yllyn ny yntrethon drey dour a'n meen flynt garow*, when we can between us bring water from the sharp flint stone. O.M. 1800. *Ry whaf dhedhy my a vra, gans myyn grow yn brás garow*, give a blow to her I will, with great stones very sharply. O.M. 2756. *Kyns ow bós marow, ha tormentys yn garow*, before I be dead, and tormented cruelly. P.C. 721. *Saw kym féns y morthelek, dhe wéth vythons dhe'n cronek, ha garow yn y dhulé*, but though they be hammered, worse they shall be for the toad, and rough in his hands. P.C. 2733. *Cryst a fue lydhys garow*, Christ was cruelly slain. R.D. 903. *Yma dour ow môs garow*, the water is becoming rough. R.D. 2298. W. *garw*. Arm. *garô*. Ir. *garbh*.

Gael. *garbh*. Manx, *yarroo*. Lat. *gravis*. Germ. *rauh*. Eng. rough. Sansc. *garva* ; fr. *garr*, to oppress.

GARRAC, s. f. A rock, a stone. A mutation of *carrac*, qd. v. *An garrac*, the rock. Llwyd, 241. W. *carreg*, y *garreg*.

GARRAS, v. a. To go, to proceed. ‡ *Dho garras*, Llwyd, 57. A late form of *cerdhes*, qd. v.

GARSE, v. a. He had loved. A mutation of *carsé*, 3 pers. s. plup. of *caré*, qd. v.

GARSEN, v. a. I had loved. A mutation of *carsen*, 1 pers. s. plup. of *caré*, qd. v.

GARSESTA, v. a. Thou hadst loved. A mutation of *carsesta*, an amplified form of *carses*, 2 pers. s. plup. of *caré*, qd. v. *A garsesta benené, war mynnyth, war ow ené, me a gerch onan dik dhys*, wouldst thou love women ? if thou wilt, on my soul, I will fetch a fair one for thee. P.C. 2838.

GARTH, s. m. A garden. It is preserved in the compound *lowarth*, qd. v. W. *gardh*, † *garth*. Arm. *garz*. Ir. *gardha*. Gael. *garadh*, *gard*. Manx, *garey*. Gr. χόρτος. Lat. *hortus*. Eng. *garth*, *yard*. Goth. *yard*, a house, an inclosure ; *aurtigard*, a garden. (Ang. Sax. *ortgearde*. Eng. *orchard*. Goth. *weingard*, a vineyard.) Sansc. *garhan*, fr. *garh*, to enclose.

GARTHOU, s. m. A goad. Corn. Voc. *stimulus*. W. *garthon*, † *gerthi*, in Oxford Glosses. (Zeuss, 1098.) Arm. *garzou*. Goth. *gazd*. O. Germ. *gart* : whence *garti*, a sceptre ; *gerta*, *gertin*, a rod, now *gerte*. Eng. *yard*.

GAS, s. f. Battle, a conflict. A mutation of *cás*, qd. v.

GAS, s. m. Hatred, enmity. A mutation of *cás*, qd. v.

GAS, pr. adj. Your, yours. *Ow Tás yuny wolowys, re bo gwerrs dheuch púp prýs worth tempacyon an tebel, ma gas bo lowyné néf*, my Father in his lights, may he be a help to you always against the temptation of the evil one, that yours may be the joy of heaven. P.C. 226. *Saw warnough agas honan, ha war gas fleches vyan, kén dhe olé why a's býdh*, but on you yourselves, and on your little children cause to weep ye shall have. P.C. 2643. An abbreviated form of *agas*, qd. v.

GASA, v. a. To leave, relinquish, suffer, permit. Written also *gasé*, 2 pers. s. imp., and 3 pers. s. fut. *gás* ; 2 pers. pl. imp. *gesouch* ; part. *gesys*, qd. v. *Maras ew dhe vodh, ow thás, gwra dhe'n payn-ma ow gasa*, if it is thy will, my Father, cause this pain to leave me. M.C. 55. *Ena Crist a's gasas, hag éth arta dhe besy*, there Christ them left, and went again to pray. M.C. 56. *Múr a foly ew dhodho, an kéth frút-ne mar a'n gás*, great folly it is to him, if he leaves that same fruit. O.M. 192. *Múr varth ambus dyogel an beys dh'y terry na'm gás*, great wonder is to me surely, that the earth will not let me break it. O.M. 372. *My a'd prys, Arluth uhel, dhe'n týr ly a ry cummyas, ma'm gasso, kyns ys myrwel ynno bós dhym dhe welas*, I pray thee, high Lord, to the earth that thou wilt give leave, that it allow me, before dying, in it to seek food for me. O.M. 377. *Dhys yth archaf, a dyrcyth, gás Adam dhe'th egery*, I command thee, O earth, allow Adam to open thee. O.M. 382. *An degvs ran dhynnuo gás*, the tenth part leave thou to me. O.M. 426. *Ny vynnyth dhe pobel Dew gasé crés dhyn yn nép tu, awos tryga yn pow-ma*, thou wilt not to the people of God allow peace to us on any side, for the purpose of dwelling in this land. O.M. 1591. *Ny fynnaf gasé onan vythol dhe vewé*, I will not leave any one of them to live. O.M.

1696. *A pe profus bynyges, ef a wodhfyé y bôs hy pechadures, ny's gassé dh'y ylyé*, if he were a blessed prophet, he would know that she is a sinner; he would not permit her to anoint him. P.C. 492. *Arluth, dhymmo vy na gâs pen na troys na vo golhys*, Lord, do not leave to me head nor foot that be not washed. P.C. 859. *Yn medh Pedyr, dhym na âs troys na leyff na vo golhys*, says Peter, do not leave foot nor hand that be not washed. M.C. 46. *Ow bennath genouch gasaf*, my blessing I leave with you. R.D. 2481. W. *gadu, gadaw, gadael.* Ir. *fagail.* Gael. *fagail.* Manx, *faagail.*

GASA, adj. Dirty. Written also *gasow.* Pryce. *Tregasa*, in Gerrans; and *Tregasow*, in St. Erme, are names of places.

GASAC, s. f. A mare. A mutation of *casac*, qd. v. *Dall yv an gasac-na*, that mare is blind. Lhwyd, 243.

GASADOW, adj. Hateful, wretched, detestable. A mutation of *casadow*, qd. v.

GASSIC, adj. Dirty, foul. Pryce. Id. qd. *gasa, gasow. Tregassic*, nom. loc.

GASSO, v. a. He may leave. 3 pers. s. subj. of *gasa*, qd. v.

GATH, s. f. A cat. A mutation of *câth*, qd v. *Bram an gâth*, the wind of a cat. C.W. 172.

GAU, s. m. Excrement, dung. Pryce. A mutation of *cau*, or *cauh*, a late form of *cauch*, qd. v.

GAVAF, v. a. I shall find. A mutation of *cavaf*, or *cafaf*, 1 pers. s. fut. of *cafos*, qd. v. *Tra vethol a rellu lês, ny gafaf omma néb tew*, any thing that will do good, I find not here on any side. C.W. 76.

GAVAL, v. a. To hold, to lay hold of, to grasp, to have. *Dho gaval*, Lhwyd, 96. W. *gavael, gavaelu.*

GAVAR, s. f. A goat. Corn. Vocab. *capra* vel *capella.* Written also *gaver.* Pl. *gever*, Lhwyd, 243; and in late Cornish, *gour. Ythawnvf bwch, ha tarow, gaver, yperges, karow, daves, war ve lavarow, hy hanow da kemeres*, I name cow, and bull, goat, steer, deer, sheep, from my words, let them take their good names. O.M. 126. *Gavar môr*, a lobster. Lhwyd, 81. Called also in Armoric *gavr-vor*, lit. a sea goat. " *Gaver* is the sea cray-fish in Cornwall, at the present day. The Jacksnipe, or Judcock, is also called *gaverhole*, the literal meaning of which is the *moor-goat*, more applicable to the large snipe which chatters as it rises, and falling with a quick motion, makes a noise like a kid." *Polwhele's Vocabulary.* (This is also called in Wales, *gavr y mynydh.* Fr. *chèvre volant.*) W. *gavyr, gaer,* pl. *geivyr, geivr.* Arm. *gavr, gaour*, pl. *gevr, geor.* Ir. *gabhar*, † *gabar* † *gabor.* Gael. *gabhar*, (pronounced *guar.*) Manx, *goayr.* Gr. κάπρος. Lat. *capra.* Fr. *chèvre.* It. Span. *cabretto.* Port. *capra.*

GAVAS, v. a. He found, he had. A mutation of *cavas*, or *cafas*, 3 pers. s. pret. of *cafos*, qd. v. *Me a gavas*, I had; *ti ryg gavas*, thou hadst. Lhwyd, 247.

GAVEL, s. m. A hold, a grasp. *Ha'n Edhewon a worras a uch Ihesus Crist un mên, leden o ha poys, ha brâs, moy agis gavel tredden*, and the Jews put over Jesus a stone, broad it was, and heavy, and large, more than the hold of three men; i. e. than three men could hold. M.C. 237. W. *gavael.* Ir. *gabhail*, † *gabal*, † *gabaul.* Gael. *gabhail.*

GAVEL, v. a. To get, to find. *Dho gavel.* Lhwyd, 72. A mutation of *cavel*, id. qd. *cafel*, qd. v.

GAWAS, v. a. To have. A mutation of *cawas*, qd. v. ‡ *Na ra chee gawas whanz warlyrch chy de contrevak, na ra gawas chwanz warlyrch gwrêg de contrevak*, do thou not entertain a desire after the house of thy neighbour, nor do thou entertain a desire after the wife of thy neighbour. Pryce.

GE, s. m. A hedge. A mutation of *ce*, qd. v. *Gyloan ge*, a hedge-sparrow. Lhwyd, 53.

GE, pron. s. Thou, thee. *Ty a vynta ge orth mâb dên*, wouldst thou with the son of man. C.W. 20. *Ythosta ge dên fûr*, thou art a wise man. 60. *Cayn dhe chardge ge a vŷdh war kerch, barlys, ha gwaneth*, Cain, thy charge will be over oats, barley, and wheat. 78. *Clow ge ow léf*, hear thou my voice. 104. *Pew a'th wrûg ge progowther*, who made thee a preacher. 170. In this word the *g* had the soft sound, as English *j*; it occurs only in late Cornish, and is a further corruption of *se*, as that is of *te.*

GE, pron. adj. Their. ‡ *Do ge gwithé*, to keep them; ‡ *Ne el e ge dibre*, he cannot eat them. Lhwyd, 244. ‡ *Kil y ge neûho*, making their nests. 245. Written also *gci*, a late abbreviated form of *agei*, id. qd. *aga.*

GEAGLE, adj. Dirty, filthy. Pryce; who quotes as an example *Tregeagle*, the dirty town. The word must have originally meant *a dirty place*, being compounded of *geag*, a mutation of *ccag*, id. qd. *cauch*, and *le*, a place.

GEAR, adj. Green, flourishing. Pryce. A corrupt form of *gwer*, qd. v.

GEAWEIL, s. m. The Gospel. Corn. Voc. *evangelium.* Written in the Ordinalia, *awayl*, qd. v. Wrongly translated by Pryce, *a tragedy.* Formed from the Latin. So also W. *evengyl.* Arm. *aviel*, † *awil.*

GEDN, s. m. A wedge. Lhwyd, 53. A late corruption of *gén*, qd. v.

GEDH, s. m. A day. *Dre dhe vôdh yn gêdh hydhyw*, by thy will in this day. P.C. 831. *Pur wyryoneth re gevsys ahanaf re'n gêdh hedhew*, very truth he has spoken of me by this day. P.C. 1588. *Me uy sensaf un bram plos an câs yn gêdh nag yn nôs*, I value not a dirty puff the case by day or by night. P.C. 2269. A corruption of *dêdh*, and is thus written to express the sound of *d*, as *g* soft, or *j* in English, which is a common sound of *d* in Irish and Gaelic. Thus *Dia* is pronounced *Jia*, and in Manx is written *Jee.*

GEEL, v. a. To do, to make. Pryce. Another form of *gil*, qd. v.

GEF, v. a. He shall have. A mutation of *céf*, 3 pers. s. fut. of irr. v. *cafos*, qd. v. *Ol dhe'n bestes ûs omma a géf bôs lour dewdhek mŷs*, all the beasts (that) are here, shall find food enough twelve months. O.M. 1060. *Pûr wŷr uy a vŷdh ragthé, na géf dên vŷth ynné*, very truly I will be for them, that not any man shall find a fault in them. O.M. 2467.

GEFE, v. a. He did find. A mutation of *cefé*, 3 pers. s. imp. of *cafos.* *Râk an torment a'u gefé, y'n colon yma neffré*, for the torment that he had is ever in my heart. R.D. 604. *Drôk dên a fue bytheueth, a wûl drôk ny'n ge'é medh yn y dhydhow*, a bad man he was ever ; to do evil he had no shame in his days. R.D. 1783. Written also *gevé*, qd. v.

GEFES, v. a. I have found. A mutation of *cefes*, 1 pers. s. pret. of *cafos*, qd. v. *A êl, ytho dhym lavar, an corf, nan gefes pâr, py le res êth*, O angel, now tell me, the body, that I found not its equal, where is it gone ? R.D. 788. *Agensow my a'u gwelas, an Arluth, nan gefes pâr,* lately I saw him, tho Lord that I found not his equal. R.D. 912. *My a grŷs bones an gwâs pystryour hu hudor brâs, nyn gefe's coweyth yn welâs,* I believe that the fellow is a wizard and a great sorcerer, I have not found his fellow in the country. R.D. 1855.

GEFFO, v. a. He may or should have. A mutation of *ceffo*, 3 pers. s. subj. of *cafos*, qd. v. *A'n geffo pows a's gwyrthyns, ha dhodho pernas cledhé,* ho that may have a coat, let him sell it, and for him buy a sword. M.C. 51. *Lemman lorch nêp a'n geffo, gorrens y scryp dyworto; ha nêp na'n geffo na nŷl, gwerthens y huyk dhe brenné anedhy dhodho cledhé,* now he that has a staff, let him put his scrip from him; and he who has not ono, let him sell his cloak to buy with it for him a sword. P.C. 919. *Me a grycs warnodho, râk paynys pan na'n gefo tyller dh'y pen,* I believe in him, for pains when he found not a place for his head. R.D. 260.

GEFYANS, s. m. Forgiveness, pardon. *Me a'n kelm yn krês an wast, may pyaso ef gefyans war pen y dhewlyn,* I will bind him in the middle of the waist, that he may pray for pardon on his knees. P.C. 1891. *Yn crêf brâs me re peches, Arluth, geffyans dhyworthys,* very grossly I have sinned, Lord, pardon from thee. R.D. 1570. Derived from *gafé*, to forgive.

GEFYN, v. a. We shall have, or find. A mutation of *cefyn*, 1 pers. pl. fut. of *cafos*. *Na gefyn, war ow cné, kyn fên neffré ow ponyé yn pup tol worth y whylas,* we shall not find, upon my soul, though we may be ever running in every hole seeking him. R.D. 549. *Fatel bydh dhynny lemyn agan Arluth na gefyn, ellas, tru, tru,* how will it be to us now, that we find not our Lord? alas! woe! woe! R.D. 731.

GEFYR, v. pass. It is found. A mutation of *cefyr*, id. qd. *cefer,* qd. v. *Mûr a gâs vyé gené trehy henna rum lauté, saw abun na gefyr ken, euch dh'y drehy hep lettyé, ha musurouch of yn lên,* much anguish it would be to me to cut that, by my truth, but since another cannot be found, go ye to cut it without stopping, and measure it faithfully. O.M. 2503.

GEFYS, part. Forgiven. The passive participle of *gafé*, qd. v. *Nêb may fe mochya geffys a gâr mochyn yn pûp lê,* he that is forgiven must will love most in every place. P.C. 513. *Ha dhym cf a leverys, dhe pêch dhys a vŷdh gefys,* and to me he said, thy sin shall be forgiven to thee. R.D. 1102. Written also *gevys,* qd. v.

GEFYTH, v. a. Thou shalt have or find. A mutation of *cefyth*, 2 pers. s. fut. of *cafos*. *Dew dhên a gefyth cna, gor y yn mês desempys,* thou wilt find two men there, put them out immediately. O.M. 333. It is also used for the third person. *Râg bôs Abel gwŷr dhegé, ef a'n gefyth yn dywedh, an ioy na dhyfyk nefré,* because Abel's tithe is true, he shall find in the end the joy that will never fail. O.M. 516. *Na wrello y vôdh gocf, y'n gefyth mûr a trystyys,* unhappy he (that) dooth not his will, he shall find much sorrow. O.M. 2094. *Hager vernans a'n par-na cf a'n gefyth,* a cruel death like that he shall have. R.D. 1985. Written also *gevyth,* qd. v.

GEGIN, s. f. A kitchen. A mutation of *cegin,* qd. v. *Ce dho'n gegin,* go to the kitchen. *Llwyd,* 252.

GEI, pron. Their. *Llwyd,* 244. An abbreviated form of *ugei,* id. qd. *aga,* qd. v.

GEIEN, s. f. A nerve, a sinew. *Llwyd,* 98. Written in the Cornish Vocabulary, *goiuen,* nervus. Pl. *geiow,* in construction *eiow,* or *icyw*. *Pûr gow a lever dhe vyn; pan sefsys hydhew myttyn, yâch êns aga icyw,* a very lie thou wilt tell, when thou gottest up this moruing, suud were their sinews. P.C. 2681. W. *gieuyn,* a nerve; pl. *giau: genyn,* a sinew. Arm. *gwazien.* Ir. *feith, feth.* Gael. *feith.* Manx, *feh.*

GEIN, s. m. The back. A mutation of *cein,* qd. v. *Cor-kyn ny gans dyaha, kyn duswcwo ny'n drccha dhywar y geyn,* let us sleep with security; though he should revive he will not raise it from off his back. R.D. 404. *A gein,* his back; *war a gein,* on his back. *Llwyd,* 230. *An heves adrô y gein,* the shirt on his back. 250.

GEL, s. f. A leech. Corn. Voc. *ghel,* sanguissuga. W. *gêl, gelen, geleu.* Arm. *gelaouen.* Ir. *dallog, + deal.* Gael. *deal, giol, gealadh.* Manx, *guillag.* Sansc. *galuká.*

GEL, s. m. Power. *Pryce.* W. *gall.*

GELAR, s. m. Anguish, pang. *Pryce.* An incorrect reading of *galar,* qd. v.

GELE, s. m. A companion, a fellow, one of two. A mutation of *celé,* qd. v.

GELEN, s. f. The elbow. *Llwyd,* 52. Another form of *elin,* qd. v.

GELER, s. f. A coffin. *Yn dour Tyber ef a fue yn geler horn gorrys down, ha mŷl dên ef a verûk dué yn dour-na râk wth hag own,* in the water of Tyber he was in a coffin of iron put deep, and a thousand men he did end in that water for horror and fear. R.D. 2320. In the other dialects it means a bier. W. *gelor.* Arm. *geler.*

GELLAS, v. a. To jest, to joke. *Evn nyng ew dha gellas, an ober-ma dha wellas; ledhys yw Abel, na sew, Eve,* it is not (time) to jest, to see this work; killed is Abel, be not angry. C.W. 90.

GELLY, v. a. To lose. A mutation of *celly,* qd. v.

GELLY, s. m. A grove. A mutation of *celly,* qd. v. *Pengelly,* the head of the grove, a place in the parish of Creed. *Pen y gelli,* is a frequent name in Wales also.

GELM, v. a. He will bind. A mutation of *celm,* 3 pers. s. fut. of *celmy,* qd. v. *Me a gelm seon lovan dha worth conna brêch an adla,* I will forthwith bind a good rope on the wrist of the knave. P.C. 2761.

GELMEN, s. m. A band, a halter. A mutation of *celmen,* id. qd. *colmen,* qd. v.

GELMY, v. a. To bind. A mutation of *celmy,* qd. v.

GELVIN, s. m. The beak, the bill of a bird. Corn. Voc. *rostrum.* W. *gylvin,* + *gelvin,* + *golbin;* *gylvant, gylv,* + *gilb.* Ir. + *gulba.*

GELVINAC, s. m. A curlew. Written by Llwyd, 240. *gylvinac.* So called from *gelvin,* a bill, its distinguishing quality. This bird is called in Welsh *gylvinhir,* or long bill, for the same reason. The root of the Welsh term *cyfylog,* a woodcock, in Cornish *cyvelac,* qd. v., is also *gylv,* a bill.

GELWEL, v. a. To call, to call for, to invoke, to name. Written also *gylwel,* qd. v. Part. *gelwys, gylwys.* In construction it changes into *celwel,* qd. v. *Yma ow celwel Ely,* he is calling Elias. P.C. 2959. *Ple clewsta gelwel Dew Cryst gans dên yn bŷs-ma genys,* where hast thou heard God called Christ by a man in this world born. O.M. 2642. *Ol mêns trespas a wrugé, dhodho cf me a'n gafsé, a menné gelwel gyryans,* all the evil he has done to him I would forgive it, if he would ask pardon. P.C. 1816. *Lemmyn worth agan gelwel, râk own desefsen merwel,* now calling us, from fear I would have desired to die. R.D. 1770. 2 pers. s. imp. *galvey*, qd. v. 3 pers. s. fut. *gelow, a elow*, qd. v. W. *galw*. Arm. *galva*. Ir. *glaodh, cnol*. Gael. *glaodh*. Manx, *knull, yll, yllee*. Sanse. *klad, cal*. Gr. καλέω, κλάιω, κλάω.

GEMERAF, v. a. I will take. A mutation of *cemeraf*, 1 pers. s. fut. of *cemeres*, qd. v. *Luen dyal war ol an veys ny gemeraf vynytha*, full vengeance on the whole world I will not take ever. O.M. 1234.

GEMERES, v. a. To take. A mutation of *cemeres*, qd. v. *An corf kêr dhe ancledhyn, dûn dh'y gemeres dhe'n lûr*, the dear body to bury, let us come to take it to the ground. P.C. 3141. *Arluth, ple'th ên alemma, dhyn dhe gemeres trygva*, Lord, where shall we go from hence, for us to take a dwelling. R.D. 2392.

GEMERYN, v. a. We shall take. A mutation of *cemeryn*, 1 pers. pl. fut. of *cemeres*, qd. v. *Mars êth arté dhyworthyn, drók yw gyné, vynytha er na whyllyn, a travyth ny gemeryn nêp lowené*, if thou wilt go again from us, I am sorry, ever until we see (thee,) from any thing we shall not take any pleasure. R.D. 2365.

GEMMER, v. a. He shall take. A mutation of *cemmer*, 3 pers. s. fut. of *cemeres*, qd. v. *Gwyn y vŷs a vo trigys yn dhe servys, rág tristys nyn d'y gemmer vynytha*, happy his lot (that) is dwelling in thy service, for sorrow will not seize him for ever. P.C. 124.

GEMMYS, adj. So much. A mutation of *cemmys*, qd. v. *Beneges re bo an Tás, a vynnas dysquedhes dhyn gwelynny a gemmys rûs, luen a vertu pûp termyn*, blessed be the Father, who would shew to us rods of so much grace, full of virtue always. O.M. 1747.

GEMYN, v. a. He will commend. A mutation of *cemyn*, 3 pers. s. fut. of *cemynny*, qd. v.

GEN, s. f. The chin. Llwyd, 89. *My a's giofjek gans un blogon, vythqueth na ve bom, a won, a rollo whaf mar gales, del ys brewaf yn dan gên*, I will smite her with a bludgeon, that never was a stroke, I know, that would give a blow so hard, as I will strike her under the chin. O.M. 2712. The plural is *genow*, the jaws, the lips, the mouth: it is generally written *ganow*, qd. v. See also the dual *dywen*. W. *gên*. Arm. *gên*. Ir. †*gen*. Gr. γένυς. Goth. *kinnus*. Germ. *kinn*. Eng. *chin*. Sanse. *hanus*, the jaw; fr. *han*, to grind, to break.

GEN, s. m. A wedge. Pl. *genow. Ty vaow, darbar lym ha pry, mryn whryl, slotyys, ha genow, ha my a fystyn agy, ow trehevel an fosow*, thou boy, prepare lime and clay, building stones, trueks, and wedges; and I will hasten within, erecting the walls. O.M. 2317. W. *gaing*, † *gen*, (in Oxford Glosses;) *cún*. Arm. *gên. euen*. Ir. †*gen*. Gr. Gael. *geinn*. Manx, *jeenys*. Lat. *cuneus*.

GEN, adj. Other. A mutation of *cen*, qd. v. *Sevys, gallus dhe gen le, dén apert ha mûr y brŷs*, he is risen, he is gone to another place, a man perfect and of much estimation. M.C. 255. *Gwythench why y, ma na vôns yn nêp maner remmuys dhe gen tyller, war beyn tenné ha cregy*, watch ye them, that they be not in any manner removed to another place, on pain of drawing and hanging. O.M. 2045.

GEN, pron. adj. Our, ours. *Hedré vy yn beys gynen, neffré trystyns ny gen bŷdh*, whilst thou art in the world with us, never will sorrow be ours. P.C. 731. *Na fyllys, a Arluth da, na font bythqueth ny gen bué*, it failed not, O good Lord, nor was a want ever ours. P.C. 916. *Arluth, mûr grûs re'th fo, rák lowené ny gen bo yn le may fuen*, O Lord, great thanks be to thee, for joy may not be ours in the place where we have been. R.D. 168. *Rák na wrello dasserchy, neffré ny gen byen ny ioy hep dhywedh*, for if he should not rise again, never should we have joy without end. R.D. 1029. *Esé dour ha ponvos brás, whárré y gen lowennas, kettel dhueth er ugan pyn*, there was care and great trouble, soon he gladdened us, when he came to meet us. R.D. 1328. *Dûn dhe menedh Olyved, yn wêdh ena ny a rêd y gen lyfryow*, let us come to the mount of Olives, also there we will read in our books. R.D. 2411. *Cûth ny gen gâs*, sorrow leaves us not. R.D. 2456. ‡ *Gen cœgar nei*, our boys; ‡*hyrlian yw gen gware nyi*, hurling is our sport. Llwyd, 245. An abbreviated form of *agan*, qd. v.

GEN, adv. Through. A mutation of *cen*, qd. v. *Drók gen y gŷk ef a fue, bŷth ny sparyaf y tenné awos our*, evil though his flesh was, I will never spare to drag him for the sake of gold. R.D. 2186.

GEN, prep. With, by. ‡ *Ma'n viuh gen liouh*, the cow is with calf. ‡ *Gen an bobl vyhodzhak*, with the poor people. Llwyd, 130. ‡ *Gen an lewar*, with the book. 241. ‡ *Hy onr gwil padn dah gen hy glawn*, she knows to make good cloth with her wool. Pryce. A late form of *gan*, qd. v.

GENAMA, pron. prep. With me. *Crist pár wêk, an caradow, a'n gorthebys, yn úr-na, te a vŷdh yn kêth golow yn paradis genama*, Christ very sweetly, the beloved, answered him, in that hour thou shalt be in the same light in Paradiso with me. M.C. 195. A poetic form of *genefvy*.

GENAU, s. m. The mouth. Corn. Vocab. os. This is properly the plural of *gén*, the chin, or jaw; but as in Welsh, it was used as a singular, and a further plural *gcnvow* was formed from it. The general form in the Ordinalia is *ganow*, qd. v. See also *Gên*. W. *genau*, pl. *gencuau*. Arm. *genaou, genou*.

GENAWED, s. m. A mouthful, a morsel. Llwyd, 5. W. *gencuaid*. Arm. *genaouad*.

GENE, pron. prep. With me. *Ow holon yntré mŷll darn, marth yw gené na squardry*, my heart into a thousand pieces, it is a wonder with me that it has not broken. M.C. 166. *Dûs gené pols dhe wandré*, come with me to walk a while. O.M. 934. *Yma gené un bé do, gorra hag eys kemyskys*, I have a good load, hay and corn mixed. O.M. 1057. *Tán ha cledhé, ynn gené lemmyn parys*, fire and sword are with me now ready. O.M. 1305. An abbreviated form of *genef*. So also W. *gen-i*. Arm. *gené*.

GENEF, pron. prep. With or by me. (*Gan-my*.) *Ha genef ef a'd yggys a lewerel gwyroneth*, and by me he prayed thee to tell the truth. O.M. 739. *Otté onma prynmer genef dhe wûl tán, degys a dré*, behold here sticks with me to make a fire, brought from home. O.M. 1314. *Colom genef vy yma*, a dove with me there is, i. e. I have a dove. O.M. 1189. *Drôg yw genef gruthyl dén*, I am sorry to have made man. O.M. 917. *Mar dha yw genef a vrŷs merwel kyns dôs drók ancow*, so well it is in my opinion to die before evil sorrow comes. O.M. 1229. Sometimes written *genaf. Yma flôch genaf genys, dre vódh an Tás Dew yn wêdh*, I have a child born, by the will of the Father, God also. O.M. 672. W. *genyv*, †*gennyf*. Arm. *ganen*, †*guenef*.

GENEN, pron. prep. With or by us. (*Gan-ny*.) *Ow tybbry genen y mu*, he is eating with us. M.C. 43. *Rág genen creçjis nêb ês, dén glán yw a bêch*, for he that is hanged with us, a man clean is of sin. M.C. 102. *May hallo genen tregé*, that he may dwell with us. O.M. 566. *Dûs genen ny*, come with us. O.M. 2378. *Ef a'n geryth genen ny*, he shall find with us. R.D. 2345. W. *genym, genym ni,* † *genhym*. Arm. *ganconp,* † *guencomp,* † *guenenmpny*.

GENES, pron. prep. With, or by thee. *(Gan-ty.) Ow broder, pûr lowenek my â genes dhe'n menedh*, my brother, very gladly I will go with thee to the mountain. O.M. 450. *Dhe vroder, ow servont lêl, prâg nagusy ef genes*, thy brother, my faithful servant, why is he not with thee? O.M. 573. *Râg genes yn pûp teller parys of dhe lafuryé*, for with thee in every place I am ready to labour. O.M. 939. Sometimes written also *genas*. *Arlath, hy a leverys, ow holon yma genas*, Lord, she said, my heart is with thee. M.C. 172. W. *genyt,* † *genhyt*. Arm. *ganez,* † *guenez,* † *guenede*.

GENNYS, pron. prep. With your. *Llwyd*, 244. A late composite of *gan*, with, and *ys* for *agys*, your.

GENOUGH, pron. prep. With or by you. Written also *genoch*, and *geneuch, (gan-chwi.) Ef a's dylyrf genoch wáy*, he will deliver them to you. P.C. 164. *Râk ow tharment a dhe scon, genoch na'm byvé trygé*, for my suffering will come soon, that with you I shall not stay. P.C. 642. *Bythqueth re luc ûs geneuch*, ever there has been a custom with you. P.C. 2034. *Me â geneuch yn lowen*, I will go with you joyfully. P.C. 3006. *Pyth yw tewlys genouch why bôs erbyn nôs*, what is purposed by you to be against night. R.D. 1286. *Geneuch why nôs ny drynyaf*, with you to go I will not grieve. R.D. 1797. W. *genych, genyeh chwi,* † *geunwch*. Arm. *ganehoch,* † *guenceoch,* † *guencochwy*.

GENOW, s. m. Wedges. Plural of *gên*, qd. v.

GENS, v. subs. They are. *Pryce.* In such phrases as *wyn gêns, na gêns*, they are not, the *g* must be joined to the preceding word, and read *nyng êns, nag êns*.

GENSY, pron. prep. With or by her. *(Gans-hy.) Ha'y bows y honon gorris a dro dhodho hy a ve, gans y eam y fye guris, hag of gensy ow tené*, and his own coat put about him it was, by his mother it was made, and he with her sucking. M.C. 161. *An golom ow devedhys, ha gensy branch olyff glâs*, the dove is come, and with her a green olive branch. C.W. 178. More frequently written *gynsy*, qd. v. W. *gandhi, ganthi,* † *genthi,* † *genti,* † *kenthy*. Arm. *gant-hi,* † *ganti,* † *ganty*.

GENSYNS, pron. prep. With them. *Llwyd*, 244. There is no authority for this form in the Ordinalia, *gansé* being always used, but it would not be incorrect, as it is the exact equivalent of W. *gandhynt*.

GENTER, s. f. A nail, a spike. A mutation of *center*, qd. v. ‡ *Guisgo an genter-ma ed eskaz vi*, knock this nail in my shoe. *Llwyd*, 230.

GENVAR, s. m. January. *Llwyd*, 16, 17. *Mis Genvar*, the month of January. W. *ionawr*. Arm. *genver*. Ir. *geanuir*. From the Latin *Januarius*.

GENY, v. n. To be born. Part. *genys, qynys. Whar? y a'n dystryppyas mar noyth genys del vyé*, anon they stripped him as naked as he was born. M.C. 130. *Yma flôch genaf genys*, there is a child born to me. O.M. 672. *Ny welys lekké bythqueth aban vîf genys*, I have not seen fairer ever sluce I was born. O.M. 1731. *Pûr wŷr ef a fue genys pûr even y Bethlem Iudi*, very truly he was born very exactly in Bethlehem Juda. P.C. 1606. *Bynyges re bo an prŷs, may fe a venen genys, an wyrhes kêr Maria*, blessed be the time that he was born of woman, the dear Virgin Mary. R.D. 153. W. *geni*. Arm. *gana*. Ir. *geiu,* † *gen,* † *geini*. Gael. *gein, gin*. Manx, *gient*. Gr. γένω, γεννάω, γίγνομαι. Lat. † *geno, gigno, gnascor*. Fr. *genère*. Goth. *kuni, keina*. Sansc. *gan, jan*.

GENZHETE, adv. Before yesterday. ‡ *De genzhete*, the day before yesterday. *Llwyd*, 249. It is a modern corruption of *eens*, before, and *de*, yesterday.

GER, s. m. A word, a saying, a report. Pl. *gerryow, gyrryow, gerryon*. *Te gêr vyth ny gevesys*, thou spakest never a word. M.C. 92. *Lavar geŷr dhymmo un gêr, mars ota nûb dén ha Du*, tell truly to me one word, if thou art the Son of God. M.C. 129. *Na leveryn un gêr gow*, let us not say a word untrue. M.C. 247. *Argyé na woy dhyn ny reys, na keusel na woy gerryow*, to argue more to us there is no need, nor speak more words. P.C. 2468. *Ow gyrryow a vŷdh previs*, my words will be proved. C.W. 60. *Der dha êr*, through thy word. C.W. 42. ‡ *An giriow-ma*, these words. *Llwyd*, 253. W. *gair,* † *geir*, pl. *geiriau*. Arm. *gêr*, pl. *gerion*. Ir. *gair, gar*. Gael. *gair*, Manx, *geirr, feigr*. (Gr. γηρύω. Lat. *garrio*. Germ. *girre*. Lith. *girru*. Russ. *graiu*.) Sansc. *gir, eirâ*, a discourse, the voice, fr. *gâr*, to cry, to shout.

GER, adj. Dear. A mutation of *cêr*, qd. v. *A myleges y'th ober, ty re'n ladhes, rum lowté, hag ef ahanan mar gêr*, O cursed in thy work, thou hast killed him, by my truth, and he so dear to us. O.M. 612. *Ow holon gêr caradow*, my dear beloved heart. O.M. 2135.

GERCH, v. a. He will bring. A mutation of *cerch*, 3 pers. s. fut. of *cerches*, qd. v. *Râk ef a gerch dhyworthyn kemmys na wordhyo Iovyn*, for he will carry from us as many as do not worship Jove. P.C. 1916. *Me a gerch onan dêk dhys*, I will fetch a fair one for thee. P.C. 2840.

GERCHEN, adj. Surrounding, about. A mutation of *cerchen*, qd. v. *Hedré vo yn y gerchen quêth Ihesu, êth yn growes prên, ny fydh dyswrŷs*, as long as is about him the cloth of Jesus, (that) went on the cross tree, he will not be destroyed. R.D. 1664.

GERCHES, v. a. To bring, to fetch. A mutation of *cerches*, qd. v. *Me a gerch dour dhys wharré, ollé ow fycher gyné yn ow dorn râk y gerches*, I will fetch water for thee soon; behold my pitcher with me in my hand to fetch it. P.C. 657. *Lavar lemyn mars yw prŷs danvon genes tûs errys dhe gerchs an vŷl losel*, say now if it is time to send with thee armed men to fetch the vile knave. P.C. 940.

GERCHO, v. a. He may fetch. A mutation of *cercho*, 3 pers. s. subj. of *cerches*. *Me a bar daras an yet, na gercho alemma chei, kyn fo mar fôl*, I will bar the door of the gate, that he may not carry hence a friend, though he be so boasting. P.C. 3050.

GERDA, s. m. Fame, renown. Cornish Vocabulary, *fama*. Literally *good word*, being compounded of *gêr*, and *da*, good. So also W. *geirda*.

GERDHES, v. a. To walk, to go. A mutation of *cerdhes*, qd. v. *Torré ha ke dhe gerdhes*, cut it, and go thy way. O.M. 204. *Dhymmo ceredhek yu weôh, ro werth dhe gerdhes yu fâs*, to me also the maimed give thou strength also to walk well. O.M. 2010.

GERENSE, s. m. Love. A mutation of *cerensé*, qd. v.

GESCY 167 GEVES

Bersabé, flour ol an bŷs, râg dhe gerensé Syr Urry a fŷdh ledhys, Bathsheba, flower of all the world, for thy love Sir Uriah shall be killed. O.M. 2122.

GERHAS, v. a. He fetched. A mutation of *cerhas,* 3 pers. s. preter. of *cerhes,* qd. v. *Dywolow yffarn a squerdyas corf Iudas ol dhe dharnow, hag anodho a gerh-as y cueff dhe dewolgow,* the devils of hell tore the body of Judas all to pieces, and from him carried his soul to darkness. M.C. 106.

GERHES, v. a. To fetch. A mutation of *cerhes,* qd. v. *Tormentors yn kettep gwâs, euch alemma gans Iudas dhe gerhes an gwâs muscok,* executioners, every fellow, go hence with Judas to fetch the crazed fellow. P.C. 961. *Dûn dh'y gerhes, cowethé,* let us come to fetch it, comrades. P.C. 2656.

GERIITDA, adj. Famous, renowned. Corn. Voc. *famosus.* Comp. of *geriit,* formed from *gér,* with the adjectival termination *iit,* as in *droegeriit,* qd. v., and *da,* good.

GERLEVER, s. m. A word-book, dictionary, or lexicon. Pryce. Comp. of *gér,* a word, and *lever,* book. W. *geirlyvyr.*

GERRES, part. Left. ‡ *Ma leinz gwrég, lacka vel zeag, gwell gerres vel kommeres,* there are many wives, worse than grains, better left than taken. Pryce. A late corruption of *gesys.*

GERRO, v. a. Allow ye. ‡ *Ha Dew lavaras, gerro ny geel dean en agan havalder warlér agan havalder,* and God said, let us make man in our likeness after our own likeness. C.W. p. 191. A late corruption of *gesouch.*

GERYN, v. a. We shall love. A mutation of *ceryn,* 1 pers. pl. fut. of *caré,* qd. v. *Nêb a geryn an moycha,* whom we love the most. C.W. 88.

GERYTH, v. a. Thou shall love. A mutation of *ceryth,* 2 pers. s. fut. of *caré,* qd. v. *Ow bolungeth mar mynnyth y collenwel hep let vŷth, dhe váp Ysac a geryth, y offrynné reys yn dhys,* my will, if thou wilt fulfil it, without any hesitation, thy son Isaac, whom thou lovest, to offer him it is necessary for thee. O.M. 1279. *Mar a'm even geryth, me a'th pŷs, dhyunno gûs crês,* if thou lovest me well, I pray thee allow to me peace. R.D. 1448.

GES, s. m. A jest, a jeer, a flout, report, mockery. *Te yn mâb Du, leun a râs, yn ges y a leverys,* thou art the Son of God, full of grace, in a jeer they said. M.C. 95. *Gûl ges ahanaf a wrêth, marth yn gynef na 'thues médh, ow kensel gow,* thou dost make a jest of me, it is a wonder with me that there is not shame speaking lies. R.D. 1390. Borrowed from the English.

GES, pron. adj. Your, yours. *Banneth an Tâs re ges bo,* the blessing of the Father be yours. O.M. 2585. *Dhe'n bédh pan y ges gorrys,* to the tomb when I sent you. R.D. 622. *Nagues ys y ges colon,* nor is joy in your heart. R.D. 1258. *Y ges bŷdh ioy na dhyfyk,* yours be joy that will not fail. R.D. 1310. *Ken leffo y ges golok,* should he come into your sight. R.D. 1802. An abbreviated form of *ages,* qd. v.

GESCY, v. a. To jest, to jeer, to deride, to mock, to flout. *Aban na dal dhe gesky, dout tân yffarn dhe'th lesky bôs dyscregyk,* since it behoves thee not to jest, fear hell fire to burn thee, being unbelieving. R.D. 1429. ‡ *Cool ge dhym, men dha gesky,* hearken thou to me, would I flout thee? C.W. 48.

GESOUCH, v. a. Leave ye. 2 pers. pl. imp. of *gasé,* qd. v. Written also *gesench. Hedré vyyn ow predery, yn glassygyon gesouch y, aga thŷr dhe wrowedhé,* while I am considering, leave ye them on a green plot, the three to lie. O.M. 2036. *Gesouch dhe vós croffolas,* leave ye off lamentations. O.M. 1662. *Gesouch vy dhe worthyby, kyns ry brues dhe vôs dyserŷs,* allow ye me to answer before giving sentence to be destroyed. P.C. 2493.

GEST, s. f. A female dog, a bitch. Pl. *gesti.* Llwyd, 14, 46, 241. W. *gâst,* pl. *geist.* In Arm. *gâst,* pl. *gisti,* is now used to designate a harlot, or common prostitute; a bitch being called *kiez,* i. e. a female dog. So Irish *banchu,* a bitch ; *gast,* old woman.

GESUI, v. a. He will advise. A mutation of *cesul,* 3 pers. s. fut. of *cesulyé,* qd. v. *Me a gesul bôs gansé prennys da gwôn yn nêp le râg an cludhva Cristunyon,* I advise that there be with them bought a good field in some place for a burial-place of Christians. P.C. 1543.

GESYS, part. Left, permitted, allowed. Part. pass. of *gasé,* qd. v. *Hag a heys dhe wrowedhé yno eff a ve gesys,* and at length to lie there it was left. M.C. 233. *Ha dhyso Dew a yrehys, may fe y tûs ol gesys dhe wîl dhodho sacryfys,* and to thee God has commanded, that all his people be permitted to make sacrifice to him. O.M. 1492. *Del hewel dhynny, omma na fydhyn gesys yn crês,* as it appears to us, here we shall not be left in peace. O.M. 1606.

GETA, pron. prep. To thee. ‡ *Me a ryn dhe why poyntya service dha tég, ha geta, rag rowlya cyn ha chattell,* I will to thee appoint a service to bear, and to thee, to rule the corn and cattle. C.W. 78. Comp. of *ge,* for *de,* to, and *ta,* thee. This form occurs only in late Cornish.

GETGORRA, v. a. To compare, to collate. *Dhe getgorra.* Pryce. A mutation of *cetgorra,* qd. v.

GEUH, v. a. Ye shall have. ‡ *Hwi a geuh.* Llwyd, 247. A mutation of *ceuh,* id. qd. *ceuch,* 2 pers. pl. fut. of *cael.* W. *chwi a gewch.*

GEVE, v. a. He had, or found. A mutatiou of *cevé,* 3 pers. s. imp. of irr. v. *cafus,* qd. v. *Cryst kymmys payn y'n gevé, angus tyn ha galarow,* Christ so much pain had, anguish sharp aud pangs. M.C. 50. *Own bôs Crist mâb Du an nêff an tebell êt a'n gevé,* fear that Christ was the son of the God of heaven seized the wicked angel. M.C. 122. *Lavar dhym, del ym kerry, pa'n vernans d'n gevé ef,* tell me, as thou lovest me, what the death he met with. O.M. 2210.

GEVEL, s. f. A pair of pincers. *Gevel-hoern,* munetorium, snuffers. Corn. Voc. lit. iron pincers. W. *gevnil,* + *gebel,* from *gavael,* to seize, grasp. Arm. *gevel.* Ir. *gäilbeal.* Gael. *geimle.* Manx, *clouw.*

GEVELYN, s. f. A cubit. A mutation of *cevelyn,* qd. v. *Kyns ys trehy war an pren re got o a gevelyn,* before cutting on the tree, too short it was by a cubit. O.M. 2520.

GEVER, s. m. An opposite position, fronting, relation. A mutation of *cever,* qd. v. *Whet kerchouch dhymmo Pilat, yn y gever, del fueff badl, y fûff tollys,* again, bring ye to me Pilate, in respect to him, as I was foolish, I was deceived. R.D. 1886.

GEVES, v. a. He had, or found. A mutation of *ceves,* 3 pers. s. preter. of *cafus. Hag ow bostyé y bôs ef Cryst gwŷr un vâp Dew a nêf yn bŷs-ma nan geves pâr,* and

GEWAR 168 GEYEN

boasting that he is Christ the true only Son of the God of heaven in this world that had not an equal. P.C. 1578. Written also *gefes*, qd. v.

GEVYANS, s. m. Pardon, forgiveness. *Da y won y vôs a râs, gevyans me ny'n býdh neffré*, well I know that he is of grace, pardon I shall never have. M.C. 104. *Arluth, gevyans dhum ené, gory pan wrugé pehé gyns corf an debel venen*, Lord, pardon to my soul! alas, when I did sin with the body of the wicked woman. O.M. 2249. Another form of *gefyans*, qd. v.

GEVYS, part. Pardoned, forgiven. *Ragon y pesys y dâs, oll y sor may fe gevys*, for us he prayed his Father, all his anger that it might be remitted. M.C. 9. *Ow thâs whêk bedhens gevys dhe'n rema aga mystyté*, my Father dear, be they pardoned to these ones their misdeeds. M.C. 185. Another form of *gefys*, qd. v.

GEVYTH, v. a. He shall have or find. A mutation of *cevyth*, 3 pers. s. fut. of *cafus*, qd. v. *Pŷr weyr ef a'n gevyth gu, pan dyffo yn ow goloc*, very truly he shall have woe, when he comes into my sight. P.C. 963. *Ef a'n gevyth war an chal*, he shall catch it on the jaw. P.C. 1181. *Lyes mâp dên yn bŷs-ma râk y gorf a'n gevyth own*, many a son of man in this world, for his body shall have fear. R.D. 2080. Written also *gefyth*, qd. v.

GEW, s. m. A lance, a spear, a javelin, a dart, a shaft. *Gew a ve yn y dhewlé gans an Edhewon gorris, ha pen lym râg y wané dhe golon Ihesus hynwys*, a spear was in his hands by the Jews put, and a sharp end to pierce him to the heart of the mild Jesus. M.C. 217. *Yn corf Ihesus caradow en gew lym ef a bechyé*, in the body of Jesus beloved the sharp spear he thrust. M.C. 218. *A'n golon yth êth dowr ha goys yn keweskis, ha ryp an gew a resas dhe dhewlé nêb a'n gwyskys*, from the heart there went a stream great, water and blood mingled, and by the spear it gushed to the hands of him that struck him. M.C. 219. Written also *giw*. *Tan, syns y'th dorn an giw-na*, take, hold iu thy hand that spear. P.C. 3010. See also *Gu*. In the Cornish Vocabulary it is written *gwayu*. W. *gwacw*, † *quacu*. Arm. *gonô*. Ir. *gath, ga*, † *gai*, † *geidh*, † *gaodh, fughn*. Gael. *fagha*. Manx, *gew, gah*. Swed. *gadd*. Sanse. *gada*, a pang; *vâgin*, an arrow.

GEW, s. m. Woe, grief, misery. Pl. *gewow*. *Dhe léf Arluth a glewaf, saw dhe face my ny welaf, er ow gewv*, thy voice Lord I hear, but thy face I do not see, for my woes. O.M. 589. *Ethinys gwêf pan vevé genys, ow terry gormenadow Dew, pellys ôn a Paradis dhe'n uôr veys er agan gew*, alas, woe is me when I was born, breaking the commandments of God, driven we are out of Paradise to the earth of the world for our misery. C.W. 76. *Dheth léf Arluth a glowaf, saw dha face me ny welaf, er ow gew*, thy voice Lord I hear, but thy face I do not see, for my woe. C.W. 84. It changes in construction into *wew*. *My a'n knouk, er y wew; otté mellow y geyn brew*, I will beat him, to his sorrow; behold the joints of his back broken. P.C. 2085. Written also *gu*, qd. v.

GEWAN, s. m. Lies, falsehood. *Au fals re scornycs gymé; wyns ûs ethom nag onan dhyochy a dustynyé pan clewscuch cows au gewan*, the false (man) has trifled with me; there is no need of any one to testify to you, when he heard you speak the lies. P.C. 1338. Plural of *gow*, qd. v.

GEWAR, s. m. Anger. *Onon gans an kêth welen yn tryff Crist a ve gorris, a'n gwyskys lasche war an pen, bum pûr gewar descthys*, one with the same rod in the hand of Christ (that) was put, struck him a lash on the head, a blow of pure anger excited. M.C. 138. W. *garwedh*.

GEWS, s. m. A speech, a word. A mutation of *cews*, qd. v. *Râg dhym yma govenek cafes dhe gews tregereth*, for my request is to obtain thy word of love. O.M. 454.

GEWS, v. a. He will speak. A mutation of *cews*, 3 pers. s. fut. of *cewsel*, qd. v. *Pyw ôs a gews mar huhel*, who art thou (that) speakest so high. O.M. 1368. *Me a gews dhodho mûr dêk*, I will speak to him very fair. P.C. 189.

GEWSEL, v. a. To speak. A mutation of *cewsel*, qd. v. *Pûr wŷr my a vyn mones dhe geusel orth Moyses, yn wêdh Aron*, very truly I will go to speak to Moses, also Aaron. O.M. 1583.

GEWSEUCH, v. a. Ye will speak. A mutation of *cewseuch*, 2 pers. pl. fut. of *cewsel*, qd. v. *Ny wodhoch pendra gewseuch*, ye know not what ye say. P.C. 443. *Teweuch, a henna na gewseuch gêr, pypenagol a wharfo*, be ye silent, of that speak not a word, whatever may happen. R.D. 670.

GEWSONS, v. a. They shall speak. 3 pers. pl. fut. of *cewsel*, qd. v. *Me a vyn y examné, ha'y dhs ha'y deskes wharré, prâg na gewsons dyougel*, I will examine him and his men, and his doctrine soon; why do they not speak clearly? P.C. 1212.

GEWSY, v. a. Thou shalt speak. A mutation of *cewsy*, 2 pers. s. fut. of *cewsel*, qd. v. *Erbyn a pyth a gewsy, ny ŷl dên vŷth gorthyby, dhe resons ŷns da ha fŷn*, against the thing thou sayest, not any man can answer, thy reasons are good aud fine. P.C. 820. *By my gewsy ken ys wêr*, never sayest thou other than true. R.D. 1195.

GEWSYS, v. a. Spoke. A mutation of *cewsys*, the preterite of *cewsel*, qd. v. *Worth golow nôs ny geusys, na ny wystrys yn scoforn*, by the light of night I spoke not, nor whispered in the ear. P.C. 1253. *Pûr wyryoneth re gensys ahanaf, re'n gêdh hedhew*, very truly thou hast spoken of me, by this day. P.C. 1537. *Y fue gynen Arluth nêf, ha worthyn ol a geusys*, the Lord of heaven was with us, and spoke to us all. R.D. 1230. *A'n bêdh ef a syrys, râk hydhew ny a geusys ol orto ef*, from the grave he is risen, for to-day we have spoken all to him. R.D. 1373.

GEWSYTH, v. a. Thou wilt speak. A mutation of *cewsyth*, 2 pers. s. fut. of *cewsel*, qd. v. *Awos an Dew a gensyth*, because of the God whom thou mentionest. O.M. 1513. *Ny geusyth, râk my wodhas bôs groutys dhym gallos brâs*, thou speakest not, for thou knewest not that there is granted to me great power. P.C. 2181.

GEYDH, s. m. A day. *Mŷns a dêf ynno, un geydh my ha'm gwrêk a vera dybry*, all that will grow in it, in one day, I and my wife will eat. O.M. 385. *Ow benneth prest ty a fŷdh, kefrys yn nôs hag yn geyth*, my blessing ever thou shalt have, equally by night as by day. O.M. 458. *Me a'n te re'n geydh hydhew*, I swear it by this day. P.C. 2684. *Agy dhe ewhé an geydh, yn paradys ty a séf*, within the evening of the day in Paradise thou shalt stand. R.D. 275. This is a corruption of *dêdh* or *dŷdh; g* soft being used for *d*, and *ey* to denote the long vowel.

GEYEN, s. f. A nerve, sinew, tendon. Written also *geien*, qd. v. *Scenys* is used for the plural, qd. v.

GEYL, v. a. He shall lose. A mutation of *ceyl*, 3 pers. s. fut. of *celly*, qd. v. *Why a geyl ow lowené a rýs dhyuch yn parathys*, ye will lose my joy (that) I gave to you in Paradise. O.M. 319.

GEYLL, s. m. A scoffing, mockery. *Pan veles y mâb dygtis gans an Edhewon mar veyll, ha'y vôs gans spern curunys, ha pêb dhodho ow cull geyll*, when she saw her son used by the Jews so vilely, and that he was with thorns crowned, and every one to him doing mockery. M.C. 165.

GEYN, s. m. The back. A mutation of *ceyn*, or *cein*, qd. v. *My a'th wheres orth y dhôn dhe yffarn kepar hag ôn war geyn lowarn py brathky*, I will help thee to bring him to hell, like as we are, on the back of a fox or mastiff. O.M. 895. *Otté mellow y geyn brew*, behold the joints of his back broken. P.C. 2086. *Gwcres, ty harlot iaudyn, ha dôk an grows war dhe geyn*, help, thou obstinate knave, and bear the cross on thy back. P.C. 2616.

GIC, s. m. Flesh. A mutation of *cic*, qd. v. *Dasserchy of a wra, par del prennas an býs-ma gans y gýk ha gans y wôs*, rise again he will, like as he redeemed this world with his flesh and with his blood. R.D. 63.

GIGEL, s. m. A distaff. A mutation of *cigel*, qd. v. *Eva, kymmer dhe gygel rág nedhé dhynny dyllas*, Eve, take thy distaff, to spin clothes for us. O.M. 367.

GIGLOT, s. f. A foolish laughter; a wanton lascivious girl. *Pryce. A giglot a lynage, ha ty war yonk a'n age, pendra wreta gans an gwâs*, O wanton of lineage, and thou so young in age, what dost thou with the fellow? P.C. 1183.

GIL, v. a. To do, to make, to work. ‡ *Dho gîl*, Llwyd, 122. ‡ *Da îl*, 231. ‡ *E vedn gys gil saw*, it will cure you. ‡ *Dry vedo hwi gil*, what will you? 244. This is a late form of *gûl*, qd. v.

GILE, s. m. A companion, a fellow, one of two. *An nýl dhodho a dellé pymp cans dyner monyys, ha hanter cans y gylé*, the one owed to him five hundred pence of money, and half a hundred the other, (lit. his companion.) P.C. 506. *Ytho mar crugé gothy agas treys, h'aga sché, gothens pûp treys y gylé ahanouch kepar ha my*, now, if I wash your feet, and dry them, let every one of you wash the feet of each other of you. P.C. 877. Written also *gclé*, qd. v.

GILEZ, pron. One another. ‡ *Dhort i gilez*, from each other. *Pryce.* A late form of *gilé*, qd. v.

GILLIS, part. Lost. *Llwyd*, 252. A mutation of *cillis*, id. qd. *collys*, qd. v.

GILLY, s. m. A grove of hazels. *Pryce.* Another form of *gclly*, qd. v.

GILWYS, part. Called. *Llwyd*, 248. See *Gylwys*.

GIRAC, s. m. The sea needle, or gar fish. *Llwyd*, 14, 33, 41. From the English.

GIRGIRIC, s. f. A partridge. *Pryce.* Written by Llwyd, *gyrgiric*, qd. v.

GIRR, s. m. The flux, the griping of the bowels. *An girr.* Llwyd, 56, 79. W. *gerí.* Gael. *gearrach.*

GITHA, v. a. To hide. *Dho githa.* Llwyd, 104. A mutation of *citha*, a late form of *cudhé*, qd. v.

GIVIA, v. a. To forgive, to pardon. *Pryce.* A later form of *gafé*, qd. v.

GIVIANS, s. m. Forgiveness, pardon. Llwyd, 171, 240. A late form of *gefyans*, qd. v.

GIVYS, part. Forgiven. *Llwyd*, 248. Written also *gevys*, and *gefys*, qd. v.

GLAN, s. f. The bank, the side, or brink of a river; the side of any thing. Corn. Voc. *ripa. Mars yw dyenkys, ellas, râk me a wêl an mên brâs war glan an bêdh fest huhel*, if he is escaped, alas, for I see the large stone on the side of the tomb very high. R.D. 522. *Gland*, for a river bank, is still used in Cornwall. W. *glan.* Arm. *glann.* Manx, *bochlane.*

GLAN, adj. Clean, pure, holy, fair, innocent. *Wy yw glân a bûb fyllé, mas nynj ouch ol da na whêk*, ye are clean from all filth, but ye are not all good nor sweet. M.C. 47. *Dên glân yw a bêch, heb fall ynno ef dyfout nyng és*, a man pure he is from sin, without doubt in him there is not a fault. M.C. 192. *Yn hanow Dew, ty môr glân, me a'th wîsk gans ow gwelan*, in the name of God, thou fair sea, I strike thee with my rod. O.M. 1675. *Why a dhyerbyn wharré dên ow tôn pycher dour glân*, ye will meet soon a man carrying a pitcher of clean water. P.C. 629. *Eychan, rág y fynner, mara kyller gans paynys mêr ow dyswul glân*, Oh, woe! for it is wished, if it could be, with great sorrows to destroy me quite. P.C. 2002. *Râk, del won, mâp Dew ôs pûr yn beys gynys a vachtyth glân*, for as I know, very Son of God thou art, in the world born of a virgin pure. P.C. 3027. W. *glân.* Arm. *glân.* Ir. *glan.* Gael. *glan.* Manx, *glen.* Gr. καλόν, γλήνη. Dor. γλάνα. Germ. *klein.* Eng. *clean.*

GLAN, s. m. Wool. *Cnêu glán*, a fleece of wool. *Llwyd*, 170. (W. *cnu gwlân, cnu o wlân.*) A later form of *gluan*, qd. v.

GLANHY, v. a. To make clean, to cleanse. Part. pass. *glanhŷs. A pûp plôs yth ouch glanhŷs, mes ol wyns ouch gulân deffry; ymu onan pûr vostyns omma a 'gys company*, from all dirt ye are cleansed, but ye are not all clean, really; there is one much defiled here of your company. P.C. 865. W. *glanhâu.*

GLANNITH, adj. Clean and neat. *Llwyd*, 95, 99. En *lannith*, cleanly. 248. W. *glanwith.*

GLANNITHDER, s. m. Cleanliness, neatness. *Llwyd*, 95, 240. W. *glanweithder.*

GLAS, s. m. The maw, or stomach. Corn. Voc. *stomacus. Lemyn ythyw cwn hŷs, ewnyn ef yn scon dh'y le.—An jawl re'th evono dh'y glas*, now it is the right length, let us adjust it soon to its place.—The devil adjust thee to his maw. O.M. 2527. *Whŷth war gam, vyngeans y'th glas*, blow athwart, vengeance in thy maw. P.C. 2716. *A harlos, yn kellep gwas, herthewch, vynyons y'ges glas*, O rascals, every fellow, push ye, vengeance in your maws. P.C. 3074.

GLAS, s. f. A country, region. *May'th ylleuch yn mês a'm glâs*, that ye go out of my country. O.M. 1587. *Gallas Moyses ha'y pobel mês a'm glâs*, gone are Moses and his people out of my land. O.M. 1628. *Ha dhywhy me re ordynas glâs nêf ynny râk trygé*, and for you I have ordained the kingdom of heaven, in it to dwell. P.C. 808. Another form of *gwlâs*, qd. v.

GLAS, adj. Blue or azure, sky coloured; gray, ash coloured; verdant, green. *Del lavaré war anow, war an pren glâs mar a le, yn pren seych ha cusadow yn erna fatel ve*, as (one) saith by mouth; on the green wood if it come, in dry and hateful wood, then how shall it be? M.C. 170. *An golom glâs hy lagas, yn mês gwra hy delyfré, lellé edhen, ren ow thâs, leverel my won ple fe*, the dove with blue eyes do thou liberate outside, a more faithful bird, by my father, I cannot say where there is. O.M. 1109, 1135. *Dynythys yn, hag yma yn hy mynn branch olyf glâs,* she is come, and there is in her beak a branch of green olive. O.M. 1122. *Dûn ganso dywhans touth brâs, râk y wor̄re yn dour glâs yw ow dysyr,* let us come with him very speedily, for to put him into blue water is my desire. R.D. 2193. In construction with feminine nouns it would strictly change into *lâs*, as in Welsh, but the rule is not always followed in Cornish, though examples are found. ‡ *Ema reiz gennam kenifra lazoun lâs râg looz,* there is given by me every green herb for food. M.C. p. 05. W. *glâs.* Arm. *glâs.* Ir. *glas.* Gael. *glas.* Manx, *glass.* In all the Celtic languages it is applied to the three colours, and it is equally indefinite in the classical. Gr. γλαυκόν. Lat. *glaucus; glastum,* woad.

GLASCOR, s. m. A kingdom, a country. *Ow colon yw clâf marthys, bôs drôg a'n par-ma codhys yn ow glascor yn torma,* my heart is wondrous sick, that such an evil is fallen in my kingdom at this time. O.M. 1570. *Ef a lâdh gans fuyryngy ol ow glascor,* he will kill with the stink all my kingdom. R.D. 2134. *Râk pâr wŷr yth hepcoras dre y ober glascor nêf,* for very truly he renounced by his work the kingdom of heaven. R.D. 2338. *A le-na yth yskynnaf yn ban bŷs yn glascor nêf,* from that place I will ascend up even to the kingdom of heaven. R.D. 2402. In construction it changes into *wlascor. Mar mynnyth bones yn eys, reys yw dhys gorrê Moyses, Aron a'th wlascor yn meys, h'aga pobel ol gansé,* if thou wilt be at ease, need is to thee to put Moses (and) Aaron out of thy country, and all their people with them. O.M. 1573.

GLASE, v. n. To become blue, to grow pale ; to be green, to flourish. *Ol an týr a bynfy yw mylleges y'th ober ; ffrut da byner re dhokko, na glasé bŷs gorfen bŷs,* all the earth thou ownest is cursed in thy deed; good fruit may it never bring, nor be verdant until the end of the world. O.M. 584. W. *glasu.* Arm. *glaza.* Ir. *glas.* Gael. *glas.*

GLASGARN, s. m. A kingdom. Llwyd, 138. This is a later form of *glascor.*

GLASSYGYON, s. m. A green, a green plot. *Hedrê vyyn ow predery, yn glassygyon genouch y, aga thŷr dhe wrowedhé,* while I am considering, leave ye them on a green plot, the three to lie. O.M. 2036. W. *glesygen.*

GLASTANEN, s. f. The oak, the scarlet oak. Cornish Vocabulary, *quercus vel jilex.* Llwyd gives *glastan, glastanan, glastennen,* as various forms. 141, 240. W. *glasdonen.* Comp. of *glâs,* green, and *tonen,* bark. Arm. *glastennen, glasten.*

GLAW, s. m. Rain. *Bedhens ebron dreys pûp tra, râk kudhé wŷns ûs furmyys, râk synsy glaw awartha, dhe'n nôr veys may fô dyllys,* let the sky be above every thing, to cover all that is created, to keep the rain above, to the earth of the world that it may be sent forth. O.M. 23. *Râg sythyn wosé henma, dew ugens dŷdh my a ôs glaw dhe godhé awartha,* for a week after this, forty days I will allow rain to fall from above. O.M. 1028. *Dûn aberedh desempys, agan gorhyl awartha gans glaw ef a vŷdh cudhys,* let us come in immediately, our ark from above with rain it will be covered. O.M. 1064. *Gallas an glaw dhe vês gullàn, ha'n dour my a grês busserys,* the rain is clean gone away, and the water I believe abated.

O.M. 1097. *Glau,* Corn. Voc. *pluvia.* W. *gwlaw,* and provincially *glaw.* Arm. *glaô.* Lat. *pluvia.* Sanse. *plu,* to flow. Gr. πλέω, βλύω, βλύζω. Lat. *pluo, fluo.* Germ. *fliesse.* Eng. *flow.* Lith. *plauju.* Russ. *plyvu.*

GLAWN, s. m. Wool. ‡ *Hy oar gwil padn dah gen hy glawn,* she knows to make good cloth with her wool. *Pryce.* A late form of *gluan,* qd. v.

GLEB, adj. Wet, moist. *Dêdh glêb,* a wet day. In construction with nouns feminine it changed as in Welsh into *lêb,* thus *ewnar lêb,* wet weather. *Ll.* 66, 243. Hence are derived the substantive *glibor,* moisture, and verb *glybyé,* to wet, qd. v. W. *gwlyb, ✝ gulip.* Arm. *gleb, glub.* Hence English *glib.* Compare also W. *gwlych,* wet. Arm. *glouech.* Ir. *fliuch.* Gael. *fliuch.* Manx, *fliugh.* Sanse. *plu,* to flow.

GLEDH, s. m. Chickweed. Llwyd, 18, *glêdh.* W. *gwlŷdh.* Ir. *flith, flaile.* Gael. *fliodh.* Manx, *flec.*

GLEDH, adj. Left, the left. A mutation of *clêdh,* qd. v. *A bûb teneven, hag a dhychow hag a glêdh,* ou every side, both on the right and on the left. M.C. 236. *Doro kenter, ha me a tak y luef glêdh gans ol ow nel,* bring a nail, and I will fasten his left hand with all my strength. P.C. 2747. *Dorn glêdh,* left hand. Llwyd, 150.

GLEDHE, s. m. A sword. A mutation of *cledhé,* qd. v. ‡ *Cans dha gledhé,* with thy sword. Llwyd, 230.

GLEN, s. m. A valley, a dale. Generally written *glyn,* qd. v.

GLENY, v. a. To cling to, to cleave to, to adhere, to stick to. Part. pass. *glenys. Y dysky nûr a'n grevyé, worto fust naweng-o glenys,* to take it off much him grieved, to him fast it was now clinging. M.C. 176. *Dhe'th scoforu whnrré yches my a re ; abarth ow Thâs lynyyes, dh'y thyller arté glencs, kepar del ve,* to thy ear soon health I will give ; ou the part of my blessed Father, to its place let it stick, like as it was. P.C. 1153. *Y'tho ow furs ha'm brustplat purpur gurow dhum strothé, dre an ŷôs a râk Pilat, worto an kŷc a glené,* my robe and my breastplate were hard purple to wring me, through the blood before Pilate, the flesh stuck to it. R.D. 2594. ‡ *Bez leddarn a glenuz ort an dzhei,* but the thieves clung to them. Llwyd, 252. Written also *glyné,* qd. v. W. *glynu.* Ir. *lean, ✝ glean.* Gael. *leanail, leantuinn, ✝ glean.* Manx, *lhiant.*

GLESIN, s. m. The herb woad. Corn. Voc. *sandix.* W. *glesyn,* what is blue ; from *glâs.* Lat. *glastum.*

GLESEUCH, v. a. Ye heard. Incorrectly for *glewseuch,* a mutation of *clewseuch,* 2 pers. pl. preter. of *clewes,* qd. v. *Arluth ot omma an gwês ol gleseuch,* a dhyallas an profus Ihesus, dampnyas dhe vôs gorrys yn growes pren,* Lord, see here the fellow, as you heard, (that) mocked the prophet Jesus, he condemned to be put on the cross tree. R.D. 1804.

GLEW, adj. Resolute, stout, sharp, acute, penetrating. *Ow bommyn yw marthys glew, ny fyn an gwês gelwel tru, na pygy cafus merci,* my blows are wondrous sharp, the fellow will not call "oh," nor pray to have mercy. P.C. 2088. *Ow stons a fue crows a pren ; kyns ên mychtern dên ha Dew ; yn le basnet war ow fen, curyn a spern lym ha glew,* my standing was a cross of wood ; before I was a king, man, and God ; instead of a helmet on my head, a crown of thorns sharp and penetrating. R.D. 2552. W. *glew.*

GLEW, v. a. He will hear. A mutation of *clew,* 3 pers-

GLIN 171 GLU

s. fut. of *clewas*, qd. v. *Na dhyscryssouch Dew a nêf, rág ef a glew agas léf*, do ye not distrust the God of heaven, for he will hear your voice. O.M. 1638. *Y wordhyé y teleth dheys, mar uskys pan glew dhe léf*, to worship him it is incumbent on thee, so quickly when he hears thy voice. O.M. 1776.

GLEWAF, v. a. I shall hear. A mutation of *clewaf*, 1 pers. s. fut. of *clewas*. *Ma ow wolon ow rannê, pan glewaf cows a'n parna*, my heart is separating when I hear talk of that kind. O.M. 2182.

GLEWAS, v. a. He heard. A mutation of *clewas*, 3 pers. s. preter. of *clewas*, qd. v. *Worth nép a glewas goryn, rák y a wor leverel*, ask of one (that) has heard, for they know (how) to say. P.C. 1260. *Me a'n glewas dyougel*, I heard him certainly. P.C. 1307. *A Thesu, mychtern a néf, ty re glewas agan léf*, O Jesus, king of heaven, thou hast heard our voice. R.D. 174.

GLEWFO, v. a. He may hear. A mutation of *clewfo*, 3 pers. sing. subj. of *clewas*. *Ot an iustys ow ôs dhyn, anodho cf gréns del vyn, pan glewfo y lavarow*, see the justice coming to us, with him let him do as he will, when he hears his words. P.C. 372.

GLEWSYUCH, v. a. Yo heard. A mutation of *clew-syuch*, 2 pers. pl. preter. of *clewas*. *An ré-ma ew gwél a rás, rág ny glewsyuch yn nép plás sawor a'n par-ma rythqueth*, these here are rods of grace, for yo have not smelt in any place savour of this sort ever. O.M. 1990. *A glewsyuch why, cowethé, del ugy an ngl horé owthenwel an pgth na vgdh*, did ye hear comrades, how the vile strumpet is calling on the thing that is not? O.M. 2727.

GLEWYUCH, v. a. Hear ye. A mutation of *clewyuch*, 2 pers. pl. imp. of *clewas*. *Oyeth sy glewyuch dhym ol, masous an dré ketep pol*, hear ye, listen to me all, masons of the town, every head. O.M. 2297. *Oyeth or oyeth yn uêdh sy glewyuch bryntyn ha kêth*, oyez, now oyez, likewise hear ye, nobles and commons. O.M. 2420.

GLEYN, s. m. The knee. *Ena Christ a's gasus, hag êth arta dhe besy war ben gleyn dheworth y dâs, del lavarsa ragon ny*, there Christ them left, and went again on his knees to his Father, as he had said for us. M.C. 56. *Mês y dhensys o mar fryn púb úr a'n trylyn dhedhé, may 'th ith war ben y dhewleyn, ha pesy yn kewlma*, but his manhood was so perfect every hour (that) he turned to them, so that he went on his knees, and prayed in this manner. M.C. 54. Another form of *glin*, qd. v.

GLIB, adj. Wet, moist. Generally written *glêb*, qd. v.

GLIBBIE, v. a. To make moist, to moisten, to wet. *Pryce*. Written also *glybyé*, qd. v.

GLIBOR, s. m. Moisture. Cornish Vocab. *humor*. W. *gwlybwr*. Arm. *glebor, glebder*. "The town of Ulubræ, mentioned by Cicero in Lit. Fam. vij. 18, appears to have been in a moist situation from the allusion to frogs." Norris's Cornish Drama, ij. 368.

GLIHI, s. m. Frost. Llwyd, 33. Written also *clihi*, qd. v. Lat. *glacies*.

GLIN, s. m. The knee. Corn. Voc. *penclin*. *Ol an re-ma ty a fýdh, ow gordhyé mara mennyth war pen dhe dhew glýn ysel*, all these thou shalt have, if thou wilt worship me low on thy knees. P.C. 136. *Pêb ol war pen y dew glýn a gân yn gordhyans dhodho*, every one upon his knees shall sing in worship to him. P.C. 247.

‡ *Pedn glin*, Llwyd, 63. W. *glîn*. Arm. *glin*. Ir. *glun*. Gael. *glan*. Manx, *glioon*. Slav. *koleno*. Sanse. *g'ânu*, fr. *jnâ*, to bend. Lat. *genu*. Gr. *γόνυ*. Goth. *kniu*. Eng. *knee*.

GLIT, s. m. A hoar frost, a rime. *Llwyd*, 131. See *Glâth*.

GLOAS, s. m. Dried cow-dung used for fuel. *Pryce*. *Me a guntell dreyn ha speru ha glôs, dha lesky heb bern, hag a wra bushe brás a voog*, I will gather briars and thorns, and dried cow-dung, to burn without regret, and will make a great cloud of smoke. C.W. 80. This word is still in use in Cornwall, and the same material is used for fuel in some parts of Wales. W. *gleiad*. Dr. O. Pughe derives the word from *glai*, glistening; I am more inclined to *golcu*, light.

GLOC, s. f. A cloak. A mutation of *clôc*. *Pan sefsys hydhew myltyn, yách êns aga icyw ; dyswêdh y a dhan dhe glôk*, when thou gottest up this morning, sound were their sinews; shew them from under thy cloak. P.C. 2682. Borrowed from the English.

GLOS, s. f. A pang, pain, anguish. *Mey fê, me re goskes pôs ; ha rum kemeres drôk glôs*, my faith, I have slept heavily; and an evil pang has seized me. R.D. 512. A contracted form of *gloys*, qd. v.

GLOW, s. m. Coal. *Pgth yw an gordhyans dhe Dew bôs leskys dhe glow luscw war an karrygy dege*, what worship is it to God that the tithe be burnt to coal-ashes on the stones? O.M. 477. ‡ *Gwell hy vyc perna nebas glow, ha hedna vedn gus tubm a dhella e a rág*, better she had bought some coal, and that will warm you behind and before. *Pryce. Huêl glow*, a coal pit. *Llwyd*, 145. W. *glo*. Arm. *glaou*. Ir. *gual*. Gael. *gual*. Manx, *geayl*. Germ. *kole*. Eng. *coal, glow*. Sansc. *gval*, to burn, to shine.

GLOW, v. a. He will hear. A mutation of *clow*, 3 pers. s. fut. of *clowas*, qd. v. ‡ *Piwa glow vi*, whom hear I? *Llwyd*, 253.

GLOWAS, v. a. He heard. A mutation of *clowas*, 3 pers. s. preter. of *clowes*, or *clowas*, qd. v. *Sera, ha me ow gwandra, me a glowas a wartha war an wedhan un êl whêk, fir ow cana*, Sir, as I was walking, I heard from above on the tree an angel sweet wisely singing. C.W. 56.

GLOWES, v. a. To hear. A mutation of *clowes*, or *clowas*, qd. v. *Worth glowes*, by hearing. *Llwyd*, 240.

GLOWSYS, v. a. Thou heardest. A mutation of *clowsys*, 2 pers. s. preter. of *clowas*, qd. v. *Drôg polat o, nêb a glowses ow cana*, an evil pullet he was, whom thou didst hear singing. C.W. 56.

GLOWYS, v. a. I heard. A mutation of *clowys*, 1 pers. s. preter. of *clowas*, qd. v. *Ef a allas dyougel, del glowys y leverel yn lyes le*, he could indeed, as I heard it said in many a place. P.C. 2874.

GLOYS, s. f. A pang, pain, anguish. *Angus brás, ha peynys tyn, ha gloys crêf a's kemeras*, great anguish, and pains, and strong pang seized her. M.C. 221. *Ma an gloys dre ow colon rák gullarow hag anken*, there is a pang through my heart for sorrows and grief. P.C. 1147. W. *glocs*. Arm. *glocz*. Sansc. *klis*, to be pained.

GLU, v. a. Hear thou. A mutation of *clu*, 1d. qd. *clew*, 2 pers. s. imp. of *clewas*, qd. v. *Cowyth, growedh an ngl tu, hag aspy ahas, ha glu, a rág hag a dencwen*, comrade, lie on one side, and look out continually, and listen, forwards and sideways. O.M. 2062.

GLUAN, s. m. Wool. Corn. Voc. *lana*. *Glân* is given by Llwyd, and *glawn* by Pryce, as late forms. W. *gwelân*, †*gulan*. Arm. *gloan*. Ir. *olann*. Gael. *olann*. Manx, *ollan*. Slav. *wlan*. Lith. *vilna*. Lat. *lana*, for *vlana*.

GLUT, s. m. Glue, viscous matter, paste. Corn. Vocab. *gluten*. W. *glûd*. Arm. *glûd*. Ir. *glaodh*. Gael. *glaodh*. Gr. γλοῖος, γλία. Lat. *gluten*. Eng. glue.

GLUTH, s. m. Dew. Llwyd, 16, 141, *glûth*. W. *gwlîth*. Arm. *gliz*.

GLUYAN, s. m. Sickness, disease. *Gwelly glûyan*, bed sickness. *Pryce*. A mutation of *clûyan*, qd. v.

GLYBOR, s. m. Wetness, moisture. *Llwyd*, 66. Another form of *glibor*, qd. v.

GLYBYE, v. a. To wet, to moisten, to make wet, to madefy. *Yma daggrow ow klybyé dhe dreys râk own kerengé, saw me a's sêch gans ow blew*, tears are wetting thy feet, for true love, but I will dry them with my hair. P.C. 482. W. *gwlybu*. Arm. *glebia, glibia, glubein, gluebein*.

GLYN, s. m. A valley through which a river flows, a woody valley, a glen. W. *glyn*. Arm. *glen*. Ir. *gleann*. Gael. *gleann*. Manx, *glion*. Scot. *glen*.

GLYNE, v. a. To cling to, to adhere to, to stick to. *Pan fue an purpur war skwych kychys dhe vês gans dyw dhorn, worto y glynes hardlych ran an kîg bîjs yn ascorn*, when the purple was on a sudden snatched away with hands, to it stuck closely a piece of the flesh even to the bone. R.D. 2597. Another form of *gleny*, qd. v.

GLYVEDHAS, s. m. Midwifery. *Benen glyvedhas*, a midwife. *Llwyd*, 103. I consider the word to be a mutation of *clyvedhas*, and connected with W. *colwynydhineth*, midwifery.

GNACIAS, v. a. Struck or knocked. A mutation of *cnacias*, 3 pers. s. preter. of *cnacié*, id. qd. *cnoucyé*, qd. v. + *E gnacias*, he knocked. *Llwyd*, 253.

GO, adv. Rather. A particle used with words to denote a progress towards, an approach, or a state short of perfection. In Welsh it is of frequent occurrence, as *pant*, a hollow, *gobant*, a little hollow. *Bron*, a hill, *govron*, a little hill. *Drwg*, bad, *go dhrwg*, rather bad. So Cornish *go dôl*, a little valley. Ir. *gabh*, progress. Sansc. *gâ*, to go.

GO, pron. adj. Their. ‡ *Ha an 'oar a drôz râg gwelz, ha an lozo rîg dasker hâz poku e cunda, ha an gwŷdh toon lavallo, ha go hâz etta go honnen, warler go henda; ha Dew gwellas tro va dah*, and the earth brought forth grass, and the herb did yield seed after its kind, and the trees yielding fruit, and their seed in themselves after their kind; and God saw that it was good. C.W. p. 190. A late corruption of *aga*, qd. v.

GOBER, s. m. A recompence, reward; fee, wages, stipend, hire. Written indiscriminately also *gobar, gobyr. A'n deppro gans cregyans da gober têk eff a'n gevyth, he that eats it with good faith, a good reward he shall obtain*. M.C. 44. *Gurŷs yw dhe temple hep sôn, agan gobyr ny a'th pŷs*, thy temple is done without noise, our wages we ask of thee. O.M. 2584. *Why a's bŷdh agas gobar eredy*, ye shall have your payment surely. O.M. 2587. *Gobar da why agas bŷdh*, a good reward ye shall have. R.D. 376. *Why a's bŷdh gobar brâs*, ye shall have a great reward. R.D. 672. W. *gobyr*. Arm. *gobr*.

GOBERNA, v. a. To hire. *Gobernes*, hired. *Pryce*.

GOC, adj. Lying, deceitful. *Menouch ef a wrûk bostyé y vôs mâp Dew, dh'y lawe, arluth an gôk*, often he did boast that he was the Son of God, be he praised! lord of the liars. P.C. 2890. *Ny vŷdh Dew nefra pûr wŷr kevys goak, trest dhymo*, God will never very truly be found a liar, trust to me. C.W. 172. This is the same word as *gauhoc, gouhoc*, from *gow*, a lie.

GOCCOR, s. m. A merchant, a trader, a dealer, a hawker, a pedler. Pl. *goccorion*. *Crist a gafas gockorion yn templys aberth yn drê, ef a rûg dhedhé yn scon môs yn mês a lena*, Christ found traders in the temples within the town, he caused them soon to go out from thence. M.C. 30. Another form of *gwicur*, qd. v.

GOCY, adj. Foolish, silly, absurd. Pl. *gocyes*. Superlative *gocyé*. *A venen, assos goky*, O woman, thou art foolish. O.M. 173. *Gortouch lymmyn gockyes, dhe'th scoforn wharré yehes my a re*, stay ye now fools, to thy ear soon health I will give. P.C. 1140. *Anyn an dên-na goky*, that man is foolish. P.C. 1662. *A Bertyl asogé mûs ha goky dres ol an dûs py ytho fôl*, O Bartholomew, thou art mad and silly beyond all the men that are fools. R.D. 972. *Hesogé goky Mathew*, and thou art foolish Matthew. R.D. 983. *Ysouch gokky ha fêllyon*, ye are silly and foolish. R.D. 1273. *Nynsouch lemmyn gokyes*, are ye not now foolish? R.D. 1136. *Ty yw. me a grŷs, an gokyé dên yn beys*, thou art, I believe, the foolishest man in the world. R.D. 1454. In construction it changes into *woky*, qd. v. The root is *côc*, qd. v.

GOCYNETH, s. m. Foolishness, folly, absurdity. *Ty a heuel muskegys, hag yn gokyneth gyllys, awos an Dew a genyyth*, thou seemest crazed, and in folly lost, because of the God (that) thou mentionest. O.M. 1512. In construction it changes into *wocyneth*. *Rum fê, mûr a wokyneth yw mones dhe lesky peyth a gl dên orto bewé*, by my faith, much of folly it is to go to burn a thing that a man can live upon. O.M. 473.

GOD, s. m. A wood. A mutation of *côd*, a contracted form of *coed*, qd. v.

GODE, s. m. Confusion. This word occurs in the following passage. *Dro re, gode thous re'th fo*, bring it, confusion be to thee. O.M. 2822. The meaning is not obvious, but evidently an imprecation. Mr. Norris suggests *gode dhons*, a good dance. I am inclined to connect it with the W. *gwaed*, blood.

GODEN, s. m. A base or foundation; the sole. Corn. Vocab. *goden truit*, planta pedis, the sole of the foot. W. *gwadyn*. Arm. *gwelen*.

GODH, s. m. A mole. Corn. Vocab. *god*, talpa. In late Cornish it was called *gûdh dhâr*. Llwyd, 160, 241. *Twrch dacar* is also one of the names in Welsh. W. *gwôdh*. Arm. *goz*. Ir. *fadh*. Gael. *fadh*.

GODH, s. f. A goose. Pl. *godhow;* (*godho*, Llwyd, 242.) *Gôdh dêk scon my a offryn dhe Dew war ben ow dewlyn, hag a's gor war y alter*, a fair goose forthwith I will offer to God upon my knees, and put it upon his altar. O.M. 1195. ‡ *Culliag godho*, a gander. Llwyd, 43. Written also *goydh*, and in the Cornish Vocabulary, *guit*, qd. v.

GODH, v. a. He will fall. A mutation of *codh*, 3 pers. s. fut. of *codha*, qd. v. *Me a lever yn torma, vynions crêf a gôdh warnas*, I say at this time strong vengeance will fall upon thee. O.M. 1498. *Mûr dhe voy ef re pechas, ha drôk warnodho a gôdh*, much the more he hath sinned, and evil will fall upon him. P.C. 2192.

GODHAL, s. m. An Irishman. Written also *gwidhal*, qd. v.

GODHALEC, adj. Irish. *Pryce.* W. *gwydhelig.* Ir. *gaodhalach.* Gael. *gaidhealach.* Manx, *gaelic, gaelg.*

GODHAS, s. m. Sediment, grounds of drink, the lees. *Lhwyd*, 15. W. *gwadhod.* Arm. *gouzia, gouziza,* to settle.

GODHAS, v. a. He fell. A mutation of *codhas*, 3 pers. s. preter. of *codha*, qd. v. *Rág own y a gangyes lyw, rág gwander y a godhas,* for fear they changed colour, for weakness they fell. M.C. 68.

GODHAS, v. a. To know. *Lhwyd*, 50. In construction it changes into *wodhas.* *Ef a wodhyé y verwy,* he knew he should die. M.C. 56. *Lemmyn mar codhas,* now if thou knewest. M.C. 92. *Taw Pedyr, te ny wodhas, yn medh Christ, pa'n dra ráf dhys,* be silent Peter, thou knowest not, says Christ, what thing I do to thee. M.C. 46. *Te a wodhyé dhe honon,* thou knewest thyself. M.C. 101. *A lan nag és a wodhfé dheuch parys a's gurellé gwell,* since there is not that knows to make them better ready for you. M.C. 158. *Dhe'n well ny wodhyens y dhystrocy,* the better they knew not (how) to destroy him. M.C. 238. *A'n dén-ma re drchevys, gallas ny wodhan pelé,* this man has risen, he is gone we know not where. M.C. 245. See also *Wodhons, Wodher, Wodhouch, &c. Godhas* is another form of *godhvos,* qd. v.

GODIIE, v. a. To fall. A mutation of *codhé*, qd. v. *Dew ugens dydh my a ás glaw dhe godhé nweartha,* forty days I will allow rain to fall from above. O.M. 1028. *Rág dout mysskyf dhe godhé,* for fear of mischief to happen. O.M. 1426.

GODHEVEL, v. a. To suffer, bear, endure. The infinitive is also written *godhaf.* *Mésk ow pobel ny vynnaf na fella agas godhaf,* among my people I will not any longer endure you. O.M. 1595. *Godhaf dhe vrûs dhe honan,* suffer thou thy judgment thyself. O.M. 2248. *Awos godherel ancow, ny nahas hy lavarow,* notwithstanding suffering death, she did not retract her words. O.M. 2760. *Arluth cúf, me yw parys godhaf gynes bôs ledhys,* dear Lord, I am ready to suffer with thee to be slain. P.C. 888. *Godheveuch omma lavur, ha gollyouch gynef ow kefyon kér colonow,* endure ye here labour, and watch with me, my dearly beloved hearts. P.C. 1024. *Ef re dhyndyles yn ta godhaf mernens yn bŷs-ma,* he has deserved well to suffer death in this world. P.C. 1343. *Ny fue ragdho y honan y'n godhefys ef, más rák kerengé máp dén,* it was not for himself he suffered it, but for the love of mankind. P.C. 3227. *Máb Maryn múr a boyn a wodhevy yn úr-na,* the Son of Mary much pain suffered at that time. M.C. 54. *Ol Ihesus a'n godhevys, ha'y wortheby ny vynnas,* Jesus endured it all, and answer him he would not. M.C. 92. *Bythqueth dén ny wodhevys payn ella dh'y golon nés,* man never suffered pain that went nearer to his heart. M.C. 172. *Dowr, ha lér, ha tân, ha gwyns, houl ha lour, ha steyr kyffris,* a Grist ow *codhaff mernens anken y a wodhevys,* water, and earth, and fire, and wind, sun, and moon, and stars likewise, at Christ suffering death, vexation endured. M.C. 211. *War y corf y wodhefys múr a peynys,* on his body he suffered many pains. R.D. 1810. W. *godhev,* † *quodeim,* in Oxford Glosses. Arm. *gouzav.* Ir. *foidhid,* † *fodaim,* † *fodam.* Gael. *foidhid, foighid.*

GODHIIIUAR, s. m. The evening. *Lhwyd,* 249. ‡ *Ha godhewhar ha metten o an kenza journa,* and the evening and the morning were the first day. C.W. p. 189. ‡ *Ha godhuhar ha metten o an nessa journa,* and the evening and the morning were the second day. 190. ‡ *Ha godhuar ha metten o an tridga journa,* and the evening and the morning were the third day. 190. ‡ *Ha godhiluar ha metten o an wheffas dydh,* and the evening and the morning were the sixth day. 192. A later form of *gurithuwer,* qd. v.

GODHO, s. m. Sediment, the lees of drink. *Lhwyd*, 147. A late corruption of *godhas,* qd. v.

GODHO, s. m. Geese. *Lhwyd*, 242. This is the same word as *godhow*, pl. of *gôdh,* qd. v. ‡ *Kulliag godho,* a gander, lit. the cock of geese. *Lhwyd*, 43.

GODHVOS, v. a. To be cognizant of, to know, to be acquainted with. Written equally common *godhfos.* Compounded of *gôdh,* = W. *gwŷdh,* knowledge, and *bôs,* to be. The inflexions are similar to those of *bôs.* *Un dra a won, a'n godhfes, a russé dhe dhydhané,* one thing that I know, if thou knewest it, could comfort thee. O.M. 151. *Godhfos gwgr ol yredy, my a vyn môs dhyncorthys,* knowing the truth all plainly, I will go from thee. O.M. 821. *My a vyn vôs garlont gurcys a urhans adró dhedhé, rág godhvos pŷth vo y hŷs,* I will that a garland be made of silver around it, to know what may be its length. O.M. 2008. *Pyw an brassé dén senges yn mŷsk ol dhy dhyskyblon, ueb a'n godhfo gorthybes,* who is esteemed the greatest man among all thy disciples, he that knows him, let him answer. P.C. 775. *Pendra wráf ny wodhes whêth, ty a'n godhvyth yn dyucedh, wogé ow môs ahanan,* what I do thou knowest not yet, thou shalt know it in the end, after my going hence. P.C. 849. *Lowenna teken godhfy,* the fairest joy thou knowest. P.C. 1042. *May rŷs y vonas ledhys, godhvedhouch kettoponon,* that he must be slain, ye know every one. M.C. 141. *Mar gwra, godhvedhys mar pŷdh, yn scon dysurcys cf a vŷdh,* if he does, if he be discovered, soon destroyed he shall be. O.M. 1520. *A Phelyp, lous ôs y'th fŷdh, ha ty gynef sollu-dhŷdh, godhfydhy gryggy yn fûs,* O Philip, thou art gray in thy faith, and thou with me a long time shouldst know how to believe well. R.D. 2381. *Godhvos,* in construction changes into *wodhvos,* qd. v. W. *gwybod.* Arm. *gouzout.* Ir. † *ceith.* Gael. *cidh.* Sansc. *vidi, kit.*

GOEF, adj. Unhappy he, miserable he. *Goef a gollas an wlás,* unhappy he (that) lost the country. O.M. 754. *Arluth warnas trogeryth, goef a ra dhe serry,* Lord on thee be love, miserable is he that doth anger thee. O.M. 1016. *Goef vŷdh nép a'm gwerthas,* miserable will he be who has sold me. P.C. 750. *Goef pan ve genys dhe'n bŷs-ma,* miserable he when he was born into this world. P.C. 871. Comp. of *goc,* id. qd. W. *gwae,* woe, and *ef,* he. *Gowy,* unhappy I; and *goy,* unhappy they; are similar compounds.

GOF, s. m. A smith. Corn. Voc. *faber* vel *cudo.* *Y hwalsons oll adró mar caffons gôff yredy,* they searched all about if they could find a smith forthwith. M.C. 154. *Yn medh an gôff, me ny wráff pûr wŷr kentrow dhe wy vydh,* says the smith, I will never make indeed nails for you. M.C. 155. *Yn nédh gurêk an gôff dhedhé, kentrow dhe wy why ny fŷll.* says the wife of the smith to them, to you nails shall not fail. M.C. 156. *Euch dhe wovyn hep lettyé worth an gôf yn Marches Row,* go to ask without delaying of the smith in Market Row.

2668. *Góf diu*, a blacksmith. Lhwyd, 58. W. *góv*, †*gof*. Arm. *gof, gov*. Ir. *gobha, gabha*, †*goba*, †*gobam*, †*gabann*. Gael. *gobha*, hence *gow chrom*, in Sir Walter Scott. Manx, *ganve*. Pers. *gava*, the renowned blacksmith of Ispahan.

GOFAIL, s. f. A smithy, a blacksmith's shop. Cornish Vocabulary, *officina*. Llwyd, 106, writes it *govail*. W. *gevail*, from *góv*, with the regular mutation of *o* into *e*. This ancient form is preserved in the instances of *gevail*, and *cegin*, but in Welsh the mutation is now generally written *y*. Arm. *govel, gofel*.

GOFEN, v. a. To ask. *A gofen*, asking. Lhwyd, 245. Another form of *govyn*, qd. v.

GOG, s. f. The cuckoo. *An góg*. A mutation of *cóg*, qd. v.

GOIDII. s. f. A goose. Lhwyd, 229. See *Goydh*.

GOIL, s. f. A sail. See *Goyl*.

GOIL, s. f. A festival. *Dédh goil*, and by contraction *degl*, a holiday. Lhwyd, 59. W. *gŵyl*, *ŵyl*, †*guil*. Arm. *gouil*. Ir. *feighil, feil*, †*fel*. Gael. *feill*. Manx, *feailley, oiel, cail*. Lat. *vigiliæ*.

GOIS, s. m. Blood. Written also *goys*, qd. v.

GOITCENIN, s. m. Dog's bane, wild or meadow saffron. Corn. Voc. *hermodactula vel tilodosa*. Comp. of *goit*, a mutation of *coit*, a wood, and *cenin*, a leek, qd. v.

GOIVEN, s. f. A nerve. Cornish Vocab. *nervus*. See *Geien*.

GOL, s. f. A sail. *Gwelan gól*, the sail yard. Lhwyd, 3. A contracted form of *goyl*, qd. v.

GOL, s. f. A holiday. Lhwyd, 18. A contracted form of *goil*, qd. v.

GOLCHY, v. a. To wash. *Yn bason bedhens gorrys, ha me a's goulch dysemnys may fóns gulán a púp plós ol*, let them be put in a basin, and I will wash them immediately, that they may be clean from all dirt. P.C. 843. *T'ommans onan dour war tán, rág wogé soper my a woulch ol agas trŷs*, let one warm water on the fire, for after supper I will wash all your feet. P.C. 853. *Saw yn tokyn ow bós gulán a goys Ihesu Nazaré, me a wolch scon ow dulé a wel dheuch kettep onan*, but in token of my being clean of the blood of Jesus of Nazareth, I will wash immediately my hands in the sight of every one of you. P.C. 2499. In all the other tenses the aspirate is softened into *h*; see *Gothy*. W. *golchi*. Arm. *golchi, gwalchi*, †*gwelchi*, †*guelhy*. Ir. *folcaim*, †*fulchaim*. Gael. *faile*.

GOLE, v. a. To hearken to, to listen to. Written also *gola*, and in construction *cola*. *Ny dál dhys kavanscusé, dre dhe wrék y vós terrys, rág orty ty dhe golé, nyl váp mam a veydh damneys*, it will not avail to make excuse through thy wife that it was broken, because that thou hearkenedst to her, a thousand mother's sons shall be damned. O.M. 323. *Rág cola worth un venen, gulán ef ré gollas an pláss*, for listening to a woman, he has quite lost the place. O.M. 419. *A synte Mari, Mathew, mar a colyth, ty a tew gans dhe whethlow*, O Saint Mary! Matthew, if thou wilt listen, thou wilt be silent with thy tales. R.D. 1368. ‡*Ty rig golla worty*; thou hast hearkened to her. Lhwyd, 242.

GOLENWEL, v. a. To fulfil. A mutation of *colenwel*, qd. v. *Rág of a vyn hep lettyé wheyl y dás y golenwel*, for he will without stopping the work of his father fulfil. O.M. 2428.

GOLES, s. m. The bottom, the lowest part. In construction *woles*. Written also *golas*. *Ha'n grows a ve drchereys, ha Ihesus fasteys ynny, ha'n pen golas delyffrys yn toll o tellys rygthy*, and the cross was raised, and Jesus fastened on it, and the lower end delivered into the hole (that) was holed for it. M.C. 184. *Ha war woles, pan ryrys, my a welas hy gwrydhyow bŷs yn uffarn dywenys*, and at the bottom, when I looked, I saw its roots even into hell descending. O.M. 781. *Deu tek a bren rág styllyow, ha compos y denwennow, brás ha crom y ben goles*, here is a fair tree for rafters, and straight its sides, large and rounded its lower end. O.M. 2443. *Ke, ty Pilat mylyges, eun yn dour dhe woles ty á*, go, thou cursed Pilate, there in the water to the bottom thou shalt go. R.D. 2196. *Golas trús*, the sole of the foot. Lhwyd, 121. W. *gwaclod*. Arm. *goeled, gweled*.

GOLEUDER, s. m. Brightness. Lhwyd, 240. Written also *golowder*, qd. v.

GOLIIAN, s. f. A knife. A mutation of *colhan*, or *collan*, qd. v. ‡*Gens e golhan*, with his knife. Lhwyd, 252.

GOLHY, v. a. To wash. In construction it changes into *wolhy*. *Gans dour gorrys yn bazon y wolhas aga garrow*, with water put in a basin he washed their logs. M.C. 45. *Henna Pedyr a sconyas Ihesus dhe wolhy y dreys; taw Pedyr, te ny wodhas, yn médh Christ, pandra rȃf dhys; mar ny'th wolhaff dre ow grás, yn néf ny wedhyth tregis; yn médh Pedyr, dhyn na ás troys na teyff na vo golhys*, that Peter refused that Christ should wash his feet; be silent Peter, thou knowest not, says Christ, what I shall do to thee; if I wash thee not by my grace, in heaven thou shalt not dwell; says Peter, to me leave not foot or hand that it be not washed. M.C. 46. *Golhy ow treys uy hyreys; homma gans daggrow keffrys re's holhas*, to wash my feet thou offeredst not; this one with tears even has washed them. P.C. 518. *Kyn na véns neffré gothys, ty ny's golhyth yn nép cás*, though they be never washed, thou shalt not wash them in any case. P.C. 853. *Y'tho mar krugé gothy agas treys h'agn scohé, golhens púp treys y gylé ahanouch kepar ha my*, now if I wash your feet, and dry them, let all wash the feet of each other of you, like as I. P.C. 877. Another form of *golchy*, qd. v., the aspirate being softened into *h*.

GOLLAS, v. a. He lost. A mutation of *collas*, 3 pers. s. preter. of *colly*, qd. v. *Rág cola worth un venen, gulán ef re gollas an pláss*, for listening to a woman he has quite lost the place. O.M. 420. *Rág an houl y lyne golow a gollas, pan éth a'n beys*, for the sun his bright hue lost, when he went from the world. P.C. 3124.

GOLLOHAS, s. m. Praise. *Yn enour dhe Dew an Tás, leverys púp gollohas, my a worhemnyn yn scon*, in honour to God the Father, let all say praise, I command forthwith. O.M. 2624. *Me a vyn mós dhe'n tempel, gollohas rág leverel, ha pigy war dhu Iovyn*, I will go to the temple, to speak praise, and to pray to god Jupiter. P.C. 356. Another form of *golochas*, qd. v.

GOLMEN, s. f. A halter. A mutation of *colmen*, qd. v.

GOLOC, s. m. Sight, look, aspect, view, appearance. *Out wearnas, harlot pen côk, scon yn més a'm golok*, out upon thee, rogue, blockhead! immediately out of my sight. O.M. 1530. *Púr wŷr ef a'n gevyth gu, pan dyffo yn ow goloc*, very truly ye shall have woe, when he comes into my sight. P.C. 964. *Ken teffo y ges golok, dhodho ny yllouch gil drók*, though he should come into your sight, to him you cannot do harm. R.D. 1861. In construction it changes into *wolow*, qd. v. *War an woolok*, on the face. P.C. 2100. W. *golwg*. Sansc. *luuc, lôk*, to see. Gr. λάω, λεύσσω. Lat. *liquco, lucco*. Germ. † *luge, leuchte*. Eng. *look, light*.

GOLOCHAS, s. m. Laud, praise. *Ol del vynny, Arluth-kêr, my a wra yn pûp tyller, hedré veyn bew yn bŷs-ma gans penys ha golochas*, all as thou wishest, dear Lord, I will do in every place, as long as we are living in this world, with penance and praise. P.C. 110. W. *goluchad*.

GOLOM, s. f. A dove. A mutation of *colom*, qd. v. *An golom glâs hy lagas, yn mês gura hy delyfré, lellé edhen, ren ow thâs, leverel ny won ple fe*, the dove with blue eyes, liberate her outside ; a more faithful bird, by my father, I cannot say where there is. O.M. 1109.

GOLON, s. f. The heart. A mutation of *colon*, qd. v. *Gans nader ythof greânheys, hag ol warbarth vynymneys, a fyne trois dhe'n golon*, by a snake I am stung, and altogether poisoned from the end of the foot to the heart. O.M. 1758. *Na gresouch a luen golon*, ye will not believe with full heart. O.M. 1857. *Ken fe y golon terrys*, though his heart may be broken. P.C. 2243.

GOLOVAS, s. m. The travails of a woman in childbirth. *Benen in golovas*, a woman in childbed. Llwyd, 131. W. *cyclychiad. Gweraig yn cyclychu*. Arm. *gwilioud, gulvoud*.

GOLOW, s. m. Light. Corn. Voc. *golov*, lux. Pl. *golowys. Pûr apert hag yn golow y leverys ow dyskas*, very open and in light I spake my doctrine. M.C. 79. *Gansé y a dhûk golow, nôs o, ny welons yn fâs*, with them they carried a light, it was night, they saw not well. M.C. 64. *Te a vydh yn kêth golow yn paredis genama*, thou shalt be in this same light in Paradise with me. P.C. 193. *Dhodho a leverys, re saffé Crist heb strevyé ol dh'y vôdh gans golowys*, to him they said that Christ had risen without striving all to his will with lights. M.C. 248. *Yn penceré gwreys perfyth dhe'n beys ol golowys glân, h'aga hynwyn y a vydh an houl, ha'n lôr, ha'n steryan*, on the fourth (day) be made perfect to all the earth bright lights, and their names they shall be, the sun, and the moon, and the stars. O.M. 34. In construction it changes into *wolow*. *Venytha na'n gefjo tam a wolow têk*, that he shall never have a bit of fair light. O.M. 552. *A Dhe Dew yth wolowys, clew galow an bobyl-ma*, O Father God in thy lights, hear the call of this people. O.M. 1831. W. *goleu*. Arm. *goleu, goulou*. Ir. *solus, soillse*, † *gle*, † *glus*. Gael. *solus, soillse*. Manx, *fullenys, soilshey*. Eng. *gloss*.

GOLOW, adj. Light, bright, shining. *Mars ôs Dew a nêf golow, dysqua lemmyn marthusow, may allyf vy y weles*, if thou art the God of bright heaven, shew now miracles, that I may see them. P.C. 81. *Râg an houl y tyw golow a gollas, pan êth a'n beys*, for the sun his bright hue lost, when he went from the world. P.C. 3123. *Prâg ys fyn Dew ow damnya, ha me mar gollow ha créf*, why will God condemn me, and I so bright and strong. C.W. 22. W. *goleu*. Ir. *follas*, † *folus*, † *glc*. Gael. *follais*.

GOLOWA, v. a. To enlighten, to give light, to illuminate, to shine. Written by Llwyd, 62, 82, 245, *gylynea, gouloua, gylynei*. In construction it changes into *colowa*. *Me ew lantorn nêf, avel tân ow collowy, moy splanna es an Dringys*, I am the lantern of heaven, like fire shining, more resplendent than the Trinity. C.W. 10. ‡ *Patl yzhi a cylywi ha trenna*, how it lightens and thunders. Llwyd, 248. W.*golewo*. Arm. *goulaoui*.

GOLOWAS, s. m. An enlightening, illumination, lightning. Llwyd, 62. ‡ *Yein kuer, tarednow, ha golowas, er, rew, gwenz, ha clehé, ha kezer*, cold weather, thunder, and lightning, snow, frost, wind, and ice, and hail. Pryce. W. *goleuad, goleuawd*.

GOLOWDER, s. m. Light, brightness. *Ha gêns bôs râg golowder yn ebbarn nêf, dha ry golow war an beys ; ha yn delna ytho*, and let them be for light in the firmament, to give light on the world; and it was so. C.W. p. 102. W. *goleuder*.

GOLOWLESTER, s. f. A light-vessel, a lamp. Cornish Vocabulary, *lampas* vel *lucerna* vel *laterna*. Comp. of *golow*, light, and *lester*, a vessel.

GOLS, s. m. The hair of the head. Cornish Vocabulary, *cesaries*. W. *gwallt*. Ir. *falt, folt*. Gael. *follt*. Manx, *folt*.

GOLSE, v. a. He had lost. A mutation of *colsé*, 3 pers. s. plup. of *colly*, qd. v. *An houl ny golsé y lyw, awos mâp dên dhe verwel*, the sun would not have lost his hue, because of a son of man to die. P.C. 3083.

GOLSOWAS, v. a. To hear, to hearken, to listen to. In construction it changes into *wolsowas*. *Tâs, ha Mâb, ha Speris Sans, wy a bys a leun golon, re wronté dheuch grâs ha whans dhe wolsowas y baconn*, Father, Son, and Holy Ghost, ye shall beseech with faithful heart, that he grant you grace and desire to hear his passion. M.C. 1. *Sucl a vynno bôs sylwys golsowens ow lavarow*, whosoever would be saved, let him hearken to my words. M.C. 2. *Aban golsté worty hy, ha gruthyl dres ow defen*, because thou hearkenedst to her, and actedst beyond my prohibition. O.M. 270. *Abram, scon golsow lemyn orth ow lavarow*, Abraham, immediately hearken now to my words. O.M. 1365. *Elcdh nêf, golsowouch dha ve lemyn*, angels of heaven listen to me now. C.W. 10. W. *goglyweed*.

GOLVAN, s. m. A sparrow. Corn. Voc. *passer*. *Golvan gê*, a hedge sparrow. Llwyd gives as the late sound *gylvan*, or *gulvan*. W. *golvan*. Arm. *golvan*. Ir. *geulbhan*. Gael. *gealbhonn*. Gr. *γόλμις*.

GOLVINAC, s. m. A curlew. Llwyd, 51. Another form of *gelvinac*, qd. v.

GOLWIDHEN, s. f. A hazel tree. Llwyd, 51. A mutation of *colwidhen*, qd. v.

GOLY, s. m. A wound, mark of a hurt. Pl. *golyow*. *Hag yn y gorff bôs gorris goleow pals leas nyjll*, and in his body that there were put plenteous wounds many thousands. M.C. 165. *Yn corf Ihesus yth csé, hag ef yn crows ow cregy, pymp nyjll strekis del iore, ha peder gwyth cans goly*, in the body of Jesus there were, and he on the cross hanging, five thousand strokes, as there were, and four times a hundred wounds. M.C. 227. *Ive saw ol dhe wolyow, a wylys vy dhe squerdyé*, are all thy wounds healed, which I saw tearing thee? R.D. 489. *Râk ty dhe weles ol ow golyow a lês yn dhe golon ty a grŷs*, because that thou sawest all my wounds openly, in thy heart thou believest. R.D. 1552. W. *gweli*. Arm. *gouli*.

GOLYAS, v. a. To watch, to be wakeful. *Yn mêdh Crist, un pols golyas ny yllouch dhum comfortyé*, says Christ, a while could ye not watch to comfort me? M.C. 55.

GONESEG   176   **GOR**

Golyouch ha pesouch yn ven, râg own an ioul ha'y vestry, watch ye and pray earnestly, for fear of the devil and his mastery. M.C. 57. *Godhevcuch omma lavur, ha gollyouch gynef,* endure ye here labour, and watch with me. P.C. 1025. *Whâth gynef un pols goylyouch,* yet with me a while watch ye. P.C. 1057. *Arluth, agan dew lagas yw marthys clâf ow colyas; golyas o agan dysyr,* Lord, our eyes are wondrous tired watching; to watch was our desire. P.C. 1068. W. *guyliad.*

GOLYAS, s. m. A watching. *En golyas a fowt dybbry a wodhevys Ihesus kêr,* the watching and want of eating dear Jesus suffered. M.C. 173. W. *gwyliad,* † *guiliat,* in Oxford Glosses.

GOLYE, v. a. To wound, to hurt. Part. *golyys. A Ihesu, ow máp, ellas, ysxyw hemma trueth brás, bôs dhe corf kêr golyys gans tebel pobel,* Oh Jesus, my son, alas ! this is a great sorrow, that thy dear body should be wounded by wicked people. P.C. 3183. W. *gweliaw, gwelio.* Arm. *goulia.*

GON, s. f. A level plain, a down, or common. Variously written *goon, gûn, gwon,* but the earlier form was *gwén,* qd. v. *Gobar da why agas bŷdh, gón Dansotha, ha Cruk heyth,* a good reward ye shall have, the plain of Dansotha, and Barrow heath. R.D. 377.

GON, s. f. A sheath. *A Peder, treyl dhe gledhé, gorré yn y won arté,* Oh Peter, turn thy sword, put it in its sheath again. P.C. 1156. Another form of *gwein,* or as written in the Cornish Vocabulary, *gurin,* qd. v.

GON, v. irr. I know. *A Arluth kymer pytê, Dew merci yn cherytê gon lour ty yw,* O Lord, take pity, God of mercy in charity I know well thou art. R.D. 1547. *Tru, y disky aban reys, alewma râg ny'm bŷdh creys, gon dhe wêr lour,* alas, to take it off since there is need, henceforth there is no peace for me, I know true enough. R.D. 1961. In construction it changes into *won,* qd. v. *Du y won y vôs a rás,* I well know that he is of grace. M.C. 104. W. *gwn, wn.* Ir. *fiun,* (†*gnia,* †*gen,* †*gne, gni,* knowledge.) Sansc. *g'na, jna,* to know. Gr. γινώσκω, γνόω. Lat. *gnosco,* †*gnoo.* Goth. *kann, kunna.* Germ. *kann, kenne.* Eng. *can, ken, know.* Lith. *zinau.* Russ. *znaiu.*

GONEDHIC, s. m. A husbandman, a farmer. Written also *gonydhic, gonythick.* Pryce. W. *gweinydhawg.*

GONEDHY, v. a. To labour, to work, to till, to cultivate, to plant, to set. *Euch, gonedheuch termyn hŷr, powes ny'gys bŷdh nêp preys,* go ye, cultivate for a long time, no rest shall ye have at any time. O.M. 1221. *An ryma yw fŷn gowedhys, ow banneth y rôf dhedhé,* these here are finely set, my blessing I give to them. C.W. 8. *Wonedhans, mŷns ês yn nêf, gwrên yn ker dhe hellyê eff dhe effarn dhe dewolgow,* let all that are in heaven work, let us go to chase him away to hell to darkness. C.W. 24. *Râg henna oll an vengens a allaf dho brudery, me a vyn gonedh derohans,* therefore all the revenge that I can think of, I will work directly. C.W. 32. W. *gweinydhu.*

GONES, v. a. To labour, to till, to cultivate. *Reys yw purrys lavyrrya, ha gones an bŷs onuna, dhe gavas dhe uy susten,* it is very necessary to labour, and till the ground here, to obtain for us sustenance. C.W. 80. Written also *gonys,* qd. v.

GONESEG, s. m. A workman, a labourer. Pl. *gonesugy. Môs dhe vyres my a vyn ow gonesugy wharé, ha dhedhé prest gorhemmyn gruthyl wheyl dêk ha prié,* I will go to see my workmen soon, and command them quickly to do fair and secure work. O.M. 2438. *Gonesugy, gonys a wreuch pûr vysy, dhym del hevel,* workmen, ye work very diligently, as it seems to me. O.M. 2447. *Gonesugy ken ugesouch why nys ty, râg sotel ouch yn pûp crêf,* workmen others than ye shall not cover it, for subtle yo are in every art. O.M. 2489. A late form of *gonidoc.*

GONIC, adj. Downy, like a level plain. *Pryce.* From *gôn,* qd. v. W. *gwaenog.*

GONIDOC, s. m. A servant. Corn. Voc. *minister.* W. *gweinidog.* Arm. *gounidoc.* From W. *gweini,* to serve. Arm. *gounid, gouncza.* Ir *fona,* †*foguam,* †*gniu.* Gael. *foghainu.*

GONS, s. f. The vagina. A mutation of *cons,* qd. v.

GONYC, s. m. Government. *Dhe vâb Seth ew dewesys genef prêst dhom servya ve ; a skeans y fŷdh lenwys, hag a gonick maga ta, ny vŷdh skeans vŷth yn bŷs, mes y aswen cf a wra der an planauth meas ha chy,* thy son Seth is chosen by me to serve me ; with knowledge he shall be filled, and with government as well ; there shall be no science ever in the world, but he shall know it, by the planets without doors and in the house. C.W. 102.

GONYS, v. a. To work, to till, or cultivate the ground. In construction it changes into *wonys,* and *conys. Towyl vŷth ny allaff yn fûs ynné sensy dhe wonys,* a tool I am not able ever well to hold in them to work. M.C. 156. *Awos bôs clâff y dhewelê toche vŷth gonys ef na gll,* because that his hands are sore, he cannot work a bit. M.C. 158. *Hedhyw yw an whefes dŷdh, aban dalletheys gonys,* to-day is the sixth day since I began to work. O.M. 50. *Dh'y teller kyus êws arté, Noc gonys may hallo,* to its former place let it go again, that Noah may till (the ground.) O.M. 1096. *Guetyeuch bones avorow ow conys yn crŷs an dré,* take ye care to be to-morrow working in the middle of the town. O.M. 2300. W. *guneud.* Arm. *great.* Ir. *gnidhim,* †*guiu,* †*dognim.* Gael. *gnathaich.* Manx, *jannoo.* Gr. γεννάω. Lat. *gigno.* Sansc. *jan.*

GONZHA, pron. prep. With him. *Llwyd,* 244. A late corruption of *ganso.*

GOON, s. f. A level plain, a down. *Y'ma goon vrâs dhymmo vy; me a's gwerth dheuch yredy a dhêk-warnugans sterlyn,* I have a large down ; I will sell it to you for thirty sterling. P.C. 1552. Another form of *gwén,* qd. v.

GOOS, s. m. Blood. In construction it changes into *woos. Me a vyn y requirya a dhewelê an kêth dên-na, y woos a dheffa scullya,* I will require it at the hands of that same man, that spilled his blood. C.W. 182. Written more frequently *goys,* qd. v.

GOOSHAC, adj. Bloody. *Pryce.*

GOPHEN, v. a. To ask. *Dho gophen,* Llwyd, 141. Generally written *govyn,* qd. v.

GOR, a prefix in composition. It denotes what is superior, intense, or excessive. W. *gor,* † *guor.* Arm. *gour.* Ir. †*for.*

GOR, v. a. To place. 3 pers. s. fnt, and 2 pers. s. imp. of *goré. An try spûs yn y anow my a's gor hep falladow,* the three grains in his mouth I will put them without fail. O.M. 871. *Nêb ûs gynef ow tybbry, a'm couryh a'm gor dhe mernans,* he that is eating with me, and my companion, will put me to death. P.C. 740. *Ugor daras dhe pryson, ha gor Ihesu ynno scon pols dhe powes,* open the door of thy prison, and put Jesus in it at once awhile to rest. P.C. 1872. *Ha gans colon dha, hep sor, gorré (gor-e) dhe'n menedh Tabor yn gordhyans dhym dh'y lesky*, and with good heart, without ill will, put it upon Mount Tabor in honour to me to burn it. O.M. 429. In construction it changes into *wor*, qd. v. *My a wor grugyer tég*, I will place a partridge fair. O.M. 1202.

GOR, s. m. A man, a male, a husband. *Goslowewch ol, a lús vús, bennath Ihesu luen a rás dheueh keffrys gór ha benen*, hear ye all, O good people, the blessing of Jesus, full of grace, to you, as well male as female. P.C. 3219. *Cryst yw pen gór ha benen*, Christ is the head of man and woman. R.D. 1396. More generally written *gour*, qd. v.

GOR, v. irr. He knows. In construction it changes into *wór*, qd. v. *Hervcydh nép a vo yn le, del wór púp dén ol yn beys*, according as any is in place, as every man in the world knows. P.C. 780. Written also *gour*, *wour*. W. *gŵyr*. Arm. *goar*.

GORA, v. a. To put, to place, to lay, to set. Written also *gorré*, and in construction *worré*, qd. v. Part. *gorys*, *gorrys*. *War penakyll y'n goras dyantell dhe esedhé*, on a pinnacle he placed him hazardous to sit upon. M.C. 13. *Ha'n tebel él, hager bréf, yn y holon a worré*, and the wicked spirit, ugly reptile, in her heart placed. M.C. 122. *Gorow ha benow yn wédh, aga gora ty a wra yn dhe worhel abervedh*, male and female also, thou shalt place them in thy ark within. O.M. 991. *Tán yn kunys gorraf uskys*, fire in the fuel I will put quickly. O.M. 1387. *Popel Ysral ny assaf, nas gorren y dh'y whýl créf*, the people of Israel I will not allow, that I put them not to their hard work. O.M. 1490. *Godhvedhys mar pýdh, yn scon dysvoreys ef a výdh, ha dhe'n mernans col gorrys*, if he be discovered, soon destroyed he shall be, and to death quickly put. O.M. 1522. *Ny's goryth hep fulladow dhe'n týr*, thou shalt not place them certainly in the land. O.M. 1870. *Marregyon, me agas pýs, gorreuch ef dhe Erod scon*, soldiers, I pray you, take him to Herod forthwith. P.C. 1614. *Dún ganso a dysympys, ha yn dour goryn an prenn*, let us come with it immediately; and in water let us put the tree. O.M. 2790. *Y'n beydh pan y'u gorsyn ny, wharré y tueth deulugy*, in the grave when we placed him, soon there came devils. R.D. 2123. *My a comond y woré yn temple dhe wrouedhé*, I command to place it in the temple to lie. O.M. 2552. W. *goru*. Arm. *gorrea*. Ir. *cuir*. Gael. *cuir*.

GORCHEMMYN, s. m. A command. Generally written *gorhemmyn*, qd. v.

GORDHY, v. a. To worship, to honour. Written also *gordhyé*. Part. *gordhys*, *gordhyys*. *An Tás Dew re bo gordhyys, synsys múr ôn dh'y garé*, the Father God be worshipped, bound much we are to love him. O.M. 1125. *Y wordhyé y teleth dheys, mar uskys pan glew dhe léf*, to worship him it is incumbent on thee, so quickly when he hears thy voice. O.M. 1775. *Ken Arluth agessa ef nyn gordhyaf býs vynary*, other Lord than him I will not worship, for ever. O.M. 1790. *Rág y dhe vynnas gordhyé fals duwow erbyn cregyans*, because that they would worship false gods against belief. O.M. 1881. *Nép a'n gordhyé, gwyn y vcys*, he that worships him, happy his lot. O.M. 1938. *Kepar ha my ef gordhyeuch*, like as me, honour yo him. O.M. 2350. *Gwyn výs nép a'n gordh yn ta*, happy he who worships him well. P.C. 156. *Synt Jovyn whék re'n carro, ha dres púp ol ré'n gordhyo*, sweet saint Jove love him, and honour him above every body. P.C. 1848. *Rág henna gordhyn neffra Ihesus néb agan pernas*, therefore let us worship for ever Jesus who redeemed us. M.C. 5. *Rág marogeth a vynné dhen cylé dhe vôs gordhyys*, for ride he would to the city to be worshipped. M.C. 28. Qu. W. *gordhi*.

GORDHYANS, s. m. Worship, adoration, honour, glory. *A Dâs, Máp, ha Spyrys Sans, gordhyans dhe'th corf wék púp prýs*, O Father, Son, and Holy Ghost, worship to thy sweet body always. O.M. 86. *Gorré dhe'n menedh Tabor, yn gordhyans dhym dh'y lesky*, put it on Mount Tabor, in honour to me to burn it. O.M. 430. *Degé warnydhy ny a offryn yn gordhyans dhe'n Tás gwella*, tithe upon it I will offer in worship to the best Father. O.M. 1184. In construction it changes into *wordhyans*. *Lemmyn Cryst agan Arluth, múr wordhyans dhys del dheguth*, now Christ our Lord, much worship to thee as is due. R.D. 150. In late Cornish it was written *gorryans*. ‡ *Rág gans te yo an michterneth, an crevder, ha'n worryans, rág bisqueth ha bisqueth*, for thine is the kingdom, the power, and the glory, for ever and ever. Pryce. Qu. W. *gordhiant*.

GOREPHAN, s. m. July. *Mis Gorephan*, the month of July. Llwyd, 74. W. *gorphenav*. Arm. *guezre*, *goueré*, *gouheré*.

GORF, s. m. A body. A mutation of *corf*, qd. v. *Dhe gorf kér gordhys re bo*, thy dear body, be it worshipped. O.M. 408. *Dún goryn y gorf yn vedh*, let us come, let us put his body in the grave. O.M. 2367.

GORFEN, s. m. The end, a conclusion. *Frut da byner re dhokko, na glasé býs gorfen beys*, good fruit may it never produce, nor grow green to the end of the world. O.M. 584. *May fén gwythys rák an bylen hag ol syhvys, trank hep gorfen*, that we may be preserved from the evil one, and all saved, time without end. P.C. 42. *Govy výth rák edregé bôs mar hager ow gorfen*, woe is me for sorrows, that my end should be so cruel. P.C. 1530. In construction it changes into *worfen*, qd. v. *Y'th whýs lavur dhe dhybry ty a wra býs y'th worfen*, in thy sweat labour to eat thou shalt, even to thy end. O.M. 274. Comp. of *gor*, prefix, and *pen*, a head. W. *gorphen*. Ir. †*forcenn*.

GORFENNE, v. a. To end, to finish, to conclude. *Prederys pêb a'y worfen, settyl allo gorfenné*, let every one think of its end, how it can end. O.M. 228. Written also *gorfen*, and *gorfenna*, and in construction *worfenna*. *Dho worfenna*, to end. Ll. 240. W. *gorphen*, *gorphenu*.

GORGYS, s. m. Distrust. *Yma dhymmo gorgys brás ahanouch, yu púr deffry*, I have great distrust of you, in very earnest. R.D. 1499. *Na gymmer hemma gorgys, rák an Arluth a geusys hydhew worthyn yn geydh splan*, do not take this distrust, for the Lord spoke to-day to us in shining day. R.D. 1501. W. *gorgas*.

GORHA, s. m. Hay. ‡ *Hwei 'ra cavas an gwás brás sigirna cusga war an gorha*, you will find that great lazy follow sleeping on the hay. Llwyd, 248. Another form of *gorra*, qd. v.

GORHEL, s. m. A vessel, a ship, an ark. *Rág henna fystyn, ke, gwra gorhel a blankos playnnyys, hag ynno lues trygva, romes y a výdh gyhvys*, therefore hasten thou, go, make a ship of planks planed, and in it many dwell-inga, rooms they shall be called. O.M. 950. *Arluth kepar del vynny, an gorhel my a'n gora,* Lord, as thou wilt, I will make the ship. O.M. 966. *Yn hanow an Tás gwella, dún abervedh desempys; agan gorhyl a warthn gans glaw ef a vydh cudhys,* in the name of the best Father, let us come in immediately; our ark from above with rain it will be covered. O.M. 1064. *Yn hanow an Tás uhel, an gorhel gnrén dyscudhé,* in the name of the Father high, the ark let us uncover. O.M. 1146. In construction it changes into *worhel,* qd. v. *Gorow ha benow yn wédh, aga gora ty a wra yn dhe worhel abervedh,* male and female also, thou shalt put them in thy ark within. O.M. 992. Written by Llwyd, *gurhal.* The oldest form was *gurchel,* as preserved in *lofgurchel,* qd. v. W. *gorchwyl,* a work, agrees in form; but the root appears to be W. *gwarch,* what incloses.

GORHEMMYN, s. m. A command. *Gorhemmyn Dew dres pûp tra, rés yw y rôs coullenwys,* the command of God above every thing, need is that it be fulfilled. O.M. 654. *Me a wra dhe gorhemmyn fest yn lowen,* I will do thy command with great pleasure. P.C. 1364. *Reys yw gúl ow gorhemmyn a dhesempys,* need is to do my command immediately. R.D. 1993. In construction it changes into *worhemmyn,* qd. v. *My a wra dhe worhemmyn yn pûp plás,* I will do thy command in every place. O.M. 1041. Compounded of *gor,* prefix, and *cemmyny,* to will. W. *gorchymmyn.* Arm. *gourchemeun,* †*gourlremen.* Ir. *forchun.* Manx, *currym.*

GORHEMMYNA, v. a. To command. Written also *gorhemmena.* Part. *gorhemmynys. Yn tressé dydh dybarth gwráf yntré an môr ha'n tyryow, hag yu týr gorhemmynaf may tefo gweydh ha losow,* on the third day I will make a separation between the sea and the lands, and I will command in the earth that trees and plants may grow. O.M. 27. *Del yw gorhemmynnys dhyn, my a's gor býs yn gorhal kefrys bestes hag edhyn,* as it is commanded us, I will put them into the ark, beasts and birds also. O.M. 1049. *Messyger, ke gorhemmyn ol dhe'n masons yn cyté may tyffons unma myttyn, war beyn cregy ha tenné,* messenger, go, command all the masons in the city, that they come here in the morning, on pain of hanging and drawing. O.M. 2277. *Fystynyn fast alemma, del gorhemynnys deffry,* let us hasten quickly hence as commanded indeed. P.C. 646. *Dhedhé me a worhemmyn, eneressycns ha bewens pel,* to them I command let them increase, and live long. O.M. 47. W. *gorchymmyn.* Arm. *gourchemen, gourchemenni.*

GORHEMMYNNAD, s. m. An injunction, a command, a commandment. Pl. *gorhemmynnadow. Serafyn, dhe Adam ke, hag arch dhodho growedhé, dre ow gorhemmynnadow,* Seraph, to Adam go, and enjoin him to lie down, by my commands. O.M. 636. *A Tás Dew gallosek fest, dhe gorhemynnadow prest ny a wra,* O Father God, most powerful, thy commands always we will do. P.C. 158. In construction it changes into *worhemmynnad. Awos an Tás Dew a'n néf, gwra y worhemmynnadow,* because of the Father God of heaven, do thou his commands. O.M. 481. *An dék gorhemmynnadow Dew,* the ten commandments of God. *Pryce's Vocab.* W. *gorchymmyniad,* pl. *gorchymmyniadau.*

GORHERY, v. a. To cover, to inclose, to hide. *Yn úrna whreuck pigadow may codho an mynydhyow warnouch, rág ewn uthekter, ha why a pýs an runyow dh' agas gorhery*

hep gow, kymmys výdh an ponveter, then ye shall make prayers, that the mountains may fall upon you, for very horror; and ye shall pray the hills to hide you, without a lie, so great will be the trouble. P.C. 2655. W. *gwarchawr,* a coverer.

GORHOLETH, s. m. Concord, agreement; delay. *Bynyges re bo an prýs, may fe gurýs an gorholeth,* blessed be the time that the agreement was made. O.M. 675. *Ha dhe welas an passyon a Ihesus hep gorholeth,* and to see the passion of Jesus without delay, which Christ suffered for us, to-morrow come ye in time. O.M. 2841. W. *gorchwyliaeth,* a transaction.

GORIB, s. m. A response, an answer. Written also *gorryb. Hemma ythew gorryb skáv, yma ow gwil ow holan clár,* this is a light answer, it maketh my heart sick. C.W. 86. *Gorryb ty a výdh oll o'th negys,* an answer thou shalt have to all thy errand. C.W. 126. W. *goreb.*

GORIBMYN, s. m. A command. *Adam, yta an puskas, edhen yn ayr, ha bestas, kekeffrys yn týr ha môr; ro dhodhans aga henwyn, y á dhe'th goribmyn,* Adam, see here the fish, birds in the air, and beasts, both in land and sea; give to them their names, they will go to thy command. C.W. 30. A late form of *gorhemmyn.*

GORIBY, v. a. To respond, to answer. *Goribow ol pûb onyn,* answer ye all every one. *Pryce.* Written also *gorryby. Pandra gowsow dhym lemyn, gorrybowh oll pûb onyn,* what say ye to me now, answer ye all, every one. C.W. 12. W. *gorebu.*

GORLAN, s. m. A sheep-fold, a church-yard. *Llwyd,* 48. A mutation of *corlan,* qd. v.

GORLENE, v. a. To quell, to quiet. It changes in construction to *worlené. Fy dheuch a vostryon plos, awos agas fus ha tros, ny wra bom y worlené,* fie on ye, O dirty boasters. notwithstanding your bragging and noise, a blow will not quell him. P.C. 2111.

GORLEWEN, s. m. The west. *An bobyl en gorlewen Kernow,* the people in the west of Cornwall. *Pryce.* W. *gorllewin.* Arm. *gourleuen.*

GORMENAD, s. m. A command. Pl. *gormenadow. Rág terry gormenadow, dhe Adam gans Dew ornys, ef a verwé,* for breaking the commands, to Adam by God ordained, he shall die. C.W. 72. *Ethlays, gwef pan vêv genys, ow terry gormenadow Dew,* alas, woe is me, when I was born, breaking the commandments of God. C.W. 76. A contracted form of *gorhemmynnad.*

GORMOLA, s. m. Praise, commendation. *Llwyd,* 77. Comp. of *gor,* prefix, and W. *mawl,* praise.

GORN, s. m. A horn. A mutation of *corn,* qd. v. *Dyson hep whethé dhe gorn, dysempys gwra y dhybry,* quietly without blowing thy horn, do thou eat it immediately. O.M. 207.

GORNEAL, v. a. To regard, to respect. *Ha, re Dhew an Drengys, Tás, ef am sett yn ban uchel, hag am gorneal mear,* and by God of the Trinity, the Father he will set me up on high, and will respect me much. C.W. 52.

GOROW, v. a. To open. ‡ *Dho gorow.* Llwyd, 43. A late corruption of *agory,* qd. v.

GORQUYTH, v. n. Be thou careful. *Hag ol rág dhe gerensé Ihesus Crista's godhevy, lymmyn gorguyth y garé, ha gwryth denater na vy,* and all for thy love, Jesus Christ suffered them, now be thou careful to love him, and take care that thou be not unnatural. M.C. 139. An-

GORTY 179 GORWEDHA

other form of *gorwyth*, 2 pers. s. imp. of *gorwythy*, qd. v.

GORRA, s. m. Hay. *Yma gené un bé da, gorra hag eys kemyskys; ol dhe'n bestes ûs omma a géf bôs lour dewdhek mýs*, I have a good load of hay and corn mixed; all the beasts that are here, shall have food enough twelve months. O.M. 1058. ‡ *Danvon rag tees dha trehé gorra*, send for men to cut hay. *Pryce's Vocab.* A late form of *guyras*, qd. v.

GORROW, s. m. The male of any kind. *A báb echen a kunda, gorow ha benow yn wédh, aga gora ty a wra yn dhe worhel abervedh*, of all sorts of species, male and female also, thou shalt put them in thy ark within. O.M. 990. *A pûp bést kemmyr wharé gorow ha benow defry*, of every beast take thou forth with, male and female really. O.M. 1022. The older form of this word was *gurruid*, qd. v.

GORRYANS, s. m. Worship, glory, adoration. A late form of *gordhyans*, qd. v. *Râg gans te yw an michterneth, ha'n crevder, ha'n worryans, râg bisqueth ha bisqueth*, for thine is the kingdom, the power, and the glory, for ever and ever. *Pryce.*

GORRYB, s. m. A response, an answer. Written also *gorib*, qd. v.

GORRYBY, v. a. To answer. Written also *goriby*, qd. v.

GORRYS, part. Placed, put. *Bolungeth Dew yw hemma, bones gorrys an spûs-ma pan dremenna a'n bŷs-ma, yn y anow bôs gorrys*, the will of God is this, that these kernels be put, when he passes from this world, in his mouth be put. O.M. 874. *Yn basom bedhens gorrys, ha me a's goulch dysempys*, let it be put in a basin, and I will wash them immediately. P.C. 842. Part. pass. of *gorra*, qd. v.

GORRYTH, s. m. A male of any kind. *Y cennath dheuch yn tyen, keffrys gorryth ha benen*, his blessing to you wholly, men and women likewise. O.M. 2837. *Nynsus gorryth na benen bŷth wel cusyl bŷs vycken a lavarré*, there is no man or woman any better advice, to eternity, who can mention. R.D. 420. A later form of *gurruid*, qd. v.

GORTOS, v. a. To await, to wait, to stop, to tarry. *Pŷth yw an ethom gortos, na cafus dustynyow*, what is the need to stay, or have witnesses? P.C. 1497. *Namnag essof ow merwel orth agas gortos*, I am almost dying, by waiting for you. R.D. 2145. *Gortos y dhôs ny a wra dhe'n brys golow*, we will await his coming to the world of light. R.D. 2412. *Omma kepar del esouch worth ow gortos*, here like as ye are waiting for me. R.D. 2435. *Gortenchlemmyn cowethé*, stay ye now, comrades. P.C. 1369. In construction it changes into *wortos*, qd. v. *Nag ens y hardh dhe wortos*, they were not bold to stay. M.C. 250. Llwyd, 85, gives as a late form *gortha*, *dho gortha*. Arm. *gortoz*.

GORTY, s. m. The man of the house, a husband. *Neb a'm grûk vy ha'm gorty, ef a rûk agan dyfen aval na wrellen dybbry*, he who made me and my husband, he did forbid us that we should not eat the apple. O.M. 181. *Rág ty dha golla orty, ho tulla dha bryas lél, ncfra gostyth dh'y gorty, me a ordayn bôs benen*, because thou didst hearken to her, and deceive thy loyal husband, ever obedient to her husband, I ordain that woman be. C.W. 66. In construction it changes into *worty*. *Hag yn wédh gura dhe'th worty, may tebro ef annodho*, and also make to thy husband, that he may eat of it. O.M. 199. Comp. of *gór*, a man, and *ty*, a house. W. *gŵr ty*.

GORTHEB, s. m. A response, an answer. Pl. *gorthebow*. *A Urry, assos gentyl, my a'd cár mûr rum peryl, râg dhe worthebow ow tèk*, O Uriah, thou art excellent, I love thee much, on my peril, for thy answers are fair. O.M. 2155. Written also *gorthyp*, qd. v. W. *gwrtheb*.

GORTHEBY, v. a. To respond, to answer. *Gortheby te ny vynsys, a ny wodhas ow mestry*, answer thou wilt not, knowest thou not my power? M.C. 144. *Crist pûr wék, an caradow, a'n gorthebys yn ûr-na*, Christ very sweetly, the beloved, answered in that hour. M.C. 193. *Dh'y gows Crist ny worthebys*, to his speech Christ answered not. M.C. 144. *Gortheb dhym, ty nychtern brás*, answer me, thou mighty king. O.M. 2229. *My a wortheb dhys wharé*, I will answer thee at once. O.M. 2835. *Yn della, a gasadow, y gorthebyth epscobow*, thus, O hatred one, dost thou answer bishops? P.C. 1266. *Mas dhe wel y'm gorthebeuch, fast prisonys why a vŷdh*, unless ye answer me for the better, fast imprisoned ye shall be. R.D. 47. Written also *gorthyby*, qd. v. W. *gwrthebu*, from *gwrth*, against, and *ebu*, to say.

GORTHEWYTH, adv. Very certainly. *Awos a gowsa dén vŷth, an keth corf-na gorthewyth ny dhassorchas*, notwithstanding what any man may say, that same body, very certainly, hath not risen again. R.D. 1035. *Yn wedhens, mar omwreyth cláff, gorthewyth te a'n prenvyth*, say they, if thou makest thyself ill, very certainly thou shalt catch it. M.C. 155. W. *gordhīwyd*, very diligently.

GORTHFEL, s. m. A snake. Corn. Voe. *coluber*. Comp. of *gorth*, which may be connected with W. *gordh*, fierce, and *fil*, or *wil*, a mutation of *mil*, an animal.

GORTHRODHY, v. a. To appoint, to substitute. *Pryce.* W. *gwrthrodhi*.

GORTHUER, s. m. Evening. *Trŷk gynen, a gouwyth kér, rág namnag yw gorthuer ha dewedhas*, stay with us, O dear companion, for it is almost evening and late. R.D. 1304. W. *gorhwyr*, extremely late; *ucher*, evening.

GORTHYBY, v. a. To respond, to answer. *Ty dyowl, gwra ow gorthyby*, thou devil, do answer me. O.M. 3 1. *Néb a'n godhfo, gorthybes*, he that knoweth it, let him answer. P.C. 775. *Ha gorthybeuch dhym yn ta, pyw a synsow why mochyn*, and answer ye me well; whom think ye greatest? P.C. 797. *Erlyn a pŷth a gewsy, ny ŷl dén vŷth gorthyby*, against what thou speakest, not any man can answer. P.C. 821. *Me a'th worthyp hep lettyé*, I will answer thee without stopping. P.C. 1237. *Dre dhe vôdh, gorthyp lemyn*, by thy will, answer thou now. P.C. 1722. *Ny a'n gorthyp ef*, we will answer for it. R.D. 1220. This is another form of *gortheby*.

GORTHYP, s. m. A response, an answer. *Me a re scon gorthyp dhys*, I will soon give an answer to thee. P.C. 512. *Ma na gaffo gorthyp vŷth, er-agan-pyn dhe cous gér*, that he may not have an answer, against us to say a word. P.C. 1839. This is another form of *gortheb*, qd. v.

GORTHYS, part. Worshipped. More correctly written *gordhys*, qd. v.

GÒRUER, s. m. A cloud, or thick mist. Llwyd, 100. A late form of *gorthuer*, qd. v.

GORWEDHA, v. a. To lie down, to be recumbent. ‡ *Na ra chee gorwedha gen guerég dén arall*, thou shalt not lie with the wife of another man. *Pryce.* *Ow corwedha*, lying down. Llwyd, 248. Though this form occurs only in late Cornish, it is etymologically more correct than the mediæval form *groweḋhé*, qd. v. W. *gorwedh*. Arm. *gourvez*.

GORWYTHY, v. a. To keep, to preserve, to guard, to be careful. *A tús kér ol cæradow, ow paynys a výdh garow, kyn vôs leskys dhe lusow; a Dhew, gorwyth am ené*, O father dear, all beloved, my pains will be cruel before being burnt to ashes; O God, keep my soul. O.M. 1356. *Gorguyth* is another form, qd. v. *Pylat justis olesé, Ihesus gorwyth dh'y dampnyé*, Pilate, a magistrate thou art, take thou care to condemn Jesus. M.C. 107. Comp. of *gor*, prefix inteus., and *gwytha*, to keep. W. *gorchadw*.

GOS, s. m. Blood. *Na dybreuch, my a gruyr, kýc gans gôs bŷs worfen beys*, eat ye not, I enjoin, flesh with blood even to the end of the world. O.M. 1220. *En Tás Dew roy dhyn bôs gwyw dhe wôs kér the resceue*, the Father God grant to us to be worthy to receive thy dear blood. P.C. 830. *Me re peches marthys trûs, gwŷr gôs Dew pan y'n gwrythys*, I have sinned wondrous sadly, when I sold the true blood of God. P.C. 1506. *Dhe'n dôr an gôs a codhas, hag a'n grûk of scon marow*, to the ground his blood fell, and made him soon dead. R.D. 1119. A contracted form of *goys*, qd. v.

GOS, pr. adj. Your. Lluyd, 231. An abbreviated form of *agos*, or *agus*, qd. v.

GOSC, v. n. He will sleep. A mutation of *cosc*, 3 pers. s. fut. of *coscé*, qd. v. *Judas ny gôsk un banné, lymmyn dywans fystyné dhum ry dhe'n fals Yedhewon*, Judas does not sleep a bit, but quickly he hastens to give me to the false Jews. P.C. 1078. *Gwythens pûp y tenewen, ha me a gôsk ryp y pen râg y wythé*, let every one keep his side, and I will sleep by his head to guard him. R.D. 418.

GOSCES, v. a. He slept. A mutation of *cosges*, 3 pers. s. preter. of *coscé*, qd. v. *Me ry goscus*, I have slept. Lluyd, 231. *Mey fe, me re gaskes pôs, ha rum kemeres drôk glôs*, my faith, I have slept heavily, and an evil pang has seized me. R.D. 511.

GOSCESYS, part. Sheltered. A mutation of *coscesys*, part. pass. of *coscusa*, qd. v.

GOSCOR, s. m. A family. Corn. Voc. *goscor, pi teilu, familia*. This is another form of *cosgor*, qd. v. Both forms exist also in W. *cosgordh*, and *gosgordh*. Arm. *cosgar*.

GOSCOTTER, s. m. Shelter. *Yn mês am ioy ha'm whekter, rês ew keskar dre terros, râg fout gwesc hu gascotter namna vyrwyn râg anwos*, away from my joy and my delight, I must wander through lands; for want of raiment and shelter, I am well nigh perishing for cold. O.M. 361. W. *gwascawd, gwascod, (gwasgodiad, gwasgodle*.) Arm. *gwasced*. Ir. *fasgadh*. Gael. *fasgadh*. Manx, *fasscad*.

GOSLOW, v. a. Hearken thou. A corrupt form of *golsow*. 2 pers. s. imp. of *golsowas*, qd. v. *Abram scon goslow lemyn orth ow lavarow a fynnaf dyryvas dhys*, Abraham, immediately hearken now to my words, (which) I will declare to thee. O.M. 1365. *Gosleuw orthyf vy wharré*, hearken thou to me presently. P.C. 496.

GOSLOWEUCH, v. a. Hearken ye. A corrupt form of *golsoweuch*, 2 pers. pl. imp. of *golsowas*, qd. v. *Gosloweuch ol, a tûs vâs; bennath Ihesu luen a râs dheuch keffrys gûr ha benen*, hearken ye all, O good people; the blessing of Jesus, full of grace, upon you, male and female likewise. P.C. 3217.

GOSOLETH, s. m. Quiet, rest. A mutation of *cosoleth*, qd. v. *Rum fey, yn ol dhe gosow, nyns ûs gyst vŷth ol, hep wow, vâs dhe dra vŷth ragtho*, by my faith in all thy words there is not a beam; without a lie, good for any thing for it. O.M. 2495.

GOSSAN, s. f. Rust, iron ochre, ferruginous earth. *Pryce*. Written also *gozan*.

GOSSE, v. n. It behoved. *Râk henna my a gossé alemma y dhylyffryé, hep gûl dodho na moy gréf*, therefore it behoved me from this place to deliver him, without doing to him any more pain. P.C. 2216. This must be a contracted form of *gothsé*, pluperf. of *góth*, qd. v.

GOSTAN, s. f. A shield, a buckler. A mutation of *costan*, qd. v.

GOSTYTH, adj. Obedient, subject. *Gostcyth dhymo y a vŷdh, kekemys ûs ynné gwrcys*, obedient to me they shall be, as much as is in them made. O.M. 53. *Kynyver bêst ûs yn tŷr, ydhyn ha puskes kefreys, yw gosteth dheuch, hag y bôs dheuch ordenys*, as many beasts as are on the earth, birds and fishes also, are subject to you very truly, and their meat to you ordained. O.M. 1217. *Râg ty dha golla orty, ha tulla dha bryas lêl, nefra gostyth dh'y gorty me a ordayn bôs benyn*, because that thou hearkenedst to her, and deceivedst thy loyal husband, ever subject to her husband I ordain that woman be. C.W. 66. W. *gostyngcdig*.

GOSYS, adj. Bloody. *A'n golon yth êth strét brûs, dour ha goys yn kemeskys, ha ryp an gyw a rexas dhe dhewlé nêb a'n gwyskis; y wholhas y dhewlagas gans y cyl lyff o gosys, dre râs an goys y whelas Ihesus Crist del o dythgtis*, from the heart there came a great stream, water and blood mingled, and by the spear it gushed to the hands of him that struck him; he washed his eyes with the one hand that was bloody; by virtue of the blood he saw how Jesus Christ was treated. M.C. 219. From *gôs*, blood.

GOT, adj. Short. A mutation of *cot*, qd. v. *An combrynsy war dhe ben, mar lêl y synsys dhe lŷn kyns ys trehy war an pren; re got o a gevelyn*, the exactness on thy head, so true thou heldest thy line before cutting on the tree, was too short by a cubit. O.M. 2520.

GOTH, s. m. Pride. Cornish Vocab. *superbia*. *Dre gôth y wrûk levercl, kyn fe dysurŷs an temple, yn tridydh y'n drehafsé, bythqueth whel na fevé quel*, through pride he did say, though the temple were destroyed, in three days he would re-build it, that it never was better. P.C. 381. *Saw an kêth Adam yw gwrŷs, me a wôr, dhe gollewel an ronys ês yn néf, der ow gôth brûs, ur voyd drethaf*, but the same Adam is made, I know, to fill up the rooms, that in heaven, through my great pride, are void through me. C.W. 36. Qu. W. *gôth*. I believe this is one of the Cornish words assumed to be Welsh, from a copy of the Cornish Vocabulary being attached in manuscript to the Liber Landavensis.

GOTH, v. n. It behoveth. *Me a vyn môs dhe'n temple, ha Dew ena y wordhyé, kepar del gôth dhymmo vy*, I will go to the temple, and worship God there, as it is incumbent on me. O.M. 1261. *Ny gôth aga bôs gorrys yn archow, râg bôs prennys gansé mernans dên bryntyn*, it behoveth not that they should be put in the treasury, because that was bought with them the death of a noble man. P.C. 1540. *Yn medhens y, ny'n gordhyn, na ny gôth dhyn y wordhyé*, say they, we will not worship him, nor ought we to worship him. M.C. 148. The preterite is *gothé. Abel pe feſté mar bel, ny gothé dhys bones hel, ow mones dhe'n sacrefys,* Abel, where hast thou been so long ? it behoved thee not to be slow, going to the sacrifice. O.M. 468. *Awos henna nyns ûs vry ; gallas hy gobyr gynsy, ha servnys yw del gothé,* for that there is no account ; her reward is gone with her, and she is served as it behoved. O.M. 2705. *Gôth* in construction changes into *côth,* qd. v. See also the subjunctive *gotho.* W. *gwedhu, gwêdh, gwedhai, ve wedhai.* Ir. *caithear.* Gael. † *caethear.*

GOTH, adj. Old, ancient. A mutation of *côth,* qd. v. *Benyn gôth,* an old woman. *An vor gôth,* the old way. Llwyd, 173, 251.

GOTH, s. m. A vein. *My re bue, war ow ené, owth emblodh, may 'th ên pûr squyth ; uskys na yllyn ponyé, del esof ow tyené, ha whŷs pûp goth ol ha lyth,* I have been, on my soul, wrestling that I was very tired ; so that I could not run immediately, and sweat every vein and limb. P.C. 2510. *Ha'n dhew-na bŷs pan vôns squyth war Crist y fôns ow cronkyé, manna gevé goth na leyth nag esé worth y grevyé,* and those two even till they were wearied, on Christ they were beating, that he had not a vein or limb that was not grieving him. M.C. 132. *Goth* is another form of *gwyth,* qd. v.

GOTHA, v. n. To fall. More correctly written *godhé,* qd. v.

GOTHEWEL, v. a. To suffer. More correctly written *godhewel,* qd. v.

GOTHMAN, s. m. A companion, a friend. A mutation of *cothman,* qd. v.

GOTHO, v. n. It would become. The subjunctive mood of *gôth,* qd. v. *Mar mynnyth cresy nag ûs dew lemyn onan, a gotho ynno cresy, ty a saw a'n trôs dhe'n pen,* if thou wilt believe that there is not a god but one, in whom thou oughtest to believe, thou shalt be healed from the foot to the head. O.M. 1761. *Dên an geffé cans davas, ha'y kentrevek saw onan, mar a's ladtré dhewortę, pa'n pŷn a gotho dhodho,* a man may possess a hundred sheep, and his neighbour only one ; if he should steal it from him, what punishment would be due to him. O.M. 2233. ‡ *Py gotho dhiu' bôs,* when it would become you to be. Llwyd, 242.

GOTHUS, adj. Proud. Corn. Voc. *superbus. Adam ty a ve gothys, pan eses yn paradys, avel harlot ow lordyé,* Adam, thou wast proud, when thou wast in Paradise, lording it like a rogue. O.M. 899. *Pa'n vernas a'n gevé ef, ha fetel veſé ledhys, râg ef o stout ha gothys, hag a ymsensy dên eréf,* what was the death that he found, and how he was killed, for he was stout and proud, and felt himself a strong man. O.M. 2221. *Taw, meleges, yn golon dell ôs dha gothys,* be silent, in heart, as thou art proud. C.W. 22. *Rág y bosta melegas, hag yn golon re othys,* because thou art cursed, and in heart too proud. C.W. 24.

GOUDHAN, s. n. A moth. Cornish Vocab. *tinea.* W. *gwidhon,* mites ; *gwyvyn,* a moth. Arm. *gaozan.* Gael. *fionag.*

GOUHOC, adj. Lying. Corn. Voc. *mendax.* The old form of *gowec,* qd. v.

GOUILES, s. m. Liquorice. Corn. Voc. *auadonia.* W. *gwylys.*

GOUR, s. m. A man, a husband. In construction it changes into *wour. Pŷth yw an gwnyl wella dhe wruthil worth an treytor-ma, yma lyes gwrêk ha gour ow treylé dhodho touth-da,* what is the best counsel to do with this traitor, there are many a woman and a man turning to him with great haste. P.C. 557. *Levereuch dhe gour an chy,* say ye to the master of the house. P.C. 633. *Dredho ef prynnys bydheuch, ol ow tûs, gour ha benen,* through it ye shall be redeemed, all my people, male and female. P.C. 768. *Levereuch a dhysempys dhe wrêk Pilat an iustis, y tue vyngeans brâs war y gour mar pŷdh ledhys Ihesu Cryst an lêl profys,* say ye immediately to the wife of Pilate the Justice, that there will come great vengeance on her husband, if be slain Jesus Christ, the faithful prophet. P.C. 1922. *Pûr wŷr a lavaraf dhys, mar pŷdh e ledhys, y tue vyngeans war dhe wour,* very truly I say to thee, if he shall be killed, there will come great vengeance on thy husband. P.C. 1940. *Gour* is to be read *gûr, (goor.)* Llwyd, 228. So it is written in the Cornish Vocabulary. See *Gûr.* W. *gŵr.* Arm. *gour.* Ir. *fear,* †*fer.* Gael. *fear.* Manx, *fer.* Gr. ἄρης, ἄρρην. Lat. *vir.* Goth. *vair.* Lith. *wyras.* (Eng. *world,* = O. H. G. *ver-alt,* age of men.) Sansc. *varas, viras,* fr. *var,* to defend.

GOUR, v. irr. He knows. It changes in construction into *wour,* under which see the examples. It is also written *gôr, wôr.* W. *gŵyr.* Arm. *goar.*

GÔV, s. m. A blacksmith. Pryce. Written generally *gôf,* qd. v.

GOVENEC, s. m. A request. *Saw kyns ys môs, ow thâs whêk, ro dhym dhe vanneth perfeth ; rág dhym yma govenek cafes dhe geus tregereth,* but before going, my sweet father give me thy perfect blessing ; for there is to me a request to have thy word of love. O.M. 453. It appears more correct to derive this, like the Welsh *govynaig,* a request, from *govyn,* to ask, than from *covio,* to remember. Though the latter is the interpretation given by Llwyd, 242. *Y ma govenec dhym,* I remember.

GOVER, s. m. A rivulet, a brook. *Moyses, kemer dhe welen, ha ty ha'th vroder Aren a-rag an debel bobel, gweask gynsy dywyth an mên, hag y rês gover fenten, mar therhyth dhodho, hep fâl,* Moses, take thy rod, and thou, and thy brother Aaron, in the presence of the wicked people, strike with it twice the stone, and a brook, a fountain, will gush, if thou wilt break it, without fail. O.M. 1845. Written in the Cornish Vocabulary, *guuer.* W. *gover,* † *guuer.* Arm. *gover, gouer, gôer.*

GOVERIC, adj. Snotty-nosed. A snotty-nosed fellow, from *gûr vurick.* Pryce.

GOVID, s. m. Affliction, trouble, grief, misery. Plural *govidion,* and corruptly *govigion.* (Llwyd, 242, *govidzhion.) Parys fest yw an spyrys, ha'n kŷc yw marthys grevyys gans cleves ha govegyon,* very ready is the spirit, and the flesh is wondrous afflicted with sickness and sorrows. P.C. 1002. *Ihesu, Arluth nêf ha beys, ha sylwadur dhyn keffrys, gâf dhymmo vy ow trespys, râk nûr yw ow govyyyyon,* Jesus, Lord of heaven and earth, pardon me my trespass, for great are my sorrows. R.D. 1154. W. *govid.*

GOVOS, v. a. To know. *Yma onan dheuch parys a arhans pûr ha fŷn gurŷs, my u's gor adrô dhodho, may haller govos dhe wŷr, ha gweles yn bledhen hŷr, py gymmys hŷs may teffo,* here is one ready for you, of silver pure, and fine made ; I will put it around it, that it may be known truly, and seen in a year long, to what length it may grow. O.M. 2102. A contracted form of *godhvos*, qd. v.

GOVY, interj. Woe is me. *Govy pan welys Eva*, woe is me when I saw Eve. O.M. 621. *Tru, govy, ellas, bôs marow Adam ow thâs gans y gorf a'm dynythys*, sad, woe is me, alas, that Adam my father is dead with his body (that) produced me. O.M. 861. *Och, govy, pan vêf genys, gans moreth ythof lynwys war dhe lerch, ow arluth whêk*, Oh, woe is me, that I was born, with sorrow I am filled after thee, my sweet lord. O.M. 2193. *Arluth, gevyans dhum ené; govy pan wrugé pehé gans corf an debel venen*, Lord, pardon to my soul; woe is me that I have sinned with the body of the wicked woman. O.M. 2250. Comp. of *go* = W. *gwae*, and *vy*, me. So *goef*, woe is he, and *goy*, woe is them. W. *gwae vi*. Ir. †*fe amai*.

GOVYN, v. a. To ask, to demand, to enquire. Written also *govynny*. In construction it changes into *wovyn*, and *wovynny*. *Ow mâp kerra, pendra vynta orthyf govyn*, my dearest son, what wilt thou ask of me? O.M. 1312. *Dew a'n danfonas dhe wofyn, prák yw genes punscié y tâs mar calcs*, God sent me to enquire, why are by thee punished his people so hardly. O.M. 1481. *Worthys me a wra govyn*, of thee I will ask. P.C. 1236. *Worthyf na wovyn lemyn, worth nép a glowas govyn, rák y a wôr leverel kemmys dhedhé re gewsys*, of me ask thou not now, ask of them who have heard, for they are able to say as much as I have said to them. P.C. 1260. *Nép ma'n rossys dhe wethé, dhtworth henna govynné (govyn e,)* him to whom thou gavest him to keep, from that one demand him. O.M. 575. *Anodho mar 'thes preder, worth y wythyes govyné (govyn e,)* of him if there is a care, from his keeper demand thou him. O.M. 609. *Ow Arluth kêr, gwynneuch orth an gciler kyns ol pan pleyt y me fe*, my dear lord, ask of the gaoler, before all, what plight he is in. R.D. 2052. *Y fôns unver yntredhé kepar ha del wovyny*, they were agreed among them in the manner as he asked. M.C. 39. *Ihesus Crist a wovynnys worth an bobyl*, Jesus Christ asked of the people. M.C. 67. *Pandra a woventé se dheworthaf ve ha'm lays, war a mynnyth govynny orth an kêth ré a's clewas*, what wilt thou ask concerning me and my laws, if thou wilt ask of the same persons that heard them. M.C. 80. *Pilat orto govynnas, yn kêth vaner-ma govyn*, Pilate of him asked, in such a manner asking. M.C. 100. W. *govyn*.

GOVYNNAD, s. m. An asking, a request, a demand. Pl. *govynnadow*, and in construction *wovynnadow*. *Ol dhe wovynnadow ty a fydh yn gwýr hep gow, otensy gynef parys*, all thy demands thou shalt have truly without a lie; see them with me prepared. P.C. 599. W. *govyniad*, pl. *govyniadau*.

GOVYS, v. a. To remember, to regard. *Adam del ôf Dew a rás bôs groythyas a wrontynf dhys, war paradys my a'th âs, saw gwra ow dra a'n govys*, Adam, as I am a God of grace, to be a keeper I grant thee, over Paradise I leave thee, but do thou remember one thing. O.M. 76. *Arloth Dew a'n nêf, an Tâs, venytha gordhyys re by, del russys moy a'n govys worth ow formyé haval dhys* Lord, God of heaven, the Father, for ever be thou worshipped, as thou hast done much of regard, by creating me like to thee. O.M. 108. The exact meaning is not evident: in the first instance *govys* may be a mutation of *covys*, and connected with *covio*, to remember; in the latter there seems to be a connection with W. *goval*, care.

GOW, s. m. A falsehood, a lie. Pl. *gewan*. In construction it changed into *wow*, and in late Cornish *ow*. *Eva dûs nês, kemer y, rág dhys ny lavaraf gow*, come nearer, take it, for I do not tell thee a lie. O.M. 183. *Na'm buef dhe wruthyl genes yn kŷk nag yn kues, hep wow*, I have not had to do with thee in flesh nor in blood, without falsehood. O.M. 659. *Tŷr sêch yn guel nag yn prâs, mar kefyth yn gwôjr hep gow*, dry land in field or in meadow, if truly thou find without falsehood. O.M. 1138. *Gow a lever an iawdyn*, the wilful man tells a lie. P.C. 367. *Mar ny fyn dynaché y gow, gans spern gwreuch y curené*, if he will not retract his falsehood, with thorns do ye crown him. P.C. 2062. *Gorrouch omma an leverow; nynges art vfdh ankevys, na tra arall, heb ow, mes omma mowns skrcfys*, put ye here the books, there is no art forgotten, nor other thing, without a lie, but here they are written. C.W. 160. W. *gau*. Arm. *gaô, gaou*, †*gou*. Ir. *go*, †*gai*, †*gaoi*, †*gau*, †*gao*, †*goo*. Gael. *go, gaoi*.

GOW, adj. Lying, false. *Kepar del ve dhe'n Justis dân leveryn war anow, a y vêdh del yw drehevys, na leveryn un gêr gow*, how it was to the Justice let us come and tell by mouth, from his grave how he is risen, let us not say a false word. M.C. 247. *Rên dhodho boxusow gans dornow ha gwelynny war an scovornow bysy, rák of dhe cows whetlow gow*, let us give him blows with hands and rods on the ears diligently, because that he hath spoken lying tales. P.C. 1302. W. *gau*. Arm. *gaô*. Ir. †*gau*. W. (W. *gau a gwir*, false and true. Ir. †*gau as fir*.)

GOWAL, adj. Complete, full. A mutation of *cowal*, qd. v.

GOWAS, v. a. To have, to obtain. *Dho gowas*, Llwyd, 64, 125. A mutation of *cowas*, qd. v.

GOWEA, v. a. To falsify, to make false, to lie hid. Llwyd, 76. From *gow*. Written also *gova*. *Meyr attomma tayr sprusan a dhêth mês an aval-ma; kemer y, ha gor y yn ban yn neb tellar dha gova*, see, here are three kernels that came out of this apple; take thou them, and lay them up in some place to hide. C.W. 134. W. *gewaw*.

GOWEU, s. m. A liar, a tale-teller. Pl. *gowygyon*. *A fals harlot, goweck pûr, ty â yn pryson yn sûr na wylly deydh*, O false knave, very liar, thou shalt go to prison surely, nor shalt see day. R.D. 55. *Adres pow palmoryon, y a fýdh mûr gowygyon, hag a lever dhe lîs gow*, across the country palmers are great story-tellers, and tell people lies. R.D. 1478. *Nyns ouch lemmyn gowygyon, ow mâs dres pow flatturyon, ow leverel an wedhow*, are ye not now liars, going through the country chattering, telling the news? R.D. 1510. This is written *gowhoc*, in the Cornish Vocabulary. ‡ *Hwedhel gûac*, a false story; pl. *hwidhlow gowigion*. Llwyd, 243. W. *gewog*.

GOWEGNETH, s. m. Falsehood, lying, deceit, guile. Abstract substantive from *gowec*. *Na wast na moy lavarow, rág gowegneth uy garaf, agan arluth yw marow*, waste thou no more words, for I do not love falsehood; our Lord is dead. R.D. 906.

GOWES, s. f. A shower. A mutation of *cowes*, qd. v.

GOWETHE, s. m. Companious. A mutation of *cowethé*, pl. of *coweth*, qd. v. *Perthcuch côf ol a'n tokyn a leverys kyns lemyn dhywy why, a gowethé*, bear ye all remembrance of the token (that) I told before now to you, O companions. P.C. 1083.

GOWLENWEL, v. a. To fulfil, to replenish. A mutation of *cowlenwel*, qd. v. *Saw ma na ŷl bôs nahen, dhe vôdh prest yn pûp hehen, y goulenwel yw ow whans*, but if it cannot be otherwise, thy will always in every thing to fulfil is my wish. P.C. 1092.

GOWLEVERIAT, s. m. A teller of lies, a liar. Corn. Vocab. *falsidicus*. Comp. of *gow*, lying, and *leveriat*, a speaker, from *leverel*, to speak.

GOWHELES, v. a. To lie to, to deceive. *Mar a talleth pertheges, ny a wra y wowheles, râk pûp ol a gâr bewé*, if he begin to be angry, we will lie to him, for all love to live. R.D. 599.

GOWR, s. m. Goats. *Devas ha'n gowr*, sheep and the goats. Llwyd, 240. This is a late plural of *gavar*, qd. v.

GOWS, v. a. Talk, speech. A mutation of *cows*, qd. v. *Râk dhe gows a bréf uffré dhe vôs dên a Galilé*, for thy speech proves ever that thou art a man of Galilee. P.C. 1408. *Dhe gows nyns yw vâs*, thy speech is not good. R.D. 613.

GOWS, s. m. To speak. A mutation of *cows*, qd. v. *Worthyf na gows na moy gêr*, speak thou not another word to me. O.M. 170. *Awos me dhe cows dhedhé*, notwithstanding that I spoke to them. O.M. 1437. *Benen, na gows muscogneth*, woman speak not folly. P.C. 1282.

GOWSE, v. a. He may speak. A mutation of *cowsé*, 3 pers. s. subj. of *cows*. *Ny a'n conclud an iaudyn, a lever y vôs Dew dhyn, na gousé moy ys march dall*, we will silence him, the wilful man, (who) says that he is a God to us, that he may not speak more than a blind horse. P.C. 1658. Written also *gowso*. *Yn certan kyn na gowso, dre luha y côth dodho drôk dyworthé*, certainly though he may not speak, by law there is due to him an evil ending. P.C. 1828.

GOWSESOW, s. m. Speeches. A mutation of *cowsesow*, pl. of *cowses*, qd. v.

GOWYTH, s. m. A companion, a comrade. A mutation of *cowyth*, or *coweth*, qd. v. *Reys yw dhe onan golyas, war y torn pûp y dhyffras y gowyth, pyno a dhalleth*, need is for one to watch, in his turn every one relieving his companion; who will begin? R.D. 410.

GOY, interj. Woe to them. *Ef yw Arluth a allos, hag a prynnas gans y vôs pobel an beys, Ihesus Cryst dhe dhasserehy, un deydh ûs ow tôs, goy kennmys na'n crŷs*, he is the Lord of power, and he has purchased with his blood the people of the world; that Jesus is risen again, a day is coming, woe to them as many as believe it not. R.D. 1187. Comp. of *go*, id. qd. W. *gwae*, woe, and *y*, them. In the same way are compounded *govy*, woe to me, and *gocf*, woe to him, qd. v.

GOYDII, s. f. A goose. *Lemyn hanwaf goydh ha yâr, a scusyf odhyn hep pâr dhe vygyens dên war an beys*, now I name goose and hen, (which) I consider birds without equal for food of man on the earth. O.M. 120. Written also *gôdh*, qd. v., and in the older orthography of the Cornish Vocabulary, *guit*. W. *gŵydh*. Arm. *gwaz*, †*gunz*. Ir. *geadh*, *gedh*, †*geidh*, *gc*. Gael. *gendh*. Manx, *guiy*. Gr. χήν (χάω, χαίνω, χάσκω.) Lat. *anser*, (*hio*, *hisco*.) Germ. *gans*. Ang. Sax. *gos*. Eng. *goose*. Sw. *gås*. Dan. *gaas*. Arm. *goas*. Russ. *gus*. Lith. *zasis*. Sansc. *hanas*, *hansi*, (*has*, to gape.)

GOYF, s. m. Winter. Corn. Voc. *hiems*. In later Cornish it was *guav*, or *gwâv*, qd. v. W. *gauav*, †*gayam*, †*gaem*, *gucv*. Arm. *goaf*, *goanv*, †*gouaff*. Ir. *geimhreadh*, †*geimrith*, †*gaim*, †*gamh*. Gael. *geamrhruith*, *gamh*. Manx, *geurey*. Gr. χεῖμα. Lat. *hiems*. Lith. *ziema*. Sansc. *himan*, (*hi*, to pour. Gr. χάω, χεἰω.)

GOYL, s. f. A sail, the sail of a ship. *Otté aperfedh gorrys, euch tenneuch a dhysempys y goyl yn ban, may hallo môs gans an guyns, ha ganso mollath an sŷns, ha Dew aban*, see him placed within; go ye, draw immediately her sail up, that he may go with the wind, and with him the curse of the saints, and God above. R.D. 2291. *Goyl ha gwern dhodho ordnys, may 'th ellé yn mês a'n wlâs; dhe un carn y fue tewlys, par may codhas yn ow bras*, sail and mast (were) for him ordained, that he might go out of the country; to a rock he was cast, so that he might fall into my judgment. R.D. 2331. Written in the Cornish Vocabulary, *guil*, qd. v.

GOYN, s. f. A sheath, a scabbard. *Gor dhe gledhé yn y goyn, dhe Pedyr Crist a yrchys, rûg dre gledhé a veuché, dre gledhé y fŷdh ledhys*, put thy sword in its sheath, Christ commanded Peter, for he that lives by the sword, by the sword shall be slain. M.C. 72. Written also *gôn*, both forms being later than *guain*, qd. v.

GOYS, s. m. Blood. *Cryst kymmys payn y'n gevé angus tyn ha galarow, ma tèth an goys ha dropyé war y fâs, an caradow*, Christ so much pain had, anguish sharp, and pangs, that the blood came and dropped on his face, the beloved. M.C. 59. *Dewugans dŷdh ow penys y spenyas y gŷk hay weys*, forty days in fasting he wasted his flesh and his blood. M.C. 10. *Garlont spern war y ben a ve gorris, may'th o squardyys adrô ol, a y ben y oys o scollyys*, a garland of thorns on his head was placed, so that was torn all about, from his head his blood was spilled. M.C. 133. *Râg galsé glân dheworto y woys, bewé ny ylly*, for his blood had gone quite from him, he could not live. M.C. 207. *Yma kên dhym dhe olé doggrow goys yn gwŷr hep mar*, there is cause to me to weep tears of blood really without doubt. O.M. 631. This is a later form of *guit*, qd. v.

GRABEL, s. m. A grappling-iron. *Teulyn grabel warnodho scherp, ha dalgenné ynno bŷth na schapyé*, let us cast a grappling-iron on him sharp, and lay hold on him, that he may never escape. R.D. 2268. *Me re tewlys dhe grabel; yn mês a'n dour an tebel corf a dhue, kyn fo mar pôs avel mên*, I have thrown two grappling-irons; out of the water the wicked body shall come, though it be heavy as stone. R.D. 2271. From the English. W. *crap*. Arm. *crap*.

GRACHEL, s. m. A heap. Llwyd, 53.

GRAMBLA, v. a. To climb. *Dho grambla*. Llwyd, 43, 145.

GRAPHY, v. a. To print, to impress. Pryce. See *Araphy*.

GRAS, s. m. Grace, thanks. Pl. *grasow*, *grassys*. *Gordhyans ha grâs dhys, a Dâs, dysechys yw an nôr veys*, glory and thanks to thee, O Father, dried is the earth of the world. O.M. 1149. *Mâb Marea, leun a râs, ol y vôdh a ve clewys*, the Son of Mary, full of grace, all his will was heard. M.C. 9. *Râg y anow a ammas dhe Ihesu leun a rasow*, for his mouth had kissed Jesus, full of graces. M.C. 106. *Benegas yw neb n wodhaffo yn whar dhodho kymmys ûs ordnys, ol en da ha'n drôk kepar*;

dhe Ihesu bedhens grassys, blessed is he that endures patiently every thing that is decreed to him, all the good and evil alike; to Jesus be thanks. M.C. 24. See the secondary forms, *rás rasow*. Borrowed from English.

GRASSE, v. a. To give thanks, to thank. *Bôs séch ha têk an awel dhe Dew y côth dhyn grassé*, that the weather is dry and fair, it behoveth us to thank God. O.M. 1148. *Dhe'n Tâs huhel yn y tron y grassaf lemmyn an câs, ty dhe vynnes dhym danfon dhum confortyé dhe vâp râs*, to the Father high on his throne, I give thanks for the case, that thou wast willing to send to me, to comfort me, thy son of grace. R.D. 508.

GRAT, s. m. A step, a stair. Corn. Vocab. *gradus*. W. *grâdh*. Ir. †*grat*. Gael. †*gradh*. All from the Latin *gradus*.

GRATH, s. m. Grace, favour. *War an Tâs Dew ny a bŷs y grâth dhyn may tanvonno*, to the Father God we pray that he may send his grace to us. O.M. 669. *Noé, dre dhe dhadder brás, ty a bew ow grâth nefré*, Noah, for thy great goodness, thou shalt ever possess my favour. O.M. 974. *Gwŷth an welen-ma yn ta, ha dén vŷth drôg dhys ny wra, ha'm grâth y rôf lemyn dhys*, keep this rod well, and no one shall do thee harm, and my grace now I give to thee. O.M. 1463. Written also *grayth*. *Ha'y holon whêk a ranné, me a lever, râg trystans, râg an grayth yn hy esé, na's gwethé an Sperys Sans*, and her sweet heart would have broken, I say, for sorrow had not the Holy Ghost protected her, for the grace that was in her. M.C. 222. W. *rhâd*. Lat. *gratia*.

GRAVAR, s. m. A barrow. *Llwyd*, 21. *Gravar dhula*, a hand-barrow. 170. (W. *berva dhwyvraich, berva dhwylaw*. Arm. *gravaz doubennek*.) *Gravar rûz*, a wheel-barrow. 240. (Arm. *gravaz rodellek*.) W.*berva*. Arm. *gravaz*. Gael. *lara, bara laimhe, bura roth*. Manx, *barrey*. Eng. *barrow*.

GRAVIO, v. a. To cut, to carve, to engrave. *Collel gravio*, Corn. Vocab. *scalprum vel scalbellum*, a graving knife. *Llwyd*, 146, writes it *gravia*; the participle is *gravys*. *Ef a vydh ancledhys yn le na fue dén bythqueth, yn alabaster gravys ; ragof y fue ordynys, maga wohŷn avel an lêth*, he shall be buried in a place where never man was, cut in alabaster; for me it was intended, as white as the milk. P.C. 3136. This word is probably borrowed more immediately from the English *grave*. The W. is *cravu*. Arm. *crava*. Ir. ‡*grabam*. Gael. *grabhail*. Manx, *grainnee*.

GRAVIOR, s. m. A carver, an engraver. Corn. Vocab. *sculptor*. W. *cravier*.

GRE, s. m. Regard, liking. *Nép a vo yn mochya gre a vŷdh an brassa henwys, herwydh nép a vo yn le, del wúr pûp dén ol yn beys*, he that is in the highest regard shall be called the greatest, according as any is in place, as every man in the world knows. P.C. 777. *Arluth why yu a dhy gre an bous, ha my dhyguysk e 1 yn súr ragouch hy ny wra*, Lord, to your liking is the robe, and that I should take it off? surely for you it will not do. R.D. 1923. 'Fr. *gre*.

GREAB, s. f. The comb of a bird; the ridge of a hill. Another form of *grib*, a mutation of *crîb*, qd. v.

GREAN, s. m. Gravel. *Polgrean*, in St. Michael Carhays, the gravel pits. Another form of *grouan*, qd. v.

GREF, s. m. Grief, complaint. *Ytho prâg na lenes ef, kafus y dhegé hep gréf, hag aban vyn y lesky*, now, why not leave him to take his tenth without complaint, and burn it, since he will. O.M. 497. From the English.

GREF, v. n. He will grieve. 3 pers. s. fut. of *grevyé*, qd. v. *Dhynny ny travyth ny gréf, aban yw y vôdh ef y lesky hep falladow*, to us there is nothing grievous, since it is his will to burn it without fail. O.M. 482.

GREFNYE, adj. Greedy, covetous, grasping. *Ny vavnaf bôs mar grefnye, dha wetha oll ow honyn ; Adam dres pûb hunyth, me a'n câr, po Dew deffan, dhe wetha heb y shara*, I will not be so greedy to keep all myself; Adam above every thing I love, or God forbid, to keep without his share. C.W. 50. This is a mutation of *crefnyé*. W. *crafain, mor grafain*.

GREG, s. f. A wife, a woman. *Greg gans gûr*, Cornish Vocabulary, *uxor*, lit. a man with a wife. An old form of *gwréc*, qd. v.

GREGOR, s. f. A partridge. *Pryce*. Another form of *grugyer*, qd. v.

GREGY, v. a. To hang, to suspend, to be hanging, to be hanged. A mutation of *cregy*, qd. v. *Gebal dhe conna a grég*, Gebal, thy neck be hanged ! O.M. 2813. *Dhe vantel gâs yn gage ; my a'n bŷdh râg ow wage, ha ty a grêk, renothas*, leave thou thy cloak in pledge, I will have it for my wages, and thou shalt be hanged, by my father. P.C. 1188.

GREGY, v. a. To believe. A mutation of *cregy*, qd. v.

GREGYANS, s. m. Belief. A mutation of *cregyans*, qd. v. *Mar tregou' why yn gregyans-na, moreth why as bŷdh ragdha*, if ye abide in that belief, sorrow ye shall have for it. C.W. 14.

GREHAN, s. m. Skin. A mutation of *crehan*, qd. v. '*Sgelli grehan*, a bat. *Llwyd*, 173.

GREIA, v. a. To cry for, to ask for. A mutation of *creia*, id. qd. *cria*, qd. v. ‡ *Dho greiah râg*, to ask for. *Llwyd*, 124.

GREIAS, v. a. He cried. A mutation of *creias*, id. qd. *crias*, 3 pers. s. preterite of *cria*, qd. v. ‡ *Dzhûan a greias awel, leddarn, loddarn*, John also cried out, thieves, thieves. *Llwyd*, 252.

GRELIN, s. m. A lake. Corn. Voc. *lacus*. It properly means a pond for beasts, a horse-pond ; being compounded of *gre*, a flock, and *lin*, a lake, as in *piselin*. W. *grelyn*. (Welsh, *gre*, a flock. Arm. *gre*. Ir. *graidh*, †*groigh*. Gael. *greigh*. Manx, *griaght*. Latin, *grex*. Sansc. *hrag*, to gather together.)

GRENS, v. a. Let them do. A contracted form of *gweréns*, 3 p. pl. imp. of *gwrey*. *Ot an Iustys ow lôs dhyn ; anodho ef gréns del vyn, pan glewfo y lavurow*, see the Justice is coming to us ; with him let him do as he will, when he hears his words. P.C. 371. *Gréns ena bôs golow*, let there be light. C.W. 190.

GRES, s. f. Belief, faith. A mutation of *crés*, qd. v. *A Iudé, gâs dhe yrés, y golou squyrdys a lés ne a welas*, O Judah, leave thy belief, his heart torn in pieces I saw. R.D. 1031.

GRES, v. a. He will believe. A mutation of *crés*, 3 pers. s. fut. of *cresy*, qd. v. *Gallas an glaw dhe vês gulân, ha'n dour, my a grés, basseys*, the rain is clean gone away, and the water, I believe, abated. O.M. 1098. Written also *greys*, qd. v.

GRESAF, v. a. I will believe. A mutation of *cresaf*, 1 pers. s. fut. of *cresy*, qd. v. *Ty a fŷdh pûr tormont sad yn gulás yffarn, del gresaf*, thou shalt have very sad torment in the region of hell, as I believe. O.M. 492. *A tne, convyth, my a'd pŷs, ny gresaf awos an beys*, O be silent, comrade, I will not believe for the world. O.M. 2752. *Dhys ny gressaf, ha me a'th peys, gás dhe wow*, I will not believe thee, and I pray thee, leave thy falsehood. R.D. 1353.

GRESOUCH, v. a. Ye will believe. A mutation of *cresouch*, 2 pers. pl. fut. of *cresy*, qd. v. *A bûr fals dyscryggygyon, tebel agas manerow, na gresouch a luen golon, bós an Tâs Dew hep parow*, O very false disbelievers, evil (are) your ways; that ye will not believe with full heart, that the Father is God without equals. O.M. 1857. *Dhymmo vy mar ny gresouch, ottengy a wél ol dheuch, kepar ha del leverys*, if ye will not believe me, behold them in the sight of you all, just as I said. P.C. 2688. Written also *grescuch*; the 2 pers. pl. of the fut. and imperative are always the same. *Na gresseuch bós treyson gures*, do not think that treason is committed. R.D. 640.

GRESSO, v. a. He may believe. A mutation of *cresso*, 3 pers. s. subj. of *cresy*, qd. v. *Dén na gresso dyougel, an kéth dén-na dhe selwel, cummen vjth na ĝl wharfos*, the man that may not believe really, that man to save not any way can exist. R.D. 2478.

GRESYN, v. a. I did believe. A mutation of *cresyn*, 1 pers. s. imp. of *cresy*, qd. v. *Me a'th pŷs dhym a gnfé, ny gresyn ly dhe vewé whêth bŷs hydhew*, I pray thee to forgive me, I did not believe thee to live yet until this day. R.D. 1549.

GRESYTH, v. a. Thou wilt believe. A mutation of *cresyth*, 2 pers. s. fut. of *cresy*, qd. v. *A venen, assos goky, na gresyth dhum lavarow*, O woman, thou art foolish, that thou wilt not believe my words. O.M. 174.

GREUCH, v. a. Make ye. An abbreviated form of *grereuch*, 2 pers. pl. imp. of *gwrey*. *Honna yw y bous nessa, ha whêth greuch y dhry omma arté dhywhy, ha dyscow y dheworto*, that is his nearest garment, and do ye yet bring him here again to you, and strip it from him. R.D. 1868. *Awos cóst arhans ung our, greuch y tenné més a'n dour, gorreuch ef yn schaih dhe'n mór*, for cost of silver or gold, do ye drag him out of the water, place him in a boat to the sea. R.D. 2232. The final aspirate was often softened into h, or omitted altogether, especially in late Cornish. (*Llwyd*, 252.) *Hag yn wêdh why, dew ha dew, a pregoth yn aweyl grew yn ol an beys*, and do ye also, two and two, preach the Gospel in all the world. R.D. 2464.

GREVYA, v. a. To grieve, to afflict. Part. *grevyys*. Fut. *gréf. Mar possé an neyll tenewen rág y scôdh hy a'n grevyé*, if he leaned on the one side for his shoulder it grieved him. M.C. 205. *Máb Du o kymmys grevyys, rág tomder ef a veesé dour ha goys na kemeskis*, the Son of God was so much grieved, for heat he sweated blood and water mixed. M.C. 58. *Dhynny ny travyth ny gréf, aban yw y vôdh ef y lesky hep falladow*, to us there is nothing grievous, since it is his will to burn it without fail. O.M. 482. Borrowed from the English.

GREYS, s. m. Strength, vigour. A mutation of *creys*, qd. v.

GREYS, s. m. The middle, centre. *Yn ewn greys an scarf tróh e*, in the just middle of the joint cut thou it. O.M. 2530. A mutation of *greys*, qd. v.

GREYS, v. a. He will believe. A mutation of *creys*,

id. qd. *crés*, 3 pers. sing. fut. of *cresy*, qd. v. *Mar kŷf tŷr esch, my a greys, dynny ny dhewhel arté*, if it finds dry ground, I believe it will not return to us again. O.M. 1131. *Kemmys na greysa, govf, yn peynys yfarn y séf bŷs gorfen bŷs*, whoever will not believe, woe to him, in the pains of hell he shall stay until the end of the world. R.D. 176.

GRIG, s. m. Heath, or ling. *Griglan* according to Polwhele is used at the present day for "heath" in Cornwall. W. *grûg*. Arm. *brûk*, *brûg*. Ir. *fraoch*, †*fraech*. Gael. *fraoch*. Manx, *freoagh*. Gr. ἐρίκη. Lat. *erica*. Fr. *bruyere*.

GRIGIS, s. m. A girdle, a belt. *Llwyd*, 15, 48. Written also *grugis*, qd. v.

GRILL, s. m. A crab fish. *Llwyd*, 46, who gives as a synonym, Arm. *grill*. A crab in Welsh is called *cranc*, which is also the name given by Legonidec, in Armoric; and W. *grill* is a chirp, or sharp noise, whence *grilliodydh*, a cricket, which is also called *gril*, in Armoric. *Gril-vôr*, or sea cricket, from its form is the Armoric term for a shrimp. Ir. *grullan*. Gael. *greollan*. Lat. *grillus*. Fr. *grillon*, a cricket.

GRISLA, v. n. To grin like a dog. *Dho grisla*. Llwyd, 141. *A grisla*, grinning. P.C. 248.

GRISYL, adj. Sharp. *Aban na fyn dewedhé, me a vyn y curuné avel mychtern Yedhewon; otté spern grisyl gyné, ha dreyn lym ha scharp ynné, a grup bŷs yn empynyon*, since he will not end, I will crown him as king of the Jews; see sharp thorns with me, and spines rough and sharp in them, (that) will pierce even to the brains. P.C. 2188. Eng. *grisly*.

GROCHEN, s. m. A skin. A mutation of *crochen*, qd. v. *Y a wŷth y vody na potré bŷs vynary, kyn fe yn bêdh mjl vlydhen, na'y grochen un wŷth terry*, they shall preserve his body, that it never decay, though it be in the grave a thousand years, nor shall his skin be once broken. P.C. 3202.

GROGAS, v. a. He hanged. A mutation of *crogas*, 3 pers. s. preter. of *crogy*, qd. v. *Ha'n Edhewon a grogas lader dhe Crist a barth clêdh*, and the Jews hung a thief to Christ on the left side. M.C. 186.

GROGEN, s. f. A skull. A mutation of *crogen*, qd. v. *Me a's ten gans ol ow nerth, may 'th entré an spikys serth dre an cen yn y grogen*, I will pull it with all my strength, that the stiff spines may enter through the skin to his skull. P.C. 2141. *Dre an grogen*, through the skull. P.C. 2558.

GRONCYE, v. a. To beat, to strike. A mutation of *croncyé*, qd. v. *May fôns hyblyth dhe groncyé*, that they might be pliant to beat. M.C. 131.

GRONEN, s. f. A grain. Corn. Vocab. *granum*. W. pl. *grawn*, sing. *gronyn*. Arm. pl. *grûn*, sing. *greûnen*. Ir. *grain*, †*grainne*. Gael. *grán*, *gráinne*. Manx, *grinc*. Lat. *granum*.

GRONTE, v. a. To grant. Part. *grontys*. *Tays ha Máb ha Speris Sans why a bŷs a'leun golon, re wronté dheuch grás ha whans dhe wolsowas y bascons*, Father, Son, and Holy Ghost, ye shall beseech with full heart, to grant you grace and desire to hear his passion. M.C. 1. *Ha kymmys a dhescryas dhodho ef a ve grontys*, and as much as he desired to him was granted. M.C. 9. *My a wront dhys*, I will grant to thee. O.M. 329. Written also *grontyé. Bós gwythyas a wrontyaf dhys*, to be a keeper I grant to thee. O.M. 74. *Ha'y grás dheuchwhy re wrontyo*, and his grace may he grant to you. O.M. 1726. *Yn ér-na yn wêdh kemeas dhe Iosep y a rontyas*, in that hour also leave to Joseph they granted. M.C. 230. Borrowed from the English.

GROW, s. m. Gravel, sand. Corn. Vocab. *grou harena*. *Nefré kyns nós alemma, ry whaf dhedhy my a wra gans myyn grow yn brás garow*, ever before going hence, give a blow to her I will, with gravel stones very roughly. O.M. 2756. " Hence the *grouan stone*, which is a sort of moorstone of a finer grain, composed of sand, fine gravel, clay and talk." Pryce. W. *gro, grawn*. Arm. *grouan, groan, grozol, grozel*. Ir. *grothal*. Gael. *grothal*.

GROWEDHE, v. a. To lie down, to recline. *My ny vennaf growedhé vynytha gans corf Eva*, I will never lie down with the body of Eve. O.M. 625. *My a kyrch an gwás wharré, bynytha rág growedhé genen ny yn tewolgow*, I will bring the fellow soon ever to lie with us in darkness. O.M. 888. *Ke yn ban wor an kunys, hag ena growedh a heys, may hylly bones leskys*, go thou up on the fuel, and there lie down at length, that thou mayest be burned. O.M. 1334. *Euch, growedhcuch, ow Arluth, may haller agas cudhé gans dylles rych*, go, lie down, my lord, that you may be covered with rich clothes. O.M. 1923. *Nans yw an voren marow, a hýs yma a'y growedh*, now is the jade dead, at length she is lying. O.M. 2759. *Na eláff výth ow crowedhé, mar pesy a léun golon*, nor any sick lying down, if he prayed with true heart. M.C. 25. *Corff Ihesus Crist yntredhé dhe'n logell a ve degys, hag a heys dhe wrowedhé yno eff a ve gesys*, the body of Jesus Christ between them to the coffin was brought, and at length to lie down in it, it was left. M.C. 233. This form is etymologically less correct than the later form *gorwedha*, qd. v., being compounded of the prefix *gor*, upon, and *gwêdh*, position. W. *gorwedh*. Arm. *gourvez*.

GROWS, s. f. A cross. A mutation of *crows*, qd. v. *Ow corf yw, re'n offeren, kepar del loverys dheuch, gwyrthys, lydhys yn grows pren*, my body it is, by the mass, like as I have said to you, sold, killed on the cross tree. P.C. 766. *Gweres, ty harlot iaudyn, ha dôk an grows war dhe geyn*, help, thou obstinate knave, and carry the cross on thy back. P.C. 2616. *Drehevouch an grows yn ban*, lift ye the cross up. P.C. 2812.

GRUAH, s. f. An old woman. Corn. Vocab. *anus*. W. *gwrâch*. Arm. *grach*.

GRUD, s. m. The jaw. Corn. Vocab. *maxilla*. In the cognate dialects it means the *cheek*. W. *grûdh*, † *grud*. Ir. *grundh*, † *gruad*. Gael. *gruaidh*.

GRUEG, s. f. A wife, a woman. Corn. Vocab. *mulier; peus gurec*, a woman's coat. *Neffré yn dour hedré vo, ny dhue dresto na varwo gour gruek na bést*, ever in the water while he is, no one goes over it that does not die, man, woman, or beast. R.D. 2227. The more common form is *gwrêc*, qd. v.

GRUEITEN, s. f. A root. Corn. Vocab. *radix*. This is an old form of *gwrydhen*, from *gwrêdh*, whence plural *gwrydhow*, qd. v.

GRUGE, v. a. To do, to make. The 3 pers. s. of the pret. is *gruc, a wruc*, or *a ryc, a rug*, which is often used as an auxiliary verb. *Ow formyé têk ha dyblans, ty rum grûk pûr havel dhys*, me create fair and bright thou hast done me, very like to thee. O.M. 88. *Néb a'm grûk vy ha'm gorty, ef a rûk dyfen, aval na wrellen dybbry, na môs oges dhe'n wethen*, he who made me and my husband, he did forbid us, that we should not eat the apple, nor go near to the tree. O.M. 181. *Ellas gweles an termyn ow arluth pan wrûk serry, pan rûk drys y worhemmyn*, alas, to see the time when I made my lord angry, when I acted against his command. O.M. 352. *An Tás a néf a'n grûk ef dhodho haval*, the Father of heaven made him like to himself. O.M. 878. *Ellas pýth yw dhym cusyl orth an dra-ma dhe wruthyl, tru govy pan y'n gruga*, alas, what counsel is there to me, to do respecting this thing? Oh, sad, when I did it. P.C. 1434. W. *gorugo, a orug*. Arm. *gra*. Ir. *rug*, † *ric*, † *rig*. Gael. *rug*. Scotch, *gar*.

GRUGIS, s. m. A girdle, a belt, a zone, a sash. Cornish Vocabulary, *cingulum* vel *zona* vel *cinctorium*. Llwyd, 4, 179, reads it *grygis*, and gives *grigis* as the late form. W. *gwregys*, † *gregys*. Arm. *gouriz*. Ir. *creas, crios*, † *cris*. Gael. *crios*. Manx, *cryss*. Sansc. *garh*, to enclose.

GRUGYER, s. f. A partridge. *Lemyn hanuaf goydh ha yâr, a sensnf edhyn hep pâr, dhe wygyens dén war an beys; hôs, payon, colom, grugyer, baryos, bryny, ha'n er, moy dredhof a výdh hynwys*, now I name goose and hen, (which) I consider birds without equal for food of man on the earth; duck, peacock, pigeon, partridge, kite, crows, and the eagle, further by me shall be named. O.M. 132. *Dhe'n Tás Dew yn mûr enor, war y alter my a wor grugyer têk ha hag awhesyth*, to the Father God in and honour, upon his altar, I will put a partridge fair great tender. O.M. 1203. Comp. of *grug* or *grig*, heath, and *yâr*, a hen; the name would be more strictly applicable, as in Welsh, to the grouse or heath-fowl. W. *grugiar*, pl. *grugieir*.

GRUPYE, v. a. To pierce. *Otté spern grisyl gymé, ha dreyn lym ha scharp yuné a grup býs yn empynyon*, see sharp thorns with me, and spines rough and sharp in them, (that) will pierce even to the brains. P.C. 2120.

GRUSSE, v. a. He had done, or would have done. 3 pers. s. plup. of *gwry*. *Un dra a won, a'n godhfes, a russé dhe dhydhané*, one thing I know, if thou knewest it, would amuse thee. O.M. 152.

GRUSSEN, v. a. I had done, or would have done. 1 pers. sing. plup. of *gwrry*. *An pýth a wrên, my ny wodhyen, râg ny wylyn; hay a quellen, my ny'n grussen, kyn fen ledhys*, the thing I did I knew not, for I did not see; and if I had seen, I would not have done it, though I had been killed. P.C. 3023. *Awos travyth ny wrussen venytha dhe guhudhas*, for the sake of any thing I would never have accused thee. O.M. 163.

GRUSSENS, v. a. They had done, or would have done. 3 pers. pl. plup. of *gwry*. *A Tás whêk, gáf dhedhé y, râg ny wodhons yn teffry, py nýl a wrôns, drôk py da, hag a codhfons yredy, ny wrussens ow dystrewy*, O sweet Father, forgive them, for they know not really, whether they do evil or good; and if they knew in truth, they would not have destroyed me. P.C. 2777. *Lemyn an toll re wrussens y a vynné dhe servyé*, now the hole they had made they would that it should serve. M.C. 180.

GRUSSES, v. a. Thou hadst done, or wouldst have done. 2 pers. s. plup. of *gwry*. *Beys vynytha y wharthes rág lowené, kepar yn beys ha dues dhe'n néf grusses yskynné*, for ever thou wouldst laugh for joy; as thou camest into the world, to heaven thou wouldst ascend. O.M. 156.

GRUSSONS, v. a. They made. 3 pers. pl. preter. of *gwrey. Grussons cunyl nag o vâs, râg may fo Ihesus dystorgs*, they took counsel (that) was not good, that Jesus should be undone. M.C. 31. *May whrussons cam dremené y vyllyk an prŷs*, that they did the evil transgression, they will curse the time. O.M. 337.

GRUSSOUCH, v. a. Ye made. 2 pers. pl. preter. of *gwrey. A's wrussouch cam tremené, cüth gwrles y dhewedh fe*, ye did an evil transgression, a grief it was to see his end. R.D. 40. *Why a vŷdh aquyttys dn râk an ouor yn torma a wrussouch dhymmo pûr wŷr*, ye shall be well requited, for the honour at this time (that) ye have done to me very truly. P.C. 312. *An pyt a wryssyuch*, the pit ye have made. O.M. 2792.

GRUSSYN, v. a. We had made. 1 pers. pl. pluperf. of *gwrey. Mâp dên my re wrûk prenné, gans gôs ow colon, na fe nep a wrussyn ny kyllys*, mankind I have redeemed with the blood of my heart, that there may be no one (that) we have made lost. R.D. 2624.

GRUSSYS, v. a. Thou madest. 2 pers. s. pret. of *gwrey. A out warnes drôk venen, worto pan wrussys colé*, Oh, out upon thee wicked woman, when thou listenedst to him. O.M. 222. *Arluth pregoth ny a wra, kepar del wrussys pûp tra, nag ûs kên Dew agesos*, Lord, we will preach, like as thou hast done everything, that there is not another God than thou. R.D. 2470.

GRUTHYL, v. a. To do, to make, to act. *Aban golsté worty hy, ha gruthyl dres ow defen*, because thou didst listen to her, and act against my prohibition. O.M. 270. *Dhe parathys seon ydh âf, râg gruthyl ol bôdh dhe vrŷs*, to Paradise soon I will go, to do all the will of thy judgment. O.M. 340. *Reys yw dhym ag dhe lyst emlodh worth an antecryst, hag of dhum gruthyl marow*, need is to me withiu the lists to fight against the antichrist, and he to put me to death. R.D. 225.

GRUYTH, s. m. Office, duty, service. Pryce. *A vynyn ryth, na tuche vy nês, na na wra gruyth na fo dhe lês, ny dhueth an prŷs, er na gyllyf dhe'n nêf dhum Tâs*, O woeful woman, touch me not nearer, nor do not make a greeting that is not for advantage; the time is not come, until I go to heaven to my Father. R.D. 876.

GRY, s. m. A cry, a call. A mutation of *cry*, qd. v.

GRYCHONEN, s. f. A spark. A contracted form of *gwrychonen*, of which the plural is *gwrychon*, qd. v. *Ty a whŷth avel cauch guâs; whŷth war gam vyngrans y'th glas, ny dryk grychonen yn fôk*, thou blowest like a dirty fellow; blow athwart, vengeance in thy maw, there remains not a spark in the forge. P.C. 2717. W. *gwreichionen*.

GRYES, v. a. He cried. A mutation of *cryes*, 3 pers. s. preter. of *cryê*, qd. v. *Me a grycs warnodho, râk paynys pan na'n gefo tyller dh'y pen*, I cried into him, for pains when he had not a place for his head. R.D. 268.

GRYGY, v. a. To believe. A mutation of *crygy*, qd. v. *Neffré of dhe dhasserchy, me ny fynnaf y grygy, bew hedré vên*, that he ever rose again, I will not believe it, as long as I may be alive. R.D. 1047. *Dhe grygy Thomas a dhué*, to believe Thomas will come. R.D. 1219.

GRYGYANS, s. m. Belief, faith. A mutation of *crygyans*, qd. v. *Ha fusta sy dhe vreder yn luen grygyans*, and strengthen thou thy brethren in full belief. R.D. 1164. *Y grygyans pûp ol gwythes, puppenagol a wharfo*,

his belief let every one keep, whatever may happen. R.D. 1537.

GRYS, s. m. Strength, force, vehemency. A mutation of *crŷs*, id. qd. v. *creys*, qd. v. *Dûn ganso a dysyompys, ha poynyn gans mûr a grŷs*, let us come with it immediately, and let us run with great strength. O.M. 2789. *Tynnouch ol gans mûr a grŷs*, pull ye all with great force. P.C. 2136.

GRYS, v. a. He will believe. A mutation of *crŷs*, 3 pers. s. fut., and 2 pers. s. imp. of *crysy*, qd. v. *Dhymmo evredhek yn wêdh, ro nerth dhe gerdhes yn fâs; ha my a grŷs yn pyrfeth aga vos gwrel a vûr râs*, to me also the maimed, give thou strength to walk well; and I will believe perfectly that they are rods of great grace. O.M. 2011. *Nêp na grŷs ynnos goef, ny fŷdh aylwys*, who will not believe in thee, woe to him, he will not be saved. R.D. 757. *Cot yw dhe dhydhyow dhe gy, nahen na grŷs*, short are thy days to thee, think not otherwise. R.D. 2038.

GRYS, v. a. To shake, to quake. A mutation of *crŷs*, qd. v. *An houl ny golsé y lyw, awos mâp dên dhe vervel, na corf dusserhy dhe vew, na dôr grŷs yn tyougel*, the sun would not have lost its hue, on account of a son of man dying; nor a body rise to life, nor the earth quake undoubtedly. P.C. 3086.

GRYSAF, v. a. I will believe. A mutation of *crysaf*, 1 pers. s. fut. of *crysy*, qd. v. *Awos lavarow trufyl, ny grysaf dhys; ty a fŷl gûl dhum crygy*, for the sake of vain words, I will not believe thee; thou wilt fail to make me believe. R.D. 1056.

GRYSSO, v. a. He may believe. A mutation of *crysso*, 3 pers. s. subj. of *crysy*, qd v. *Ha kekymmys a'n gwello, hag yno ef a grysso, bôs ynches dhodho yw reys*, and as many as may see it, and in him believe, need is that there be health to him. R.D. 1707.

GU, s. m. A lance, a spear, a javelin. *Yw saw ol dhe wolyow a wylys vy dhe squerdyé, a wrûk an gu ha'n kentrow, dhe kŷc precius dafolé*, are all thy wounds healed which I saw tearing thee? which the spear and the nails made, deforming thy precious flesh. R.D. 491. *Gans gu lym y a'n gwanas dre an golon*, with a sharp spear they pierced him through the heart. R.D. 1117. *Gans gu gwenys me a fue*, with a spear I was pierced. R.D. 2603. The same as *gew*, qd. v.

GU, s. m. Woe, grief, misery. Pl. *guow. Euch alemma, tormentors, dhe gerhas an gwâs muscok; pûr wŷr of an gevyth gu, pan dyffo yn ow goloc*, go hence, executioners, to fetch the crazy fellow; truly he shall have woe, when he comes into my sight. P.C. 963. *Syttyouch dalhennow yn cam, ha dûn ny lôth brâs lês yn epscop Syr Cayfas yu gwîth a prŷs er y gu*, lay hold on the rogue, and let us come with him in great haste, even to bishop Sir Caiaphas, in a turn of time for his woe. P.C. 1130. *Why pryncys an dewolow, scon egercuch an porthow; py mar ny wrcuch y fŷdh guow kyns tremené*, ye princes of the devils, immediately open the gates; if ye do not, there shall be woes before passing. R.D. 90. Written also *gew*, qd. v. It enters into composition with pronouns, as *goef*, woe to him; *gow*, woe to me; *govy*, woe to them. W. *gwae*. Arm. *gwa*, †*goa*. Ir. †*fe*. Gr. *oùai*, *ηόοs*. Lat. *væ*. Sanse. *ghus*, fr. *ghu*, to cry.

GUAC, adj. Lying, false. ‡ *Hucdhel gûac*, a false story; pl. *huidhlou gawigion*. Llwyd, 243. *Gûac*, a liar. 240. A late orthography of *gowec*, qd. v.

GUAF, adj. Chaste. Corn. Voc. *castus*. Unknown elsewhere.

GUAHALECH, s. m. A peer, a satrap. Corn. Vocab. *satrapa*. This may be related either to W. *gwalch*, a hero; or *gwledig*, a prince.

GUAILEN, s. f. A rod. *Guailen ruifanaid*, Cornish Vocabulary, *sceptrum*, a sceptre. An old form of *gwelen*, qd. v. Written also *gunylen*.

GUAINTOIN, s. m. The spring. Cornish Vocabulary, *ver*. Llwyd, 170, gives *guninten*, as a later form. W. *gwanwyn*, † *guiannuin*, † *gualianuyn*, † *guayanuhin*, † *guaiannun*; the root being *gwaint*, smart, vigorous. (Cf. Eng. *quaint, wanton*.) In Armoric the spring is called *nevez-amzer*, lit. new time. In Irish and Gaelic, *earrach*, which may be compared with Gr. ἔαρ. Lat. *ver*.

GUAN, adj. Weak. Cornish Vocabulary, *debilis*. *Guan a scient*, encrguminus, possessed with a devil; lit. weak of mind or knowledge. See *Gwan*.

GUAR, s. m. The neck. Cornish Vocabulary, *collum*. See *Gwar*.

GUARAC, s. m. A charter, a patent. Cornish Vocabulary *diploma*, derived from *gwara*, to bend; and it is a literal translation of *diploma*, a doubled, or bent document. For the same reason a bow was called *guarac*. See *Gwarac*.

GUAS, s. m. A servant. Corn. Vocab. *guas bathor far*, sollers. The Latin gives the equivalent only of *far*, it should have been *nummularius servus sollers*, a clever coiner's servant. See *Gwâs*.

GWAV, s. m. Winter. A late form of *goyf*, qd. v., and is written by Llwyd, *gwâv*.

GUAYLEN, s. f. A rod. Cornish Vocabulary, *virga*. Written also *guailen*, being the older form of *gwelen*, qd. v.

GUBER, s. m. A reward, recompense, salary. ‡ *Mîr Dzhuan, medh e vester, ybma de giber*, yes John, said his master, here thy wages. Llwyd, 251. A later form of *gobyr*, qd. v.

GUBMAN, s. m. Sea tang, or wrack. Llwyd, 9, 42. A corrupt form of *gumman*, qd. v.

GUDRA, v. a. To milk. Llwyd, 17. ‡ *Buket gudra*, a milk pail. 95. ‡ *Dhort gudra an deves ha'n gover*, from milking the sheep and the goats. 240. W. *godro*. Arm. *gozro, gôrô*. Ir. *crúdh*. Cf. Sansc. *gotra*, a hurdle, or enclosure for kine; *gotrá*, a herd of kine.

GUCCY, adj. Foolish. ‡ *Henna ythew trevath brâs, ny dhe vonce mar gucky, may 'thew kellys dhyn an plas*, that is a great pity, that we should be so foolish, that the place is lost to us. C.W. 74. *Me a'n to war ow ena, gucky ythos*, I will swear it on my soul, thou art foolish. C.W. 166. This is a late form of *gocy*, qd. v.

GUDZH, s. m. Blood. Llwyd, 10, 54. ‡ *Dylla gudzh*, to let blood. 120. A late corruption of *goys*, qd. v.

GUDZHYGAN, s. f. A black pudding, a blood pudding. From the Welsh *gwaedogen*. Llwyd, 10. Arm. *gwadegen*.

GUDH, s. f. A mole. *Gûdh dhâr, gûdh dhaor*. Llwyd, 160, 241. *Pil gudhar*, a mole hill. 64. A later form of *gôdh*, qd. v.

GUDH, s. f. A goose. Llwyd, 43. A later form of *gôdh*, or *gûydh*, qd. v.

GUDHO, v. a. He may hide. A mutation of *cudho*, 3 pers. s. subj. of *cudhé*, qd. v. *Rág lŷf brâs my a dhoro, a gudho ol an nôr berys, mŷns dên ûs yn berys may fo, kyns ôs due an lŷf, budhes*, for I will bring a great flood, (that) may cover all the earth of the world, that all men that are in the world may be drowned before the end of the flood. O.M. 982.

GUEDEU, s. f. A widow. Corn. Voc. *vidua*. The later form is *gwedho*, qd. v.

GUEID, s. m. Work. Corn. Voc. *opus*. The old form of *gwŷth*, qd. v.

GUEIDVUR, s. m. A workman. *Gueidvur argans*, argentarius, a workman in silver. *Gueidvur cober*, erarius, a workman in copper. *Veidvur ti*, architectus, a builder. Corn. Vocab. Compounded of *gueid*, work, and *gour*, a man. This is the old form of *gwythor*, qd. v.

GUEIN, s. f. A sheath, a scabbard. Corn. Voc. *vagina*. The old form of *gôn*, qd. v. W. *gwain*. Arm. *gouin, gouhin*. Ir. *faigin*. Gael. *faigean*. Manx, *fine*. Lat. *vagina*. Fr. *gaine*. It. *guaina*.

GUELI, s. m. A bed. Corn. Vocab. *lectum vel lectulum*. Written also *gwely*, qd. v.

GUEN, s. f. A plain, a field. Corn. Voc. *campus*. The old form of *gwôn*, qd. v.

GUENENEN, s. f. A bee. Corn. Vocab. *apis*. Plural *guenen*. ‡ *Ma leias gwrêg lacka vel zeag, gwell gerres vel kommeres; ha ma leias bennen pokar an guenen, y vedn gueras degê tees dendle pêth an bês*, there are many wives worse than grains, better left than taken; and there are many women like the bees, they will help men to get the wealth of the world. *Pryce*. Derived from *gwané*, to sting, or pierce. W. *gwenynen*, plural, *gwenyn*. Arm. *gwenan, gwenanen*.

GUENNOL, s. f. A swallow. Corn. Voc. *hirundo*. Llwyd, 65, derives *gwennol*, as if *gwenvol*, white-belly, but *b* never changes into *n* in composition; I am more inclined to derive it from *gwen*, white, and *ol*, the rump. In late Cornish it was called ‡ *tshycuc*, i. e. house cuckoo. W. *gwennol*. Arm. *guenneli*. Ir. *ainleog*, † *fainleag*, † *fannall*. Gael. *ainleag*. Manx, *gollan-geayee*.

GUENOIN, s. m. Poison. *Guenoin reiat*, veneficus, a giver of poison, a poisoner. Corn. Voc. Llwyd, 171, writes the word *gwenwyn*. W. *gwenwyn*. Arm. *contamm*. Lat. *venenum*.

GUENUUIT, adj. Sagacious, skilful. Corn. Voc. *sagax vel gnarus*. Llwyd, 143, writes it *gwenwit*. Perhaps compounded of *gwen*, desirable, and *gwŷdh*, knowledge.

GUERET, s. m. The ground. Corn. Voc. *humus*. Llwyd, 66, *gweret*. The later form was *gwyrras*, qd. v. W. *gweryd*.

GUERN, s. m. A mast. Corn. Voc. *malus*. See *Gwern*.

GUERNEN, s. f. An alder tree. Corn. Voc. *alnus*. See *Gwernen*.

GUESBEUIN, s. m. A primate. Corn. Vocab. *primas*. Llwyd, 128, reads the word *gweshevin*.

GUEUS, s. f. The lips. Corn. Vocab. *labia*. Llwyd, 75, *gweus*. It is properly a lip. W. *gweus, gwevus*. Arm. *gnoéûz, gwez, geûz*. Ir. *pus*.

GUHIEN, s. f. A wasp. Corn. Vocab. *vespa*. This word is unknown elsewhere. The equivalent in Welsh being *cacynen*. Arm. *gwezpeden*.

GUHIT, s. f. A daughter-in-law. Corn. Vocab. *nurus*. This in later orthography would be as written by Llwyd, 101, *guhidh*. W. *gwaudh*. Arm. *gouhez*, † *guhedh*. Sansc. *vadhu*.

GUHUDHAS, v. a. To accuse. A mutation of *cuhudhas*, qd. v. *Awos travyth ny wrussen venytha dhe guhudhas*, because of any thing I would not ever accuse thee. O.M. 164.

GUIAT, s. m. A web, cloth woven. Corn. Vocab. *tela*. The old form of *gwiad*, qd. v.

GUIBEDEN, s. f. A gnat. Corn. Vocab. *scinifes*. To be read *gwibeden*, Llwyd, 96. The latest form was *gwiban*, qd. v. W. *gwibedyn*, *gwiban*, †*groydbedyn*, pl. *gwibed*.

GUICGUR, s. m. A merchant. Corn. Vocab. *mercator vel negotiator*. This is written in the Ordinalia, *gwicor*, qd. v.

GUID, s. m. A vein. Corn. Vocab. *vena*. This in later orthography was written *gwyth*, qd. v.

GUIDEN, s. f. A collar. Corn. Voc. *cutulus*. As this is an unknown Latin term, I propose reading *catulus*, a collar, which are often made of twigs. The word would therefore be cognate with W. *gwden*. Ir. *gad*, *gada*, *feith*. Gael. *gad*. Eng. *a with*. Sansc. *vêsta*, a reed.

GUIDEN, s. f. A tree. Corn. Vocab. *arbor*. The old form of *gwedhen*, qd. v.

GUIDTHIAT, s. m. A keeper. Corn. Voc. *custos*. The old form of *gwithias*, qd. v.

GUIL, s. f. A sail. Corn. Voc. *velum*. The older form of *goyl*, qd. v. W. *hwyl*, †*huil*. Arm. *gwêl*, *gwil*. Ir. *seol*, †*sool*, †*fial*. Gael. *seol*. Manx, *shiaull*. Lat. *velum*. Germ. *segel*. Eng. *sail*.

GUIL, v. a. To do, to make. A later form of *gúl*, qd. v. Written by Llwyd, 41, 251, *gwil*.

GUILAN, s. f. A kingfisher. Corn. Voc. *alcedo*. This is a wrong interpretation, as it properly means *a gull*. See *Gwilan*.

GUILLUA, s. f. A watch station. Corn. Vocab. *vigilia*. Comp. of *guilia*, the old form of *golyas*, to watch, and *va*, a place. W. *gwȇlva*.

GUILSCHIN, s. m. A frog. Corn. Voc. *rana*. Written by Llwyd, 136, *gwilskin*, who also gives *kwilken*, as a late form. Borrowed probably from the old English *wilkin*. *Wilky*, a toad or frog, is also found as an obsolete term.

GUILTER, s. m. A mastiff. Corn. Voc. *molossus*. This is probably the W. *gwylltiur*, one who frightens.

GUIN, s. m. Wine. Corn. Vocab. *vinum*. *Guinfellet*, acetum, vinegar. See *Gwin*.

GUINBREN, s. m. A vine. Corn. Vocab. *vitis*. See *Gwinbren*.

GUINS, s. m. Wind. Corn. Vocab. *ventus*. The old form of *gwyns*, qd. v.

GUIRION, adj. True. Corn. Vocab. *verax*. See *Gwirion*.

GUIRLEVERIAT, s. m. A speaker of truth. Cornish Vocabulary, *veridicus*. Comp. of *guir*, or *gwir*, true, and †*leveriat*, a speaker. So †*gouleveriat*, a teller of lies, qd. v.

GUIRT, adj. Green, flourishing. Corn. Vocab. *viridis*. This must be read *gwirdh*, as written by Llwyd, 174. The late form was *gwêr*, qd. v. W. *gwyrdh*, m., *gwerdh*, f. Arm. *gwer*. Ir. *fear*, *feur*, *fer*, †*urde*. Gael. *feur*. Lat. *viridis*. Sansc. *harit*, *hari*.

GUIS, s. f. An old sow that has had many pigs. Pryce. Corn. Voc. *scroffa*. W. *banwes*. Arm. *gwiz*, *gwêz*. Ir. *ceis*.

GUISC, s. f. Vesture, clothing, raiment. Corn. Vocab. *vestis* vel *vestimentum* vel *indumentum*. W. *gwisg*, †*guisc*. Arm. *gwisc*. Ir. *cosc*. Gr. ἐσθος, ἐσθὴς. Lat. *vestis*. Goth. *wasti*. Germ. †*wad*. Eng. *weed*. Sansc. *vastis*, fr. *vas*, to cover, to clothe. See *Gwisc*.

GUISCTI, s. m. A wardrobe. Corn. Vocab. *vestiarium*. Comp. of *guisc*, clothes, and *ti*, a house.

GUISTEL, s. m. A hostage, a pledge, surety. Cornish Vocabulary, *obses*. W. *gwystyl*. Arm. *gwestl*, †*goestl*. Ir. *gustal*, *giall*, *geal*. Gael. *gustal*, *geall*. Manx, *gioal*. Old Germ. *gisal*. Sansc. *visti*.

GUIT, s. m. Blood. Corn. Vocab. *sanguis*. This word read by Llwyd, 144, *gûyd*, is the oldest form of *goys*, qd. v. W. *gwaed*, †*gwael*. Arm. *gwâd*, *goad*, †*gwed*, †*goed*. Sansc. *vasis'tr*.

GUIT, s. f. A goose. Corn. Vocab. *auca*. *Chelioc guit*, anser, a gander. The old form of *goydh*, qd. v.

GUIT, adj. Wild, savage. In *guitfil*. W. *gwydh*, †*guid*. Arm. *gwez*, *goez*. Ir. *fiadh*. Gael. *fiadhaich*. Manx, *feie*.

GUITFIL, s. m. A wild beast. Cornish Vocab. *fera*. Comp. of *guit*, wild, and *mil*, a beast. W. *gwydhvil*.

GUL, v. a. To do, to make. *Arluth nêf, roy dhym gûl du yn pûp ober a wrellyn*, Lord of heaven give me to do well in every work that I do. O.M. 444. *My re bredyrys gûl prat, râg y wythê erbyn hâf*, I have thought of doing a thing, to keep it against summer. O.M. 467. *Gwyn y vȇs pan ve gynys a allo gûl dhys servys*, happy is he that is born that may do thee service. O.M. 1477. *Pan vynnouch agis honon, wy a gîl gûll da dhedhê*, when ye will yourselves, ye may do good to them. M.C. 37. In construction it changes into *wûl*, and *cûl*. *Ny sconnyaf yn nêp maner a wûl ol dhe voluneth*, I will not refuse in any manner to do all thy will. O.M. 1292. *Ha'y vôs gans spern curunys, ha pêb dhodho ow cûll geyll*, and that he was with thorns crowned, and every one at him scoffing. M.C. 165.

GULAN, adj. Clean, pure. *Tan, resyf dheworthyf ve, ow degê ha'm offryn gulân*, take, receive from me my tithe and my offering pure. O.M. 504. *Râg colê orth un venen, gulân of re gollas an plas*, by listening to a woman, clean he has lost the place. O.M. 920. *Ha gans towal ha lŷn gulan my a's sêch ketteb onan*, and with a towel and clean linen I will dry them every one. P.C. 836. The same word as *glân*, qd. v.

GULAT, s. f. A region, a country, one's country. Corn. Vocab. *patria*. The old form of *gwlâs*, qd. v. W. *gwlâd*. Arm. *glâd*, an estate.

GULEIT, s. m. Roast meat. Corn. Vocab. *arsura*. W. *golwyth*.

GULEN, v. a. To demand, to require. Llwyd, 124.

GULHY, v. a. To wash. Llwyd, 245. Generally written *golhy*, qd. v.

GULI, s. m. A wound. Pl. *gullyow*. Pryce. Generally written *goly*, qd. v.

GULLAN, s. f. A gull. Llwyd, 240. Pl. *gulles*. ‡ *Mi rig gwelaz an karnow idzha an gulles ha'n idnen môr aral kil y ge neitho*, I saw the rocks where the gulls and other sea birds make their nests. 245. See *Gwylan*.

GULLAS, s. m. The bottom. Pryce. Another form of *golas*, qd. v. *Trogullas*, the lower town.

GULOW, s. m. Light. ‡ *Ha po thera Dzhûan en gwilli, thera tol en tâl an tshei ; ha ev a welaz gulow*, and when John was in bed, there was a hole in the top of the house ; and he saw a light. *Llwyd*, 252. A later form of *golow*, qd. v.

GUMMAN, s. m. Sea weed, or wrack. W. *gwyman*. Arm. *goemon*. Ir. *feamuin*. Gael. *feamain*. Manx, *famlagh*. Fr. *goemon*.

GUMMYAS, s. m. Leave, permission. A mutation of *cummyas*, qd. v. *War an beys meystry, luen gummyas yma dhymmo*, power over the world, full permission there is to me. O.M. 410.

GUN, s. m. A gown. ‡ *Ha genz hedna Dzhûan genz e golhan trohaz, der an tol, méz a kein gûn an manah pis pûr round*, and with that John with his knife cut, through the hole, out of the back of the monk's gown, a piece very round. *Llwyd*, 252. W. *gŵn*. Ir. *gunna*, †*fuan*. Gael. *gún*. Manx, *goon*. Celtic, *guanacum*. Varro.

GUN, s. f. A down, or common. Pl. *guniow*. Llwyd, 15. ‡ *Keow lshoy uûn*, hedges of the field in the Down. 242. Written also *gón*, qd. v.

GUN, s. f. A scabbard. *Llwyd*, 15, 169. Another form of *gôn*, id. qd. *guein*, qd. v.

GUNDE, v. a. To crucify. *Pryce*. *Y fedh othom annedhé dhe gundé mâb dên defry, may fo rŷs un deydh a due guthyl crows annedhé y*, there will be need of them to crucify the Son of Man, truly ; that it may be necessary (on) a day that will come to make a cross out of them. O.M. 1950. This is not a Celtic word, and not to be found in the other dialects, but is borrowed from the obsolete English *gunde*, to break to pieces. (See Wright's Dictionary of Obsolete and Provincial English.)

GUNITHIAT, s. m. A labourer. *Gunithiat creu*, agricola. Corn. Vocab. This is an old word derived from a verb, identical with W. *gwncyd*, *gwneuthur*, to make. Ir. *gnithim*, +*gniu*, +*dogniu*. Gael. *gnathaich*. Manx, *jannoo*.

GUR, s. m. A man, a male, a husband. Corn. Vocab. *vir*. *Gur gans grueg* vel *freg*, maritus, a husband ; lit. a man with a wife. *Greg cans gur*, uxor, a wife ; lit. a woman with a husband. *Gur priot*, sponsus, a bridegroom. *Gur iovenc*, adolescens, a young man. In the Ordinalia it is generally written *gour*, qd. v.

GUR, s. m. An end, extremity. A mutation of *cur*, qd. v.

GURBULLOG, adj. Mad, insane. Corn. Vocab. *insanus*. Comp. of *gur*, or *guor*, over, and *pullog*, *bullog*, the adjective of *pull*, = Welsh, *pŵyll*, reason, sense. W. *gorphwyllog*.

GURCATH, s. m. A he cat, a tom cat. *Llwyd*, 241. Comp. of *gûr*, male, and *câth*, a cat. W. *gwrcath*. Arm. *targaz*.

GURCHMENNIS, s. m. A bidding, a charge, or command. *Llwyd*, 85. The same word as *gorhemynnad*, in a later form, qd. v. W. *gorchymyniad*.

GURCHUER, s. m. The evening. *Llwyd*, 172. One of the various forms of *gurthuwer*, qd. v.

GURHAL, s. m. A ship. *Lew gurhal*, a ship's rudder, *Llwyd*, 48, 97. Generally written in the Ordinalia, *gorhel*, qd. v.

GURHEMIN, s. m. A command. *Gurhemin ruif*, edictum, a king's decree. Cornish Vocabulary. Another form of *gorhemmyn*, qd. v.

GURHHOG, s. m. A great grandfather's father. Corn. Vocab. *attavus*. This word, like *hengog* and *dipog*, appears to be compounded with *cog*. The Welsh has *caw*, m., *cawes*, f., in a line of affinity descending : son or daughter of the fourth degree ; *gorchaw*, *gorchawes*, of the fifth. (Zeuss.) The Welsh equivalent of *gurhog* is *gorhendad*, and his father, *hengaw*, a great grandfather's grandfather.

GURIS, s. m. A girdle, a belt, a sash. *Pryce*. Another form of *grugis*, qd. v.

GUROW, adj. Male, of the male kind. ‡ *Della Dew a wrés dên en havalder e honnen, en havalder Dew e gwres ef, gurow ha benow ef a wrés an gy*, so God made man in his own likeness, in the likeness of God created he them ; male and female created he them. C.W. p. 192. This is a late form of *gurruid*, qd. v.

GURRA, v. a. To place, to put, to set. *Llwyd*, 68. *War an fordh dyllas a lés a ve gurris dhe ragdho*, on the road clothes abroad were placed before him. M.C. 29. *Gurris ve yn y golon yn delnia gûl*, it was put in his heart to do thus. M.C. 89. Another form of *gorré*, or *gora*, qd. v.

GURRIA, v. a. To worship, to adore. ‡ *An bobl ry urria*, the people did worship. *Llwyd*, 49. A late corruption of *gordhyé*, qd. v.

GURRUID, s. m. A male. Cornish Vocabulary, *mas* vel *masculum*. This is the old form of *gorryth*, qd. v. W. *gwrryw*, from *gwr*, male, and *rhyw*, kind. Ir. *fircan*. Gael. *firionn*. Manx, *fyrryn*.

GURTIUHER, s. m. Evening. Corn. Vocab. *vespera*. This word variously written *gorthewar*, *gathewer*, *guhuar*, *godhihuar*, occurs in the two versions of the first chapter of Genesis. It is written by Llwyd, 172. *gûrchûer*. It seems to be compounded of *gurth*, id. qd. W. *gor*, *gordh*, intense, and W. *hŵyr* or *uehcr*, evening. The Welsh has also *echwydh*, and *godechwydh*.

GURTHID, s. m. A spindle. Cornish Vocab. *gurhthit*, fusus. Llwyd, 62. writes the word *gurthyd*. W. *gwerthyd*. Arm. *gwerzid*. Ir. *fearsaid*, †*fersaid*. Gael. *fearsaid*. Cf. Lat. *verto*, *verticillus*, *versatilis*. Med. Lat. *vertebrum*, *verteolus*.

GURWEDHA, v. n. To lie down. *Llwyd*. Written also *gorwedha*, qd. v.

GURYN, s. f. A crown. A mutation of *curyn*, qd. v.

GURYN, v. a. To wring, to squeeze. *Me a'n dalhen fest yn tyn, ha gans ow dornow a'n guryn na sowennu*, I will hold him very tightly, and with my hands will squeeze him that he thrive not. P.C. 1132. Borrowed from the English.

GURYS, s. m. Glass. *Pryce*. *Ottensy purys, a's guyskens a dhesempys adro dhodho ef mar myn ; maga gwyn avel an gurys, dyeth vyé bones rcys gueth a'n par-ma dhe iaudyn*, behold it ready ; let him put it on immediately about him, if he will ; as white as the glass, it were a pity to be given a cloth of this sort to the wilful man. P.C. 1790. Llwyd, 18, gives *gweder*, qd. v., 'as the Cornish for *glass*.

GURYS, part. Made. To be read *gwrys*, qd. v.

GUS, s. m. A wood. A mutation of *cûs*, qd. v.

GUS, pr. adj. Your. An abbreviated form of *agus*, qd. v. ‡ *En metten pan a why sevel, why rez cawse dha guz tâz, ha guz damma wor aguz pedndowlin,—Bednath Dew, ha'n bednath war a vee, ne a pidge dhu Dew*, in the morning when you rise, you must say to your father, and

GUTHYL 191 GWAIL

your mother, on your knees,—The blessing of God, and a blessing upon me, I pray to God. *Pryce.*

GUSCAS, s. m. Fellows. *Pryce.* Used in late Cornish as an irregular plural of *gwâs.*

GUSCENS, v. a. They slept. A mutation of *cuscens,* 3 pers. pl. imperf. of *cuscy. Pylat a yrchys dhedhé monas dhe'n corf, ha gwythé tam na guskens,* Pilate charged them to go to the body, and be careful that they slept not a bit. M.C. 241.

GUSCYS, s. m. A covert, a shelter. *Ny won vŷth pe 'dh âf lemyn, nymbus gwesc guskys na chy, ow holan ol dhe dynmyn râg moreth a wra lerry,* I know not where I shall go now, there is not for me clothes, shelter, nor house; my heart all to pieces for grief will break. O.M. 356. W. *gwascawd, cysgod.* Arm. *gwasceed.* Ir. *fosgadh,* † *fasgad.* Gael. *fasgadh.* Manx, *fastee.*

GUSEL, v. a. To speak. A mutation of *cusel,* id. qd. *cewsel,* qd. v. *Pylat yn ta a wodhyé y dhe gusel dre envy,* Pilate well knew that they spoke through envy. M.C. 127.

GUSIGAN, s. f. A bladder. *Llwyd,* 240. W. *chwysigen.* Arm. *chouczigel.* Lat. *vesien.*

GUSTLE, v. a. To associate, to confederate. *Ena Pylat pan glewas yn delma y dhe gewsell, prederow a'n kemeras râk own y dhe leverell, ha dh'y wotyé drys an velds a ogas hag a bell, may teffé tûs gans nerth brâs er y lyn rag gustlé bell,* then Pilato when he heard them speak in this manner, thoughts seized him for fear they should tell, and publish it through the country near and far off, so that men should come with great strength against him to confederate long. M.C. 249. W. *gwystlo,* to pledge : *cysgylltu,* to join.

GUSTYTH, adj. Obedient, subject. *Y rôf hynwyn dhe'n puskes, porpos, sowmens, syllycs, ol dhym gustyth y a vŷdh,* I give names to the fishes, porpoises, salmons, congers, all to me obedient they shall be. O.M. 137. *Rag ty dhe gola worty, ha colle dhe bryes len, nefré gustyth dh'y gorty me a orden bûs benen,* because thou hast hearkened to her, and deceived thy faithful spouse, ever obedient to her husband I ordain woman to be. O.M. 295. Written also *gostyth,* qd. v.

GUSYL, s. f. Counsel, advice. A mutation of *cusyl,* qd. v. *A vroder ow banneth dhys, râg dhe gusyl yw pûr dha,* O brother, my blessing on thee, for thy counsel is very good. O.M. 1828. *Un gusyl da ha perfeyth dhym ty a rôs,* a counsel good and perfect to me thou hast given. R.D. 2142.

GUTHEL, s. m. Furniture. Corn. Voc. *supellex.* Read by Llwyd, 151, *gwadhel.* This is the Welsh *gwadhol,* a dower, or portion given with a wife upon marriage, and of which household furniture was an important part. Arm. *argoulou.*

GUTHOT, s. m. Corn. Corn. Vocab. *fer,* i. e. *far.* The last syllable is probably the same as *yd,* corn, qd. v.

GUTHYL, v. a. To do, to make. *Yn medhens, mar omwrcyth clâff, gordhewyth te a'n prenvyth, awos guthyl wheyl mar scaff yn cthom dhyn mar fyllyth ; y worthebys ne vannaff aga guthyl, war ow fŷdh,* say they if thou feignest thyself ill, assuredly thou shalt catch it, in respect of doing a work so light in need to us if thou wilt fail; he answered, I will not make them on my faith. M.C. 155. *Dûs yn râk, yma dhym toul guthyl may fe dhe wôs yeyn,* come forth, I have a tool that will make thy blood cool. P.C. 1622. In construction it changes into *cuthyl* and *wuthyl. Dhe Ihesus Cryst betegyns ow cuthyl drôk ha belyny,* to Jesus Christ nevertheless doing hurt and villainy. M.C. 96. *An Edhewon ny wodhyé an prennyer py fêns keffis dhe wuthyl crows ancdhé,* the Jews knew not the sticks where they would be found to make a cross of them. M.C. 151.

GUUER, s. m. A brook. Corn. Voc. *rivus.* An old form of *gover,* qd. v.

GUW, s. m. A spear, a lance, a javelin. *Kerchyn Longys, an gwâs dal, gans guw dhe wané an gal yn y golon,* let us fetch Longius, the blind fellow, to pierce the villain with a spear in his heart. P.C. 2917. *Pan fo guw yn y dhulé,* when there is a spear in his hands. P.C. 2922. *Pan wylys vy y wané dre an golon gans an guw,* when I saw him pierced through the heart with the spear. R.D. 432. The same word as *gew,* qd. v.

GUYDH, s. f. A goose. *Llwyd,* 43, 241. This is the sound of the old form *guit,* as written in the Cornish Vocabulary, qd. v. *Celiog glûydh,* a gander. See *Goydh.*

GUYLYS, s. m. Liquorice. Corn. Voc. *libestica.* Written also *gwules,* qd. v.

GUYN, adj. White. Corn. Voc. *albus.* See *Gwyn.*

GUYRAF, s. m. Corn. Vocab. *fenum.* The old form of *gorra,* qd. v., which is found in the Ordinalia. W. *gwair.* Ir. *fewr,* † *fer.* Gael. *feur.* Manx, *faiyr.* Gr. φορβή. Lat. *herba.* Sanse. *harit,* verdure.

GUYS, s. f. An old sow that has had pigs, more than once. *Llwyd,* 146, 211. See *Guis.*

GWADN, adj. Weak. *Llwyd,* 76. A late corruption of *gwan,* qd. v.

GWADNGYRTI, s. f. A concubine. *Llwyd,* 252.

GWADHEL, s. m. Furniture, household stuff. *Llwyd,* 158. See *Guthel.*

GWAE, s. m. Woe, grief, misery. *Pryce.* The form found in the Ordinalia is *gu,* qd. v. W. *gwae.*

GWAETH, adj. Worse. *Llwyd,* 243. More generally written *gwêth,* qd. v.

GWAG, adj. Empty, hungry, vain, void, vacant, at leisure. *Ny wodhen râg ponvotter, py 'dh cen yn gwcel py yn côs ; ow holon gwâk dyvotter, rum kymmer hag awel bûs,* we know not, for trouble, whether we shall go into a field, or into a wood ; my heart is become empty, and desire of food has seized me. O.M. 365. *Lemyn dyfreth ôf, ha gwâk, pûr wŷr dres ol tûs an beys,* now wretched I am, and empty, very truly above all men of the world. O.M. 593. ‡ *Ha 'thera an noar heb roath ha gwâg,* and the earth was without form and void. C.W. p. 189. ‡ *Rag an Arleth na vedn sindzhy e dipeh, nêb es komeres e hanno en gwâg,* for the Lord will not hold him sinless, who taketh his name in vain. *Pryce. Gwâg,* at leisure, having nothing to do. *Llwyd,* 19. W. *gwâg.* Arm. *gulâg.* Ir. † *guag,* † *cuacca,* † *coca.* Gael. *caoch, fas.* Lat. *vacuus.*

GWAG, s. m. A void, a vacuum ; hunger. *Llwyd,* 57. Pl. *gwagion,* caves, cells, graves. "When the tinners hole into a piece of ground, which has been wrought before, though filled up again, they call it *holing in gwâg.*" *Pryce.* W. *gwâg.*

GWAIL, s. m. Stalks. *Awos henna ny wraf vry, na anothans y bŷs voy me ny scttyaf gwail gala,* of that I will make no account, nor of them ever more will I set the stalks of straw. C.W. 98. This is the plural of *gwailen*, which is generally written *gwelen*, qd. v.

GWAITH, s. m. A work, a deed. *Llwyd*, 108. Written also *gwýth*, qd. v.

GWAL, s. m. A wall. It is preserved in *Tregwal*, in Sennan, the walled Town. *Pryce.* W. *gwal, gwawl.* Ir. *fal, bala.* Gael. *bala.* Manx, *balla, boal, boalley, vawl, voalley.* Gr. cΛap. Lat. *vallum, vallus.* Lith. *wolus.* Germ. *wall.* Russ. *wal.* Eng. *wall.* Fr. *val.* Sansc. *valan, vallas*, fr. *val*, to cover, to maintain.

GWALIIT, s. m. The hair of the head, a bush of hair. *Pryce.* This is rather a Welsh word, but the old form *gols*, qd. v. is preserved in the Cornish Vocabulary. *Blew* was generally used in Cornwall, as *blew an pen*, the hair of the head.

GWAN, adj. Weak, feeble, infirm, poor. *Arté Iudas ow trylé gwan wecor ny'n gevé pâr, ny ĝl dên vŷth amontyé mĝns a gollas yn chyffar*, again Judas turning, a weak trader, obtained not an equivalent; not any man can compute all (that) he lost in the bargain. M.C. 40. *Galsof coyth ha marthys gwan, dynythys ew ow deweydh*, I am become old, and wondrous weak; my end is arrived. O.M. 855. *Yn crês an chy rês vyé kafus gyst crêf na vo gwan*, in the midst of the house it would be necessary to have a strong beam, that it be not weak. O.M. 2482. *Why a'n gwylvyth yn yer worth agas yuggé, ol tûs an brys, crêf ha gwan, ye shall see him in the sky judging you, all the men of the world, strong and weak, P.C. 1334. *Pan welaf ow nûb mur wan, ow town kemys velyny*, when I see my son so weak, bearing so much abuse. M.C. 100. W. *gwan*. Arm. *gwan*. Ir. *fann*. Gael. *fann*. Lat. *vanus*. Gr. εὖνις. Goth. *wans*. Germ. *wahn*. Lith. *wienas*. Eng. *wan*. Sansc. *vanda*.

GWAN, s. f. A going through, or penetrating, a thrust, a stab, a prick; a sting. *Llwyd*, 41, 154, *gwân*. W. *gwân*.

GWANAN, s. f. A bee. Pl. *gwenyn*. *Llwyd*, 13, 15, 53. *Cawal gwanan*, a bee hive. A later form of *gwencnen*, or *guenenen*, qd. v.

GWANDER, s. m. Weakness, infirmity, debility. *Râg gwander war ben dowlyn hy a'n gwelas ow codhé*, for weakness on his knees she saw him falling. M.C. 171. *Râg dhodho ef na ylly dôn an grows râg gwander*, for he could not bear the cross on him for weakness. M.C. 173. *Râg gwander ef re codhas*, for weakness he has fallen. P.C. 2618. W. *gwander*. Arm. *gwander*.

GWANDRE, v. a. To wander, to walk about. *Dên yonk whêk, gwandré a wrêth, me a'th pŷs, pyno a whylyth, dhymo lavar*, sweet young man, thou art walking about, I pray thee, whom seekest thou, tell me. R.D. 1639. *Me a'th pŷs, ke aberth yn pow dhe wandré un pols byan*, I pray thee, go within the country, to walk a little while. R.D. 1634. *Sterran gwandré*, a planet, lit. a wandering star. *Llwyd*, 121. Borrowed from the English.

GWANE, v. a. To thrust, to penetrate, to pierce, to stab, to stick. Imp. *gwân*. Part. *gwaneys, gwenys, gwynys*. *Gew a ve yn y dhiwlé gans an Edhewon gorris, ha pen lyn râg y wané dhe golon Thesus hynwys*, a spear was placed in his hands by the Jews, and a sharp end to pierce him to the heart of the mild Jesus. M.C. 217. *Dhe'n marreg worth y hanow y a yrchys may whané*, to the soldier by his name they commanded that he should pierce. M.C. 218. *Yn pren crows bedhens gorrys, ha dyulef kelmys, ha gwenys dre an golon*, on the cross tree let him be put, and feet and hands bound, and pierced through his heart. P.C. 2376. *Kerchyn Longys an gwâs dal gans guw dhe wané an gal yn y golon*, let us fetch Longius, the blind fellow, to pierce the villain with a spear in his heart. P.C. 2917. *Gans gu lym y a'n gwanas, dre un golon may resas*, with a sharp spear they pierced him, so that it passed through the heart. R.D. 1117. *Gans nader ythof guanheys*, I am stung by a snake. O.M. 1756. *Doro dhe luef yn woly guynys may fueff dre an golon*, put thy hand in the wound where I was pierced through the heart. R.D. 1540. In later Cornish the infinitive was written *gwana*. *Dho gwana tardha*, to bore through. *Llwyd*, 117. W. *gwanu*. Arm. *gwana*. Ir. *guin*. Gael. *guin*. Sansc. *vâna*.

GWANETH, s. m. Wheat. *Cayn, dhe chardge ge a vŷdh war kerch, barlys, ha gwaneth, dhe wethyll an dega lcal*, Cain, thy charge shall be over oats, barley, and wheat, to make the true tithe. C.W. 78. *Bara gwaneth*, wheaten bread. W. *gwenith*; compounded of *gwen*, white, and *ith*, id. qd. *ŷd*, corn. Arm. *gwiniz*. (Ir. *cruithncachd*. Gael. *cruincachd*. Manx, *cornacht*.) The colour has given the name in other languages. White is in Sansc. *sweta*. Goth. *hveit*. O. H. Germ. *huiz, wiz*. Ang. Sax. *hvít*. Lith. *kwetys*. Hence we find *wheat* called in Goth. *hvaitei*. Lith. *kwecio*. Cf. also Slav. *shito*, and Gr. σῖτον.

GWAR, s. f. The neck. Corn. Voc. *collum*. In Welsh *gwar* is the nape of the neck, which was called in Cornish *pol kil*, and in Armoric, *choug ar chil*.

GWARA, s. m. Wares, merchandize. *Yn chy Dew mars ues marchas, me a's chas yn mês pûp gwâs, hag a tevyl aga gwara*, if there is a market in God's house, I will drive them out, every fellow, and overturn their wares. P.C. 318. Borrowed from the English.

GWARAC, s. m. That which is bent, a bow. *My ny dorraf bŷs vycken an acord ûs lemyn gureys yntré my ha lynneth dên, bŷs vynytha ef a veys: yn record yw token len, ow gwarak a fŷdh scityys yn ban yn creys an ebren, na allo bones terrys*, I will not break for ever the agreement that is now made between me and the race of man; for ever it shall be: in record my bow is a faithful sign, that shall be set up in the midst of the sky, that it may not be broken. O.M. 1244. This is the same word as *guarac*. (The root is *gwar*, generally written in Welsh *gŵyr*, bending. Arm. *gŵâr, gour*.) W. *gwarog, gwarcy, gwary*. Arm. *gwarek, gonrek*.

GWARDY, s. m. A playhouse, a theatre, a scene. *Llwyd*, 163. Comp. of *gwaré*, a play, and *ty*, a house. W. *chwarendy*.

GWARE, s. m. A play, a dramatic exhibition, a comedy; sport, pastime, game. Written also *gwary*. Pl. *gwariow*. *Ef a wra ow shyndyé, mar clew vŷth agan gwary*, he will hurt me, if he shall hear of our sport. O.M. 2134. *An gwary yw dúc lynmyn*, the play is now ended. O.M. 2830. *Rum fey henna yw gwary da*, on my faith that is good game. P.C. 1375. *Dûn yn râk gans an gwary*, let us come on with the play. P.C. 1388. *Ens pôp ol war tuhé tre, an gwary yw dywydhys*, let all go home, the play is ended. P.C. 3238. *Kettel dhueth er agan pyn, ny gen bo whans gwariow*, when he came to meet us, we had no want of pastimes. R.D. 1330. "*Gwary-mcers* signify "great plays;" by this name the rounds, or amphitheatres, wherein these Interludes wore represented, are called *Westward;* but the right name of these Interludes is *Gwaré-mirkl*, a miracle play." *Pryce.* W. *gware, chwareu.* Arm. *choari.* Ir. *gair, gaire,* joy, laughter. Gael. *gaire.*

GWARE, v. a.   To play, to act in a play, to perform a comedy. Written also *gwary*. Part. *gwaryes*. *Dho gwaré*, to play. *Lhwyd*, 82. *An kéth jorna-ma ew dédh, dhe'n Tâs Dew re bo grassyes, why a wellas lean matters gwarryes, ha Creation oll an bŷs,* this same day is a day, to God the Father be thanks, (that) ye have seen many matters acted, and the Creation of the whole world. C.W. 184. *Gwarê peliow*, to play at bowls. *Pryce.* W. *gware, chwareu.* Arm. *choari.*

GWARNYA, v. a. To warn, to give notice to, to caution. Part. *gwarnyys, gwarnys*. *Del rebechsé, ow nacha Du leun a râs, hag cf gwarnyys del vyé,* so he had sinned in denying God, full of grace, as he had been warned. M.C. 86. *Cryst worth an goyn a warnyas, dre onan bôs treson guris,* Christ at the supper gave notice that treachery was done by one. M.C. 42. *Te a wodhyé dhe honon, pe dre gen ré vés gwarnys,* thou knewest thyself, or by some others thou wast warned. M.C. 101. *Me a dhue dh'agas gwarnyé,* I will come to warn you. P.C. 606. *Mc a's gwarnyas,* I have warned you. P.C. 757. *Mar ny'n guarnyaf scon wharré,* if I will not warn him soon. P.C. 1968. *Me a's gwarn, youynk ha hên,* I warn ye, young and old. P.C. 2031. *My a wra dhe worhemmyn, hag a warn dhe wysterdens,* I will do thy command, and will warn the architects. O.M. 2416. From the English.

GWARHAS, s. m. The top or summit. *Guarhas ganow,* the palate, lit. the top of the mouth. *Lhwyd,* 111. A late form of *gwartha*, qd. v.

GWARRA, adj. Higher. *Gueal Gwarra,* the higher field, in Lambourne. *Pryce.*

GWARRHOG, s. m. Cattle of all kinds. *Lhwyd,* 115. A corrupt form of *gwarthec,* qd. v.

GWARROE, v. a. To cover. *Pryce.* W. *gwarthu.*

GWARTH, adj. High. Comp. *gwarthah*. Sup. *gwartha*. *Pryce.* W. *gwarth.*

GWARTHA, s. m. The top, or summit. *My a vyn lemyn tyldyé gwartha an gorhyl gans gueth, ha henna a ra greythé na dheffo glaw aberredh,* I will now cover the top of the ark with a cloth, and this will keep that the rain may not come in. O.M. 1074. *A vyne gwarthé y ben war y gorf bŷs yn y droys, squardyys oll o y grohen, hag cf cudhys yn y woys,* from the very top of his head on his body to his feet, torn was all his skin, and he hidden in his blood. M.C. 135. *A wartha,* from above, qd. v. W. *gwarthav,* †*gwartha.* Arm. *gorré.*

GWARTHEC, s. m. Cattle of all kinds, horned cattle. *Dûn aberredh desempys; agan gorhyl a wartha gans glaw ef a vŷdh cudhys; merch, guarthec, môch ha deves, dreuch aberredh desempys,* let us come in immediately; our ark from above, with rain it will be covered; horses, cattle, pigs, and sheep, bring ye within forthwith. O.M. 1063. W. *gwartheg.* Ir. *ccathra.* Gael. †*ccathra.* Dr. Owen Pughe, in his Dictionary, derives it from *gwarth,* high, and defines it to be "what serves to cover, to make equivalent; a medium of exchange or traffic; and cattle being that medium amongst the Britons, the term came to imply the animals themselves in the aggregate."

2 D

GWAS, s. m. A youth, a servant, one of the common people, a mean person, a fellow, a rogue, a rascal. Pl. *gwesyon,* or *gwesion.* Lhwyd, 242. *Kyrchouch dhe drê an guâs, may hallo cané ellas, nefré yn tewolgow tew,* bring ye home the fellow, that he may sing 'alas' ever in thick darkness. O.M. 544. *Venytha ny dhôf a'n plen er na'n prenné an guâs-na,* never will I come from the place until that fellow catches it. O.M. 2152. *Deuch yn râg yn kettep guâs,* come forward, every fellow. P.C. 1350. *Máp an guâs gôf,* son of the smith fellow. P.C. 2479. *Ef o harlot, tebel wâs, worewth lader vyé,* he was a vile man, a wicked fellow, at last a thief he was. M.C. 38. *Arrow lour dhynny yma, ha gwesyon stout yn torma, a'n caché uskys,* arms enough to us there are, and stout fellows at this time, that will catch him quickly. P.C. 616. W. *gwâs,* †*guas;* pl. *gweision,* †*gweisson.* Arm. *gwaz,* †*goas.* Ir. *gas.* Mod. Lat. *vasus, vassalus, vassallus.*

GWASAÑAETH, s. m. Attendance, service, bondage, slavery. *Ythové an Arluth de Dew, néb a's drôs dhe vés a'n tŷr Mizraim, dhe vés a'n chy gwasanaeth,* I am the Lord thy God, who brought thee out of the land of Egypt, out of the house of bondage. *Pryce.* W. *gwasanaeth.* Arm. *gwazoniez,* †*goazonies.*

GWAYAH, v. a. To move, to crawl, to creep. *Ha'thera an noar hep compoester, ha gwâg, ha tewlder war bedgeth an downder, ha Sperys Dew rig gwayah war bedgeth an dowrow,* and the earth was without form and void, and darkness on the face of the deep, and the Spirit of God did move on the face of the waters. C.W. p. 189. *Ha Dew lavaras, gweréns an dowrow, dry râg por mear an tacklow gwayah es tôn bewnas,* and God said let the waters bring forth abundantly the moving creatures that bear life. 191. *Ha Dew rig gwercy an puskas brâs, ha kenefra tra bew és a gwayah,* and God made great fishes, and every thing living that moveth. 191. W. *chwyvo, chwimio.* Arm. *finca.*

GWAYN, s. m. Gain, advantage. *May caffons y agn gweayn war Ihesus Cryst dh'y ladhé,* that they might find their advantage over Jesus Christ to kill him. M.C. 114. Borrowed from the Old French, *guain.* It. *guadagno.*

GWAYNIA, v. a. To gain, to procure. *Gwra, O malcyrn, an tacklow-na gen an gwella krender el bôs predrys an marthusyon aga termen, ha'n tacklow a vyn gwaynia klôs dhys râg newra,* do, O king, those things which with the best strength may be thought the wonders of their time, and the things will gain glory to thee for ever. *Pryce.*

GWAYTHE, v. a. To work, to labour. Another form of *gwethel,* or *guthyl,* qd. v. W. *gweithio.*

GWAYTHY, v. a. To make worse, to worst, to damage, to break, to destroy. Derived from *gwayth,* id. qd. *gwéth,* worse. The verbal form is *fethy,* qd. v. W. *gwaethu.*

GWAYW, s. m. A spear, a lance, a javelin. *Hoch-wayu,* venabulum, a hog-spear. Corn. Voc. This is the old form of *gêw,* or *gu,* qd. v. W. *gwaew.*

GWEADER, s. m. A weaver. *Lhwyd,* 13, 240. ‡ *Why lader gwender, lavarro' gâs pader, ha ro man do higa an cáth,* you thief of a weaver, say your prayer, and give up to play the cat. *Pryce.* From *gweia,* to weave, qd. v. W. *gwcadur, gwcawdyr.* Arm. *gwccr.* Ir. *fighcadoir.* Gael. *fighcadair.* Manx, *fidder.*

GWEAL, s. m. A field. *An bestes, ha'n ohan, ha'n dewidgyow oll yn gweall,* the beasts and the oxen, and all the sheep in the field. C.W. 78. The same word as *gwél*, qd. v.

GWEAL, v. a. He shall see. *Dew vâb yma dhym genys, tevys ydhyns dha denes; why oll a's gweall*, two sons there are to me born, and they are grown to men; you all see them. C.W. 78. *Gans dhe lagasow a lês, ty a weall pûb tra omma*, with thy eyes abroad thou wilt see every thing here. C.W. 52. A later mode of writing *gwél*, 3 pers. s. fut. of *gweles*, qd. v.

GWEDEN, adj. Weak. *Pryce.* A late corruption of *gwan*.

GWEDER, s. m. Glass. *Llwyd*, 18, 175. W. *gwydyr*. Arm. *gwezr, gwer*. Lat. *vitrum*.

GWEDNHOGIAN, s. f. A wart. *Llwyd*, 172. A corrupt form of *gwennogen*. Arm. *gwennaen, gwenanen*. W. *gwenan*, a blister under the skin.

GWEDRAN, s. m. A glass to drink with. *Gwedran a vein*, a glass of wine. *Llwyd*, 242. W. *gwydryn*. Arm. *gweren*.

GWEDII, s. m. Trees. This is a plural aggregate, and is written also *gwcydh*, and *gwydh*. *A lena y'n hombronkyas uchel war ben un menedh, ha dhodho y tysquedhas our, hag archans, gwels, ha gwêdh*, from thence he led him high on top of a mountain, and to him he shewed gold, and silver, grass and trees. M.C. 16. *Hag yn tŷr gorhemmennaf may tefo gwcydh ha losow*, and in the land I command that trees and plants grow. O.M. 28. (W. *gwŷdh*, †*guid*. Arm. *gwez*.) Written in the Cornish Vocabulary, *guit*, (see *Luworch-guit*,) which is the old form of *gwydh*, qd. v.

GWEDH, s. f. A form, shape, fashion. It is only found in the compound *ynwedh*, also, (qd. v.) which is the same as the W. *un wêdh*, of the same form. W. *gwêdh*. Arm. *giz, kiz*. Ir. *caidh, aidhe*, †*fuad*. Manx, *kiadd*. Gr. εἶδος. Lat. *visus*. Lith. *weidas*. Russ. *wid*. Sansc. *vidhas*, fr. *vidh*, to distinguish.

GWEDHEN, s. f. A tree. Plural *gwêdh, gwcydh*. *Pûp gwedhen tefyns a'y sâf, ow tôn hy frût, ha'y delyow*, let every tree grow from its stem, bearing its fruit and its leaves. O.M. 29. *Warnedhy yma gwedhen, whel gans lues scoren, sow nôth ol ŷns hep dylyow*, on it there is a tree, high with many boughs, but they are all bare without leaves. O.M. 775. *Mŷr gwell orth an wedhen; mŷr pandra wylly ynny, kefrys gwrydhyow, ha scoren*, look better at the tree; look, what thou canst see in it, besides roots and branches. O.M. 800. In Llwyd's time it was written *gwedhan*. ‡ *Gwedhan lavalow*, an apple tree. 10. ‡ *Gwedhan cnyfan*, a hazel tree. 51. W. *gwydhen*. Arm. *gwezen*.

GWEDHIO, adj. Deprived, destitute, widowed, solitary. *Gûr gwedho*, a widower. *Gwrêg wedho*, a widow. *Llwyd*, 174, 241. Written in Cornish Vocabulary, *guedeu*, qd. v. W. *gwedhw*. Arm. *goullô*. Ir. *feab*, †*fedhb*. Slav. *wedowa*. Gr. ἤθεος. Lat. *viduus*. Sansc. *vidhas*, fr. *vidh*, to separate. Cf. also Sansc. *vidhavâ*, a widow, fr. *vi*, without, and *dhava*, a husband.

GWEDHRA, v. n. To wither. Part. *gwedrys*. Llwyd, 43, 60. This form is borrowed from the English. W. *gwidh*, withered.

GWEEL, s. m. Rods. A plural aggregate. Written also *gwêl*, whence s. *gwelen*, a single rod. *Ef a yrhys dhym kyrhas a mount Tabor gweel a rûs*, he ordered me to fetch from mount Tabor the rods of grace. O.M. 1957. *Arluth kêr, dhymmo gweeres gans dhe weel yn nêp maner*, dear Lord, help me with thy rods in some way. O.M. 2006. *My a grŷs yn pyrfeth aga vos gweel a vûr rûs*, I will believe perfectly that the yare rods of great grace. O.M. 2012. W. *gwiail*. Arm. *gwial*. Gael. *faill*.

GWEF, interj. Woe to him. *Ha Ihesus a worthebys, a'n scudel diblry a wra, gwef vŷth pan veva genys a dor y vam dh'en bŷs-ma*, and Jesus answered, he that eats from my dish, woe to him that ever he was born from his mother's womb to this world. M.C. 43. Another form of *goef*, qd. v. In later times we find it used for *govy*. ‡ *Ethlays, gwef pan vevé genys, ow terry gormenadow Dew*, alas, woe to me that I was born, breaking the commandments of God. C.W. 76.

GWEFF, adj. Worthy, deserving. *A ow cows why a'n clewas, leverouch mar pŷth savvys; ol warbarth y n armas, gweff yw dhe vonas ledhys*, ye heard him speaking, say if he shall be saved; altogether they cried out, he is deserving to be killed. M.C. 95. A various form of *gwyw*, qd. v.

GWEITHIUR, s. m. A workman. This is Llwyd's reading, 41, of *gueiduur*, qd. v.

GWEL, s. m. A sight, a vision. *Arluth Ihesu, ro dhym an grâs par may feyf gwyw, dhe gafos spas gynes hydhuw yn nêp pids, may bomê vu, ha gwêl a'th fâs*, Lord Jesus, give me the grace, as I may be worthy to find occasion, with thee to-day, in some place, that I may have a view and sight of thy face. R.D. 842. *Ny berraf gwêl ahanas*, I will not bear the sight of thee. C.W. 88. *Mr a wolch scon ow dulê, a wêl dheuch kettep onan*, I will wash immediately my hands in the sight of every one of you. P.C. 2500. *Dhymmo vy mar ny gressouch, ottengy a wêl ol dheuch, kepar ha del leverys*, if ye will not believe me, behold them in the sight of you all, just as I said. P.C. 2689. W. *gwêl*. Arm. *gwêl*.

GWEL, s. m. Rods. Plural aggregate, whence *gwelen*, a rod. Written also *gweel*, qd. v. *Otté an gwêl dheragon, glâs ow tevy*, see the rods before us, growing green. O.M. 1984. *An rê-ma yw gwêl a rûs*, these are rods of grace. O.M. 1995.

GWEL, s. m. A field. *Tŷr sêch yn gwêl nag yn prâs nar kefyth yn gwŷr hep gow, yno gweet in-ta whelas bôs dhe'th ly ha dhe'th kynyow*, dry land in field or meadow if truly thou wilt find without deceit, in it take good care to seek food for thy breakfast, and for thy dinner. O.M. 1137. *Nyns ûs yn gwêl nag yn prâs tûs veve, saw uy, my a greys*, there are not in field nor in meadow men living, except us, I believe. O.M. 1151. *Râg may feuchevy sostoneys, euch dhe wonys gwêl ha lôn*, that ye may be maintained, go to till field and plain. O.M. 1164.

GWELAS, s. m. A sight, a vision, or seeing. *Llwyd*, 175. W. *gwelad, gweled*.

GWELDZHOW, s. m. A pair of shears. *Llwyd*, 243. W. *gwellaiv*, † *guillihim*. (Oxf. Gloss.) Arm. *gwcltré, gwcntlé*, †*gwcltlé*. Sansc. *vil*, to cut, to divide. Gr. ὀλλύω, †ἐλω. Lat. *vello*. Goth. *vilva*.

GWELEN, s. f. A rod, a yard, a man's yard. Written also *gwelan*, pl. *gwêl* or *gweel*, and *gwelynny*. *Yn y lêff dhychow yn wêdh gwelen wyn a ve gorris*, in his right hand also a white rod was put. M.C. 136. *Onon, gans an kêth welen yn lyff Cryst a ve gorrys, a'n gwyskys lasche war an pen*, one with the same rod in the hand of Christ (that) was put, struck him a lash on the head.

GWELES 195 GWELVAN

M.C. 138. *Gwelen a pren a wrâf synsy*, a rod of wood I will hold. O.M. 1444. *Yn hanow Dew, ty mór glán, me a'th refsek gans ow gwelan*, in the name of God, thou fair son, I strike thee with my rod. O.M. 1676. *My a wél tyyr gwelen*, I see three rods. O.M. 1729. *Beneges re bo an Tás a vynnas dysquedhes dhyn gwelynny a gemmys rás*, blessed be the Father (that) would shew to us rods of so much grace. O.M. 1747. *Am lemyn dhe'n gwellynny, a barth an Tás veneges*, kiss now the rods, on the part of the blessed Father. O.M. 1791. *Gwelan* means also a yard measure. (So Welsh *llath*, a rod, a yard.) *Gwelan gól*, the sail yard. *Lhwyd*, 3. W. *gwialen*. Arm. *gwalen*.

GWELES, v. a. To see, to behold, to look upon. Written also *gwelas*. 3 pers. sing. fut. *gwél*. Part. *gwelys*. *Ellas gwelcs an termyn, ow Arluth pan wrûk serry*, alas, to see the time, when my Lord was offended. O.M. 351. *My â dhe'n yet desempys, may callaf gweles ken ta*, I will go to the gate immediately, that 1 may see further good. O.M. 794. *Cannas ôs, hep danger, nyns ûs font ynnos gwelys*, thou art a messenger, without delay, there is not a fault in thee soon. O.M. 2293. *Na nŷl oges nag yn pel, ny's gwelaf ow trenygé*, neither near nor far, I see her not flying over. O.M. 1142. *Pan welaf ow máb mar wan*, when I see my son so weak. M.C. 166. *Ny fŷf dén dhodho bythqueth, na ny wylys kyns lymman y lyn*, I was never a man to him, nor have I seen before now his form. P.C. 1239. *Mar a's gwél, cf a wra môs dhe cudhé*, if he sees you, he will go to hide. P.C. 1003. *Mar ethuk yw dhe weles, may tyglyn an tebeles, pan y'n gwellons kettep pen*, so horrid it is to see, that the devils will wince, when they see it every head. P.C. 3046. *Fynytha hedré vyncy, unma ny'm gwelyth arté*, ever whilst thou livest, here thou shalt not see me again. O.M. 244. *A'n gwelesta a dhyragos, a alsesta y ascnfos*, if thou shouldst see him before thee, couldst thou know him. R.D. 861. *Warbarth ol del y'n gwelayn dhyragon ow cows worthyn*, all together as we have seen him before us speaking to us. R.D. 1210. *Hydhew, a tryckes yn tré, dhyragos ty a'n gwelsé*, to-day, if thou hadst staid at home, before thee thou wouldst have seen him. R.D. 1382. *Ha kekenmys a'n gwello, hag ynno cf a grysso, bós yaches dhodho yw reys*, and whoever sees it, and believes in him, need is to him that he be healed. R.D. 1706. *Ef pan welas tan na ylly y dolla*, when he saw that he could not deceive him a jot. M.C. 13. *Y hwalsons oll a dro mar caffons gúf yredy, onan y welsons eno*, they searched all about if they could find a smith readily, one they saw there. M.C. 154. *Pu yw néb a welcuch wy*, who is he whom ye see? M.C. 69. *Dh'y your hy a dhunvonas a Cryst kepar del welsé*, to her husband she sent of Christ as she had seen. M.C. 123. *A na wylta ol mŷns ês orth dhe vlamyé, seost thou not all that are blaming thee?* M.C. 120. *Ow trvones wy a'm gwylwyth heb nêb mar*, ye shall see me coming without any doubt. M.C. 93. *Yn aga herwydh ydh esé un marreg, Longis hynryg, dall o, ny wely banna*, in their company there was a soldier, named Longius, blind he was, he saw not a glimpse. M.C. 217. *Dall én, ny welyn yn fâs, ow bôs mar wyl ow pewé*, I was blind, I saw not well, that 1 was living so vile. M.C. 220. *Ihesus Cryst, del welsouch, a ve ledhys*, Jesus Christ, as ye saw, was killed. M.C. 255. *Own múr a's kemeras râg an marthus re welsens*,

great fear seized them for the miracle they saw. M.C. 254. *Me a lever dheuch deffry, pyw penag a'm gwellha vy, cf a wylfyth ow Thás*, 1 tell you truly, whoever shall see me, he will see my Father. R.D. 2385. *Pûr wŷr y tue vyngeans tyn warnouch, man gweller a ver termyn*, very truly sharp vengeance will come upon you, as will be seen in a short time. P.C. 1040, 1963, 2200. Welsh, *gweled*. Arm. *gwelet*. Sansc. *vlôks*. Old Irish, † *fell*, whence † *fili*, a seer, a prophet, a poet. Mod. Ir. *file*. Gael. *file, filidh*. W. *gweledydh*.

GWELHE, v. a. To shew. *Pandra yw henna dhyso; gwelhé ny yllyth dhymno pûr wŷr hep mar*, what is that to thee? thou art not able to shew him to me very truly without doubt. R.D. 1643. W. *gwylchu*, to appear.

GWELL, adj. Better. The irregular comparative of *da*, or *más*. Superl. *gwella*. *Bedhens gwerthys, ha bôs den rág y rané dhe wohosogyon yn bŷs, gwell vya ys y seolyé*, let it be sold, and be for us to distribute it to the poor in the world, it would be better than to spill it. M.C. 36. *Râg gwell deves vyttetth wŷn nyns â yn agas ganow; yn pow-ma nyns ûs gwell gwŷn*, for any better drink of wine will not go into your mouth; in this country there is no better wine. O.M. 1912. *Dén yn bŷs-ma ny'n musyr gwell*, no man in this world will measure it better. O.M. 2514. *Gwel yw dhyn dôn*, it is better for us to bring. P.C. 2298. W. *gwell*. Arm. *gwell*. Cf. also Gr. οὖλων. Lat. *valens, validus*. Goth. *waila*. Russ. *vclu*. Germ. *wohl*. Eng. *well*. Sansc. *valitas*, from *val*, to uphold.

GWELLA, adj. The irregular superlative of *da*, or *más*. *Dre weres agan Dew ny, a néf an Arluth gwella*, by the help of our God, the best Lord of heaven. O.M. 536. *Doro dhym an gwŷn gwella*, bring me the best wine. O.M. 1094. *Urry ow marrck gwella, my a vynsa dhe pysy*, Uriah, my best soldier, I would pray thee. O.M. 2139. Arm. *gwella*. In Welsh it is not used, *gorau* being the term employed.

GWELLA, v. a. To make better, to mend, to improve. *Gordhyans dhys ha lowené! dhe Dás kér a crehys gwella dhe chér*, worship to thee and joy! thy dear Father has commanded to better thy condition. P.C. 1050. *Duech dhym seon; par-ma allo ow colon gwella ow chér*, come ye to me forthwith; so that my heart may better my condition. R.D. 2242. W. *gwella*. Arm. *gwellaat*.

GWELLS, s. m. Grass, herbs of all sorts; straw, litter. *A lena y'n hombronkyas uchel war ben un menedh, ha dhodho y tysquedhas ovr, hag archans, gwels, ha gwêdh*, from thence he led him high on top of a mountain, and to him shewed gold and silver, grass, and trees. M.C. 16. *Sew olow ow thryys, lyskys, ny dŷf gwels na flour yn bŷs yn kéth fordh-na may kyrdhys*, follow thou the prints of my feet, burnt; no grass nor flower in the world will grow in that same road that I walked. O.M. 713. *Gwrêns an noar dry râg gwells, ha losow, toan hás*, let the earth bring forth grass, and herbs, yielding seed. M.C. p. 93. ‡ *Ky gufr vel an guelz*, as green as grass. *Lhwyd*, 248. *Girelz*, straw, id. 27. W. *gwellt*.

GWELV, s. f. A lip. Pl. *gwelvans*. Llwyd, 7, 75. W. *gwevyl, gwevl*. Arm. †*gweol*. Ir. *giall*. Gael. *gial*. Fr. *gucule*. Eng. *gill*.

GWELVAN, v. n. To weep. *Lhwyd*, 14. The common form in the Ordinalia is *olé*, qd. v. W. *gwylo, wylo*.

Arm. *gwela.* Ir. *guil.* Gael. *guil.* Manx, *gull.* Gr. κλαίω. Lat. *fleo.*

GWELY, s. m. A bed, a couch. Pl. *gwelyow.* (Llwyd, 242, writes it *gweliaw.*) *Growedh yn gwely a hŷs, may hyllyf genes coské,* lie down in the bed at length, that I may sleep with thee. O.M. 2127. *Yn del-ma ef a'n dythgtyas, may eyn o y wely,* in this manner he treated him, that healthy was his bed. M.C. 235. It is written in the Cornish Vocab. *gueli.* W. *gwely,* † *gueli.* Arm. *guelé.*

GWEN, s. m. The anus. *Ellas na dhelleys a'm gwén dh'y lesky un luhesen ha crak taran,* alas that I did not discharge to burn him a flash of lightning, and a clap of thunder. R.D. 292. *Rum gwên.* R.D. 2084. *Tol ow gwén.* R.D. 2355.

GWEN, adj. White. This is the feminine form of *gwyn,* which was used with nouns feminine, as *Trewen,* the white town. The rule was not always observed in Cornish, (see *Llwyd,* 243,) but in Welsh it continues indispensable. W. *gwen,* f. In Armoric, *gwenn* is the only form for masculines and feminines.

GWENAN, s. f. A blister, a small pock, a wen. *Llwyd,* 78, 132. W. *gwenan.* Arm. *gwenaen.* Ir. *fuinc.* Gael. *foinne.*

GWENAR, s. f. Venus, the goddess of love. *De gwenar,* dies Veneris, Friday. *Llwyd,* 54. (W. *dydh gwener.* Arm. *digwener.*) W. *gwener.* Arm. *gwener.* From the Latin, *Venere.*

GWENGALA, s. m. September. *Mis gwen-gala,* the month of September. *Lhwyd,* 148. In late Cornish it was corruptly sounded *miz-gwedn-gula.* Comp. of *gwen,* white, and *cala,* straw. Arm. *gwen gôlô.* The month is called in Welsh *medi,* which means also a reaping.

GWENS, s. m. Wind. *Ll.* 153. *Ycin kuer, tarednow, ha golowas, er, rew, gwens, ha cleké, ha kezer,* cold weather, thunders, and lightning, snow, frost, wind, and ice, and hail. *Pryce.* Generally written *gwyns,* qd. v.

GWENYN, s. m. Bees. *Llwyd,* 43. A plural aggregate, from which is formed the singular *gwenynen,* or as it is written in the Corn. Vocab. *guenenen,* qd. v. W. *gwenyn.* Arm. *gwenan.* The root is *gwané,* to sting.

GWENYS, part. Pierced, stabbed, stung. *Yn pren crows bedhens gorrys, ha treys ha dyulef ketmys, ha gwenys dre an golon,* on the cross tree let him be put, hands and feet bound, and pierced through the heart. P.C. 2376. *Gans ga gwenys ha marow dre an golon me a fue,* with a spear pierced and killed through the heart I was. R.D. 2603. *Gwenys ôv der an asow, ha'n sêth gallas dredhof,* pierced I am through the ribs, and the arrow is gone through me. C.W. 114. *Gwenys* is the part. pass. of *gwané,* qd. v., and is also written *gwynys,* qd. v.

GWER, adj. Green, verdant. ‡ *Delkio gwêr,* green leaves. *Llwyd,* 18, 61. A late form of *gwyrdh,* or as written in the Cornish Vocabulary, *guirt,* qd. v.

GWERAS, s. m. The ground, the earth. Written also *gwyrras. Ow thâs pan ew e marow, me a vyn y anclydhyas; dún alemma heb falladow, goryn an corf yn gweras, gans solempnyly ha cân: mês an dôr ew a ve gwrŷs, hag arta dhe'n kêth gwyrras y fydh trylys,* since my father is dead, I will bury him; let us come from hence without fail; let us put the body in the ground with solemnity and song: out of the earth he was made, and again to the same earth he shall be turned. C.W.

150. A later form of *gwrref,* or as written in the Cornish Vocabulary, *guercl,* qd. v.

GWERCHES, s. f. A virgin. *Venytha me a grŷs dhe vôs a werches genys, Máp Dew, agan dysprynnyas,* for ever I believe thee to be born of a Virgin, Son of God, our Redeemer. P.C. 403. *Néb vyé a humthan der an Sperys Sans, dendhys a'n gwerches Vary,* who was conceived by the Holy Ghost, born of the Virgin Mary. *Pryce.* It is also written in the Ordinalia, *gwyrches,* qd. v.

GWERDHOUR, s. m. A channel of water. *Warbarth ol gweel Bchethlen, ha coys Penryn yn tyen, my a's re lemyn dheuch why, hag ol gwerdhour,* together all the field of Bohellan, and the wood of Penryn, wholly, I give them now to you, and all the water courses. O.M. 2591. Comp. of *gover,* a rivulet, and *dowr,* water.

GWERDHYA, v. a. To worship. *Rág henna y côth dhymo gans colon púr aga gwerdhya,* therefore it behoveth me with pure heart to worship them. C.W. 142. A later form of *gordhyu,* qd. v.

GWERDHYANS, s. m. Worship, glory. *Ha rág henna gwrén ny canu, yn gwerdhyans dhe'n Tás omma,* and therefore let us sing, in worship to the Father here. C.W. 180. A late form of *gordhyans,* qd. v.

GWEREN, s. f. A tankard. Arm. *gweren.* Llwyd, 5, derives the word from W. *gwirod,* liquor. It may however be formed like the Armoric, from *gwer,* glass.

GWERES, s. m. A guarding against, assistance, help. Written also *gweras. May whello an debeles ow gweres menouch dhedhé,* that the wicked ones may see my frequent help to them. O.M. 1850. *Reys yw dhych dry gweres gynef vy dh'y gemeres,* need is to you to bring help with me to take him. P.C. 596. *Gwyn vŷs ynno nép a grŷs, rák dhe weres yn parys dhe'th servygy yn bŷs-ma,* happy be that believes in him, for thy help is prepared for thy servants in this world. P.C. 2707. *An emprour rew danfonas a whylas yn pow gweres,* the emperor has sent me to seek help in the country. R.D. 1646. *Rág púp tra ol a fydh da, dre weres agan Dew ny,* for every thing will be good, by the help of our God. O.M. 535. W. *gwared.* Arm. *gwarez.*

GWERES, v. a. To assist, to help, to heal. *A Dhew a niff, dhe pysy a luen colon, gweres ny,* O God of heaven, I pray thee with full heart, help us. O.M. 1608. *Gweres dychhans, my a'd bŷs, ow fysadow dres púp tra,* help thou quickly, I pray thee my prayers above every thing. O.M. 1829. *Dew an niff, dre y versy, me a bŷs d'agan gweres,* the God of heaven, through his mercy, I pray to help us. O.M. 732. *My a's gweres, púp huny, mar mynnyuch perfyth creny,* I will help you, every one, if ye will believe perfectly. O.M. 2017. *H'ow gwereseuch, cowethé, ow corré tumbyr yn ban,* and help me comrades, putting the timber up. O.M. 2478. *Tyr Maria, me a grŷs, púr ylwys a'n gweresas,* dear Mary, I believe very fortunately helped him. M.C. 230. It changes in construction into *weres,* qd. v. *My a wra dhyso parow pup ár ol rág dhe weres,* I will make to thee an equal always to keep thee. O.M. 101. *A ow máp kêr, na portha wher, Dew a'th weres,* O my dear son, do not complain, God will help thee. O.M. 1358. *Dûs a lena, ty Gebal, gor an pren yn mês gans mal, ha'th weresas Amalek,* come from thence, thou Gebal, put the tree outside with a will, and let Amalek help thee. O.M. 2781. W. *gwared.*

GWERES, s. m. A horse covering. *Pryce.* Perhaps connected with W. *gwerchyr*, a covering. Arm. *goulcher.*

GWERHY, v. a. To sell. ‡ *Gwerhav an marh-na*, I will sell that horse. ‡ *Gwer an dên an marh-na*, the man will sell that horse. ‡ *E ma'n dên a gwerhy an marh*, the man is selling the horse. ‡ *E ryg gwerhy*, he did sell. *Mi ven gwerhy*, I will sell. ‡ *Mi a'i gwerha*, I will sell it. *Lhwyd*, 246. ‡ *Gwerhez*, sold. A late form of *gwerthy*, qd. v.

GWERHAS, s. f. A virgin. *Gans aga garm hag olva Ihesus Cryst a ve mevyys, may fynnas dyyskynna yn gwerhas ha bôs genys*, with their cry and lamentation Jesus Christ was moved, that he would descend into a virgin and be born. M.C. 4. *Du dre vertu an Tâs dhynny a dhyttyas gweras, en mâb dre y skyans brâs, pan gemert kÿc a werhas*, God by the virtue of the Father for us provided help, the Son by his great knowledge, when he took flesh of the virgin. M.C. 3. This is another form of *gwerches*, or *gwyrches*, qd. v.

GWERN, s. f. An alder, an alder tree, a mast of a ship. Pl. *gwernow*. *Goyl ha gwern dhodho ordnys, may 'th ellê yn mês a'n wlâs, dhe un carn y fue teulys, par may codhas yn ow brâs*, sail and mast (were) ordained for him, that he might go out of the country, to a rock he was cast, so that he fell into my judgment. R.D. 2311. *Yma peyk dhym provys, ha lovanow pûb ehan; deffrans sortow a wernow, yma parys pûr effan*, there is pitch provided by me, and ropes of every kind; different sorts of masts are ready very plainly. C.W. 166. Written in the Cornish Vocabulary, *guern.* W. *gwern.* Ir. *fearn,* †*fern.* Gael. *fearn.* Manx, *farney.* Anc. Gaul *vern.* Cf. *Vernodubrum*, the name of a river in Gaul, mentioned by Pliny, iij. 4. (W. *gwerndhwyyr.*)

GWERNEN, s. f. An alder tree. *Lhwyd*, 42, 241. Corn. Voc. *quernen*, alnus. W. *gwernen.* Arm. *gwernen.*

GWERNIC, adj. Marshy, swampy, moorish. Derived from *gwern*, which, as in Welsh, signified also a swamp, or boggy ground, and gave the name to *alder trees*, as being properly *swamp trees.* Hence the names of places, *Guarnick*, and *Gwarnick.* W. *gwernog.*

GWERRA, v. a. To sell. ‡ *Gorah ow thees dha'n fear, dha gwerra ludnow*, put my men to the fair to sell bullocks. *Pryce.* A late form of *gwerthê.*

GWERTHE, v. a. To sell, to vend. Part. pass. *gwerthys. Dhe'n Edhewon y ponyas y Arluth râg gwerthê*, to the Jews he ran to sell his Lord. M.C. 38. *Dremas yw cf lean a râs, nêb re werthys, yn mêdh e*, exceedingly good is he, full of grace, whom I have sold, sayeth he. M.C. 103. *Fest yn crêf me re bechas, Ihesus dhe wy ow querthê*, very greatly I have sinned, selling Jesus to you. M.C. 104. *Onan ahanouch haneth rum gwerthas dhom yskerens*, one of you this night has sold me to my enemies. P.C. 737. *Lavar dhymmo, oma vy nêp a'th werthas dhe'n Hudhewon dhe ladhê*, tell me, am I he who hath sold thee to the Jews to kill thee? P.C. 755. *Gwerthens y hugk, dhe brennê anedhy dhodho cledhê*, let him sell his cloak, to buy with it for him a sword. P.C. 922. *Yma gwon vrâs dhymmo vy, me a's gwerth dheuch yredy, a dhek-warnugans sterlyn*, there is a large down to me, I will sell it to you now for thirty sterling. P.C. 1533. *Iudas fals a leverys, trehans dynar a vonê, en box oll bedhens gwerthys, ha vôs den rag y rannê*, the false Judas said, three hundred pence of money I let the box all

be sold, and be for us to share it. M.C. 36. Welsh, *gwerthu.* Arm. *gwerza.* Lat. *verto.* Compare also the substantives; W. *gwerth.* Arm. *gwerz.* Ir. *feart,* †*fert.* Gr. ἀρετή. Lat. *virtus.* Goth. *wairthi.* Germ. *werth.* Eng. *worth.* Sansc. *vartis;* from *var*, to prefer.

GWERWELS, s. m. Feeding ground, or pasture *Lhwyd*, 113. Comp. of *gwer*, green, and *gwels*, straw. It properly means *grass*, which in Welsh is *glaswellt*, and *gwellt glâs.*

GWERYBY, v. a. To answer. *Cayn, dhymo, py ma Abel, ow gweryby uskys gwra*, Cain, where is Abel, do thou quickly answer me. C.W. 84. A late corruption of *gorthyby*, qd. v.

GWERYSON, s. m. Guerdon, reward. *Mar a kÿl bones yacheys, ty a fÿdh dhe lyfreson, hag an ow dhe weryson, neffrê dhe vôdh a vÿdh gwrÿs*, if he can be healed, thou shalt have thy liberty, and the gold thy reward; ever shall thy will be done. R.D. 1677. Formed from the word *guerdon*, according to the sense, but the form approaches near the French *guerison*, a cure.

GWESC, s. f. A covering, a garment, dress, a husk, a pod. Pl. *gwescas. Ny won vÿth pe 'dh âf temyn, nymbus gwesc, guskys, na chy, ow holan ol dhe dymmyn râg moreth a wra lerry*, I know not where I shall go now, I have not clothes, shelter, nor house; my heart all in pieces for grief will break. O.M. 356. *Râg fout gwesc ha goscotter, namna vyrwyn râg anwos*, for want of clothes and shelter, I am almost dying with cold. O.M. 361. Written also *gwisc*, and in Cornish Vocabulary, *guisc*, qd. v.

GWESCA, v. a. To dress, to put on, to clothe, to wear. Part. *gwescys. An Princis esu yn pow gans Iudas a dhanvonas tûs ven gweskis yn arvow krpar ha del êns dhe'n gâs*, the princes that were in the country with Judas sent bold men, clothed in armour, just as if they were going to the battle. M.C. 64. *Adam, attoma dyllas, hag Eva, dh'ages quethê; fystenouch, bedhens gweskes*, Adam, behold here clothes, and Eve, to clothe you; make ye haste, let them be worn. C.W. 72. In Lhwyd's time it was written *gwesga.* ‡ *Gwesgas*, worn. 246. See *Guiscy.*

GWESCEL, v. a. To strike, to beat, to knock, to drive. *Râg henna war an chal hy gwescel genef yw mal, ha browy hy esely*, therefore on the jaw to smite her the will is with me, and bruise her limbs. O.M. 2734. *Mês mara kewsys yn ta, ha'n gwirioneth y synsy, prâg omgweskyth yn delma, nyng yw mernas belyny*, but if I have spoken well, and hold the truth, why dost thou strike me thus, it is not but duty. M.C. 82. *Y a wiskis Cryst gans gwyn, awel fôl y a'n scornyê, hag a'n gweska fest yn tyn, beteggyns gêr ny gewsy*, they clothed Christ with white, like a fool they scorned him, and struck him very sharply, nevertheless he spoke not a word. M.C. 114. *Râg an spykis o garow, pan vôns gweskis dh'y sensy*, for the spikes were rough, when they were driven to hold him. M.C. 159. ‡ *Bedhes gwescys dhiueth, ken gweskal enweth, râg hedna yw an gwella point a skians oll*, be struck twice, before striking once, for that is the best of all knowledge. *Lhwyd*, 251. See *Gwyscy.*

GWESION, s. m. Fellows, mean fellows. *Lhwyd*, 242. *Saw nyns o torn da, danvon gwesyon a'n par-ma gans arvow dhum kemeres*, but it was not a good turn, to send fellows like these with arms to take me. P.C. 1299. Plural of *gwâs*, qd. v.

GWESPER, s. m. Vespers, evening service, evening *Erbyn bonas henna guris nans o prŷs gwesper yn wlâs*, against this was done, it was now the time of evening service in the country. M.C. 230. W. *gosper*. Arm. *gousper*, †*guesper*. Ir. *feascor*, †*fescor*. Gael. *feasgar*. Manx, *fastyr, asbyrt*. All from the Latin *vesperus*. Gr. ἑσπέρος.

GWESYS, v. a. To speak, to say. *Ytho migtern olesé, yn medh Pilat yn erna ; gwyr re gwesys yredy, yn medh Cryst, migtern oma*, now art thou a king ? says Pilate then ; truth thou hast spoken truly, says Christ, a king I am. M.C. 102. If not a misprint for *gewsys*, it is the same as W. *gwedyd*.

GWET, v. a. Take thou care. *A bûp kynde edhen vâs, y'th worhel guet dew gorré*, of every kind of good birds, take care to put two in thy ark. O.M. 980. *Oll an edhyn ow nyge, guet copel may kemery*, of all the birds flying, be careful that thou take a couple. O.M. 1024. This is written also *gweyl*, and is to be read *gwêth*, being the 2 pers. s. imp. of *gwythé*, qd. v.

GWETH, s. f. A course, a turn, or time. *Dûn ny ganso toth brâs bŷs yn epscop syr Cayfas yn gweth a prŷs er y gu*, let us come with him in great haste even to bishop Caiaphas, in a turn of time for his woe. P.C. 1130. *Teir gweth*, thrice ; *milgweth, milweth*, a thousand times ; *deweth*, twice ; *sylgweth*, on a Sunday ; *bisgweth*, ever. Llwyd, 162, 132. Written also *gwyth*, qd. v.

GWETH, s. m. A cloth, a garment. Generally written *gweth*, qd. v.

GWETH, adj. Worse. Used as the comparative of *drôc*. *An ioul ynno re dreesé, may'dh o gwêth agis cronek*, the devil in him had dwelt, so that he was worse than a toad. M.C. 47. *Mar passé a'n neyll tenewen, râg y scôdh hy a'n grevyé, ha whâth a wre an pren, war dheclarek war a'n gorré*, if he leaned on the one side, for his shoulder it grieved him, and yet worse did the wood, if he laid it backwards. M.C. 205. *Ty a vydh mernuns calcs ; gwêth ôs ys ky*, thou shalt have a hard death ; thou art worse than a dog. R.D. 2026. It changes in construction to *wêth*. *Saw kyn fêns y morthelck, dhe wêth vythons dhe'n eronek*, but though they be hammered, they shall be worse for the toad. P.C. 2732. W. *gwaeth*. Arm. *gwaz*. (Ir. *measa*, †*messa*.)

GWETHA, adj. Worst. Used as the superlative of *drôc*. Llwyd, 243. *Dôn ny ganso toth brâs bŷs yn epscop syr Cayfas yn gwetha prŷs er y gu*, let us come with him in great haste, even to bishop sir Caiaphas, in the worse time to his woe. P.C. 1130. It is doubtful whether this is the correct rendering, as *yn gweth a prŷs*, might mean in a turn of time. W. *gwaethav*. Arm. *gwasa*.

GWETHE, v. a. To make worse, to impair, to damage. *Duon agas lavarow, ha hyreth bôs Cryst marow, pûr wŷr a gl ow gwethé*, grief of your speeches, and sorrow that Christ is dead, very truly may hurt me. R.D. 1416. W. *gwaethu*.

GWETHE, v. a. To keep, to preserve. *Bôst a wrêns tyn ha deveth y'n gwethens worth y ehen*, a boast they made firm and shameless, that they would keep him against his efforts. M.C. 242. *Oynment o a gymmys râs, may wethé eorf heb pedry*, the ointment was of so much virtue, that it kept a body without rotting. M.C. 235. Another form of *gwythé*, qd. v.

GWETHE, v. a. To work, to labour, to make, to do. *Gwethé godhyans aga meyn orth Ihesus a omgammé*, doing worship they made wry their faces towards Jesus. M.C. 198. *Krêf yw gurydhyow an spedhes, may'dhyno ow dynovrech terrys, worlê menouch ow guethé*, strong are the roots of the briars, that my arms are broken, working often at them. O.M. 689. *Gwethé* is formed from *gwêth*, id. qd. *gwŷth*, qd. v., a work or deed. W. *gweithio*.

GWETHYL, v. a. To do, to make. *Gans pêeh pûr wŷr an bŷs ew hagrys, ny allaf sparya na moy heb gwethyl mernans, a ver spys, war pobel oll menas ty*, with sin very truly the world is deformed, I can spare no more, without bringing death, in a short time, ou all the people but thee. C.W. 164. *Mara kŷll dheworth an da dhe wethyl drôk agan dry*, if he can bring us from the good to do wrong. M.C. 21. Another form of *guthyl*, qd. v.

GWETHYN, adj. Weaved. *Yn scorgŷs prenyer esé yn dewlé an dew Edhow, hag yn fast kelmys dhedhé kerdyn gwethyn yn mesk cronow, may fôns hyblyth dhe gronkyé*, scourges of rods were in the hands of the two Jews, and fast bound to them cords weaved among thougs, that they might be pliant to beat him. M.C. 131. *Gwethyn* is a plural form, and the singular would be *gweth*, derived from *gwea*, id. qd. *gwia*, to weave.

GWEYL, s. m. A vision, a sight. *A weyl ol dhe'n arlythy, my a's pe dhyso wharé*, in the sight of all the lords, I will pay to thee forthwith. P.C. 1558. Another form of *gwel*, qd. v.

GWEYL, v. a. To do, to make. ‡ *Hy oar gweyl padn dah gen hy glawn*, she knows to make good cloth with her wool. ‡ *Na dál dên gweyl trevon war an treath*, men ought not to make houses on the sand. Pryce. *Cayn hag Abel, te a wôr, ornys gns dha l'ewnt Tabor dha weyl offren dehogall*, Cain and Abel, thou knowest, are ordered to Mount Tabor to make an offering truly. C.W. 90. Another form of *gûl*, qd. v.

GWEYTTENS, v. a. Let them take care. *Saw gweytyens pûp may tweko ganso lorch py eledhé da*, but let every one take care that he bring with him a staff or good sword. P.C. 942. 3 pers. pl. imp. of *gwythé*, qd. v.

GWEYTTEUCH, v. a. Take ye care. *Me a dhue dh'agas gwarnyé, ha gweytyeuch bôs tûs parys gans battya ha elydhydhow*, I will come to warn you, and take ye care that men are ready with staves and sword. P.C. 607. *Gweytyeuch ol er agas fŷdh*, be ye all careful on your faith. R.D. 373. 2 pers. pl. imp. of *gwythé*, qd. v.

GWEYTH, v. a. Take thou care, be careful. *Lymmyn gorquyth y garé, ha gweyth denater na vy*, now be thou careful to love him, and take care that thou art not unnatural. M.C. 139. *Gweyt bôs a râg yn voward, ma na vy synsys coward*, take care to be forward in advance, that thou be not held a coward. O.M. 2156. *Fystyn, ow duf whêk avy, gweyl an harlot na seapyo*, hasten my sweet captain mine, take care that the knave escape not. P.C. 990. This is the 2 pers. s. imp. of *gwythé*, qd. v., *ey* being used to express the long vowel.

GWIA, v. a. To weave, to knit. Llwyd, 163. W. *gwen*. Arm. *gwea*. Ir. *figh*. Gael. *figh*. Manx, *fee*. Lat. *vieo*. Eng. *weave*. Sansc. *ve*. (Gr. ἤ-τριον. Lith. *udis*, a texture.)

GWIAD, s. m. A weaving, a knitting ; a thing woven, or knitted. Corn. Voc. *guiat*, tela. W *greenad*. Arm. *gwiad*.

GWIADER, s. m. A weaver. Written also *gwiader*, Llwyd, 163, and *gweader*, qd. v.

GWIBAN, s. f. A fly, an insect. *Llwyd*, 71, 240. W. *gwiban*.

GWIC, s. f. A village; a cave, a bay, or creek of the sea. It is preserved in the names of *Gweek*, in Wendron, and the two *Gwcegs*, in Mawgan. W. *gwig*. Arm. *gwic*. Ir. *fich*. Gr. οἶκος. Lat. *vicus*. Germ. *wik, wih*. Sansc. *vaikas*, from *vic*, to occupy.

GWICGUR, s. m. A merchant, a dealer, or trader. Corn. Vocab. *guicgur*, mercator *vel* negotiator. Written also *gwiccor*, pl. *gwiccorion*. *Gwickur hên*, an old merchant. C.W. p. 193. *Arté Iudas ow trylé gwan wecor nym gevé par, ny ýl dên výth amontyé mýns a gollas yn chyffar*, again Judas turning a poor trader did not get an equivalent, nor can any man reckon all he lost in the bargain. M.C. 40. *Why gwycoryon, euch yn mês ydh esouch ow kuthyl ges a Dhu hag e sans cglos*, ye traders go out, ye are making a jest of God, and of his holy church. P.C. 331. *Kewsewch lemman gwyccoryon, del ouch why synsys gweryon, pendra gewsys an dên-ma*, speak now, traders, as ye are esteemed true men, what did this man say. P.C. 1304. Comp. of *gwie*, and *gûr*, a man. W. *gwicawr, gwicor*, a hawker, a pedlar; pl. *gwicorion*.

GWIDN, adj. White, pale. ‡ *Codna gwidn*, a weasel, lit. white neck. (It is called *bronwen*, white breast, in Welsh.) ‡ *Hernan gwidn*, a white herring. *Llwyd*, 65, 111, 241. A late corruption of *gwyn*, qd. v.

GWIDNAC, s. m. A whiting fish. *Llwyd*, 43. A late corruption of *gwynac*, qd. v.

GWIDRAN, s. m. A drinking glass. *Gwidran a win*, a glass of wine. *Pryce*. Written also *gwedran*, qd. v.

GWIDHAL, s. m. An Irishman. Pl. *gwidhili*. Llwyd, 242. A later form was *godhal*, qd. v. W. *gwydhcl*. Ir. *gaoidheal*, †*gaedel*. Gael. *gaidheal*.

GWIDHEN, s. f. A tree. Written in Cornish Vocabulary, *guiden*. It is generally written in the Ordinalia, *gwedhen*, qd. v.

GWIDHENIC, adj. Abounding in wood, woody.

GWIHAN, s. f. A periwinkle. *Llwyd*, 13, 240. W. *gwichiad*. Ir. *faechog, faochog*. Gael. *faoch, faochag*. Manx, *feochaig*.

GWILAN, s. f. A gull. *Llwyd*, 241. It is wrongly rendered in the Cornish Vocabulary, *guilan* alcedo, a kingfisher. W. *gwylan*. Arm. *gwelan*. Ir. *faoillean*, †*foilenn*. Gael. *faoillean, aoillean*. Manx, *foillan*. Fr. *goelan*.

GWILI, s. m. A bed. ‡ *Mós dho wili*, go to bed. *Llwyd*, 15, 231. ‡ *Lian gwili*, a sheet. 81. ‡ *Ha po'thera Jowan yn gwili*, and when John was in bed. 242. Written in Pryce's Vocabulary, *gwillé*. *Gwillé plév*, a feather bed; *gwillé cala*, a straw bed. Both are late forms of *gwely*, qd. v.

GWILLEW, s. m. A beggar. *Llwyd*, 68. W. *gwilliad*, a vagrant.

GWIN, s. m. Wine. Corn. Vocab. *guin*, vinum; *guin fellel*, acetum. Botler, *fystyn hep lettyé, doro dhym an gwýn gwella*, butler, hasten without stopping, give me the best wine. O.M. 1904. *Rág gwell dewes vylteth wŷn nyns â yn agas ganow; yn pow-ma nyns ûs gwel gwŷn*, for no better drink of wine will go into your 1904. *Kens môs eyf ten gwŷn pymeth*, before going mouth; in this country there is no better wine. O.M. drink thou a draught of spiced wine. O.M. 2294. *Mar ny goryth médh py gwýn, ke dhe fenten dhe evé*, if thou shalt not find mead or wine, go to the fountain to drink. O.M. 2436. *Gwedran a win*, a glass of wine. *Llwyd*, 242. W. *gwin*, †*guin*. Arm. *gwin*. Ir. *fion*, †*fin*. Gael. *fion*. Manx, *feeyn*. Gr. οἶνος. Lat. *vinum*.

GWINBREN, s. m. A vine. Corn. Voc. *guinbren*, vitis, lit. a wine tree, being compounded of *gwin*, and *pren*, a tree. W. *gwinwydhen, gwinien*. Arm. *gwinien*. Ir. *fincamhain*, †*finnain*, †*fine*. Gael. *fionain*, †*fionan*. Manx, *feeyney*.

GWINIC, adj. Boggy, swampy, fenny, marshy. From *gwén*, a meadow.

GWINYS, part. Stung. *Llwyd*, 248. Written generally *gwynys*, qd. v.

GWINZAL, s. m. A fan for winnowing. *Llwyd*, 60. Derived fr. *gwyns*, wind. W. *gwyntyll*. Ir. *geidval, geoithrean*, from *geoth*, wind. Gael. *beantag*. Lat. *ventilo*, to fan, or winnow.

GWIR, adj. True. Corn. Voc. *guir*, verus. Pl. *guirion, gweryon*. *Hen yw gwŷr ef a galsé pûp tra y dhyweul arté moy ys na fe*, this is true, he cou ld destroy every thing, more than it was. R.D. 977. *Keuscuch lemman guykcoryon, del ouch why synsys gueryon, pendra geusys an dên-ma*, speak now, traders, as ye are accounted true (men,) what said this man. P.C. 1305. *Yn médh Cryst, an kueff colon, pár wŷr te re leverys*, says Christ, the dear heart, very truly thou hast spoken. M.C. 100. *Gwŷr vrês yw honna*, that is true decision. P.C. 515. *Rum fay, gwŷr yw agas cows* by my faith, your speech is true. P.C. 1345. *Yw gwŷr dhym a leveryth*, is it true (which) thou sayost to me? P.C. 1941. *Ylho bedhyth mylyges, pár wŷr drŷs ol an bestes*, now thou shalt be cursed very truly above all the beasts. O.M. 312. *Ty a drŷg nefré, awos ol dhe wŷr dhegé, yn tewolgow brás*, thou shalt dwell ever, notwithstanding all thy true tithe, in great darkness. O.M. 557. W. *gwir*, †*guir*. Arm. *guir*, †*quir*. Ir. *fior*, †*fir*. Gael. *fior*. Manx, *feer*. Gr. †ἦρος. Lat. *verus*. Germ. *wahr*. Eng. *very*. Lith. *wiernas*. Russ. *wiernyi*. Sansc. *varyas*, excellent, from *var*, to prefer.

GWIR, s. m. That which is true, truth. *Arluth, gwŷr a leversouch, y a gowsys yntredhé*, Lord, you have spoken the truth, they said amongst them. M.C. 50. *Osé máb Du, leun a rás, lemyn gwŷr lavar dhyn*, art thou the son of God, full of grace? now tell us the truth. M.C. 100. *Onan ha try ôn yn gwŷr, en Tás, ha'n Map, ha'n Spyrys*, one and three we are in truth, the Father, the Son, and the Spirit. O.M. 3. *Godhfos gwŷr ol yredy, my a vyn môs dhyworthys*, knowing all the truth plainly, I will go from thee. O.M. 821. W. *gwir*. Arm. *guir*.

GWIRAS, s. f. Liquor, wassail, drink. *Nyns yw Ely a gylwa; seches dhodho yma, ef a'n gevé drôk wyras; ottensé gynef parys, bystel, eysel kymyskys, wassel mars ûs seches brás*, it is not Elias (that) he called; he is thirsty, he has had bad liquor; behold it with me ready, gall (and) vinegar mixed; wassail, if there is great thirst. P.C. 2975. W. *gwirawd*.

GWIRDER, s. m. Truth, verity, veracity. *My a wél tŷgr gwelen, ny welys tekké rum fay, bythqueth aban véf genys; yn gwyrder an thyr gwelen yw dysguydhyans ha token a'n try person yn drynsys*, I see three rods, I never saw fairer, on my faith, since I was born; in truth, the three rods are a declaration and a token of the three persons in Trinity. O.M. 1752.

GWIRION, adj. Truly right, true, truth-telling, just, innocent. Corn. Voc. *guirion*, verax. *Nynsus dên orth ow servyé, lên a gwyryon, me a greys, yn ol an beys saw Noe, ha'y wrêk, ha'y flehes kefrys*, there is no man serving me, faithful and true, I believe, in all the world, but Noah, and his wife, and his children likewise. O.M. 930. *Pûr wêsr y tue vyngeans tyn, mar pŷdh an gwyryon dysergs, warnouch, war agas flechys*, very truly, sharp vengeance will come, if the innocent he destroyed, upon you, upon your children. P.C. 1938. *A Dhu, aso why bylen, ow ladhé gwyryon hep kên*, O God, ye are wretches, killing the innocent without cause. P.C. 2625. *My a'n pŷs a luen golon, yechés dhymmo a dhunfon, kepar del ôs Dew gwyryon, ha mûr dhe râs*, I pray him with full heart, to send health to me, like as thou art true God, and great thy grace. R.D. 1717. W. *gwirion*. Arm. *guirion*. Ir. *firinneach*, †*firian*, †*firion*. Gael. *firinneach*. Manx, *firrinach*.

GWIRIONETH, s. m. Truth, veracity. *Mar keus ken es gwyryoneth*, if he speak other than truth. P.C. 1461. *Lavar dhynny guyryoneth, hep feyntys na falsury*, tell thou the truth to us, without deceit or falsehood. P.C. 1477. *Pûr wyryoneth re gcusys ahanaf, re'n gêdh hedhew*, very truth thou hast spoken of me, by this day. P.C. 1587. *Me a worthyp dhys warré an gwyryoneth yredy*, I will answer thee presently the truth surely. P.C. 1974. Written also *gwyroneth*. *Lavar my dh'y bysy a leverel gwyroneth*, say that I beseech him to tell the truth. O.M. 702, 740. *My a lever gwyroneth*, I tell the truth. P.C. 735. W. *gwirionedh*. Arm. *gwirionez*. Ir. *firinne*. Gael. *firinn*. Manx, *firrinys*.

GWISC, s. f. A covering, a garment, dress; husk, pod. Corn. Vocab. *guisc*, vestis vel vestimentum vel indumentum. W. *gwisg*, †*guise*. See *Guise*.

GWISCE, v. a. To put on, to clothe, to dress; to wear. Part. *gwiscys*. *Y a wiskis Cryst gans greyn, avel fôl y a'n scornyé*, they clad Christ with white, like a fool they scorned him. M.C. 114. *Kyng ys y vôs alemma, yn gwyn ef a vŷdh gwyskys*, before going hence, in white he shall be clothed. P.C. 1780. *Ottensy parys, a's gwyskens a dhesempys adro dhodho ef mar wyn*, behold it ready, let him wear it immediately about him, if he will. P.C. 1788. *Hag yn gwyn ef re'n gwyscas*, and in white he has clothed him. P.C. 1844. *Aban yw y queth gwyskys*, since his cloth is put on. P.C. 2133. *Y'n y dhyllas arté an harlot a vŷdh gwyskys*, in his clothes again the knave shall be dressed. P.C. 2533. *Pilat, gynef nyns yw mêdh, awos gwyské an queth, a fue yn kerehyn Ihesu*, Pilate, I am not ashamed, because of wearing the cloth, (that) was about Jesus. R.D. 1936. *Dyllas rûdh yn an codhfos, prûk y's gwyskyth*, red clothes in our knowledge, why wearest thou them? R.D. 2549. W. *gwisgaw*. Arm. *gwiska*.

GWISCEL, v. a. To strike, to knock. ‡*Gwisco' an genter-ma ed eskaz vi*, knock this nail in my shoe. Lhwyd, 230. See *Gwyskel*.

GWITH, s. m. A keeping, protection, care, caution. *A syre na blamyouch ny, a nyngesé alwheow warbarth yn ges guŷth why ha dyen an darasow*, O sir, blame us not, were not the keys together in your keeping, and the doors secure. R.D. 651. ‡*Kemer with na rey gara an vor yôth rag an vor nowedh*, take thou care that thou lovest not the old way for the new way. Lhwyd, 251. W. *cadw*.

GWITHE, v. a. To keep, to preserve, to guard. *Henna a ra gwythé, na dheffo glaw abervedh*, that will keep, that the rain may not come in. O.M. 1075. *My re brederys gûl prat, rûg y wythé erbyn hôf*, I have thought of doing a thing, to keep it against summer. O.M. 488. *Gwŷth an gwelen-ma yn ta*, keep thou this rod well. O.M. 1461. *Banneth an Tâs ragas bo, hag ef prest ragas gwytho venytha yn cosoleth*, the blessing of the Father be on thee, and may it always preserve thee for ever at rest. O.M. 1724. *Arluth an nêf, gwŷth ow enef, rûk pûp drôk tra*, Lord of heaven, guard my soul, from every evil thing. P.C. 263. *Cryst, mychtern an Yedhewon, na'n laddro an Cristenyon, gwytheuch war pcyn*, Christ, King of the Jews, that the Christians steal him not, guard ye, under penalty. R.D. 366. *Me a'n gwŷth, kyn tassorcho*, I will keep him, though he should rise again. R.D. 379. *Gwythens pûp y tenewen*, let every one keep his side. R.D. 417. *Y grygyans yûp ol gwythes, puppenagol a wharfo*, his belief let every one keep, whatever may happen. R.D. 1537. *Dho gwitha*, to keep. Lhwyd, 140. ‡ *An dzhyi a kymeras an vor noweth, ha Dzhûan a gwithas an vor gôth*, they took the new way, and John kept the old way. 252. W. *cadw*. Ir. *coimhcad*. Gael. *coimhead*. Manx, *caddey*. Sanse. *kad*.

GWITHES, s. m. A keeper, a guardian. Pl. *gwithysy*. *Nep ma'n ressys dhe wethé, dheworth henna govynné, (govyn e,) py ûr fûf vy y wythes*, he to whom thou gavest him to keep, ask him of that one, what time was I his keeper? O.M. 576. *Hag ordeynench gwythysy dh'aga aspyé vysy, war peyn brâs, d'agé gwythé*, and appoint ye guards to watch them diligently, under great penalty, to keep them. O.M. 2038. *Mara pewaf, why a vêdh ow chyf privé gwythysy*, if I live, ye shall be my chief private guards. O.M. 2397. W. *ceidwad*. Ir. *coimhcadaidhe*, *coimheuduigh*. Gael. *coimhcadaiche*.

GWITHIAS, s. m. A keeper, a guardian. A later form of *gwithiad*, which in Corn. Voc. is written *guidthiat*, qd. v. *Adam del ôf Dew a râs, lôs greythyas a werontyuf dhys war paradys*, as I am a God of grace, to be a keeper I grant to thee over Paradise O.M. 75. *Anodho mar 'dh ês preder, worth y wythyas govynné (govyn e,)* of him if there is anxiety, ask him of his keeper. O.M. 600. *Seth, ow mâp, my a dhanfon dhe yet parathys yn scon, dhe Cherubyn, an gwythyas*, Seth, my son, I will send to the gate of Paradise forthwith, to the Cherub, the guardian. O.M. 602.

GWLAS, s. f. A country, a region, a kingdom. *Tâs a wrûk pûp gwlâs, ha dên a pry*, Father, (that) hath made every country, and man of earth. R.D. 309. *Adam, ke yn mês a'n wlâs, troha ken pow dhe vewé*, Adam, go out of the country, towards another land to live. O.M. 343. *Ty a fŷdh pûr tormot sad yn gwlâs yffurn, del gresaf*, thou shalt have very sad torment in the region of hell, as I believe. O.M. 492. *Nyns yw ow gwlâs a'n bŷs-ma, hag a pe hy, ow servons bŷth ny'm gassé, dhe'n Yedhewon ow gwerthé; na'm bues gwlâs ynno deffry*, my kingdom is not of this world, and if it were, my servants would never leave me, selling me to the Jews; my kingdom is not in it really. P.C. 2010. *Gwlâs* is a later form of *gwlâd*, which in the Cornish Vocabulary is written *gulat*, qd. v. W. *gwlâd*. Arm. *glâd*.

GWLASCOR, s. f. A kingdom. *Dhe'n Crystynnyon ol adro, yntredhé gasaf ow râs, yn ow gwlascor may leffo bewnans neffré,* to the Christians all around, among them I leave my grace, in my kingdom that they may ever find life. R.D. 1585. *Pyw a ylta gy bones, pan yw mar rûdh dhe dhyllas, yn gwlascor néf,* who caust thou be, when thy clothes are so red, in the kingdom of heaven? R.D. 2513. *Yma ow trylé duffry ol an wlascor a Iudi,* he is turning really all the country of Judæa. P.C, 1594. *Arluth Cryst me a'th pyssé a prydiry ahané, pan vysé yn dhe wlascor,* Lord Christ, I would pray thee to think of me, when thou shalt be in thy kingdom. P.C. 2908.

GWLEZOW, s. m. Gads, wedges, such as tinners use. *Pryce.*

GWODHAS, v. a. To know. *Gwodhav,* or *me a vyn gwodhas,* I will know. *Gwidhi,* or *ti a wydhy,* thou shalt know. *Ev a wôr,* he will know. *May gwothfo ev,* that he may know. *Gwon, mi a won,* or *wi a wôr,* I know. *Ti a wôr,* thou knowest. *Ev a ûr, ev a wyr,* he knoweth. *Ni a wydhen,* or *wodhen,* we know. *Gwedhoh,* or *hwi a wedhoh,* ye know. *Gwedhans,* they know. *Gwedhun,* or *my a wydhun,* I knew. *Ti a wydhys,* thou knewest. *Ev a wydhys,* he knew. *Ni a wedhyn,* we did know. *Gwydhoh,* or *hwi a wydhoh,* ye did know. *Gwydhans,* and *gweians,* they did know. *Llwyd,* 247. This is the late form with its inflexious of the irr. verb *godhfos,* qd. v.

GWON, s. f. A field. *Me a gesul bûs gansé prennys da gwon yn nép le râg an cladhva Crystunyon,* I advise that there be with them bought a good field in some place, for the burial-place of Christians. P.C. 1544. Written in the Cornish Vocabulary, *guen. Gôn, goon,* and *gun,* are also various forms, pl. *guniow.* W. *gwaen,* † *gwaun,* † *gwoun.* Arm. *geun,* † *gueun.* Ir. *fonn.* Gael. *fonn.* Manx, *fenyn, foain.* Lat. *fundus.* Germ. *fani, vern.* Gr. πεδίον. Sansc. *puttan,* fr. *pat,* to extend. Gr. πετάω, πιτνάω. Lat. *pateo, pando.*

GWORHEMMEN, v. a. To command. Part. *gworhemminys. Llwyd,* 249. A late form of *gorhemmys,* qd. v.

GWORHEMMYNIAS, s. m. A command. Pl. *gworhemmynadow.* This is formed from *gworhemmynad,* of which *gworhemmynias* is a later corruption. *Llwyd,* 242. See *Gorhemmynad.*

GWORRIA, v. a. To worship, to glorify. A later corruption of *gordhyé,* qd. v.

GWORYANS, s. m. Glory, renown. *Llwyd,* 63. A late corruption of *gordhyans,* qd. v.

GWOSE, prep. After. *Gwosé-ma,* henceforth, hereafter; corrupted in Llwyd's time into ‡ *udzhema. Gwosé-na,* after that: ‡ *udzhena. Gwosé* was also corrupted into *gwodzhi.* Llwyd, 249. The general form in construction is *wosé,* qd. v. W. *gwedi,* † *guetig,* † *gueti.* Arm. *goudé.* Ir. *feasda.* Gael. *feasd.* Sansc. *pus'c'at.*

GWRA, v. a. Do thou; he will do. 2 pers. s. imp., and 3 pers. s. future of *gwrey,* qd. v. *Dysempys gwra y dhybry,* do thou eat it immediately. O.M. 208. *Ty dyowl, gwra ow gorthyby,* thou devil, do answer me. O.M. 301. *Na wra na moy pecha,* do thou sin no more. M.C. 34. *Del won, yn un fystyné, me a's gwra,* as I know, in a hurry, I will make them. M.C. 158. It changes in construction into *qura,* and *wra. Râg the ladhé dén mar qura, ef a'n geryth seyth kemmys,* for if a

---

man will kill thee, he shall get it seven times as much. O.M. 598. *Ow holan ol dhe dymmyn râg moreth a wra terry,* my heart all in pieces for grief will break. O.M. 358.

GWRADNAN, s. f. A wren. A corrupt form of *gwrannan,* which is formed from the English. *Llwyd,* 9, 167, 240.

GWRAGEDH, s. m. Wives, women. *Kemer dhe wrêk, ha'th fichas, h'aga gwragedh gor gansé,* take thy wife, and thy children, and put their wives with them. O.M. 976. *Deuch abervedh, ow flehys, h'ages gwragedh maga ta,* come in, my children, and your wives as well. C.W. 176. Plural of *gwrêc,* or *grêg. Gwragedh vohosugion,* poor women. *Llwyd,* 243. W. *gwragedh.* sing. *gwraig.* Arm. *gragez,* siug. *grêc,* or *grée.*

GURAH, s. f. An old woman. *Llwyd,* 4, 43, 173, *gurâh.* W. *gurâch.* Arm. *grâch.*

GWREANS, s. m. Work, workmanship, creation. *Me a wôr, hag a leall gryfs, gwreans Dew y vôs hemma,* I know, and truly believe, the work of God to be this. C.W. 154. *Praga na wreta predery, y festa formys devery, der y wreans tu omma,* why dost thou not consider, that thou wast formed by his workmanship here. C.W. 16. *Yn bŷs-ma, râg dhe wreans, ty a berth gossythyans, ken na brodar,* in this world, for thy deed thou shalt bear punishment, though thou art a brother. C.W. 82. Written also *gwryans.*

GWREAR, s. m. A maker, a creator. *Meur wordhyans dhys ow formys, ha gwréar a oll an bŷs,* much glory to thee my former, and maker of all the world. C.W. 102. *Unpossyble nyug ew tra dha wréar oll an bŷs-ma,* impossible is not a thing to the Creator of all this world. C.W. 172. *Mars ew bôdh Dew y honyn, ueb ew gwréar noer ha néf,* if it is the will of God himself, who is the maker of earth and heaven. C.W. 178. *Me a credy yn Dew an Tâs ollgallusec, gwréar an néf, ha an noar,* I believe in God the Father Almighty, maker of heaven and earth. *Pryce.*

GWREC, s. f. A wife, woman. Written also *gwrêg;* pl. *gwragedh,* qd. v. *Mŷns a déf yany un geydh, my ha'м gwrêk a wra dybry,* all that will grow in it, in one day I and my wife will eat. O.M. 386. *Ma yma lys gwrêk ha gour ow treylé dhodho touth da,* there are many a woman and man turning to him in good haste. P.C. 559. *Ty dhe honan dhe balas, dhe wrêk genes dhe nedhé,* thou thyself to dig, thy wife with thee to spin. O.M. 346. *En debell wrêk casadow,* the wicked wife of evil countenance. M.C. 150. *Gwrêg wedhow,* a widow. *Llwyd,* 174. *Gwrêg brederys,* a careful woman. *Prederys ew an wrêg-na,* careful is that woman. Written in the Cornish Vocabulary, *gruęg, greg.* and *freg.* W. *gwraig,* † *gurhie,* in Oxford Glosses, † *greyc.* Arm. *grêg.* Ir. † *gruag,* † *frag,* † *fvace.* Gael. † *gruag.* Lat. *virago, virgo.*

GWREDH, s. m. A root. Pl. *gwredhiow.* Written also *gwreydh,* qd. v.

GWREDHAN, s. f. A single root, a root. *Llwyd,* 9, 136.

GWREDHAV, v. a. I will do. *Gwerhâv vi,* or *mi werhâv, Llwyd,* 246. A late form of *gwráf,* 1 pers. s. fut. of *gwrey,* qd. v.

GWREGE, v. a. To do, to make. *Dewsull-blegyow, pan esé yn myśk y abestely, y wrég dhe ré anedhé môs dhe'n dré,* Palm Sunday, when he was among his apostles, he caused some of them to go to the town. M.C. 27. Written also *gwrugé*, qd. v.

GWRELLE, v. a. To do, to make, to create. *A ban nag ës a wodhfé dheuch parys a's gurellé gwell*, since there is not (that) knows for you ready to make them better. M.C. 158. *Deuch genef, ha holyouch ve, godhvedhouch na wrellouch tros*, come with me, and follow me, see ye that ye make not a noise. M.C. 63. *An Edhewon yntredhé a rúg may werellons terry aga mordhosow*, the Jews among them caused that they should break their thighs. M.C. 229. *Pûp ûr ol oberedh da, gwyn blys kymmys a'n gwrello*, always good works, happy they as many as do them. O.M. 605. See also *Wrello, &c.*

GWREIDHEN, s. f. A root. Written in the Cornish Vocabulary, *gruciten*, radix. Plural, *gwreidhow*. The form met with in the Ordinalia, is *gwrydhyow*, qd. v. The late form of *gwreidhen* was *gwredhen*.

GWRES, s. m. Heat. W. *gwrês, grês*. Arm. *grouez*. Ir. † *gris*, † *grcs*. Gael. † *gris*. Sansc. *gris'ma*.

GWREY, v. a. To do, to make, to create. 2 pers. s. imp., and 3 pers. s. fut. *gwra*, qd. v. Part pass. *gwrys*. *Avel Du y fedhyth gurys*, like to God thou shalt be made. M.C. 6. *Me a'd wra arluth brâs*, I will make thee a great lord. M.C. 16. *Te ny wodhus pandra 'râf dhys*, thou knowest not what I shall do to thee. M.C. 46. *Oll mýns ûs ef a 'ra*, all that is he will do. M.C. 60. *Pyth yw an drôk re wrussys*, what is the evil (that) thou hast done? M.C. 101. *Moycha dhodho drôk a wre, hena redha an gwella grâs*, he that did most hurt to him was the best fellow. M.C. 112. *Hag ol drôk suel a wressé*, and all was wrong that he had done. M.C. 119. *Me ny wrâf kentrow dhewy*, I will not make nails for you. M.C. 155. *Lemyn an toll re wrussens*, but the hole they had made. M.C. 180. *Gonys oll a wréns yn fast*, they all did labour fast. M.C. 202. *Hag a dhychow lader brâs cregy a 'russons yn wêdh*, and on the right a great thief they did hang also. M.C. 186. *An gorhel gwrên dyscudhé*, the ark let us uncover. O.M. 1146. *Arluth, hen yw re nebes, mar quréñ flôch výth denythy*, Lord, this is too little, if we do any children produce. O.M. 390. *Gwréns Dew y vêdh, ha'y vynnas*, let God do his will and his pleasure. O.M. 1153. *Gwreuch why trestyé yn y grâs*, do ye trust in his grace. O.M. 1659. *Yn delma pan wressé*, in this manner when he had done. M.C. 48. *Pandra wrêth*, what art thou doing? C.W. 64. *Prâg y wresta yn della*, why didst thou so? C.W. 64. *Omma ny wreuch trega*, here ye shall not dwell. C.W. 72. *Ow negysyow ydheu gurýs, par dell wrussouch dhym orna*, my errands are performed as you did command me. C.W. 136. *Na wreuch terry an deffan*, do not ye break the prohibition. C.W. 156. *Pan wressouch gwyll an lester*, when ye did make the vessel. C.W. 176. *Ges a wressens anodho*, a jest they made of it. C.W. 176. *Nêb na whytho, gréns funnyé gans y lappa*, he that does not blow, let him fan with his lap. P.C. 1243. See also *Wren, Wressen, Wrûk, &c.* The Cornish and Armoric have substituted *r* for *n*. W. *gueneud*, † *guru*. Arm. † *groaff, gréat*, (part.) Ir. *gnídh*, † *gniu*, † *dogniu*. Gael. *gnathaich*. Manx, *jannoo*.

GWRIDNIAS, part. Pressed, squeezed. Llwyd, 138. A late corruption of the part. of *guryn*, qd. v.

GWRUGE, v. a. To do, to make. Preterite *gwrúg*, or *gwrúk, a wrûk, a wrûg*, and by contraction *rûk*, or *rûg*.

Ef a wrûk ow husullyé, frût annedhy way torren, he did advise me that I should break off fruit from it. O.M. 217. *Pan wrugé dres ow dyfen, fest yn týn ef ru'm sorras*, when he acted against my prohibition, very grievously he provoked me. O.M. 423. *Er na vrys arlu treyles a'n kêth doer kyns a wrugaf*, until thou art again turned to the same earth (from which) I first made thee. C.W. 70. *Ow frýns kêr, ty a wrûg pûr dhrocg ober*, my dear husband, thou hast done a very wicked act. C.W. 94. *Pan rûg dheuch ow holyé*, when I caused you to follow me. M.C. 50. *Nêb a'm grûk vy ha'm gorty, ef a rûk agan dyfen, aval na wrellen dybbry*, he (that) made me and my husband, he did forbid us, that we should not eat the apple. O.M. 182. *Ef a rûk agan dyfen*, he did forbid us. O.M. 182. See also *Wrûg*, and *Rûg*. W. *gorugo*; preterite, *gorug, a orug*. Arm. *gra*, make thou; *ra*, he made. Ir. *rug*, † *ric*, † *rig*. Gael. *rug*. Scotch, *gar*.

GWRUTHYL, v. a. To do, to make. *A mcys óf, ow predyry pandra allaf dhe wruthyl*, I am puzzled, thinking what I may do. O.M. 194. *Reys yw y wruthyl porrys*, very necessary it is to do it. O.M. 649. *Me a vyn môs alemma, dhe wruthyl ow nygyssow*, I will go hence, to do my errands. O.M. 1004. Written by Llwyd 245, 250, *gwrythyl, gwrithil, g'rithil*.

GWRY, s. m. A seam. *Lemmyn Pilat, jewdy, cafus an bows-na hêp gwry ûs y'th kerehyn me a vyn*, now Pilate, I tell you, have that robe without seam, (that) is about thee, I will. R.D. 1921. W. *gweuiad*; (*gwnio*, to sew; *ggruiam*, in Oxford Glosses.) Arm. *gri, groui*, a seam; *griu*, to sew.

GWRYANS, s. m. Work, creation. *Deuch yn scon, may huth-thuho ow colon, agan gwryans nu'm bo mêdh*, come ye forthwith, that my heart may be exalted, that our work may not be a shame to me. R.D. 1877. Written also *gwreans*, qd. v., and derived from *gwrey*.

GWRYCHON, s. m. Sparks. *Hag a'th whyp war an wolok, may whylly gwrychon ha môk, dhe dhew-lagas a dre dro*, and whip thee on the face, that thou wilt see sparks and smoke, round about thy eyes. P.C. 2101. A plural aggregate, of which the singular is *gwrychonen*, or by contraction *grychonen*, qd. v. W. *gwreichion*.

GWRYDHYE, v. a. To take root, to be rooted. Part. *gwrydhyys*. *Yn gordhyans dhe'n Tâs a nêf, my a vern agan plunsé, ha tregouch dh'y ordenauns ef, gwrydhyouch, ha tyvouch arté*, in worship to the Father of heaven, I do plant ye; and dwell ye in his ordinance; take ye root, and grow again. O.M. 1804. *Yma tra varth wharvedhys haneth, an kêth gwêl-ma yn dôr y môns ol gwrydhyys, ha'n thýr dhe onan yw unyys*, there is a wondrous thing happened to night; these same rods in the earth they are all rooted, and the three joined in one. O.M. 2084. W. *gwreidhio*. Arm. *grisienna, growienna, grienna*.

GWRYDHYOW, s. m. Roots. *Kréf yw gwrydhyow an spedhes, may 'thyw ow dywvrech terrys, worté menouch ow quethé*, strong are the roots of the briars, that my arms are broken, working often at them. O.M. 687. *Ha war woles pan vyrys, my a welns hy gwrydhyow bfýs yn yffarn dywenys*, and on the bottom when I looked, I saw its roots even into hell descending. O.M. 782. *Mýr gwel orth an wedhen, mýr pandra wylly ynny, kefrys gwrydhyow ha scorn*, look better at the tree, look, what dost thou

GWYLVYTH 203 GWYNNEC

see in it, also at the roots and branches. O.M. 802. *Gwrydhyow* is formed from a sing. *gwrŷdh*, whence also *gwrydhou*, a single root. W. *gwraidh*, pl. *gwreidhion*; *wreidhyn*, a single root. Arm. *grisien, gourien, gwouien, grien*; pl. *grisiou, grisiennou.* Irish, *freamh.* Gael. *freumh.* Manx, *fraue.* Gr. ῥίζα. Lat. *radix.* Germ. *kraut,* † *reute.* Eng. *root.* Sansc. *radus,* a point; from *rad,* to penetrate.

GWRYTH, s. m. Service. *Râk henna dhe'n bŷs y tuyth, râg dôn dustiny ha gwryth dhe'n lendury yn pûp prŷs,* for that I came to this world, to bear testimony and service to the truth at all times. P.C. 2024.

GWYDN, adj. White. *Llwyd*, 10. A late corruption of *gwyn,* qd. v.

GWYDNAC, s. m. A whiting fish. *Llwyd,* 10. A later form of *gwynnec,* qd. v.

GWYDH, s. m. Trees, shrubs. ‡ *Ha an noar a drôs râg gwels, ha'n losow râg dascor hâs warler e eunda, ha an gwŷdh tôn avulow, ha go hâs etta go honnen, warler go launda,* and the earth brought forth grass, and the herb did yield seed after its kind, and trees bearing fruits, whose seed is in themselves, after their kind. C.W. p. 199. This in the old orthography would be *guit*, and thus we find it written in the Cornish Vocabulary. See *Guitfil,* and *Luworeh-guit,* which Llwyd, 174, writes *lyworch gwŷdh*. W. *gwydh*, † *guit.* Arm. *gwez.* See *Gwêdh.*

GWYDH, adj. High, conspicuous. Pryce gives this as a Cornish word, but I believe without authority.

GWYDHEN, s f. A tree, a single tree. Generally written *gwedhen,* qd. v.

GWYLFYM, v. a. I shall see. *Llwyd,* 246, gives this form as the 2 fut. of *gweles. Mar gwylfym,* if I shall see. *Mar gwylfydh,* if thou shalt see. *Mar gwylyf e,* if he shall see. *Mar gwylfon,* if we shall see. *Mar gwelfo,* if ye shall see. *Mar gwylfyns,* if they shall see.

GWYLL, v. a. To do, to make. *Râg dha garengu lemyn me a vyn gwyll Paradys,* for thy love now I will make Paradise. C.W. 28. *Ahanas tenaf asan, hag a honna me a vyn gwyll dhys pryas,* from thee I will draw a rib, and of it I will make for thee a wife. C.W. 30. *Perth côv dhe gwithé sans an dŷdh Sabboth; wheh dydhiow te wra whêl, hag a wra mŷns ês dhys dhe wyll,* remember to keep holy the Sabbath day; six days shalt thou labour, and do all that thou hast to do. *Pryce.* This is a late form of *gûl,* qd. v.

GWYLLOUCH, v. a. Ye shall see, 2 pers. pl. fut. of *gweles. Arluth worth an gwâs myrouch; ne a grŷs pan y'n gwyllouch dhyragoch why, dhudho ny ylleuch gûl drôk, hedrê ve y gys golok,* Lord, look ye at the fellow; I believe, when you see him before you, you will not be able to do him harm while he is in your sight. R.D. 1912.

GWYLLS, adj. Wild, savage. *Dhe'n edhya gwyls râg nycthy tellyryow esa parys, dhe Gryst y ben py sensy tyller vŷth nyng o keffys,* to the wild birds to nestle places were ready, to Christ his head to hold never a place was found. M.C. 206. *Gans lŷf uy wrâf hyuytha ladhé an dûs gwyls na dôf,* with flood I will never destroy mankind, wild nor tame. O.M. 1254. *Me a vyn môs dhe wandra, bestas gwylls dhe aspea, hag a vyn gans ow sethow ladha part anodhans y,* I will go to wander, to look for wild beasts, and I will with mine arrows kill some of them. C.W. 108. W. *gwyllt,* † *guilt.* Ir. *geilt, fuol.* Gael. † *geilt,* † *fuol.*

GWYLLY, v. a. Thou shalt see. 2 pers. s. fut. of *gweles,* qd. v. *Ha war scon del y'n gwylly, ef a'th saw hep ken gly ol a'th elevos yn tyen,* and as soon as thou shalt see him, he will heal thee, without other remedy of all thy malady entirely. R.D. 1694.

GWYLLYF, v. a. I may see. 1 pers. s. subj. of *gweles,* qd. v. *Drewh e dhyuuno mo'n gwyllyf, na row vŷdh pan y'n kyffyf a dhesempys,* bring ye him to me that I may see him; he shall die immediately, when I get him. R.D. 1776.

GWYLSYN, v. a. We saw. 1 pers. pl. preter. of *gweles,* qd. v. *Ny gen bo whans gwariow, a lês ol y wolyow adhyragon pan gwylsyn,* we had no desire of pastimes, all his wounds disclosed when we saw before us. R.D. 1332.

GWYLVYTII, v. a. He shall see. 3 pers. sing. fut. of *gweles,* qd. v. *Ha deydh brues dheuch ef a dhue, ha why a'n gwylvyth yn yer worth agan yuggé,* and the day of judgment he will come to you, and ye shall see him in the sky judging you. P.C. 1332. *Ef a nêf dhe pen try dêdh, ha henna ny a'n gwylvyth gans dew lagas,* he will rise at the end of three days, and we shall see him with (our) eyes. R.D. 53.

GWYLY, s. m. A bed, a couch. *Dues, ow howethes Eva, growedh yn gwyly a hŷs,* my companion Eve, lie in bed at length. O.M. 653. *El a'n leverys dedhy haneth ha hy yn gwyly, pûr dhyfun, mŷns re gruays,* an angel said it to her this night, and she in bed quite awake; he said the whole. P.C. 2203. This is another form of *gwely,* qd. v.

GWYLYS, v. a. I have seen. 1 pers. s. preter. of *gweles,* qd. v. *Râk an kêth dên-ma lythqueth ny'n servyes war ow ené, na, rum fay, my ny'n gwylys,* for this same man never have I served, upon my soul, nor by my faith, have I seen him. P.C. 1286. *An eledh omma yw gwyn, avel an houl pan dhynehyn, yn ken lyw ny's gwylys wheth,* the angels here are white, like the sun when it shines, in other colour I have not seen them. R.D. 2534.

GWYLYS, part. Seen. Part. pass. of *gweles,* qd. v. *Spyrys a vewnans ynno, vynytha na vo gwylys,* that the spirit of life in it never more shall be seen. O.M. 986.

GWYN, adj. White, fair, pleasant, glorious, blessed. *I bcyn o mar grîf ha tyn, caman na ylly lewé, hib dascor y eueff gwyn, bythqueth yn lân revewsé,* his pain was so strong and sharp, so that he could not live without yielding his glorious soul, (that) had ever lived pure. M.C. 204. *Un flôch yonk, gwyn y dhyllas, eyll o, ha y ny wodhyens,* a young child, white his apparel, an angel he was, and they knew it not. M.C. 254. *Môs dhe wolhy ow dulé a dhesempys me a vyn omma yn dour, may fôns y gwyn ha glân lour a vostethes,* go to wash my hands immediately I will here in the water that they may be white and clean enough from dirt. R.D. 2205. In construction it changes into *wyn,* and *whyn. I vam whêk, Marya wyn, pûb ûr fystené a wre,* his sweet mother, blessed Mary, every hour made haste. M.C. 171. *Ef a vŷdh anclethys yn le na fue dên lythqueth, yn alabauster gravys; ragef y fue ordynys maga whyn avel an lêth,* he shall be buried in a place where never man was, cut in alabaster; for me it was intended, as white as the milk. P.C. 3138. *Gwyn* with *bŷs* is used, as in Welsh, to express a happy state, as *gwyn ow bĵs*, happy I. (W. *gwyn fy mĵd.*) See *Bĵs*. The feminine form of *gwyn* was *gwen*, qd. v. W. *gwyn*, m., *gwen*, f. Arm. *gwenn*. Irish, *fionn*, *fenn*, †*fin*, †*find*, *ban*. Gael. *fionn*, *ban*. Manx, *ben*. Anc. Gaulish, *vind*. (Cf. *Vindobona*, *Vindonissa*.) Sanso. *pándu*.

GWYN, s. m. White, a white colour, that which is fair or white. *I a wyskis Cryst gans gwyn, avel fôl y a'n scornyé*, they clothed Christ with white, like a fool they scorned him. M.C. 114. *Kyng ys y vôs alemna, yn gwyn of a vĵdh gwyskys*, before his going hence, in white he shall be clothed. P.C. 1780. *Hag yn gwyn ef re'n gwyskas*, and in white he has clothed him. P.C. 1844. W. *gwynn*. Arm. *gwenn*.

GWYNNA, v. a. To make white, to whiten. *Iosep dhe Gryst a wynnas y arrow, ha'y dheffrech whêk, yn vaner del yn vhas, hag a's ystynnas pûr dêk*, Joseph for Christ made white his legs, and his sweet arms, in manner as was usual, and stretched them out very fairly. M.C. 233. W. *gwynnu*. Arm. *gwenna*.

GWYNNEG, s. f. A whiting fish. In late Cornish corrupted into *gwynluac*. W. *gwyniad*. Arm. *gwennek*, *gwennik*. Ir. *fuincog*. Gael. *fionnag*.

GWYNS, s. m. Wind. *Dour ha lêr, ha tân, ha gwyns, houl, ha loer, ha steyr kyffrys*, water and earth, and fire and wind, sun, and moon, and stars likewise. M.C. 211 *Gwrĵs da vyé eafus tân, râk marthys yeyn yw an gwyns*, it would be well done to have a fire, for wondrous cold is the wind. P.C. 1215. *Euch tennuch a dhysempys y goyl yn ban, may hallo môs gans an gwyns*, go ye, draw immediately her sail up, that she may go with the wind. R.D. 2292. *Gwyns adro*, a whirlwind. W. *gwynt*. Arm. *gwent*. Ir. *gwoth*. Gael. *gaoth*. Gr. ἄητος. Lat. *ventus*. Goth. *winds*. Lith. *wésis*. Sanse. *váta*, *vahanta*; from *vah*, to go.

GWYNYS, part. Pierced. Part. pass. of *gwané*, qd. v. *A Thomas, doro dhe luef yn woly gwynys may fues dre an golon*, O Thomas, put thy hand into the wound where I was pierced through the heart. R.D. 1540.

GWYRCHES, s. f. A virgin, a maid. *Onan yw an, Tâs a nêf, arall, Cryst y un vaaw ef, a vĵdh a wyrches genys*, one is the Father of heaven, another, Christ his one Son, who shall be of a virgin born. O.M. 2663. Written also *gwerches*, qd. v., and *gwyrhes*. *Bynnyges re bo an prĵs, may fe a venen genys, an wyrhes kêr Maria*, blessed be the time that he was born of woman, the dear Virgin Mary. R.D. 154. W. *gwyryn*. Arm. *gwerch*, *gwerchez*, †*gwerches*. Irish, †*gearait*, †*gerait*, (*geirrseach*, a girl.) Lat. *virgo*. Sanse. *virada*.

GWYRRAS, s. m. The ground, earth. *Més a'n dôr ev a ve gwrĵs, hag arta dhe'n kêth gwyrras y fĵdh trylyes*, out of the earth he was made, and again to the same earth he shall be turned. C.W. 160. This is a later form of *gwered*, or as written in the Cornish Vocabulary, *gueret*, qd. v. W. *gweryd*.

GWYRTHY, v. a. To sell. *Mas lemmyn rĵs yw porris batayles kyns ys coské, a'n geffo powes, a's gwyrthyns, ha dhodho pernas cledhé*, but now it is very necessary to battle rather than sleep, he that has a coat, let him sell it, and buy for him a sword. M.C. 51. *Pyth yw an ethom ryé an onyment kêr y skullyé, ef a galsé bôs gwyrthys a try cans dyner ha moy*, what is the need to spill the precious ointment? it might have been sold for three hundred pence and more. P.C. 535. *Ow corf yw, re'n offeren, gwyrthys, lydhys yn grows pren*, my body it is, by the mass, sold, killed on the cross tree. P.C. 766. *Me re pechés marthys trûs, gwyr gôs Dew pan y'n gwyrthys*, I have sinned wondrous sadly, the true blood of God, when I sold it. P.C. 1507. Another form of *gwerthy*, qd. v.

GWYSCEL, v. a. To beat, to strike. Participle, *gwyscys*. *Dew a erchys dhys, Moyses, dhe welen y kemeres, ha gwyskel an môr gynsy*, God has commanded thee, Moses, to take thy rod, and to strike the sea with it. O.M. 1605. *Arluth, lavar dyssempys dhymny, mars yw bôdh dhe vreys my dhe wyskel gans cledhé nêp ûs worth dhe dalhenné*, Lord, say immediately to us, if it is the wish of thy judgment, that I strike with the sword him that is seizing thee. P.C. 1140. *Gans queth me a vyn eudhé y fâs, hag onan a'n gwĵsk; yn ûr-na, ef dysmegys py gansé y fue gwyskys*, with a cloth I will cover his face and one shall strike him ; in that hour let him declare, by whom he was struck. P.C. 1371. *Yn hanow Dew, ty môr glân, me a'th wĵsk gans ow gwelan*, in the name of God, thou fair sea, I will strike thee with my rod. O.M. 1676. *Pan vo gwyskys an bugel, y fy an deves a bel, hag ol an flok a dhybarth*, when the shepherd is smitten, the sheep will flee far, and the flock will separate. P.C. 893. *Y cudhé scon me a wra; gwyskys lemmyn nêp cowyth, may hallo ef dysmygy pyne a'n gwyskys, a'n barth clêdh*, I will presently cover him ; let some comrade now strike, that he may shew who struck him on the left side. P.C. 1377. *Gans pûb colmen may'th ellé, pan vryskens, yn môs an crow*, with every knot that the blood might come out, when they struck. M.C. 131. W. *gwasgu*. Arm. *gwascu*. Irish, *faisg*. Gael. *faisg*. Manx, *faaste*.

GWYTH, s. m. Act, or motion ; work. *Ow ham wĵth brâs, gáf dhym a Tâs dre dhe vertu*, my great evil deed forgive me, O Father, by thy virtue. P.C. 3020. Written in the Cornish Vocabulary, *gueid*, opus. W. *gwaith*, †*gweith*. Ir. †*fecht*. Lat. *factum*.

GWYTH, s. m. Course, turn, or time. *Tressé gwĵth, hag ef yn cren, y pesys, Du dylyr vy*, the third time, and he trembling prayed, God deliver me. M.C. 57. *Pymp mĵll strekis, del iové, ha peder gwĵth cans golhy*, five thousand strokes, so they were, and four times a hundred wounds. M.C. 227. *Go-vy vĵth pan ĵth dhodho, pan ôf fythys dhyworto ter-gwĵth lydhew*, woe is me. that I ever went to him, when I am worsted by him three times to-day. P.C. 147. *Saw râk Peder caradow, lyes gwĵth me re besys*, but for beloved Peter, many times I have prayed. P.C. 884. Written also *gwêth*, and *gweyth*. W. *gwaith*, †*gweith*. Arm. *gwech*, *gwez*, †*guez*, †*guciz*. Ir. *feacht*, †*feet*, *faoi*, *fa*. Gael. *fáth*, *fa*. Lat. *vice*. Goth. *wiko*. Russ. *wick*. Germ. *woche*. Eng. *week*. Sanse. *vicis*, fr. *vic*, to remove.

GWYTH, s. m. A vein. Pl. *gwythy*. *Neb a vynna a ylly nevera oll y yseren, hay skennys kĵfe ha gwythy pan esa yn crows pren*, whosoever would might number all his bones, his sinews, flesh, and veins, when he was on the crosstree. M.C. 183. This is written in the Cornish Vocabulary, *guid*, qd. v., and for the singular, *gôth* was also used, qd. v. W. *gwĵth*, *gwythen*, *gwythien*, †*guithenn*. Arm. *gwazen*, *gwazien*. Ir. *feith*. Gael. *feith*.

GWYTHOR, s. m. A workman, a worker. Pl. *gwythor-*

yon. Syr, arluth whêk, mûr y râs, yma ow conys dhyuwhy chyf gwythoryon ol an gwlâs, a wodher dhe dysmegy, Sire, sweet lord, of much grace, there are working for you all the chief workmen of the land who can be mentioned. O.M. 2331. Written in the Cornish Vocabulary, *guciduwr.* W. *gweithiwr.* " Marium plerique Mamurium, nonnulli Vecturium, opificem utpote ferrarium, nuncuparunt." Trebell. Poll. quoted by Zeuss, 180.

GWYTHRES, s. f. Action, deed, fact, work. *Ihesus Cryst a leverys y vôs scryfys yn lyfrow yn pûb gwythres y côth dhys gordhyé dhe Dhu, ha'y hanow,* Jesus Christ said that it is written in books, in every action it behoveth thee to worship God, and his name. M.C. 17. *A Dûs del ôn dhe wythres, a bol hag a lyys formys,* O Father, as we are thy work, made of clay and mire. O.M. 1069. W. *gweithred.*

GWYTHY, v. a. To work, to labour. Part. *gwythys. Out warnouch, a dhew adla, pendra wreuch ow repryfa, ha my omma yn ow hel; y a vŷdh gwythys cales, hedré vyns yn ow gwlâs,* out upon you, O two knaves, why do ye reprove me, and I here in my hall ? they shall be hard worked, as long as they are in my kingdom. O.M. 1502. W. *gweithio.*

GWYW, adj. Apt, fit, proper, due, deserving, worthy. *Nep a rella yn ketella, mernans yw gwyw dh'y vody,* whoever will act in that way, death is due to his body. O.M. 2242. *Gwyw yw yn lên dhe servyé,* it is worth while to serve thee faithfully. O.M. 2001. *Gwyn bŷs a allo bôs gwyw lên dhe'th gordhyé,* happy he that can be worthy faithfully to worship thee. P.C. 284. *Yn pren crows gruwch y worré, del yw e greyw dyougel,* on the crosstree do ye put him, as he is deserving truly. P.C. 2358. W. *gwiw, wiw.* Arm. †*guiu,* † *uiu.* Irish, *fiu.* Gael. *fiu.* Manx, *feeu.*

GY, s. m. Water, a river, a brook. It is preserved in the names of places, as *Boswor*gy, the house on the river. It is the same as the Welsh *gŵy*, which occurs so frequently in the names of rivers in Wales, as Con*wy*, El*wy*, Myn*wy*, Og*wy*, Dis*wy*, &c. W. *gŵy; gŵyg, wyyg,* †*uisc,* a stream. Arm. *gwaz, oaz.* Irish, *gais, uisge.* Gael. *gais, uisge.* Manx, *ushtey.* Sansc. *g'as,* to flow.

GY, s. m. A house. *Lemyn Noy y'th worhel ke, ty hag ol mryny dhe gy,* now Noah, go into the ark, thou and all within thy house. O.M. 1018. *Kerch y dhe gy, mar mynnyth,* bring them to the house, if thou wilt. P.C. 2282. *Dûn yn kerch gans an prysnes; ke dhe gy, kerch y yn môs, môs alemma ma hyllyn,* let us come away with the prisoners; go to the house, bring them out, that we may go hence P.C. 2200. *A-gy,* in the house. *Gy* is the secondary mutation of *chy,* qd. v., and is the only instance in the Corn. Language. This mutation is quite unknown to Welsh and Armoric, but there is an exact parallel in Manx, as *chiarn,* a lord, *nyn jiarn,* our lord. In both cases *ch* is a corruption of *t.*

GY, pron. subs. Thou, thee. *Me a lever ow mâp dhys, Dew dhymmo vy a erchys, may fydhé gy offrynnys dhodho of war an alter,* I tell thee my son, God hath commanded me that thou be offered to him upon the altar. O.M. 1327. *Ha dhyso gy ydhesé benenes lour,* and to thee there were women enough. O.M. 2246. *Dreys pûp huny pûr wyr ôs gy bynyges,* above every one very truly thou

art blessed. P.C. 417. *Saw dhe vôdh dhe gy Arluth bedhens gurŷs yn pûp termyn,* but thy will to thee, Lord, be it done at every time. P.C. 1039. *Ogé gy, a cowyth da, onan a dûs an dên-ma,* art thou, O good fellow, one of the people of this man ? P.C. 1234. *Ahanas gy un demma my ny sensaf yn torma,* of thee one halfpenny I do not hold at this time. P.C. 2263. *Me a vyn degy adro, ha dhe worré gy dhe'n fo, a dhesempys,* I will carry round, and put thee to flight immediately. P.C. 2314. *Gy* is another form of *sy,* and both corruptions of *ty,* or *ti,* qd. v.

GY, pron. subs. Ye, you. *Ow mebyon, my a gy peys, yn mês whêth dylleuch iryssé, mar kêf tŷr sŷch, me a greys, dynny ny dhewhel arté,* my sons, I pray you, send out yet a third; if it shall find dry land, I believe it will not return to us again. O.M. 1129. A later form of *chwi,* and agrees exactly with the Manx, *jee,* as bee-jee, be ye; *jean-jee,* do ye, &c.

GY, pron. subs. They, them. ‡ *Ha gwréns an gy bôs rág tavasow, ha rág termeniow, ha rág journiow, ha rág bledheniow,* and let them be for signs, and for seasons, and for days, and for years. C.W. p. 190. ‡*Ha Dew rig go benigas an gy,* and God did bless them. 192. ‡ *Gava do ny agan cammow, pokara ny gava an gy nêb ês camma warbyn ny,* forgive us our trespasses, as we forgive them that trespass against us. *Pryce.* Llwyd, 244, 252, writes the word phonetically, *dzhei;* as *mêdh an dzhei,* say they. This is a later form; *y* being always used in the Ordinalia.

GYBEDDERN, s. m. A beetle, or mallet. *Llwyd,* 84.]

GYBMAR, v. a. Take thou. A late corruption of *gymmer,* a mutation of *cymmer,* qd. v.

GYC, s. m. Flesh. See *Gic.*

GYC, s. m. Noise. ‡ *Sottall lower ôe, me a greys; hag a vyn môs, heb gwill gyc, yn wedhan pûr smoth heb mycke, avel call wheak asnynes,* I am subtle enough, I believe; and I will go, without making a noise, into the tree very smoothly without discovery, like a sweet angel adorned. C.W. 40.

GYDREVA, adv. The third day hence. *Llwyd,* 249. This seems to be a corrupted compound from *gŷdh,* day, and *treva,* third. W. *tradwy.* Gr. τη τρίτη.

GYDH, s. m. A day. *Pan o pûr holerch an gŷdh, y tefenas un marrek,* when tho day was far on, there awoke a soldier. M.C. 244. *Yn kêth gŷdh-na pûr avar, ha'n houl nowydh drehevys,* on that same day very early, and the sun newly risen. M.C. 252. *Gwyn veys ha quellen an gŷdh,* happy I, should I see the day. O.M. 1013. A corruption of *dŷdh,* qd. v.

GYDIAS, s. m. Judgment. *Llwyd,* 74. A contracted form of *gyhudhas,* a mutation of *cyhudhas,* or *cuhudhas,* qd. v.

GYDHIHWAR, s. m. The evening. *Llwyd,* 52, 65. ‡ *Mi vedn gyz gwelaz arta gydhihwar,* I will see you again in the evening. 244. One of the various forms of *godhihuar,* or *gurthuwer,* qd. v.

GYE, v. a. To spear, to pierce with a lance. *Pan fo guw yn y dhulé, me a hyrch dhodho hertyé, hag a'n gy ewn dh'y golon,* when there is a spear in his hands, I will enjoin him to thrust, and he shall pierce him right to the heart. P.C. 2234. Formed from *guw,* a spear.

GYF, v. a. He shall have. A mutation of *cêf,* 3 pers. s. fut. of *cafos,* qd. v. *Ef a glŷf yn Araby, yn mount Tabor, gwelynny a plansas Moyses, hep mar,* he will find in Arabia, in Mount Tabor, rods which Moses planted, without doubt. O.M. 1930. *Ena why a gûf asen hag ebel yn un golmen*, there ye shall find an ass and foal in a halter. P.C. 176. *Ny gûf medhek a'n saweya*, he finds not a leech (that) can cure him. R.D. 1648.

GYFFE, v. a. He may have. A mutation of *cyffé*, 3 pers. s. subj. of *cafos*, qd. v. *Warnedhy pren be tewlys, ol an bows pyw a'n gyffé*, on it a lot was cast, all the coat who should have. M.C.190. *Gyfyé* is another form, qd.v.

GYFFY, v. a. Thou shalt have. A mutation of *cyffy*, 2 pers. s. fut. of *cafos*, qd. v. *Fystyn ow dûf whêk a vy, gweyt an harlot na scapyo; drok handlé, del om kyry, pan guffy dalhen ynno*, hasten, my sweet captain mine, take care that the knave escapes not; handle him roughly, as thou lovest me, when thou shalt have hold in him. P.C. 992.

GYFYANS, s. m. Forgiveness, pardon. *Rág y servonnth yn nêp plâs nys tefyth fout a gyffyans*, for his servants in no place will there be a want of pardon. O.M. 1808. *A'y gyfyens ny rôf bram*, for his forgiveness I care not a jot. P.C. 2779. *Pedar, guffyens ty a vydh, rák dhe eddrek yw perfyth*, Peter, pardon thou shalt have, for thy repentance is perfect. R.D. 1159. *Pûp crystyon ol yn wêdh a vynno pygy gyfyans, y's kyrhaf gans ow eledh*, every Christian also (that) will pray for pardon, I will bring them with my angels. R.D. 1576. From *gafé*, to forgive.

GYFFE, v. a. He would have. A mutation of *cyfyé*, 3 pers. s. subj. of *cafos*, qd. v. *Nyn gyfyé dên gallos dhe'n mernans y worré ef; ragon y fynnes nerwel ha môs yn bêdh*, man would not have power to put him to death; for us he would die, and go into the grave. R.D. 966. Another form of *guffé*, qd. v.

GYFYN, v. a. I did have. A mutation of *cyfyn*, 1 pers. s. imperf. of *cafos*, qd. v. *Yn y worthyp ny gufyn fout vyth ol yn nêp terwyn, kên dh'y ladhé*, in his answer I did not find any fault at all at any time, cause to kill him. R.D. 1850.

GYFYS, part. Pardoned, forgiven. *Ha rák henna, warbarth, ol y fichas gwlân dedhy hy y feydh gufys*, and for that, together all her sins clean to her shall be forgiven. P.C. 520. Part. pass. of *gafé*, qd. v.

GYGEL, s. m. A distaff. See *Gigel*.

GYHYDHA, v. n. To accuse. A mutation of *cyhydha*, or *cuhudha*, qd. v.

GYHYDHAS, s. m. Judgment. A mutation of *cyhudhas*, or *cuhudhas*, qd. v.

GYL, v. a. He shall be able. 3 pers. s. fut. of *gally*, qd. v. *Why a gûf bohosugyon pûp ûr warnoch ow carmé; pan vynnoch agus honon, why a gyl gûl da dhedhé*, ye will have the poor always on you calling; when ye will yourselves, ye may do good to them. P.C. 546. *A gil, Thomas, fest yn ta; mâp Dew daserchy a wra pan y rynno*, Thomas, very well it may be; the Son of God will rise when he pleases. R.D. 641. It changes in construction to *gîl*, qd. v.

GYLE, s. m. A companion. See *Gilé*.

GYLL, v. a. He will lose. A mutation of *cyll*, 3 pers. s. fut. of *cylly*, qd. v.

GYLLY, v. n. To lose. A mutation of *cylly*, qd. v. *Pan rûk drys y worhemmyn, ow ertech grûk dhe gylly*, when I acted against his command, it caused me to lose my heritage. O.M. 354.

GYLLY, v. n. To go, to become. Part. *gyllys*. *Whêth ow cufyon dyfunouch, ha kês-colon ol pesowch na gyllouch yn temptacion*, again my dears, awake, and with one heart all pray, that ye enter not into temptation. P.C. 1077. *Ny dhueth an prŷs, er na gyllyf dhe'n nêf dhum tâs, may tewhyllyf arté dhum gwlâs*, the time is not come, until I go to heaven to my Father, that I may return again to my country. R.D. 878. *An êl dhyn a leverys worth an bêdh, y vûs yn ban dasserchys, ha dhe nêf golow gyllys gans mûr cledh*, the angel said to us at the tomb, that he was risen up, and to the bright heaven gone with many angels. R.D. 1065. *Yma dhymmo vy dnon, gyllys lemmyn y'm colon*, there is sorrow to me, gone now into my heart. R.D. 2247. The preterite is *gallas*; other tenses are *galsof*, *galsé*, *galsons*, qd. v.

GYLLYF, v. n. I may be able. 1 pers. s. subj. of *gally*, qd. v. *Me a'n herth gwell ha gyllyf, na vlamyouch vy kyn fyllyf, rák dul ôf, ny welaf man*, I will thrust it the best I can; blame me not, though I should fail, for I am blind, I see not at all. P.C. 3012. W. *gallwyv*.

GYLM, v. a. He will bind. A mutation of *cylm*, 3 pers. s. fut. of *cylmy*. *Me a gylm an ngl wharré; ottê ow lovan gyné rág y gylmy. Ha me a gylm y gylé, alemma kyns tremené*, I will bind the one soon; behold my rope with me to bind him. And I will bind the other, before passing from hence. P.C. 2785.

GYLMY, v. a. To bind. A mutation of *cylmy*, qd. v.

GYLSEN, v. a. We lost. A mutation of *cylsen*, 1 pers. pl. preter. of *cylly*, qd. v. *Nang ew mêr a for pûr wŷr, aban gylsen sight an tŷr*, it is now much of way very truly, since we lost sight of the land. C.W. 178.

GYLVAN, s. m. A sparrow. *Gylvan gê*, a hedge-sparrow. Llwyd, 53, 114, 240. A later form of *golvan*, qd. v.

GYLVINAC, s. m. A curlew. Llwyd, 240, 241. So called from W. *gylvin*, a beak. W. *gilvinhir*, a curlew. Gael. *guilbinn*, *guilbneach*, *guilbirneach*. Irish, *filbin*, a lapwing.

GYLWEL, v. a. To call. *My a'th pŷs, gynes mar plêk, war lowyn sgêwel mercy*, I pray thee, if it pleases thee, on Jove to call mercy. P.C. 1807. *Uthyk mûr yw dhe areth, lemen worth agan gylwel*, very horrid is thy speech, now calling us. P.C. 955. *En Tâs a nêf yn gylwyr*, the Father of heaven I am called. O.M. 1. (W. *gelwir*.) *Hag ynno lues trygva, romes y a vŷdh gylwys*, and in it many dwellings, rooms they shall be called. O.M. 952. *Yowynk ha lous, kyn fo tollys dre y dennos, mercy gylwys*, young and grey, though he may be deceived by his witchery, let him call for mercy. P.C. 20. *Y'n gylwys mâp Dew, yn prôf ahanaf way portho côf, pan deffé dh'y welascor ef*, I called him the Son of God, in proof that he might bear remembrance of me, when he should come to his kingdom. R.D. 271. *Pûb onan ol a ylwys. Arluth Du, yw me henna*, every one of them all cried out, Lord God, am I he? M.C. 43. *Nyns yw Ely a gylwa*, it is not Elias (whom) he called. P.C. 2973. Another form of *gelwel*, qd. v.

GYLYWA, v. a. To shine. *Dho gylywa*. Llwyd, 62. The same as *golowa*, qd. v.

GYMERES, v. a. A mutation of *cymeres*, qd. v.

GYMMYN, v. a. He shall commend. A mutation of *cymmyn*, 3 pers. s. fut. of *cymmyny*, qd. v. *A Dâs yntré dhe dhewlé my a gymmyn ow ené, gwŷthé ef rág tarofvan*,

O Father, into thy hands I commend my soul, preserve it from terrors. O.M. 2363.

GYMMYS, adj. So much. A mutation of *cymmys*, qd. v. *Pûr vysy a veydh dhedhé, ha dhe gymmys a ve gwrġs*, very hard it shall be for them, and for as much as has been done. O.M. 336. *Ha gweles yn bledhen hŷr, py gymmys hŷs may teffo*, and see in a long year, to what length it may grow. O.M. 2104.

GYN, s. m. A back. *Au mŷl dynul re dorrow mellow y gŷn*, may a thousand devils break the joints of his back. P.C. 2619. A contracted form of *geyn*, a mutation of *ceyn*, or *cein*, qd. v.

GYN, pron. adj. Our. *Dho gyn honyn*, to ourselves *Lhwyd*, 244. An abbreviated form of *agyn*, or *agan* qd. v.

GYN, prep. With. Used only in composition, as *gyné*, *gynen*, &c.

GYNDAN; s. m. Debt. A mutation of *cyndan*, qd. v. ‡ *Ny vedn e nevra dôs vês a gyndan*, he will never get out of debt. *Lhwyd*, 230.

GYNE, pron. prep. With me. *Drók yw gyné, na venta cammen tryle yn maner têk*, I am sorry that thou wilt not turn thy way in a fair manner. P.C. 1292. *Ottê try pren gyné vy*, behold three lots with me. P.C. 2849. An abbreviated form of *gynef*, and is also written *yené*.

GYNEF, pron. prep. With me. *Y'ma gynef flowrys têk*, I have fair flowers. P.C. 258. *Gynef yma fardhel pûr dha, war ow keyn*, I have a very good burden on my back. O.M. 1616. *Dueeh gynef warbarth ol, me ngas peys*, come with me together all, I pray you. R.D. 2307. Comp. of *gyn*, 1d. qd. *gan*, or *gans*, and *me*. Written also *genef*, qd. v.

GYNEN, pron. prep. With us. *Hedré vy yn beys gyneu, neffré trystyns ny gen bydh*, whilst thou wilt be in the world with us, we shall never have sorrow. P.C. 730. *Rĝs yw dheuch whéth, bĝs ma fo gwrġs an dywedh, gynen lufuryé*, ye must yet, until the end be accomplished, labour with us. P.C. 1831. Written also *genen*, qd. v.

GYNES, pron. prep. With thee. *My â gynes yn lowen*, I will go with thee gladly. P.C. 191. *Dyrwê dhym nêp reson a'th tyskes omma dyson, may hyllyn gynes dysky*, show to me some reason of thy teaching here quietly, that we may learn with thee. P.C. 1250. Written also *genes*, qd. v.

GYNES, v. a. To sow, to plant. *Lhwyd*, 149. Another form of *gonys*, qd. v.

GYNNADAR, s. m. A sower, a seedsman. *Lhwyd*, 148, 240.

GYNOUCH, pron. prep. With ye, or you. *Yn lowen gynouch my û*, joyfully I will go with you. P.C. 1835. Written also *gynouch*. *Ytho gynouch me a trŷk, y ges bydh ioy na dhufyk, deuch lavaraf*, now with you I will stay, you shall have joy (that) will not fail, I say to you. R.D. 1309. These are various forms of *genouch*, qd. v.

GYNS, adv. Before. A mutation of *cyns*, qd. v. *Mar ny vgdh Pilat marow dhe gyns, ny won pyth a wrâf*, if Pilate be not dead before, I know not what I shall do. R.D. 1843.

GYNSY, pron. prep. With her, or it. (*Gans-hy.*) *Dew a erchys dhys Moyses dhe welen y kemeres, ha gwyskel an môr gynsy*, God has commanded thee Moses, thy rod to take, and strike the sea with it. O.M. 1665. *Gallas hy gobyr gynsy, ha servyys yw del gothé*, her reward is gone with her, and she is served as she ought. O.M. 2764. Welsh, *gandhi*, † *genthi*, † *kenthy*, † *genti*. Arm. *gant-hi*, † *ganti*, † *ganty*.

GYNYS, part. Born. *Yn wedhen me a welas yn ban whel worth scoren flôch byan nowydh gynys*, in the tree I saw high on a branch, a little child newly born. O.M. 800. *Yn wêdh ol râg agan lês, y fue gynys a wyrhes kêr Maria*, also all for our advantage, he was born of the virgin dear Mary. R.D. 1199. This is the same as *genys*, part. of *geny*, qd. v.

GYNZHANS, pron. prep. With them. *Lhwyd*, 244. Though this form is not found in the Ordinalia, *gansé* being always used, it agrees nearer with the W. *gan-dhynt*.

GYRGYRIC, s. f. A partridge. *Lhwyd*, 5, 117, 241, derives this from *cor-yâr*, a dwarf-hen. It occurs only in late Cornish, and more probably is a corruption of the older term *grugyer*, qd. v.

GYRHAS, v. a. To fetch, to bring. A mutation of *cyrhas*, qd. v. *Dûn dhe gyrhas Salamon, ha goryn cf yn y dron, avel mychtern yn y se*, let us go to fetch Solomon, and let us put him in his throne, like a king in his seat. O.M. 2371. *Heil Arluth, me re gyrhas dhys dhe dré mâb Adam, a fals kudry, may hallo genen tregê*, hail, Lord, I have fetched home to thee the son of Adam, the false deceiver, that he may dwell with us. O.M. 564.

GYRYN, s. f. A crown. ‡ *Tau gyryn*, to the crown. *Lhwyd*, 249. A mutation of *cyryn*, or *curyn*, qd. v.

GYS, pron. adj. Your. *Euch, ponetheuch termyn hŷr, powes ny gys bydh nêp preys*, go ye, labour for a long term; rest ye shall not have at any time. O.M. 1222. *Euch lemmyn yn paradis kepar del y gys prynnys marthys yn tyn*, go ye now into Paradise, like as I have redeemed ye, wondrous painfully. R.D. 180. ‡ *Hwei el dendel gyz bownas ybma*, ye may get your living here. *Lhwyd*, 251. ‡ *Mi vedn gyz gwelas arta gydhihwar*, I will see you again in the evening. 344. ‡ *Ew hodda gyz hâr hwei*, is that your sister? 244. *Gys* is an abbreviated form of *agys*, qd. v. In later Cornish it was contracted into *'z*, as ‡ *an lydrow adro'z garrow*, the stockings on your legs. ‡ *An esyizow adro'z treiz*, the shoes on your feet. ‡ *An manak adro'z dorn*, the glove on your hand. *Lhwyd*, 250.

GYSENZIII, v. a. To lay. *Lhwyd*, 245.

GYSIGAN, s. f. A bladder. *Lhwyd*, 25, 172, writes it *gyzigan*. W. *chwysigen*. Arm. *chouezigen*, *chouezigel*. Lat. *vesica*.

GYSSEUCII, v. a. Ye left, or have left. *Syr Pilat dhys lowené, corf Cryst, a gysseuch gyné, yn bêdh gallas*, Sir Pilate, joy to thee, the body of Christ, (which) you left with me, is gone to the tomb. R.D. 38. 2 pers. pl. preter. of *gasé*, qd. v.

GYSSYS, v. a. Thou leftest, or hast left. *A Tûs, &s ow Dew kêr, prâg y'm gyssys tuch dheworthys yn nêb maner*, O Father, thou art my dear God, why hast thou left me a moment from thee in any manner? P.C. 2957. 2 pers. sing. preterite of *gasé*, qd. v.

GYST, s. m. A joist, a beam. Pl. *gystys*. *Yn crês an chy rês vyé kafus gŷst crêf na vo grean*, in the midst of the house it would be necessary to have a strong beam, that it may not be weak. O.M. 2482. *Saw levercuch* dhym defry, pren dhé gŷst ple kefyn ny, a vo compes avel sheft, but tell ye me seriously, a tree for the beam where shall we find, which may be straight like a shaft. O.M. 2492. *Lemyn dreheveuch an gist, yw gwrŷs crowes, war duscodh Cryst, dh'y dôn dhe drê,* now lift ye the beam, (that) is made a cross, on the shoulders of Christ, to carry it home. P.C. 2564. *Sytteuch gystys worth an yet,* put ye beams against the gate. P.C. 3067. Written also *jyst,* qd. v. W. *dist.* Gael. *dist.* Scot. *geist, gest.*

GYTHEFFIA, v. a. To propose, to offer. *Lhwyd,* 102, *gytheffias,* offered. *Gytheffys dhyu',* offered to you. 242. ‡ *Rag dout na vedho na mwi gytheffiaz dhyu', rhag an dzhedhma,* lest there be no more offered to you this day. 250.

GYVYANS, s. m. Forgiveness, pardon. *Ol mêns trespas a wrugé, dhodho cf me a'n gafsé, a menné geluel gyvyans,* all the evil he has done, to him I would forgive it, if he would ask pardon. P.C. 1816. This is another form of *gyfyans,* qd. v.

GYW, adj. Deserving, worthy, able. *Râg own y a gangyes lyw, râg gwander y a godhas, yn trevyth y nyng êns gyw dhe wethyl dris y vynnas,* for fear they changed colour, for weakness they fell, in nothing were they able to act beyond his will. M.C. 68. *Ha Pilat dhe war breder a leverys dhe Ihesu ; ol an dûs-wa a lever dhe vôs creqis te yw gyw,* and Pilate presently said to Jesus; all these men say that thou art deserving to be hanged. M.C. 129. *I frynys o brâs ha créf yn ioy dhedhy trylys yw, râg migternas yw yn néf, dhe vôs gordhyys hy yw gyw,* her pains (that) were great and strong are turned into joy for her, for she is queen in heaven, to be worshipped she is worthy. M.C. 226. Another form of *gwyw,* qd. v.

H.

THIS letter, sounded as in English, is not only an aspiration, but a distinct letter, and has two separate offices. First, it is employed to aspirate initial vowels after certain words preceding:—thus *gallaf,* I am able ; *ny allaf,* I am not able; *may halluf,* that I may be able. *Gallouch,* ye are able; *ny allouch,* ye are not able ; *may hallouch,* that ye may be able. Secondly: in Cornish *h* is frequently used as a substitute for the guttural *ch*:—thus *whêh* for *chwêch,* six ; *marh* for *march,* a horse ; *golhy* for *golchy,* to wash ; *dh'y huhudha,* for *dh'y chuhudha,* to accuse her ; *yn y holon* for *yn y cholon,* in her heart. Cf. Gr. χεῖμα, χθὲς, with the Lat. *hiems, heri.*

HA, conj. And. Before a vowel *hag. Tâs ha mâb,* father and son. *Dên hag ancval,* man and beast. It is used with *kepar,* like, as, when it has no equivalent in English: thus, *kepar ha dew,* like a god. O.M. 290. *Kepar hag ôn,* like as we are. O.M. 894. *Kepar ha my,* like me. O.M. 2350. *Kepar ha del leverys,* as I said. P.C. 2690. *Gwell ha gyllyf,* the best I can. P.C. 3012. *Kepar ha me a welas,* as I saw. R.D. 1076. It is often found joined with other words, as *han, (ha-an)* and the ; *hath, (ha-ath)* and thy ; *hay,* and his ; *hammy,* and me. It is sometimes found written *a.* W. *a, ag, ac,* †*ha,* †*hac.* Arm. *ha, hag.* Ir. *acus, agus.* Gael. *agus.* Manx, *as.* Lat. *ac.*

HA, interj. Ah, alas. *Pryce.*

HABADIN, s. m. Bondage, slavery. *Me yw an Arluth dhy Dew, nêb a's drôs dhe vês a'n tŷr Mitzraim, dhe vês a'n chy habadin,* I am the Lord thy God, who brought thee out of the land of Egypt, out of the house of bondage. *Pryce.*

HABAL, adj. Apt, fit. *Pryce.*

HABLYS, s. m. Preparation. *Deyow hablys,* the Thursday of preparation. Maundy Thursday. *An dŷdh o deyow hablys, may fenné Ihesus sopyé gans an rê yn y servys war an bês re dhewessé,* the day was the Thursday of preparation, that Jesus would sup with those in his service on the world (whom) he had chosen. M.C. 41. Written also *hamlos.* *Kerch a'n fenten dhym dour clêr dhe dhygtyé bôs dhynny ny erbyn soper, kepar del yw an vaner dwyow hamlos,* fetch clear water for me from the fountain, to prepare food to us for supper, like as it is the custom on Thursday of the preparation. P.C. 654. W. *dydh iau cablyd.* Arm. *iaou-gamblid, inou-amblid.* In W. *cablyd* means blaspheming, and *maundy* may be derived from the old English, *maund,* or *maunder,* to murmur. In Med. Lat. *capitilavium* is the name of Palm Sunday ; and metaphorically a *chiding,* or *castigation.* Cf. old Irish, *caplat, caplait.*

HABLYTH, adj. Pliant. *Pryce.* Incorrectly for *hyblyth,* qd. v.

HACRA, adj. More or most foul. This is both the comparative and superlative of *hager,* and is generally written in the Ordinalia, *hacré. Yn della war a whyrfith, mŷl wêth a vŷdh an dywedh, ha hacré es an dalleth,* if it happen so, a thousand (times) worse will be the end, and more odious than the beginning. R.D. 350. *An hacré mernans a vo, me a vyn ordyne dhodho* the most cruel death that may be, I will ordain for him. R.D. 2005. *Bynnyges re by, dhe'n harlot pan fynsys ry an hakeré mernans yn beys ; rák hacré mernans cys em-ladhé y honan ny gaffé dên, my a grŷs,* blessed be thou, to the villain when thou wouldest give the cruelest death in the world ; for a more cruel death than to kill himself no man may find, I believe. R.D. 2071.

HACTER, s. m. Deformity. *Oll dha splender, ha'th tecter, y trayl scon dhys dha hacter, ha mêr uthec byllen,* all thy splendour, and thy beauty shall be turned immediately to deformity, and most ugly foulness. C.W. 22. A contracted form of *hacrder,* the abstract substantive of *hager.*

HAD, comp. pron. And thy, *(ha-ad.) Dhe dhrwyth awos plegyé, rág haneth me re welas y to venions had ladhé,* thou shalt promise on account of pleasing (me,) for to-night I have seen that vengeance would come and slay thee. M.C. 123.

HAF, s. m. Summer. Corn. Voc. *estas. Pûp gwedhen tefyns a'y sâf, ow tôn hy frût ha'y delyow, ha'n losowys erbyn hâf degyns hâs yn erberow,* let every tree grow from its stem, bearing its fruit and its leaves, and let the plants against summer produce seed in gardens. O.M. 31. *My re bredyrys gîl prat, rág y wyllé erbyn hâf,* I have thought of doing a thing, to keep it against summer. O.M. 488. *Tormentores, dhymmo deuch, py vyngeans ha geuch why agas bŷdh kyns dôs hâf,* executioners, come to me, or surely vengeance ye shall have before summer comes. R.D. 1763. In later Cornish it was pronounced *háv*, as in Welsh. (*Ll.* 41.) *Ha fruites war bûb gwedhan y teyf gwáf ha háv keffrys*, and fruits on every tree shall grow winter and summer likewise. C.W. 28. W. *háv*, †*ham*. Arm. *han, hanv,* †*háf*. Ir. *samh, samhradh.* Gael. *samh, samhradh.* Manx, *sourcy*.

HAG, conj. And. Used before vowels, as *ha*. (qd. v.) is before consonants.

HAGEN, adv. But, but yet, notwithstanding. *Lhwyd*, 172. W. *hagen*. "*Tebyg yw genyv i hagen*, it appears likely to me nevertheless." (Mabin. j. 259.) Arm. *hagon, hogen.* Ir. *ceana, acht ceana.* Gael. *ceana, a cheana*.

HAGENZOL, adv. And also, furthermore, moreover. *Lhwyd*, 135, 249.

HAGER, adj. Ugly, deformed, rough, foul, evil, naughty, fierce, cruel. Comp. *hacrah*. Sup. *hacra*. *Hag y ce dhé ben develyn, ha hager mowys a wre*, and they went on their knees, and made ugly mouths. M.C. 196. *Y'ma ow tegenayré hager gowes, war ow fédh*, there is coming down a fierce shower, on my faith. O.M. 1080. *Gory vgth rák edregé, bôs mar hager ow gorfen*, woe to me ever for sorrows, that my end should be so cruel. P.C. 1530. *Hager awel hag awel tég*, foul weather and fine weather. Pryce. *Hager oberow*, evil deeds. *Lhwyd*, 252. W. *hagyr, hagr*. Arm. *hacr*. Eng. haggard.

HAGRY, v. a. To make ugly, or unseemly; to defile. Part. *hagrys*. *Noy, mar lenwys ow an bỹs lemyn a skerewynsy, may'thew dewedh devethys unna a gỹk pûp hynyth; gans péch pûr wỹr ow hagrys, ny allaf sparya na moy*, Noah, so full is the world now of wickedness, that an end is come in it of flesh of every kind; with sin very truly it is defiled, I can forbear no more. C.W. 164. W. *hagru*. Arm. *hacraat*.

HAI, pron. subs. She. *Lhwyd*, 56, 67, 244, thus writes *hi*, or *hy*, qd. v.

HAIL, adj. Generous, liberal, bountiful. Corn. Vocab. *largus*. W. *hael*, †*hail*, †*hel*. Arm. *heal, hel*, † *hail*, †*hacl*. Ir. *fail, fial*. Gael. *fial*. Manx, *feoilt*.

HAIN, comp. pron. And our. *Lhwyd*, 244. Comp. of *ha*, and, and *ein*, our, which is the Welsh form, the Cornish being *agan*.

HAIZ, s. m. Barley. *Pryce*. W. *haidh*. Arm. *heiz*.

HAL, s. m. A salt marsh, a moor. Plural, *halow*. *Och, tru, tru, shyndyys ỗf gans cronck du, ha whethys gans y venym, ow coské yn haus yn hál*, Oh, sad, sad! I am hurt by a black toad, and blown by his venom, sleeping down in the moor. O.M. 1780. *Neffré na wrello dybry, lemyn fleryé ha peddry, kepar ha seym py lyys haal*, that she may never eat, but stink and rot, like train oil, or salt-marsh mud. O.M. 2708. It enters into the names of many places in Cornwall, as *Penhale, Penhallow*. So also *Pennal*, in Merioneth. W. *hál*. Arm. *hál*.

HAL, s. m. A hill. Pl. *halow*. *Hál bian*, a little hill. *Lhwyd*, 172. ‡ *An lyzûan bian gen i'ar nedhez, ez a tivi rn an halow ncî, ez kreiez Plêth Maria*, the small plant with the twisted stalk, (which) grows on our hills is called *Plêth Maria*. 245. A late form of *alt*, or *als*, qd. v.

HALAN, s. m. The calends. *Dew halan gwáv*, All Saints' day, lit. the calends of winter. *Lhwyd*, 45. W. *dydh calan gauav*. *Halan* is a mutation of *calan*, qd. v.

HALLAF, v. a. I shall be able. A mutation of *gallaf*, 1 pers. s. fut. of *gally*, qd. v. *Ny gewsyth, rák ny wodhas bôs grontys dhym gallos brás hedhow may hallaf dynys*, thou dost not speak, for thou knowest not that there is granted to me great power, this day that I may choose. P.C. 2183.

HALLAN, v. a. I may be able. A mutation of *gallan*, 1 pers. s. subj. of *gally*. *Alemma rág ny'm bỹdh creys, gon dhe wỹr lour, ny wclaf vy ydh hallan sawyé ow bewnans, mars dre mûr our*, henceforth there will be no peace for me, I know well enough; I do not see that I can save my life, unless by much gold. R.D. 1962. *Dóg vy besyn dhodha, may hallan ve attendya pan vaner lew ythewa*, lead me to it, that I may see what manner of lion it is. C.W. 114. It is also the 1 pers. pl. *Mynstrells, growch dheny peba, may hallan warbarth downssyn*, minstrels, do ye pipe to us, that we may together dance. C.W. 184.

HALLE, v. a. He might be able. A mutation of *gallé*, 3 pers. s. imperf. of *gally*. *Dheworté un lam bechan ydh éth, pesy may hallé*, from them a little space he went, that he might pray. M.C. 53. *Yn della ef a tynné, may hallé dre baynys brás merwel rág dhe gerensé*, so he would, that he might with great pains die for thy love. M.C. 70.

HALLER, v. pass. It is possible. A mutation of *galler*, 3 pers. s. pres. passive. *Ymu onen dheuch parys, a avans pûr ha fỹn gwrỹs; my a's gor adro dhodho, may haller govos dhe wỹr, ha gweles yn bledhen hỹr py gymmys hỹs may teffo*, here is one ready for you, of silver pure, and fine made; I will put it round it, that it may be known truly, and seen in a long year, to what length it may grow. O.M. 2102. *Me a'n kelm, hag a cach an cercot vrás dhe vês ús adro dhodho, may haller ry yfle gras*, I will bind him, and snatch the large surcoat away, (which) is about him, that it may be possible to give an evil grace. P.C. 2076.

HALLO, v. a. He may be able. A mutation of *gallo*, 3 pers. s. subj. of *gally*. *Dh'y teller kyns êns arié, Noc gonys may hallo*, to its former place let it go again, that Noah may till (the ground.) O.M. 1096. *Dûn dhe gyrhas Salamon, ha gorỹn ef yn y dron avel mychtern yn y se, may hallo vôs kerenys*, let us come to fetch Solomon, and let us place him on his throne, like a king in his seat, that he may be crowned. O.M. 2374.

HALLONS, v. a. They may, or might be able. A mutation of *gallons*, 3 pers. pl. subj. of *gally*. *Ol au brys a rós dhedhé, may hallons ynno bewé, h'aga ficchys vynytha a dheffo anedhé y*, all the world he gave to them, that they might in it live, and their children afterwards (that) should come from them. O.M. 2832. *Arluth, yma dour tommys lour, may hallons bôs golhys agu trỹs yn kettep pol*, Lord, there is water warmed enough, that may be washed their feet every one. P.C. 840. *An prysners kettep onan dyewhy yn rák dyssenipys may hallons bones brugys*, the prisoners every one bring ye forth immediately, that they may be judged. P.C. 2234.

HALLOUCH, v. a. Ye shall be able. A mutation of *gallouch*, 2 pers. pl. fut. of *gally*. *Golyouch ha pesuuch ow this may hallouch môs dh'y asedh*, watch ye and pray my Father that ye may be able to go to his seat. M.C. 52. *Deuch geneff, ha holyouch ve, godhvedhouch na rell-*

2 F

ouch trôs, ha me a ra dhe Crist anmô, may hallouch y aswonvos, come ye with me, and follow me, see that ye make not a noise, and I will kiss Christ, that ye may be able to know him. M.C. 63.

HALOIN, s. m. Salt Cornish Vocabulary, *sal*, where it is also written *halein*. In late Cornish it was pronounced *holan*, and *holan*. Welsh, *halen*. Arm. *halen, holen, choulen*. Ir. *salann*. Gael. *salann*. Manx, *sollan*. Lat. *sal*. Gr. ἅλς, ἅλας. Goth. *salt*. Lett. *sahls*. Slav. *solu*. Eng. *salt*.

HALOINER, s. m. A salt-maker, a salter. Corn. Voc. *sulinator*. Welsh, *halenwr*. Arm. *halennour, holenner, choalenner*. Irish, *salanoir*.

HALSAN, v. a. I should be able. A mutation of *galsan*, 1 pers. s. plup. of *gally*. *Yn erna re sent deffry ydh halsan rowlya pûr gay, ha bôs stately dhom dewys*, then by the saints truly I should be able to rule very gaily, and be stately in my godhead. C.W. 46. *My hall, Serra, dheuch granty, a callen dôs dhe'n pryck-na, ydh halsan bôs pûr very*, I may, Sir, to you grant, if I could come to that degree, I should be very merry. C.W. 44.

HAM, adj. Wrong. *Ow ham wôth brâs, gûf dhym, a Tâs, dre dhe vertu*, my great evil deed forgive me, O Father, by thy virtue. P.C. 3029. The regular aspirate mutation of *cam*, qd. v.

HAM, comp. pron. And my. *My ham gwrêk ham flôch byhan*, me and my wife and my little child. O.M. 397. Comp. of *ha* and *am*; it may be written for distinction *ha'm*, though not so marked in the Ordinalia.

HAMBROKKYA, v. a. To wash. *Llwyd*, 77.

HAMLOS, s. m. Preparation. *Duyow hamlos*, Maundy Thursday. *Kepar del yw an vaner duyow hamlos*, like as it is the custom on Maundy Thursday. P.C. 654. Written also *hablys*, qd. v.

HAMMY, comp. pron. And me. *(Ha-my.)* *Aban vynnyth pûp huny ladhé ol an nôr vôs-ma, saw unsel ow tâs hamuy, lâdh ny gansé maga ta*, since thou wilt kill every one who is on the earth of this world, save only my people and me, kill us with them as well. O.M. 971.

HAN, s. m. A song. *Râg henna my a's temptyas dhe behé, may fe ellas aga hân kepar ha my*, for that I tempted them to sin, that "alas" might be their song like as mine. O.M. 310. The regular aspirate form of *cân*, qd. v.

HAN, comp. art. And the. *(Ha-an.)* For distinction this may be written *ha'n*.

HANADZHAN, s. m. A sigh. (*Ll.* 8, 159.) W. *ochenaid, uchenaid*. Arm. *huanat, chuanat*. Ir. *cagnach, osnadh*. Gael. *osnag, osnad, uchanaich*. Manx, *osnec*. Sansc. *us'na*.

HANAF, s. m. A drinking-cup. Corn. Vocab. *hanapus*. Llwyd, 33, 45, gives *hanath* as the late form. Arm. *hanap, hauaf*, a measure for grains and liquids. Med. Lat. *hanafas, hanapus*. Fr. *hanap*. Eng. *hanaper, hamper*.

HANDERU, s. m. A cousin german. *Pryce*. W. *cevnder, cevnderw, + ceintiru*, pl. in Oxford Glosses. Arm. *cevenderv, cenderv*.

HANETH, adv. This night, to-night. *Py le y'n gevyth of chy, râg yn nôs haneth dybry bôs Pask omma of a vyn*, where shall he find a house? for in this night, eat the Passover meal here he will. P.C. 671. *El a'n leverys dedhy haneth, ha hy yn gwyly pûr dhefun, mêns re gewsys, an* angel said it to her this night, and she in bed quite awake, all that I have said. P.C. 2203. *Ple ma haneth a wor dên vôth*, where is there to-night any man who knows? R.D. 849. W. *heno, + henoid*. Arm. *henoz*. Ir. *a-nocht, + innocht*. Gael. *a-nôchd*. Manx, *nocht*. Lat. *hâc nocte*.

HANEU, s. f. A sow. *Llwyd*, 159, 241. An erroneous reading of *bancu*, qd. v.

HANIC, adj. Summerly. *Pryce*.

HANOW, s. m. A name. Pl. *hynwyn, henwyu*. *Ke yn râk, del y'm kyrry, yn hanow Dew awartha*, go before, as thou lovest me, in the name of God above. O.M. 538. *Py hanow y fÿdh gylwys*, what name shall he be called? O.M. 676. *Me a'th pÿs gans dhe ganow, lavar dhymmo dhe hanow*, I pray thee with thy mouth, tell me thy name. R.D. 233. *Py hanow ôs benen vâs*, what name art thou, good woman? R.D. 1697. *Ow hanow yw vernona*, my name is Veronica. R.D. 1703. *Aga hynwyn y a vÿdh an houl, ha'n lôr, ha'n steryan*, their names shall be the sun, and the moon, and the stars. O.M. 35. *Ro dhodhans aga henwyn*, give them their names. C.W. 30. Written also *anow*, qd. v. W. *henw, enw*. Arm. *hanô, + hanu*. Irish, *ainim, ainm*. Gael. *ainm*. Manx, *enm*. Gr. ὄνομα. Lat. *nomen*.

HANS, s. m. A hundred. *Try hans cevelyn da an lester a vÿdh a hÿs*, three hundred cubits good the ship shall be in length. O.M. 955. The regular aspirate mutation of *cans* after *try*. So W. *tri chant*.

HANTER, s. m. A half, a moiety. *Gansé y a'n hombronkyas yn prôs hanter nôs*, with them they led him at the season of midnight. M.C. 76. *Try hans kevelyn da an lester a vÿdh a hÿs, ha hanter cans kevelyn yn-wêdh ty a vera y lês*, three hundred cubits good the vessel shall be in length, and half a hundred cubits also thou shalt make its width. O.M. 957. *Yn della hy a begyas bys hanter dÿdh yredy*, so it ceased till mid-day surely. M.C. 201. *Myruch worth an vorvoran, hanter pÿsk ha hanter dên*, look ye at the mermaid, half fish and half man. P.C. 2404. *Wosé try deydh ha hanter*, after three days and a half. R.D. 226. W. *hanner, + hanther*. Arm. *hanter*.

HANWAF, v. a. I will name. 1 pers. s. fut. of *henwel*, qd. v. *Lemyn hanwaf goydh ha yâr, a sensaf edhyn hep pâr dhe vygyens dên war an boys*, now I name goose and hen, (which) I esteem birds without equal for food of man in the world. O.M. 129. *Ythanwaf (ydh-hanwaf) bûch ha tarow, ha march yw bêst hep parow, dhe vâp dên râg ymweres*, I name cow and bull, and horse, (which) is a beast without equal, for the son of man to help himself. O.M. 123.

HANYS, pron. prep. From thee. *Mester da, der dha gymmyas, me a wêl un todn pûr vrâs hanys yn bush ow plattya*, good master, by thy leave, I see a very great bullock from thee in the bush couching. C.W. 112. This is not the common form, which is *ahanas*, qd. v. W. *hanot*. The root is *han*, from, or out of.

HAR, s. m. Slaughter. Llwyd, 45, 65, *hâr*. Another form of *ar*, qd. v.

HARDLYCH, adv. Closely. *Pan fue an purpur war skwych kychys dhe vês gans dyw dhorn, worto y ganes hardlych run a'n kÿc bÿs yn ascorn*, when the purple was on a sudden snatched away with two hands, to it there stuck closely a piece of the flesh even to the bone. R.D. 2597. Ang. Sax. *heardlice*. Eug. *hardly*.

HARDH, adj. Strong, bold, close. *Ha me a wyth hardh na fe dên fyth ol anedhé dhe wûl dhe Dhew sacrifyth*, and I will take good care that there be not any man of them to make sacrifice to God. O.M. 1517. *My a's gwŷth gans mûr enour na vo hardh dên yn bŷs-ma, kyn fe mychtern py empreour, aga gorra alemma*, I will keep them with great honour, that there be no strong man in this world, though he be king or emperor, to take them hence. O.M. 2054. *Yn della ydh il codha a tûs warnan yn torma, na fên hardh dh' aga gwythé*, so the people may fall upon us at that time, that we may not be able to keep them. P.C. 2297. *Pûr hardh dûn dhodho wharré, gorryn ef yn bêdh arté; du yw y lyw*, very boldly let us come to him soon, let us put him in the grave again; black is his hue. R.D. 2099. W. *hardh*. Arm. *harz*.

HARENGA, s. m. Love, affection. A mutation of *carenga*, qd. v.

HARFEL, s. m. A viol. Corn. Voc. *fiala*. From the Latin, *harpa*.

HARFELLÔR, s. m. A fiddler. Corn. Vocab. *fidicen*; where a female fiddler is called *fellores*, fidicina.

HARHA, v. a. To bark, to cry out at one, to bay like a dog. Lhwyd, 34, 77. Another form of *harthy*, qd. v.

HARLOT, s. m. A vile mau, a rogue, a villain; used as a term of reproach. *Ef o harlot, tebel wâs, wotewedh lader vye*, he was a vile man, a wicked fellow, at last a thief he was. M.C. 38. *Ha dhe Iesus y honon an harlot a leverys*, and to Jesus himself the scoundrel said. M.C. 81. *Avel harlot ow lordyé*, lording it like a rogue. O.M. 901. *An harlot brâs*, the great villain. O.M. 907. This is the frequent meaning of the word in old English; (see Chaucer,) and its original meaning was a bold stripling, a servant, or a hoiden, which shews that it was borrowed from the W. *herlod*, a stripling.

HARLUTRY, s. m. Corruption, rottenness. *An môr brâs yn cut termyn adro dhom tŷr a bŷdh dreys, râg y wetha pûr elyn orth harlutry prest pûb preys*, the great sea in a short time about my earth shall be brought, to keep it very clean from corruption at all times. C.W. 8.

HARLYTH, adv. Exactly. *Ottvé musurys da, dên yn bŷs ny'n musyr gwel; harlyth my a'n trehy omma, hag ewnné gans ol dhe nel*, behold it well measured; no man in the world will measure it better; I will cut it exactly here, and adjust it with all thy strength. O.M. 2512.

HAROW, adj. Rough, rugged, sharp, severe. *Suel a vynno bôs sydwys golsowens ow lavarow, a Ihesu del ve helbeys war an bŷs avel carow, ragon menouch rebekis ha dyspresiys yn harow*, whosoever would be saved, let him hearken to my words, of Jesus how he was hunted on the world like a deer; for us often reproached and despised cruelly. M.C. 2. A mutation of *garow*, qd. v.

HAROW, interj. Sad ! alas ! *Out, out, harow, harow, mar ny vŷdh Pilat marow, dhe gyns ny won pŷth a wraf*, out, out, alas, alas ! if Pilato be not slain, I know not what rather I shall do. R.D. 1841. W. *haro*.

HARTHY, v. a. To bark, to cry out, to bay like a dog. Llwyd, 13, 29. W. *arthu*, *cyvarth*. Arm. *harza*. Gael. *comhart*.

HAS, s. m. Seed. *Pûp gwedhen tefyns a'y sâf, ow tûn hy frût ha'y delyow, ha'n losowys, erbyn hâf, degyns hâs yn erberow*, let every tree grow from its stem, bearing its fruit and its leaves, and let the plants against summer produce seed in gardens. O.M. 32. *War bûp frût, losow ha hâs, a vo ynny hy tevys*, over all fruit, herbs, and seed, that may be grown in it. O.M. 77. *Ol a'n edhyn ow nygé gwet copel may kemery, anedhé dhe sawyé hâs*, of all the birds flying, be careful that thou take a couple, to save seed from them. O.M. 1025. *Me yw mychtern re wruk câs, ol râg dry Adam ha'y hâs a tebel seuth*, I am a king that has suffered, all to bring Adam and his seed from evil plight. R.D. 2518. W. *hâd*. Arm. *hâd*. Lat. *satus*, *satio*. Goth. *seths*. Germ. *saat*. Eng. *seed*. Sansc. *sâtis*, from *su*, to produce.

HAS, v. a. He will leave. A mutation of *gâs*, 3 pers. s. fut. of *gasé*. *A ow mâp kêr, na porth a wher, Dew a'th weres; ef Dew a râs a'n covath ny hâs*, O my dear son, do not complain; he a God of grace will not leave thee from remembrance. O.M. 1359.

HASSAF, v. a. I will leave. A mutation of *gasaf*, 1 pers. s. fut. of *gasé*. *Dhe vâp Ysac a geryth, y offrynné reys yw dhys, war venedh a dhysguedhaf dhyso gy, del lavaraf, a'n covath bŷth ny hassaf, mar gurêth dhym an sacrufys*, thy son Isaac whom thou lovest, it is necessary for thee to offer him upon a mountain which I shall shew to thee, as I say, from remembrance I will not leave thee, if thou wilt make to me the sacrifice. O.M. 1283.

HAT, s. m. A hat. Llwyd, 62, observes that *debr dowr*, (i. e. solla pluvialis) which some use, seems a late invented word. W. *het*, *hetan*. Ir. *hata*. It is not a Celtic term, but Teutonic. Ang. Sax. *hæt*. Germ. *hut*. The primary meaning is a cover; whence a thimble is called in German, *finger-hut*.

HATH, comp. pron. And thy. *(Ha-ath.) Attebres, ty ha'th worty, a'n wedhen ha'y avalow*, if thou atest, thou and thy husband, of the tree and its fruits. O.M. 175. *Ha ny ow tôs a le-na, my ha'th vam kekyffrys*, and we coming from that place, I and thy mother also. O.M. 715. W. *ath*, *a'th*.

HAUNSEL, s. m. Breakfast. Llwyd, 17. *Gweág âv, ra ve gawas haunsel*, I am hungry, shall I have breakfast ? Pryce. Borrowed from the English, *handsel*.

HAUS, adv. Downwards, down. *Ellas, och, tru, tru, shyndyys ôf gans cronek du, whethys gans y venyn, ow coské yn haus yn hâl*, alas, Oh, sad, sad, I am hurt by a black toad, and blown by his venom, sleeping down in the moor. O.M. 1780. ‡ *In hauz*. (Llwyd, 248.) W. *yn is*.

HAV, s. m. Summer. *Ha fruites war bûb gwedhan y tyyf, gwâv ha hâv keffrys*, and fruits upon every tree shall grow, winter and summer alike. C.W. 28. A later form of *hâf*, qd. v.

HAVAL, adj. Like; similar, resembling. Super. *havalla*. *Ny a'd wra ty dhên a bry, haval d'agan fase wharé*, we make thee man of clay, like to our face presently. O.M. 60. *Ow formyé têk ha dyblans, ty rûm grûk pûr havel dhys*, forming me fair and bright, thou hast made me very like to thee. O.M. 68. *An Tâs a nêf a'n grûk ef dhodho haval*, the Father of heaven made him like to himself. O.M. 878. W. *haval*. Arm. *hevel*, *henvel*, *hanval*, *hanouul*. Ir. *samhail*, *amhail*. † *samal*, † *amal*. Gael. *samhail*. Manx. *oil*. Gr. ὁμαλός. Lat. *similis*. Sansc. *sama*. Goth. *sama*. Slav. *sumu*. Eng. *same*.

HAVALDER, s. m. Likeness, similitude, resemblance. Pl. *havaldrow*. *Ha Dew laveras, gerro ny geel dên en agan havalder, warlêr agan havalder*, and God said let us make man in our own image, after our likeness. C.W. p. 192. *Te nyn wra dhys honon havalder trehys vŷth, na havalder a travyth ês yn nêf a wartha*, thou shalt not make to thyself the likeness of any things, nor the likeness of any thing in heaven above. Pryce. *Ha gurêns an gy bôs rág havaldrow, ha rág termeniow, ha rág journiow, ha rág bledheniow*, and let them be for likenesses, and for seasons, and for days, and for years. C.W. p. 190.

HAW, comp. pron. And my. *(Ha-ow.) Pûr apert hag yu golow y leveris ow dyskas, ow lahys, ha'w lavarow*, very openly and in light I spake my doctrine, my laws, and my words. M.C. 70. *Rág omsawya ow honyn, keffrys ow gwrêk ha'w flehys, an lester a vŷdh genyn*, to save myself, also my wife, and my children, the vessel shall be with us. C.W. 172.

HAWLSONS, v. a. They shouted. *Pylat artê a gowsas, a Ihesus pŷth a vŷdh guris; y hawlsons gans golon vrâs dhe'n mernans bedhens gorris*; Pilate, again said, "With Jesus what shall be done?" they shouted with great heart, "let him be put to the death!" M.C. 126. *Y hawlsons gans moy colon, bedhens ef yn crows ledhys*, they exclaimed with greater heart, let him be slain on a cross. M.C. 128. This is the 3 pers. pl. preterite of *helwy*, qd. v.

HAWZ, s. f. A duck. Pryce gives this as the late form of *hôs*, qd. v. Pl. *higi*. See also Llwyd, 241.

HAYS, s. m. Seed. A late orthography of *hâs*, qd. v.

HE, s. m. The skin. Corn. Voc. *cutis*. W. *hiv*.

HE, adv. Easily. It is used in the three British dialects as a prefix in composition, to denote feasibility. Thus, *hegar*, amiable; *hewel*, visible. It is also written *ho*, as in *hogil*, feasible; and *hy*, as in *hyblyth*, pliant. W. *hygar*, †*hegar*; *hywel*, †*hewel*; *hyblyg*, †*heblyg*. Arm. *hegar*. It is analogous to εὖ in Greek, as εὐπλεκής. W. *hyblyg*; εὔβουλος, W. *hybwyll*. In old Irish, the form was †*so*, †*su*. Gael. *so*. Sansc. *su*.

HEB, prep. Without, destitute, or void of. *Máb dên hel ken ys bara, nyn gevas oll y vewnas*, the Son of Man without other than bread hath not taken all his life. M.C. 12. *Gwâs, te a dhêk an grows heb ncow*, fellow, thou shalt bear the cross without a lie. M.C. 174. Written equally common *hep*. *Pysyn may fyyn scrvysy dh'agan arluth hep parow*, let us pray that we may be servants to our Lord without equals. O.M. 236. *Warnedhy yma gwedhen, uhel gans lues scoren, saw nôth ol gns hep dylyow*, on it there is a tree, high with many a branch, but they are all bare without leaves. O.M. 777. W. *heb*, †*hep*. Arm. *heb*, *hep*. Ir. †*sech*. Gr. ἰκάς. Lat. *secus*. Zend, *haca*.

HEBFORD, adj. Without a road. Corn. Vocab. *inviam*. Comp. of *heb*, without, and *ford*, or *fordh*, a road.

HEBMA, pron. adj. This. ‡ *Rág hedna me a wra, byn-ytha wosn hebma, yn eborn y fŷdh gwelys an gabm dhavas yn teffry*, for that I will cause, ever after this, in the sky that there shall be seen the rainbow manifestly. C.W. 182. A late corruption of *hemma*, qd. v.

HEBRENCIAT, s. m. A leader. *Hebrenchiat luir*, dux, a captain : *hebrenchiat plui*, presbyter, an elder, lit. "the leader of a parish." Corn. Voc. (*ch* for *k*.) W. *hebryngiad*. Arm. *ambrouger*. The verbal form in the Ordinalia is *hembronc*, qd. v.

HECCA, s. m. Richard, Dick. A man's name. Pryce.

HECHEN, s. m. A tribe, family, kind, sort. *Me a'n clewas ow tyffen na vo reys, awos hechen, trubit vŷth dhe syr Cesar*, I heard him forbidding that there be given, for any consideration, any tribute to sir Cæsar. P.C. 1574. Variously written *hehen*, *cehen*, *chen*, qd. v.

HED, s. m. Length, longitude. Llwyd, 231. The old form of *hês*, or *hŷs*, qd. v. W. *hŷd*, †*hit*, and provincially in Wales, *feed*. Arm. *hêd*. Ir. *fad*, *fvadh*, †*fot*. Gael. *fad*. Manx, *fud*.

HED, pron. adj. That, that same. *Hêd* is an abbreviated form of *hedda*, and only occurs in late Cornish. ‡ *Hêd yw*, that is. Llwyd, 232.

HEDDA, pron. adj. That, that same. A further corruption of *hedna*, as this is of *henna*. Llwyd, 10, 73, 244. ‡ *Udzha hedda*, afterward. 124.

HEDNA, pron. adj. That, that same. A corruption of *henna*, qd. v. ‡ *Bedhez gwesgyz dhiweth, ken gweskal enweth, rág hedna yw an gwella point a skians oll*, be struck twice before striking once, for that is the best point of wit of all. Llwyd, 251.

HEDRA, s. m. October, the month of October. Llwyd, 10, 105. W. *hydrev*, the ingathering, harvest, autumn, October; so defined by Dr. Owen Pughe, who derives the word from *hyd*, to, and *trêv*, town, home. Dr. Davies derives it from *hydhvrêv*, the belling of deer, the rutting season, October; and this agrees with the Armoric, *hêrê*, *hezrê*.

HEDRE, conj. Whilst, as long as. *Y'th whŷs lavur dhe dhybry ty a wra, bŷs y'th worfen, spern ha spedhes ow tevy, hedrê vy may fo anken*, in thy sweat thou shalt labour to eat, even to thy end, thorn and briars growing, as long as thou mayst be until death be. O.M. 276. *I'ynytha hedrê vywy, umma ny'm gwelyth artê*, ever whilst thou livest, here thou shalt not see me again. O.M. 243. *Y a vŷdh gwythys calas, hedrê vŷns y yn ow gwlás*, they shall be hard worked, as long as they are in my kingdom. O.M. 1503. *Hedrê vyyn ow predery, yn glass-ygoyon gesouch y aga thŷr dhe wrowedhê*, while I am considering, leave them on the sward the three to lie. O.M. 2035. W. *hŷd-tra*. Arm. *endra*.

HEDH, adj. Feasible, easy, free from difficulty. Llwyd, 58. W. *hawdh*, *hêdh*. Arm. *eaz*, *acz*. Ir. *sith*. Gael. *sith*.

HEDH, s. m. Tranquillity, peace. W. *hêdh*, †*hed*. Arm. *eaz*. Ir. *sith*, †*sid*. Gael. *sith*. Manx, *shee*.

HEDHWCH, s. m. Peace, quietness, tranquillity. *Têg yw hedhwch*, fair is peace. Motto of the family of Noye. Pryce. W. *hedhwch*.

HEDHY, v. a. To stretch out, to reach at, to reach, to fetch. Written also *hedhes*. *Stôp an wedhen trocha'n dôr, may hyllyf aga hedhes*, bend the tree towards the ground, that I may reach them. O.M. 202. *Heedh ow bool dhymmo touth ta*, reach me my axe quickly. O.M. 1001. *Gwyn veys ha quellen an gŷdh, may fe yrhys dhym hedhy*, gladly I would see the day, that it is enjoined me to reach. O.M. 1014. *Hêdh e dhe'n dôr, my a'd pŷs, scon ef a vŷdh amendyys*, reach it to the ground, I pray thee, soon it shall be amended. O.M. 2521. *Cowethê, hedheuch cunys, ha me a wheŷth gans mûr greys, may tewê an tân veharrê*, comrades, reach ye wood, and I will blow with much force, that the fire may kindle soon. P.C. 1219 *Hedhouch cercot a baly*, reach ye a surcoat of satin. P.C. 1784. *Ila why tynneuch agas try, bŷs may hedho dhe'n tol*, and pull ye three, until it reaches to the hole. P.C. 2764. *Y fylly moy ys tresheys, dhe'n toll guris hy na hedhê*, it failed more than a foot length, to the hole made that it reached not. M.C. 180. *Yn spong orth gevlen fast dhe Grist hy a ve hedhys*, in a sponge on a rod quickly to Christ (it) was reached. M.C. 202. ‡*E ryg hedhas râg e erêh*, he stretched forth his arm. *Lhwyd*, 250. This is derived from *hêd*, length. Welsh, *hydu*, (2 pers. imp. *hwda*, pl. *hwdiwch*.) Arm. *heda*.

HEDHY, v. a. To make peace, to cause quiet, to tranquillize, to be at peace, to rest, to cease, to stop. *Orden dhe'th tûs hy knoukyé gans meyn, na hedhens nefré erna varwen eredy*, order thy people to beat her with stones that they never stop until she die quite. O.M. 2677. *Ha gans meyn gurreuch hy knoukyé, erna wrello tremené; ernytha na wrench hedhy*, and with stones do ye beat her, until she die; never do ye stop. O.M. 2696. *Na hedhyn, râg yma war agan toul knoukyé fast bys may feyn squeyth*, we will not stop, for it is on our design to strike hard until we be weary. O.M. 2697. *May fo gôs y vlevennow, ha'y corf ol kyns ys hedhy*, that his hairs may be bloody, and his body all before leaving off. P.C. 2096. Derived from *hêdh*, peace. W. *hedhu*.

HEDHYW, adv. To day, this day. *Hedhyw me a dhesyr dre ow grath dalleth an beys*, this day I desire by my grace to begin the world. O.M. 5. *Hedhyw yw an whefes dydh aban dallethys gonys*, this is the sixth day since I began to work. O.M. 49. It is written as often *hedhew*. *Pûr wyryoneth re gowsys ahanaf, re'n gêdh hedhew*, very truth thou hast spoken of me, by this day. P.C. 1588. *Ioy dheuch guthyl da hedhew*, joy to ye to do well to-day. R.D. 825. *Hydhew, hithu, hithou, hithyou*, are other various forms. In the Corn. Voc. it is written *hedheu*, hodie. Welsh, *hedhyw, hedhi*, † *hediw*. Arm. *hizio, hisio, hirio*, † *endez*, (answering to the late Cornish form ‡ *yn dzhedh*, Lhwyd, 65.) Ir. *aniudh*, † *indiu*, † *hindiu*. Gael. *an diugh*. Manx, *jiu*. Lat. *hodie, (hoc die.)*

HEEIt, adj. Long. This is the English pronunciation of *hir*, qd. v.

HEGAR, adj. Amiable, lovely, pleasing. *Arté Iudas ow trylé, gwan wecor nyn gevé par, ny gl dén vgth amontyé myns a gollas yn chyffar*, worth *Ihesu ef a feelé, kepar ha pan ve hegar; yn deweedh ny acordyé y golon gans y lavar*, again Judas turning; a weak trader (that) found not an equivalent, nor can any man compute how much he lost in the bargain; Jesus he flattered, as when he was amiable; in the end his heart accorded not with his word. M.C. 40. Compounded of the prefix *he*, and *cary*, to love. W. *hygar*, † *hegar*. Arm. *hegar*, † *hocar*. Gaul. *su-caros*.

HEHEN, s. m. Kind, sort, particular, effort. *Saw ma ny gl bôs na hen, dhe vôdh prest yn pûp hehen y goulenwel yw ow whans*, but if it cannot be otherwise, thy will always in every thing to fulfil is my wish. P.C. 1001. *Yn dyspyt dh'aga hehen*, in spite of their efforts. P.C. 2527. *Me â geneuch yn lowen, mar callen guthyl hehen a socor nag a servys*, I will go with you gladly, if I can do any sort of help or of service. P.C. 3007. *Pûb hehen*, every one. Lhwyd, 244. Variously written *hwhen, echen, ehen*, qd. v.

HEIN, s. m. The back. A mutation of *cein*, qd. v. *Mester whêk, dhys lowyné, otté an asen gené, ha'n ebel dhyso kefrys; var y heryn, râg dhe eunyé, dyllas me a vyn lesé; yskyn yn ban mars yw prŷs*, sweet master, joy to thee! behold the ass with me, and the foal for thee also; on her back to ease thee, clothes I will spread; mount up if it is time. P.C. 220. *Asgarn an hein*, spina dorsi, the back bone. *Lhwyd*, 153.

HEIRNIOR, s. m. A workman in iron, a blacksmith. Corn. Voc. *ferrarius*. W. *haiarnwr*. Arm. *houarnour*. See *Hoern*.

HEL, s. m. A hall. Corn. Voc. *aula*. *Pendra wreuch ow repryfa, ha my omma yn ow hel*, what do ye reproving me, and I here in my hall. O.M. 1501. *Rôf dhys ow thour, hel ha chammbour*, I give thee my tower, hall, and chamber. O.M. 2410. *Otté dynythys an gwâs omma gynen bŷs y'th hel*, behold the fellow come here with us, even to thy hall. P.C. 1203. *Wolcom Cayfas, ty hag ol dhe gowethé y'm hel*, welcome Caiaphas, thou and all thy companions in my hall. P.C. 1581. From the English. Ir. *all, halla*. Ang. Sax. *sel*. Fr. *salle*.

HEL, adv. Slow, tardy. *Abel, pe festé mar bel, ny gothé dhys bones hel, ow mones dhe'n sacrefys*, Abel, where hast thou been so long? thou oughtest not to be slow, going to the sacrifice. O.M. 461.

HELHIA, v. a. To hunt, to drive, to pursue. *Gans an êl yn pûr dhefry, my ha'm gwerêk râg gûl foly, helhys warbarth a fuen ny yn mês scon a paradys*, by the angel in very earnest, I and my wife for doing folly driven together we were quickly out of Paradise. O.M. 709. *Suel a vynno bôs sylwys, golsowens ow lavarow, a Ihesu del ve helheys war an bŷs avel carow*, whosoever would be saved, let him hearken to my words, of Jesus, how he was hunted on the world like a deer. M.C. 2. Another form is *hella*, qd. v. W. *hela*, † *helgha*, in Oxford Glosses. Irish, *sealg*, † *selg*. Gael. *scalg*. Manx, *shelg*. Heb. *shalach*. Cf. the name of British tribe, Σελγοῦαι.

HELHIAT, s. m. A pursuer, a persecutor. Corn. Voc. *persecutor*. W. *helydh*.

HELHWUR, s. m. A hunter. Corn. Voc. *venator*. Comp. of *helhia*, and *gour*, a man. In late Cornish it was written *hellier*. *Helhiat*, written by Lhwyd, 119, *heliad*, is another form of the agent. W. *heliwr*. Ir. *sealgaire*. Gael. *scalgair*. Manx, *selgeyr*. Old Celtic, Σελγοῦαι.

HELIGEN, s. f. A willow. Cornish Vocab. *salix*. Pl. *helic*. In late Cornish it was written and pronounced *helagan, helak, hellik*, Lhwyd, 16, 143. *Heligan*, a place of willows, is the name of a place in Cornwall as it is of a parish in Flintshire, *Helygen*, or *Halkin*. *Penhelyg*, the head of the willows, is also a common name of places in Wales and Cornwall. W. *helygen*, pl. *helyg*. Arm. *halegen*, pl. *halec*. Ir. *saileog, seileach*. Gael. *seileach*. Manx, *sheillach*. Lat. *salix*. Ang. Sax. *welig*. Eng. *willow*.

HELLA, v. a. To hunt, to chase, to drive out. *Down warbarth, an naw order, hellyn yn mês Lucyfer a dhescempys mês a'n nêf*, let us come together, the nine orders, let us chase Lucifer immediately out of heaven. C.W. 22. *Wonethans, myns ês yn nêf gwrên yn kerth y hellyé eff dhe effarn, dhe dewolgow*, let them work, all that are in heaven, let us chase him away to hell to darkness. C.W. 24. *Mchal, yskydniow, cal splan, hellouch Adam gans clodha dân, ha'y wrêg mês a Baradys*, Michael, descend, angel bright, chase Adam with a sword of fire, and his wife out of Paradise. C.W. 70. *Aban omma towles dychles, haq a Paradys hellys, me a vyn dhalleth palas, râg gweas boos dhymo ve ha dhom fichys, ha dyllas*, since I am thrown out of happiness, and from Paradise hunted, I will begin to dig, to get meat for me and my children, and clothes. C.W. 76. Another form of *helhia*, qd. v. W. *hela*.

HELLIER, s. m. A hunter, a huntsman. *Pryce*. Another form of *helhwur*, qd. v.

HELLYN, v. a. We may. A mutation of *gellyn*. 1 pers. pl. subj. of *gally*. *Lemyn, Eva, ow fryas, henna ytho dhe folly gy, råg henna paynes pûr vrås yma ornes ragan ny, may hellyn kyny dredha*, now, Eve, my spouse, that was thy folly, for very great pains are ordained for us, that we may lament for it. C.W. 74. Another form of *hyllyn*, qd. v.

HELLYRCHY, v. a. To hunt, to pursue, to persecute. *Assevyé plygadow gencf gruthyl bôdh dhe vrŷs, a callen hep kelladow, ha doul ow vôs hellyrchys*, it would be agreeable to me to do the will of thy mind, if I could without losses, and fear of my being persecuted. O.M. 2118.

HELWY, v. a. To halloo, to cry out, to shout. *Y helwys a lewn golon, gans mûr ioy ha lowené, yn hanow Du yntredhon benegas yw neb a dhe*, they cried from a full heart, with much joy and gladness ; in the name of God blessed is he that cometh amongst us. M.C. 30. *Y helwys en Edhewon, bedhens ef yn crows gorris ; yn médh Pylat me ny won reson prâg y fŷdh dampnys ; y hawlsons gans uoy colon, bedhens ef yn crows ledhys*, the Jews cried, let him be put on a cross; said Pilate, I know no reason why he should be condemned; they shouted with greater heart, let him be slain on a cross. M.C. 128. Written also *hylwy*, qd. v.

HEM, pron. dem. This. *Gwyr a gewsyth, icvody ; hem yw marth hep falladow, råk an darasow deffry dycn ol ŷns ha'n fossow*, truth thou sayest, I tell you; this is a miracle without fail, for the doors indeed are all entire and the walls. R.D. 654. An abbreviated form, before a vowel, of *hemma*.

HEMBRYNCY, v. a. To lead, to conduct, to bring, to convey. *Ow arluth kêr cûf colon, pyw ytho a's hembronk dh'y, mar ny wrâf vy nag Aron aga ledya venary*, my dear lord of heart-loved, who is it then (that) will lead them to it? if I do not nor Aaron lead them ever. O.M. 1874. *Yn ewn fordh dh'y may 'dh yllyn, may fven hembrynkys, pesyn en Tâs Dew, luen a vercy*, in the right road to it that we may go, that we may be led, we will pray the Father God, full of mercy. O.M. 1073. *Cowethé, dhym lawreuch yn scon prâg ydh hembrenkych ow enewalles dhe vês*, comrades, tell me directly why are ye leading my animals away. P.C. 204. *Danvon tâs dh'y aspyé, mar a'n kefons yn nep chy, ha'n kelmyns treys ha dulé, ha'n hembrynkys bŷs dhynny*, send thou men to watch him; if they find him in any house, let them bind him feet and hands, and bring him to us. P.C. 584. *Hembrynkewch an harlot gwâs*, bring ye the knave fellow. P.C. 1195. *Syngys mâr ôn dhe Iudas, râk ef a'n hembroneas pûr compys bŷs yn losel*, much beholden we are to Judas, for he conducted me very straight to the rogue. P.C. 1205. Written also *hombroncy*, qd. v. (See *Hebrenciad*.) W. *hebryng*. Arm. *ambrouc*.

HEMERES, v. a. To take, to capture. A mutation of *cemeres*, qd. v. *Tâs ûs dhym ow tevones, yw gans ow thraytor dyskis, fatel dôns dh'ow hemeres, ha del vedhaff hombronkis*, folk are coming to me, (that) are by my betrayer taught, how they should come to take me, and how I may be led. M.C. 61.

HEMMA, pron. dem. This, this here. *Bolungeth Dew yw hemma*, the will of God is this. O.M. 673. *Tan hemma, gor gansé y, ha henna yw pymveré*, take this, put it with them, and that is the fourth. P.C. 2850.

Na gymer hemma gorgys, rák an arluth a gewsys hydhew worthyn yn geydh splan, take thou not this distrust, for the Lord spoke to us to-day in bright day. R.D. 1501. *Hemma yw dcaul ymskemunys*, this is a devil accursed. R.D. 2088. *Råk me a dûp bôs hemma an kêth mâp êth alemma, yw mychtern a lowené*, for I think this is the same son (who) went hence who is the king of joy. R D. 2508. The fem. form is *homma*, qd. v. *Hemma* is an euphonized form of *hen-ma*, comp. of *hen*, this, and *yma*, here. W. *hwn-yma*. Arm. *he-man*.

HEN, pron. dem. This. *Hen yw djdh a boweswa dhe pâp dén a vo sylwys ; yn dysquydhyeus a henna ny a bowes desempys*, this is a day of rest to every man that may be saved; in declaration of that we will rest forthwith. O.M. 145. *Arluth, hen yw re nebes*, Lord, this is too little. O.M. 389. *Wogé hen-ma ty a wêl mâp Dew owdh esedhé a barth dyow dhe'n Tâs Dew, arluth huhel*, after this thou shalt see the Son of God, sitting on the right hand of Father God, Lord on high. P.C. 1327. *Hen yw agan cryggans*, this is our belief. R.D. 954. *Hen yw gwŷr*, this is true. R.D. 977. *Me a glewas leverel an arlont y dhe denné war y ben gans kymnys nell, ma 'tèth an dreyn ha cropyé dhen empyunyon, dre an tell ; henno (hen-o) payn a vir byté esa Crist ow codhcvel*, I heard say that they drew the garland on his head with so much strength that the thorns went and pierced to the brains through the holes; this was pain of great pity (which) Christ was enduring. M.C. 134. The feminine form is *hon*, qd. v. W. *hwn*, m., *hon*, f. Arm. *hen*. Ir. *sin*, † *sin*. Gael. *so*. Manx, *shoh*.

HEN, adj. Old, ancient, antique. *Ol ny a pŷs, yowynk ha hên, war Dhu pâp prŷs mercy gan kên, may fên gwythys råk an bylen, hag ol sylwys, trank heb gorfen*, all we pray, young and old, to God always mercy with pity, that we may be preserved from the evil one, and all saved, time without end. P.C. 39. *Me a's qwarn, yowynk ha hên, my ny gafuf yno kên may cothfo dhym y dampné*, I warn ye, young and old, I find not in him a cause that it is incumbent on me to condemn him. P.C. 2031. W. *hên*. Arm. *hên*. Ir. *sean*. Gael. *seann*. Manx, *shenn*. Anc. Gaul. *seno*. (*Seno-magus*, Oldfield.) Gr. ἕνη. Lat. *senex*, *senis*. Goth. *sincigs*, *sinista*. Lith. *senas*. Zend, *hana*. Sanse. *sanas*, exhausted, fr. *sâi*, to fail. O.H. Germ. *sini-scalc*. Eng. *sene-schal*.

HEN, adj. other. The aspirate mutation of *cen*, qd. v. *Saw ma ny ŷl bôs wa hen, dhe vôdh prest yn pâp hehen y godenweel yw ow whans*, but if it may not be otherwise, thy will always in every thing to fulfil is my wish. P.C. 1090. *Henno ay anvodh, ny wréns y na hen scyle, lymyn synvyé aga bôdh*, this was against his will, they made no other ground, but followed their will. M.C. 175.

HENBIDIAT, adj. Sparing. Corn. Voc. *parcus*. Zeuss derives it from the same root as *ped*, in Welsh, *arbed*, *arbedu*, to spare. with the intensive particle *hen*, or *en*. Lhwyd, 113, reads it *henbidhiat*.

HENDAS, s. m. A grandfather. Pl. *hendasow*. *Whâth ken-thew ow hendas Cayn pûr drôk dén accomplys, me a'n kymar yn dysdayn, mar ny vedhaf ve prevys whâth mêr lacka*, yet although my grandsire Cain is a very bad man enough accounted, I take it in disdain, if I shall not be proved yet much worse. C.W. 106. *Ha'm hendas Cayn whâth ew bew, yn defyth yn mŷsk bestes yma ef prest ow pewa*, and my grandsire Cain is yet alive, in the desert among beasts he is now living. C.W. 108. A later form of *hendad*, or as written in the Cornish Vocabulary, *hendat*, avus. Compounded of *hên*, old, and *tâs*, a father. *Gans crehen an bestes-na me a wra dyllas dhymo, par del wrûg ow hendasow*, with the skins of those beasts I will make clothes for myself, so as my ancestors did. C.W. 108. W. *hendad*, † *hendat*. A grandfather is also called in Welsh, *taid*, and *tâd cu*; and in Armoric, *tâd coz*, an old father.

HENATH, s. m. A proceed, generation. *Râg me an Arluth dhy Dew yw Dew a sor, hag a dry pehasow an tasow war an flehes bŷs au tressa, ha'n peswerra henath, nêb ma na ello perthy ve*, for I the Lord thy God am a jealous God, and will bring the sins of the fathers upon the children unto the third and fourth generation of them that do not honour me. Pryce. W. *hanaeth*, fr. *hanu*, to be descended from, or proceed.

HENGOG, s. m. A great great grandfather, a grandfather's father, or ancestor in the fourth degree. Cornish Vocabulary, *abavus*. *A soweth, gweles an prŷs, Cayn ow hengyk ew marow; ragdha te a vŷdh ledhys, a fals lader casadow*, ah, alas, to see the time, Cain my progenitor is dead! for this thou shalt be slain, O false hateful thief. C.W. 122. Comp. of *hên*, old, and *cóg*. This latter is peculiar to Cornish, and appears to be contained in the compounds *dihog*, and *gurhhog*. The W. has *caw*, m. *caves*, f. in a line of affinity descending; a descendant of the fourth degree; *gorchaw*, *gorchawes*, of the fifth, and *hengaw*, *hengawes*, of the sixth. The Welsh equivalent of *hengog* is *hendaid*, and in Armoric, *tâd-iou*.

HENNA, pron. dem. The one there, that one, that. *Arluth Du, y a armas, pu a ŷl henna bonas*, Lord God they cried, who can that one be? M.C. 42. *Mar a tybbryth a henna, yw hynwys pren a skyens, yn mês alemma ty â*, if thou wilt eat of that, (which) is called the tree of knowledge, out of this place thou shalt go. O.M. 81. *Yn dysquydhyens a henna ny a bowes desempys*, in declaration of that we will rest forthwith. O.M. 147. *Y volungeth yw henna*, his will is that. O.M. 2352. *Arluth, leverel dym gwra, mars ôf vy an kêth henna*, Lord, do thou tell me, if I am that same. P.C. 742. *Gans henna*, therewith. *Rag henna*, therefore. Comp. of *hen*, this, and *yna*, there. The feminine form is *honna*, qd. v. W. *hwn-yna*, *hynna*. Arm. *hen-nez*.

HENROSA, v. a. To dream. *Pûr wŷr me a henrosas, ha war ow kŷn a'n clewas yn mês a'n bêdh ow sevel; mars yw dyenkys ellas, râk me a wêl an mên brâs war glan an bêdh fest huhel*, very truly I have dreamed, and on my back I heard him out of the tomb rising; if he is escaped, alas! for I see the great stone on the side of the tomb very high. R.D. 517. Formed from *henros*, or *hunrus*, a dream, qd. v.

HENS, adv. Before. A mutation of *cens*, qd. v. ‡ *Ha po ti ha dha wrêg an moiha bian warbarh; nenna greu' terhi an dezun ha na hens*, and when thou and thy wife are most merry together; then do ye break the cake, and not before. Lhcyd. 252.

HENWEL, v. a. To name, to nominate, to call. Part. *henwys*, *hynwys*. *A Dâs, ty re dhrôs dhymmo ascorn a'm kŷk ha corf o par may fo ow howethes; my a's henow tyrago*, O Father, thou hast brought to me (what) was a bone of my flesh and body, so that it might be my companion; I will name her Virago. O.M. 115. *Drêfen un wŷth dhe henwel, lydhys ôf pûr dhyogel*, because of once naming thee, I am killed very certainly. O.M. 2724. *A glewsynych why cowethê del ugy an rŷl horê ow thenwel (owdh-henwel) an pyth na vŷdh*, heard ye comrades, how the vile strumpet is calling the thing that exists not? O.M. 2729. *Ydh henwaf beuch, ha tarow, oll an chattel debarow, aga henwyn kemerans*, I will name them cow and bull, all the cattle feeding, let them take their names. C.W. 30. *Ryp crows Ihesus ydh esê un dên henwys Sentury*, by the cross of Jesus there was a man named Sentury. M.C. 208. *Yn aga henwydh ydh esê un marreg Longis hynwys*, in their party there was a soldier named Longius. M.C. 217. *Ha Dew a henwys an golow dêdh*, and God called the light day. C.W. p. 189. *Kepar ha del ambosas, ny hynwys dhym saw Pedar*, like as he promised, he named to me none but Peter. R.D. 918. *Henwa*, name thou; *henwassis vi*, I had been called; *henwir vi*, I shall be called; *henwer vi*, let me be called. 247. Formed from *hanow*, a name. Lhwyd, 247. W. *henwi*. Arm. *henwel*, *hanvel*, *hanouein*.

HENWYN, s. m. Names. *Ydh henwaf beuch, ha tarow, oll an chattel debarow, aga henwyn kemerans*, I will name the cow and bull, all the cattle feeding, their names let them take. C.W. 30. The plural of *hanow*, qd. v., and is also written *hynwyn*, qd. v.

HEPAR, adj. Without equal, unequalled, incomparable. *Me a grŷs a lavassen scon war ow breuth y'n latthen, râk me a lever dheuch, an corf hepar, renothas, ef re dhustruak*, I believe we might venture at once, on my judgment, to kill him; for I tell you, the incomparable body, by my father, he has destroyed. R.D. 1639. Comp. of *hep*, without, and *pâr*, an equal.

HEPCOR, v. a. To renounce, to lay aside, to dispense with. *Pan wrêth hepcor an bewnans hep guthyl na moy cheyson, a hûch an cledh ha'n sêns ty a dhue dhe nêf dhum tron*, when thou shalt put away life, without doing any more occasion, above the angels and saints, thou shalt come to heaven to my throne. R.D. 459. *Ha maga fuer drôk deffry mones dhe hepcor an ioy bŷth na dhufŷk*, and as it would be an evil indeed to go to reject the joy (that) will never fail. R.D. 1433. *An carna (carn-na) a ygoras, del o destnys dhodho ef, râk pûr wŷr ydh hepcoras dre y ober glascor nêf*, that rock opened, as it was fated for him, for very truly he renounced by his work the kingdom of heaven. R.D. 2337. W. *hepcor*.

HEPMAR, adv. Without doubt, doubtless. Written also *hemmar*. Lhwyd, 248.

HEPPAROW, adj. Without equals, incomparable. Ll. 232. It is properly a combination of the two words, *hep*, without, and *parow*, pl. of *pâr*, an equal.

HERCH, v. a. He will command. 3 pers. s. fut. of *archa*, qd. v. *Arluth, why a herch dhodho an queth dysky dhywortо, hep na moy gêr*, Lord, you shall command him to take off the cloth from him, without any further word. R.D. 1947.

HERDHYA, v. a. To thrust, to push. Written also *herdhyê*. *Mam Ihesus, Marya wyn, herdhya an gyw pan welas yn y nâb yn tynewyn, dre an golon may resas*, the mother of Jesus, Mary blessed, when she saw the spear thrust in her son in the side, through the heart that it passed. M.C. 221. *Pan fo guw yn y dhulê, me a hyrch dhodho hertyê, hag a'n gy ewn dh'y golon*, when there is a spear in his hands, I will enjoin him to thrust, and to pierce him right to his heart. P.C. 2923. *Tan, syns y'th dorn an giu-na, ha herdhyé gans nerth yn ban*, take, hold in thy hand that spear, and thrust it with force upwards. P.C. 3011. *Me a'n herdh gwel ha gyllyf*, I will thrust it the best I can. P.C. 3012. *Gwrewch y herdhyé aperfeth*, do yo push it in. R.D. 2286. *Lemmyn herdhcuch hy dhe ves*, now push ye her out. R.D. 2295. W. *hyrdhu, hyrdhio.*

HERENSE, s. m. Love, affection. A mutation of *eerensé*, qd. v. *Aban na vynta eresy, ty a kyl ow herensé ; vynytha hedré vynvy, uvima ny'm gwelyth arté*, since thou wilt not believe, thou shalt lose my love; ever whilst thou livest, here thou shalt not see me again. O.M. 242.

HERN, s. m. Iron. *Ellas, och, tru, yn ow calon asyw bern, pan welaf ow map Ihesu adro dh'y pen curyn spern; treys hu dywlef a pup tu fast tackyes gans gentrow hern*, alas! oh, sad! in my heart there is sorrow, when I see my son Jesus, about his head a crown of thorns; feet and hands on every side, fast fixed with nails of iron. P.C. 2038. A contracted form of *hoern*, qd. v.

HERNAN, s. f. A pilchard. Pl. *hěrn. Hernan gwyn*, a herring. Llwyd, 33, 65, 240. ‡ *Pan a priz rág hěrn*, what price for pilchards? *Pryce*. This is borrowed from the English *herring*; which is called in W. *penwag, ysgadan*. Ir. *sgadan*, † *scatan*. Gael. *sgadan*. Manx, *scaddan*. O.H. Germ. *schade*. Eng. *shad*. Sausc. *skad*, to bound.

HERNIA, v. a. To iron, to shoe horses. ‡ *Whelas poble tha trehé ithen ; môs dh'au gôv dha hernia an verh*, seek people to cut furze; go to the smith to shoe the horses. *Pryce.* Another form is *wrennyé*, qd. v.

HERWYDH, s. m. Agency, power, company. *Gwyth an gwelen-ma yn ta ; hedré vo yn dhe herwydh, fythys neffré ny vedhyth*, keep this rod well; as long as it is in thy power, thou shalt never be overcome. O.M. 1464. *Yn aga herwydh ydh esé un marrey Longius hynwys*, in their company there was a soldier named Longius. M.C. 217. It is frequently used, as in Welsh, as a preposition; in respect of, according to. *Herwydh y volungeth ef, ow map, y fydh gwrés*, according to his will, my son, it will be done. O.M. 1320. *Herwydh dhe grath, na'm byma peyn yu gorfen*, according to thy grace, let there be not to me punishment to the end. O.M. 2253. *Dydh brues y wevéh ysedhé ol an bys-ma rák iuggé pup ol herwydh y ober*, the day of judgment ye shall sit to judge all this world, every one according to his work. P.C. 816. *Ytho why kemercuch e, ha herwydh ayns lahu, gwerëch y iuggyé*, now take ye him, and according to your law, do ye judge him. P.C. 1978. W. *herwydh, †herwyd*, † *erguid*. Arm. *hervez*, †*heruez*. Ir. †*archuit*. Its component parts must be W. *ar* on, and *gwydh*, presence.

HES, s. m. Longitude, length of place or time, duration. *Arluth cúf, ol hennn gulán, try hés ow fal mar a'm be, my ha'm gwrëk ha'm flôch byhan bysy ugdh dhe sostené*, dear Lord, all that entirely, if I have three lengths of my spade, me and my wife, and my little child, it will be hard to support. O.M. 396. *Mar callo trylyé dhe hés lavar Crist pan vo clewys*, that he might turn at length the word of Christ when it was heard. M.C. 109. Written also *heys*, and *hýs*, qd. v.

HES, s. f. A swarm. Written by Llwyd, 14, 28, *hez*, as the late pronunciation. Welsh, *haid*. Arm. *hêd*. Ir. *saith*. Gael. *sgaoth*.

HESCEN, s. f. A bulrush, a sedge, a reed. Corn. Voc. *heschen, canna vel arundo*. The word is preserved in the names of *Penesken*, a place in Ruanlanihorn ; *Goon hoskin*, in St. Enoder; and *Goon hoskyn*, in St. Peran Sabulo. W. *hesgen*, pl. *hěsg*, † *sescand*. Arm. *hescen*, pl. *hěsc*. Ir. *scisg*. Gael. † *seasg*.

HESP, s. m. A lock. Corn. Vocab. *sera*. W. *hespen*. Eng. *hasp*.

HETHEN, s. f. A bird. Corn. Vocab. *avis vel volatile*. See *Edhen*.

HETHEU, adv. To-day. Corn. Voc. *hodie*. See *Hedhyw*.

HEUL, s. m. The sun. Written in the Cornish Vocabulary, *hewul, sol*. The orthography in the Ordinalia is *houl*, qd. v. W. *haul*, † *heul*. Arm. *heol*. Ir. † *soil*. Gr. ἥλιος, σείρ, σείριον. Lat. *sol, sirius*. Goth. *sauil*. Lith. *saulé*. Sansc. *súris, súryas*, fr. *sur*, to shine.

HEVEL, adj. Similar, like. Comp. of *he*, and *mal*, similar. It is generally written *haval*, and *avel*, qd. v.

HEVELEP, adj. Like, similar, equal. Used also as a substantive. Likeness, similitude. *Ty re dhysverug credy hevelep dhom face vy, Urry, nép o marrek lên*, thou hast destroyed verily the likeness to my face, Uriah, who was a trusty knight. O.M. 2337. Written also *hyvelep*, qd. v. W. *cyfelyb*. Arm. *hevelep*.

HEVELEPTER, s. m. Likeness, similitude. *Pryce*.

HEVELES, s. m. Likeness. *Pryce*. W. *heveliad*.

HEVIS, s. m. A shirt, a smock, a jacket. Corn. Vocab. *colobium*. Written by Llwyd, 4, 33, 45, *hevez*. ‡ *An hevez adro y gein*, the shirt on his back. 230. W. *hevys*. Arm. *hivis*. Ir. † *caimse*. Gael. *caimis*. All from the Latin, *camissa*. Fr. *chemise*.

HEWEL, adj. Easily seen, visible, conspicuous. Generally used as a verb impersonal. *Ty a hewel muskegys*, thou seemest crazed. O.M. 1151. *Del hevel dhynny, onima ny fydhyn gesys yn crês*, as it appears to us, here we shall not be left in peace. O.M. 1605. *Del hevel dhymmo pir wêr hon yw cusyl da*, as it appears to me, very truly this is good advice. O.M. 2266. *Gonys a wrewch pir vysy dhym del hevel*, you work very diligently as it appears to me. O.M. 2449. *By ny hewel dre lahu, y côth dhodho bôs dampnys*, it never appears by law, that he ought to be condemned. P.C. 2383. *Bôs y servont nag ôs gryw, da ydh hewel*, to be his servant thou art not worthy, it appears well. R.D. 1000. Comp. of *he*, easily, and *gwêl*, sight. W. *hyvel*, †*hewel*, †*hignel*. Arm. *huel*, a man's name.

HEWIL, adj. Watchful, vigilant. Corn. Vocab. *hewuil*, vigil ; *hich hewuil*, pervigil. Comp. of *he*, easily, and *gwilio*, to watch. W. *hywyl*, †*heuil*.

HEYN, s. m. The back. See *Hein*.

HEYS, s. m. Longitude, length of place or time, duration, while. *Heys Crist y a gemeras a'n neyl lef bys yn ybvn, woorth an lês y a dullas dew dull yn growes heb kên*, the length of Christ they took from the one hand even to the other, on the breadth they bored two holes in the cross without pity. M.C. 178. *Corf Ihesus Crist yntredhé dhe'n logell a ve degys, hag a heys dhe wrowedhé ynno of a ve gesys*, the body of Jesus Christ, between them to the coffin was brought, and at length to lie there it was left. M.C. 233. *Try heys dhe bál*, three lengths of thy spade. O.M. 392. *Heys ol ow cruchen scorgyys*, all the lengths of my skin scourged. R.D. 2538. Written also *hés*, and *hŷs*, qd. v.

HI, pron. subs. She, her, it. In the Ordinalia it is generally written *hy*, which is also the orthography of the possessive, but easily determined by the context. *Dh'y gour hy a dhanvonas a Crist kepar del welsé*, to her husband she sent, of Christ as she had seen. M.C. 123. *Pan o an kentrow lemmys, hy a's dûk dhe'n Edhewon*, when the nails were sharpened, she carried them to the Jews. M.C. 160. *Y bows y honon gorris a dro dhodho hy a re*, his own coat put about him it was. M.C. 161. *Ottensy umma, ry hanow dhedhy hy gwra*, behold her here, do thou give a name to her. O.M. 103. *Aban golsté worty hy*, since thou hearkenedst to her. O.M. 269. *Euch wharé dh'aga scyssé, kyns hy bôs nôs*, go at once to possess them, before it be night. O.M. 2769. *Nyns yw ow gwlás a'n bŷs-ma, hag a pe hy, ow servons bŷth ny'm gassé*, my kingdom is not of this world, and if it were, my servants would never have left me. P.C. 2011. In the two following examples, which are common British idioms, the first *hy* is the possessive, and the latter the substantive. *Nefré gustyth dh'y gorty ne a orden bôs benen, may mohchaho hy huth hy*, ever obedient to her husband I ordain woman to be, that her affliction may be increased. O.M. 297. *Rŷs ew dhym kewsel defry orth ow gwrêk kyns môs a dré ; mars ellen hep cows orty, hy holon hy a torsé*, I must speak really to my wife before going from home ; if I should go without speaking to her, her heart would break. O.M. 2174. W. *hi*. Arm. *hi, ezi*. Ir. *si, hi, i*. Gael. *si, i*. Manx, *ee*. Goth. *hi*. Gr. *ἥ*. Lat. *ea*. Sansc. *ê, ê'sa*.

HICH, adv. Very. *Ilich hewuil*, pervigil, very watchful. Corn. Vocab. *Ilich* is an intensive particle. W. *uch*. Arm. *uch, us, uz, † ut, † ud*. Ir. *os, ois, † uas, † suas, † soos*. Gael. *os, suas, † uchd*. Manx, *hcoss, seose*. Germ. *hoch*. Sansc. *ut*.

HIDHEW, adv. To-day. *Hidhew gwra gans skians fyr*, to-day with prudence act thou well. Pryce. Llwyd, 65, 249, 251, writes the word *hidhû* ; both being various forms of *hedhyw*, qd. v.

HIG, s. m. A hook, or crook. Llwyd, 176, who also writes it *ig*, qd. v. W. *hic, higell*. Arm. *higen, igen*.

HIGA, v. a. To play at a game. ‡ *Why lader giveader, lavarro' guz pader, ha ro man do higa an gâth ; gra owna guz furu, hidhow, po avorow, ha why ell bôz dean dah whdîh*, you thief of a weaver, say your prayer, and give up to play the cat ; do mend your ways, to-day or to-morrow, and you may be a good man yet. *Pryce's Cornish Rhymes*. W. *hiciaw*.

HILLIV, v. a. I may be able. Llwyd, 247. A later form of *hyllyf*, qd. v.

HILWY, v. a. To halloo, to shout, to cry loudly. Written also *helwy*, and *hylwy*, qd. v.

HINS, s. f. A way, a course, a career, a journey. It occurs in the compounds *camhinsic*, and *eunhinsic*, qd. v. W. *hynt*, † *hint*. Arm. *hcnt*. Ir. *sead*, † *set*, † *innleach*. Gael., *ionad*. Goth. *sinths*.

HINWYS, part. Named. Llwyd, 248. Written also *hynwys*, qd. v.

HIR, adj. Long, tall, prolix, tedious, dilatory. Corn. Vocab. *longus*. Comp. *hirra*, *(hirré.)* Superl. *hirra*, *(hirré.)* *Pandra yw dhe nygys, mar hŷr fordh dôs may fynsys*, what is thy errand, that thou wouldst come so

long a way ? O.M. 734. *My a welas yn paradys fenten rás, ha warnydhy un wedhen, hŷr gans mûr a scorewnow*, I saw in Paradise a fountain of grace, and over it a tree, tall, with many boughs. O.M. 839. *Kymmer dyso ow enef, rág hŷr lour ew ow bewnans*, take my soul to thee, for long enough is my life. O.M. 848. *Yn dôr my a vyn palas tol, may fo ynno cudhys, ha'y wûl hŷr ha doun ragdho*, in the earth I will dig a hole, that he may be covered in it, and make it long and deep for him. O.M. 867. *Gans squyr compes, ha scannt lyn, na vo hyrré crumsyn, na vŷth cotta war nép cor*, with straight square, and scant line, that it may be not longer, I undertake, nor any shorter in any way. O.M. 2511. W. *hir*. Arm. *hir*. Ir. *sior*, † *sir*. Gael. *sior*. Lat. *serus*. Sansc. *c'ira*.

HIRENATH, s. m. A length of time, a long time, duration. *Hirenath bew ôv yn bŷs-ma, may'dh ôv squyth a lavyr brás és dhymo pûb nôs ha dŷdh*, a length of time I have lived in this world, that I am weary with the great labour (that) is to me every night and day. C.W. 126. W. *hiriani*. Arm. *hirnez*.

HIRETH, s. m. Longing, an earnest desire, regretting, regret. *Saw bytegyns, pan y'th welaf, bôs hep hyreth my ny allaf*, but nevertheless, when I see thee, to be without yearning I am not able. P.C. 3176. *Yma dhymmo hyreth tyn yn ow colon pûp termyn, ha morethek*, there is to me sharp longing in my heart always, and sorrowful. R.D. 747. *Rûk hyreth galsof pûr cláf*, for longing I am become very ill. R.D. 775. *Ydh esen dre hyreth war dhe lerch owdh ymwedhé*, we were through great longing after thee pining. R.D. 1169. W. *hiraeth*. Arm. *hirrez*.

HIRGERNIAD, s. m. A blower of the long horn, a trumpeter. Llwyd, 167. Formed regularly from *hirgorn*.

HIRGORN, s. m. A trumpet. Corn. Voc. *tuba*. Bardh *hirgorn*, tubicen, a trumpeter. Comp. of *hír*, long, and *corn*, a horn.

HISOMMET, s. m. A bat. Corn. Voc. *hihsomet*, vespertilio. This may possibly be a wrong reading of a word connected with the Welsh term *ysllum*. The common name of a bat in Cornish was *asgelly-grohen*, leather wings, qd. v.

HITADVER, s. m. The harvest. Corn. Vocab. *messis*. Comp. of *hit*, the old form of *ŷs*, corn, and *adver*, restoration. W. *hadadver*, from *hád*, seed, and *adver*.

HIVIN, s. m. Yew, a yew tree. Corn. Voc. *taxus*. W. *yw, ywen*, † *eu*. Arm. *ivin, ivinen*. Ir. *iubhar, ibhar, iodha*, † *ibar*, † *eo*. Gael. *iubhar*. O.H.G. *iva*. N.H.G. *eiben-baum*. Eng. *yew*. Fr. *if*. Span. Port. *iva*.

HLO, s. m. A child. This word is given by Llwyd, as a mutation of *flô*, or *flôh* ; but there is no trace of *f* being a mutable letter in the earlier Cornish of the Ordinalia. *Gen hlô*, with a child ; *an hlô-na*, that child. *A'n hlôh*, of the child; *dh'an hlô*, to the child. 230, 242.

HO, adv. Feasibly, easily. Another form of *he*, or *hy*, qd. v.

HOALEA, v. a. To weep, to lament, to bewail. Llwyd, 60. A later form of *gwelvan*, or *olé*, qd. v. W. *gwylo*. *wylo*. Arm. *gwela*. Ir. *guil*. Gael. *guil*. Manx, *guil*. Gr. *κλαίω*. Lat. *fleo*.

HOAR, s. f. A sister. Llwyd, 15. Written also *hoer*, qd. v.

HOCYE, v. a. To delay, to be dilatory. *Torré yn ow*

feryl vy hep hokyé, break it off at my risk without delaying. O.M. 198. *Ha why dreheveuch ybeyn, may farwé an dhew vylen, qwyk hep hokkyé bedhens gvorŷs*, and do ye raise the other, that the two villains may die, quick without delaying let it be done. P.C. 2828. *Me a'n kerch dheuch hep hokyé*, I will fetch him to you without delaying. R.D. 1891.

HOCH, s. m. A pig, a hog. Corn. Vocab. *porcus*. W. *hwch*, f., a sow. Arm. *houch, hoch*, m., a hog. Gr. ὗς. Lat. *sus*. Germ. *sau*. Eng. *sow*. Sansc. *sús*, produced, *súkaras*, a pig; from *sú*, to produce, to be prolific.

HOCHWAYU, s. m. A hog-spear. Corn. Vocab. *hochwyu*, venabulum. Comp. of *hôch*, and *gwayu*, id. qd. gew, a spear, qd. v. W. *hwchwaew*.

HODDA, pron. adj. That there, that. ‡ *Ew hodda gys hôr hwci*, is that your sister? *Llwyd*, 67, 244. ‡ *Hodda nag ew vâs*, that (woman) is not good. *Pryce's Vocab*. This is a further corruption of *hodna*, as that is of *honna*, qd. v.

HODNA, s. m. A neck. A mutation of *codna*, qd. v. *Ter i hodna*, about her neck. *Llwyd*, 230, 249.

HOEDEN, s. f. A romp, a hoiden. *Pryce*. W. *hoeden*.

HOER, s. f. A sister. Written in the Cornish Vocabulary, *wuir*, soror. *Calmana ow hoer fysten, gâs ny dhe vôs a lc-ma, par del osta ow fryas, ha'w hoer, aburth mam ha tâs*, Calmana, my sister, hasten, let us be gone from hence; as thou art my spouse, and my sister, on the side of mother and father. C.W. 96. In late Cornish it was contracted into *hôr*. W. *chwaer*, †*chwior*; prov. *hwaer*. Arm. *choar*. Ir. *suir*. Gael. *piuthar (piuar.)* Manx, *shuyr*. Gr. κάσις. Lat. *soror*. Goth. *svistar*. O.H.G. *suestar*. Germ. *schwester*. Lith. *sesser*. Sel. *sestra*. Zend, *khauhar*. Pers. *khuaher*. Sansc. *swasar*, fr. *sú*, to produce.

HOERN, s. m. Iron. *Ebil hoern*, clavus, a nail; *gevel hoern*, munctorium, snuffers; lit. iron pincers; *padel hoern*, sartago, a frying pan; lit. an iron pan. Coru. Vocab. In the Ordinalia it is written *hôrn*, and *hern*, qd. v. W. *haiarn*. Arm. *houarn*, †*haiarn*, †*hoiarn*. Ir. *iarrun*. Gael. *iarunn*. Manx, *iaarn*. Germ. *isarn*. Eng. *iron*.

HOET, s. f. A duck. Corn. Voc. *aneta*. *Celioec hoet*, a drake. The later form was *hôs*, qd. v. W. *hwyad*. Arm. *houad, houed*. Gr. ὑάς, ὑάεν.

HOGEN, adj. Mean, vile, evil; mortal. *Aban goistê worty hy, ha grulhyl dres ow defen, mylyyê a wráf defry an nôr y'th whythres hogen*, since thou hearkenedst unto her, and actedst beyond my prohibition, I will assuredly curse the earth in thy evil deed. O.M. 272. *Ow blonogath yw henna, may tockans omma pûr splan frutcs dhom bôdh, râg magu scyl a dheyg bewnans hogan*, that is my will, that they produce here very fine fruits to my will, to feed those that bear a mortal life. C.W. 8.

HOGEN, s. f. A pork pasty. *Pryce*.

HOGUL, adj. Feasible, easy. *Ellas vîgh pan rûk colé mar hogul worth ow eskar; kemys drûk ús ow codhé ha dewedhes hag avar*, alas, that I ever listened so readily to my enemy; so much evil is falling, both late and early. O.M. 627. Comp. of *ho*, id. qd. *he* and *hy*, feasibly, and *gûl*, to do.

HOH, s. f. A sow. *Hôh vedho*, a drunken sow. *Llwyd*, 241, 242. A later form of *hôch*, qd. v., and it agrees in meaning with the Welsh.

HOI, pron. subs. They. *Henwer hoi*, let them be named. *Llwyd*, 247. This pronoun in the Ordinalia is invariably written *y*, qd. v. W. *hwy, hwynt*, †*wy*, †*wynt*. Arm. *hi*, †*y*. Ir. *siad, iad*, †*é*. Gael. *iad*. Manx, *ad*. Gr. ὅι. Lat. *hi, ii*.

HOL, adj. All. *Môs dhe'n menydh me a vyn, ha gwyl an dega lemyn, ha lesky hol-ma pûr glân*, I will go to the mountain, and make the tithe now, and burn all this very clean. C.W. 80. Generally written *oll*, or *ol*, qd. v. W. *holl, oll*. Arm. *holl, oll*.

HOLAN, s. m. Salt. *Llwyd*, 15, 143. A late form of *halen*, or *haloin*, qd. v. W. *halen*. Arm. *halon, holan*.

HOLAN, s. f. A heart. *Ow holan ol dhe dymmyn râg moreth a wra terry*, my heart all to pieces for grief will break. O.M. 359. More generally written *holon*, qd. v.

HOLERCH, adv. Late. *Pan o pur holerch an gĝdh, y tefenas un marrek, del dêth a'n nêf war y fŷdh ef a welas golow têk*, when the day was far advanced, there awoke a soldier, as it came from heaven on his face he saw a fair light. M.C. 244. Comp. of *ho*, feasibly, and *lerch*, a footstep.

HOLHAS, v. a. He washed. A mutation of *golhas*, 3 pers. sing. preterite of *golhy*, qd. v. *Whêth aban dhuthé y'th chy, golhy ow treys ny hyrsys, homma gans daggrow keffrys rê's holhas yn surredy*, yet since I came into thy house, to wash my feet thou hast not offered; this one with tears even has washed them surely. P.C. 520.

HOLLAN, s. m. A knife. A mutation of *collan*, qd. v. *Râk ow colon ow honan gans ow hollan me a wân*, for my own heart with my knife I will pierce. R.D. 2043. Llwyd, 253, writes it *holhan*.

HOLON, s. f. A heart. The regular aspirate mutation of *colon*, qd. v., *h* being substituted for *ch*. *Ow hôlon gêr caradow*, my dear beloved heart. O.M. 2135. *Mars ellen hep cows orty, hy holon hy a torsê*, if I should go without speaking to her, her heart would break. O.M. 2174. *Ha resys gois hy holon*, and the blood of her heart is run out. C.W. 2748. *Dh'agas prennê me a rôs gôs ow holon*, to purchase you I gave the blood of my heart. R.D. 166.

HOLYE, v. a. To come after, to follow. *Aban rûg dheuch ow holyé*, since I caused you to follow me. M.C. 50. *Pedyr, Andrew, ha Iowan, yn medh Crist, deuch holyouch ve bŷs yn menedh*, Peter, Andrew, and John, says Christ, come follow me even to the mount. M.C. 53. *Deuch grueff, ha holyouch ve, godhvedhouch na rellouch trôs*, come ye, and follow me, know that ye make not a noise. M.C. 63. *Saw Pedyr Crist a holyas abell avel un ownek, dhe dyller an prins Annas*, but Peter followed Christ far off like a coward, to the place of prince Annas. M.C. 77. *Benenas prest a holyas Ihesu Crist yn un gurmé; Ihesus wortê a veras, hag a leveris dhedhê*, women close followed Jesus Christ bewailing; Jesus looked on them, and said to them. M.C. 168. The root is *ôl*, a trace, or footstep. W. *oli*. Arm. *heulia*.

HOMBRONCY, v. n. To lead, to conduct, to bring, to convey. *A lena y'n hombronkyas uchel war ben un menedh*, from thence he led him high on top of a mountain. M.C. 15. *Iudas êth yn y negis, en ioul yw e'n hombronky*, Judas went on his errand, the devil it was (that) guided him. M.C. 62. *Ihesus a ve hombronkys, ha war y lyrch múr a lu*, Jesus was led forth, and after him a great crowd. M.C 163. Written also *hembryney*, qd. v., both forms being later than *hebrency*, as preserved in the substantive *hebrenciat*, qd. v.

HOMMA, pron. subs. This female here, this one, this. *Dew teka wél yw homma, gorf a gollas an wlâs*, God, the most fair sight is this, unhappy he (that) lost the country. O.M. 753. *Golhy ow treys ny hyrsys, homma gans daggrow keffrys re's holhas yn surredy*, to wash my feet thou hast not offered, this (woman) with tears even has washed them surely. P.C. 519. *Rum fey, homma yw cusyl da*, by my faith, this is good advice. P.C. 1549. Comp. of *hon*, this, and *ma*, here. W. *hon-yma*. Arm. *hou-man*.

HON, pron. subs. This female, this. Used with substantives feminine, as *hen* is with masculines. *Llwyd*, 232. *Rum fey, hon yw cusyl fýn*, by my faith, this is fine advice. O.M. 2041. *Benneth an Tás Dew re'th fo; rág súr, del hevel dhymmo, pûr wŷr hon yw cusyl da*, the blessing of God the Father be on thee; for surely, as it appears to me, very truly this is good advice. O.M. 2207. W. *hon*.

HONAN, s. m. Self, one's own person, the same person or thing. Used with pronouns possessive, as *self* is in English. Written indiscriminately *honon*, and *honyn*. *My a vyn môs ow honan war an pynakyl yn ban dhe yaedhé*, I will go myself upon the pinnacle above to sit. P.C. 87. *Rák ow colon ow honan gans ow hollan me a wán*, for my own heart with my knife I will pierce. R.D. 2042. *Godhaf dhe vrûs dhe honan*, suffer thine own judgment. O.M. 2248. *Adam ke yn mês a'n wlâs, troha ken pow dhe vewé, ty dhe honyn dhe balas, dhe wrêk genes dhe nedhé*, Adam, go out of the country, towards another land to live; thou thyself to dig, and thy wife with thee to spin. O.M. 345. *N'yns yw da bones un dên y honan, heb cowyth py cowethes*, it is not good that a man should be by himself, without a male or female companion. O.M. 94. *An ré-ma yw oberys, del vynsyn agan honan*, these are wrought, as we would ourselves. O.M. 16. *Pan vynnoch agas honon, why a gŷl gûl da dhedhé*, when ye will yourselves, ye can do good to them. P.C. 545. *Gwell yw dhywhy why mones ages honan dhe'n dhew eno*, it is better for you to go yourself to the two lads. R.D. 642. W. *hûn, hunan*; plural, *hunain*. Arm. *unan*, †*hunan*. Irish, *fein, hein*, †*fenine*. Gael. *féin, hein*. Manx, *hene*.

HONNA, pron. subs. That female there, that one, that. Used with feminines, as *henna* is with masculines. *Dhymmo vy why a rôs gwrêk, honna yw ol dhe vlamyé*, to me you gave a wife, she is all to blame. O.M. 266. *Gwrên un alter lêk ha da, may hyllyn sacryfyé dhodho war an kêth honna*, let us make an altar fair and good, that we may sacrifice to him upon that same. O.M. 1172. *My a vŷr scon orth honna*, I will look immediately at that. O.M. 1251. *Gwŷr vrês yw honna*, that is a true decision. P.C. 515. *Del levaraf yn torma, honna yw an fordh wella*, as I say at this time, that is the best way. R.D. 582. Comp. of *hon*, this, and *na*, there. W. *hon-yna,honna*. Arm. *houn-nez*.

HONWA, v. a. To name, to call. *Llwyd*, 43. A later form of *henwel*, qd. v.

HONYS, part. Named. *Cherubyn, an uchella ty a vŷdh, dôs a rág uskys;* Seraphyn *inwedh honys*, Cherubyn, the highest thou shalt be, come forth quickly; Seraphyn likewise named. C.W. 4. Probably a contracted form of *honwys*, part. of *honwa*.

HOR, s. m. A ram. Pl. *hyrroz*. ‡*Hor diu*, a black ram; ‡*hyrroz dyon*, black rams. *Llwyd*, 243. A late abbreviated form of *hordh*, qd. v.

HOR, s. f. A sister. *Dhe'th hôr*, to thy sister. ‡ *Yw an vôz-na agys hôr*, is that maid your sister ? *Llwyd*, 232, 246. A contracted form of *hoer*, qd. v.

HORDH, s. m. A ram. Corn. Voc. *aries*. In late Cornish this was abbreviated into *hor*, pl. *hyrroz*. Welsh, *hwrdh*, pl. *hyrdhod*. Arm. *tourz*, pl. *tourzed*, †*urz*. *Myharen* is also a ram in Welsh. Manx, *heurin*, a hegoat.

HORF, s. m. A body. A mutation of *corf*, qd. v. *Ow horf a ve yw henma*, this is my body. M.C. 44. (W. *vy nghorf i yw hwn yma*.)

HORN, s. m. Iron. *Knouk an hôrn tys ha tas*, strike the iron, tick-a-tack. P.C. 2719. *Yn trok a hôrn crêf, yn dour Tyber ef a sêf*, in a box of strong iron, in the water of Tiber he shall stay. R.D. 2136. *Yn dour Tyber ef a fue yn geler hôrn gorrys down*, in the water of Tiber he was in a coffin of iron put deep. R.D. 2320. A contracted form of *hoern*, qd. v.

HORVEN, s. f. A prop, a support. Pl. *horvenow*. *Nans yw groundyys genef vy sol a brŷs gans horvenow, mar ny fystyn pûp huny, why a's bŷdh drôg vommennow*, now they are grounded by me long ago with supports ; if every one hastens not, ye shall have bad blows. O.M. 2322.

HOS, s. f. A duck. *Lemyn hanwaf goydh ha yâr; hôs, payon, colom, grugyer, moy dredhof a vŷdh hynwys*, now I name goose and hen; duck, peacock, pigeon, partridge, further by me are named. O.M. 132. A later form of *hoel*, qd. v.

HOS, s. f. A boot. Corn. Voc. *ocrea*. W. *hôs*, hose, a stocking. Arm. *heûz*. Ir. *as, asa*, a shoe. Med. Lat. *hosa*.

HOSAN, s. f. Hose, a stocking, long hose. Pl. *hosaneu*. Corn. Voc. *calcias*, breeches. W. *hosan*. Ir. *osan*. Gael. *osan*. Manx, *oashyr*.

HOT, s. m. A hat. Corn. Voc. *caputium*. W. *het, hetan, hod, hotan, hotyn*.

HOUL, s. m. The sun. *Tewolgow brâs a ve guris, an houl a gollas y fŷth*, great darkness was made, the sun lost its face. M.C. 200. *Dowr ha lêr, ha tân, ha gwyns, houl ha lour, ha steyr keffrys*, water and earth, and fire, and wind, sun and moon, and stars also. M.C. 211. *Hemma yw tewolgow brâs, an houl y lyw re gollas*, this is great darkness, the sun has lost his brightness. P.C. 2992. *An houl ny golsé y lyw*, the sun would not have lost its brightness. P.C. 3083. Another form of *heul*, qd. v.

HOULDREVAL, s. m. Sunrise. *Llwyd*, 5. Comp. of *houl*, the sun, and *dreval*, a contracted form of *drehevel*, to rise, qd. v.

HOULSEDHAS, s. m. Sunset, the west. *Llwyd*, 104. ‡ *Po rez deberra an bez, vidn heerath a sew ; po res dal an vor, na oren pan a tu, dhuyran, houlzedhas, po gledh, po dihow*, when thou comest into the world, length of sorrow follows ; when thou beginnest the way, it is not known which side, east, west, or north, or south. *Pryce*. Comp. of *houl*, the sun, and *sedhé*, to sit down, to settle.

HUDHOW 220 HULE

HOUTYN, adj. Big, large, haughty. *Na lader, kyn fe vŷth mar vrâs quallok, na mar houtyn a'y vody*, he shall not steal, though he be ever so great a braggart, or so big of his body. O.M. 2069. From the Fr. *hautain*.

HOW, comp. pron. And my. *(Ha-ow.) Ny vern tra vŷth assayé, h'ow gwereseuch, cowethé, ow corré tumbyr yn ban*, it is of no consequence to try, and help me, comrades, putting the timber up. O.M. 2479.

HOWETHES, s. f. A female companion. *A dâs, ty re dhrûs dhymmo ascorn a'm kŷk, ha corf, o par may fo ow howethes*, O Father, thou hast brought to me bone of my flesh and body, (that) was meet that she should be my companion. O.M. 113. *Dues, ow howethes Eva, growedh yn gwyly a hŷs*, come, my companion Eve, lie down in the bed at length. O.M. 652. The regular aspirate mutation of *cowethes*, qd. v., *(h for ch.)*

HUC, s. f. A cloak. *Lemman lorch nêp a'n geffo, gorrens y scryp dyworto, ha nêp na'n geffo na nŷl, gwerthens y hugk dhe brenné anedhy dhodho cledhé*, now he who has a staff, let him put his scrip from him; and he who has not one, let him sell his cloak to buy with it for him a sword. P.C. 922. *Me a grŷs a lavassen scon, war ow breuth, y'n latthen, râk, by my hûk, me a lever dheuch an cas*, I think we might venture at once, on my judgment, to kill him, for by my cloak I will tell you the case. R.D. 1837. W. *hug, hugan*. Ir. †*fuan*.

HUCH, adv. Above, over. *Syrys me re wrûk scrifé agas cheson dh'y ladhé, tackeuch e a huch y ben*, Sirs, I have written your accusation to put him to death; tack it above his head. P.C. 2793. *Pan wrêth hepcor an bewnens, hep guthyl na moy cheyson, a huch an eledh ha'n sêns, ty a dhue dhe nêf dhum trôn*, when thou shalt put away life, without suffering any more trouble, over the angels and the saints, thou shalt come to heaven to my throne. R.D. 461. Written also *uch*, qd. v.

HUCHOT, adv. Upward. Corn. Vocab. *sursum*. From *huch*, high. W. *uchod*. Gael. †*uchd*.

HUDER, s. m. A deceiver, hypocrite, a juggler, a sorcerer. *My re gyrhas dhys dhe dré mâb Adam, a fals huder, may hallo genen tregé*, I have brought home to thee the son of Adam, the false deceiver, that he may dwell with us. O.M. 565. *Yn mês gynen ty a dhue, râk dhyso gy marth yw e; lavar dhyn mars ôs huder, drôk na ŷl dên vŷth dhe wûl*, out with us thou shalt come, for with thee it is a wonder; tell us if thou art a sorcerer, that no man is able to do harm to thee. R.D. 1831. *Me a grŷs bones an gwâs pystryour, ha hudor brâs, ny'n gefes cowyth yn wlâs*, I believe the fellow is a wizard, and a great sorcerer, I have not found his fellow in the country. R.D. 1854. Formed from *hûd*, enchantment, of which the later form was *hûs*, qd. v.

HUDOL, s. m. A sorcerer. Corn. Vocab. *magus*. W. *hudol*.

HUDHA, v. a. To cover, to hide. *Hellouch Adam gans cledha dân, ha'y wrêg mês a Baradys, ha dew queth dodhans gwera doen, dh'aga hudha pûb season, aga notha na vo gwelys*, drive ye Adam with a sword of fire, and his wife out of Paradise; and two garments make them carry, to cover them at all seasons, that their nakedness may not be seen. C.W. 70. The regular asp. mut. after *aga* of *cudha*, or *cudhé*, qd. v., *(h for ch.)*

HUDHOW, s. m. A Jew. Plural, *Hudhewon*. Pryce. More generally written *Edhow*, and *Yudhow*, qd. v.

HUDHY, v. n. To swell, to be swollen, to be puffed up, to be exalted. Part. *hudhys*. *Ow colon yw mûr hudhys, nyns ûs peyn orth ow greffya*, my heart is greatly exalted, no pain is afflicting me. R.D. 483. *Deuch yn scon, may hudhdhaho ow colon, agan gwerjans na'm bo mêdh*, come ye forthwith, that my heart may be exalted, that our work may not be a shame to me. R.D. 1877. Another form of *hwedhy*, qd. v.

HUGENS, num. adj. Twenty. *Aban omu dasserchys, dew hugens deydh dyvydhys bŷdh, pan fo nôs*, since I am risen, forty days ended will be, when it is night. R.D. 2437. More generally written *ugans*, qd. v.

HUHEL, adj. High, lofty. *A Dâs Dew Arluth huhel, my a'th wordh gans ol ow nel*, O Father God, high Lord, I worship thee with all my strength. O.M. 509. *Pyw ôs, a genos mar huhel, lavar dhymmo dyowgel*, who art thou (that) talkest so high? speak to me truly. O.M. 1368. *Huhel ydhos ysedhys, ha dyantel*, high thou art seated, and dangerously. P.C. 93. *Ot omma menedh huhel*, see here a high mountain. P.C. 125. *Me a wêl an mên brâs war glan an bêdh, fest huhel*, I see the large stone, on the side of the tomb very high. R.D. 522. Another form of *uchel*, qd. v.

HUHELDER, s. m. Loftiness, height, highness. *A Tâs kêr yn huhelder, ty a formyns nêf ha bys, râk luen ôs a hunelder, hag a allus kekeffrys*, O dear Father in height, thou hast created heaven and earth; for thou art full of greatness, and of power likewise. R.D. 423. Another form of *uchelder*, qd. v.

HUHELTAT, s. m. A patriarch. Corn. Voc. *patriarcha*. The literal meaning is "high father," being compounded of *huhel*, high, and *tât*, the old form of *tâs*, a father. So W. *ucheldad*.

HUHELVAIR, s. m. A viscount. Corn. Voc. *vicecomes*. Comp. of *huhel*, high, and *mair*, a steward.

HUHELWUR, s. m. A nobleman. Corn. Vocab. *clito*. Comp. of *huhel*, high, and *gour*, a man. So W. *uchelwr*.

HUHON, adv. High, above. *An Tâs Dew, dre'n Spyrys Sans dhe'n bŷs danvonas sylwyans; a huhon Mâp Dew a scyf*, the Father God, through the Holy Ghost, has sent salvation to the world; on high the Son of God will stand. R.D. 2612.

HUHUDHAS, v. a. To accuse. *Dhe'n tyller Crist re dethyé, ha'n Edhewon o dygnas; ydh esa an venyn gansé parys êns dh'y huhudhas*, to the place Christ came, and the Jews were opposing; the woman was with them; they were ready to accuse her. M.C. 33. The regular aspirate mutation after *y* fem. of *cuhudhas*, qd. v., *(h for ch.)*

HUIBREN, s. f. A cloud. Corn. Voc. *nubes*. Another form of *ebron*, qd. v. W. *wybren*. Arm. †*coabren*.

HUII, num. adj. Six. ‡ *Ma huîh biuh dhodho, dew mark, ha trei cans lodn daves*, he has six cows, two horses, and three hundred sheep. Llwyd, 244. A late form of *whêh*, qd. v.

HUIR, s. f. A sister. Corn. Voc. *soror*. Another form of *hoer*, qd. v.

HUIS, s. m. An age. Corn. Voc. *seculum*. Written also *oys*, qd. v.

HULE, s. f. An owl. Corn. Vocab. *noctua vel strix*. Llwyd, 241. The later form was *ula*. Latin, *ulula*. The W. equivalent is *dylluan*, which may be formed form *dall*, blind, and *huan*, sun, i. e. blinded by the sun.

HUMDHAN, v. a. To brood, to be breeding, to conceive, to be conceived. *Me a credy yn Dew an Tás olgallusek, gurêar an nêf, ha'n 'oar; hag yn Iesu Christ, y náb y honan, an Arluth ny, nêb vyc a humdhan der an Spyrys Sans, genys a'n gwerches Vary,* I believe in God the Father almighty, maker of heaven and earth; and in Jesus Christ his own son, our Lord, who was conceived by the Holy Ghost, born of the Virgin Mary. Pryce. *Ma hy a humdhan,* she is breeding. *ibid.* A late form of *ymdhoyn,* comp. of *ym,* reflective particle, and *doyn,* to bear. W. *ymdhwyn.*

HUN, s. f. Sleep, slumber, drowsiness. *Hun desimpűl,* lethargia, a lethargy, lit. a sudden sleep. Corn. Vocab. *My a vyn lemyn coské ; yma hûn orth ow gryvyé, marthys yn erda,* I will now sleep; sleep is heavy on me wondrous greatly. O.M. 1921. *Cosel my re bowesas, assyw whêk an hûn myttyn,* I have rested softly ; sweet is the morning sleep. O.M. 2074. *Me re goskes pôs, ha rum kemeres drôk glôs ; dre ow hûn me a welas nêb cse aberth yn bêdh, gans can ha mûr a cledh, dhe wernans y tassorchas,* I have slept heavily, and an evil pang has seized me; in my sleep I saw him that was in the grave, with a hundred and more of angels, to life he has risen. R.D. 513. Written also *huyn. Rák me a welas dre huyn pûr wŷr y tue mernans lyn, mara pydhê ef ledhys,* for I saw during sleep very truly that sharp death will come, if he be slain. P.C. 1950. *Elhæ gans un huyn re bên tullys,* by a sleep we have been deceived. M.C. 246. W. *hûn.* Arm. *hûn.* Ir. *suan.* Gael. *suan.* Manx. *saveen.* Gr. ὕπνον. Lat. *somnus.* Lith. *sapnas.* Sel. *spanie.* Sansc. *svapnas.*

HUNELDER, s. m. Greatness. *A Tás kêr yn huhelder, ty a formyas nêf ha bcys ; rák luen ôs a hunelder, hag a allus kekeffrys,* O dear Father on high, thou hast created heaven and earth; for thou art full of greatness, and of power likewise. R.D. 425.

HUNRUS, s. m. A dream. *My re welcs y'm hunrus a dhyragof êl dyblans,* I have seen in my dream before me a bright angel. O.M. 1954. The verb is *henrosa,* to dream, qd. v. Arm. *hunvré.*

HUNY, s. m. One, an individual. *Pŷth yw an othom dynny cafus lafur a'n par-na, aban vynnyth pûp huny ladhê ol an nôr vŷs-ma,* what is the need to us to have such labour, since thou wilt kill every one on the earth of this world ? O.M. 969. *Ol y pobel ymôns y orth y syrcé pûp huny, ha'n môr a pûp tu dhedhê,* all his people, they are following him every one, and the sea on every side to them. O.M. 1689. *Syndys ve dre govaytis ; yn della yw leas huny,* he was hurt through covetousness ; so is many a one. M.C. 62. *Huny* is formed from *un,* one ; which is used in Welsh, as *pob un, llawer un. Hini* is similarly used in Armoric, as *ann hini bráz,* (W. *yr un brás,)* the great one. *Va hini,* (W. *vy un i,)* mine. *Da hini,* (W. *dy un di,)* thine.

HURE, v. a. To anoint, to embalm. *Gás vy lemmyn dh'y huré, yn queth kyns ys y vaylé, gans alocs, mer keffrys, hag y a wŷth y cody, na potré bŷs vynary, kyn fe yn bêdh mŷl vlydhen,* leave me now to embalm him, before wrapping him in cloth, with aloes, myrrh also ; and they shall preserve his body, that it never decay, though it be in the grave a thousand years. P.C. 3196. Written also *uré,* qd. v.

HUSULYE, v. a. To counsel, to advise. *Ef a wrûk ow husullyé, frút annedhy may torren, moy es Dew ny a vyé,* he did advise me, that if I should break off fruit from it, more than God we should be. O.M. 217. The regular asp. mutation after *ow,* of *cusulyé,* qd v., *(h* for *ch.)*

HUTYC, adj. Glad, joyful. *Duwon yn y corf a'n meck, ny vŷdh hutyk y golon,* sorrow in his heart choaks him, his heart will not be glad. O.M. 2818. More correctly *hudhyc,* from *hudhy,* to exalt.

HUTH, s. m. Affliction. *Nefré gustyth dh'y gorty me a orden bôs benen, may mohchaho hy huth hy, dre wûl ow gorhemmyn trôch,* ever obedient to her husband I ordain woman to be, that her affliction may be increased, though breaking my commandments. O.M. 297. The regular aspirate mutation after *hy,* fem. of *cûth,* qd. v. *(h* for *ch.)*

HUTHYC, adj. Horrible, terrible, frightful. *Fystynyn fast dh'agan pow, rák devones dewolow dhe'n terogé ; y môns ow cryé huthyk,* let us hasten quick to our country, for devils are coming to the land ; they are crying horribly. R.D. 2304. More generally written *whyc,* qd. v.

HUVEL, adj. Humble. Corn. Voc. *humilis.* Sup. *hyvela,* most humble. Pryce. W. *huvyll, uvell.* Arm. *vuel.* Ir. *umhal,* † *umal,* † *humal.* Gael. *umhal.* Manx, *inlev.* à Lat. *humîlis.*

HUVELDOT, s. m. Humility. Corn. Voc. *humilitas.* W. *huvylldod, uvelldod.* Arm. *vueldet.* Ir. † *umaldoit.*

HUYHUI, pron. subs. Ye, or you. *Dheuh huyhui,* unto you. Llwyd, 244. A reduplicate form of *hwi,* or *why,* answering to the Welsh *chwychwi.*

HWALSONS, v. a. They searched. *Wháth dhedhé kentrow nyngo Ihesus yn crows rág synsy ; y hwalsons ol adro mar caffons gôff yredy,* yet there were not to them nails to hold Jesus on the cross; they searched all around if they could find a smith truly. M.C. 154. This would have been more correctly *hwilsons,* or *hwelsons,* being the 3 pers. pl. preterite of *hwila,* or *whela,* qd. v.

HWANNEN, s. f. A flea. Corn. *pulex.* In late Cornish, it was corrupted into *whannon, hwadnen,* pl. *whidden.* Pryce; Llwyd, 132. W. *chwannen,* pl. *chwain.* Arm. *choanen, choenen,* pl. *choenn.*

HWANS, s. m. Desire, longing, appetite. *E-ma hwans dhymmo,* there is a desire to me, i. e. I desire. Llwyd, 250. In the Ordinalia it is always written *whans,* qd. v.

HWARFO, v. a. It may happen. *Tra bynag a wharfo,* whatever may happen. Llwyd, 230. Generally written *wharfo,* qd. v.

HWARY, v. a. To play. *Dho hwary,* to play. Llwyd, 245. Another form of *gwary,* qd. v. Welsh, *chwareu.* Arm. *choari.*

HWATH, adv. Yet, again, over and above. This is Llwyd's orthography of *wháth,* qd. v.

HWEC, adj. Sweet, pleasant, dear. Comp. *hwecah.* Llwyd, 26, 68, 243, who writes it *hwég.* In the Ordinalia it is always written *whêk,* qd. v.

HWECTER. s. m. Sweetness, pleasantness. Llwyd, 240. See *Whecter.*

HWEDA, v. a. To vomit, to spew. Llwyd, to shew the corrupt pronunciation of his time, writes it *hwedzha,* 10, 177. W. *chwydu.* Arm. *choueda.* Ir. *sceith.* Gael. *sgeith.* Manx, *skeah.*

HWEDH, s. m. A swelling, a puffing up, a swell. *Ll.* 167. *A'n goys-na dagrennow try dre y dew lagas ydh êth,* *nyg o comfort na yly a wrello y holon huedh,* of that blood, three tears there went through her two eyes, it was not comfort nor cure that made her eyes to swell. M.C. 225. W. *chŵydh.* Ir. *at, siat.* Gael. *at, seidcadh.* Manx, *att, gatt.*

HWEDHY, v. a. To swell, to puff up. Part. *hwedhys.* Llwyd, 18, 248. W. *chwydho,* S. W. *hwydho.* Arm. *chouéza.* Gr. *οἰδέω.* Sansc. *aidh.*

HWEFFAS, adj. Sixth. Llwyd, 20. Written also *whêffes,* qd. v.

HWEG, adj. Sweet, dear, pleasant. Llwyd, 47, 156. Written also *hwêc,* and *whêc,* qd. v.

HWEGER, s. f. A mother-in-law. Corn. Voc. *socrus.* W. *chwegyr.* Gr. *ἑκυρά.* Lat. *socrus.* Goth. *svaihro.* Sel. *svekru.* O.H. Germ. *suigar.* Sansc. *swasru.*

HWEGOL, adj. Dear. Llwyd, 47. Written also *whegol* qd. v. W. *chwegol.*

HWEH, num. adj. Six. *Hwch dinair,* sixpence. Llwyd, 148. Generally written *whêh,* qd. v.

HWEI, pron. s. Ye, you. ‡ *Rhago' hwei,* for you. Llwyd, 177, 244, thus writes *chwi,* or *hwi,* to shew that it was sounded in his time, as *i* in the English words, *fight, tire.* In the Ordinalia it is written *why,* qd. v.

HWEL, s. m. A work, a mine. Pl. *hwêliow. Dên hwêl,* a workman. *Hwêl stên,* a tin mine ; *hwêl glow,* a coal pit. *Bêst hwêl,* a labouring beast. *An hwêl a cudhas scent,* the work fell short. Llwyd, 251. *Mein hwcyl,* work-stones, or stones for building, is given by him, 242, as an instance of the inflexion of the genitive case. It is written also *whêl,* qd. v., and the word is in common use at the present day for a mine in Cornwall. Thus, *Wheal Basset, Wheal West Seton, &c.*

HWELLAM, v. a. I may see. ‡ *Mai hwellam,* that I may see. Llwyd, 246, *hwellas, hwello, &c.* See *Whello.*

HWERO, adj. Bitter. Llwyd, 26, 42. Comp. *hwerwa.* 243. It is also written *wherow,* qd. v. Welsh, *chwerw.* Arm. *chouerô.* Ir. *scarbh,* + *serb.* Gael. *searbh.* Manx, *sharroo.*

HWERTHIN, s. m. Laughter, a laugh. Corn. Vocab. *risus.* The radical form is *hwarth,* or as it is written *wharth,* qd. v. W. *chwerthin, chwarth, chwardh.* Arm. *choarzin, choarz.* Irish, *gaire,* + *faithre.* Gael. *gaire.* Manx, *gear.* Sansc. *hars,* to rejoice.

HWERTHIN, v. a. To laugh. Llwyd, 141. He also gives *huerhin* as the late form. *A hwerhin,* laughing. 29, 248. In the Ordinalia it is written *werthyn,* qd. v. W. *chwerthin.* Arm. *choarzin.*

HWES, s. m. Sweat, perspiration. *Hwês,* Llwyd, 157. Written also *wheys,* and *whŷs,* qd. v. W. *chwŷs.* Arm. *choues.* Gr. *ἰδος.* Lat. *sudor.* Germ. *schweiss.* Eng. *sweat.* Sansc. *swaidas,* fr. *svid,* to sweat.

HWESA, v. a. To sweat, to perspire. Llwyd, 157, *dho hweza.* Written also *wesa,* qd. v. W. *chwysu.* Arm. *chouezi.*

HWETTAG, num. adj. Sixteen. Llwyd, 147. Written also *whettac.* These are both late forms ; being compounded of *whêh,* six, and *dêg,* ten, the correct form would be *hwedhec,* or *whedhec,* agreeing with the Armoric, *chouezec.*

HWETH, s. m. A puff, a blast of wind, a gale, breath. *Pryce.* Written also *whêth,* qd. v. W. *chwŷth.* Arm. *chouez.* Ir. *seid ; gaoth,* + *gaith,* + *gaid ; fath,* + *fed.*

Gael. *seid, gaoth, fead.* Manx, *sheid, geiach, geay, fed.* Sansc. *svâsa.* â *rad. svas,* to blow.

HWETHA, v. a. To blow. Llwyd, 245. Part. *hwethys,* Llwyd, 60, also writes *dho hwethia.* In the Ordinalia it is written *whethê,* qd. v. W. *chwythu.* Arm. *choueza.*

HWETHVIANS, s. m. A bubble. *Hwethvians an dour,* a bubble of water. Llwyd, 45.

HWEVRAL, s. m. February. Llwyd, 31 ; who also instances *hwerval,* 59, as a corrupted form. W. *chwevror.* Arm. *chouevrer.* Ir. *fvabhra,* + *febrai.* All from the Latin, *februarius.*

HWI, pron. s. Ye, or you. Llwyd, 246. ‡ *Dry vedo hwi gil,* what will you ? 244. Generally written in the Ordinalia, *why,* qd. v.

HWIGAN, s. f. The crumb, or soft of bread. Llwyd, 87.

HWIGEREN, s. m. A father-in-law. Corn. Voc. *socer.* W. *chwegrwn.* Gr. *ἑκυρὸς.* Lat. *socer.* Goth. *svaihra.* Sel. *svekar.* Lith. *szessur.* Germ. *schwaeher.* Sansc. *swasura.*

HWIL, v. a. To make, to do. *Dho hwil,* to make. Ll. 246. This is a corruption of *wil,* or *wîl,* the regular mutation of *gîl,* qd. v.

HWILA, v. a. To seek, to search for. Llwyd, 69. It is written also *hwilas.* ‡ *Me a vedn môs dha hwillaz hwêl dha il,* I will go to seek work to do. 251. This is a later form of *chwila.* In the Ordinalia the forms used are *whela,* and *whelas,* qd. v. W. *chwilio, chwilied.* Arm. *chouilia.* Manx, *shalee.*

HWILEN, s. f. A beetle. Corn. Vocab. *scurabœus.* W. *chril, chwilen.* Arm. *chouil.* Ir. *cuil.*

HWILIOG, s. m. A searcher, a seeker, a conjuror. *Pryce.* W. *chwiliog.*

HWIRNORES, s. f. A hornet. Corn. Vocab. *scrubo, (crabo)* W. *chwyrnores,* from *chwyrnu,* to buzz loudly. It is also called in Welsh, *chwiliores.* Arm. *chouiliorez.*

HWITEL, s. m. A tale, a story. Pl. *hwitlow.* Llwyd, 288. He also gives as a various form *hwedhel,* plural, *hwidhlow.* 243. It is the same word as *whethel,* qd. v.

HY, pron. s. They, them. *Euch, ow dew êl, dhum servons lêl, yn pryson cus ; hep ygery, na fos terry, drew hy yn mês,* go ye, my two angels, to my faithful servants, who are in prison ; without opening, or breaking wall, bring ye them out. R.D. 318. *Otê omma alwhedhow ; drew hy dhymmo hep lettyê, ha me a's ygor wharrê an darasow agan naw,* see here keys ; bring ye them to me without delay, and I will open them soon, our nine doors. R.D. 637. The general form of this pronoun is *y,* qd. v. In Llwyd's time the sound had been corrupted into *gy,* and *dzhei,* 244. W. *hwy, wy, hwynt,* + *wynt.* Arm. *hi,* + *y.* Ir. *siad, iad,* + *e.* Gael. *iad.* Manx, *ad.* Ang. Sax. *hi.* Gr. *οἱ.* Lat. *ii.*

HY, pron. adj. Her, its. Used only with nouns feminine. *Saw n'u wedhen dhym yma hy bôs sychys marthys vrâs,* but of the tree there is to me great wonder that it is dried. O.M. 756. *My a welas hy gierydhyow,* I saw its roots. O.M. 782. *Nôth yw ol hy scorennow,* all its boughs are bare. O.M. 780. *An golom glâs hy lagas,* the dove blue (as to) her eye. O.M. 1109. *Mars ellen hep cows orty, hy holon hy a torsê,* if I should go without speaking to her, her heart would break. O.M. 2174. *Mar mynnyth hy dystrewy, orden dhe'th tûs hy knoukyê gans meyn,* if thou wishest to destroy her, order thy people to beat her with stones. O.M. 2675. W. *ei,* which, as in Cornish, requires to be followed by the asp. mutation; thus, *ei chalon hi a dor'sni*, her heart would have broken. Arm. *he*, which follows the same rule, as *hi a werzo he zi*, she will sell her house, *(z = th.)* Ir. *a*. Gael. *a*. Manx, *e*.

HY, pron. s. She, her, it. This is the form invariably in the Ordinalia, but Llwyd writes it *hi*, under which see it explained.

HYBEN, pron. The other one of two. *Doro kenter, ha me a tak y luef glêdh gans ol ow nel.—Ny a dyl tol râk hyben a dhysempys hep anken, râg tempré an harlot fôl,* bring thou a nail, and I will fasten his left hand, with all my strength.—I will bore a hole for the other, immediately without trouble, to tame the mad rascal. P.C. 2749. *Na ny lever bôs Dew ken, saw an Tâs a nêf yn ban; ha ty voren myrch hyben a wra dew dhys dhe honan,* we say not that there is another God, but the Father of heaven above; and thou jade girl, the other makest a god to thee thyself. O.M. 2649. Written also *yben,* qd. v. Arm. *eben,* when feminine only.

HYBLYTH, adj. Pliant, flexible. *Hag yn fast kelmys dhedhé kerdyn gwedhyn yn mêsk cronow, may fôns hyblyth dhe gronkyé,* and fast bound to them were cords pinited among thongs, that they might be pliant to beat. M.C. 131. Comp. of *hy,* feasibly, and *plêth,* a plait. W. *hybleth*.

HYC, s. m. A fish-hook. Corn. Vocab. *hamus*. Written also *hig,* qd. v. Arm. *higen*.

HYDHEW, adv. To-day. *Me a grês ny re pechas hydhew brâs worth y ladhé,* I believe we have sinned to-day greatly by killing him. P.C. 2994. *An corf êth hydhew yn pry,* the body went this day into the earth. R.D. 21. One of the various forms of *hedhyw,* qd. v.

HYHY, pron. s. She, her, she herself. *Deso benyn, yn medha, Iowan dhe vâb me a wra, na bŷth moy ken mam neffré es hyhy te na whela,* to thee woman, said he, John thy son I will make; nor evermore other mother than her seek thou not. M.C. 198. A reduplicate, and emphatic form of *hy,* or *hi*. W. *hyhi*.

HYL, v. a. He will be able. *Deuch gynef, me a dhyswé chy dh'agas mester wharré râg parusy y soper; effan, may hŷl pûp mâp bron, ef hag ol y dhyskyblon, cafus y ês hep danger,* come ye with me, I will shew a house for your master, presently, for preparing his supper; large, that every son of the breast may, he and all his disciples, take his ease without delay. P.C. 676. A mutation of *gŷl,* 3 pers. s. fut. of *gally,* qd. v.

HYLL, s. m. A recess, a back, the nape of the neck. *Heb cows gêr y clamderys, y codhas war bol y hŷll,* without saying a word she fainted, she fell on the back of her head. M.C. 165. *Hŷll,* or *hîl,* is the regular aspirate mutation of *cil,* qd. v., after *y* feminine, *(h* for *ch.)*

HYLLER, v. pass. It is possible. *Râg y hyller ervyré, hay welas, y vôs prest worth dhe vetyé, dhe vêth dhys ha belyny,* for it is possible to observe, and to see him, that he is ready meeting thee, for shame to thee and villainy. M.C. 20. The same as *haller,* a mutation of *galler,* pres. impers. passive of *gally,* qd. v.

HYLLY, v. a. Thou mayest be able. *Ny a whŷth yn dhy vody sperys may hylly bewé,* we blow in thy body a spirit that thou mayest live. O.M. 62. *Ke yn ban war an kunys, hay ena growedh a heys, may hylly bones leskys,* go thou up on the fuel, and there lie at length, that thou mayest be burned. O.M. 1335. A mutation of *gylly,* 2 pers. s. subj. of *gally,* qd. v.

HYLLYF, v. a. I may be able. *Stop an wedhen trocha'n dôr, may hyllyf aga hedhes,* bend the tree towards the ground, that I may reach them. O.M. 202. *Hedheuch dhymmo ow kledhé, râk may hyllyf y ladhé,* reach ye to me my sword, for that I may kill him. R.D. 1960. A mutation of *gyllyf,* 1 pers. s. subj. of *gally,* qd. v.

HYLLYN, v. a. We may be able. *Da vye dhyn môs ganso, may hyllyn y acusyé,* it would be well for us to go with him, that we may accuse him. P.C. 1625. *Dyswé dhym nêp meystry brâs, may hyllyn dyso cryggy,* shew us some great power, that we may believe thee. P.C. 1771. A mutation of *gyllyn,* qd. v.

HYLWY, v. a. To halloo, to cry out, to shout. *Y hylwys en Edhewon, lahys ês yn pow a dro, may rôs y ladhé yn scon mygtern nêb a omwrello,* the Jews cried out;—there are laws in the country about, that he must be slain forthwith, whoever would make himself a king. M.C. 121. Another form of *helwy,* qd. v.

HYLY, s. m. Brine, salt water, sea water. *An corf-ma mylyges yw, ytho ef a gôdh dhynny; dhe vôs yn dôr nyns yw gwyw, nag yn dour, nag yn hyly,* this body is accursed, now it falls to us; to be in earth it is not worthy, nor in water, nor in brine. R.D. 2318. Derived from *hâl,* salt. W. *heli*. Arm. *heli*. Ir. *saile*. Gael. *saile*. Manx, *saailey*.

HYNADZHA, v. a. To groan, to sigh. Lhoyd, 62, 159. A late form of a word agreeing with W. *ochencidio*. Arm. *huanada*.

HYNADZHAS, s. m. A groan, a sigh, a howling. Ll. 62. This is a late corrupt form. W. *uchenaid*. Arm. *huanad*. Ir. *osnadh*. Gael. *osnadh, osnag, uchannich*. Manx, *osnec*. Sansc. *usna*.

HYNSE, s. m. Sex. *Ow holon gêr caradow, Dew ruth ros flour hy hynsé, ef a vŷdh hep falladow marow râg dhe gerensé,* my dear beloved heart, God hath given thee the flower of her sex, he shall be, without fail, dead for thy love. O.M. 2136. Probably a mutation of *cynsé,* id. qd. *cunda,* qd. v.

HYNWYN, s. m. Names. *Aga hynwyn y a vŷdh an houl, ha'n lôr, ha'n steryan,* their names shall be the sun, and the moon, and the stars. O.M. 35. *Ro dhedhé aga hynwyn; y a dhue dhe'th worhemmyn,* give to them their names, they will come at thy command. O.M. 120. Plural of *hanow,* qd. v.

HYNWYS, part. Named, called. *Yn secund dŷdh y fynna gruthyl ebron nêf hynwys,* on the second day I will make the sky called heaven. O.M. 18. *Bargos, bryny, ha'n er, moy dredhof a vŷdh hynwys,* kite, crows, and the eagle further by me shall be named. O.M. 134. O.M. 134. The participle passive of *henwel,* qd. v. It is also the 3 pers. sing. preterito. *Ny hynwys dhym saw Pedar,* he named to men none but Peter. R.D. 916.

HYNWYS, adj. Mild, placid, kind, gentle. *Gew a we yn y dhewlé gans an Edhewon gorris, ha pen lym râg y wunné, dhe golon Ihesus hynwys,* a spear was in his hands by the Jews placed, and a sharp end to pierce him to the heart of the mild Jesus. M.C. 217. Welsh, *hynaws*.

HYR, adj. Long. See *Hir*.

HYRCHI, v. a. He will command. *Pan fo guw yn y dhulé, me a hyrch dhodho hertyé, hag a'n gy ewn dh'y golon*, when there is a spear in his hands, I will command him to thrust, and he shall pierce him right to his heart. P.C. 2923. 3 pers. s. fut. of *archa*, qd. v.

HYRCHYS, v. a. He commanded. *Hcil mestrigi, Cayphas re hyrchys dhywhy a dhôs dhe Ierusalem*, hail masters, Cainphas hath enjoined you to come to Jerusalem. P.C. 1648. The same as *yrchys*, 3 pers. sing. preterite of *archa*, qd. v.

HYRSYS, v. a. Thou offeredst. *Ty a wél an venen-ma; whet aban dhuthé y'th chy, golhy ow treys uy hyrsys; homma gans daggrow keffrys re's holhas yn surredy*, thou seest this woman; ever since I came into thy house, to wash my feet thou hast not offered; this one with tears has washed them, surely. P.C. 518. A softened form of *hyrchsys*, 2 pers. sing. preterite of *archa*, qd. v.

HYS, s. m. Longitude, length of place or time, duration. *Adam, cummyas scon a fydh, hŷs dhe baal luen dhe drehy*, Adam, permission shall be forthwith, to cut full the length of thy spade. O.M. 380. *Ha gweles yn bledhen, hŷr, py gymmys hŷs may teffo*, and to see in a year long to what length it may grow. O.M. 2104. *Lemyn ydhyw ewn hŷs*, now it is the right length. O.M. 2525. *Nans yw an voren marow, a hŷs yma a'y growedh*, now is the jade dead, at length she is lying. O.M. 2750. Written also *hês*, and *heys*. W. *hŷd*, †*hit*; S. W. *feed*. Arm. *héd*. Ir. *fad*, *feadh*, †*fot*. Gael. *fad*. Manx, *fud*.

HYSSEAS, conj. Until. *Gans dour gorris yn bathon y wolhas aga garrow, hysseas ys gureg pûr wyn, del vynna Du caradow*, with water put into a basin he washed their legs, until he made them very white, as God the loveable would. M.C. 45. W. *hŷd at*.

HYVEL, adj. Humble, obedient. Sup. *hyvela*, most obedient. Pryce. Written also *huvel*, qd. v.

HYVELEP, s. m. A likeness. *Ow hanow yw Vernona; fas Ihesu gynef yma yn hyvelep gurŷs a'y whŷs, ha kekemmys a'n gwello, hag ynno a grysso, bôs yaches dhodho yw reys*, my name is Veronica; I have the face of Jesus, in a likeness made by his sweat; and whoever beholds it, and believes in him, need is that there should be health to him. R.D. 1705. Written also *hevelep*, qd. v., and it is the same as *eyvelep*, or *cevelep*. W. *cyfelyb*. Arm. *hevelep*.

HYVLA, v. a. To be humble, to be obedient, to obey. Llwyd, 102. Ir. *umhlaigh*. Gael. *umhlaich*.

I.

This letter is immutable. Its proper sound in all the Celtic dialects is the same as in French and Italian. When short as in the English words, *sin*, *fin*, and when long as *ee* in *deed*, *seed*. In the Ordinalia *y* is constantly used for it, with the same sound. In latest Cornish it was often sounded as the diphthong *ei*, or *i* in the English words, *fight*, *sign*. Thus *hwi*, you, became *hwei*; *tri*, or *try*, three, *trei*, &c.

I, pron. s. They, them. *I helwys a leun golon*, they cried from a full heart. M.C. 30. *I éth yn un fystene dhe'n tyller gansé o ordnys*, they went in a hurry to the place (that) was ordained by them. M.C. 176. In the Ordinalia it is always written *y*, qd. v.

I, pron. adj. His, her, its. *I vam, pan y'n drehevys, ha'y vôs devethys dhe oys*, when his mother had reared him, and he was come to age. M.C. 10. *Rág i frenna*, to buy it. Llwyd, 231. ‡*War i lêr* after him. ‡*Ter i hodna*, about her neck. 249. Generally written *y*, and *ky*, qd. v.

IA, adv. Yea, yes. Used to express assent in answering a discriminating question. Llwyd. 61. W. *ie*, †*ieu*. Arm. *ia*, †*ya*. Irish, *cadh*, *seadh*. Gael. *cadh*, *seadh*. Manx, *she*. Ang. Sax. *gea*, *geae*. Germ. *ja*. Eng. *yea*.

IACH, adj. Healthy, sound, well. Corn. Vocab. *sanus*. *Pan sefsys hydhew myttyn, yach êns aga icyw; dyswedh y a dhan dhe glôk*, when thou gottest up this morning, sound were their sinews; shew thou them from under thy cloak. P.C. 2081. *Mydhyggyeth a vŷdh gurŷs, may fo yach a pûp cleves*, a remedy shall be made, that he may be well from every disease. R.D. 1671. W. *iach*, †*iacc*. Arm. *iach*.

IACHE, v. a. To render sound, to make well or whole, to heal, to cure; to become sound or well, to be healed or cured. Part. *iachrys*, *iachŷs*. *Ny dhebbraf bôs, bones marow an profes a alsé ow yaché*, I will not eat food, because the prophet is dead (that) could have healed me. R.D. 1687. *Mar ny allaf bôs yachrys, ny won pyth wráf*, if I cannot be cured, I know not what I shall do. R.D. 1501. *Mar a kŷl bones yacheys, ty a fŷdh dhe lyfreson*, if he can be healed, thou shalt have thy liberty. R.D. 1673. *Bôs ow mâp dhymmo savoyys, ow colon yw yachŷs*, that my son is saved to me, my heart is healed. O.M. 1361. W. *iachau*. Arm. *iachaat*. Irish, *ic*. Gael. *ic*. Gr. *ίάομαι*.

IACHES, s. m. Health, soundness, sanity. *Kekemmys a'n gwello, ac ynno cf a grysso, bôs yaches dhodho yw reys*, whoever sees it, and believes in him, need is that there should be health to him. R.D. 1708. Another form of *ieches*, qd. v.

IAG, s. m. A cure, a remedy. *Hemma yw iag a'n pla, y gurf yw krehyllys da ganso*, this is a cure of the plague; his body is rattled well by it. P.C. 2817. Ir. *ic*. Gael. *ic*.

IAR, s. f. The female of birds, a hen. Written in the Cornish Vocabulary, *yar gallina*. *Lemyn hanwaf goydh ha yâr, a sensaf edhyn hep pâr dhe vygyens dên war an beys*, now I name goose and hen, (which) I hold birds without equal for food of man in the world. O.M. 129. *Iâr gini*, a guinea hen. Llwyd, 88. Pl. *yér*. 243. "A pullet is still called *mabyer*, in Cornwall." Polwhele. W. *iêr*, *giar*, pl. *ieir*, *gieir*. Arm. *iar*, pl. *iêr*. Ir. *cearc*. Gael. *ceare*, Manx, *kiark*.

IAR, s. m. A stalk. ‡*An lyzûan bian gen t'ar nedhez ez a tivi en an halow nei, ez kreiez Pléth Maria*, the small plant with the twisted stalk (which) grows on our hills, is called *Pléth Maria*. Llwyd, 245.

IDN, num. adj. One. ‡*Ha na ve idn frôth na mikan na trawaran nôr vez*, and there was no anger, nor strife, nor dispute between them afterwards. Llwyd, 253. A late corruption of *un*, qd. v.

IDNAC, card. num. Eleven. *Llwyd,* 176. A corrupted form of *unnec,* qd. v.

IDNE, s. m. A fowler. Cornish Vocabulary, *auceps.* Formed from *edhen,* or *edn,* a bird. The final *e* in *idné,* as in *euré,* denotes an agent, answering to *ai,* in Welsh. Cf. W. *casai,* a hater; *cardotai,* a beggar; *dyhudhai,* a pacifier; *magai,* a nourisher, &c.

IDNIC, s. m. A young bird, a chicken. Written also in the Cornish Vocabulary, *ydnic,* qd. v.

IDZHA, v. subs. There is. ‡ *Idzha'n leauh dha'n dén yync-na,* has that young man got the ague ? *Llwyd,* 242. A corrupted form of *ydhyw.* W. *ydyw, ydi.*

IDZHIN, v. subs. We are. ‡ *Ni idzhin a gwelas,* we are seeing, or we see. *Llwyd,* 240. A corruption of *ydhon,* reduplicate form of *ón,* 1 pers. pl. pres. of irr. v. *bós,* to be. W. *ydym.*

IDHEN, s. f. A bird. *Llwyd,* 29. Another form of *edhen,* qd. v. In late Cornish it was used for the plural. ‡ *Ni rig gwelas an karnow idzha an gullez ha'n idhen mór aral kil y ge ncitho,* I saw the rocks where the gulls and other sea birds make their nests. *Llwyd,* 245.

IDIIIO, s. m. Ivy. *Llwyd,* 15, 65. W. *eidhew, eidhiorwg, eiñorwg.* Arm. *ilio, iliarek.* Ir. *eidhean, idho, iodha.* Gael. *eithean.* Manx, *hibbyn.* Lat. *hedera.* Fr. *lierre.*

IDHOW, s. m. A Jew. Pl. *idhewon.* Llwyd, 242. More generally written *Edhow,* qd. v.

IECHES, s. m. Health, soundness, sanity. *Me a'n pŷs a luen golon yeches dhymmo a dhanvon,* I pray him with full heart to send health to me. R.D. 1716. Written also *iches. Am lemyn dhe'n gwellymny, a barth an Tás veneges, hag y a wra credy a pup cloves dhys jches,* kiss thou now the rods, on the part of the blessed Father, and they will surely from every disease cause to thee health. O.M. 1794. *A Dás Dew, dre dhe veray, danfon jehes dhymmo vy a'm cloves may 'thóf grevyys,* O Father God, through thy mercy, send health to me from my disease, that I am afflicted with. O.M. 2030. W. *iechyd,* † *icchuit.* Arm. *icched,* † *icchet.* Ir. *easaooth.*

IEIN, adj. Cold as ice, frigid. The Cornish Vocabulary wrongly interprets it, as a substantive, *frigus. A dhysempys gwrcuch lán du, rák yeyn fest yw an awel,* immediately make ye a good fire, for very cold is the weather. P.C. 1209. *Dús yn rák, yma dhyn toul guthyl may fe dhe wós yeyn,* come thou forth, I have a tool that will make thy blood cool. P.C. 1622. *Gwésk war an mŷn, bommyn dreys keyn, mar pedhé yeyn, ny dhue dhe gur,* smite thou on the edge, blows over the back, if it be cold, it will not come to the end. P.C. 2729. Written also *ién,* or *yén. Y gelmy fast why a wra, gans lovan ha chaynys yn,* bind him fast you shall, with rope and cold chains. P.C. 2069. W. *iain,* † *icin.* Arm. *ién,* † *icin.*

IENDER, s. m. Cold, frigidity, coolness. *Rág, rum fay, rák oeen anwos, ny glewaf yender dhum troys ; ydhesnf ow clamderé,* for, by my faith, on account of very chilliness, I do not feel the cold to my feet ; I am benumbed. P.C. 1223. *Bewa ydhesaf púb ér yn tomder ha yender rêw,* living I am always in heat and cold of frost. C.W. 120. W. *ieinder.* Arm. *iender.*

IEU, s. f. A yoke. Corn. Vocab. *jugum.* W. *iau,* † *iou.* Arm. *ieu, iad, ieb, geó.* Latin, *jugum.* Greek, ζυγὸς. Sause. *yuga ; (yug,* to join.)

IEU, s. m. Jupiter, Jove. *Dédh Ieu,* and contractedly *Dé Ieu,* dies Jovis, Thursday. *Llwyd,* 54. Written also *iow.* W. *iau, iou,* † *iob, (dydh iau.)* Arm. *iaou, iou, (diziaou, diziou.)* Lat. *Jove.* Gr. Ζεύ.

IEY, s. m. Ice, frost. Corn. Voc. *glacies.* W. *iâ,* † *jaig.* Ir. *aigh,* † *aig.* Gael. *eigh.*

IEYW, s. m. Sinews. *Púr gow a lever dhe vyn ; pan sefsys hydhew myttyn, ydeh éns aga ieyw,* a very lie thou wilt tell; when thou gottest up this day in the morning, sound were their sinews. P.C. 2681. This is a mutation of *gcyow,* pl. of *gcien,* qd. v.

IFARN, s. m. Hell, the infernal region. *Dywolow yfarn a squerdyas corf Iudas ol dhe dharnow,* devils of hell tore the body of Judas all to pieces. M C. 106. *Ty a fŷdh púr tormot sad yn gwelás yffarn, del gresaf,* thou wilt have sad torment in the region of hell, as I believe. O.M. 492. *Púr wŷr y fydhons dampnys dhe tán yfarn, droka le,* very truly they will be condemned to the fire of hell, the worst place. P.C. 3004. *Gorreuch ef yn schath dhe'n mór ; an schath a'n dék dhe yfern,* place ye him in a boat to the sea; the boat will carry him to hell. R.D. 2235. *Porth yfarn me a torras,* the gate of hell I have broken. R.D. 2574. W. *ufern.* Arm. *ifern.* Irish, *ifearn,* † *ifurnn.* Gael. *ifrinn.* Manx, *niurin.* All from Latin, *inferna.*

IG, s. m. A hook, fish-hook. *Llwyd,* 33, *ig. Yg hôrn,* an iron hook. 242. Written in the Cornish Vocabulary, *hyc,* qd. v. Arm. *igen.*

IGANS, s. m. A score, twenty. *Llwyd,* 27. ‡ *Trei igans,* sixty. ‡ *Trei igans ha dég,* seventy. A later form of *ugans,* qd. v.

IGANSVES, adj. Twentieth. Another form was *igansvath.* Llwyd, 243. W. *ugeinved.* Arm. *ugentved.*

IL, v. a. To make, to do. A mutation of *gil,* qd. v. ‡ *Do hwilas hwel do il,* to seek for work to do. *Llwyd,* 251.

ILL, v. a. He will be able. A mutation of *gill,* 3 pers. s. fut. of *gally,* qd. v. *Nynsyw henna mád, na ny il bós yn della, dén dhe verwel awos cous lavarow da,* that is not good, nor can it be so, a man to die because of speaking good words. P.C. 2400. *Ty a ll,* thou canst. *Llwyd,* 247. Written more generally *gll,* qd. v.

ILIN, s. m. Elbow. *Llwyd,* 15. Generally written *elin,* qd. v.

IM, comp. pron. Into my. *Llwyd,* 244. See *Ym.*

IMPINION, s. m. The brain. Corn. Voc. *cerebrum. Me a's ten gans ol ow nerth, may'dh entré an spikys serth dre an cen yn y grogen ha scullyé y ympynnyon,* I will pull with all my strength, that the stiff spines may enter through the skin into his skull, and scatter his brains. P.C. 2142. *An dreyn bŷs yn ympynyon éth yn y pen,* the thorns even into his brain went to his head. R.D. 1011. Written also *empinion,* under which see it explained.

IMPOC, s. m. A kiss. Corn. Voc. *osculum.* W. *impog, poc.* Arm. *poc.* Irish, *póg,* † *boc.* Gael. *póg.* Manx, *puag.*

IN, prep. In. *In nép le,* in some place. *Llwyd,* 244. Written also *en,* and *yn,* qd. v.

INGUINOR, s. m. A craftsman. Coru. Vocab. *opifex.* Probably formed from the French, *ingénieur.*

INNIAS, s. m. A repulse, a denial. Pl. *inniadow.* See *Ynnias.*

INTER, prep. Between. *Intré,* Llwyd, 249. See *Ynter.*

INWEDH, adv. Also. *Torré yn ow feryl vy, hag inwedh*

gwra dhe'th worty may lebro of annodho, pluck it at my risk, and also cause to thy husband that he may eat of it. O.M. 199. More frequently written *ynwedh*, qd. v.

IORCH, s. m. A roe buck. Corn. Vocab. *yorch*, caprea. W. *iwrch*. Arm. *iourch*. Gr. ἴορκος. It is quoted by Scapula in a line from Oppian :—καὶ ἰόρκους ὀρυγάς τε, καὶ αἰγλήεντας ἰόρκους.

IORCHES, s. f. A roe. Llwyd, 46. W. *iyrches*. Arm. *iourches*.

IOT, s. m. Stirabout, hasty pudding. Corn. Voc. *puls*. W. *uwd*, †*iot*. Arm. *ioud*, *iôd*, *iôt*. Ir. †*ith*.

IOUENC, adj. Young. *Gûr iouenc*, adolescens, a young man. Corn. Vocab. This word is variously written *iungk, iouenc, yonk, yowynk*, qd. v. *Ty mar yonk, pendra wreta gans an gwâs*, thou, so young, what dost thou with the fellow ? P.C. 1184. *Ol ny a pŷs, yowynk ha hên, war Dhu pûp prŷs mercy gan kên*, all we pray, young and old, to God always, mercy with pity. P.C. 39. W. *ieuanc*, †*iouenc*. Arm. *iaouanc*. Sause. *yuvan*. Lat. *juvenis*.

IOW, s. m. Jupiter, Jove. Another form of *Ieu*, qd. v. See also *Dûyow*.

IRA, v. a. To anoint, to grease. Llwyd, 245. In the Ordinalia it is generally written *uré*, qd. v. W. *iraw*.

IRAT, s. m. Ointment Llwyd, 176. Written in the Cornish Vocabulary, *urat*, qd. v.

IRCH, s. m. Snow. Corn. Voc. *nix*. The late form was *er*, qd. v. W. *eira, eiry*. Arm. *erch*.

IS, s. m. Corn, a berry. ‡ *Is lara*, bread corn ; ‡ *pedn iz*, an ear of corn ; ‡ *iz saval*, standing corn ; ‡ *iz diu*, a hurtle-berry. Llwyd, 61, 148, 153, 168. The late form of *ŷs*, qd. v.

ISA, adj. Lowest. *Trév isa*, the lowest town, in St. Enoder. *Isa coit*, the lowest wood. W. *isav*.

ISCEL, s. m. Broth. Corn. Vocab. *iskel*, jus. The late form was *isgal*. Llwyd, 74. W. *isgell*. From the Lat. *jusculum*.

ISEL, adj. Low, humble, lowly. Sup. *isella*, qd. v. *Y popel ny vŷdh sparyys, yssel y fedhons gwythys, keffrys yn nôs haq yn geydh*, his people shall not be spared, low they shall be kept, by night and by day also. O.M. 1515. *Ol an rê-ma ty a fŷdh, ow gordhyé mara mennyth, war pen dhe dhew glŷn yseal*, all these thou shalt have, if thou wilt worship me low on thy knees. P.C. 136. In late Cornish it was generally written *ual*. Llwyd, 46. *Gwâs isal*, humble servant. Comp. *isala*. *Ty isala*, lower house. W. *isel*. Arm. *izel*. Ir. *isiol, iscal*, †*isil*. Gael. *iosal, injil*.

ISELDOR, s. m. The lowest or deepest part, the bottom. Llwyd, 68. W. *iselder*. Arm. *izelder*.

ISELLA, adj. Lowest. Superlative of *isel*, qd. v. *Arluth, henna me a wra, a'n gor yn pyl ysella yn mŷsk pryves*, Lord, that I will do, put him in the lowest pit among reptiles. R.D. 2010. Arm. *izela*. W. *isav*.

ISION, s. m. Chaff, husks of corn. Llwyd, 111. See *Usion*.

ISOT, adv. Downwards. Corn. Voc. *deorsum*. W. *isod*, †*issol*.

ISPAC, s. m. A bishop. Llwyd, 7, 57. The late form of *epscop*, qd. v.

ITTA, prop. In. ‡ *Po terra vi itta o gwili*, when I was in my bed. Llwyd, 252. A late corruption of *yn*.

ITH, comp. pron. In thy. *Ith torn*, in thy hand. Ll. 230. Generally written *yth*, qd. v.

ITHEU, s. m. A firebrand. Corn. Voc. *titio*. Supposed to be a wrong reading of *tewen*, qd. v.

ITHIC, adj. Huge, large, very great, exceeding, strenuous. Llwyd, 68, 155, 249. *Ithik tra*, most of all, very much. 122. Generally written in the Ordinalia, *uthec*, qd. v.

IUH, adv. Above, over. Llwyd, 158. A late form of *uch*, qd. v.

IUHAL, adj. High, lofty. A late form of *uchel*, qd. v. ‡ *Mar iuhal*, so high. Llwyd, 248.

IUNC, adj. Young. ‡ *Dean iunk*, a young man. Llwyd, 74. A late form of *iouenc*, qd. v., and is variously written *iungk, iynk, iyngk*.

IVRE, s. m. Darnel, tares. Llwyd, 15. Welsh, *evrau, evré*. Fr. *ivraie*.

IWIN, s. m. A finger nail. Plural, *iwinas*. Llwyd, 176. A late form of *ewin*, qd. v.

IYNCAR, s. m. A young man. Llwyd, 41. English, *younker*.

J.

THIS letter was an entire stranger to the Celtic languages, and when it occurs in old manuscripts it is used for I. It is used in a few Cornish words to express a very modern corruption of the sound of *di*, as *jowl* for *diowl*; and in the loan of foreign words. With regard to Armoric, Legonidec observes :—" Cette articulation est toute moderne, et on ne l'emploie que par un relâchement dans la prononciation. Dans les livres anciens, les mots qui commencent aujourd'hui par J sont écrits par I, et l'on prononce encore aussi souvent *iaô, iaved*, et *iaritel*, que *jaô, javed, jaritel*." J is also used in Manx for *di*, as *Jee*, God. Ir. *Dia*.

JAMMES, adv. Ever, always, continually. *My a vyn gruthyl castel, ha drehevel dhym ostel, ynno jammes ráy trygé*, I will make a village, and build for myself a mansion, in it ever to live. O.M. 1711. *Heil pryns Annas, dhychy gammas mûr lowené*, hail prince Annas, ever to you (be) much joy. P.C. 933. *Aban osa mar gortes, ny a wra del leveryth ; ha pûp onan ol jammes neffré parys dhys a vŷdh*, since thou art so courteous, we will do as thou sayest ; and every one ever will be prepared for thee. R.D. 677. Fr. *jamais*.

JAUDYN, s. m. An obstinate wilful fellow, a rascal. *Gow a lever an iaudyn*, the wilful man tells a lie. P.C. 367. *Py hanow yw an iaudyn dhymmo a dhanfonas e*, what is the name of the fellow he has sent to me. P.C. 1091. *Dyeth vyé bones reys queth a'n par-na dhe iaudyn*, it were a pity that a cloth of this sort should be given to a wilful man. P.C. 1792. *Nyns yw saw un plos iaudyn*, he is nought but a foul rascal. P.C. 1894.

JAWL, s. m. A devil. *An jawl re'th ewno dh'y glas*, the devil adjust thee to his maw. O.M. 2527. ‡*gor scon, abarth an jawl, dhe dharasow*, open thou at once, in the devil's name, thy doors. R.D. 80. *Yn ban dhe néf Ihesu a wrûk yskynné, worth an iawl râk a's gwytho yn pûp le*, up to heaven Jesus did ascend, from the devil that he might keep them in every place. R.D. 2641. Another form of *dewol*, qd. v. W. *diawl*.

JEFFO, v. a. He may have. *Arluth, henna why ny wreuch ; an hagkré mernans whyleuch ma'n jeffo ef,* Lord, that do you not; seek the most cruel death that he may have it. R.D. 1973. A corruption of *geffo,* (by softening the *g,*) which is a mutation of *ceffo,* 3 pers. s. subj. of *cafos,* qd. v.

JENVAR, s. m. January. *Mis Jenvar,* the month of January. Written by Llwyd, 67, *genivar,* qd. v.

JEVAN, s. m. A devil. *Me a lever dheuch yn scon, tynnyn ef yn ban war lon, máp an jevan,* I tell you, forthwith, let us draw him up on the wave, the son of the evil one. R.D. 2282. *Re fethas an fals jevan hydhyw terguyth,* he has overcome the false demon this day three times. P.C. 154.

JEVES, v. a. He had. *Mara jeves vel dybbry, me a wôr gwŷr yredy nag yw c Dew,* if he has had a desire to eat, I shall know true, clearly, that he is not a God. P.C. 47. *Máp dén hep ken ys bara, býth nyn jeves ol bewnes, leman yn lavarow da a dhuc dhyworth drenses,* Son of man, without other than bread, hath never had all life, but in good words that come from trinity. P.C. 66. *Neb a vo y gorf golhys, nyn jeves ethom golhy saw y treys na vóns scehys, râg gwlán yw ol yredy,* he whose body is washed, hath not need of washing except his feet, that they be not dried, for he is all clean truly. P.C. 802. *Pendra ny venté kensel ? dout an jeves an losel, mar keus, y vôs concludyys,* why wilt thou not speak ? a fear the knave has had, if he speaks, that he will be silenced. P.C. 1776. I consider this word to be a corruption of *geves,* qd. v. A mutation of *ceves,* or *cefes,* 3 pers. s. preter. of *cafos.*

JEVODY, adv. I tell you. *Râg dout y vones ledhys, my ny vynnaf, jevody,* for fear of his being killed, I will not, I tell you. R.D. 594. *Gwŷr a geusyth, jevody,* thou sayest truth, I tell you. R.D. 653. *Lemyn Pilat, jevody cafus an bows-na hep gwry, ûs yth kerchyn, me a vyn,* now Pilate, I tell you, have that robe without seam, (that) is about thee, I will. R.D. 1920. Borrowed from the French, *je vous dis.*

JORNA, s. m. A day. Pl. *jorniow. An kynsa jorna,* the first day. C.W. 6. *An keth jorna-ma,* this same day. Ibid. 184. Written also *journa,* and by Llwyd, 27, *jwna.* ‡ *Ha godhewhar ha metten o an kensa journa,* and the evening and the morning were the first day. C.W. p. 189. ‡ *Ha gwrêns an gy bôs râg tavazow, ha râg termenions, ha râg journiow, ha râg blodhedniow,* and let them be for signs, and for seasons, and for days, and for years. p. 90. From the French, *journee.*

JOVE, v. subs. They were. *In corf Ihesus ydhesé, hag ef yn crows ow cregy, pymp mýll strekis del jové, ha peder gwŷth cans goly,* in the body of Jesus there were, and he on the cross hanging, five thousand strokes as there were, and four times a hundred wounds. M.C. 227. It may possibly be a corruption of *gevé,* he had, a mutation of *cevé,* 3 pers. s. imperf. of *cafos.*

JOVYN, s. m. Jove. *Mar a'th caffaf, re Jovyn, y'th ladhaf kyns ys vyttyn a'm dew lurf,* if I find thee, by Jove, I will kill thee before morning with my hands. O.M. 1532. *Râg henna, dhys my a de, gordhyé Jovyn veneges,* therefore I swear to thee, to worship the blessed Jove. O.M. 1812. *Gorf nép a wordh Jovyn, ha serry Dew awartha,* unhappy he who worships Jove, and angers God above. O.M. 1589.

JOWAN, s. m. John, a man's name. *Deso benyn, yn medha, Iowan dhe vâb me a wra,* to the woman he said, I will make John thy son. M.C. 198. *Iowan y vam a sensy Maryn, Crist del arsé,* John considered Mary as his mother, as Christ had commanded. M.C. 199. W. *Ioan, Icuan, Evan.* Arm. *Ian, Iann.* Ir. *Eoin.*

JOWL, s. m. A devil. Pl. *jowlow. Gans an Jowl y fûns tullys,* by the devil they were deceived. C.W. 74. *A soreth ! te dha gregy dha'n Jowl brâs, hay anfugy,* alas ! thou to believe the great devil, and his hypocrisy. C.W. 76. A later form of *jwel,* qd. v.

JYST, s. m. A joist, a beam. Pl. *jystys. War lew a dhellar, daras ty a wra, port ef a vŷdh hemrys; jystys dredho ty a pyn a lês, râg na vo digys,* on the hinder side, a door thou shalt make, a port it shall be called ; beams through it thou shalt nail broadways, that it may not be opened. C.W. 164. Written also *gŷst,* qd. v. W. *dist.* Gael. *dist.* Scot. *geist, gest.*

L.

THIS letter is radical, and immutable in all the Celtic languages, except in Welsh, where it is secondary, and a mutation of *ll.* The Welsh radical *ll* has an aspirate sound, now peculiar to that language, but the *l* was strongly aspirated in the Anglo-Saxon, as we find there *hlaf,* a loaf; *hlæfdig,* a lady ; *hlaword,* a lord.

LA, s. m. A hand. *Lwyd,* 242. An abbreviated form of *lau,* or *lav,* id. qd. *lýf,* qd. v.

LAC, adv. Loose, remiss, lax, out of order, naughty, bad. Comp. *lacca,* worse. *Alemma býs yn Tryger, war ow fay lacka mester ny alsen y dhycrbyn,* from hence to Treguer, on my faith, a worse master I should not be able to meet him. P.C. 2275. *Me a'n kymer yn dysdayn, mar ny vedhaf ve prevys whàth mêr lacka,* I take it in disdain, if I shall not be proved yet much worse. C.W. 106. *Ma lias gwrêg lackn vel seag,* there are many wives worse than grains. Pryce. W. *llac.* Ir. *lag.* Gael. *lag.* Manx, *lhag.* Lat. *laxus, lassus.*

LACCA, s. m. A pit, a well. *Lwyd,* 132. According to Pryce, it also means a *rivulet ;*—" which we still call a *luke,* and *leak,* or *leake ; Landleake,* the church on the rivulet." See also *Lagen.* Welsh, *llùch,* †*laich,* a lake. Arm. *louch, lagen.* Ir. *loch.* Gael. *loch.* Manx, *logh.* Gr. λάκκος. Lat. *lacus.*

LACCA, v. n. To faint away. *Prethy ny allaf pella ; me a vŷdh sûr dha lacka, mes te dhym a lavara,* I can hold no longer; I shall be sure to faint, except thou tell it to me. C.W. 46 W. *llaccâu.*

LACE, v. a. To lick, or slap ; to throw about; to cudgel; to lace or lash. *Me a'th lak,* I will lace thee. Pryce. W. *llachio.*

LACIE, v. a. To lace together, to fasten. *Aban yw an pren tellys, bedhens an ebyl gorrys dredhé, râg aga lacié,* since the wood is bored, let the pegs be put through them, to fasten them. P.C. 2575. From the English, *lace.*

LACHA, s. m. Law. *Dyswrŷs a vŷdh ol Iudy, ha kellys an lacha ny,* undone will be all Judea, and lost our law.

LADH 228 LAFURYE

R.D. 11. *Ty a wra y worré scon a dhescmpys yn pryson, an casadow, bys may hallo bôs juggys, ha dre laeha bôs dampnys dhe vôs marow, though shalt put him forthwith immediately in prison, the hateful one, till he may be tried, and by law condemned to be put to death.* R.D. 1981. The more general form is *laha,* qd. v. Arm. *lezen,* † *lesen,* † *laes.* Irish, *lagh.* Gael. *lagh.* Manx, *leigh.* Lat. *lex, lege.* Mod. Lat. *laga.* Ang. Sax. *lak, laga.* Germ. *lage.* Isl. *lag, laug.* Swed. *lagh, lag.* Eng. *law.*

LAD, s. m. Liquor. Corn. Voc. *liquor.* W. *llaith,* subs. and adjective. Arm. *leix.* Irish, *fliuch.* Gael. *fliuch.* Manx, *fliugh.* Lat. *latex.* Sansc. *layat, (li,* to become liquid.)

LADER, s. m. A thief, a robber, a pillager, a plunderer. Pl. *ladron, laddron.* Corn. Voc. *latro. An Edhewon a grogas lader dhe Gryst a'n barth clêdh, hag a dhychow lader brâs cregy a russons yn wêdh, ha Crist yn crês, leun a râs, leun y golon a voreth, gans laddron y tewedhas, del yw scrifys ay dhewedh,* the Jews hung a robber on the left side of Christ, and on the right a great robber they hung also, and in the middle Christ full of grace, his heart full of sorrow, with robbers he ended, as it is written of his end. M.C. 186. *Dywedh o, ha lader pûr,* shameless he was, and a very thief. M.C. 191. *An puré lader yn pow,* the veriest thief in the country. P.C. 1174. *An laddron a'n dyalas dre lyes torment ahas,* the thieves mocked him through many detestable torments. R.D. 1424. *An purré laddron yn pow,* the veriest thieves in the country. M.C. 90. W. *lleidr,* plural, *lladron.* Arm. *laer,* pl. *lacroun.* Ir. *sladthoir,* † *ladar,* † *ladron.* Goth. *lheidr.* Lat. *latro,* pl. *latrones.* Sansc. *lut,* to rob. Gr. λάθρα, furtively.

LADRA, v. a. To steal, to rob. Written also *laddré.* 3 pers. s. fut. *lader. Mar tue wêp gwâs ha laddré en gwcel dheworthyn pryvé, mêdh vgdh ol d'agru rhen,* if any fellow comes and steals the rods from us secretly, all shame it will be to our efforts. O.M. 2064. *Na lader, kyn fe vgdh mar vrâs quallok,* he will not steal, though he be ever so great a braggart. O.M. 2007. *Mar a's ladré dheworto, pan pyn a pydn dhodho,* if he steal it from him, what punishment is due to him? O.M. 2232. *Gwreuch y pûr fast, ma un allons y laddra yn mês a'n bêdh,* make ye them very fast, that they may not steal him out of the tomb. R.D. 35. *Mar ny wrer y wythé, y dhyskyblon yn pryvé a'n lader yn mês a'n beydh,* if it be not guarded, his disciples privily will steal him out of the tomb. R.D. 343. *Dhyworthyn dên na'n laddro, by na porth dout,* that a man may steal him from us, never entertain fear. R.D. 380. *Y laddré mar whylé dên, ef a'n pren,* if a man seek to steal it, he shall catch it. R.D. 370. W. *lladratta.* Arm. *laera.*

LADUIT, s. m. Nothing. Corn. Voc. *nihil.*

LADII, s. m. A cut, a cutting off, a killing, slaughter. *Onon esa yn preson, Barabas ydho gylwys, presonys o ef dre dreyson, ha râg dén-lâdh kekyffrys,* there was one in prison, Barabbas was he called; he was imprisoned for treason, and for manslaughter also. M.C. 124. *Dhe vôs dén-lâdh yw anken,* to be the killing of a man is a misfortune. O.M. 2335. W. *llâdh,* † *lâd.* Arm. *laz.* Ir. *slaighe,* † *slaod.* Germ. *schlacht.* Ang. Sax. *slæge.* Sansc. *slath.*

LADHE, v. a. To kill, to slay. 2 pers. sing. imp. *lâdh.* Part. *ledhys. Ol warbarth y a ylwys, te Pylat lâdh e, lâdh e, mernans an grows desympys; Pylat a yewsys arté, drcdhouch why brthens ledhys,* all together they cried out ;— " Thou Pilate, kill him! kill him! the death of the cross forthwith!" Pilate again said ;—" By you let him be killed." M.C. 142. *Râg dhe ladhé dén mar qura, ef a'n gevyth scyth kemmys a paynys in nôr bŷs-ma,* for if a man shall kill thee, he shall get seven times as much of pains in the earth of this world. O.M. 598. *Râg dhe verkyé my a gwra, yn bŷs dén vŷth na'th ladho,* for I will mark thee, in the world that no man slay thee. O.M. 603. *A mylegys y'th ober, ty re'n ladhes,* O cursed in thy deed, thou hast killed him. O.M. 1533. *Mar a'th enffaf, re Jovyn, y'th ladhaf kyns ys vyttyn, a'm dew luef,* if I catch thee, by Jove, I will kill thee before morning with my hands. O.M. 2226. *Saw un marrek a'n ladhas, ha dhe'n dôr scon a'n goras,* but a horseman slew him, and soon drove him to the earth. O.M. 2226. *Y dhadder yw drôk tylys, pan y'n ladhsons dybyté,* his goodness is ill requited, when they have killed him without pity. P.C. 3008. *Me a gryfs a lavassen scon war ow breuth yn latdhen,* I think we might venture at once, on my judgment, to kill him. R.D. 1836. W. *llâdh,* † *lâd;* † *ladam* cædo. (Oxf. Gloss.) Arm. *laza.* Gr. ληίζω, λάζομαι. Lat. *lædo.*

LADHVA, s. f. Slaughter, murder. *Râg an ladhva o mar vrâs, ny yll Dew dhymo gava,* for the murder was so great, God cannot forgive me. C.W. 98. W. *lladhva.*

LAFROC, s. m. Breeches. Corn. Voc. *femoralin. Lafrocwn* perizomata *vel* campestria, drawers. Lhcyd, 13, 45, gives *lavrak* as the late form, for a pair of breeches. *Lafrocwn* of the Cornish Vocabulary, he reads *lafroc pan,* cloth breeches. 118. Arm. *lavrek.* W. *llavrog,* having large buttocks. The root is the W. *llavr,* the breech.

LAFUR, s. m. Labour, toil, work. Written also *lafyr,* and *lavur. Gwyn bŷs vones dhym fethys lafur ha duwon an bŷs,* joyful that for me is vanquished the labour and sorrow of the world. O.M. 851. *Pyth ew an othom dynny cafus lafur a'n par-na,* what is the need for us to have such labour? O.M. 968. *Y'th whŷs lavur dhe dhybry ty a wra, bŷs yth worfen,* in thy sweat thou shalt do labour to eat, even to thy end. O.M. 273. *Heb mûr lavur defry benytha nys tevyth flôch,* without great labour indeed shall never children be to her. O.M. 299. *Ty re fue fest lafur brâs,* thou hast had very great labour. R.D. 2628. *Hirnath bew ôn yn bŷs-ma, ma ythov squyth a lavyr brâs ês dhymo pûb nôs ha dýdh,* a length of time I have lived in this world, that I am weary with the great labour (that) is to me every night and day. C.W. 126. W. *llavur.* Arm. *labour.* Ir. † *lubhra.* Lat. *labor.*

LAFURYE, v. a. To labour, to toil, to work. *Môs dhe balas my a eyn, râg susten'd vevenans dhyn, rŷs yw porrys lafurryé,* I will go to dig, to sustain life for us, to labour is very needful. O.M. 683. *Râg genes yn pûb teller, parys ôf dhe lafuryé,* for with thee in every place I am ready to work. O.M. 940. *Pan vo ol dhyn lafurryyé, agan wheyl a vŷdh mothow,* when all is laboured by us, our work will be failing. O.M. 1225. *Reys yw dhyso lafurrya,* it is necessary for thee to work. O.M. 1208. *Nans ôn lafuryys ganso, hag an ysxyly pûr squyth,* now we are oppressed with it, and our limbs are very weary.

O.M. 2823. W. *llavurio*. Arm. *laboura*. Lat. *laboro*.

LAGADEC, adj. Full of eyes, quick of sight. *Lhuyd*, 105, gives *lagadzhac* as the late corrupt form. W. *llygadog*. Arm. *lagadec*.

LAGAS, s. m. An eye. Pl. *lagasow*. As is the general case with pairs, the dual form *dew lagas* is often used instead of the plural. *An golom glás hy lagas*, the dove with blue eyes. O.M. 1109, 1135. *Lemyn gans ow dew lagas me a wêl*, now with my eyes I see. P.C. 410. *Agan dew lagas yw marthys cláf ow colyas*, our eyes are wondrous sore in watching. P.C. 1065. *Me a tru warê yn y dhew lagas*, I will spit soon in his eyes. P.C. 1400. *A-rák agan lagusow, a-lês ol y wolyow ny u welas*, before our eyes, displayed all his wounds we saw. R.D. 1492. A later form of *lagat*.

LAGAT, s. m. An eye. Corn. Voc. *oculus*. Pl. *legeit*, oculi. *Bleu en lagat*, palpebre, eyelashes. *Bleu en lagat*, pupilla, the pupil, (lit. life) of the eye. (W. *mablygad*. Arm. *map an lacad*.) This is the oldest orthography. W. *llygad*, † *licat*. Arm. *lagad*. Sansc. *laks*. or *lauc*, to see.

LAGEN, s. f. A pond, a pool, a lake. Corn. Voc. *stagnum*. Arm. *lagen*.

LAHA, s. m. Law. Pl. *lahys*. *An debel dús a gewsys, dhynny yma laha may rûs y vonas ledhys, rág máb Du cf a omwra*, the evil folk said :—"Surely, we have a law that he must be killed, for he makes himself the Son of God." M.C. 143. *Ambosow orth tryher gwreys, annedhé nyns ês laha*, promises made by the mighty, of them there is no law. O.M. 1235. *Gwês da, crocer dhym yma, a awcon múr a laha*, I have a crozier-bearer, a good fellow, who knows much law. P.C. 1457. *Lemmyn me agis pûs oll a baynis Crist predcry, ha na vo gesys dhe goll an lahys a rûg dhynny*, now I pray you all to think of Christ's pains, and that to loss be not left the laws he made for us. M.C. 182. *Yma un goás marthys prout, ol an cyté ow trylyé, hag an lahes ow syndyé*, there is a fellow wondrous proud, turning all the city, and violating the laws. P.C. 580. Another form of *lacha*, qd. v.; *ch* being softened into *h*.

LAHVELET, s. m. A rudder. *Pryce*. This form must be corrupt. It is connected with Welsh, *llywedydh*, a guider, from *llyw*, a rudder, which is also preserved in the Cornish, *leu*, qd. v.

LAIAN, adj. Faithful. Corn. Vocab. *fidelis*. The form used in the Ordinalia is the contracted one of *lén*, qd. v.

LAIG, s. m. A layman. *Lluyd*, 75. Another form of *leic*, and *lêc*, qd. v.

LAINES, s. f. A nun. Corn. Voc. *nonna*. W. *lleian*. Arm. *leanez*, † *leanes*. (W. *lleiandy*, a nunnery. Arm. *leandi*.)

LAIT, s. m. Milk. Corn. Voc. *lac*. The old orthography of *leyth*, or *léth*, qd. v., as written in the Ordinalia. W. *llacth*. Arm. *leaz, lez*. Irish, *lachd*, † *laith*. Gael. *lachd*. Lat. *lac, lacte*.

LAITTY, s. m. A milkhouse, a dairy. A local name. Comp. of *lait*, milk, and *ty*, a house.

LAM, s. m. A leap, a stride; a space of time or place; a slip, fall, trip, sliding; chance, accident. *Ny lettys saw un un lam, ow kafus banneth ow mam*, I stopped only a space, receiving the blessing of my mother. O.M. 470. *Dheworté un lam bechan ydh éth pesy may hallé*, he went from them a little space that he might pray. M.C. 53. *A lorels, re's bo drók lam*, O rascals! be it an evil step for ye! P.C. 1125. *Me a wra y concludyé war un lam*, I will shut him up in a trice. P.C. 1464. *Kenter scon dre dhe dew trôs my a's gwysk, may fo drók lam*, nails soon through thy two feet I will drive, that it may be an evil chance. P.C. 2782. *Ty a fydh cowal drók lam*, thou shalt have a fully bad leap. P.C. 2913. W. *llam*. Arm. *lamm*. Irish, *leum*, † *leim*. Gael. *leum*. Manx, *lheim*.

LAMME, v. a. To leap, to jump, to bound, to stride, to step. *Lemmel* was also used for the infinitive. *War ow fay hemma yw deaul ymskemunys, yn mês a'n dôr y lammas*, on my faith this is a devil accursed, out of the earth ho has jumped. R.D. 2000. *A'n bédh pan dhucth ha lammé, y fyys yn un vrammé, own kemerys* from the grave when he came and leaped, thou fleddest in terror, seized by fear. R.D. 2093. W. *llammu*; † *lammam*. salio. (Oxf. Gloss.) Arm. *lammout, lemel*, † *lamma*. Ir. *leim*. Gael. *leum*. Manx, *lheim*. Sansc. *laip*. Goth. *hlaupa*. Ang. Sax. *hleapa*. Germ. *laufé*. Eng. *leap*. Gr. λείπω. Lat. *labor*.

LAN, s. f. A church, an inclosure. The primary meaning was a piece of ground enclosed for any purpose; an area to deposit any thing in; hence a yard; a churchyard. With the sense of a yard, we have in Welsh, *corlan*, a sheepfold; *gwinllan*, a vineyard; *perllan*, an orchard; *ydlan*, a stackyard, &c. With the sense of a church, it enters into most of the names of parishes in Wales, as *Llangadwaladr, Llandudno, Llangernyw*, &c., and wherever the Welsh were resident, as in Cornwall, where we have *Lanmorran, Landuwenac, Lanreath*, &c., and in Britanny, there are *Lanbaol, Langoat, Laniliz*, &c. Again in Scotland, we have *Lanbride, Lanmorgan*, &c., and in England, *Lancant, Lanbeach, Langar*, &c. W. *llan*. Arm. *lan*. Ir. † *lann*, † *land*. Gael. † *lann*. Manx, *lhan, lhannce*.

LAN, adj. Clean, pure, fair, holy. A mutation of *glán*, qd. v. *I beyn o mar greff ha tyn, canan na ylly bewé heb dascor y eneff gwyn; bythqueth yn lán reversé*, his pain was so strong and keen, that he could not live any way without parting with his pure soul; over holy he had lived. M.C. 204. W. *glán, lán*.

LANHERCH, s. m. An open place in a wood, a sheltered area, a glade, a forest. Corn. Vocab. *saltus*. W. *llanerch*. It is the name of several places in Wales, as *Llanerch y medh, Llanerch Aeron*, &c.; and in Cornwall, as *Laurack*; and in Scotland, as *Lancrk*, and *Lanrick*.

LANWES, s. m. Fulness, satiety, glut. *Ty a wra wogé hemma gorré an tús a le-na bŷs yn tyreth a dhynwa lanwes leyth ha mêl kefrys*, thou shalt after this bring the people thence to a land that produces fulness of milk, and honey also. O.M. 1430. Welsh, *llanwed, llonaid*, † *loneit*. Irish, *lainne*, † *lanad*. Gael. *lanachd, lainc*. Manx, *laneid*.

LAOL, v. a. To say, to speak, to tell. *Lluyd*, 54. ‡ *Thera vi idol*, I say. 71. ‡ *Dho idol gow*, to tell a falsehood. 150. ‡ *Emá radn a lôl*, some say. 250. It occurs only in late Cornish. Welsh, *llolio*, to prate, to tattle. Sansc. *lal*, to prate.

LAPPIOR, s. m. A dancer. Corn. Voc. *saltator*. Formed from the English, *leaper*.

LAPPIORES, s. f. A female dancer, a dancing woman. Corn. Voc. *saltatrix*. From *lappior*, with the feminine termination.

LAVAR 230 LAWE

LAS, adj. Blue; grey; green. The feminine mutation of *glâs*, qd. v. *Losowan lâs*, a green herb. *Mola lâs*, a fieldfare. Llwyd, 168.

LAST, s. m. Nastiness. *Gans an Edhewon war hast drôk dhewus a ve dythgtys, tebell lycour mûr y lâst, eysyll bestyll kemyskis*, by the Jews in haste a bad drink was dighted, evil liquor, great its nastiness, vinegar, gall mixed. M.C. 202. Arm. *lastez*, filth.

LATH, s. m. Milk. Llwyd, 75. *Lâth* is a contracted form of *leath*, ld. qd. *leyth*. See *Lait*.

LATHYE, v. a. To lay or place. *H'ow gwereseuch, cowethé, ow corré tumbyr yn ban, may haller aga lathyé, yn crês an chy rês vyé knfus gyst crêf na vo gwan*, and help me, comrades, putting the timber up, that they may be laid, in the middle of the house it would be necessary to have a strong beam (that) is not weak. O.M. 2480. *Hay gîl troys a ve gorris poran war ben y gelé, worth an groves y fôns lathyys, gans kenter gwyskis dredhé*, and one of his feet was placed right over the other, on the cross they were laid, with a nail struck through them. M.C. 179.

LAU, s. f. A hand. Corn. Vocab. *manus*; which also furnishes us with another form, *lof*, dual, *duilof*, as *lien duilof*, a towel. The forms preserved in the Ordinalia are *lef, luef*; dual, *dewlucf, dyulef, dulé, dyulé, deulé*. W. *llaw*, † *lau*, † *lof*, whence *llovrudh*, redhanded; *llovi*, to handle; *rhaglovydh*, a vice-gerent; *unllovyauc*, one-handed. Arm. † *lao*, † *la*. Irish, *lamh*, † *lam*, † *laam*. Gael. *lamh*. Manx, *lauc*. Goth. *lofa*. Scottish, *loof*. Eng. *luff*. Sansc. *labh*, to seize. Gr. λάβω, λαμβάνω.

LAUN, adj. Full. Pryce. Generally written *leun*, and *luen*, qd. v.

LAUNTIER, s. m. A lamp. Llwyd, 81.

LAUR, adv. Enough, sufficiently. Llwyd, 144. Generally written *lour*, qd. v.

LAUTE, s. m. Loyalty, good faith, truth. *Cowyth whêk by my lauté, ty a fŷdh mêns a vynny*, sweet comrade, by my truth, thou shalt have all thou wilt. P.C. 580. *Del ôs cowyth da, lavar a pilé osa, er dhe lauté*, as thou art a good companion, say whence thou art, on thy truth. P.C. 2180. Written also *leauté*, and *lewté*. Derived from the Old French, *loiauté*.

LAVALOW, s. m. Apples, fruits. ‡ *Gwedhan lavalow*, an apple tree. Llwyd, 10. ‡ *Ha Dew laveras, gwerens an noar dry râg gwells, ha losow toen hâs, ha'n gwecdh toen lavalow warler e cunda*, and God said, let the earth bring forth grass, and herbs yielding seed, and the trees yielding fruit after their kind. Gen. j. 11. (M.C. p. 93.) "*L*. is premised, for what I have observed, only in the word *lavalow*, apples; which is but a very late corruption of *avalow*." Llwyd, 231.

LAVAR, s. m. Utterance, speech, voice; a saying; a word; a proverb. Corn. Vocab. *sermo* vel *locutio*. Pl. *lavarow, levarow*. *Mâb dên heb ken ys bara nyn gevas oll y veunas lemmen yn lavarow da, a dhé dheworth an dromas; dre worthyp Crist yn ûr-na lemmyn ny a gîl gwelns, lavar Dû maga del wra nêb a vynno y glewas*, the Son of Man without other than bread hath not taken all his life, but in good words that come from the Supremely Good. By Christ's answer then we may now see, how God's word feeds whosoever will hear it. M.C. 12. *Del leveryth, my a grŷs y fŷdh agan enefow dre levarow Dew mygys*, as thou sayest, I believe that our souls will be fed by the words of God. P.C. 76. *Whêt y lavar a fue, crês ol dhywhy why*, ever his speech was, "Peace to you all." R.D. 1361. *An lavar gôth ew lavar gwîr*, the old saying is a true saying. Pryce. Welsh, *llavar*. Arm. *lavar*. Irish, *labhairt, labhradh*, † *labar*, † *labrad*. Gael. *labhairt*. Manx, *loayr*. Sansc. *lapan*, (lap, to speak.) Cf. also Latin, *labrum*. Span. *palabra*. Port. *palavra*. Eng. *palaver*.

LAVARY, v. a. To speak, to say, to tell, to pronounce, to declare. The infinitive is generally *leverel*, qd. v. Part. *leverys*. *Hag êth arta dhe besy, del lavarsa ragon ny*, and he went again to pray as he had said for us. M.C. 56. *En prins scon a leveris, te Crist, lavar dhym ple ma dhe dûs*, the prince straightway said, "Thou Christ, tell me where are thy people?" M.C. 78. *Crist un gêr ny lovery*, Christ would not say a word. M.C. 96. *Hag y lavarsons dhodho*, and they said to him. M.C. 154. *Râg dhys ny lavaraf gow*, for I do not tell thee a lie. O.M. 180. *Lavar dhymmo dyongel*, tell thou to me clearly. O.M. 1369. *Dysempys arch ha lavar*, forthwith command thou and say. P.C. 61. *Nyns ûs gorryth na benen bŷth well cusyl bys vycken a lavarré*, there is not male or female ever better advice to eternity (that) could mention. R.D. 422. For examples of the other tenses see *Leverel*. W. *llavaru, lleva'u*. Arm. *lavarel*. Irish, *labhair*. Gael. *labhair*. Manx, *loayr*. Sansc. *lap*.

LAVASY, v. a. To dare, to venture, to attempt. *Portheres gentyl mars ôs, me a'th pŷs a lavasos dry ow cowyth aberveth*, portress, gentle as thou art, I pray thee that thou wouldst venture to bring my companion within. P.C. 1226. *Me a grŷs a lavassen scon war ow breuth y'n lathhen*, I think we might venture at once, on my judgment, to kill him. R.D. 1835. *Mar levesyn y knoukyé ol dhe brevyon, y wrên dhodho ef hep mar*, if I might venture to knock him all to pieces, I would do it to him without doubt. R.D. 1892. W. *llavasu*. Ir. *lamham*, † *luisim*.

LAVERYANS, s. m. A tongue or language. Pryce.

LAVIRIA, v. a. To work, to labour. ‡ *Dera vi laviria*, I do labour. Llwyd, 246. A late form of *lafuryé*, qd. v.

LAVIRIANS, s. m. Labouring, labour. ‡ *Buz, gen nebas lavirians, eye venja dendle go booz, ha dillaz*, but, with little labour, they would get their meat, and clothes. Pryce. W. *llavuriant*.

LAVRAC, s. m. A pair of breeches. Llwyd, 13, 45. *Lavrak pan*, cloth breeches. 118. A later form of *lafrog*, qd. v.

LAVUR, s. m. Work, labour, toil. *Heb mûr lavur defry benytha nys levyth flôch*, without great labour indeed she shall never bear children. O.M. 299. *Awos lavur na dewon nefré ny fallaf dheuchwhy*, because of labour nor sorrow, I will never fail you. O.M. 2405. *Godheveuch omma lavur*, endure ye here labour. P.C. 1024. Written also *lafur*, qd. v.

LAWAN, s. m. Birds, fowls. *Yn tân ty a wra lesky, ha kêth pagya-ma defry yn effarn, why drôg lawan*, in fire thou shalt burn, and this homicide surely in hell, ye wicked fowls. C.W. 124.

LAWE, s. m. Laud, praise, request. *Yn enour Dew, dh'y lauwé, cuch dh'y drehy hep lettyé*, in honour of God, to his praise, go ye to cut it without delaying. O.M. 2504. *Ny vyn Dew kêr, dh'y lauwé, na fella my dhe wewé omma genouch*, dear God, to his praise, will not that I should live any longer here with you. O.M. 2359. *Wogé hen-ma ly a wêl Máp Dew owdh esedhé a bart dyow, dh'y lawé, dhe'n Tâs Dew, Arluth huhel,* after this thou shalt see the Son of God sitting on the right side, to his praise, of the Father God, Lord high. P.C. 1329.

LAWEN, adj. Joyful, glad. *Pryce.* Generally written *lowen,* qd. v.

LAWENES, s. m. Joy, gladness, delight. *Llwyd,* 62. A later form of *lowené,* qd. v. W. *llawenydh.*

LAWENIC, adj. Cheerful, glad, merry. *Llwyd,* 13, 42. Generally written *lowenec,* qd. v.

LAWER, adj. Many, much; several. *Lawer flowrys a bûb chan yn plâs-ma yia tevys,* many flowers of every kind in this place shall grow. C.W. 28. ‡ *Pysgos lawer,* many fishes. *Llwyd,* 248. The word is variously written *lower, lawr,* and *lour,* qd. v. W. *llawer.* Ir. *lear, lor,* †*lar,* †*ilar,* †*hilar.* Gael. *leor.* Manx, *liooar.* Gr. πλήρης. Lat. *plêrus, plures.*

LAWETHAN, s. m. Fiends. *Belsebuc ha lawethan, dylleuch luhes ha taran quyt a'n losco,* Beelzebub and fiends send forth lightnings and thunder, that it burn him quite. R.D. 128. *Ha my caugeon lawethan, merwel a wrén ow cûl tân yn dan un chek,* and my dirty fiends, we will die making a fire under the kettle. R.D. 139.

LAWN, adj. Clean, clear, open. A corruption of *lân,* a mutation of *glân. Trelawn,* an open town. It may however be connected with W. *llawnt.* Eng. *lawn.*

LAYS, s. m. Laws. A contracted form of *lahys,* pl. of *laha,* qd. v.

LAYS, s. m. Green. Pren *lays,* a green tree. *Pryce.* A late form of *lâs,* a mutation of *glâs,* qd. v. It was finally written *lase,* as *Goonlase,* the green down, in St. Agnes. *Borlase,* the green top or summit.

LE, s. m. A place, space, spot, situation, stead. *A'm bewnans del yw scrifys yn lyffrow en lcas le,* of my life as it is written in many a place. M.C. 73. *Ihesus a dhedhoras, hag êth yn le may fynné,* Jesus ascended, and went to the place that he would. M.C. 243. *Ha ny ow tôs a le-na,* and we coming from that place. O.M. 714. *Offrynnyé an kêth mols-ma, yn le Ysac, y settya war an alter dhe lesky,* (I will) offer this same sheep; instead of Isaac (I will) set it on the altar to burn. O.M. 1385. *My a vyn gûl yn della, py le penag y's kyffyn,* I will do so, wherever I find it. P.C. 1551. *Omma aberth yn pen wlâs, le na fue denses bythqueth,* here within the head countrry, where manhood never was. R.D. 2531. W. *lle,* †*loc.* Arm. *lech.* Ir. *loc.* Gael. *loc.* Lat. *locus.* Gr. λέχος. Ang. Sax. *lenh, lege.* Eng. *lay.* Russ. *lug.* Fr. *lieu.*

LE, adj. Less, smaller. Used as the comparative of *bechan.* Superl. *leia,* qd. v. *Dêk-warn-ugens a moné; me ny vennaf cafus lê yn gwyryoneth,* thirty of money; I will not take less in truth. P.C. 594. *Mêr lê,* much less. *Llwyd,* 91. ‡ *Na reugh eva rê, mes eva rag guz zchaz; ha hedna, muy po lê, vedna gwitha corf en chaz,* do not drink too much, but drink for your thirst; and that, more or less, will keep the body in health. *Pryce.* Welsh, *llai.* Irish, *lugha,* †*laigiu,* †*lu.* Gael. *lugha.* Manx, *sloo.* Old Celtic, *lugu,* in *Lugu-dunum,* Lyons; *Lugu-ballium,* Carlisle; &c. Greek, ἐλαχύς, ἐλαχίων. Eng. *less.* Sansc. *laghu,* (lic, to diminish.)

LEADAN, adj. Large. *Llwyd,* 76. See *Ledan.*

LEAL, adj. Faithful, true, loyal. *Llwyd,* 59. *Me a byes dhe'n leal Drenges, ha drevo omma yn beys dha vûs leal servant dhodho,* I pray to the faithful Trinity, and while I am here in the world, to be a loyal servant to it. C.W. 102. The general form in the Ordinalia is the contracted one of *lêl,* qd. v. Arm. *leal.* Span. *leal.* It. *leale.* Fr. †*leall.* Scot. *leil.* From the Lat. *legalis.*

LEANA, v. a. To fill to fill up. *Dho leana. Llwyd,* 68. A late form of *lenwel,* qd. v.

LEAS, adj. Many, frequent, much. *Yn lyffrow yn leas le, dre brofusy leverys,* in books in many places by prophets spoken. M.C. 73. *Herodes a wovynnys orth Ihesus Crist leas tra,* Herod asked of Jesus Christ many a thing. M.C. 111. *Goleow pals leas mŷll,* plenteous wounds many thousands. M.C. 165. *Ha leas ganso ena dodho a dhûk dustuny,* and many with him there to him bare witness. M.C. 208. Written also *lias,* and *lues,* qd. v. W. *lliaws,* †*liaus.* Arm. *lies, (a-lies,* often.) Ir. *liachd,* †*lia.*

LEAS, s. m. Breadth. ‡ *Maûz a leas,* to go abroad. *Llwyd,* 129. A late form of *lês,* qd. v.

LEASDER, s. m. Plenty, abundance. *Pryce.*

LEATH, s. m. Milk. *Llwyd,* 75. *Leath crêv,* raw milk. *Leath cowles,* sour milk. ‡ *Es leath luck gen veu,* is there milk enough with the cow? *Pryce.* Another form of *lêth,* or *leyth,* which are again later forms of *lait,* qd. v.

LEAUH, s. m. A calf. ‡ *Ma'n viuh gen leauh;* the cow is in calf. *Llwyd,* 230. A late corruption of *loch,* qd. v.

LEAUII, s. m. The ague. ‡ *Idzha'n lêauh dhe'n dén yynk-na,* has that young man the ague? *Llwyd,* 242. Arm. *lench, lêch,* the rickets.

LEB, adj. Wet. The feminine mutation of *glêb,* qd. v. *Cewar lêb,* wet weather. *Llwyd,* 243.

LEB, pron. rel. Who, which, what. *Llwyd,* 134. A late corruption of *neb,* qd. v.

LEBBA, adv. Here. *Llwyd,* 248. A more recent corruption of *lebma.*

LEBMA, adv. Here. ‡ *A lebma,* from hence. *Llwyd,* 65. A late corruption of *lemma,* qd. v.

LEBMA, v. a. To sharpen. *Llwyd,* 41. A late corruption of *lemma,* qd. v.

LEBMAL, v. a. To leap, to hop, to dance. *Llwyd,* 143, 245. A late corruption of *lemmel,* qd. v.

LEBMEN, adv. Now. *Llwyd,* 251. Written also *lehmyn,* being late corruptions of *lemmyn,* qd. v.

LEC, adj. Lay. *Anson whansek ol dhe pysy, lettrys ha lêk, war Dhu mercy,* we are desirous to pray, lettered and lay, to God for mercy. P.C. 38. *Otié omma skyber dêk, ha cala lour war hy luer, pynag vo lettrys py lêk a weles an chy, nym dêr,* see here a fair room, and straw enough on its floor; whoever he may be, lettered or lay, (that) hath seen the house, I am not concerned. P.C. 681. Another form of *leic,* qd. v.

LEDAN, adj. Broad, wide, ample, spacious, extensive. *Yn amendys a'd pehasow, orden bôs gnereys temple golow, brás ha ledan,* in amends of thy sins, order to be made a brilliant temple, great and ample. O.M. 2261. *Ha'n Edheuon a worras a uch Ihesus Crist un mên, leden o, ha poys, ha brás, moy agis gavel tredden,* and the Jews put above Jesus Christ a stone, broad it was, and heavy, and large, more than the grasp of three men. M.C. 237. W. *llydan*, †*litan*. Arm. *ledan*. Irish, *leathan*, †*lethan*, †*litan*, †*litan*. Gael. *leathan*. Manx, *llcan*. Greek, πλατύς. Lat *latus*. Sansc. *parthus;* (*parth*, to expand.) Goth *braids*. Lith. *platus*. Ang. Sax. *brad*. Germ. *breit*. Eng. *broad*.

LEDANLES, s. f. A plaintain. *Llwyd*, 121. Called in the Corn. Voc. *enlidan*, qd. v. Comp. of *ledan*, broad, and *les*, a herb. Arm. *ledanlus*. W. *llydan y fordh*.

LEDR, s. m. A cliff, a steep hill. Written also *ledra*. *Lam ledra*, the cliff, or steep spot of ground. *Pryce*. This may however be compared with W. *llam y lladron*, the robbers' leap; a precipice in Merioneth, where thieves were thrown down. W. *llethyr, llethr*, a cliff.

LEDRYS, part. Stolen. Part. pass. of *ladra*, qd. v. *Mur ny fedhé ef gwythys, gans y lûs y ffydh leddrys*, if he be not guarded, by his people he will be stolen. R.D. 354. Written by Llwyd, 354, *ledres*. *Po marh ledres*, when a horse is stolen.

LEDYA, v. a. To lead. *Pyw ytho a's hembronk dhy, mar ny wraf vy nag Aron aga ledya venary*, who then will lead them to it, if I nor Aaron do not conduct them ever? O.M. 1876. Borrowed from the English.

LEDZНEC, s. f. A heifer. *Llwyd*, 3, 240.

LEDHYS, part. Killed, slain. Part. pass. of *ladhé*, qd. v. *El a'n nêf ôf, danfenys rág gwythé na ve ledhys dhe váp Ysac*, an angel from heaven I am, sent to preserve that he be not killed thy son Isaac. O.M. 1373. *Mar codhfo an casadow, dystouch y fycn ledhys*, if the villain knew, immediately I should be killed. O.M. 2120.

LEF, s. f. A voice, sound, cry. *Dhe léf, Arluth*, a glewaf, thy voice, Lord, I hear. O.M. 587. *Ty re glewas agan léf*, thou hast heard our voice. R.D. 174. *Uthyk yn clewas y léf*, it is terrible to hear his voice. R.D. 2340. *Orto ef y a sedhas, may clewo léf Ihesus whêk*, on it they sat, that they might hear the voice of sweet Jesus. M.C. 77. Welsh, *llêv*. Arm. *lef, lev*. Cf. Lat. *clamo*, to cry out.

LEF, s. f. A hand. *Gwlân ef re gollas an plâs, a'm léf dhychow a wrussen dh'y wythé an geffo grâs*, he has quite lost the place, (which) with my right hand I had made to keep it if he had the grace. O.M. 421. *Hag yn y léff dhychow yn wêdh gwelen wyn a ve gorris*, and in his right hand also a white rod was put. M.C. 136. Written also, to express the long *ê, leyf*, and *luef*. See the dual form *dywlef*. The earlier forms were *lau* and *lof*, qd. v.

LEFA, v. a. To cry aloud, to shout. *Ow bannath dhyso, Gryffyn, ty a lyfes yn dhe fê; mar ny gevyth médh py gwyn, ke dhe fenten dhe evê*, my blessing on thee, Gryffyn, thou shoutedst in thy faith; if thou findest no mead or wine, go to the fountain to drink. O.M. 2434. W. *llevain*. Arm. *lefa*.

LEGAST, s. m. A lobster. Pl. *legesti*. *Llwyd*, 33, 242. Dr. Davies's Welsh-Latin Dictionary, 1632, gives *llegest*, polypus piscis, as a Welsh word, and quotes the Liber Landavensis, as his authority. It is not however the Welsh name, which is *cimwch*, and is another instance, with *côth*, and many others, of words taken from the Cornish Vocabulary, and mistaken for Welsh. "In the Welsh Dictionary, *legast* is rendered *Polypus* out of the Liber Landavensis; but erroneously I suppose, seeing it is manifestly the Latin *Locusta*, and that it is at this day used in that sense in Cornwall. One sort of this *Legast*, (called otherwise by the Cornish, *Gavar-môr,*) the Western English called anciently *Legster*, afterwards *Lengster*, and now *Long Oyster*." Llwyd, 5. Arm. *legestr*. Fr. *langouste*.

LEGRADZ, s. m. A reading, a varying, a changing. Pl. *legradzhow*. Pryce.

LEGRIA, v. a. To read, to vary, to change. *Pryce*.

LEHAN, s. m. A tile, a slate. *Llwyd*, 161. The diminutive of *léh*, or *lêch*, a slab, or flat stone. W. *llêch, llechen*. Arm. *leach*. Irish, *leac*, †*liac*. Gael. *leac*. Manx, *leac*.

LEHE, v. a. To lessen, to diminish. Part. *lehcys, lehŷs*. *Yowynk ha loys, kyn fo tollys dre y deunos, mercy gylwys; scon y gallos a vŷdh lehŷs*, let young and grey, though they be deceived by his witchery, call for mercy; soon his power shall be lessened. P.C. 21. *Penys a reys rûg y terros, may fo lehcys mûr a y gallos dre ow fynys*, penance is necessary for his lands, that may be diminished much of his power through my pains. P.C. 44. Written also *leyhé*, and *lyha*, qd. v.

LEIA, s. m. Least. *Dha'n leiah, en leinh*, at least. *Ll* 91. Written also *lyha*, qd. v. It is used as the superlative of *bechan*. W. *lleiav*. Ir. +*lugimen*.

LEIC, s. m. A layman. Corn. Voc. *laicus*. The older form of *léc*, qd. v. From the Latin.

LEID, s. m. A tribe, a family. Corn. Vocab. *progenies* vel *tribus*. *Luyte* written in the MS. by another hand, and read by Llwyd, 4, 166, *leith*. W. *llwyth*. Ir. *slead, sleachd, sliochd*, †*lucht*, †*luct*. Gael. *sluagh, luchd*. Manx, *sluight, slei*. Sansc. *laukas*. Gr. λαός, λειτός. Goth. *lauihs*. Germ. *leute*. Slav. *liúd*.

LEL, adj. Faithful, loyal, true. Comp. and superl. *lellé*. *Lavar, ple ma Abel, dhe vrodcr, ow servont lél*, say thou, where is Abel, thy brother, my faithful servant. O.M. 572. *An golom glâs hy lagas, yn mês gueva hy delyfré; lellé edhen, ren ow thâs, leverel ry won ple fê*, the dove blue as to her eyes, do thou liberate out; a more faithful bird, by my father, I cannot say where there was. O.M. 1111. *Mars ôs profus lél*, if thou art a faithful prophet. O.M. 1799. Used also adverbially. *Me a worthyp dhyso lél*, I will answer thee faithfully. P.C. 1751. *Râg kemmys a'n crŷs, hag a vo lél vygydhys, sylwel a wra*, for as many as believe it, and are faithfully baptized, he will save. R.D. 1143. A contracted form of *leal*, qd. v.

LEMMA, v. a. To sharpen, to whet. Part. *lemmys*. *Pan o an kentrow lemmys, hy a's dûk dhe'n Edhewon*, when the nails were sharpened, she brought them to the Jews. M.C. 160. *Gans ow boell nowydh lemmys, my a squat pûb peis tymber*, with my axe newly sharpened, I will hew every piece of timber. C.W. 168. W. *llymmu*. Arm. *lemma*. Ir. *liomham*. Gael. *liomh*. Manx, *shliu*.

LEMMA, adv. Here, this place. *Llwyd*, 248. Comp. of *le*, a place, and *ma*, here. *A lemma*, from this place, hence. *Euch a lemma pûr thôth brâs, del y'm kerreuch, ages dew*, go ye hence with great speed, as ye love me, ye two. O.M. 542. W. *lle-yma*.

LEMMYN, adv. Now, even now, at present, but. Written indiscriminately *lemen, lemen, lemmen, lemyn, lemmyn*, and *lymmyn*. *Mars ôs Dew a nêf golow, dysqua lemman marthusow may allyf vy y weles*, if thou art the God of bright heaven, show now miracles, that I may see them. P.C. 82. *Salmon, lemen ke y'th tour,* Solomon, now go into thy palace. O.M. 2389. *Ellas, bythqueth kyns lemmen, y vôs gwŷr Dew ny wydhen,* alas ! ever before now I did not know him to be true God. P.C. 1913. *Ny won vyth pe'dh âf lemyn,* I know not ever where I shall go now. O.M. 355. *Lemmyn, yacheys uban ôs, yn la ty a ğl godhfôs nag êns Dew byth lemmyn ef,* now, since thou art healed, thou mayest know well there is not any God but he. R.D. 1749. *Nyns yw gulân lemmyn mostys,* it is not clean, but dirty. R.D. 1927. The oldest form is *luman,* qd. v. The component parts are *le,* a place, and *man,* id. qd. *ma,* here.

LEMMEL, v. a. To leap, to jump. *Llwyd,* 245. The inflected tenses are formed from *lammê,* qd. v.

LEN, s. f. A blanket, a cloak, a whittle. Pl. *lennow,* ‡ *lednow.* Corn. Voc. *sagum.* ‡ *Pandra vedhoh why geil rag lednow rag 'as flo,* what will you do for whittles for your children ? *Pryce.* W. *llen,* †*lenn.* Arm. *lenn.* Ir. *leine,* †*leann,* †*lenn.* Gael. *leine.* Manx, *lheiney.* Lat. *lana.*

LEN, s. m. A ling fish. Pl. *lenesow.* *Y rôf hynwyn dhe'n puskes, porpus, sowmens, syllyes, ol dhym gustyth y a vŷdh; lenesow ha barfusy, pysk ragof ny wra skusy, mar cordhaf Dew yn perfyth,* fishes, porpoises, salmons, congers, all to me obedient they shall be; lings and cods, a fish from me shall not escape, if I worship God perfectly. O.M. 138. W. *lling.* Arm. *lean.* Ir. *lang, long.* Gael. *long.*

LEN, adj. Full. *Dhe kekemmys na'm gwello, hag yn perfyth a'n cresso, ow lên beuneth me a pŷs,* to as many as shall not see me, and shall perfectly believe it, my full blessing I pray. R.D. 1556. *Lên a râs,* full of grace. *Llwyd,* 232. A contracted form of *leun,* qd. v.

LEN, adj. Faithful, trusty, true, honest. *Nyns ûs dên ori ow servyê, lên ha gwyryon, me a greys,* there is not a man serving me, trusty and true, I believe. O.M. 930. *Del oma marrek lên,* as I am a trusty knight. O.M. 2150. *Gwyw yw yn lên dhe servyê,* it is worth while to serve thee faithfully. O.M. 2608. *Râk dhe vôs, geyler, mar lên,* because, gaoler, thou art so trusty. R.D. 91. *Gensy prest dew venyn lên esa worth y homfortyê,* with her at hand were two loyal women, comforting her. M.C. 167. A contracted form of *laian,* qd. v., as written in the Cornish Vocabulary. It seems to be derived from the French, † *loiau.*

LENA, adv. That place, there. *A lena,* from that place. *An Edhewon yntredhê a rûg may wrellons terry aga morthosow wharê, hag a lena aga dry,* the Jews among them caused that they should break their thighs anon, and bring them thence. M.C. 229. *Ef a rûg dhedhê yn scon monas yn mês a lenê,* he made them forthwith go out from thence. M.C. 30. *(Lenê* is to be read *lena.* Llwyd, 227.) Comp. of *le,* a place, and *na,* there. W. *lle-yna.*

LENCY, v. a. To swallow, to absorb. *Dreath lenky,* a quicksand. *Llwyd,* 160. It occurs also in the compound *dadlyncy. Clunk,* to swallow, is still used in Cornwall. W. *llyncu,* †*lunca.* Arm. *lonca.* Ir. *slugadh.* Gael. *sluig.* Manx, *lhuggey.*

LENDURY, s. m. Cleanness, cleanliness, good faith, truth. *Râg henna dhe'n bŷs y twyth, rag dôn dustiny ha gwryth dhe'n lendury yn pûp prŷs,* for that I came to the world, to bear testimony and service to the truth at all times. P.C. 2025. *Gwyryoneth a reys bôs dreys abervedh yn mater-ma, ha lendury kekeffrys, râg ymsywê y a wra,* truth must be brought within this affair, and good faith also, for they follow each other. P.C. 2449. A mutation of *glendury,* from *glander,* id. qd. W. *glendid,* cleanness, purity, from *glân,* clean, pure.

LENN, v. a. To read. *Dho lenn.* Pryce. Arm. *lenn, lenna.* W. *llên,* literature. Arm. *lenn.* Gael. *leughadh.*

LENNER, s. m. A reader. Pl. *lenneriow.* Pryce. Arm. *lenner.* W. *llenwr,* a scholar; *dar-llenwr,* a reader.

LENWEL, v. a. To fill, replenish, to fulfil, to become full. Part. pass. *lenwys, lynwys. Lemmen pan yw nêf dhyn gwrŷs, ha lenwys a eledh splan,* now when heaven is made to us, and filled with bright angels. O.M. 10. *Mar lenwys ew an bŷs lemyn a skerewynsy,* so full is the world now of wickedness. C.W. 162. *Ha Dew râg aga benigya, ha laveras, bedhouch lên a hâs, lue grew cressyn ha lenwel an dour en môr,* and God did bless them, and said, be ye full of seed, and do ye increase and fill the water in the sea. M.C. p. 94. *Ha Dew râg aga benigya, ha Dew laveras dhodhans, bedhow lên a hâs, ha cressyouch, ha lenouch an 'oar,* and God did bless them, and God said to them, be ye full of seed, and multiply, and replenish the earth. Ibid. p. 95. W. *llenwi,* †*llewni.* Arm. *leunia.* Ir. *lion,* †*lin.* Gael. *lion.* Manx, *lhieen.*

LER, s. m. A floor, a pavement, a ground floor, the ground, earth. Pl. *lerow, lerriow.* Llwyd, 242. *Dowr ha lêr, ha tân ha gwyns, houl ha lour, ha steyr kyffrys,* water and earth, and fire and wind, sun and moon and stars likewise. M.C. 211. *An mêan lêr,* the foundation stone. Llwyd, 60. Written also *lear, leur,* and *luer;* and in the Cornish Vocabulary, *lôr,* qd. v.

LER, s. m. A trace, a footstep. *War i lêr,* after him. *Llwyd,* 124, 249. A late abbreviated form of *lerch.*

LERCH, s. m. A trace, vestige, footstep. Generally used with *war,* on, to express the preposition *after.* *A tûs vâs, why re welas, fetel formyas Dew an Tâs nêf ha nôr war lerch y vrŷs,* O good people, ye have seen how God the Father created heaven and earth after his judgment. O.M. 2827. *Saw me, war lerch drehevel, a's dyerbyn dyogel yn Galilê ol warbarth,* but I, after rising, will meet you certainly in Galilee altogether. P.C. 896. *Gans moreth ydhof lynwys war dhe lerch, ow arluth whêk,* with sorrow I am filled after thee, my sweet lord. O.M. 2195. *Dûn war y lerch,* let us come after him. P.C. 663. *Mûr yw ow fyenasow war y lerch ef,* great are my anxieties after him. R.D. 1072. *Dûn alemma, marrougyon, war aga lerch fystynyn,* let us come hence, knights, after them let us haste. O.M. 1641. *(Ol,* a footstep, is similarly used in Welsh, as, *ar vy ol,* after me ; *ar dy ol,* after thee ; &c.). Written also *lyrch.* W. *llyr.* Arm. *lerch.* Ir. *lorg,* †*lorc.* Gael. *lorg.* Manx, *lurg.*

LES, s. m. Commodity, profit, advantage, good, benefit, interest, service. Corn. Vocab. *commodum.* *An Tâs Dew gordhyys re bo, a's ordnes dhym râg ow lês,* the Father God be worshipped, who has appointed her to me for my benefit. O.M 116. *Na wra gruyth na fo dhe lês,* do not an action that is not for advantage. R.D. 876. *Lemmyn môs dhe dharyvas tra na wra lês,* but to go to assert a thing of no benefit. R.D. 952. *Nêp a formyas môr ha tîr, hag ol pûp tra yn wêdh ol râg agan lês,* who created sea and land, and all things also

2 ι

for our advantage. R.D. 1198. W. *llês*. Ir. *leas*, †*les*. Gael. *leas*.

LES, s. m. A court, a hall. *Lés-newydh*, new court, the name of a hundred in Cornwall. Written also *lis*, qd. v.

LES, s. m. Breadth, width, latitude. *A lés*, abroad. *Try heys dhe bâl kemery; a drûs musury trylles (try lês,)* three lengths of thy spade thou shalt take ; athwart thou shalt measure three breadths. O.M. 393. *Hanter kans kevelyn yn-vedh ty a wra y lés*, half a hundred cubits also thou shalt make its width. O.M. 958. *Worth an lés y a dollas dew doll yn grows*, according to the width they bored two holes in the cross. M.C. 178. *War an fordh dyllas a lés a ve gurris dhe ragdhé*, on the road raiment was placed abroad before them. M.C. 29. *An dour a uger a lés*, the water will open wide. O.M. 1666. *Me a wêl dhe wolyow warbarth a lés*, I see thy wounds altogether disclosed. R.D. 1317. W. *llèd*, †*llet*. Arm. *lèd*. Irish, *leithne*, †*lethit*. Gael. *leud*. Manx, *lheead*.

LES, s. m. An herb. Corn. Vocab. *herba*. *Lôs* and *lûs* must have been other forms, whence the plurals, *losow* and *lusow*, (‡*luzu*.) *Avel olow aga threys, sŷch ŷns ol kepar ha leys*, like the prints of their feet, they are all dry like herbs. O.M. 761. *Hag yn týr gorhemmennaf may tefo gwvdh ha losow*, and I command in the earth that trees and herbs grow. O.M. 28. *Ha'n losowys erbyn hâf drygns hâs yn erberow*, and let the plants against summer produce seed in gardens. O.M. 31. W. *llys*, *llws*. Arm. *lez*, *louzou*, †*lus*. Ir. *lus*, †*lub*. Gael. *lus*. Manx, *lus*.

LESC, s. m. A cradle. Llwyd, 53. Ir. *lusca*. W. *llûsg*, a drag.

LESCY, v. a. To burn, to be burning. *Gorré dhe'n menedh Tabor, yn gordhyans dhym dh'y lesky*, put it upon Mount Tabor, in worship to me to burn it. O.M. 430. *Pûr wŷr leskys of a vŷdh*, very truly burnt it shall be. O.M. 433. *Me a'n gor war an alter, hag a'n lésk gans tân prynner*, I will put him on the altar, and will burn him with a fire of wood. O.M. 1290. *Ow paynys a vŷdh garow kyn vôs leskys dhe lusow*, my pains will be cruel, before being burnt to ashes. O.M. 1355. *A nyns esó ynnon ny agan colon ow lesky*, ah, was not in us our heart burning ? R.D. 1322. Another form of *losey*, qd. v.

LESDERTH, s. m. Feverfew. Corn. Vocab. *febrifugia*. Read by Llwyd, 87, *lés derthen*. The latter like the W. *dyrton*, *y dhyrton*, is formed from the Lat. *tertiana*.

LESDUSHOC, s. m. Betony. Cornish Vocab. *betonica*. Comp. of *lés*, and adj. *dushoc*, id. qd. W. *twysog*, tufted, from *twys*, a tuft or spike, which is characteristic of the herb.

LESE, v. a. To make broad, to widen, to expand, to spread. *Otté an asen gené, ha'n ebel dhyso keffrys ; war y heyn rág dhe eyasyé dyllas me a vyn lesé*, behold the ass with me, and the foal for thee also, on her back to ease thee, clothes I will spread. P.C. 221. W. *lledu*. Arm. *leda*.

LESENGOC, s. m. Marigold, or sunflower. Corn. Voc. *solsequium*. Comp. of *lés*, and *en*, intens. part., and *côch*, red. Marigold is called in Welsh, *rhudhos*, from *rhûdh*, red.

LESIC, adj. Bushy. *Pryce*. It occurs in the name *Trelesic*, in St. Earth, and is formed from *lés*, a herb. W. *llyseuawg*, abounding with plants.

LESLUIT, s. m. Horehound. Corn. Voc. *marrubrium*. Comp. of *lés*, and *luit*, grey. *Lotles* is compounded of the same elements, qd. v. Ir. *laithlus*.

LESSERCHOC, s. m. Clotbur, hog's-herb. Corn. Vocab. *lappa*. Comp. of *lés*, and *serchoc*, id. qd. W. *serchog*, loving. This is read by Tonkin, in Pryce's Vocabulary, *les-en-hoc*, lit. hog's-herb.

LESTER, s. f. A vessel of any kind, a ship. Corn. Voc. *navis*. Pl. *lestri*, *listri*. *Luu lîstri*, classis, a fleet. Ibid. *Tryhans kevelyn da an lester a vŷdh a hŷs*, three hundred cubits good the ship shall be in length. O.M. 956. *Pûp maner bôs yn býs-ma, ûs dhe dybry may teleth, rág dê'n ha bêst maga ta, yn dhe lester ty a fêdh*, all manner of food in this world, which ought to be eaten, for man and beast as well, in thy ship thou shalt have. O.M. 996. *Gwarnys ŷf guns Dew an Tâs, dhe withyl an lester-ma*, warned I am by God the Father, to make this ship. C.W. 168. *Clut lestri*, a dish-clout. Llwyd, 116. See also *encoislester*, and *goloulester*. W. *llestyr*, pl. *llestri*. Arm. *lestr*, pl. *listri*. Ir. *leaster*, †*lester*. Gael. *leastar*.

LESTEZIUS, adj. Lousy. Llwyd, 115. It is probably the Arm. *lastezuz*, which has the same meaning.

LET, s. m. Hindrance, hesitation, delay. *Tyorryon, tyeuch an temple hep let, na dheffo glaw dhe'n styllyow*, tilers, cover ye the temple without delay, that the rain come not to the rafters. O.M. 2487. *Ke yn kerch dynehans hep let*, go thy way quickly without stopping. R.D. 116. *Vynytha, hep na moy let*, evermore, without any further delay. R.D. 2283. Not Celtic, being the old English, *let*.

LETSHAR, s. m. A frying pan. Llwyd, 61, 144.

LETTRYS, adj. Lettered. *Asson whansek ol dhe pysy, lettrys ha lêk, war Dhu mercy*, we are desirous all to pray, lettered and lay, to God for mercy. P.C. 38. *Otté omma skyber dêk, ha cala lour war ky lucr ; pynak vo lettrys py lêk, a wéles an chy, nym dêr*, see here a fair room, and straw enough on its floor ; whoever he may be, lettered or lay, (that) has seen the house, I am not concerned. P.C. 688.

LETTYA, v. a. To stop, to delay, to hinder or prevent. *Ny lettys saw un lam*, I stopped only a space. O.M. 470. *A dâs, colon caradow, ny vynnaf lettya pella*, O father, dear heart, I will not stop longer. O.M. 722. *Fystyn, hep lettyé, doro dhym an gwŷn gwella*, haste thou, without stopping, bring me the best wine. O.M. 1903. *Mara qureth aga lettya*, if thou wilt prevent them. O.M. 1495. *My a worthep dhys wharé, yn certan na vy lettyys*, I will answer thee at once ; certainly that thou be not delayed. O.M. 2236. *Lavar dhynny dhe volungeth, na vên lettyys gans whethlow*, tell us thy will, that we be not delayed with tales. P.C. 2054.

LETHER, s. m. A letter, an epistle. Plural, *letherow*. Pryce. See *Lither*.

LETHEREN, s. f. A letter, a character of the alphabet. See *Litheren*.

LEU, s. m. A lion. Corn. Voc. *leo*. *Yta an sêth tennys, ha'n bêst yma gweskys, y vernans gallas ganso ; dôg ve besyn dhodho, may hallan ve attendya pa'n vaner lew ylh-ewa*, lo the arrow is shot, and the beast is struck ; its death is gone with it ; lead me to it that I may observe what manner of lion it is. C.W. 114. W. *llew*. Arm. *leon*. Irish, *leon*, †*leo*. Gael. *leomhann*. Manx, *lion*.

Gr. λέων. Lat. *leo, leone*. Basque, *lcoya, leu*. Sansc. *lūnakas*, a ferocious beast, from *lū*, to cut.

LEU, s. m. The rudder of a ship. Corn. Vocab. *clavus*. *Leu pi obil*, a rudder or peg. *Lew gurhal*, the rudder of a ship. Llwyd, 48. W. *llyw*.

LEUN, adj. Full, replete, complete. *Máb Marea, leun a rás, oll y védh a ve clewys*, the Son of Mary, full of grace, all his wish was heard. M.C. 9. *Y box rych leun a yly, hy a vynnas y derry*, her box rich full of salve, she wished to break it. M.C. 35. *Ha Crist yn crés, leun a ras, leun y golon a voreth*, and Christ in the middle, full of grace, his heart full of sorrow. M.C. 186. Written also *luen*, and contractedly *lén*, qd. v. W. *llawn*. Arm. *leûn*. Ir. *lán*. Gael. *lán*. Manx, *lane*. Gr. πλέον, πολύς. Lat. *plenus*. Goth. *fulls*. Lith. *pilnas*. Sansc. *pulas*, from *pal*, to heap up.

LEUR, s. m. A floor, pavement, ground floor, ground, earth. *Eff o Crist a dhéth dhe'n leur, máb Du ha dén yw kyffris*, he was Christ (that) came to the earth, the Son of God and Man he is likewise. M.C. 8. Written also *luer*, and *lér*, and in the Cornish Vocabulary, *lor*, qd. v.

LEUTE, s. m. Loyalty, truth. *Ow arluth, by my leuté, my a der crak ow conné*, my lord, by my truth, I will break my neck, crack. O.M 2183. Written also *lauté, loute, leaute*. *Ny guffen, war ow louté, compossé pren yn nep le*, we may not get, upon my truth, a straighter tree in any place. O.M. 2576. *Gwell yw un dén dhe vervel, ages oll an bobyl léi dhe vós kellys, rum lauté*, better it is that one man die than all the faithful people to be lost, by my truth. P.C. 448. *Rum lenuté, dún a dhystouch*, by my truth, let us come immediately. R.D. 1243. From the old French, *loiaute*.

LEUUIT, s. m. The master, or pilot of a ship. Corn. Voc. *gubernator vel nauclerus*. This word is read by Llwyd, 97, *lewyidh*. It is the same as W. *llywydh*, a ruler, or director, from *llyw*, a rudder.

LEVAR, s. m. A book. Pl. *leverow, lyfrow*. *Múr o an payn dar ken dhe váb Du, múr y alloys, del lever dhyn an levar, kymmys payn ny ve a y oys*, great was the pain beyond other to the Son of God, great his power, as saith the Book to us, so much pain was not of his age. M.C. 135. *Yn lewyr yma scrifys, dre cledhé nep a vewo, ef a vyru yn súr dredho*, in the Book it is written; he who lives by the sword, he shall surely die by it. P.C. 1157. *An levar-ma*, this book. Llwyd, 244. *Gorrouch omma an leverow, nyng és art vgth ankevys*, put here the books, there is not any art forgotten. C.W. 158. Written also *liver*, qd. v.

LEVARVA, s. f. A library, a bookcase. *Pryce*. Comp. of *levar*, a book, and *ma*, a place.

LEVEN, adj. Smooth, even, level. Llwyd, 65. W. *llyvn*. Arm. *lampr*. Ir. *sleamhan*, †*slemn*. Gael. *steamhuinn*. Manx, *lhian*. Lat. *lhian*. Lat. *levis, lenis, planus*.

LEVEREL, v. a. To speak, to say, to tell. *A leverel gwyroneth*, to say the truth. O.M. 702. *My a lever dhys*, I will tell thee. O.M. 305. *Ha'n él dhym a leverys*, and the angel said to me. O.M. 844. *Ef a wra tyn dhe punsnyé, my levery och, ellas*, he will severely punish thee, that thou wilt say, "Oh! alas!" O.M. 1528. *Del levaraf dhyuchwhy why*, as I say to you. O.M. 1653. *Ny won pandra leveryn*, I know not what I may say. O.M. 2532. *Mar a lever dén vgth*, if any man say. P.C. 179.

Levereuch dhym, cowethé, tell me, comrades. P.C. 319. *Del leveryth a vgdh gwrgs*, as thou sayest, it shall be done. F.C. 450. *Mara leversys henna*, if thou saidst that. P.C. 1762. *Pan leverta dhym*, when thou tellest me. P.C. 2017. *Ty re leverys an gwgr*, thou hast said the truth. P.C. 2019. *Kyn leverryf gwgr*, though I should say truly. P.C. 1481. *Leveryn oll dhodho*, we will all say to him. P.C. 2880. *Arluth, gwgr a leversouch*, Lord, you have spoken true. M.C. 50. *Dún leveryn war anow, a'y védh del yw drehevys, na leverys un gér gow*, let us come, let us tell by mouth, from his grave how he is risen, let us not say a false word. M.C. 247. *Tgr Marea, cleyr ha whar, a dhéth dhe'n bédh leverys*, the three Maries, clear and gentle, came to the tomb mentioned. M.C. 252. *Yn enour dhe Dew an Tás, leveryys púp gollokas my a worhemmyn yn scon*, in honour to God the Father, he said all praise I command forthwith. O.M. 2634. Another form of *lavary*, qd. v.

LEVERIAT, s. m. A speaker. *Gow-leveriat*, a teller of lies. Corn. Voc. W. *llavarydh*, a speaker; *llevariad*, a speaking.

LEVERID, s. m. Sweetmilk. Corn. Vocab. *lac dulce*. Read by Llwyd, 4, 75, *leverith*. W. *llewrith*. Arm. *livriz*, †*lefrith*. Ir. *leamhnacht*, †*lemnachd*.

LEVESYN, v. a. I might venture. 1 pers. sing. subj. of *lavasy*, qd. v.

LEWEN, s. f. A louse. *Lewen-ki*, Corn. Voc. *cinomia*, a dog-fly. Literally, a dog-louse, from *lewen*, id. qd. *lowen*, and *ci*, a dog.

LEWENIC, adj. Glad, merry, cheerful, frolicksome. Llwyd, 65, 75. Another form of *lowenec*, qd. v.

LEWIADER, s. m. A steersman, the pilot of a ship. *Pryce*. W. *llywiadur*.

LEWILLOIT, s. m. The spleen. Corn. Voc. *splen*. In the Irish Glosses to Gildas's Lorica, *lu leith* occurs as the name of the spleen. See Stokes's Irish Glosses, 4to, 1860, p. 150.

LEWTE, s. m. Loyalty. *Páb ér, te dhén, gwra lewté*, always, thou man, do loyalty. M.C. 175. See *Leute*.

LEYF, s. f. A hand. *Yn médh Pedyr, dhym na ás troys na leyff na vo golhys*, said Peter; "leave thou not to me foot nor hand that be not washed. M.C. 46. The same word as *léf*, qd. v.

LEYHY, v. a. To make smaller, to diminish, to lessen. Part. *leyhys*. *Dhe vestry a vgdh leyhgs neffré war an envrow*, thy power shall be diminished ever over the souls. P.C. 143. *Comfortys yw ow colon, pan clewys ow teryfus bones leyhgs dhe pascyon*, my heart is comforted, when I heard (thee) declaring thy Passion to be alleviated. R.D. 505. Written also *lyha*, qd. v. W. *lleiháu*, from *llai*, (Corn. *lé*,) less.

LEYS, s. m. An herb. *Avel olow nga threys, sých gns ol kepar ha leys*, like the prints of their foot, they are all dry like herbs. O.M. 761. The same word as *lés*, qd. v.

LEYS, s. m. Breadth. See *Lés*.

LEYSCY, v. a. To burn. *Púp pystryor y cothé dre reson da y trysky*, every sorcerer it would be incumbent for reason good to burn him. P.C. 1768. The same word as *lescy*, qd. v.

LEYTH, s. m. A limb. *Ha'n dhew-na, býs pan vóns squyth, war Crist y fóns ow cronkyé, manna gevé goth na leyth nag esa worth y grevyé*, and those two, until they were weary, were beating Christ, so that he had not vein or limb that was not grieving him. M.C. 132. The same word as *lýth*, qd. v.

LEYTH, s. m. Milk. *Ty a wra wogé hemma gorré an tús a le-na býs yn tyreth a dhynwa lanwes leyth ha mêl kefrys*, thou shalt after this bring the people thence even to a land that produces fulness of milk and honey also. O.M. 1430. Written also *léth*. *Ef a vǵdh ancledhys yn le na fue dên bythqueth, yn alabaster gravys; ragof y fue ordynys, maga whyn avel an léth*, he shall be buried in a place where never man was, cut in alabaster; for me it was intended, as white as the milk. P.C. 3138. The earlier form was *lait*, qd. v.

LI, s. m. A breakfast. *Týr sêch yn gwêl nag yn prûs, mar kefyth yn gueǵr hep gow, ynno gwcet in-ta whelas bôs dhe'th ly ha dhe'th kynyow*, dry land in field or in meadow, if thou wilt find truly without deceit, in it take good care to seek food for thy breakfast, and for thy dinner. O.M. 1140. *Aruth ow tevos a Spayn, ydh egen yn crês Almayn orth un prys-ly*, Lord, coming from Spain, I was in the midst of Germany, at a breakfast meal. R.D. 2149. *Sáv aman, kemar dha li, ha ker dha'n hûl, môr trig a metten travyth ne dâl*, get up, take thy breakfast, and go to the moor, the seatide for the morning is nothing worth. Pryce's Corn. Proverbs. W. *llith*, a bait, a mash.

LIAS, s. m. A multitude, a great many. W. *lliaws*.

LIAS, adj. Many, much, frequent. *Lias termen*, many times, often times. *Lias onon*, many a one. *Maga lias*, as many. Llwyd, 122, 232. In the Ordinalia, it is generally written *leas*, and *lues*, qd. v.

LIASDER, s. m. Plenty, abundance. Llwyd, 51.

LIDZHU, s. m. Ashes. Llwyd, 10, 48. A late corruption of *lusow*, qd. v.

LIEN, s. m. A linen cloth. *Lien duilof*, manutergium vel mantile, a towel. *Lien gueli*, sindo, bed linen. Corn. Voc. *Urys da yw credy, lemmyn mayl e yn lyen*, well embalmed he is indeed, now wrap him in linen. P.C. 3204. *Crýs yn Cryst, del y'th coscaf; form a y fûs a dhyaquedhaf, dhym del y'n rôs yn lyen*, believe in Christ, as I tell thee; the form of his face I will shew, to me as he gave it on linen. R.D. 1693. W. *lliain*, †*licin*. Arm. *lian*. Ir. *lin*. Gael. *lion*.

LIF, s. m. A flood, a deluge, inundation. Pl. *lifow*. *Rág lýf brâs my a dhoro, a gudho oll an nôr beys, nûjns dên ûs yn beys may fo kyns bôs dué an lýf budhes*, for I will bring a great flood that will cover all the earth of the world, that every man that is in the world may be drowned before the flood is ended. O.M. 981. *Dûn oll dhe'n gorhyl lôth da gans lýf na wrellen budhy*, let us come all to the ark quickly, by the flood that we be not drowned. O.M. 1048. *Naus yw an lyfow basseys, pan ûs gweydh ow teschê*, now are the floods abated, when the trees are drying. O.M. 1127. W. *lliv, lli*. Arm. †*liv*. Ir. †*lia*, †*li*. Lat. *lues,—luvium*. Sansc. *li*, to make liquid.

LIFERN, s. m. The heel or ankle bone. Corn. Voc. *talus*. Read by Llwyd, 160, *livern*. Perhaps it should be *ufern*. W. *ufarn, ucharn, fêr, fern, bigvorn, migvorn*, all mean ankle. Arm. *ufern*. Ir. †*odbrann*. Gael. *aobrann*. Manx, *abane*.

LILIE, s. m. A lily. Corn. Vocab. *lilium*. Arm. *lili*. Ir. *lile*. Gael. *lili*.

LILL, s f. A goat. It occurs in the local name of Tre-lill, in St. Ewe. W. *llill*.

LIN, s. m. Flax, linen. Corn. Vocab. *linum*. *My a woulch oll agns trýs, ha gans towal a lýn gulán, my a's sêch ketteb onan a bôp mostethes ha lǵs*, I will wash all your feet, and with a towel of clean linen I will wipe them every one from all dirt and mire. P.C. 836. W. *llin*. Arm. *lin*. Ir. *lin, lian*. Gael. *lin, lion*. Manx, *licen*. Gr. λίνον. Lat. *linum*.

LIN, s. m. A pool, a pond. *Pisc-lin*, vivarium, a fish pond. Corn. Voc. Written also *lyn*, qd. v. W. *llyn*, †*linn*. Arm. *lenn*. Ir. *linn*. Gael. *linne*.

LIN, s. f. The moon. It occurs only in the composite *di-lin*, Monday, being as in the other Celtic dialects, borrowed from the Latin. W. *llûn, dýdh-llûn*. Arm. *lun, dilun*. Ir. *luan*. Gael. *luan*. Gr. σελήνη. Lat. *luna*.

LINAZ, s. f. A nettle. Llwyd, 178. The late form of *linhaden*.

LINHADEN, s. f. A nettle. Corn. Voc. *urtica*. Arm. *linad, lenad; linaden, lennden*. The Welsh name is *danadlen*; linseed being *llinhad*. See *Coiclinhat*.

LINIETH, s. m. Lineage, a race. *War y corf y wodhefys mûr a peynys râk savvyé lynnyeth mâp dên*, on his body he suffered many pains to save the race of the son of man. R.D. 1810. *Mâb Jared ydhové, hep gow, sevys a lynnyeth pûr vrâs ydhové*, the son of Jared I am, without a lie, sprung from a lineage very great I am. C.W. 152. Written also *lynneth*, qd. v.

LININ, s m. A string. Corn. Voc. *filum*. W. *llinyn*. Arm. *linen*. Ir. *lin*.

LIS, s. m. A court, a hall, or palace, a court of justice. Written also *lês*, qd. v., as *Lês newydh*, new court. W. *llýs*. Arm. *lez*, †*les*, †*lis*. Ir. *leas, lios*, †*lis*. Gael. *lios*. Manx, *liass*.

LISTRI, s. m. Vessels. Pl. of *lester*, qd. v. *Luu listri*, classis, a fleet, lit. a host of ships. Corn. Voc.

LITHER, s. m. A letter, an epistle. Pl. *litherow*. W. *llythyr*. Arm. *lizer*. Lat. *litera*.

LITHEREN, s. f. A letter, a single letter, a character of the alphabet. Corn. Voc. *litera*. W. *llythyren*. Arm. *lizeren*. Ir. *litir*, †*liter*. Gael. *litir*.

LITHRIAD, s. m. A fall, a trip. Pryce. W. *llithriad*.

LIU, s. m. A colour, dye, or hue. Corn. Voc. *color*. *Liu melet*, minium, red colour. Ibid. *An houl ny golsé y lyw, awos nâp dên dhe vervel*, the sun would not have lost its hue, because of a son of man to die. P.C. 3083. *Râg an houl y lyw golow a gollas, pan êth an beys*, for the sun his bright hue a gollas, when he went from the world. P.C. 3123. *Gorryn ef yn bêdh arté, du yw y lyw*, let us put him into the grave again; black is his hue! R.D. 2101. W. *lliw*, †*liou*, †*liu*. Arm. *liou, liu, liv*. Ir. *li*. Gael. *lidh, li*. Sansc. *lig*, to paint.

LIUE, v. a. To colour, to paint. *Whet avar prýs soper yw, tân brâs an oan re a lyw, kyns y vôs medhen restys*, it is yet early time for supper, the great fire will brown the lamb too much, before it be roasted soft. P.C. 697. W. *lliwio*, ‡*llivo*. Arm. *liva, liuein*.

LIUOR, s. m. A painter, a dyer. Corn. Voc. *pictor*. W. *lliwiwr*, ‡*llivwr*. Arm. *liver*.

LIVAN, s. f. The leaf of a book. Llwyd, 33, 111. From the English.

LIVER, s. m. A book. Corn. Voc. *liber vel codex*. Pl. *livrow, lyffrow, lyfryow*. Written also *levar* and *lyvyr*, qd. v. *Liver bian*, a little book. Llwyd, 78. W. *llyvyr*. Arm. *levr*, †*leor*. Ir. *leabhar*, †*lebor*, †*libar*. Gael. *leabhar*. Manx, *lioar*. All from Lat. *liber*.

LLU, s. m. A host, an army. Corn. Voc. *exercitus. Luu listri,* classis, a fleet : lit. a host of ships. *Ibid.*

LO, s. m. An inlet of water, a pool, a pond, standing water. Preserved in the local names, *Looe,* and *Duloe,* black pool ; names of parishes, in Cornwall. W. *llwch,* pl. *llychau,* † *laichou,* in Oxf. Gloss. Arm. *louch.* Ir. *loch.* Gael. *loch.* Manx, *logh.* Gr. λάκκοϛ. Lat. *lacus.*

l.O, s. m. A spoon, a spattle. Pl. *lew.* Llwyd, 48. W. *llwy,* † *louhi.* Arm. *loa.* Ir. *liach.* Gael. *liadh.* Manx, *lheegh.*

LOBMAS, s. m. A lesser sort of bream, a shad-fish. Llwyd, 41.

LOC, s. m. Sight, presence. *Fystyneuch, a dhew pen côk, dreuch an prysners ol y'm lok a dhesempys,* make haste, O ye two blockheads, bring all the prisoners to my presence immediately. P.C. 2329. This word must be the root of *goloc,* the sight, and agrees with W. *llwg,* in *golwg,* sight, and *amlwg,* evident. Sansc. *laukas,* aspect ; from *lauc,* to appear.

LOCII, s. m. A calf. Corn. Voc. *vitulus. Loch euhic,* hinnulus, a hind-calf. *Ibid.* The latest form was *leauh,* qd. v. W. *llo.* Arm. *leûe, lue.* Ir. *laogh,* † *loegh,* † *loig.* Gael. *laogh.* Manx, *lheiy.*

LODER, s. m. A hose, a stocking. Corn. Voc. *caliga.* Pl. *lodrow,* ‡ *lydraw.* Llwyd, 3. W. *llawdyr,* pl. *llodrau.* Arm. *loer,* † *lezrou.*

LODN, s. m. The young of a cow or sheep, a young ox, a bullock, a steer, a wether. Pl. *lodnow. Mester da, der dhe gymmyas, me a wêl un lodn pûr vrâs hanys yn bush ow platiya,* good master, by your leave, I see a very great bullock from thee in the bush couching. C.W. 112. *Ke yn mês a'n lester scon, dheth wrêg ha'th flehys kefrys, edhyn, bestes ha pûb lodn,* go forth from the ship immediately, thy wife and thy children also, birds, beasts, and all cattle. C.W. 180. *Te nyn wra chan a whêl, te nyn dhy odh, nyn dhy merch, nyn dhy dên whêl, nyn dhy môs whêl, nyn dhy lodnow,* thou shalt not do any manner of work, thou nor thy son, nor thy daughter, nor thy manservant, nor thy maidservant, nor thy cattle. Pryce. *Tri cans lodn davas,* three hundred sheep. *Ll.* 244. In Welsh it is also applied to the young of horses, and other animals. W. *llwdn,* plur. *llydnod.* Arm. *loen,* † *loezn,* pl. † *loznet.* Gael. *loth.* Manx, *lhiy, lhuan.* Sansc. *latva,* a horse.

LOE, s. m. A rule. Corn. Voc. *regula.* W. *llyw.*

LOER, s. f. The moon. *Dowr ha lêr, ha tûn, ha gwyns, houl ha locr ha steyr keffrys,* water and earth, and fire, and wind, sun and moon, and stars too likewise. M.C. 211. *Yn peswera dydh bydh gwrÿs, an houl, ha'n loer, ha'n stêr yn wêdh kekyffrys,* in the fourth day shall be made, the sun, and the moon, and the stars too likewise. C.W. 8. *An houl ha'n locr, kekeffrys oll warbarth ew confithys,* the sun and the moon likewise, all together are consenting. C.W. 150. Written also *lôr, loos, lour,* and by Llwyd, *lûr.* In the Cornish Vocabulary, *luir,* qd. v.

LOER, adj. Many, much. *Râg governyé ow bewnans yma loer orth bôdh ow brÿs,* for governing my life, it is much according to the will of my mind. O.M. 90. Another form of *lower,* qd. v.

LOF, s. f. A hand. Corn. Voc. *manus.* Dual, *duilof. Lien duilof,* munutergium *vel* mantile, a towel. *Ibid.* The same authority gives the other form, *lau,* qd. v.

LOFGURCHEL, s. m. An utensil. Corn. Voc. *utensilia.* Comp. of *lof,* the hand, and *gurchel,* id. qd. *gorhel,* a vessel, qd. v.

LOGEL, s. f. A depository, or place for holding any thing, a cupboard, a drawer, a pocket, a chest, a little coffer, a coffin. Corn. Vocab. *loculus. Corff Ihesus Crist yntredhé dhe'n logell a ve degys, hag a heys dhe wrowedhé ynno ef a ve gcays,* the body of Jesus Christ between them to the coffin was borne, and at length to lie in it it was left. M.C. 233. *Teulewch whey agas dyw dorn war an logol, ynno an corf mylyges, dhe'n dour ganso ny a reys,* throw ye your two hands on the coffin, in it the accursed body, to the water with it we will run. R.D. 2179. W. *llogell.* From the Latin.

LOGODEN, s. f. A mouse. Corn. Voc. *clissemus* vel *mus* vel *soorex. Logoden-fer,* sura, the calf of the leg. *Ibid.* "This, which is literally the mouse of the leg, is a strange combination, but it is borne out by the Greek, μῦς, which means 'mouse,' and '*muscle*'; the Latin is not very different, and the W. *llygoden* means 'mouse,' and *llywethan,* 'muscle.'" *(Norris's Cornish Drama.)* W. *llÿg,* pl. *llygod,* † *locot,* s. *llygoden.* Arm. *logoden,* pl. *logod.* Ir. *luch.* Gael. *luch.* Manx, *lugh.*

LOGOSAN, s. f. A mouse. Pl. *logos. Ydh henwaf beuch ha tarow ; march ha casak hag asen ; ky ha câth, logosan,* I name cow and bull; horse and mare and ass ; dog and cat, mouse. C.W. 32. The late form of *logoden,* which was finally corrupted into *lygodzhan.* ‡ *Lygodzhan vrâs,* a rat, i. e. a great mouse. Llwyd, 3, 96. ‡ *Logaz,* mice. 19. A rat is called in Welsh, *llygoden frengig,* a French mouse, and also in Irish, *luch fhrancach.*

LOIN, s. m. The loin ; a grove, wood, bush. Pl. *loinow.* Pryce. W. *llwyn.* Ir. *luan.* Gael. *luan.*

LOMMEN, s. f. A mess of meat. *Lommen cowl,* a mess of pottage. Pryce. W. *llymaid,* a sup.

LONATH, s. m. The reins, kidneys. Llwyd, 30, 138. Arm. *lonech, lounech, loncz.* W. *elwlen.*

LOOD, s. m. Slime, sludge. Pryce.

LOOS, adj. Grey, hoary. *Râg dry flehys, ty a vew may sota loos,* for bearing children, thou shalt live until thou art grey. C.W. 28. Written also *lous,* qd. v.

LOOSECH, s. m. Hire. Pryce.

LOOW, s. m. Lice. Pryce. The plural of *louen,* qd. v.

LOR, s. m. A floor, a pavement. Corn. Voc. *pavimentum* vel *solum.* Other forms are *lôr, luer, lûr,* qd. v. W. *|llawr,* † *laur.* Arm. *leûr,* Ir. *lâr.* Gael. *lâr.* Manx, *laare.* Basque, *lurra.* Ang. Sax. *flor, flore.* Eng. *floor.* Germ. *flur.*

LOR, s. f. The moon. *Aga hynwyn y a vydh an houl, ha'n lôr, ha'n steryan,* their names shall be the sun, and the moon, and the stars. O.M. 36. *An lôr yn nôs, houl yn geydh,* may rollons y golow splan, the moon in night, sun in day, that they may give their bright lights. O.M. 39. A contracted form of *locr,* id. qd. *luir,* qd. v.

LORCH, s. f. A staff. Corn. Voc. *baculus. Leverouch ow dyskyblon mar a fyllys dheuch travyth, pan wrugé ages danvon hep lorch na scryp nôs na deydh,* say, my disciples, if any thing was wanting to you, when I sent you without staff or scrip, night or day. P.C. 914. *Lemman lorch nép a'n geffo, gorrens y scryp dyworto,* now he who has a staff, let him put his scrip from him. P.C. 919. *Saw gucytyens pûp may tokco ganso lorch, py cledhé da,* but let every one take care that he bring with him a staff, or a good sword. P.C. 943. In late Cornish it was abbreviated into *lor*. *Lor vrâs*, a club, or baton. *Lhwyd*, 44, 48. Arm. *lorchen*. Ir. *lorg*. Gael. *lorg*.

LORDEN, s. m. A lurdane, a clown, a blockhead. *Kemer hy, ty plos lorden, syns war dhe keyn an grows pren, take it*, thou dirty lurdane, hold the cross-tree on thy back. P.C. 2585. The old English, *lurdan*.

LOREL, s. m. A vagrant, a vagabond, a rascal. *Y a vŷdh gwythys calas, hedré vyns y yn ow gwlâs; râg nyns ouch mas dew lorel*, they shall be worked hard as long as they are in my kingdom; for ye are naught but two vagabonds. O.M. 1504. *A lorels, re's lo drôk lam*, Oh rascals! he it an evil leap for ye! P.C. 1125. *A pûr lorel*, O very knave. P.C. 1381.

LOS, adj. Gray, hoary. *Ha nêp a's tefo gallos, a vŷdh gans yowynk ha lôs henvys tûs vrâs pûp termyn*, and those who have power will he by young and gray called great people always. P.C. 789. *Scullyns y wôs, râk yonk ha lôs, sylwel mar myn*, he has shed his blood, for young and gray, if he will save. R.D. 333. *Thomas, crŷs dhym, kyn ôf lôs*, Thomas, believe me, though I am gray. R.D. 965. A contracted form of *loys*, qd. v.

LOS, adj. Mean, sluggish, idle. *Pryce*. W. *llêsg*. Arm. *laosk, losk*. Ir. *lcasg, + lesc, + losg*. Gael. *lcasg*. Lat. *laxus*.

LOSC, s. m. A burning, inflammation, a searing, cornsmut. *Lhwyd*, 178. Corn. Vocab. *arsura* vel *ustulatio*. W. *llôsg*. Arm. *losk*. Ir. + *losc*.

LOSCY, v. a. To burn, to inflame, to be burning. *Belsebuc ha lawethan, dyllcuch luhes ha taran quyt a'n losco*, Beelzebub and fiends, send forth lightning and thunder, that it burn him quite. R.D. 130. *Me a wrûg oblashion brâs, hag a loscas lower a ŷs*, I have made a great oblation, and have burned much corn. C.W. 86. *Yn tân ty a wra losky, ha'n keth pagya-ma defry yn cffarn, why drôg lawan*, in fire thou shalt burn, and this same homicide truly in hell, yo wicked fowls. C.W. 124. Written also *lescy*, qd. v. W. *llosgi*. Arm. *lcski*. Ir. *loisg, + losc*. Gael. *loisg*. Manx, *loshl*.

LOSEL, s. m. A vile idle fellow, a scoundrel, a rascal, a knave. *Lavar lemyn mars yw prŷs danvon genes tûs erys dhe gerches an vŷl losel*, say now if it is time to send armed men with thee to bring the vile knave. P.C. 940. *Syngys mûr ôn dhe Iudas, râk ef a'm hembroncns pûr compys bŷs yn losel*, much beholden we are to Judas, for he conducted me very straight to the rogue. P.C. 1200. Old English, *losel*.

LOSOW, s. m. Plants, herbs. *Hag yn tŷr gorhemmennaf may tefo gwcydh ha losow*, and I command in the earth that trees and plants grow. O.M. 28. *War bûp frût losow ha hâs, a vo ynny hy tevys*, over all fruit, herbs, and seed, that are grown in it. O.M. 77. This is a plural aggregate, and a further plural *losowys* is formed from it. *Ha'n losowys erbyn hâf degyns hâs yn erberow*, and let the plants against summer produce seed in gardens. O.M. 31. *A losowys ol an bŷs mar whêk savor ny dhothé bŷs vynary*, from all herbs of the world so sweet a scent would not come for ever. O.M. 1742. *Lés* is another form, qd. v. W. *llysiau*. Arm. *louzou*.

LOSOW, s. m. Ashes. *Lhwyd*, 242. More correctly *lusow*, qd. v.

LOST, s. m. A tail, the rump. *A Dhew a râs, serponnt yw hy, euth hy gwelas. A'n lôst kymmer dhedhy yn ban,* *y'th torn hep gêr, sens dhe honan, dhys lavaraf*, O God of grace, it is a serpent, it is horrid to see it.—By the tail take it up in thy hand, without a word; hold it thyself I tell thee. O.M. 1454. *Lhwyd*, 4, 10, 116. *Lost-slavan*, the dirty tail. *Pryce*. W. *llôst*. Arm. *lost*. Ir. + *los*. Gael. + *los*.

LOSTEC, adj. Having a large tail, hence the name of a fox. *Lhwyd*, 179. W. *llostog*. Arm. *lostec*. Ir. + *loisi*, a fox. A heaver is called in W. *llostlydan*, broad-tail.

LOSTVAN, s. m. A burning. *Whet yma mûr a lostvan yn ow colon ow honan ol ragdho ef*, there is yet much burning in my heart of myself, all for him. R.D. 1249. This must be read *loscvan*, from *losc*, a burning.

LOTLES, s. f. Mugwort. Corn. Voc. *artemisia*. Comp. of *lot*, grey, and *lés*, an herb. *Lesluit* is from the same roots.

LOTINOW, s. m. Bullocks. *Yn dewellens pechadow gûl alter da vyé, ha dhodho agan lothnow warnedhy sacryfyé*, in atonement of sins, to make an altar would be good, and to him our bullocks upon it to sacrifice. O.M. 1175. Incorrectly for *lodnow*, pl. of *lodn*, qd. v.

LOUEN, s. f. A louse. Corn. Voc. *pediculus*; where it is also written *lewen*. In late Cornish, *luan*, pl. *lou, loow*. W. *lleuen*, pl. *llau*. Arm. *laouen, leuen*, pl. *laou, leu*.

LOUNDREZ, s. m. London. *Pryce*. W. *llundain*. Fr. *londres*.

LOUR, adv. Enough, sufficiently. *Râg hŷr lour ew ow bewnans*, for long enough is my life. O.M. 848. *Ol dhe'n bestes ûs omma a gêf bôs lour dewdhek mŷs*, all the beasts (that) are here shall find food enough twelve months. O.M. 1060. *My a'n musur lour yn ta*, I will measure it well enough. O.M. 2507. *Arvow lour dhynny y ma*, arms enough to us there are. P.C. 614. *Ny a's ten, may fôns lour hŷr*, we will stretch it, that it be long enough. P.C. 2760. *Henna yw lour dhynny*, that is enough for us. R.D. 2375. W. *llwyr*.

LOUS, adj. Grey, hoary. *A Phelip lous ôs y'th fŷdh*, O Philip, thou art grey in thy faith. R.D. 2379. The same as *loys*, qd. v.

LOVAN, s. f. A rope, a cord, a string. Corn. Voc. *funis* vel *funiculus*. Pl. *lovanow*. *Lovan cryff rag y sensy*, a strong rope to hold him. M.C. 105. *Kymer dhymmo ve kunys, gans lovan bedhens strothys, ha war dhe keyn doga ef*, take a load of fuel for me, with a rope let it he bound, and on thy back carry it. O.M. 1207. *Worth an pôst yn le may mn, y gelmy fast why a vra gans lovan ha chaynys yên*, to the stake, in the place where he is, ye shall bind him fast with rope and cold chains. P.C. 2060. *Dismas, dodho a dhyow, kelmouch fast gans lovonow ef yn pren crous*, Dismas, to him on the right, bind him fast with ropes on the cross-tree. P.C. 2520. *Me a gelm seon lovan dha worth connu brêch an adla*, I will bind forthwith a good rope around the wrist of the knave. P.C. 2761. W. *llyvan*. Arm. *louan*. Ir. + *lomna*, + *loman*. Gael. *lomna, liomhain*. Manx, *louyn*.

LOVANNAN, s. f. A small rope, a cord. *Lhwyd*, 164. W. *llyvanen*.

LOVENNAN, s. f. A weasel. Corn. Voc. *mustela*. In Welsh, *lloven, llovenan*, is the name of a fish, a burbot; and so also is *louanek*, or *leonek*, in Armoric. *Llowlenan* is one of the names of a weasel in Welsh.

LOWARTH, s. m. A garden. *Pylat êth yn mês ay hell yn un lowarth a'n gevo, ogas o, nyng esa pell*, Pilate went out of his hall into a garden which he had, near it was, it was not far. M.C. 140. *Ena un lowarth esé, ha ynno bédh ve parys*, there was a garden there, and in it a grave was prepared. M.C. 233. This is the same word as W. *lluarth*, the first meaning of which is *a camp*, being compounded of *llu*, an army, and *garth*, or *gardh*, an inclosure, a garden. *Cadlas* is a similar instance; the first meaning being a *camp*; comp. of *cád*, battle, and *clás*, an inclosure; the common meaning at the present day is a *stack-yard*. The first element however of *lowarth* may possibly be identical with the old Irish, *lub*, an herb. In the Cornish Vocabulary it is written *luworth*, qd. v. Arm. *liors*, a garden.

LOWAS, s. f. Lightning. *Llwyd*, 3, 62. A late form of *luchas*, or *luwhas*, qd. v.

LOWEN, adj. Glad, joyful, merry. Corn. Voc. *letus. Me a wra fest yn lowen dhé nygys býs yn gorfen*, I will do very joyfully thy errand even to the end. O.M. 719. *Pan wrugé dres ow defen a mês a parathys lowen an él wharé a'n goras*, when he acted against my prohibition, out of happy Paradise the angel soon put him. O.M. 923. *My â gynes yn lowen*, I will go with thee gladly. P.C. 191. The comparative was written *lowenné. Púr lowen re'n Arluth Dew, ha lowenné a pe bew*, very gladly, by the Lord God, and more gladly, if he were living. P.C. 3158. W. *llawen*. Arm. *laouen*, † *louen*. Ir. *loinneach*. Gael. *loinneach*. Sansc. *la, las*, to enjoy. Gr. λάω, λαύω. Lat. *lætor, ludo*.

LOWENDER, s. m. Joy, mirth. *Clow ge ow léf, maym bové grás wogé hemma dhe'th welas yn lowender gans dha eledh awartha uchel yn néf*, hear my voice, that I may have grace hereafter to see thee in joy, with thy angels above, high in heaven. C.W. 104.

LOWENE, s. m. Joy, bliss, gladness, mirth. *Ow arluth, lowené dhys; ow otté ve devethys arté dhe dré*, my lord, joy to thee! Behold me come again home. O.M. 2211. *Arluth Dew kêr, clew ow léf, ha gor vy dhe lowené*, dear Lord God, hear my voice, and place me in bliss. O.M. 1896. *Mýr lowené oll an býs*, see thou the joy of all the world. P.C. 131. *Ma'gas bo lowyné néf*, that yours may be the joy of heaven. P.C. 226. *Lowenna tekca gothfy*, the fairest joy thou knowest. P.C. 1042. W. *llawenydd*. Arm. *levenez*. Ir. *lainne*. Gael. *loinn*.

LOWENEC, adj. Glad, joyful, merry. *Ha warnodho a ysedh él benegas lowenek*, and on it sat an angel blessed joyful. M.C. 244. *Gans henna y a drulyas comfortis ha lowenek*, with that they returned, comforted and joyous, M.C. 257. *Ow broder, púr lowenek, my â genes dhe'n menedh*, my brother, very gladly I will go with thee to the mountain. O.M. 449. *Ny a ýl bós lowenek gwelas Ihesu gallosek Arluth a rûs*, we may be joyful to see Jesus the powerful Lord of grace. R.D. 1333. *Ef a gewsys lowenek*, he spake cheerfully. R.D. 1848. W. *llawenog*.

LOWENHE, v. a. To cause to rejoice, to make glad, to gladden, to comfort; to be glad. Written also *lowenny. Ow colon yw marthys cláf, lowenhé me ny allaf*, my heart is wondrous sick, I cannot be glad. P.C. 1427. *Esé dour ha ponvos brás; wharré y 'gen lowennas, kettel dhueth er agan pyn*, there was concern and great trouble; soon he gladdened us, when he came to meet us. R.D. 1328. *Múr fest y 'gen lowenhas*, very much he gladdened us. R.D. 1444. *Lavar dhym mar a kyllyth yn nép poynt ow lowenhé*, tell me if thou canst in any point gladden me. R.D. 1090. *Mar têk yw dhe dheryvas, dredhos ydh óf lowenhýs*, so fair is thy declaration, through thee I am rejoiced. R.D. 2618. *Me a ýll bós lowenheys*, I may be rejoiced. C.W. 70. W. *llawenhâu*. Arm. *laouenaat*.

LOWER, adj. Many, much. *Au bedhow yn lower le apert a ve egerys*, the tombs in many places were opened wide. M.C. 210. *Me a wrúg oblashion brás, hag a loskas lower o ýs*, I have made a great oblation, and have burnt much corn. C.W. 86. W. *llawer*. Ir. *lear, lor*, † *lar*, † *ilar*, † *hilar*. Gael. *leor*. Manx, *liooar*. Gr. πλήρης. Lat. *plérus, plures*.

LOWERN, s. m. A fox. Corn. Voc. *vulpes. My a'th whores orth y dhón dhe yffarn, kepar hag ón, war geyn lowarn py brathky*, I will help thee to bring him to hell, as we are, on the back of a fox or a mastiff. O.M. 895. W. † *lowern*. Arm. *louarn, loarn*. Though now obsolete in Welsh, the names of a fox being *llwynog, cadnaw*, and *madyn*, the word is preserved in the name of a place, called in Liber Landavonsis, 251, † *crucou lcuirn*, † *crucou leugirn*, the hillocks of the foxes.

LOWERNES, s. f. A fox bitch, a vixen. *Pryce*. Arm. *louarnez, loarnez*.

LOWR, adv. Downward. *Llwyd*, 54. The same word as *luer*, and *lúr*, qd. v.

LOYS, s. f. A pang. A mutation of *gloys*, qd. v. *Hy a wolas kymmys, gans mar vêr nerth ha galloys, a'n fynten may trehevys ran yn ban du droka loys*, she wept so much, with so great strength and power, that from the fountain a part was raised upwards, worst pang. M.C. 224.

LOYS, adj. Gray, hoary. *Yn býs-ma rak dry ascor, ty a vew býs may fy loys*, in this world to bring offspring, thou shalt live till thou be gray. O.M. 72. *Yowynk ha loys, kyn fo tollys dre y deunos mercy gylwys*, let young and gray, though they be deceived by his subtility, call for mercy. P.C. 19. A later form of *luit*, qd. v.

LU, s. m. A great multitude, a host, an army. Corn. Voc. *llu*, exercitus ; *luu listri*, classis, a fleet, i. e. a host of ships. *Ihesus a ve hombronkis, ha war y lyrch múr u lu dre volder tebel Iustis, rag y chasyé, kyn dho Du*, Jesus was conducted, and after him a great multitude, by order of an evil Justice, to chase him, though he was God. M.C. 163. W. *llu*, (= *lug*.) Ir. *sluagh*, † *sluag*, † *slog*. Gael. *sluagh*. Manx, *sleigh*. Gaulish, *slogos* (in *Catu-slogi*.) Gr. λόχος.

LUAN, s. f. A louse. *Llwyd*, 16, 115, *lúan*. The late form of *louen*, qd. v. Pl. *lou, loow*.

LUAN, adj. Cheerful. *En lúan*, cheerfully. *Llwyd*, 248, 252. Another form of *lowen*, qd. v.

LUAR, s. m. A garden. *Llwyd*, 33, 66. A late form of *lowarth*, qd. v.

LUARN, s. m. A fox. *Llwyd*, 241. The same as *lowern*, qd. v.

LUAS, adj. Much, many. Written indiscriminately *lues, leas*, and *lias. Crist a besys del redyn yn delma yn luas le*, Christ prayed, as we read thus in many places. M.C. 204. *Ha'n corfow esa ynné a ve yn ban drehevys, hag éth poran dhe'n cyté, gans luas y fóns gwelys*, and the bodies (that) were in them, were raised up, and went straight to the city, by many they were seen. M.C. 210. *Gevy oyl ol ow pewé, ow codhaf lues galar*, unhappy ever living, enduring much sorrow. O.M. 633. *Ke nyg a-uch lues pow*, go thou, fly over many a country. O.M. 1136. See also *Lyes*.

LUC, adv. Enough, sufficiently. ‡ *Es leath luck gen veu*, is there milk enough with the cow? *Pryce*. It occurs only in late Cornish.

LUCHAS, s. f. Lightning. *Nango hanter dýdh yn wlâs, po moy, del yma seryfis, dorgis esa ha luchas, ha'n tewolgow kekyffrys*, now it was mid-day in the land, or more, as is written, earthquake there was, and lightning, and the darkness likewise. M.C. 209. The same as *luhet*, qd. v.

LUDER, s. m. A lord lieutenant, a peer, or viceroy. *Pryce*. W. *llywawdwr*.

LUDNOW, s. m. Bullocks, cattle. ‡ *Ha Dew gwrâs bestes an noar warlêr go hâs, ha'n ludnow warlêr go hâs*, and God made the beasts of the earth after their seed, and the cattle after their seed. C.W. p. 191. ‡ *Gorah ow thees dha'n fêr dha gwerra ludnow*, put my men to the fair to sell bullocks. *Pryce*. The plural of *lodn*, qd. v.

LUDZH, adj. Grey. *Llwyd*, 46, 231. *Lúdzh* is a late corruption of *loys* or *luit*, qd. v.

LUED, s. m. Mire, filth. *Pryce*. Who also gives *luth* as another form. W. *llaid*. Arm. *louz*. Ir. *lathach*, † *loth*. Gael. *lathach*. Manx, *laagh*.

LUEDIC, adj. Miry, filthy, stinking. *Llwyd*, 132. W. *lleidiog*.

LUEF, s. f. A hand. *Pandra synsyth y'th luef lemyn*, what holdest thou in thy hand now? O.M. 1442. *Ow dyw-lucf colm ha'm garrow gans lovan*, tie thou my hands and my legs with a rope. O.M. 1346. *Doro kenter, ha me a tnk y luef glêdh*, bring thou a nail, and I will fasten his left hand. P.C. 2747. One of the various forms of *lof*, qd. v.

LUEN, adj. Full, abounding, great, abundant. *Pûr luen yma dhym ow whans*, very great is my want to me. O.M. 91. *Kepar del ôs luen a rûs*, as thou art full of grace. O.M. 106. *Luen tregereth me a pŷs*, abundant mercy I pray. R.D. 1148. Another form of *leun*, qd. v.

LUER, s. m. A floor. *Ottê omma skyber dêk, ha cala lour war hy luer*, see here a fair room, and straw enough on its floor. O.M. 680. *An arhans, kettep dyner, me a's deghes war an luer*, the silver, every penny, I have brought on the floor. P.C. 1515. Another form of *lôr*, qd. v.

LUERN, s. m. A fox. Llwyd, 179, *lúern*. Id. qd. *lowern*, qd. v.

LUES, adj. Many, much. Written also *luas*, qd. v.

LUF, s. f. A hand. *Rag colê orth un venen, gulân ef re gollas an plâs a'm lûf dhychow a wrussen*, for listening to a woman, he has clean lost the place, (which) with my right hand I had made. O.M. 921. A contracted form of *luef*, qd. v.

LUGARN, s. m. A lamp, a light, a candle. Corn. Voc. *lichinus*. W. *llygorn*. Arm. *letern*. Ir. *lochran*, † *luacharnn*, gen. *lochairnn*. Gael. *lochran*. Goth. *lukarn*. Lat. *lucerna*. Zeuss, 28, points to Locarno, near the head of Lago Maggiore, as exhibiting the Gallic form of the word; while Lucerne, at the foot of the lake of the same name in Switzerland, gives the Latin form.

LUHAS, adj. Many. *Ay ben y oys o scoliys, hag ynno fest luhas tol gans an dreyn a ve tellys*, from his head his blood was spilt, and in it very many holes were bored by the thorns. M.C. 133. More generally written *luas*, qd. v.

LUHESEN, s. f. A flash of lightning. *Ellas, na dhellcys dh'y lesky un luhesen ha crak taran*, alas ! that I sent not forth to burn him a flash of lightning, and a clap of thunder. R.D. 295. W. *llucheden*. Arm. *lucheden*.

LUHET, s. f. Lightning. Corn. Vocab. *fulgur*. In the Ordinalia it is written *luhes*. *Dylleuch luhes ha taran a'n losco*, send ye forth lightning and thunder that it burn him. R.D. 129. *Ellas dhynny ny dâl man duello luhes na taran dh'y lesky ef*, alas! it avails us not a bit to discharge lightning nor thunder to burn him. R.D. 296. Another form is *luchas*, qd. v. W. *lluched*. Arm. *luched*, † *luffet*.

LUID, s. m. A battle array. Corn. Voc. *procinctus*. *Hebrenchiat luid*, dux, a captain, or leader of an army. Ibid. W. *lluedh*, *lluydh*.

LUIR, s. f. The moon. Corn. Voc. *luna*. In the Ordinalia it is variously written *loer*, *lôr*, qd. v., and by Llwyd, *lûr*. W. *lloer*. Arm. *loar*, *loer*.

LUIT, adj. Grey, hoary, greyish white. *Les-luit*, Corn. Voc. *marrubrium*, horehound. This is the oldest form of the word, and is the same as *lot*, in *lot-les*. qd. v. The later form of the Ordinalia is *loys*, qd. v. W. *llwyd*, † *luit*. Arm. *loued*. Ir. *liath*. Gael. *liath*. Manx, *lheeah*. Latin, *luteus*.

LUMAN, adv. Now, at present. Corn. Voc. *nunc vel modo*. In the Ordinalia it is variously written *lemyn*, *lemmyn*, *lemmen*, *lymmyn*, and *lemman*, qd. v. W. *llyman*, *llyma*.

LUR, s. m. The ground, the earth. *Dhe'n lûr*, to the ground, downwards, down. *An gwêl a râs dhyworth an lûr gwrâf dhe drehy*, the rods of grace from the ground I will cut them. O.M. 1987. *Dyeskyn a'n vŷnk dhe'n lûr*, descend thou from the post to the ground. P.C. 2868. *Dûn dh'y gymeres dhe'n lûr*, let us come to take it down. P.C. 3141. *Del ôs formyas dhe'n nêf, ha'n lûr*, as thou art Creator to the heaven and the earth. R.D. 843. *Hag yn gorhel brâs gorrys gynen may teffo dhe'n lûr*, and in a great ship placed with us that he may come to the abyss. R.D. 2330. Id. qd. *lôr*, qd. v.

LUR, s. f. The moon. *Llwyd*, 17, 82. A contracted form of *luir*, qd. v.

LUSOW, s. m. Ashes, or the remains of anything burnt. *Pyth yw an gordhyans dhe Dew, bôs leskys dhe glow lusow war an caryeg degê*, what is the worship to God, that the tithe be burnt to coal ashes on the stones? O.M. 477. *Ow paynys a vŷdh garow kyn vôs leskys dhe lusow*, my pains will be cruel before being burnt to ashes. O.M. 1355. This was finally corrupted into *lidzhu*. Llwyd, 10, 48. W. *lludw*. Arm. *ludu*. Ir. *luaith*. Gael. *luath*. Manx, *leoie*.

LUSOW, s. m. Herbs. *Llwyd*, 242. See *Losow*.

LUWORCHGUIT, s. m. A shrub. Corn. Voc. *virgultum*. *Luworch* is most probably an error for *luworth*, id. qd. *lowarth*, a garden, and *guit*, being *gwŷdh*, shrubs, the meaning will be "garden shrubs."

LUZ, adj. Gray, hoary. A later corruption of *loys*, qd. v. ‡ *Karreg luz en kuz*, the gray rock in the wood, was the Cornish name of St. Michael's Mount.

LY, s. m. A breakfast. See *Li*.
LYC, adv. Enough, sufficiently. *Pysgos lyk*, fish enough. *Llwyd*, 248. It occurs only in late Cornish, and is also written *luc*, qd. v.
LYDDRYS, part. Stolen. *Re Vahun y tóf yn wêdh, mars yu c lyddrys a'n bêdh, why a's bydh ages ancow*, by Mahound I swear also, if he is stolen from the tomb, ye shall have your death. R.D. 611. The part. pass. of *ladra*, qd. v.
LYDROW, s. m. Stockings. ‡ *An lydrow adro's garrow*, the stockings on your legs. *Llwyd*, 250. The plural of *loder*, qd. v.
LYDHYS, part. Killed, slain. *Lydhys ôf pûr dhyogel*, I am killed very certainly. O.M. 2725. *Kepar del leverys dheuch, gwyrthys, lydhys yn grows pren*, like as I have said to you, sold, killed on the cross tree. P.C. 766. *Cryst a fue lydhys garow*, Christ was cruelly slain. R.D. 903. Part. pass. of *ladha*, qd. v.
LYEN, s. m. Literature, learning, erudition, scholarship. *Mâb lyen*, a clergyman, a clerk, a priest. *My a vyn lemyn ordné mâb-lyen, ow sêl pryvé, dhe vôs epscop yn temple*, I will now ordain a priest, my privy seal, to be bishop in the temple. O.M. 2600. *Ow mâp-lyen, kerch Annas an pryns, may hyllyf clewas pŷth yw an gussyl wella dhe wruthil*, my clerk, fetch Annas the prince, that I may hear what is the best counsel to do. P.C. 553. W. *llên*. Arm. *lenn*.
LYEN, s. m. Linen. See *Lien*.
LYES, adj. Many. *Ma yma lyes gurêk ha gour ow treylé dhodho touth-da*, there are here many a man and woman turning to him speedily. P.C. 657. *Annodho del yw scryfys yn lyfryow, yn lyes le*, of him as it is written in books, in many places. P.C. 740. *Lyes prŷs wogé merwel*, many times after dying. P.C. 1755. *Ef re trylyas lyes cans yn mês a'n fey*, he has turned many hundreds out of the faith. P.C. 1995. Written indiscriminately *leas, lias, luas*, and *lues*. See *Leas*.
LYF, s. m. A flood, a deluge. See *Lif*.
LYFFROW, s. m. Books. Plural of *lyvyr*, qd. v.
LYFRESON, s. m. Liberty. *Mar a kŷl bones yacheys, ty a fŷdh dhe lyfreson, hag an our dhe weryson*, if he can be healed, thou shalt have thy liberty, and the gold thy guerdon. R.D. 1676. Fr. *livraison*.
LYGADZHAC, adj. Eyed. ‡ *Ydn lygadzhac*, one-eyed. Llwyd, 10. A late corruption of *lagadec*, qd. v.
LYGODZHAN, s. f. A mouse. ‡ *Lygodzhan wrâs*, a rat, a great mouse. *Llwyd*, 3. A late corruption of *logosan*, qd. v.
LYHA, adj. Least. *Ahanouch nêb yw mochya, ha'n brasa gallos dodho, bydhens kepar ha'n lyha*, of you he who is the greatest, and has the greatest power, let him be like as the least. P.C. 794. Written also *leia*. It is used as the superlative of *bechan*. W. *lleiav*.
LYHY, v. a. To make less, to lessen, to diminish. *Am dhedhé a dhesempys yn hanow an Tâs an nêf, try person un Dew hennys, ha sâr y lyha dhe grêf*, kiss them immediately in the name of the Father of heaven, three persons one God named, and surely he will lessen thy pain. O.M. 1772. *Pûr wŷr, mar lyha ow grêf, my a'n fŷth dysosy*, very truly, if he will lessen my pain, I shall be bound to him. O.M. 1787. *Yn dan dryys may fo pottyys, ha y vertu a vŷdh lyhŷs dre an mostethus hep fâl*, under feet that it may be put, and its virtue will be lessened by the dirt, without fail. O.M. 2808. Written also with the aspirate. *Och gony, mones mar pel; ugan meystry dyougel Cryst a lycha*, Oh, woe is me! to go so far; our power truly Christ will lessen. P.C. 1909. Written also *leyhy*, qd. v.
LYHWEDHA, v. a. To shut, to lock. *Llwyd*, 48. A late corruption of *alwedha*, from *alwedh*, a key, qd. v. Arm. *alchouexa*.
LYM, adj. Keen, sharp, acute, pointed. *Gew a ve yn y dhewlé gans an Edhewon gorris, ha pen lym rag y wané*; a spear was in his hand placed by the Jews, and a sharp point to pierce him. M.C. 217. *Otté spern grisyl gyné, ha dreyn lym ha scharp ynné, a grup bŷs yn empynyon*, see sharp thorns with me, and spines acute and sharp in them, that will pierce even to the brains. P.C. 2119. *Gans gu lym y a'n gwanas*, with a sharp spear they pierced him. R.D. 1117. *Curyn a spern lym ha glew*, a crown of thorns sharp and stiff. R.D. 2582. W. *llym*, f. *lem*. Arm. *lemn*.
LYMMYN, adv. Now, but. *An gwary yw dué lymmyn*, the play is ended now. O.M. 2839. *Iudas ny gôsk un banné, lymmyn dywans fystyné dhum ry dhe'n fâls Yedhewon*, Judas does not sleep a bit, but quickly hastens to give me to the false Jews. P.C. 1079. *Gorteuch lymmyn, gockyes; dhe'th scoforn wharré yehes my a re*, stay now, fools, to thine ear soon health I will give. P.C. 1140. Another form of *lemmyn* or *lemman*, qd. v.
LYN, s. m. Humor, liquor, juice, water; standing water, a lake, a pool, a pond. *Mam Ihesus, Marya wyn, herdya an gyw pan welas yn y mâb yn tenewyn, dre an golon may resas; ha dhe'n dôr an goys ha'n lyn annodho dell deveras, angus brâs, ha peynys lym, ha gloys crêff a's kemeras*, the mother of Jesus, Mary blessed, when she saw the spear thrust into her son in the side, so that it ran through the heart; and how to the ground the blood and water dropt from him, great anguish, and sharp pains, and a strong pang seized her. M.C. 221. Written in the Cornish Vocabulary, *lin*, qd. v. W. *llyn*, †*linn*. Arm. *lenn*. Ir. *linn*. Gael. *linne*.
LYNNETH, s. m. Offspring, progeny, race. *Ha nefré y fŷdh avry, yntré dhe lynneth dhe sy, ha lynneth benen pup preys*, and ever there shall be enmity between thy offspring and the offspring of the woman always. O.M. 315. *My ny dorraf bys vycken an acord ûs lemyn gwreys yntré my ha lynneth dên*, I will not break for ever the agreement (that) is now made between me and the race of man. O.M. 1242. Another form of *linieth*, qd. v.
LYNNIC, adj. Moist, wet. *Pryce*. W. *llyniog*.
LYNWYS, part. Filled. *Och, govy, pan vêf genys; gans moreth ydhof lynwys war dhe lerch ow arluth whêk*, Oh, alas, that I was born! with sorrow I am filled after thee, my sweet lord. O.M. 2194. Part. pass. of *lenwel*, qd. v.
LYRCH, s. m. A trace, a footstep, a vestige. *War lyrch mâb dên dhe becha*, after the son of man did sin. M.C. 7. *Dysquedhyens war lyrch anken bedhé mygtern yn dewedh*, a declaration after sorrow that he was a king at last. M.C. 236. *War y lyrch ef mûr ow hyreth*, after him great (is) my longing. R.D. 836. Written also *lerch*, qd. v.
LYS, s. m. Mud, mire. *Gans towal a lŷn gulân, my a's sêch kettep onan a bôp mostethes ha lŷs*, with a towel of clean linen I will dry them every one from all dirt

LYVYR 242 MA

and mire. P.C. 838. A contracted form of *lyys*, qd. v.

LYSCY, v. a. To burn. Part. *lyscys*. *Tân an iowl mûr dh'y lysky, na dheffo na moy yn pow*, the fire of the great devil to burn him, that he may come no more into the country. R.D. 2175. *Sew olow ow thryys lyskys*, follow thou the prints of my feet burnt. O.M. 711. *Ow coské yn haus yn hâl, lyskys ôf a'n kîl dhe'n tâl*, sleeping down in the moor, I am burnt from the nape to the forehead. O.M. 1781. Written also *lescy*, and *loscy*, qd. v.

LYSTEN, s. f. A towel, napkin. *Flôch byan nowydh gynys, hag ef yn quethow maylys, ha kylmys fast gan lysten*, a little child newly born, and he (was) in cloths swathed and bound fast with a napkin. O.M. 808. *Hag yn crcys hy varennow un flôch maylys gans lysten*, and in the middle of its branches, a child swathed with napkins. O.M. 840.

LYSUAN, s. f. A herb, a plant. Pl. *lusow, lusu, losow, losowes, lysywys*. Llwyd, 65, 243. ‡ *Ha Dew laveras, gwrêns an 'oar dry râg gwêls, ha lusu doan hâs*, and God said, let the earth bring forth grass, and herbs bearing seed. C.W. p. 190. ‡ *Ha an 'oar a drôs râg gwels, ha'n losow rig dasker hâs pokar e cunda*, and the earth brought forth grass, and the herbs did produce seed after their kind. Ibid. ‡ *Ema reis gennam kemeffra lousuan glâs râg bôs*, every green herb is given by me for meat. Ibid. ‡ *An lysûan bian gen i'ar nedhcx, ez a tivi en an halow nei, ez kreiz Plêth Maria*, the small plant with the twisted stalk (which) grows on our hills, is called Pleth Maria. Llwyd, 245. The radical form is *lys*, or *lus*, or as written in the Cornish Vocabulary, *les*, qd. v. W. *llysicuyn*, plur. *llysiau*, from sing. *llys*. Arm. *louzaouen, lezeuen*, pl. *louzou, lezeu*; sing. †*lus*. Ir. *lus*. Gael. *lus*. Manx, *lus*.

LYTTHYN, v. a. We should have killed. *Gory vgth pan y'n lytthyn*, woe is me, when we ever killed him. P.C. 2998. To be read *lydhyn*, being 1 pers. pl. subj. of *ladhé*, qd. v.

LYTTRY, v. a. Thou mayst steal. 2 pers. sing. subj. of *ladra*, qd. v. *Ha me a vŷth na'n lyttry, na cous ef dhe dhasserchy un gêr tuch vyth*, and I will take care that thou steal him not, nor say that he has arisen one word at any time. R.D. 58.

LYTH, s. m. A limb. *Uskys na yllyn ponyé, del esof ow tyené, ha whŷs pûp gôth ha lŷth*, I could not run immediately, I am panting so, and sweat every vein and limb. P.C. 2512. *Dre mûr hyreth ydhof pûr squyth, ha'm corf dhe wêdh, yscarn ha lŷth*, through great longing I am quite weary, and my body also, bones and limb. R.D. 848. Written also *leyth*. *War Crist y fôns ow cronkyé, manna gevé gôth na leyth nag esa worth y grevyé*, on Christ they were beating, so that he had not vein nor limb (that) was not grieving him. M.C. 132. Not a Celtic word, being the old English *lith*, a joint or limb. Ang. Sax. *lith*. Goth. *lithus*.

LYTHER, s. m. A letter, an epistle. Pl. *lytherow*, letters, learning. Llwyd, 13, 59, 80. The same as *lither*, qd. v.

LYVYR, s. m. A book. Pl. *lyfryow, lyffrow*. *Yn lyvyr yma scrufys bôs eledh worth dhe wythé*, in a book it is written that angels are guarding thee. P.C. 95. *Yn lyfryow scryfys yma bôs collenwys lowené a ganow an fiechys da*, in books it is written that joy is fulfilled from the mouths of good children. P.C. 435. *Dûn dhe'n menedh Olyved, yn wêdh ena ny a rêd y gen lyffrow*, let us come to the Mount of Olives, also there we will read in our books. R.D. 2411. *Yn êr-na del redyn ny, yn lyfrow del yw scrifys*, then as we read, in books as it is written. M.C. 206. Written also *levar*, and in the Cornish Vocabulary, *liver*, qd. v.

LYW, s. m. A hue, a colour. Written in the Cornish Vocabulary, *liu*, qd. v.

LYYS, s. m. Mire, dirt. *A Dâs, del ôn dhe wythres, a bol hag a lyys formys, bŷdh dymny nerth ha gweres*, O Father, as we are thy work, made of clay and mire, be to us strength and help. O.M. 1070. *Neffré na wrello dgbry, lemyn fleryé ha peddry kepar ha seym py lyys haal*, that she may never eat, but stink and rot like train oil or salt-marsh mud. O.M. 2708. A later form of *lued*, qd. v.

M.

This letter, sounded as in English, is a mutable radical initial in the six Celtic dialects, and changes into *mh* or *v*. Thus C. *mam*, a mother; *y vam*, his mother. W. *mam, ei vam*. Arm. *mam, he vamm*. Manx, *moyrn*, pride; *e voyrn*, his pride. In Irish and Gaelic, the secondary form is written *mh*, but pronounced as *v*, as *muir*, sea; *môr*, great; *a mhuir mhôr*, (*a vuir vôr*) the great sea. In Welsh, Irish, and Manx, *m* is also a secondary letter, being the nasal mutation of *b*. Thus W. *bara*, bread; *vy mara*, my bread. Ir. *bron*, sorrow; *ar mron*, our sorrow. Manx, *bea*, life; *nyn mea*, our life. Cf. also Gael. *bean*, a woman; pl. *mnai*.

MA, s. f. A place, a space, a state. In common use as an affix in composition, as *trigva*, a dwelling place; *morva*, a place on the sea, a marsh. *Ma* is similarly used in Welsh, as *trigva, morva*, &c. W. *ma, man*. Arm. *mann*. Ir. *magh*, †*mag*, †*magen*. Gael. *magh*. Coptic, *ma*.

MA, pr. subs. I, me. This form only occurs in composition. *Ty ny wodhas lemyn pedra wrama dhys*, thou knowest not now what I do to thee. P.C. 856. *Omma pols powesouch hedré vyma ow pygy*, here a while rest ye while I am praying. P.C. 1013. *Ellas, pan fema gynys*, alas, when I was born! R.D. 2207. *Herwedh dhe grath ha'th pytê, na'm byma peyn yn gorfen*, according to thy grace and thy pity, let there not be to me pain at the end. O.M. 2254. See *Me*, and *My*.

MA, pr. adj. My, mine. Llwyd, 244. *Ma tâs*, my father. *Dho va vam*, to my mother. Pryce. The form of this pronoun in the Ordinalia is *ow*, qd. v. W. *mau, my*, †*mi*. Arm. *ma*. Irish, *mo*. Gael. *mo*. Manx, *my*. Sansc. *mâmaka*. Gr. ἐμός, ἐμή. Lat. *meus, mea*. It. *mio*. Fr. *mon, ma*. Germ. *mein*. Scot. *ma*. Eng. *my*.

MA, v. imp. There is, it is. *Lavar ple ma Abel dhe vroder*, say where is Abel thy brother. O.M. 571. *My a wôr ple ma onan*, I know where there is one. O.M. 2561. *Ellas govy, ma ow dyllas ow tewy*, alas, woe is me, my clothes are blazing. O.M. 2633. *Ma yma lyes gwrêk hâ gour ow treylé dhodho touth-da*, there are here many women and men turning to him speedily. P.C. 557. It often has *y* preceding. *Ow tybbry genen y ma*, he is eating with us. M.C. 43. *Arluth, hy a leveris, ow holon y ma genas*, Lord, she said, my heart is with thee. M.C. 172. It is used with dative pronouns, to denote possession, in accordance with the Latin idiom, *est mihi*. *Yma dew dhyn parys*, we have two ready. M.C. 51. *An debel dûs a gewsys, dhymny y ma laha may rŷs vonas y ledhys*, the wicked people said, we have a law that he must be killed. M.C. 143. The plural is *môns*, *y môns*, qd. v. W. *mae, y mac. (Y mae genyv,* I have.) Arm. *ma*.

MA, adv. Here, in this place. An abbreviation of *yma*, qd. v. It is joined to substantives, when it has the power of a demonstrative pronoun. *Mars ôs Mâb Du, leun a râs, an veyn-ma gwra bara dhys*, if thou art the Son of God, full of grace, make these stones bread for thee. M.C. 11. *An ré-ma yw oberys del vynsyn agan honan*, these are wrought, as we ourselves would. O.M. 15. *Ef a'n gevyth seyth kemmys a paynys yn nôr bŷs-ma*, he shall have seven times as much of pains in the earth of this world. O.M. 600. This idiom is in common use in Welsh, as *y dŷn yma*, this man ; *y vlwydhyn yma*, this year. So also in Armoric, *ann dûd-ma a zo pinvidik*, these people are rich. A similar idiom obtains in Irish, as *an t-aite so*, this place ; lit. the place here. Cf. also the French, *cette maison-ci*.

MA, conj. If, that, so that. *Ma ny gaffaf branchys vâs, me a dhystryp ow dyllas, hag a's set y dan y treys*, if I find not good branches, I will take off my clothes, and put them under his feet. P.C. 249. *Ow Tâs, ma ny gyl bones may treylyo mernens dhe vês*, my Father, if it cannot be that death be turned away. P.C. 1069. *Cryst kymmys payn yn gevê, angus tyn ha galarow, ma têth an goys, ha dropyê war y fas, an caradow*, Christ, so much pain had he, keen anguish and pangs, that the blood came, and dropped on his face, the beloved. M.C. 59. *Lyes trefeth y'n clewys, ma na ŷl y dhynaché*, many times I heard him, so that he cannot retract it. P.C. 1725. *Pŷs e dhym ma'n danfonno*, pray him that he send him to me. R.D. 1020. W. *mal*. Arm. *ma*. Ir. *ma*. Gael. *ma*. Manx, *my*.

MAB, s. m. A son, a male child, a boy, a male, a mau. Pl. *mebion, mebbion*. Cornish Vocabulary, *filius*. *Mab aflavar*, infans, an infant. *Mab meidrin*, alumpnus, a foster-son. *Muister mebion*, pædagogus, a schoolmaster. Ibid. *Tâs, ha Mâb, ha'n Speris Sans, wy a bŷs a leun golon*, Father, Son, and Holy Ghost, ye shall beseech with a full heart. M.C. 1. *War lyrch mâb dên dhe becha*, after that the son of man sinned. M.C. 7. *Pan welas y mâb dygtis gans an Edhewon mar veyll*, when she saw her son treated so vilely by the Jews. M.C. 165. *Râg y fŷdh mâp yn Bethlem genys a dhyspreen an bŷs*, for there will be a son born in Bethlehem (that) will redeem the world. O.M. 1934. *Nyns us mâb glŷ yn wlâs-ma*, there is not a smith in this country. P.C. 2724. *Map lyen*, a clergyman. P.C. 553. *Caym hag Abel, ow mebbyon, cuch sacryfyeuch yu soon yn menedh dhe'n Tâs an nêf*, Cain and Abel, my sons, go sacrifice forthwith in the mount to the Father of Heaven. O.M. 437. *A vryes, hep falladow, mebyon ha myrhes kefrys*, O spouse, without failings, sons and daughters likewise. O.M. 1038. Llwyd, 243, gives *meib*, as another plural, and Jordan has *mybyon*. C.W. 144. W. *mâb, † mâp;* pl. *meibion, † meib*. Arm. *mâb, mâp;* pl. *mibien*. Ir. *mac*. Gael. *mac*. Manx, *mac*.

MABM, s. f. A mother. ‡ *Ow molath dhys râg henna, ha molath dha vabm gansa te a vŷdh magata*, my curse to thee for that, and the curse of thy mother with it, thou shalt have as well. C.W. 88. A late corruption of *mam*, qd. v.

MACHTETH, s. f. A virgin, a maid. *Mâp Dew pûr, ha dên keffrys, a vachteth gulân dynythys*, Son of very God, and man also, of a pure virgin born. P.C. 1727. *Râk del won, mâp Dew ôs pûr, yn beys gynys a vachtyth glân*, for, as I know, very Son of God thou art, in the world born of a pure virgin. P.C. 3027. Written *mahteid*, virgo, in the Cornish Vocabulary. There is nothing similar in Welsh or Armoric. Ir. *moidhidean*. Gael. *maighdean*. Manx, *moidyn*. Ang. Sax. *mǽgdh*. Eng. *maid*.

MADAM, v. a. I will. ‡ *Me vadam*, Llwyd, 240. A late corruption of *mynnaf*.

MADERE, s. m. The herb madder. Corn. Voc. *sinitia*. Ang. Sax. *mæddere*.

MADRA, v. a. To study, to consider. ‡ *Buz mar crown gy predery, pan dâl go gwary, ha mudra ta, pen drig seera ha damma*, but if they should consider what ought to be their play, and study well, what did their father and mother. *Pryce*.

MAEN, s. m. A stone, a block of stone. Pl. *meyn, myyn*. *Maen flent*, a flintstone. Llwyd, 150. *Ty vaow darbar lym ha pry, meyn wheyll, slodyys, ha genow*, thou boy prepare lime and clay, building stones, trucks, and wedges. O.M. 2318. *Trehesy meyn*, stone cutters. O.M. 2411. *Orden dhe'th tûs hy knoukyé gans meyn*, order thy people to beat her with stones. O.M. 2677. *An veyn-ma gwra bara dhys*, these stones make thou bread for thee. M.C. 11. The contracted form of *mên* is generally used in the singular, qd. v. W. *maen, †main*. Arm. *maen, mean*. Hence Lat. *mœnia*, walls.

MAERDUIT, s. m. A steward. Corn. Voc. *dispensator*. Comp. of *maer*, or *mair*, qd. v., and *buit* (W. *bwyd*) the old form of boys, qd. v.

MAES, s. m. An open country, a plain field, a field. The general form in use was the contracted one of *mês*, qd. v.

MAGA, v. a. To feed, to nourish. 2 pers. s. imp. *mâg*. Part. *megys, migys*. Llwyd, 248. *Leman why a ŷll gweles lavar Du maga del vera neb a ŷll y kemeres*, now ye may see how the word of God will feed whoever can take it. P.C. 71. *A mester kêr caradow, del leveryth, my a grŷs y fŷdh agan encfow dre levarow Dew mygys*, O dear beloved master, as thou sayest, I believe that our souls will be fed by the words of God. P.C. 76. W. *magu*. Arm. *maga*.

MAGA, conj. So much, as much, as, so. It aspirates the initial following. *Maga ta*, as well, also. *Maga gwyn avel an gurys*, as white as the glass. P.C. 1790. *Lyes gwŷth y wrûk bostyé yn try gêdh y wûl arta maga ta bythqueth del fue*, many times he boasted, in three days to make it again as good as ever it was. P.C. 2443. *Yn alabauster gravys, maga whyn avel an lêth*, cut in alabaster as white as the milk. P.C. 3138. *Ha maga fuer drôk deffry mones dhe hepcor an ioy bŷth na dhyfyk*, and as it would be an evil truly to go to reject the joy that never fails. R.D. 1432. *Saw an corf-na, byw a pe, an emperour ef sawsd, maga têk bythqueth del fue*, but that body, if it were living, would cure the emperor, as well as ever he was. R.D. 1650. *Hag a'n dydhgithyas pûr lowen maga têk del rebyé*, and dighted it very gladly as fair as it had been. M.C. 71. *Ef a doys a dhesympys maga town ty del wodhyé*, he swore forthwith as deep an oath as he knew. M.C. 85. *Dén ha bêst maga ta*, man and beast also. O.M. 995.

MAGLEN, s. f. A springe, gin, snare, halter. Corn. Voc. *laqueus*. W. *magl, maglen, maglai*. Lat. *macula*.

MAHTHEID, s. f. A virgin. Corn. Voc. *virgo*. The old form of *machteth*, qd. v.

MAIDOR, s. m. A victualler. Corn. Voc. *caupo*. To be read *maithor*. W. *maethwr; maethu*, to feed.

AIR, s. m. A mayor or chief. Corn. Voc. *præpositus*. Written also *maer*, as *maer-buit*, qd. v. W. *maer*, †*mair*. Arm. *maer*, †*mair*. Ir. *maor*, †*maer*. Gael. *maor*. Lat. *major*. Fr. *maire*.

MAISTER, s. m. A master. Corn. Voc. *magister*. *Maister melvion*, pædagogus, a schoolmaster. *Ibid.* Regularly formed from the Latin, by the mutation and consequent disappearance of the *g*. In the Ordinalia generally written *mester*, qd. v. Welsh, *meistyr*. Arm. *maester*, †*mester*. Ir. *maighistir*. Gael. *maighstir*.

MAITHES, s. f. A maid. ‡ *An seithas dýdh yw an Sabbath an Arluth de Dhew, enna ty na wra chan a wheel, ty, ha'th vâb, ha'th verh, de gwâs, ha de maithes*, the seventh day is the Sabbath of the Lord thy God, in it thou shalt do no manner of work, thou, and thy son, and thy daughter, thy manservant, and thy maidservant. Pryce. A later form of *machteth*, qd. v.

MAL, conj. As, like as, so, so that. Llwyd, 178, 240. ‡ *Gwra perthy de tâs, ha de mam, mal de dydhiow bedhens hir war an tir, néb an Arluth de Dhew ryes dees*, do thou honour thy father, and thy mother, that thy days may be long in the land which the Lord thy God giveth thee. Pryce. *Avel* is another form, qd. v. W. *mal*, †*amal, (amal itercludant*, ut subigant. *Juv. Gloss.) val, vel*. Arm. *evel*. Ir. *amhail*, †*amail*, †*amal*. Gr. ὁμαλός. Lat. *similis*.

MAL, s. m. Will, desire. *Rág henna war an chal hy gweskel genef yw mal*, for that, on the jaw to smite her the will is with me. O.M. 2734. *Dús a le-na, ty Gebal, gor an pren yn més gans mal*, come away thou Gebal, carry the tree outside with a will. O.M. 2780. *Dhe gafus gynen yw mal*, to take thee there is with us a desire. P.C. 1178. *Mal yw gynef dhe gafus*, tho will is with me to take thee. P.C. 1531. *Me a wra gans bones mal*, I will with good will. P.C. 2629. *Cous ganso genen o mal*, to talk with him the will was with us. R.D. 1488. *An preys mall ow genef*, the time is welcome with me. C.W. 142.

MAL, s. m. A joint. Llwyd, 240. Pl. *mellow, melyow*. *Mar ny'n gorraf, an myl dyawl re dorro mellow y gyn*, if I do not take him, may a thousand devils break the joints of his back. P.C. 1619. *My a'n knouk ef er y wew, otté mellow y geyn brew*, I will beat him for his grief; see the joints of his back broken. P.C. 2086. *Y vellow kettep onan dyscnvylsys yns ertan*, his joints every one are strained certainly. P.C. 2770. W. *mâl*, in *cymmal*. Arm. *mell; (mellow-kein*, the spine.)

MALAN, s. m. The evil principle, the evil one, the devil. *Hou geiler, avarth malan, dús yn rág ha'th vaw keffrys*, ho, gaoler, in the fiend's name, come forward, and thy servant too. P.C. 2235. *How hale kettep onan, gesouch hy a barth malan yn morter skuat dhe godhé*, lo! haul every one, let it, in the fiend's name, into the mortise crack to fall. P.C. 2851. W. *mallon*. The root is W. *mall*, evil, a malady, debility. Arm. *fall*. Ir. *mall*, †*feal*. Gael. *mall, feall*. Sause. *malan*. Gr. μέλαν. Lat. *malum, malignum*.

MALAN, s. f. The Goddess Malan. *Rák why á scon ahanan dhe Pilat, re synt Malan, rák y ma owth yscdhé*, for ye shall go immediately from us to Pilate, by Saint Malan, for he is sitting. P.C. 2341. W. *malan*. This was the name of a celebrated ancient British Goddess, who was invoked with imprecations in any perilous crisis. She was also called Andras. See the "Biographical Dictionary of Eminent Welshmen."

MALBEW, adv. In any wise, in any way. *Saw a pôn ny dewyow gwerýs, ny veas malbew serrys, me a wôr henna yn ta*, but if we were made gods, thou wouldst in no wise be angry, I know that well. C.W. 60. *Malbew edrek ês dhymmo, an chorle Abell ûs ledhys*, is there in any way sorrow to me, that the churl Abell is killed? C.W. 94. *Ny sparyaf anodhans y malbew onyn a vo têg*, I will not spare of them in any wise one that is fair. C.W. 106.

MALEGAS, part. Accursed. *Ha'n serpent tregans yna, nefra ny dhê a le-na rág ydhew malegas brás*, and let the serpent stay there, never shall he come thence, for he is greatly accursed. C.W. 68. A late form of *mylegės*, qd. v.

MALOU, s. m. Mallow. Corn. Voc. *malva*. Arm. *malô, malv*.

MALYE, v. a. To wrap. *Dhyworthé ma 'gan bo grás, aga malyé my a vyn yn cendel hag yn ourlyn*, from them that we may have grace, I will wrap them in fine linen and silk. O.M. 1750. Written also *maylé*, qd. v.

MAM, s. f. A mother, the womb. *Mam teilu*, materfamilias, the mistress of the family. Corn. Voc. *Mam gwenen*, a stock of bees. Pryce. *Dhe vanneth dhym mûr a blêk, ha banneth ow mam yn wêdh*, thy blessing pleases me much, and the blessing of my mother likewise. O.M. 456. *Ha gwerýs nôth oll, rág an pêch a pehns ow thás hu'm mam*, and all made bare, for the siu (that) my father and mother sinned. O.M. 759. *Rág orty ty dhe golé, mýl vâp mam a výdh damnrys*, for that thou hearknedst to her, a thousand mother's sons shall be damned. O.M. 324. *Govy výth pan vêf genys*, a dor ow mam dynythys, *na vythqueth pan denys bron*, woe is me that I was born, from the womb of my mother brought, or ever sucked the breast. O.M. 1754. *Y vam pan y'n drchevys*, his mother when she reared him. M.C. 10. *Gans y vam y fyê guris*, by his mother it was made. M.C. 161. W. *mam*. Arm. *mamm*. Manx, *mummig*. (Ir. †*mam*, a breast.) Gr. μάμμα. Pers. *mama*. Span. *mama*. Syr. Carn. *mama*. Eng. *mama*. (Lat. *mamma*, a breast.) Sansc. *ma*. Gr. μαῖα. Coptic, *maa*. Malay, *maa*. *Mam*, a mother, is confined to the three British Dialects of the Celtic; the equivalent in the Erse being Ir. *mathair*. Gael. *mathair*. Manx, *moir*. Gr. μήτηρ. Lat. *mater*. Sansc. *mátar*; the primary meaning being a *maker*, from *má*, to form or fashion. Lith. *mote, motina*. Russ. *mater, mat*. Germ. *mutter*. Eng. *mother*.

MAM, comp. pron. That—me. *My a'd pcys, arluth uhel, dhe'n týr ty a ry cummyas, ma'm (ma-ym) gasso kyns ys myrwel, ynno bós dhym dhe welas*, I pray thee, high Lord, that thou wilt give leave to the earth, that it allow me before dying, to seek for myself food in it. O.M. 377.

MAMAID, s. f. A nursing or foster-mother, a nurse. Corn. Voc. *altrix* vel *nutrix*. To be read as by Llwyd, 101, *mammaith*. Comp. of *mam*, and *maith*, ld. qd. *macth*, nurture. W. *mammaeth*. Irish, *muime*. Gael. *muime*.

MAN, s. f. A space, a spot, a trifle, nought. *A vâp, ny*

MANEG 245 MAR

dâl koles man, an pŷth a dhue gwelis veydh, O son, it avails not to conceal any thing, the thing that comes will be seen. O.M. 653. *Arluth whêk, ny amonnt man an pyt a wrussyuch,* sweet lord, the pit (that) you made avails not any thing. O.M. 2791. *Nyns yw henna man,* that is not any thing. P.C. 2339. *Rak dall ôf, ny welaf man,* for I am blind, I see not at all. P.C. 3014. W. *man.*

MAN, s. m. A stone. *Kyn fe dyswrys an temple dhe'n dôr, na safê mân, me a'n dreha artê kyns pen trydydh,* though the temple should be destroyed to the ground, that a stone does not stand, I will build it again before the end of three days. P.C. 345. *Mân pobas,* a bakestone. *Llwyd,* 48. A contracted form of *mean,* qd. v.

MAN, comp. conj. That—him, it; that, so that, as. *(Ma— yn.) Nep ma'n ressys dhe wethé, dheworth henna govynné (govyn e,)* he to whom thou gavest him to keep, from that one demand him. O.M. 574. *Un deydh a dhue yredy, ma'n talvedhaf oll dhywchy,* a day shall come surely, that I will repay it all to you. P.C. 269. *Pûr wŷr y tue vyngcans tyn warnouch, ma'n gueller a ver termyn,* very truly sharp vengeance will come upon you, as will be seen in a short time. P.C. 1940. *Me a'n knouk fest dybyté, ma'n geffo pûp ol bysné, ow myres worth y vody,* I will beat him hard without pity, that all may have shuddering, looking at his body. P.C. 2092.

MAN, adv. Upwards. A mutation of *ban. Drehevys man,* roused up. *Ro nian do higa,* give up to play. *Pryce.* See *Anan.*

MAN, v. s. He will. Another form of *men* or *myn,* 3 pers. s. fut. of *menny* or *mynny,* qd. v. *Mar man Dew, râg an gwella my a lever yn templa wharé servys dhodho ef,* if God will, for the best I will say in the temple service forthwith to him. O.M 2620.

MANACH, s. m. A monk. Corn. Voc. *monachus.* In late Cornish the guttural was softened into *h.* ‡ *Gûn an manah,* the gown of the monk. ‡ *Hi a kynsilias gan ndwyn vanah,* she plotted with a certain monk. ‡ *Ha e glywas an manah laveral,* and he heard the monk speak. *Llwyd,* 252. W. *mynach,* † *monach,* pl. † *menchi.* Arm. *manach, monach.* Ir. *manach.* Gael. *manach.* All from the Latin.

MANAES, s. f. A nun, a female recluse. Corn. Vocab. *monacha vel monialis.* W. *mynaches,* † *manaches.* Arm. *manaches.*

MANAF, v. a. I will. A late form of *mennaf,* 1 pers. s. fut. of *menny. Râg henna, benyn vâs Eva, genas ny vanaf flattra, na ny vanaf usya gow,* therefore, good woman Eve, with thee I will not flatter, nor will I use a lie. C.W. 48.

MANAL, s. m. A handful, a gripe. *Manal ŷs,* a sheaf of corn. *Llwyd,* 33, 241. From the Latin *manipulus.*

MANAN, conj. Unless, if not. *(Ma—na'n.) Camen Pylat pan welas na ylly Crist delyffré, manan geffo ef sor brâs dheworth oll an gowethé, râg henna ef a juggyas Ihesu dhedhé dh'y ladhé,* Pilate, when he saw that he could not any way deliver Christ, unless he should have great anger from all the assemblage, for that he adjudged Jesus to them to kill him. M.C. 150.

MANEG, s. f. A glove. Pl. *manegow. Dre ow thrŷs y tûth un smat gans kentrow d'aga gorré; y fue ow manegow plut, spyggys brâs dre ow dywlé,* through my feet a fellow came with nails to put them; my smooth gloves were great spikes through my hands. R.D. 2589. *Llwyd,* 15, 47, 243, writes it *manag, manak, manck,* pl. *menik.* ‡ *An manak adro'z dorn,* the glove on your hand. 250. W. *maneg,* pl. *menig.* Arm. *manec, maneg,* pl. *manegou.* Ir. *maineog,* † *manic.* Gael. *manaig.* All from the Lat. *manica.*

MANERLICH, adj. Valiant. *My a'd pŷs, messyger, dôg manerlich ow baner del vynny bôs rewardyys,* I pray thee, messenger, carry my banner valiantly, as thou wishest to be rewarded. O.M. 2200.

MANNO, adv. Often, many times. *Llwyd,* 143. A late corruption of *menouch,* qd. v.

MANNO, comp. conj. That not. *Besy yw dhys bôs vuell, ha spernabyll y'th servys, manno allo an tebell ogas dhys bonas trylys,* it is needful for thee to be humble, and despicable in thy service, that the evil one may not be turned near thee. M.C. 19. It would have been more correctly written *manna, (ma-na.)*

MANS, adj. Maimed, lame. Cornish Vocab. *mancus.* Arm. *mank, monk, mons.*

MANSEC, adj. Stony. *Killy-mansek,* the stony grove. *Pryce.*

MANTEDH, s. m. Stone in the bladder or kidneys. *Clevas y mantedh,* the disease of the stone. *Llwyd,* 80.

MANTEL, s. f. A mantle, a cloak. Corn. Voc. *mantellum. Dhe vantel gûs yn gage, my a'n bŷdh râg ow wage,* the mantle leave thou in pledge, I will have it for my wages. P.C. 1186. *Dyskyn y vantel wharré, râg yn y dhyllas artê an harlot a vŷdh gwyskys,* let us take off his mantle soon, for in his clothes again the knave shall be dressed. P.C. 2531. W. *mantell.* Arm. *mantel.* Ir. † *matal.* Gael. *manntal.* Germ. *mantel.*

MANULE, s. m. A manual book. *Llwyd,* 86. Lat. *manuale.*

MANYN, s. m. Butter. *Llwyd,* 45. An abbreviated form of *amenen,* qd. v.

MAOS, v. n. To go. ‡ *Maos a leaz,* to go abroad. ‡ *Maos dhan dre,* to go home, to return. *Llwyd,* 129, 137. A late form of *môs,* qd. v.

MAOZ, s. f. A maid. *Llwyd,* 38. A later form of *mowes,* qd. v.

MAP, s. m. A son. See *Mâb. Meppig,* a little son, qd. v.

MAR, conj. If. It often takes *a* after it, and aspirates the initials following. *Mar a tybbryth a henna,* if thou eat of that. O.M. 61. *An kêth frût-na mar a'n gâs,* that same fruit if he leaves it. O.M. 192. *Mar a pe,* if it was. O.M. 211. *Ena tûs mar a kafuf,* if I find the people there. O.M. 341. *Mar qurên flôch vŷth denythy,* if we do children ever produce. O.M. 390. *Mar myn Dew,* if God wills. O.M. 650. *Mar tue nêp gwâs ha laddré,* if any fellow comes and steals. O.M. 2064. *Mar pedhaf kelmys lemmyn,* if I shall be bound now. O.M. 1349. *Mara peys pell,* if it drops long. O.M. 1082. *Mar a crustê leverel,* if thou didst say. P.C. 1758. Before vowels *mars* is always used, qd. v., or rather an *s* is prefixed as *mar sos, &c.,* and also after *mar a. Mara sosé mâp Dew mûr,* if thou art the Son of the great God. P.C. 2867. Arm. *mar.* Ir. *mar.* Gael. *mar.*

MAR, adv. So, so much as. *Mar dha yw genef a vrŷs, mervel kyns dôs drôk ancow,* so well it is, in my opinion, to die before evil sorrow comes. O.M. 1229. *Mar vûr me re pechas,* so greatly I have sinned. P.C. 1519. *Ha saw ny gynes yn wêdh, na'm beyn mar hager dhywedh na mar garow,* and save us with thee also, that we may not have so cruel an end, nor so rough. P.C. 2895.

It softens the initial following. W. *mor.* Ir. *mar.* Gael. *mar.*

MAR, s. m. A doubt, a doubting. *Yma kên dhym dhe olé daggrow goys yn gwŷr, hep mar,* there is cause to me to weep truly tears of blood, without doubt. O.M. 631. *Nys tevé tûs vŷth, hep mar, roow mar dhu,* never have people received, without doubt, gifts so good. O.M. 2597. *Me a wodhvyth yn ûr-na pŷth yw dhe gallos, hep mar,* I shall know in that hour what thy power is, without doubt. P.C. 64.

MAR, adj. Much, many. *Syngys mâr ôn dhe Iudas, râk ef a'm hembroncas pûr compys bŷs yn losel,* much obliged we are to Judas, for he conducted me very straight to the rogue. P.C. 1204. A contracted form of *mear*, qd. v.

MARADGYON, s. m. Wonders. *Pryce.* A late corruption of *marthegion*, qd. v.

MARBURAN, s. f. A raven. Corn. Voc. *corvus*. More correctly *marchvran*, qd. v.

MARCH, s. m. A horse. Corn. Voc. *equus*. Pl. *merch*. *Ydhanvonf buch ha tarow, ha march yw bêst hep parow dhe vâp den râg ymweres,* I name cow and bull, and horse, (that) is a beast without equals for the son of man to help himself. O.M. 124. *Na gousé moy ys march dall,* that he speak no more than a blind horse. P.C. 1658. *Merch, gwarthck, mô ch, ha deves, dreuch abervedh desempys,* horses, cattle, pigs, and sheep, bring ye within forthwith. O.M. 1065. In late Cornish it was softened into *marh.* W. *march,* pl. *meirch.* Arm. *march.* Ir. † *marc,* pl. *mairc.* Gael. † *marc.* Ancient Gaulish, *marcos,* pl. *marci.* (τριμαρκισία, in Pausanias.) Cf. Eng. *mare, marshall.*

MARCHAS, s. f. A market. Pl. *marchasow. Yn chy Dew marsus marchas, me a's chas yn mês pûp gwâs, hag a tevyl aga guara,* if there is a market in God's house, I will drive them out, every fellow, and will overturn their wares. P.C. 316. *Yn chy Dew ny goth marchas termyn vŷth ol war nêp cor,* in the house of God a market is not becoming at any time, on any account. P.C. 2419. *Euch dhe wovyn, hep lettyé, worth an gôf yn marchas row,* go ye to ask without delaying, of the smith in Market Row. P.C. 2668. W. *marchnad.* Arm. *marchad.* Ir. and Gael. *margadh.* Manx, *mergee.* Lat. *mercatus.*

MARCHVRAN, s. f. A raven. *Gwŷr dhym ty a dharyvas, an varchvran-na dh'y whelé; yma war garynnyas brâs ow lybry fest dybytê,* truth to me thou hast told, to look for that mven; it is upon great carrion, eating fast without pity. O.M. 1106. Comp. of *march,* a horse, and *brân,* a crow. *March* is used similarly in Welsh to strengthen the meaning; as *march-daran,* loud thunder; *marchleidyr,* an arrant thief; *marchvorion,* the large winged ants, &c. A raven is called in Welsh, *cigvran.* Legonidec gives *malvran,* as the Armoric synonym, which seems connected with W. *mulvran,* a cormorant.

MARH, s. m. A horse, a steed. Pl. *merh.* Llwyd, 243. ‡ *Marh bian,* a little horse, or colt. 57. *An marh-na,* that horse. ‡ *Po marh ledres,* when a horse is stolen. 232. ‡ *Ma marh dhy bredar vi,* my brother has a horse. 242. In ‡ *buzl verh,* horse dung; ‡ *rên verh,* horse hair; Llwyd considers *verh,* to be a genitive case singular, an anomaly in the British dialects. I am more inclined to consider it as the regular plural form. ‡ *Mous dha'n gôv dha herniah an verh,* go to the smith to shoe the horses. *Pryce.* This is a later form of *march,* qd. v.

MARHAR, s. m. Mercury. *De Marhar,* dies Mercurii, Wednesday. Llwyd 15, 54. W. *mercher, dŷdh mercher.* Arm. *mercher, di-mercher.* Lat. *mercurius.*

MARHAS, s. f. A market. Pl. *marhasow. Ef re dhystcrug an marhas; yma ow kûl maystry brâs,* he has destroyed the market; he is doing great violence. P.C. 376. *Why gwycoryon, euch yn mês; ydhesouch ow kuthyl ges a Dhu hag e sans eglos, yn ow thy a piyadow pan wrcuch agas marhasow, ha fowys, dhe laddron plos,* ye traders, go out; ye are making a jest of God and his holy church, in my house of prayers when ye make your markets, and a den for foul thieves. P.C. 335. ‡ *Telhar marhas,* a market place. Llwyd, 61. Another form of *marchas,* qd. v., *ch* being softened into *h.*

MARHEG, s. m. A horseman, knight, cavalier; hence a soldier in general. Written also *marrec,* pl. *marregion, marrogion, marrougion. Pan dethens y bŷs yn bêdh, ydh éth un marrck dh'y ben, hag arall dh'y dreys yn wêdh, yrvys fast bŷs yn dheweu,* when they came to the grave, one soldier went to his head, and another to his feet also, armed quite to the jaws. M.C. 242. *Ha war tu trê fystenens kefrys marrck ha squyer,* and let knight and squire hasten towards home. O.M. 2003. *Del oma marrek lên, venytha ny dhôf a'n plen, erna'n prenné an gwâs-na,* as I am a trusty knight, I will never come from the place until I take that fellow. O.M. 2150. *Marreyyon me agas pŷs gorrcuch ef dhe Erod scon,* horsemen, I pray you, take him to Herod soon. P.C. 1613. *Euch lemmyn ow marreggyon yn bêdh,* go now, my knights into the tomb. R.D. 301. *Dûn alemma marrougyon,* let us go hence knights. O.M. 1039. *En varogyon a guskas myttyn,* the soldiers slept at morning. M.C. 243. This must have been originally *marchce.* W. *marchawg,* † *marchauc.* Arm. *marchec, marhec.* Ir. *marcach.* Gael. *maraach.* Manx, *markiagh.*

MARNAS, s. m. Death. Llwyd, 72, 76. A later form of *mernans,* qd. v.

MARNAS, conj. Unless, except. Written also *marnes. Hep gûl dyel a ver speys war pêp ol marnas ty,* without executing vengeance in a short time on all except thee. O.M. 946. *Nyns â dên vŷth vynytha a'n kêth rê-na dhe'n tŷr sans, marnas Calef ha Iosué,* not any man shall ever go of those same to the holy land, except Caleb and Joshua. O.M. 1880. *Marnes dredhos, Vernona, ny'm bŷdh gweres,* unless through thee, Veronica, there will be no help to me. R.D. 2220. *Râk me a wôr lour, denses, marnes dre an luen duses, omma ny sêf,* for I know well enough, manhood, unless through the full Godhead, here will not remain. R.D. 2515.

MARNY, conj. If not, unless. (*Mar-ny.*) *Tokyn dhyuch marny dhyswé,* a token to you unless I show. P.C. 343. *Arlothes kêr my a wra agas nygys fystyné, dyspyl dhe vyrch Thedama marny'n gwarnyaf scon wharré,* dear lady, I will hasten your errand, despite thy daughter Thedama, if I do not warn him very soon. P.C. 1968. *Marni,* Llwyd, 249.

MAROGETH, v. a. To act as a horseman, to ride. *Ow messyger, kyrch ow courser dhe varogeth,* my messenger, fetch my courser to ride. O.M. 1900. *My a vyn a dhysempys marogeth waré bŷs ty,* I will immediately ride, presently, even to it. O.M. 1971. *Marogeth my ny alla, yma cleves y'm body,* I cannot ride, there is a disease in my body. O.M. 2145. This would have been more correctly written *marhogeth, marchogeth*, and is the same as W. *marchogaeth.* Arm. *marchecaat.* Ir. *marcaidh.* Gael. *marcaich.* Manx, *mark.*

MAROW, adj. Dead, deceased, lifeless. *Yn grows gans kentrow fastis, peynys bŷs pan ve marow*, fastened on a cross with nails, tortured till he was dead. M.C. 2. *Ena un lowarth esé, ha ynno bêdh ve parys dên marow râg recevé*, there was a garden there, and in it a tomb was prepared to receive a dead man. M.C. 233. *Yn més alemma ty â, hag a fŷdh marow vernans*, out of this place thou shalt go, and shalt die the death. O.M. 84. *Kyn feva ledhys marow dre mûr peyn ha galarow, ny'th ty nahaf bynary*, though I be killed dead by great pain and sorrows, I will never deny thee. P.C. 905. W. *marw,* † *maru*, pl. *meirw.* Arm. *marô*, † *maru.* Ir. *marbh.* Gael. *marbh.* Manx, *marroo*, pl. *merroo, mcirroo.* Old Celtic, *marvos.* Sansc. *marías, (mar* to die.*)* Lat. *mortuus.* Lith. *mirtas.* Sansc. *mâras*, death. Gr. μόρος. Lith. *maras.* Cf. *morimarusa*, the dead sea, in Macrobius.

MARS, conj. If. Used before a vowel, as *mar* is before a consonant. *Da yw yn més dyllo brân, mars ûs dôr sêch war an beys*, it is good to send forth a crow, if there is dry ground on the world. O.M. 1100. *Hy a wra aspyé, mars ûs dôr sêch yn nêp pow*, she will look out, if there is dry land in any country. O.M. 1116. *Cowyth, profynn an styllyow, mars êns compos dhe'n fosow*, comrades, let us try the rafters, if they are straight to the walls. O.M. 2472. *Mars ellen hep cous orty, hy holon hy a torsé*, if I should go without speaking to her, her heart would break. O.M. 2173. *Mars euch lemyn més a dré, nefré ny dhebraf vara*, if yon go now away from home, I will never eat bread. O.M. 2185. *Neffré mars êth ahanan*, if thou wilt ever go from us. O.M. 2652. *Yn chy Dew mars ues marchas*, in the house of God if there is a market. P.C. 316. *Arluth, leverel dym gwra, mars ôf vy an kêth henna*, Lord, do thou tell me, if I am that same. P.C. 742. *Mars yw dhe vôdh*, if it is thy will. P.C. 1088. In the Ordinalia the *s* is joined to the next word, as *mar ses, mar syw, &c.*

MARS, conj. Unless, except. Another form of *marnas.* *Hag a'n doro dhe anken, mars ny a wra ymdenné*, and will bring us to sorrow, unless we do refrain. O.M. 226. *Yma dout dhym pûr dhuffry mars ef a'n creys, nug usy aberth yn fus*, there is fear to me, unless he believe it, that he is not within the faith. R.D. 1217. *Ny welaf vy ydh hallan sawyé ow bewnans, mars dre mûr our*, I do not see that I can save my life, unless by much gold. R.D. 1964. *Mars Cryst a weres deffry*, unless Christ helps indeed. R.D. 2132.

MARTESEN, adv. Perhaps, possibly. *Pûp cowyth ol prydyrys, martesen vŷdh yn y urŷs desmygy pren vûs ple fô*, let every comrade consider, perhaps it will be in his mind to shew where there may be a good tree. P.C. 2541. *Dyswé ran a'th veystry ; hag yn ûr-na martesen dhe'th lavarow y cresen, hag a'th carvyth bynary*, shew a portion of thy power, and then perhaps we might believe thy words, and love thee for ever. P.C. 2870. Arm. *martezé.* Derived, by Legonidec, from *mar*, if, *te*, should come, and *se* or *ze*, that, "if that should happen."

MARTH, s. m. A wonder, miracle, marvel, prodigy. Pl. *marthow. Yn mêdh Pylat, marth a'm bes, kymmys drôk a wodhevyth*, says Pilate, it is a marvel to me, how much evil thou endurest. M.C. 120. *Mûr a varth brâs yw henna dhym*, much of great wonder is that to me. M.C. 157. *Marth yw gené*, it is a wonder to me, i. e. I am surprised. *Marth yn teffry ûs dhym lemmyn*, a wonder really there is to me now. O.M. 1300. *Yma marth dhym a un dra*, there is a wonder to me of one thing. O.M. 1395. *Ahanas marth a'n gefes*, a wonder of thee has seized him. O.M. 1484. *Pyth yw an marth a wharfé*, what is the wonder which has occurred ? R.D. 1263. *Tewolgow brâs a ve guris, an houl a gollas y feth, ha moy marthus me a grŷs, ys an rê-na ve yn wêdh*, great darkness was made, the sun lost his face, and I believe there were also more wonders than those. M.C. 200. Arm. *marz.*

MARTHEGION, s. m. Wonders. Written also *marthogion. Yma mûr a varthogion a'n kêth gyst-ma warvethys*, there are many wonders by this same beam wrought. O.M. 2546. *Yma dhym mûr varthegyon*, there are to me many wonders. P.C. 770. *Nag-ues ioy y 'ges colon lemyn dar nêp marthegyon ûs wharfethys*, there is not joy in your heart now, through some wonders (that) have happened. R.D. 1259. This is a corruption (*g* soft,) of *marthusion*, pl. of *marthus.*

MARTHUS, s. f. A wonder, a miracle. Pl. *marthusow, (marthusion) marthegyon. Scruth own mûr a's kemeras, râg an marthus re welsens*, a shiver of great fear seized them at the marvel they saw. M.C. 254. *Saw an wedhen, dhym ymu hy bôs sychys marthys vrâs*, but the tree, it is to me a great wonder that it is dry. O.M. 756. *Mars ôs Dew a nêf golow, dysqua lemman marthusow, may allyf vy y welés*, if thou art the God of bright heaven, shew now miracles, that I may see them. P.C. 82. See *Varthegyon.*

MARTHUSEC, adj. Wonderful, marvellous. *Arluth, assyw varthusek, pan dhueth, Ihesu gallosek, dh'agan myras*, Lord, it is wonderful, when thou comest, Jesus powerful, to see us. R.D. 1177.

MARTHYS, adj. Wonderful, marvellous, miraculous. *Galsof coyth ha marthys gwan*, I am become old and wondrous weak. O.M. 855. *Ow colon yw marthys clâf*, my heart is wondrous sick. O.M. 1337. *Yma hûn orth ow gryvyé marthys yn vrûs*, sleep is grieving me wondrous greatly. O.M. 1922. *Râk marthys ycyn yw an gwyns*, for wondrous cold is the wind. P.C. 1215. *Kepar del y 'gys prynnys, marthys yn tyn*, like as I have redeemed ye wondrous painfully. R.D. 181.

MARU, s. m. Marrow. *Lloyd*, 15, 87. W. *mêr.* Arm. *mél.* Ir. *smior.* Gael. *smear.* Manx, *smuir.* O. Norse, *smior*, butter. Germ. *schmier.* Eng. *smear.* Sansc. *mraks*, to anoint.

MARWEL, v. n. To die, to become dead. *Me a grŷs y kemersé wêth an vŷl kyngys marwel*, I believe the vile (man) would take it yet, before dying. P.C. 324. *Pan varwo, gorry (gor-y) hep ful yntré y dhŷns ha'y davas*, when he dies, put them without fail between his teeth and his tongue. O.M. 825. *Ellas, na varwen yn wêdh*, alas, that I die not also. P.C. 2046. *Pan o Ihesus Cryst dampnys, aberth an crows may farwé*, when Jesus Christ was condemned, upon the cross that he should die. M.C. 151. Written also *merwel*, and *myrwel*, qd. v.

MAS, conj. But, unless. *Râg nyns ouch mas dew lorel*, for ye are nought but two vagabonds. O.M. 1504. *Ny fue ragdho y honan y'n godhefys ef, nus râk kerengé máp dên*, it was not for himself he suffered it, but for love of the son of man. P.C. 3228. *Mas dhe wel y'm gorthebouch fast prysonys why a vŷdh*, unless ye answer me the better, fast imprisoned ye shall be. R.D. 47. *Wy yw glán a bûb fyltê, mas nynj ouch ol da na whêk*, ye are pure from every foulness, but ye are not all good nor sweet. M.C. 47. *Mas lemmyn rŷs yw porrys batayles kyns ys coské*, but now it is needful, very needful, to battle rather than sleep. M.C. 51. Written also *mes*. Fr. *mais*. Sp. *mas*.

MAS, adj. Good, beneficial. In construction it changes into *vás*, and *fás*. *Del ogé dên más*, as thou art a good man. O.M. 1767. *Lavar dhymmo, cowyth más*, tell me, good fellow. P.C. 602. *An dûs vás a dheserya dhedhé gwlás néf o kyllys*, the good folk desired for themselves the country of heaven, (that) was lost. M.C. 4. *Kymmys yn bŷs ús vás, ty a fŷdh*, as much as is good in the world, thou shalt have. M.C. 16. *Dhymmo evredhek yn wêdh, ro nerth dhe gerdhes yn fás*, to me also, tho maimed, give power to walk well. O.M. 2010. *Mar ny wonedhons yn fás, y a's tevyl anfugy*, if they do not work well, they shall have sorrow. O.M. 2327. *Más* is a later form of *mâd*, or as written in the Corn. Vocab. *mat; bennen vnt*, a good woman. W. *mâd*, †*mat*. Arm. *mâd, mat*. Ir. *math, maith*, †*maid*. Gael. *math*. Manx, *mie*.

MATERN, s. m. A king, a sovereign. *Llwyd*. 140. Written also in late Cornish, *materyn*. ‡ *Cara, gordhya, ha owna Dew, an mateyrn, ha'n lahes, en guz plew ; owna Dew, parthy muteyrn, ha cara goz contrevogion*, love, worship, and fear God, the king, and the laws, in your parish ; fear God, honour the king, and love your neighbours. *Pryce*. The older form is *mychtern*, qd. v. W. *mydeyrn*.

MATERNAS, s. f. A queen. *Pryce*. A late form of *michternas*, qd. v.

MATOBERUR, s. m. A foul reproachful act. Such is the explanation given by Llwyd, 128, under *probrum*. An evident mistake ; it should have been placed under the next word *probus*, good ; being compounded of *mât*, good, and *oberur*, a worker.

MAUR, adj. Great, large, big. Corn. Voc. *magnus*. In the Ordinalia it is generally written *meur*, and *múr*, qd. v. W. *mawr*, †*maur*. Arm. *meûr*. Ir. *mór*, †*már*. Gael. *mór*. Manx, *mooar*. Gaulish, *máros*. Gr. μάρος. Sansc. *mara*. Germ. *mehr*. Eng. *more*.

MAW, s. m. A boy, a child, a lad, a youth, a servant. *Dhodho ef me a'n vossaw, epscop pryns doctor ha maw, dhe'n iustis Pylat arté, euch ganso yn kettep pen*, to him I will scud him, bishop, prince, doctor, and boy, to the justice Pilate again, go with him every head. P.C. 1794. *Lemmyn taw, dhys ny fynnaf bones maw*, now be silent, I will not be a servant to thee. P.C. 2281. *Gwask dhe waw a'n scoveron, pan fy ef, gans múr a nel*, strike thy servant on the car, when he is so, with much force. P.C. 2287. Another form of *mâb*, qd. v.

MAY, conj. That. It aspirates the initials following. *An gusyl o may fe dris dhe rág Crist pehadures*, the counsel was that a sinful woman should be brought before Christ. M.C. 32. *Me a ra dhe Crist ammé may hallouch y asweonvos*, I will kiss Christ that ye may be able to know him. M.C. 63. *Pandra yw dhe nygys, mar hŷr fordh dús may fynsys*, what is thy errand, that thou wouldst come so long a way ? O.M. 734. *Yn keth fordh-na may kyrdhys*, in that same road that I went. O.M. 713. *Yn pow may 'dh ê, ef a sawyé an glevyon*, in the country that he was, he healed the sick. M.C. 25. *Yn le may 'dh ên, yn trevow, yn splan me a's derevas*, in the place that I was, in towns clearly I declared them. M.C. 79. *En gŷdh o devow hablys, may fenné Iesus sopyé*, the day was Maunday Thursday, that Jesus would sup. M.C. 41. *Rág an termen re devé, may fŷdh an begel kyllys*, for the time has come that the shepherd shall be lost. M.C. 48. *Clew ge ow lêf, maym bové grás wosé hemma*, hear thou my voice, that there be to me grace hereafter. C.W. 104. W. *mai*. Arm. *maz*.

MAYLE, v. a. To wrap, to swathe. Written also *maylyé*. Part. pass. *maylys, maylyes*. *Máb Dew o nêb a wylsys, avel flôch byhan maylys*, the Son of God it was whom thou sawest, like a little child swathed. O.M. 810. *Iosep whêk, reseew e dhys, hag yn cendal glán maylyé*, sweet Joseph, receive him to thee, and wrap him in clean linen. P.C. 3156. *Lemmyn mayl e yn lyen*, now wrap thou him in linen. P.C. 3204. *Me a'n mayl scon, war ow feydh*, I will wrap him soon on my faith. P.C. 3205. *Scon me a re clout dhodho, may ro'n maylé war an dôr*, soon I will give him a clout, that shall wrap him on the earth. R.D. 388. *Gás vy lemmyn dh'y huré, yn queth kyns ys y vaylé*, let me now to embalm him, before wrapping him in a cloth. P.C. 3197.

MAYN, s. m. A mean, a medium. *Rág bonas 'gan pêch mar vâr, mayn yntredhé a ve gurys*, because our sin was so great, a mean was made between them. M.C. 8. Ir. †*medon*. Med. Lat. *medianus*. Fr. *moyen*. See *Mein*.

MAYN, s. m. A friend, an intimate. Pl. *mayny*. *Me a wór dhe gollenwel an romys ên yn néf, der ow góth brás, a voyd dredhaf, ha'w mayny*, I know to fill up the rooms that in heaven, through my great pride, are void by me and my friends. C.W. 36.

MAYTETH, s. f. A maiden. ‡ *Ow lêf oll yta changys avel mayteth yn devery*, my voice is all changed like to a maiden truly. C.W. 40. *Me a wêl un mayteth whêg ow sedha*, I see a sweet maiden sitting. C.W. 132. This is a late form of *machteth*, qd. v. *Maythys* is another form. ‡ *Te nyn kymmer kyrath warlyrch y den whêl, nyn warlyrch y maythys*, thou shalt not take a longing after his man-servant, nor his maid. *Pryce*.

ME, pr. s. I, me. In construction it changes into *ve*. *Deuch geneff ha holyouch ve, godhvedhouch an rellouch tros, hu me a ra dhe Crist amiué, may hallouch y asweonvos*, come ye with me, and follow me, see that ye do not make a noise ; I will kiss Christ, that yo may be able to know him. M.C. 63. *Me yw máb Du yredy, Crist a leveris dhedhé*, I am the Son of God indeed, Christ said to them. M.C. 197. *Pa'n dra a woventé se dheworthaff ve ha'm lahys*, what thou wouldst ask of me and my laws. M.C. 80. *Me a welas*, I saw. O.M. 804. *Me a vyn môs*, I will go. O.M. 1252. Written equally common *mi*. Arm. *me*. Ir. *mi*. Manx, *mee*. Gr. μέ. Lat. *me*. Goth. *mik*. Germ. *mich*. Eng. *me*. Fr. *moi*. Span. *me*. It, *mi, me*. Sansc. *ma, me*.

ME, s. m. May. *Mis mé*, the mouth of May. *Llwyd*, 14, 84. W. *mai*. Arm. *mae, me*. Gael. *màigh*. From the Lat. *maius*.

MEAN, s. m. A stone. *Méan pobas*, a bake stone. *Méan bian*, a little stone or pebble. *An méan lêr*, the foundation. *Mé an plymon*, a plumstone. Llwyd, 45, 60, 110. Another form of *maen*, qd. v.

MEAR, adj. Great, large, big; many, much. *Púr vear*, very abundantly. Pryce. A late form of *maur*, qd. v., and written also *mêr*, qd. v.

MEAS, s. m. A field. *A meas, yn meas*, abroad, without, out. *Dôs a méas*, to go out. Llwyd, 129. A later form of *macs*, or *mês*, qd. v.

MEAWL, s. m. Bad luck, mischief. *How geyler plos, re'th fo meawl*, ho! dirty jailor, a mischief to thee. R.D. 70. Written also *meul*, qd. v.

MEBION, s. m. Sons, boys. *Maister mebion*, pedagogus, a schoolmaster, lit. a master of boys. Corn. Voc. *Ow mebyon, my a gy peys, yn mês whêt dyllcuch'tryssé*, my sons, I pray you, send outside yet a third. O.M. 1129. Plural of *máb*, qd. v.

MECHIEC, adj. Stinking. Llwyd, 132.

MEDDONS, v. a. They will. Llwyd, 246. A late corruption of *mennôns*, 3 pers. pl. fut. of *menny*, qd. v.

MEDE, v. a. To reap, to mow. Corrupted in late Cornish into *medgé*. ‡ *Whelas megouzion dha medgé an ís*, look for reapers to reap the corn. Pryce. Written also *midi*, qd. v.

MEDER, s. m. A reaper, a mower. "A mower is still called *meader, meter*, in Cornwall." Polwhele. W. *medwr*.

MEDINOR, s. f. A hinge. Corn. Voc. *cardo*. Arm. *mudurun*.

MEDRA, v. a. To behold. ‡ *Bydh ware dhym na vova dên, rág me ny allaff medra*, be cautious for me that it be not a man, for I can not discern it. C.W. 112. This is a late corruption of *mira*, qd. v. Llwyd, 231.

MEDRY, v. a. To be able. ‡ *Mar nys medra dheffa previ pew a ryg an badober, mi a vedn krêg ragta*, if I cannot prove who did the evil deed, I will be hanged for it. Llwyd, 252. W. *medru*. Ir. *feidir, eidir*. Gael. *murrach*.

MEDJI, s. f. Shame, bashfulness. *Médh vfjdh ol d'agen chen*, all shame it will be to our class. O.M. 2066. *Arluth, golhy mara qurêth ow threys, dhym y fyé médh*, Lord, if thou dost wash my feet, it would be a shame to me. P.C. 846. *My ny fedhaf rák médh dôs yn mfjsk ow brudereth*, I shall not for shame come among my brethren. P.C. 1429. *A wûl drók nyn gefê médh yn y dhydhow*, to do evil he had no shame in his days. R.D. 1784. W. *cuweydh*. Arm. *mez*.

MEDIJ, s. m. Mead, a fermented liquor made with honey and water. *Ow bannath dhyso Gryffyn, ty a lefes yn dhefé; mar ny gevyth médh py gwfjn, ke dhe fenten dhe evé*, my blessing to thee, Gryffyn, thou shoutedst in thy faith; if thou find not mead or wine, go to the fountain to drink. O.M. 2434. Written in the Cornish Vocabulary, *medu, meddou*, medum. W. *médh*, †*med*. Arm. †*mez*. Ir. *meadh*, †*med*. Gael. *meadh*. Gr. μέθυ. O.H.G. *metu*. Lith. *medus*, (honey.) Sansc. *madhu; mada, mad*, to intoxicate.

MEDHA, v. a. To be ashamed. *Mar ny vedhaf ow desyr, neffré ny'n geelaf omma, medhan, un spyes*, if I shall not have my desire, I will not see him one while here, I should be ashamed. C.W. 60. Arm. *meza*.

MEDHAL, adj. Soft, mollient, tender. *Ow spyrys ny drîje nefré yn corf máp dên vfjth yn beys, ha reson yw ha praga, rág y vôs kfje medhel gurfjs*, my spirit shall not dwell always in the body of any soul of man in the world; and reason is, and why, for that he is made of soft flesh. O.M. 928. In Llwyd's time it was pronounced *meddal*. 29. And so it was when Jordan wrote. *Rág y vôs kfjg meddal gurfjs*, for that he is made of soft flesh. C.W. 162. W. *medhal*. Arm. *pezel*, †*mezel*. Ir. †*muadh*. Manx, *mecley*. Sansc. *pésala*.

MEDHALDER, s. m. Softness, tenderness, mildness, gentleness. Written by Llwyd, 240, as pronounced in his time *medalder*. W. *medhalder*.

MEDHDAS, s. m. Drunkenness, intoxication. Llwyd, 52. W. *medhwdod*.

MEDIIEC, s. m. A physician. Corn. Voc. *medicus*. *Dhodho gueyt may taufenny Cryst, bfjs yn daras y chy, dres pûp medhek del yw flour*, to him take care that thou send Christ, even to the door of his house, as he is the flower above every leech. R.D. 1632. *An emprour re'u dunfonas a whylas yn pow gweras; dhodho yma cloves brás, ny gfjf medhek a'n sawya*, the emperor has sent me to seek help in the country; he has a great malady, he finds not a leech who can cure him. R.D. 1048. W. *medhyg*. Arm. *mezek*. From the Latin.

MEDHECNAID, s. m. Physic, medicine. Corn. Voc. *medecina*. A later form is *mydhygycth*, qd. v. W. *medhyginiaeth*. Arm. †*mezekiez*.

MEDHES, v. a. To speak, to say. *Eva, ny allaf medhes, rág owen ty dhom kuhudhé*, Eve, I cannot speak, for fear thou shouldst accuse me. O.M. 159. *Kyn fallens oll, me a vedh, yn médh Pedyr, y'th servis; yn médh Crist yn nôs haneth, kyns ys boys colyck clewys, Pedyr, te a'm nách terqweth*, though all fail, says Peter, I shall be in thy service; says Christ, this very night before a cock is heard, Peter, thou shalt deny me thrice. M.C. 49. *Yn medhens y, ny'n gordhyn*, say they, we will not worship him. M.C. 148. *Yn médh an g6ff, me ny wrdjff pûr wfjr kentrow dhewy vfjth; yn medhens, mar omwereyth cláff; gordhewyth le a'n prenvyth*, says the smith, I will not very truly make nails for you ever; say they, if thou makest thyself sick, very diligently thou shalt pay for it. M.C. 155. *Kemmys ew gans y murnys, aga holon ew terrys rág enrow, medhaf y dy*, so much is it by them mourned, their hearts are broken for grief, I say to thee. C.W. 98. It only occurs in the present tense, which is thus inflected; *medhaf, medhys, médh;* pl. *medhon, medhoh, medhens.* (See Llwyd, 247.) W. *medhyd*. Arm. *cmez, emê*. Ir. *meadhair*, talk or speech. Gael. *meadhair, meaghar*. Sansc. *mach*.

MEDHO, adj. Drunken, intoxicated. *Gwás medho*, a drunken fellow. *Hôh vedho*, a drunken sow. Llwyd, 243. W. *medhw*. Arm. *mezo*. Ir. *meisgeach*, †*mesec*. Gael. *misgeach*. Manx, *meshtal*.

MEEC, v. a. He will choke. To be read *méc*, 3 pers. s. fut. of *megi*, qd. v.

MEER, v. a. Look thou. A late form of *mír*, 2 pers. s. imp. of *miras*, qd. v.

MEERO, v. a. Look ye. A late form of *mirouch*, 2 pers. pl. imp. of *miras*, qd. v.

MEGI, v. a. To make smoke, to smother, to stifle, to suffocate, to choke. Part. *megis*. 3 pers. s. fut. *méc*. *Na war rág ef ny ylly posé, rág owen bôs megis*, nor forward could he lean, for fear of being suffocated. M.C.

MELDER 250 MELLYA

206. *Caehaf ybɩn pûr anwhêk, duwon yn y gorf a'n meek, ny vŷdh hutyk y golon,* I will seize the other very sharp; sorrow in his body will choke him; his heart will not be glad. O.M. 2817. Derived from *môg* or *môe,* smoke, qd. v. W. *mygu.* Arm. *mouga.* Ir. *much,* †*muc.* Gael. *much.*

MEGIN, s. f. A pair of bellows. Pl. *meginow.* Llwyd, 243. Written also *mygɩnow. Ny wôn gôf yn oll Kernow, a whytho gans mygenow bŷth well,* I know not a smith in all Cornwall, who can blow with the bellows ever better. P.C. 2713. W. *megin,* pl. *meginau.* Arm. *megin,* pl. *meginou.*

MEGOUSION, s. m. Reapers. ‡ *Whelas megouzian dha medgé an îs,* to look for reapers to reap the corn. *Pryce.* This is found only in late Cornish. It is a corruption of *medwoision,* pl. of *medwas;* comp. of *medi,* to reap, and *gwâs,* a servant. So W. *medelwas, medelweision.*

MEGYS, part. Bred, nurtured. *Lhuyd,* 248. Part. pass. of *maga,* qd. v.

MEHIL, s. m. A mullet. Corn. Voc. *mullus.* Plural, *mehilly.* The latest form was *mehal. Pryce.* Arm. *mel,* pl. *meli.*

MEHIN, s. m. Lard, the fat of bacon. Corn. Voc. *lardum.* W. *mehin.*

MEIB, s. m. Sons. One of the plurals of *mâb,* qd. v. *Lhuyd,* 243.

MEIDRIN, s. m. Nurture, fosterage. *Mâb meidrin,* alumnus, a foster-son. Corn. Voc. *Meidrin* is to be read *meithrin,* being the W. *meithrin,* from *maeth,* nurture, and *trin,* to manage.

MEIN, s. m. Stones. *Mein whŷyl,* work stones, i. e. stones for building. *Trehesi mein,* stone cutters. *Lhuyd,* 242. Plural of *maen,* qd. v.

MEIN, s. m. An edge, margin, the lip, the mouth. (See *Meyn.*) *Gwethé godhyans aga meyn; orth Ihesus a omgamé,* the worst their mouths knew; to Jesus they bent themselves. M.C. 196. Written also *mîn,* qd. v. W. *mîn.* Arm. *mîn.* Ir. *mên.*

MEIN, prep. Within, in. *Oll mein y chy,* all in the house. *Lhuyd,* 231. Written also *meyny,* qd. v. W. *mewn,* †*mywn,* †*ymynen.* Arm. † *en metou.* Ir. †*inmedon,* † *immedon.* Lat. *in medium.*

MEITH, s. m. Whey. *Lhuyd,* 149. W. *maidh.* Ir. *meadhg, meidhg,* †*medhg.* Gael. *meog, meug.* Old French, *mégue.* Germ. *matten.* Sansc. *mai,* to churn.

MEL, s. m. Honey. Corn. Voc. *mel. Ty a wra wogé hemma gorré aw lûs a le-na bŷs yn tyreth a dhynwa lanwes leyth ha mêl kefrys,* thou shalt after this bring the people thence, to a land (that) produces fulness of milk and honey also. O.M. 1430. *An luef a'm grûk me a wêl, hay odor whekké ys mêl, ow lôs wurnaf,* the hand (that) made me I see, and his odour sweeter than honey, coming upon me. R.D. 144. *Criban mêl,* a honey comb. *Lhuyd,* 59. W. *mêl.* Arm. *mêl.* Ir. *mil.* Gael. *mil.* Manx, *mill.* Gr. μέλι, μέλιτος. Goth. *milith.* Lat. *mel.* Fr. *miel.* It. *mele.*

MELDER, s. m. Sweetness. *Dhe nêp yw ioy ow colon, ha'm melder kepar ha kens,* to the one (that) is the joy of my heart, and my sweetness as formerly. R.D. 457. *Datherehys ûf a vernaus, ow melder, ty a yll y atendyé, lôs geufr ow cous kettep gêr,* risen I am from death, my sweetness; thou mayest attend to it, that my speech is true, every word. R.D. 476.

MELEGES, adj. Cursed. *Taw Lucifer meleges, yn colon del ôs tha gothys,* be silent, cursed Lucifer, in heart as thou art proud. C.W. 22. *Râg bosta meleges, hag yn colon re odhys,* because thou art cursed, and in heart too proud. C.W. 34. Another form of *myleges,* qd. v.

MELEN, adj. Of the nature of a beast, brutal, cruel. In construction *velen. Scrifys yw, ha ken me ny'n lavarsen, corf Ihesus ha'y asely y dhe denna mar velen, nêb a vynna a ylly nevera oll y yseren,* it is written, and otherwise I should not have said it, Jesus's body, and his limbs that they drew so brutally, whoever would might number all his bones. M.C. 183. *Crog ro'm bo, er an dhewen, neffré mars êth ahanan, er na'n prenny yn feleu, ha nacha oll the gous guldn,* may hanging be to me, by the gills, if thou shalt ever go from us, until thou shalt pay for it cruelly, and clean deny all thy talk. O.M. 2653. More correctly written *milen,* qd, v., being derived from *mil,* a brute. W. *milain.*

MELEN, adj. Yellow. Llwyd, 243, gives this an instance of the feminine of *melyn,* qd. v. This rule however obtains in Welsh only, there being not the least trace of of it in the Cornish Ordinalia.

MELET, s. m. Red lead. *Liu melet,* minium. Corn. Voc. Gr. μίλτος.

MELHUES, s. f. A lark. *An velhues,* the lark. A later form of *melhuel.* "*Alauda.* Pliny tells us was a Gaulish word, denoting the same bird which the Romans had formerly from its crest called *galerita.* (Quæ ab apice Galerita appellata quondam, postea Gallico vocabulo etiam Legionis nomen dederat alaudæ. Pl. Nat. Hist. ix. 37.) That the Cornish *melhuel,* or, which is all the same, *y velhuel,* is the same with this Celtic *alauda,* I make not the least doubt; but it may be questioned whether the Romans changed *y velhuel* into *alauda;* or the Cornish an old Celtic word which might be *alawi,* into *nelhuel.* To me both seem to have corrupted *uchelhed,* or according to the Cornish pronunciation, *ewholet,* i. e. *altivola;* for a lark is yet called with us (in Welsh,) by a word of the same signification, *uchedydh.*" Llwyd, 11. See *Ehidil.* A lark is also called in Welsh, *hedydh, ehedydh;* i. e. the flyer, *par excellence.* Another name is *meilierydh,* that which rises high; which may be connected with the Cornish *melhuel.*

MELHYONEN, s. f. A violet. Corn. Voc. *vigila.* W. *meillionen,* plur. *meillion.* Arm. *melshen, melshon.* Ir. *fal-chuaeha.* Gael. *fuilchuach.*

MELIAS, v. a. To reduce to powder, to grind. *Lhuyd,* 245. W. *malu.* Arm. *mala.* Ir. *meil,* † *mrl.* Gael. *meil.* Manx, *beihll.* Gr. μύλλειν. Lat. *molo.* Goth. *malan.* Germ. *mahlen.* Sansc. *mal.*

MELIN, s. f. A mill. Corn. Vocab. *molendinum. Hâl melin,* the mill moor; *nom. loc.* In late Cornish written *belin,* qd. v. W. *melin.* Arm. *melin, milin.* Ir. *muileann,* † *muileand,* † *muilenn,* † *mulenn.* Gael. *muilean.* Manx, *myllin, mwillin.* Gr. μύλα. Lat. *molu, molendinum.* Med. Lat. *molina.* Goth. *moulin.* Ang. Sax. *mylen.* Germ. *muhle.* Lith. *malunas.* Fr. *moulin.* Sp. *molino.* Sansc. *malanan.*

MELLYA, v. a. To meddle with. *Dew a rôs y worhemmyn pûr dhefry dres pûp tra na wrellan mellya worty,* God gave his commandment very truly above every thing that I should not meddle with it. C.W. 46. *Gwayt na fo gansy mellyes, me a'th chardg a uch pûb tra,* take care that it be not meddled with, I charge thee above all things. C.W. 28. *Worthaf ve ny dâl bôs mellyes a us pûb tra,* with me it behoveth not to be meddled with above every thing. C.W. 118. W. *ymhel.* Arm. *emellout.* Fr. *mcler.*

MELLOW, s. f. Joints. Plural of *mâl,* qd. v.

MELWIOGES, s. f. A tortoise. Corn. Voc. *testudo.* W. *melwioges,* a snail.

MELYEN, s. f. A snail, or slug. Corn. Voc. *limax.* The late corrupted form was *molhuiddzhan.* Llwyd, 79. W. *malaen, melyen, malwen, malwoden,* pl. *malwod.* Arm. *melchoueden, nielfeden,* pl. *melchoued.* Ir. † *mcle,* a sluggard. Dr. Owen Pughe derives the word from *malw,* that has power to extend; *mâl,* ductile. The root however may be Arm. *melv,* snot, slime. W. *mevl,* nastiness. In Irish a snail is *seilchide, seilighide.* Gael. *seilcheag,* from *svile,* spittle. Gr. σιαλος. Lat. *saliva.*

MELYN, adj. Of the colour of honey, yellow. *Ow Arluth, parys yw an stede gay, yn wêdh an courser melyn; pan vynny, yskyn,* my lord, ready is the gay steed, likewise the yellow courser; when thou wilt, mount. O.M. 1065. *Pe le era why môs, moz dêg, gans agas bedgeth gwyn, ha agas blew melyn,* where are you going, fair maid, with your white face, and your yellow hair. Pryce. *Cranag melyn,* a yellow frog. *Ridh velyn,* a deep yellow, (W. *rhûdh velyn.* Arm. *ruz velen.)* Llwyd, 62, 136. Written in the Cornish Vocabulary, *milin.* W. *melyn,* † *milin,* f. *melen.* Arm. *melen.* Med. Lat. *melinus.*

MELYNOY, s. m. The yelk of an egg. Llwyd, 175. Comp. of *melyn,* yellow, and *oy,* an egg. W. *melynwy.* Arm. *melen-vi.*

MEN, s. m. A stone. Plur. *mŷn. Gwêsk gynsy dywyth an mên,* strike thou with it twice the stone. O.M. 1844. *May hallo bôs anclcdhys yn bêdh mên, dhe vôdh mars yw,* that he may be buried in a stone tomb, if it be thy will. P.C. 3116. *Ewnyn an mên warnodho,* let us adjust the stone over it. P.C. 3207. *Warnodho yma mên brâs dres oll an mŷn,* on it there is a great stone, over all the stones. R.D. 400. A contracted form of *maen,* qd. v.

MEN, adj. Strong, powerful, strenuous, eager. In construction *ven,* and *fen. Golyouch ha pesouch yn ven, râg own an ioul hay vestry,* watch ye and pray strongly, for fear of the devil and his power. M.C. 57. *An princis esa yn pow gans Judas a dhanvonas tûs ven givsskis yn arvow, kepar ha del êns dhe'n gâs,* the princes (that) were in the country, sent with Judas strong men clad in armour, as if they were going to the battle. M.C. 64. *Ihesus a ve danvenys, ha dheworth an prins Annas gans tûs ven a dhesympys bŷs yn ebscop Cayphus,* Jesus was sent, and from the prince Annas, with strong men immediately unto bishop Caiaphas. M.C. 88. *Me a wêl un dên ow lôn pycher dour lôth men,* I see a man carrying a pitcher of water (with) eager haste. P.C. 662. After the adverbial particle *yn,* the initial is aspirated, as *yn fen,* strongly, qd. v. This may possibly be the root of *anuein,* invalidus, in the Cornish Vocabulary, qu. *anveu.* Gr. μένος, strength.

MENAS, conj. Except, besides. *Ny vannef orth êl na moy dôs dhe'n stat-ma menas me,* I will not that an angel more come to this state besides me. C.W. 10. *Ny alluf spurya na moy, heb gwethyl mernans a ver spyes war pobel oll menas ty,* I cannot spare more without inflicting death in a short time upon all the people except thee. C.W. 164. *Der lyvyow a dhower pûr vrâs, ny ve un mâb dên sparys, menas Noe, y wrêg, hay flehys,* by floods of water very great, not one son of man was spared, except Noah, his wife, and his children. C.W. 184. A later form of *mernans,* qd. v.

MENDZHA, v. a. He would. Llwyd, 246. A late corruption of *mensé,* qd. v., 3 pers. s. plup. of *menny,* qd. v.

MENEDH, s. m. A mountain. Pl. *menedhiow.* Written also *menydh, mynydh,* pl. *menydhyow, mynydhyow. Mâb Marya leun a râs dhe'n menedh Olyff ydh êth,* the Son of Mary, full of grace, went to the mount of Olives. M.C. 52. *A vês dhe'n drê ydhesé menedh uchel yredy,* outside the town there was a mountain high indeed. M.C. 162. *Môs dhe'n menydh me a vyn,* I will go to the mountain. C.W. 80. *Dûn alemma, eowyhé, war menydhyow dhe wandré, ha dhe pigy,* let us come hence, comrades, on the mountains to walk, and to pray. P.C. 108. *Yn ûr-na whreuch pysadow, may codhdho an mynydhyow warnouch râg own uwhether,* in that hour ye shall make prayers, (that the mountains may fall upon you, for very horror. P.C. 2652. *Menedh bian,* a little mountain, a hill. Llwyd, 49. Written in the Cornish Vocabulary, *menit,* mons. Welsh, *mynydh,* † *minid, mwnt,* (*mwn,* a spire.) Arm. *menez.* Ir. *monadh.* Gael. *monadh.* Lat. *mons, monte.* Chin. *mon.*

MENEN, s. m. Butter. An abbreviated form of *amenen,* qd. v.

MENESTROUTHY, s. m. Minstrels, musicians. *Ol an tekter a wylys, ny ĝl taves dên yn bŷs y leverel bynytha, a frût da ha floures lêk, menestrouthy ha cân whêk,* all the beauty (that) I saw, the tongue of man can never tell, of the good fruit and fair flowers, minstrels and sweet song. O.M. 770.

MENISTROR, s. m. A butler, a manciple. Corn. Voc. *pincerna.* W. *menestyr.* From the Lat. *minister.*

MENJAM, v. a. I will. A very late corruption of *mennaf.* Pryce.

MENNY, v. a. To will, to wish. *Er y byn mennaf mones,* I will go to meet him. P.C. 232. *Ow gordhyé mar a mennyth,* if thou wilt worship me. P.C. 135. *Yma ow kûl maystry brâs, râk mennas cafos enor,* he is doing great violence, for he wished to get honour. P.C. 378. *Dhodho ef me a'n gafsé, a menné gelwel gyvyans,* to him I would forgive it, if he would ask pardon. P.C. 1816. *Mara mennouch yn della,* if you will so. P.C. 2377. *Na ken myghtern ny vennyn ys Cesar, caffos neffré,* no other king than Cæsar we wish to have ever. M.C. 148. *Bedheus ena gorris, y fense bôs dre vestry,* let it be put there, that he would bo through mastery. M.C. 188. *A Tâs, dre dhe luen weres dhe pygy mensen,* O Father, through thy full help, I would pray thee. R.D. 444. *Ny fensen awos travyth yn della bôs wharfedhys,* I would not for any thing that it should happen so. P.C. 1942. Written also *mynny,* qd. v.

MENOU, adv. Very little. Pryce. Written also *minow,* qd. v.

MENOUCH, adj. Frequent. Used also adverbially. Frequently, often, many times. *Ragon menouch rebekis, ha dysprcsijs yn harow,* for us (he was) often reproached, and despised cruelly. M.C. 2. *Krêf yw gwrydhyow an spedhes, may'dhyne ow dyw-vrech terrys, worté menouch ow quethé,* strong are the roots of the briars, that my arms are broken, working often at them. O.M. 689. *May*

May whellō an debeles ow gweres menouch dhedhé, that the wicked may see my frequent help to them. O.M. 1850. *Menouch ef a wrûk bostyé,* often he did boast. P.C. 2888. R.D. 338. W. *mynych, (yn vynych.)* Ir. *minic, †menic, †inmenic.* Gael. *minig.* Manx, *mennick.* Goth. *maenig.*

MENS, s. m. Magnitude, greatness, quantity. *Pûp dên ol degyns ganso y pŷth an mêns a allo, war aga keyn fardellow,* let every man take with him his thing, the quantity (that) he can, burdens on their back. O.M. 1892. *Cowyth whêk, ty a fŷdh mêns a vynny,* sweet comrade, thou shalt have all that thou wilt. P.C. 500. *Ol mêns trespas a wrugé, dhodho ef me a'n gafsé,* all the amount of trespass he has done, to him I would forgive it. P.C. 1814. Written also *nŵns,* qd. v. W. *maint, †meint.* Arm. *ment.* Ir. *meid, †meit.* Gael. *meud.* Gr. μένεθος. Goth. *mahts.* Germ. *macht.* Eng. *might.* Fr. *maint.* Snsc. *mahatvan.*

MENTA, v. a. Thou wilt. *Mar menta,* if thou wilt. *Lhuyd,* 251. Comp. of *men,* 3 pers. s. fut. of *menny,* and *te,* thou.

MENTE, s. f. Mint, the herb mint. Corn. Voc. *mintc.* W. *mintys.* Arm. *ment.* Ir. *miontas.* Gael. *meannt, meannd.* Anc. Gaulish, *menta.* "Montastrum Græci lalamintheu, Hispani creobula, Galli *mentam.* Apulej. Madaur, p. 219."

MENWIONEN, s. f. An ant, or emmet. Corn. Vocab. *formica.* Perhaps the correct reading is *meuwionen.* W. *mywionen, bywionyn, môr,* pl. *myuion, bywiou, morion. Morgrugyn,* pl. *morgrug,* is another term in Welsh. Arm. *merienen, merionen,* plur. *merien, merion.* Ir. *†moirb.* Gael. *†moirb.* Lat. *myrmex.*

MENYS, adj. Small, little. *Ha'y brewy mar venys avel skyl brâg,* and bruise her as small as malt dust. O.M. 2620. *Agen flehys kekeffrys, whâth ke'dhyns y mar venys, me a dhôg ran war ow keyn uakes lemyn,* our children likewise, yet since they are so small, I will carry some on my back immediately now. C.W. 100. Written also *minis,* and *munys,* qd. v. W. *mân; mwnes,* small particles. Arm. *nan.* Ir. *mion.* Gael. *min.* Maux, *myn.* Gr. μυνὸς. Lat. *minus, minuus.* Goth. *mins.* Sanse. *minas.*

MEPPIG, s. m. A little son, a child. *Lemmyn ma dhyuny meppig whêg yn gwyly,* now there is to us a sweet child in the bed. *Lhuyd,* 253. Diminutive of *mâb,* qd. v. W. *mebyn.*

MER; adj. Great, big, large. *A néf uhel an Tâs mêr, re'th ordené ty ha'th wrêk pan vy marow, yn y cucr,* the great Father of high heaven, may he ordain thee and thy wife, when thou diest, into his court. P.C. 684. A contracted form of *meor,* qd. v.

MERAS, v. a. To see, to behold. 2 pers. s. imp. *mêr. Pylat a worhemynnys meras Crist marow nara o,* Pilate commanded to see Christ if he were dead. M.C. 215. *Dhe veras worth Crist y êth, hag ef yn crows ow cregy,* to look on Christ they went, and he on the cross hanging. M.C. 216. *Cayn, ow broder, mêr ha preder, henna yw moog whêg,* Cain, my brother, look and consider, that is sweet smoke. C.W. 80. *Merouch py na ve towlys yn clêdh dhe vones pedrys,* see ye where he is thrown into the ditch to be rotten. C.W. 82. Written also *miras,* qd. v.

MERCH, s. f. A daughter. *Yn dŷdh-na te nyn wra chan a whêl, te nyn dhy vâb, nyn dhy merch, nyn dhy dên whêl, nyn dhy môs whêl,* on that day thou shalt not do any manner of work, thou nor thy son, nor thy daughter, nor thy workman, nor thy workwoman. Pryce. In the Ordinalia it is generally written *myreh,* qd. v. W. *merch.* Arm. *merch.* Lith. *wyrénê.* Lat. *virgo.* Sansc. *virá.*

MERCH, s. m. Horses. *Merch, gwarthek, môch, ha deves,* horses, cattle, pigs, and sheep. O.M. 1065. Plural of *march,* qd. v.

MERH, s. m. Mars, March. *Mis merh,* the month of March. *De-Merh,* (W. *dydh Mawrth.* Arm. *di-meurs.* Ir. *dia-mart.* Gael. *di-mairt.* Manx, *jemayrt.)* Tuesday. *Lhwyd,* 54, 86. W. *mawrth.* Arm. *merch, meurs.* Ir. *marl, †mairt.* Gael. *mart.* Manx, *mayrt.* All from the Lat. *mars, martius.*

MERH, s. f. A daughter. ‡ *Enna chee na wra chan a whel, chee ha de mâb ha de merh, de gwâs ha de maithes,* then thou shalt not do any manner of work, thou and thy son, and thy daughter, thy servant, and thy maid. *Pryce.* A later form of *merch,* the guttural *ch* being softened into *h.* Lhwyd, 242, gives this word as an instance of inflexion, thus *merch,* a daughter, *an vyrh,* of the daughter. As there is no instance of an inflected case in the Ordinalia, *myrh, an vyrh,* must be considered as mere various readings. See *Myrch.*

MERNANS, s. m. Death, decease. *Râk me a welas dre huyn pûr wŷr y tue mernans tyn mara pydhé ef ledhys,* for I saw during sleep very truly that sharp death will come, if he should be slain. P.C. 1060. *Dre y vernans yredy, oll an bŷs a fŷdh sylwys,* through his death truly, all the world will be saved. O.M. 817. *Me a vyn aga sywa, dhe'n mernans agu gorra, kekeffrys byau ha brâs,* I will follow them, to put them to death, as well small and great. O.M. 1094.

MERTHURYE, v. a. To martyr. Part. *merthuryys, mertheryys. Y whylsyn y verthuryé, hag yn grows pren y squerdyé,* we saw his being martyred, and on a crosstree his being torn. R.D. 1282. *Fatel fue Cryst mertheryys, râk kerengé tûs an boys why a welas yn tyen,* how Christ was martyred, for love of the people of the world, ye have seen entirely. P.C. 3220. Arm. *merzeria.* W. *merthyru,* from *merthyr,* a martyr. Arm. *merzer, †martir.* Ir. *martirach, †martir.* Gael. *martaraeh.* All from the Latin, *martyr.*

MERWEL, v. a. To die, to become lifeless. *Mar dha yu genef a wrŷs, merwel kyns dôs drôk ancow,* as well it is in my opinion to die before tho evil sorrow comes. O.M. 1230. *Gwell yw un dên dhe verwel ages ol an bobyl lêl,* better it is that one man should die than all the faithful people. P.C. 446. *Merwel a wrên ow oûl tân,* we will die making a fire. R.D. 139. *Reson o râg oll an wlâs ef a wodhyé y veruy,* (the) reason was that for all the country he knew that he should die. M.C. 56. *Mar ny wrêf, hep falladow, mûr a'n bobyl a verow,* if thou dost not, without failings, many of the people will die. O.M. 1803. *Ev a vervys,* he died. *Lhwyd,* 230. Written also *marwel,* qd. v. W. *marw.* Arm. *mervel.*

MES, s. m. A field. *Yn mês, a vês,* abroad, without doors, outside. *Dhe vês,* away. *Mar a tybbryth a henna, yw hynwys pren a skyens, yn mês alemma ty â,* if thou eat of that, (which) is named the tree of knowledge, out of this place thou shalt go. O.M. 83. *Euch yn mês*

MESTERNGES 253 MEVIYS

a dhysympys, go ye out immediately. O.M. 318. *Pan wrugé drea ow defen, mês a paruthys lowen, an êl wharé a'n goras*, when he acted against my prohibition, out of happy Paradise, the angel soon put him. O.M. 923. *Marseuch lemyn mês a dré, nefré ny dhebraf vara*, if you will go now from home, I will never eat bread. O.M. 2185. *Ke dhe vês omscumunys dhe dhyvcyth vêth yn tewolgow*, go thou away, accursed, to a wilderness ever into darkness. M.C. 17. *T'is Crist dhe vês a fyas*, the people of Christ fled away. M.C 77. A contracted form of *maes*, qd. v.

MES, conj. But. *Mes y dhensys o mar feyn pûb ûr a'n trylya dhedha*, but his manhood was so delicate (that) he always turned him to it. M.C. 54. *Mes bedhens guris dhe vynnas*, but let thy will be done. M.C. 55. *Reson y a rey ragdhé, mes war fals yth êns growndys*, reasons they gave for it, but on falsehood they were grounded. M.C. 116. Written also *mas*, qd. v.

MESC, s. m. The midst, the middle. *Yn mêsc*, in the middle, among. *Yn mêsk flechys Ysrael, dysky laha Dew huhel a vra dhedhé, deydh ha nôs*, among the people of Israel, teach the law of the high God he does, day and night. O.M. 1553. *Mêsk ow pobel ny vynnaf na fella agas godhaf, euch alemma dhe ken pow*, among my people I will not any longer endure you ; go ye hence to another land. O.M. 1594. *Kerdyn gwethyn yn mêsk cronow*, cords plaited among thongs. M.C. 131. Written also *mfsc*, qd. v.

MESCAT, adj. Mad, furious, foolish. *Lhwyd*, 42, 143, 172. A late form of *muscoc*, qd. v.

MESCATTER, s. m. Madness, insanity, folly. *Lhwyd*, 71, 85.

MESCLEN, s. f. A muscle shell, fish. Corn. Voc. *muscla*. The latest form was *bezlen*. W. *masgyl, mesglyn*, a shell, or husk. Arm. *mesklen*, a muscle. The Welsh name of a muscle is *cragen lâs*, i. e. a blue shell.

MESEN, s. f. An acorn. Corn. Voc. *glans*. W. *mesen*, pl. *més*. Arm. *mezen*, pl. *mez*. Ir. *meas*. Gael. *meas*. Manx, *mess*. In the British dialects it now means acorns only, but in the Erse, all tree fruit. Ang. Sax. *mæstc*, acorns, nuts, &c. Eng. *mast*. Goth. *mais*, food. Germ. *mast*.

MESIC, adj. Belonging to a field. *Pryce*. W. *maesawl*.
MESLAN, s. m. A mastiff dog. *Lhwyd*, 93, 240.
MESTER, s. m. A master. Pl. *mestrisi*. *A master kêr, my a vra pûp tra kepar del vynny*, O master dear, I will do every thing like as thou wishest. O.M. 2045. *Lowené dhys, a vester, yn mêdh Iudas an braithky*, joy to thee, O master, says Judas the hound. M.C. 65. *Ha'n tebel êl, hager bríf, yn y holon a worré, war y mester yenions créf y lo, Ihesus mar ladhé*, and the evil angel, ugly reptile, put into her heart that strong vengeance would come on her lord, if he killed Jesus. M.C. 122. *Lemyn nyns es mestrysy yn wlâs-ma, pûr wfr, saw ny, ow masones yn pow-ma*, now there are not masters in this country, very truly, save us, masoning in this land. O.M. 2468. *Mestrysy* was also corrupted into *mestrygy*. *Heil doctours ha mestrigi*, hail, doctors, and masters. P.C. 1047. *Mestrygy, wolcom y'm tour*, masters, welcome to my palace. P.C. 1711. Written in the Cornish Vocabulary, *maister*, qd. v.

MESTERNGES, s. f. A kingdom. *Yn mêdh Ihesus, nyng-ugy ow mesternges yn bfs-ma*, says Jesus, my kingdom is not in this world. M.C. 102. An erroneous reading of *myglernes*, qd. v.

MESTRES, s. f. A mistress. ‡ *A vester ha a vestres rôs dhem tesan, ha laveras dhem*, my master and my mistress gave to me a cake, and said to me. *Lhwyd*, 253. W. *meistres*. Arm. *maestres*. Ir. *mighistreas*. Gael. *banmhaighstir*. Med. Lat. *magistressa*. It. *maestressa*. Fr. *maîtresse*. Eng. *mistress*.

MESTRY, s. m. Mastery, force, power, violence. *A ny wodhas ow mestry, bôs dhymmo may fês ledhys*, knowest thou not my power, that it rests with me whether thou shalt be killed ? M.C. 144. *Dês a'n grows hep pystegé, ha ny a grfs dhe vestry, hag a'd syns mester neffré*, come from the cross without magic, and we will believe in thy power, and hold thee a master always. M.C. 107. Written also *maystry*, qd. v.

METIN, s. m. The morning. Corn. Voc. *mane*. *Godhewhar ha metten o an kensa journa*, the evening and morning were the first day. C.W. p. 189. *Metten da dhe why*, good morning to you. *Pryce*. Generally written in the Ordinalia *myttyn*, qd. v. W. *meityn*. Arm. *mintin*. Ir. *mainne*, † *matin*. Gael. *mainnc*. Manx, *vaidyn*. Lat. *matutina*. It. *mattina*.

METOL, s. m. Steel. *Lhwyd*, 47. From the Eng. *metal*. The equivalents are W. *dûr*, † *dira*, in Oxf. Gloss. Arm. *dir*. Ir. *dûr*. Gael. *dur*. Sansc. *dharas*, firm. Gr. ὄηρὸϛ. Lat. *durus*.

METHEN, adj. Full, complete. *Whet avar prfs soper yw, tân brâs an oan re a lyno, kyns y vôs methen restys*, it is yet early supper time, a great fire will colour the lamb too much, before it be quite roasted. P.C. 698. W. *ammeuthyn*, dainty.

METHIA, v. a. To feed, to nourish, to cherish, to foster, to nurse. *Lhwyd*, 42, 245. W. *maethu*; fr. *maeth*, nourishment. Arm. *macz, meaz*. Ir. † *maes*, † *maise*.

METHIC, s. m. A physician. *Lhwyd*, 240, 241. Another form of *medhic*, qd. v.

MEUCH, adv. Quickly, soon. *Lyvyreuch whet, pan 'dh euch mar freth, pyro a whyleuch ?—Ihesu rum feydh a Nazareth, ny'n gevyth meuch*, say ye again, when ye are so bold, whom seek ye ?—Jesus, by my faith, of Nazareth, we shall find him quickly. P.C. 1118. W. *môch*. Ir. *moch*. Gael. *moch*. Manx, *mochey*. Lat. *mox*.

MEUL, s. m. Mischief, bad luck. *Fysteneuch dh'agas kregy ; degouch genouch pûp huny whyppys da, ragas bo meul*, make haste, hanging to ye ! bring with you every one good whips, bad luck to ye ! P.C. 2048. Written also *meaul*, qd. v. W. *mevl*. ("*Mcvl i'r llygoden untwll*, bad luck to the mouse with one hole." Welsh Adage.) Arm. *melv*. Ir. *meubhal*; † *mebul*. Gael. *masladh*, † *meabhal*.

MEUR, adj. Great, much. *Ot omma menedh huhel ha me a dhysqué dhys guel a vcur a pow*, see here a high mountain, and I will shew thee a sight of much country. P.C. 127. *Kyn y'n carra vyth mar veur, awos y ladhé ny'm duer*, though he may love him ever so much, for killing him no concern is to me. R.D. 1697. Another form of *maur*, qd. v.

MEVE, comp. pron. He is. *Awatta, ef a gowsas, agis mygtern ple mevé*, behold, he said, your king where he is. M.C. 147. A poetic form of *ma-ve*.

MEVIYS, part. Moved. *Gans agu garm hag olva Ihesus*

MIDZHI 254 MILGY

Crist a ve meviys, with their cry and lamentation Jesus Christ was moved. M.C. 4. Formed from the English, with the regular change of *o* into *e*.

MEYN, s. m. A mouth. (See *Mein*.) *Hag ydh êns dhe dowolyn, hag y kewsens dhe scornyé, hag a gamma aga meyn, pûb onon râg y eysyé*, and they went on their knees, and spoke him to scorn, and wried their mouths, each of them to extol him. M.C. 137. *Hag y ee dhe ben dewolyn, ha hager mowys a wre; gwethé godhyans aga meyn; orth Ihesus a omgamé*, and they went on their knees, and made ugly mouths; the worst their mouths knew; to Jesus they bent themselves. M.C. 196.

MEYN, s. m. Stones. Plural of *maen*, qd. v.

MEYNY, prep. Within, in. *Lemyn Noy y'th worhel ke, ly hag oll meyny dhe gy*, now Noah, go thou into thy ark, thou and all within thy house. O.M. 1018. Another form of *mein*, qd. v., if not the same as *mayny*, qd. v.

MEYR, adj. Much, great. *Ruth veyr a dûs a'n sewyas, pûb eyr paris dh'y vlamyé*, a great company of people followed him, always ready to accuse him. M.C. 108. Another form of *mear*, qd. v.

MEYS, s. m. A field. *A meys ôf ow predyry, pandra allaf dhe wruthyl*, I am abroad thinking, what I shall be able to do. O.M. 193. *Mar mynnyth bones yn cys, rys yw dhys gorré Moyses, Aron a'th volascor yn meys, ha'ga pobel ol gansé*, if thou wilt be at ease, need is to thee to put Moses (and) Aaron out of thy country, and their people all with them. O.M. 1573. Another form of *mês*, to express the long *ê*.

MEYSTRY, s. m. Mastery, power, a great thing, a wonder. *Eva, war an beys meystry lucn gummyas yma dhymmo, Eve*, power over the world, full permission there is to me. O.M. 409. *Dyswé dhym nêp meystry brâs, may hyllyn dyso crygy*, shew us some great power, that we may believe in thee. P.C. 1770. Another form of *mestry*, qd. v.

MI, pron. s. I, me. In construction *vi*. *Môs dhe balas my a vyn*, I will go to dig. O.M. 681. *My â dhe'n yet descympys*, I will go to the gate immediately. O.M. 793. *Colom genef vy yma; yn onour Dew my a wra war an alter hy gorré*, a dove with me there is; in honour of God I will on the altar place it. O.M. 1189. *Torré yn ow feryl vy*, pluck it at my risk. O.M. 197. *Tan henna dheworthef vy*, take that from me. O.M. 206. *Dhestrirya yw a gowsas Arluth prag y hysta vy*, Lord why hast thou forsaken me is (what) he said. M.C. 201. Written also equally common *me*, qd. v.

MICAN, s. m. A morsel. *Pryce.*

MICAN, s. m. Spite, pique, animosity. ‡ *Ha na ve idn frôth na mikan na trauaran nôr vez*, and there was no anger nor strife, nor dispute between them henceforth. Llwyd, 253. W. *mic, mig, migen.*

MICHTERNETH, s. m. A kingdom. See *Mychterneth*.

MIDIL, s. m. A reaper. Corn. Vocab. *messor.* Arm. † *midil.* W. *medel*, a reaping, a company of reapers. Gael. † *meithle.* Manx, *mheil.*

MIDZHAR, s. m. A reaper. Llwyd, 13, 90. A late corruption of *mider* or *meder.* W. *medwr.* Arm. *meder.*

MIDZHI, v. a. To reap. Llwyd, 15, 20. A late corruption of *midi.* W. *medi.* Arm. *medi, midi.* Ir. *methil.* Sanse. *mas.* Gr. *μαάω.* Lat. *meto.* Goth. *maita.* Germ. *mähe,* † *metze.* Eng. *mow.*

MIGINAU, s. m. A pair of bellows. Llwyd, 13, 60. A late form of *meginow*, pl. of *megin*, qd. v.

MIGYS, part. Bred. Llwyd, 248. Part. pass. of *maga*, qd. v.

MIHAL, s. m. Michael, a proper name. Llwyd, 12. *Mihâl, yskynyouch, êl splan, hellouch Adam gans cledha dân, ha'y wrêg mês a Baradys*, Michael, descend angel bright, chase Adam with a sword of fire, and his wife out of Paradise. C.W. 70. W. *mihangel.*

MIL, s. f. A thousand. Pl. *miliow.* Used also as an adjective. *Hag yn y gorf bôs gorris golcow pals leas mŷl*, and that in his body were put plenteous wounds many a thousand. M.C. 165. *Eledh dherygthy a sêf, leas mŷl y bôdh a syw*, angels before her stand, many a thousand her will shall follow. M.C. 226. *Mŷl puns a our da*, a thousand pounds of good gold. P.C. 212. *T'culel pren mŷl well vyé*, to throw lots would be a thousand (times) better. P.C. 2847. *Mŷl vêth a vŷdh an dywedh*, a thousand (times) worse will be the end. R.D. 348. *Mŷl dên cf a wrûk dué*, a thousand men he did end. R.D. 2321. *Syth mŷl ha sŷth cans blydhen*, seven thousand and seven hundred years. R.D. 2494. *Ev a drayl dheso dha lês moy es millyow a bynsow*, it will turn to thee to profit more than seven thousands of pounds. C.W 54. *Ha disquedhes truath dhe milliow nêb es ow cara, ha gwythé ow gurhemynadow*, and shew mercy unto thousands that love me, and keep my commandments. Pryce. W. *mil.* Arm. *mil.* Irish, *mile.* Gael. *mile.* Manx, *millcy.* Mod. Gr. *μίλιον.* Lat. *mille.* Basque, *milla.*

MIL, s. m. An animal, a beast. Corn. Voc. *animal.* Pl. *miliow*, cattle. *Guitfil*, fera, a wild beast. *Morvil*, cetus, a whale. Corn. Voc. *Ha gorêns an gy kymeres gallus dres an puscas an môr, ha dres an edhen an ebarn, ha dres an miliow, ha dres oll an bês*, and let them have power over the fish of the sea, and over the fowl of the air, and over the cattle, and over all the world. C.W. p. 192. W. *mil.* Arm. *mil.* Ir. † *mil.* Gael. *miol, mial.* Manx, *meeyl.*

MILDIR, s. m. A mile. *Syth mŷl ha sŷth cans blydhen, un dên kyn fo ow kerdhes, ow tôs kyn spedyé yn geydh dew ugans myldyr perfeyth, omma ny alsé bones*, seven thousand and seven hundred years, if a man should be travelling, and though he sped in one day's coming forty miles complete, he could not be here. R.D. 2497. W. *milldir.* Comp. of *mil*, a thousand, and *tir*, ground.

MILEN, adj. Of the nature of a brute, brutish, brutal, cruel. *Pûr vylen y a'n pyltyé, hag yn spytys a'n scornyas; moycha dhodho drôk a wre, henna vedha an guellu gwâs*, very brutally they pelted him, and in spites scorned him; whoso did most evil to him, that one was the best fellow. M.C. 112. Written also *melen*, qd. v. W. *miluin.*

MILGY, s. m. A hound, a greyhound. *Bencn a wella dhe flôch, mŷl wŷth dychtys ages brôch gans nêb milgy*, woman, seest thou thy son? a thousand (times) worse treated than a badger by some hounds. P.C. 2927. W. *milgi*, a greyhound. Comp. of *mil*, a beast, and *ci*, a dog. Though a greyhound is now called *cu* by the Irish, formerly *cu* meant any dog, or dog only, and a greyhound was called *cu mhil*, or *mil chu.* So Gael. *miol chu*, a greyhound.

MILPREV, s. m. The Druid's or serpent's egg. *Llwyd*, 110. The *ovum anguinum* of Pliny. Comp. of *mil*, a thousand, and *prév*, a reptile. It was a common belief in Cornwall in Llwyd's time that the glass beads which are frequently found in Cornwall, and Wales, and called by the Welsh *glain neidyr*, were the work of snakes; and it is a common belief now in Wales that on a certain day of the year an immense number of snakes come together and make these beads with the foam of their mouths. This agrees substantially with Pliny's account, and has descended from the Druids.

MILGWETH, adv. A thousand times. *Llwyd*, 232. Written also *milweth* and *milwyth*, qd. v.

MILIN, adj. Yellow. Corn. Vocab. *fulvus* vel *flavus*. More correctly written *melyn*, qd. v.

MILL, s. f. A poppy. Corn. Voc. *papaver*. W. *mill*, a violet. "*Môr beraidh a'r mill*, as fragrant as the violet." *Welsh Adage.*)

MILVIL, card. num. A thousand thousand, a million. *Dhynny gweres ny dâl man; mylvyl dyaul a vyé gwan er-y-byn ef*, nothing avails to help us; a million devils would be weak against him. R.D. 132. *Evé, ydh esé gynef moy ages mylvyl enef yn brôs pûr dék*, drink thou, there are with me more than a million souls in very fair broth. R.D. 141. W. *milvil*.

MILWYTH, adv. A thousand times. *Wolcom iudas, par mon fay, wolcom mylwyth yn ow hel*, welcome Judas, by my faith, welcome a thousand times in my hall. P.C. 937. Written by Llwyd, *milweth, milwyth*, 232, 248. Comp. of *mil*, and *gwŷth*, a time. W. *milwaith*.

MIN, s. m. A kid. Corn. Voc. *hedus*. In late Cornish, *myn* and *mynnan* were used, qd. v. W. *myn, mynnan*. Arm. *menn*. Ir. *meanann*, plur. *meann*; †*mend*, plur. †*mind*. Gael. *mean*. Manx, *mannan*.

MIN, s. m. An edge, extremity, the lip, the mouth. *Gwask war an mŷn, re'th fo drôk pŷn; bommyn dreys kyn, mar pêdh e ycyu, ny dhue dhe gyr*, strike thou on the edge, bad pain be to thee; blows over the back, if it be cold, it will not come to measure. P.C. 2727. Llwyd writes it *min*, 41, and *meen*, 227. So also in the Dramas. *Ha'y veen môn hay scorcnnow*, and out of its slender top and its branches. O.M. 2444. *A vyne gwarthé y ben war y gorf bŷs yn y droys, squardyys oll o y grohen*, from the highest point of his head, on his body unto his feet, all his skin was torn. M.C. 135. See *Mein*.

MINFEL, s. m. Yarrow. Corn. Voc. *millefolium*. W. *minvel*. Both from the Latin. The proper Welsh name is *mildhail*, comp. of *mil*, a thousand, and *dail*, leaves.

MINNE, pron. s. I also. *Llwyd*, 244. W. *minnau*, †*minne*. Ir. *mesi, misi*. Gael. *mise*. Manx, *mish*.

MINNY, v. a. To will. *Pryce*. Generally written *menny*, and *mynny*, qd. v.

MINOUCH, adj. Frequent. *Pryce*. See *Menouch*.

MINOW, adj. Little, small. *Pryce*. The same as *menow*, qd. v.

MINYS, adj. Little, small. *Poccys minys*, measles. *Ll*. 160. ‡ *Der tacklow minnie ew brês tees gonvethes avel a tacklow brâs; drefen en tacklow brâs ma an gy mennow hedha go honnen, bus en tacklow minnis ema an gy suyah hâs go honnen*, by small things are the minds of men discovered, as well as by great matters; because in great things they will stretch themselves, but in small matters they will follow their own nature. *Pryce*. Written also *munys*, and *menys*, qd. v.

MIRAS, v. a. To look at, to see, to behold. Written also *mires*. 2 pers. s. imp. *mir*. *Dew, mŷr orth ow offryn, ha ressef dhys ow degé*, God, look at my offering, and take to thee my tithe. O.M. 505. *My a vŷr scon orth henna*, I will immediately look at that. O.M. 1251. *Me a vyn môs dhe vyras*, I will go to see. O.M. 1399. *Ny alluf myres y'th fath, râk golowder*, I cannot look in thy face for the light. O.M. 1412. *Ow scoforn trechys myrouch dhe vês dhyworth ow pen*, see ye my ear cut off from my head. P.C. 1144. *Myrcuch worth an vorvoran*, look ye at the mermaid. P.C. 2403. *Mŷr worto*, look at it. R.D. 1729. *Prest y keffy, pan vyré, hemma yw mygtern Edhewon*, readily he found, when he looked, this is the king of the Jews. M.C. 187. *Ha war woles pan vyrys, my a weles hy gwrydhyow*, and at the bottom when I looked, I saw its roots. O.M. 781. Arm. *mirout*. Lat. *miro, miror*. Fr. *mirer*.

MIRAS, s. m. The look, aspect, mien, visage. *Llwyd*; 43, 58. W. *mir, miré*.

MIS, s. m. A month. Corn. Voc. *mensis*. *Yma gené un bê da, gorra hag eys kennyskys, ol dhe'n bestes üs omma a glŷ bês lour dewdhek mŷs*, I have a good load, hay and corn mixed; all the beasts (that) are here shall have food enough twelve months. O.M. 1060. *Rewardys ty a vŷdh a dhyworthyf vy, rum fŷdh, kyns pen vŷs*, rewarded thou shalt be by me, on my faith, before the end of the month. P.C. 1046. *Mis gorephan*, the month of July; *mis du*, November, or the black month; *mis kevardhiu*, December. *Llwyd*, 53, 74, 100. W. *mis*. Arm. *miz*. Ir. *mios*, †*mis, mi*. Gael. *mios*. Manx, *mec*. Gr. μείν, μήν. Lat. *mensis*. Sansc. *mas, mâsas*. Zend, *maonh*. Goth. *mena*. Lith. *menu*. Eng. month. Fr. *mois*.

MISCEMERAS, v. a. To err, to mistake, to wander. Part. *miscemeres*. Llwyd, 57, 248. Comp. of Eng. *mis*, and *cemeres*, to take. W. *camgymeryd*.

MISCOGGAN, s. m. A fool. *Pryce*. From *muscoe*, qd. v.

MISCYMERIANS, s. m. An error, a mistake. *Llwyd*, 57.

MO, pron. adj. My, mine. *Pryce*. Generally written *my*, qd. v.

MOAREN, s. f. A blackberry. *Llwyd*, 18. See *Moyr*. W. *mwyaren*.

MOC, s. m. Smoke, fume. *Hag a'th whyp war an wolok, may whylly gurychon ha môk dhe dhewlagas a dre dro*, and will whip thee on the face, that thou mayst see sparks and smoke round about thy eyes. P.C. 2101. *Ow lesky yn tân yn môk*, burning in fire, in smoke. R.D. 1458. W. *mwg*, †*muc*. Arm. *moug, môg*. Ir. *much*. Gael. *muig, smuid*. O.N. *mugga*. Ang. Sax. *smoca, smic*. Eng. smoke.

MOCH, s. m. Pigs. *Merch, gwarthek, môch, ha deves, dreuch abervedh desempys*, horses, cattle, pigs, and sheep, bring ye within forthwith. O.M. 1065. *Tremoch*, pigstown, is the name of a place in the parish of Mabe; so *Mochdrev*, in Denbighshire, and Montgomeryshire. W. *môch*, s. *mochyn*. Arm. *môch*. In the three British dialects it is a plural aggregate; but the singular is designated by Ir. *muc*. Gael. *muc*. Manx, *muc*.

MOCHA, adj. Greatest, most. Written also *mochya*. *Py le vŷdh an guêl plynsys, may fôns mocha onowrys*, ha'n guella may wrôns tevy, where shall the rods be planted, they may be most honoured, and may grow best? O.M. 2033. *Lavar dhymmo a ver spys, py nŷl o mocha sengys an kêth dên-ma dhe cara,* tell thou to me, in a short space, which one was most bound to love this man? P.C. 510. *Nêb may fe mochya geffys, a gâr mochya, yn pûp le,* he that is forgiven most, will love most in every place. P.C. 513. *Nêb a vo yn mochya gre a vsydh an brassa henwys,* he (that) is in the highest degree, shall be called the greatest. P.C. 777. These are various form of *moycha*, qd. v.

MOCHAHE, v. a. To make greater, to enlarge, to increase; to be increased. *May mohchaho hy huth hy, dre wûl ow gorhemmyn trôch, na heb mûr lavur defry benytha nys tevyth flôch,* that her affliction may be increased, through breaking my commandment, not without great labour indeed shall she ever have a child. O.M. 297. W. *mwyhâu*. Arm. *muia*.

MOD, s. m. A place. *Pryce.* A mutation of *bôd*, qd. v.

MODEREB, s. f. An aunt. *Modereb abarh mam,* matertera, an aunt on the mother's side; *modereb abarh tat,* amita, an aunt on the father's side. Corn. Vocab. W. *modryb,* plural, *modrybedh,* †*modrepet*. Arm. *moereb, mouerb,* pl. *mocrebed.* Ir. *maithrean.* Gr. μητρυιά.

MODERUY, s. f. A bracelet. Corn. Voc. *armilla.* W. *modrwy,* comp. of *môd,* †*maut,* which is the old form of W. *bawd,* a thumb, (Arm. *meûd,*) and *rhwy,* a ring. The W. *modeedh,* an inch, is similarly compounded of *môd,* a thumb, and *mêdh,* measure. An armlet or bracelet is in Welsh, *breichrwy*.

MOEL, adj. Bare, bald. *Pryce. Moelvré, (moel-bré)* the bare hill, is the name of several places in Cornwall, as *Mulberry,* in Lanivett; *Mulfra,* in Madern; *Mulvera,* in St. Austle. It is also very frequent in Wales, as *Moelvré,* in Llangadwaladr, Denbighshire ; *Moelvré,* in Bettws Abergele ; and *Moelvré,* in Anglesey, with many others. W. *moel.* Arm. *moel.* Ir. *maol.* Gael. *maol.* Manx, *meayl.*

MOELII, s. f. An ousel, a blackbird. Corn. Voc. *merula.* Welsh, *mwyalch.* Arm. *moualch.* "The Gaulish name 'Αλκιμοεννίς, a place on the left bank of the Upper Danube, in Ptolemy, appears to be the same word, with the component parts transposed; it was doubtless so called from the river *Alcmona* or *Alchmona* by the historians of Charlemagne. There are also German names of rivers and places derived from animals, such as Ebraha, Uraha." Zeuss, 1113. Many rivers in Wales are called from the names of animals, as *Iwrch, Twrch, Alarch, Elain,* &c.

MOI, adj. More. *Llwyd,* 249. See *Moy*.

MOICHA, adj. Greatest. *Llwyd,* 253. See *Moycha*.

MOIIA, adj. Greatest, most. ‡ *Ha po ti ha da wrêg an moiha lûan warbarh ; nenna greuh terhi an dezan, ha na hens,* and when thou and thy wife are most merry together, then break the cake, and not before. *Llwyd,* 252. A late form of *moycha*, qd. v.

MOIN, adj. Slender, fine, thin. *Pryce.* A later form of *moin,* qd. v.

MOII, s. m. Pigs. *Crow môh,* a pigsty. *Cig môh,* bacon. *Llwyd,* 15, 76. A later form of *môch*, qd. v.

MOLA, s. f. An ousel. ‡ *Mola dhiu,* a blackbird; ‡*mola lâs,* a fieldfare. *Llwyd,* 85, 168. A later form of *moch,* qd. v.

MOLENEC, s. m. A goldfinch. *Pryce.* A corruption of *melenec,* from *melen,* yellow. W. *melynog.* Arm. *melenec.*

MOLEYTHY, v. a. To curse. *An ioul a trylyas sperys, hag êth dh'y tyller tythy ; tergweyth y fe convyetys ; ewn yn dhyn y voleythy,* the devil lost heart, and went to his place quickly, thrice was he convicted ; right it is for us to curse him. M.C. 18. *Genef lower y a sorras, hag a'm molythys mûr vrâs,* with me they have been greatly angered, and have cursed me very greatly. C.W. 98. Another form of *molletha,* qd. v.

MOLHUIDAN, s. f. A dew or naked snail, a slug. *Pryce.* Written by Llwyd, *molhuidzhon,* 10, 48, being the corrupt pronunciation of his day. It is the same word as W. *malwoden.* Arm. *melehouèden.*

MOLLETH, s. f. An imprecation, curse, reproof. Written also *mollath* and *molloth,* pl. *mollathow, mollothow. Ow molleth a rôf dhyso, molleth ow eledh kefrys,* my curse I give to thee, the curse of my angels also. O.M. 585. *War nêp a'n grûk ow molleth,* my curse on him that did it ! R.D. 964. *May hallo môs gans an gwŷns, ha ganso molleth an sŷns, ha Dew aban,* that he may go with the wind, and with him the curse of the saints, and God above. R.D. 2293. *Na whela agen nea, mâb molathow, par del ôs,* seek not to deny us, son of curses as thou art. C.W. 92. *Lenwys a volothow,* filled with curses. C.W. 108. W. *melldith.* Arm. *malloz,* †*millie.* Ir. *mallachd,* †*maldach.* Gael. *mallachd.* Manx, *mallacht.* All from Lat. *maledictio.*

MOLLETHA, v. a. To curse, to imprecate, to execrate. *Llwyd,* 84. Written also *mollethia,* and *molythia.* The form in the Ordinalia is *mylygé,* qd. v. W. *melldithio.* Arm. *millisien.* Ir. *malluigh.* Gael. *mallaich.*

MOLLETHANS, s. m. A cursing, imprecating, reviling, slandering. *Llwyd,* 84. W. *melldithiad.* Arm. *milligaden.* Ir. *mallughadh.* Gael. *mallachadh.*

MOLLETHEC, adj. Accursed. *Bôs Iudas ef a vodhyé pûr hager ha molothek ; an ioul ynno re drocsé, may 'tho gwêth agis cronek,* he knew that Judas was very ugly and accursed; the devil had dwelt in him, that he was worse than a toad. M.C. 47.

MOLS, s. m. A wether sheep. Corn. Voc. *vervex. Yn gordhyans dhodho omma, offrynnyé an kêth mols-ma ; yn le Ysac y settya war an alter dhe lesky,* in worship to him here, (I will) offer this same sheep ; in stead of Isaac (I will) put it on the altar to burn. O.M. 1384. In late Cornish it was pronounced *moulz.* *Llwyd,* 172. W. *môllt,* pl. *myllt.'* Arm. *maout, meut.* Ir. †*molt.* Gael. *mult.* Manx, *molt,* pl. *muilt.* Mod. Lat. *molto, multo, muto.* Fr. *mouton,* †*moulton.* Eng. *mutton.*

MOLYTHIA, v. a. To curse. *Llwyd,* 68. Another form of *molletha,* qd. v.

MON, adj. Slender. *Dew, teka bren râg styllyow, ha compos y denwennow ; brâs ha crom y ben goles ; ha'y veen môn, ha'y scorennow my a vyn trehy tennow ha lathys têk ha corbles,* God, the fairest tree for rafters, and straight its sides ; large and rounded its lower end ; and its point slender, and its branches I will cut into beams, and fair laths, and joists. O.M. 2443. A contracted form of *moyn,* id. qd. *muin,* qd. v.

MONE, s. m. Money. Plur. *monyys. Dêk warnugens a moné, me ny vennaf cafus le, yn gwyryoneth,* thirty (pieces) of money, I will not take less, in truth. P.C.

593. *An nýl dhodho a dellé pymp cans dyner monyys, ha hanter cans y gylé*, the one owed to him five hundred pence of monies, and half a hundred the other. P.C. 505. Written by Llwyd, 115, 253, *monnah, mona.* ‡ *Dry dre an mona, ha perna moy,* bring home the money, and buy more. *Pryce.* W. *mwnai.* Arm. *mouneiz.* Ir. *monadh.* Lat. *moneta.* Med. Lat. *moneia.* Fr. *monnaie.* Eng. money.

MONEDH, s. m. A mountain. *Llwyd*, 93. Pl. *monedhiow. Monedh brâs,* a great mountain. *Pryce.* A later form of *menedh,* qd. v.

MONES, v. a. To proceed, to go. *Rum fey mŷr a wokyneth yw mones dhe lesky peyth a ŷl dên orto bewé,* by my faith a great folly it is to go to burn a thing (that) a man can live upon it. O.M. 475. *Wharé my a vyn mones,* forthwith I will go. O.M. 730. *Ny gothé dhys bones hel, ow mones dhe'n sacrefys,* thou oughtest not to be slow, going to the sacrifice. O.M. 468. *War lyrch dhe vones dhe dré,* after thy going home. O.M. 830. In M.C. it is generally written *monas. Oll monas y a vynné bŷs yn mont a Galvary,* all they would go even to the Mount of Calvary. M.C. 162. *Môs* is a contracted form of this word, qd. v. W. *myned, mynd.* Arm. *moned, mond.*

MONS, v. irr. They are. Used with nouns plural, as *ma* is with nouns singular. *Ow popel vy grevyys brâs gans Pharow yw mylyges, y môns dhymo ow cryé,* my people, greatly aggrieved by Pharaoh, (who) is accursed, they are to me crying. O.M. 1418. *Me a wôr ple môns parys, râg an recsyon ordenys,* I know where they are ready, for the fellows ordered. P.C. 2579. *Râg ny wodhons py gymmys y môns y ow peché,* for they know not how much they are sinning. M.C. 185. W. *maent, y maent.*

MOR, s. m. Sea. Corn. Voc. *marc. Mor difeid,* pelagus, the main sea. *Mor tot,* oceanus, the ocean. *Spaven mor,* equor, smooth sea. Ibid. *Yn tressé dŷdh dybarth gorûf yutré an môr ha'n tyryow,* on the third day I will make a separation between the sea and the lands. O.M. 26. *Dûn alemma dhe'n môr ruydh,* let us come hence to the Red Sea. O.M. 1622. *Vŷth ny yllyn tremend an môr-ma,* we shall never be able to cross this sea. O.M. 1649. *Ty môr glân, me a'th wysk gans ow guelan,* thou fair sea, I strike thee with my rod. O.M. 1675. *Saw guet may wrylly cresy lemyn yn Tâs a wrûk néf, tŷr ha môr, ha dên a bry,* but take care that thou do believe now in the Father (that) hath made heaven, earth, and sea, and man of clay. O.M. 1786. W. *môr.* Arm. *môr.* Ir. *muir.* Gael. *muir.* Manx, *muir.* Anc. Gaulish, *mori,* (*Moricambe, Moridunum, Morimarusa.*) Slav. *more.* Lat. *marc.* Sansc. *miras,* (mi, to flow.)

MOR, adv. So. *Mor uhel,* so high. *Pryce.* Generally written *mar,* qd. v.

MOR, s. m. Berries. *Llwyd*, 94. A plural aggregate, from whence is formed the sing. *moran. Moran dhiu,* a blackberry, pl. *môr diu. Llwyd*, 94. *Moran cala,* a strawberry. 44. *Moran,* a bramble berry. 240. *Môr* is a contracted form of *moyr,* qd. v.

MORDEN, s. m. A wooden mallet, a beetle. *Pryce. War gîs vy dhe dhchesy gans morben bom treirysy dhe'n vŷl hora war an tual,* soon let me strike, with mallet, a terrible blow to the vile strumpet on the forehead. O.M. 2704.

MORCATH, s. m. A sea-cat, skate, or ray fish. *Pryce.*

W. *morgath, câth vôr.* Arm. *morgaz.*

MORDHOS, s. m. The thigh. Plur. *mordhosow. An Edhewon yntredhé a râg may wrellons terry aga morthosow wharé, hag a lena aga dry,* the Jews among them caused that they should break their thighs presently, and bear them thence. M.C. 229. The oldest form was *mordoit,* wrongly written in the Cornish Vocabulary, *morboit,* femur vel coxa. In late Cornish it was corrupted into *morraz.* W. *mordhwyd,* † *morduit,* † *mordwyt,* † *morduith.* Arm. *morzed, morzad.*

MOREC, adj. Of the sea, maritime. *Pryce.* W. *morawg.* Arm. *morec.*

MOREN, s. f. A maid, a damsel, a girl, a wench, a jade. *Asota gokky, Androw, an voran re geusys gow, na preder ken,* thou art foolish, Andrew, the girl has told a lie, do not think otherwise. R.D. 1044. *Na ny lever bôs Dew ken, saw an Tâs a néf a ban; ha ty voren myrch hyben a wra dew dhys dhe honan,* we say not that there is another God, but the Father of heaven above; and thou, jade girl, the other makest a god to thyself. O.M. 2649. *Yn dyspyt dh'y dâs ha'y vam, an voren a vŷdh ledhys,* in spite of his father and mother, the jade shall be killed. O.M. 2741. Written in the Cornish Vocabulary, *moroin,* puella. W. *morwyn.* Lat. *virgo, virgine.*

MORETH, s. m. Grief, sorrow. *Ow holon ol dhe dymmyn râg moreth a wra terry,* my heart all to pieces for grief will break. O.M. 358. *Gans moreth ydhof lynwys war dhe lerch, ow arluth whék,* with sorrow I am filled after thee, my sweet lord. O.M. 2104. *Pan predyryf a'y passyon, moreth a'm kymmer yn scon ragdho,* when I think of his passion, grief takes me immediately for him. R.D. 1083.

MORETHEC, adj. Grieved, sorrowful, sad, doleful, miserable. *My a ŷl bôs morethec, guelas ow mâp mar anwhek dychtys del yw,* I may be mournful, seeing my son so roughly treated as he is. P.C. 3187. *Yma dhymmo hyreth tyn yn ow colon pup termyn ha morethek,* there is to me sharp longing, in my heart always, and sorrowful. R.D. 749. *Peynys a'd wra morethek yn yffarn down pûb termyn,* pains will make thee miserable in deep hell always. M.C. 60. *Tûs Crist dhe vês a fyas, pûp a'y du pûr vorethek,* the people of Christ fled away, each on his (own) side very mournful. M.C. 77.

MORGI, s. m. A sea dog, a dog-fish. ‡ *Dibra morgi en mis Men, râg dho goil maw,* eat a dog-fish in the month of May, for to make a boy. *Pryce.* Comp. of *môr,* sea, and *ci,* a dog. W. *morgi.* Arm. *morgi.*

MORHOCH, s. m. A porpoise. Corn. Voc. *delphinus.* Lit. a sea hog, being compounded of *môr,* sea, and *hôch,* a hog. W. *morhwch.* Arm. *morhouch.* Ir. *muc mhara,* † *mucc mora.* Gael. *muc-bhiorach,* lit. a sharp-pointed pig; *muc mhara* being the Gaelic term for a whale.

MORLENOL, s. m. The tide, or influx of the sea. *Llwyd,* 42. Comp. of *môr,* sea, and *lenol,* for *lenwel,* to fill. W. *morlanw.* Ir. *lan mara.*

MORNADER, s. f. A lamprey. Corn. Voc. *murena* vel *murenula.* Lit. a sea-snake, being comp. of *môr,* the sea, and *nader,* a snake. W. *morneidyr.*

MOROGETH, v. a. To be a horseman, to ride. *An asen a ve kerchys; warnedhy râg esedhé dyllas pan a ve gorrys, râg morogeth a vynné dhe cyté dhe vôs gordhyys,* the she-ass was fetched; on her for sitting clothes of cloth were placed, for he would ride to the city to be worshipped. M.C. 28. An incorrect form of *marogeth*, qd. v.

MOROIN, s. f. A girl. Corn. Voc. *puella*. Written in the Ordinalia *moren*, qd. v.

MORRAS, s. m. The thigh. *Lhuyd*, 12, 59. A late form of *mordhos*, qd. v.

MORTRIG, s. m. The ebb of the sea. *Sâv aman, kemmer dha li, ha ker dha'n hât; mortrig a metten travyth ne dâl*, get up, take thy breakfast, and go to the moor ; the ebb sea of the morning is nothing worth. "This proverb is spoken in St. Just, in Penwith, where are both fishermen and tinners." *Pryce*. See *Trig*.

MORTHELEC, adj. Hammered, well beaten. *Saw kyn fêns y morthelek, dhe wêth vydhons dhe'n cronek, ha garow yn y dhulé*, but though they be hammered, they shall be worse for the toad, and rough in his hands. P.C. 2731.

MORTHOL, s. m. A hammer, beetle, or maul. Plur. *mortholow*. *Morthol bian*, a little hammer. *Lhuyd*, 84. *Heedh ow bool dhymmo touth da, ow thardar, ha'm mortholow*, reach ye my axe quickly, my auger and my hammers. O.M. 1002. W. *morthwyl, morthwyl*, †*morthol*. Arm. *morzol*. Med. Lat. *martellus*.

MORVA, s. f. A place near the sea, a marsh, a moory or fenny place. *Pryce*. It is preserved in the name of a parish, *Morva*, in Penwith. Comp. of *môr*, sea, and *ma*, a place. W. *morva*.

MORVIL, s. m. A whale. Corn. Voc. *cetus*. Pl. *morvilow*. ‡ *Ha Dew rig gorês an morvilow brâs, ha kencfra tra bew ês a gwayah, neb rig an dowrow dry râg pûr vear warlerh 'go hâs*, and God created great whales, and every living creature (that) moveth, which the waters brought forth abundantly after their kind. C.W. p. 191. Comp. of *môr*, sea, and *mil*, a beast, being the sea-beast *par excellence*. W. *morvil*.

MORVOREN, s. f. A mermaid. *Dên yw hanter morvoron, benen a'n pen dhe'n colon*, human is half a mermaid, woman from the head to the heart. P.C. 1742. *Myreuch worth an vorvoran, hanter pýsk ha hanter dên*, look ye at the mermaid, half fish and half man. P.C. 2403. Comp. of *môr*, sea, and *moren*, a maid. W. *morvorwyn*. Arm. *môr-chrêg, mari moryan*. Ir. *moruadh*, †*muirmora*. Gael. *maighdean-ruhara*. Manx, *ben varrey*.

MOS, v. a. To proceed, to go. *Saw kyns ys môs, ow thâs whêk, ro dhym dhe vanneth perfeith*, but before going, my sweet father, give me thy perfect blessing. O.M. 451. *Môs dhe balas me a vyn*, I will go to dig. O.M. 681. *My a vyn môs dhyworthys*, I will go from thee. O.M. 822. *Môs a wrên ny dhe'n castel*, we were going to the village. R.D. 1471. *Yma dour yn môs garow*, the water is going rough. R.D. 2298. *Kyng-ys y vôs alemma, yn gwyn ef a vgdh gwyskys*, before his going hence, in white he shall be clothed. P.C. 1779. A contracted form of *mones*, qd. v.

MOS, s. f. A maid. Pl. *musy*. *Gwra yn della, me a'th peys, me a dhôg an vôs a'm dorn*, do so I pray thee, I will lead the maid in my hand. C.W. 100. *Yn dýdhna le nyn wra chan a whêl ; te nyn dhy vâb, nyn dhy merch, nyn dhy dên whêl, nyn dhy môs whêl*, in that day thou shalt do no manner of work, thou nor thy son, nor thy daughter, nor thy man-servant, nor thy maid-servant. *Pryce*. A contracted form of *mowes*, qd. v.

MOSE, v. a. To remove, to send away, to drive away.

Dhodho ef me a'n vossaw, epscop, pryns, doctor ha maw, dhe'n iustis Pylat arté euch ganso yn kettep pen, to him I will send him ; bishop, prince, doctor, and boy, to the magistrate Pilate again go with him, every head. P.C. 1793. *Arluth, me a wra henna ; parys yw genef pûb tra dha vosé dhodhans alemma*, Lord, I will do that ; every thing is ready with me to drive them from hence. C.W. 70. "Hence we have our western term *to vease away*." Pryce. W. *mudo*.

MOSTETHES, s. m. Filth, dirt. *Ha'y vertu a vgdh lyhgs dre an mostethes hep fal*, and its virtue will be lessened by the dirt, without fail. O.M. 2809. *Gans towal a lýn gulân, my a's sêch kettep onan a bôp nostethes ha lýs*, with a towel of clean linen I will dry them every one from all dirt and mire. P.C. 838. *Môs dhe wolhy ow dulé a dhenympys me a vyn omma yn dour, may fôns y gwyn ha glân lour a vostethes*, go to wash my hands immediately I will, here in water, that they may be white and clean enough from dirt. R.D. 2206.

MOSTYS, adj. Filthy, dirty, defiled. *An bous,—y dysyryé nynsyw dhys, nynsyw gulân lemmyn mostys*, the robe,— it is not for you to desire it ; it is not clean but dirty. R.D. 1927. *Mes ol nyns ouch gulan deffry ; yma onan pûr vostyys omma a'gys company*, but ye are not all clean really ; there is one much defiled here of your company. P.C. 867.

MOTHOW, adj. Failing. *Pandra amount dhyn gonys, mar serryth orth dên hep wow, pan vo dhyn lafurryys, agan whcyl a vgdh mothow*, what avails it to us to cultivate, if thou art angry with man, without a lie ; when all is laboured by us, our work will be failing. O.M. 1226.

MOURDER, s. m. Greatness, bigness. *Lhuyd*, 84. From *maur*, great, qd. v. W. *mawrder*.

MOURERIAC, adj. High-worded, high-flown, vaunting. *Lhuyd*, 84. Comp. of *maur*, great, and *geriac*, wordy.

MOUROBRUR, adj. Magnificent, sumptuous. *Lhuyd*, 84. Comp. of *mour*, great, and *obrur*, worker.

MOUSEGY, v. a. To stink, to be loathsome. *A arluth, mûr gras re'th fo, râk lowené ny gen bo yn le may fuen ; lemmyn pocvau ha lesky, ow flcryé, ow mousegy, kepar ha kuen*, O Lord, great thanks be to thee, for joy may not be ours in the place where we have been ; but pleasant and burning, smelling, stinking like as dogs. R.D. 171. From *musae*, stinking, qd. v. Arm. *moueza*.

MOWES, s. f. A maid. Plur. *mowysy*. *Mar mynnyth cufus mowes, my a'd wor bys dhedhy*, if thou wilt have a maid, I will soon bring thee to her. R.D. 2071. *Ha mowysy gans golow yn lanterns, hep falladow, fystencuch fust alemma*, and maids with light in lanterns, without fail, make ye haste quick hence. P.C. 944. *Mar a mennyth, kerch dhodho a dhysempys, may geffo un mowes*, if thou wilt, fetch to him immediately, that he may have a maid. P.C. 1876. Arm. *maouez, mouez*. Span. *moza*.

MOWLS, s. m. A wether sheep. *Lhuyd*, 27. A late form of *mols*, qd. v.

MOWNS, v. irr. They are. ‡ *Lower y mowns y ow murnya*, enough they are mourning. C.W. 98. A late form of *môns*, qd. v.

MOWYS, s. m. Ugly faces. *Gans mowys y a'n scornyns ; yn y fâs y a drewys*, with ugly faces they scorned him ; they spat in his face. M.C. 95. *Hag y ec dhe ben dewlyn, ha hager mowys a wre,* and they went on their knees, and made ugly faces. M.C. 196. Not Celtic, being the Old English *mowes.*

MOY, adj. More, greater, bigger. *Ef a wrûk ow husullyé, frut annedhy may torren, moy es Dew ny a vyé,* he did advise me, if I should gather fruit from it, greater than God we should be. O.M. 219. *Cafos moy dhys aban rês, try hcys dhc bâl kemery,* since it is needful for thee to have more, thou shalt take three lengths of thy spade. O.M. 391. *Mar tue moy, nys tevyth man,* if more will come, it will not be enough. O.M. 390. *Moy pêch o pan dyspresyas ys delo pan y'n gwerthé,* greater sin it was when he misprized him than when he sold him. M.C. 104. *Na byth moy ef ny gaffas prag may fe rŷs y dampnyé,* nor any more did he find why there should be need to condemn him. M.C. 116. *Dysk y dynchaus, hep na moy cous dhym hydhew,* take it off quietly, without any more talk to me to day. R.D. 1940. *Mar strechyn omma na moy, ny agan bŷdh y dregé,* if we remain here any more, we shall not be able to bear it. P.C. 3001. (See also *Voy.*) W. *mŵy.* Arm. *mui,* † *muy.* Ir. *mo,* † *maa,* † *maa,* † *moa,* † *moo.* Gael. *mo.* Manx, *moo.* Ang. Sax. *ma.* Scot. *ma, may, maa, mae.* Eng. + *mo,* † *moe.* Sansc. *mah,* to increase. "One thing is tolerably clear about the Celtic forms, that they have lost a vowel-flanked *g :* cf. Sansc. *mahíyáns ;* Osc. *mais ;* Latin, *major,* for *mag-ios ;* Goth. *maiza ;* Gr. μείζων, from μεγίων." Stokes's Irish Glosses. 129.

MOYA, adj. Greatest. Llwyd, 243. A later form of *moycha,* qd. v.

MOYAR, s. m. Berries, such as grow in clusters, called acini. Llwyd, 94. *Moyar diu,* blackberries. In late Cornish it was contracted into *môr,* whence the sing. *moran.* W. *mwyar.* Arm. *mouiar, mouar.* Ir. *smeur.* Gael. *smeur.* Manx, *smair.* Gr. μόρον. Lat. *morum.*

MOYCHA, adj. Greatest, most. *Moycha dhodho drôk a wre, henna vedha an gwella gwâs,* whosoever did most evil to him, that one would be the best fellow. M.C. 112. *Hag cf moycha yn y beyn, yn y fâs y a drewé,* and he most greatly in his pain, they spat in his face. M.C. 196. *Nêb a geryn an moycha,* whom I loved the most. C.W. 90. Written also *mocha,* and *mochya,* qd. v. W. *mŵyav,* † *mwyhav.* Arm. *muin.* Ir. † *maam.*

MOYRBREN, s. m. A mulberry tree, a bramble bush. Corn. Voc. *morus.* Comp. of *moyr,* id. qd. *moyar,* and *pren,* a tree. W. *merwydhen,* a mulberry tree ; *miar, miaren,* a bramble. Arm. *mouar, mouaren,* a mulberry.

MOYS, s. f. A table. *Ha'n gwŷn esa war en foys (voys) ef a rannas yntredha,* and the wine that was on the table he divided among them. M.C. 45. A later form of *muis,* qd. v.

MOYS, comp. conj. More than. (*Moy—ys.*) *Me ny gafn moys kyns reson gans gwŷr dh'y vrusy,* I have no more than before reason with truth to judge him. M.C. 117.

MUCH, s. f. A daughter. Corn. Voc. *filia.* Probably an abbreviated form of *myrch,* in the same way as *uch* is used in Welsh pedigrees for *verch.* See *Myrch.*

MUI, adj. Greater, more. *Mui brâs,* greater. Llwyd, 84. *Muy vel,* more than. 248. Another form of *moy,* qd. v.

MUIN, adj. Slender, fine, thin. Corn. Vocab. *gracilis.* The older form of *moin,* and *môn,* qd. v. W. *muin,* † *mein.* Arm. *moan, moen.* Ir. *min.* Gael. *mín.* Gr. μανός.

MUIS, s. f. A table. Corn. Voc. *mensa.* The later form was *moys,* qd. v. W. *mwys,* † *muis.* (W. *clemuis,* Lib. Land. 155. = Lat. *clemens:* W. *monwys,* = Lat. *monensis.*) Ir. *meis,* † *mias.* Gael. *mias.* Goth. *mês.* Lith. *miesa.* Gr. μάζα. Lat. *mensa.*

MUNYS, adj. Small, little. *Yn lyfryow scryfys yma, bôs collenwys louené a ganow an flechys da, ha'n rê munys ow lené,* in books it is written, that joy is fulfilled from the mouths of good children, and little ones sucking. P.C. 438. Written also *menys,* qd. v.

MUR, adj. Great, much, many. *Mûr a foly ew dhodho, an kêth frût-na mar a'n gâs,* it is a great folly in him, if he leaves that same fruit. O.M. 191. *Mûr varth a'm bûs dyogel, an beys dh'y terry na'm gâs,* great wonder is surely to me, that the earth will not leave me to break it. O.M. 371. *Dhe vanneth dhym mûr a blêk,* thy blessing pleases me much. O.M. 455. *Kyn wylly mûr wolowys,* though thou see much light. O.M. 717. *Hŷr, gans mûr a scorennow,* tall, with many boughs. O.M. 838. *May 'thens mûr a lûs dyswrcys,* so that many men are destroyed. O.M. 1560. *Gans can ha mûr a cledh dhe vcwnans y tassorchas,* with a hundred and more of angels to life he was risen. R.D. 515. Written in the Cornish Vocabulary, *maur,* qd. v.

MURRIAN, s. m. Ants or emmets. Llwyd, 61. *Crig murrian,* the hill of ants, is the name of a place, in the parish of Filley. Sing. *murrianen.* Llwyd, 96, 240. W. *mor, morion,* sing. *morionen.* Arm. *merien, merion,* sing. *merienen, merionen.* Ir. + *moirb.* Gael. + *moirb.* Lat. *myrmex.*

MURS, conj. Unless. *Dén fŷth ol murs dre pystry yn try deydh ny'n dhrehafsé,* any man, unless through sorcery, in three days would not raise it. P.C. 1764. Generally written *mars,* qd. v.

MUS, adj. Mad. *A Bertyl, asogé mûs, ha goky dres ol an dûs yw yw fol,* O Bartholomew, thou art mad beyond all the men who are fools. R.D. 971.

MUSAC, adj. Stinking, ill smelling. Pryce. W. *mŵs.* Arm. *mouezuz.*

MUSCEGY, v. a. To grow mad, or distracted, to be raving. Part. *muscegys. Ty a hewel muskegys, hag yn gokyneth gyllys, awos an Dew a geunyth,* thou seemest crazed, and in folly gone, because of the God whom thou mentionest. O.M. 1511. *Thomas, ty yw muskegys hag yn muscokneth gyllys,* thou art mad, and in madness gone. R.D. 1127. *A Thomas, nyns yw goky, ydh esas ow nuskegy yw mês a fordh,* O Thomas, he is not foolish, thou art raving out of the way. R.D. 1466.

MUSCOC, adj. Mad, distracted, amazed. *Tormentors, yn kettep guas, euch alemma gans Iudas dhe gerhas an guas muscok, ugy ow ymwryl mâp Dew,* executioners, every fellow, go hence with Judas to fetch the crazed fellow, (that) is making himself a son of God. P.C. 961. Ir. *meisgeach,* † *mesce,* intoxicated. Gael. *misgeach.*

MUSCOCNETH, s. m. Madness, folly. *Ty yw muskegys, hag yn muscokneth gyllys,* thou art mad, and in madness gone. R.D. 1128. *Benen na gows muscocneth, râk an kêth dên-ma bythqueth ny'n servyes,* woman, do not speak folly, for this same man I never served. P.C. 1283. *Anodho dycheth vyé, y wokyneth na agé, ha'y muscochneth,* of him it were a pity his folly not to leave, and his madness. P.C. 1990.

MUSURE, v. a. To measure. *Euch dh'y drehy hep lettyé, ha musurouch ef yn lên*, go ye to cut it, and measure it faithfully. O.M. 2506. *My a'n musur lour yn ta, na bertheuch own a henna*, I will measure it well enough, do not ye have fear of that. O.M. 2507. *Ottevé musurys da, dên yn bŷs ny'n musur guel*, see it well measured; no man in the world will measure it better. O.M. 2513. *Cafos moy dhys aban rês, try heys dhe bâl kemery, a drus musury trylles, ha gwet na wra falsury*, since it is necessary for thee to have more, three lengths of thy spade thou shalt take; athwart thou shalt measure three breadths, and take care, that thou doest no deceit. O.M. 393. *May hallo bôs musurys*, that it may be measured. O.M. 2566. *My re wrâk y vusuré rág an kêth wheil-na dewyth*, I have measured it for this same work twice. O.M. 2568. *Myserouch tol dh'y dhulé*, measure ye a hole for his hands. P.C. 2740. W. *mesur*, † *misur*. Arm. *musur*. Ir. *mensaire*, † *mesur*. Gael. *meusair*. Lat. *mensura*. Med. Lat. *mesura*. Fr. *mesure*. Eng. *measure*. Sansc. *mas*, to measure.

MUSY, s. f. Maids. *Llwyd*, 242. Plural of *môs*, qd. v.

MY, pron. suhs. I, me. See *Mi*.

MYC, s. m. A discovery, detection. *Me ne vedhaf confedhys, om bôs ynof folsury; sottal lower ôv, me a grŷs; hag a vyn môs heb gwil gyck, yn wedhan pûr smoth heb myck avel êl whêk assyncs*, I shall not be convicted that there is in me deceit; I am subtle enough, I believe; and will go without making a noise, into the tree very smoothly without detection, like a sweet angel adorned. C.W. 40.

MYCHTERN, s. m. A sovereign, a king. *Aban yw mychtern Faro budhys, ha'y ost ol ganso, ny am bŷdh crês dhe vewé*, since king Pharoah is drowned, and all his host with him, we shall have peace to live. O.M. 1712. *Ow arluth ker caradow, mychtern ôs war ol an bŷs*, my dearly beloved lord, king thou art over all the world. O.M. 2114. *Lavar dhymmo vy yn scon, mars ôs mychtern Yedhewon*, tell me forthwith if thou art the king of the Jews. P.C. 1583. *A vynnech ol assentyé rák pask my dhylyfryé Ihesu, mychtern Yedhewon*, will ye assent for passover I should liherate Jesus, king of the Jews? P.C. 2039. *Cesar yw agan arluth mychtern, Cæsar is our lord king*. P.C. 2221. W. *mychteyrn*, comp. of † *mycht*, id. qd. Ir. *mocht*, great, and *teyrn*, a king. Sansc. *mahat*, great.

MYCHTERNES, s. f. A queen. *I feynys o brâs ha creff yn ioy dhedhy trylys yw, rág mygternas yw yn nêf, dhe vôs gordhyys hy yw gyw*, her pains (that) were great and strong are turned iuto joy for her, for she is queen in heaven, to be worshipped she is worthy. M.C. 226.

MYCHTERNETH, s. m. Sovereignty, dominion, royalty, a kingdom. *Mychterneth war aga tûs a fe arlythy a y yus kyns ys lemyn*, dominion over their people lords have had over them before now. P.C. 785. *Aberth yn bêdh del re'th worsyn, pen vychterneth, dre dhe eledh bŷdli socor dhym*, within the tomb, as we have put thee, head of royalty, by thy angels be succour to us. R.D. 315. *Del yw ef pen mychterneth, me a grŷs yn mês a bêdh hydhew a sêf*, as he is head of sovereignty, I believe out of the grave that to-day he will rise. R.D. 712. Written also *mychternes*. *In mêdh Ihesus, nyngugy ow mygternes yn bŷs-ma*, says Christ, my kingdom is not in this world. M.C. 102.

MYDZHOVAN, s. f. A yoke. *Llwyd*, 74.

MYDHYGYETH, s. m. A remedy, a cure. *Mydhygyeth a vŷdh gwrŷs, may fo yâch a pûp clêves, mar crŷs y vôs Dew a'n nêf*, a cure shall be made, that he may be sound from all disease, if he will believe that he is God of heaven. R.D. 1670. From *medhec*, qd. v.

MYGENOW, s. f. A pair of bellows. P.C. 2713. See *Megin*.

MYGILDER, s. m. Warmth. *Llwyd*, 162, 240. From adj. *mygil*, warm. W. *muygyl*. Arm. *mougur*.

MYGYS, part. Nourished, fed, reared, bred. *A mester kêr caradow, del leweryth, my a grŷs y fŷdh agan enefow dre levarow Dew mygys*, O dearly beloved master, as thou sayest, I helieve that our souls shall he fed by the words of God. P.C. 76. *Ny dâl dhodho y naché, rák ef yw a Galilé, ha 'y dên, ganso prest mygys*, he ought not to deny him, for he is of Galilee, and his man, always brought up with him. P.C. 1282. Part. pass. of *maga*, qd. v.

MYHTERNETH, s. m. Sovereingty. *Llwyd*, 240. A late form of *mychterneth*, qd. v.

MYIN, s. m. Stones. *Fôs a vyin*, a stone wall. *Llwyd*, 230. Plural of *mean*, qd. v.

MYL, card. num. A thousand. See *Mil*.

MYLYGE, v. a. To curse. Part. *mylygys, mylyges, mylcges*. *Aban golsté worty hy, ha gruthyl dres ow defen, mylygé a wrâf defry an nôr y'th whythres hogen*, since thou hearkenedst to her, and actedst beyond my prohibition, I will assuredly curse the earth in thy evil deed. O.M. 271. *Ytho bedhyth mylyges, pûr wŷr drys ol an bestes a gerdho war an nôr vcis*, now thou shalt be accursed, very truly above all the heasts that walk on the carth of the world. O.M. 311. *May whrussons cam dremené, y vyllyk an prŷs*, that they did the evil transgression, they will curse the time. O.M. 338. *A mylyges y'th obcr, ty re'n ladhes rum loncté*, O cursed in thy deed, thou hast killed him by my truth. O.M. 610. *Ty Sathnas, deavel mylygys*, thou Satan, devil accursed! P.C. 137. This seems derived immediately from the Latin *maledico*, as W. *melldigo*. See also *Mollethia*.

MYN, v. a. He will. 3 pers. s. fut. of *mynny*, qd. v. *Mar myn Dew*, if God wills. O.M. 650.

MYN, s. m. A kid. *Llwyd*, 241. Written in the Cornish Vocabulary, *min*, qd. v.

MYNES, v. a. To go. *Llwyd*, 241. Generally written *mones*, qd. v.

MYNGAR, s. m. A horse collar, a yoke. *Llwyd*, 164. W. *mynwar; mynci*, a hame. Ir. *muince*. A horse collar made of twisted straw, and called *munger* is still in use in Cornwall.

MYNIC, adj. Stony. *Carvynik*, the stony town, in Gorran. From *mcyn*, stones. W. *maenawg*.

MYNNAN, s. f. A kid. *Llwyd*, 241. W. *mynnan*. See *Min*.

MYNNAS, s. m. Will, purpose, intention. *Mes bedhens guris dhe vynnas, Arluth Du, dhe vôdh del vr*, but let thy will be done, Lord God, thy pleasure as it may he. M.C. 55. *Gans levarow a'n scornyas; gallus o grantis dhedhé dhe wrthyll aga mynnas, yn della ef a vynné*, with words the scorned him; power was granted to them to do their will; even so he would. M.C. 70. *Gwrêns Dew y vôdh, ha'y vynnas, py-penag vo yn y vreys*, let God do his pleasure and his will, whatever may he in

MYRCH 261 MYTTYN

his mind. O.M. 1153. W. *mynnad.* Arm. *mennad.*

MYNNES, v. a. To purpose, to will, to wish. *Arluth, mar callé wharfos, gynen ty dhe vynnes bôs omma pûp ûr,* Lord, if it could be with us that thou wouldst be here always. R.D. 2440. *Suel vynno bôs sylwys, golsowens ow lavarow,* whoever would be saved, let him hearken to my words. M.C. 2. *Ihesus Crist a ve mevyys, may fynnas dijskynna yn gwerhas ha bôs genys,* Jesus Christ was moved that he would descend into a virgin and be born. M.C. 4. *Y vôs kyllys ny vynna,* he would not that he should be lost. M.C. 7. *Ihesus Crist par del vynnas, dhodho ef a worthebys,* Jesus Christ as he would, unto him he answered. M.C. 11. *Ow honoré mar mynnyth,* if thou wilt worship me. M.C. 16. *Pema nêb a vyn dhe guhudha,* where is he that will accuse thee? M.C. 34. *Pan vynnouch agis honon, wy a gîl gûll da dhedhé,* when ye wish yourselves, ye can do good to them. M.C. 37. *Doyn dhyn dustuny a wra, mygtern a fyn bôs synsys,* he will bear witness to us, that he would be held a king. M.C. 111. *Rûg henna ef a vynsé gwethé Crist,* therefore he wished to protect Christ. M.C. 127. *Mar mynnouch, me a'n chasty,* if ye wish, I will chastise him. M.C. 127. *Gortheby te ny vynsys,* thou wouldst not answer. M.C. 144. *Y ny vynsans y ranné,* they would not divide it. M.C. 190. *Mar a mynné amendyé,* if he would amend. P.C. 1862. *Me a grŷs y fynsco dhe comparya lemyn genof,* I believe that thou wouldst compare thyself with me. C.W. 16. *Mar mynta bôs exaltys,* if thou wilt be exalted. C.W. 48. *Dên a vynta ge gûl a bry,* man thou wilt make of earth. C.W. 20. *Ny vynnys cola orth dhe da,* thou wilt not hearken to thy good. *Ny vynsan dhe'th cusulya,* I would not advise thee. C.W. 50. For more examples, see the mutations *vynna,* &c. Written also *menny,* qd. v. W. *mynnu.* Arm. *menna.* Irish, *miannadh.* Gael. *miannach.* Manx, *mian.* Gr. μενω. Goth. *man.* Lith. *menu.* Russ. *mniu.* Germ. *meinen.* Ang. Sax. *menan.* Eng. *mean.* Sanse. *man.*

MYNS, s. m. Magnitude, size, quantity, multitude, number, all. *Rûg ydhewel dhym bôs da yn kynsa dŷdh mŷns ûs gwrŷs; bedhens ebron dreys pûp tra, râk kudhé mŷns ûs formyys,* for it appears to me to be good all that is made on the first day: let the sky be above every thing, to cover all that is created. O.M. 20. *Ke kymmer mŷns a vynny,* go, take as much as thou wilt. O.M. 403. *Gallas an porthow brewyon, hag ol mŷns o,* gone are the gates to pieces, and all that there was. R.D. 127. *A Adam, dhyso crês l yn wêdh dhe ol ow fleches mŷns yw gwyryon,* O Adam, peace to thee l also to all my children, as many as are innocent. R.D. 163. *Yn mêdh Pylat worth an mŷns, a'n pêch provas ris yw ry,* says Pilate to the multitude, it is necessary to give proof of the crime. M.C. 117. W. *maint,* † *meint.* Arm. *ment.* Ir. *meid,* † *meit.* Gael. *meud.*

MYNYDH, s. m. A mountain. Pl. *mynydhyow.* See *Menedh.*

MYRAS, v. a. To behold. See *Miras.*

MYRCH, s. f. A daughter, a young woman, a girl, a maid, a virgin. Pl. *myrches. Na ny lever bôs Dew ken, saw an Tâs a nêf yn ban; ha ty voren myrch hyben a wra dew dhys dhe honan,* we say not that there is another God, but the Father of heaven above; and thou, jade girl, the other makest a God to thee thyself. O.M. 2648. *A pûr voren plos myrch gal ty a verow cowal,* O very jade, dirt, daughter of evil, thou shalt die quite. O.M. 2736. *O vryes, hep falladow, mebyon, ha myrhes kefrys,* O spouse, without fail, sons and daughters likewise. O.M. 1038. *Myrches a Ierusalem, na clouch, na na wreuch drem warnaf vy, nag onan vŷth,* daughters of Jerusalem, weep not, nor make lament on me, not any one. P.C. 2639. Written also *merch,* qd. v.

MYRWEL, v. a. To die. *My a'd pcys, Arluth uhel, dhe'n tŷr ty a ry cummyas, ma'm gasso kyns ys myrwel ynno bôs dhym dhe welas,* I pray thee, high Lord, that it allow me before dying to seek for myself food in it. O.M. 377. More generally written *merwel,* qd. v. Llwyd, 247, gives another form, *myrwy.*

MYSC, s. m. The midst, the middle. *Yn mŷsk,* among. *My a welas hy gurydhyow bŷs yn yffarn dywcnys yn mŷsk mûr a tewolgow,* I saw its roots even into hell descending, in midst of great darkness. O.M. 784. *Pyw an brassé dên senges yn mŷsk ol dh'y dhyskyblon,* who is esteemed the greatest man amongst all thy disciples? P.C. 774. *Senseuch ef yn agan mŷsk,* hold ye him in our midst. P.C. 1374. *Mar ny vŷdh an whethlow due yn agcs mŷsk,* if the idle tales be not finished amongst you. R.D. 1401. *In agis mŷsk pan esen, lahys Du dhcuch ow tysky,* when I was among you, teaching to you the laws of God. M.C. 75. Written also *mêsc,* qd. v. W. *mŷsg.* Arm. *mesg.* Ir. *measg.* Gael. *measg* Manx, *mest.* Sansc. *maks,* to mix. Lat. *miscco.*

MYSHEVY, v. a. To do mischief, to injure, to destroy. Part. *myshevyys. Nyns ûs bewé na fella, ydhon warbarth myshevyys,* there is no living any longer, we are altogether destroyed. O.M. 1704.

MYSHYF, s. m. Mischief, harm, evil. *Myshyf lemmyn codhys worthyn, nyns ûs bewé,* evil now has fallen upon us, there is no living. O.M. 1707. From the English.

MYSTERDEN, s. m. An architect. Its proper meaning is superintendant, or head man, being compounded of *myster,* a master, and *dên,* a man. *Syr arluth, my a wra dhe worhemmyn ol yn lyen, hag a warn dhe vysterdens avorow dhys may teffens yn kettep pen,* Sire lord, I will do thy command all entirely, and will warn the architects that they come to thee to-morrow, every head. O.M. 2416, 2431.

MYTERN, s. m. A king. *Clevas an mytern,* king's evil. Llwyd, 156. A later form of *mychtern,* qd. v. W. *mydeyrn.*

MYTERNES, s. f. A queen. Llwyd, 138. A later form of *mychternes,* qd. v.

MYTERNETH, s. m. Sovereignty. Pryce. A later form of *mychterneth,* qd. v.

MYTTYN, s. m. The morning. *Cosel my re bowesus, assyw whêk an hûn myttyn,* I have rested softly, sweet is the morning sleep. O.M. 2074. *Ke, gorhemmyn ol dhe'n masons yn cyté may tyffons umma myttyn war beyn crcgy ha tenné,* go, command all the masons in the city, that they come here in the morning, on pain of hanging and drawing. O.M. 2270. *Pan sefsys hydhew myttyn, yâch êns aga icyw,* when thou gottest up this morning, sound were their sinews. P.C. 2680. *En varogyon a guskas myttyn, ha'n gŷdh ow tardhé,* the soldiers slept at morning, and the day breaking. M.C. 243. Written also *metin,* qd. v.

MYYN, s. m. A mouth. *Dynythys yw, hag yma yn hy myyn branch olyf glâs*, she is come, and there is in her beak a branch of green olive. O.M. 1122. Another form of *mîn*, qd. v.

MYYN, s. m. Stones. *Gans myyn gwreuch hy knoukyé erna wrello tremené*, with stones do ye beat her until she does die. O.M. 2094. *Ry whaf dhedhy my a wra gans myyn grow yn brâs garow*, give a blow to her I will, with gravel stones very sharply. O.M. 2756. Written also *meyn*, being the plural of *maen*, qd. v.

N.

This letter is a primary initial, and immutable in Cornish, and in the other Celtic languages. In Welsh and Irish, it is also a secondary letter, being the nasal mutation of *d*. Thus W. *davad*, a sheep; *vy navad*, my sheep. Ir. *duil*, desire; *ar nuil*, our desire.

NA, adv. No, not, neither, nor, that not. *Gans gloteny of pan welas cam na ylly y dolla*, with gluttony when he saw that he could not a whit deceive him. M.C. 13. *Me ny'th dampnyaf yredy, ha na wra moy pecha*, I will not condemn thee indeed, and do thou not sin any more. M.C. 34. *Ef ny ylly dre dhewsys godhaff na nŷll drôk na da*, he could not through godhead endure either evil or good. M.C. 60. *Yn médh Pedyr, dhym na ûs troys na leyff na vo golhys*, says Peter, leave not to me either foot or hand that it be not washed. M.C. 46. *Aban na fyn dewedhé*, since he will not end. P.C. 2115. Before vowels *nag* is used qd. v. W. *na*. Arm. *na*. Ir. *na*. Gael. *na*. Gr. *ve, vŋ*. Lat. *ne, ni*. Goth. *ni, nih*. Sclav. *nc*. Fr. *ne*. Scot. *na*. Span. It. Eng. *no*.

NA, adv. There. An abbreviated form of *ena*, and subjoined to substantives to express the demonstrative pronoun *that*; *an dên-na*, that man, lit. the man there. *Ny dŷf guels na flour yn bŷs yn kéth fordh-na may kyrdhys, ha ny ow tôs a le-na*, neither grass nor flower in the world will grow in that same road that I walked, and we coming from that place. O.M. 714. *Y vôs Dew ha dên yn wlân dhe'n kéth tra-na cryggyans rén*, that he is God and man clearly, to that same thing belief we give. P.C. 2406. *Dre worthyp Crist yn ûr-na*, by the answer of Christ in that hour. M.C. 12. *Pan glewas an lavarow-na*, when he heard those words. M.C. 147. The same idiom prevails in Welsh, as *y dŷn yna*, that man; *y lle yna*, that place. So also in Armoric, as *an dra-ze*, that thing.

NABOW, v. a. He will know. *Me a'n nabow dyougel, ydh o fe deaul kyns merwel, aberth yn nôr*, I know it certainly, that he was a devil before dying, within the world. R.D. 2120. *Nabow* is an abbreviated form of *anabow*, 3 pers. s. fut. of a verb agreeing with W. *nabod, adnabôd*, Arm. *anavout*. The infinitive used in Cornish is *answonvos*, qd. v.

NACHA, v. a. To deny, to refuse, to forswear. Written also *naché*. Part. pass. and preterite *nechys*. *Pedyr y umdennas yn ûr-na del rebechsé, ow nacha Du leun a râs, hag ef gwarnyys del vyé*, Peter went out in that hour, as he had sinned, denying God full of grace, and he warned as he had been. M.C. 86. *Ef a nachas y arluth a dhesympys*, he denied his Lord forthwith. M.C. 84. *Kyns ys boys colyek clewys, te a'm nâch tergweth*, before that a cock is heard, thou wilt deny me thrice. M.C. 49. *Kyns ys bôs kullyek kenys, ter gwyth y wrêch ow naché*, before that the cock hath crowed, three times you will deny me. P.C. 904. *Ne ny'n nachaf*, I will not deny him. P.C. 910. *Ny'm nâch mar a'n pesaf ef*, he will not deny me if I will pray him. P.C. 1166. *Y'n nachen ef a'm guarnyas*, he warned me that I should deny him. P.C. 1420. *Govy vŷth pan y'n nechys*, alas, when I ever denied him. P.C. 1428. The guttural was often softened into *h*, and the word written *naha*, qd. v. W. *naca, nuccâu, nagu*. Arm. *nacha*. Lat. *nego*.

NADEDH, s. f. A needle. Llwyd, 10, 41, writes it *nadzhedh*, to express the corrupt sound of his day. W. *nydwydh, nodwydh*, † *notuid* in Oxf. Gloss. Arm. *nadoz, nadoué*. Ir. *snathad*. Gael. *snathad*. Manx, *snaid, sned*.

NADELIC, s. m. A birthday, the Nativity. *Deu Nadelic*, natalis (Christi,) Christmas day. Llwyd, 97. (W. *dŷdh nadolig*.). ‡ *Flôh vye gennes en Mis-Merh; ni trehes e bigel en Miz-East; e a roz towl dhe proanter Powel, miz-du ken nadelik*, a child was born in the month of March; we cut his navel in the month of August; he gave a fall to the parson of Paul, the black month before the Nativity. *Pryce's Cornish Riddles*. W. *nadolig*. Arm. *nadelec*. Ir. *nodhlag*, † *notluicc*. Gael. *nollnig*. Manx, *nolig*. All from the Lat. *natalicius*.

NADER, s. f. A snake, a viper, an adder. Corn. Voc. *vipera, vel serpens vel anguis*. *Gans nader ydh ôf guanheys, hag ol warbarth vynymmcys a fyne trois dhe'n golon*, by an adder I am stung, and altogether poisoned from the end of the foot to the heart. O.M. 1750. *Môrnader*, a lamprey. Llwyd, 96. W. *nadyr, nudr, neidyr*. Arm. *aer*. Ir. *nathair*. † *nathir*. Gael. *nathair*. Lat. *natrix*. Goth. *nadr*. Germ. *natter*. Ang. Sax. *nœddre*. The English word *adder* seems to be a mistake arising from the confusion between *a nadder* and *an adder*; so also *a newt* and *an eft*.

NAG, adv. No, not, nor. Used before vowels as *na* is before consonants. *Dal na bodhar ny asé nag omlanas nag onen*, blind nor deaf he left not that was not cured, not one. M.C. 25. *Prâg nag usy ef genes*, why is he not with thee ? O.M. 573. *Nag ûs fordh dhymmo dhe vôs sylwys*, nor is there a way for me to be saved. P.C. 1523. *Me a'n te war ow fŷdh, na nŷl yn nôs nag yn geydh nyn gevyth crês*, I will swear it to thee on my faith, no one, in night nor in day, hath peace. P.C. 1881. W. *nag*. Arm. *nag*.

NAHA, v. a. To deny, to refuse, to forswear. Written also *nahé*. Part. *nehys*. *Tan ow fŷdh, ny'th nahaff kyn fên ledhys*, on my faith, I will not deny thee though I be slain. O.M. 2129. *My ny allaf dhe nahé*, I cannot deny thee. O.M. 2129. *Awos godhewel ancow, ny nahas hy lavarow*, notwithstanding suffering death, she did not retract her words. O.M. 2761. *Ny'th ty nahaf bynary*, I will never deny thee. P.C. 907. *Ty a'n nahas*, thou didst deny him. R.D. 1351. *Na borth dout, ny vŷdh nehys*, bear not doubt, thou shalt not be denied. C.W. 42. Another form of *nacha*, qd. v.

NAHEN, adv. Otherwise. *Saw ma ny ŷl bos nahen, dhe*

vôdh prest yn pûp hchen y goulenwel yw ow whans, but if it be cannot otherwise, thy will always in every thing to fulfil is my wish. P.C. 1090. Nyns ûs dên vŷth a bŷs-ma a vra gúl dhym yn torma crygy nahen, there is not any man of this world, (that) shall make me now believe otherwise. R.D. 1126. Cot yw dhe dhydhyow dhe gy, nahen na grŷs, short are thy days to thee, think not otherwise. R.D. 2038. Comp. of na, nog. and hen for chen, being the regular aspirate mutation of cen, which is required after na. So W. créd, believe thou; na chréd, believe thou not.

NAM, s. m. An exception, defect, fault, blemish, offence, sin. Ha Iowan otté dhe vam ; yn della syns hy hep nam hedrévy why, and John, behold thy mother; so hold thou her, without exception, as long as thou livest. P.C. 2929. Honna o drôg préf, heb nam, a dullas Eva dhe vam, that was a wicked reptile, without exception, (that) deceived Eve thy mother. C.W. 138. W. nam. Arm. nam.

NAM, comp. pron. That not—me. (Na that not—me me.) Mûr varth a'm bûs dyogel, an brys dh'y terry na'm gâs, great wonder is surely to me, that the earth will not let me break it. O.M. 372. Nans yw lemmyn tremenes nêp dew-cans a vledhynnow, na'm buef dhe wruthyl genes, now there are gone by some two hundred years, that I have not had to do with thee. O.M. 658. My a vôr yn ta lemmyn, na'm bês bewé na filla, I know well now, that there is not living for me longer. O.M. 1884. Rák ow thorment a dhê scon, genouch na'm byvé trygé, for my suffering will come soon, that with you I shall not stay. P.C. 542. Genouch aban na'm bŷdh cres, dhyworthcuch mennaf mones adro yn pow, with you since there will not be peace for me, from you I will go about in the country. R.D. 1133. Dhe kckemmys na'm guello, hag yn perfyth a'n cresso, ow lên benneth me a pŷs, to as many as shall not see me, and shall perfectly believe it, my full blessing I pray. R.D. 1544. Tormentores, deuch yn scon, agan guryans na'm bo mêdh, executioners, come ye forthwith, that our work may not be a shame to me. R.D. 1878. W. na'm.

NAM, adv. Now. Lhwyd, 249.

NAMNA, adv. Almost, all but, well nigh. Namnag before vowels. Y golon namna dorré, his heart almost broke. M.C. 87. Ràg fout gwesc ha goscotter, namna vyrwyn râg anvos, for want of clothes and shelter, we are all well nigh perishing for cold. O.M. 302. Râg own namnag ôf pûr dhal, for fear I am well nigh quite blind. O.M. 1056. Namnag yw ow colon trôch, almost is my heart broken. P.C. 3185. Namna'n dullas, it almost blinded ns. R.D. 42. Namna'gan dallas golow, the light almost blinded ns. R.D. 302.

NAN, adv. Not, that not. Yn drog-gras dh'y dâs Adam, venytha nan geffo tam a wolow têk, in requital to his father Adam, that he shall never have a bit of fair light. O.M. 551. Hag ow bostyé y bôs ef Cryst gwŷr un vâb Dew a nêf, yn bŷs-ma nan geves pâr, and boasting that he is Christ, the one true son of God of heaven, in this world that hath not an equal. P.C. 1578. Agensow my a'n gweles, an Arluth nan geves pâr, lately I saw him, the Lord that hath not an equal. R.D. 912. Arm. nann.

NAN, comp. pron. Not him. (Na—'n.) Ef a doys a dhesympys maga town ty del wodhyé gans Cryst na vyé tregis, na bythqueth ef na'n guelsé, he swore forthwith as deep an oath as he knew, that he was not staying with Christ, and that he had never seen him. M.C. 85. Mars mar a pedha degis gans y dús, na'n caffan ny, yn urna bŷdh leverys ef dhe scvell dre vestry, but if he be carried away by his people, that we should not find him, then it will be said, that he arose through power. M.C. 240. Nêp na'n gordhyo del dhegouth nyns yw dén fûr, del gresaf, he that does not worship him as he ought, is not a wise man, as I believe. P.C. 215. Nêp na'n synso y sylwyas a dhu goef, he that does not hold him his Saviour, O God, woe is he! R.D. 614.

NAN, adv. comp. Not the. (Na—an.) En grows whêth nynj-o parys, na'n Edhewon ny wodhyé an prennyer py féns kefis dhe wruthyll crows anedhé, the cross was not yet ready, nor did the Jews know, whore the timbers should be found to make a cross of them. M.C. 151.

NANS, s. m. A valley, dale, ravine. Corn. Voc. vallis. Pl. nansow. In êr-na dhe'n menydhyow why a erch warnouch codhé ; yn ketella an nansow wy a bŷs ragas cudhé, in that hour ye shall bid the mountains to fall upon you; likewise the vallies ye shall pray to hide you. M.C. 170. It is preserved in the names of many places in Cornwall. Pennans, (W. Pennant,) in Creed. Trenans, (W. Trenant,) in St. Austell. Nans, in Illogan. Nans Avallen, (W. Nant Avallen,) the valley of the apple tree. Nans a Gollan, (W. Nant y gollen,) the valley of the hazel, &c. W. nant, a ravine, a brook. Arm. † nant. Now obsolete, but preserved in the names of places in Britanny, as Bronantcar, Nantes. The equivalent used in Armoric is traon, traoun, and more anciently in Buhez Nonn, tnou. Cf. also the Gaulish name Nantuates, in Cæsar. Nant is also used in Switzerland for a water-fall, as Nant d'Arpenaz, Nant d' Orli.

NANS, adv. Now. Used before vowels. A'n nêf my a dhêth yn nans, Eva wêk, gwella dhe cher, from heaven I am come now, sweet Eve, to better thy condition. O.M. 165. Nans yw tremenes nêp dew-cans a vledhynnow, now are gone by some two hundred years. O.M. 656. Nans yw hy prŷs a rey brwrys, now it is time to give judgment. P.C. 2471. Erbyn bonas henna guris, nans o prŷs gwesper yn wlâs, against that was done, it was now vesper-time in the country. M.C. 230.

NAS, adv. Not; that not—him, her, it, them. (Na—as.) Popel Ysral ny assaf, na's gorren y dhy whŷl cref, the people of Israel I will not allow, that I put them not to hard work. O.M. 1490. Ha'y holon whêk a ranné, me a lever, râg trystans, rag an grayth yn hy csé na's gwethé an Spyrys Sans, and her sweet heart would have parted, I say, for sorrow, had not the Holy Ghost protected her for the grace that was in her. M.C. 222. Râk y tue dydhyow may fenygouch an torrow na's tevé vythqueth flches, for the days will come, that ye shall bless the wombs, (that) have never borne children. 2647.

NASCRA, s. f. The womb. Bynuges re bo an prŷs may wrûk dhe dhôn y'm nascra, blessed be the time that I bore thee in my womb. R.D. 486. Probably connected with W. asgré, the heart, the bosom. Arm. asgre, ascre.

NATER, s. f. Nature. Ha'n enef del dascorsé erbyn nater gans un cry, and how he gave up the soul against nature with a cry. M.C. 206. From the English.

NATURETH, s. m. Natural affection. *Moreth an sêth, ha pytet, natureth o ha denseth*, grief (was) the arrow, and pity, natural affection it was and humanity. M.C. 223.

NATH, comp. pron. Not thy. (*Na—ath.*) *Râk dhe verkyé my a gura yn bŷs dên vy'th na'th ladho*, for I will mark thee in the world, that no man slay thee. O.M. 603. W. *na'th*.

NAUN, s. m. Hunger. Corn. Voc. *famis*. Written in the Ordinalia *noun*. *Arluth cûf, ol henna gulán try hês ow fûl mar a'm be, my ha'm gwrêk ha'm flôch byhan bysy vŷdh dhe sostené ; mar tue moy nys tewyth man, râg nown y wrôns elamderé*, dear Lord, all that quite three lengths of my spade if I have, me, and my wife, and my little child it will be hard to support ; if more come, it will not be enough, they will faint from hunger. O.M. 400. W. *newyn*. Arm. *naoun*. Ir. †*nuna*.

NAVYTH, adv. Never. (*Na-bŷth.*) *A Simon, na gous un gêr, navyth, navyth yn awher ny sevys nês*, O Simon, speak not a word ; never, never, unhappily, he has not risen again. R.D. 1020.

NAW, card. num. Nine. *Dew a rôs dhyn an naw ran râg bewé orto*, God gave to us the nine parts to live upon it. O.M. 493. *Ioseph yn dan naw alwcdh ha Nichodemus yn wêdh gurcuch y pûr fest*, Joseph under nine keys, and Nichodemus also, make yo them very fast. R.D. 31. *Drewhy dhymno, hep lettyé, ha me a's ygor wharré an darasow agan naw*, bring yo them to me, without delaying, and I will open soon our nine doors. R.D. 639. *Naw eans*, nine hundred. *Naw degves*, nineteenth. *Naw pons*, nine pounds. *Llwyd*, 251. W. *naw*. Arm. *naû*. Ir. *naoi*, † *noi*, † *noe*. Gael. *naoi*. Manx, *nuy*. Gr. ἐννέα. Lat. *novem*. Isl. *niu*. Swed. *nio*. Sansc. *navan*.

NAWNJ, adv. Now. A corruption of *nans*, the final *s* being changed into *j* or *g* soft. *Crows Ihesus nawnj-o parys ; y êth dh'y ladhé yn scon*, the cross of Jesus was now ready ; they went to slay him forthwith. M.C. 160. *Ynircdhé pows Ihesus a ve dyskis ; y dysky mûr a'n grevyé ; worto fast nawng-o glenys*, among them the coat of Jesus was removed ; its being removed grieved him much ; it was now clinging close to him. M.C. 176.

NAWNZAC, card. num. Nineteen. *Llwyd*, 176, writes it ‡ *nowndzhak*. A corruption of *nawntek*. Arm. *naontek*. This number is very differently expressed in Welsh by *pedwar-ar-bymtheg*, i. e. four on fifteen. Ir. *naoi-dheag*. Gael. *naoi-dheug*. Manx, *nuy-jeig*. Gr. ἐννεα-καί-δεκα. Lat. *novemdecim*.

NEA, v. a. To deny, to refuse. *Râg henna voyd a lema ; na whela agen nea, mâb molathow par del ôs*, wherefore begone from hence ; seek not to deny us, son of curses as thou art. C.W. 92. A late form of *naha* or *nacha*.

NEB, pron. Whoever, who, whom, who, any, any one, some, every. Written also *nêp*. *Godhaf paynys pan vynnas, nêb na ylly gûll peches*, when he was willing to suffer pains, he that could not commit sin. M.C. 3. *Lemyn ny a fill gwelas lavar Du manga del vera nêb a vynno y glewas*, now we may see how the word of God will feed whoever will hear it. M.C. 12. *Pan omsettyas dhe dempté guthyll pêch nêb na ylly*, when he set himself to tempt him who could not commit sin. M.C. 20. *Yn nêb chan a servys*, in every kind of service. *Dre nêb fordh a govaytis*, through some way of covetousness. M.C. 15.

Nêb a whelcuch why me yw, I am he whom ye seek. M.C. 68. *Nêb dew eans a vledhynnow*, some two hundred years. O.M. 657. *Nêb na whytho, grêns fannyé*, he that blows not, let him fan. P.C. 1243. *Worth nêp a glewas govyn*, ask thou of some one who has heard. P.C. 1260. W. *nêb*, †*nep*. Arm. *neb*, †*nep*. Ir. *neach*, † *nech*, † *neich*, † *neb*. Gael. *neach*. Lat. *nemo*.

NEBES, s. m. Some portion, somewhat, a little, a few, a small number. *Arluth, hen yw re nebes, mar gurên flôch vŷth denythy*, Lord, this is too little, if we do any children produce. O.M. 389. *Dhe'n Arluth dhe will yma dre dhe vôdh gansé nebes*, the Lord has to do, by thy will, something with them. P.C. 208. *Yma dhymmo nebes dhe leverel dhys*, I have somewhat to say to thee. P.C. 495. *Nebes servys te a wra*, a little service thou shalt do. P.C. 3009. W. *nebaved*. Arm. *nebeûd*.

NEBTRA, s. m. Something. Corn. Voc. *aliquid*. (*Nêb—tra.*) W. *nebtra*, nothing. *Llwyd*, 99. Arm. *netra*.

NEBYN, pron. s. Some one, any one, certain. *Llwyd*, 175. (*Neb—un.*) ‡ *Hei a kynsilias gen nebyn vanah a erra en tre*, she consulted with a certain monk (that) was in the town. 252. W. *nêb un*.

NECHYS, part. Denied. *Yn lowen dhys kemer e, râg nechys by ny bedhyth*, gladly take him to thee, for thou shalt never be denied. P.C. 3130. Part. pass. of *nacha*, qd. v. It is also the preterite.

NEDELIC, s. m. Christmas day. *Llwyd*, 17. Another form of *Nadelic*, qd. v.

NEDH, s. m. Nits. *Nêdh* is a plural aggregate, whence the sing. *nedhan*, f. a single nit. *Llwyd*, 78. W. *nêdh*, s. *nedhen*. Arm. *nez*, s. *nezen*. Ir. *sneadh*, *snidh*, † *sned*. Gael. *sneadh*, *snidh*. Manx, *snieug*. Sansc. *niksâ*. Gr. κόνιν, κόνιδ-ος. Lat. *lens*, *lendis*. Slav. *gnida*. N.H.G. *nisse*. Lith. *glinda*. Ang. Sax. *hnitu*. Eng. *nit*.

NEDIIE, v. a. To spin, to turn, to twist. Part. *nedhes*. *Adam, ke yn mês a'n volâs, troha ken pow dhe vewé ; ty dhe honyn dhe balas, dhe wrêk genes dhe nedhé*, Adam, go out of the country, towards another land to live ; thou thyself to dig, thy wife with thee to spin. O.M. 346. *Eva kymmer dhe gygel, râg nedhé dhynny dyllas*, Eve, take thy distaff, to spin for us clothes. O.M. 368. *Guns kegel a dhesempys, nedhé dyllas me a wra*, with distaff immediately I will spin clothes. O.M. 416. *An lysúan bian gen i'ar nedhes*, the small plant with the twisted stalk. *Llwyd*, 245. W. *nydhu*. Arm. *neza*. Ir. *sniomh*. Gael. *sniomh*. Manx, *sneeu*. Sw. *sno*. Gr. *νήθω*, *νήw*. Lat. *neo*.

NEDHOW, s. m. News. *Nynsouch lemmyn gowygyou, ow môs dres pow flatturyon, ow leverel an nedhow*, are ye not now liars, going through the country chattering, telling the news ? R.D. 1512. A contracted form of *newydhow*, pl. of *newydh*, qd. v.

NEF, s. m. Heaven. Corn. Vocab. *celum*. *An dûs rês a dheserya dhedhé gulâs nêf o kyllys*, the good people desired for them the country of heaven (that) was lost. M.C. 4. *En Tâs a nêf y'm gylwyr*, the Father of heaven I am called. O.M. 1. *Y lavaraf, nêf ha tŷr bedhens formyys orth ow brŷs*, I say, heaven and earth be formed according to my mind. O.M. 8. *Arloth Dew a'n nêf, an Tâs*, Lord God of heaven, the Father. O.M. 105. *A le-na ydh yskynnaf yn ban bŷs yn glascor nêf*, from that place I will ascend up even to the kingdom of heaven. R.D. 2402. In late Cornish it was pronounccd *nêv.* Llwyd, 45. W. *nèv, †néff.* Arm. *env, † nef.* Ir. *neamh, † nem.* Gael. *neamh.* Manx, *niau.* Slav. *nebo.* Lott. *debbes,* (for *dnebbes.*) Sansc. *nabhas.* Gr. νέφος. Lat. *nubes.*

NEFFRE, adv. Ever, for ever. *Dhe vestry a vŷdh ledhys neffré war en encvow,* thy mastery shall be destroyed for ever over the souls. M.C. 17. *War agan flehys yn frâs ha warnan bedhans neffré,* on our children greatly and on us be it for ever. M.C. 149. *Benyges nefré re by,* blessed ever be thou. O.M. 819. Borrowed from the English.

NEGIS, s. m. Business, errand, message. Written also *neges, negys,* plur. *negyssyow,* and *nygys,* pl. *nygyssow,* qd. v. *Iudas êth yn y negis,* Judas went on his business. M.C. 62. *Me a grŷs yn ta spedyé om negis hancth yn nôs,* I believe that I shall speed well in my business this very night. M.C. 63. *Agis negis pyth yw e,* your business, what is it? M.C. 69. *Gorryb ty a vŷdh oll a'th negys,* an answer thou shalt have to all thy errand. C.W. 126. *Ow negyssyow ydhew gurŷs,* my businesses are performed. C.W. 136. W. *neges.* Lat. *negotium.*

NEHYS, part. Denied, disavowed. *Râg henna gwreuch amendya, agis foly bŷdh nehys,* therefore do ye amend, your folly shall be disavowed. C.W. 170. Part. pass. of *naha,* qd. v.

NEI, pron. v. We, us. Llwyd uses this form to express the sound of *ni* in his time. ‡ *Ragon nei,* for us. ‡ *En an halow nei,* on our hills. 245.

NEID, s. m. A nest. Corn. Voc. *nidus.* This is the old form of *neith,* as written by Llwyd, 99, pl. *neithow,* 242, 245. ‡ *Mi'rig gwelaz an karnow idzha en gullez ha'n idhen môr aral kil y ge neitho,* I saw the rocks (on which) the gulls and other sea birds make their nests. Pryce writes it *nŷth.* W. *nŷth.* Arm. *neiz.* Ir. *nead.* Gael. *nead.* Manx, *edd.* Gr. †ναός. Lat. *nidus.* Sansc. *nida,* (*nad* to sit.)

NEIHUR, adv. Last night, yesterday evening. Pryce. Written by Llwyd, 242, *nehuer.* ‡ *Ma agen ost nci destriez nehuer, ha nei dal krêg ragta,* our host was killed last night, and we shall be hanged for it. W. *neithiwyr.* Arm. *neizur.* Gr. νύκτωρ. Lat. *nocte-hesterna, nocte heri.*

NEIL, pron. s. One of two, one or the other, one. *Iudas êth a dhesympys a neyl tu dhe omgregy,* Judas went forthwith on one side to hang himself. M.C. 105. *Heys Crist y a gemeras a'n neyll léf bŷs yn yben,* the length of Christ they took from the one hand to the other. M.C. 178. *Mar possé a'n neyll tenewen râg y scôdh hy a'n grevyé,* if he leant on the one side, for his shoulder it grieved him. M.C. 205. *A dystouch mars ty a dhêg a neyl pen dhe dour Cedron, cachaf yben pûr anwhek,* if thou wilt immediately carry the one end to the water of Cedron, I will seize the other very sharp. O.M. 2815. *Na neile,* neither of the two. Llwyd, 98. Generally written in the Dramas *nŷl,* qd. v. W. *naill; ail,* second. Arm. *an eil.* Ir. *nail, † aile, † aill, † naile, † uaill.* Gael. *nall, null.*

NELL, s. m. Might, power, strength. *Me a glewas leverel an urlont y dhe denné war y ben gans kymmys nell ma 'téth an dreyn ha cropyé dhe'n empynnyon dre an tell,* I have heard say that they drew the garland on his head with so much strength that the thorns went and pierced to the brains through the holes. M.C. 134. *My â gans*

ol ow nel yn dûr dhe dhallath palas, I will go with all my strength to begin to dig in the ground. O.M. 369. *Y vôs mâp Dew mûr y nel lemyn ny a wôr yn ta,* that he is the Son of God, of great power, now we know well. P.C. 1911.

NEMBES, comp. v. There is not. *Worthys me nembes nygys, na by le ês devethys,* with thee I have no business, nor whence thou art come. C.W. 42. Id. qd. *nimbes,* qd. v.

NENA, adv. Then, now, moreover. Llwyd, 167, 249. *An oyl a vercy in nena a vŷdh kevys,* the oil of mercy in that time will be found. C.W. 138. *Dowt sor Dew nyngesa dhodhans nena, me a wôr gwŷr,* the fear of God's anger was not on them then, I know truly. C.W. 176. Written also *nenna.* ‡ *Nenna an dzhei a varginiaz rág bledhan moy, rág pokâr guber,* then they bargained for a year more, for the same wages. Llwyd, 251. An abbreviated form of *an ena.*

NENBREN, s. m. The roof of a chamber. Corn. Voc. *laquear.* More properly as in Welsh, "the upper roof beam," being comp. of *nen,* (Arm. *nein,*) a ceiling, and *pren,* a beam. W. *nenbren.*

NENNA, adv. Thence, from that place. Llwyd, 69, 71. An abbreviation of *anenna,* comp. of *a'n, (a—an)* from the, and *enna,* there.

NENNIS, s. f. The island. More correctly *an ennis,* qd. v.

NEP, pron. adj. Whoever, who, what. Written indiscrinately *nêb,* qd. v.

NEPPETH, s. m. Any thing, something, somewhat. *Grannut dhe'th whythres, my a'd peys, nep-peyth a oel a vercy,* grant to thy workmanship, I pray thee, some of the oil of mercy. O.M. 327. *Me a'th pŷs, Arluth a râs, a dhanfon dhynny cannas, may bên nepith ascwonfos fatel yw dhye,* I pray thee Lord of grace, to send a messenger to us, that we may be knowing something how it is to thee. R.D. 769. (*Nêp—peth.*)

NERTH, s. m. Might, power, strength, force. *Dre y nerth brâs, ha'y skyveth, ena golmas dewolow,* through his great strength, and his skill, there he bound devils. M.C. 212. *Gans mar vêr nerth ha gallows,* with so much strength and power. M.C. 224. *Bŷdh dynny nerth ha gweres,* be thou to us strength and help. O.M. 1071. *Dhymmo evredhek yn wêdh, ro nerth dhe yerdhes yn fûs,* to me also, the maimed, give thou power to walk well. O.M. 2010. *Y cussylyaf leverel dôs nerth warnan ha'y dhôn dhe vês,* I advise to say that a force come on us, and bore him away. R.D. 570. *An Yedhewon gans nerth pûp ir ygé kerhyn,* the Jews with violence always are about them. R.D. 885. W. *nerth.* Arm. *ners.* Irish. *neart, † nert.* Gael. *neart.* Manx, *niart.* Anc. Gaulish, *nerto-máros.* W. *nêr,* the mighty one. Gr. ἀνήρ. Lat. *nero.* Sansc. *nar.*

NES, adj. Nearer, near; again. As in Welsh, it is used as a comparative to *agos,* and often adverbially. *Bythqueth dên ny wodhevys payn alla dh'y golon nês,* never man endured pain that went nearer to his heart. M.C. 172. *Prâg na dhueté nês râg cous orthyf,* why dost thou not come nearer, to speak to me? O.M. 149. *Sâf ena, na nês na dhûs na fella, râg ny vynnaf,* stand thou there, come thou not nearer nor further, for I will not. O.M. 1404. *Dús nês, hag ysé gené,* come thou near, and sit with me. P.C. 579. *Dên a vo marow ny dhuwew nês*, a man (that) is dead will not revive again. R.D. 949. *Navyth, navyth yn a wher ny sevys nês*, never, never, unhappy, he has not risen again. R.D. 1021. W. *nês*. Arm. *nês*. Sans. *naddhas*, (*nah* to draw near.) Germ. *nahe*. Eng. *nigh*.

NESHEVIN, s. m. A neighbour. Corn. Voc. *propincus*. W. *nesevin*; regularly formed from *nesav*, nearest.

NESSA, adj. Nearest, next, hithermost, second. Used as in Welsh for the superlative of *agos*. *Honna yw y bous nessa, dyscow y dhewerto*, that is his nearest garment, strip it from him. R.D. 1607. *Omma nessa dhom thrôn ve*, here next to my throne. C.W. 4. *Prâg y 'rustu y ladha, hag êv dha vrodar nessa*, why didst thou kill him, and he thy nearest brother? C.W. 122. ‡ *Ha Dew a grias an ebbarn nêv, ha godhuhar ha metten o an nessa journa*, and God called the sky heaven, and the evening and the morning were the second day. C.W. p. 190. *Nessa seithan*, next week. ‡ *En nessa tshei*, in the next house. Llwyd, 250, 252. W. *nesav*. Arm. *nesa*.

NESSE, v. a. To draw near, to approach. *Ow nessé yma an preys, may fydh mâp Dew ynno reys dhe'n fuls Yedhewon dygnas*, drawing near is the time, that the Son of God shall be given in it to the false Jews to be afflicted. P.C. 1006. W. *nesu*. Arm. *nesaat*.

NEV, s. m. Heaven. *An nêv*, the heaven. Llwyd, 45. A later form of *nêf*, qd. v.

NEVER, s. m. A number. *Yn blydhen y a vye bedcrow kenever, hag a owleow esé yn corf Ihesus worth never*, in a year there would be as many paternosters as were of wounds in the body of Jesus by number. M.C. 228. Written also *niver*, qd. v.

NEVERA, v. a. To number, to count, to reckon. *Scrifys yw, yn suredy, ha ken me ny'n lavarsen, corf Ihesus ha'y asely y dha denna mar velen, nêb a vynna a ylly nevera oll y yscren, ha'y skennys, kîc, ha gwythy, pan cen yn crows pren*, it is written of a surety, and otherwise I should not have said it, the body of Jesus and his limbs they drew so brutally, whosoever would might number all his bones, and his sinews, flesh, and veins, when he was on the cross-tree. M.C. 183. Written also *nivera*, qd. v.

NEVRA, adv. Ever. Llwyd, 176. ‡ *Na nevra*, never. ‡ *Na vedn e nevra*, he never will. 101. A late form of *nefré*, qd. v.

NEWYDH, s. m. That which is new, a new thing. Pl. *newydhow*, news. Written also *newedh*, pl. *newedhow newodhow*. *Newedhow me re elewes, bones Ihesus bynygys, ow tôs omma dhe'n cité*, news I have heard that Jesus blessed is coming here to the city. P.C. 229. *Lemmyn a abesteleth lavaraf dheuch newodhow; Ihesu dasserchys a'n bêdh, me a'n gwelas ugynsow*, now, O apostles, I will tell you news; Jesus is risen from the tomb, I saw him lately. R.D. 894. Written also *nowydh*, qd. v.

NEWYDH, adj. Now, fresh, late, recent. *Ena un lowarth esé, ha ynno bêdh ve parys, dên marow râg reeevé, newydh parrys nynjo usyys*, there was a garden there, and in it a tomb ready to receive a dead man, newly prepared, it had not been used. M.C. 233. More generally written *nowydh*, qd. v. W. *newydh*, + *neguid*, + *nowit*. Arm. *ncvez*, + *ncuez*, + *nowid*. Ir. *nuadh, no, + nuide, + nuie, + nue, + nu*. Gael. *nuadh*. Manx, *noa*. Sans. *navas*. Gr. *νέος, νέιος*. Lat. *novus*. Goth. *niwis*. Germ. *neu*. Lith. *naujas*. Russ. *novyi*. Eng. *new*.

NEWNGO, comp. v. Now was. *Newngo devethys an prŷs, may 'tho ogas dh'y dhewedh*, now the time was come that he was near to his end. M.C. 200. Compounded of *newng*, a corruption of *nans*, and *o* was.

NEYL, pron. s. One of two. See *Nril*.

NEYS, v. a. He will fly. *Marth dhym a'n deusys yma; mar uskys del dhueth omma; êl bŷth ny neys*, wonder to me if this is the Godhead, so swiftly as he came here; an angel never flies. R.D. 2504. *Neys* is the 3 pers. s. fut. of a verb *nygé*, which is only found in the corrupted form of *nygé*, qd. v.

NI, pron. s. We, us. *Lemmyn ny a gîll gwelas*, now we may see. M.C. 12. *An bewnans ny re gollas, hag yn reêdh agan flechys, omdhychtyn, trussen an wlâs, fyan na veny kefys*, we have lost our life, and also our children; let us dight ourselves, let us cross the country; let us flee that we be not taken. M.C. 246. *Ny a vyn formyé an bŷs, par del ôn try hag onan*, we will create the world, as we are three and one. O.M. 11. *Lâdh ny gansé magé ta*, kill thou us with them as well. O.M. 972. *Y gous ny dâl dhynny ny*, it behoves us not to say it. R.D. 568. *Orthin ni*, to us. Llwyd, 245. W. *ni*. Arm. *ni*. Ir. *sinn*. Gael. *sinn*. Manx, *shin*. Gr. *νώι*. Lat. *nos*. Sans. *nas*.

NI, adv. Not. *Y vôs kyllys ny vynna*, that he should be lost he would not. M.C. 7. *Yn oll an bŷs ny ylly dên cafos kymmys anfwth*, in all the world a man could not find so much misfortune. M.C. 225. *War an beys ny gns parow*, on the earth there are not equals. R.D. 1820. *Ni ôr dên vŷth*, no man at all knows. Llwyd, 244. *Ni* in Welsh, *ni* softens some initials following, and aspirates others. *Aban na fyn dewedhé, me a vyn y curuné*, since he will not end, I will crown him. P.C. 2115. In Irish *ni* also aspirates, as *ni chairigedar*, he does not accuse. (W. *ni cherydha*.) Before vowels in Cornish *ni* assumes a *g*, as *nig o*, he was not. *Nyg o comfort na yly a wrello y holon huedh*, there was not comfort nor remedy that could make her heart swell. M.C. 225. *Ni tra vŷth*, nothing. Po ni, unless. Llwyd, 99. W. *ni, nid*. Arm. *na*. Ir. *ni*, +*nid*. Gael *ni*. Manx, *ny*. Lat. *ni*.

NIJA, v. a. To fly, to swim. ‡ *Ha Dew lavares, grêns an dowrow dry râg por meer an tacklow gwuyah ês dôn bownas, hag an edhen ês a nija dres an noar a lês en ebbarn nêv*, and God said, let the waters bring forth abundantly the things moving that have life, and the fowl that flieth above the earth abroad in the firmament of heaven. C.W. p. 191. Llwyd writes it *nyidzha*, to swim. 99. Both various forms of *nygé*, qd. v. It is written also in Arm. *niju*.

NIM, comp. pron. Not me. *Vynythu hedré vyvy, umma ny'm geelyth arté*, ever whilst thou livest, here thou shalt not see me again. O.M. 244. *Ow arluth my a'n te dhys, ny'm prêf dên war gowardy*, my lord, I swear it to thee, no man shall prove me of cowardice. O.M. 2161. *Ow servons bŷth ny'm gassé*, my servants would have never left me. P.C. 2012. *Hag a pe, ow thüs dhewy ny'm delyrfsens yn delma*, and if it were, my people would not have given me up to you in this manner. M.C. 120. In these instances 'm represents the 1st pron. susbtantive. *Nym* is often used with the verb substantive to denote possession, when 'm represents the pro-

NOETH 267 NOTHA

noun adjective, or possessive. Thus *ny'm bŷdh tregé*, it will not be mine to stay. *Nymbes (ni—am—bôs,) whans,* it is not mine that there should be a desire. *A'y frut dybry ny'm bes whans,* I have no wish to eat of its fruit. O.M. 171. *Ny won vyth pe'dh âf lemyn ; nymbus greese, guskys, na chy,* I know not where I shall go now ; I have not clothes, shelter, nor house. O.M. 357. *Vytheth powes my ny'm bŷdh, mar vrew ew ow ysayly,* I shall never have rest, so bruised are my limbs. O.M. 1011. *Alemma râg ny'm bŷdh creys,* henceforth peace will not be mine ; or I shall have no peace. R.D. 1960. *Genouch mc nvm bŷdh tregé,* with you I shall not stay. M.C. 37. W. *ni'm, †nem.* Arm. *nem ; († nem boe quet,* non sunt mihi ; *† nem bezo,* non erit mihi.) Ir. *† nim ; † nim charatsa indfshir,* (W. *ni'm carant y gwêfr,*) the men love me not.

NIUL, s. m. A fog, a mist, a little cloud. *Llwyd,* 57. W. *niwl.* Ir. *ncubhal, neul, † niul.* Gael. *neul.* Gr. νεφέλη. Lat. *nebula.* O. H. Germ. *nebel.*

NIVER, s. m. A number. *Abel, râg dhe offryn kêr, ty a vŷdh genen nefré, ha dewolow hep nyver pŷp ûr orthys ow scrynkyé,* Abel, for thy dear offering, thou shalt be ever with us, and devils without number always grinning at thee. O.M. 569. Written also *never,* qd. v. W. *niver, † nimer.* Arm. *niver..* Irish, *numhir.* Gael. *nuimhir.* All from the Lat. *numerus.*

NIVERA, v. a. To number, to count, to reckon. Part. *nivyrys.* Written also *nyfyrys. Yma câs brâs wharfedhys, ha codhys war dhe pobel; ny yllons bôs nyfyrys, an tús yw marow yn wys,* there is a great misfortune happened and fallen on thy people ; they cannot be numbered, the people (that) are dead, in truth. O.M. 1544. *Ha me yn wêdh a'n guelas, ha ganso ef company brâs ; orth y syreé lyes guas, ny allons bôs nyfyrys,* and I also saw him, and with him a large company ; many fellows following, they could not be numbered. R.D. 558. *Nivera,* reckon thou ; *nivyrys,* reckoned. *Llwyd,* 248. Written also *nevera,* qd. v. W. *niveru.* Arm. *nivera, niveri.*

NOADHO, s. m. News. *Llwyd,* 242. A late corruption of *nowedhow,* pl. of *nowedh,* or *nowydh,* qd. v.

NOAR, s. f. The earth. Generally contracted into *nôr,* qd. v.

NOATH, adj. Naked, bare. *Llwyd,* 63, 101. A late form of *north,* qd. v.

NAOTHA, s. m. Nakedness. *Pryce.* See *Notha.*

NOD, s. m. A mark, a token, a characteristic. *Llwyd,* 241. The late form of this word was *nôs* or *nôz.* W. *nôd.* Arm. *neuz.* Ir. *nod.* Lat. *nota.*

NODEDEC, adj. Notable, noted. Corrupted in late Cornish into ‡ *nodzhedzhek. Pryce.* W. *nodedig.* Ir. *† noitheach.*

NODEN, s. f. Thread, yarn. Corn. Vocab. *filum.* W. *woden.* Arm. *neuden.* Ir. *snath.* Gael. *snath.* Manx, *snaie.*

NOETH, adj. Naked, bare, uncovered, void, destitute of. Written also *noyth,* and contractedly *nôth,* qd. v. *Drefen ow bôs noeth hep quetl, ragos ydh yth dhe gudhé,* because of my being naked, without a cloth, I went to hide from thee. O.M. 260. *Pyw a dhysquedhes dhyso dhe vôs noeth corf, trôs, ha brech,* who disclosed to thee that thou art naked (as to) body, foot and arm ? O.M. 262. *Wharé y a'n dystryppyas mar noyth genys del vyé,* anon they stripped him as naked as he was born. M.C. 130. W. *noeth.* Arm. *noaz.* Ir. *nochd, † nocht.* Gael. *nochd.* Lat. *nudus.* Goth. *naquaths.* Lith. *nogns.*

NOI, s. m. A nephew. Corn. Voc. *nepos.* W. *nai.* Arm. *ni.* Ir. *† nia, † nine.* Gael. *† nia.* Lat. *nepos.* Fr. *neveu.* Germ. *neffe.* Ang. Sax. *nefu.* Eng. *nephew.* Sansc. *naptar.*

NOIT, s. f. A niece. Corn. Voc. *neptis.* W. *nith.* Arm. *niez.* Ir. *† nigh, † ni, † necht.* Gael. *† nigh.* Lat. *neptis.* Fr. *nièce.* Germ. *nichte.* Eng. *niece.* Sansc. *naptri.*

NOR, s. f. Earth. *Aban vynnyth pŷp huny ladhé ol an nôr vŷs-ma,* since thou wilt kill every one in the earth of this world. O.M. 970. *A tûs vâs, why re welas fetul formyas Dew an Tâs néf ha nôr, war lerch y vrŷs,* O good people, ye have seen how God the Father created heaven and earth after his judgment. O.M. 2627. *Danfenys a néf dhe'n nôr,* sent from heaven to earth. P.C. 1952. *Ny dogoth dhynny ladhé dén vŷth ol yn nôr bysma,* it behoves us not to kill any man in the earth of this world. P.C. 1982. *Môr, nôr, h'an néf,* sea, earth, and the heaven. R.D. 1976. *Aberth yn nôr,* within the earth. R.D. 2122. An irregular mut. of *dôr,* qd. v.

NOS, s. m. Night. Corn. Voc. *nox. Ow benneth prest ty a fŷdh, kefrys yn nôs hag yn geydh,* my blessing thou shalt have, equally by night and by day. O.M. 458. *Dysky lahu Dew huhel a wera dhedhé deydh ha nôs,* teach the law of God the High he does to them day and night. O.M. 1555. *Kyns hy bôs nôs,* before it be night. O.M. 2769. *Worth golow nôs ny gewys,* by the light of night I spoke not. P.C. 1253. *Râg yn nôs haneth dybry bûs pâsk omma ef a vyn,* for in this very night, eat the paschal food here he will. P.C. 671. *Gansé y a'n hombronkyas yn prŷs hanter nôs,* with them they conducted him at the time of midnight. M.C. 76. W. *nôs.* Arm. *nôs.* Ir. *nocht.* Gael. *nochd.* Manx, *noght.* Gr. νύξ, νυκτὸς. Lat. *nox, noctis.* Goth. *nahts.* Lith. *naktis.* Sansc. *nic, nakta.* Germ. *nacht.* Russ. *noch.* Slav. *nosch.* Ang. Sax. *niht.* Eng. *night.*

NOS, s. m. A mark, a token. *Llwyd,* 231. A later form of *nôd,* qd. v.

NOTYE, v. a. To note, to observe, to denote, to make known. *Ihesus ganso o keris, ha nynjo hard dh'y notyé,* Jesus was loved by him, and it was not hard to note it. M.C. 214. *Rag own y dhe leverel ha dh'y notyé drys an wlâs,* for fear that they should say, and make it known through the country. M.C. 249. *Bôdh Pylat y a notyas yn le may 'th êns rag henna,* the will of Pilate they made known in the place they were in for that reason. M.C. 251. *Yowynkes menouch a vera yn yowynkneth mûr notyé,* youths often do in youth much to be noted. P.C. 434.

NOTH, adj. Naked, bare, void. *Agan corfow nôth gallus, gans deyl agan cudhé gwrên,* our bodies are become naked, with leaves let us cover ourselves. O.M. 253. *Warnedhy yma gwedhen, uhel gans lues scoren, saw nôth ol gns hrp dylyow,* on it there is a tree, high with many boughs, but they are all bare without leaves. O.M. 777. *Arluth lemmyn a's dysken, dyragouch nôth y fyen,* Lord, now if I take it off, before you naked I should be. R.D. 1942. A contracted form of *noeth,* qd. v.

NOTHA, s. m. Nakedness. *Mehal, yskynnyow, êl splan ; hellouch Adam gans cledha dân ha'y wrêg mês a Barndys ; ha dew queth dodhans gurra doen, dh'aga hudha, aga notha na vo gwelys*, Michael, descend, angel bright; chase Adam with a sword of fire, and his wife out of Paradise; and two garments to them do thou bear, to cover them, that their nakedness may not be seen. C.W. 70. W. *nowthedh.* Arm. *noazded.*

NOTHLEN, s. f. A winnowing sheet. Pl. *nothlennow. Ha bedhouch war colonow, rák Satnas yw yrvyrys, avel ys y'nothlennow dh'agas kroddré, me a grýs,* and be ye of cautious hearts, for Satan is desirous, as corn in winnowing sheets, to sift you, I believe. P.C. 881. W. *nithlen;* from *nithio,* (Arm. *niza.* Ir. *nigh.* Gael. *nigh.* Manx, *nice.* Sansc. *nigh,)* to winnow, and *llen,* a sheet.

NOWEDHANS, s. m. Novelty. Written by Pryce, *nowedzhans.* W. *newydhiant.*

NOWN, s. m. Hunger. *Rág nown y wróns clamderé,* from hunger they will faint. O.M. 400. Written in Corn. Voc. *naun,* qd. v.

NOWNSEC, card. num. Nineteen. Written by Llwyd, 176, *nowndzhak.* See *Nawnzac.*

NOWYDH, adj. New, fresh, recent. *Flóch byan nowydh gynys,* a little child newly born. O.M. 806. *Hy a dhesefsé scorné gans an epscop, ha'y dollé dhe wordhyé dewow nowydh,* she would wish to strive with the bishop, and delude him to worship new gods. O.M. 2732. *Luhys nowydh ow lesky,* teaching new laws. M.C. 107. *Ganso mar callo clewas whelth nowydh, a vo coyntis,* if he might hear from him the new story that was recounted. M.C. 109. *Ha'n houl nowydh drehevys,* and the sun newly risen. M.C. 252. Written also *nowedh,* and *newydh,* qd. v.

NUM, comp. pron. Not mine. Id. qd. *nim,* qd. v.

NY, pron. subs. We, us. See *Ni.*

NY, adv. Not. See *Ni.*

NYETHY, v. a. To make a nest, to nestle. *Yn ér-na del redyn ny, yn lyffrow del yw scrifys, dhe'n edhyn gwêls rág nythy tellyryow esa paris, dhe Crist y ben py senzy, tellyr výth nyngo kefis,* then as we read in books as it is written; for the wild birds to make nests places were ready; for Christ where he might lay his head, no place was found. M.C. 206. The substantive is written by Pryce, *nğth,* and by Llwyd, *neith,* and in the Corn. Voc. *neid,* qd. v. W. *nythu.* Arm. *neizia.*

NYGE, v. a. To fly; to swim, to float. *Ol an edhyn ow nygé, guet copel may keniery,* of all the birds flying, be thou careful that thou take a couple. O.M. 1024. *Saw an edhyn bynceges, y a ng quyc hag uskys,* but the blessed birds, they will fly quickly and readily. O.M. 1068. *Agan gorhel re nyggyas, re'n sawyé, Arluth huhel,* our ark hath floated, may it save us, High Lord. O.M. 1087. *Colom whék, glás hy lagas, ke ng a-uch lues pow,* sweet dove, blue her eye, go fly above much country. O.M. 1136. *Me a'n gwelas ow nygé, gauso nuír a gowethé,* I saw him flying, with him many companions. R.D. 552. Written also *nija,* qd. v. Arm. *nija.* In Welsh *neidio* means to jump or leap; (cf. Sansc. *nat,* to dance,) *hedeg* and *ehedeg* being the terms for *flying. To swim* is in W. *novio.* Arm. *neui, ncuni.* Ir. *snamh.* Gael. *snauh.* Manx, *snaue.* Gr. *νέω.* Lat. *no, nato.*

NYGETHYS, s. m. That which flieth, a bird. *Gorreuch an fals nygethys gans Abel a desempys dhe'yssedhé,* put ye the false bird with Abel forthwith to dwell. O.M. 914.

NYGYS, s. m. Business, an errand. Pl. *nygyssow. Ny wou ua fordh dhum nygys,* I know not the way to my errand. O.M. 699. *My a wra fest yn lowen dhe nygys,* I will do very joyfully thy errand. O.M 720. *Pandra yw dhe nygys,* what is thy business? O.M. 733. *Ow banneth dheuchwy púp prýs, mar dha y wreuch ow nygys,* my blessing on ye always, so well ye do my errand. O.M. 912. *Me a vyn môs alema dhe wruthyl ow nygyssow,* I will go hence to do my errands. O.M. 1044. Written also *negys,* qd. v.

NYL, pron. s. One of two, one or the other, one. *Clewys a'n nğl tenewen,* I heard on one side. O.M. 214. *Na nğl oges nag yn pel, ny's gwelaf ow trenygé,* neither near nor far, I see her not flying over. O.M. 1142. *Py nğl o mocha sengys an kéth dén-ma dhe caré,* which one of the two was most bound to love this same man? P.C. 510. *Ha nép na'n geffo na nğl, gwcrthens y hugk dhe brenné aneidhy dhodho clodhé,* and he who has not one, let him sell his cloak to buy with it for him a sword. P.C. 921. A contracted form of *neyl,* or *neil,* qd. v.

NYM, comp. pron. Not me. See *Nim.*

NYN, adv. Not. *Ken arluth agesso ef, nyn gordhyaf bys vynary,* other Lord than him, I will not worship for ever. O.M. 1789. *Me a'n te dhys war ow fýdh, na nğl yn nós nag yn geydh nyn gevyth crés,* I swear to thee on my faith, that no one in night nor in day hath any peace. P.C. 1882. *Máp dén hep ken ys bara býth nyn geves ol bewnes,* the son of man, without other than bread, hath not had all life. P.C. 69. *Býth nyn gevyth fout a ioy, nép a ğl gwrlas dhe fas,* never shall he have lack of joy, who can see thy face. R.D. 1561. *A wúl drók nyn gcfé médh, yn y dhydhow,* to do evil he had not shame in his days. R.D. 1783. Before vowels *nyns* is used, qd. v.

NYN, comp. pron. Not him. *(Ni—'n) Bythqueth me ny'n aswonys,* I never knew him. M.C. 84. *Yn medhcns y, ny'n gordhyn;* na ny góth dhyn y wordhyé, they say, we do not worship him; nor does it behove us to worship him. M.C. 148. *Otté vé musurys da; dén yn býsmy'n mwyr guel,* behold it well measured; no man in the world will measure it better. O.M. 2514. *Awos owen brás lavarow, agan Arluth hep parow, me ny'n nachaf war ow fay,* for fear of big words, our Lord without equals, I will not deny him, on my faith. P.C. 910. *Ny'n saw dén vğth,* no man shall save me. R.D. 1988.

NYNS, adv. Not. Used before vowels, as *nyn* is before consonants. The *s* is often placed before the succeeding word in the MSS. as *nyw syw* for *nyns yw,* or joined into one word. *Nynsyw da bones un dén y honan,* it is not good that a man should be alone. O.M. 93. *Nynsus parow dhys yn bcys,* there are not equals to thee in the world. O.M. 435. *Rusken nynsesé a'n býyn dhe'n bén,* bark there was none, from the point to the stem. O.M. 779. *Anuedhé nynses laha,* of them there is not law. O.M. 1236. *Rág nynsouch mas dew lorel,* for ye are not but two vagabonds. O.M. 1504. *Nyns á dén vğth vynytha a'n kéth ré-na dhe'n tír sans,* not any man shall go over of those same to the holy land. O.M. 1878. *Neffré dhe dré my nynsaf,* I will never go home. R.D. 811. *Iohan nynsos lemmyn flóch,* John thou art not now a child. R.D. 1363. *Thesu omma nynsugy, rák sevys yw,* Jesus is not here, for he is risen. R.D. 782. *Nyns* was often corrupted into *nyng* or *nynj,* as *nyngew, nyngesé, &c. Dén vğth nynges, yn medhky,* there is no man at all, says she. M.C. 34. *Býth nyngéns y cowethé,* they were never comrades. M.C. 41. *Nyn-gew ragos dhe ladhé*, it is not for thee to slay. M.C. 123. *Whath kentrow dhedhé nyngo, Ihesus yn crows rág aynsy*, still there were not to them nails, to hold Jesus on the cross. M.C. 154. *Ihesus ganso o keris, ha nyn-jo hard dh'y notyé*, Jesus was loved by him, and it was not hard to note it. M.C. 214. *Ogas o, nyn-gesa pell*, it was near, it was not far. M.C. 140.

NYNY, pron. s. We, us. *A Dâs veneges re by; lemyn saw ol ôn nyny agan dysses*, O Father, be blessed; now we are all cured of our diseases. O.M. 2024. A reduplicate form of *ni*. W. *nyni*.

NYS, adv. Not. *Fest yn tyn hy a wolé, dhe wherthyn nys tera whans*, very bitterly she wept, to laugh a desire did not arise. M.C. 222. *Na heb mûr lavur defry benytha nys tevyth flôch*, nor without great labour indeed shall a child ever be to her. O.M. 300. *Râg y servonnth yn nêp plâs nys tesyth fout a gyffyans*, for his servants in no place will there be a want of pardon. O.M. 1808. W. *nis*.

NYS, comp. pron. Not—him, her, it, them. *(Ni—'s.) Ota cowes pûr ahas, ny's pyrth dên mara peys pell*, behold a shower very terrible, man cannot bear it if it drops long. O.M. 1082. *Ny nŷl ogas nag yn pell, ny's quelaf ow trenygé*, neither near nor far, I see her not flying over. O.M. 1142. *Ef a wodhfyé y bôs hy pechadures, ny's gassé dh'y ylyé*, he would have known that she is a sinner; he would not have permitted her to anoint him. P.C. 493. *Mar ny's cafaf scon dhum dues*, if I do not find them come soon to me. R.D. 647. *Yn ken lyw ny's gwylys whêth*, in other colour I have never seen them. R.D. 2534.

NYSE, v. a. To fly; to swim, to float. 3 pers. s. fut. *nŷs*, or *neys*, qd. v. The general form in use was *nygé*, qd. v., by the common corruption of *s* into *g* soft, or *j*.

NYTH, s. m. A nest. Pl. *nythow*. *Nŷth yâr*, (W. *nyth iâr*,) a hen's nest. *Pryce*. Written by Llwyd, *neith*, and in Cornish Vocabulary, *ncid*, qd. v.

NYTH, comp. pron. Not—thee, *(Ni—ath.) Me ny'th dampnyaf yredy*, I do not condemn thee indeed. M.C. 34. *Mar ny'th wolhaff dre ow grâs*, if I wash thee not by my grace. M.C. 46. *Ny'th nahaff kyn fên ledhys*, I will not deny thee though I be slain. M.C. 49. *Cleves vŷth ny'th kemersé*, no illness had taken thee. M.C. 157. *Ny'th ty nahaf bynary*, I will never deny thee. P.C. 907.

O.

This letter had the same sound as in English; when short as in *for, pot, sort*, and when long as in *bone, cone, lone*. It is a mutable vowel in the three British dialects, changing into *e*. Thus C. *corn*, a horn; *cernial*, a hornblower; *Cernow*, Cornwall. In Welsh, it now changes into *y*, but anciently *e*. Thus W. *corn*, pl. *cyrn*, † *cern*; *Cernyw*, Cornwall. Arm. *corn*, pl. *cern*.

O, pron. subs. He, him, it. It is only used in composition with prepositions, as *ganso*, with him or it; *orto*, to him or it; *ynno*, in him or it, &c. W. *o*.

O, v. subs. He was. 3 pers. s. preterito of *bôs*. *Ol y doul ef o tewlys ganso yn nêf rág tregé; Ihesus ganso o keris, ha nynj-o hard dh'y notyé*, all his plan was formed to dwell with him in heaven; Jesus was loved by him, and it was not hard to note it. M.C. 214. *My a wôr prâg o ganso*, I know how it was with him. O.M. 185. *An brassa egé yn pow guns pûp ol ty o gylwys*, the greatest that was in the country by every body thou wast called. R.D. 1096. *Ydh o ow fous ha'm brustplat purpur garow dhum strothé*, my robe and my breastplate were hard purple to wring me. R.D. 2591. W. *oedh*. Arm. *oa*.

O, v. subs. Ye are. *Yn mês duegh why hep terry chy, ha hep alwhedh; gylwys ô why, pen arlythy, gordheugh an bêdh*, come ye out without breaking house, and without a key; ye are called, chief lords, honour ye the tomb. R.D. 325. An abbreviated form of *oh*, which again is a softened form of *och* or *ouch*, qd. v.

OAN, s. m. A lamb. Pl. *oin, ean, ennvs*. *Whet avar prŷs soper yw; tân brâs an oan re a lyw kyns y vôs methen restys*, it is yet early supper time; the great fire will brown the lamb too much before it be quite roasted. P.C. 697. Written in Corn. Voc. *oin*, qd. v.

OAR, s. f. The earth. *An 'oar*, the earth. *Llwyd*, 66. *An 'oar*, is for *an noar*, and that again an euphonic mutation of *an doar*. See *Doar*.

OBBA, adv. Here. *Pryce*. Written by Llwyd, 65, 248, *ybba*; being the latest corruption of *omma*, qd. v.

OBEL, adv. Afar off, aloof. *Pryce*. Generally written *a bel*. See *Pell*.

OBER, s. m. A work, deed, operation. Plur. *obcrow, oberedh*. *Arluth nêf, roy dhym gîl da yn pûp ober a wrellyn*, Lord of heaven, give me to do well in every work that I do. O.M. 445. *Eddrek mûr a'n kemeras râg an ober re weressé*, great sorrow seized him for the work he had done. M.C. 220. *Râk agan drôk ober kens*, for our evil deed before. P.C. 2002. *Wogé ow da oberow*, after my good works. R.D. 2599. *Pup urol oberedh da, guyn bŷs cymmys a'n gwrello*, always good works, happy as many as do them. O.M. 604. *Dhe gîl drôk tra, ha dynaché oberow da*, to do evil things, and to reject good works. P.C. 13. W. *ober*. Arm. *ober*, † *euber*, pl. *euffrou*. Ir. *obair*. Gael. *obair*. Manx, *obbyr*. Lat. *opere*.

OBERETH, adj. Full of works. *Oberëth dremas a ŵŷff, yn êr-na rych ef a vŷdh; drok dhên yn gŷdh-na goef, dhe Gryst a fŷdh a'n barth clêdh*, full of works the very good shall come, then rich he shall be; the wicked man on that day, woe to him; on the left side to Christ he shall be. M.C. 259.

OBEROR, s. m. A worker, a workman. Corn. Vocab. *operarius*. *Droch-oberor, maleficus*, an evil-worker. Comp. of *ober*, and *gôr*, a man. Arm. *oberer, oberour*.

OBERWAS, s. m. A work servant, or follow. *Pryce*. Comp. of *ober*, and *gwâs*, a servant.

OBERY, v. a. To work, to labour, to make. Part. and preterite, *obcrys*. *Pûr ryel an rê-ma yw oberys, del vynsyn agan honen*, very royal these are wrought, as we would ourselves. O.M. 15. *Mar pue drôk a oberys, trôch y hy gans dhe gledhé*, if it was evil that she did, kill her with thy sword. O.M. 291. *Ha kemmys a'n gordhyo ef, gans mûr ioy y tue dhe'n nêf dre y dhadder oberys*, and as many as worship him, with great joy they shall come to heaven, by his goodness made. R.D. 1224. W. *oberu*. Arm. *ober*. Lat. *opero*.

OBIL, s. m. A peg. Corn. Voc. *clavus*. Another form of *Ebil*, qd. v.

OBMA, adv. Here, in this place. *Llwyd*, 65, 248. ‡ *Yn haval dhynmo obma ymadge dean gwregaf shapyn*, in likeness to me here the image of man I did form. C.W. 182. A late corruption of *omma*, qd. v.

OCH, v. subs. Ye are. *Euch, whyleuch dhymmo Pilat; godhfedheuch ma na veuch bad; lús ôch a prys*, go seek for me Pilate; see that ye be not foolish; ye are men of account. R.D. 1775. More generally written *oueh*, qd. v.

OCH, interj. Oh. *Och, tru, tru, me re behas, ha re dorras an dyfen*, Oh, sad, sad, I have sinned, and have broken the prohibition. O.M. 249. *Mar ny dhue dhum confortyé, ow mornyng vydh och ha tru*, if he will not come to comfort me, my mourning will be "oh" and "sad." R.D. 438. *Ha'y gàn u vydh och, goef, dhe'n bŷs-ma pan fue genys*, and his song shall be "oh"; woe is he, to this world when he was born. R.D. 2313. W. *ach*. †*oia*, †*oi*. Arm. *ah*, †*ach*. Ir. *o, ogh, ugh*. Gael. *och*. Manx, *ogh*.

ODGHA, prep. After. ‡ *Odzha henna*, afterwards. *Pryce*. Written by Llwyd, *udzha*, being a corruption of *wogé*, qd. v.

ODION, s. m. An ox, a bullock. Corn. Voc. *bos*. In late Cornish corrupted into *udzheon, odgan. Pryce*. W. *eidion*. Arm. *ejenn, ijenn, yjenn*.

ODN, card. num. One. *Pryce*. A late corruption of *on*, id. qd. *un*, or *onan*, qd. v.

ODZII, v. subs. Ye are. ‡ *Hwi odzhi a gweles*, ye are seeing. *Llwyd*, 240. A late corruption of *ysouch*, qd. v.

ODHIWORTO, comp. pron. From him. *Llwyd*, 244. More correctly *adhiworto*, qd. v.

ODHOM, s. m. Want, necessity, need. Pl. *odhommow*. *Pydh ew an odhom dynny ca fus lafur a'n par-na*, what is use for us to have labour of that sort? O.M. 967. *Na porth dout, me fi genes, mar pydh odhom dhe'th weres*, have no fear, I will go with thee, if it will be necessary to help thee. R.D. 596. *Deuch yn rág ketep onan lemyn yn ow odhommow*, come ye forth every one now in my necessities. O.M. 2684. Written also *edhom*, qd. v.

ODHIOMEC, adj. Necessitous, needy, poor. Pl. *odhomcgyon*. *Rák ty yw Dew gallogek, dhe pûp a vo odhomnck, warnos a pyssé mercy*, for thou art a mighty God, to all who are needy, on thee who call for mercy. R.D. 2377. *Ha'y ow kúl kemmys da pûp úr dhe odhomegyon*, and thou doing so much good always to the needy. P.C. 2636. Written also *edhomog*, qd. v.

OEL, s. m. Oil. *Pryce*. Borrowed from the English.

OER, s. m. An hour. *Pryce*. Another form of *our*, qd. v.

OEZENZ, v. subs. They were. *Llwyd*, 245. A late form of *esens*, qd. v. W. *oedhent*.

OEZYH, v. subs. Ye were. *Llwyd*, 245. A late form of *esouch*, qd. v. W. *oedhych*.

OEZYN, v. s. We were. *Llwyd*, 245. A late form of *esen*, qd. v.

OF, v. subs. I am. 1 pers. s. pres. of irr. v. *bós*. *Glán óf a wós an dremas*, I am clean from the blood of the supremely good. M.C. 140. *Parys óf dhe lafuryé*, I am ready to act. O.M. 040. *Why re leverys ow bós, ha pûr wŷr yn della óf*, ye have said I am, and very truly so I am. P.C. 1494. *Lemmyn ydh óf vy yachgs a púp dyses*, now I am healed from every disease. R.D. 1741. Written in late Cornish *ôv. Llwyd*, 245. W. *ŵyv*. Arm. *ounn*, †*óf*. Ir. †*am*. Sansc. *asmi*. Gr. εἰμί. Lat. *sum*.

OFEREN, s. f. The mass. *An bara-ma kymereuch dheuch lemman yn kettep pen, hag anodho ol dybreuch; ow corf yw, re'n oferen, kepar del leverys dheuch*, this bread take yo to you now every head, and of it all eat, my body it is, by the mass, like as I said to you. P.C. 764. W. *oferen*. Arm. *ofvren*.

OFERGUGOL, s. m. A cope. Corn. Vocab. *casula*. Comp. of *ofer* for *oferiat*, a priest, and *cugol*, a hood.

OFERIAT, s. m. A priest. Corn. Vocab. *presbiter*. W. *ofiriad*. From the Lat. *offero*, to offer.

OFFRYN, s. m. An offering. *A Dás Dew, twen a byté, tan resyf dheworthyf ve ow drgé, ha'm offryn glán*, O Father God, full of pity, take, receive from me my tithe and my offering pure. O.M. 504. *An Tás a wûrk ow formyé, a'm offryn re woffé grás*, the Father who created me, to my offering may he acknowledge favour. O.M. 530. *Ple ma an offryn, a dás, a vydh leskys dhe Dhew rás, rág y wordhyé*, where is the offering, O father, (that) shall be burnt to the God of grace, for worshipping him? O.M. 1316. W. *offrwm*.

OFFRYNE, v. a. To offer. Part. *offrynnys*. *Hag ol agas gwŷr dhegé dhodho gwetyeuch offrynné, ha'y lesky del yrchys ef*, and all your true tithe, to him take ye care to offer, and burn, as he hath enjoined. O.M. 441. *My ny vynnaf offrynné ol ow degé*, I will not offer all my tithe. O.M. 500. *Degé ol agan edhyn, bestes yn wedh maga ta, warnydhy my a offryn yn gordhyans dhe'n Tás guella*, tithe of all our birds, beasts also as well, I will offer upon it, in worship to the best Father. O.M. 1183. *Ow máp Y'sac offrynnys ef a vydh war an mencdh*, my son Isaac offered he shall be on the mountain. O.M. 1287.

OGAS, adj. Near, neighbouring. Written also *oges* and *ogos*. *Manno allo an tebell ogas dhys bonas trylys*, that the evil one may not be turned near thee. M.C. 19. *Pylat éth yn mês a'y hell yn un lowarth a'n gero; ogas o, nyng-esa pell*, Pilate went out of his hall into a garden (that) he had; near it was, it was not far. M.C. 140. *Ha dh'y notyé drys an wlás a ogas hag u bell*, and to make known through the country, anear and afar. M.C. 249. *Pûr oges yw dhe ancow*, very near is his death. P.C. 2660. *Rág fals Iudas, nép a'm guerthas, ogas yma*, for false Judas. who has sold me, is near. P.C. 1102. In late Cornish it was used as a substantive. *Ogas*, a neighbour. *Llwyd*, 173. It is also written by him *agos*, qd. v. W. *agos*. Arm. *egos*. Ir. *agus*, †*acus*, †*ocus*, *focus*. Gael. *fogus*. Manx, *aggys*, *faggys*. Gr. ἐγγύς. Lat. *angustus*.

OGE, v. subs. Thou art. *Mars ogé Crist máb Davy, dés a'n grocs heb pystegé*, if thou art Christ the son of David, come from the cross without magic. M.C. 197. *Moyses, del ogé dén más, my a'd pŷs ow sawyé*, Moses, as thou art a good man, I pray thee to heal me. O.M. 1767. *Ogé, gy, a cowyth da, onen a dûs an dén-ma*, art thou, O good fellow, one of the people of this man? P.C. 1234. A corrupted form of *osé*, qd. v.

OGO, s. f. A cave, a cavern. "Caves along the shore

OLEWNE 271 OMA

are still called *ogos* in Cornwall by the present inhabitants." *Polwhele's Vocabulary.* W. *ogov.* Arm. *caff.* Ir. *uagh, cuas.* Gael. *uagh.* Manx, *oghe, ooig.* Lat. *cavea.*

OH, s. m. An ox. Pl. *ohan.* ‡ *Gora an ohan en arder*, put the oxen in the plough. *Pryce.* The singular was not in use, but *ohan* was used for the plural of *odion*, or ‡ *udzheon.* W. *ých*, pl. *ychen.* Arm. pl. *ochen, ohen.* Ir. *agh*, †*sngh.* Gael. *agh.* Sansc. *uksha.* Goth. *auhs.* Germ. *ochs, ochse.* Ang. Sax. *oxa.* Eng. *ox.*

OH, v. sub. Ye are. *Lhuyd*, 245. A late form of *óch*, qd. v.

OH, interj. Oh, woe is me. *Lhuyd*, 249. A later form of *och*, qd.v.

OI, s. m. An egg. *Lhuyd*, 110. Plur. *oiow.* Pryce. *Melin-oi*, the yelk of an egg. *Lhuyd*, 175. Written also *oy*, qd. v.

OILET, s. m. A frying pan. Corn. Voc. *frixorium.* Unknown to the other dialects.

OIN, s. m. A lamb. Corn. Voc. *agnus.* Written in the Ordinalia *oan*, and *ûn*, qd. v. Pl. *ean.* W. *oen*, pl. *wyn.* Arm. *oan*, pl. *ein.* Ir. *uan.* Gael. *uan.* Manx, *eayn.* Lat. *agnus.* Cf. also Gr. *οἴν.*=Lat. *ovem.*

OIR, adj. Cold, frigid. Corn. Voc. *frigidus.* W. *oer.* Ir. *fuar.* Gael. *fuar.* Manx, *feayr.*

OIS, v. subs. Thou art. ‡ *Ti ois a gweles*, thou art seeing. *Lhuyd*, 246. The general form is *ôs*, qd. v.

OIV, s. m. I am. *Lhuyd*, 247. A late form of *ôf*, qd. v.

OL, s. m. A mark, trace, impression, footstep. Pl. *olow. Me a wêl ôl treys ow thás*, I see the impression of the feet of my father. C.W. 128. *Sew olow ow thryys lyskys*, follow the prints of my feet, burnt. O.M. 711. *Avel olow aga threys, sýeh ýns ol kepar ha leys*, like the prints of their feet, they are all dry like herbs. O.M. 700. W. *ôl.* Arm. *cul.* Ir. †*ol.* Gael. *ail.*

OLAS, s. f. A hearth. *Lhuyd*, 15. ‡ *Hy oar gwil padn da gen hy glawen, ha el hy yla a delveth gowas tân*, she knows to make good cloth with her wool, and on her hearth she ought to have fire. *Pryce.* W. *aelwyd.* Arm. *aoled, oaled.* Ir. *callagh.* Gael. *teallach.* Manx, *chiollagh.*

OLE, v. a. To weep, to wail, to lament, to cry. *Yma kên dhym dhe olé daggrow goys yn gwŷr hep mar*, there is cause to me to weep tears of blood, truly without doubt. O.M. 630. *Na allaf gueles yn fâs, kymmys daggrow re olys*, I cannot see well, so many tears I have wept. P.C. 2608. *Myrches a Jerusalem, na olouch, na na wreuch drem warnaf vy, nag onan výth*, daughters of Jerusalem, weep not, nor make lament on me, not any one. P.C. 2640. *Kên dhe olé why a's býdh*, cause to weep ye shall have. P.C. 2644. *Garmé a wrêth, na ôl na scrýg*, cry out thou dost ; weep not nor shriek. R.D. 853. Written also *wolé*, qd. v. W. *wylo, gwylo.* Arm. *gwela.* Ir. *guil.* Gael. *guil.* Manx, *gull.* Gr. *κλαίω.* Lat. *fleo.*

OLEU, s. m. Oil. Corn. Vocab. *oleum.* Also *an olive. Gwedhan oleu*, (W. *olewydhen*,) an olive tree. *Lhuyd*, 106. W. *olew*, †*oleu*; *eli.* Arm. *oleou*, †*olco*; *eôl, cúl.* Ir. *ola.* Gael. *ola, uillidh.* Manx, *ooil.* Gr. *ἔλαιον.* Lat. *oleum.* Goth. *alév.*

OLEUBREN, s. m. An olive tree. Corn. Voc. *olea vel oliva.* (*Oleu-pren.*) W. *olewydhen.* Arm. *olivezen.*

OLEWEN, s. f. An olive, a single olive. *Lhuyd*, 106.

OLIPHANT, s. m. An elephant. Corn. Voc. *elephans.* The late form was *olifans* Lhuyd, 241. Arm. *olifant.* W. *clifant*, pl. *elifeint*, in Mabinogion. The animal is well designated by the W. *cawrvil*, lit. a gigantic beast.

OLL, adj. All, every. *Mâb Marca leun a râs, oll y vôdh a ve clewys*, the son of Mary full of grace, all his wish was heard. M.C. 9. *Mâb dên heb ken ys baru nyn gevas oll y vewnas*, the Son of Man without other than bread hath not had all his life. M.C. 12. There being no difference in sound, it is written as often *ol. Yn peswerè, gwereys perfyth dhe'n brys ol golowys glân*, on the fourth, be made perfect to all the earth bright lights. O.M. 34. *My a wra dhyso parow pûp ûr ol râg dhe weres*, I will make to thee an equal every hour to help thee. O.M. 101. W. *oll*, †*ol, holl.* Arm. *oll, holl.* Ir. *oll, uile*, †*huile.* Gael. *uile.* Manx, *ooilley.* Gr. *ὅλος.* Goth. *alls.* Germ. *all.* Eng. *all.*

OLGALLUSEC, adj. Almighty. *Me ew henwis Dew an Tâs, olgallusec dres pûp tra*, I am called God the Father, almighty above every thing. C.W. 1. *Me a credy yn Dew an Tâs olgallusec, gwrêar an nêf, hag an 'oar*, I believe in God the Father almighty, maker of heaven and earth. *Pryce.* Comp. of *oll*, and *gallusec*, mighty. W. *ollalluog, hollalluog.* Arm. *hollchalloudek.*

OLGALLUSTER, adj. Almighty. *Me a credy yn Dew an Tâs olgalluster, gwrêar an nêf, hag an 'oar*, I believe in God the Father, almighty, maker of heaven and earth. *Hag a'n barth dychow dorn Dew olgalluster yma ow sedhè*, and on the right hand of God the Father almighty he is sitting. *Pryce.*

OLVA, s. f. A weeping, lamentation. *An dús vâs a dheserya dhedhè guläs nêf o kyllys, gans aga garm hag olva Ihesus Crist a ve mevrys*, the good people desired for themselves the country of heaven (that) was lost ; with their cry and lamentation Jesus Christ was moved. M.C. 4. W. *wylva, gwylva.* Arm. *gwelvan.*

OM, pron. My, mine ; in my, from my ; me. *Me a gris yn ta spedyé om negis haneth yn nôs*, I believe I shall speed well in my business this very night. M.C. 63. *Mês mara keweys yn ta, ha'n gwyryoneth y synsy, prâg om gwysgeth yn delma, nyngyw mernas belyny*, but if I have spoken well, and have held the truth, why dost thou strike me thus ? it is nought but villainy. M.C. 82. *Yn mêdh an gôff, clevas brâs ês om devleff devethys*, says the smith, a great disease is come on my hands. M.C. 156. *Drok handlé, del om kyry, pan gyffy dalhen ynno*, handle him roughly, as thou lovest me, when thou shalt have hold in him. P.C. 991. *Why am gwêl ow terlentry, splanna ês an Tâs defry ; henna cressouch om bosuf*, ye see me glittering, brighter than the Father truly ; this believe ye that I am. C.W. 18. *Om corf ve gwresays honna*, of my body was she made. C.W. 30. (See also *dom, dhom*, to my.) Written also *ym*, qd .v. W. *ym.*

OM, a particle used in composition to form reflexive verbs. As *cregy*, to hang ; *omgregy*, to hang one's self. *Gwrey*, to make ; *omwrey*, to make one's self. *Em* and *ym* are similarly used in Cornish, qd. v. W. *ym*, †*em*, †*im*, †*om.* Arm. *en em*, †*em.* Ir. †*imme*, †*im*, †*imm*, †*imb.*

OMA, v. subs. I am. *Ha del oma marrek lên*, and as I am a trusty knight. O.M. 2150. *Lavar dhymmo hrp lettyé, oma vy nêp a'th werthas dhe'n Hudhewon dhe*

OMLANA 272 OMWETHE

ladhé, tell me without delaying, am I he who hath sold thee to the Jews to kill. P.C. 755. *Aban oma dasserchys, dew hugens deydh dyvythys bĕdh pan fo nôs*, since I am risen, forty days ended will be when it is night. R.D. 2436. *Gwŷr re gewsys yredy, yn mêdh Crist, mychtern oma*, thou hast spoken truly indeed, says Christ, a king I am. M.C. 102. An enlarged form of *ôf*, qd. v.

OMBROVY, v. a. To prove one's self. *(Om—provy.) Ydh ombrovas gwan dyack may'dh ôf poyntyes dhe bayn brâs*, I have proved myself a weak husbandman, so that I am appointed to great pain. C.W. 68.

OMDENNA, v. a. To withdraw one's self, to go out, to depart. *Dre virtu an scrifé, pêb dhe vês a omdennas*, by virtue of the writing every one withdrew himself out. M.C. 33, 68. *Pedyr a omdennas yn ûr-na del rebechsé*, Peter went out in that hour that he had sinned. M.C. 86. Comp. of *om*, and *tenna*, to draw. Written also *ymdenna*, qd. v. Welsh. *ymdynnu*. Arm. †*emtenna*. Buhez, 4. 3.

OMDESEVY, v. a. To throw one's self down, to fall. *Ahanas ydhew scrifys bôs eledh worth dhe wythé rûg own yn dh'omdescvys, dhe droys worth meyn dhe dochyé*, of thee it is written that angels are guarding thee, for fear it is that thou fall, (and) dash thy foot against a stone. M.C. 14. Comp. of *om*, and *desevy*, to throw down, qd. v.

OMDHAL, v. a. To hold one's self, to repress ; to withstand, to resist, to repugn ; to strive, to quarrel, to fight. Llwyd, 51, 139, 141, 249. Comp. of *om*, and *dal*, to hold. W. *ymdhal*.

OMDHYCHTYE, v. a. To dight or prepare one's self. *An bewnans ny re gollus, hag yn wêdh agan flechys; omdhychtyn, trussen an wlâs, fyan na veny kefys*, we have lost our life, and also our children ; let us dight ourselves, let us cross the country, let us flee that we be not taken. M.C. 246. Comp. of *om*, and *dychtyé*, to dight, qd. v.

OMGAMMA, v. a. To bend one's self, to make wry. *Hag y ee dhe ben dewlyn, ha hager mowys a were ; gwethé godhyans aga meyn, orth Ihesus a omgamé*, and they went on their knees, and made ugly faces ; the worst their mouths knew, to Jesus they made wry. M.C. 196. Comp. of *om*, and *camma*, to bend. W. *ymgammu*.

OMGREGY, v. a. To hang one's self. *Iudas êth a dhesempys a wryl tu dhe omgregy ; cafus daffar pûr parys, lovan crŷff rûg y sensy*, Judas went forthwith on one side to hang himself ; he found convenience very ready, a strong rope to hold him. M.C. 105. Comp. of *om*, and *cregy*, to hang. Written also *ymgregy*, qd. v. W. *ymgrogi*.

OMGWÊDHE, v. a. To cover one's self. *Agen corfow nooth gallas; omgwedhen ny gans deel glâs*, our bodies are become naked ; let us cover ourselves with green leaves. C.W. 62. Comp. of *om*, and *gwedhé*, another form of *cudhé*, qd. v.

OMLADH, v. a. To cut off mutually, to fight. *Urry, ow marrek quella, my a vynsa dhe pysy, gor ost genes yrvys da, dhe omladh, del y'm kerry*, Uriah, my best knight, I would pray thee, take with thee a host well armed, to fight, as thou lovest me. O.M. 2141. Comp. of *om*, and *ladhé*, to cut. Written also *emladh*, qd. v. W. *ymladh*.

OMLANA, v. a. To cleanse one's self, to become clean.

Ihesu Crist yn pow may'the, ef a sawyé an glevyon, dal na bodhar ny asé, nag omlanas nag onon, Jesus Christ in the country that he went ; he healed the sick ; blind nor deaf he left not (that) was not cured, not one. M.C. 25. Comp. of *om*, and *glanhy*, to cleanse, qd. v. W. *ymlanhâu*.

OMMA, adv. Here, in this place. *Omma ny wreuch why trygé, euch yn mês a dhyaympys*, here ye shall not stay, go out immediately. O.M. 317. *Ol dhe'n bestes ûs omma a gêf bôs lour dewdhek mŷs*, all the beasts (that) are here shall have food enough twelve months. O.M. 1059. *How otté an pren omma, nyns ûs tecka yn wlâs-ma*, ho ! behold this piece of wood, there is not a fairer in the country. P.C. 2558. *Prâg na dhôns genas omma*, why came they not here with thee? M.C. 78. *Mŷns ûs omma cuntullys*, all that are gathered here. M.C. 92. "O is often pronounced in Cornish, as in the English words, *honey, money*, &c. For *omma*, here, *newodhow*, news, &c. are read *ymma, newydhow*." Llwyd, 228. W. *yma*, †*ynan*, (in the place.) Arm. *ama, ma*.

OMMELY, v. a. To turn aside, to remove. *En benenas yn delma yntredhé a leverys ; dheworth an bêdh an meynma dhypny pu a'n ommelys*, the women thus said among themselves, these stones from the tomb, who has removed them for us. M.C. 253. *Me a'th wisk, harlot jawdyn, may'dh onelly dhe'th kylban*, I will strike thee, rogue, rascal, that thou fall on thy back. C.W. 82. Written also *umhelys*, qd. v. W. *ymchwelyd*.

OMSAWYA, v. a. To save one's self. *Râg omsawya ow honyn, keffrys ow gwrêk ha'w flehys, an lester a vŷdh genyn, der weras Dew, uskys gurŷs*, for saving myself, also my wife and children, the ship shall be by us, through the help of God, quickly made. C.W. 172. Comp. of *om*, and *sawyé*, to save.

OMSCEMYNY, v. a. To excommunicate, to curse. l'art. *omscemynys*. *Ke dhe vês, omscumunys, dhe dhyveyth vêth yn tewolgow*, go thou away, accursed, to a wilderness ever into darkness. M.C. 17. *Omskemynys lower ydhoré, nyngew reis skemyna moy*, accursed enough I am, there is not need to curse more. C.W. 88. *A gan Cain onskemynys ow nâb Abel yw ledhys*, Oh, by Cain the accursed my son Abel is killed. C.W. 90. Written also *ymscemyny*, qd. v.

OMSETTYA, v. a. To set one's self. *Te na yllyth omwethé un prês yn geydh na pechy, pan omsettyas (dhe demptyé guthyl pêch nêb na ylly*, thou canst not keep thyself a moment in the day that thou wilt not sin, when he set himself to tempt Him who could not commit sin. M.C. 20. Comp. of *om*, and *settya*, to set.

OMWERAS, v. a. To help one's self. *Cooth yw ef hag avlethys, panna ylla omweras, y vaw ny venna bôs*, complaisant he is and witty, why could he not take care of himself, his boy I will not be. C.W. 84. Comp. of *om*, and *gweres*, to help. Written also *ymweres*, qd. v.

OMWETHE, v. a. To keep or preserve one's self. *Te na yllyth omwethé un prês yn geydh na pechy*, thou canst not keep thyself a moment in the day that thou wilt not sin. M.C. 20. *Kyns yn ta ef a ylly tûs a bôb drôk ol sawyé ; lemmyn gans ol y vestry ragon ny wôr omwethé*, before well he was able to save people from every ill, now with all his power he knows not how to keep himself from us. M.C. 194. *An dên-ma re drehevys, gallas ny wodhan pelé lemman na veny ledhys nyng-is*

ONI 273 ORTO

furdh dhe omwethé, this man has arisen, he has gone we know not where; now there is no way to keep ourselves that we be not slain. M.C. 245. Comp. of *om*, and *gwethé*, to keep. Written also *ymwythé*, qd. v.

OMWRELLE, v. a. To make one's self, to pretend, to feign. *Y hylwys en Edhewon, lahys ês yn pow a dro, may rŷs y ladhé yn scon mychtern néb a omwrello*, the Jews cried out;—the laws in the country about are, that he must be slain forthwith who would make himself a king. M.C. 121. *Rág mychtern a omwrello, dhe Sesar yw contrary*, for he that would make himself a king is hostile to Cæsar. M.C. 146. Comp. of *om*, and *gwrellé*, to make. Written also *ymwryl*, qd. v.

OMWREY, v. a. To make one's self, to pretend, to feign. *Dhynny yma laha, may rŷs y vonas ledhys, rág máb Du ef a omwra*, we have a law, that he must be killed, for he makes himself Son of God. M.C. 143. *Yn medhens, mar omwreyth clâff, gordhewyth te a'n prenvyth*, say they;—if thou makest thyself sick, very diligently thou shalt pay for it. M.C. 155. *Mars ota mar fúr war an bŷs del omwressys, lemmyn dyswa ha wra cúr*, if thou art so wise in the world, as thou madest thyself, now shew and work a cure. M.C. 191. Comp. of *om*, and *gwrey*, to make. Written also *ymwrey*, qd. v.

ON, v. subs. We are. 1 pers. pl. pres. of *bós*. *Onan ha try ón yn gwŷr, en Tás, ha'n Máp, ha'n Spyrys*, one and three we are in truth, the Father, and the Son, and the Spirit. O.M. 3. *A Dás del ón dhe wyth res, a bol hag a lyys formys, bŷdh dynny nerth ha gweres, rág warnas prest ny a bŷs*, O Father, as we are thy work, made of clay and mire, be to us, strength and help, for to thee we ever pray. O.M. 1069. *An Tás Dew, re bo gordhyys; aynsys múr ón dh'y garé*, the Father God be worshipped; we are much bound to love him. O.M. 1126. *A Dás, veneges re by; lemyn saw ol ón nyny agan dysses*, O Father, be blessed; now we are all cured of our diseases. O.M. 2024. *Dynnythys ón hep danger*, come we are without delay. P.C. 1860. W. *ŷm*. Arm. *omp*.

ON, s. f. An ash. Lluyd, 240. Called also *onnan*, or *onnen*, and *enwedhan*. (See Onnen.) W. *on*. Arm. *ounn*.

ONAN, s. m. One, an individual, a single person or thing. *Onan ha try ón yn gwŷr*, one and three we are in truth. O.M. 3. *Scon a onan a'th asow, my a wra dhyso parow*, forthwith from one of thy ribs, I will make to thee an equal. O.M. 99. *Awot omma onan da ragon ordenys parys*, behold here is a good one, intended for us ready. O.M. 1719. *Dén a'n geffé cans davas, ha'y kentrevek saw onan*, a man may possess a hundred sheep, and his neighbour only one. O.M. 2231. *Onan ahanouch haneth rum gwerthas dhom yskerens*, one of you this night has sold me to my adversaries. P.C. 736. *Ny gloveys drôk nag onan ef the wûl bythqueth yn beys*, no one has heard any evil that he has done in the world. P.C. 2435. Written also *onen*, and *onon*. See *Un*.

ONEST, adj. Honest, honourable, decent. *Rág mychtern nag emperour onest my vŷdh ow gwelas*, for a king or emperor it would not be decent to see me. R.D. 1946. W. *gonest, onest*. Arm. *onest*. Lat. *honestus*.

ONI, v. imp. We are. *(On—ni.)* *Del ony onen ha try, Tás ha Máp yn trynyté*, as we are one and three, Father and Son in Trinity. O.M. 57. *Yn úr-na y fŷdh clewys, del ony gansé brewys*, in that hour it will be heard, as we are wounded by them. R.D. 573.

ONNEN, s. f. An ash tree, a single ash. Corn. Vocab. *fraxus*. An ash in general was *on*, qd. v. The term used for the plural was *envydh*, comp. of *on*, ash, and *gwŷdh*, trees. W. *on, onnen*, pl. *yun*. Arm. *onn, ounn, ounnen*, pl. *ounnennou, ounn*. Ir. *fuinscan, oinswann*, †*uinsenn*, †*huinnius*. Gael. *uinseann*. Manx. *ungin*. Gr. γελασσνέν, (centunculum herba Gallis.) Dioscor. 3,120.

OOL, v. a. He shall weep. *Ty a'n ool, ha lyas mŷl, kyn 'dhota skynnys yn wharth*, thou shalt weep, and many thousands, though thou art fallen into laughter. C.W. 168. Another form of *ól*, 3 pers. s. fut. of *olé*, qd. v.

OR, v. irr. He knows, he knows how, he is able. ‡ *Ni ór dén véth*, no one at all knows. Lluyd, 244. ‡ *Piwa ór*, who knoweth? 252. ‡ *Mi ór*, I can; *mi ór mós*, I can go. ‡ *N'or mi*, I cannot. 124. ‡ *N'ora vi screfa na mui*, I can write no more. 250. A late form of *wór*, qd. v.

ORCHINAT, s. m. A shoe. Corn. Voc. *calciamentum*. More exactly translated by the Fr. *chaussure*. W. *archenad*, apparel, including shoes; *archen*, a shoe. Arm. *archennad*, †*archen*.

ORD, prep. Of, by, on, in, with. *Mar a mynnyth govynny ord en kéth re a's clewas*, if thou wilt ask of the same persons (that) heard them. M.C. 80. *Ha'y ŷll léff a ve tackis ord en growes fast may 'thesé*, and one of his hands was nailed on the cross, so that it was fast. M.C. 179. An orthographical variation of *orth*, qd. v.

ORDENE, v. a. To order, to ordain, to appoint. Written also *ordeyné, ordyné, ordné*. Part. *ordenys, ordnys*. *Nefré gustyth dh'y gorty, me a orden bôs benen*, ever obedient to her husband, I ordain woman to be. O.M. 296. *Yma gorhyl créf ordnys*, there is a strong ship ordained. O.M. 1040. *Awot omma onan da, ragon ordenys parys*, behold here a good one, intended for us ready. O.M. 1720. *Hag ordeyneuch guythyny dh'aga aspyé*, and appoint guards to watch them. O.M. 2038. *Orden dhe'th tús hy knoukyé*, order thou thy people to beat her. O.M. 2676. *Kepar del ordenas ow dhis dymmo vy yn lowené*, as my Father ordained for me in joy. P.C. 809. *Me a vyn lemyn ordné*, I will now ordain. O.M. 2509. *Ordneuch bar dhe ysedhé*, order ye a bar to be placed. P.C. 2225. *Me a'th cusulsé ordyné tûs dhe wythé bêdh an treytor yw marow*, I would advise thee to order men to guard the grave of the traitor (that) is dead. R.D. 336. *Me a ordyn ragdho cales paynys may geffo*, I will ordain for him pains that he have. R.D. 1986. Borrowed from the English. So W. *ordeinio*.

ORRACH, s. m. Dung. Pryce. Ir. *otrach*. Gael. *otrach*.

ORS, s. f. A boar. Corn. Voc. *ursus*. W. *arth*. Arm. *ours*. Ir. †*ursa*. Gr. ἄρκτος. Lat. *ursus, ursa*. Sansc. *arksas*.

ORTE, comp. pron. By or upon them. *Ny vynnaf orta bones na pel ena yn dyses*, I will not that they be any longer there in misery. O.M. 1431. *Orté*, thereon. Lluyd, 244. Comp. of *orth*, and *é*, which is always used in composition for *y* them. Written also *worté*, qd. v. W. *wrthynt*. Arm. *out hô*. Ir. †*friu*, †*friusom*.

ORTO, comp. pron. By or upon him, or it. *(Orth—o.)* *Rum fey, múr a wokyneth yw mones dhe lesky peyth a ŷl dén orto bewé*, by my faith, a great folly it is to go to burn a thing (that) a man can live upon it. O.M. 475.

ORTHYN 274 OSTEL

Govyn orto mar a'm bŷdh, ask of him if I shall have. O.M. 693. *A'n bêdh ef a syrcys, râk hydhew ny a geusys ol orto ef*, from the tomb he has risen, for to-day we have spoken all to him. R.D. 1374. Written also *worto*, qd. v. W. *wrtho*, †*wrthaw*. Arm. *out-hann*, †*outaff*. Ir. †*fris*.

ORTY, comp. pron. By or upon her. *(Orth-hy.) Râg orty ty dhe golé, mŷl vâp mam a vcydh damncys*, because thou hearkenedst to her, a thousand mother's sons shall be damned. O.M. 323. *Rŷs ew dhym kewsel defry orth ow gwrêk kyns môs a drê ; mars cllen hep cous orty, hy colon hy a torsé*, I must speak really to my wife before going from home ; if I should go without speaking to her, her heart would break. O.M. 2173. Written also *worty*, qd. v. *wrthi*. Arm. *out-hi*, †*outy*. Ir. †*fric*.

ORTII, prep. At, by, to, for, with. *Y lavaraf, nêf ha tŷr, bedhens formyys orth ow brŷs*, I say, heaven and earth, let them be created by my judgment. O.M. 8. *Ha, Dew, mŷr orth ow offryn*, and, God, look at my offering. O.M. 505. *Râg colé orth un venen gullân ef re gollas an plâs*, for listening to a woman he has completely lost the place. O.M. 919. *Ke wêth tressé treveth dh'y, ha mŷr gwel orth an wedhen*, go yet the third time to it, and look thou better at the tree. O.M. 800. *Pŷth yw an cusyl wella orth an dra-ma*, what is the best advice for this thing ? R.D. 15. *Orth* is used with the infinitive mood to form the participle active when governing pronouns, which are placed between in their adjectival forms. *An avel, orth y dyrry*, the apple plucking it. O.M. 195. *Ow scollyé ugan gwara, ha'n fêr, orth y tystrywy*, scattering our wares, and the fair, destroying it. P.C. 342. *Ow colon yw mûr hudhys, nyns ûs pcyn orth ow greffya*, my heart is greatly exalted, no pain is afflicting me. R.D. 484. *Us whêt dhe'th corf galarow, na torment orth dhe greffyé*, are there yet pains to thy body, or torment afflicting thee ? R.D. 488. *Orth y sywé lyes gwâs, ny yllons bôs nyfyrys*, following him many fellows, they could not be numbered. R.D. 557. *Namnag esof ow merwel, orth agas gortos*, I am almost dying, waiting for you. R.D. 2146. Written also *worth*, qd. v. W. *worth*. Arm. *ouch, oud* †*ouz,* † *oz*.

ORTHEUCH, comp. pron. Of, from, to you. *(Orth— chwi.) Yma dhymmo mûr dysyr, a wodhfes ortheuch an gwŷr ; pyw ouch, levereuch henna*, I have a great desire to know of you the truth ; who are ye ? tell that. R.D. 195. *Mear a rês dhe why ; ow ry cusyl dhym, ortheuch me a vyn cola*, much thanks to you ; giving counsel to me, to you I will hearken. C.W. 52. Written also *worthouch*, qd. v. W. *wrthych*. Arm. *ouzouch*, †*ozoch*, †*ouzouchuy*. Ir. †*frib*, †*fribsi*.

ORTHYF, comp. pron. Of, from, to, against me. *(Orth— mi.) Eva prâg na dhucté nês râg cous orthyf*, Eve, why comest thou not nearer, to speak to me ? O.M. 150. *Ow mâp kerra, pendra vynta orthyf govyn*, my dearest son, what wilt thou ask of me ? O.M. 1312. *Serry orthyf ny rês dhys*, to be angry with me thou needest not. O.M. 2524. Written also *orthaf*. *Orthaff mar mynnyth colé*, if thou wilt listen to me. M.C. 175. *Golsowoch a der dro orthaf ve, mŷns ês omma*, hearken ye round about to me, all that are here. C.W. 104. Written also *worthyf*, qd. v. W. *wrthyc*. Arm. *ouz-in*. Ir. †*friumm*, †*frimsa*.

ORTHYN, comp. pron. Of, from, to, against us. *(Orth—*

ni.) Lavar dhymmo, ty venen, an frût ple russys tyrry; mara pe a'n kêth echen o dyfynnys orthyn ny, tell me, thou woman, where didst thou break off the fruit, was it of that same sort which was forbidden to us ? O.M. 212. Written also *worthyn*, qd. v. W. *wrthym*. Arm. *ouz-omp*. Ir. †*frinn*, †*frinni*.

ORTHYS, comp. pron. Of, from, to, against thee. *(Orth —ti.) Dewolow hep nyver, pûp ûr orthys ow scrynkyé*, devils without number always grinning at thee. O.M. 570. *Noc, râk kerengé orthys, my ny gemeré neffré trom dyal war ol an veys*, Noah, for love to thee, I will never take heavy vengeance on all the world. O.M. 1207, 1231. Written also *worthys*, qd. v. W. *wrthyt*. Arm. *ouz-id*. Ir. †*frit*, †*friut*, †*fritso*, †*fritsu*.

OS, v. subs. Thou art. 2 pers. s. pres. of *bós*. *Yn mêdh an lader arall, drôk dhên ôs kepar del vês*, says the other robber, a bad man thou art as thou hast been. M.C. 192. *Arloth Dew a'n nêf, an Tâs, kepar del ôs luen a râs, venytha gordhyys re by*, Lord, God of heaven, the Father, as thou art full of grace, for ever be thou worshipped. O.M. 106. *A Dâs, benyges del ôs, dhe arhadow me a wra*, O Father, blessed as thou art, thy commands I will do. O.M. 1033. *Pyw ôs a gews mar huhel, who art thou (that) speakest so high ?* O.M. 1368. *Nyns yw aga Dew pleysys genes gy, pan ôs punsys, ty ha'th pobel, mar cules*, their God is not pleased with thee, when thou art punished, thou and thy people, so severely. O.M. 1563. W. *wyt*. Arm. *oud*.

OSA, v. subs. Thou art. 2 pers. s. pres. of *bós*. Written equally common *osé*. *A Seth, osa dynythys agy dhe yet Paradys, lavar dhym pandra wylsta*, O Seth, thou art come within the gate of Paradise, tell me what thou sawest. O.M. 763. *Arluth, veneges re by, del osé Dew hep pches*, Lord, blessed be thou, as thou art God without sin. O.M. 1796. *Kepar del osé sylwyas*, as thou art a Saviour. P.C. 394. *Del osa Dew dhyn ha pen*, as thou art God to us, and head. P.C. 732. *Aban osa mar gortes, ny a wra del leveryth*, since thou art so courteous, we will do as thou sayest. R.D. 675. *A nyns osé pryeryn, ufercth yw dhys govyn pyw yw an marth a wharfé*, if thou art not a stranger, it is idleness for thee to ask what is the wonder which has occurred. R.D. 1261. *Osé* is a composition of *ôs*, thou art, and the pronoun *te* ; with the common corruption into *se*. It was also written *osta*. W. *wyt-ti*.

OSAV, v. subs. I am. A late corruption of *esof*, qd. v. Written by Llwyd, 245, *ossav* and *ossam*.

OST, s. m. An army, a host. *Urry, ow marrek guella, my a vynsa dhe pysy, gor ost genes yrvys da dhe omladh, del y'm kerry*, Uriah, my best knight, I would pray thee, take with thee a host well armed to fight, as thou lovest me. O.M. 2141. Borrowed from the English.

OST, s. m. A host, an innkeeper. ‡ *An ost an tshei*, the host of the house. Llwyd, 252. Borrowed from the English.

OSTA, v. subs. Thou art. *(Os—te.) Gwra yn della, me a'th pŷs, par del osta jowl willy*, do so, I pray thee, as thou art a wily devil. C.W. 31. *Pew osta dhe ês yn wedhan awartha gans trôs ha câs*, who art thou that art in the tree above, with noise and song ? C.W. 42. See also *Ydhosta*.

OSTEL, s. m. An inn, a mansion. *My a vyn gruthyl castel, ha drehevel dhym ostel, ynno jammes râg ircgé*, I will make a village, and build myself a mansion, in it ever to dwell. O.M. 1711. W. *ostyl.* Fr. *hôtel,* †*hostel.* Eng. *hostel, hotel.*

OSTES, s. f. A hostess. ‡ *Ybma ma gen ostez nci, ha yynk eu hei,* here is our hostess, and young is she. *Llwyd,* 252.

OSTIA, v. a. To lodge at an inn. ‡ *Nenna médh e vester ; Kelmer uith na rey ostia en tshei lebma vo dén kôth demi- dhyz dhe bennen iynk,* then says his master ; take care that thou do not lodge in a house where an old man is married to a young woman. *Llwyd,* 251.

OSY, v. subs. Thou art. *Wolcom, ow máp ôs yn nêf, wolcom fest osy gynef, ysé dhymmo a dhyow,* welcome, my son, thou art in heaven, very welcome thou art to me, sit on the right to me. R.D. 2627. Another form of *osa,* qd. v.

OT, adv. Lo, behold. *Ot omma menedh huhel,* see here a high mountain. P.C. 125. *Ot an justys ow tôs dhyn,* see the magistrate coming to us. P.C. 370. *Arluth, ot omma an gwês,* Lord, see here the fellow. R.D. 1803. *Ot en corf yn trok gorrys,* behold the body in a box placed. R.D. 2183. An abbreviated form of *otté,* qd. v.

OTA, adv. Lo, behold. *Ota saw bôs war ow kŷn,* see the load of food on my back. O.M. 1053. *Ota cowes pûr ahas,* behold a shower very dreadful. O.M. 1081. Another form of *otté,* qd. v.

OTA, v. subs. Thou art. *Lavar gwîr dhymmo un gêr, mars ota máb dén ha Du,* tell me truly one word, if thou art son of man and God. M.C. 129. *Orth Crist ef a wovynnys, te dhén, a blé ota gy,* of Christ he asked ; thou man, whence art thou ? M.C. 144. *Te Crist mars ota mar fûr war an bŷs del omwressys, lemmyn dyswa ha gwra cûr,* thou Christ, if thou art so wise, in the world as thou madest thyself, now shew and work a cure. M.C. 191. Written also *oté. Ytho mychtern oté sc, yn médh Pylat yn êr-na,* art thou a king, says Pilate then. M.C. 102. *En Edhewon dre envy a gewsys Crist râg syndyé, Pylat Iustis oté se ? Ihesus, gorweyth y dampnyé,* the Jews through envy said, to hurt Christ ; Pilate art thou a Justice ? take thou care to condemn Jesus. M.C. 107. The same word as *osa,* but containing the older form of *ôs,* (*ot—te.*) W. *wyt—ti.*

OTTE, adv. Lo, behold, see. *Adam, otté an puskes, ydhyn an nêf, ha'n bestes, kefrys yn tŷr hag yn môr,* Adam, see the fishes, birds of the heaven and the beasts, equally in land and in sea. O.M. 117. *Otté omma vé kunys, ha fast ef gynef kelmys, pûr wŷr, a dâs,* behold here a load of fuel, and fast it is bound by me, very truly, O father. O.M. 1299. *Arluth, otté ny genouch,* Lord, behold us with you. R.D. 1879. *Otté an corf casadow ow tôs y ban,* see the hateful carcase coming up. R.D. 2278. Another form of *wetté,* qd. v.

OTTE, v. subs. Ho is. *Llwyd,* 245. A form agreeing with W. *ydi.* Ir. *ata.*

OTTEFE, adv. Behold him or it. (*Otte—fe.*) *Ottefé lemmyn keffys ; dûs dhum arluth dyssempys,* behold him now taken ; come thou to my lord immediately. R.D. 1902. Written also *ottevé. Ottevé musurys da, dên yn bŷs ny'n musyr guel,* see it well measured, no man in the world will measure it better. O.M. 2513. *Ottevé ow crewedhé ; my re wrûk y vusuré rag an kêth wheîl-ma dewyth,* see it lying ; I have measured it for this same work twice. O.M. 2567.

OTTENSE, adv. Behold him or it. *Ottensé, kemereuch e, ha crousyouch ef a ver spys ; my ny gafaf, rum lauté, dh'y ladhé kên fŷth yn beys,* behold him, take ye him, and crucify him in a short time ; I find not, by my truth, any cause in the world to kill him. P.C. 2165. *Nyns yw Ely a gylwu, seehes dhodho yma ; ef a'n gevé drôk wyras ; ottensé gynef parys, bystel cysel kymyskys,* it is not Elias (that) he called ; he is thirsty ; he has found it a bad liquor ; behold it with me ready, gall (and) vinegar mixed. P.C. 2975.

OTTENSY, adv. Behold her, or it. *Scon a onan a'th asow my a wra dhyso parow pûp ûr ol râg dhe weres ; Adam ottensy umma, ry hanow dhedhy hy gwra, dhe'th pâr rak hy kymmeres,* forthwith from one of thy ribs, I will make to thee an equal, every hour to help thee ; Adam, behold her here ; do thou give a name to her, to take her for thy equal. O.M. 102. *Ottensy parys, a's gwys- kens a dhesempys adro dhodho ef mar myn,* behold it ready, let him wear it immediately about him if he will. P.C. 1787.

OTTENSY, adv. Behold them. *Ol dhe wovynnadow ty a fŷdh yn gwŷr hep gow ; otensy gynef parys,* all thy demands thou shalt have truly, without a lie ; see them all with me ready. P.C. 601. Written also *ottengy. Dhymmo vy mar ny gresouch, ottengy a wêl ol dheuch, kepar ha del leverys,* if ye will not believe me, behold them in the sight of you all, just as I said. P.C. 2689.

OTTOMA, adv. See here. (*Otte—omma.*) *Ow ottoma an trôk hôrn ; teuleuch why agas dyw dorn war an logol,* ho ! see here the iron box ; throw ye your two hands on the coffin. R.D. 2177.

OTHVAS, v. a. To know. *An Tâs, ef ny vynsé worth dén vythol bôs mar fûr dha othvas a drôk ha da,* the Father, he would not that any man should be so wise to know of evil and good. C.W. 48. A late form of *wodhfos,* qd. v.

OTHYS, adj. Proud, haughty. *Râg y bosta meleges, hag yn golon re othys, der reson dhys me a breif,* because that thou art accursed, and in heart too proud, through reason I will prove to thee. C.W. 24. A mut. of *gothys,* qd. v.

OUCH, v. subs. Ye are. 2 pers. pl. pres. of *bôs. Dew vody dha ouch yn gwŷr,* two good bodies ye are truly. O.M. 2461. *Wolcom fest ouch yn chymma,* ye are very welcome in this house. P.C. 1207. *Yma dhymmo mûr dysyr a wodhfes ortheuch an gwŷr ; pyw ouch ? levereuch henna,* I have a great desire to know of you the truth ; who are ye ? tell ye that. R.D. 196. *Nyns ouch lem- myn gouygyon, ow môs dres pow, flatturyon, ow leverel an nedhow,* are ye not now liars ? going through the country, chatterers, telling the news. R.D. 1510. W. *ŷch.* Arm. *óch.*

OUNTER, s. m. An uncle. *Llwyd,* 114. This was a later form, agreeing with the Arm. *conter.* The oldest form was *ewiter,* qd. v. W. *ewythr.*

OUR, s. m. Gold. *Me a vynsé a talfens mŷl puns dho- dho a our da,* I would they were worth a thousand pounds to him of good gold. P.C. 212. *Ny welaf vy ydh hallan sawyé ow bewnans, mar dre mûr our,* I see not that I can save my life, unless by much gold. R.D. 1964. *Ha dhodho y tysquedhas our hag archans, gwels, ha gwêdh,* and to him he shewed gold and silver, grass, and trees. M.C. 16. *Awos cost arhans nag our, greuch y tenné mês a'n dour*, notwithstanding the cost of silver and gold, do ye drag him out of the water. R.D. 2231. *Besaw our*, a gold ring. Llwyd, 242. W. *aur*, S. W. *oyr*; †*eur*. Arm. *aour*. Ir. *or*. Gael. *or*. Manx, *airh*. Lat. *aurum*.

OUR, s. f. Hour. *Râg dry Adam a yfarn me a dhûk curyn a spern nêp try our adro dhum pen*, for the purpose of bringing Adam out of hell, I wore a crown of thorns some three hours about my head. R.D. 2555. *Hanter our*, half an hour. The common form was the contracted one of *ûr*, qd. v. In late Cornish it was written *owr* and *owr*. Llwyd, 66. W. *awr*. Arm. *eur, heur*. Ir. *uair*. Gael. *uair*. Manx, *oor*. Gr. ὥρα. Lat. *hora*. Fr. *heure*. Sansc. *haura*, a period. Goth. *jer*. Germ. *jahr*. Eng. *year*.

OURLYN, s. m. Silk. *Dhyworthé ma'gan bo grûs, aga malyé my a vyn gans mûr a reonté brâs yn cendel hag yn ourlyn*, from them that we should have grace, I will wrap them with very great care in fine linen and in silk. O.M. 1752. Comp. of *our*, gold, and *lin*, flax. W. *eurlin*.

OW, pron. adj. My, mine. It aspirates the initials of words following when mutable. *A Dâs, ty re dhrôs dhymmo ascorn û'm kŷk ha corf o pur may fo ow howethes*, O Father, thou hast brought to me bone of my flesh and body (that) was meet that she should be my companion. O.M. 113. *Torré yn ow feryl vy*, break it off at my risk. O.M. 197. *Banneth ow mam, ha banneth ow thâs kefrys*, the blessing of my mother, and the blessing of my father likewise. O.M. 471. *Ty dyowl, gwra ow gorthyby*, thou devil, do answer me. O.M. 301. *An sarf re rûk ow thollé*, the serpent did deceive me. O.M. 286. *Rûk ow colon ow honan gans ow hollan me a wân*, for my own heart with my knife I will pierce. R.D. 2042.

OW, a particle used in the formation of participles, by placing it before the infinitive mood; thus *cané*, to sing; *ow cané*, singing; *lesky*, to burn, *ow lesky*, burning. It changes the initials of verbs following when sonants into surds; thus *gûl* to do, *ow cûl*, doing; *dysky*, to teach, *ow tysky*, teaching; *bewé*, to live, *ow pewé*, living. *A meys ôf ow predyry pandra allaf dhe wruthyl*, I am puzzled thinking what I may do. O.M. 193. *Ow cafus banneth ow mam*, receiving the blessing of my mother. O.M. 471. *Fystyn duwhans, gueres vy ow tôn a plôs casadow*, hasten thou quickly, help me bringing the foul villain. O.M. 892. *Yma ow cûl sacryfys*, he is making a sacrifice. O.M. 1556. *Pan esa Crist ow pesy*, when Christ was praying. M.C. 62. *Ef a clewas en colyek ow cané*, he heard the cock crowing. M.C. 86. *Yn kŷg yn goys ow pewé*, in flesh, in blood living. M.C. 256. Before vowels *owdh* is the form used. *Rûk yma owdh yscûhé*, for he is sitting. P.C. 2342. *My re bue owdh emlodh*, I have been wrestling. P.C. 2509. *Ha'n bedhow owdh cgery, me a's guêl*, and the graves opening, I see them. P.C. 2999. This particle is derived from the preposition *worth*, by, which was always used when pronouns were governed. *Worth ow duwenhé*, grieving me. R.D. 1413. *Yn pûp tol worth y whylas*, in every hole seeking him. R.D. 551. See *worth* and *orth*. *Wrth* is similarly used in Welsh. In Armoric *o*, †*oz*, and *och* before vowels.

OW, interj. Ho. Used to call attention. *Aha, Belsebuc, aha; ow otté un purvers da lemyn wharfedhys*, aha! Beel-sebub, aha! ho! see a good purchase now obtained. O.M. 882. *Ow ottoma an trôk hôrn*, ho! see here the iron box. R.D. 2177.

OWN, s. m. Fear, dread. *Eva, ny allaf medhes, râg own ty dhom kuhudhé*, Eve, I cannot speak, for fear (lest) thou shouldst accuse me. O.M. 160. *A Dhew a rûs, serponni yw hy; euth y gwelas; own a'm bus vy, crenné a wrâf*, O God of grace, it is a serpent; horrid to see it; fear is upon me, I do tremble. O.M. 1452. *Na bertheuch own a henna*, do ye not entertain a fear of that. O.M. 2508. *Ny'm bues own vŷth annodho*, there is to me not any fear of him. R.D. 365. ‡ *Ma own dho vi*, (W. *mae arnav own*,) there is fear to me; I am afraid. Llwyd, 164. W. *own*, †*ovun*. Arm. *aoun, eun*. Ir. *obhan, uabhan*, †*omun*, †*homon*. Gael. *uabhan, uamhan*.

OWNA, v. a. To fear, to dread, to be afraid. Llwyd, 245. *Cara, gordhya, ha owna Dew; an mateyrn, ha'n lahes, en gus plew; owna Dew, parthy mateyrn, ha cara gos controvogion*, love, worship, and fear God; the King, and the laws, in your parish; fear God, honour the King, and love your neighbours. Pryce. W. *ovni*.

OWNA, v. a. To amend, to correct, to rectify. ‡ *Gwreuch owna gys furu*, do ye amend your ways. Llwyd, 250. ‡ *Ownow*, amend ye. Pryce. A late form of *cwna*, qd. v.

OWNEC, s. m. A timid person, a fearful fellow, a coward. *Gueyl bês a râg yn voncard, ma na vy synsys coward, nag awos dên vŷth ownek*, take thou care to be forward in advance, that thou be not held a coward, nor for any man be thou a fearful person. O.M. 2158. *Saw Pedyr Crist a holyas abell avel un ownek*, but Peter followed Christ from afar, like a coward. M.C. 77. W. *ovnog*. Arm. *aounik*.

OY, s. m. An egg. Pl. *oyow*. *Râg henna whela neb jyn, po an vyadge ny dâl ôy*, therefore seek out some gin, or the voyage will not be worth an egg. C.W. 36. *A'n premas me ny rôf ôy*, for the promise I will not give an egg. C.W. 100. *Yth oll agen vyadge, re'n jowl brâs, ny dâl vŷth ôy*, all our voyage, by the great devil, is not worth an egg. C.W. 150. *Oy godho*, a goose egg; *oyow cdhen*, birds' eggs; *melyn oy*, the yelk of an egg. Pryce. Written in the Cornish Vocabulary *uy*, qd. v.

OYETH, adv. Hear, hearken. *Oyeth sy glewyuch dhym ol masons an dré, ketep pol*, hear, listen ye to me all the masons of the town, every head. O.M. 2297. *Oyeth or oyeth yn wêdh, sy glewyuch bryntyn ha kêth, an mychtern a worhemmyn*, hear, now, hear, likewise hearken ye, nobles and commons, the king commands. O.M. 2419. *Oyeth* is the old Norman French *oiez*. It is still used by the town crier in the Town of Aberconwy, in North Wales, who repeats *hoyz, hoyz, hoyz*, three times before commencing every notice, which is now always given in Welsh. The custom has continued since the English colony was planted there by Edward I.

OYREC, adj. Golden, bright like gold, red, ruddy, shining. Llwyd, 142. W. *curog*.

OYS, s. f. Age, process of time; an age, a period of time. *I vam pan y'n drehevys, ha'y vûs devedhys dhe oys, gull penans ef a pesys*, when his mother had reared him, and he was come to age, to do penance he prayed. M.C. 10. *Mûr o an payn dar ken, dhe vûs Du mûr y alloys, del lever dhyn an levar, kymmys payn ny ve a'y oys*, great was the pain beyond other to the Son of God, great His might, as saith the Book to us, so much pain was not of his age. M.C. 135. Written in the Cornish Vocabulary, *huis*, seculum. It was corrupted in late Cornish into ‡ *oydge*, C.W. 152; and ‡ *uz*, Llwyd, 42. ‡ *Ogc côth*, old age; *oos younk*, youthful age. *Pryce*. W. *oed*, † *oet*. Arm. *oed*, † *oad*. Ir. *aes*, *aos*, † *ais*, † *oes*. Gael. *aois*. Manx, *eash*. Gr. ἔτος. Lat. *aetas*. Goth. *aiws*. Sansc. *ayus*. Seculum is in Welsh *oes*, † *ois*, pl. *oesoedh*, † *oisoud*. *Yn oes oesoedh*, † *i ois oisoud*, in secula seculorum, for ever and ever.

OYS, s. m. Blood. A mutation of *goys*, qd. v. *A'y ben y oys o scolliys*, from his head his blood was spilt. M.C. 123. The general form is *woys*, qd. v.

OYV, v. subs. I am. ‡ *Oyv a gweles*, I am seeing, I see. ‡ *Oyv a moz*, I am going. Llwyd, 246, 247. A late form of *ôf*, qd. v. W. *ŵyv*.

OZHOZ, v. subs. Thou art. ‡ *Ozhos tox*, thou art coming. Llwyd, 247. A late corruption of *assos*, qd. v.

P.

THIS letter in Cornish is both a radical initial and secondary. When primary it changes into *b* and *ph*, (generally written *f*) as in the other Celtic dialects. Thus *pen*, a head; *y ben*, his head; *ow fen*, my head. W. *pen*, *ei ben*, his head, *ei phen*, her head. Arm. *penn*, *he benn*, his head; *he fenn*, her head. Ir. *paisde*, a child; *ar baisde*, our child; *mo phaisde*, my child. Manx, *padjer*, a prayer; *nyn badjer*, our prayer; *e phadjer*, his prayer. The Welsh only has a further mutation into the nasal *mh*, as *vy mhen*, my head. When secondary *p* in Cornish is a mutation of *b* as in Armoric. Thus *bewé*, to live; *ow pewé*, living. Arm. *breur*, a brother, *ho preur*, your brother. This mutation is unknown to Welsh initials, but occurs in the middle and the end of words, as *gwypo*, he may know, from *guylod*; *cyfelypach*, more like, from *cyfelyb*, like.

PA, pron. adj. What, which. Used in asking questions. Llwyd, 244. *Pa an dra*, what thing? *Pa an marh*, what horse? 240. *Pa le*, what place, where? In late Cornish it also meant *why*. ‡ *Pa'n dreu hedna, mêdh Dzhuan*, why will you not give that, says John. Llwyd, 251. In construction it changes into *ba*. The general form in the Dramas is *pe*, and *py*, qd. v. W. *pa*, † *pi*, † *py*. Arm. *pe*. Ir. *ca*, *co*. Gael. *cia*. Manx, *que*. Sansc. *ka*. Lat. *quæ*.

PA, adv. When, at what time. *Otté ha coynt o an guas, pa na vynné gorthyby, a dhyrak an arlythy, dhe resons an doctors brâs*, see how cunning the fellow was, when he would not answer, in the presence of the lords, to the reasons of the great doctors. P.C. 1820. *A Dhew yssé fuef goky, pa na vynnan vy crygy a'n bêdh y vôs dasserchys*, O God I was indeed a fool, when I would not believe that he was risen from the grave. R.D. 1566. An abbreviated form of *pan*, qd. v. Arm. *pa*.

PADEL, s. f. A pan. Corn. Voc. *padel hoern*, sartago, a frying pan. In late Cornish written *padal*, Llwyd, 15, 241. W. *padell*, † *patel*. Arm. *pedel*. From the Lat. *patella*.

PADER, s. m. A pater, the paternoster, the Lord's prayer. *Pader an Arluth*. Pl. *pederow*. *Púb tedholl nêb a vynné leverel pymthek pader a leun golon rag gordhyé pascon agan arluth kêr, yn blydhen y a vyé a bederow kenever hag a owleow esé yn corf Ihesus worth never*, he that would every day say fifteen paternosters with a full heart to worship the Passion of our dear Lord, in a year there would be as many paternosters as there were of wounds in the body of Jesus by number. M.C. 228. Borrowed from the Lat. *pater*. So W. *pader*. Arm. *paderen*. Ir. *paidir*. Gael. *paidir*. Manx, *padjer*.

PADN, s. m. Cloth of linen, or wool. ‡ *Hy ôar gwil padn da gen hy glawn*, she knows to make good cloth with her wool. *Pryce*. A corruption of *pan*, qd. v.

PADZHAR, card. num. Four. ‡ *Padzhar iganz ha deg*, fourscore and ten, ninety. Llwyd, 15, 100. A late corruption of *pevvar*, qd. v.

PADZHWERA, num. adj. Fourth. Llwyd, 134. A late corruption of *pevveré*, qd. v.

PAGYA, s. m. Homicide. *Yn tân ty a vera lesky, ha'n kêth pagya-ma defry yn effarn, why drôg lawan*, in fire thou shalt burn, and this same homicide truly in hell, ye wicked fowls. C.W. 124.

PAHAN, comp. pron. What tho. *Levereuch dhym hep lettyé, pahan chesyon a's bues why erbyn Ihesu Nazaré, pan vynnouch y dhystrewy*, tell ye me without delaying what accusation have ye against Jesus of Nazareth that yo would destroy him. P.C. 1070. Comp. of *pa*, what, and *an*, the, *h* being inserted as in W. *paham*, (*pa—am*) for what, or why. *Puhan pleyt yma Pilat yn le may ma*, what (is) the plight in which Pilate is in the place where he is? R.D. 2057.

PAL, s. m. A spade, a shovel; a mattock. It changes in construction into *bâl* and *fâl*. *Cafes moy dhys aban rês, try heys dhe bâl kemery*, since it is necessary for thee to have more, three lengths of thy spade thou shalt take. O.M. 392. *Arluth cûf, ol henna gulân try hês ow fâl mar a'm be, my ha'm gwrêk ha'm flôch byhan bysy vydh dhe sostené*, dear Lord, all that quite, if I have three lengths of my spade, me and my wife, and my little child, will be hard to support. O.M. 396. W. *pâl*. Arm. *pâl*. Manx, *fuayl*. Lat. *pala*.

PALADOR, s. m. A shaft; the shaft of a mine. *Pryce*. W. *paladyr*, a shaft, the trunk of a tree. Sansc. *palati*, a tree.

PALAS, v. a. To dig, to delve. *Kepar del fuvé dremmas, yn dôr my a vyn palas tol may fo ynno cudhys*, like as he was a very good man, in the earth I will dig a hole, that he may be covered in it. O.M. 865. *Mós dhe balas my a vyn râg sustené vewnans dhym*, I will go to dig, to sustain life to us. O.M. 681. W. *palu*. Arm. *pala*. Gael. *pleadh*. Lat. *palo*.

PALCH, adj. Weak, sickly, amending poorly. *Pryce*.

PALF, s. f. The palm of the hand. Corn. Voc. *palma*. W. *palv*. Arm. *palf*, *palv*. Lat. *palma*.

PALMOR, s. m. A palmer. Pl. *palmoryon*. *Adres pow palmoryon, y a fydh mûr gowygyon, hag a lever dhe tûs gow*, across country palmers, they are great story-tellers, and tell people lies. R.D. 1477.

PALORES, s. f. A Cornish chough, or a red-legged crow. Corn. Voc. *graculus*. W. *palores*.

PALS, adj. Plenteous. *Pan welas y mâb dygtis gans an Edhewon mar veyll, hag yn y gorf lôs gorris goleow pals leas myls, hep cows gêr y clamderis*, when she saw her son treated by the Jews so vilely, and that in his body were put plenteous wounds many thousands; without saying a word she fainted. M.C. 165. Gael.

pailt. Manx, *palchey.* Arm. †*splet,* multitudo. Buh. Nonn, 10, 4.

PALY, s. m. Satin, velvet. *Hedhouch cercot a buly, dhodho me a vyn y ry, râg ef dhym dhe lafuryé,* reach a surcoat of satin ; to him I will give it, for that he has worked for me. P.C. 1784. W. *pali.*

PAN, s. m. Cloth, linen or woollen cloth. Pl. *pannow.* *An asen ow quandré, warnedhy râg escdhé dyllas pan a ve gorrys ; râg morogeth a vynné dhe'n cylé dhe vôs gordhijs,* the she-ass was fetched ; on her to sit raiment of cloth was put, for he would ride to the city to be worshipped. M.C. 28. *Nynsyw cryggy dhe beggars, hag a fo aga dyllas cloutys gans dyvers pannow,* it is not (right) to believe beggars, whose clothes are patched with divers cloths. R.D. 1509. *Lavrok pan,* cloth breeches. Llwyd, 118, 241. Lat. *pannus.*

PAN, adv. When, at what time. As in Welsh it softens the initials following. *Lemmen pan yw nêf dhyn gworgs, ha lenwys a eledh splan,* now when heaven is made to us, and filled with bright angels. O.M. 9. *My pan esen ow quandré,* when I was walking about. O.M. 213. *Why re dhweth dhym gans arvow, gans fustow ha clydhydhyow kepar ha pan veué vy an puré lader yn pow ; pan dyskys yn eglusyow ny wrûg dên fyth ow sensy,* ye have come to me with arms, with staves, and swords, as if I were the veriest thief in the country ; when I taught in the churches no man did seize me. P.C. 1173. *Why re dhrôs dhym an dên-ma, kepar ha pan dreylé ef en dûs dhyworth Dew an nêf,* ye have brought this man to me, as though he turned the people from the God of heaven. P.C. 1853. *Bys pan,* until that. *Yn grows gans kentrow fastis, prynys bŷs pan vé marow,* fastened on a cross with nails, tortured till he was dead. M.C. 2. *A ban,* from the time when, since. *Ny strechyaff pell a ban nag es a wothfé dheuch paris a's gwrellé gwell,* I will not delay long, since there is none that knows how to prepare them for you better. M.C. 158. W. *pan.* Arm. *pa.* Ir. *cuin,* †*céin.* Gael. *cuin.* Manx, *cuin.* Lat. *quando.* Goth. *hwan.* Germ. *wann.* Ang. Sax. *hwænne.* Eng. *when.*

PAN, comp. pron. What the. *(Pa—an.) Lavar dhym, del y'm kerry, pa'n vernans a'n gevé ef,* tell thou me, as thou lovest me, what death did he meet with. O.M. 2219. *Mar a's ladtré dheworto, pa'n pŷn a godho dhodho,* if he steal it from him, what punishment is due to him. O.M. 2233. *Lavar lemyn pa'n drôk vo a dhysquydhysta dhynny,* tell me what (is) the evil thou shewest to us ? P.C. 338.

PANAN, s. m. A parsnip. Plur. *panes.* Llwyd, 240, 243. W. *panas.* Arm. *panes.* Fr. *panais.* Lat. *pastinaca.*

PANDRA, s. f. What thing. *(Pa—an—tra.) Pandra yw a vynnouch wy,* what is it that ye would ? M.C. 67. *Pandra wrêth,* what art thou doing ? O.M. 257. *Saw pandra wrama govyn,* but what shall I ask ? O.M. 698. *Lavar dhym pandra wylsta,* tell me what thou sawest. O.M. 765. *Mŷr pandra wylly ynny,* look what thou canst see in it. O.M. 801. *Pandr' ew henna dhynny ny,* what is that to us ? M.C. 105. Written also *pendra,* qd. v.

PANNA, pron. adj. What. ‡*Panna huêl allosti guil,* what work canst thou do ? Llwyd, 251. A late form of *pan,* qd. v.

PANYN, pron. adj. Which one, whether of them. *(Pa—an—un.)* Llwyd, 244.

PAPAR, s. m. Paper. Llwyd, 47. From the English. The Welsh generally call paper, *papyr,* (Arm. *paper.* Gael. *paipear.* Germ. *papyr.* Fr. *papier,*) but they have also *pabwyr,* for a rush, regularly formed from the Lat. *papyrus.*

PAR, s. m. A peer, a match, an equal, a fellow ; sort, kind. Pl. *parow. Lemyn hanwaf goydh ha yâr, a sensaf edhyn hep pâr dhe vygyens dên war an beys,* now I name goose and hen, (which) I consider birds without equal for food of man on the earth. O.M. 130. *Nynsus pâr dhys yn bŷs-ma,* there is not an equal to thee in this world. O.M. 2010. *Yn bŷs-ma nan geves pâr,* that had not his equal in this world. P.C. 1578. *Ydhanwaf bûch ha tarow, ha march yw bêst hep parow, dhe vâp dên râg ymweres,* I name cow and bull, and horse (that) is without equals for the son of man to help himself. O.M. 124. *Râk dhe saye me a vyn, py pâr maw ôs yn torma,* for I will try thee, what sort of a lad thou art now. P.C. 2309. *Râk ny glewsyuch yn nêp plâs savour a'n pâr-ma vythqueth,* for ye have not smelt in any place savour of this sort ever. O.M. 1991. *Ma ow wolon ow ranné, pan glewaf cous a'n pâr-na,* my heart is breaking, when I hear talk of that kind. O.M. 2182. The word is still used in Cornwall among the miners, as a pare or gang of men. W. *pâr.* Arm. *pâr.* Ir. *peire.* Gael. *paidhir.* Manx, *piyr.* Lat. *par.*

PAR, adj. Equal, meet. *A Dôs, ty re dhrôs dhymmo ascorn a'm kŷk* (ha) *corf o par may fo ow howethes,* O Father, thou hast brought to me bone of my flesh and body, (that) was meet that it should be my companion. O.M. 113. Arm. *pâr.*

PAR, adv. Like as, so. *Ny a vyn formyé an bŷs, par del ôn try hag onan,* we will create the world, like as we are three and one. O.M. 12. *Arluth henna me a wra, a'n gor yn pyt ysella yn mijsk pryves, par ma'n geffo mûr a pŷn,* Lord, I will do that, and put him in the lowest pit among reptiles, so that he may have much pain. R.D. 2012. *Tormentores, dueeh dhym scon, par ma allo ow colon guella ow cher,* executioners, come to me forthwith, so that my heart may better my condition. R.D. 2241.

PARADYS, s. m. Paradise. Written also *parathys. Helhys warbarth a fuen ny yn mês scon a paradys,* driven together we were quickly out of Paradise. O.M. 710. *Pan wrugé dres ow defen, mês a paravays lowen an êl wharé a'n goras,* when he acted against my prohibition, out of happy Paradise the angel soon put him. O.M. 923. W. *paradwys.* Arm. *paradoz,* †*paradoes,* †*paradis.* Ir. *parralhas.* Gael. *pàras.* Manx, *pargis.* Lat. *paradeisus.*

PARC, s. m. An inclosure, a field, a park. Pl. *parcow.* Pryce. Preserved in the names of many places. *Park en vrân,* the crow's field. *Park hale,* the moor field. *Park hoskin,* sedge field. W. *parc.* Arm. *parc.* Ir. *pairc.* Gael. *pairc.* Manx, *pairk.* Fr. *parc.* Ang. Sax. *pearrac.* Eng. *park.*

PARCHEMIN, s. m. Parchment. Corn. Vocab. *pergamenum vel membranum.* Borrowed from the French form, *parchemin.* Called in Welsh *memrwn,* from Lat. *membrana.*

PAREZ, adj. Ready, prepared. *Llwyd*, 113. A late form of *parys*, qd. v.

PARH, s. m. A part, a side. Corn. Voc. *modereb a barh mam*, matertera, aunt on the mother's side; *a barh tat, amita*, on the father's side. Another form of *parth*, qd. v. See also *Barh*.

PARHY, v. a. To divide. Written by Llwyd, 55, *parri, dho barri*.

PARLEDII, s. m. A parlour. *Llwyd*, 13.

PAROT, adj. Ready, prepared. Corn. Voc. *coctus*. The old form of *parys*, qd. v. W. *parod*. From the Lat. *paratus*.

PAROW, s. m. An equal. *Scon a onan a'th asow my a wra dhyso parow pûp ûr râg dhe weres*, forthwith from one of thy ribs I will make to thee an equal, always to help thee. O.M. 100. *Pysyn may fyyn scrvysy dh'agan Arluth hep parow*, let us pray that we may be servants to our Lord without equal. O.M. 236. *Nynsus parow dhys yn beys*, there is not an equal to thee in the world. O.M. 435.

PARTHI, s. m. A part, side, division. *Yn nef y fedhaff tregis a'n barth dychow gans am câr*, in heaven I shall dwell on the right side with my Father. M.C. 93. *Am lemyn dhe'n gwellynny, a barth an Tâs veneges*, kiss thou now the rods, on the part of the blessed Father. O.M. 1792. *A barth an pla*, in the name of the plague. P.C. 1348. *Pan êth dreyn yn empynnyon a pûp parth dre a grogen*; when the thorns went into the brain, on every part through the skull. R.D. 2558. *A barth a wollas*, on the bottom. C.W. 124. *A barth awartha*, on the higher side. C.W. 146. *Scrif ol remma dhy arhadow parth chy agan colonnow, ny dhy bŷs*, write thou all these thy commands within our hearts, we beseech thee. Pryce. W. *parth*, †*part*, †*pard*. Arm. *pars*, †*pers*. Ir. *part*, †*pairt*. Gael. *pairt*. Lat. *pars, parte*. Sanse. *parth*, to spread.

PARTHY, v. a. To honour, to respect. *Cara, gordhya, ha owna Dew, an mateyrn, ha'n lahes, en 'gus plew; owna Dew, parth an mateyrn, ha cara 'gus contrevogyon*, love, worship, and fear God, the King, and the laws, in your parish; fear God, honour the King, and love your neighbours. Pryce. W. *parchu*.

PARUSY, v. a. To make ready, to prepare. Part. *parusys. Râg yma bôs parusys dhyso, ha dhedhê kefrys*, for there is food prepared for thee, and for them also. P.C. 458. *Deuch gynef, me a dhyswê chy dh'agas mester wharré râk parusy y soper*, come ye with me, I will shew a house for your master presently to prepare his supper. P.C. 675. *Râg yma bous lour omma erbyn soper, a pewa ol parusys*, for there is meat enough here against supper, if it be all made ready. P.C. 690. Formed from *parus*, or *parys*. W. *parotôi*.

PARYS, adj. Prepared, ready. *Râg genes yn pûp teller, parys ôf dhe lafuryê*, for with thee in every place I am ready to act. O.M. 940. *Tân ha cledhê yma genê lemmyn parys*, fire and sword are with mo now prepared. O.M. 1306. *Prest hep danger vedhaf parys*, soon without delay I shall be ready. O.M. 1910. *Dewdhek lyggyon yn un ro vyê a'n nêf danvenys, ha moy, a mynnen dhymmo pesy ow thâs pûr barys*, twelve legions in a gift would be sent from heaven, and more, if for myself I would pray my Father. M.C. 72. A later form of *parot*, qd. v.

PAS, s. m. A cough. *Llwyd*, 30, 168, *pâz*. W. *pâs, pestech*. Arm. *pâs, pâz*. Ir. *cás, casachd*. Gael. *casad*. Latin, *tussis*. Fr. *toux*. Eng. cough. Sansc. *cas*, to cough. Germ. *keiche*. Lith. *kosta*. Gr. †κοίζω.

PASC, s. m. Easter, the Passover. *Euch yn drê, hag ordeneeh bôs pâsk dhynny hep lettyê*, go ye into the town, and order the paschal food for us, without delaying. P.C. 618. *Me agas pŷs, râk pask may fo dyllyfrys Barabas hep skullyê y wôs*, I pray you, that for passover that delivered be Barabbas, without shedding his blood. P.C. 2368. *Thomas, ydhos pûr woky, dresen na fynnyth cryyg an Arluth dhe dhasserchy dn pask vyltyn*, Thomas, thou art very stupid, because thou wilt not believe the Lord to have risen Easter-day in the morning. R.D. 1108. *Râg pasch o dhedhê, dŷdh uchel y a sensy*, for it was Easter to them; a high day they held it. M.C. 229. W. *pâsg, pâsc*. Arm. *pasc*. Irish, *caisg*, †*casc*. Gael. *caisg*. Manx, *caisht*. Scotch, *pasche*. From Lat. *pascha*.

PASWARDHAC, eard. num. Fourteen. *Llwyd*, 134. A corruption of *peswardhec*, qd. v.

PASWERA, num. adj. Fourth. *Llwyd*, 243. A corruption of *peswerê*, qd. v.

PATLA, adv. How, by what means. *Llwyd*, 135. Written also *fatla*, qd. v. A late form of *paltel*, qd. v.

PATSHAN, s. m. The haunch, or buttock. *Llwyd*, 48.

PATTEL, adv. How, by what means. *Llwyd*, 231. Written also *fattel*, qd. v. ‡ *Patl yzhi a cylywi*, how it lightens. *Llwyd*, 248. Comp. of *pa*, what, and *del*, manner. W. *pa dhelw, pa dhull*.

PAUGEN, s. f. A sock. Corn. Voc. *pedula*. W. *pawgen*; comp. of *paw*, a foot, and *cen*, a covering.

PAUN, s. m. A peacock. Corn. Voc. *pavo*. Written also *payon*, qd. v. W. *paun, pawan*. Arm. *paun*. Fr. *paon*. Lat. *pavo, pavone*.

PAW, s. m. A foot. *Râk bôs ow arluth mar clâf, a Dhew, ple tôf, na ple ydh âf, ny won ple toulaf ow paw*, because of my lord being so sick, O God, where I shall come, or where I shall go, I know not where I shall cast my foot. R.D. 1666. *Ty geyler scon, ty ha'th vaw, kymereuch er an dhyw baw, ha gorreuch ef yn dôr down*, thou gaoler, forthwith, thou and thy boy, take (ye) him by the two feet, and put him in deep ground. R.D. 2076. W. *pawen*. Arm. *paô*.

PAYN, s. f. Pain. Pl. *paynys. Dre conquest a dhylyfras mês a payn an cnefow*, by the conquest (that) delivered the souls out of pain. R.D. 2630. *Ow paynys a vŷdh garow kyn vôs leskys dhe lusow*, my pains will be cruel before being burnt to ashes. O.M. 1354. *Nyngew ow faynys bechan, ûs lemmyn war ow sensy*, my pains are not little, (that) now are holding me. M.C. 166. *Lemmyn me agis pŷs oll a baynys Crist predery*, now I pray you all of Christ's pains to think. M.C. 182. Written also *peyn*, qd. v.

PAYNES, s. f. A peahen. *Llwyd*, 241. W. *peunes, paenes*. Arm. *paunez*.

PAYON, s. m. A peacock. *Hôs, payon, colom, grugyer, bargos, bryny, ha'n er moy dredhof a vŷdh hynwys*, duck, peacock, pigeon, partridge, kite, crows, and the eagle further by me shall be named. O.M. 132. Another form of *paun*, qd. v.

PE, v. subs. A mutation of *be*, 3 pers. s. subj. of *bôs*, qd. v. *A pe vôdh Dew yn della*, if God's will were so. O.M. 2356. *A pe ve dên drôk*, if he were a bad man. P.C. 2909. *Dhe vôdh mar pe genes*, if thy will be with thee. R.D. 441. *Saw yn della mar a pe*, but if it were so. R.D. 1022. *Saw an corf-na byw a pe, an emperour ef sawsé*, but that body if it were living would have cured the emperor. R.D. 1657.

PE, pron. What, which. *Lemmyn merouch pe nyle a'n dûs a vŷdh delyffris*, now see ye which of the two men shall be delivered. M.C. 125. *An dên-ma re drehevys, gallas ny wodhan pe le*, this man has arisen, he is gone we know not where. M.C. 245. *Pe penag ol a wylly*, whatsoever thou seest. O.M. 745. Written also *pa*, qd. v. W. *pa*. Arm. *pe*.

PE, adv. Where, in what place. *Pe ma, yn mêdh Crist dhydhy, nêb a vyn dhe guhudha*, where, says Christ to her, is he that will accuse thee ? M.C. 34. *Abel, pe festé mar bel*, Abel, where hast thou been so long ? O.M. 467. *Ny won vŷth pe'dh âf lemyn, nymbus gwesc, guskys, na chy*, I know not where I shall go now, I have not clothes, shelter, nor house. O.M. 355. Written also *py*, qd. v.

PE, conj. Or. *Llwyd*, 44. Generally written *po*, qd. v. Arm. *pe*.

PEB, pron. s. Every one, each one, all. *Dre virtu an scrifé pêb dhe vês a omdennas*, by virtue of the writing every one withdrew. M.C. 33. *Tûs Crist dhe vês a fyas, pêp a'y du phr vorethek*, the people of Christ fled away, each one on his (own) side very sorrowful. M.C. 77. *Ha pêb dhodho ow cûll geyll*, and every one doing guile to him. M.C. 165. *Prederys pêb a'y worfen*, let every one think of its end. O.M. 227. *Pêb ol war pen y dew glŷn a gân yn gordhyans dodho*, every one on his knees will sing in worship to him. P.C. 247. W. *pawb*, † *paup*. Ir. *ceach*, † *cach*. Gael. *gach*. Manx, *ynch*. Lat. *quisque*.

PEBA, v. a. To bake. *Llwyd*, 17. ‡ *Es an bara pebes luck*, is the bread baked enough ? *Pryce*. Another form of *pobas*, qd. v. W. *pobi*. Arm. *pobi*. Sansc. *pach*. Gr. πέπτω.

PEBA, v. a. To use a pipe, to pipe, to play a tune. *A barth an Tâs, menstrels a rûs, pebouch wharé*, in the name of the Father, minstrels of grace, pipe immediately. O.M. 2846. *Mynstrels, grouch dhe ny pcba, may hallan warbarth downssya*, minstrels, do ye pipe to us, that we may together dance." C.W. 184. Another form of *piba*, qd. v.

PEBAN, s. f. A little pipe, a flageolet. See *Piban*.

PEDER, s. m. A baker. Corn. Voc. *pistor. (Peba— gour.)* W. *pobwr*. Arm. *pober*.

PECAR, adv. Equally, like as, as. *A bûb sort oll a leverow cgwall unna ew gorrys, pekar ydhew an soriow gorrys unna der devyes*, of every sort of books equally in them are put, as are the sorts put in them by pairs. C.W. 160. Id. qd. *pocâr*, qd. v.

PECH, s. m. Sin, offence, transgression. *Bŷth ny allaf yn ow rôs dhe will pêch vŷth y cachyé*, I shall never be able in my net to catch him to do any sin. P.C. 55. *A'n ladhas mûr yw y bêch*, who killed him, great is his sin. P.C. 3162. *Dhe pêch dhys a vŷdh gcfys*, thy sin will be forgiven thee. R.D. 1102. *Ol pêch Adam pan prennas*, when he redeemed all the sin of Adam. R.D. 2562. *Gáf dhem ow fêch, my a'd pŷs*, forgive me my sin, I pray thee. O.M. 2726. W. *pêch*.

PECHA, v. a. To sin, to commit sin, to transgress, to offend. Written also *peché*. *War lyrch mâb dên dhe becha, reson prâg y fe prynnys yn Ihesus Crist dhe ordna yn nêff y vonas tregys*, after the son of man sinned, the reason why he was redeemed is that Jesus Christ ordained that he should dwell in heaven. M.C. 7. *Te na yllyth omwethé un prês yn geydh na pechy*, thou canst not keep thyself a moment in the day that thou wilt not sin. M.C. 20. *Ha'n virtu an pregoth o mâb dên dhe asé peché*, and the virtue of the sermon was that the son of man left sinning. M.C. 23. *Ha na wra na moy pecha*, and do thou sin no more. M.C. 34. *Fest yn crêff me re bechas, Ihesus dhe wy ow querthé*, very strongly I have sinned, selling Jesus to you. M.C. 104. *Hag an aval devethys, drcdhy Adam may pechsé*, and the apple had come from it, that Adam had sinned by. M.C. 152. *Ny wrûk an dên-ma vythqueth war an bŷs-ma drokoleth, na ny peches war nêp cor*, this man has never done evil deed in this world, nor sinned in any sort. P.C. 2905. W. *pechu*. Arm. *pcchi*. Lat. *pecco*.

PECHAD, s. m. Sin, offence, transgression. Pl. *pechadow*. *Yn dewellens pechadow, gûl alter da vyé*, in atonement for sins, to make an altar would be good. O.M. 1173. *Hag henna dhe'th pechadow dha gy, dha'n doer a wra cruppya*, and that for thy sins, on the earth thou shalt creep. C.W. 66. For the singular the later form *pechas*, qd. v. was generally used. W. *pechawd, pechod*. Arm. *pechod*, † *pechct*. Ir. *peacadh*, † *peccat*. Gael. *peacadh*. Manx, *peccah*. All from the Lat. *peccatum*.

PECHADUR, s. m. A sinner, a transgressor. See the later form *pehadur*. W. *pechadur*. Arm. *pecher*. Ir. *peacach, peacthach*, † *pecthad*. Gael. *peacair, peacach*. Manx, *peccach*. Lat. *peccator*.

PECHADURES, s. f. A female sinner. *A pe profus bynyges, ef a wodhfyé y bôs hy pechadures* ; *ny's gassé dh'y ylyé*, if he were a blessed prophet, he would have known that she is a sinner ; he would not have permitted her to anoint him. P.C. 491. *Pechadores es hep gow, an brassa egé yn pow, gans pûp ol ty o gylwys*, thou art a sinner without a lie, the greatest that was in the country by every body thou wast called. R.D. 1094. *My re buc pechadores a pechas marthys yn frâs*, I have been a sinner (that) sinned wondrous greatly. R.D. 1097. Written also *pehadures*, qd. v. W. *pechadures*. Arm. *pecherez*. Fr. *pecheresse*.

PECHAS, s. m. Sin, offence, transgression. Pl. *pechasow*. *Godhaff paynys pan vynnas, nêb na ylly gûl pechas*, when he was willing to suffer pains, who could not commit sin. M.C. 3. *Leun a bechas, ny won ken, dhe wethyll agis meystry*, full of sin I know not other, to do your power. M.C. 75. *Râk henna warbarth ol y fechas gwûlân dedhy hy y feydh gyfys*, for that together all her sins clean to her will be forgiven. P.C. 528. *My re bechas, hag a henna a clow mcrsy war Dew agan Tâs may affo an pechasow*, I have sinned, and for that I cry mercy of God our Father, that he may pardon our sins. O.M. 1866. *Yn dewyllyens pechasow*, in atonement of sins. P.C. 826. A late form of *pechad*, qd. v., and written also *pehas*, qd. v.

PECHYE, v. a. To thrust, to dart. *Yn corf Ihesus caradow en gew lym ef a bechyé pûr ewn yn dan an asow, dre an golon may'thesé*, in the body of loveable Jesus the sharp spear he darted very right under the ribs, so that it was through the heart. M.C. 218.

PEDAR, card. num. Four. Used with nouns feminine, as *peswar* is with masculines. *Dyllas Crist a ve rynnys, pedar ran guris anedhê, gans peswar marreg a brŷs, dhe bûb marreg ran may fe,* the clothes of Christ were divided, four parts made of them, by four soldiers of account; to every soldier that there might be a part. M.C. 190. *In corff Ihesus ydh esê, hag ef yn crows ow cregy, pymp mŷll strekis del iové, ha peder gwŷth cans goly, ha tryugons moy gansé, ha pymthek, pûr wŷr êns y,* in the body of Jesus there were, while he was hanging on the cross, five thousand strokes as there were, and four times a hundred wounds, and three score more with them, and fifteen, very truly were they. M.C. 227. *Fenten bryght avel arhans, ha pedyr stryth vrâs defry, ow resek a-dyworty,* a fountain bright like silver, and large streams indeed, flowing from it. O.M 772. W. *pedair,* † *pedeir.* Arm. *peder.* Ir. † *cethcora,* † *ceteora.* Sansc. *katasras.* Lith. *keturios.*

PEDN, s. m. A head, summit, extremity. ‡ *A, chorll côth, te pedn pilles, fatla vynta ge henna, y fŷdh an bŷs consumya,* Ah! old churle, thou bald pate, how wilt thou have this to be, that the world will be consumed ? C.W. 108. ‡ *Aylas, me yw marow, ha'w fedn squattyes pûr varow, why a'n gwêl inter dew ran,* alas, I am dead, and my head broken very cruelly, you see it in two parts. C.W. 124. ‡ *Pedn yz,* an ear of corn. Llwyd, 34. ‡ *Pedn braos,* a jolt-head. ‡ *Blew an pedn,* hair of the head. 49. ‡ *Pedn-pral marh,* a horse's skull. 59. ‡ *Pedn dhrog,* wicked. 84. ‡ *Pedn rydh,* red-headed. 142. ‡ *Bar an pedn,* top of the head. 172. ‡ *Pedn diu,* a boil. 136. (W. *pendhuyn,* lit. a black-head.) "The Cornish now call a kind of boteh or boil, "Blackhead." They also call a tomtit *pednpaly;* and say *pednamene,* head to feet; as in many Cornish huts, large families lie, husband, wife, and children, (even grown up) of both sexes, in one bed." *Polwhele.* ‡ *Pedn diu,* blackheads, young frogs, or tadpoles. *Pryce. Pedn* is a late corruption of *pen,* qd. v.

PEDNZIVIG, adj. Noble, principal. Pl. ‡ *pednzivigian,* nobility, gentry. *Llwyd,* 108. A late corruption of *pendevig,* qd. v.

PEDREN, s. f. The breech, the buttock. Pl. *pedrennow. Me a'n knouk fest dybyté, man geffo pûp ol bysné, ow myres worth y vody, del wascaf y peydrennow, may fo gôs y vlewennow, ha y corf ol kyns ys ready,* I will beat him hard without pity, that all may have shuddering, looking at his body, as I shall strike his buttocks, that his hair may be bloody, and all his body, before leaving off. P.C. 2004. W. *pedrain,* pl. *pedreiniau.*

PEDREVAN, s. f. A lizard, eft, or newt. *Llwyd,* 240. *Pedrevan an dour,* a water lizard. 143. Llwyd, 75, gives another form *pedrevor,* and reads *pedresif,* for *wedresif,* qd. v. He also gives *peder chwilen,* as a Welsh synonym.

PEDRY, v. a. To rot, to become rotten, to putrify. Part. *pedrys. Oynment o a gymmys râs, may wethê corf heb pedry,* the ointment was of so much virtue, that it kept a body without putrefying. M.C. 235. *Neffré na wrello dybry, lemyn fleryê ha peddry kepar ha scym py lyys haal,* that she may never eat, but stink and rot, like train-oil or salt-marsh mud. O.M. 2707. *An kêth gwâs-ma gorreuch why yn drôk pryson dhe peddry,* this same fellow put ye in a bad prison to rot. R.D. 2002. *Merouch pymava towlys, yn clêdh dhe vonas pedrys,* see ye where he is thrown, in a ditch to be rotten. C.W. 82. W. *pydru.* Lat. *putreo.*

PEDYR, s. m. Peter; a man's name. Written also *peder. Peder, Androw, ha Iowan, dûn ahanan hep falladow,* Peter, Andrew, and John, let us go hence, without delay. P.C. 464. W. *Pedr.*

PEDII, v. subs. He shall or will be. *Mara pêdh e lêl juggys,* if he be fairly judged. P.C. 1344. *Mar pêdh e yeyn, ny dhue dhe gur,* if it will be cold, it will not come to the end. P.C. 2729. A mutation of *bêdh,* qd. v.

PEDHA, v. subs. He should be. *Mars mara pedha degis gans y dûs na'n caffan ny, yn ûr-na bŷdh leverys ef dhe sevell dre vestry,* but if he be carried away by his people, so that we should not find him, then it will be said that he arose through power. M.C. 240. A mutation of *bedha,* 3 pers. s. subj. of *bôs.*

PEDHAF, v. subs. I shall or will be. *Mar pedhaf kelmys lemmyn,* if I shall now be bound. O.M. 1349. *Maru pedhaf bew vledhen,* if I shall be living a year. O.M. 2386. A mutation of *bedhaf,* qd. v.

PEDHIGLA, v. a. To roar like a lion, to bellow. *Llwyd,* 142. A *pedhigla,* bellowing. 248.

PEDHOUCH, v. subs. Ye will be. *Yn ûr-na, der vaner da, marn pedhouch repentys, an kêth plâg a wra voydya,* in that hour, after a good manner, if ye will repent, that same plague shall be made void. C.W. 170. A mutation of *bedhouch,* qd. v.

PEDHYN, v. s. We shall or will be. *Yn ûr-na me a weyl, mar a pedhyn ny abel dhe wîl defens a râk tues,* then I shall see, if we shall be able to make a defence before people. P.C. 2305. A mutation of *bedhyn,* qd. v.

PEG, s. m. Pitch. *Râg henna fystyn, ke, gura gorhel a blunkos playnnyys, hag ynno lues trygva, romes y a vŷdh gylwys; a-vês hag agy yn ta gans pêk bedhens stanch wrŷs,* therefore hasten thou, go, make a ship of planed planks, and in it many dwellings, rooms they shall be called; without and within well with pitch let them be made staunch. O.M. 954. *A vês hag agy yn ta gans peyk bedhans stanch gwrŷs,* without and within well with pitch let them be made staunch. C.W. 104. *Yma peyk dhym provyes, ha lowonow pûp chan, deffrans sortow a vernow yma parys pûr effan,* there is to me pitch provided, and ropes of every kind, different sorts of masts, here are ready very plainly. C.W. 166. W. *pŷg.* Arm. *pec, peg.* Ir. *pic,* † *bi.* Gael. *pic.* Manx. *pick.* Lat. *pix, pice.* Fr. *poix.*

PEG, s. f. A prick, a smart, a smarting. *Pryce.* The verb is written *piga,* qd. v. W. *pîg.* Arm. *pic.* Gael. *pioc.*

PEG, s. m. A small piece, a bit. *Ef a'n gevyth war an chul; dên vythol na dhoutyans peg,* he shall catch it on the jaw; let not any man doubt a bit. P.C. 1182. Borrowed from the English.

PEGANS, s. m. Necessaries of life, money, instruments. *Fystenouch troh an daras, râg omma ny wreuch trega; agas toules dha'th ballas, h'ages pegans dha nedha, y towns parys,* make ye haste through the door, for here ye shall not dwell; your tools for delving, and your instruments to spin, they are ready. C.W. 72. *Cuntell warbarth ow fegans, me a vyn môs pûr uskys,* gather thou together my necessaries, I will go very quickly. C.W. 94. *Degen genan agen pegans,* let us carry with us our necessaries.

C.W. 96. *Victual erall dhyn yma, ha pegans lower dha vewa*, other victuals to us there are, and necessaries enough to live. C.W. 108. Probably a corrupt plural of *péth*, qd. v.

PEGY, v. a. To pray, to beseech. *Ha dhe'n Tâs gwrén oll pegy, na skydnya an kêth vengeans warnan ny, nag en flechys*, and to the Father let us all pray, that the same vengeance may not fall on us, nor our children. C.W. 160. More generally written *piggy*, and *pygy*, qd. v.

PEGYA, v. a. To cease. *In'della hy a begyas bys hanter dydh yredy*, so it ceased until mid-day indeed. M.C. 201. The interpretation is doubtful, and is arrived at by comparing the word with W. *peidio*; in the same way as C. *nija*, to fly, = W. *neidio*.

PEH, s. m. Sin, offence, transgression. Llwyd, 52, 115. A late form of *péch*, qd. v.

PEHAD, s. m. Sin, offence, transgression. Pl. *pehadow*. Llwyd, 242. A late form of *pechad*, qd. v.

PEHADUR, s. m. A sinner. Pl. *pehadoryon*. *Kyn nag óff dén skentyll púr, par del von lavaraff dhys, yntré Du ha pchadur acordh del ve kemerys*, though I am not a very learned man, even as I know I will tell to thee, between God and sinner how accord was taken. M.C. 8. *Ihesu Crist mûr gerensé dhe vôb dén a dhyswedhas, a'n uchelder may 'thesé dhe'n bys pan deyskynnas, pchadoryon râg perna o descvijs dre Satnas*, Jesus Christ shewed much love to the son of man, when he descended to the world from the height that he was, to redeem sinners who were felled by Satan. M.C. 5. Another form of *pechadur*, qd. v.

PEHADURES, s. f. A female sinner. *An gusyl o may fe dris dhe rág Crist pehadures, ol dh'y vôdh may rollo brés anedhy, del re dhe grés*, the counsel was that a sinful woman should be brought before Christ, that he might give judgment upon her according to his will as some believed. M.C. 32. Another form of *pechadures*, qd. v.

PEHAS, s. m. Sin, offence, transgression. Pl. *pehasow*. *Arluth, veneges re by, del osé Dew hep pehas*, Lord, blessed art thou, as thou art God without sin. O.M. 1796. *Yn amendys a'd pehosow, orden bôs gureys temple golow, brás ha ledan*, in amendment of thy sins, order to be made a brilliant temple, great and broad. O.M. 2259. *Moy yw ow gwan oberow, hag yn wêdh ow fehasow es tell ew dha versy, Dew*, greater are my evil deeds, and likewise my sins, than so is thy mercy, God. O.W. 84. Another form of *pechas*, qd. v.

PEHE, v. a. To sin, to transgress. *Och, tru, tru, my re behas, ha re dorras an dyfen*, Oh, sad, sad, I have sinned, and have broken the prohibition. O.M. 249. *Râg henna my a's temptyas dhe behé*, for that I tempted them to sin. O.M. 308. *Saw my a greys hy bós séch, ha gurjys nôth ol rág an pêch a pehas ow thás ha'm mam*, but I believe that it is dry, and all made bare, for the sin which my father and mother sinned. O.M. 759. *Gory pan wrugé pché gans corf an debel venen*, woe is me, when I have done sin with the body of the wicked woman. O.M. 2250. Another form of *peché*, qd. v.

PEIS, s. f. A coat, a jacket. Corn. Voc. *tunica*. Generally written in the Dramas, *pows*, qd. v. See also *Peus*. W. *pais*, a coat, a petticoat. Ir. †*ceis*. Cf. Dutch *pey*, and Eng. *pea-jacket*.

PEL, s. f. A sphere, a ball, a bowl to play with. Pl. *peliow*. *Pêl-ma*, this ball. *Ny ol devethes war týr glâs dho gwaré peliow, râg 'gun ehas*, we are all come upon green land, to play at bowls for our health. Pryce. W. *pêl*. Arm. *pellen*. Lat. *pila*. Sansc. *pal*, *pil*, to throw a ball.

PELE, adv. Where, in what place. (*Pe—le.*) *An dên-ma re drehevys, gallas ny wodhan pelé*, this man has arisen, he has gone, we know not where. M.C. 245. *Del ôs cowyth da, lavar a pilé osa*, as thou art a good companion, say whence thou art. P.C. 2170. Llwyd, 248, gives as the earliest form *pyléch*, then *pléch*, then *ple*.

PELE, s. m. A spire, a steeple. *Carn pele*, the spire rock. Pryce.

PELEZ, adj. Bald. ‡ *Pedn pelez*, a bald head. Pryce. Written also *pilez*, qd. v.

PELIHA, pron. inter. Which or whether of the two. Llwyd, 178, *peliha*.

PELL, adj. Distant, remote, far, long. Comp. *pellah*, †*pellach*, *pella*. *Pylat êth yn mês a'y hell yn un lowarth a'n gero, ogas o, nyng esa pell*, Pilate went out of his hall into a garden which he had, near it was, it was not far. M.C. 140. *Ny strechyaff pell*, I will not delay long. M.C. 158. *Ha dh'y notyé drys an wlâs, a ogas hag a bell*, to make it known through the country, anear and afar. M.C. 249. *Bewé pel a wrûk yn beys*, I lived long in the world. R.D. 210. *Ny iuggyn mones nêp pel, lemmyn bys yn un castel henwys Emmaus*, we do not think to go any distance, but so far as a village called Emmaus. R.D. 1294. W. *pell*. Arm. *pell*.

PELLA, adj. Farther, longer. The comparative of *pell*. Originally written *pelluch*, (Llwyd, 243,) the guttural being softened into *h*, and generally omitted. *Ny allaf pella trega*, I cannot stay longer. O.M. 2190. *Ny vennaf pella lettyé*, I will not longer delay. P.C. 1612. *Lemmyn me a greys yn ta y fynnaf vy môs pella enouch haneth*, now I believe well, that I shall go further than you to-night. R.D. 1297. *Nymbus bywé na fella*, living is no longer for me. R.D. 2210. W. *pellach*. Arm. *pelloch*.

PELLDER, s. m. Distance, remoteness. *Râg henna dûn a lema, yn pelder dheworth ow thás*, therefore let us go hence, to a distance from my father. C.W. 98. *Aban ew pûb tra parys, dûn ny yn kerth kekeffrys, pelder adro yn bys*, since every thing is ready, let us go away likewise, afar off about in the world. C.W. 100. W. *pellder*. Arm. *pellder*, *pelder*.

PELLEAR, adv. A long time. (*Pell—ear*, au hour.) Pryce.

PELLEN, s. f. A ball of thread or yarn, a round body, a bowl. Corn. Vocab. *globus*. W. *pellen*. Arm. *pellen*. Gael. *peileir*.

PELLIST, s. m. A pilch or pelisse. Corn. Voc. *pellistgur*, pellicia, a leathern pilch, lit. a man's pelisse; *pellisiker*, mastruga, a fur coat. W. *pilysyn*. Lat. *pellicia*.

PELLY, v. a. To render distant, to remove far off, to drive away. Part. *pellys*. *Ethlays, gwef pan vevé genys, ow terry gormenadow Dew, pellys ôn a Baradys dha'n noer veys er agan gow*, alas, woe is me when I was born, breaking the commandments of God, driven we are from Paradise to the world for our woe. C.W. 76. W. *pellu*. Arm. *pellaat*. Lat. *pello*.

PEMDHAC, card. num. Fifteen. Llwyd, 135. Written also *pymthec*, qd. v.

PEMP, card. num. Five. *Llwyd*, 18, 135. ‡ *Pemp degvas*, fifteenth. Written also *pymp*, qd. v.

PEMPAS, num. adj. Fifth. *Llwyd*, 135. ‡ *Ha gothuhar ha metten o an pempas jorna*, and the evening and the morning was the fifth day. M.C. p. 95. C.W. p. 191. A later form of *pympes*, qd. v.

PEN, s. m. An extremity, end, conclusion; head, a chief, beginning, the upper part, a summit. Pl. *pennow*. Cornish Vocabulary, *caput*. *A lena y'n hombronkyas uchel war ben un menedh*, thence he led him high on top of a mountain. M.C. 16. *Gans queth y ben y quedhens, gwelas banna ny ylly*, with a cloth his head they covered so that he could not see a jot. M.C. 96. *Hu hager fest an dygtyas, corf ha pen, treys ha devolé*, and very foully treated him, body and head, feet and hands. M.C. 130. *Aga fen y a sackyé*, their heads they wagged. M.C. 195. *Cayphas a'n droys arté dhe Pylat o pen Iustis*, Caiaphas brought him again to Pilate (that) was chief justice. M.C. 119. *Ha'n pen arall o pytel*, and the other end was pity. M.C. 223. *May'th êth war ben y dhewlyn*, so that he went on his knees. M.C. 54. *Del osa Dew dhyn ha pen*, as thou art God to us, and head. P.C. 732. *Kyns pen vys*, before the end of a month. P.C. 1646. *Me a dhybarth ynterthoch, hag a wra dheuch pennow couch*, I will separate between you, and make your heads red. P.C. 2326. *Kyns pen sythyn*, before the end of a week. R.D. 30. *Ev yw pen côk*, he is a block-head. R.D. 2017. *Del lavaraf, pen bronnen*, as I say, rush-head. R.D. 2096. *Pen ha duscoudh*, head and shoulders. R.D. 2500. ‡ *Pennow tiys*, heads of the people, chief men. *Llwyd*, 128. *Pennow ys*, ears of corn. *Pryce*. W. *pen*, †*penn*. Arm. *penn*. Ir. *ccann*, †*cenn*. Gael. *ccan*. Manx, *cione*. (Cf. W. *penmawr*; Ir. †*cenmar*, *capito*, i. e. great head; W. *noethben*; Ir. *nochtchenn*, barehead.—The Erse form is also preserved in Welsh, in the compound *talcen*, a forehead; and in the simple form *cyn*, †*cen*, chief, foremost, head.) Cf. also Lat. *finis*. Sansc. *phan*, to end.

PENAG, adv. Soever. Answering to *cunque* in Latin. *Gwrêns Dew y vôdh ha'y vynnas, py penag eo yn y vreys*, let God do his will and his pleasure, whatever may be in his mind. O.M. 1154. *Pup-penag-ol a vo ef*, whosoever he may be. P.C. 23. *My a vyn gúl yn della, py le penag y's kyffyn*, I will do so, wherever I find it. P.C. 1551. *A henna na geuseuch gêr, py-penag-ol a wharfo*, of that speak not a word, whatever may happen. R.D. 671. *Pyw penag a'm gwella vy, ef a wylfyth ow thâs*, whoever shall see me, will see my Father. R.D. 2383. Used also without a pronoun. *Penag a wryllyf ammé, henna yw ef*, whomsoever I shall kiss, that is he. P.C. 1084. Written also *pynag*, qd. v. W. *pynag*. Arm. *pennag*.

PENCANGUER, s. m. A centurion, the head of a hundred men. Corn. Voc. *centurio*, (*pen—can—gur*, pl. of *gour*.)

PENCAST, s. m. The Pentecost, Whitsuntide. *Llwyd*, 32, 116, 241. Arm. *pentekost*. From Lat. *pentecoste*. Ir. *cincighis*. Gael. *cuingis*. Manx, *kingeesh*. From Lat. *quinqungesima*.

PENCLIN, s. m. The knee. Corn. Voc. *genu*. More correctly written *penglin*. See *Glin*.

PENCLUN, s. m. The hip, the haunch. Corn. Vocab. *clunis*. See *Clun*.

PENDEVIG, s. m. A prince, one of the highest rank, a chief man, a nobleman. Corn. Voc. *princeps*. Pl. *pendevigion*. Written later *pensevic*, qd. v. In Llwyd's time it was corrupted into ‡ *pednzhivig*, pl. *pednzhivigion*. 128. Comp. of *pen*, head, and *dwi*, to rule. W. *pendevig*. Arm. *pinvidic, pinouic*.

PENDIWEN, s. f. A reed. *Llwyd*, 43. Arm. *penduen*. *Pendhu* in Welsh is the "brownwort." Comp. of *pen*, head, and *du*, black.

PENDRA, s. f. What thing, what, why. *Ow mâp kerra, pendra vynta orthyf govyn*, my dearest son, what wilt thou ask of me? O.M. 1311. *Pendra wreuch ow repryfa*, why do ye reprove me? O.M. 1500. *Pendra wrâf ny wodhes whêth*, what I will do, thou knowest not yet. P.C. 848. *Pendra reys dhynny dhe gûl*, what is necessary for us to do? P.C. 1354. *Pendra ny venté keusel*, why wilt thou not speak? P.C. 1775. Another form of *pandra*, qd. v.

PENDRUPPIA, v. a. To nod, or shake the head. *Llwyd*, 135. W. *pendwmpian*.

PENGARN, s. m. A gurnet fish. *Llwyd*, 135. Pl. *pengarnas*. *Y rôf henwyn dha'n puskas, dhe wyan, pengarnas, selyas*, I will give names to the fishes, to breams, gurnards, congers. C.W. 32. W. *pengarn, pengernyn*.

PENGUCH, s. m. A head covering, an upper garment. Corn. Voc. *penguchgrec*, *mastruga*, a fur coat; lit. a woman's cloak. W. *penguwch*.

PENNAGEL, pron. Whoever. *Pennagel ew na lavara*, whoever says not. C.W. 14. *Ha pennagel a wra henna*, and whoever shall do that. C.W. 118. A late form of *penag-ol*, qd. v.

PENPRAL, s. m. A skull. *Penpral marh*, a horse's skull. *Pryce*.

PENRYN, s. m. A promontory, cape, head-land. *Why a's bŷdh agas gobyr eredy, warbarth ol gueel Behethlen, ha coys Penryn yn tyen, my a's re lemyn dheuch why, ye* shall have your reward surely, together all the field of Bohellan, and the wood of Penryn, wholly I give them now to you. O.M. 2589. W. *penryn*. It forms the name of many places; as *Penryn Blathaon*, Caithness, in Scotland; *Penryn Rhionydh*, the point of Galloway; *Penryn Penwyth*, Land's End, in Cornwall; *Penryn Creudhyn*, in North Wales, &c. Comp. of *pen*, a head, and *rhyn*, a point, or cape.

PENS, s. f. A pound in money, twenty shillings. ‡ *Ena dzhei a varginiaz râg trei penz an vledhan guber*, then they agreed for three pounds a year wages. *Llwyd*, 251. A late form of *puns*, qd. v.

PENSEVIC, s. m. A prince. *Lucyfer yw ow hanow, ow howetha yw tanow, pensevic yn néf omma, why a vôr yn ta henna, ow bosaf gwell es an Tâs*, Lucifer is my name, my companions are fires, a prince in heaven I am, ye know well that, that I am better than the Father. C.W. 10. Written by Llwyd, 99, *penzivik*, pl. *pendzhivigion*, 128. A late form of *pendevig*, qd. v.

PENTEILU, s. m. The head of the family, the master of the house. Corn. Voc. *paterfamilias*. Comp. of *pen*, head, and *teilu*, qd. v., a family. W. *penteulu*.

PENVO, comp. v. When it may be. *(Pan—bo.)* *Ha penvo reys degevy, gorouch y dha'n Mount Tabor*, and when it is necessary to give tithe, put them to the Mount Tabor. C.W. 78. *Gans dén penvo convedhys*, by man when he is discovered. C.W. 118.

PENYS, s. m. Penance. *Ol del vynny, Arluth kêr, my a wra yn pŭp tyller hedré veyn bew yn bŷs-ma, gans penys ha golochas*, all as thou wishest, dear Lord, I will do in every place, as long as we may be alive in this world, with penance and praise. P.C. 116. W. *penyd*. Arm. *pinigen*, (fr. Fr. *punition*.) Ir. *peanas*, †*pennait*, †*pennit*. Gael. *peanas*. Manx, *panys*.

PENYS, v. a. To do penance. *Penys a reys rag y terros, may fo leheys mûr a'y gallos*, it is necessary to do penance for his arrogance, that much of his power may be diminished. P.C. 43. *Dew ugans dŷdh ow penys y speynas y gŷk ha'y woys*, two score days doing penance, he spent his flesh and blood. M.C. 10. W. *penydu, penydio*. Lat. *pœniteo*.

PÊP, pron. s. Every one. *War pêp ol marnas ty*, upon all except thee. O.M. 948. The same as *pêb*, qd. v.

PEPYNAG, pron. s. Whatsoever, whatever. *My a vyn aga threhy, pepynag ol a wharfo*, I will cut them, whatever may happen. O.M. 1736. Written also *pepenag*. *Rês yw syvel y vôdh ef, pepenag vo*, it is necessary to follow his will, whatever it be. O.M. 662. *Pepenagol may'th ello*, wherever he may go. P.C. 630. *(pe—penag.)* W. *pa—bynag*.

PER, s. m. A caldron, a kettle, a boiler, a furnace. Corn. Voc. *lebes*. W. *pair*, †*peir*. Arm. †*pér*. Ir. *coire*. Manx, *coirrey*. Sanso. *charu*.

PER, s. m. Pears. A plural aggregate, of which the sing. is *peran*. *Gwedhan peran*, a pear tree. Llwyd, 133. W. *pêr, peren, peran, peranen*. Arm. *pér, peren, pír*. Ir. *piorra*. Gael. *peur*. Lat. *pyrum*. Fr. *poire*. Eng. *pear*.

PERAG, adv. For what, wherefore, why. Llwyd, 249. Comp. of *pe*, what, and *râg*, for. Generally contracted into *prâg*, qd. v. W. *parag*, *pyrag*. Arm. *perae, perag*.

PERAN, s. f. A pear. Pl. *pêr*, qd. v. *Gwedhan peran*, a pear tree. Llwyd, 133.

PERBREN, s. m. A pear tree. Corn. Vocab. *pirus*. (*Pêr—bren*.) W. *perbren*. Arm. *peren, gwezen-bêr*. Irish, *crann piorra*. Gael. *craobh pheuran*.

PERCOU, v. a. Remember thou, bear thou remembrance. ‡ *Perco dhe gwithé sans an dŷdh Sabboth*, remember thou to keep holy the Sabbath day. Pryce. ‡ *En hâv percou gwâv*, in summer remember winter. Gwavas family motto. A corruption of *perth*, bear thou, 2 pers. sing. imp. of *perthy*, qd. v., and *côv*, memory, qd. v.

PERFO, v. a. He may do. *Râg my a vŷdh an kynsa, bom yn vyag a rollo, hag a perfo ow meystry*, for I will be the first that will give a blow on the journey, and perform my mastery. O.M. 2164. 3 pers. s. subj. of a verb = W. *peri*, to cause.

PERFYTH, adj. Perfect, complete, in perfection. Written also *perfeth*, and *perfeyth*. *Yn peswerê, gweres perfyth dhe'n beys ol golowys glân*, on the fourth be made perfect to all the world bright lights. O.M. 33. *Ro dhym dhe vanneth perfeth*, give me thy perfect blessing. O.M. 452. *Un gusyl da ha perfyth dhym ty a rôs*, a counsel good and perfect to me thou hast given. R.D. 2142. *Dew ugans myldyr perfyyth*, forty miles complete. R.D. 2497. W. *perfaith*, à Lat. *perfectus*. Arm. *peurchreat*. Ir. *foirfeachd*. Gael. *foirfe*.

PERHEN, s. m. A possessor, owner, proprietor. Llwyd, 124. *An harlot, foul y berhen, awos kemmys drôk a wrên, a'n beys ny fyn tremené*, the rascal, foul his owner,

notwithstanding so much harm as we do, from the world will not pass. P.C. 2112. *Ty losel, foul y perhen, systyn dhe vrêch war an prên*, thou knave, foul his owner; stretch out thy arm on the wood. P.C. 2752. W. *perchen*. Arm. *perchen*. Manx, *berchagh*.

PERNA, v. a. To take, to lay hold of; to buy, to purchase, to redeem. Part. *pernys*. *May fynnas dyskynna yn gwerhas, ha bôs genys gins y gŷk agan perna*, that he would descend into a virgin, and be born with his flesh to redeem us. M.C. 4. *Dhe'n bŷs pan deyskynnas pehadoryon râg perna a desevijs dre Satnas; râg henna gordhyn neffré Ihesus nêb agan pernas*, to the world when he descended to redeem sinners who were felled by Satan, therefore let us ever worship Jesus who redeemed us. M.C. 5. *Dew dhê'n Crist a dhanvonas dhe berna boys ha devras*, Christ sent two men to buy food and drink. M.C 42. *Ow horf a ve yw henna, yn mêdh Crist, ragouch wy pernys a berth yn bŷs-ma*, my body is this, says Christ, bought for you within this world. M.C. 44. *A'n geffo pows a's gwyrthyns, ha dhodho pernas cledhé*, he that hath a coat, let him sell it, and buy for him a sword. M.C. 51. *Ny a'n pernas dheworthys*, we bought him from thee. M.C. 105. *Dheworthaf drôk a'n perna*, may the evil one take him from me! O.M. 617. ‡ *Na'rcuh e berna*, do not buy it; ‡ *mi a bernav*, I will buy. Llwyd, 244, 247. Another form of *prenné*, qd. v. W. *prynu*. Arm. *perna, pernein*.

PERNAR, s. m. A buyer, a purchaser, a redeemer, a ransomer. Llwyd, 137. W. *prynwr*. Arm. *prener, pernour*.

PERS, adj. Partial. Llwyd, 113. Arm. †*pers, a bers*. W. *parth, o barth*.

PERSEIT, s. m. A jug with two ears. Corn. Voc. *amfora*. Comp. of *per*, and *saith*, a pot, qd. v.

PERTHEGES, v. n. To bear, suffer, to be angry. Pryce. *Mâs yw dhe cusyl, deffry; mar scon dhodho del ymmy, kychouch ef yn vryongen, ha dalynnouch mûr calvs, ma na allo pertheges yn dyspyl ol dh'y echen*, good is thy counsel, really; as soon as thou kissest him, catch him in the throat, and hold him very hard, that he cannot endure it, in spite of all his efforts. P.C. 1009. *Mar a tulleth pertheges, ny a wra y wowheles, râk pŭp ol a gâr bewé*, if he begin to be angry, we will lie to him, for every one loves to live. R.D. 598.

PERTHY, v. a. To bear, carry, sustain, entertain. *My a lever dhys Urry, na borth dout ahanaf vy nefré; râg ny fydh kên dhe perthy, my a lever dheuchwhy why*, I tell thee, Uriah, bear no doubt of me ever; for there will be no reason to bear it, I say unto you. O.M. 2208. *My d'n musur lour yn ta, na bertheuch own a henna*, I will measure it well enough, do not ye have fear of that. O.M. 2508. *Pertheuch côf ol a'n tokyn a leverys kyns lemyn dhywy why, a gowethé*, all bear remembrance of the token (that) I told before now to you, O companions. P.C. 1081. *Na berth dout, ny vŷdh nehys*, do not bear a doubt, it shall not be denied. C.W. 42. *Ty a berth gossythyans, ken na brodar*, thou shalt suffer punishment, though a brother. C.W. 82. Another form of *porthy*, qd. v.

PERTHY, v. a. To honour, to respect. *An tresa, ha'n pemera henath nêb ma na ello perthy ve*, the third and fourth generation of them that do not honour me. Pryce. *Gwra perthy de tâs, ha de mam, mal de dydhiow*

PESWAR   285   PEVEVA

bcdhens hŷr war an tŷr, nêb an Arluth de Dew ryes dees, do thou honour thy father, and thy mother, that thy days may be long in the land which the Lord thy God hath given thee. *Pryce.* A corruption of *perchy*, id. qd. W. *parchu, perchi.*

PERVEDH, s. m. The inward part, the middle region. *A bervedh*, within. *A bûb echen gorow ha benow yn wêdh, agn gora ty a wra yn dhe gorhel a bervedh*, of every kind male and female also, thou shalt put them in thy ark within. O.M. 992. *Henna a wra guythé, na dheffo glaw a bervedh*, that will keep that the rain may not come in. O.M. 1076. *Ke a bervedh yn castel a dhyragof*, go within the village before me. P.C. 195. W. *pervedh.* Lat. *per medium.*

PERYL, s. m. Peril, danger, risk. *Torré yn ow feryl vy, hag ynwêdh gwra dhe'th worty, may lebro ef annodho*, break it off at my risk, and also cause to thy husband that he may eat of it. O.M. 197. *Da yw, na dhout perill*, it is good, fear not danger. C.W. 44. W. *perygl;* â Lat. *periculum.* Arm. *pirill.* Ir. *peireacuil.* Gael. *peireagal.*

PES, s. m. Pease, pulse. *Llwyd*, 121, 150, *péz*; ‡ *cuthu péz*, pease-cods. W. *pŷs.* Arm. *pêz, piz.* Ir. *pis, peasair.* Gael. *peasair.* Manx, *pishyr.* Sansc. *pêshi.* Lat. *pisa.* Fr. *pois; pesierc*, a field of peas.

PES, v. subs. Thon shouldst be. *Râk pûr wŷr gynen mar pés, ny a vyé pûr attês, ha lowen mûr*, for very truly if thou shouldst be with us, we should be very much at ease, and very glad. R.D. 2442. A mutation of *bés*, 2 pers. s. subj. of *bôs.*

PESACH, adj. Rotten. *Pryce.*

PESAD, s. m. A prayer, invocation. Pl. *pesadow. Pan o y besadow guris, dhe'n dowdhek y leverys, koscouch lemmyn mars ew prŷs, powesouch, wy yw grewjs*, when his prayers were done, he said to the twelve; sleep now if it is time, rest, ye are weighed down. M.C. 61. Written also *pysad, pysadow*, qd. v. From *pesy*, to pray.

PESC, s. m. Fish. *Llwyd*, 18. *Pesc sâl*, salt fish. 143. Written also *pysc*, qd. v.

PESGWYTH, adv. As often as. *Pryce. An gam dhavas, pesyrwyth may gwella why hy, remembra ahanaf why me a wra bŷs venary*, the rainbow truly as often as ye see it, remember you I will for ever. C.W. 182. Comp. of *pe*, what, and *gwŷth*, a time.

PESTRIORES, s. f. A female sorcerer, a witch. *Llwyd*, 241. *Out warnas, a pûr vŷl scout, hep dhout pestryores stout, kyn fy mar prout, ty a'n pren*, out upon thee! O most vile scont; without doubt a stont witch; though, thou art so proud, thou shalt catch it. O.M. 2668. Written also *pystriores*, qd. v.

PESWAR, card. num. Four. Used with nouns masculine, as *pedar* is with feminines. *Dyllas Crist a ve rynnys, prdar ran yuris anedhé, gans peswar marreg a brys, dhe bûb marreg ran may fé*, the clothes of Christ were divided, four parts were made of them, by four soldiers of worth; to every soldier that there might be a part. M.C. 190. *Y êth yn un fystene, peswar marrek greys êns*, they went in a hurry, four armed soldiers they were. M.C. 241. *Pandra wrên agan peswar, what shall we four do?* R.D. 563. *Awos bôs ny peswar smat, guythé an bêdh ny ylayn*, though we be four fellows, we could not keep the tomb. R.D. 602. W.

pedwar, †petguar, †petuar. Arm. *pevar.* (Cf. Πετουάρια, oppidum Parisorum Britanniæ populi; apud Ptol.) Ir. *ceathair, † cethir.* Gael. *ccithir.* Manx, *kiare.* Gr. Dor. πέτορα. Lat. *quatuor.* Goth. *fidvor.* Lith. *keturas.* Sansc. *chatur.*

PESWARDHEC, card. num. Fourteen. Written by Llwyd, 134, *pazwardhak.* W. *pedwar-ar-dheg.* Arm. *pevarzek.* Ir. *ceathar deag.* Gael. *ceithirdeug.* Manx, *kiare-jcig.* Lat. *quatuordecim.*

PESWERE, num. adj. Fourth. *Yn pesweré gwreys perfyth dhe'n beys ol golneys glân*, on the fourth, be made perfect to all the earth bright lights. O.M. 33. *An pesweré a gewsys, na whelyn gwevyé an powo*, the fourth said, let us not seek to flee the country. M.C. 247. *Yn peswera dŷdh bŷdh gwrŷs an houl, ha'n loer*, on the fourth day shall be made the sun and the moon. O.W. 8. Written also *pysweré*, qd. v. W. *pedweerydh, † petguaril, † petgunred.* Arm. *pevaré, pevarved.* Ir. *ceathramhadh, † cethramad.* Gael. *ceathramh.* Manx, *kiarroo.*

PESY, v. a. To pray, to supplicate, to beseech, to implore. *Mar pesy a leun golon*, if he prayed with a full heart. M.C. 25. *Golyouch ha pesouch ow thâs, may hallouch môs dh'y asedh*, watch ye and pray my Father, that ye may be able to go to his seat. M.C. 52. *Dheworté un lam bechan ydh êth pesy may hallé*, from them he went a little distance that he might pray. M.C. 53. *Yn maner-ma y pesys râg an kêth ré re'n crowsé*, in this manner he prayed for those same that crucified him. M.C. 185. *An lader a'n barth dychow a besys yn ketelma*, the thief on the right side prayed thus. M.C. 193. *Ha pesyn râg y ené*, and let us pray for his soul. O.M. 2368. *Ny'm nâch, mar a'n pesaf ef*, he will not deny me, if I pray to him. P.C. 1166. The 3 pers. s. fut. is written *peys*, qd. v. Another form is *pysy*, and by the common corruption of *s* into *g*, *pigy*, and *pygy*, qd. v. W. *pedi.* Arm. *pedi, † pidi;* â Lat. *peto.* Goth. *bidyan.* Germ. *beten.* Ang. Sax. *biddan.* Eng. *bead, bid.*

PETH, s. m. A thing, a something, an article. Plur. *pethow*, things, riches, wealth. *Bo clewns, bo pêth kescar, po dre breson presonys*, be it sickness, be it poverty, be it imprisoned in prison. M.C. 24. ‡ *Pêth tshyi*, household stuff, furniture. *Llwyd*, 158. ‡ *Es kêz? ez po neg ez ? ma sêz kêz, dro kêz; po neg ez kêz, dro pêth ez*, is there cheese? is there or is there not? if there is cheese, bring cheese; or if there is not cheese bring what there is. *Cornish Proverb, in Pryce's Vocabulary.* ‡ *Ha'n Dew euhella vedn ry pêth yw gwella ol râg why*, and the God supreme will give what is best of all for you. *Ibid.* Written also *peyth*, and *pŷth*, qd. v. W. *pêth.* Arm. *pez, †pet.* Ir. †pet. Sansc. *pêtva*, a particle, or atom.

PEUS, s. f. A coat, a petticoat. *Peus grec*, toral, a woman's coat. Corn. Vocab. Another form of *peis*, qd. v.

PEVA, comp. v. It should be. *Râg yma bous lour omma erbyn soper, a peva ol parusys*, for there is meat enough here against supper, if it should be all made ready. P.C. 600. *Genas a peva tastys, maga fûr te a vea yn pûb poynt avella*, by thee if it should be tasted, as wise thou wouldst be as he. C.W. 48. Comp. of *pe*, a mutation of *be*, 3 pers. s. subj. of *bôs*, and *va* for *ve*, he.

PEVEVA, comp. v. Where was it? *Dên nês, gâs ve dh'y wellas, maras ew aval da; lavar peveva kefys*, come nearer, let me see it, if it be a good apple ; say where was it found. C.W. 54. Comp. of *pe*, where, *ve*, a mutation of *be*, was, and *va* for *ve*, it.

PEW, v. a. To own a thing, to possess. *Lemmyn dyskudh ha lavar pyw an pren a bew hep mar pous Ihesu an Nazaré*, now shew thou aud say which lot shall possess without doubt the coat of Jesus of Nazareth. P.C. 2853. *Henna a's pew, why a wôr kettep onan py pren yw e*, that shall have it, ye know every one which lot it is. P.C. 2855. *Re synt iovyn me a's pew*, by St. Jove I have it. P.C. 2858. *War tu a'y vam a'n pewo, y ben a vynnas synsy*, on the side of his mother (that) owned him, his head he would hold. M.C. 207. (See also *Bew*.) W. *piau*. Arm. *piaoua*.

PEW, pron. s. Who. *Pew osta dhe es yn wedhan awartha gans trôs ha cân*, who art thou (that) art in the tree above with noise and song ? C.W. 42 *Pew an Jowl pandra vŷdh gwrŷs*, what the devil shall be done ? C.W. 106. *Pew a'th wrûg ge pregowther*, who made thee a preacher ? C.W. 170. Written also *pu*, and *pyw*, qd. v.

PEWAS, s. m. A recompense, a reward. *Pryce*.

PEWE, v. a. To live, to be alive. A mutation of *bewé*, qd. v. *Dall ên, ny welyn yn fâs ow bôs mar veyl ow pewé*, blind I was, I saw not well, that I was living so vilely. M.C. 220. *Mara pewyf*, if I live.

PEYL, s. m. The knot of a bow. *Yta an sêth compys, ten hy yn ban bys an peyl, pardell ôs archer prevys, hag a ladhas moy es mîl a vestas kyns es lemyn*, the arrow is right, draw it up to the knot, as thou art a proved archer, and hast killed more than a thousand of beasts before now. C.W. 112. Another form of *pêl*, qd. v.

PEYN, s. f. Pain, agony, torment, anguish. Pl. *peynys*. *Herwedh dhe grath ha'th pyté, na'm byma peyn yn gorfen*, according to thy grace and pity, let there not be pain to me at the end. O.M. 2254. *Pylat a yrchys dhedhé war beyn kylly an bewnans*, Pilate commanded them on pain of losing their life. M.C. 241. *Colon dên a ŷll crakyé a vynna prest predery an paynys brâs a'n gevé, ha'n dyspyth heb y dylly*, a man's heart might break (that) would readily consider the great pains that he had, and the spite without deserving it. M.C. 139. *Y beynys o crêf ha brâs warnodho heb y dylly*, his pains were strong and great upon him without deserving them. M.C. 56. *I feynys o brâs ha crêff yn ioy dhedhy trylys yw*, her pains (that) were great and strong, are turned into joy for her. M.C. 226. *Flehys wûr ha benenas a Ierusalem yn drê a wôr bôs ow frymys brâs, ragoff na whelcuch olé*, children many and women of Jerusalem at home, who know that my pains are great, seek ye not to weep for me. M.C. 168. W. *poen*. Arm. *poen*. Ir. *pian*. Gael. *pian*. Manx, *pian*. Gr. ποινά. Lat. *pœna*.

PEYNE, v. a. To pain, to torture. Written also *peynyé*. Part. *peynys*. *Why a dhêth yn arvow dhom kemeres, dhom syndyé, dhom peynyé bŷs yn crow*, ye are come in arms to take me, to hurt me, to torture me even unto death. M.C. 74. *En Edhewon yntredhé a whelas dustuneow râg peyné Crist ha syndyé*, the Jews amongst them sought witnesses to torturo and hurt Christ. M.C. 90. *Yn grows gans kentrow fastys, peynys bŷs pan ve marow*, fastened on a cross with nails, tortured till he was dead. M.C. 2. *Natur scyle, me a syns, arluth*

da mar pŷdh peynys, ol y sogeté, kyn fôns sŷns, râg y beyn dhe vôs grevijs, nature will cause, I hold, if the goud Lord be pained, all his subjects, though they were holy, to be grieved for his pain. M.C. 211. W. *poeni*. Arm. *poania*, *poenein*.

PEYS, v. a. He will pray. 3 pers. s. fut. of *pesy*, qd. v. *My a'd peys, arluth uhel*, I pray thee, high Lord. O.M. 375. *Ow mebyon, my a gy peys, yn mês whêtla dylleuch tryssé*, my sons, I pray you, send outside yet a third. O.M. 1129. *Me a'th peys, gâs dhe wow*, I pray thee, leave thy lie. R.D. 1354. *Ow dewolow, deuch gynef warparth ol, me agas peys*, my devils, come with me together all, I pray you. R.D. 2308. *Pŷs* is another form, qd. v.

PEYSY, v. a. To drop. *Pryce*. *Ota cowes pûr ahas, ny's pyrth dên mara peys pel ; a wronnd an dôr stremys brâs ow lewraga gans mûr nel*, behold a shower very detestable, man will not bear it, if it drops long ; great streams around the earth, thickening with much violence. O.M. 1082.

PEYTH, s. m. A thing. *Rum fey, mûr o wokyneth yw mones dhe lesky peyth a ŷl dên orto bewé*, by my faith, much folly it is to go to burn a thing which a man can live upon. O.M. 474 *Pan dra ny vyn Dew gûl vry ahanaf, na sowyny an peyth a wrehaf ny wra*, why will not God make account of me, nor prosper the thing that I do. O.M. 521. The same as *pêth*, and *pŷth*, qd. v.

PEZEALLA, adj. How many, so many as. *Llwyd*, 135.

PI, conj. Or. Corn. Vocab. *goscor pi teilu*, family or household ; *leu pi obil*, a rudder or peg ; *penguch grec pi pillistker*, a woman's cloak or pelisse. *Heb cowyth py cowethes*, without a fellow or helpmate. O.M. 95. *Mar ny gevyth mêdh py gwŷn, ke dhe fenten dhe vvé*, if thou wilt not find mead or wine, go to a fountain to drink. O.M. 2435. Another form of *po*, qd. v.

PIB, s. f. A pipe, a tube, a musical pipe, a flute. Corn. Voc. *musa*. Llwyd, 60, 163, *pib*. W. *pib*. Arm. *pib*. Ir. *piob*. Gael. *piob*. Manx, *piob*. Fr. *pipe*. Germ. *pfeife*. Eng. *pipe*, *fife*.

PIBA, v. a. To pipe, to play on a pipe, or flute. *Menstrels pybych (pibeuch) bysy, may hyllyn môs dhe dhonssyé*, minstrels, pipe diligently that we may go to dance. R.D. 2645. W. *pibaw*, *pibo*.

PIBAN, s. f. A little pipe, a tube, a pipe, a flute, a flageolet. *Llwyd*, 14, 163, 167. *An biban*, the pipe. 231. Dimunitive of *pib*. W. *piben*. Arm. *piben*.

PIBYDH, s. m. A piper. Thus Llwyd, 164, writes *piphit*, tibicen, in the Cornish Vocabulary. W. *pibydh*.

PIDN, s. m. A peg, or pin. *Llwyd*, 48, 115. A late corruption of *pin*, borrowed from English.

PIDNIAN, s. m. The brain. *Llwyd*, 240. A late corruption of *impinion*, qd. v.

PIDZHI, v. a. To pray. *Llwyd*, 109, 231. Written in the Ordinalia, *pigy*, qd. v.

PIDZHAD, s. m. A prayer. Plur. *pidzhadow*. Llwyd, 127. A late corruption of *pysad*, qd. v.

PIGA, v. a. To prick, to prickle, to sting. *Llwyd*, 132. W. *pigaw*, *pigo*. Arm. *pica*. Lat. *pungo*. Sanc. *pice*.

PIGOL, s. f. A mattock, a pick, or pickaxe. *Llwyd*, 86, 142. Arm. *pigol*. W. *piccell*, a javelin.

PIGY, v. a. To pray, to supplicate. *Dûn alemma, cowythé, war menydyow dhe wandré, ha dhe pigy*, let us come hence, compauions, on the mountains to wander, and to pray. P.C. 109. *Amen, pigyn yn perfyth,* Amen, let us pray perfectly. P.C. 199. *Me a vyn môs dhe'n tempel, gollohas râg leverel, ha pigy war dhu Iovyn,* I will go to the temple to speak praise, and pray to god Jupiter. P.C. 357. Another form of *pesy,* qd. v.

PIL, s. m. A mound, a little hill, a hillock. *Pil gudhar,* a molehill. Llwyd, 64. *Pil teil,* a dunghill. 154. W. *pil, pill.* Arm. *pill.*

PILES, adj. Bare, bald. ‡ *Pedn pilez,* bald head. Llwyd, 45. ‡ *A chorll côth, te pedn pylles, fatla vynta ge henna, y fŷdh an bŷs consumys,* ah! old churle, thou bald pate, how wilt thou have that to be, that the world shall be consumed. C.W. 168. "A certain kind of oats are called *pillis,* because it has no husks." Pryce. W. *pilio,* to make bare, to peel, to pare.

PILLEN, s. f. A fringe. Corn. Vocab. *fimbrium.* W. *pilyn.* Arm. *pil, pilen.* Irish, *bile, pillin.* Gael. *bile, pillin.* Eng. *pillion.*

PILM, s. m. Flying dust like flour. Pryce.

PIN, s. m. Pine. *Gwedhan pin,* a pine tree. Pryce. Arm. *pin.* Lat. *pinus.*

PINBREN, s. m. A pine tree. Corn. Voc. *pinus.* Comp. of *pin,* and *pren* a tree. W. *pinbren, pinwydhen.* Arm. *pinen.*

PIRGIRIN, s. m. A stranger. Corn. Vocab. *peregrinus.* W. *percrin.* Arm. *pirchirin.* From the Latin.

PISA, v. a. To make water, to piss. *Pitshar pisa,* an urinal. Llwyd, 87. W. *pisaw, piso.* Fr. *pisser.* Germ. *pissen.*

PISAS, s. m. Urine. Llwyd, 177. W. *pis, pisw.*

PISC, s. m. Fishes. Corn. Voc. *piscis.* Pl. *puskes. Y rêf hynwyn dhe'n puskes, porpus, sowmens, syllyes, ol dhym gunlyth y a vŷdh, lenesow ha barfusy, pŷsk ragof ny ura skusy, mar cordhyaf Dew yn perfyth,* I will give names to the fishes, porpoises, salmons, congers, all to me obedient they shall be ; lings and cods, a fish from me shall not escape, if I worship God perfectly. O.M. 139. *Myrcuch worth an vorvoran, hanter pŷsk ha hanter dên,* look ye at the mermaid, half fish and half man. P.C. 2404. W. *pŷsg,* †*pisc,* pl. *pysgod.* Arm. *pesc,* pl. *pesced.* Ir. *iasg.* Gael. *iasg.* Manx, *ceast.* Lat. *piscis.*

PISCADUR, s. m. A fisherman. Corn. Voc. *piscator.* W. *pysgotter, (pysgod-gwr.)* Arm. *pesketer.* Ir. *iascairc.* Gael. *iasgair.* Manx, *ecasteyr.* Lat. *piscator.*

PISCLIN, s. m. A fishpond. Corn. Vocab. *vivarium.* Comp. of *pisc,* and *lin,* a pond. W. *pysgodlyn.*

PISGETTA, v. a. To fish, to catch fish. Llwyd, 120. W. *pysgotta.* Arm. *pesketa.*

PISY, v. a. To pray, to supplicate. *Do bisy,* to pray. Llwyd, 231. ‡ *Thera vi war as pisi,* I desire you. 250. The same as *pysy,* qd. v.

PIWA, pron. s. Who. *Piwa yw an dên-na,* who is that man? *gûwa bennac,* whoever. Llwyd, 244. A later form of *pew* or *pyw,* qd. v.

PIYADOW, s. m. Prayers. *Why guycoryon, cuch yn mês; ydh enough ow kuthyl ges a Dhu hag e sans eglos, yn ow thy a piyadow pan wrcuch agas marhasow, ha fowys dhe laddron plos,* ye traders, go out; ye are making a jest of God and his Church, in my house of prayers when ye make your markets, and a den for foul thieves. P.C. 334. W. *pyadow,* pl. of *pesad,* qd. v. A variation of *pijadow,* which is a corrupted form of *pesadow,* pl. of *pesad,* qd. v.

PLA, s. m. A plague, a pest, an evil, a devil. *Dh'agan gwythé, rág máp an pla agan temptyé pûr fyyl a wra,* to preserve us, for the son of evil will very craftily tempt us. P.C. 10. *A barth an pla,* in the name of the fiend. P.C. 1348. *Ty yw máp an pla,* thou art the son of the evil one. P.C. 1763. *Hemma yw iag an pla,* this is a cure of the plague. P.C. 2817. W. *pla.* Irish, *plaig.* Gael. *plaigh.* Lat. *plaga.* Gr. πλαγά.

PLANCEN, s. f. A plank, a board. Pl. *plances, plancos, plancys.* Llwyd, 33, 160, 243. *Rág henna fystyn, ke, gwra gorhel a blankos playnyys, hag ynno lues trygva,* therefore hasten thou, go, make a ship of planks planed, and in it many dwellings. O.M. 950. *Gans ow boell nowydh lemmys me a squat pûb pcis timber hag u playn oll an plankes, hag a sell pûb plankyn sûr,* with my axe newly sharpened I will hew every piece of timber, and will plane all the planks, and will set every plank sure. C.W. 106. *Plancys zaban,* deal planks. Llwyd, 242. W. *planc.* Arm. *plankcn.* Gael. *plang.*

PLANS, s. m. A plant. Llwyd. 121. W. *plant.* Arm. *planten.* Ir. *planda.* Gael *plannt.* Lat. *planta.* Fr. *plante.*

PLANSY, v. a. To plant. Written also *plansé.* Part. *plynsys. In gordhyans dhe'n Tás a'n nêf, my a wra agas plansé,* in worship to the Father of heaven, I will plant ye. O.M. 1892. *Môs dhe blansé my a vyn yn dôr an dŷr guelen-ma,* I will go to plant these three rods in the ground. O.M. 1887. *Ef a gŷf yn Araby, yn mount Tabor, guelynny a plansas Moyses hep mar,* he will find in Arabia, in Mount Tabor, rods (that) Moses planted without doubt. O.M. 1032. *Dôg alena tŷr guelen a wrûk Moyses dhe plansé,* bring thou thence the three rods (that) Moses planted. O.M. 1946. *Py le vŷdh an guel plynsys, may fôns mocha onowrys, ha'n guella may wrôns levy,* where shall the rods be planted, that they may be most honoured, and that they may grow best? O.M. 2032. W. *plannu.* Arm. *planta.* Ir. *planndaigh.* Gael. *planntaich.* Lat. *planto.*

PLAS, s. m. A palace, a large house, a mansion, a place. Llwyd, 111. *Rág colê orth un venen, gulán ef re gollas an plás, a'm lûf dhychyow a wrussen,* for listening to a woman, he has clean lost the mansion, with my right hand (that) I have made. O.M. 920. *Ha pan deffasta dha'n plás, ty a gŷf yn yet un êl a ro gorthib dhys,* and when thou comest to the place, thou shalt find an angel (that) will give thee an answer. C.W. 126. W. *palas, plâs.* Ir. *palas.* Lat. *palatium.*

PLAT, adj. Flat, splay. *Dre ow thrŷs y tûth un smal gans kentrow d'aga gorré; y fue ow munegow plat, spygys brás dre ow dyvcté,* through my feet there came a fellow with nails to put them; my gloves were flat, great spikes through my hands. R.D. 2589. ‡ *Trûszplat,* splay-footed. Llwyd, 121. Arm. *plad, plat.* Fr. *plat.*

PLATII, s. m. A place. *Môs dhe blansé my a vyn en gueel gans rcouté vrás yn nêp plath têk hag ylyn,* I will go to plant the rods with great care, in some fair and clean place. O.M. 2060. *Yn plath may môns y a séf, dredho ef pan ŷns plynsys,* in the place where they are they shall stand, through him when they are planted. O.M. 2091.

PLATTYA, v. a. To couch, to squat. *Mester da, der dha gymmyas me a wêl un lodn pûr vrás hanys in bush ow plattya,* good master, by thy leave, I see a very great bullock from thee in the bush couching. C.W. 112.

PLE, adv. Where, in what place. A contraction of *pe*, what, and *le*, a place. *Lavar dhymmo, ty vencn, an frût ple russys tyrry,* tell me, thou woman, where didst thou break off the fruit ? O.M. 210. *Me a wôr ple ma onan,* I know where there is one. O.M. 2561. *Râk bôs ow arluth mar clâf, a Dhew, ple tôf, na ple ydh âf, ny won ple toulaf ow paw,* because of my lord being so ill, O God, where shall I come, or where I shall go, I know not where I shall cast my foot. R.D. 1665. *Arluth, ple 'dh ên alemma,* Lord, where shall we go from hence ? R.D. 2391. W. *pu le, ple.* Arm. *pelcch.*

PLEG, s. m. A flexion, a bend, a plait, a fold, a double. *Iosep dhe Gryst a vynnas y arrow ha'y dheffrech whêk, yn vaner del yn whas, hag a'n ystynnas pûr dêk; adro dh'y gorff y trylyas sendall rych yn luns plêg,* Joseph for Christ made white his logs and sweet arms, in manner as was usual, and stretched them out very fairly; around his body he wrapped linen rich in many a fold. M.C. 232. W. *plŷg.* Arm. *plêg.* Lat. *plica.*

PLEGAD, s. m. Desire, wish. Plural, *plegadow. En Edhewon yntredhê a whelas dustuncow râg peyné Crist ha syndyé; ny gewsys dhe blegadow, saw war Dhu y a vynné dre envy leverel gow,* the Jews amongst them sought witnesses to torture and hurt Christ; they spake not to (their) wishes, but of God they would through envy utter a lie. M.C. 90. *Mars ew an newodhow da, ty a vŷdh rewardys, ha'm holon yn wêdh gansé ty a vŷdh prest dhe'th plegadow,* if thy news be good, thou shalt be rewarded, and my heart also with it thou shalt have ready to thy desires. C.W. 54. *An lester ydhew gurŷs, têk ha da dhom plegndow,* the ship is made, fair and good to my wishes. C.W. 174. W. *plygiad.*

PLEGADOW, adj. Inclined, desirous. *Me a beys dhe wrear nessow, may fôn pûb êr plegadow dhe vones y servant ef yn bŷs-ma, heb falladow, ha drevon bew,* I pray to the Creator of Heavens that I be every hour desirous to be his servant in this world, without deceit, and while I live. C.W. 152. W. *plygadwy.*

PLEGYE, v. a. To plait, to fold, to bend, to incline, to bow, to wrap. *Pan dhucth yn râk an plosck, ef a gewsys lowenck, dhum plekgyé,* when the dirty fellow came forward, he spoke cheerfully, to influence me. R.D. 1849. *Arluth,* why a herch dhodho an queth dysky dhy-worto, hep na moy gêr; râk hedrê vyuch ow pleghyé, dhywhy bŷth ny's dŷsk neffrê,* Lord, you command him to take the cloth from him, without any further word; for as long as you are yielding he will never take it off for you. R.D. 1950. Written by Llwyd, 68, *plegya,* dho *plegya. Plegy* is another form. ‡ *Na ra chee plegy an dôr dothynz, na ge worry,* thou shalt not bow down to them, nor worship them. Pryce. W. *plygu.* Arm. *plega.* Lat. *plico.*

PLEGYE, v. a. To please. Written also *plecyé.* 3 pers. s. fut. and 2 pers. s. imp. *plêc. Râg bythqueth my ny welys benen dhym a well plekyé,* for never have I seen a woman that pleases me better. O.M. 2108. *An chy yn ta dhym a plêk,* the house pleases me well. P.C. 683. *Lavar fûr, mûr dhym a'm plêk,* speak thou wisely, much it will please me. P.C. 1737. *Hag yn ûr-na ty a plêk dhe'n arlythy,* and then thou wilt please the lords. P.C. 1900. *Ny blêg dhyn golok anodho,* the sight of it doth not please me. C.W. 54.

PLEME, comp. v. Where is. *Plemé, dhymmo levereuch,* where is it, tell ye me. R.D. 46. *Awatta, ef a gowsas, agis mychtern plemé ve,* behold, said he, your king, where he is. M.C. 147. Comp. of *ple,* where, and *me* for *ma,* there is.

PLAYN, adj. Full, complete. *Pan deffa an termyn playn a pymp mŷl ha pymp cans vledhen, un oyl a vercy yn nena a vŷdh keyys,* when the full time shall come of five thousand and five hundred years, the oil of mercy in that time shall be found. C.W. 138. Fr. *plein.*

PLEN, s. m. A plain, a field. *Del oma marrek lên, venythé ny dhôf a'n plên, crna'n prenné an guâs-na,* as I am a trusty knight, never will I come from the field until I take that fellow. O.M. 2151. From the English.

PLENTYE, v. a. To make plaint, to complain. *Dhe'n tyller Crist re dethyé, ha'n Edhewon o dygnas; ydh esa an venyn gansé; paris êns dh'y huhudhas; hedré vôns y ow plentyé, Ihesus yn dôr a scryfas,* to the place came Christ, and the Jews (that) were opposed; the woman was with them; ready were they to accuse her; while they were complaining, Jesus wrote in the ground. M.C. 33.

PLETH, s. f. A plait, a braid, a wreath. *Na ôl na scryg, nêp a whyleth, sychsys y treys gans dhe dhyw plêth,* weep not nor shriek, whom thou seekest, thou didst dry his feet with thy two plaits. R.D. 854. ‡ *An lysûan bian gen i'ar ncdhez, ez a livi en an halow nci, ez kreicx Plêth Maria,* the small plant with the twisted stalk (that) grows on our hills is called "Mary's Plait." Llwyd, 245. "The present Cornish still say to *plethan,* for to braid, or plait." Polwhele. W. *plêth.* Ir. *filleadh.* Gael. *pleat.*

PLEW, s. m. A parish. Llwyd, 113. Written also *plui,* and *ply,* qd. v.

PLISCIN, s. m. An eggshell. Llwyd, 163. Diminutive of *plisg.* W. *plisgyn.* Arm. *pluscen.*

PLISG, s. m. A husk, a shell, a paring. Llwyd, 132. W. *plisg.* Arm. *plusg.* Ir. *plaosg.* Gael. *plaosg.* Manx, *bleayst.*

PLIV, s. m. Feathers. Llwyd, 122. Written also *plyv,* qd. v.

PLOM, s. m. Lead. Llwyd, 8, 122, gives the late form *plobm.* ‡ *Plobm rŷdh,* red lead. 91. W. *plwm.* Arm. *ploum.* Lat. *plumbum.*

PLONTYE, v. a. To plant. *Me a'th pŷs, gâs dhe wow; na whylé plontyé whethlow, del y'th pesaf,* I pray thee, leave thy lie ! seek not to plant idle tales, as I pray thee. R.D. 1355. Another form of *plansy,* qd. v.

PLOS, s. m. Dirt, filth; a weed, any thing noisome; a foul offender, a villain. Pl. *plussyon,* qd. v. *Fystyn dwwhans, guerees vy, ow tôn a plôs casndow,* hasten thou quickly, help me, bringing the hateful villain. O.M. 801. *Adam plos a dhewfsé wnrnan conquerryé neffré,* Adam the villain would have desired to conquer us always. O.M. 908. *A pûr voren, plôs, myrch gal, ty a verow cowal,* O very jade, dirt, daughter of evil, thou shalt die entirely. O.M. 2736. *Me a's goulch dysempys, may fôns gulân a pûp plos ol,* I will wash them immediately, that they may be clean from all dirt. P.C. 844. Used also adjectively. *Ha fowys dhe laddron plos,* and dens for foul thieves. P.C. 336. *Dhe Dhew plos te gey ny re nan nŷl dhyn bôs na dewes,* thy foul God of thine gives us not either meat or drink. O.M. 1809. *Nyns yw saw un plos iaudyn,* he is not but a dirty rascal. P.C. 1894. *Fy dheuch, a vosteryon plos,* fy on ye, O dirty boasters. P.C. 2100. Derived by Llwyd, 33, from Lat.

pulvis. W. *llach.*

PLOSEC, adj. Foul, filthy, villainous, wicked. *Re iovyn, arluth an brys, del leveryth a vŷdh gurŷs dhe'n plosek gwâs aftythys,* by Jove, Lord of the world, as thou sayest, it shall be done to the foul wretched fellow. P.C. 451. *Pan dhueth yn râk an plosek, ef a gewsys lowenrk,* when the dirty fellow came forward, he spoke cheerfully. R.D. 1847.

PLUFOC, s. m. A bolster. Corn. Vocab. *pulvinar.* W. *plucog,* †*plumauc.* The root is *pluv,* feathers.

PLUI, s. f. A parish. Corn. Voc. *hebrenchiat plui,* the leader of a parish. Written in the Ordinalia *plu,* and in late Cornish *plew. Ha râg bôs agas wheyl lêk, my a re dhyuch plu Vuthek,* and because your work is fair, I will give you the parish of Vuthek. O.M. 2463. *An antecryst yn lyes plu a treyl pobyl dhyworth Dew yn pûp le may kerdho cf,* the antichrist in many a parish will turn people from God in every place that he may go. R.D. 247. *Il'a nyns yw ef a parth Dew, bysy vyê ol an blu râk y wythé,* and if he is not on the side of God, all the parish should be diligent to keep him. R.D. 2106. W. *plûyv.* Arm. *ploué, pleû,* †*ploe.* From the Lat. *plébe.*

PLUMAN, s. f. A plum. ‡ *Gwedhan pluman,* a plum tree. Llwyd, 131. ‡ *Mean pluman,* a plum stone. *Pryce.* Borrowed from the English. In Welsh, *eirinen.*

PLUMBREN, s. m. A plum tree. Corn. Voc. *plumbus.* Comp. of *plum,* and *pren,* a tree.

PLUSSYON, s. m. Dirty fellows, villains, wretches. *Teweuch râk médh, dew adla; ymdhysquedhas ny vynna dhe plussyon, a welouch why,* be silent for shame, ye two knaves; he would not show himself to wretches, see you. R.D. 1497. Plural of *plôs,* qd. v.

PLUVEN, s. f. A feather, a pen. Corn. Voc. *penna.* The singular of *plûv,* written by Pryce, *plyv.* Llwyd, 244, writes the sing. *plyven;* an *blyven-ma,* this pen. W. *plûv, plu,* †*plum;* sing. *pluven, pluen.* Arm. *plû;* sing. *pluen.* Ir. *clumh,* †*clum.* Gael. *cluimh.* Manx, *clooie.* Lat. *pluma.*

PLYGADOW, adj. Inclined, agreeable. *Pûp ober ol yn bŷs-ma a wrên re bo plygadow,* all the work in this world (that) we do, may it be agreeable. O.M. 1008. *Ow arluth kêr caradow, mychtern ôs war ol an bŷs; assevyê plygadow genef gruthyl bôdh dhe vrŷs,* my dearly beloved lord, king thou art over all the world; it would be agreeable to me to do the will of thy mind. O.M. 2115. Another form of *plegadow.*

PLYGYE, v. a. To bend, to incline, to bow the knee. *Ha y grâs dheuchwhy a wronnîyo, nefré dhe blygyé dhodho, yn dalleth hag yn dywedh,* and his grace may he graut to you, ever to bow down before him, in the beginning and in the end. O.M. 1727. Another form of *plegyé,* qd. v.

PLYNCEN, s. f. A plank, a board. Plur. *plyncennow. Y dreys ha y dulé yn ten gans kentrow worth an plynken bedhens tackys,* let his feet and his hands firmly with nails to the plank be fastened. P.C. 2517. *Cowyth, profwyn an styllyow, mars êns compes dhe'n fosow, may haller agu lathyê gans corblen, lunys, tennow, hag a's ly gans plynkennow, may fo ivy myres worté,* comrades, let us try the rafters, if they are straight to the walls, that they may be laid with joists, laths, beams, and cover them with planks, that there may be a joy to look at them. O.M. 2475. Written also *planken,* qd. v.

PLYNCH, s. m. A start. *Scolkyouch dhy an dan dava, râg mar a's guêl, ef a wra môs dhe kudhé war un plynch,* lurk ye after him under silence, for if he sees you, he will go to hide at a start. P.C. 1004. From the Old English, *blench,* to start. *Norris.*

PLYNCHYE, v. n. To start, to stir. *Wharé y a'n dystryppyas mar noyth genys del vyê, hag worth pôst fast a'n colmas, unwyth na ylly plynchyé,* anon they stripped him as naked as he had been born, and bound him fast to the post, so that not once could he stir. M.C. 130.

PLYNSYS, part. Planted. *Yn plath may môns y a sêf, dredho ef pan ŷns plynsys,* in the place where they are they shall stand, through him when they are planted. O.M. 2092. *Na nahaf, epscop goky, râg an thyyr guelen defry a ve gans Davyd plynsys,* I will not recant, foolish bishop, for the three rods truly were by David planted. O.M. 2057. Participle pass. of *plansy,* qd. v.

PLYSG, s. m. A husk, or shell. Llwyd, 132. See *Plisg.*

PO, conj. Whether, either, or. *Bo clewas bo pêth kescar, po dre breson presonys,* be it sickness, be it poverty, or imprisoned in a prison. M.C. 24. *Lemmyn merouch pe nyle a'n dûs a vŷdh delyfris, po Cryst, leverouch scyle, po Barabas, dén blanys,* now see ye which of the two men shall be delivered; whether Christ, say ye the grounds, or Barabbas, a man blamed? M.C. 125. A mutation of *bo,* qd. v. *Pe* is similarly used in Armoric, and *ba* and *fa* in Old Irish; as *imb'i cein fa in accus beosa,* whether I am afar or near; *imp' oge fa lanamnas,* whether celibacy or matrimony. *Zeuss,* 674. All being adaptations of the verb substantive.

PO, adv. If. Llwyd, 249. *Po cen,* if otherwise, else. 150. *Po ni, ponag,* if not, unless. 99. ‡ *Po na venno' hui gil an della-na moi,* if you will do so no more. 249. W. *po.*

PO, comp. v. When there is or may be. A contraction of *pa fo.* Llwyd, 249. ‡ *Po marh ledres,* when a horse is stolen. 232. ‡ *Ha po ti hu da werég an moiha lúan warbarh, nenna g'reu' terhi an dezan, ha na henz,* and when thou and thy wife are most merry together, then do ye break the cake, and no sooner. 252.

POAN, s. f. Pain, anguish, torment. Llwyd, 55. Generally written *pryn,* qd. v.

POB, pron. adj. Every, all. Written in the Ordinalia *pôp,* qd. v. *Pôb bledhan,* every year. Llwyd, 135. *War edhyn, bestes pôp prŷs, gallos a fŷdh warnedhé,* over birds, beasts, at all times power shall be over them. O.M. 1213. *Ha gans towal a lŷn gulân, my a's sêch, ketteb onan, a bôp mostethes ha lŷs,* and with a towel of clean linen, I will dry them every one from all dirt and mire. P.C. 838. *Ens pôb ol war tuhé trê, an guary yw dywydhys,* let all go towards home, the play is ended. P.C. 3238. Another form is *pûb,* or *pûp,* qd. v. W. *pôb,* †*pop.* Arm. *pôb,* †*pcb.* Ir. *cach,* †*gach.* Gael. *gach.* Manx, *gach.*

POBAS, v. a. To bake. *Dho pobas,* Llwyd, 120. ‡ *Mân pobas,* a bakestone. 48. *Ty pobas,* a bakehouse. 121. ‡ *Ma gurég vi a pobas metten, ha hei 'ra guil tezan rugez, do dôz dre do da werég,* my wife is baking to-morrow, and she will make a cake for thee, to take home to thy wife. 251. Another form is *peba,* qd. v. W. *pobi.* Arm. *pobi.* Sanse. *pach.* Gr. πέπτω.

POBEL, s. f. A people, people. Corn. Voc. Written also *popel* and *pobyl. Ihesus Crist a wovynnys worth an bobyl a dhêth dy gans an fals yn y scrwys, pandra yw a vynnouch wy,*

Jesus Christ asked of the people that came thither with the false one in his service, What is it that ye would? M.C. 67. *Rŷs yn porris dhe onon merwel rág pobyl an wlás, pobyl Thesus y honon na vóns tregis gans Satnas,* it is right needful for one to die for the people of the country, that the people of Jesus himself may not dwell with Satan. M.C. 80. *Ow popel vy grevyys brás gans Pharow yw mylyges, ymóns dhymo ow cryé,* my people greatly aggrieved by Pharaoh, (that) is accursed, they are to me crying. O.M. 1416. *Ny vynnyth dhe pobel Dew gasé crés dhyn yn nép tu,* thou wilt not to the people of God allow peace to us on any side. O.M. 1507. W. *pobyl, pobl.* Arm. *pobl.* Ir. *pobal, † popul.* Gael. *poball.* Manx, *pobble.* Lat. *populus.*

POC, s. m. A push, a shove. *Pock,* a shove, is still used in Cornwall. W. *pwg.*

POCAR, adv. As, like as, such, like, so as, equally. *Llwyd,* 134. ‡ *Nenna an dzhei a varginiaz rág bledhan moy, rág pokár guber,* then they bargained for a year more, for the same wages. 251.

POCARA, adv. As, like as, so as. *Llwyd,* 150, 248.

POCCUIL, s. m. A kiss. Corn. Voc. *basium.* The root is *poc,* whence *impog,* qd. v. Pryce gives the form *poccan.* W. *poc, pocan, pocyn.* Arm. *poc.* Ir. *póg, † bóc ;* dim. *pogan.* Gael. *póg.* Manx, *paag.*

POCCYS, s. m. A pox, a disease. *Poccys frenc,* lues venerea. *Llwyd,* 82. *Poccys minis,* small pox, measles. 169. Borrowed from the English.

POCEN, adv. Or else, otherwise. *Llwyd,* 249. (*Po—cen.*) *Na dhout peril, benen vás, poken y whressan fyllell, hag y fea péch pŷr vrás,* doubt not danger, good woman, otherwise I should work deceit, and should sin a very great sin. C.W. 44. *Cool ye dhym, mar mynta bós exaltys, poken venary why a vŷdh avel fichys,* hearken to me, if thou wilt be exalted, otherwise for ever you will be like children. C.W. 48.

POCVAN, s. m. A pox, a disease, sickness. *Rák lowené uy 'gen bo yn le may fuen, lemmyn pocvan ha lesky,* for joy may not be ours in the place where we have been, but disease and burning. R.D. 170. *Tán ha mók ha pocvan brás,* fire and smoke, and great sickness. R.D. 2341. *Pocvan pŵp ŵr ha rynny, skrymba brás a'n dewolow, cf a'n gevyth genen ny,* disease always and horror, great outcries of devils, he shall find with us. R.D. 2343. *Pocvan brás,* the great pox. *Pryce.*

PODAR, adj. Rotten, corrupt, good for nothing. *Llwyd,* 133. W. *pwdyr.* Lat. *putris, putre.*

PODDRAC, s. f. A witch, a sorcerer or sorceress. *Pryce.*

PODRE, v. n. To become rotten, or putrid, to rot, to be corrupted. *Gás vy lemmyn dh'y huré yn queth kyns ys y vaylé gans aloes, mer keffrys, ha y a wŷth y vody, na potré bŷs vynary, kyn fe yn bédh mŷl vlydhen,* leave me now to embalm him, before wrapping him in cloth, with aloes, myrrh also; and they will preserve his body, that it never be corrupted, though it be in the grave a thousand years. P.C. 3200. *Lemmyn omma ty a drŷk, bys pan pottro ol dhe gŷk,* now here thou shalt stay, until when all thy flesh may rot. R.D. 2022. Another form is *pedry,* qd. v.

PODRETH, s. m. Rottenness, a sore. Pl. *podrethes. Vythqueth na ve bom a won a rollo whaf mar gales, del y's brewaf yn dan gén ; kekyfrys kŷc ha crohen del vêdh lwen a bodrethes,* never was a stroke I know (that) would give a blow so hard, as I will strike her under the chin ; flesh and skin also, as they will be full of sores. O.M. 2714. W. *pydredh.*

PODZHER, s. m. A little dish or porringer. *Llwyd,* 46. A late corruption of the English word *porringer.*

POEN, s. f. Pain. Pl. *poenow,* and contractedly *ponow,* qd. v. The general form for the singular is *peyn,* qd. v.

POENYS, part. Pained, grieved. *Pryce.* Generally written *peynys,* qd. v.

POES, adj. Weighty, heavy, grievous. *Pryce.* Generally written *poys,* qd. v.

POESDER, s. m. Weight. *Pryce.* W. *pwysder.*

POESYGYS, adj. Torrid, or extremely hot. *Pryce.*

POL, s. m. A pond, a pool ; stagnant water, a miry place ; mire, mud, slime ; a well, a pit. Corn. Vocab. *puteus. Pol kil,* occipitum, the nape, or hinder part of the head. *Llwyd,* 104. *Heb cows gér y clamderis, y tethas war bol y hŷll,* without saying a word she fainted, she fell on the back of her head. M.C. 165. *Pol down,* a deep pit, a gulf. *Llwyd,* 44. *Poll,* mud. 80. *Pol grean,* a gravel pit. *Pryce.* W. *pwll.* Arm. *poull.* Ir. *pol.* Gael. *poll.* Manx, *poyl.* Eng. *pool.*

POL, s. m. The poll, the head. *Oyeth ay glewyuch dhym ol, masons an dré, kettep pol,* hear ye, listen to me all, masons of the town, every head. O.M. 2398. *Arluth, yma dour tommys lour, may hallons bós golhys aga trŷs, yn kettep pol,* Lord, there is water warmed enough, that their feet may be washed, every head. P.C. 841, 3054. From the English.

POLAN, s. f. A small pond, a pool, stagnant water. *Llwyd,* 154. *Pollan troilla,* a whirlpool. 61. Diminutive of *pol,* qd. v.

POLIA, adv. Where. *Llwyd,* 252. A late corruption of *pelé.*

POLS, s. m. A space of time, a while. *Dús gené pols dhe wandré,* come thou to walk with me a while. O.M. 934. *Yma dhymmo dhe wruthyl un pols byhan tacklow pryvé,* I have to do a little while private matters. P.C. 91. *Ow dyskyblon ysedhouch, hag omma pols powesouch, hedré vyma ow pygy,* my disciples, sit ye, and rest here a while, whilst I am praying. P.C. 1012.

PON, v. subs. We should be. *Saw a pony (pón—ny) dewyow guerŷs, ny veas mal bew serrys,* but if we were made gods, thou wouldst in no wise be angry. C.W. 60. A mutation of *bôn,* 1 pers. pl. subj. of *bós,* qd. v.

PONAG, conj. Except, unless. *Llwyd,* 249. (*Po—nag.*)

PONFOSYC, adj. Troubled, vexed. *Bós trest dhywhy pendra wher, ha ponfosyc agan cher may 'thouch serrys,* what is the care that ye are sad, and troubled as to your cheer, that ye are sorrowful. R.D. 1256. From the subs. *ponfos,* or *ponvos,* qd. v.

PONI, conj. Unless. *Llwyd,* 249. (*Po—ni.*)

PONOW, s. m. Pains. *Ny a'th dég, bŷs gorfen vŷs, yn ponow dhe werowedhé,* we will carry thee, till the end of the word, in pains to lie. O.M. 904. *Yn néf agas encfow neffré a trŷg hep ponow,* in heaven your souls ever shall dwell without pains. P.C. 8. A contracted form of *poenow,* pl. of *poen,* qd. v.

PONS, s. f. A bridge. Corn. Voc. *pons. Nyns ús pons war dour Cedron,* there is not a bridge over the waters of Cedron. O.M. 2804. *Degruch an pren a dhyhons war dhour Cedron may fo pons,* carry ye the tree quickly, over the waters of Cedron that it may be a bridge. O.M. 2811. W. *pont.* Arm. *pont.* Lat. *pons, ponte.* Fr. *pont.*

PONSTER, s. m. Quackery, giving improper medicines. *Pryce.*

PONVOS, s. m. Trouble, vexation, heat. *Esé dour ha ponvos brás, wharré y'gen lowennas, kettel dhueth er agan pyn,* there was concern and great trouble; soon he gladdened us, when he came to meet us. R.D. 1328. Written also *ponfos,* whence *ponfosyc,* qd. v.

PONVOTTER, s. m. Trouble, vexation. *Ny wodhen râg ponvotter py'dh een yn gweel py yn côs,* I knew not for trouble whether I was in a field or in a wood. O.M. 363. *Genen ny y fýdh dhe dhrôn yn ponvotter venary,* with us shall be thy throne in trouble for ever. O.M. 898. Written also *ponveter. Ha why a pŷs an runyow dh'agas gorhery hep gow, kymmys výdh an ponveter,* and ye shall pray the hills to hide you, without a lie, so great will be the trouble. P.C. 2656.

PONYE, v. a. To run. *Wotewedh lader vye, dhe'n Edhewon y ponyas Crist y arluth râg gwerthé,* at last he was a thief, to the Jews he ran, to sell Christ his lord. M.C. 38. *Dre un scochfordh y ponyas, cafos y mâb mar callé,* through a cross-road she ran, if she could get her son. M.C. 164. *My re bue owdh emlodh, may'th ên pûr squyth, uakys na yllyn ponyé,* I have been wrestling till I was very much tired, that I could not run immediately. P.C. 2510. *Na gefyn war ow ené, kyn fên neffré ow ponyé, yn pûp tol worth y whylas,* we shall not find upon my soul, though we be ever running, in every hole seeking him. R.D. 550. Written by Llwyd *punnia,* qd. v.

POOC, s. m. A heap or stack of hay, or turf. *Pryce.* Written also *pouk.* This is still in common use in Cornwall. *Polwhele.*

POOT, v. a. To kick like a horse. This word is now used in Cornwall. *Polwhele.* (W. *pwtio,* to butt, or thrust.)

POP, pron. adj. Every, each. Written also *pôb,* qd. v.

POPEL, s. f. People. Corn. Voc. *populus.* Written also *pobel,* qd. v.

POPTI, s. m. A bakehouse. Corn. Voc. *pistrinum.* W. *pobty,* comp. of *pobi,* to bake, and *ty,* a house.

PÔR, adv. Very. *Pôr dha,* very good. Llwyd, 259. Generally written *pûr,* qd. v.

PORAG, adv. Why, wherefore. *Pryce.* A late form of *perag,* qd. v.

PORAN, adv. Straightly, rightly. *Ha'y ŷll troys a ve qorris poran war ben y gelé; worth an grows y fôns lathys, gans kenter guyskis dredhé,* and one of his feet was put right over the other; on the cross they were laid, with a nail struck through them. M.C. 179. *Ha'n corfow csa ynné a ve yn ban drehevys, hag êth poran dhe'n cyté; gans luas y fôns gwelys,* and the bodies (that) were in them were raised up, and went straight to the city; by many they were seen. M.C. 210. *Why a sêdh warbarth genaf mŷna a golla orthaf ve, poran ryb ow thenewan,* ye shall sit together with me, all that hearken to me, close by my side. C.W. 14.

PORCHEL, s. m. A little pig. Corn. Vocab. *porcellus.* W. *porchell.* Arm. *porchel.* Borrowed from the Latin.

PORHAL, s. m. A barrow pig, a hog. Pl. *porhelli, porelli.* Llwyd, 84, 124, 242. The late form of *porchel.*

POROGGA, v. a. To read. *Pryce. Dho porogga,* lego. Llwyd, 77. Pryce has wrongly understood Llwyd, the meaning being to steal. From the English *prog.*

PORPOS, s. m. A plaice fish; a porpoise. *Pryce.* Pl. *porpesow.* Llwyd, 114.

PORRAN, s. f. A leek. *Pryce.* Arm. *pour, pouren.* Lat. *porrum.* Fr. *porreau.*

PORRYS, adj. Very necessary. Written indiscriminately also *porres,* and *porris. Pan vyn an Tâs yn della, reys yw y wruthyl porrys,* when the Father wills so, need it is to do it, very needfully. O.M. 649. *Râg sustené veunans dhyn, rŷs yw porrys lafurryé,* to sustain life for us, very needful it is to labour. O.M. 683. *Reys yw y vôs gw̃yr porrys,* very needful it is that it should be true. P.C. 1074. *Ow bôs scrrys nynsyw marth; ages bones ol warbarth porrys worth ow duwenhé,* that I should be angry is no wonder; you being altogether willed to grieve me. R.D. 1413. *Râg an lays dhynny ês, a vyn y dampnyd porres,* for we have laws, that will needs condemn her. M.C. 32. *Reys yw porris heb strevyé lôdh ow thâs dhe vôs sewijs,* it is needful, very needful, that my Father's will should be followed without striving. M.C. 73. Apparently compounded of *pôr,* id. qd. *pûr,* very, and *rrys,* need.

PORTAL, s. m. The threshold, entry, portal; a porch. Llwyd, 13, 80, 173.

PORTH, s. m. A door, a gate, an entrance. Corn. Voc. *janua* vel *valva.* Pl. *porthow. Er ow fyn travyth ny sêf; porth yfarn me a torras,* against me nothing will stand; the gate of hell I have broken. R.D. 2574. *Eneff Crist dhe yffarn êth, hag a dorras an porthow,* the soul of Christ went to hell, and broke the gates. M.C. 212. *Skon egereuch an porthow,* immediately open ye the gates. R.D. 98. *Râk an porthow lep dywedh a výdh ygerys yn wêdh, may'th ello abervedh an mychtern a lowené,* for the everlasting gates shall be opened also, that may enter in the King of joy. R.D. 101. W. *porth.* Arm. *porz, pors.* Lat. *porta.* Fr. *porte.*

PORTH, s. m. A port, a sea port, a harbour, a bay. It is preserved in the names of many places in Cornwall, as *Porth Carnow, Porthlunoy, Porthgwiden, Porthollan, &c.* Every part of the coast of Cornwall is indented by secluded and romantic coves, still provincially called *porths.* In late Cornish it was corrupted into *porh* and *por.* Llwyd, 20. Hence *Porbean, Porkellis, &c.* W. *porth.* Arm. *porz, pors.* Lat. *portus.* Fr. *port.*

PORTHER, s. m. A door-keeper a porter. *Pryce.* W. *porthawr.* Arm. *porsier.* Ir. *portair.* Gael. *portair.*

PORTHERES, s. f. A female door-keeper, a portress. *Portheres gentyl mars ôs, me a'th pŷs a lavasos dry ow cowyth abervedh,* portress, if thou art kind, I pray thee to venture to bring my companion within. P.C. 1225. W. *porthores.* Arm. *porsierez.*

PORTHY, v. a. To bear, to carry; to bear with, to endure, to sustain, to suffer. 2 pers. s. imp. *porth. Arluth, porth côf yn deydh dywedh a'm enef vy,* Lord, bear thou remembrance at the last day of my soul. O.M. 1272. *A ow mâp kêr, na porth a wher,* O my dear son, do not bear grief. O.M. 1357. *Na porth own výdh, na vêdh trest,* bear thou not fear for ever, be not sad. O.M. 1467. *Y'n gythrys mâp Dew, yn prôf ahanaf may portho côf, pan deffé dh'y wlascor ef,* I called him the Son of God, in proof that he would keep remembrance of me, when he should come to his kingdom. R.D. 272. *Ef a porthas hep a wher mûr a peyn war y corf kêr, râk tûs an bỹs*, he bore, without complaining, much pain on his dear body, for the people of the world. R.D. 738. *Râk na'n guela, dhym a nêp tu, kueth a portha ; ny gansen tru*, for that I see him not, to me on any side, I feel sorrow ; I would not sing, "alas!" R.D. 866. *Rág henna an vuscogyon orto a borthas avy*, for that the madmen bore hatred towards him. M.C. 26. *An gwás a vynsé lesky agan ysow yn tefry, ny yllan porthy henna*, the fellow would have burnt our corn indeed, I could not bear that. C.W. 82. W. *porthi*.

PORUIT, s. m. A wall. Corn. Voc. *paries*. W. *parwyd*. From the Lat. *paries, parietc*. Fr. *paroi*.

POS, adj. Heavy. *Me re goskes pós, ha rum kemeres drôk glós*, I have slept heavily ; and a bad pang has seized me. R.D. 511. *Pós re teulseuch agas clún*, heavily have ye thrown your haunch. R.D. 523. *Yn mês a'n dour an tebel corf a dhue, kyn fo mar pós awl mên*, out of the water the wicked body shall come, though it be heavy as stone. R.D. 2274. A contracted form of *poys*, qd. v.

POSE, v. a. To lean, to incline, to rest on, to rest one's weight on. *Na war rág ef ny ylly posé, rág own bós megis*, nor was he able to lean forwards, for fear of being stifled. M.C. 206. *Warnans na bossé y ben, rág an arlont a usyé, mar possé a'n neyll tenewen, rág y scódh hy a'n grevyé*, on them he could not lean his head, for the garland (that) he wore ; if he leant on the one side, for his shoulder it grieved him. M.C. 205. A contracted form of *powesy*, qd. v.

POSSYGYON, s. m. Heaviness, drowsiness. *Yma un possygyon brás war ow'wholon ow codhé*, there is a great heaviness falling on my heart. O.M. 526. *Rŷs yw dhym porrys coské, possygyon yn pen yma*, it is very necessary for me to sleep, there is drowsiness in the head. O.M. 1906.

POST, s. m. A post, a pillar. Corn. Vocab. *columpna. Worth an póst yn le may ma, y gelmy fast why a wra*, to the post, in the place that he is, ye shall bind him fast. P.C. 2058. *A harlot ymskemunys, worth póst ty a vŷdh kelmys, dhe wodhaf an strecusow*, O knave accursed, to a post thou shalt be bound, to feel the blows. P.C. 2071. *Hag worth póst fast a'n colmas, unwyth na ylly plynchyé*, and to a post they bound him, so that once he could not flinch. M.C. 130. W. *póst*. Arm. *post*. Ir. *posta*. Gael. *post*. Lat. *postis*. Fr. *poste*.

POT, s. m. A bag, a pudding. ‡ *Pot guidn*, a white pudding. *Pryce*. W. *poten*. Ir. *putóg*. Gael. *putag*.

POTRO, v. a. He may rot. 3 pers. s. subj. of *podré*, qd. v.

POUS, s. f. A pound, a pound in money, a piece of money. *Pryce*. A pound in money was also *puns*, qd. v.

POW, s. m. A region, country, land, province. *Tra ny vŷdh yn pow adro, na wodhfo dhe dharryvas*, there is not a thing in the country round which he will not know to publish. O.M. 189. *Adam, ke yn mês a'n wlás troha ken pow dhe vewé*, Adam, go out of the country towards another land to live. O.M. 344. *Yn pow-ma nynsus guel gwŷn*, in this country there is no better wine. O.M. 1914. *Yn ol dhe gosow nynsus gŷst rŷth ol, hep wow, vás dhe dra vŷth ragtho, nag yn wlásma yn nêp pow*, in all thy woods there is not a beam, without a lie, good for any thing for it, nor in this country in any part. O.M. 2498. *Ow môs dres pow*, going over the country. R.D. 1511. *Pow isal*, a low or flat level country. *Dên pow*, a country fellow, a clown. *Dên o piwa an pow*, a man of what country was he? Llwyd, 46, 53, 142. *Pow-dár*, the region of oaks, is the name of one of the hundreds of Cornwall. W. *pau*, from the the Lat. *pagus* ; (hence also W. *powys*, †*poguis*, = Fr. *pays;* so also Ital. *paesé*, from Latin *pagense.*) Arm. †*pou*.

POWES, s. m. Rest, quiet, repose. *Vytheth powes my ny'm bŷdh, mar vrew ew ow yssyly*, there is never rest to me, so bruised are my limbs. O.M. 1011. *Euch gonetheuch termyn hŷr, powes ny'gys bŷdh nêp preys*, go ye, work a long time, rest ye shall not have at any time. O.M. 1222. W. *powys*, †*poues*. Arm. *paouez*, *poez*, †*poues*. Ir. †*piss*. Gael. *fois*. Gr. παύω, to rest.

POWESVA, s. f. A place of rest, rest. *Hen yw dŷdh a bowesva dhe púp dên a vo sylwys ; yn dysquydhyens a henna, ny a bowes desempys*, this is a day of rest to every man that may be saved ; in declaration of that wo will rest forthwith. O.M. 145. *Aga sona me a wra, may fo 'n sythvas dŷdh henwys an dŷdh a bowesva a búb dên a vo sylwys*, I will bless them, that the seventh day may be called the day of rest to every man that will be saved. C.W. 32. Comp. of *powes*, rest, and *ma*, a place. Arm. *paouezvan*. W. *gorphwysva*.

POWESY, v. n. To be in a state of rest or repose, to rest. Written also *powes*. 2 pers. s. imp. and 3 pers. s. fut. *powes*. *Wosé cous ha lafuryé, an vaner a vyé da kemeres croust hag evé, ha powes wosé henna*, after talk and labouring, the custom would be good, to take food and drink, and rest after that. O.M. 1002. *Côsk war dhe tor, ha powes*, sleep on thy belly and rest. O.M. 2070. *Coscl my re bowesas, assyw whék an hún myttyn*, I have rested softly ; sweet is the morning sleep. O.M. 2073. *Yn dysquydhyens a henna, ny a bowes desempys*, in declaration of that, we will rest forthwith. O.M. 148. *Squyth ef dre vêr lafuryé, powes my a vyn defry*, weary I am through much labouring, rest I will really. O.M. 2050. *Koscouch lemmyn mars ew prŷs ; powesonch, wy yw grevijs*, sleep ye now, if it is time ; rest, ye are weighed down. M.C. 61. *En benenas, leun a rás, gans an bêdh fast powessens*, the women full of grace rested quite on the tomb. M.C. 254. *Pols dhe powes*, to rest awhile. P.C. 1873. *Powes lemmyn, losel wás*, stop now, idle fellow. P.C. 2718. W. *powyso*. Arm. *paoueza*.

POWS, s. f. A coat, a gown, a robe. It changes in construction into *bows*, and *faws*. *An geffo pows a's gwyrthyns, ha dhodho pernas cledhé*, he that hath a coat, let him sell it, and buy for himself a sword. M.C. 51. *Ha'y bows y honon gurris adro dhodho hy a ve ; gans y vam a fŷé guris, hag ef gensy ow tené ; kepar Ihesus del devys, yn dclla an bows a wré*, and his own coat it was about him ; it was made by his mother while he was with her sucking ; as Jesus grew up, so she made the coat. M.C. 161. *Pan do!hyans dhy, yntrcdhé pows Ihesus a ve dyskis*, when they came thither, among them the coat of Jesus was stript. M.C. 176. *Ydho ow fous ha'm brustplat, purpur gurow dhum strothé*, my robe and my breastplate were hard purple to wring me. R.D. 2591. In the Cornish Vocabulary, the older form is *peis*, and *peus*, qd. v. W. *pais*, †*peis*. Ir. †*ceis*.

POYNT, s. m. A point. *Och, my re bue boches coynt*,

PRAT 293 PREF

hag êth yn râk ré a poynt, Oh, I have been little cunning, and went forward too much point blank. P.C. 3032.

POYNY, v. a. To run. *Dûn ganso a dysympys, ha poynyn gans mûr a grŷs, ha yn dour goryn an pren*, let us come with it immediately, and let us run with great strength, and in the water let us put the tree. O.M. 2789. Another form of *ponyé*, qd. v.

POYS, adj. Heavy, grievous. *Gûll penans ef a pesys, henna ganso nynjo poys*, to do penance he prayed, that with him was not grievous. M.C. 10. *Ha'n Edhewon a worras a uch Ihesus Crist un mên; leden o, ha poys, ha brás, moy agis gavel tredden*, the Jews placed above Jesus Christ a stone; broad it was, and heavy, and large, more than the hold of three men. M.C. 237. Written also *pós*, qd. v. It was finally corrupted into *puz*, qd. v. In the other dialects it is a substantive. W. *pwys*. Arm. *pouez*. Lat. *pondus, pensus*. Fr. *poids, pese*. It. *peso*.

PRAG, adv. Wherefore, why. Written also *prâc*. *War lyrch mâb dên dhe becha, reson prâg y fe prynnys yw Ihesus Crist dhe ordna yn nêff y vonas tregys*, after the son of man sinned, the reason why he was redeemed is, that Jesus Christ ordained that he should dwell in heaven. M.C. 7. *Mes mara kewsys yn ta, ha'n gwrconeth y synsy, prâg omgwysketh yn delma*, but if I have spoken well, and have held the truth, why dost thou strike me thus? M.C. 82. *My ny won leverel prâk gans pûp na vedhaf ledhys*, I cannot tell why by every one I shall not be slain. O.M. 595. A contracted form of *perag*, qd. v.

PRAGA, adv. Why, wherefore. *Pylat a vynnas scrifé a vewnans Crist acheson, praga dampnys rebee, hag a'n scrifas y honon*, Pilate would write of the life of Christ an accusation why he was condemned, and he wrote it himself. M.C. 187. *Ow spyrys ny drŷc nefré yn corf mâp dên vŷth yn beys, ha reson yw ha praga, râg y vôs kŷc medhel gurŷs*, my spirit shall not dwell always in the body of any son of man in the world; and the reason is and why, because he is made of soft flesh. O.M. 927. An enlarged form of *prâg*.

PRAL, s. m. A skull. *Pen pral march, (½ pedn pral marh,)* a horse's skull. Llwyd, 62.

PRAONTER, s. m. A priest. Llwyd, 127. Another form of *pronter*, qd. v.

PRAS, s. m. A meadow. *Tŷr sêch yn guel nag yn prâs, mar kefyth yn gwêr hep gow, ynno gueet in-ta whelas bôs dhe'th ly ha dhe'th kynyow*, dry land in field or in meadow if truly thou find without deceit, in it take good care to seek food for thy breakfast and for thy dinner. O.M. 1137. *Nynsus yn guel nag yn prás tûs vew saw ny, my a greys*, there are not in field nor in meadow men living, except us, I believe. O.M. 1151. "In present Cornish a small common is called a *prâs*." Polwhele. Arm. *prad*. Lat. *pratum*. Fr. *pré*.

PRAT, s. m. An act or deed, a cunning trick. *My re bredyrys gûl prat, râg y wythé erbyn hâf*, I have thought of doing a trick to keep it against summer. O.M. 487. *Desefsen dodho ry what; dhynny ef a wrûk an prat, hag a fyes dhyworthyn*, we wished to give him a blow; to us he did the trick, and fled from us. R.D. 605. *Pûr uskes gwrâf an pratt*, very soon I will do the deed. C.W. 38. *Na barth dout a'n bratt es gwryes*, bear thou no doubt, of the trick (that) is done. C.W. 54. W. *praith*. Ang. Sax. *prætt*, craft, subtilty.

PRATHEC, adj. Meadowy. *Pratheck*. Pryce.

PRE, adv. Very. *Pryce*. A corruption of *per*, for *pûr*, qd. v.

PRECYONS, adv. Altogether. *Drôg yw genef gruthyl dên, precyons ha haval dhum fâs*, I am sorry to have made man, altogether like to my face. O.M. 418. *Drôg yw genaf gwythil dên, preshyons haval dhom honyn*, I am sorry to have made man, altogether like to myself. C.W. 160. Derived by Pryce from *prés*, a time.

PREDER, s. m. Anxiety, solicitude, care, thought. Pl. *prederow*. *Anodho mar 'th ês preder, worth y wythyes govynné*, if there is anxiety to thee respecting him, ask him of his keeper. O.M. 608. *Arluth, dout dhymmo yma, ha preder mûr a un dra*, lord, a fear there is to me, and much anxiety about one thing. R.D. 20. *Ha Pylat dhe war breder a leveris dhe Ihesu*, and Pilate, after thinking, said to Jesus. M.C. 129. *Ena Pylat pan glewas yn delma y dhe gewsell, prederow a'n kemeras, râg own y dhe leverell*, then Pilate, when he heard that they spoke thus, thoughts took him for fear that they would say. M.C. 249. Written also *pryder*, qd. v. W. *pryder*. Arm. *preder*.

PREDERY, v. a. To think, to be thoughtful, to study, to meditate, to think of, to consider. Written also *predyry, prydery*, and *prydyry*, qd. v. *Ha'n ioul henna pan glewas, y demptyé a bredcrys*, and the devil when he heard that, thought to tempt him. M.C. 11. *Crist, Mâb an Arluth uchell, y demptyé pan prederys*, when he thought to tempt Christ, the Son of the high Lord. M.C. 19. *Arluth, pan dyffy dhe'th pow, predery ahanaff gura*, Lord, when thou shalt come to thy country, do think of me. M.C. 193. *A meys ôf ow predyry*, I am outside thinking. O.M. 193. *Prederys pêb a'y worfen*, let every one think of his end. O.M. 227. *Hn'y daggrow a dhewere, anodho pan predery*, and her tears dropt when she thought of him. M.C. 231. *Cayn whêk, preder a'd enef*, sweet Cain, think of thy soul. O.M. 479. *My re bredyrys gûl prat*, I have thought of doing a trick. 487. *Ny yw colon predyry an tekter a's bedheuch why*, heart cannot conceive the enjoyment ye shall have. P.C. 32. *Why a preder a'y passyon*, ye shall think of his passion. P.C. 3223. *Pan predyryf a'y passyon*, when I think of his passion. R.D. 1083. *Me ne brederaf gwell for*, I do think of a better way. C.W. 90. *Prâg na bredersys*, why didst thou not consider? C.W. 24. W. *pryderu*. Arm. *prederiaz*.

PREDERYS, adj. Thoughtful, studious, pensive, solicitous, careful, diligent. *Gûr prederys*, a careful husband; *gwrêc bredcrys*, a diligent wife; *prederys ew an wrêg-na*, diligent is that wife. Llwyd, 243. Written also *pryderys*, qd. v. W. *pryderus*. Arm. *prederiuz*.

PREDN, s. m. Wood, a tree. Llwyd, 10, 79. A late corruption of *pren*, qd. v.

PREF, s. m. Any small animal, a vermin, an insect, a worm, a reptile. Written also *prêv*, qd. v. Pl. *prevyon, preves*. *Ha'n tebel êl, hager brêf, yn y holon a worré*, and the evil angel, ugly reptile, put into her heart. M.C. 122. *Dhe wrôk ha'th flehas kefrys, edhyn, bestes, ha prevyon, cresseuch, coullenweuch an beys*, thy wife and thy children also, birds, beasts, and reptiles, increase, fill the earth. O.M. 1160. *Hag oll an bestes yn bŷs*, *gans prevas a bûb sortow*, and all the beasts of the world, with reptiles of all sorts. C.W. 8. *Prév'nôr*, earth worm. *Llwyd*, 82. The oldest form was *prif*, qd. v. See also *pryf*. The W. form at present is *pryv*, but in the old Juvencus Glosses, *prem*.

PREF, s. m. A proof. *Pryce.* Pl. *prevas*, qd. v. W. *pruvv*.

PREF, v. a. He will prove. 3 pers. s. fut. of *preva*, qd. v. *Ny'm prêf dên war gowardy*, no man shall prove me of cowardice. O.M. 2161. *Ha'y ober a prêf henna*, and his work proves that. P.C. 214. *Me a'n prêf*, I will prove it. R.D. 12.

PREGOTH, s. m. A sermon, a preaching. *Ihesu Crist yn pow a dro, pûb eroll pregoth a wre, ha'n virtu an pregoth o mâb dên dhe asé peché*, Jesus Christ about in the country at all times made a preaching, and the virtue of his preaching was that the son of man left off sinning. M.C. 23. *Thomas, ty û dhe Cynda, hag ena pregoth a wra yn ow hanow*, Thomas, thou shalt go to India, and there shalt make a preaching in my name. R.D. 2458. W. *pregoth*, from the Latin, *predicatio*. Arm. *prezec*.

PREGOWTHER, s. m. A preacher. Written also *pro-gowther*, qd. v.

PREGOWTHY, v. a. To preach. *An lays a bregowthys, lemmyn dyswé mars ŷns da*, the laws that thou preachedst, shew now if they are good. M.C. 78. Written also *pregewthy*. *Taw, an êl a bregewthy a'n wedhen hag a'y vertu*, be silent, the angel preached of the tree, and of its virtue. O.M. 220. W. *pregethu*. Arm. *prezegi*.

PREN, s. m. A tree, wood, timber, a piece of wood, a lot. Pl. *prennyer, prynnyer*, and *prynner*, qd. v. *Mar a tybbryth a henna yw hynwys pren a skyens*, if thou eat of that (which) is named the tree of knowledge. O.M. 82. *Guclen a pren a wrâf synsy*, a rod of wood I do hold. O.M. 1444. *Pren dhe gŷst ple' kefyn ny*, timber for a beam where shall we find? O.M. 2493. *Gorré dhe'n mernans, gorré yn pren crous a dhywempys*, put him to death, put him on the cross-tree forthwith. P.C. 2162. *Teulel pren mĝl wel vyé*, to throw a lot would be a thousand (times) better. P.C. 2847. *In scorgijs prennyer esé yn dewlé an ij Edhow*, in the scourges of sticks (that) were in the hands of the two Jews. M.C. 131. *En grows whâth nynio parys, na'n Edhewon ny wodhyé an prennyer py fêns kefús dhe wuthyll crows anedhé*, the cross was not yet ready, nor did the Jews know where the timbers would be found to make a cross of them. M.C. 151. *Per-bren*, a pear tree. *Moyr-bren*, a mulberry tree. *Pinbren*, a pine-tree. W. *pren*. Arm. *prenn*. Ir. *crann.* Gael. *crann.* Manx, *croan*.

PREN, v. a. He shall expiate. 3 pers. s. fut. of *prenné*, qd. v. *Kyn fy mar prout, ty a'n pren*, though thou art so proud, thou shalt pay for it. O.M. 2069. *Ef a'n pren, yn ta del y'n dyndylas*, he shall pay for it, as he has well deserved it. P.C. 1346.

PRENEST, s. m. A window. *Llwyd*, 21. Arm. *prenest, prenestr*. W. *fenestr*.

PRENIC, adj. Wooden, woody. *Pryce.*

PRENNE, v. a. To take; to buy, to purchase; to redeem, to expiate, to pay for. *Dh'agas prenné me a rôs gôs ow holon*, to purchase you I have given the blood of my heart. R.D. 165. *Guerthens y hugk dhe brenné anedhy dhodho cledhé*, let him sell his cloak to buy with it for him a sword. P.C. 922. *Me a gesul bôs gansé prennys da gwon yn nêp le*, I advise that there be with them bought a good field in some place. P.C. 1544. *My a's pren dhyworthys*, I will buy it from thee. P.C. 1555. *Ol pêch Adam pan prennas*, when he expiated all the sin of Adam. R.D. 2562. *Venythé ny dhôf a'n plen, erna'n prenné an gwâs-na*, never will I come from the place, until I take that fellow. O.M. 2152. *Erna'n prenny yn felen*, until thou expiate it cruelly. O.M. 2653. *Mar omwreyth clâf, gordhewyth te a'n prenvyth*, if thou makest thyself sick, very diligently thou shalt pay for it. M.C. 155. *Hy frenné bŷth nyns yw bern*, to buy it is no concern. R.D. 2234. W. *prynu*, †*prena*. Arm. *prena*. Ir. *crean*, †*cren.* Gael. *cean-naich*.

PRENNE, v. a. To fasten with a piece of wood, to bar. *Dûn tôth brâs dhe prenné agan yettys, râg mar tue dh'agan porthow, ef a ter an darasow*, let us come in great haste to bar our gates, for if he comes to our doorways, he will break the doors. P.C. 3039. W. *prenio*. Arm. *prenna*.

PRENNYER, s. m. Pieces of wood. Plural of *pren*, qd. v.

PRES, s. m. A stated time; time, season; a meal time; a meal. *Te na yllyth omwedhé un prés yn geydh na pechy*, thou canst not keep thyself a moment in the day that thou wilt not sin. M.C. 20. *Pêb brés*, at all times, continually. ‡ *Prez*, Llwyd, 18, 161. ‡ *Prez búz*, a repast, a meal. 57, 137. Written also *preys*, and more frequently *prŷs*, qd. v.

PREST, adv. Readily, quickly, soon; always, ever; at hand, near; very. *Dhe Dhu ny gôth dhys temptyé yn nêb ehan a servys, lemmyn prest y honoré*, thy God it behoves thee not to tempt, but in every kind of service always to honour him. M.C. 15. *Del yw scrifys, prest yma adro dhynny ganso try*, as it is written, there are always about us with him three. M.C. 21. *Gensy prest ij venyn lên esa worth y homfortyé*, with her at hand were two loyal women, comforting her. M.C. 167. *Prest y keffy pan vyré*, readily he found when he looked. M.C. 187. *Ha'n scherewys prest a bell dhe worth an gwîr a fyé*, and the wicked were very far from the truth. M.C. 203. *Ow benneth prest ty a fŷdh*, my blessing thou shalt ever have. O.M. 457. W. *prest*. Arm. *prest*. Lat. *præsto*.

PRETHY, v. a. To bear, to forbear, to hold out. *Pryce.* A late form of *perthy*, qd. v.

PREVA, v. a. To prove, to try. *Llwyd*, 128, 252. 3 pers. s. fut. *prêf*. Part. *prevys*. *Dre dha gous ydhew prevys dhe vôs dên a Galylé*, by thy speech it is proved that thou art a man of Galilee. M.C. 85. *Henna yn scon ny a wra dre'n lahn a'n prêf yn ta*, that we will soon do through the law (that) will prove it well. P.C. 2381. This is another form of *provi*, qd. v.

PREVA, adv. Truly. *Yn preva*, in truth. *Pryce.* *Râg leverel yn prevé, my ny vynnaf offrynné ol ow degé*, to speak truly, I will not offer all my tithe. O.M. 490.

PREVAN, s. f. A small worm, a worm. *Llwyd*, 164. Diminutive of *prêv*.

PREVAS, s. f. Proofs. *Yn mêdh Pylat worth an mŷns, a'n pêch prevas ris yw ry*, says Pilate to the multitude, it is necessary to give proofs of the crime. M.C. 117. Plur. of *prêf*, or *prôf*, qd. v.

PREYS, s. m. A time, a season. *Mar kûf carynnyas, warnedhé y trŷg pûp preys*, if it shall find carrion, it will always stay on it. O.M. 1104. Another form of *prŷs*, qd. v.

PRI, s. m. Mould or earth, clay. *An corf êth hydhew yn pry*, the body went this day into the earth. R.D. 21. *Tás a wrûk pûp gulás, ha dên a pry*, Father (that) made every country, and man of earth. R.D. 310. *Máp dên a bry yn perfyth me a vyn y vôs formyys*, the son of man of earth perfectly I will that he be formed. O.M. 55. *Ty vaow, darbar lym ha pry*, thou boy prepare lime and clay. O.M. 2317. *Pul pri*, a clay pit. Llwyd, 43. W. *pridh*. Arm. *pri*. Ir. *criadh*, †*criad*. Gael. *creadh*. Manx, *cray*.

PRIAN, s. m. Clayey ground. "Hence the lodes, soft clayey veins of tin, &c. are called *prian*." Pryce. W. *pridhyn*.

PRIDERYS, adj. Pensive, anxious, troubled. Corn. Voc. *sollicitus*. See *Pryderys*.

PRIDIT, s. m. A poet. Corn. Voc. *poeta*. W. *prydydh*, from *prydu*, to compose.

PRIES, s. m. and f. A spouse, a married man or woman, a husband, a wife. It changes in construction into *bries*, and *fries*. *Eva, prág y whrusté sy tullé dhe bryes hep kên*, Eve, why didst thou deceive thy husband without mercy? O.M. 278. *Gans dhe bryes kêr Eva*, with thy dear wife Eve. C.W. 88. *Pries; ow fries*, my husband. Llwyd, 231. A later form of *priot*, qd. v.

PRIF, s. m. A worm. Corn. Vocab. *vermis*. Prifpren, *eruca*, a caterpillar, lit. a timber-worm. It also means any small animal, a vermin, an insect. Written also *prŷf*, plur. *pryves*; and *prêf*, pl. *prevyon*, *preves*, qd. v. W. *prŷv*, †*prem*, in Juvencus Glosses. Arm. *prev*. Ir. *crumh*, †*cruim*, *cnumh*. Gael. *cnuimh*. Lat. *vermis*. Goth. *vaurm-s*. Eng. *worm*. Sansc. *karmi*.

PRIMUSDOC, adj. Blear-eyed. Corn. Vocab. *lippus*. "Not clearly written, but it must be the Armoric *pikousek*, from *pikouz*." Zeuss. "This odd word is abridged in the first syllable as in *prinid*; the *s* may be *f*, and *d* looks quite as much like *cl*. Cf. Gaelic *prab* and *prabach*." Norris.

PRINID, adj. Bought. *Caid prinid*, emptius, a bought slave. Corn. Voc. It is strictly the participle passive of *priny*, or *prynny*, to buy. W. *prynedig*, *prynwyd*.

PRIOT, adj. Married. *Gur priot*, sponsus, a bridegroom, or married man. Corn. Voc. The later form was *pries*, qd. v. W. *priod*, †*priawt*. Arm. *pried*, †*priet*. Sansc. *priya*, a husband.

PRIS, s. m. Price, value, worth, account, esteem. *Mars ós máp Dew a múr prŷs, dyyskyn, ha dhe'n dôr ke*, (*Mars ós máp Dew a vûr brŷs, dyskyn ha dhe'n dôr ke*, M.C. 14) if thou art the Son of God of great worth, descend and go to the ground. P.C. 99. *Trevow a brŷs, castilly brás hag huhel*, towns of price, castles large and high. P.C. 132. Written by Llwyd, *priz*, 30, 128. *Pan a priz rag hoarn*, what price for pilchards? Pryce. W. *pris*. Arm. *priz*. Gael. *pris*. Manx, *prios*. Lat. *pretium*. Fr. *prix*. Eng. *price*.

PRIT, s. m. Hour, time. Corn. Voc. *hora*. The later form was *prys*, qd. v. W. *prŷd*, †*pryt*. Arm. *pred*, †*pret*.

PRIVE, adj. Firm, secure. Pryce. *Mara pewaf, why a védh ow chyf privé guythygy*, if I live, you shall be my chief private guards. O.M. 2397.

PRIVETH, adj. Private. *Yn priveth*, privately. Pryce.

PRIVIA, v. a. To bleat. *Ma'n dhavas a privia*, the sheep is bleating. Llwyd, 248. A mutation of *brivia*, qd. v.

PROF, s. m. A proof. *Why a wra y aswonvos dédh brús, hag a'n kûf yn próf*, you will acknowledge it on the day of judgment, and have it in proof. P.C. 1496. *Y'n gylwys, máp Dew, yn próf ahanaf may portho côf, pan deffé dh'y wlascor ef*, I called him the Son of God, in proof that he should keep remembrance of me, when he should come to his kingdom. R.D. 271. *Prôf ny wra*, he will not give proof. R.D. 1200. Written also *préf*. W. *praw*.

PROFUIT, s. m. A prophet. Corn. Voc. *propheta*. The later form was *profus*. W. *prophwyd*, from the Latin ; (*wy = ê*.)

PROFUS, s. m. A prophet. Pl. *profusy*, and by the corruption of the *s*, *profugy*. *Moyses, mar ós profus lél*, Moses, if thou art a faithful prophet. O.M. 1799. *Ef yw an profus Ihesu, a lever y vôs máp Du a nêf huhel*, he is the prophet Jesus, (that) says that he is the son of God, of high heaven. P.C. 325. *A'm bewnans del yw scrifys yn lyffrow yn leas le, dre brofusy leverys*, of my life as it is written in books in many places, spoken by prophets. M.C. 73. *Mars osa Crist máp Duveth, pen drcs ol an profugy*, if thou art Christ the Son of David, head over all the prophets. P.C. 1480. Written also *profeth*. *Ke, a profeth, cowyth whêk*, go, O prophet, sweet companion. P.C. 1895. A later form of *profuit*, qd. v.

PROGATH, s. m. A sermon. Llwyd, 16, 50. A late form of *pregoth*, qd. v.

PROGATHAR, s. m. A preacher, an orator. Llwyd, 19, 50. Written also *progowther*. *Pew a'th wrûg ge progowther, dha dhesky omma dhe ny*, who made thee a preacher, to teach here to us? C.W. 170. W. *pregethwr*. Arm. *prezeger*. Ir. †*preaccoire*.

PRON, s. m. A breast. *Dyskynnouch, ketep máp pron; oté an gwêl dheragon glûs ow tevy*, alight ye, every son of the breast, behold the rods before us growing green. O.M. 1963. An irregular mutation of *bron*, qd. v.

PROUNDER, s. m. A priest, a parson. Corn. Vocab. *sacerdos*. Written also *pronter*. Llwyd, 143. Plur. *pronteryon*. *Rág y vôs war bronteryon mester brás a berth yn wlâs, gurris ve yn y golon yn delwa gûl*, because of his being over priests a great master in the land, it was put into his heart to do thus. M.C. 89. *Pronter berric*, a gorbellied priest. Pryce. The latest form was *proanter*. ‡ *E a roz towl dho proanter Powl, miz-du ken Nadclik*, he gave a throw to the parson of Paul, the black month before the Nativity. Pryce. Derived by Zeuss from the Lat. *præbendarius*.

PROVY, v. a. To prove, to try. *An ioull dhe Adam kewsys, a'n avel te kemer tam, avell Du y fedhydh gurŷs, pan y'n provas nynjo mâd*, the devil said to Adam; of the apple take thou a bit; like God thou shalt be made; when he proved it, it was not good. M.C. 6. *Cowyth profyym an styllyone, mars êns compes dhe'n fosow*, comrade, let us try the rafters, if they are straight to the walls. O.M. 2471. *Ydh ombrovas gwan dyack, may 'thôf poyntyes dha bayn brás, dha byt efarn*, I have proved myself a weak husbandman, that I am appointed to great pain, to the pit of hell. C.W. 68. The substantive is *próf*, qd. v. W. *provi*. Arm. *proui*. Ir. *formhadh*. Manx, *prow*. Lat. *probo*.

PROVYEHA, v. a. To provoke. *Llwyd*, 75.

PROW, s. m. Gain, advantage. *A harlot gans dhe whethlow, annedhé ty ny fýdh prow, war ow ené*, O knave, with thy tales, thou shalt have no gain from them, on my soul. P.C. 2658.

PRY, s. m. Earth, clay. See *Pri*.

PRYAS, s. m. and f. A spouse. See *Pries*.

PRYC, s. m. State, rank, degree. *My hall, Sera, dheuch gramercy, a callen dôs dhe'n pryck-na, ydh alsan bôs pûr very*, I may, Sir, to you thank, if I could come to that degree, I might be very merry. C.W. 44. *My a sylly in ûr-na, a callan dôs dhe'n prick-na, y fea bargayn pûr fûr*, I perceived in that hour, if I could come to that degree, it would be a' very wise bargain. C.W. 58.

PRYDER, s. m. Care, anxiety, thought. Pl. *pryderow. Govy, ny won pendra wrâf; gallas ow calon pûr clâf dre pryderow*, woe is me, I know not what I shall do ; gone is my heart very sick through cares. P.C. 2611. *Gyllys ôf yn pryderow, mûr yw ow fyenasow*, gone I am in thoughts ; great are my anxieties. R.D. 16. Written also *preder*, qd. v. W. *pryder*. Arm. *preder*.

PRYDERYS, adj. Mournful, pensive. *Llwyd*, 92, 151. Written also *prederys*, qd. v. W. *pryderus*. Arm. *prederiux*.

PRYDYRY, v. a. To have a thought, to think, consider. *Pan prydyryf a'y passon, nyns â ioy výdh y'm colon*, when I think of his Passion, joy will never enter into my heart. R.D. 759. *A Ihesu, luen a verey, ahanan gura prydyry*, O Jesus, full of mercy, do thou think of us. R.D. 772. *Pûp cowyth ol prydyrys, mar tesen vfýdh yn y vrýs desmygy pren vâs ple fo*, let every comrade consider, perhaps it will be in his mind to shew where there is a good tree. P.C. 2540. *Arluth Cryst, me a'th pyssé a prydiry uhané, pan tysé yn dhe wlascor*, Lord Christ, I would pray thee to think of me, when thou shalt be in thy kingdom. P.C. 2907. Written also *predery*, qd. v.

PRYDZHAN, v. n. To boil. ‡ *Ma'n dzhei a rostia ha prydzhan*, they are roasting and boiling. *Llwyd*, 248. A mutation of *brydzhan*, a corruption of *brydian*. See *Brudias*.

PRYERYN, s. m. A stranger. *A nyns osé pryeryn, usereth yw dhys govyn pyth yw an marth a wharfé a un profus bynyges*, if thou art not a stranger, it is idleness for thee to ask what is the wonder (that) has occurred to a blessed prophet. R.D. 1261. The oldest form in the Cornish Vocabulary is *pirgirin*, qd. v. W. *pererin*. Arm. *pirchirin*. From the Lat. *peregrinus*.

PRYF, s. m. Any small animal, a worm, a reptile. Pl. *pryvcs*, qd. v. *Ha'n serpent a welta ydhew an very prýf-na a wrûg an Jowl dha entra uny hy râg temptya dheth vam Eva*, and the serpent thou seest is the very same reptile, (that) the Devil did enter into her, to tempt Eve. C.W. 132. See *Prîf* and *Prif*.

PRYGWYTH, s. m. A small space of time, a little while. *Peder, ny wolsys yn fâs ; un prygwyth gynef golyas kyns ys dôs ow torment tyn*, Peter, thou hast not watched well; a little while with me watch before my sharp torment comes. P.C. 1055. Comp. of *pry* for *prŷd*, a season, and *gwŷth*, a time.

PRYNNER, s. m. Pieces of wood, sticks. Pl. of *pren*, qd. v. *Me a'n gor wan an alter, hag a'n lésk gans tân prynner*, I will put him on the altar, and burn him with a fire of sticks. O.M. 1290. *Otté omma prynner genef dhe wûl tân, degys a dré*, behold here pieces of wood with me to make a fire, brought from home. O.M. 1314. *My a vyn war an alter gorré lemmyn an prynner*, I will upon the altar put now the wood. O.M. 1323. Written also *prynnyer*. *A Dew kér, assoma squyth, prynnyer derow ow trehy*, O dear God, I am weary, cutting oak sticks. O.M. 1010. *En prynnyer a ve kerhys en grows scon dythgtis may fe*, the timbers were fetched that the cross might be prepared forthwith. M.C. 153.

PRYNNY, v. a. To buy, to purchase, to expiate, to pay for. Part. *prynnys*. *Môs dhe vyres me a vyn an corf a'm prynnes yn tyn, mar tassorhas*, I will go to see the body (of him that) redeemed me painfully, if it has risen again. R.D. 686. *Ef yw arluth a allos, hag a prynnas gans y wôs pobel an beys*, he is the Lord of power, and has purchased with his blood the people of the world. R.D. 1184. *Dredho ef prynnys bydheuch, ol ow tûs, gour ha benen*, through it ye shall be redeemed, all my people, man and woman. P.C. 767. *Reson prâg y fe prynnys yw Ihesus Crist dre ordna yn néf y vonus tregys*, the reason why he was redeemed is that Jesus Christ ordained that he should dwell in heaven. M.C. 7. Written also *prenné*, qd. v.

PRYS, s. m. A stated time, a while ; time, season ; meal time, a meal. *Gansé y a'n hombronkyas yn prŷs hanter nôs heb wow bŷs yn aga fryns Annas*, they led him with them at the time of midnight, without a lie, even to their prince Annas. M.C. 76. *Erbyn bonas henna guris, nans o prŷs gwespar yn wlâs*, against that was done, it was now vesper-time in the land. M.C. 230. *Gordhyans dhe'th corf wék pûp prŷs*, worship to thy sweet body, at all times. O.M. 86. *Arluth, me a'th peys a dhybry gynef un prŷs, dre dhe wôdh, ha'th dyskyblon, rág yma bôs parusys dhyso ha dhedhé kefrys*, Lord, I pray thee to eat a meal with me, by thy will, and thy disciples, for there is food prepared for thee, and for them also. P.C. 466. *Me a's gor alemma un prŷs kyns nôs*, I will bring them hence a while before night. P.C. 2334. *Ha why kelmoch an dew gam yn dyw crous kyns bôs prŷs bôs*, and do yo bind the two rogues on two crosses before it is meat time. P.C. 2784. *Ydh egen yn crés Almayn orth un prŷs-ly yn pûr wŷr pan fûf gylwys*, I was in the midst of Germany at a breakfast meal, very truly when I was called. R.D. 2149. Written also *prês*, and *preys*, qd. v., and in the Corn. Voc. *prit*, qd. v.

PRYVES, s. m. Any small animals, reptiles, worms. *Arluth, henna me a wra, a'n gor yn pyt ysella yn mýsk pryves*, Lord, that I will, (and) put him in the lowest pit among reptiles. R.D. 2011. Plur. of *prýf*, qd. v.

PRYVIA, v. a. To do or solicit another man's business, to procure. *Llwyd*, 129.

PRYWETH, s. m. A space of time, a time, a while. *An Tás Dew, Arluth a van, re'm gorré dhe gosoleth, ow enef ha'm corf dhe'n gulan, Amen, pysys pûp pryweth*, the Father God, Lord above, may he put me to rest ; my soul and my body to the ground, Amen, I have prayed at all times. O.M. 860. Another form of *prygwyth*, qd. v.

PU, pron. s. Who, which, what. *An harlot a leverys, pu a woras yt colon cows yn delma worth iustis*, the scoundrel said, who put it in thy heart to speak thus to a Justice? M.C. 81. *Dhe worth an bêdh an meyn-ma dhynny pu a'n ommelys*, these stones from the grave who hath moved them for us ? M.C. 253. Written also *pyw*, qd. v.

PUB, pron. adj. Each, every, all. Written indiscriminately *pûp*. *Yn pûb gwythres y côth dhys gordhyé dhe Dhu ha'y hanow*, in every work it behoves thee to worship thy God, and his name. M.C. 17. *Wy a gûff bohosogyon pûb êr warnouch ow carmé*, ye will have the poor always calling on you. M.C. 37. *Dybbry boys ef ny rynnas, lymmyn pûb êr ol olé*, he would not eat food, but weep always. M.C. 67. *Nêb yw arluth drys pûp tra*, who is Lord above every thing. O.M. 623. *Ha mŷr a pûp tenewen, aspy yn-ta pûp cchen, whythyr pûp tra ol bysy*, and look thou on every side, examine well every particular, search out every thing diligently. O.M. 746. Another form of *pôb*, qd. v.

PUB, pron. s. Every one, each individual. *My ny won leverel prâk gans pûp na vedhaf ledhys*, I cannot tell why by every one I shall not be slain. O.M. 596. *Drou e dhymmo dhe tackyé a uch y pen gans mûr greys, may ballo pûp y redyé, gour ha benen kekyffrys*, bring ye it to me to fasten above his head with much strength, that every one may read it, man and woman likewise. P.C. 2809. Another form of *pêb*, qd. v.

PUE, v. subs. He was. *Mar derré, hy leverys, kepar ha dew y fedhé ; mar pue drôk a oberys, trôch y hy gans dhe gledhé*, if I broke it off, she said, like a god I should be ; if it was evil (that) she did, kill her with thy sword. O.M. 291. A mutation of *bue*, qd. v.

PUL, s. m. A pit, a pond, a muddy pool, dirt, mire. Lhwyd, 43. *Pul doun*, a deep pit, the bottomless pit. *Pul stean*, a tin pit. *Pryce*. Another form of *pol*, qd. v.

PULLAN, s. m. A pit, a pond. *Pullan troillia*, a ditch, moat, or trench. *Pryce*. Diminutive of *pul*. Written also *polan*, qd. v.

PUNNYA, v. a. To run. *Dho punnia kerr*, to run away. Lhwyd, 53, 61. Another form of *ponyé*, qd. v.

PUNS, s. f. A pound in weight, or money. Pl. *pynsow*. *Me a vynsé a talfens mŷl puns dhodho a our da*, I would they were worth a thousand pounds to him of good gold. P.C. 212. *Otté myr gynef parys, cans puns, ha henna yw mûr*, behold myrrh with me ready, a hundred pounds, and that is much. P.C. 3144. *Merouch, merouch orth hemma ; otomma avall dhŷs, mar gwrêth tastya anodha, ev a drayl dheso dha lês, moy es millyow a bynsow*, look, look at this, here is an apple for thee, if thou wilt taste of it, it will turn to thee to profit, more than thousands of pounds. C.W. 54. W. *punt*. Ir. *pontu, † pond*. Gael. *punnd*. Manx, *punt*. Lat. *pondus*.

PUNSYE, v. a. To punish. Part. *punsys*. *Ty a vŷdh punsys pûr tyn râg dhe dhrôg a ver dermyn*, thou shalt be punished very severely for thy evil in a short time. O.M. 1000. Borrowed from the English.

PUI', pron. adj. Each, every. See *Pûb*.

PUPPENAC, comp. pron. Wherever, whosoever, whatever. *Puppenagol a vo ef*, whosoever he may be.

P.C. 23. *Puppenak ma fo redys an awayl-ma, tavethlys hy a vŷdh pûr wŷr neffré*, wherever may be read this Gospel, she shall be talked of very truly ever. P.C. 550. *Y grygyans pûp ol guythes, puppenagol a wharfo*, his belief let every one keep, whatever may happen. R.D. 1538. Comp. of *py*, where, who, what, and *penac*, soever.

PUR, adj. Pure, clean, undefiled, right, very. Sup. *purra*, qd. v. *An barth cleydh nêb o cregis, dyveth o ha lader pûr*, he that was hung on the left side, shameless he was and a very thief. M.C. 101. *Mars osa Crist mâp Davydh, mâp Dew pûr ha dên yn wêdh, dre dhe vôdh gorthyp lemyn*, if thou art Christ, the Son of David, Son of very God, and man also, by thy will answer now. P.C. 1721. *Pûr wyryoneth re geusys ahanaf, re'n gêdh hedhew*, very truth thou hast spoken of me, by this day. P.C. 1587. W. *pûr*. Arm. *peur*. Ir. *pur*. Lat. *purus*.

PUR, adv. Very, quite. *Ytho bedhyth mylyges, pûr wŷr drys ol an bestes* now thou shalt be accursed, very truly above all the beasts. O.M. 312. *Râg own namnag ôf pûr dhal*, for fear I am well nigh quite blind. O.M. 1056. *Yn pûr defry, nêp a rella yn ketella*, very positively, whoever has acted in that way. O.M. 2230. *Lydhys ôf pûr dhyogel*, I am killed very certainly. O.M. 2725. *Pûr oges yu dhe ancow*, very near is thy death. P.C. 2660. *Pûr ryes*, very necessary. W. *pûr*. Arm. *peur*. Ir. *fior*. Gael. *fior*. Manx, *feer*. Lat. *per*.

PUR, s. m. Snivel, snot. Lhwyd, 3, 33, 95, *pûr*. W. *poer*, spittle. Arm. *burudik*, snivel. Lat. *pus, pure*.

PURCENIAT, s. m. An enchanter, a sorcerer, a wicked man. Written by Lhwyd, 84, *purkeniat*, and 241, *purcheniat*. Comp. of *pûr*, very, and *ceniat*, a singer.

PURPUR, s. m. Purple, a purple robe. *An quêth têk a ve dyskis, ha'n purpur ryche a usyé*, the fair cloth was stript off, and the purple (that) he used. M.C. 161. *Ot omma gynef, hep fal, quêth rûdh, purpur pal, dhe wyské adro dhodho*, behold here with me, without fail, a red cloth, a purple pall to clothe around him. P.C. 2128. W. *porphor*. Arm. *pourpr*. Ir. *corcur*. Gael. *corcur*. Fr. *pourpre*. From the Lat. *purpura*.

PURRA, adj. Veriest. Superlative of *pûr*, qd. v. *Dhom pcynyd bŷs yn crow, kepar ha del veva ve an purra lader yn pow*, to torture me even unto death, as if I were the veriest robber in the land. M.C. 74. *Kepar ha pan vevé vy an puré lader yn pow*, as if I were the veriest robber in the land. P.C. 1174.

PURRYES, adj. Very necessary. *Reys yw purryes lavyrrya, ha gones an bŷs omma, dha gawas dhe ny susten*, needful, very needful it is to labour, and till the earth here to get for us sustenance. C.W. 80. Generally written *porrys*, qd. v.

PURVERS, v. a. A purchase. *Ow otté un purvers da lemyn wharfedhys ; avos ol roweth Adam, bŷs dhyn umma yn un lam ef a vŷdh kyrhys*, behold a good purchase now obtained ; notwithstanding all the bounty of Adam, to us here in a trice he shall be brought. O.M. 882.

PUSCES, s. m. Fishes. *Buskes, hag edhyn*, beasts, fishes, and birds. O.M. 43. *Adam, otté an puskes, ydhyn an nêf, ha'n bestes*, Adam, behold the fishes, birds of heaven, and the beasts. O.M. 117. *Puskes brâs*, great fishes, whales. C.W. p. 191. The singular is written *pysc*, qd. v.

PUSORN, s. m. A bundle, a fardle; the burden of a song. *Mara kyllyn y gafus, vynytha na dheppro bous, me a'n kelm avel pusorn*, if I can find him, that he may never eat food, I will bind him like a bundle. R.D. 542. *Ha ty Tulfryk, pen pusorn, dalleth dhynny ny cané,* and thou Tulfric, the end of a song begin to sing to us. R.D. 2353.

PY, pron. adj. Who, which, what. *Py hanow y fydh gybrys*, what name shall he be called? O.M. 676. *Lavar dhymmo kyns mones py tyller. yma Moyses, ha py côst yma trygys*, tell me before going, in what place is Moses, and in what coast he is dwelling. O.M. 1551. *Lavar dhymmo a ver spys py ngl o mocha sengys an kêth dên-ma dhe curé*, tell me in a brief space, which one was most bound to love this same man? P.C. 510. *Py le y fydh e keffys*, where will he be found? R.D. 702. *A Bertyl, asogé mûs, ha goky dres ol an dûs py ydho fôl*, O Bartholomew, thou art mad and stupid beyond all the men who are fools. R.D. 973. Written also *pa* and *pe*, qd. v. *Py* is also an old Welsh form.

PY, adv. Where, in what place, whither. *Nan Edhewon ny wodhyé an prennyer py fens kefis dhe wuthyll crows anedhé*, nor did the Jews know, where the timbers could be found to make a cross of them. M.C. 151. *Ow mâp, py 'dh êth dhe vroder*, my son, where is thy brother gone? O.M. 606. *Arluth cúf, lavar dhynny yn kêth trê-ma py fynny bôs pask dhynny ordyné*, dear Lord, tell us in this same town where wilt thou paschal food order for us. P.C. 622. *Saw levereuch, cowethé, py kefer pren dh'y crousyé*, but say, companions, where shall be found a tree to crucify him? P.C. 2535. Written also *pe*, qd. v.

PY, conj. Either, whether, or. *Heb cowyth py cowethes*, without a male or female companion. O.M. 95. *Ny wodhen râg ponvotter, py 'dh een yn gweel py yn côs*, I know not from trouble whether I should go into a field or into a wood. O.M. 364. *War geyn lowarn py brathky*, on the back of a fox or mastiff. O.M. 805. *Mar ny gevyth mêdh py gwfyn, ke dhe fenteu dhe evé*, if thou find not mead or wine, go to a fountain to drink. O.M. 2435. Another form of *po*, qd. v.

PYB, pron. adj. Each, every, all. Lhuyd, 251. *Pyb hehen*, every one. 244. See *Púb*.

PYCAR, adv. As, like as. Lhuyd, 71, 112. Generally written *pocâr*, qd. v.

PYCEN, adv. Or otherwise. Pryce. See *Poceu*.

PYDH, v. subs. He will be. A mutation of *bydh*, 3 pers. s. fut. of *bôs*. *Mar qura, gothvedhys mar pydh, yn seon dyswreys ef a vydh*, if he does, if it will be discovered, soon destroyed shall he be. O.M. 1520. *War y gour, mar pydh ledhys*, on her husband, if he shall be slain. P.C. 1922.

PYGY, v. a. To pray, to supplicate. *Ow dyskyblon, y-sedhouch, hag omma pols powesouch, hedré vyma ow pygy*, my disciples, sit and have rest a while, whilst I am praying. P.C. 1013. *Ow arlothes gyné dre dhynnarch agas pygys na wrellouch cammen ladhé an profus a Nazaré*, my lady by me through command prayed you that you do not unjustly kill the prophet of Nazareth. P.C. 2195. *Kemmys a fynno crygy ha'y pygy ef*, whoever will believe and pray to him. R.D. 285. *Râg kueth pygyth, garmé a wrêth*, for grief thou prayest, cry out thou dost. R.D. 852. *Ha pygyn Dew gallosek*, and we will pray to mighty God. R.D. 2394. A corrupted form of *pysy*, qd. v.

PYJAD, s. m. A prayer, a supplication. Pl. *pyjadow*. *Mercy yw stos dhe nêp a'n pfys, puppenagol a vo ef, pyjadow a luen colon, a wor dhe vês tempacion*, mercy is extended to whoever prays for it, whosoever he may be; prayers of a full heart to put away temptation. P.C. 24. *Yn ûr-na whreuch pyjadow, may codhdho an mynydhyow warnouch râg cwn uthekder*, in that hour ye shall make prayers, that the mountains may fall upon you, for very horror. P.C. 2651. Written by Lhuyd, 127, *pydzhadow*.
‡ *Pydzhadow an Arluth*, the Lord's Prayer. Pryce. A corrupted form of *pysad*, qd. v.

PYLE, adv. Where, in what place, whence. *Ny won pylé*, I know not where. C.W. 154. *Worthys me nembes negys, na bylé ês dcvethys*, with thee I have no business, nor whence thou art come. C.W. 42. Properly two words, *py*, what, and *le*, a place, and often contracted into *ple*, qd. v.

PYLLES, adj. Bald. ‡ *Pedn pylles*, bald-pate. C.W. 168. See *Piles*.

PYLTA, adv. Much. *Pylta gwel*, much better. Lhuyd, 249.

PYMENT, s. m. Drink, liquor. *Yn pow-ma nynsus guel gufyn, râg hemma yw pyment ffyn; yuf, ow arluth hep parow*, in this country there is no better wine, for this is fine liquor; drink my lord, without equals. O.M. 1915. Written also *pymeth*. *Kens môs cyf ten guyn pymeth, ha dhe seafé ydh êth yn ow nygys, my a gryfs*, before going, drink a draught of spiced wine, and thou more lightly wilt go in my errand, I believe. O.M. 2294.

PYMP, card. num. Five. *In corff Ihesus ydh esé, hag ef yn crows ow eregy, pymp mgll strekis del iové, ha pedergwyth cans goly*, in the body of Jesus there were, and he on the cross hanging, five thousand strokes as there were, and four times a hundred wounds. M.C. 227. *An ngl dhodho a dellé pymp cans dyner monyys, ha hanter cans y gylé*, the one owed to him five hundred pence of money, and half a hundred the other. P.C. 505. *Maria, mfyr ow pym woly*, Mary, see my five wounds. R.D. 867. Written also *pemp*, qd. v. W. *pymp*, † *pump*. Arm. *pemp*. Ir. *cúig*, † *coic*. Gael. *cuig*. Manx, *queig*. Æol. Gr. πέμπε. Anc. Gaulish, *pempe*. Πεντάφυλλον, Ῥωμαίοι κίγκεφδλιουμ, Γάλλοι πεμπέδουλα. Dioscorides. 4, 42. Latin, *quinque*. Sansc. *panc'a*. Goth. *fimf*. O.H.G. *vinf*. Germ. *fimf*.

PYMPES, adj. Fifth. *Yn pympes dydh me a vyn may fo formyys dre ow nel bestes, puskes, hag edhyn, tfyr hn môr dhe goullenwel*, on the fifth day I will that be made by my power beasts, fishes, and birds, earth and sea to fill. O.M. 41. *In pympas dydh, orth ow brfys an puskes hep falladow, hag ol edhyn kekeffrys, me a's gura dhom plegadore*, in the fifth day by my judgment, the fishes without failings, and all the birds likewise I will make them to my wishes. C.W. 8. W. *pymmed*, † *pimphet*. Arm. *pemved*. Ir. *cuigeadh*, † *cuigedh*. Gael. *cuigeadh*. Manx, *queigoo*.

PYMTHEC, card. num. Fifteen. *In corff Ihesus ydh esé, hag ef yn crous ow eregy, pymp mgll strekis del iové, ha pedergwyth cans goly, ha tryugons moy gansé, ha pymthck, pûr wfyr êns y*, in the body of Jesus there were, and he on the cross hanging, five thousand strokes as there were, and four times a hundred wounds, and three score more with them, and fifteen, very truly were they. M.C. 227. *Pûb tédh oll nêb a vynnê leverel pymthek pater*, he that would every day say fifteen paternosters. M.C. 228. W. *pymtheg*, †*pymdec*. Arm. *pemzek*. Ir. *cuigdeag*. Gael. *cuig-deug*. Manx, *queig-jeig*. Lat. *quindecim*.

PYN, s. m. The head. A mutation of *pen*, qd. v. This is a solitary instance in any of the three British dialects, of an inflected genitive case, by changing the vowel. It occurs however only in the compound prepositions, *erbyn*, or *warbyn*, when the possessive pronoun is inserted, and the initial undergoes the regular mutation. *Er ow fyn*, against me. R.D. 1919, 2573. *Er dhe byn*, against thee. O.M. 1350. *Er agas pyn*, against ye. P.C. 180. *Er aga fyn*, against them. M.C. 96. See *Erbyn*. This agrees exactly with the ancient Irish forms; as *cenn*, a head; *ar chenn*, lit. to the head, in front of, against; *ar mo chiunn*, before me; *ar a chiunn*, before him; *ar ar chiunn*, before us; &c. Zeuss, 577, 618. See also Norris's Cornish Grammar, 234.

PYN, s. f. Pain, punishment. *Mar a's ladtré dheworto pa'n pŷn a gotho dhodho*, if he steal it from him, what punishment is due to him? O.M. 2233. *Guask war an mŷn, re'th fo drôk pŷn*, a harlot púr, strike on the edge, bad pain be to thee, O very rogue. P.C. 2727. A contracted form of *peyn*, qd. v.

PYN, v. a. He shall fasten. *Trester dredho ty a pyn adrus, râg na vo degees*, beams through it thou shalt nail across, that it may not be shut. O.M. 903. 3 pers. s. fut. of *pyné*, id. qd. W. *pinio*, to pin, to peg, or fasten.

PYNAG, pron. s. Whosoever, whatsoever. *Yma un ponygyon brâs war ow wholon ow codhé, pynag ové, ren ow thâs*, there is a great heaviness falling on my heart; whatever it may be, by my father. O.M. 528. *Ny fynnaf gasé onan vyth-ol dhe vevé, pynag a wharfo an cas*, I will not leave any one of them to live, whatever the case may be. O.M. 1698. *Pynak vo, lettrys py lêk, a weles an chy, nŷm dêr*, whoever he may be, lettered or lay, that has seen the house, I am not concerned. P.C. 681. *Ny a'n gura dhys wharré, a dhyssempys hep lettyé, pynag a fo*, we will do it for thee soon, immediately without stopping, whatever it may be. R.D. 2000. Used also adverbially. *Py nŷl pynag-ol may fo, me a wra y concludyé war un lam*, what one soever he may be I will shut him in a trice. P.C. 1402. Written also *penag*, qd. v. W. *pynag*. Arm. *pennag*.

PYPRYS, adv. Always, at all times. Llwyd, 249. A contracted form of *púb—prŷs*.

PYR, adv. Very. *Pyr havel dhys*, very like thee. Llwyd, 242. Comp. *pyrra*. *Pyrra fool ne ve gwelys*, a verier fool was not seen. C.W. 174. Generally written *púr*, qd. v.

PYRCAT, s. m. A pulpit, a pleading place. Llwyd, 141, 158.

PYRFYTH, adj. Perfect. *Ty a wylfyth yn pyrfyth merkyl têk gurŷs*, thou shalt see perfect a fair miracle done. O.M. 1449. Written also *pyrfeth*. *May hyllyn môs dhe'n tyreth yw ordnys dhyn yn pyrfyth*, that we may go to the land (that) is ordained for us perfectly. O.M. 1679. *My a grŷs yn pyrfeth*, I believe perfectly. O.M. 2011. Another form of *perfyth*, qd. v.

PYRTII, v. a. He will bear. *Otn cowes púr ahas, ny's pyrth dên mara peys pel*, behold a shower very dreadful, man will not bear it if it drops long. O.M. 1082. 3 pers. s. fut. of *porthy*, qd. v.

PYS, v. a. He will pray. 3 pers. s. fut. of *pysy*, qd. v. *Gweres dynchans, my a'd pŷs, ow fysadow dres pûp tra*, help quickly, I pray thee, my prayers above every thing. O.M. 1829. *Agan gobyr, ny a'th pŷs*, our wages we ask thee. O.M. 2584. *Arlythy, my agas pŷs*, lords, I pray you. O.M. 2346. *Mercy yw stos dhe nêp a'n pŷs*, mercy is extended to whoever prays for it. P.C. 22. It is also the 2 pers. s. imp. *Pŷs gans colon dywvsyk*, pray thou with undoubting heart. R.D. 1370. *Pŷs e, dhym ma'n danfonno*, pray thou him, that he may send him to me. R.D. 1620.

PYS, part. Paid. *Rák henna an gwella us dascor mŷns moné yw pŷs*, therefore it is the best to give up all the money (that) is paid. P.C. 1538. Borrowed from the English.

PYS, s. m. The world, world—creation. *Drôk pŷs of, re'n geydh hydhew, mar uskys ef dhe verwel*, ill-fated I am, by this day, that he should die so soon. P.C. 3089. A mutation of *bŷs*, qd. v.

PYSAD, s. m. A prayer, a supplication. Pl. *pysadow*. It changes in construction into *bysadow*, and *fysadow*. *Gweres dynchans, my a'd pŷs ow fysadow dres pûp tra*, quickly, I pray thee, my prayers above all things. O.M. 1830. Written also *pesad*, qd. v.

PYSAF, v. a. I shall or will pray. 1 pers. s. fut. of *pysy*, qd. v.

PYSDER, s. m. Heaviness. Llwyd, 240. Formed from *pŷs*, id. qd. *poys*, heavy.

PYSC, s. m. A fish. Pl. *puskes*. See *Pisc*.

PYSGADYR, s. m. A fisherman. Llwyd, 120, 240. *Pysgadyr an mytêrn*, a kingfisher. 65. W. *pysgotwr*, (*pysgod*, plur. of *pŷsc*,—*gŵr*, a man.) Arm. *pesketer*. Ir. *iascaire*. Gael. *iasgair*. Manx, *ceasteyr*. Lat. *piscator*.

PYSGETTA, v. a. To fish. Llwyd, 120. W. *pysgoin*. Arm. *peskela*.

PYSSE, v. a. He would pray. 3 pers. s. subj. of *pysy*, qd. v.

PYST, adj. Blackish, dull, stupid. Pryce. *What vyngeans dhys, a pen pyst, ple clewsta gelwel Dew Cryst gans dên yn bŷs-ma genys*, what vengeance to thee, O blockhead, where hast thou heard the calling God Christ by man in this world? O.M. 2641. Probably a mutation of *pôst*, a post.

PYSTEGE, s. m. Witcheries. *Ré dhe Gryst a lovery, aberth yn crows pan evé, mars ogé Crist Máb Davy, dês a'n grows hep pystegé*, some to Christ said, on the cross when he was; if thou art Christ the son of David, come from the cross without witchcraft. M.C. 197. The plur. form of *pystye*, qd. v.

PYSTRY, s. m. Witchcraft, magic, sorcery. *Mura leversys henna, certan ty yw mâp an pla; dên fŷth ol, mur dre pystry yn try deydh ny'n dhrehafsé*, if thou saidst that, certainly thou art the son of the fiend; no mau, unless through sorcery, in three days would raise it. P.C. 1764. Arm. *pistri*.

PYSTRYOR, s. m. A wizard, sorcerer, magician. *Pûp pystryor y cothé dre reson da y leysky*, every sorcerer it is incumbent for good reason to burn him. P.C. 1766. *Me a grys bones an gudn pystryour ha hudor brâs*, I believe the fellow is a wizard and a great sorcerer. R.D. 1854.

PYSTRYORES, s. f. A female sorceress, a witch. Written also *pestryores*, qd. v.

PYSTYC, s. m. Witchery, magic, sorcery. Pl. *pystygé*, or *pystegé*, qd. v. *Fystynyn fast dh'agan pow, râk devoues dewolow dhe'n terogé; y môns ow cryé huthyk; dún yu kerch râk dout pystyk scon hep lettyé*, let us hasten quick to our country, for devils are come to the lands; they are crying horribly; let us come away, for fear of witchcraft, soon without delaying. R.D. 2305. Ir. *piscog*. Gael. +*piscog*. Manx, *pishag*. Arm. *pistig*, a sharp pain.

PYSWERE, num. adj. Fourth. *Tan hemma, gor gansé y, ha henna yw pymweré*, take this, put it with them, and this is the fourth. P.C. 2851. Written also *peswerê*, qd. v.

PYSY, v. a. To pray, beg, entreat. 3 pers. s. fut. and 2 pers. s. imp. *pŷs*, qd. v. *Pysyn may fyyn servysy dh'agan arluth hep parow*, let us pray that we may be servants to our Lord without equals. O.M. 235. *Lavar, annes ow vôs vy a'm bewnens, may dh'y bysy a leverel gwyroneth*, say thou, that I, being wearied of my life, pray him to say the truth. O.M. 701. *Amen, pysys pûp pryweth*, Amen, I have prayed at all times. O.M. 860. *Consder gentyl, y'th pysof a ry dhymmo cusyl dha*, gentle counsellor, I pray thee to give me good advice. O.M. 1566. *Saw vyner re dhewhylly, genes my a wra pysy*, but always that thou wilt return, with thee I will pray. O.M. 2197. *Dhyuch lavara, ow dyskyblyon, pysouch toythda ol kes-colon*, to you I say, my disciples, pray forthwith, all with one heart. P.C. 2. *Why, a'm cofun vy, hep gow, pysouch may fe ve evys*, you, in remembrance of me without deceit, pray that it may be drunk. P.C. 288. *Lyes gusth me re beays*, many times I have prayed. P.C. 864. *Me a'n kelu yn krês an wast, may pysso ef gefyens war pen y dheulyn*, I will bind him in the middle of the waist, that he may pray for pardon on his knees. P.C. 1890. *Me a'th pyssé a prydiry uhané*, I would pray thee to think of me. P.C. 2909. Written also *pesy*, qd. v.

PYTH, s. m. A thing, an article, a substance. Plur. *pythow*. *An pŷth a screfys, screfys, yn médh Pylat dhe-dhé y*, the thing (that) I have written, I have written, says Pilate to them. M.C. 188. P.C. 2804. *An pŷth a dhue yn dyweth*, the thing will come at last. O.M. 671. *Me a wothfyth yn ŵr-na pŷth yw dhe gallos, hep mar*, I shall know in that hour what is thy power, without doubt. P.C. 64. *Why wôr pŷth yw gwella dheuch dhe wruthyl*, ye know what is best for you to do. P.C. 408. *Heuna yw pŷth a dhynrys*, that is what I choose. P.C. 3017. As in Welsh it is constantly used as an interrogative pronoun. *Pŷth yw an gordhyans dhe Dew*, what is the worship to God? O.M. 476. *Aron whêk, pŷth a cusyl a rêth dhym*, sweet Aaron, what counsel givest thou to me? O.M. 1813. *Pŷth cw an othom dynny cufus lafur a'n par-na*, what is the need to us to have labour of that sort? O.M. 967. Written also *pêth*, qd. v.

PYTH, adv. Ever. A mutation of *bŷth*, qd. v.

PYTHESTA, comp. v. Where art thou. *Adam, pythesta? Golsow dhymmo, ha dês nês*, Adam, where art thou?

300

Hearken to me, and come nearer. C.W. 54. Comp. of *py*, where, *es* for *ôs*, thou art, and *ta* for *te*, thon.

PYTHWETH, adv. Ever. *A Dûs kûf y'th wholowys, an sarf re rûk ow thollé; dh'y falsury y cresys; pythweth re rûg ow syndyé*, O Father dear in thy lights, the serpent hath deceived me; her falsehood I believed; ever she hath injured me. O.M. 288. A mutation of *bythweth*, id. qd. *bythgweth*, qd. v.

PYW, pron. s. Who, whom. *Pyw a dhysquedhes dhyso dhe vôs noeth*, who disclosed to thee thy being naked? O.M. 261. *Pyw ôs a gews mar huhel*, who art thou (that) talkest so high? O.M. 1368. *Pyw ytho a's hembronk dhy*, who then will lead them to it? O.M. 1874. *Pyw a fî henna bones*, who can that be? P.C. 771. *Pyw a synsow why mochya, nêp a serf py a dheber*, whom think ye greatest, him that serves, or that eats? P.C. 708. *Pyw ouch, levereuch heuna*, who are ye, tell that. R.D. 196. *Me a'th pŷs, pyw a whylyth*, I pray thee, whom seekest thou? R.D. 1040. Written also *pu*, qd. v. W. *pwy*, +*pui*. Arm. *piou*, +*piu*. Ir. *cia*. Gael. *co*. Manx, *quoi*. Lat. *qui*.

PYW, comp. v. Who or which is. (*Pyw—yw*, is.) *Lemmyn dyskudh ha lavar pyw an pren a bew hep mar pous Ihesu an Nazarê*, now shew thou and say which is the die (that) owns without doubt the coat of Jesus of Nazareth. P.C. 2853. *Pyw mychtern a lovené*, who is the king of joy? R.D. 106. *Pyw henna gans deusys môs re dhueth mar uskys dhe'n wlâs*, who is that with Godhead good (that) hath come so swiftly to the country? R.D. 2486.

PYWPENAG, pron. Whosoever. *Me a lever dheuch deffry, pyw-peung a'm gwrllha vy, ef a wyfyth ow thâs*, I say to you truly, whoever seeth me, seeth the Father. R.D. 2383. Written by Llwyd, 134, *piwha bennac*.

Q.

This letter is not a regular member of the British alphabet, but is used in a few Cornish words with *u* following to express the sound of *cw*, as *quellen, qura, qurêth, bysqueth*, for *cwellen, cwra, cwrêth, byscweth, &c*. That it was in early use is proved by an inscription on a stone in Golval, near *Penzance*, where the British name *Cynedhav* is written *Quenctav*. (Llwyd, 228.) It was used always in Armoric for *k*, until Legonidee's time; as *quegin*, a kitchen; *quelen*, holly; for *kegin, kelen, &c*. It is never used in Welsh, Irish, or Gaelic; but it has a place in the Manx alphabet, with regular mutations into *wh*, and *g*, as *quing hrome*, a heavy yoke; *e wching*, his yoke; *ayn guing*, their yoke. The Irish *cuig*, five; *cuigeal*, a distaff, &c., are written in Manx, *queig, quiggal*.

QUALLOC, s. m. A boaster, a braggart. *Na lader, by my vallok, kyn fe vŷth mar vrâs quallok, ua mar howlyn a'y vody*, he shall not steal, by my belt, though he be ever so great a braggart, or so big of his body. O.M. 2068.

QUANDRE, v. a. To walk about, to wander. *My pan cscu ow quandré, clewys a'n ugl tenewen un êl ow lulleth cané a uchaf war an werdhen*, when I was walking about, I heard on one side an angel beginning to sing above on the tree. O.M. 213. Borrowed from the English.

QUEDHENS, v. a. They covered. Another form of

cudhens, 3 pers. pl. imperf. of *cudhé*, qd. v. *Gans quêth y ben y quedhens guelas banna na ylly*, with a cloth his head they covered, that he could not see a drop. M.C. 96.

QUELLEN, v. a. I should see. A mutation of *gwelen*, 1 pers. s. subj. of *gweles*, qd. v. *A Dew kêr, assoma sqwyth, wyn veys a quellen un wyth an terwyn dhe dhercedhé*, O dear God, I am weary, happy (my) lot, if I should see once the time to end. O.M. 685. *Gwyn veys a quellen an gydh, may fe yrhys dhym kedhy*, happy my lot if I should see the day, that it has been enjoined me to reach. O.M. 1013. *Mar a quellen drôk dhum flehys na duan, ow colon a vydh terrys*, if I should see evil to my children or sorrow, my heart will be broken. P.C. 1944.

QUELSE, v. a. He had seen. A mutation of *gwelsé*, 3 pers. s. pluperf. of *gweles*. *Ef a doys a dhesympys maga town ty del vodhyé, gans Crist na vyé tregis na bythqueth na'n quelsé*, he swore forthwith as deep an oath as he knew, that he had not been staying with Christ, nor that he had ever seen him. M.C. 85.

QUELYN, v. a. We shall see. A mutation of *gwelyn*, 1 pers. plur. fut. of *gweles*, qd. v. *Arluth kêr, gura yn lowrn; hedré vy yn beys gynen, neffré trystyns ny 'gen bydh; del osa Dew dhyn ha pen, mara quelyn dhys ankew neffré ny a vydh dhe weyth*, dear Lord, be joyful; whilst thou art in the world with us, we shall never have sorrow; as thou art God to us, and Head, if we shall see grief to thee, we shall ever have it also. P.C. 733.

QUERTH, v. a. Thou wilt do. *Mar querth, me a ter dhe pen dhys awartha*, if thou wilt, I will break thy head for thee above. R.D. 921. Incorrectly for *quréth*, qd. v.

QUERTHE, v. a. To sell. A mutation of *gwerthé*, qd. v. *Fist yn criff me re bechas, Ihesus dhe wy ow querthé*, very strongly I have sinned, selling Jesus to you. M.C. 104. *Rág ow querthé Crist dhywhy, me re pechas marthys mûr*, for (in) selling Christ to you, I have sinned wondrously greatly. P.C. 1517.

QUETH, s. m. A cloth. Pl. *quethow*. *Dresen ow bôs noeth hep quêth, ragos ydh yth dhe gudhé*, because of my being naked without a cloth, I went to hide from thee. O.M. 259. *Yn wedhen me a welas yn ban uhel worth scoren, flôch byen nowydh gynys, hag ef yn quethow maylys, ha kylmys fast gans lysien*, in the tree I saw up high on a branch, a little child newly born, and he was swathed in cloths, and bound fast with a napkin. O.M. 807. *Ot omma gynef, hep ful, quêth rûdh, purpurpal, dhe wyské adro dhodho*, behold here with me, without fail, a red cloth, a purple pall, to clothe around him. P.C. 2128. *Y vôs mâp Dew da y syw, pan dorras quêth an templ*, that he was the Son of the good God it follows, when the cloth of the temple was rent. P.C. 3086.

QUETH, s. m. A time, or course. A mutation of *gwêth*, qd. v, as in *bythqueth*, ever, qd. v. Written also *qujth*, qd. v.

QUETHE, v. a. To work, or labour at. A mutation of *gwethé*, qd. v. *Krîf yw gwrydhyow an spedhes, may thyw ow dywvrech terrys, worté menouch ow quethé*, strong are the roots of the briars, that my arms are broken, working often at them. O.M. 689.

QURA, v. a. He will do. A mutation of *gwra*, 3 pers. s. fut. of *gwrey*, qd. v. *Mar qura, gothvedhys mar pydh, yn scon dyswrrys ef a vydh*, if he will do, if it he discovered, soon destroyed he shall be. O.M. 1520.

QURETA, v. a. Thou wilt do. A mutation of *gwra*, 3 pers. s. fut. of *gwrey*, qd. v. and *te*, thou. *Dysmyg lemmyn, ty guâs smat, pyw a rôs dhyso an wat; ha mar a qureta, me a wra y gudhé ef*, declare now, thou brave fellow, who gave thee the blow; and if thou wilt do, I will cover him up. P.C. 1385.

QURETH, v. a. Thou wilt do or make. A mutation of *gwrêth*, 2 pers. s. fut. of *gwrey*, qd. v. *A'n covath bydh ny hassaf mar qurêth dhym an sacryfys*, from remembrance I will never leave thee, if thou wilt make to me the sacrifice. O.M. 1284. *Mara qurêth aga lettya*, if thou wilt prevent them. O.M. 1495. *Golhy mara qurêth ow treys*, if thou wilt wash my feet. P.C. 845.

QUREUCH, v. a. Ye will do. A mutation of *gwreuch*, 2 pers. pl. fut. of *gwrey*, qd. v. *Ytho mar qureuch ow wylas, gesouch ow thús us gené dhe vôs quyt dhe tremené*, now if ye do seek me, allow my people (that) are with me to pass quite away. P.C. 1121.

QUREVA, v. a. He will do. A mutation of *gureva*, comp. of *gwra*, 3 pers. s. fut. of *gurey*, and *ve*, he. *Mar a quereva yn della, crysy dhodho ny a wra, y vôs profus bynygys*, if he will do so, we will believe him, that he is a blessed prophet. P.C. 2882.

QUUDHAS, v. a. He covered. *Un quêth têk hy a drylyas adro dhodho desympys, ha warnans hy a'n quuthas, rág gwythé na ve storvys*, a fair cloth she wrapt around him immediately, and over him she covered him, to keep him that he should not be starved. M.C. 177. Another form of *cudhas*, 3 pers. s. preter. of *cudhé*, qd. v.

QUYTH, s. m. A time, a course. *Hayl Cayfas, syr epscob stonel, dêk can qujth dhys lowené*, hail, Caiaphas, bold Sir, bishop; ten hundred times joy to thee. P.C. 574. A mutation of *gwyth*, id. qd. *gwêth*, qd. v.

QUYTH, adv. Free. *Dhe vês y a dhelyffras Barabas, quyth may 'th ellé*, they delivered out Barabbas, that he should go free. M.C. 150. From the English, *quit*.

R.

This letter is an immutable radical in all the Celtic languages, except the Welsh. There it is secondary, being the soft mutation of *Rh*, which is the radical form as in Greek; thus *rhôdh*, a gift; *ei rôdh*, his gift. There are traces of the aspirated *rh* in Irish also, but it is rejected from modern grammars. It is also found in ancient Gaulish words, as *rheda*, a chariot; and the proper names *Rhedones*, *Rhenus*, *Rhodanus*, &c.

RA, v. a. He will do or make. An abbreviated form of *wra*, a mutation of *gwra*, 3 pers. s. fut of *gwrey*, qd. v. Used as an auxiliary with infinitives. *Drow e dhymmo dysempys, ha my a ra y dybry*, bring it to me immediately, and I will eat it. O.M. 248. *Arluth, warnas tregeryth; goef a ra dhe serry*, Lord, mercy on thee, woo is he that angers thee. O.M. 1016. *Pyth a vynnouch why dhe ry ? ha me a ra dheuch spedyé, ow enfos Crist yredy*, what are ye willing to give ? and I will speed you, taking Christ forthwith. M.C. 39.

RA, v. a. He will give. *Me a ra*, I will give. *Pryce*. Generally writen *re*, qd. v.

RAC, prep. For. Written also *rág*, qd. v.

RACCA, s. m. A play, a comedy. Corn. Voc. *comedia*. W. *rhaca*, a spectacle, or show.
RACCAN, s. m. A rake. *Llwyd*, 33, 136. W. *rhacan*. Ir. *raca*. Ir. *racn*. Gael. *rac*.
RACH, s. m. Care. *Pryce*. *Me a wŷsk, ha henna gans mûr a rach, may dhys tenno a uel cor*, I will strike, and that with much care, that it be drawn out for thee in the best way. P.C. 2722. W. *rhwech*, urgency.
RADN, s. f. A share, a portion. ‡ *Dha radn a'n ryna*, to some of those. C.W. 170. ‡ *Radn ehan a bûb sortow*, some kind of all sorts. C.W. 180. ‡ *E-ma radn a lôl*, some say. *Llwyd*, 250. A late corruption of *ran*, qd. v.
RADNA, v. a. To divide, to distribute. *Llwyd*, 55. A late corruption of *ranné*, qd. v.
RAF, v. a. I will do. An abbreviated form of *wráf*, a mutation of *gwrâf*, 1 pers. s. fut. of *gurey*. *Tavo, Pedyr, te ny wodhas, yn mêdh Crist, pan dra râf dhys*, be silent, Peter, thou knowest not, says Christ, what thing I do to thee. M.C. 46.
RAFARIA, interj. Strange, wonderful! *Llwyd*, 91. Id. qd. *refaria*, qd. v.
RAFSYS, part. Hurried to, carried. *Ennoc ydhof hynwys, dhe'n plâs-ma y fûf rafsys yn kêfc, yn kuews*, Enoch I am named, to this place I was carried in flesh, in blood. R.D. 198. Probably formed from the English *ravished*.
RAG, s. m. A front, a presence. Written also *râc*. *Ke yn râk, del y'm kyrry*, go in front as thou lovest me. O.M. 537. *Ymôns a râg pel gylys*, they are in front far gone. O.M. 1636. *Deuch yn râg ketep onan*, come forth, every one. O.M. 2083. *Yn ûr-na me a wryl mur a pedhyn ny abel dhe wûl defens a râk tues*, then I shall see if we be able to make a defence before people. P.C. 2306. *Dre an gôs a râk Pilat worto an kîfe a glené*, through the blood in the presence of Pilate the flesh struck to it. R.D. 1593. W. *rhâg*. Arm. *râg*. Ir. *roimh*, †*re*, †*ria*, †*rcs*, †*rias*. Gael. *roimhe*. Manx, *roish*.

RAG, prep. Before, for, on account of, because of, for the purpose of, from. *Dhe'n bŷs pan dryskynnas, pehadoryon râg perna o descvijs dre Satnas ; râg henna gordhyn neffra Ihcsus nêb agan pernas*, to the world when he descended to redeem sinners (that) were felled by Satan ; therefore let us ever worship Jesus who redeemed us. M.C. 5. *En scherevys a sorras râg bonas Crist honoris*, the wicked were angered because that Christ was honoured. M.C. 31. *Râg bós dhedhé ioy mar vrâs, ha my pûp ûr ow lesky, râg henna my a's temptyas*, because they had joy so great, and I was always burning, for that I tempted them. O.M. 306. *Râg nown y wróns clamderé*, for hunger they will faint. O.M. 400. *Râg dhe offryn kêr ty a vŷdh genen neffré*, because of thy dear offering, thou shalt be ever with us. O.M. 567. *Gordhyans dhys, a Dhew a rûs, pan danfenys dhe cannas râg Pharo dh'agan guythé*, glory to thee, O God of grace, when thou sentest thy messenger to keep us from Pharaoh. O.M. 1671. W. *rhâg*. Arm. *rág*.

RAG, adv. Because, for. Written indiscriminately also *râc*. *Râg orty ty dhe golé, mŷl vâp man a veydh damneys*, because thou hearkenedst to her, a thousand mother's sons shall be damned. O.M. 324. *Râk ny allas dên yn beys anodho gûl defnydh vâs*, for no man in the world has been able to make a good use of it. P.C. 2547. *Râg ef a glew agas lêf*, for he will hear your voice. O.M. 1658. *Râk ty dhe wcles ol ow golyow a lês, yn dhe golon ty a grŷs*, because thou hast seen all my wounds openly, in thy heart thou believest. R.D. 1551. W. *rhâg*.

RAGAS, comp. pron. May it be yours. *Banneth an tôs ragas bo, hag ef prest ragas gwytho venytha in cosoleth*, may the blessing of the Father be yours, and may he always keep you ever in rest. O.M. 1723. *Ow benneth ol ragas bo*, my blessing be on you all. P.C. 265. *Ragas bo meul*, may a curse be yours. P.C. 2048. *Ragas bo crês ha mûr ioy*, may yours be peace and great joy ! R.D. 1285. Comp. of the optative particle *re*, and *agas*, your.

RAGGORYS, part. Put forth. *Pryce*. Comp. of *râg*, and *gorys*, placed, qd. v.

RAGLEVERYS, part. Aforesaid, before mentioned. *An sêth yw râg-leverys a's gwyskis tyn gans mûr angus*, the arrow aforesaid struck her sharp with much anguish. M.C. 224. Comp. of *râg*, and *leverys*, spoken.

RAGOF, pron. prep. For, from, or before me. *(Râg-my.) Pŷsk ragof ny wra skusy, mar cordhyaf Dew yn perfyth*, a fish from me shall not escape, if I worship God perfectly. O.M. 139. *Ef a vŷdh anclcdhys yn le na fue dên bythqueth, yn alabaster gravys ; ragof y fue ordynys, naqa whyn avel an lêth*, he shall be buried in a place that man never was, in alabaster carved ; for me it was intended, as white as the milk. P.C. 3137. *Flehys mûr ha benenas, rayoff na wheleuch olé*, children many and women, for me seek ye not to weep. M.C. 168. W. *rhagov*, †*ragof*. Ir. *romhaın*, †*remum*, †*rium*, †*rinmat*. Gael. *rium*. Manx, *roym*.

RAGON, pron. prep. For, from, or before us. *(Râg-ny.) Ragon y penys y dâs, oll y sor may fé gevys*, for us he prayed his Father that all his wrath might be remitted. M.C. 9. *Del levaraf vy dhywchy, cf a emblodh ragon ny*, as I say to you, he will fight for us. O.M. 1661. *Gueyteuch dygtyé bôs ynny, lour dh'agan soper ragon*, take ye care to prepare food in it, enough for our supper for us. P.C. 640. *Ens dew a'm dyscyblyon dhe'n castel ûs a ragon a dhysempys*, let two of my disciples go to the village (that) is before us immediately. P.C. 174. *Lemmyn gans ol y vestry, ragon ny wôr omvethé*, now with all his power he knows not how to keep himself from us. M.C. 194. W. *rhagon*. Ir. *romhaınn*, †*remuind*. Gael. *riunn*. Manx, *roin*.

RAGOS, pron. prep. For, from, or before thee. *(Râg-ty.) Nyng-ew ragos se ladhé*, it is not for thee to slay. M.C. 123. *Drefen ow bôs noeth hep quêth, ragos ydh ŷth dhe gudhé*, because I am naked without a cloth, I went to hide from thee. O.M. 260. *Couyth, my a wra ragos moy es yn della*, comrade, I will do for thee more than that. P.C. 1232. *Bŷth nynsyw ragos dhe arluth avel ôs gy*, never it is for thee, for a lord as thou art. R.D. 1930. W. *rhagot*, †*ragot*. Ir. *romhad*, *romhat*, †*re-mut*, †*romut*. Gael. *riut*. Manx, *royd*.

RAGOUCH, pron. prep. For, from, or before ye. *(Râg—chui.) Olouch râg agis flechys, ha ragouch agis honon*, weep ye for your children, and for yourselves. M.C. 169. *Ow horf a ve yw hemna yn mêdh Crist, ragouch uy pernys aberûh yn bŷs-ma*, my body of me is this, says Christ, for you bought within this world. M.C. 44.

Ha me a pŷs ragouch ow thâs, may feuch sylwys dre y luen râs, and I will pray my Father for you, that ye may be saved through his full grace. P.C. 27. *Râg hemma yw ow gôs fŷn, hag a vŷdh ragouch skullys,* for this is my last blood, and it shall be shed for you. P.C. 825. W. *rhagoch,* † *ragoeh.* Ir. *romhaibh,* † *remuib.* Gael. *ribh.* Manx, *rhymbiu, reue.*

RAGOUN, adv. For fear of, lest that, lest. *Llwyd,* 248. Properly two words, *râg,* for, and *own,* fear. *A meys ôf ow predyry, pandra allaf dhe wruthyl, an avel orth y dyrry, râg own genes bones gŷl,* I am puzzled thinking, what I may do, by plucking the apple, for fear of there being guile with thee. O.M. 196. W. *rhag own.*

RAGTHE, pron. prep. For, from, or before them. *(Râg —y.) Saw Syr Urry ow ledhys, ha dhe votteler kekyfrys; govy ragthé,* but Sir Uriah is killed, and thy butler also; woe is me for them! O.M. 2216. *Pûr wŷr my a vŷdh ragthé, na gêf dên vŷth fout ynnê yn nep fôs vŷth,* very truly I will be for them, nor shall any man find a fault in them, in any wall. O.M. 2456. *Reson y a rey ragthé, mês war fals ydh êns growndys,* reasons they gave for them, but on falsehood they were grounded. M.C. 118. W. *rhagdhynt,* † *raedunt.* Ir. *rompa,* † *trempu.* Gael. *riu.* Manx, *rhymboo, roue.*

RAGTHO, pron. prep. For him or it. *(Râg—o.) Yn dôr my a vyn palas tol may fo ynno eudhys, ha'y wîl hŷr ha doun ragtho,* in the earth I will dig a hole, that he may be covered in it, and make it long and deep for him. O.M. 867. *Yn ol dhe gosow nynsus gŷst vŷth ol hep wow vâs dhe dra vŷth ragtho,* in all thy woods there is not a beam, without a lie, good for any thing for it. O.M. 2407. *Ny fue ragtho y honan y'n godhefys ef, mas râk kerengê mâp dên,* it was not for himself he suffered it, but for the love of mankind. P.C. 3226. W. *rhagdho, rhagtho,* † *racdaw;* † *racdam,* in Juvencus Glosses. Ir. *roimhe,* † *reme.* Gael. *ris.* Manx, *roish.*

RAM, comp. pron. By my. *(Re—am.) Ny wodhyan guthell na ken, ram lea' lowta,* I knew not how to do otherwise, by my loyal truth. C.W. 76. Written also *rum,* qd. v.

RAM, comp. pron. Hath—me. *(Re—am.) Ty ram tullas ve heb kên,* thou hast deceived me without pity. C.W. 62. Generally written *rum,* qd. v.

RAN, s. f. A part, a portion, share, division. *Wharé y soras Iudas, ny gewsy dre geryté, lemen râg cafos ran erâs a'n pencon mar a callé,* anon Judas was wroth, he spoke not through charity, but to get a large share of the pay if he could. M.C. 38. *Pedar ran guris anedhé gans pewcar marreg a brŷs, dhe bûb marreg ran may fe,* four parts were made of them, by four soldiers of worth, to every soldier that there might be a part. M.C. 190. *A ol dhe drevas an degves ran dhymmo gâs,* of all thy tillage leave the tenth part to me. O.M. 426. *Worto y glynes hardlych ran a'n kŷe bŷs yn ascorn,* to it adhered closely a portion of the flesh even to the bone. R.D. 2598. W. *rhan,* † *ran.* Arm. *rann.* Ir. *rann, roinn, ruinn.* Gael. *rann, roinn.* Manx, *ranney.*

RAN, v. a. They will do. An abbreviated form of *wrân,* a mutation of *gwrân,* 3 pers. pl. fut. of *gwrey.* ‡ *Dzhyi a rân,* they shall do. *Llwyd,* 246.

RANNE, v. a. To part, to share, to divide, to break, to be broken. Part. pass. *rynnys.* 3 pers. s. fut. *ran.* *Ma ow wolon ow ranné, pan glewaf cous a'n pâr-na,* my heart is breaking, when I hear talk of that kind. O.M. 2181. *Me a vyn lemmyn ranné yntredhon ol y dhyllas, ha my a's ran dŷch wharré,* I will now divide between us all his clothes, and I will soon divide them for you. P.C. 2841. *Dre pûr hyreth ow colon marth yw na ran,* through very regret it is a wonder that my heart breaks not. R.D. 1440. *Ha'n gwŷn esa war en foys ef a rannas yntredhé,* and the wine (that) was on the table he divided among them. M.C. 45. *Dyllas Crist a ve rynnys, pedar ran guris anedhé; y bous ef o'mar dêk guris, y ny vynsans y ranné,* the clothes of Christ were parted, four parts were made of them, his coat was so fairly made, that they would not part it. M.C. 190. *Ha'y dagrow a dheveré a'y dew lagas pûr dhewhans, ha'y holon whêk a ranné, me a lever, râg trystans, râg an grayth yn hy esé nus gwethé an Spyrys sans,* and her tears dropt from her eyes very copiously, and her sweet heart would have broken, I say, for sorrow, had not the Holy Ghost protected her, for the grace that was in her. M.C. 222. W. *rhannu;* † *rannam,* partior, in Oxford Glosses. Arm. *ranna.*

RANNY, v. a. To vex, to torment. *Pryce. Hag ydh êns dhe ben dovolyn, hag y kewsens dhe scornyé, hag a gamma aga meyn pûb onon râg y eysyé; lowenê dhys, le yw dheyn myglern, rŷs yw dhe wordhyé; ken o dhadho mûr a bayn, may'th ethens worth y ranné,* and they went on their knees, and spake to scorn him, and wried their mouths, every one to exalt him; this was great pain to him, that they should go to torment him. M.C. 137.

RAS, s. m. Grace, thanks, worth, value, excellence, virtue. A mutation of *grâs,* qd. v. *Dre râs an goys y whelas Iheasus Crist del o dythgtis,* by the virtue of the blood he saw how Jesus Christ was treated. M.C. 219. *Oynment o a gymmys râs may wethê corf heb pedry,* the ointment was of so much virtue, that it kept a body without rotting. M.C. 235. *Dên apert, ha mûr y râs,* a man clearly, and great his worth. M.C. 243. *Mêr râs dhe why, Eal Dew,* much thanks to you, Angel of God. C.W. 136, 142. W. *rhâd,* † *rat.* Ir. *rath,* † *rad.* Gael. *rath.* Lat. *gratia.*

RASOW, s. m. Graces, excellencies. A mutation of *grasow,* pl. of *grâs,* qd. v. *Gans unnient dhodho esa, ha spyeis a vûr rasow,* with ointment (that) he had, and spices of great virtues. M.C. 234. *Mar ny fŷn dre y rasow ow gueres a termyn ver,* if he will not, through his graces, help me in a short time. R.D. 705.

RE, pron. s. *Pandra wowenté se dhewortha f ve ha'm lays? mar a mynnyth, govynny orth an kêth rê n's elevas; an rê-na a gî dhe dhysky yn della y re dhyskas,* what wouldst thou enquire of me and my laws? if thou wilt, enquire about them from those same that heard them; those can teach thee as they have learned. M.C. 80. *Gans rê a gymmys colon en loven a ve tennys,* by some with so much heart the rope was pulled. M.C. 181. *Rê erell,* some others. M.C. 195. *Rê a'n Edhewon tebell a leverys,* some of the wicked Jews said. M.C. 203. *An rê-ma yw oberys,* these are wrought. O.M. 15. *An rê munys ow tené,* the little ones sucking. P.C. 438. *Py gans ken rê yw dyskys,* or by other persons is taught. P.C. 2002. W. *rhai,* † *rei.* Arm. *rê.*

RE, s. m. A running. *Me a vyn setyé eolm re, may fastyo an eolm wharré adro dhum bryangen a dhysempys dhum tagé,* I will put a running noose, that the knot choak me. P.C. 1525. W. *rhe.* Ir. *ra*, +*rai*; *ria.* Gael. *ruith.* Sansc. *ri, ray.*

RE, v. a. He will give. 3 pers. s. fut. of *rey*, qd. v. *Gura ol del leverys, ha gráth dhyso my a re,* do all as I have said, and grace I will give to thee. O.M. 1472. *My a's re dheuch yn lueu ro,* I will give them to you in full gift. R.D. 675.

RE, prep. By, through. Used only in imprecations. *Mar a'th caffuf, re Iovyn, y'th ladhaf kyns ys vyttyn, a'm dew luef,* if I find thee, by Jove, I will kill thee before morning with my hands. O.M. 1532. *Re Dew an Tâs,* by God the Father. O.M. 1919. *Re Dew Tâs, ow Arluth kér,* by God the Father, my dear Lord. O.M. 2274. *Ef a'n pren, re Synt Iovyn,* he shall pay for it, by Saint Jove. P.C. 368. *Re Varia,* by Mary. Llwyd, 249. *Re* is an abbreviated form of *dre;* so *ro* in Gaelic is used for *troinh.*

RE, adv. Excessively, too, too much. *Hen yw re nebes,* this is too little. O.M. 389. *Ny yllyr re dhe wordhé,* it is not possible too much to worship thee. O.M. 1852. *Re got o a gevelyn,* it was too short by a cubit. O.M. 2520. *Hag éth yn râk re a poynt,* and went forward too much. P.C. 3032. *Ha re prl ny re strechyas,* and too long we have stayed. R.D. 721. W. *rhy,* +*re,* +*ry,* +*ro.* Arm. *ré,* +*ra.* Irish, *ro,* +*ra,* +*ru.* Gael. *ro.* Manx, *ro.*

RE, a particle, used in construction, which when placed before the preterite tense turns it into the preterperfect. *Ty re dhrús dhymmo,* thou hast brought to me. O.M. 111. *Och, tru, tru, my re behas, ha re dorras an dyfen,* Oh, woe, woe, I have sinned, and have broken the prohibition. O.M. 249. *Agan gorhel re nygyas,* our ark has floated. O.M. 1087. *Yn ketella ty re wrûk, ha dheworth Urry re dhûk y un wrêk,* in that way thou hast acted, and from Uriah hast taken his only wife. O.M. 2243. *My re vevas termyn hŷr,* I have lived a long time. O.M. 2345. It is also placed before the preterpluperfect. *Pedyr a omdennas yn ûr-na del re bechsé,* Peter withdrew then as he had sinned. M.C. 86. *En Edhewon betegyns gúl tol arall ny vynné, lemyn an tol re wrussens, y a vynné dhe servyé,* the Jews nevertheless would not make another hole, but the hole they had made they would that it should serve. M.C. 180. *Ha dhodho a leverys re saffé Crist heb strevyé,* and to him said that Christ had risen incontestably. M.C. 248. This particle is an abbreviated form of *rug,* did, and though not in the present day, it was formerly used in Welsh also, and placed before the perfect, pluperfect, and second future tenses. (See *Dosparth Edeyrn Davod Aur,* p. 130.) The most ancient form in Welsh was *ro,* as in *roluncas,* gutturavit; *rogulipias,* olivavit; *roricavit,* sulcavissent. Quoted by Zeuss, 420, from the Luxemburgh Glosses.

RE, a particle, used in construction, and placed before a subjunctive tense to give it an optative sense. *Ventytha gordhyys re by,* ever be thou worshipped. O.M. 107. *Amen, yn della re bo,* Amen, so be it. O.M. 462. *Bynyges re bo an prŷs, may fe gurŷs an gorholcth,* blessed be the time that the agreement was made. O.M. 674. *Y grâs re dhanvonno dhyn, an Tâs Dew a wrûk pûp tra,* may he send his grace to us, the Father God (that) made every thing. O.M. 1188. *Ha'y grâs dheuchehy re wronntyo,* and his grace may he grant to you. O.M.

1726. *Banneth an Tâs re-ges bo,* may the blessing of the Father be yours! O.M. 2585.

REA, interj. O strange! wonderful! *Rea rea, rea reva, rea suas.* Llwyd, 112, 249. *Rea* is probably an abbreviated form of *reva,* id. qd. W. *rhyvedh,* a wonder.

REAL, adj. Royal, kingly. *A callen dôs dhe'n pryck-na, ydh alsan bôs pûr very; henna vea reall dra, ha maga fûr accomptys,* if I could come to that degree, I might be very merry; that would be a royal thing, and being accounted as wise. C.W. 44. Written also *ryal,* qd. v.

REB, prep. By, nigh, near to. Llwyd, 117, 130. *Reb an lán,* by the fire. 249. *Ha môs reb keow Chy wôn,* and going by the hedges of the House of the down. 252. A later form of *ryb,* qd. v.

REBBON, pron. prep. By or near unto us. Llwyd, 243. A later form of *rybbon,* or *rybon,* qd. v.

REBE, v. s. He has been. 3 pers. s. preterite of *bôs,* with the verbal particle *re* prefixed. *Agan crcgy ny yw mall, râg ny rebé luddron drês,* our hanging is deserved, for we have been froward robbers. M.C. 192. Written also *rebea,* and *rebce. Pan ethons oll dhe weary, ancombrys y rebea,* when all were gone out, not of one mind were they. M.C. 34. *Pylat a vynnas scrifé a vewnans Crist acheson, praga dampnys rebee,* Pilate would write of the life of Christ an accusation, why he was condemned. M.C. 187. *Bythqueth dremas rebee,* he was ever a good man. M.C. 214. *Dal o, ny wely banna, ef rebea dén a brŷs,* he was blind, he saw not a drop, he was a man of worth. M.C. 217.

REBECIS, part. Reproached, rebuked. *Ragon menouch rebekis, ha dysprcsijs yn harow,* for us he was often reproached and despised cruelly. M.C. 2. Arm. *rebech.*

REBECHSE, v. a. He had sinned. *Pedyr a omdennas yn ûr-na del rebechsé,* Peter withdrew then as he had sinned. The part. *re,* and *bechsé,* a mutation of *pechsé,* 3 pers. s. plup. of *pechy,* qd. v.

REBEN, v. s. We have been. 1 pers. pl. preterite of *bôs,* with the verbal particle *re* preceding. *Marrek arall a gowvas, gowy vŷth pan vcyn genys; tru,* a Dhu, *elhas, elhas, gans un huyn re-bén tullys,* another soldier said; woe is me that we were born! sad, O God, alas, alas, by a sleep we have been deceived. M.C. 246.

REBYE, v. s. He had been. 3 pers. s. plup. of *bôs,* with the verbal particle *re* prefixed. *Crist a settyas yn tyen an scovern arté dhe drê, hag a'n dythgthtyas pûr lowen maga têk del rebyé,* Christ set the ear completely home again, and made it right gladly as fair as it had been. M.C. 71.

RED, s. f. A ford. Pryce. Written in Corn. Voc. *rid,* qd. v.

REDANAN, s. f. A brake, or fern. Llwyd, 240. The sing. of *reden.*

REDEBELL, adj. Very wicked. *Ah, redebell, dowethy; gorta ha bŷdh dhym rowlys,* ah, very evil one, come hither, and be by me ruled. C.W. 40. *(Re—tebel.)*

REDEGVA, s. f. A course or race. Corn. Voc. *cursus.* Properly a race-course, being comp. of *redec,* (W. *rhedeg,)* to run, and *ma,* a place. W. *rhedegva.*

REDEN, s. m. Fern. Corn. Voc. *filix.* It is properly a plural aggregate, of which the singular would be *redenen,* pronounced in Llwyd's time *redanan. Celioc reden,* a grasshopper, (W. *ceiliog rhedyn,)* lit. cock of the fern. W. *rhedyn.* Arm. *raden.* Ir. *raithneach,* +*rath.*

REME 305 RENA

Gael. *raineach.* Manx, *rhennaeh.* Lat. *ratis,* in Marcoll. Burd. 25.
REDI, v. a. To read. Written generally *redyé.* *En lybell a ve tackis worth en growes fast may 'th esé, hag a uch pen Crist gorrys, may hylly péb y redyé,* the libel was fixed on, so that it was fast on the cross, and put above the head of Christ, that every one might read it. M.C. 189. *Crist a benys, del redyn yn delma yn lues le,* Christ prayed, as we read thus in many places. M.C. 204. *Yn ketella ydhyw reys, del redyer yn lyes le,* so it is necessary, as it is read in many places. P.C. 1168. From the English.
REDIC, s. m. A radish. Corn. Vocab. *raphanum.* W. *rhudhwgl.* Manx, *rahgyl.* Formed from the Latin, *radix, radice.*
REDIOR, s m. A reader. Corn. Voc. *lector.*
REDIORES, s. f. A female reader. Corn. Voc. *lectrix.*
REFARIA, interj. By Mary. *Re Faria, piwa glow vi,* by Mary, whom do I hear ? Lhuyd, 253. More correctly *Re Varia.*
REGETH, v. n. He hath gone. *Yn y golon fast regeth mûr a gerensé worthys,* into his heart there hath gone much love towards thee. M.C. 115. *Regeth* is another form of *reseth,* qd. v., with the common substitution of *g* soft for *s.*
REGIHTEN, s. f. A burning coal. Corn. Vocab. *pruna.* W. *rhysyn.* Arm. *regezen.*
REI, v. a. To give, to grant, to present. Part. *reis. Ef a galsé bôs guyrthys a try cans dyner ha moy, ha réna galser dhe rey dhe vochesegyon yn boys,* it might have been sold for three hundred pence and more ; and those might have been given to the poor in the world. P.C. 537. *Ow nessé yma an preys, may fydh mâp Dew ynno reys dhe'n fals Edhewon dygnas,* the time is approaching, that the Son of God shall be given in it to the false Jews to oppose. P.C. 1097. *Guel ys ol tûs an bys-ma, y reyth kusyl,* better thau all the men of this world, thou givest counsel. P.C. 472. *Reson y a rey ragthé, mes war fals ydh êns growndys,* reasons they gave for it, but on falsehood were they grounded. M.C. 118. A varied form of *roi,* qd. v.
REIAT, s. m. A giver. *Guenoin reiat,* a giver of poison. Coru. Voc.
REIS, s. m. Need, necessity. See *Reys.*
RELLA, v. a. He shall have done. An abbreviated form of *wrella,* a mutation of *gwrella,* 3 pers. s. 2 fut. of *gwrellé. Yn pûr defry, nêp a rella yn ketella, mernans yw gwyw dh'y vody,* very truly whoever shall have acted in that way, death is due to his body. O.M. 2240. *Tra veth oll a rella lês, ny gavaf omma nêb tu,* any thing at all that will do good, I find not here on any side. C.W. 76.
RELLOUCH, v. a. Ye will do. An abbreviated form of *wrellouch,* (qd. v.,) a mutation of *gwrellouch,* 2 pers. pl. of *gurey. Deuch geneff, ha holyuuch ve, gothvedhouch na rellouch trôs,* come ye with me, and follow me, see that ye make not a noise. M.C. 63.
REM, comp. pron. May—me. *(Re—my.) An Tâs Dew, Arluth a van, ré'm gorré dhe gosoleth,* the Father God, Lord above, may he put me to rest. O.M. 858.
REME, comp. pron. These. *An ré mé ew guél a râs,* these are rods of grace. O.M. 1080. More correctly *ré-ma.* See *Ré.*

REMENAT, s. m. The remainder, the rest. Pl. *remenadow.* Llwyd, 139, 249. *Gorra an dra-ma dha'n remenat,* add this to the rest. 242.
REMMA, comp. pron. These. *(Ré—ma.) Ty nyn râs plegy dhe remma,* thou shalt not bow down to these. *Arluth, kemer truath warnan ny, ha scrif ol remma dhy arhadow parch chy agan colonow, ny dhy bŷs,* Lord have mercy upon us, and write all these thy commandments in our hearts, we beseech thee. Pryce. *An remma,* those. Lhuyd, 244. W. *y rhai yma.*
REMUFE, v. a. He moved. *Mar remufé, y pen crak me a torsé,* if he moved, his head, crack I would break. R.D. 396. Formed from the English.
REN, comp. pron. Hath—him, it, us. *(Re—'n.) Fest pel my ré'n servyas ef,* very long I have served him. O.M. 852. *Dhe tâs kêr re'n danvonas dhe'th servyé,* thy dear Father hath sent us to serve thee. P.C. 167. *Del yw ty ré'n leverys,* as it is, thou hast said it. P.C. 1325. *Mychtern erod re dhanfonas Ihesu dhys, hag yn guyn cf ré'n guysceas,* king Herod has sent Jesus to thee, and in white he hath clothed him. P.C. 1844. *My ré'n collas dredho,* I have lost it through him. P.C. 149. *Yn maner-ma y pesys, râg an kêth ré ré'n crowsé,* in this manner he prayed, for those same that crucified him. M.C. 185. Arm. *ren.*
REN, comp. pron. May—him, us. *(Re—'n.) Agan gorhel re nygyas, ré'n sawyé, Arluth huhel,* our ark has floated, may it save us, high Lord. O.M. 1088. *Ha peaym râg y ené, may fo Dew luen a byté ré'n kyrho dhodho dh'y wlath,* and let us pray for his soul, that God, full of pity, may carry him to him to his kingdom. O.M. 2370. *Synt Iovyn whêk ré'n carro, ha dres pûp ol ré'n gordhyo,* may sweet saint Jove love him, and honour him above every body. P.C. 1848.
REN, comp. prep. By the. *(Re—an.) My a'n trêch, ré'n Arluth Dew,* I will cut it, by the Lord God. O.M. 2537. *Ow cerf yw, ré'n offeren,* my body it is, by the mass. P.C. 764. *Me a'n te, ré'n geydh hydhew,* I will swear it by this day. P.C. 2484.
REN, s. m. The mane, horse hair. Lhuyd, 73. *Rên verh,* the mane of a horse. 242. W. *rhawn.* Arm. *rein.* Ir. *ron, roinne.* Gael. *ron, roinne.* Manx, *renaig.*
REN, v. a. We will give, let us give. 1 pers. pl. fut. and imp. of *rei. Kyn na vynno dysmegy, dûn yn râk gans an gwary, ha rên dhodho boxusow gans dornow ha gwelyny war an scovernow,* since he will not tell, let us come forward with the play, and let us give him blows with hands and rods on the ears. P.C. 1389. *Y vôs Dew ha dên yn wlân dhe'n tra-na cryggyans rên,* that he is God and man clearly, to that same thing we will give belief. P.C. 2406.
REN, v. a. I would give. 1 pers. s. subj. of *rei. A'y vestry ef ny rên bram ; yn dyspyt dh'y dâs ha'y vam, an woren a vŷdh ledhys,* for his power I would not give a puff ; in spite of his father and his mother, the jade shall be killed. O.M. 2730.
RENA, comp. pron. The people there. *(Ré—na.) Pandra yw a vynnouch wy ? En ré-na a worthebys, Ihesus yw a'n confluns ny,* what is that ye would ? Those answered, it is Jesus whom we would take. M.C. 67. *An ré-na a gîl dhe dhysky yn della y ré dhyscas,* those can teach thee as they have learned. M.C. 80. W. *rhai yna,*

RENCIA, v. a. To snore, to snort. *Dho renkia*, Llwyd, 17, 140. W. *rhwncian*. Arm. *rochal*. Ir. *roncam*. Lat. *rhoncisso*.

RENCIAS, s. m. A snoring, a snorting. Llwyd, 140. W. *rhwnc*. Arm. *roch*. Lat. *rhoncus*.

RENNIAT, s. m. A sharer, a carver. Corn. Voc. *discifer*. From *ranné*, to share.

RENOTHAS, interj. By my father, indeed. More correctly written *ren ow thâs*. *Yma un posygyon brâs war ow wholon ow codhé, pynag vové, ren ow thâs*, there is a great heaviness falling on my heart; whatever it may be, by my father. O.M. 528. *Lellé edhen, ren ow thâs, leverel ny wôn ple fe*, a more faithful bird, by my father, I cannot say where there is. O.M. 1111. *Mgl wel vyé renawthas, yn bys-ma genys na ve*, a thousand (times) better it would be, by my father, that he had never been born into this world. P.C. 751. *Me a'n te dhys, renothas*, I swear it to thee, by my father. P.C. 851. *Ty a grêk, renothas*, thou shalt be hanged, by my father. P.C. 1188.

REOL, s. f. A rule, rule, order. *Pryce*. Written also *rowl*, qd. v. W. *rheol*. Arm. *reol*. Ir. *riaghal*, †*riagul*, †*riagol*. Gael. *riaghladh*. Manx, *reill*. Lat. *regula*.

REONTE, s. m. Care. *Dhyworthé ma'gan bo grâs, aga mulyé ny a vyn gans mâr a reonté brâs yn cendel hag yn ourlyn*, from them that ours may be the grace, I will wrap them with very great care in fine linen and in silk. O.M. 1751. *Dyworto mu'm boma grâs, môs dhe blansé ny a vyn en gueel gans reonté vrâs yn nêp plath têk hag ylyn*, from him that mine may be the grace, I will go to plant the rods with great care in some fair and clean place. O.M. 2079. Perhaps *reouté*. Fr. *royauté*.

RES, s. m. Need, necessity. *Yn mês a'm ioy ha'm wheker rês ew keskar dre terros*, away from my joy and my delight there is necessity to wander through lands. O.M. 360. *Arluth cúf, dhe archadow y wruthyl rês yw dhymmo*, dear Lord, thy commands, need is to me to do them. O.M. 998. *Yn pûp teller dhym may fo rês, prest hep danger vedhaf parys*, in every place that there may be need for me, soon without delay I shall be ready. O.M. 1000. *Scrry orthyf ny rês dhys*, to be angry with me there is no need to thee. O.M. 2524. Written also *reys*, qd. v.

RES, v. a. I gave. 1 pers. s. pret. of *rei*. *Aban rês an brûs unweyth, ny fymnaf y ry dywoyth*, since I gave the judgment once, I will not give it twice. P.C. 2495. Written also *rgs*, qd. v.

RES, comp. pron. Has—them. *(Re—'s.) Golhy ow treys ny hyrwys; homma gans daggrow keffrys rês holhas*, to wash my feet thou offeredst not; this one with tears even has washed them. P.C. 520.

RES, comp. pron. May—yours; may—theirs. *(Re—'s.) A loreis, re's bo drôk lam, syttyouch dalhennow yn cam*, O rascals, may yours be an evil step! set hands on the rogue. P.C. 1125. *En Edhewon skyntyll kêth, re's leffo mûr vylyny, dhe veras worth Crist y êth, hag ef yn crous ow cregy*, the same learned Jews, may much harm come to them, to look on Christ they went, whilst he was hanging on the cross. M.C. 216.

RESEC, v. a. To run, to flow, to rush out, to slide away, to pass, to go. *Fenten bryght avel arhans, ha pedyr streyth vrâs defry, ow resek a dyworty*, a fountain bright as silver, and four springs large indeed, flowing from it. O.M. 773. *Guask gynsy dywyth an mên, hag y rês gover fenten mar therhyth dhodho hep ful*, strike thou with it twice the stone, and a brook, a fountain, will gush, if thou break it, without fail. O.M. 1845. *Marow yw an voron gans ow whaffys sol a breys, ha resys gois hy holon*, dead is the jade by my blows a long time past, and the blood of her heart has run out. O.M. 2748. *A'n golon ydh êth stret brâs, dour ha goys yn kemeskis, ha ryp an gyw a resus dhe dhewlé néb a'n gwyskis*, from the heart there went a great stream, water and blood mixed, and ran down by the spear to the hands of him that struck him. M.C. 219. *Resec* is a later form of *redec*, as preserved in *redegva*. W. *rhedeg*, †*redec*. Arm. *redec*. Ir. *rioth*, *rith*. Gael. *ruith*, †*roid*. Manx, *ratch*. Sansc. *ru*, *rôtum;* ri, *rotum*.

RESETH, v. a. He is gone. *Ow colon res-eth yn cláf, ow clewes dhe lavarow*, my heart is gone sick, hearing thy words. P.C. 1027. *Lavar dhymmo vy yn scon, ple res-eth dhe dhyskyblon, prâg na dhevons y yn chy*, tell me now immediately, where are gone thy disciples, why came they not into the house. P.C. 1246. *Reseth* is compounded of the verbal particle *re* with *s* added before a vowel, and *êth*, he went. Generally written *re-seth*. *Regeth* is a later form.

RESSYS, v. a. Thou gavest. 2 pers. s. pret. of *rei*. *Nêp ma'n ressys dhe wethé, dheworth henna govynné*, to whom thou gavest him to keep, ask for him from that one. O.M. 575. Written also *russys*, and *rysnys*, qd. v.

RESTYE, v. a. To thrust. *Ol ow ysyly yn ten, hag a wêl dhe lyes plu; yn golon dre'n tenewen, dhe restyé syn-gys ow gu*, all my limbs stretched, and in the sight of many a parish; in heart through the side I felt my spear thrust. R.D. 2586.

RETII, v. a. Thou wilt give. 2 pers. s. fut. of *rei*. *Aron whêk, pyth a cusyl a rêth dhym orth am wreysyl, a sôn an debel bobel*, sweet Aaron, what counsel wilt thou give me for my judgment, at the noise of the wicked people? O.M. 1814. Writen also *rcyth*, qd. v.

RETII, comp. pron. Hath—thee. *(Re—'th.) Myns ús omma cuntullys, pûr apert y re'th flamyas*, all that are here gathered, very openly they have blamed thee. M.C. 92. *Herodes re'th tenyrchys*, Herod hath greeted thee. M.C. 115. *Aberth an bêdh del re'th worsyn*, within the grave as we have put thee. R.D. 312.

RETII, comp. pron. May—thine. *(Re—'th.) Benneth an Tâs Dew re'th fo*, may the blessing of God the Father be thine. O.M. 2265. *A nêf uhel an Tâs mâr re'th ordené, ty ha'th wrêk, pan vy marow*, may the great Father of heaven ordain thee and thy wife, when you die, into his court. P.C. 685. *A vyl losel, re'th fo crôk*, O vile rogue, may hanging be thine. P.C. 2007.

REUCII, v. a. Give ye. 2 pers. pl. imp. of *rei*, qd. v. *Pûr ankensy gans dornow dhodho war an scovornow, reuch boxescow trewysy*, very painful with hands to him on the ears give ye sad blows. P.C. 1362.

REUCII, v. a. Do ye. An abbreviated form of *wreuch*, a mutation of *gwreuch*, 2 pers. pl. imp. of *gwrey*, qd. v. *Na reuch eva re*, do not ye drink too much. *Pryce*. ‡ *Na reuh a berna*, do not ye buy it. Llwyd, 244.

REV, s. f. A spade, a shovel. Llwyd, 79, 11. *Rêv tân*, a fire shovel. 18. W. *rhaw*. Ir. *ruamh*. Gael *ruamh*. Manx, *reuyr*, to dig.

REV, s. m. An oar. *Llwyd*, 138. A later form of *ruif*, qd. v.

REVADAR, s. m. A rower, an oarsman. *Llwyd*, 14, 138. A late form of *ruifadur*, qd. v.

REVE, interj. Wonderful! strange! *Rea revé*. Llwyd, 112, who also writes it *reva*, 249. W. *rhyvedh*.

REVEN, s. f. Rome, the city of Rome. *Pryce*. From the Lat. *romana*. W. *rhuvain*. Arm. *rom*. Ir. *romh*. Gael *roimh*. Manx, *raue*.

REVENUER, s. m. A Roman. *Pryce*. (*Reven—gour*.) W. *rhuveinivr*.

REW, s. m. Frost, ice. Corn. Voc. *reu*, gelu. *Defalebys ov pür vear, hag overdevys gans blew ; bewa ydhesaf pûb er yn lomder ha yender rew, nôs ha dýdh*, deformed I am very much, and overgrown with hair; I do live continually in heat and coldness of frost, night and day. C.W. 120. ‡ *Yein kuer, tarednow, ha golowas, er, reu, gwenz, ha elehé, ha kezer*, cold weather, thunder, and lightning, snow, frost, wind, and ice, and hail. *Pryce*. W. *rhew*, †*reu*, †*rogu*, †*rou*. Arm. *reô*, †*riou*. Ir. *reo*, †*reud*. Gael. *reo, reodh*. Manx, *rio*. Gr. κρύοs. Lat. *frigus*.

REW, s. m. A line, a row. *Fleches Ebbrow, dûn yn un rew scon hep lettyé erbyn Ihesu, ni'b yno guŷr Dew, ow tôs dhe'n drê*, children of Hebrews let us come in a row immediately without delaying, to meet Jesus, who is true God, coming to the town. P.C. 239. *Mar gwreuch orthaf colu, why a's bŷdh wosa hemma joies nêf yn un rew*, if ye will hearken to me, ye shall have hereafter the joys of heaven in one stretch. C.W. 156.

REW, comp. pron. Hath—my. (*Re—ow*.) *An emprour re'u danfonas a whylas yn pow gueras ; dhodho yma clevos brâs, ny gŷf medhek a'n saweya*, the emperor has sent me to seek help in the country; he has a great disease, he finds not a leech (that) can cure him. R.D. 1645.

REWLE, v. a. To rule, to order. Written also *rewlyé*. Part. *rewlys*. *Iovyn roy dhys bôs dên mâs ha lén rewlyé dhe wlascor*, may Jove grant to thee to be a good man, and just to rule thy kingdom. P.C. 1707. *Ena rewlys o an beys, ha lyes onon dhe wêl*, there the world was kept in order, and many a one to see. P.C. 2411. *Argyé na moy dhyn ny reys na kewsel na moy gerryow ; a'u rewlens ef un iustis, hag ol an comners an pow*, to argue more is not necessary to us, nor to speak more words; let the magistrate rule it, and the commoners of the country. P.C. 2469. Written later *rowlia*, qd. v. W. *rheoli*.

REYS, s. m. Need, necessity. *Pan vyn an Tâs yn della, reys yw y wruthyl porrys*, when the Father so wills it, very needful it is to do it. O.M. 649. *Dhe vâp Ysac a geryth, y offrymné reys yw theys, war venedh a dhysqurdhaf*, thy son Isaac, whom thou lovest, it is necessary for thee to offer him on a mountain that I will show. O.M. 1280. *Pendra reys dhynny dhe gûl*, what is necessary for us to do? P.C. 1354. *Kettel tersys an bara, awwonys Cryst a gara, mar dha del reys*, as thou brakest the bread, I knew Christ (whom) I love, so well as it behoveth. R.D. 1320. *Avos travyth nyns o reys môs dhe worré dhe'n mernes mâp Dew a'u nêf*, because of any thing there was not need to go to put to death the Son of God of heaven. R.D. 1252. *Reys o dhodho dysquedhas y dhewlé*, need there was to him to shew his hands. M.C. 157. W. *rhaid*, †*reit*.

Arm. *réd*, †*ret*. Ir. *riachdanach*, †*ret*, †*reit*, †*re*. Gael. †*riachdanas*.

REYS, v. a. He will run. *Dhe'n dour ganso ny a reys*, to the water with it we will run. R.D. 2181. Another form of *rês*, 3 pers. s. fut. of *resec*, qd. v.

REYS, part. Given. See *Rei*.

REYTH, v. a. Thou wilt give. 2 pers. s. fut. of *rey*, or *rei*, qd. v. *Guel ys ol tûs an blys-ma, del ôs dalleth a pûp tra, y reyth kusyl*, better than all the people of this world, as thou art the beginning of every thing, thou wilt give counsel. P.C. 472. *Ihesus a gewsys pûr dêk ; Iudas ow ry te a vyn dre dhe vay a reyth mar whêk, dhe nêb a'm tormont mar dhyn*, Jesus said very fairly; Judas, thou wilt give me, by the kiss (that) thou givest so sweetly, to those who will torment me so keenly. M.C. 66. Written also *réth*, qd. v.

RHAG, prep. For, before, from. *Llwyd*, 245. *Rhag danyn dhcuh*, to send to you. 242. Generally written *râg*, qd. v.

RHAGDAS, s. m. A forefather, an ancestor. Pl. *rhagdasow*. Llwyd, 84. Comp. of *rhag*, before, and *tâs* a father.

RHEDHIC, s. m. A radish. *Llwyd*, 136. See *Redic*.

RHEI, v. a. To give, to grant, to yield. *Llwyd*, 50, ‡ *Mi vedn rhei dhiu an gwella*, I will yield to you; lit. I will give you the best. The same idiom obtains in Welsh, *rhoi y goreu*. *Rhei* is generally written *rei* or *rey*, and *ry*, qd. v.

RHYN, s. m. What is pointed, a point of land, a cape, a promontory, a hill. Pl. *rhynyow*. It is preserved in the local name *Penrhyn*. (W. *penrhyn*.) The later form was *run*, qd. v. "*Rhyn* is now pronounced *reen*." Pryce. W. *rhyn*. Arm. *rûn, reûn*. Ir. †*rinn*, †*rún*, †*rind*. Gael. *roinn, riun*. Gr. ῥίν.

RHYNEN, s. f. A little hill, a hillock. *Llwyd*, 49, 172. Diminutive of *rhyn*.

RHYTTIA, v. a. To rub. *Llwyd*, 61. *Dho rhyttia'n dha*, to rub well. 118. W. *rhwtio*. Arm. *ruza, reûza*.

RID, s. m. A ford. Corn. Voc. *vadum*. W. *rhyd*, †*rit*. Arm. *rodo*, †*roton*.

RID, adj. Free, unconstrained. Corn. Voc. *benen rid, femina*, an unmarried woman. Written also *ruid*, qd. v. W. *rhŷdh*.

RIDAR, s. m. A riddle, a sieve. *Llwyd*, 52, *ridar a kasher*. "A sieve is still called *a casier*." Pryce.

RIDH, adj. Red. *Pryce*. See *Rudh*.

RIDHVELYN, adj. A deep yellow, tawny. *Llwyd*, 62. Comp. of *ridh*, red, and *melyn*, yellow. W. *rhydhvelyn*.

RIG, v. a. He did. An abbreviated form of *grûc*, 3 pers. s. pret. of *gwrey*. Generally used as an auxiliary. *Mi rig dós*, I came. *Llwyd*, 171. *Mi rig gwelas*, I saw. 245. *Ty rig gotta worty*, thou didst hearken to her. 242. *Ha Sperys Dew rig gwayath war bedgeth an dowrow*, and the Spirit of God did move on the face of the waters. C.W. p. 180. It was shortened again into *ry*, (qd. v.,) and in the Ordinalia *re* is the form generally used. *Oruc* was similarly used in Welsh.

RINC, s. f. A quail. Corn. Voc. *coturnis*. W. *rhinc*.

RINE, s. m. The channel of a river. *Pryce*. Written also *ryne*.

RISC, s. m. The bark, or rind of a tree. *Llwyd*, 32, 51. *E risk*, its bark. 244. Written also *rusc*, qd. v. W. *rhisg*.

RITAN, s. f. The weasand or windpipe. *Llwyd*, 165.
RIW, s, m. Sort, kind, sex. *Gurriw*, male kind. *Benenriw*, female kind. *Pryce*. *Neb riu guerrus vel guerras véth*, some sort of help than no help at all. *Ibid*. W. *rhyw*, †*riu*.
RO, s. m. A gift, a present. Pl. *roow, rohow*. *Dewdhec legyon yn un ro vyé a'n néf danvenys*, twelve legions in a gift would be sent from heaven. M.C. 72. *A wovynnys corf Ihesus worto yn ro*, and begged the body of Jesus from him as a gift. M.C. 215. *Rág henna Pylat a rós dhe'n worogyon uga ro*, therefore Pilate gave to the soldiers their gift. M.C. 250. *Dhe dheank yn della a'n paynys o créff ha brás, ha cufos rohow mar dha*, to escape thus from the pains (that) were strong and great, and get gifts so good. M.C. 251. *Rág dhe roow prest yw da*, for thy gifts are always good. O.M. 2314. *Ow ry dhym ro a'n pár-na*, giving me a gift of that sort. O.M. 2316. W. *rhodh, rho*. Arm. *ró*.
RO, v. a. Give thou. 2 pers. s. imp. of *rei*, or *ry*. *Ro dhedhé aga hynwyn*, give to them their names. O.M. 120. *Ro dhym dhe vanneth perfyth*, give me thy perfect blessing. O.M. 452. *Ro nerth dhe gerdhes yn fás*, give thou strength to walk well. O.M. 2010. *Ro dhym cusyl avel dén*, give me advice like a man. O.M. 2672. W. *rho*. Arm. *ró*.
ROATH, s. m. Form, figure. *Ha 'thera an noar heb roath, ha gwág*, and the earth was without form, and void. C.W. p. 189. W. *rhith*. Arm. *reiz*. Ir. *rochd, croth, †cruth*. Gael. *riochd*.
ROF, v. a. I will give. 1 pers. s. fut. of *rei*, or *ry*. *Y róf hynwyn dhe puskes*, I will give names to the fishes. O.M. 135. *Ha'm grath a róf dhys*, and my grace I will give thee. O.M. 1463. *Róf dhys ow thour*, I will give thee my palace. O.M. 2110. *A'y gyfyans me ny róf bram*, for his forgiveness I will not give the least value. P.C. 2779. W. *rhôw*.
ROLLO, v. a. He should give. 3 pers. s. subj. of *rei*, or *ry*. *An gusyl o may fe dris dhe rág Crist pehadures, ol dhi'y vódh may rollo brés*, the counsel was that a female sinner should be brought before Christ, that he might give judgment upon her all according to his will. M.C. 32. *My a vfidh an kynsa bom a rollo*, I will be the first that will give a blow. O.M. 2163. *Me a's gufsk yans un bloyon, vylhqueth na ve bom a won a rollo whaf mar gales, del y's brewaf yn dan gén*, I will strike her with a bludgeon, so that never was a stroke I know (that) will give a blow so hard, as I will strike her under the chin. O.M. 2711. Written also *rollé*. *I éth ha Ihesus gansé, bfis yn Pylat o Iustis, anotho brés may rollé, dre y vrés may fo ledhys*, they went and Jesus with them, even to Pilate (who) was Justice, that he might give judgment on him, by his judgment that he might be slain. M.C. 98.
ROLLONS, v. a. They should give. 3 pers. pl. subj. of *rei*, or *ry*. *An lór yn nós, houl yn geydh, may rollons y golow splan*, the moon in night, sun in day, that they may give their bright light. O.M. 40.
ROM, comp. pron. By my. *Huhel ydhos ysedhys, ha dyantel, rom lauté*, high thou art seated, and dangerously, by my truth. P.C. 94. Another form of *rum*, qd. v.
ROM, comp. pron. Hath—my. *Lemmyn devé ken termyn; ow thás rom growntyas dhe wy*, but another time

has come; my Father has granted me to you. M.C. 75. More generally written *rum*, qd. v.
ROM, comp. pron. May—mine. *(Re--'m.) Crog rom bo, cr an dhewen, neffré mars éth ahanan, crna'n prenny yn felen ha nacha ol dhe gows gulán*, may a hanging be mine, on the gills, if ever thou shalt go from us, until thou shalt pay for it cruelly, and clean recant all thy talk. O.M. 2051. So also *ram* in Armoric. †*Doe ram pardono*, may God pardon me. (*Buhez Nonn*, 44, 4.)
ROOZ, adj. Red. ‡*Pedn rooz*, a red head. *Pryce*. A late form of *rúdh*, qd. v.
ROS, s. f. A moor, a mountain meadow, peatland, a common. *Llwyd*, 32, *rós*. It is preserved in the names of many places in Cornwall, as *Penrose, Trerose, Roswarne, &c*. It is very commonly used thus also in Wales. W. *rhós*. Arm. *ros*. Gael. *ros*.
ROS, s. f. A circle, a wheel. *Llwyd*, 32, 141, 241. *Gravar rós*, a wheelbarrow. 170. W. *rhôd*. Arm. *ród*. Ir. *rhatha, †roth*. Gael. *roth, †raith*. Lat. *rota*. Lith. *ratas*. O.H.G. *rad*. Sansc. *rathyan*.
ROS, s. f. A net. *Awos ol ow gallos, byth ny allaf yn ow rós dhe wúl péch vfith y cachyé*, notwithstanding all my power, I shall never be able in my net to catch him to do sin. P.C. 54. A later form of *ruid*, qd. v.
ROS, v. a. He gave. 3 pers. s. pret. of *rey*, or *ry*. *Rág néb a'n grúk ny a bry a rós dhyn defennadow*, for he who made us of clay gave us prohibitions. O.M. 238. *Dhymmo vy why a rós gwrék*, to me you gave a wife. O.M. 265. *Dh'agas prenné me a rós gós ow holon*, to purchase you I gave the blood of my heart. R.D. 165. *Un gusyl da ha perfeyth dhym ty a rós*, a counsel good and perfect to me thou gavest. R.D. 2143. W. *rhoes*.
ROSONS, v. a. They gave. 3 pers. pl. pret. of *rei*, or *ry*. *Wogé ow da oberow, dywes a yrhys dedhé; dhym rosons byslyl wherow, byth ny fynnys y evé*, after my good works I asked them for drink; they gave me bitter gall, I would never drink it. R.D. 2601. W. *rhoisout*.
ROSTIA, v. a. To roast, to toast. Part. *rostias*. *Llwyd*, 165. ‡*Ma'n dzhyi a rostia ha prydzhan*, they are roasting and boiling. 248. W. *rhostio*. Arm. *rosta*. Ir. *rosta*. Gael. *roist*. Germ. *rüsten*. Fr. *rôtir, †rostir*.
ROWETH, s. m. Bounty, liberality. *Ow otté un purvers da lemyn wharfedhys; awos ol rowcith Adam, bfis dhyn umma yn un lum ef a vfidh kyrhys*, behold a good purchase, now obtained; notwithstanding all the bounty of Adam, to us in a trice he shall be brought. O.M. 884. From *ro*, a gift.
ROWL, s. m. A rule, rule, government. *Ena me a dhék an rowl*, there I shall bear the rule. C.W. 32. *Changys yw an rowl lemyn, ellas, orth an prff cola*, the rule is now changed, alas, by hearkening to the reptile. C.W. 78. *Néb yma a'n dhrwollow a dhéth més an néf golow genef ve, ow tón rowl vrás*, some there are of the devils (that) came out of bright heaven with me, bearing great rule. C.W. 146. Another form of *reol*, qd. v.
ROWLER, s. m. A ruler, a governor. *Mar gwréth henna, honorys ty a vfidh bfis venary, ha pen rowler warnan ny*, if thou wilt do that, honoured thou shalt be for ever, and chief ruler over us. C.W. 38. *Henna Pylat pan welas kymmys cowsys er y byn, rowlors ha tús ryche yn wlds, resons mar fól, ha mar dyn*, when Pilate saw that, that so many spoke against him, rulers and rich people in the country, reasons so foolish and so sharp. M.C.

100. W. *rheolwr.* Ir. *riaghalloir, riaghlaighthcoir.* Gael. *riaghlair, riaghladair.*

ROWLIA, v. a. To rule, to direct. *Llwyd,* 138, *dho rowlia. Yn êr-na, re sent deffry, ydh halsan rowlya pûr gay,* then, by the saints truly, I could rule very gaily. C.W. 46. *Me a vyn dhe why poyntya service dha dég hay geta rûg rowlya rys ha chattel,* I will to you appoint a service to bear, and to thee to rule the corn and cattle. C.W. 78. *Ha Dew gurás dew golow brâs, an brassa golow dhe rowlia dýdh, ha an behanna golow dhe rowlia an nós,* and God created two great lights, the greater light to rule the day, and the lesser light to rule the night. C.W. p. 190. *Kyn na wôr hy cowss banna, me a's rowl hy del vanaf,* since she knows not to speak a jot, I will rule her as I will. C.W. 38. *Gorta, ha bŷdh dhym rowlys,* stop thou, and be by me ruled. C.W. 40. W. *rheoli.* Arm. *reolia.*

ROUNSAN, s. f. An ass. ‡ *Na ra chee gawas whans warlyrch chy de contrevak, na ras gawas whans warlyrch gwrêg de contrevnk, na e dên whêl, na e môs whel, na e udzheou, na e rounsan, na traveth an pew ef,* thou shalt not covet the house of thy neighbour, nor his manservant, nor his maidservant, nor his ox, nor his ass, uor any thing that is his. *Pryce.* Goon *rounsan,* the ass's down, in St. Enoder. *Ibid.*

ROWMANN, adv. Lay os aside or down. *Pryce.* (*Ro—aman.*)

ROY, v. a. May he give. 3 pers. s. opt. of *rei,* or *ry.* qd. v. *Seth a vŷdh y ewn hanow, a'n Tâs a'n nêf caradow roy dhodho grath dh'y servyé,* Seth shall be his just name, may the Father of heaven beloved give to him grace to serve him. O.M. 680. *Iovyn roy dhys bôs dên más,* may Jove grant thee to be a good man. P.C. 1706. *Iovyn roy dheuch mûr onour warbarth ol kyng-ys merwel,* may Jove give to you great honour all together before ye die. P.C. 1712.

ROYS, part. Given. *Ha gevys may fe dhodho kyffrys y bêch hay fyllyé degis na ve dheworto gulás néf, ha roys dhe gen ré,* and that might be forgiven to him as well his sin and his filth, that the kingdom of heaven might not be taken from him, and given to others. M.C. 23. Another form of *roys,* qd. v.

ROZELLEN, s. f. A whirl for a spindle. *Llwyd,* 172. W. *rhodellen.*

RU, s. f. A street, or paved way. Written also *rew.* Pryce. "Truru, now *Truro,* three streets." Arm. *rû.* Fr. *rue.*

RUAN, s. f. A river. *Polruan,* the pool of the river, in Lanteglos juxta Fowey. *Pryce.*

RUDDOC, s. m. A roblu redbreast. *Pryce.* W. *rhudhog,* from *rhûdh,* red.

RUDH, adj. Red, crimson. Corn. Voc. *rud, ruber. Ot omma gynef hep fâl gwêth rûdh, purpur pal, dhe wyské adro dhodho,* behold here with me, without fail, red cloth, a purple pall, to clothe around him. P.C. 2128. *Pyw henna gans deusys más re dhueth mar uskys dhe'n wlás, guyskys yn rûdh,* who is that with Godhend good, (that) hath come so swiftly to the country, clothed in red? R.D. 2489. *Pyw a ylta gy bones, pan yw mar rûdh dhe dhyllas yn gulascor néf,* who canst thou be, when is thy clothing so red in the kingdom of heaven? R.D. 2512. W. *rhûdh,* †*rud.* Arm. *ruz.* Ir. *ruadh.* Gael. *ruath.* Gr. ἐρευθος. Lat. *rutilus.* Goth. *rodun* Germ. *roth.* Fr. *rouge.* Scotch, *roy.* Eng. *red.* Sanso. *rohida.*

RUG, v. a. He made or did. An abbreviated form of *wrûg,* 3 pers. s. pret. of *gwrey.* Written indiscriminately *rûc.* Often used as an auxiliary verb. *Yn mêdh Crista bnn rûg dheuch ow holyé, daver vŷth vy ny dhecsyuch dhe worré trewyth ynné,* says Christ, since I made you follow me, ye carried no conveniences to put any thing in them. M.C. 50. *Orth Pylat ol y setsans, ha warnodho a rûg cry,* on Pilate they all set, and to him cried. M.C. 117. *An grows y a rûg gorré war scôdh Ihesus dh'y dôn dhy,* the cross they did put on the shoulders of Jesus to carry it thither. M.C. 162. *Néb a'm grûk vy ha'm gorty, ef a rûk agan dyfen aval na wrellen dybbry,* he that made me and my husband, he did forbid us that we should not eat the apple. O-M. 182. *An sarf re rûk ow thollé, dh'y falsury y cresys, pythwcth re rûg ow syndyé,* the serpent hath deceived me; her falsehood I believed, ever she hath hurt me. O.M. 286. *Ellas gweles an termyn, ow arluth pan wrûk serry, pan rûk drys y worhemmyn, ow eriech grûk dhe gylly,* alas to see the time, when I did anger my Lord, when I acted against his command, I lost my heritage. O.M. 363. *Ellas vŷth pan rûk colé mor hogul worth ow eskar,* alas ever when I hearkened so readily to my enemy. O.M. 627. *Oruc,* or *orug,* was similarly used in Welsh.

RUID, s. f. A net. Corn. Vocab. *rethe.* The later form was *rôs,* qd. v., and it was finally corrupted into *ruz,* plur. *ruzow. Pryce.* W. *rhwyd.* Arm. *roued,* †*roed.* Lat. *rete.*

RUID, adj. Free, unmarried. *Gur ruid,* mas vel masculum, a male; lit. a free man. Written also *rid,* qd. v. W. *rhŷdh, rhwydh.* Arm. *rouez.* Ir. *reidh,* †*reid.* Gael. *reidh.* Manx, *rea.*

RUIF, s. m. What impels or directs, au oar, a ruler, a king. Corn. Voc. *remus.* It had both meanings in Cornish as in Welsh. *Gurhemin-ruif,* edictum, a king's decree. Corn. Voc. The latest form was *rév,* qd. v. W. *rhwyr.* Arm. *roev, ref.* Ir. *ramh,* †*ram.* Gael. *ramh.* Lat. *remus.*

RUIFADUR, s. m. A rower, an oarsman. Corn. Voc. *remex* vel *nauta. Llwyd,* 138, *ruivadur.* Comp. of *ruivad,* a rowing, from *ruif,* an oar, and *gour,* a mau. W. *rhwyvadur, rhwyvwr.* The latest form was *rcvadar,* qd. v. Arm. *roevier, roevier, rouanow, rouanvour.* Ir. *ramhadoir, ramhaire.* Gael. *ramhair.*

RUIFANAID, s. m. A kingdom. Corn. Voc. *regnum. Guailen ruifanaid,* sceptrum, a sceptre; lit. the rod of a kingdom. *Ibid.* Road by Llwyd, 133, 145, *ruyvanedh. O pa an ruivanedh,* of what country. 53. W. *rhwyvaniad, rhwyvaniaeth.*

RUIFANES, s. f. A female ruler, a queen. Corn. Voc. *regina. Llwyd,* 138, *ruivanes.* W. *rhwyvanes.* Arm. *ruanes.*

RUM, comp. pron. May—me. (*Re—m.*) *An Tâs a wrûk ow formyé, a'm offryn re woffé grás; ha pan wryllyf tremené a'n bŷs, rum gorré dh'y wlâs,* the Father (that) did form me, to my offering may he acknowledge favour; and when I shall pass away from the world, may he bring me to his country. O.M. 532. Written also *rom,* qd. v.

RUM, comp. pron. He hath—me. (*Re—'m.*) *Ty rum*

grük pûr havel dhys, thou hast made me very like to thee. O.M. 83. *Fest yn tyn ef rum sorras,* very grievously he hath provoked me. O.M. 424. *Ha'm pen ol hy rum uras,* and all my head she has anointed. P.C. 526. *Onan ahanouch haneth rum gwerthas dhom yskerens,* one of you this night has sold me to my enemies. P.C. 737. Though now obsolete this idiom was formerly common in Welsh. *Rhym (rym, rum,) gorug yn vedhw vêdh Tren,* the mead of Tren made me drunk. *Llywarch Hên.* 90. *Llam rym daearawd,* the step that was decreed to me. *Llam rym gallas,* the step that befel me. *Ibid. Rhodri mawr, rhwym llawr, rym lloves,* great Rodri, the ground binds him, who extended bounty to me. *Il. Prydydh Môch.*

RUM, comp. pron. By my. (*Re—'m.*) *Rum fey,* by my faith. O.M. 473. *Ty re'n ladhas, rum lowté,* thou hast killed him, by my faith. O.M. 611. *Mara pedhaf bew vledhen, my a'n taluyth dhyuch, rum pen, pypenagol a sconyo,* if I shall be alive a year, I will pay it to you, by my head, whoever may object. O.M. 2387. Written also *rom.* Gael. *rium.*

RUN, s. m. A hill. Plur. *runyow. Yn úr-na whreuch pyjadow may codhdho an mynydhyow warnouch rág ewn uthekter, ha why a pýs an runyow dh'agas gorhery, hep gow, kymmys vŷdh an ponvoter,* in that hour ye shall make prayers, that the mountains may fall upon you, for very horror ; and ye shall pray the hills to hide you, without a lie, so great will be the trouble. P.C. 2654. Another form of *rhyn,* qd. v.

RUNEN, s. f. A little hill, a hillock. Corn. Voc. *collis.* Diminutive of *rún.* Written by Llwyd, *rhynen,* qd. v.

RUSC, s. m. The bark, or rind of a tree. Corn. Vocab. *cortex.* Written by Llwyd, *risc,* qd. v. W. *rhisg,* †*risc.* Arm. *rusc.* Ir. *rusg,* †*rúsc.* Gael. *rúsg.* Manx, *roost.*

RUSCEN, s. f. The bark, or rind of a tree. *Warnedhy yma gwedhen, uhel gans lues scoren, saw nôth ol ŷns, hep dylyow ; hag adro dhedhy rusken nyns esé a'n blŷn dhe'n bèn, nôth yw ol hy scorennow,* in it there is a tree, high with many a bough, but they are all bare, without leaves ; and about it bark there was none from the point to the stem ; all its boughs are bare. O.M. 778. W. *rhisgen.* Arm. *rusken.*

RUSSE, v. a. He would do. An abbreviated form of *wrussé,* a mutation of *gwrussé,* 3 pers. s. subj. of *gwrey. Ewn prág na dhueté nês ráy cous orthyf*? *un dra a won, a'n gothfes,* a *russé dhe dhydhané,* Eve, why wilt thou not come nearer to speak to me ? one thing I know, if thou knewest it, (that) would amuse thee. O.M. 152.

RUSSONS, v. a. They made or did. *Hag a dhychow lader brâs cregy a russons yn wêdh,* and on the right a great thief they did hang also. M.C. 186. An abbreviated form of *wrussons,* a mutation of *gwrussons,* 3 pers. pl. pret. of *gwrey.*

RUSSYS, v. a. Thou didst, or hast done. An abbreviated form of *wrussys,* a mutation of *gwrussys,* 2 pers. s. pret. of *gwrey. Venytha gordhyys re by, del russys moy a'n govys, worth ow formyé, haval dhys,* for ever be thou worshipped, as thou hast done much of regard, by creating me like to thee. O.M. 108. *Lavar dhymmo, ty venen, an frût ple russys tyrry,* tell me, thou woman, where didst thou pluck the fruit ? O.M. 210. *Ty re gam wrûk credy, ha re'n drós dhe vûr anken, pan russys dhodho dybry ha tastyé frût an wedhen,* thou hast done evil verily, and hast brought him to much sorrow, when thou madest him to eat and taste the fruit of the tree. O.M. 283.

RUTE, s. m. The herb rue. Corn. Voc. *ruta.* From the Latin. Written by Llwyd, 142, *ryte.* W. †*ryt.* Arm. *rû.* Ir. *ruith, raith.*

RUTH, s. f. A multitude, a crowd. *Rág henna y tanvonas Crist dhodho ef may'n dampné ; ruth veyr a dûs a'n sewyas, pûb cyr paris dh'y vlamyé,* therefore he sent Christ to him that he might condemn him ; a great crowd of people followed him, always ready to accuse him. M.C. 108.

RUTH, comp. pron. Hath—thee. (*Re—'th.*) *Ow holon gêr caradow, Dew ruth rôs flour hy hynsé,* my dear beloved heart, God hath made thee the flower of her sex. O.M. 2136.

RUY, s. m. A king, a sovereign ruler. Corn. Voc. *rex.* An abbreviated form of *ruif.* W. *rhwŷv, rhi,* †*rig.* Arm. *roue,* †*roen.* Irish, *righ, ri,* †*rig.* Gael. *righ.* Manx, *ree.* Lat. *rex, rege.* Goth. *reiks.* Sansc. *raj.* Fr. *roi.*

RUYDH, adj. Red, crimson. *Dûn alemma dhe'n môr ruydh, tûs, venenes, ha flehys,* let us come hence to the Red Sea, men, women, and children. O.M. 1622. *Byry yw dheuch fystyné kyns ys y dhe tremené an môr ruydh,* diligently you must hasten, before that they pass the Red Sea. O.M. 1635. Another form of *rûdh,* qd. v.

RUZ, s. f. A net. *Llwyd,* 28, 140. *Scath rûz,* a fishing boat, lit. a net boat. 53. Pl. *ruzow.* A late form of *rôs,* qd. v.

RY, v. a. To give, to grant, to present, to bestow. *Ry hanow dhedhy hy gwra,* do thou give her a name. O.M. 103. *Cortes ûs drys tûs an bŷs, ow ry dhym ro a'n parma,* courteous thou art above all the people of the world, giving me a gift of this sort. O.M. 2316. *Rŷs yw dhyso dyogel ry dour dhynny dhe evé,* need is to thee certainly to give to us water to drink. O.M. 1801. *Hedhouch cercot a baly ; dhodho me a ryn y ry,* reach ye a surcoat of satin ; to him I will give it. P.C. 1785. *Aban rês an brûs unwyth, ny fynnaf y ry dywyth,* since I gave the judgment once, I will not give it twice. P.C. 2496. *Desyfsen dodho ry what,* we wished to give him a blow. R.D. 604. The infinitive is written also *rey,* or *rei,* qd. v., part. *reys.* For the different tenses see the Grammar.

RY, a particle used before verbs of various tenses. *Llwyd,* 238. ‡ *My a adzhan,* I know. *Me ry gollas,* I have lost ; *me ry goscus,* I have slept. 231. It is a later form of *re,* qd. v. W. †*ry.*

RYAL, adj. Royal, kingly. *Y a vŷdh ryal ha splan, cannasow dhem danvenys, rág ow servia bŷs viccan me a vyn may fôns nevra,* they shall be royal and resplendent, messengers to me sent, for serving me, the world's sovereign, I will that they ever be. C.W. 4. Written also *real,* qd..v. W. *rhiawl.* Arm. *real.* Ir. *rioghamhail.* Gael. *rioghail.* Manx, *recoil.* Lat. *regalis.* Fr. *royal.*

RYB, prep. Beside, by the side of, by, near, nigh to. Written also *ryp. Gans henna a'n Edhewon onan yn ban a sevys, hag a rôs ryb an scovern box dhe Grist a dhesympys,* with that one of the Jews rose up, and straightway gave Christ a buffet beside the ear. M.C. 81. *Ryp crows Jhesus ydh esé un dén hencys Sentury,* beside the cross of Jesus there was a man named Sentury. M.C. 208. *A'n golon ydh êth stret brâs, dour ha goys yn kemeskis, ha ryp·an gyw a resas dhe dhewlé nêb a'n greyskis*, from the heart there went a great stream, water and blood mixed, and ran down by the spear to the hands of him (that) struck him. M.C. 219. *Lader óf a fue iuggys, ha ryp Ihesu Cryst gorrys yn crous a pren*, I am a thief (that) was judged, and placed beside Jesus Christ on a cross of wood. R.D. 266. *Guythens pûp y tencwen, ha me a gósk ryp y pen rág y wythé*, let every one guard his side, and I will sleep by his head to guard him. R.D. 418. This word is peculiar to Cornish, and probably an adaptation of the Lat. *ripa*.

RYBON, pron. prep. Beside us. (*Ryb—ny*.) *Rág yma bós parusys dhyso, ha dhedhé kefrys, yn plás ús omma rybon*, for there is food prepared for thee, and for them likewise, in a place that is here beside us. P.C. 460. Written by Llwyd, 244, *rybbon*.

RYD, s. m. A ford. *Llwyd*, 169. See *Rid*.

RYDII, adj. Red, ruddy, crimson. *Llwyd*, 91, 141. *Reden rydh*, red fern. 299. See *Rûdh*.

RYDHIC, adj. Reddish. *Llwyd*, 13. W. *rhudhog, rhudh-yg*.

RYG, v. a. He made or did. *E ryg hedhas rág*, he stretched forth. *Llwyd*, 250. More generally written *rúg*, qd. v.

RYGO, v. a. Ye will do. A corrupted form of *wrugouch*. a mutation of *gwrugouch*, 2 pers. pl. fut. of *gwrugé*. ‡ *Po rygo hwei môs*, when you go. *Llwyd*. 253.

RYGTHE, v. a. To command. *Llwyd*, 73.

RYGTHY, pron. prep. For or before her. (*Rág—hy*.) *Ha'n grous a ve drehevys, ha Ihesus fasteys ynny, ha'n pen golas delyffrys yn tol o tellys rygthy*, and the cross was lifted, and Jesus fastened on it, and the lower end delivered into a hole that was bored for it. M.C. 184. See also *Derygthy*, W. *rhagdhi*, †*racdi*. Ir. *roimpe, roimpi*, †*reimpe*. Gael. *rithe*.

RYNA, pron. s. The people there, those. *Dha ran a'n rŷna ef a vynsa disklosya an destruction brâs ha'n lyw*, to some of them he would disclose the great destruction and the flood. C.W. 170. ‡ *Ha rynêy vedn dirra bedn moar ha gwenz*, and those will last against sea and wind. Pryce. Another form of *rê-na*, qd. v. W. *rhai yna*, and colloquially *rheiny*.

RYNE, s. f. The channel of a river. Id. qd. *ruan*. Pryce.

RYNNA, v. a. To grin. *Dho rynna*. Pryce.

RYNNY, s. m. A shivering, horror. *Pocvan púp úr ha rynny, skrymba brâs a'n dewolow ef a'u gevyth genen ny, a púp drôk maner ponow*, sickness always and horror, great outcry of devils, he shall have with us, pains of all evil sorts. R.D. 2343. W. *rhynnu*.

RYNNYS, part. Shared, divided. *Dyllas Crist a ve rynnys, pedar ran guris anedhé gans pedwar marreg a ûrfys, dhe bâb marreg ran may 'sé*, the clothes of Christ were divided, four parts made of them by four soldiers of worth, to every soldier that there was a portion. M.C. 190. Part. pass. of *ranné*, qd. v.

RYS, s. m. Need, necessity. *Rŷs yw dhym porrys coské*, need is to me greatly to sleep. O.M. 1905. *Rŷs yw gruthyl dyogel vôdh agan arluth sefryn*, it is necessary to do certainly the will of our sovereign lord. O.M. 2188. *Rŷs yw dheuch gynen lafuryé*, need is to you to labour with us. P.C. 1829. *Rŷs yw porrys dhe onon merwel rág pobyl an wlâs*, it is needful, right needful for one to die for the people of the country. M.C. 80. A contracted form of *rrys*, qd. v.

RYS, v. a. I gave. 1 pers. s. pret. of *rei*, or *ry*. *Omma ny wreuch why trygé, euch yn mês a dhynympys; why a geyl ow lowené a rŷs dhyuch yn parathys*, here ye shall not dwell, go out immediately; ye will lose the joy (that) I gave you in Paradise. O.M. 320. Written also *rés*, qd. v. W. *rhois*.

RYSSYS, v. a. Thou gavest. 2 pers. s. pret. of *rei*, or *ry*. *Bythqueth bay dhym ny ryssys, ha homma vŷth ny sestyas, aban duthé yn chy dhys, pûp úr ol ammé dhum treys*, never a kiss thou gavest me, and this one has never ceased, since I came into thy house, continually to kiss my feet. P.C. 522.

RYTII, adj. Woeful, sorrowful. *A vynyn ryth, py le ydh êth? râk kucth pygyth, garmé a wrêth*, O woeful woman, whither goest thou? for grief thou prayest, cry out thou dost. R.D. 851. *A vynyn ryth, na tuche ve nês; na na wra gruyth na fo dhe lês*, O woeful woman, touch me not nearer; nor do a service that may not be for advantage. R.D. 875. See also *Wryth*, sorrow.

RYTII, comp. pron. May—thine. (*Re—'th*.) *Ow banneth prest ty a fŷdh, kefrys yn nôs hag yn geydh, ha mŷns ús yn beys ryth fo*, my blessing thou shalt ever have, equally by night and by day, and all (that) is in the world may it be thine. O.M. 459. Written also *reth*, qd. v.

RYTH, adj. Open, plain, flourishing. Whence *Goonreeth*, the open downs, in Gluvias. Pryce. W. *rhŷdh*.

S.

THIS letter in Cornish and Welsh is an immutable radical. In Armoric it is mutable, changing in construction into *z*, as *seched*, thirst, *ar zeched*, the thirst. In Irish and Gaelic it is also mutable, changing into *sh*, which is pronounced as *h*, and into *t*. Thus *sliochi*, issue; *a shliocht*, his issue; *ar tliocht*, our issue. The same mutation occurs also in Manx, as *sooill vie*, a good eye; *e hooill*, his eye; *y tooill*, the eye.

SA, v. a. Stand thou. *Sa ban, Noe, ow servont kêr*, stand up, Noah, my dear servant. O.M. 933. An abbreviated form of *sáf*, qd. v.

SABAN, s. f. A fir tree, a pine. Written *zaban*, by Llwyd, 33. *Aval zaban*, the cone of a pine. 51. *Plankys zaban*, deal boards. 242. From the Lat. *sapinus*. Fr. *sapin*. The oldest term was *sibuit*, qd. v. Called in Welsh, *fynnidwydh*.

SACRA, v. a. To consecrate. *My a vyn lemyn ordné mâb-lyen, ow sêl pryvé, dhe vôs epscob yn temple; an laha dhe venteyné, servys dhe Dew dhe gané, y sacra scon my a wra*, I will now ordain a priest, my privy soul, to be bishop in the temple; the law to maintain, service to God to sing, I will consecrate him forthwith. O.M. 2604. *Yrverys eu, rum lewté sol-a-dhydh dhe avonsyé an kynsé benfys a'm been; dhe epscop gurâf dhe sacré; kymmer dhe vytour wharé, ha bŷdh yn dhe servys lên*, it is thought of, by my truth, for a long time, to advance thee to the first benefice I may have; to a bishop I will consecrate thee; take thy mitre forthwith, and be faithful in thy service. O.M. 2614. W. *segru.* Lat. *sacro.*

SACH, s. m. A sack, a bag. Corn. Voc. *sach diawol,* demoniacus one possessed with the devil. (W. *sâch diawl.*) In late Cornish softened into *zâh,* Llwyd, 30. W. *sâch.* Arm. *sach.* Ir. *sacc.* Gael. *sac.* Manx, *sack.* Gr. σάκκος. Lat. *saccus.*

SADARN, s. m. Saturn. *De Sadarn,* Saturday. *Ll.* 64. W. *sadwrn, dŷdh sadwrn.* Arm. *disadorn.* Ir. *dia sathuirn.* Gael. *di sathuirne.* Manx, *jesarn.* All from the Lat. *dies saturni.*

SAF, v. a. Stand thou. 2 pers. s. imp. of *sevel,* qd. v. *Adam, sâf yn ban yn clôr, ha treyl dhe gîk ha dhe woys,* Adam, stand up clearly, and turn to flesh and to blood. O.M. 65. *Ke growedh war an dôr gulân, ha côsk, bŷth na sâf yn ban, crna fo cowethes gwrês,* go thou, lie down on the earth clean, and sleep, nor ever stand up, until a helpmate be made. O.M. 97. *Moyses, sâf cna, na nês, na dhûs na fella, râg ny vynnaf,* Moses, stand there, not nearer, and come no further, for I will not. O.M. 1403. The final was softened into *v* in later times. *Sâv yn ban yn cloer,* stand up in clearly. C.W. 28. W. *sâv,* +*sâf.* Arm. *sab.*

SAF, s. m. A stand, a standing, a stem. *Pûp gwedhen tefyns a'y sâf, ow lôn hy frût hn'y delyow,* let every tree grow from its stem, bearing its fruit and its leaves. O.M. 29. *A dâs whêk ol caradow, ou dywluef colm ha'm garrow, gans louan fast colmennow, na allan sevel am sâf,* O sweet father, all beloved, tie my hands and my legs with a rope, fast knots, that I may not be able to stand on my standing. O.M. 1348. *Râk hyreth galsof pûr clâf, ny allaf syvel a'm sâf,* from regret I am become ill, I am not able to stand on my standing. R D. 776. W. *sâf.* Arm. *sab, sav.*

SAFE, v. a. He had stood. 3 pers. s. plup. of *sevel,* qd. v. *E'n deskyens del vyê, ha dhodho a leverys re saffê Crist heb streoyê ol dh'y vôdh gans golowys,* they taught him how it was, and said that Christ had risen incontestably, all to his will with lights. M.C. 248. *Tokyn dhyuch murny dhysevê; kyn fe dyserŷs an temple dhe'n dôr na safê mân, me a'n dreha artê kyns pen trydydh, rum lautê, tekê ages kyns y van,* a token to you indeed I will shew; if the temple be destroyed to the ground, that a stone should not stand, I will build it again before the end of three days, by my truth, fairer than it was up before. P.C. 345.

SAIR, s. m. An artificer, a wright, an artisan. Corn. Vocab. *sair-pren,* lignarius, a carpenter or woodman. (W. *saer pren, prensner.*) W. *saer.* Ir. *saor,* +*sacr.* Gael. *saor.* Manx, *seyir.* Lat. *faber.*

SAITHOR, s. m. A diver, a cormorant. Corn. Vocab. *mergus* vel *mergulus.* The literal meaning is *a shooter,* from its rapid diving. (W. *saethwr.*) The root is *saith,* id. qd. *sêth,* an arrow.

SAL, adj. Salted, salt. Written by Llwyd, *zâl.* 13. *Pêsk zal,* salt fish. 143. W. *hallt.* Arm. *soll.* Ir. *saillte,* +*salt.* Gael. *saillte.* Manx, *sailt, hailt.* Lat. *salsus.*

SALLA, v. a. To salt, to season with salt. Llwyd, 245. Part. *sellis,* 143. W. *halltu.* Arm. *sulla.* Ir. *saillim.* Gael. *saill.*

SALVER, s. m. A saviour. Llwyd, 143. Arm. *salver.* The proper terms in Cornish are *sylwadur,* and *sylwyas,* qd. v.

SAM, s. m. A burden. Pryce. Arm. *samm.*

SANS, s. m. A holy person, a saint. Llwyd, 30, 241. Pl. *sansow,* and *sŷns,* written by Llwyd, 243, *seins. Râg pan yskynnyf dhe nêf, me a fyn cafus gynef kekeffrys cledh ha sŷns,* for when I ascend to heaven, I will have with me also angels and saints. R.D. 190. *Tebel dên yw; Dew na sŷns ny'n câr,* he is a wicked man; God and saints love him not. R.D. 2114. *Cowethyans en sansow,* the communion of saints. Pryce. W. *sant.* pl. *saint.* Arm. *sant,* pl. *sent.* Ir. *sanct,* +*sancht; san.* Gael. +*san.* Lat. *sanctus.*

SANS, adj. Holy, sacred, sanctified. *An Spyrys Sans,* the Holy Ghost. *A Dâs, Mâp, ha Spyrys Sans, gordhyans dhe'th corf wêk pûp prŷs,* O Father, Son, and Holy Ghost, glory to thy sweet body at all times. O.M. 85. *An Sperys Sans yw tressa,* the Holy Ghost is the third. O.M. 2664. *Nyns â dên vŷth vynytha a'n kêth rê-na dhe'n tŷr sans,* not any man shall go over of those same to the holy land. O.M. 1870. *Why guycoryon, euch yn mês; yth crouch ow kuthyl ges a Dhu hag e sans eglos,* ye traders, go out; ye are making a jest of God and his holy church. P.C. 333. *Pensans, (Penzance,)* Holyhead. This is a later form of *sanct,* which is preserved in the local names, *Lansant, (Lezant,)* holy church; *Sant Crêd, (San creed,)* holy faith.

SANT, s. m. A banquet, food, any thing eaten with bread. Corn. Voc. *daps* vel *obsonum* vel *ferclum.* W. *saig.*

SARF, s. f. A serpent. *A Dâs kûf y'th wholowys, an sarf re rûk ow thollê, dh'y falsury y creays, pythueth re râg ow syndyê,* O dear Father in thy lights, the serpent hath deceived me; her falsehood I believed, ever she hath injured me. O.M. 286. *Un sarf yn guedhen yma, bêst uthyk hep falladow,* there is a serpent in the tree, an ugly beast, without failings. O.M. 797. W. *sarf.* Sanso. *sarpa.* Lat. *serpens.*

SART, s. f. An urchin, a hedgehog. Written in the Cornish Vocabulary, *sort,* qd. v. In late Cornish, *zart.* Llwyd, 56. W. *sarth.*

SASNEC, adj. English, Saxon. The late form given by Llwyd is *Zaznak.* Another form is *Sowsnac,* 23, 42. W. *sacsneg.* Arm. *saoznek.* Ir. *sagsonach.* Gael. *snsunnach.*

SAVAL, v. n. To stand. *Is saval,* standing corn. Llwyd, 147. A late form of *sevel,* qd. v.

SAW, adj. Safe, sound, healed. *A Dâs, veneges re by; lemyn saw ol ôn ny ny agan dysses, hep mar,* O Father, mayst thou be blessed; now cured we are all of our diseases, without doubt. O.M. 2024. *A Arluth whêk, saw ûf ha têk a pûp cleves,* O sweet Lord, I am healed and fair from all disease. P.C. 415. *Yw saw ol dhe wolyow a wylys vy dhe squerdyê,* are all thy wounds healed, (that) I saw tearing thee ? R.D. 489. *Ha henna saw ugas gura n pûp cleves yn bŷs-ma,* and that will make you sound from all disease in this world. R.D. 1599.

SAW, s. m. A load, a burden. *Otn saw bôs war ow kŷn; Jafet degyns saw aral,* behold a load of food on my back; let Japhet bring another load. O.M. 1053. *Kemer y, ty plôs lorden, syns war dhe keyn an grous pren, yma lour dhe saw dhyso,* take it, thou dirty lurdane, hold the cross-tree on thy back, it is enough for a load for thee. P.C. 2587. W. *sawch*.

SAW, adv. Save, except, but, only. *Ow broder, pûr lowrnek my â genes dhe'n menedh; saw kyns ys môs, ow thâs whêk, ro dhym dhe vanneth perfeth,* my brother, very gladly I will go with thee to the mountain, but before going, my sweet father, give to me thy perfect blessing. O.M. 451. *Caym ny lettys saw un lam, ow kafus banneth ow mam,* Cain, I stopped only a space, obtaining the blessing of my mother. O.M. 470. *Dhe lêf, Arluth, a glewaf, saw dhe face my ny welaf,* thy voice, Lord, I hear, but thy face I see not. O.M. 588. *Dên a'n geffé cans davas, ha'y kentrevek saw onan,* a man may have a hundred sheep, and his neighbour only one. O.M. 2231. Eng. *save*.

SAWAN, s. f. A hole in the cliff through which the sea passeth. *Sawan davis*, sheep's hole. *Pryce*. W. *sawell*.

SAWARN, s. m. A smell, a savour. *Drôg sawcarn*, a stink or ill savour. *Llwyd*, 60. A late form of *sawor*, qd. v.

SAWELL, adj. That giveth health, healthful. *Pryce*.

SAWOR, s. m. A smell, a savour, odour. *Byneges yw an guél-ma, pan ûs sawor mûr da ow tevos annedhé y; a losowys ol an bŷs, mar whêk smyllyng, my a grŷs, ny dhothé bŷs venary*, blessed are these rods, for the savour is very good, coming from them; from all the herbs of the world, such sweet smelling, I believe, would never have come. O.M. 1740. *An ré-ma ew guél a râs, râg ny glewsyuch yn nêp plâs sawor a'n par-ma vythqueth,* these are rods of grace, for you have not smelt in any place savour of this kind ever. O.M. 1191. W. *sawyr, sawyr, sawr.* Arm. *saour.* Manx, *soar.* Lat. *sapor.* Fr. *saveur.*

SAWS, s. m. An Englishman, a Saxon. Plur. *sawsen.* *Pryce.* Written by Llwyd, 42, 242, *sowes,* plur. *sowsen. Pow an Sowsen,* the country of the Saxons or Englishmen, England. W. *sais,* plur. *saeson.* Arm. *saoz,* plur. *saozon.* Ir. *sagsonach.* Gael. *sasunnach.* Manx, *sostynach.* Lat. *saxo, saxones.*

SAWSAC, adj. Healthy. *Pryce. Bos-sawsack,* the healthy dwelling, in Constenton.

SAWSNEC, s. f. The English language. *Pryce.* ‡ *Zouznak,* Llwyd, 42. W. *saesnaeg.* Arm. *saoznek.* Ir. *sacsanach.*

SAWMENT, s. m. Preservation, keeping. *Dew pillar manaf poyntya, râg an purpos-ma wharé; bryck a vŷdh onyn anotha, ha marbel a vŷdh y gela, râg sawment y a vŷdh gurŷs dha'n leverow,* two pillars I will appoint for this purpose by and by,; brick shall be one of them, and marble shall be the other, for preservation they shall be made to the books. C.W. 158.

SAWTHENY, v. a. To mislead. *Pryce.* Part. *sawthenys. Pûr ewn pan vo ow soppyé, me a dhue dh'agas guarnyé, ha gueytyruch bês tûs parys gans battys ha clydhydhow, y wêdh lanters gans golow, ma na veny sawthenys,* very exactly when he is supping, I will come to warn you, and take care that men be ready with staves and swords, also lanterns with light, that we may not be misled. P.C. 610.

SAWYE, v. a. To save, to preserve, to heal, to cure, to be healed or cured. 2 pers. s. imp. and 3 pers. s. fut.

saw. Part. *sawyys, sawys. Mar mynnyth cresy nag ûs Dew lemyn onan, a gotho ynno cresy, ly a saw a'n trûs dhe'n pen,* if thou wilt believe that there is not a god but one, in whom thou oughtest to believe, thou shalt be healed from the foot to the head. O.M. 1762. *Lemyn guyn ow beys, aban y'm sawyas ef,* now I am happy, since he hath healed me. O.M. 1775. *Kepar del osé sylwyas, me a'th pŷs a sawyé ow dew lagas,* like as thou art a Saviour, I pray thee to heal my eyes. P.C. 396. *Me agas saw yn lowen,* I will cure you gladly. P.C. 405. *Dhe fay re wrûk dhe sawyé,* thy faith hath made thee whole. P.C. 531. *Mars ogé Cryst mâp Dew kêr, ymsaw soon yn nêp maner na vy marow; ha saw ny gynes yn wêdh,* if thou art Christ, the Son of dear God, save thyself in some way, that thou be not dead; and save us with thee also. P.C. 2894. *Ny gŷf medhek a'n sawya,* he finds not a leech that can cure him. R.D. 1640. *Ple ma Iesu, dhe pygy a leverel dhymmo vy; ef a'n sawsé yn teffry a pûp dyssevys yn bŷs-ma,* where is Jesus, I pray thee to tell me; he would cure him really from all disease in this world. R.D. 1651. *Ha sawyys ty a vŷdh a'th cleves,* and healed thou shalt be of thy disease. R.D. 1712. *Sawyys yw ow ysyly,* healed are my limbs. O.M. 1797. *Bôs ow mâp dhymmo sawyys,* that my son is saved to me. O.M. 1380. *Dre grath an gueel vôs sawrys,* to be cured by the grace of the rods. O.M. 2019. *Henna Iudas pan welas Crist an bewnans na sawyé,* when Judas saw that, that he would not save the life of Christ. M.C. 103. Ir. *sabhalaim.* Gael. *samhail.*

SCABER, s. f. A barn. Pl. *scaberyow, scaberias.* *Pryce.* More correctly written *scibor,* qd. v.

SCABERIA, v. a. To sweep. *Pryce.* See *Scibia.*

SCABERIAS, s. m. A sweeper. *Pryce.*

SCAF, adj. Light in weight, nimble. Written also *scâv.* Comp. *scafé. Yn medhens, mar omwreyth clâff, gordhewyth te an prenvyth, awos guthyll whcyll mar scâff yn ethom dhyn mar fyllyth,* say they, if thou makest thyself sick, very diligently thou shalt pay for it, on account of doing work so light if thou wilt fail us in need. M.C. 155. *Hemma ydhew gorryb scâv,* yma ow gwîl ow holon clâv, this is a light answer, it maketh my heart sick. C.W. 86. *Kens môs cyf ten guŷn pymeth, ha dhe scafé ydh éth yn ow nygys, my a grŷs,* before going drink a draught of spiced wine, and more nimbly thou wilt go in my errand, I believe. O.M. 2295. W. *ysgavn,* † *scamn;* († *scamnogint,* levant, Juvencus Glosses.) Arm. *scan, scanv.* Ir. *scrimncach.*

SCALA, s. m. A dish. Corn. Vocab. *patera.* Germ. *schale.*

SCANNTLYN, s. m. A measure. *My a'n musur lour yn ta, na berthewch own a henna, ow arluth whêk, Dew a wôr, gans squyr compes ha scanntlyn na vo hyrré esumsyn na vŷdh cotta war nêp cor,* I will measure it well enough, do not have a fear of that, my sweet Lord, God knows, with straight square and a measure that it be not longer, I undertake, nor shorter in any part. O.M. 2510. From the old English *scanteloun,* a carpenter's measure.

SCARCEAS, s. m. A shark fish. Llwyd, 33, *skarkeas.*

SCARF, s. m. A joint. *Ny gl an gŷst yn y blâs, re hŷr ew a gevelyn; yn ewn greys an scarf trohé, ha compys mar ny vêdh e, ny won pandra leveryn,* the beam will not go into its place, too long it is by a cubit, in the just middle of the joint cut it, and if it will not be straight, I know not what I may say. O.M. 2530.

SCARFE, v. a. To join. *Hedhé dhe'n dôr, my a'd pŷs, soon ef a vŷdh amendyys, my a'n scarf yn ta wharé,* reach it to the ground, I pray thee, soon it shall be remedied, I will soon join it well. O.M. 2523.

SCAT, s. m. A buffet, a box, a blow. *Llwyd,* 49. "This word is still in use in Cornwall and Devon." *Polwhele.*

SCATH, s. m. A boat. Plur. *scatha. Gorreuch ef yn schath dhe'n môr; an schath a'n dêk dhe yfern,* put yo him in a boat to the sea; the boat shall carry him to hell. R.D. 2233. *Vynytha, hep na moy let, an corf yn schath ny a set, a dhesempys,* evermore without any further delay, we will put the body into a boat, immediately. R.D. 2284. *Lemmyn pûp ol acltyes dorn yn kêth schath-ma dh'y tenné,* now let every one put his hand on this same boat to draw it. R.D. 2352. *Scath rûs,* a net or fishing boat. *Scath kîr,* a long boat. *Llwyd,* 53. *Portscatha,* the harbour of boats, in Gerrans. *Polscatha,* the pool of boats. *Pryce.* W. *ysgraf.* Arm. *scaf.* Ir. †*sgaffa,* †*scuf.* Gael. *sgoth.* Lat. *scapha.* Fr. *esquif.* Eng. *skiff.*

SCAVDER, s. m. Levity, lightness. *Llwyd,* 240. W. *ysgavnder.* Arm. *scanvder.*

SCAVEL, s. f. A bench, a stool. Corn. Voc. *scabellum. Ha'n noar yu tordh a wolas, scon worth compas a vŷdh gwrŷs; honna a vŷdh ow scavell drôs,* and the earth likewise below immediately by compass shall be made, that shall be my footstool. C.W. 1. *Scavell an gow,* the bench of lies. *Pryce.* W. *ysgavell.* Arm. *scabel.* Ir. †*sgabhal.* Lat. *scabellum.*

SCAWEN, s. f. An elder tree. Llwyd, 144, 240, gives the forms *scavan, scawan.* Pl. *scaw.* The word is preserved in the local name *Boscawen,* the abode of the elder tree. "*Scaw* is still in use for an elder in Cornwall." *Polwhele.* W. *ysgawen,* †*scawen.* Arm. *scaô, scav, scaven.* Lat. *scobies.* Hence Eng. *skewer.*

SCEANS, s. m. Knowledge, wit. *Skeans benyn yn brotall,* woman's wit is brittle. C.W. 86. *Dhe vâb Seth ew dewesys genaf prest dhom servya ve; a skeans y fŷdh lenwys,* thy son Seth is chosen by me readily to serve me; with knowledge he shall be filled. C.W. 102. Another form of *scians,* qd. v.

SCEANS, adj. Pleasant, witty, merry. *Llwyd,* 78.

SCELLI, s. m. Wings. An abbreviated form of *ascelli,* plur. of *ascell.* ‡ *Sgelli grehan,* leather wings, a bat. *Llwyd,* 31. "A bat is now called a *leatherwing,* in Devonshire." *Polwhele.*

SCEMYNA, v. a. To excommunicate, to curse. Part. *scemynys. Omskemynys lower ydhové, nyngew reis skemyna moy,* accursed enough I am, there is not need to curse more. C.W. 88. *Der henna proder yn ta, ef a fyll der gêr arta dhe'th destrowy, skemynys,* therefore consider well, he can by a word again destroy thee, accursed. C.W. 16.

SCENT, adj. Scant, sparing. *Saw ydhové wondrys trobles, skant ny welaf un banna,* but I am wondrous troubled, scarce do I see a glimpse. C.W. 106. *Ha an huêl a cydhas skent,* and the work fell short. *Llwyd,* 251. Borrowed from English.

SCENTELETH, s. m. Knowledge. Written also *skentuleth. Ow bennath y'th chy re bo, mar luen ôs a skenteleth,* may my blessing be in thy house, so full thou art of knowledge. P.C. 1804. *Cussyllyouch uenouch Ihesu a gasé y wokyneth, ha treylé dhe skentuleth, ow tynvedh na ganno tru,* advise ye often Jesus to leave his folly, and turn to wisdom, that he may not sing "sad" at last. P.C. 1809.

SCENTYL, adj. Learned, wise. *Kyn nag ôff dén skentyll pûr, par del won lavaraff dhys yntré Du ha pehadur acordh del ve kemerys,* though I am not a very learned man, even as I know I will tell to thee between God and sinner how accord was taken. M.C. 8. Written also *scyntyl,* qd. v.

SCENYS, s. m. Sinews. *Corf Ihesus ha'y asely y dhe denna mar velen, nêb a vynna a ylly nevera oll y yscren, ha'y skennys, kŷc, ha gwythy, pan esa yn crows pren,* the body of Jesus and his limbs they drew so brutally, whoever would might number all his bones, and his sinews, flesh and veins, when he was on the cross-tree. M.C. 183. W. *gewyn,* a sinew.

SCES, s. f. A shade, a shadow. *Llwyd,* 176, *skez.* The late form of *scôd,* qd. v.

SCEVARN, s. m. The ear. *Llwyd,* 44. See *Scovern.*

SCEVENS, s. m. The lungs, lights. Corn. Voc. *sceuens, pulmo.* In Llwyd's time *skephans,* 27, 132. From *scaf,* light. W. *ysgyvaint,* †*skeueynt.* Arm. *scevent, scrent.* Ir. *sgamhan,* †*scaman.* Gael. *sgamhan.* Manx, *scowan.*

SCHAF, adj. Rapid. *Mŷr worto hag u ver spys a'th trôk ly a vŷdh yacheys pûr quyk ha schaf,* look at it, and in a short time thou shalt be cured of thy evil, very quick and rapidly. R.D. 1731.

SCHEREWNETH, s. m. Wickedness. *Ha satnas gans y antell, ha'y scherewneth, ha'y goyntys, Crist mâb an Arluth uchell y dempiyé pan prederis,* and Satan with his danger, and his wickedness, and his cunning, when he thought to tempt Christ, the Son of the High Lord. M.C. 19. *Golyouch ha pesouch ow thâs may hallouch môs dh'y ascdh, na vedhouch temtijs dygnas gans gow ha gans scherewneth,* watch ye and pray my Father that ye may be able to go to his seat, that yo be not tempted to molest with falsehood and with wickedness. M.C. 52.

SCHEREWYNSY, s. m. Wickedness. *Noe, mar luen yw an beys lemyn a scherewynsy, may 'thew dhweth dynythys,* Noah. so full is the world of wickedness, that the end is come. O.M. 942. *Noy, mar lemeys ew an byes lemyn a skerewynsy, may 'thew dewedh develhys.* C.W. 102.

SCHEREWYS, s. m. Wicked men. *En scherewys a sorras râg bonas Crist honoris, ha bôs y ober mar vrâs, ha dris an bŷs ol notijs,* the wicked men were augered because that Christ was honoured, and that his work was so great and noted through all the world. M.C. 31. *Ha'n scherewys prest a bell dhe worth au gwŷr a fye,* and the wicked men were very far from the truth. M.C. 203. *An scherewes a dregas yn yffarn yn tormont crêff,* the evil ones dwelt in hell in strong torment. M.C. 213. *Arluth, lavar dyssempys dhynny, mars yu bôdh dhe vrcys ha bolenegoth an Tâs, ny dhe wyskel gans cledhé nêp ûs worth dhe dalhenné, scherewys drôk aga guâs,* Lord, say immediately to us, if it is the will of thy mind, and the wish of the Father, that I strike with a sword him that is holding thee, the servant of the wicked villains. P.C. 1142. *Scherewys* is a plural form, from the Old English *shrew,* which had the meaning of *wicked.*

SCHYNDYE, v. a. To hurt, to injure. *Aga fleyr a gl schyndyé, ha ladhé mûr Yedhewon*, their stink may injure and kill many Jews. P.C. 1547. Written also *shyndyé*, and *syndyé*, qd. v.

SCIANS, s. m. Knowledge, skill, art, science, wisdom. *Ha dhynmo grâs ha skyans dhe dhcrevas par lavarow*, and to me grace and knowledge to declare by words. M.C. 1. *En mâb dre y skyans brâs pan gemert kŷg a werhas*, through the Son's great wisdom, when he took flesh of a virgin. M.C. 3. *Saw a'n frût ny fŷdh kymmyas yw pren a skeyens hynwys ; mar a tybbryth a henna yw hynwys pren a skeyns, yn mês alemma ty â, hag a fŷdh marow vernens*, but of the fruit there will not be permission, (that) is named the tree of knowledge ; if thou wilt eat of that (that) is named the tree of knowledge, out of this place thou shalt go, and shalt die. O.M. 80. A later form of *scient*, qd. v.

SCIANTOLETH, s. m. Prudence. *Llwyd*, 240. Id. qd. *scentuleth*, qd. v.

SCIBER, s. f. A barn, any large room. Plur. *sciberion, sciberyow. Levereuch dhe gour an chy, agas mester dhe dhanvon py plâs ydh yllé dybry, ef hag ol y lyskyblon ; hag ef a dhyswé dhynchy un skyber efan yn scon*, say ye to the man of the house, that your master sends, where he may eat, he and all his disciples ; and he will shew you a large room forthwith. P.C. 638. *Otté omma skyber dêk, ha cala lour war hy luer*, see here a fair room, and straw enough on its floor. P.C. 670. Written by Llwyd, 66, *skibor*. The plural is preserved in the local name of *Skiberion*, the barns, in Mawgan. W. *ysgubor*, †*esculaur*. Arm. *skiber*. Ir. *sciobal*. Gael. *sgiobal*. The root is W. *ysgub*, a sheaf. Ir. *scuab*. Gael. *sguab*. Manx, *skeab*. Ang. Sax. *sceaf*. Eng. *sheaf*. Lat. *scopa*.

SCIBIA, v. a. To sweep, to brush. *Llwyd*, 172, *dho skibia*. W. *ysgubo*. Arm. *scuba*. Ir. *sguaba*. Gael. *sgob*.

SCIDAL, s. f. A little dish. *Llwyd*, 46. Id. qd. *scudel*, qd. v.

SCIENT, s. m. Knowledge, wisdom. Corn. Voc. *gunn a scient*, energuminus, weak of mind: *diskient*, insipiens, foolish. From the Lat. *scientia*.

SCIENTOC, adj. Wise. Corn. Voc. *sapiens*. Written by Llwyd, 118, *skientic*, skilful, expert. From the subs. *scient*.

SCILLY, v. a. To cut off. "Hence the *Scilly Isles*, cut off from the insular continent." *Pryce*.

SCINAN, s. f. A pin. *Llwyd*, 41. It must be the same word as *scinen*.

SCINEN, s. f. An ear-ring. Corn. Voc. *inauris*.

SCIRAN, s. f. A bough or branch of a tree. Pl. *scirow*. Llwyd, 63. Written also *scoren*, qd. v. W. *ysgyren*.

SOITH, adj. Weary, tired, jaded, faint. *Llwyd*, 67. Generally written in the Dramas *squyth*, qd. v.

SCLANDRY, v. a. To offend, to slander, to accuse. Part. *sclandrys. Arluth, leverel dym gura, mars ôf vy an kêth henna, na vo dên aral sclandrys*, Lord, tell me if I am that same, that another man may not be accused. P.C. 743. *Kyns bôs un nôs tremenys, why a vŷdh pûr wŷr sclandrys ahanaf ketep mâp bron*, before one night be passed, ye will be very truly offended for me, every son of the breast. P.C. 891. *Kyn fôns y ol sclandrys, neffré avos bôs ledhys, my ny wrâf dhe dhyflasé*, though they be all offended, ever because of being killed, I will not displease thee. P.C. 899. Borrowed from the English.

SCOCHFORDH, s. f. A cross-road. *Dre un scochfordh y ponyas, cafos y mâb mar callé*, through a cross-road she ran, if she could get her son. M.C. 164.

SOOD, s. f. A shade, a shadow. Corn. Voc. *umbra*. The latest form was *skez*. W. *ysgawd*. Arm. *sceûd*. Ir. *scath*. Gael. *sgiath*. Manx, *scaa*. Goth. *skadus*. Gr. σκότος, σκιά, σκιάδιον. Ang. Sax. *scad, scead, sced*. Eng. *shade*.

SCODEC, adj. Shady. *Llwyd*, 176. W. *ysgodawg*. Arm. *scodek*. Ir. *scathach*. Gael. *sgiathach*.

SCODU, s. f. A shoulder. Dual, *discodh*, the two shoulders, the shoulders. *An grows y a rûg gorré war scôdh Ihesus dh'y dôn dhy*, the cross they did put on the shoulder of Jesus to bear it thither. M.C. 162. *Mar possé a'n neyll tenewen, râg y scôdh hy a'n grevyé*, if he leant on the one side, for his shoulder it grieved him. M.C. 205. Written also *scoudh*, qd. v. The oldest form was *scuid*, qd. v.

SOOL, s. f. A school. Corn. Voc. *scola*. From the Latin.

SCOLCHYE, s. f. A sculking. *Why a dhêth dhym yn arvow, dre dreyson yn un scolchyé, gans boclers ha cledhydhyow*, ye have come to me in arms through treason, sculkingly, with bucklers and swords. M.C. 74. From the English.

SCOLHEIC, s. m. A scholar. Corn. Voc. *scholásticus*. W. *ysgolhaig*, †*escoleyc*, †*scolheic*. Arm. *scolaer*. Ir. *sgolaire*. Gael. *sgoilear*.

SCOLLYE, v. a. To spill, to shed, to pour, to scatter. Part. *scollyys, scollys. Pan wreta mar coynt fara, ow scollyé agan guara, ha'n fêr orth y tystrywy*, when thou actest so rudely, scattering our wares, and the fair destroying it. P.C. 341. *En kêth oynement a scollyas warnaf, râk ow anclydhyas, hy a'n grûk dre kerensé*, the same ointment she poured on me for my burial, she did it through love. P.C. 547. *Myschef a gôdh tyn ha créf, râk y wôs a vŷdh scollys*, mischief will fall sharp and strong, for his blood (that) shall be shed. P.C. 2460. *A'y ben y oys o scolijs, hag ynno fest luhas tol gans an dreyn a ve tellys*, from his head his blood was spilt, and in it very many holes were bored by the thorns. M.C. 133. Written also *scullyé*, qd. v.

SCON, adv. Soon, immediately, forthwith. *Adam, cummyas scon a fŷdh hŷs dhe baal luen dhe drehy*, Adam, leave shall be forthwith to cut full the length of thy spade. O.M. 379. *Ow dâs fest lowenek vŷdh, mar scon a'n bŷs tremené*, my father will be very joyful, if he soon passes from the world. O.M. 834. *Mester yn scon my a vera*, master, I will do it immediately. O.M. 1005. *Ellas, na allaf yn scon keusel worthys*, alas, that I cannot at once speak to thee. R.D. 761.

SCONYA, v. a. To refuse, to deny, to reject. Written also *sconyé. Dre sor kyn fêns y terrys, dhe sconya my ny alla*, though they be broken in anger, I am not able to refuse. O.M. 1238. *Ny sconnynf yn nêp maner a wûl ol dhe voluneth*, I will not refuse in any manner to do all thy will. O.M. 1291. *Mara pedhaf bew vledhen, my a'n talvyth dhyuch, rum pen, pypenngol a sconyo*, if I be alive a year, I will pay it to you, by my head, whoever may refuse. O.M. 2368. *Me a gews dhodho mûr dêk, na sconyer pendra wreny*, I will speak to him very fair, that what we do may not be refused. P.C. 190.

Er dhe byn ny wrûf sconyé, against thee I will not refuse. P.C. 500. *Henna Pedyr a sconyas, Ihesus dhe wolhy y dreys*, that Peter refused, that Jesus should wash his feet. M.C. 46. *Betegyns te ny sconyth*, nevertheless thou dost not refuse. M.C. 120.

SCOREN, s. f. A branch, a bough. Pl. *scorennow*. Corn. Voc. *scorren*, ramus. *Mŷr pandra woylly ynny kefrys gworydhyow ha scoren*, look what canst thou see in it besides roots and branch. O.M. 802. *Cherubyn, êl Dew a rûs, yn wedhen me a welas, yn ban uhel worth scoren*, cherub, angel of the God of grace, in the tree I saw, high up on a branch. O.M. 805. *Nôth yw ol hy scorennow*, bare are all its boughs. O.M. 780. *Hŷr gans mûr a scorennow*, tall with many boughs. O.M. 838. W. *ysgyren*. Arm. *scourren*.

SCORNYE, v. a. To contend, to strive. Written also *scornê*. *Hy a dhesefsê scornê gans an epscop, ha'y dollé dhe wordhyé newow nowydh*, she would wish to strive with the bishop, and delude him to worship new gods. O.M. 2730. *An fals re scoruyes gynê*, the false (man) has striven with me. P.C. 1335. *Ny dâl dhys scornyé gynê*, it behoves thee not to strive with me. R.D. 105. *Me a'th pŷs, scornyé gynen lemyn na wra*, I pray thee, do not make mockery with us now. R.D. 918.

SCOUDH, s. f. A shoulder. *War ow scoudh me a vyn y dhôn dhe drê*, on my shoulder I will carry it home. P.C. 658. *Me a's dêk fest yn lowen râg y dhyffres a anken; dro hy dhymmo war ow scoudh*, I will carry it very gladly, to shelter him from pain; bring it to me on my shoulder. P.C. 2623. Written also *scôdh*, qd. v. The oldest form was *scuid*, qd. v.

SCOUL, s. m. A kite. Corn. Voc. *milvus*. Arm. *skoul*. W. *ysgwel, ysglyv*, rapacious.

SCOVARN, s. f. The ear. Corn. Voc. *scouarn*, auris. Written also *scovern, scovorn, scoforn*. Pl. *scovornow*. *Pedyr a'n neyl tenewen yn mês a dennas cledhé, hag a drohas ryb un pen scovern onan anedhé; Crist a scityas yn tyen an scovern artê dhe drê*, Peter from the one side drew forth a sword, and cut beside the head an ear of one of them; Christ set the ear completely home again. M.C. 71. *Cowethé, guercsouch, ow scoforn trechys myrouch dhe vês dhyworth ow pen*, companions, help, see my ear cut off from my head. P.C. 1144. *Dhe'th scoforn wharré yches my a re*, to thy ear soon healing I will give. P.C. 1150. *Pûr aukensy gans dornow dhodho war an scovornow reuch boxsesow trewysy*, very painful with hands to him on the ears give ye sad blows. P.C. 1361. *Ha rên dhodho boxsusow gans dornow ha guelynny war an scovornow*, and let us give him buffets with hands and rods on the ears. P.C. 1391. W. *ysgywarn*, †*eskeuarn*. Arm. *scouarn*.

SCOVARNOG, s. m. A hare. Corn. Voc. *lepus*. From *scovarn*, the ear. Its large ears being a distinguishing quality. So Gr. λαγωὸς, from λάγ, great, and οὖς, ear. W. *ysgyvarnog*. Arm. †*skouarnek*. Irish, *sciberneog*. Gael. *sgiobarnag*. (The root is lost to the Erse.) Llwyd, writes the word *scowarnak*, and *scowarnog*, as the common pronunciation of his time. *Scowarnog bian*, a leveret or little hare. 78. In many parts of Wales it is now colloquially called a *scywarnog*. "A hare is still called *a scavernick*, throughout the west of Cornwall." *Polwhele*.

SCOVVA, s. f. A tent, a pavilion. *Moyses whêk, ny a dreha ragon chy pols dhe wonys; râg ny a ŷl gûl scovva ow cortes vôs goskesys*, sweet Moses, we will raise for us a house, a while to labour; for we may make a tent waiting to be sheltered. O.M. 1717.

SCREFA, v. a. To write. *Ha'n pŷth a screfys screfys, yn mêdh Pylat dhedhê y*, and what I have written, I have written; says Pilate to them. M.C. 188. *Mês omma monens screfys*, but here are written. C.W. 160. *Arluth, kemer truath warnan ny, ha screfa ol remma de arhadow parth chy agan colonow*, Lord, have mercy upon us, and write all those thy laws in our hearts. *Pryce*. *Scrêf*, write thou. Llwyd, 248. ‡*N'ora vi screfa na mui*, I can write no more. 250. Another form of *scrifa*, qd. v.

SCRÊFT, s. m. Scripture. Llwyd, 146. W. *ysgrythyr*.

SCRIFE, v. a. To write. 2 pers. s. imp. *scrif*. Part. *scrifys*. *Me a'th pŷs, scrif ow enê, pan vŷf marow, yn dhe rôl*, I pray thee, write my soul, when I am dead, in thy roll. P.C. 421. *Me re wrûk scrifê agas cheson dh'y ladhé*, I have written your accusation to kill him. P.C. 2791. *Na scrif mychtern Yedhewon, saw scrŷf ynno an bylen dhe leverel y vôs ef*, write not king of the Jews, but write on it, the villain said that he was. P.C. 2798. *An pŷth a scrifys, scrifys; na ken ny scrifaf neffré*, what I have written I have written; no otherwise will I ever write. P.C. 2808. *Yn levyr yma scrifys*, in a book it is written. P.C. 1157. *Hag yn ol an kêth henna, nynsus y hanow scryffys*, and in all that same his name is not written. O.M. 2646. *Ihesus yn dour a scryfas*, Jesus wrote on the ground. M.C. 33. *Pylat a vynnas scrifê a vewnans Crist acheson, praga dampnys rebee, hag a'n scrifas y honon*, Pilate would write of the life of Christ an accusation, why he was condemned, and he wrote it himself. M.C. 187. W. *ysgrivo, ysgrivenu*. Arm. *scriva*. Ir. *scriobh*, †*scrib*. Gael. *sgriobh*. Manx, *scrieu*. Lat. *scribo*.

SCRIFE, s. m. A writing. *Hedre vôns y ow plentyé, Ihesus yn dour a scryfas, ha dre vertu an scrifé, pêb dhe vês a omdennas*, while they were complaining of her, Jesus wrote on the ground, and by virtue of the writing, every one out withdrew. M.C. 33. W. *ysgriv*. Ir. *scriobh, scriobhadh*. Gael. *sgriobh, sgriobhadh*. Manx, *screeuee*.

SCRIVEN, s. f. A writing. Corn. Voc. *scriuen danuon*, epistola, a letter missive. W. *ysgriven*; *ysgriven danvon*. Manx, *screeuyn*.

SCRIVINAS, v. a. To scratch, to claw. Llwyd, 145, *dho scrivinas*. W. *ysgravino*. Arm. *scrapa*.

SCRIVINIAT, s. m. A writer. Corn. Voc. *scriuiniat*, scriptor. W. *ysgrivenydh, ysgrivenwr*. Arm. *scrivaner*.

SCRIVIT, s. m. A writing. Corn. Voc. *scriuit*, scriptum. Written by Llwyd, 146, *scrividh*. W. *ysgriviad*. Arm. *scrid, scrit*.

SCRUTH, s. m. A shiver, a horror. *En benenas leun a rûs gans an bêdh fast powessens; worth an pen y a welas dhe'n bêdh ow leveris kens un flôch yonk, gwyn y dhyllas, eyll o, ha y ny wodhyens; scruth own mûr a's kemeras râg an marthus re welsens*, the women full of grace leaned quite on the tomb; they saw at the head of the tomb, (that) is before mentioned, a young child, white his raiment; it was an angel, and they knew it not; a shiver of great fear seized them at the marvel (that) they saw. M.C. 254. W. *ysgryd*. Arm. *skrija*.

SCRYGE, v. n. To shriek. *A vynyn ryth, py le ydh éth? râg kueth pygyth, garmé a wrêth; na ôl na scrŷg, nép a whyleth, sychsys y treys gans dhe dhyw pléth*, O woeful woman, where goest thou? for grief thou prayest, cry out thou dost; weep not nor shriek, whom thou seekest thou driedst his feet with thy two plaits. R.D. 853. W. *ysgrechio*; from *ysgrech*, a shriek. Ir. *screach*. Gael. *sgreach*. Manx, *scrach*. Eng. *screech*.

SCRYMBA, s. m. An outcry. *Pocvan pûp ûr ha rynny, skrymba brâs an dewolow, ef a'n gcvyth genen ny a pûp drôk maner ponow*, sickness always, and horror, great outcry of the devils, he shall find with us, and all evil sorts of pains. R.D. 2344. W. *ysgarm*. Arm. *scrimpa*, to neigh.

SCRYNCYE, v. a. To snarl, to grin. *Abel, râg dhe offryn kêr, ty a vŷdh genen nefré; ha dewolow hep nyver, pûp ûr orthys ow scrynkyé*, Abel, because of thy dear offering, thou shalt be ever with us; and devils without number always grinning at thee. O.M. 570. W. *ysgyrnygu*. Arm. *scrina*.

SCUATTYA, v. a. To break, to burst, to smite. *Dho skwattia*, Llwyd, 117, 142. See *Squattya*.

SCUBILEN, s. f. A whip, a scourge. Corn. Voc. *flagrum* vel *flagellum*. W. *ysgubell*; dim. of *ysgub*, a besom. Arm. *scubelen*.

SCUDEL, s. f. A dish, a platter. Corn. Voc. *discus*. *Pûb onan a ylwys, Arluth Du, yw me henna? Ha Ihesus a worthebys; a'm scudel dyblyry a wra; gwef oŷth pan veva genys a dor y vam dhe'n bŷs-ma*, every one exclaimed; Lord God am I that one? And Jesus answered; out of my dish he is eating; woe to him that ever he was born from his mother's womb to this world. M.C. 43. W. *ysgudell*. Arm. *scudell*. Manx, *skual*. From the Lat. *scutellus*.

SCUDII, s. f. A shoulder. Llwyd, *scûdh*, 11, 16. Written also *scôdh*, and *scoudh*, qd. v.

SCUID, s. f. The shoulder. Corn. Voc. *scapula*. Written in the Dramas *scôdh*, and *scoudh*, qd. v., and the duals *dywscodh*, and *duscodh*. W. *ysgwydh*. Arm. *scoaz*, †*sconce*. (Ir. †*scoid*, the nape.) Sansc. *skaudha*.

SCUIDLIEN, s. m. A hood. Corn. Voc. *superhumale*. Lit. a shoulder-linen. Comp. of *scuid*, and *lien*, a cloth. W. *ysgwydhlian*.

SCULLYE, v. a. To shed, to spill, to pour, to scatter. Part. *scullys*. *Yma gynef flowrys têk, yn onor dhum arluth whêk aga scullyé yn danno*, I have fair flowers, in honour to my sweet Lord, (I will) scatter them under him. P.C. 260. *Me a vyn môs dhe uré ow arluth, treys ha dewlé gans onement kêr, ha war y prn y scullyé*, I will go to anoint my Lord, feet and hands with precious ointment, and pour it upon his head. P.C. 476. *Eveuch lemyn ol an guŷn, râg hemma yw ow gôs fŷn, hag a vŷdh ragouch skullys yn dewyllyens pechusow*, drink ye now all the wine, for this is my last blood, and will be shed for you, in atonement of sins. P.C. 829. *Cres ys a hos Dew a allos y vones dhyn; scullyns y wôs râg yonk ha lôs, sylwel mar mym*, we believe that he is God of power to us; he shed his blood for young and gray, if he will save. R.D. 333. Written also *scollyé*, qd. v. The root is *scul* or *scyl*, qd. v. W. *chwalu*. Arm. *scula*. Ir. *scaoil*. Gael. *sgaoil*. Manx, *skeayl*. Scotch, *skail*, *skell*. North of England, *scale*.

SCUSY, v. n. To escape, to get free. *Y rûf hynwyn dhe'n puskes, porpus, sowmens, syllyes, ol dhym gustyth y a vŷdh; lenesow ha barfusy, pŷsk ragof ny wrv skusy, mar cordhyaf Dew yn perfyth*, I will give names to the fishes, porpoises, salmons, congers, all to me obedient they shall be, lings and cods, a fish from me shall not escape, if I shall worship God perfectly. O.M. 139.

SCUTH, s. m. A plight. *Me yw mychtern re wrûk cûs ol râg dry Adam ha'y hâs a iebel scuth; mychtern ôf a lowené, ha'n victory éth gyné, yn arvow rûdh*, I am a king (that) hath done battle all for the purpose of bringing Adam from evil plight; I am a king of joy, and the victory hath gone with me, in red arms. R.D. 2519. *Ha fattel duthys yn ban, dre dhe gallos dhe honan, ha war dhe corf mar drôk scuth*, and how camest thou up through thy own power, and on thy body such evil plight? R.D. 2570.

SCUYTHI, v. n. To tire, to grow weary. *Dho skuythi*, Pryce. See *Squythé*.

SCWYTH, s. m. A jerk, switch, or twitch. Pryce. See *Squych*.

SCYDNYA, v. n. To descend, to fall down. *Ha dhe'n Tâs gurên oll pegy, na skydnya an kêth vengeans yn nêb termyn warnan ny, nag en flechys*, and to the Father let us all pray, that the same vengeance may not fall down at any time upon us, nor our children. C.W. 160. *Ty a ool ha lyns mŷl, kyn 'thota skydnys yn wharth*, thou shalt weep and many thousands, though thou art fallen into laughter. C.W. 168. *Mar ny wreuch, vengeans pûr vrâs a skydn warnouch kyns na pell*, if ye will not, very great vengeance will fall upon you before long. C.W. 172. A late corruption of *dysskynné*, qd. v.

SGYGGYOW, s. m. Shoes. *Moyses, sâf ena, na nês na dhûs na fella, râg ny vynnaf; dheworthys dŷsk dhe 'skyggyow dhe vês, sevel war tŷr venrges a wrêth, del lavaraf dhys*, Moses, stand there, nor nearer, come not; from thee take off thy shoes, stand on hallowed ground thou dost, as I tell thee. O.M. 1400. *Eskygyow* is a corrupted form of *esgidiow*, plur. of *esgid*, qd. v.

SCYL, s. m. What is scattered, dust, waste. *Me a re gans mŷr a râs wharé lemyn strokyus vrâs pûr ewn war an brest a râg, bŷs may codhé hy dhe'n dôr, ha'y brewy guyls yn dar clor mar venys avel skyl brâg*, I will give with much pleasure soon now great strokes, very exactly on the breast in front; until she fall upon the earth, and bruise her, in fierce pain, as small as malt dust. O.M. 2720. *Te nyn râs towlé hanow an Arluth dhy Dew dhe skul, râg an Arluth nyn syns hemma leal, nêb ês towlé y hanow dhe skul*, thou shalt not throw the name of the Lord thy God to waste, for the Lord will not hold him faithful, who throweth his name to waste. Pryce. W. *chwâl*.

SCYLE, s. f. Base, foundation, groundwork. *Yn mêdh Plat, scyle vûs, me ny gafé, rum lowté; na bŷth moy ef ny gaffas prâg may fe rŷs y dampnyé*, says Pilato, good grounds I have not found, by my loyalty; nor any more did he find why there was need to condemn him. M.C. 116. *Lemmyn merouch pe nyle a'n dûs a vŷdh delyffrys, po Crist, leverouch scyle, po Barabas, dên blamys*, now see ye which of the two men shall be delivered, whether Christ, say ye the grounds, or Barabas, a guilty mau. M.C. 125. *Pylat a gewsys arté, dredhouch why bedhens ledhys, râg ynno me ny gaffé scyle vâs may fo dampnys*, Pilate said again, by you let him be killed, for in him I have not found good grounds that he should be condemned. M.C. 142. *Pan êth Pylat dh'y redyé, scyle nynj o nag onan*, when Pilate went to read it, there was no ground not one. M.C. 187. As *nyle* is written for *neyl* or *ncil*, and *pascon* for *passon*, so *scyle* must be for *seyl* or *seil*, the oldest form of which was *sel*, qd. v. W. *sail*, † *seil*.

SCYLE, v. a. To lay a foundation, to found, to cause. *Natur scyle, me a syns, Arluth da mar pŷdh peynys, ol y soyeté kyn fôns sŷns, râg y bryn dhe vôs grevijs*, nature will cause, I hold, if the good Lord be pained, all his subjects, though they were holy, for his pain to be grieved. M.C. 211. W. *seitio*.

SCYLUR, s. m. A scholar. Pl. *scylurion*. Llwyd, 146, 242.

SCYNTYLL, adj. Learned, knowing, wise. *Gans dên skyntyll a wodhyé me a glevas leverel*, by a learned man that knew I have heard say. M.C. 134. *En Edheuon skyntyll kêth, re's teffo mûr velyny, dhe veras worth Crist y êth, hag ef yn crous ow cregy*, the same learned Jews, may much harm come to them, to look on Christ they went, while he was hanging on the cross. M.C. 216. Another form of *scentyl*, qd. v.

SCYWARNAC, s. m. A hare. *Llwyd*, 22, 240. A late form of *scovarnec*, qd. v.

SE, s. f. A seat. *Heyl, ow arluth yn dhe se*, hail, my lord, in thy seat. O.M. 905. *Dûn dhe gyrhas Salamon, ha goryn ef yn y drôn, avel mychtern, yn y se*, let us come to fetch Solomon, and put him on his throne, like a king in his seat. O.M. 2393. *Yssé yn dhe see yn wêdh, a bewé dhe tâs Daveth, râg ef a'n kemynnys dhys*, sit in thy seat also, (which) thy father David possessed, for he has bequeathed it to thee. O.M. 2302. *A Tâs bynyges y'th se*, O Father, blessed on thy seat. R.D. 2619. *Asedh* is another form, qd. v., and for the verb, see *sedha, ysedhé*. W. *sêdh, se*. Ir. *saide*, † *suide*. Gael. † *saide*. Lat. *sedes*. Gr. ἕδος. Lith. *sodas*. Sansc. *sadas*.

SE, pron. s. Thee. *Dh'y gour hy a dhanvonas, a Crist kepar del welsé ; yn kerdh delma dre gannas ; nyng ew ragos se ladhé, Crist yw synsys mûr dremas*, to her husband she sent, of Christ as she had seen, away thus by a messenger ; it is not for thee to slay, Christ is held very exceeding good. M.C. 123. More generally written *sy*, qd. v., both being variations of *te*, or *ti*.

SEAG, s. m. Grains of malt after brewing. ‡ *Ma lciaz gwrêg lackn vel zeag, gwell gesses vel kommeres*, there are many wives worse than grains, better left than taken. *Pryce*. W. *socg*.

SECERDER, s. m. Security. *Llwyd*, 60. From *seccr*, id. qd.ᵃ W. *sicr*, certain. Irish, *sacair*. Gael. *socair*. Manx, *shickyr*. Lat. *securus*.

SECH, adj. Dry, dried, parched, withered. *Saw my a greys hy bôs sêch, ha gurfjs nôth ol râg an pêch a pehas ow thâs ha'm mam*, but I believe that it is dry, and all made bare, for the sin (that) my father and mother sinued. O.M. 757. *Ha hy a wra aspyé, mars ûs dôr sêch yn nêp pow*, and she will see, if there is dry land in any country. O.M. 1116. *Tyr sêch yn guél nag yn prâs*, dry land in field or meadow. O.M. 1137. *Bôs sêch ha têk an awel, dhe Dew y coth dhyn grassé*, that the weather is dry and fair, it behoveth us to give thanks to God. O.M. 1147. Written indiscriminately *sŷch*, qd. v.

SECHE, v. a. To make dry. 3 pers. s. fut. *sêch*. Part. *sechys*. *Yma daggrow ow klybyé dre dreys, râk ewn kerengé, saw me n's sêch gans ow blew*, tears are wetting thy feet for true love, but I will dry them with my hair. P.C. 484. *My a woulch ol agas trŷs, ha gans towal a lŷn gulân my a's sêch ketteb onan*, I will wash all your feet, and with a towel of clean linen dry them every one. P.C. 837. *Y'tho mar kruyé golhy agas treys, h'aga seché, golhens pûp treys y gylé ahanouch, kepar ha my*, now if I have washed your feet, and dried them, let every one wash each other's feet of you, like as I. P.C. 676. *Nêb a vo y gorf golhys, nyn jevcs ethom golhy saw y treys na vôns sechys, râg gulân yw ol yredy*, he whose body is washed hath not need of washing only his feet that they be not dry, for he is all clean truly. P.C. 863. Written also *syché*, qd. v.

SECHES, s. m. Thirst, drought. *Scches dhodho yma, ef a'n gevé drôk wyras*, there is thirst to him, he has had a bad relief. P.C. 2975. *Ottensé gynef parys, bystel, cysel kymyskys, wassel, mars ûs secches brâs*, behold them with me ready, gall (and) vinegar mixed; wassail, if there is great thirst. P.C. 2978. *Seches dhymmo vy yma*, thirst to me there is. P.C. 2979. W. *syched*. Arm. *sched*. Lat. *siccitas*.

SECHTER, s. m. Dryness, drought. *Llwyd*, 240. W. *sychder*. Arm. *sechder*.

SECHYS, adj. Dry, dried, withered. *Dôr sechys*, dry land. *Pryce*. See *Sychys*.

SEDHE, v. n. To seat one's self down, to sit. 3 pers. s. fut. *sêdh*. Part. *sedhys*. *Taw, sedhé vyn ty, Phelip*, be silent, wilt thou sit, Philip. R.D. 995. *Te a sêdh*, thou shalt sit ; *why a sêdh*, ye shall sit. C.W. 6. Other forms are *asedhé, csedhé*, and *ysedhé*, qd. v. W. *sedhu*. Arm. *azeza*. Ir. † *suide*. Lat. *sedeo*. Gr. ἔζω, ἴζω. Goth. *sitan*.

SEDHEC, s. m. A seat. *Tâs Crist dhe vês a fyas, pêb a'y du pûr vorethck ; saw Pedyr Crist a holyas abell, avel un ownck dhe dyller an prins Annas ; ena ydhesé sedhek, orto y asedhas, may clewo lêff Ihesus whêk*, the people of Christ fled away, each on his (own) side very mournful, but Peter followed Christ from afar, like a coward, to the place of the prince Annas ; there was a seat there, on it he sat down, that he might hear the voice of sweet Jesus. M.C. 77.

SEDHVA, s. f. A sitting place, a seat. *Pryce*. Generally written *asedhva*, qd. v.

SEF, v. n. He shall stand. 3 pers. s. fut. of *sevel*, qd. v. *Del sevys mâb Du a'y vêdh, yn êr-nn dhe'n tressa dŷdh, yn della ol ny a sêf dêdh brues, drôk ha da yn wêdh*, as the Son of God arose from the tomb, then, on the third day, so shall we all wise on doomsday, good and bad alike. M.C. 259. *Râk me a wôr lour denses, marnes dre an luen dueces, omma my sêf*, for I know well the manhood, except through the full Godhead, here will not remain. R.D. 2516. W. *saiv*.

SEFSYS, v. n. Thou stoodest up. 2 pers. s. preterite of *sevel*, qd. v. *Pan sefsys hydhew myttyn, yâch êns aga ireyw*, when thou gottest up this day in the morning, their sinews were sound. P.C. 2680.

SEGERIS, adj. Empty, void of, vain. *Llwyd*, 60.

SEGYR, adj. At leisure, having nothing to do. *Llwyd*, 169. W. *segur*. Lat. *securus*.

SEGYRYS, adj. At leisure. *Llwyd*, 169.

SEH, adj. Dry. A late form of *sêch*. Finally softened into *zêh*. Llwyd, 150.

SEHAR, s. m. Drought, dryness. *Llwyd*, 12, 240, *zehar*. A late form of *sechter*, qd. v.

SEHAS, s. m. Thirst. A later form of *seches*. Written by Llwyd, 26, *zehaz*.

SEHA, v. a. To dry, to wipe; to be dry, to be thirsty. *Dho seha*, Llwyd, 43, 162. A later form of *seché*, qd. v.

SEHYS, adj. Dry, thirsty. *Pryce*. A later form of *sechys*, qd. v.

SEINS, s. m. Saints. *Llwyd*, 243. Generally written *sŷns*, qd. v.

SEIT, s. m. A pot. Corn. Voc. *olla*. The latest form was *zeath*, Llwyd, 106. W. *saith*.

SEITAG, card. num. Seventeen. *Llwyd*, 148. Comp. of *seith*, seven, and *dég*, ten. The correct form would be *sritek*. Arm. *seitek*. (W. *dau-ar-bymtheg*, two upon fifteen.) Ir. *seacht-deag*. Gael. *seachd-deug*. Manx, *shiaghtjeig*. Lat. *septendecim*.

SEITH, card. num. Seven. *Caym ny vedhyth yn della, râg dhe ladhé dén mar qura, ef a'n govyth scyth kemmys a paynys yn nôr bŷs-ma*, Cain, thou shalt not be so, for if a man does kill thee, he shall get it seven times as much of pains in the earth of this world. O.M. 509. *My ny won pycé cammen; sŷth mŷl ha sŷth cans blydhen un dén kyn fo ow kerdhes, ow tôs kyn spedyé yn geydh dew uguns myldyr perfeyth, omma ny alsé bones*, I know not who he is at all; seven thousand and seven hundred years, if a man should be travelling, and though he sped coming in a day forty miles complete, here he could not be. R.D. 2494. W. *saith*, †*seith*. Arm. *seiz*. Ir. *seacht*, †*secht*. Gael. *seachd*. Manx, *shiacht*. Gr. ἑπτά. Lat. *septem*. Sansc. *saptan*. Zend, *hapte*. It. *sette*. Span. *siete*. Fr. *sept*. Goth. *sibun*. Germ. *sieben*. Ang. Sax. *seofa*, *seofan*. Eng. *seven*.

SEITHAS, num. adj. Seventh. Llwyd, 148, 243.

SEITHUN, s. f. A week. Corn. Voc. *scithum*, obdomada. Written also *sythyn*. *Râg sythyn wosé hemma, dew ugens dŷdh my a fix glaw dhe godhé awartha*, for a week after this, forty days I will allow rain to fall from above. O.M. 1026. *Lavar lemmyn, ha ty a vŷdh rewarddys, may leverry, me a grŷs, kyns pen sythyn*, speak now, and thou shalt be rewarded, if thou wilt say, I believe, before the end of the week. R.D. 30. Written by Llwyd, *seithan*, and derived by him from the Lat. *septimana*, 33. ‡ *An dzhyrna-ma war seithan*, this day seven night. 249. *Nesaa seithan*, next week. 250. Arm. *seizun*. Ir. *seachdmhain*, †*sechtmaine*. Gael. *seachduin*. Manx, *shiaghtin*. Fr. *semaine*. In W. *wythnos* is a week, lit. eight nights.

SEITHVES, num. adj. Seventh. *Râg bones ol lêk ha da, yn wheddydh mŷns yw formyys, aga sona ny a wra, may fe scythves dŷdh hynwys*, for that all is fair and good, in six days all that is created, bless them we will, that it may be called the seventh day. O.M. 144. *A Cayn, mâb Adam, ythové sevys, yn sŷthvas degré*, from Cain the son of Adam, I am raised in the seventh degree. C.W. 104. *Râg henna an Arluth a benigas an seithvas dŷdh, hag a'n uchelhas*, therefore the Lord blessed the seventh day and hallowed it. *Pryce*. Comp. of *scith*, seven, and *med*, a measure. W. *seithved*. Arm. *seizved*. Ir. *seachtmhadh*. Gael. *seachdamh*. Manx *shiaghtoo*.

SEL, s. m. A foundation, base, or groundwork. Corn. Voc. *fundamentum*. This is the oldest form of *scyle*, qd. v. W. *sail*. Arm. *sôl*. Lat. *solum*.

SELDA, s. m. A cellar. *Llwyd*, 47. Lat. *cella*.

SELL, s. m. A view, a prospect. *Pryce*. Written also *syll*, qd. v.

SELLI, s. m. An eel. Corn. Voc. *anguilla*. Pl. *selyes*. *Y rôf henwyn dhe'n puskes, dhe wyan, pengaruas, selyas*, I will give names to the fishes, to breams, gurnards, congers. C.W. 32. Written also *syllyas*, qd. v. W. *llyswen*; (*sil*, pl. *silod*, fish fry.) Arm. *sili*, *silien*.

SELLIC, adj. Conspicuous, remarkable, in open view. *Crug sellick*, the conspicuous barrow, in Veriau. *Pryce*.

SELLYS, adj. Salted. *Llwyd*, 143. Part. pass. of *salla*, qd. v.

SELWEL, v. a. To save. *Bôdh dhe vâb yw yn della, râk selwel kemmys yw da, aban fue Adam formys*, the will of thy son is so, for to save as many as are good, since Adam was created. P.C. 2953. *Dén na gresso dyougel, an kéth dén-na dhe selwel cammen vŷth na ŷl wharfos*, the man that believeth not really, that same man to save not any way can exist. R.D. 2479. Written also *sylwel*, qd. v.

SEMLANT, s. m. Semblance, form, appearance. *Pahan pleyt yma Pilat, yn le may ma, ha pan semlant ús ganso; lavar ol an guŷr dhymmo fatel me fa*, in what plight is Pilate, in the place where he is, and what appearance is with him? tell all the truth to me how he is. R.D. 2060. Borrowed from the English.

SENDAL, s. m. Fine linen. *A dro dh'y gorff y trylyas sendall rych yn luas plêg*, around his body he wrapped linen rich in many a fold. M.C. 232. Written also *cendal*, qd. v. W. *sindal*. Eng. †*sendal*. Span. *cendal*.

SENED, s. m. A synod. Corn: Voc. *sinodus*. From the Latin. W. *senedh*.

SENGYS, part. Bound, obliged, held, esteemed. *Lavar dhymmo, a ver spys, py nŷl o mocha sengys an kéth dénma dhe caré*, tell thou me, in a short space, which one of the two was most bound this man to love? P.C. 510. *Pyw an brassé dén senges yn mŷsk ol dhy dhyskyblon*, who is esteemed the greatest man among all thy disciples? P.C. 773. A corrupted form of *sensys*, part. pass. of *sensy*, qd. v. Written also *syngys*, qd. v.

SENS, s. m. Saints. *Pan weréth hepcor an bewneus, hep guthyl na moy cheyson, a huch an eleth ha'n séns, ty a dhue dhe néf dhum trôn*, when thou shalt put away life, without suffering any more trouble, above the angels and the saints, thou shalt come to heaven to my throne. R.D. 461. Written also *sŷns*, being the plural of *sans*, qd. v.

SENSY, v. a. To hold, esteem, value; to apprehend, catch, seize. 2 pers. s. imp. *sens*. Part. *sensys*. *Lemyn hanwaf goydh ha yâr, a sensaf edhyn hep pâr dhe eyygens dén war an beys*, now I name goose and fowl, (which) I esteem birds without equal for food of man on the earth. O.M. 130. *A'n lost kymmer dhedhy yn ban, y'th torn hep gêr sens dhe honan*, by the tail take it up, in thy hand without a word hold (it) thyself. O.M. 1455. *Ken agesouch venytha ny zenzen*, otherwise than you, ever we do not consider. O.M. 2358. *Senseuch ef yn agan mŷsk*, hold ye him in our midst. P.C. 1374. *Pan dyskys yn eglusyow ny wrûg dén fŷth ow sensy*, when I taught in the churches, no man ever seized me. P.C. 1176. *Wharé y a'n kemerce, hag a'n sensys yntrethé*, presently they took him, and held him among them. M.C. 70. *Tonvyl vŷth ny allaf yn fâs ynno sensy, dhe wonys*, any tool I cannot well hold in them to work. M.C. 156. *Hag yntré en Edhewon an grows fast a ve sensys*, and among the Jews the cross was fast held. M.C. 181. *Râg Pasch o dhedhé, dŷdh uchel y a sensy*, for it was the Passover to them, a high day they held it. M.C. 229. Written also *synsy*, qd. v. The second *s* became corrupted into *g*, as *sengys* for *sensys*, and in Llwyd's time that was the prevailing sound. Hence he writes it *sendzha, dho sendzhé*, to hold; *sendzhys*, held, obliged. ‡ *Sendzhys ôn ni a huci*, we are obliged to you. 252.

SERA, s. m. Sir, a father. *Me a vyn môs dhom sera*, I will go to my father. C.W. 86. Another form of *sira*, qd. v.

SERCHOG, adj. Loving, attached. Corn. Vocab. *les serchog*, lappa, clot bur. W. *serchog*.

SERRY, v. a. To provoke, to anger, to offend; to become angry, or displeased. Part. *serrys*. *Eva kyns del vy serrys, my a wra ol del vynny*, Eve, rather than thou be angry, I will do all as thou wishest. O.M. 245. *Ellas, gwelcs an termyn ow arluth pan wrûk serry*, alas, to see the time when I made my lord angry. O.M. 352. *Pan dorassa an aval, an Arluth a fue serrys*, when he had plucked the apple, the Lord was angered. O.M. 880. *Gorf a ra dhe serry*, woe to him (that) angereth thee. O.M. 1010. *Pandra amount dhyn gonys, mar serryth orth dên*, what avails it to us to cultivate, if thou be angry with man. O.M. 1224. *Serry dhys na dâl*, it avails thee not to be angry. R.D. 1405. *Ow bôs serrys nyns yw marth*, that I am angry is not a wonder. R.D. 1411. Written also *sorry*, qd. v.

SERTH, adj. Stiff, hard. *Me a's ten gans ol ow nerth, may 'th entré an spikys serth dre an cen yn y grogen*, I will pull it with all my strength, that the stiff spines may enter through the skin into the skull. P.C. 2140. W. *serth*.

SERVIS, s. m. A servant. Pl. *servisy*. *Fysyn may fyyn servysy dh'agan Arluth hep parow*, let us pray that we may be servants to our Lord without equals. O.M. 235. *Gordhyans ha grâs dhe Dew ow Thâs, luen a vercy, pan danvonas yn onor brâs dhym servysi*, glory and thanks to God my Father, full of mercy, when he hath sent in great honour servants to me. P.C. 172. *An Tâs Dew roy dhym bôs gwyw dhe vôs lên servysy dhys*, may God the Father grant to us to be worthy to be faithful servants to thee. P.C. 713. The plural was also corrupted into *servygy*. *Mâp Dew ôs ha dên un weydh, sawo ol dhe lên servygy*, Son of God thou art, and man likewise, save all thy faithful servants. P.C. 279. Llwyd, 242, gives the pl. *servisi*, and the late form *servidzhi*. Lat. *servus*.

SERVYE, v. a. To serve. 3 pers. s. fut. *serf*. *Bydhens kepar ha'n lyha; ha nêp a dheppro kensa, kepar ha nêp a servyo*, let him be like the least; and he who eats first like him who serves. P.C. 796. *Pyw a synsow why mochya, nêp a serf py a dheber*, whom think ye greatest? him who serves or who eats. P.C. 799. *Yn creys me re ysedhas avel servont ow servyé*, I have sat in the midst like a servant serving. P.C. 804. From the English.

SESTYA, v. a. To cease, to desist. *Bythqueth bay dhym ny ryssys, ha homma vŷth ny sestyas, abân duthé yn chy dhys pûp ûr ol ammé dhum treys*, never a kiss to me didst thou give, and this one has never ceased, since I came to thy house, continually to kiss my feet. P.C. 523. Lat. *sisto*.

SETTYA, v. a. To set, to set by, to value, to esteem. *Crist a settyas yn tyen an scovern arté dhe drê*, Christ set the ears completely home again. M.C. 71. *Orth Pilat ol y setsans, ha warnodho a rûg cry*, ou Pilate they all set, and to him cried. M.C. 117. *An houl, ha'n lôr, ha'n stergan, my a set a huch an gwcydh yn creys an cbron avan*, the sun, and the moon, and the stars, I will set over the trees in the midst of the sky above. O.M. 27. *Awos henna ny wrâf cry, na anothans y bŷs voy me ny settyaf guail gala*, of that I will not make account, nor them will I value ever more the stalk of a straw. C.W. 98. *Mark Dew warnaf yw settys*, the mark of God is set on me. C.W. 116.

SETH, s. f. An arrow. Pl. *sethow*. *Dre y holon ydh êth sêth, y mâb syndis pan welsé; moreth an sêth ha pytel; natureth o ha denseth*, through her heart there went an arrow, when she saw her son hurt; grief (was) the arrow, and pity, natural love it was and humanity. M.C. 223. *Gor ow sêth dhe denewen, may hullan tenna dhodho*, put thou my arrow to the string that I may shoot at it. C.W. 112. *Yta an sêth tennys, ha'n bêst yma gweskys*, behold the arrow shot, and the beast is struck. C.W. 114. *Me a vyn môs dhe wandra, bestas gwylls dhe aspeas, hag a vyn gans ow sethow ladha pûb anothans y*, I will go to walk about, to look for wild beasts, and will with mine arrows kill every one of them. C.W. 108. W. *saeth*. Arm. *saez, sez*. Ir. *soighead*. Gael. *saighead*. Manx, *side*. Lat. *sagitta*. It. *saetta*.

SETH, v. n. He went. *Py le re sêth*, where is it gone? R.D. 789. Read *res-êth*, the *s* being prefixed to a vowel after *re*. So after *a*, in *mar a sêth é*, if he is gone. R.D. 538.

SETHAN, s. f. An arrow. Dim. of *sêth*. Llwyd, 143, *zethan*.

SETHAR, s. m. An archer, a shooter; a sea mew, cob or gull. Llwyd, 14, 30, 76, *zethar*. A late form of *saithor*, qd. v.

SEUYAD, s. m. A tailor. Corn. Voc. *sartor*. Formed from the English *to sew*, with the usual termination to denote the agent.

SEUYADES, s. f. A female tailor, a sempstress. Llwyd, 241.

SEVEL, v. n. To stand up, to rise, to stand; to raise up. 3 pers. s. fut. *sêf*, qd. v. Part. *sevys*. *Scrifys yw yn leas le, yt allos y vôs gorrys kyffris sevell ha codhé, ha ganso kyn fês tewlys, te a ŷll sevel arté*, it is written in many a place, that it is put in thy power as well to stand as to fall, and though thou hast been cast down by him, thou wilt be able to stand again. M.C. 22. *Gans henna a'n Edhewon onan yn lun a sevys*, with that one of the Jews stood up. M.C. 81. *Ena hy a ve sevys yn ban ynter benenas*, there she was raised up among (the) women. M.C. 172. *Eledh dherygthy a sêff*, angels before her shall stand. M.C. 226. *Râg Ihesus dhe leverel yn tressa dŷdh y sevy*, for Jesus had said that he would rise on the third day. M.C. 238. *Ha dhodho* a *leverys re saffé Crist hep strevyé*, and to him (they) said that Christ had risen without contending. M.C. 248. *Del sevys Máb Du a'y védh, yn êr-na dhe'n tressa dýdh yn della ol ny a séff dédh brues, drók ha da yn wédh*, as the Son of God rose from his tomb, then, on the third day, so shall we all arise on doomsday, good and bad likewise. M.C. 259. *Dýsk dhe 'skyggyow dhe vôs, sevel war týr veneges a wrêth*, take off thy shoes, stand on blessed ground thou dost. O.M. 1407. *Ha'n mór a púp tu dhedhé, ow sevel avel dyw fôs*, and the sea on every side to them, standing like two walls. O.M. 1690. *Sevyn yn ban, dên ahanan seon alcmma*, let us stand up, let us come hence soon from here. P.C. 1099. *Lemmyn ow abesteleth, sevouch yn agus crygyans; aban óf sevyn a'n bédh, gothfedheuch y's býdh sylvans*, now my apostles, stand in your belief; since I am risen from the tomb, know ye that he have salvation. R.D. 1572. *Sevouch yn agys crygyans*, stand in your belief. R.D. 2389. W. *sevyll*. Arm. *sevel*. Ir. *seas*. Gael. *seas*. Manx, *shass*.

SEVI, s. m. A strawberry. *Llwyd*, 19, 61. *Delkiow sevi*, strawberry leaves. *Rág delkiow sevi gura muzi tég*, for strawberry leaves make maidens fair. *Pryce*. W. *syvi*. Arm. *sivi*. Ir. *súbh lair*. Gael. *súbhag lair*.

SEVYLLIAC, s. m. A sneak, a loiterer. *Adam, ma ow lordyn avel dûk yn Paradys, ha me sevyllyak omma yn efarn, yn tán púb prýs, yn ponvan brás ow lesky*, Adam is lording like a duke in Paradise, and I a loiterer here in hell, in fire always, in great pain burning. C.W. 34. W. *sevylliog*.

SEW, v. a. Follow thou. 2 pers. s. imp. of *sewyé*, qd. v.

SEW, s. m. A bream. Pl. *sewion*. *Carnsew*, the bream rock. *Pryce*.

SEWYE, v. a. To follow, to pursue. Written also *sewé*. 2 pers. s. imp. *sew*. Part. *sewyys, sewys*. *Dhe'n menedh Olyff ydh éth, ha'y dhyscyplys a'n sewyas*, to the mount of Olives he went, and his disciples followed him. M.C. 52. *Reys yw porris, heb strevyé bódh ow thâs dhe vôs sewyys*, it is needful, very needful, that the will of my Father should be followed without striving. M.C. 73. *Ha ny a'd cuwyll, na âs lemyn y vódh heb sewyé*, and we advise thee, leave not his will without following (it.) M.C. 116. *Sew olow ow thryys, lyskys*, follow thou the prints of my feet, burnt. O.M. 711. *Banneth sewes, bowler*, let a blessing follow thee, butler. O.M. 1917. *A dhyrnyouch me a pýs ow bones ymskemunys, me mar a'n sewys bythqueth*, before you I pray that I may be cursed, if I have ever followed him. P.C. 1416. *Benet sewys*, let a blessing follow. P.C. 3015. Written also *syweé*, qd. v. This word is borrowed from the English, which, though now obsolete in this sense, was by Wickliff and writers of his age almost invariably used for "follow." Thus Wickliff has in 1 Peter, iij. 11. "Seke he pees, and parfytli *sue* it." So in Matth. viij. "Whanne Jhesus was come down fro the hill, myche puple *sueden* him.—*Sue* thou me and lete the dede men birie her dede men. " So in *Life of Thomas Becket*.—"Faste he *suede* aftor hem, he and othere mo." l. 15. "The pley he *suede* of houndes, and of haukes also ynouz." l. 191.

SEYCH, adj. Dry. *War an pren glays mar a tê, yn pren scych ha casadow yn êr-na fatel ve*, on the green wood if it come, in dry and hateful wood how would it be? M.C. 170. Another form of *sêch* or *sých*, qd. v.

SEYF, v. n. He will stand. *A huhon máp Dew a seyf*, on high the Son of God will stand. R.D. 2612. Another form of *séf*, qd. v.

SEYM, s. m. Grease, train-oil. *Wâr gás vy dhe dhchesy gans morben lom trewysy dhe'n vśl hora war an tnal, neffré na wrello dybry, lemyn fleryé ha peddry, kepar ha scym py lyys hnal*, soon let me strike with mallet a terrible blow to the vile strumpet on the forehead, that she may never eat, but stink and rot, like train-oil or salt-marsh mud. O.M. 2708. W. *snim, swyv*. Arm. *soav, son*. Ir. *snim*. Gael. *saill*. Manx, *sayll*. Lat. *sebum*. Fr. *suif*.

SGAV, adj. Light, nimble. *Llwyd*, 11. Id. qd. *scáf*, qd. v.

SGELLIGREHAN, s. m. A bat. *Pryce*. See *Scelligrehan*.

SHAGGA, s. m. A cormorant, a shag. *Llwyd*, 51, 89. From the English.

SHANOL, s. m. A channel, a gutter, kennel. *Llwyd*, 46.

SHIMBLA, s. m. A chimney; a hearth, or fireside. *Llwyd*, 60.

SHYNDYE, v. a. To hurt, to injure. Part. *shyndyys*. *Ellas, Moyses, och, tru, tru, shyndyys óf gans cronck du, ha whethys gans y venym, alas, Moses*, Oh, sad, sad, hurt I am by a black toad, and blown by his venom. O.M. 1778. *Ow artuth whêk ol, lêdh e, ken ef a wra ow shyndyé, mar clew vyth agan guary*, my all sweet lord, kill him, else he will hurt me, if he shall ever hear of our sport. O.M. 2133. Written also *schyndyé* and *syndyé*, qd. v.

SIAN, s. m. The sea shore, a strand. *Llwyd*, 81, *zian*.

SIBUIT, s. m. A fir tree. Corn. Voc. *abies*. This in the orthography of the Dramas would be written *sibwydh*, being compounded of *sib*, (Lat. *sapus*) and *gwydh*, a tree. Called also *saban*, qd. v. W. *sybwydh*. Arm. *sup, sapr, sapren*. Med. Lat. *sapus, sappus, sappetus*.

SICER, s. m. Cider. Corn. Vocab. *sicera*. W. *suger*. Arm. *sidr, sistr*.

SICH, adj. Dry. *Llwyd*, 150. *Pen sich-nans*, the head of the dry valley, in Gwennap. *Pryce*. Generally written *sých*, qd. v.

SICHOR, s. m. Dryness, drought. Corn. Voc. *siccitas*. Arm. *sechor*.

SIGER, adj. Hollow, full of holes. *Llwyd*, 47.

SIGYR, adj. Sluggish, lazy. *Llwyd*, 151. *An gwás brás sigyr-na*, that great lazy fellow. 248. W. *segur*. Lat. *securus, socors*.

SIHY, v. a. To dry. *Pryce*. A late form of *sychy*, qd. v.

SIL, s. m. Sunday. *Llwyd*, 54. Plur. *siliow*. Written also *sul*, qd. v.

SILGUETII, s. m. Sunday tide, the sunday, on a sunday. *Llwyd*, 249. Comp. of *sil*, sunday, and *gwéth*, a time.

SIL, s. un. A view, or prospect. *Pryce*. See *Syll*.

SILLI, s. f. An eel. *Llwyd*, 241. Pl. *sillies*, 243. *Y róf hynwyn dhe'n puskes, porpus, sowmens, syllyes, ol dhym gustyth a y védh*, I will give names to the fishes, porpoises, salmons, eels, all to me obedient they shall be. O.M. 136. Written also *selli*, qd. v. Arm. *sili*.

SIM, s. m. A monkey. Corn. Voc. *simia*. From the Latin. W. *simach*.

SINSY, v. a. To hold. Generally written *sénsyé*, and *synsyé*, qd. v.

SINSIAT, adj. Tenacious. Corn. Vocab. *tenax*. From *sinsy*, to hold, with the ordinary termination.

SIRA, s. m. Sir, a sire, a father. Llwyd. 114. ‡ *Ha madra ta, pan drig scera ha damma*, and study well, what did father and mother. *Pryce. Sira wyn*, a grandfather. *Llwyd*, 44.

SIW, s. m. A bream. Plur. *siwion*. Written by Pryce *sew*, and by Llwyd, *ziw*.

SLEV, adj. Skilful, expert, cunning. *Llwyd*, 118.

SLEYVETH, s. m. Skill, cunning. *Enuf Crist dhe yffarn êth, hag a dorras an porthow, dre y nerth brâs ha'y sleyveth ena gobmas dewolow*, the soul of Christ went to hell and broke the gates, through his great strength and his skill there he bound the devils. M.C. 212.

SLODYYS, s. m. Sledges, trucks. *Ty, vaow, darbar lym ha pry, meyn wheyl, slodyys, ha genow, ha my a fystyn agy, ow trchevel an fosow*, thou boy, prepare lime and clay, building stones, trucks, and wedges; and I will hasten within, raising the walls. O.M. 2318.

SLOTTEREE, s. m. Rainy weather, foul, and dirty; a slattern. *Pryce*.

SLYNTYA, v. n. To slide, to glide along. *Ha te, prŷf, a wra cruppya, ha sleyntya war doar a heys*, and thou reptile, shalt creep, and slide on the ground along. C.W. 66. *Me a vyn dallath cruppya, ha slyntya war doer a heys*, I will begin to creep, and slide upon the earth along. C.W. 68. *Slyncya*, is another reading. Eng. *slink*.

SMAT, s. m. A friend, a brave fellow, a soldier. *Dysmyg lemmyn, ty guas smat*, declare now, thou brave fellow. P.C. 1392. *Rág cf gans cam a gerch dhywcorthyn Adam hag Eva, ha lyes smat*, for he with wrong will fetch from us Adam and Eve, and many friends. P.C. 3036. *Lowené dhys Syr Pilat, awos bôs ny pescar smat, goythé an bêdh ny ylsyn*, joy to thee, Sir Pilate, though we be four brave fellows, we could not keep the tomb. R.D. 603. *Dre ow thrýs y tûth un smat gans kentrow d'aga gorré*, through my feet a soldier came with nails to put them. R.D. 2587.

SNIT, s. m. A snipe. "*Snite* is still used in Cornwall for a snipe." *Polwhele*. W. *ysnid, ysnilcn*.

SNOD, s. m. A fillet, a ribband. Corn. Voc. *vitta*. W. *ysnoden, noden*. Arm. *neuden*. Ir. *snaidhm, † snath*. Gael. *snaim*. Scotch, *snood*. Lat. *nodus*.

SOA, s. m. Suet, tallow. *Pryce*. W. *sûyv*. Arm. *soav, soa*. See *Seym*.

SOATH, adj. Fat, greasy. *Nansoath*, the fat valley, in Ludock. *Pryce*.

SOCH, s. f. A ploughshare. Corn. Voc. *vomer*. Softened into *zôh*, in Llwyd's time, 18, 177. W. *swch, † such*. Arm. *souzh*. Ir. *soc*. Gael. *soc*. Manx, *sock*. Lat. *soccus*. Fr. *soc*.

SOG, adj. Moist, wet. *Pryce*; who derives hence *Rowgan*, the moist valley, in Stephens. Written also *sug*, qd. v.

SOL, s. f. A foundation. *Pryce*. Id. qd. *sel*, qd. v. Used with *dŷdh*, a day, and *prŷs*, time, to express a length of time. *Nansyu groundyys genef vy sol (a) brŷs gans horvennow*, they are now begun by me long ago with scaffolds. O.M. 2322. *Yrverys cw, rum leveté, sol a dhŷdh dhe avonsyé a'n kynsé benfys a'm been*, it has been thought of, on my truth, for a long time to advance thee to the first benefice I have. O.M. 2612. *Rág varow yw an voron gans ow whaffys sol a breys*, for the jade is dead by my blows a long time past. O.M. 2747. *Néb rum gwerthas sollabreys*, who hath sold me some time ago. P.C. 746. *Ny fue golhys sol-a-dhêdh*, it has not being washed a long time. R.D. 1929.

SOLER, s. m. A groundroom, an entry, a gallery, a stage of boards in a mine. *Pryce*. Corn. Voc. *solarium vel solium*. From the Latin. W. *seiler*.

SOLS, s. m. Corn. Voc. *pecunia*. Written by Llwyd, 115, *zoulz*, a shilling. W. *swllt*. From the Lat. *solidus*. Mod. Lat. *soldus*. It. *soldo*. Fr. *sou*.

SON, s. m. A sound, a noise, report, speech. *Aron whêk, pŷth a cusyl a rêth dhym orth am vrcsyl, a són an debel bobel*, sweet Aaron, what advice givest thou in my dispute, at the noise of the wicked people. O.M. 1815. *Hep whethé corn na gûl són*, without blowing a horn, or making a noise. P.C. 1358. *Pŷth yw an whethlow ha'n són a glowaf aberth yn pow*, what are the tales and the report that I hear within the country? R.D. 608. *Gâs dhe són*, leave off thy noise. R.D. 1010. *Kymer, toul e yn pryson, na sparyé, kyn wrello són*, take thou, throw him into prison, spare him not, though he make a noise. R.D. 2016. W. *són, sŵn, sain*. Arm. *son, soun*. Ir. *soin, † son, † sian*. Gael. *son*. Manx, *sheean*. Lat. *sonus*. Gr. *åwòv*.

SONA, v. a. To bless, to hallow, to sanctify, to consecrate, to charm. Written also *soné*. 2 pers. s. imp., and 3 pers. s. fut. *sôn*. Part. *sonys*. *Aga sona ny a wra*, we will bless them. O.M. 143. *A Dhew, lemyn gwyn ow bŷs, ow vle sonys hep whethlow*, O God, now happy is my lot, my being blessed without deceit. O.M. 466. *My a'd pŷs, ow sona gura kyns ys môs*, I pray thee, do bless me before I go. O.M. 723. *Lemyn agan soné gura kyns ys bones ancdhys*, now do thou bless us before it is inhabited. O.M. 1721. *Dal óf, ny allaf gueles, són vy gansé, hep dangvr*, blind I am, I cannot see; bless thou me with them without delay. O.M. 2008. *Són vy kyns môs*, bless thou me before going. O.M. 2167. *Du a sonas an bara dhe rág y abestcly*, God blessed the bread before his apostles. M.C. 44. *An rŷ-ma ew oll têk gurŷs, me a'y sôn war barth heb gow*, these are all made fair, I will bless them together without a lie. C.W. 10. *Sonys bêdh do hanow*, hallowed be thy name. *Pryce*. W. *swyno*. Ir. *sona, † sên*. Gael. *sona*. O.N. *signa*. O.H.G. *segen*. Lat. *signo*.

SOR, s. m. Anger, wrath, ill will, grudge, grumbling. *Ragon y peays y dâs oll y sor may fe gevys*, for us he prayed his Father that all his wrath might be remitted. M.C. 9. *Na dhegouch sor yu golon war néb a vyn ow sawyé*, do not ye bear anger in heart against any one (that) would save me. M.C. 37. *Dhe Herodes ydh esa pûr wŷr worth Pylat sor brâs*, to Herod there was very truly against Pilate great anger. M.C. 110. *Dre sor kyn fêns y terrys*, though they be broken in anger. O.M. 1237. W. *sor*.

SORDYA, v. n. To arise, to be raised. Part. *sordyys*. *Bresel crêff a ve sordyys en grows pu ellé dh'y dôn*, a strong contest was raised, the cross who should go to bear it. M.C. 160. *Ternoys y sordyas bresel gans an Edhewon goky*, the day after there arose a contest among the foolish Jews. M.C. 238. Lat. *exordior*.

SORN, s. m. A small space, a corner. *Belsebuc whêk, wheyth dhe corn, ha galvy drê a pûp sorn an dhewolow,* sweet Beelzebub, blow thy horn, and call home from every corner the devils. P.C. 3056. *A dhysempys whylewh e, mar as êth e dhe cudhé yn nêp bós, tewl, py yn sorn,* immediately seek yo for him, if he has gone to hide in some bush, hole, or in a corner. R.D. 539. W. *sorn.*

SORRAS, s. m. A grudge, grumbling. *Pryce.* W. *sorrad.*

SORRY, v. n. To be angry, or offended ; to render angry, to provoke. 2 pers. s. imp., and 3 pers. s. fut. *sor. En scheremys a sorras râg bonas Crist honoris,* the wicked were angry for that Christ was honoured. M.C. 31. *Moy es Dew ny a cyé, bŷs vynytha na sorren,* greater than God we should be, that we should never be offended. O.M. 220. *Y won dhe wŷr Dew an Tâs re sorras drewyth brnen,* I know truly, God the Father a sorry woman hath angered. O.M. 256. *Râg ow fehas pandra wrûf, may te sorré, a dâs whêk,* for my sin what shall I do, that thou shouldst be angry, O sweet Father. O.M. 2258. *Râg henna me a sorras, hag a tôs na worên neffré,* for that I was angry, and swore that I never would. P.C. 1421. *Bŷth na sor,* never be thou angry. C.W. 90. *Râg me an Arluth dhy Dew yw Dew a sor,* for I the Lord thy God am a God that will be offended. *Pryce.* Sorry is another form, qd. v. W. *sorri.*

SORT, s. m. A hedgehog. Corn. Voc. *hyricus* vel *crinatius.* Written also *sarl.* Arm. *sort.* Fr. *sourd,* a salamander. W. *sorth, swrth,* slothful, rough. The proper name in W. is *draenog,* prickly.

SOS, v. subs. Thou art. *Os* assumes an *s* as a prefix after *mar* and *mara,* as *mar sôs,* if thou art ; of which *mar sosa, mar sota, mar sosé, mar a sosé, mar sogé,* are various forms. For convenience they may be read *mars ôs, mars osa, mars ota, mars osé, maras osé, mars ogé.* See *Mars, &c.*

SOTEL, adj. Subtle, clever. *Gonesugy ken agesouch why ny's ty, râg sotel ouch yn pûp crefl,* other workmen than you shall not cover it, for skilful ye are in every art. O.M. 2490.

SOTH, v. a. To flatter. *Pûb ér dhe dhên gura lewté, beva dên yonk bo dên côth, orthaf mar mynnyth colé, neffré gans an fals na soth,* always do thou loyalty to mau, be he a young man or an old man, if thou wilt listen to me, ever with the false do not flatter. M.C. 175. From the Old English, *soothe,* to flatter.

SOTH, s. m. Suite. *Arluth, otté ny genouch, del fursym yn ta genouch, yn agas soth ; lavar dhynny bôs dhe vrŷs, ha ny a'n gura ef uskys, kepar del gûth,* Lord, behold us with you, as we fared well often in your suite, tell us the will of thy mind, and we will do it immediately, like as it is becoming. R.D. 1881.

SOUL, s. m. Stubble. Llwyd, 11, 155, gives the late form *zoul.* W. *sonyl, sovl.* Arm. *soul.* Lat. *stipula.*

SOWETH, interj. More the pity, sadly, unhappily, alas. *A na wylw ol mŷns es orth dhe vlamyé yn soweth, hag ow ry dhys bozow tres, beteyns te ny sconyth,* seest thou not all the multitude (that) is blaming thee unhappily, and giving thee froward blows ? nevertheless thou dost not refuse. M.C. 120. *A soweth, te dha gregy dha'n jowl brâs, ha'y anfugy,* ah, sad, thou to believe the great devil, and his hypocrisy. C.W. 70. *Fensen ow bosaf marow, soweth, bytheth bôs formyys,* would that I were dead ; alas that I ever was made. C.W. 92. *Soweth an prŷs,* accursed be the time. C.W. 120. *Ah, soweth, gweles an prŷs,* ah, unhappily to see the time. C.W. 122. W. *ysyweith,* comp. of *y sy,* that is, and *gweeth,* worse. Arm. *siouaz,* † *suez.* Ir. *saoth,* † *saith,* tribulation.

SOWLS, s. m. A shilling. Llwyd, 151, *zowls.* A late form of *sols,* qd. v.

SOWS, s. m. An Englishman, a Saxon. Plur. *sowson.* Llwyd, 242, *sowzon.* Pow *an Sowson,* England. 42. Written also *saws,* qd. v.

SOWSNEC, s. f. The English language. Llwyd, 42, ‡ *zouznak,* and 32, ‡ *znznak.* W. *saesnaeg.* Arm. *saoznek.* Written also *sawsnec,* qd. v.

SOWYNNE, v. a. To prosper, to flourish, to thrive. Written also *sowené.* 3 pers. s. fut. *sowyn. Pan dra ny vyu Dew gûl vry ahanaf, na sowyny an peyth a wrehaf ny wra, ha pûp âr chatel Abel, y a sowyn nŷl blêk guel ; Abel a'n pren râg henna,* why will not God make account of me ; nor thrive the thing (that) I do will not ; and always an article of Abel's will thrive a thousand fold better ; Abel shall pay for that. O.M. 520. *Venytha na sowyny, tan hemma war an challa,* that thou mayest never thrive, take this on the jaw-bone. O.M. 539. *Me a'n dalhen fest yn tyn, ha gans ow dornow a'n guryn na sowenno,* I hold him very tightly, and with my hands squeeze him that he thrive not. P.C. 1133. *Ny sowynaf, gon yn ta, nefra yn bŷs,* I shall not prosper I know well, ever in the world. C.W. 98. *Henna ew marrudgyon brâs, an nocr ny sowennas yn for my wrûg ev kerras,* that is a great wonder, the earth hath not flourished in the way I made him go. C.W. 128.

SPAS, adv. Whilst, until. *Llwyd,* 55, 249.

SPAVEN, s. m. Smoothness. Corn. Voc. *spaven mor* equor, smooth sea. W. *yspai, yspailh,* what is clear and open.

SPECCIAR, adj. Spotted, speckled. *Llwyd,* 33. Borrowed from the English.

SPEDHES, s. m. Briars, brambles. *Y'th whys lavur dhe dhybry ty a wra, bŷs y'th worfen ; spern ha spedhes ow tevy, hedré vy may jo anken,* in thy sweat labour to eat thou shalt, even to thy end ; thorns and briars growing, whilst thou shalt be until death be. O.M. 275. *Crêf yw gwrydhyow an spedhes, nay'th yw ow dyno-vrech lerrys worté wenouch ow quethé,* strong are the roots of the briars, that my arms are broken, working often at them. O.M. 689. *Spedhes* is a plural aggregate, of which the sing. would be *spedhen.* W. *yspydhaden,* † *ispidatenn.* Ir. *sciathach.* Gael. *sgithench.* Manx, *skaig.*

SPENCER, s. m. A butler. *Pyw a symsow why mochya, nép a serf py a dheber ? A nynsyw nép a dheppro ? yw sûr del heuel dymmo ; moy yw arluth es spencer,* whom think ye greatest, him (that) serves, or (that) eats ? is it not he that eats ? sure it is as it seems to me ; greater is the lord than the butler. P.C. 802. The obsolete English term.

SPERN, s. m. Thorns. *Spern ha spedhes ow tevy,* thorns and briars growing. O.M. 275. *Gans spern gurêch y curené,* with thorns do yo crown him. P.C. 2064. *Otté spern grisyl gynné, ha dreyn lym ha scharp ynné, a grup bŷs yn empynyon,* see sharp thorns with me, and spines pointed and sharp in them, (that) will pierce even to the brains. P.C. 2116. *Pan wclaf adro dh'y pen euryn spern,* when I see about his head a crown of thorns. P.C. 2934. *Me a dhuk curyn a spern nêp try our adro dhum pen,* I wore a crown of thorns some three hours around my head. R.D. 2554. *Spern* is a plural aggregate, the singular being *spernan.* Llwyd, 240. *Spernan wyn,* a white thorn. 110. *Spernan diu,* a black thorn. Arm. *spern, spernen.*

SPERNABYL, adj. Willing to be despised. *Besy yw dhys bôs vuell ha spernabyll y'th servys, manno allo an tebell ogas dhys bôs trylys,* it is needful for thee to be humble and willing to be despised in thy service, that the evil one may not be turned near to thee. M.C. 19. Formed probably from the Old English, *asperne,* to disregard. Lat. *aspernor.*

SPERIS, s. m. A spirit. *Tays ha Mâb ha'n Speris Sans vry a bŷs a leun golon,* Father, Son, and Holy Ghost, ye shall beseech with a full heart. M.C. 1. *An ioul a trylyas speris, hag êth dh'y tyller bythy,* the devil turned spirit, and went to his place quickly. M.C. 18. Written also *spyrys,* qd. v.

SPIRIT, s. m. A spirit. Corn. Voc. *spiritus.* The oldest form of *speris,* and *spyrys,* qd. v. W. *yspryd.* Arm. *sperel.* Ir. *spiorad,* † *spirut.* Gael. *spiorad.* Manx, *spyryd.* All from the Lat. *spiritus.*

SPLAN, adj. Bright, resplendent, splendid, clear, lucid. Comp. *splanna.* *Lemmen pan yw nêf dhyn gwrŷs, ha lennys a clêdh splan, uy a vyn formyé an bŷs,* now when heaven is made to us, and filled with bright angels, we will form the earth. O.M. 10. *Ny yllyn syvel yn ban râk own anodho, y wolow o mâr a splan,* I could not stand upright for fear of him, his light was very brilliant. R.D. 535. *Râk an Arluth a geusys hydhew worthyn yn geydh splan,* for the Lord spoke to us to-day in clear day. R.D. 1503. *Yn le may 'th ên, yn trewow yn splan me a's derevas,* in the place that I was, in towns clearly I declared them. M.C. 79. *Oll gans our terlentry ydhesaf, splanna es an houl,* all with gold glittering I am, more resplendent than the sun. C.W. 10, 14. *En splan,* clearly. Llwyd, 248. The last form was *spladn.* 48. W. *ysplan.* Arm. *splan.* Lat. *splendidus.*

SPLANDER, s. m. Brightness, splendour, clearness. Llwyd, 33. *Oll dhe splander ha'th tekter y treyl skon dhys dhe hacter, ha môr utheck byllen,* all thy splendour and beauty shall be turned immediately to deformity and most ugly foulness. C.W. 22. W. *ysplander.* Arm. *splander.* Lat. *splendor.*

SPLANNA, v. n. To be bright, to shine, to glitter. Llwyd, 62. W. *ysplanna.* Arm. *splanna.* Lat. *splendeo.*

SPRUS, s. m. Grains, kernels. A plural aggregate, of which the singular is *sprusan,* f. *Attoma tayr sprusan dryes mês a Baradys dhe why; a aval y fôns terrys, a dhêth a'n wedhan defry ew henwys, gwedhan a wenans: an êl a ornas dhe ny, pan vo dewedh dhê'th dhydhyow, ha'th vôs gyllys a lema, gora sprusan y'th ganow, ha'n dhew arall pûr dhybblans yn dha dhew freig; mês an spris y fŷdh tewys gwedhan a vŷdh pûr precyous,* here are three kernels brought out of Paradise to you; out of an apple they were broken (that) came from the tree truly, that is called the Tree of life: the angel commanded to us, when were ended thy days, and thou wert gone from hence, to put one kernel in thy mouth,

and the two others very distinctly in thy nostrils; out of the kernels there shall grow a tree, (that) shall be very precious. C.W. 140. Written also *spûs.* *Kemer tyyr spûs a'n aval a dybrys Adam dhe dâs,* take three kernels of the apple (which) Adam thy father ate. O.M. 823. *An try spûs yn y anow me a's gor,* the three grains in his mouth I will put. O.M. 870. *Bolungeth Dew yw hemma, bones gorrys an spûs-ma yn y anow,* the will of God is this, that these kernels be placed in his mouth. O.M. 874. Arm. *splus,* sing. *splusen.*

SPYRYS, s. m. A spirit. *Onan hu try ôn yn guyr, en Mâp, ha'n Mâp, ha'n Spyrys,* one and three we are in truth, the Father, and the Son, and the Spirit. O.M. 4. *A Dâs, Mâp, ha Spyrys Sans, gordhyans dhe'th corf wêk pûp prŷs,* O Father, Son, and Holy Ghost, glory to thy sweet body always. O.M. 85. *Ow spyrys ny drŷc nefré yn corf mâp dên vŷdh yn beys,* my spirit shall not always dwell in the body of any son of man in the world. O.M. 925. *Marow yw pûp tra cêf spyrys a wenans ynno,* dead is every thing (that) there was the spirit of life in it. O.M. 1000. A later form of *spirit,* qd. v.

SQUARDYE, v. a. To tear, to rend, to break to pieces; to be torn, to be rent, to be broken to pieces. Part. *squardyys.* *Garlont spern wâr y ben a ve gorris, may'th o squardijs adro ol,* a garland of thorns was put on his head, so that it was torn all about. M.C. 133. *Ow holon yntré mŷll darn marth yw gené, na squardthy,* it is a wonder to me that my heart does not break into a thousand pieces. M.C. 166. *Oll warbarth may 'th êns squardis,* that they were altogether torn. M.C. 181. *A wotta omma nêb ŷll tempell Du dowstoll squardyé, ha dh'y vûdh y dhrehevell,* behold here one that can tear to pieces the temple of God, and raise it at his will. M.C. 195. *Veyll an tempyll a squardyns yntré dew,* the voil of the temple was torn in two. M.C. 209. Written in the Dramas, *squerdyé,* qd. v.

SQUAT, adv. Suddenly. *How, hale kettep onan, gesouch hy, a barth Malan, yn morter skuat dhe godhé, ho! haul every one, let it, on Malan's part, into the mortiso crack to fall.* P.C. 2816. "*Squat* is a word used by the miners, the squat of a load, a broad heap." *Pryce.*

SYUATTYA, v. a. To pluck, or tear to pieces, to smite, to strike, to hew. 3 pers. s. fut. *squat.* Part. *squattyys.* *Squattyys ew dha ampydnyon,* smashed are thy brains. C.W. 124. *Gans ow boell nowydh lemmys me a squat pûb peis tymber,* with my axe newly sharpened, I will hew every piece of timber. C.W. 166. Llwyd, 55. *squattia;* 117, 142, *dho skuattia, dho skuattya.* Arm. *skeja.*

SQUENIV, adj. Unchaste. Corn. Voc. *incestus.* "This word appears to be the negative of *gwaf,* chaste; which is cognate with the Gael. *geanm.* The two forms would then be theoretically *gnanv, disgueniv,* or perhaps *gnanu, disguenm,* in analogy with *laian, dislaian.*" Norris's Cornish Drama."

SQUERD, s. m. A rent, any thing torn. *Pryce.* "*Squard* is still used in Cornwall for a rent in the garment." *Polwhele.*

SQUERDYE, v. a. To tear, to rend, to break to pieces. Part. *squerdys, squyrdys.* *Dyeth mûr yw dhym skuerdyé na terry pous an plos wês; iculcl pren mŷl wel ryé, pan vôns squerdys ny vŷdh vâs,* it is a great pity to me to tear or rend the coat of the dirty fellow; to throw dice would be a thousand (times) better, when it is torn it will not be good. P.C. 2845. *Dywolow yffarn a squerdyas corf Iudas ol dhe dharnow*, devils of hell tore the body of Judas all to pieces. M.C. 100. *Yw saw ol dhe wolyow a wylys vy dhe squerdyé*, are all thy wounds healed (that) I saw tearing thee? R.D. 496. *Y golon squyrdys a lés me a welas*, his heart torn in pieces I saw. R.D. 1032. *Un profus lyynygce, yn grous ha dhynverrch a lés, squerdys y treys ha'y dhewlé*, a blessed prophet on a cross, and his arms extended, torn his feet and his hands. R.D. 1266. Written also *squardyé*, qd. v. Arm. *scarza*.

SQUYCH, s. m. A jerk, switch, or twitch. *Pan fue an purpur war skwych kychys dhe vés gans dyw dhorn, worto y glyncs hardlych ran a'n kŷc bŷs yn ascorn*, when the purple was with a jerk snatched away with hands, to it adhered closely a piece of the flesh even to the bone. R.D. 2594.

SQUYTH, adj. Weary, tired, fatigued. *A Dew kér assoma squyth, wyn weys a quellen un wŷth an termen dhe dhevedhé*, O dear God I am weary, happy should I see once the time to end. O.M. 684. *Squyth ŷf dre vér lafuryé*, I am weary through much labouring. O.M. 2049. *Nans on lafuryys ganso, hag an yssyly pûr squyth*, now we are oppressed with it, and our limbs are very weary. O.M. 2824. *Ha'n dhew-nu, bŷs pan vôns squyth, war Crist y fôns ow cronkyé*, and those two until they were tired, were beating Christ. M.C. 132. Arm. *skuiz, squiz*.

SQUYTHENS, s. m. Weariness, fatigue. *Me a vyn môs dhe uré ow Arluth, treys a dewlé gans onement kér, ha war y pen y scullyé, a pûp squythens y sawyé, hag ylyé y wewyon*, I will go to anoint my Lord, feet and hands with precious ointment, and shed it upon his head; from all weariness cure him, and anoint his bruises. P.C. 477. Arm. *skuizder*.

SQUYTHEYS, adj. Weary, made weary. *A él, me a lever dhys, ow thâs ew côth ha squythreys; ny garsé pellé bewé*, O angel, I will tell thee, my father is old and weary; he would not wish to live longer. O.M. 737.

STAGEN, s. f. A lake, a pool. Llwyd, 33. Lat. *stagnum*.

STEAN, s. m. Tin. Llwyd, 154. *Hwél stean*, a tin-work. 60. *Pul stean*, a tin pit. Pryce. *Stean San Aynes an gwella stean en Kernow*, the tin of St. Agnes the best in Cornwall. Ibid. Written also contractedly *stên*. *Hwél stén*. Llwyd, 145. W. *ystaen*. Arm. *stean*. Ir. *stan*. Gael. *staoin*. Manx, *stainney*. Lat. *stannum*. Fr. *étain*.

STEFENIC, s. f. The palate. Corn. Voc. *palatum*. Read by Llwyd, 111, *stevnig*. Pryce gives *stevaic* as the reading. W. *ystwaig*. Arm. *stan, stuon, stavn, stafn*.

STELLA, adv. Always, continually. Llwyd, 70, 148, 178.

STEN, s. f. A milkpail. Llwyd, 240. W *ystên*.

STENER, s. m. A tinner, a pewterer. Plur. *stennerion*. Pryce. *Ry dha stener dec pens en bledhan*, give to a tinner ten pounds a year. Ibid. Written also *stynnar*. W. *ystaenwr*. Arm. *staener, stener*.

STENOR, s. f. A water wagtail. Llwyd, 93, 240. From *stên*, a milkpail. This bird has various names in Welsh, as *tinsigl, sigl-din y gŵys, brith yr ôy*, and in connection with the dairy, *brith y vuches*.

STEREN, s. f. A star. Corn. Voc. *stella*. Plur. *stér, steyr, steryan*. *Dowr ha lér, ha tán, ha gwyns, houl, ha lour, ha steyr kyffris, a Gryst ow codhaff mernans, anken y wodhevys*, water and earth, and fire, and wind, sun and moon, and stars likewise, at Christ suffering death, sorrow they suffered. M.C. 211. *Yn peswere gwereys perfyth dhe'n beys ol golowys glân, h'aga hynwyn y a vŷdh an houl, ha'n lór ha'n steryan*, on the fourth be made perfect, to all the earth bright lights, and their names they shall be the sun, and the moon, and the stars. O.M. 36. *An planats ês awartha, ha'n stér yn wêdh maga ta*, the planets (that) are on high, and the stars also as well. C.W. 156. Written by Llwyd, *sterran*. *Sterran loski*, a blazing star, or comet. *Sterran gwandré*, a planet. 121. *Sterrian moya*, the greatest stars. 224. W. *seren*, †*scirena*, in Oxford Glosses, plur. *sêr*. Arm. *steren, stiren*. Ir. †*rean*. Gael. †*stcorn*. Gr. ἀστήρ. Lat. *astrum, sidera*. Goth. *stairno*. Isl. *stiorna*. Ang. Sax. *sterra*. Eng. *star*.

STEVEL, s. f. A chamber; a dining room. Corn. Voc. *stewel*, triclinum. Llwyd, 4, 166. W. *ystavell*, †*estavell*, pl. †*stevill*, in Juvencus Glosses. Lat. *stabulum*.

STEVYA, s. m. A crowd, a company. *Yn un stevya oll y éth bŷs yn Pylat o Iustis*, in a crowd they all went to Pilate (who) was magistrate. M.C. 239. Cf. It. *stivar*, from Lat. *stipare*, to cram full. Eng. *stevedor*.

STICEDN, s. m. A pale, post, or stake. Llwyd, 112.

STIFAC, s. m. A cuttle fish. Llwyd, 148, 274. W. *ystifiog*. Lat. *sepia*.

STIL, s. m. A beam, a rafter. Llwyd, 165. Pl. *stilliow*. *Dew tek a bren râg styllyow, ha compos y denwennow, brâs ha crom y ben golcs*, lo the fairest tree for rafters, and straight its sides, large and rounded its lower end. O.M. 2441. *Cowyth, profyyn an styllyow, mars êns compes dhe'n fosow*, comrade, let us try the rafters, if they are straight to the walls. O.M. 2471. *Tyewch an temple hep let, na dheffo glaw dhe'n styllyow*, roof ye the temple without delay, that the rain come not to the rafters. O.M. 2488. W. *estyll*, planks; sing. *astyllen*. Lat. *stilus*.

STILLEN, s. f. A hedge in a mine, or stream work. Pryce.

STIRAN, s. f. A slap. ‡*Dho rei stiran war an vôh*, to give a slap on the cheek. Llwyd, 117.

STLAF, s. m. A stammerer. Corn. Voc. *blesus*. Arm. *stlabeza*, to pronounce ill.

STOC, s. m. The stock of a tree, a trunk. Corn. Voc. *stirbs*. Gael. *stoc*.

STOL, s. f. A stole, a scarf. Corn. Voc. *stola*. W. *ystola*. Arm. *stôl*. From the Latin. *Stollof*, Corn. Voc. *manuale*, a sleeve or hankerchief; lit. a scarf or dress for the hand; being compounded of *stôl*, and *lôf*, a hand. *Manuale* was used in the middle ages to signify a handkerchief, or napkin, or sleeve covering the hands.

STONS, s. m. A standing. *Ow stons a fue crows a pren; kyns ên mychtern, dên ha Dew*, my standing was a cross of wood; before I was a king, man and God. R.D. 2579.

STORC, s. m. A stork. Corn. Voc. *ciconia*. From the English. (W. *chwibon*.)

STRAIL, s. m. Tapestry. Corn. Voc. *tapeta*. *Strail-elester*, matta, a mat of sedge or rushes. Ibid. W. *ystruill*. Lat. *stragula*.

STRECHYE, v. n. To stop, to stay, to tarry. Written also *streché*. 2 pers. s. imp., and 3 pers. s. fut. *streeh*. *Farwel, ow arluth gwella, my vynna streché pella*, farewell, my best lord, I will not stay longer. O.M. 2268. *Bŷs yn epscop fystynyn; streché na woryllyn*, let us hasten to the bishop; let us not stop any longer. P.C. 1135. *Ny wrên strechyé na fella*, we will not stop any longer. P.C. 2334. *Mar strechyn omma na moy, ny agan bŷdh y dregé*, if we stay here any more, we shall not endure it. P.C. 3001. *Ke yn kereh dywhans hep let, na strech hep mar*, go thou away quickly without delay, tarry not, doubtless. R.D. 117. *Ha re pel ny re strechyas*, and too long we have stayed. R.D. 721. *Ty ha'th vaw na strech lemmyn*, thou and thy boy, stay not now. R.D. 1991. *Yn un fystené me a's gwra; ny strechyaf pell*, in a hurry I will make them; I will not tarry long. M.C. 153. Eng. stretch.

STREIL, s. m. A horse-comb. Corn. Voc. *strigil* vel *strigulus*. Formed from the Latin, by the regular mutation of *g* into its secondary form *gh*, which having no sound was omitted.

STREKING, s. m. A buckle. Corn. Voc. *fibula*. W. *ystraig*.

STREST, s. m. A shaft, or upright stem of a pillar. Pryce.

STRET, s. m. and f. A fresh spring, a stream. Corn. Voc. *latex*. *A'n golon ydh êth strêt brâs, dour ha goys yn kemeskis, ha ryp an gnw a resas dhe dhewlé nêb a'n gwyskis*, from the heart there went a great stream, water and blood mixed, and ran down by the spear to the hands of him that struck him. M.C. 219. Written also *strêth*, or *streyth*. *Fenten bryght avel arhans, ha pedyr streyth wrâs defry, ow resck a dywonty, worté myres may 'th o whans*, a fountain bright as silver, and four large streams indeed flowing from it, that there was a desire to look at them. O.M. 772. Ir. *sroth*, + *sruth*. Gael. *sruth*. Manx, *stroo*. W. *frwd*, † *frut*. C. † *frot*. Arm. *froud*. Latin, *fretum*. Sansc. *srotas*, (*sru*, to flow.) Germ. *srut*; "nomen multis fluviis commune." *Wachl*.

STREVYE, v. a. To strive, to contend. *Reys yw porris heb strevyé bûth ow thâs dhe vôs sewys*, it is needful, that the will of my Father should be followed without striving. M.C. 73. *Ha dhodho a leverys re saffé Crist heb strevyé*, and said to him that Christ had risen incontestably. M.C. 248. From the English.

STRIC, adj. Active, nimble, swift. Llwyd, 47, 68, 170, *strîk*.

STRIF, s. m. Strife, contention. *Hag ol kerehys dodho dh'y wlâs hep stryf ha kâs*, and all brought to him to his land without strife and hatred. P.C. 30. Arm. *strif, striv*. Eng. *strife*.

STRIFOR, s. m. A wrangler, a causer of strife. Corn. Voc. *contentiosus*.

STRIWE, s. m. A sneezing. Llwyd, 154, *strihwe*.

STRIWI, v. a. To sneeze. Llwyd, 154, *dho striwhi*; 248, *a striwi*, sneezing. W. *ystrewi*. Arm. *strevia*, *striourin*. Irish, *sraoth*. Gael. *sreoth*. Manx, *strciyr*. Lat. *sternuto*.

STROC, s. m. A stroke, a blow. Pl. *streeis*. *Yn corf Ihesus ydh esé, hag ef yn crows ow cregy, pymp mŷll streckis del iové, ha pedergreyth cans goly*, in the body of Jesus there were, while he was hanging on the cross, five thousand strokes as there were, and four times a hundred wounds. M.C. 227.

STROCOS, s. m. A stroke. Pl. *strocosow*. *Ef a vynsé gûl deray, hag a rôs strokosow tyn, saw un marrek a'n ladhas*, he wished to do a deed, and he gave sharp strokes, but a soldier killed him. O.M. 2225.

STROTIIE, v. a. To bind, to gird, to wring. *Kymer dhymmo ve kunys, gans lovan bedhens strothys, ha war dhe geyn doga ef*, take firewood for me, with a rope let it be bound, and on thy back carry it. O.M. 1207. *Ydh o ow fous ha'm brustplat purpur yarow dhum strothé, dre an gôs a rûk Pilat worto an kŷc a glené*, my robe and my breastplate were hard purple to wring me, through the blood before Pilate the flesh stuck to it. R.D. 2502.

STUL, s. m. Epiphany, Twelfth day. *Degl stûl*, the holiday of the Epiphany. Llwyd, 57. W. *ystwyll*. From the Lat. *stella*, a star. Called in Armoric, *goucl an steren*.

STULL, s. m. A rafter, or style. Pl. *stullyow*. This word is still in use in Cornwall. Timber placed in the backs of levels, and covered with boards or small poles to support rubbish, is called *a stull*. See *Stil*.

STUT, s. m. A gnat, a small fly. Corn. Voc. *culex*.

STYNNAR, s. m. A tinner, a pewterer. Llwyd, 154. Id. qd. *stener*, qd. v.

SUBEN, s. f. A mass, a morsel. Corn. Voc. *offa*. W. *sob, soban, sopen*. Arm. *souben*. Eng. *sop*.

SUDRONEN, s. f. A drone. Corn. Voc. *fucus*. Arm. *safronen*. (W. *begegyr*.)

SUEL, pron. Such, he that, that, those, who, as many as. *Suel a vynno bôs sylwys, golsowens ow lavarow*, as many as would be saved, let them hearken to my words. M.C. 2. *Pûr apert hag yn golow y leveris ow dyskas, ow lays ha'w lavarow, suel a vynna y elewas*, very openly, and in light I spake my doctrine, my laws and my words, (to) as many as would hear them. M.C. 70. *En Edhewon a armé, treytour pûr y vôs keffys, hag ol drôk suel a wressé*, the Jews cried out that he was found a very traitor, and all evil that he had done. M.C. 119. *Gowyn worthyn, hep lettyé, py suel a vynnyth deffry*, ask thou of us, without delaying, whatever thou wilt truly. P.C. 502. Written also contractedly, *sûl*. *Yn nêp tol fyan dhe'n fo alemma, bŷs may 'th ello, sûl â dhe'n nêf*, into some hole let us flee away hence, until he goes, who is going to heaven. R.D. 136. W. *sawl*. Arm. *seûl*. Ir. *samhail*. Gael. *samhuil*.

SUG, adj. Moist. Pryce; from which derives hence *Tresugan*, the moist or bog dwelling, in St. Columb Major. Written also *sog*, qd. v.

SUIDNAN, s. f. A draught, or portion. Llwyd, 65, *súidnan*.

SUIF, s. m. Tallow. Corn. Voc. *aruina*. In late Cornish *soa*. W. *sŷyv*. Arm. *soav, soa*. Lat. *sebum*. Fr. *suif*. See also *Scym*.

SUL, s. m. The sun. Used only with *dêdh*, as *dêdh sûl*, Sunday, from the Lat. *dies solis*. *Lavar dhyn mars ôs huder, drôk na ŷl dên vŷth dhe wûl, na nŷl dhé weyth na dhê sûl; gorthyp lemmyn hep a whêr*, tell us if thou art a sorcerer, that no man is able to do harm to thee, neither on work-day or Sunday; answer us now without a murmur. R.D. 1833. *My ny garaf streché pel na nŷl dhê wŷth na dhê sûl*, I love not to stay long, neither on work-day or Sunday. R.D. 2250. Written also *sil*, qd. v. W. *súl*. Arm. *sul*. Ir. *sul*. Gael. +*sol*, +*sul*. Lat. *sol*.

SULL, s. m. A prospect, or view. *Pryce*. Written also *sell* and *syll*, qd. v.

SURGYA, v. n. To rise. *Dho surgya*. Pryce. Lat. *surgo*. Eng. *surge*.

SY, pron. s. Thou, thee. *Eva, prág y whrusté sy tullé dhe brycs hep kên*, Eve, why didst thou deceive thy husband without pity. O.M. 277. *Prág y tolsté sy hep kên*, why didst thou deceive her without pity. O.M. 302. *Hen ew an oel a versy o dedhyncys dyso sy dheworth an Tás Dew a'n nêf*, this is the oil of mercy (that) was promised to thee by the Father God of heaven. O.M. 842. *Par del y'th prynnys yn kêr, ha fasta sy dhe vreder yn huen gryggyans*, like as I bought thee dearly, strengthen thou also thy brethren in full belief. R.D. 1103. *Sy* is another form of *ty*, softened sometimes into *gy*, qd. v. *aud* is used after verbs, and for emphasis after the compound pronoun. It is also found with a plural verb. *Oyeth sy glewyuch dhym ol masons an dré, ketep pol ; guetynuch bones avorow ow conys yn crŷs an dré*, hear ye, listen to me all masons of the town, every head; take ye care to be to-morrow working in the middle of the town. O.M. 2207.

SYCH, adj. Dry. *Avel olow aga threys, sŷch gns ol kepar ha lcys*, like the prints of their feet, they are all dry like herbs. O.M. 761. *Mar kâf tŷr sŷch, my a greys, dynny ny dhewhel arté*, if it shall find dry ground, I believe, it will not return to us again. O.M. 1131. Written also *sêch*, qd. v. W. *sŷch*, m. *sêch*, f. Arm. *sech*. Ir. *siuc*, +*svec*. Gael. *seac*, + *sic*. Lat. *siccus*. Gr. σαυκόσ. Lith. *sausas*. O. Slav. *suchu*.

SYCHE, v. a. To make dry, to dry, to wipe. Part. *sychys*. *Dew, têk a sell yw homma, goef a gollas an wlâs ; saw an wedhen, dhym yma hy bôs sychys marthys vrâs*, God, fair to look at is this, woe to him (that) lost the country ; but the tree, it is to me a great wonder that it is dried. O.M. 756. *Na ôl na scryg, nêp a whyleth sychsys y treys gans dhe dhyw pléth*, weep not nor shriek, he whom thou seekest thou driedst his feet with thy two plaits. R.D. 554. Written also *seché*. W. *sychu*. Arm. *secha*.

SYGAL, s. m. Rye. *Lhvyd*, 147. Arm. *segal*. Ir. *seagul*. Gael. *seagal*. Manx, *shoggyl*. Gr. σεκελή. Lat. *secale*. Fr. *seigle*. (Called in W. *rhŷg*. Ang. Sax. *rygc*.)

SYGALEC, s. f. A field of rye. *Pryce*. Arm. *segalec*.

SYGAN, s. f. Sap, juice, moisture. *Lhvyd*, 13, 157. W. *sig*. Arm. *sún*. Ir. *sugh*. Gael. *sugh*. Manx, *soo*. Lat. *succus*. Sansc. *saikas*. Fr. *suc*.

SYHYS, part. Dried. *Gothy ow treys ny hyrsys ; homma gnus duggrow keffrys re's holhas ; gans y blewo y fons syhys*, to wash my feet thou hast not offered ; this one with tears even has washed them; with her hair they were dried. P.C. 521. A softer form of *sychys*, part. pass. of *syché*, qd. v.

SYL, s. m. The sun. *Pryce*. Generally written *súl*, qd. v.

SYL, adv. Although, albeit. *Lhvyd*, 57, 79, 234, 249.

SYLGWETH, adv. On a Sunday. Llwyd, *zylgueth*. Comp. of *syl*, and *gwêth*, a time. W. *sulgwaith*.

SYLL, s. m. A view, a prospect. Written also *sell*. W. *syll, sêl*. Arm. *sell*. Ir. *suil*, an eye. Gael. *scall, scall-*adh*, a view; *suil*, an eye. Manx, *sooill*, an eye.

SYLLY, v. a. To view, to behold, to observe. *Agy dhe'n yet gor dhe ben, ha y sylryth ol na gen, pe-penag-ol a teylly*, within the gate put thy head, and thou shalt behold all not otherwise, whatsoever thou seest. O.M. 744. *My a sylly yn úr-na, a callen dús dhe'n prúck-na, y fyé bargyn púr fúr*, I saw then, if I could come to that degree, it would be a very wise bargain. C.W. 58. W. *syllu, selu*. Arm. *sellout*. Ir. *sillim*. Gael. *seall*. Manx, *shilley*.

SYLWADUR, s. m. A saviour. Written also *sylwader*, and *sylwador*. *Ty yw sylwador an beys*, thou art the Saviour of the world. P.C. 304. *Ytho dasserchys yn Ihesu agan sylwadur*, now is risen Jesus our Saviour. R.D. 800. *Ihesu Arluth nêf ha beys, ha sylwadur dhyn keffrys*, Jesus, Lord of heaven and earth, and Saviour to us also. R.D. 1152. *Ihesu a ladhas nêp o dhyn sylwader*, Jesus he has slain who was to us a Saviour. R.D. 2008. Arm. *salver*. Lat. *salvator*.

SYLWANS, s. m. Salvation. *Ef a yrhys dhym kyrhus a mount Tabor gucel a rás, ma'm vedhen drédhé sylwans*, he ordered me to bring from Mount Tabor the rods of grace, that I may have salvation through them. O.M. 1958. *Aban ôf sevys a'n bêdh, godhfedhcuch y's bŷdh sylwans*, since I am risen from the tomb, ye know that ye have salvation. R.D. 1574. *May fo dhe Dhu dhe wordhyans, ha sylwans dhe'n enevow*, that there may be to God the glory, and salvation to the souls. M.C. 1. Written also *sylwyans*.

SYLWEL, v. n. To save; to be saved. Part. *sylwys*. *Dew a alsé hep mervel gíl dhe púp dên ol sylwel dres an beys ol*, God could without dying have caused every man to be saved over all the world. R.D. 975. *Rák kemmys a'n crŷs, ha a vo lêl vygydhys, sylwel a wra*, for as many as believe it, and are faithfully baptized, shall be saved. R.D. 1144. *Yma dhynmo vy duon, gyllys lemmyn y'm colon, yn della Dew dhum sylwel*, there is sorrow to me, gone now into my heart, so God save me! R.D. 2248. *Dre y vernans yredy ol an bŷs a fŷdh sylwys*, through his death clearly all the world will be saved. O.M. 818. *Nêp na grŷs ynnos, goef ny fŷdh sylwys*, he that believes not in thee, miserable he! be will not be saved. R.D. 758. Arm. *salvi*.

SYLWYANS, s. m. Salvation. *Yn Cryst reys yn dhys crygy y vôs cf arluth dhynny, ha sylwyans dhe tús an bŷs*, in Christ it is needful for thee to believe, that he is Lord to us, and Salvation to the people of the world. R.D. 1711. *May tyffouch ol dhe sylwyans, sevouch yn agys cryggyans*, that ye may come all to salvation, stand ye in your belief. R.D. 2388. *An Tás Dew dré'n Spyrys Sans dhe'n beys dhanvonas sylwyans*, God the Father, through the Holy Ghost, has sent salvation to the world. R.D. 2611.

SYLWYAS, s. m. A Saviour. *Ihesu, máp rás, agan sylwyas, dues gueres my*, Jesus, son of grace, our Saviour, come, help us. R.D. 307. *Nêp na grŷs y bôs sylwyas, goef genys y vonas a brŷs benen*, he that believes him not to be a Saviour, woe to him that he was born from the womb of woman. R.D. 2418.

SYNDYE, v. a. To hurt, to injure. Part. *syndys*. *Syndys ve drc govaytis ; yn della yw lcas huny*, he was hurt through covetousness ; so is many a one. M.C. 62. *Why a dhêth dhym yn arvow dhom kemeres, dhom*

SYPPOSIA 328 SYWETH

syndyé, dhom peynyé bŷs yn erow, ye are come to me in arms, to take me, to hurt me, to torture me even unto death. M.C. 74. *Dre y holon ydh êth sêth, y mâb, syndys pan welsé,* through her heart there went an arrow, when she saw her son hurt. M.C. 223. *Dh'y falaury y cresys, pythueth re rûg ow syndyé,* her falsehood I believed, ever she hath hurt me. O.M. 288. Written also *schyndyé* and *shyndyé,* qd. v.

SYNGY, v. a. To hold, to esteem, to value; to apprehend, to bind, to oblige. Part. pass. *syngys. Syngys mûr ôn dhe Iudas,* much obliged we are to Judas. P.C. 1203. *Ny a'n gor wharré dhe Pylat fast bŷs yn tré, hag ef syngyns guyryoneth,* we will take him soon, to Pilate speedily, even to the city, and let him judge the truth. P.C. 1801. *Ty vaw, lemyn syng-é fast,* thou boy, now hold him fast. P.C. 1883. *Vynythа syngys ôf dhys,* ever bound I am to thee. R.D. 96. *Yn golon, dre'n tencwen, dhe revtyé syngys ow gu,* in the heart, through the side, I felt my spear thrust. R.D. 2586. A corrupted form of *synsy.*

SYNS, v. a. Hold thou. 2 pers. s. imp., and 3 pers. s. fut. of *synsy,* qd. v. *Tan, syns y'th dorn an giu-na, ha herthyé gans nerth yn ban,* take, hold thou in thy hand that spear, and thrust it with force upwards. P.C. 3010. *Natur scyle me a syns arluth da mar pŷdh peynys, ol y vogcté kyn fôns sŷns rûg y beyn dhe vôs grevys,* nature will cause, I hold, if the good lord be pained, all his subjects, though they be saints, to be grieved for his pain. M.C. 211.

SYNS, s. m. Saints. *Gwreuch y herthyé a perfeth, gans mollath Dew ha'y elwdh ha sŷns keffrys,* do ye push it in, with the curse of God, and his angels, and saints also. R.D. 2288. *Mollath an sŷns, ha Dew aban,* the curse of the saints, and God above. R.D. 2293. Plural of *sans,* qd. v.

SYNSY, v. a. To hold, to esteem, to value; to apprehend, to catch; to bind, to oblige. 2 pers. s. imp. and 3 pers. s. fut. *syns.* Part. pass. *synsys. Bedhens ebron dreys pûp tra, rûk synsy glaw awartha,* let there be a sky above every thing, to hold the rain above. O.M. 23. *Synsys mûr ôn dli'y garé,* we are much bound to love him. O.M. 1126. *Pandra synsyth y'th luef lemyn,* what holdest thou in thy hand now? O.M. 1442. *Guelen a pren a wrâf synsy,* a rod of wood I do hold. O.M. 1444. *H'agas mychtern ef synscuch, hedré vyweli byw yn bŷs-na,* and for your king esteem him, as long as ye are alive in this world. O.M. 2350. *Pyw a synsow why mochya,* whom think ye greatest? P.C. 798. *Synsew e fast, hep lettyé,* hold ye him fast, without delaying. P.C. 1086. *Del ouch why synsys gueryon,* as ye are esteemed true men. P.C. 1305. *Mara quréth, my a syns dhe vûs dremas,* if thou wilt do, I will hold thee to be a good man. P.C. 1773. *Syns war dhe keyn an grous pren,* hold the cross tree on thy back. P.C. 2586. *Nep na'n synso y syhwyas, a Dhu, goef,* he that holds him not his Saviour, O God, woe to him. R.D. 614. *Dhe'n Edhewon dyrryvys del o.y fynnas synsy,* to the Jews he declared how it was that he would hold him. M.C. 62. W. *synnio.* Lat. *sentio.* Fr. *sentir.*

SYPPOSIA, v. n. To sleep, to repose. *Dho syppozia,* Pryce. ‡ *Lebmen an hostez an twhei, hei a kymsilinz gen ucbyn vanah a crra en tre, a dho destria an dén kôth en guilti en termen an noz, a resta an dzhyi syppozia ; ha a fout gorra war an vertshants,* now the hostess of the house, she consulted with a certain monk that was in the town to destroy the old man in bed at night, while the rest of them were sleeping, and to lay the blame on the merchants. Lhwyd, 252.

SYTTYA, v. a. To set, to place, to lay. Part. pass. *syttys. Ha ny a dlysycé yn wêdh an corf a sytscuch yn bêdh yw Ihesu mâp Maria,* and we will shew also the body (that) ye placed in the tomb is Jesus, the Son of Mary. R.D. 629. *Tummasow kekyffris adro dhe dhewen gans nerth brâs a ve syltys,* thumps likewise about his jaws with great force were laid. M.C. 138. *Syltyyn an pren yn y plas,* let us set the wood in its place. O.M. 2573. Written also *settya,* qd. v.

SYTH, card. num. Seven. *Sŷtli mŷl ha sŷth cans blydhen, un dén kyn fo ow kerdles, ow tôs kyn spedyé yn gcydh dew ugans myldyr perfeyth omma ny alsé bones,* seven thousand and seven hundred years, if a man should be walking, and though he sped in one day's coming forty miles complete, here he could not be. R.D. 2494. A contracted form of *scith,* qd. v.

SYTHVAS, adj. Seventh. *Aga sona me a wra, may fo 'n sythvas dŷdh hennys an dŷdh a boveswa,* I will bless them, that the seventh day may be called the day of rest. C.W. 32. Written also *seithves,* qd. v.

SYTHYN, s. f. A week, seven-night. See *Scithyn.*

SYVEL, v. n. To stand, to rise. *Yn sûr gans ow dew lagas ow syvel me a'n guelas,* surely with my eyes I saw him rising. R.D. 530. *Ny yllyn syvel yn ban, rûk own anodho,* I could not stand upright for fear of him. R.D. 533. Another form of *sevel,* qd. v.

SYW, v. zubs. He is. *Mar syw, mara syw, mar sywa,* if he is. See *Mars* and *Yw.*

SYWE, v. n. To follow. 2 pers. s. imp., and 3 pers. s. fut. *syw.* Written also *syrvyé. Rês yw syvé y vôdh ef, pepenag ~o,* need it is to follow his will, whatever it be. O.M. 661. *My a vyn aga sywé, ha warbarth aga ladlé,* I will follow them, and together kill them. O.M. 1630. *Lemmyn gwreuch ol ow syvé,* now do ye all follow me. O.M. 1674. *Mar kefyn déu a'n par-na, ny a'n syw bŷs yn y chy,* if we find a man of that sort, we will follow him even to his house. P.C. 648. *Y vôs mâp Dew da y syw, pan dorras quêth an tempel,* that he is the Son of the good God it follows, when the cloth of the temple was rent. P.C. 3087. *Na wréns y na hen scyle lymmyn synvyé aga bôdh,* they made no other ground but followed their will. M.C. 175. The same word as *sewyé,* qd. v.

SYWETH, interj. More the pity, alas. *Ah syweth,* Lhwyd, 65, 106. The same as *soweth,* qd. v.

T.

This letter in Cornish, Welsh, and Armoric, is both a primary initial, and a secondary mutation. When a radical initial it changes into *d,* and *th,* as *tâs,* a father; *y dâs,* his father; *ow thâs,* my father. W. *tâd ; ci dâd ;*

his father ; *ei thâd*, her father. (The Welsh also has a further mutation into the nasal *nh*, as *vy nhâd*, my father.) Arm. *tád ; he dâd*, his father ; *va zâd*, my father ; the aspirate form being represented by *z*. When secondary *t* in Cornish and Armoric is the aspirate mutation of *d* as *da*, good ; *pûr dha*, very good ; *maga ta*, as good ; *yn ta*, well. *Dôn*, to bear ; *ow tôn*, bearing. *Due, y due*, he will come. Arm. *dourn*, a hand ; *he zourn*, his hand ; *hô tourn*, your hand. This mutation is not found in the initials of Welsh words, but occurs in other places, as *cretto*, he may believe, from *credu ; gatto, (na atto,)* he may leave, from *gadael ; caletach*, harder, from *caled*. In the Erse languages, *t* is also both primary and secondary. When primary it has the same mutation in Irish as in Cornish, thus Ir. *tir*, land ; *ar dir*, our land ; *a thir*, his land. In Manx, *t* changes into *h* and *dh*, as *taggloo*, discourse ; *e haggloo*, his discourse ; *nyn dhaggloo*, our discourse. When secondary, *t* is a mutation of *s*, as Ir. and Gael. *suil*, an eye ; *e shuil*, his eye ; *an tiul*, the eye. Manx, *sooill, e hooill, y tooill*.

TA, adj. Good. The aspirate mutation of *da*, qd. v. *Ha mŷr a pûp tenewen ; aspy yn ta pûp echen*, and look thou on every side ; examine well every particular. O.M. 747. *Avês hag agy yn-ta gans pêk bedhens stanchurŷs*, without and within well let it be staunched with pitch. O.M. 953. *Degê ol agan edhyn, bestes yn wêdh maga ta, warnydhy my a offryn*, tithe of all birds, beasts also as well, I will offer upon it. O.M. 1182.

TA, pron. s. Thou. This form is only found in composition in the Dramas, the simple forms being *te* and *ti* or *ty*, qd. v. *Lavar lemyn pan drôk vo a ver tu a dhyagwydhyata dhynny, pan wreta mar coynt fara*, tell thou now what evil is there on any side (which) thou shewest to us, when thou actest so rudely ? P.C. 339. *Pendra leverta a'n flechys ûs ow canê*, what sayest thou of the children (that) are singing ? P.C. 432. *A'n guelesta a dhyragos, a alsesta y aswonfos*, if thou shouldst see him before thee, couldst thou know him ? R.D. 861.

TA, pron. adj. Thy, thine. *Ta honan*, thyself. Llwyd, 244. Another form of *te*, or *ty*, qd. v.

TABM, s. m. A piece, a morsel. *Ev a gowzys dhym mar dêk ny wodhyan tabm y naha*, he spoke to me so fair, I knew not how to deny him a jot. C.W. 56. A late corruption of *tam*, qd. v. "*Tabm* is still used in Cornwall for a bit of bread and butter." *Polwhele*.

TAC, v. a. He will choke. 3 pers. s. fut. of *taga*, qd. v. *Ty geyler, dûs yn râk, ha mar ny dhueth, my a'th tâk, hag a ver spys*, thou jailer, come forth ; and if thou wilt not come, I will throttle thee, and in a short time. R.D. 1990.

TACCYE, v. a. To tack, to fasten. Written also *taccé*. Part. *tacryys, taccys*. 3 pers. s. fut. *tac*. *Us tryr spik vrûs genes gurŷs, râk takkyé an fals profus yn pren crous*, hast thou three great spikes made, for fastening the false prophet on the cross tree ? P.C. 2672. *Doro kenter, ha me a tak y luef glêdh*, give thou a nail, and I will fasten his left hand. P.C. 2747. *Tackeuch e a hugh y ben*, fasten ye it above his head. P.C. 2793. *Treys ha dynclef a pûp tu fast tackyes gans kentrow hern*, feet and hands on every side fast fixed with nails of iron. P.C. 2938. *Ynny hy bedhens tackyys*, on it let him be fastened. P.C. 2164. *Worth an plynken bedhens tackys*, on the planks let them be fastened. P.C. 2518. Borrowed from the English.

TACEL, s. m. A thing, an instrument, a tool. Pl. *tacklow*. *Dôs gené pols dhe wandré, ha dyso my a lever yntrethon tuclow pryvé*, come with me to walk about a while, and I will tell thee between ourselves private things. O.M. 936. *Yma dhymmo dhe wruthyl un pols lyhan tacklow pryvé*, I have to do a little while some private matters. P.C. 92. *Mêr a dacklow*, many things. C.W. 56. W. *tacyl*, pl. *taclau*.

TAD, s. m. A father. Llwyd, 114, thus reads *tat*, in the Cornish Vocabulary.

TADDER, s. m. Goodness. Llwyd, 240. More correctly *dader*, qd. v.

TADVATH, s. m. A nurser, a breeder. Llwyd, 101, thus reads *tatvat* in the Cornish Vocabulary.

TAER, adj. Potent, powerful. *Pryce*. W. *taer*.

TAG, s. m. A choking, a strangling. *A molath dhe'n hôr fen kam, ha thâg yn wêdh ganso*, a curse to the crooked headed strumpet, and a choking too with it. C.W. 58. W. *tâg*. Arm. *tâg*.

TAGA, v. a. To stifle, to strangle, to choke, to throttle. 3 pers. s. fut. *tâc*, or *tâg*. Part. *tegys*. Llwyd, 157. *Me a vyn setyé colm ré, may fastyo an colm wharré adro dhum bryangen, a dhysempys dhum tagé*, I will put a running knot, that the knot may fasten soon around my throat, immediately to choke me. P.C. 1528. *Mal yu gynef dhe gafus dhe vôs gynen dhe terrus, yn dhe pêch râk dhe tagé*, I am glad to take thee to go with us to (our) lands, in thy sin for strangling thyself. P.C. 1533. *Wor tyweth whet crôk a'th tâg*, at last hanging will choke thee yet. P.C. 1818. W. *lagu*. Arm. *taga*. Ir. *tacht*. Gael. *tachd*. Manx, *tachd*.

TAHUA, s. m. A sea calf, a seal. Llwyd, 120, 241.

TAIR, card. num. Three. Used with feminines only, as *tair deleian*, three leaves ; *tair bledhan*, three years. Llwyd, 243. Another form of *teir*, qd. v.

TAIRDHAC, card. num. Thirteen. *Pryce*. Written by Llwyd, 166, *tardhak*. See also *Tredhec*.

TAIRNANT, s. m. A fomentation, or poultice. Corn. Voc. *malagma*.

TAISH, s. m. A mole, spot, or freckle. *Pryce*. Fr. *tache*.

TAL, s. m. The front, forehead ; end or top. Corn. Voc. *frons*. *Ow coské yn haus yn hâl, lyskys ûf a'n kŷl dhe'n tâl*, sleeping down in the moor, I am burned from the nape to the forehead. O.M. 1781. *Wheys yw ow thâl, dhyso gy ow fystené*, my forehead is sweating, hastening to thee. O.M. 2086. *Wâr gâs vy dhe dhehesy gans morben bom trewysy dhe'n vŷl hora war an taal*, soon let me strike with mallet a terrible blow to the vile strumpet on the forehead. O.M. 2705. *Dew a settyas mark warnas yn an corn dhe dâl omma*, God hath set a mark on thee in the horn of thy forehead here. C.W. 100. *Te a'n gwél yn corn ow thâl*, thou seest it in the horn of my forehead. C.W. 118. *Tâl an chy*, the top of the house. Llwyd, 252. *Kodna tâl*, forehead. 61. W. *tâl*. Ir. †*tal*. Gr. τέλος. Sanse, *tal*, to end.

TAL, adj. High, tall, eminent. *Pryce*. *Tal carn*, the high rock, in St. Allen. W. *tal*.

TAL, v. a. He will pay. 3 pers. s. fut. of *taly*, qd. v.

TALBUM, s. m. A capon. *Pryce*.

TALCH, s. m. Bran. Corn. Voc. *furfures*. W. *talch*.

TALGEL, s. f. A pantry, a buttery. Corn. Voc. *sigillum, cellarium*. W. *talgell*, a pantry. Arm. *talgel*, a scal.

TALHAC, s. m. A rock fish. Corn. Voc. *rocea*. Called by Llwyd, 241, *a roach*. W. *talawg*, having a large forehead.

TALLETH, v. n. To begin. The aspirate mutation of *dalleth*, qd. v. *My pan esen ow quaudré, clewys a'n ngl tenewen un êl ow dalleth cané*, when I was walking about, I heard on one side an angel beginning to sing. O.M. 215. *Mar a talleth pertheges*, if he begin to be angry. R.D. 598.

TALLIC, s. m. That which is placed high, a garret. Pryce. *Botallack (Bodtallic,)* the high dwelling. W. *bodtalog*, nom. loc.

TALLYOUR, s. m. A large dish, a platter. *Ow tybbry gynef yma a'n tallyour yn kêth bôs-ma nêb rum guerthas sollabreys*, he is eating with me from my plate in this same food, who hath sold me some time ago. P.C. 754. Written by Llwyd, 76, *talhiar*.

TALON, s. m. The belly. Corn. Voc. *venter*. W. *talon*.

TALSOCH, adj. Dull, stupid. Corn. Voc. *hebes*. Comp. of *tâl*, a forehead, and Arm. *souch*, dull.

TALVES, adj. Worth, of value. *Bôs talves*, to be worth. Llwyd, 160.

TALY, v. a. To pay, to requite, to recompense. 3 pers. s. fut. *tâl*, and *talvyth*. Part. *tylys*, qd. v. *Mara pedhaf bew vledhen, my a'n talvyth dhyuch, rum pen, pypenagol a sconvo*, if I shall be living a year, I will pay it to you, by my head, whoever may object. O.M. 2387. *Me a vynsé a talfens mîl puns dhodho a our da*, I would they were worth a thousand pounds to him of good gold. P.C. 211. *Un deydh a dhue yredy, ma'n talvedhaf ol dhywhy, kenmys cnor dhym yw gurys*, a day will come surely, that I will repay it all to you, as much honour as to me is done. P.C. 269. *Hag ef a dalvyth dhys whêth, y honoré del wrusseys*, and he will repay thee yet, as thou hast honoured him. M.C. 115. *Syr, Arluth, Dew tâl dhyso*, Sire, lord, God reward thee. O.M. 2605. *Ow box mennaf dhe terry a dâl mûr a voné da*, my box I will break, (that) is worth much good money. P.C. 486. (Sce *Dâl*.) W. *talu*. Arm. *tallout*. Ir. *tuill*, *diol*. Gael. *diol*.

TAM, s. m. A morsel, a bite, a piece, a jot, a bit. Pl. *tymmyn*. *Ellas, pan dhybrys an tam*, alas, when I ate the morsel. O.M. 762. *Dhe escarn ol ketep tam gans ow bom a fydh brewys*, thy bones all, every bit, with my blows shall be bruised. O.M. 2743. *A'n aval te kemer tam*, of the apple take thou a bit. M.C. 6. *Ha gwythé tam na guskens*, and to take care that they slept not a whit. M.C. 241. *Ow holan ol dhe dymmyn râg moreth a wra terry*, my heart all to pieces for grief will break. O.M. 357. W. *tam*. Arm. *tamm*. Ir. *tnom*. Gael. *teum*. Gr. τόμος.

TAN, s. m. Fire. Corn. Voc. *ignis*. Pl. *tanow*. *Tân ha cledhé yma lemmyn parys*, fire and wood are now ready. O.M. 1305. *Dufydh nerth an flam ha'n tân*, assuage the power of the flame and the fire. O.M. 2637. *Otté an tân ow lesy*, behold the fire kindling. P.C. 693. *Tommuns bnan dour war tân*, let one warm water on the fire. P.C. 833. *Ow lesky yn tân ha môk*, burning in fire and smoke. R.D. 281. *Lucyfer yw ow hanow; penscvic yn nêf onuma; ow howethé ew tanow*, Lucifer is my name; a prince in heaven I am; my companions are fires. C.W. 10. W. *tân*. Arm. *tân*. Ir. *teine*, †*tenc*. Gael. *teine*. Manx, *chenney*.

TAN, v. a. Take thou. *Adam, ystyn dhym dhe dhorn, tan henna dheworthef vy*, Adam, reach to me thy hand, take thou that from me. O.M. 206. *Tan, resyf dheworthyf ve ow degé ha'm offryn gulân*, take, receive from me my tithe and my offering pure. O.M. 504. *Tan hemma war an challa*, take this on the jaw. O.M. 540.

TAN, comp. art. To the. *Tan gyryn*, to the crown. Llwyd, 249. More correctly *dan*, (*do—an*.)

TAN, prep. Under, beneath, below. *Yn médh Pedyr, tan ow fêdh, ny'th nahaf, kyn fên ledhys*, says Peter, on my faith, I will not deny thee, though I should be slain. M.C. 49. *Hen yw an erfs, tan ow fêdh*, that is the middle, on my faith. O.M. 2534. *En gew lym ef a bechyé pûr cren yn dan an asow dre an golon may'th esé*, the sharp spear he darted very right under the ribs, so that it was through the heart. M.C. 218. (Sce *Dan*.) W. *tan*, *dan*. Arm. *didan*, *indan*.

TANFENNY, v. a. Thou shalt send. A mutation of *danfenny*, 2 pers. s. fut. of *danfon*, or *danvon*, qd. v. *Dhodho gweyl may tanfenny*, take care that thou wilt send to him. R.D. 1630.

TANFONAS, v. a. He sent. A mutation of *danfonas*, 3 pers. s. pret. of *danfon*, or *danvon*, qd. v. *Ha gynef y tanfonas y té dheuch pare vcuch wâr*, and by me he sent that he would come to you, as ye were aware. R.D. 913.

TANFONNO, v. a. He may send. A mutation of *danfonno*, 3 pers. s. subj. of *danfon*, qd. v. *War an Tâs Dew my a bîs, y grath dhyn may tanvonno*, to the Father God we pray, that he may send his grace to us. O.M. 669. *Danvencuch why dhe Pylatt gans messeger may tanfonno dhyuch yn scon Cryst, myehlern an Ycdhewon*, send ye to Pilate by a messenger, that he send to you forthwith Christ, the King of the Jews. R.D. 1596.

TANOV, pron. prep. Under me. Llwyd, 244. (*Tan—vy*.) W. *tanov*.

TANOW, adj. Thin, slim, slender, lean; few, scarce. *Thomas, ty â dhe Cynda, hag ena pregoth a wra yn ow hanow, ha gura dhys moy servygy; yn wlâs-na ow lên grysy tîs yw tanow*, Thomas, thou shalt go to India, and there shalt preach in my name, and make for me more servants; in that country my true believers are few persons. R.D. 2462. Written by Llwyd, 162, *tanow*, and 15, 64, *tanaw*. ‡ *Davaz tanow*, a lean sheep. 83. W. *tenau*. Arm. *tanaô*. Ir. *tanaidhe*, *tana*. Gael. *tana*. Manx, *thanney*. Lat. *tenuis*. Sansc. *tanu*.

TANOWDER, s. m. Thinness, scantiness, scarcity. Written by Llwyd, 136, 240, *tanawder*. Arm. *tanawder*.

TANTER, s. m. A suitor. Corn. Voc. *procus*. This may be read *tawter*, and would then be borrowed from the English *touter*.

TAPER, s. m. A taper, a wax candle. Corn. *cereus*. From the English.

TARAD, s. m. What pervadeth, a piercer, an auger, a whimble. *Tarad y cued*, wood-pecker. Pryce. (W. *taradyr y coed*.) Written also *tardar*, qd. v.

TARAN, s. f. Thunder. Corn. Vocab. *tonitruum*. Pl. *tarennow*. *Belscbuc ha lawcthan, dylleuch luhes ha taran guyt a'n losew*, Beelzebub and fiends, send forth lightnings and thunder, that it burn him quite. R.D. 129.

Ellas, na dhelleys a'm gwêen dh'y lesky un luhesen, ha crak taran, alas, that I sent not forth a lightning to burn him, and a clap of thunder. R.D. 204. *Ellas, dhynny ny dâl man duello luhes na taran dh'y lesky ef*, alas, it avails us not a bit to discharge lightning nor thunder to burn him. R.D. 296. ‡ *Ycin kuer, tarednow, ha golowas,* cold weather, thunders, and lightning. *Pryce*. W. *taran*. Arm. *curun*, thunder ; *taran*, lightning. Ir. *toran*. Gael. *torrun*. Manx, *taarnagh*. Hence the name of *Taranis*, a god of the ancient Gauls, mentioned by Lucan.

TARDAR, s. m. An auger, borer, whimble. *Hecdh ow bool dhymmo towth da, ow thardar, ha'm mortholow ; me a vyn môs alema, dhe wruthyl ow nyggyssow,* reach thou to me my axe quickly, my auger, and my hammers ; I will go hence to my errands. O.M. 1002. Written also by Pryce, *tarad.* W. *taradyr*, † *tarater*, in Oxf. Glosses. Arm. *tarar, tarazr*. Ir. *tarar*. Gael. *taradh.* Manx, *tharrar.* Fr. *tarière.* Lat. *terebra.* Sansc. *tar*, to penetrate.

TARDH, s. m. A breaking forth, an eruption. *Dŷdh tardh*, break of day. *Pryce.* (Arm. *tarz an deiz*.) W. *tardh*. Arm. *turz*.

TARDHA, adv. Through. *Dho gwana tardha*, to bore through. Llwyd, 117. W. *tardh*.

TARDHIAC, card. num. Thirteen. Llwyd, 166. Another form of *tredhec*, qd. v.

TARDHIE, v. a. To pervade, to break out, to emanate; to penetrate, to bore, to pierce. *Yn ûr-na y a colmas y dhefreth fast gans cronow, yn goys yn mês may tardhas, del fastsens en colmennow*, then they bound his hands fast with thongs, so that the blood sprang out, so they fastened the knots. M.C. 76. *En varogyon a guskas myllyn, ha'n gŷdh ow tardhé, ha Ihesus a dhedhoras, hag êth yn le may fynné*, the soldiers slept at morning, while the day was breaking, and Jesus arose and went whither he would. M.C. 243. W. *tardhu*. Arm. *tarza*.

TARNEIDZHA, v. a. To swim over. Llwyd, 166. Comp. of *tar*, over, (Ir. *tar*,) and *neidzha* or *nija*, to swim. Ir. *tarsnamham*.

TARNEWHON, s. m. The loin. Llwyd, 82. A late corruption of *teneween*, qd. v.

TAROFAN, s. m. A phantom, fright, terror. Written in the Cornish Vocabulary, *taruuluan*, phantasma; which Llwyd, 120, reads *tarnytuan*. *A Dâs yntré dhe dhewelé my a gymmyn ow enê, gwŷth e râg tarofan,* O God, into thy hands I commend my soul, preserve it from fright. O.M. 2364. Written also *tarosfan*. *Tarosfan a dhue defîry war tûs vâs, pan vôns yn chy, h'agn darasow degrys*, a phantom will come indeed upon good people, when they are in the house, and their doors shut. R.D. 1450. W. *tarwutan*, a scarecrow ; from *tarv*, fright, and *hutan*, a delusion.

TAROW, s. m. A bull. *Ydhanwaf bûch ha tarow, ha march yw bêst hep parow dhe vâp dên râg gymweres*, I will name cow and bull, and horse, (that) is a beast without equals for the son of man to help himself. O.M. 123. *Ydh henwaf beuch, ha tarow, oll an chattall debarow aga henwyn kemerans,* I name cow, and bull, and all the cattle feeding, their names let them take. C.W. 30. W. *tarw*, pl. *teirw*. Arm. *taro, tarv*, plur. *tirvi*. Ir. *tarbh*. Gael. *tarbh.* Manx, *tarroo*, pl. *terroo, teiroo*. Anc. Gaul. *tarvos*. Gr. ταῦρος. Lat. *taurus*.

TARTII, s. m. A breaking out, an eruption. *Pryce.* See *Tardh*.

TAS, s. m. A father. Pl. *tasow*. *An Tâs ha'n Mâb, ha'n Spyrys*, the Father, and the Son, and the Spirit. O.M. 1. *An Tâs a nêf a'n grûk ef dhodho haval*, the Father of heaven made him like to himself. O.M. 878. *An Tâs Dew a wrûk pûp tra*, God the Father made every thing. O.M. 1168. *Del yrchys agan tâs dhyn*, as our Father commanded us. O.M. 448. *Saw kyns ys môs, ow thâs whêk, ro dhym dhe vanneth perfeth*, but before going, my dear father, give me thy perfect blessing. O.M. 451. *Ragon y pesys y dâs, oll y sor may fe gevys*, for us he prayed the father that all his wrath might be remitted. M.C. 9. *My yw Dew dhe tassow, Abram, Ysac, ha Iacob yn wêdh kejfrys*, I am the God of thy fathers, Abraham, Isaac, and Jacob likewise. O.M. 1409. *Tâs gwyn*, a grandfather, Llwyd, 3 ; but in Welsh *tâd gwyn* is a stepfather ; and *taid, tâd da*, is a grandfather ; W. *tâd cu;* and Arm. *tâd cûn*, a great grandfather. *Tâs* is a later form of *tâd*, or as written in the Cornish Vocabulary, *tat*, pater. W. *tâd*, † *tât*. Arm. *tâd.* Ir. *athair.* Gael. *athair.* Manx, *ayr.* The Irish term *athair*, † *athir*, is supposed to have lost an initial *p*, and to be derived from the Sansc. *pâ*, to protect, nourish ; whence Sansc. *pilar*. Gr. πατήρ. Lat. *pater.* Eng. *father.* The Welsh *tâd* has its equivalent in Sansc. *tâtu*, (carissime.) The Irish form is lost to the British Dialects, though there seems a trace of it in W. *athrach, (athr—ach*, lineage ;) *cywathrach*, affinity. Cf. also the infantine terms, W. *tada.* Arm. *tata.* Gael. *taid, taididh.* Manx, *jeid.* Gr. τέττα. Lat. *tata.* Eng. *dad, daddy.* Gipsy, *dad, dada.* Port. *taita.* Hindoo, *dada.* Russ. *tiatia.* Fin. *tant*.

TASSERCHY, v. a. To rise again, to arise. The aspirate mutation of *dasserchy*, qd. v. *Ef a tasserch dyougel lyes prŷs wogé merwel*, he will rise indeed many days after dying. P.C. 1754. *Pan bostyas dhe pen try deydh y tasserchy dhe veenans*, when he boasted at the end of three days that he would rise again to life. R.D. 375. *Me a'n gwŷth kyn tassorcho*, I will keep him, though he should rise again. R.D. 379. *Nêb esé aberth yn bêdh gans can ha mûr a eledh, dhe veenans y tassorchas*, he that was within the tomb, with a hundred and more of angels, to life has risen. R.D. 516.

TASSERHY, v. a. To rise again, to arise. The aspirate mutation of *dasserhy*, qd. v. *Ef a leverys yn wêdh, try dêdh wogé môs yn bêdh, dhe veenans y tasserhy*, he said also, three days after going into the grave, to life that he would rise again. P.C. 1747. *Môs dhe vyres me a vyn an corf a'm prynnes yn tyn, mar tassorhas*, I will go to see the body (of him that) redeemed me painfully, if it has risen again. R.D. 687.

TASURN, s. m. A pile of wood, a wood-rick. *Pryce.* W. *tâs, dâs.* Arm. *tes.* Fr. *tas*.

TAT, s. m. A father. Corn. Voc. *pater.* Read by Llwyd, 114, *tâd*. The old form of *tâs*, qd. v.

TATVAT, s. m. A foster father. Corn. Voc. *altor vel nutritor*. To be read as by Llwyd, 101, *tadvath*. W. *tadmaeth*, + *taidmaeth* ; comp. of *tâd*, a father, and *maeth*, nutrition.

TAVAS, s. m. A tongue, a language ; a token. Plur. *tavasow*. *Ol an tekter a vylys, ny gl tavas dên yn bŷs y leverel bynytha*, all the beauty (that) I saw, the tongue of man in the world can not tell it ever. O.M. 767. *Kemer tyyr spûs a'n aval a dybrys Adam dhe dâs, pan varwo gorry hep fal yntré y dhŷns ha'y davas,* take thou three kernels of the apple (that) thy father Adam ate, when he dies put them without fail between his teeth and his tongue. O.M. 826. *Tavas rê hir,* too longue-tongued, a blab. *Llwyd,* 80. *Tavas nadar,* (W. *tavod y neidr,)* the herb addor's tongue. 107. *An lavar côth yw lavar gwir, bêdh dorn re ver dhe'n tavas re hir, mês dên heb davas a gollas y dir,* the old saying is a true saying, there will be too short a hand to too long a tongue, but a man without a tongue lost his land. 251. *Côth tavasow,* ancient tongues. *Pryce. Cam thavus,* a crooked token, a rainbow. ‡ *Râg hedna me a wra benytha wosa helma, yn eborn y fŷdh gwelys, an gabm thavas yn teffry,* therefore I will make ever hereafter, in the sky it shall be seen, the rainbow truly. C.W. 182. ‡ *Cabm-thavas en mettyn, glaw bôs etten,* a rainbow in the morning, rain is in it. *Pryce.* ‡ *Ha gurenz an gy bôs râg tavasow, ha râg termeniow,* and let them be for signs, and for seasons. C.W. 190. The old form was *tavot,* qd. v.

TAVASEC, adj. Having a tongue, tongued; full of words, verbose, prating. *Llwyd,* 81. W. *tavodiog.* Arm. *teodec.*

TAVASETH, s. m. A tongue, or language. *Tavaseth Kernuak,* the Cornish language. *Pryce.* W. *tavodaeth.*

TAVETIILYS, part. Spread abroad, spoken of. *En kêth oynement a scollyns wearnaf, râk ow anclydhyas, hy a'n grûk dre kerensé; puppenak ma fu redys an awonylma, lavethlys hy a vŷdh pûr wŷr neffré,* the same ointment she poured on me, for my burial, she did it through lore; wherever may be read this gospel, spoken of she shall be very truly ever. P.C. 551. Part. pass. of a verb *tavethly.* W. *lavellu,* to spread, from *tavell,* a spread, a tablet. Ir. *tabhaill.* Lat. *tabella.*

TAVOT, s. m. A tongue. Corn. Vocab. *tauot,* lingua. The old form of *tavas,* qd. v. Welsh, *tavaved, tavod,* † *tafaut.* Arm. *teod.* It is supposed to be one of the elements of the corrupt Gaulish plant—name ταρβη-λοθάξιον, which Zeuss reads ταρβοταβάτιον, ox-tongue, comp. of W. *tarw*; Ir. *tarbh,* † *tarb,* and *tavaved,* tongue.

TAVOLEN, s. f. The dock plant. Corn. Voc. *dilla.* In later Cornish, *tavolan.* Llwyd, 15, 240. W. *tavolen, tavol.* Arm. *teol.*

TAW, v. n. Be thou silent. 2 pers. s. imp. of *tewel,* qd. v. *Taw, an êl a bregewthy a'n wedhen, hag a'y vertu,* be thou silent, the angel preached of the tree, and of its virtue. O.M. 229. *A tavo, cowyth, my a'd pŷs,* O be silent, comrade, I pray thee. O.M. 2751. *A dhesempys lemmyn, taw,* immediately now, be silent. P.C. 2280. W. *taw.* Arm. *tað.*

TAWAF, v. n. I will be silent. 1 pers. s. fut. of *tewel,* qd. v. *Awos owa my ny tauwaf, ny a'n prêf gufr a gousaf kyns ys dybarth,* from fear I will not be silent, I will prove it true (what) I speak before separating. R.D. 923. W. *taweav.*

TAWO, v. n. He may be silent. 3 pers. s. subj. of *tewel,* qd. v. *Tewel avel un bobba a wrûk, pan fue acussys; nêp a tawo yn pow-ma dhyrag iug ny fŷdh iuggys,* hold his tongue like an idiot he did, when he was accused; he that is silent in this country before a judge will not be tried. P.C. 2387. W. *tawo.*

TE, pron. s. Thou, thee. *An ioul dhe Adam kewsys, a'n aval te kemer tam,* the devil said to Adam, of the apple take thou a bit. M.C. 6. *Taw, Pedyr, te ny wodhas, pan dra râf dhys,* be silent Peter, thou knowest not what thing I do to thee. M.C. 46. *Mûr a onour te a fŷdh, te yw myglern curunys,* great honour thou shalt have, thou art a crowned king. M.C. 136. *Sawe te ha me kyffris agan bewnans may fên sûr,* save thyself and me likewise, that we may be sure of our life. M.C. 191. In the Dramas it is written *ty.* See *Ti.*

TE, pron. adj. Thy, thine. This is the radical form of *de,* which became used as the primary, and changed into *dhe.* See *De.*

TE, v. a. He will swear. 3 pers. s. fut. of *toy,* qd. v. *Me a'n te dhys renothas,* I swear it to thee, by my father. P.C. 851. *Me a'n te dhys, war ow fŷdh,* I swear it to thee, on my faith. P.C. 1880. *Yn della mar a whyrfeth, mŷl wêth a vŷdh au dynoedh, me a'n te, re sant iouyn,* if it happen so, a thousand (times) worse the end will be, I swear it, by saint Jove. R.D. 340.

TE, v. n. He will come. The aspirate mutation of *de,* qd. v. 3 pers. s. fut. of *dôs. Ha gynef y tanfonas y te dheuch paré vcuoh wôr, kepar ha del ambosas,* and by me he sent, that he will come to yon, as ye are aware, and as he promised. R.D. 914. *Ol warbarth y a armas, mar te venions ha codhé, war agan flehys yn frâs, ha warnan bedhans neffré,* all together they cried, if vengeance come and fall, on our children greatly, and on us be it ever. M.C. 149.

TEBEL, adj. Evil, wicked, foul. Pl. *tebeles. Râg ef o tebel edhen, nêb a glewnys ow cané,* for he was an evil bird, whom thou heardest singing. O.M. 223. *A debel venyn hep râs, ty rum tullas hep kên,* O evil graceless woman, thou hast deceived me without pity. O.M. 251. *Y a dreylfyth, hag a wordh dewow tebel,* they will turn and worship evil gods. O.M. 1818. *Hedré vo yn dhe herwydh, fythys neffré ny vedhyth gans tebeles war an beys,* as long as it is in thy power, thou shalt never be overcome by the wicked in the world. O.M. 1466. *May whello an debeles ow gweres menouch dhedhé,* that the wicked may see my frequent help to them. O.M. 1849.

TEBRO, v. a. He may eat. A mutation of *debro,* 3 pers. s. subj. of *debry,* qd. v. *Hag ynwedh gwra dhe'th worty may tebro ef annodho,* and also make to thy husband that he may eat of it. O.M. 200.

TEBRY, v. a. To eat. A mutation of *debry,* qd. v. *Ow tebry,* eating.

TEBYAS, v. a. To think, to suppose. *Llwyd,* 225. Written also *tibias,* qd. v.

TEC, adj. Fair, clear, beautiful, agreeable, pretty, pleasant. Written also indiscriminately *têg,* qd. v.

TECA, adj. Fairest. Superlative of *têc* or *têg. Lowenna tekca gothfy,* the fairest joy thou knowest. P.C. 1042.

TECACH, v. a. Fairer. Comp. of *têc,* or *têg,* of which *tecah* was a later form,(Llwyd, 243,) and this is generally written *teca, tceé,* or *teccé,* in the Dramas. *Trekké alter yn nêp pow ny alsê dên aspyé,* a fairer altar in any country a man could not see. O.M. 1177. *Me a'n dreha arté kyns pen trydydh teké ages kyns y van,* I will raise it up again before the end of three days fairer than before. P.C. 348. *Otté an pren omma, nyns ûs tecka yn velâs-ma,* behold the timber here, there is not fairer in this country. P.C. 2559. *Tecké ys houl yw y lyw,* fairer than the sun is her huc. M.C. 226. W. *tecaah.*

TECEN, s. m. A short space of time, a little while. *Rág tcken*, for a little while. *Lluyd*, 115, 249. W. *ticyn*. Arm. *tacen*. Gael. *tacan*.

TECTER, s. m. Fairness, clearness, beauty. *Ol an tekter a wylys ny gl taves dén yn býs y leverel bynytha*, all the beauty I saw, the tongue of man in the world cannot tell it ever. O.M. 766. *Ny yno colon predyry an tekter a's bedheueh* why, heart is not to conceive the delight ye will have. P.C. 33. *Myhal, yn scon gorr'y dhy, yn tekter hag yn múr ioy, dre péch a fue kellys kyns*, Michael, put them forthwith there, in delight and in much joy, (that) was lost before through sin. R.D. 186.

TEDH, s. m. A day. *Púb tédh oll néb a vynné leverel pymthek pater*, he that would every day say fifteen paternosters. M.C. 228. An irregular mutation of *dédh*, qd. v.

TEDHA, v. a. To melt, to thaw, dissolve, liquefy; to become melted. *Llwyd*, 54. W. *todhi*. Arm. *teúzi*. Ir. *tinam*. Gael. *taisich*.

TEDNA, v. a. To draw, to pull, to shoot. ‡ *An pleasure és dhym yn býs ydhere gans gwarack tedna*, the pleasure (that) is to me in the world is to shoot with a bow. C.W. 106. ‡ *Dho tedua*, to draw; ‡ *tedna cledha*, to draw a sword. *Llwyd*, 55, 156. A late corruption of *tenna*, qd. v.

TEEN, s. m. The breech. ‡ *Pedn ha teen*, head and tail. *Pryce*. See *Tin*.

TEER, s. m. Land. *Pryce*. See *Tir*.

TEERA, v. a. To land, to come to shore. *Pryce*. W. *tirio*.

TEES, s. f. People, folk. *Pryce*. A late orthography of *tús*, qd. v.

TEFENAS, v. n. He awoke. A mutation of *defenas*, 3 pers. s. preterite of *defena*, id. qd. *dyfuny*, qd. v. *Pan o púr holerch an gýdh, y tefenas un marrek*, when the day was very well advanced there awoke a soldier. M.C. 244.

TEFFO, v. n. He may come. A mutation of *deffo*, 3 pers. s. subj. of irr. v. *dôs*. *Yn plâs-ma me a worto antecryst býs may teffo, er-y-byn ydh áf dhe'n beys*, in this place I will stay until antichrist comes; against him I will go to the world. R.D. 239. *Ken teffo y'gra golok, dhodho ny yllouch gúl drôk*, though he should come into your sight, to him ye cannot do harm. R.D. 1861. *En Edheuon skyntyll kéth, re's teffo múr vylyny, dhe veras worth Crist y éth, hag ef yn erous ow cregy*, those same learned Jews, may much disgrace be to them, to look on Christ they went, and he hanging on the cross. M.C. 216. Written also *teffé*. *An grous I a rúg gorré war scôdh Ihesus dh'y dôn dhy, dhe Ihesus Crist may teffé ol an gréff ha'n belyny*, the cross they put on the shoulder of Jesus to bear it thither, that to Jesus Christ might come all the grief and shame. M.C. 162. *May teffé tús gans nerth brás*, that men should come with great strength. M.C. 249.

TEFFONS, v. n. They may come. A mutation of *deffons*, 3 pers. pl. subj. of irr. v. *dós*. *Ke, gorhemmyn dhe'n cyté may teffons omma wharré war beyn aga bôs dyswrýs*, go thou, command the city, that they come here soon, on pain of their being destroyed. O.M. 2408. Written also *teffens*. *Hag a warn dhe vysterdens avorow dhys may teffens yn ketep pen*, and will warn the archi-tects that they come to thee to-morrow, in every head O.M. 2714.

TEFFRY, adv. Seriously. The aspirate mutation of *deffry*, qd. v. *Ow tás a vy, marth yn teffry ús dhym lemmyn*, my father mine, a wonder really there is to me now. O.M. 1309.

TEFIGIA, v. n. To tire, to be tired. *Llwyd*, 245. W. *difygio*. From the Lat. *deficio*.

TEFO, v. n. He may grow. 3 pers. s. subj. of *tevy*, qd. v. *Hag yn týr gorhemmenaf may tefo gwcydh ha losow*, and in the earth I will command that trees and plants grow. O.M. 28. *May haller govos dhe wýr, ha gweles yn bledhen hýr py gymmys hýs may teffo*, that it may be known truly, and seen in a year long, to what length it may grow. O.M. 2104.

TEFONES, v. n. To come. A mutation of *devones*, qd. v.

TEFYNS, v. n. Let them grow. 3 pers. pl. imp. of *tevy*, qd. v. *Púp gwedhen tefyns a'y sýf, ow tôn hy frút ha'y delyow*, let every tree grow from its stem, bearing its fruit and its leaves. O.M. 29.

TEG, adj. Fair, clear, beautiful, pretty, pleasant, fine, agreeable. Corn. Voc. *pulcher*. Written indiscriminately *tée*. Comp. *tevach*, *tecah*, *teca*, *tecé*. Super. *teca*, *tecé*. *Honna yo ol dhe vlamyé, a dorras an aval ték*, she is all to blame (that) plucked the fair apple. O.M. 267. *Bôs séeh ha ték an awel dhe Dew y côth dhyn grassé*, that the weather is dry and fair, it behoves us to thank God. O.M. 1147. *Y bous ef o mar dék guris y ny vynsaus y ranné*, his coat was made so fair that they would not part it. M.C. 190. *Tég awel*, a calm. *Llwyd*, 84. *Maw tég*, a comely boy; *môz dég*, a fair maid. 243. W. *tég*. Ir. *teide*, *teth*. Gael. †*teth*. Sansc. *téghas*, splendour.

TEGENSYWE, v. n. To descend. *Yma ow tegensywé hager gonees, war ow fédh*, there is coming down a fierce shower, on my faith. O.M. 1079. A mutation of *degensywé*, which is probably the same word as *degenow*, qd. v.

TEGES, part. Strangled, choked. *Llwyd*, 157. Part. pass. of *taga*, qd. v.

TEGLENE, v. n. To unloose, to give way. A mutation of *deglené*, qd. v.

TEHEN, s. f. A fire-brand quenched. *Llwyd*, 164. More correctly *tewen*, qd. v.

TEIL, s. m. Muck, manure, dung, dirt, mire. *Llwyd*, 59. *Pil teil*, a dung-hill, 154. W. *tail*. Arm. *teil*.

TEILU, s. m. A family, a household. Corn. Voc. *familia*. *Pen teulu*, the master of a house; *mam teulu*, the mistress of a house. *Ibid*. W. *teulu*, †*telu*, comp. of *ty*, a house, and *llu*, a host. Ir. *teaghlach*, †*teglach*. Gael. *tenghlach*. Manx, *lucht thie*.

TEIR, card. num. Three. Used with nouns feminine, as *tri* is with masculines. *Ferror, lowené dhys! ús teyr spik vrás genes gurýs*, smith, joy to thee! are there three great spikes with thee made? P.C. 2670. Written also *tyyr*, or *týr*. *My a wél tyyr guelen gay*, I see three gay rods. O.M. 1729. *Ancdhé ty a wylfyth týr gwedhen tevys wharré*, from them thou wilt see three trees grown presently. O.M. 828. W. *tair*, †*teir*. Arm. *teir*. Ir. †*teora*, †*teoir*. Sansc. *tisras*. Zend, *tisaró*.

TEIRGWETH, adv. Three times, thrice. *Llwyd*, 162. Comp. of *teir*, and *gwéth*, a time. Written also *tergwyth*, qd. v. W. *teirgwaith*. Arm. *teir-gwcz*.

TEITHIOC, s. m. A servant. Corn. Voc. *vernaculus*.

W. *teithiog*, characteristic, peculiar; *brenhin teithiog*, a king of acknowledged right.

TELEIN, s. f. A harp. Corn. Voc. *cithara*. W. *telyn, telan*; from *tel*, what is drawn tight. Arm. *telen*.

TELEINIOR, s. m. A player on the harp, a harper. Corn. Voc. *citharista*. W. *telynawr, telyniwr, telyniwr*. Arm. *telenner*.

TELETH, v. imp. It behoveth. A mutation of *deleth*, 3 pers. s. fut. of *dely*, qd. v. *Y wordhyé y teleth dhys, mar uskys pan glew dhe lêf*, to worship him it behoveth thee, so quickly when he hears thy voice. O.M. 1775. *Dew vylyges, y teleth warbarth aga bôs gorrys*, two wicked ones, it behoveth that they should be put together. P.C. 2553.

TELYWCH, v. a. Pay ye. 2 pers. plur. imp. of *taly*, qd. v. *Pilat a'n ladhas, hep fal wearnodho telywch dial, rák ef o Crist mychtern nêf*, Pilate killed him, without fail, take ye retribution of him, for he was Christ, the King of heaven. R.D. 1753.

TELL, s. m. Holes. *Gans dên skyntyll a wodhyé me a glewas leverel, an arlont y dhe denné war y ben gans kymmys nell, ma teth an dreyn ha cropyé dhe'n empynnyon dre an tell*, by a learned man that knew I have heard say, that they drew the garland on his head with so much force that the thorns came and penetrated to the brains through the holes. M.C. 134. *Ellas bones dhe treys squerdys, ol dhe yscarn dyscavylsys; tel y'th dywluef*, alas, that thy feet are torn; all thy bones stretched; holes in thy hands. P.C. 3174. Plural of *toll*, qd. v.

TELLER, s. m. A place. Pl. *tellyryow*. *Dhe'n nedhyn gwyls rág nyethy tellyryow esa paris, dhe Crist y ben py sensy, teller vjth nyngo kefys*, for the wild birds to make nests places were prepared; for Christ, where he might lay his head, no place was found. M.C. 206. *Rág genes yn pûp teller parys ôf dhe lafuryé*, for with thee in every place I am ready to labour. O.M. 939. *May rollo yn nêp teller dour dhe evé dhedhé y*, that he may give in some place water to them to drink. O.M. 1823. Written also *tiller* or *tyller*, qd. v. And by Llwyd, *telhar; telhar marhas*, a market place. 61. Lat. *tellus, tellure*.

TELLY, v. a. To bore a hole, to penetrate. 3 pers. s. fut. *teyll*. Part. pass. *tellys*. *Hag ynno fest luhas tol gans an dreyn a ve tellys*, and in it very many holes were bored by the thorns. M.C. 133. *Dew droys Ihesus caradow, ha'y dhyw leyff y a delly*, the feet of Jesus the loveable, and his hands they bored. M.C. 159. *Rág y dreys y a vynnas telly, dh'y worré yntien*, for his feet they would bore (a hole) to put them tightly. M.C. 178. *Y delly soon my a wra*, I will soon bore it. P.C. 2570. *Me a teyll tol rág an nŷl*, I will bore a hole for the one. P.C. 2743. *Me a dŷl tol rák hyben*, I will bore a hole for the other. P.C. 2749. The preterite and subjunctive are formed from *tolly*, qd. v. W. *tyllu*. Arm. *toulla*. Ir. *toll*. Gael. *toll*.

TEMMIG, s. m. A small part, a portion; a particle, a fragment. Pl. *temmigow*. Llwyd, 243. *En demigow*, piecemeal. 113. Diminutive of *tam*, qd. v. W. *temig*.

TEMPEL, s. m. A temple, a church. Pl. *templys*. Llwyd, 242, 249. W. *teml*. Arm. *tempel*. Ir. *teampul*. Gael. *teampull*. Manx, *chiamble*. Lat. *templum*.

TEMPRE, v. a. To temper, to soften, to tame. *Me a wra y tempré*, I will tame him. P.C. 1892. *My a dŷl tôl rák hybeen, rág tempré an harlot fôl*, I will bore a hole for the other, to tame the mad rascal. P.C. 2751. Borrowed from the English.

TEN, s. m. A pull, a draught, a drawing, a draught of horses. *Kens môs eyf ten gufyn pymeth, ha dhe scafé ydh éth yn ow wygys, my a grŷs*, before going, drink thou a draught of spiced wine, and more nimbly thou wilt go in my errand, I believe. O.M. 2294. W. *tyn*. Arm. *tenn*.

TEN, s. m. A beam. Pl. *tennow*. *A'y veen môn, ha'y scorennow my a vyn trehy tennow, ha lathys têk, ha corbles*, out of its slender stem, and its branches, I will cut beams, and fair laths, and joists. O.M. 2445. *Cowyth, profyyn an styllyow, mars êns compos dhe'n fosow, may haller aga lathyé gans corbles, lasys, tennow*, comrade, let us try the rafters, if they are straight to the walls, that they may be laid with joists, laths, beams. O.M. 2474.

TEN, adj. Stretched, tight, straight, firm. *Rág y dreys y a vynnas telly dh'y worré yn ten*, for his feet they would bore (a hole) to put them tightly. M.C. 178. *Y dreys ha'y dulé yn ten gans kentrow worth an plynken bedhens tackys*, his feet and his hands firmly with nails to the planks be fastened. P.C. 2516. *Ol ow yeyly yn ten, hag a wêl dhe lyes plu*, all my limbs stretched, and in the sight of many a parish. R.D. 2583. Written also *tyn*, qd. v.

TEN, v. a. He will draw. 3 pers. s. fut. of *tenna*, qd. v. *Me a's ten gans ol ow nerth*, I will pull it with all my strength. P.C. 2139. *Wharré ny a'n ten yn ban*, soon we will draw him up. R.D. 2259.

TENA, v. a. To suck. Written also *tené*, a mutation of *dena*, qd. v. *Yn lyfryow scrufys yma, bôs collenwys lowené a ganow an flechys da, ha'n ré nunys ow tené*, in books it is written, that joy is fulfilled from the mouths of good children, and little ones sucking. P.C. 438.

TENEWEN, s. m. What is stretched or extended; a bowstring; the flank; a side. Corn. Voc. *latus*. Pl. *tenwennow, tynwennow*. *Clewys a'n nŷl tenewen un êl ow talleth cané*, I heard on one side an angel beginning to sing. O.M. 214. *Cowyth, growedh a'n nŷl tu, hag aspy ahas ha glu, a rág, hag a denewen*, comrade, lie on one side, and watch continually, and listen, forwards and sidewards. O.M. 2063. *Dre tek a bren rág styllyow, ha compos y denwennow*, lo the fairest tree for rafters, and straight its sides. O.M. 2440. *Knoukyouch ef del dyndylas, may cosso y tynwennow*, strike ye him as he has deserved, that his sides may itch. P.C. 2084. *Namma fue ow colon tróch, pan wylys gorré an gu yn golon dre'n tenewen*, my heart was almost broken, when I saw the lance put into the heart through the side. R.D. 1246. *Why a sêdh warbarth genef, mŷns a gola orthyf ve, poran ryb ow thenewan*, ye shall sit together with me close by my sides. C.W. 14. *Gor ow sêth dhe denewan, may hallan tenna dhodha*, put thou my arrow to the string, that I may shoot at it. C.W. 112. W. *tenewyn*.

TENNA, v. a. To pull, to draw, to drag, to draw a bow, to shoot. Writ. also *tenné*. 3 pers. s. fut. and 2 pers. imp. *ten*. Part. pass. *tennys*. *War brŷn tenné ha cregy*, on pain of drawing and hanging. O.M. 2046. *Ny a's ten may fôns lour hŷr*, we will stretch them that they be long enough. P.C. 2700. *Me a wŷsk may dhys tenno a uel cor*, I will strike that it be drawn out for thee in the best way. P.C. 2723. *Greuch y tenné mês a'n dour*, do yo drag him out of the water. R.D. 2232. *Euch tenneuch a dhysempys y goyl yn ban*, go ye, draw immediately her sail up. R.D. 2290. *Pedyr a'n neyl tenewen yn mês a dennas clêdhé*, Peter from the one side drew out a sword. M.C. 71. *Gans ré a gymmys colon eu loven a ve tennys*, by some the rope was pulled with so much heart. M.C. 181. *Pan dêth leyff' Crist war an toll dre an nerth may tensons hy*, when the hand of Christ came on the hole through the strength that they drew it. M.C. 182. *Scrifys yw yn suredy, ha ken me nyn tavarsen, corff' Ihesus ha'y ascly y dhe denna mar velen, nêb a vynna a ylly nevera oll y yserren*, it is written of a surety, and otherwise I should not have said it, that they drew the body of Jesus so brutally, whoever would might number all his bones. M.C. 183. *Ahanas tennaf asen, me a vyn, a'th tenewan*, I will draw a rib from thee, I will, from thy side. C.W. 30. *Gor ow sêth dhe denewan, may hallan tenna dhodho*, set my arrow to the string, that I may shoot at it. C.W. 112. *Yta an sêth tennys, ha'n bêst yma gwyskys*, the arrow is shot, and the beast is struck. C.W. 114. *Yta an sêth compys, ten hy yn ban lys an peyl*, the arrow is right, draw thou it up to the knot. C.W. 112. Written also *tynné*, qd. v.

TER, v. a. He will break. 3 pers. s. fut. of *terry*, qd. v. *Râg mar tue dh'agan porthow, ef a ter an darasow*, for if he comes to our gates, he will break the doors. P.C. 3041. *Ow colon ynnof a ter pûr even dre fyenasow*, my heart in me will break very really through troubles. R.D. 707.

TER, prep. About, around. *Ter i hodna*, about her neck. Llwyd, 249. Also *between*, when it is an abbreviated form of *ynter*, qd. v.

TERGWEYTH, adv. Three times, thrice. *Tergueyth y fe convyctijs, even yn dhym y voleythy*, thrice was he convicted, right it is for us to curse him. M.C. 18. *Govy vgth pan gth dhodho, pan bf fythys dhyncorto tergwyth hydhew*, woe is me, that I went to him, when I was vanquished by him three times to-day. P.C. 147. *Re fethas an fals icvan hydhew tergoyth*, he has conquered the false demon this day three times. P.C. 155. Written by Llwyd, *teirgweth*, qd. v.

TERIII, v. a. To break, to bruise. Llwyd thus writes *terry*, qd. v.

TERLENTRY, v. a. To shine, to be resplendent, to glitter. *Oll gans our ow terlentry ydhesaf, splanna es an houl devery*, all with gold glittering I am, more resplendent than the sun indeed. C.W. 10. *Why a'n gwêl ow terlentry, splanna es an houl devery*, ye shall see him glittering, more resplendent than the sun indeed. C.W. 14.

TERMYN, s. m. A term, time, season. *Ellas gweles an termyn, ow arluth pan wrûk serry*, alas to see the time when my lord was angered. O.M. 351. *Pan vo termyn denythys*, when the time is come. O.M. 813. *Euch, gonethcuch ternyn hŷr, pows ny 'gys bŷdh nêp preys*, go ye, cultivate for a long time, rest ye shall not have any time. O.M. 1221. *Dynythys yw ow thermyn am bewnans yn bŷs-ma*, come is my term of my life in this world. O.M. 1885. *A ver dermyn*, in a short time. O.M. 1601. (See *Dermyn*.) Written at a later period *termen*, pl. *termeniow*. C.W. p. 190. *An termen-ma*, this time; *lias termen*, frequently; *termen hep diwedh*, time without end. Llwyd, 118, 143, 173. W. *term*.

TERNEWAN, s. m. A side. ‡ *Ternewan an awan*, the bank of a river. Llwyd, 3. A late corruption of *tenewen*, qd. v.

TERNOS, adv. The day following. *En Edhewon ny vynné bôs an laddron ow eregy ternos, râg pasch o dhedhé, dŷdh uchel y a sensy*, the Jews wished not that the robbers should be hanging the day after, for it was Easter to them; a high day they held it. M.C. 229. Written also *ternoys*. *Ternoys y sordyns bresel gans an Edhewon goky*, the day after there arose a quarrel between the foolish Jews. M.C. 238. W. *tranoeth*. Arm. *trónôz*.

TEROGE, s. m. Lands. *Fystynyn fast dh'agan pow, râk devones dewolow dhe'n terogé ; y niôns ow cryê huthyk*, let us hasten quick to our country, for devils are come to the lands; they are crying horridly. R.D. 2303. A corrupted form of *terros*, pl. of *tir*, qd. v.

TERROS, s. m. Lands, territory, country. Pl. of *tir*, qd. v. Llwyd, 243. *Yn mês a'm ioy ha'm wheleter, rês ow keskar dre terros, râg fout gwesc ha goscotter namna vyrwyn râg anwos*, away from my joy and my delight, need is to wander through lands; for want of clothes and shelter, I am well nigh perishing for cold. O.M. 300. Written also *terrus*. *Mal yw gynef dhe gafus, dhe vôs gynen dhe terrus*, I am glad to have thee, to go with us to (our) lands. P.C. 1532. *Mal yw genen dhe gafus, dhe vôs lemyn dhe terrus, ha dhe peyn kepar ha ny*, we are glad to have thee, to go now to (onr) country, and to pain, like us. O.M. 554.

TERROS, s. m. A boasting, bragging, arrogance, vanity. Pl. *terrygy*. *Penys a reys râg y terros, may fo leheys mûr a y gallos dre ow fynys*, penance is necessary for his arrogance, that much of his power may be lessened by my pains. P.C. 43. *Dûn alemma, cowythé, war menydhyow dhe veudré, ha dhe pigy ow thâs kêr dre y vôdh dh'agas gwythé râg terrygy*, let us come hence, comrades, on the mountains to walk, and to pray my dear Father by his will to keep you from your vanities. P.C. 112.

TERRY, v. a. To break, to make a rupture, to cut, to pluck off. 3 pers. s. fut. *ter*. Part. pass. *terrys*. *Ow holan d dhe dymmyn râg moreth a wra terry*, my heart all to pieces for grief will break. O.M. 356. *Dre sor kyn fêns y terrys, dhe sconya my ny alla*, though they be broken in anger, I am not able to resist. O.M. 1237. *Gorhemmyn Dew a terrys, dre henna y fûf dampnys dhe vôs neffré yn yfern*, the command of God I broke, through that I was condemned to be ever in hell. R.D. 212. *Eva prâg y whrusté sy tullé dhe bryes hep kên, an aval worth y derry*, Eve, why didst thou deceive thy husband without pity, by plucking the apple? O.M. 279. *A dhyregcuch me a ter torth a vara*, before you I will break a loaf of bread. R.D. 1313. *Kettel tersys an bara, aswonys Crist a gara*, as thou brakest the bread, I knew Christ (whom) I love. R.D. 1318. Another form of *torry*, qd. v.

TERRY, s. m. A breaking. *Terri an dêdh*, the break of day. Llwyd, 52, 54. W. *toriad y dŷdh*.

TERVYNS, s. m. A tempest. *Porth yfarn me a torras, hag a dhrôs lyes enef a vêr drôk, tervyns, ha chs*, the gate of hell I broke, and brought many souls from great evil, tempest, and torment. R.D. 2577.

TERYFAS, v. a. To declare. *Confortys yu ow colon, pan clewys ow teryfas, bones leyhys dhe pascyon a fue tyn, garow, ha brás*, my heart is comforted, when I heard (thee) declaring, that thy Passion was alleviated, which was sharp, cruel, and great. R.D. 504. A mutation of *deryfas*, id. qd. *derevas*, qd. v.

TES, s. m. Heat, warmth. Corn. Voc. *fervor*. W. *tês*. Arm. *tez*. Ir. *teas*, †*tes*. Gael. *teas*. Manx, *chias*. Sansc. *teghas*.

TESAN, s. f. A cake. ‡ *Ma gurég vi a pobas netten, ha hy ra guil tesan rages, dho dhûs drê dho da wrég*, my wife is baking to-morrow, and she will make a cake for thee, to come home to thy wife. ‡ *Ha an dzhei a wyras an naw pens en desan*, and they placed the nine pounds in the cake. *Lhwyd*, 251. W. *teisen*. Ir. *caise*.

TESCY, v. a. To teach. *Ef a dhueth a Galylé, lays nowydh ow tesky, lens ganso ow trylé*, he came from Galilee, teaching new laws, turning many with him. M.C. 107. The asp. mutation of *descy*, id. qd. *desca*, qd. v.

TESEHE, v. a. To dry. *Nans yu an lyfow basseys, pan ûs gwcydh ow tèschè*, now the floods are abated, when the trees are drying. O.M. 1128. The asp. mutation of *deschè*, id. qd. *dyschy*, qd. v.

TEST, s. m. A witness. *A Pylat, wolcom ôs fest, râk me a'th câr, Dew yn tést, pan y'th welaf*, O Pilate, thou art most welcome, for I love thee, God (being) witness, when I see thee. R.D. 1812. Written in the Cornish Vocabulary, *tist*, qd. v.

TESTYNY, s. m. A witnessing, testimony. *Me ew lantorn nêf, avel tân ow collowy, moy splunna es an drengys, heuna degouche destynny, ow bosnf prynce pûr gloryous*, I am the lantern of heaven, like fire shining, more resplendent than the Trinity, (of) that bear ye witness, that I am a prince very glorious. C.W. 10. Written in the Cornish Vocabulary, *tistuni*, qd. v.

TETYVALY, interj. Tittle-tattle. An expression of contempt. *Tety-valy, bram an gáth, nynges yddree dhymmo whûth, awos an kêth ober-na*, tittle-tattle, the wind of a cat, there is not sorrow to me yet, on account of that same act. C.W. 94.

TETH, v. n. He came. The asp. mutation of *dêth*, qd. v. *Cryst kymmys payn y'n gevé, angus tyn ha galarow, ma têth an goys ha dropyé war y fás an caradow*, Christ had so much pain, keen anguish and pangs, that the blood came and dropped on his face, the beloved. M.C. 59. *Ynny bonas gorys ragon ny Cryst a vynné, ha war an pren frût degis, may fe sur dh'agan sawyé, may têth frut may fèn kellys rág Adam dhe altamyé*, on it for us Christ wished to be put, and borne a fruit on the tree, that he might be sure to save us, so that the fruit, whereby we were lost, came to redeem Adam. M.C. 153.

TETHAN, s. f. A little breast, teat, or dug; an udder. *Lhwyd*, 3, 84, 170, 240. The diminutive of *têth*. (See also *Tidy*.) W. *têth, did*. Arm. *tez*. Ir. *cioch, did*. Gael. *cioch*. Manx, *cug*. Sansc. *chuchi*. Gr. τιτθὸς. Mod. Lat. *tetina*. Fr. *teton*. It. *tetta*. Span. *teta*. D. *tet*. Germ. *zitze*. Ang. Sax. *tit*. Eng. *teat*. Basque, *titia*.

TETHONS, v. n. They came. A mutation of *dethons*, qd. v.

TEUL, s. m. Deceit, fraud, guile. *Ysouch gokky ha fellyon, ha teul yn agas colon râk fout crygy*, ye are silly and foolish, and deceit in your heart for want of believing. R.D. 1274. Written also *toul* and *tull*, qd. v.

TEUL, s. m. A throw, a cast. See *Tewl*.

TEVOS, v. n. To come. *Byneges yu an guêl-ma, pan ûs sawor mûr da ow tevos annedhé y*, blessed are these rods, when a very good savour is coming from them. O.M. 1741. A mutation of *devos*, qd. v.

TEVY, v. a. To grow. 3 pers. s. fut. *tif*, qd. v. Part. pass. *tevys, tefys*. *War bûp frût, losow, ha hás, a vo ynny hy tevys*, over all fruit, herbs, and seed, that may be in it grown. O.M. 78. *Oté an gwêl dheragon glâs ow tevy*, see the rods before us growing green. O.M. 1985. *I'y le vŷdh an guêl plynsys, may fêns mocha onowrys, ha'n guella may wróns tevy*, where shall the rods be planted, that they may be most honoured, and may grow best? O.M. 2034. *Kepar Ihesus del devys, yn della an bows a wre*, as Jesus grew, so she made the coat. M.C. 161. With the pronominal characteristic preceding it signifies *to have*. *Heb nûr lavur defry benytha ny's tevyth flôch*, without much labour indeed never shall she have a child. O.M. 300. *Mar ny wonethons yn fás, y a's tevyth aufugy*, if they work not well, they shall have grief. O.M. 2328. *Ny a gl lour bones prout, ny's tevê tús vŷth hep mar roow mar dha*, we may be proud enough, people have never had gifts so good. O.M. 2597. *Ha nêp a's tefo gallos a vŷdh gans yowynk ha lôs henwys tús vrâs pûp termyn*, and those who may have power will be by young and old called great people always. P.C. 788. *Râk y tuc dydhyow may fenygouch an torrow na's tevê vythqueth flehes*, for the days will come that ye will bless the wombs (that) have never had children. P.C. 2647. (See also *Tefo, Tefyns, Teyf*.) Written also *tyvy*, qd. v. Welsh, *tyvu*. Arm. *tevaat*. Sansc. *tu*.

TEVYL, v. a. He will throw. *Yn chy Dew marsues marchas, me a's chas yu mês pûp guás, hag a tevyl aga guara*, in the house of God if there is a market, I will drive them out every fellow, and will overthrow their wares. P.C. 318. Another form of *tewl*, 3 pers. s. fut. of *tewlel*, qd. v. W. *tavl*.

TEW, adj. Thick, gross, fat, foggy. *Lhwyd*, 54, 102, 120, 153. *Belsebuk hn Satanas, euch atemma, pûr thôth brâs, del y'n kyrreuch, ages dew, ha kyrchouch dhe drê an guás may hallo cané ellas nefré yn tewolgow tew*, Beelzebub and Satan, go hence, with very great speed, as ye love me, you two, and bring home the youth, that he may sing "alas" ever in thick darkness. O.M. 540. W. *tew*, †*teu*. Arm. *teô*. Ir. *tiugh*, †*tiug*. Gael. *tiugh, liu*. Manx, *chioo*. Germ. *zahe*. Ang. Sax. *toh*. Eng. *tough*. Scot. *teuch*. O.N. *thykkr*. Swed. *tiocht*. Eng. *thick*.

TEW, s. m. A side. *Tra vethol a rella lês, ny gavnf omnna nêb tew*, any thing at all that will do good, I shall not find here on any side. C.W. 76. More generally written *tu*, qd. v.

TEWAL, adj. Dark, dusky, obscure. *Lhwyd*, 44, 45, 162. W. *tywyll*. Arm. *tewel, teval*. Irish, *teinheal*, †*temel*. Sansc. *tama*, darkness. Slav. *tma*.

TEWDER, s. m. Thickness, grossness, fatness. *Lhwyd*, 240. W. *tewder*. Arm. *teoder*.

TEWEL, v. n. To be silent, to hold one's tongue. 3 pers. s. fut. *tew*. 2 pers. s. imp. *taw*, qd. v. *Ydh hevel bôs falsury gynes, pan wreta tewel*, it seems there is falsehood in thee, when thou wilt be silent. P.C. 1320.

Tewel avel un bobba a wrûk pan fue aeussys, hold his tongue like an idiot he did, when he was accused. P.C. 2385. *Mar asos fûr, ty a tew, hag a ynden*, if thou art wise, thou wilt be silent, and wilt withdraw. R.D. 984. *Teweuch râk wêdh, dew adla*, be ye silent for shame, two knaves. R.D. 1495. (See also *tawaf, tawo*.) W. *tewi*. Arm. *tevel*. Ir. *tamham*, †*tua*. Gael. *tamh*. Lat. *taceo*.

TEWEN, s. m. A quenched firebrand. Corn. Vocab. *ticio*. Where it is read by Zeuss *itheu*, and by Llwyd, *tehen*. The former reading agrees with the Armoric, and the latter with the Welsh. W. *tewyn*. Arm. *eteô, etef*, pl. *eteviou, etivi*. Ir. *athainne*. Gael. *aithine*. Lat. *titio, litione*. Fr. *tison*.

TEWHYLLYF, v. n. I may return. *Ny dhueth an prŷs, vrna gyllyf dhe'n nêf dhum Tâs may tewhyllyf arté dhum gullas dhe gous worthys*, the time is not come, until I go to heaven to my Father, that I may return again to my country, to speak to thee. R.D. 879. A mutation of *dewhyllyf*, 1 pers. s. subj. of *dewhel*, qd. v.

TEWL, s. m. A cast, a throw, design, purpose. *Pryce*. Written also *toul*, qd. v. W. *tavyl*. Arm. *taol, talm*. Ir. *tubhal, tuilmh*. Gael. *tabhuil*.

TEWL, s. m. A hole. *A dhysempys whylewh e, maras êth e dhe cudhé yn nêp bós, tewl, py yn sorn*, immediately seek ye him, if he has gone to hide in some bush, hole, or corner. R.D. 539. Another form of *toll*, qd. v.

TEWL, v. a. He will throw. *Yn beydh pan y'n gorsyn ny, icharré y tueth deulugy ; warnan codhas, hag a'n teul ef sron yn ban*, when we put him in the grave, presently there came devils ; they fell on us, and throw him forthwith upwards. R.D. 2126. 3 pers. s. fut. of *tewlel*, qd. v. W. *tavl*.

TEWLDER, s. m. Darkness. *Ha'th era an noar heb roath, ha gwâg, ha vêdh an tewlder war bedgeth an dounder ; and the earth was without form, and void, and darkness was on the face of the deep. Ha dhe deberhee an golow dhurt an tewlder*, and to divide the light from the darkness. C.W. p. 189, 191. Written also *tulder*. Derived from *tewal*, dark. Arm. *tcoualder, tevalder*.

TEWLEL, v. a. To throw, to cast, to purpose, to design. 3 pers. s. fut. *tewl*, qd. v. Part. pass. *tewlys*. *Kyn fynnyf war an bŷs-ma tewlel vyngcans na dyal*, if I should wish upon this world to cast vengeance or flood. O.M. 1250. *Ha teulcuch e dral ha dral yn Bessedé pûr gowal*, and throw ye it piece by piece into Bethsaida very completely. O.M. 2782. *Teulel pren vsŷl vel vyé*, to throw a die would be a thousand (times) better. P.C. 2847. *Pyth yw teulys genouch why bôs erbyn nôs*, what is purposed by you to be against night? R.D. 1286. *A cowethé, tculyn gravel warnodho*, O comrades, let us cast a grappling-iron on him. R.D. 2268. *Me re teulys dew grabel*, I have cast two grappling-irons. R.D. 2271. *Dhe un carn y fue teulys*, to a rock he was cast. R.D. 2333. *Gans Iudas del o tewlys drey Ihesus an del vynné*, with Judas it was so arranged to bring Jesus as he would. M.C. 41. *Ha whâth an Ioul a dewlys towll ken manner mar eallé*, and still the devil cast a plan otherwise if he could. M.C. 15. *Toula* is another form, qd. v. W. *tavlu*.

TEWOLGOW, s. m. Darkness, obscurity. *May hallo cané ellas nefré yn tewolgow tew*, that he may sing "alas" ever in thick darkness. O.M. 546. *Hemma yw tewolgow brâs ; fattel êny war tu tré*, this is great darkness ; how shall we go towards home? P.C. 2090. *Hag anodho a gerhas y eneff dhe dewolgow*, and from him fetched his soul to darkness. M.C. 106. Written in the Cornish Vocabulary *tiwulgou*, tenebre. Llwyd, 224, makes it an irregular plural of *tewal*, but I am more inclined to derive it from the W. *tywyllwch*.

TEWRAGA, v. n. To thicken. *Ota cowes pûr ahas, ny's pyrth dên mara peys pel, a wronnd an dôr stremys brâs, ow tewraga gans mûr nel*, behold a shower very dreadful, man cannot bear it if it drops long, great streams cover the earth, thickening with much violence. O.M. 1082. So rendered by Pryce, who derives it from *tew*. I think it more likely to be a mutation of *dewraga*, another form of *dewrasa* agreeing with W. *dyvrycio*, to hasten.

TEWY, v. a. To burn, to blaze, to flame, to kindle. *Ellas, govy, ma ow dyllas ow tevey dheworth pren Cryst*, my a grŷs, alas, woe is me, my clothes are blazing from the wood of Christ, I believe. O.M. 2633. A mutation of *dewy*, id. qd. *dywy*, qd. v.

TEWYNNYE, v. n. To shine, to glitter. *Dên apert, ha mûr y râs, golow eleyr ow tewynnyé*, a man clearly and great his grace, a clear light shining. M.C. 243. A mutation of *dewynnyé*, id. qd. *dywhynny*, qd. v.

TEYF, v. n. He will grow. 3 pers. s. fut. of *tevy*. *Lower flowrys a bûb chan yn le-ma yta tevys, ha frutes war bûb gwedhan y teyf gweáf ha hâv keffrys*, abundant flowers of every kind are grown, and fruits on every tree shall grow winter and summer alike. C.W. 28. *Hag y triff a'n kêth sprûs-na un gwedhan wosa henna, na berth dowt, a vŷdh pûr dêk*, and there will grow from these same kernels a tree hereafter, bear no doubt, (that) will be very fair. C.W. 134. Written also *tŷf*, qd. v.

TEYL, v. a. He will bore a hole. 3 pers. s. fut. of *telly*, qd. v. *Me a teyl tol râg an nŷl, nynsus guês a west dhe Heyl a'n tollo guel*, I will bore a hole for the one ; there is not a fellow west of Hayle (that) can bore it better. P.C. 2743.

TEYR, card. num. Three. See *Teir*.

TI, s. m. A house. Corn. Voc. *domus*. *Why gwyeoryon, euch yn mês, ydhesouch ow kuthyl ges a Dhu, hag e sans eglos, yn ow thy a pygadow pan wreueh agas marhasow, ha fowys dhe laddron plos*, ye traders go out, ye are making a jest of God and his holy church, in my house of prayers when ye make your markets, and a den for foul thieves. P.C. 334. The letter *t* in this word came to have the sound of *ch* before the vowel *i* or *y*, as in Erse ; the same as in English *church* ; and to express this sound *ty* is always written *chy* in the Ordinalia, qd. v. The original form is preserved in the local names, *Tywardreath, Tywarnhaile, Tybister, &c.* W. *ty*, † *ti*, † *tig*. Arm. *ti*. Ir. *teach, tigh*, † *teg*. Gael. *tigh*. Manx, *tie*. Gr. τοίχος, τείχος, τέγος. Lat. *tectum* ; *tego*, to cover. Sansc. *tég*.

TI, pron. s. Thou, thee. *Del ony onan ha try, Tâs ha Mâp yn trynyté, ny a'd wra ty dhên a bry ; ha'n bewnans pan y'n kylly, dho'n dôr ty a dreyl arté*, as we are are one and three, Father and Son in Trinity ; we make thee, man, of clay ; and the life when thou losest it, to the earth thou shalt turn again. O.M. 59. Written indiscriminately *te* and *ty*. W. *ti*. Arm. *te*. Ir. *tu*. Gael. *tu*. Manx, *(too)* oo. Gr. σὺ, σέ. Lat. *tu, te*. Sansc. *tvâ, tava, te*.

TIAH, v. a. To swear. *Llwyd*, 74. *Na râs tiah gow warbyn de contreveck*, thou shalt not swear falsely against thy neighbour. *Pryce.* Written also *tyé*, qd. v.

TIBIANS, s. m. Thought, opinion. *Pryce.* See *Tybians*.

TIBIAS, v. a. To think, to believe. *Pryce.* See *Tybias*.

TICCIDEW, s. m. A butterfly. *Llwyd*, 34, 112. W. *gloyn Duw* (carbo Dei.) Ir. *dealan De*. Gael. *deallan De*.

TIDI, s. m. A breast, pap, or teat. *Llwyd*, 84, 112. (See *Tethan*.) W. *did*. Ir. *did*. Eng. *diddy*.

TIES, s. m. Folk, people. *Pennow ties*, chief people. *Llwyd*, 128. A late form of *tús*, qd. v.

TIHA, prep. Towards. *Pryce.* See *Tyha*.

TIN, s. m. A bottom, the breech. *Ty a wôr guel bremmyn brâs dyllo menouch mês a'th tŷn*, thou knowest better how to do dirty work. P.C. 2105. *Whyp an tŷn, kymer an pen*, breech whip, take thou the head. R.D. 2081. *Râk yn mês yma y pen pûr hŷr aves dhwn tŷn*, for its end is out very long behind me. R.D. 2357. W. *tin*. Ir. *tón*. Gael. *tòn*. Manx, *thoin*.

TIOC, s. m. A husbandman, a farmer, a ploughman, a rustic. Pl. *tiogow*. Corn. Voc. *pobel tiogou*, vulgus, the common people. In Jordan and Llwyd's time it was pronounced *tiak*. *Ydhom provas gwan dyac*, I am proved a weak husbandman. C.W. 68. ‡ *Panna hweêl allosti guil, mêdh an tiak*, what work canst thou do, said the farmer. 251. W. *taiog*. Arm. *tick*. Ir. *tighearnach*. Gael. *tuathanach*.

TIOGOU, s. m. The rabble. Corn. Voc. *pobel tiogou*, vulgus. *Tiogou* is the pl. of *tiog*, id. qd. W. *taiog*, rude, rustic.

TIN, s. m. A fortified place, a castle. Another form of *din*, qd. v. Hence *Tintagel*, in Cornwall; and *Tinsyliwy*, *Tindaethwy*, in Wales.

TIR, s. m. Land, earth, soil, ground. Corn. Voc. *terra*. Pl. *tiryow*, *terros*. *Mychtern ôf war wlâs ha tŷr, yn henna y sûf genys*, king I am over land and earth, in that I was born. P.C. 2020. *Pepenag vo a'n barth wŷr, a cleufyth ow voys yn tŷr*, whoever is of the true side, will hear my voice on earth. P.C. 2026. *Nêp yw arluth tŷr ha môr*, who is Lord of earth and sea. P.C. 2422. *Yn tressé dŷdh dybarth gwrâf yntré an môr ha'n tyryow*, on the third day I will make a separation between the sea and the lands. O.M. 26. *Tir devrae*, watery ground, a fen. *Llwyd*, 112. (See *Terros*.) W. *tir*. Arm. *tir*, *ter*. Ir. *tir*. Gael. *tir*. Manx, *cheer*. Lat. *terra*.

TIRA, v. a. To land, to come to land, to come ashore. Written by Pryce, *teera*. W. *tirio*.

TIRETH, s. m. Land, earth, country. *Ha mar ny wrer y wythê, y dhyskyblon yn pryvé a'n lader yn mês a'n brydh, hag a lever yn pûp le y vôs dasvewys arté, ha gyllys dhe ken tyreth*, and if it is not guarded, his disciples privily will steal him out of the tomb, and will say in every place, that he is revived again, and gone to another country. R.D. 346. *Gallas ýf dhe ken tyreth, ha ganso mûr a eledh*, gone he is to another land, and with him many angels. R.D. 763. *Dhys ydh archaf, a dyreyth, gâs Adam dhe'th egery*, I command thee, O earth, allow Adam to open thee. O.M. 381.

TIS, s. f. Folk, people. *Llwyd*, 63, 223. *Ow this*, my people. 249. Generally written in the Ordinalia, *tús*, qd. v.

TIST, s. m. A witness. Corn. Voc. *testis*. Written in the Ordinalia, *test*, qd. v. W. *tŷst*, †*test*. Arm. *test*.

Ir. *test*. Gael. *teist*. Lat. *testis*.

TISTUNI, s. m. A witnessing, testimony. Corn. Voc. *testimonium*. Written also *testyny*, qd. v. W. *tystioliaeth*; *testun*, a theme. Arm. *testeni*. Ir. *teastughadh*, †*tesias*, †*testemin*, †*testimin*. Gael. *teisteanas*, *teistcas*.

TITHE, pron. s. Thou also. *Llwyd*, 244. W. *tithau*, †*titheu*. Ir. *tusa*, †*tussu*. Gael. *tusa*. Manx, *uss*. Lat. *tute*.

TITHIA, v. a. To hiss. *Dho tithia*. *Llwyd*, 150. W. *chwithrwd*.

TIWLDER, s. m. Darkness, obscurity. *Llwyd*, 240. Id. qd. *tewlder*, qd. v.

TIWULGOU, s. m. Darkness. Corn. Voc. *tenebrae*. Written in the Ordinalia *tewolgow*, qd. v.

TIWY, v. a. To kindle, to light. *Pryce*. Written also *tewy*, qd. v.

TO, s. m. The covering of a house, a roof, a thatch. Corn. Voc. *tectum*. Hence *ty*, to roof, qd. v. W. *to*. Arm. *to*. Ir. *tuighe*. Gael. *tugh*, *tubh*. Manx, *thoo*.

TO, v. a. He would come. *Dhodho bŷs pan danvonas Crist, y to dhe Galylé*, until when Christ sent to him, that he would come to Galilee. M.C. 87. *Ha'n tebel êl, hager brêf, yn y holon a worré war y mester venions crêf y to, Ihesus mar ladhé*, and the evil angel, ugly reptile, put into her heart that strong vengeance would come on her lord, if he slew Jesus. M.C. 122. A mutation of *do*, 3 pers. s. fut. of *dôs*, qd. v.

TO, v. a. He will swear. 3 pers. s. fut. of *toy*, qd. v.

TOCCO, v. a. He may bring. *Saw gweytyens pûp may tokco ganso lorch, py cledhé da*, but let every one take care that he bring with him a staff, or a good sword. P.C. 943. A mutation of *docco*, 3 pers. s. subj. of *doga*, qd. v.

TODN, s. f. A lay. ‡ *Aras an kenza an todn*, plough first the lay. *Pryce*. A corrupted form of *ton*, qd. v.

TOEN, v. a. To bear, or carry. *Râg yma ef deffry, ow toen ol agan maystry*, for he is truly bearing all our power. P.C. 3077. A mutation of *doen*, qd. v.

TOF, v. n. I shall come. *Râk bôs ow arluth mar clâf, A Dhew, ple tâf, na ple ydh âf, my won ple toulaf ow paw*, because of my lord being so ill, O God, where I shall come or where I shall go, I know not where I shall cast my foot. R.D. 1665. A mutation of *dôf*, qd. v.

TOF, v. a. I will swear. 1 pers. s. fut. of *toy*, qd. v.

TOIM, adj. Hot, warm. Corn. Voc. *calidam*. W. *twym*. Arm. *tuemm*, *tomm*. Ir. *timeach*.

TOIMDER, s. m. Heat, warmth. *Pryce*. Written in the Cornish Vocabulary *tumder*, and in the Ordinalia *tomder*, qd. v. W. *twymder*. Arm. *tomder*, †*tuimder*.

TOLCORN, s. m. A flute or fife. Corn. Voc. *linthuus* (for *lituus*). Lit. a horn with holes, being comp. of *toll* and *corn*, a horn. W. *tolgorn*.

TOLL, s. m. A hole, a perforation. Pl. *toll*, qd. v. *Hag ynno fest luhas toll gans an dreyn a ve tellys*, and in it very many holes were bored by the thorns. M.C. 133. *Worth an lês y a dollas dew doll yn grows heb kên*, according to the width they bored two holes in the cross without pity. M.C. 178. *Yn dôr my a vyn palas tol, may fo ynno cudhys*, in the earth I will dig a hole, that he may be covered in it. O.M. 865. *Yn nêp tol fyen dhe'n fo alemma*, into some hole let us flee away hence. R.D. 134. W. *twll*. Arm. *toull*. Ir. *toll*. Gael. *toll*. Manx, *towl*. Sansc. *talla*.

TOLLA, v. a. To deceive, to delude. Written also *tollé*. Part. *tollys*. *Râg ty dhe gola worty ha tollé dhe bryes lên*, because thou hast hearkened to her, and deceived thy faithful spouse. O.M. 294. *Prâg y tolsté sy hep kên, worth hy thempté dhe dyrry an frût erbyn ow dyfen*, why didst thou deceive her pitilessly, by tempting her to pluck the fruit against my prohibition? O.M. 302. *Hy a dhesefsé scorné gans an episcop, ha'y dolle dhe wordhyé dewow nowydh*, she would wish to strive with the bishop, and delude him to worship new gods. O.M. 2731. *Gans gloteny ef pan welas cam na ylly y dolla*, when he saw with gluttony that he could not a whit deceive him. M.C. 13. *Gorthyp vy na vâf tollys*, answer thou me, that I be not deceived. P.C. 2008. Written also *tullé*, qd. v.

TOLLEC, adj. Full of holes, perforated, hollow. *Llwyd*, 47. W. *tyllog*. Arm. *toullec*. Ir. *tolltach*. Gael. *tollach*.

TOLLOR, s. m. A receiver of toll. Corn. Voc. *theolenarius*. W. *tollwr*, from *toll*, a toll. Arm. *tell*. Gr. τέλον. Germ. *zoll*. Eng. *toll*.

TOLLY, v. a. To make a hole, to perforate. *Worth an lês y a dollas dew doll yn grows heb kên*, according to the width they bored holes in the cross without pity. M.C. 178. *Me a tryl tol râg an nâl, nynsus guâs a west dhe Heyl a'n tollo guel*, I will bore a hole for the one; there is not a fellow west of Hayle, (that) can bore better. P.C. 2745. *Tolla*, bore thou. *Llwyd*, 248. The other tenses are inflected from the other form *telly*, qd. v.

TOM, adj. Hot, warm. *Llwyd*, 18. Another form of *toim*, qd. v.

TOMALS, s. m. Quantity, much of anything. *Llwyd*, 134. W. *talm*. Ir. *tamal*. Manx, *tammylt*.

TOMDER, s. m. Heat, warmth. *Mâb Du o kymmys greeijs, râg tomder ef a wesé dowr ha goys yn kemeskis*, the Son of God was so much grieved; from heat he sweated water and blood mingled. M.C. 58. *Bewa ydhesaf pûb car yn tomder ha yender rew, nôs ha dâdh*, I do live continually in heat and cold of frost, night and day. C.W. 120. *Yn pŷt-ma y wrêth trega genaf ve a barth a wollas, hag a losky yn tomder tân*, in this pit thou shalt dwell with me on the lower side, and shalt burn in heat of fire. C.W. 124. Another form of *toimder*, qd. v.

TOMMA, v. a. To make warm, to warm. Part. *tommys*. *Tommans onan dour war tân, râg wogé soper my a woulch ol agas trŷs*, let one warm water on the fire, for after supper I will wash all your feet. P.C. 833. *Arluth, yma dour tommys lour, may hallons bôs gelhys aga trŷs yn kettep pol*, Lord, there is water warmed enough, that may be washed their feet every one. P.C. 839. W. *twymo, twymno*. Arm. *tomma*. Ir. *teagham*.

TON, s. f. A wave. *Otté an corf casadow ow lôs y ban; me a lever dheuch yn scon, tynnyn ef yn ban war ton*, see tho hateful carcase coming up; I tell you forthwith let us draw him up on the wave. R.D. 2281. W. *ton*, pl. *tonnau*, †*tonnou*, in Juvencus Glosses. Arm. *ton*. Ir. *tonn*. Gael. *tonn*. Manx, *tonn*.

TON, s. f. Unploughed land, a meadow, a lay. *Cressewch, coullenweuch an brys avel kyns, kettep nâp pron; râg may fewch why sostoneys euch dhe wonys guel ha ton*, increase ye, fill the world as before, every son of the breast; that ye may be sustained, go to till the field and lay. O.M. 1164. W. *ton*.

TON, v. a. To bear, or carry. *Pûp gwedhen tefyns a'y sâf, ow tôn hy frût, ha'y delyow*, let every tree grow from its stem, bearing its fruit and its leaves. O.M. 30. *Fystyn duwhans, gurres vy ow tôn a plos casadow*, hasten thou quickly, help me bringing the foul villain. O.M. 892. A mutation of *dôn*, qd. v.

TONEC, s. m. A flock, a drove, a herd. *Llwyd*, 64. *Gans henna y a drylyas, confortis ha lowenek, hag êth tûs Crist râg whelas, hag a'e eafos morethek; y lavarsons ol en câs; ydh ethons yn un tonck bŷs yn Galyté dh'y whelas, ha dhe gows worth Ihesus wêk*, with that they turned, comforted and joyous, and went to seek the people of Christ, and found them mournful; they told all the case; they went in one flock to Galilee to seek him, and to speak to Jesus sweet. M.C. 257.

TONNEL, s. f. A cask. Corn. Voc. *dolium*. W. *tunell*. Arm. *tonel*. Ir. *tunna*. Gael. *tunna*. Manx, *tunnry*. Fr. *tonneau*. M.H.G. *tonne*. Eng. *tun*.

TONS, v. n. They shall come. A mutation of *dôns*, qd. v.

TOON, v. a. To bear, or carry. *Nyns yw marth cûth ken y'm bo, ow toon an pren a dhe dro*, it is no wonder if I have sorrow, carrying the tree about. O.M. 2820. Another form of *toen*, or *tôn*, qd. v.

TOOTH, s. m. Haste. Pryce. *Tooth-du*, immediately. Written also *tôth*, qd. v.

TOP, s. m. A top, summit, height. *Me a wêl goodly wedhan, ha'y thop pûr uchel yn ban bes yn nêf ma ow tevy*, I see a goodly tree, and its top very high, aloft, even to heaven it is growing. C.W. 132. *Yn top an wedhan dêk ydh esa un mayteth whêk*, on the top of the fair tree, there was a sweet virgin. C.W. 138. W. *top*. Ir. *top*. Gael. *top*.

TOR, s. f. A prominence; a bulge, a belly, the womb; the swell of mountain, a mountain. Corn. Voc. *venter*. Pl. *torrow*. *Tormentours, an kêth guas-ma gans skorgys ha whyppys da gwrêch y cronkyé tor ha keyn*, executioners, this same fellow, with good scourges and whips do ye smite him, belly and back. P.C. 2057. *Govy vŷth pan vêf genys, a dor ow mam denyhys, woe is me when I ever was born, out of my mother's womb brought. O.M. 1754. *Côsk war dhe tor, ha powes*, sleep on thy belly, and rest. O.M. 2070. *Râk y tue dydhyow, may fenygouch an torrow, nas tevé vythqueth flehes*, for the days will come that ye will bless the wombs that never bare children. P.C. 2646. *Tor an dorn*, the palm of the hand. *Llwyd*, 111. *Tor brâs*, big bellied. 171. *Torr* remains as the name of many hills in Cornwall. Torr Point, in Anthony. Rough-*torr* is the name of a place in St. Breward; and *Helmintor*, the moory stony hill, in Lanlivery. W. *tor*. Arm. *tôr*, *teûr*. Ir. *turr*. Gael. *torr*.

TORCH, s. m. A hog. Corn. Voc. *nagalis*. W. *twrch*. Arm. *tourch*. Ir. *torc*. Gael. *torc*.

TORCHAN, s. f. A torch. *Llwyd*, 69.

TORMA, s. m. This time. *A wylsta ken yn torma ys del egé agensow*, seest thou else at this time, than as it was just now? O.M. 795. *Y'n guraf ytho scon yn torma*, I will do it now immediately at this time. O.M. 1275. Comp. of *torm*, ld. qd. *termen*, qd. v., and *ma*, here.

TORN, s. m. A turn, a winding. *Saw nyns o torn da denvon guesyon a'n pâr-ma gans arvow dhum kemeres*, but it was not a good turn to send fellows of this sort with arms to take me. P.C. 1298. *I yes torn da yn bys-ma rc wrúk dhe vohosugyon*, many a good turn in this world he has done to the poor. P.C. 3107. *Reys yn dhe onan golyas ; war y torn púp y dhyffras y gowsyth, paw a dhalleth*, need is that one should watch ; in his turn every one protecting his comrade, who will begin ? R.D. 409. *Torn an vor*, the turning of the way, is the name of a place in St. Agnes. W. *turn, twrn.* Ir. *turna*. Gael. *túrn*. Sansc. *túrni*, velocity.

TORN, s. m. A hand. *A'n lóst kymmer dhedhy yn ban, y'th torn hep gér sens dhe honan*, take it up by the tail, in thy hand, without a word, hold it thyself. O.M. 1455. A mutation of *dorn*, qd. v.

TORNEWAN, s. m. A side. *Llwyd*, 82. ‡ *Tornewan an awan*, the side of a river. 141. A late corruption of *tenewen*, qd. v.

TORRY, v. a. To break, to bear, to break off. *Torr-e yn ow feryl vy*, break it off at my risk. O.M. 197. *Ef a wrúk ow husullyé frút annedhy may torren*, he did advise me that I should gather fruit from it. O.M. 218. *My ny dorraf bys vycken an acord*, I will never break the agreement. O.M. 1239. *Mars ellen hep cows orty, hy holon hy a torsé*, if I should go without speaking to her, her heart would break. O.M. 2174. *Fôs ny torras, na war dharas ny dhue dhynny*, he broke not a wall, nor through door will he come to us. R.D. 329. *An prysners gaisons yn wédh, ny torsans chy*, the prisoners are gone also, they broke not the house. R.D. 662. *Terry* and *tyrry* are also other forms, qd. v. W. *torri*. Arm. *terri*.

TORROG, adj. Bigbellied, frequent. *Pryce*. W. *torrog*. Arm. *torrec*. Ir. *torrach*. Gael. *torrach*. Manx, *torrach*.

TORTH, s. f. A loaf. *Yssedheuch a termyn ver, a dhyrageuch me a ter torth a vara*, sit ye for a short time, before you I will break a loaf of bread. R.D. 1314. *An Arluth Ihesu guella, a dhyragon torth vara ef a torras*, the Lord Jesus, the best, before us a loaf of bread he broke. R.D. 1490. W. *torth*. Arm. *tors*. Ir. *tort*. Gael. *tort*. Med. Lat. *torta*. Fr. *tourte*. Eng. *tart*.

TOS, v. n. To come. *Ot an justys ow tôs dhyn*, see the magistrate coming to us. P.C. 370. *An lucf a'm grúk me a wél, ha'y odor whekké ys mél ow tôs warnaf*, the hand (that) made me I see, and his odour sweeter than honey coming upon me. R.D. 145. A mutation of *dôs*, qd. v.

TOS, v. a. He swore. *Y'n nachen ef a'm guarnyas ; râk henna me a sorvas, hag a tôs na wrên neffré*, he warned me that I should deny him ; for that I was angry, and swore that I never would. P.C. 1422. A contracted form of *toys*, preterito of *toy*, qd. v.

TOT, adj. Extended. Corn. Voc. *mor tot*, occanus. W. *tawd*.

TOTTA, adv. Immediately. *Me a vyn alemma môs dhom gwrêk ha'm flehes totta*, I will go hence to my wife and children immediately. O.M. 1036. A contracted form of *tôth da*.

TOTH, s. m. Haste, despatch. *Hy cemercs me a wra ugy dhe'n gorhyl tôth brás*, I will take her inside the ark with great speed. O.M. 1124. *Peder, conyth, dún tôth da, agan nyggys guren bysy*, Peter, companion, let us come quickly, our errand let us do diligently. P.C. 643. *Peder, me a wél un dên ow tôn pycher dour, tôth men dùn war y lerch*, Peter, I see a man carrying a pitcher of water, very hastily let us come after him. P.C. 662. Written also *touth*, and *toyth*. *Me a vyn y dhôn dhe drê, ha fystyné gans touth brás*, I will carry it home, and hasten with great speed. P.C. 660. *Ow dyskyblyon, pyscuch toyth da, ol kes colon*, my disciples, pray ye forthwith, all with one heart. P.C. 2. W. *tûth*.

TOUL, s. m. A throw, a cast, purpose, design. *Ha whâth an Ioul a dewlys towll ken maner mar callé dre néb fordh a govaytis guthyll dh'y gowsys treylé*, and yet the Devil cast a plan otherwise if he could through some way of covetousness cause his speech to turn. M.C. 15. *Ol y doul ef o tewlys ganso yn néf rág tregé*, all his plan was formed to dwell with him in heaven. M.C. 214. *Na hedhyn, rág yma war agan toul knoukyé fast bys may fryn squeyth*, we will not stop, for it is on our design to strike hard until we be weary. O.M. 2698. *Henna me a wra, râk ny won yn beys guel toul dhyn dhe wruthyl dhe'n kaugeon*, that I will do, for I know not in the world a better trick for us to do to the dirty fellow. P.C. 2920. W. *tavl*.

TOUL, s. m. Deceit, fraud, guile. *Hep toul púr wŷr me a grŷs, dredhos y fydhyn sylwys*, without deceit very truly I believe, through thee that we shall be saved. P.C. 286. Written also *teul*, and *tull*, qd. v.

TOUL, s. m. A hole. *Pendra wráf, orth en ioul mar ny gaffaf toul war nép cor*, what shall I do, for the devil if I shall not find a hole in some place. R.D. 2131. Another form of *tol*, qd. v.

TOU'LA, v. a. To throw, or cast. 2 pers. s. imp. *toul*. Part. *toulys*. *Toul an grous dhe'n dôr dhe worowedhé*, throw thou the cross to the ground to lie. P.C. 2661. *Rum fay, lemmyn a'n caffen, er an ascal, y'n toulsen yn creys un tán*, by my faith, now should I get him, by the wing, I would throw him into the midst of the fire. R.D. 290. *Plc tôf, na plc ydh áf, ny won plc toulof ow paw*, where I shall come, or where I shall go, I know not where I shall cast my foot. R.D. 1665. *Aban óv dhe dhrók towlys*, since I am to evil thrown. C.W. 68. Llwyd, 66, *dho towla ; 62, dho towla e mês*, to pour out. Another form of *tewlel*, qd. v. W. *tavlu*.

TOUR, s. m. A tower, fort, palace. *Llwyd*, 168. *Lemyn púp dyyskynnes, saw kyns ys yn tour moncs levereuch dhym*, now let every one alight, but before going to the palace speak ye to me. O.M. 2030. *Rôf dhys ow thour, hel ha chammbour ; vedhaf dhe wour*, I will give to thee my palace, hall and chamber ; I will be thy husband. O.M. 2110. *Salmon, lemen ke y'th tour*, Salmon, now go into thy palace. O.M. 2389. Written in the Cornish Vocabulary, *tur.* W. *tŵr*. Arm. *tour*. Ir. *tor, tur*. Gael. *túr*. Manx, *toor*. Lat. *turris*. Fr. *tour*. Eng. *tower*.

TOVYS, part. Grown. *Dew váb y ma dhym genys, ha tovys ydhyns dhe denes*, I have two sons born, and grown they are to manhood. C.W. 78. Another form of *tevys*, part. pass. of *teva*, qd. v.

TOWAN, s. m. A sandy shore-bank, a strand. Preserved in the names of many places in Cornwall, from their position ; and in Wales, as *Towyn*, in Merionethshire, and *Towyn*, opposite Aberconwy. W. *tywyn*. Arm. *teven, tún*.

TOWN, adj. Deep. *Ef a doys a dhesympys maga town ty*

del wodhyé, he swore forthwith as deep an oath as he knew. M.C. 85. A mutation of *down*, qd. v.

TOWN, v. a. To bear. *Ow holon yntré myll darn marth yw gené na squardhy, pan wclaff ow máb mar wan, ow town kemys velyny*, it is a wonder with me that my heart does not break into a thousand pieces, when I see my son so weak, suffering so much villainy. M.C. 166. A mutation of *down*, another form of *doyn*, or *dón*, qd. v.

TOWTH, s. m. Haste, dispatch. *Ow cannas whék, dhe'n beys toneth, lowenna tekca gothfy*, my sweet messenger, to the world quick, the fairest joy thou knowest. P.C. 1041. Another form of *tóth*, qd. v.

TOY, v. a. To swear, to take an oath, to adjure. 1 pers. s. fut. *tóf*; 3 pers. s. fut. *to*, and *te*, qd. v. *Re Vahun, y tóf yn wédh, mars yw e lyddrys a'n bédh, why a's býdh ages ancow*, by Mahound I swear also, if he is stolen from the grave, ye shall have your death. R.D. 610. *Oll dha lyvyr nyn dál cáth, me a'n to, war ow ena*, all thy labour is not worth a cat, I swear it, on my soul. C.W. 168. *Neffra ny výdh dewedhys, me a'n to, war ow honssyans*, it will never be finished, I swear it, on my conscience. C.W. 174. *Ef a doys a dhesympys maga town ty del wodhyé*, he swore immediately as deep an oath as he knew. M.C. 85. This verb is also written *tyé*, from the subs. *ty*, qd. v., and in later Cornish *tiah*. W. *tyngu*. Arm. *toui*. †*A huy a toche*, would ye swear? †*A te touhe*, wouldst thou swear? *Buhez Nonn*. 160.

TRA, s. f. A thing. Pl. *traow*. *En Tás a néf y'm gylwyr, formyer púp tra a výdh gwrýs*, the Father of Heaven I am called, the Creator of every thing that is made. O.M. 2. *Un dra a won, a'n godhfes, a russé dhe dhydhané*, one thing I know, if thou knewest it, would amuse thee. O.M. 151. *Kynyver dén us yn wlás, na tra yn býs ow pevé*, as many men as there are in the land, or thing in the world living. O.M. 1030. *Marow yw púp tra esé spyrys a vewnans ynno*, dead is every thing (that) there was the spirit of life in it. O.M. 1089. *Bydhaf byay war an dra*, I shall be diligent on the matter. P.C. 1932. *Pa'n dra a wounté se*, what thou wouldst ask. M.C. 80. *Herodes a wouynnys orth Ihesus Crist leas tra, ha trevyth ny worthebys*, Herod asked of Jesus Christ many things, and he answered nothing. M.C. 111. A late plural was *trehys*. *Te nyn wra dhys honan havalder trehys výth*, thou shalt not make to thyself the likeness of any things. Pryce. W. *tra*. Arm. *tra*.

TRA, conj. As, like as, even as; so that. Llwyd, 178, 248. Written also *tre, dre, tro*, and *try*. W. *tra*. Arm. *tra*. Ir. *trath*. Gael. *trath*.

TRA, prep. Beyond, over. *Tra mór*, beyond the sea. Pryce. Written *tre* in composition. W. *tra*. Arm. *tre*. Gael. *thar*. Lat. *trans*.

TRAHA, prep. Towards. *Traha'n dór*, towards the ground; *traha'n darras*, towards the door. Pryce. A late form of *troha*, qd. v.

TRAHES, s. m. A cutter. Pl. *trahesi mein*, stone-cutters. Llwyd. 242. More correctly *trches*, qd. v.

TRAILIA, v. a. To turn. ‡*Ol dha splendar ha'th tectar, y trayl skon dheis dha hacter ha mêr utheck byllen*, all thy splendour and beauty, shall be turned immediately to deformity, and most ugly foulness. C.W. 22. ‡*Dén cóth o e, ha guadn, a trailia an bér*, an old man he was,

and weak, turning the spit. Llwyd, 252. ‡*Ha trailins y gein dha an toul*, and he turned his back to the hole. Ibid. ‡*Dho trailia a dhethar*, to turn back. 140. A later form of *treylé*, qd. v.

TRAITH, s. m. The sandy beach of the sea, sands. Written in the Cornish Vocabulary *trait*, harena. Written later *treath*, which is preserved in the local name *Treath*, in Menackan. *Tywardreath*, the house on the sands. *Pentraeth*, the head of the sands. W. *traeth*. Arm. *traez*, †*treiz*. Ir. *traigh, tracht*. Gael. *traigh*. Manx, *traih*. Cf. Lat. *tractus, trajectus*.

TRANC, s. m. A space of time, time. *Ol ny a pýs, youynk ha hên, war Dhu púp prŷs, mercy gan kên, may fên guythys rák an bylen, hag ol sylwys, trank hep gorfen*, all we pray young and old, to God always, mercy with pity, that we may be preserved from the evil one, and all saved, time without end. P.C. 42. *Me a's kymmer yn lowen, hag a gúl trank hep worfen dhys y guerthé, dhe ancledhyns Crystenyon*, I will take it gladly, and will time without end sell it to thee to bury Christians. P.C. 1562. W. *tranc*.

TRAVYTH, s. m. Any thing. (*Tra—býth*.) *Dhymny ny travyth ny gréf, aban yw y vódh ef y lesky hep falladow*, to us not any thing is grievous, since it is his will to burn it without fail. O.M. 482. *Awos travyth ny wrussen venytha dhe guhudhas*, because of any thing I would not ever accuse thee. O.M. 163. *Travyth ny wréth gorthyby erbyn dustenyow lél*, thou answerest nothing against trusty witnesses. P.C. 1317.

TRAWARAN, s. m. Dispute, dissension. ‡*An bara dzhei a dhabraz, ha na ve idn fróth, na mikan, na trawaran nôr vez*, the bread they ate, and there was not any anger, nor strife, nor dispute henceforth. Llwyd, 253. Comp. of *tra*, a thing, *war*, upon, and *ran*, a division.

TRAWETHAC, adj. Doleful, mournful. Llwyd, 81, who also writes it *trawedhak*, 92, 116. From *traweth*, id. qd. *trueth*, qd. v.

TRAWYTHES, adj. Rare, scarce. Llwyd, 136.

TRE, s. f. A dwelling place, a homestead, a home, a town. *Levereuch dhym, cowethé, pyw henna a dhue dhe'n tré, war keyn asen hag ebel, ow môs war tu a'n temple*, tell me, companions, who is that (that) is coming to the town on the back of an ass and foal, going towards the temple? P.C. 320. *Ef yw an brofus Ihesu, divithys a Naznré, tré a wlascor Galilé*, he is the prophet Jesus, come from Nazareth, a town of the kingdom of Galilee. P.C. 329. *Hemma yw tewolgow brás, fatel êny war tu tré*, this is great darkness, how shall we go towards home? P.C. 2007. *Hydhew a tryckes yn tré, dhyragos ty a'n guelsé byw yn point da*, to-day, if thou hadst staid at home, before thee thou wouldst have seen him alive, in good condition. R.D. 1381. *Arluth, ny â dhy wharré, rák ny yllyn yn nép tré trygé dres nós*, Lord, we will go to it directly, for we cannot in any town stay over night. R.D. 2404. *Tré, dré*, at home, *adré*, homewards. Llwyd, 248. Homewards is expressed by *tua thré*, in South Wales, and *adré*, or *adrev*, in North Wales. *Tré* is an abbreviated form of *trév*, qd. v.

TRE, a particle used in composition. Over. It is the same as W. *tra*, and answers to the Latin *trans*. *Tremenes*, to pass over. (Lat. *transire*.) *Trenija*, to fly over, (Lat. *transvolo*.) *Tremor*, foreign. (Lat. *transmarinus*.) Llwyd, 250. See *Tra*.

TRE, prep. Between. *Llwyd,* 249. A late abbreviated form of *yntré,* qd. v.

TREATII, s. m. The sandy beach of the sea, sands. ‡ *Na dâl dên gwîl treven war an dreath,* a man ought not to make houses on the sand. *Pryce.* Another form of *traith,* qd. v.

TREBATH, s. m. That which has three feet, a tripod, a trivet, a three-footed stool ; a brand-iron, a brandice. *Llwyd,* 19, 166. The late form of *tribedh,* qd. v.

TREBE, conj. Until, as far as, till when. *Pryce.* Llwyd, 240.

TREBYTCHYA, v. a. To tumble, to stumble, to trip. *Pryce. Whath pûr browt trebytchya,* yet very proud falling. C.W. 20. *Ow carma yma an bêst, me a'n gwêl ow trebytchya,* the beast is crying, I see it tumbling. C.W. 114. From the French *trebucher.*

TRECH, s. m. A stem, the trunk of a tree. Corn. Voc. *truncus.* Arm. *trehjen.*

TRECHY, v. a. To cut, to make an incision, to break off. 3 pers. s. fut. *trêch.* Part. pass. *trechys.* Ny a'n *trêch, del levereth,* we will cut it, as thou sayest. O.M. 2533. *Cowethé, guerevouch ; ow scoforn trechys myrouch quyt dhe vês dhyworth ow pen,* companions, help ye ; see my car cut quite from off my head. P.C. 1144. *Otté genef vy bony, me a'n trêch wharré gynsy,* behold I have an axe, I will cut it soon with it. P.C. 2565. Another form of *trochy,* qd. v.

TREDDEN, s. m. Three men. *Ha'n Edhewon a worras a uch Ihesus Crist un mên; leden o, ha poys, ha brâs, moy agis gavel tredden,* and the Jews put above Jesus Christ a stone ; broad it was, and heavy, and large, more than the hold of three men. M.C. 237. Comp. of *tre* for *tri,* three, and *dên,* a man. W. *tridyn.*

TREDNA, s. m. Thunder. *Llwyd,* 164. A late form of *trenna,* qd. v.

TREDZHA, adj. Third. *Llwyd,* 162. A late corruption of *tressa,* qd. v.

TREDHEC, card. num. Thirteen. *Llwyd,* 166. *(Tri-déc.)* W. *tri-ar-dhec.* Arm. *trizék.* Ir. *trideag.* Gael. *tri-deug.* Manx, *three-jeig.* Lat. *tredecim.*

TREFFIA, v. a. To spit. *Dho treffia,* Llwyd, 154. A late form of *trewé,* qd. v.

TREGA, v. a. To dwell, to inhabit, to abide, to stay, to tarry. Written also *tregé.* Part. *tregys. My a vyn gruthyl castel, ha drchevel dhym ostel, ynno jammes râg tregé,* I will make a village, and build for me a mansion, in it ever to dwell. O.M. 1711. *Ha tregouch dh'y ordrnanns ef,* and abide ye in his ordinance. O.M. 1893. *Ny allaf pellu trega,* I cannot longer stay. O.M. 2190. *Try hag onan ow trega yn un deweys,* three and one dwelling in one Godhead. O.M. 2665. *Reson prâg y fe prynnys yw Ihesus Crist dhe ordna yn nêf y vonas tregys,* the reason why he was redeemed is that Jesus Christ ordained in heaven that he should dwell. M.C. 7. *Mar ny'th wolhaff dre ow grâs, yn nêf ny vedhyth tregys,* if I wash thee not by my grace, in heaven thou shalt not dwell. M.C. 46. *An scherewes a dregas yn yffarn yn tormont crêff,* the evil ones dwelt in hell in strong torment. M.C. 213. *Tregans an chorle nêb yma,* let the churl remain where he is. C.W. 150. Written also *trigu,* qd. v.

TREGE, adj. Third. *Meneuch fest y wrûk bostyé, an tregé deydh dasvewé kyn fe ledhys war garow,* very often he did boast, to revive on the third day, though he were killed so cruelly. R.D. 339. *Ow arluth yn bêdh gallas, hydhew yw an tregé deydh,* my Lord went into the tomb, to-day is the third day. R.D. 681. *En tregé deydh yw hydhew,* the third day is to-day. R.D. 691. A corrupted form, with *g* soft, of *tressé,* qd. v.

TREGER, s. m. A dweller, an inhabitant. Pl. *tregerion.* Pryce. W. *triger.*

TREGERETH, s. m. Compassion, pity, mercy, love. *Rág dhym yma govenek, cafes dhe geus tregereth,* for I have a request, to obtain thy speech of love. O.M. 454. *An oyl a versy o dydhyscys dhymmo vy gans an Tâs, a'y dregereth, pan vêf chacys gans an êl,* the oil of mercy was promised to me by the Father, of his pity when I was driven by the angel. O.M. 705. *Arluth, warnas tregereth ; goef a ra dhe serry,* Lord, on thee (be) love ; woe is he (that) doth anger thee. O.M. 1015. *Luen tregereth me a pŷs,* abundant mercy I pray. R.D. 1148. W. *trugaredh ;* from *trugar,* compassionate ; comp. of *tru,* wretched, and *caru,* to love. Arm. *trugarez.* Ir. †*trocaire.* Gael. *trocair.* Manx, *trocuirys.*

TREGVA, s. f. A dwelling place, habitation. *Ena Crist a dhelyffras a breson Adam hag Evef, suel a wressa bôdh y dâs, ma'n geffo tregva yn nêf,* there Christ delivered Adam and Eve from prison, (and) whoso would do his Father's will, that he might have a dwelling-place in heaven. M.C. 213. Written also *trigva,* qd. v.

TREHE, conj. Until that. *Llwyd,* 178.

TREHES, s. m. A cutter, a tailor. Pl. *trehesi. Ke gorhemmyn dhe'n cyté may teffons omma wharé, war beyn aga bôs dywnrŷs, masons ha karpentoryon, trehesy meyn, tyorryon, an temple may fe coul wreys,* go thou, command the city, that there come here soon, on pain of their being destroyed, masons and carpenters, stonecutters, tilers, that the temple may be fully built. O.M. 2411. ‡ *Pendra veddo why geil râg lednow râg as flô?—E seera vêdh trehes, sarra whêg,* what will you do for whittles for your child?—His father shall be a tailor, sweet sir. *Pryce.*

TREHEVEL, v. a. To raise up. *Hag yn triddydh dyowgel ef a wra y trehevel, kyn fe terrys, ol a'y le,* and in three days certainly he will build it, though it be broken all from its place. P.C. 353. A mutation of *drehevel,* qd. v.

TREHEVYS, part. Raised up. *Hy a wolas kymmys gans mar vêr nerth ha galloys, a'n fynten may trehevys ran yn ban du droka loys,* she wept so much, with so great strength and power, that from the fountain a part was raised upwards, worst pang. M.C. 224. A mutation of *drehevys,* part. pass. of *drehevel,* qd. v.

TREHY, v. a. To cut. Part. *trehys. Assoma squyth prynnyer derow ow trehy,* I am weary, cutting oak sticks. O.M. 1010. *Me a vyn trehy teunow,* I will cut beams. O.M. 2445. *Euch dh'y drehy, hep lettyé,* go ye to cut it, without delaying. O.M. 2505. *Râk an pren yw trehys da, ny alsé vŷth bones guel,* for the tree is well cut, it could never have been better. P.C. 2569. A softened form of *trochy,* qd. v.

TREI, card. num. Three. *Trei cans,* three hundred. *Trei igans,* sixty. *Trei igans ha dêg,* seventy. Llwyd's orthography of *tri,* qd. v. 149, 244.

TREIN, s. m. A nose. Corn. Voc. *nasus.* In late Cornish the form was *trôn.* W. *trwyn.* † *trein,* (Taliesin ; see Llwyd, 230.) Ir. *sron,* an Iron. Gael. *sron, sroin.* Manx, *stroin.* Gr. *ῥίν.*

TREIS, s. m. Foot. *Llwyd*, 250. Written also *treys*, qd. v.

TRELEBBA, conj. Even to. ‡ *Râg 'dhové an Arluth de Dew ew Dew a sŷr, a dry pehnasow an tasow war an flehas trelebba an tridga ha padgwerra henath*, for I am the Lord thy God, (that) is a jealous God, and will bring the sins of the fathers upon the children even to the third and fourth generation. *Pryce.*

TREMENE, v. n. To pass, to pass over, to die. Part. *tremenys, tremenes*. 3 pers. s. fut. *tremyn*. *Nans yw lemmyn tremenes nép dew-cans a vledhynnow*, now there are gone by some two hundred years. O.M. 656. *Pan fo tryddydh tremenys, ty a dhascor dhe enef*, when three days are passed, thou shalt give up thy soul. O.M. 845. *Ha guns myyn gureuch hy knoukyé, er-na wrello tremené,* and with stones beat ye her, until she die. O.M. 2695. *Vŷth ny yllyn tremené an môr-ma*, we shall never be able to pass over this sea. O.M. 1648. *Dresof ef a tremenas*, over me he passed. R.D. 525. *Mâb Dew a bremyn a'n beys*, the Son of God shall pass from the world. P.C. 747. *Ol y beyn y'n tremensé ha trylys ens yn ioy brâs*, all his pain had passed him, and they were turned into great joy. M.C. 258. Arm. *tremeni;* part. *tremenet*. W. *tramwy*. Ir. *tairreimnim*.

TREMENES, v. a. To traverse, to frequent a place much. *Llwyd*, 250. Comp. of *tre*, id. qd. *tra*, over, and *mones*, to go. W. *tramwy*. Lat. *trameo*.

TREMOR, adj. Transmarine, foreign. *Llwyd*, 250. Comp. of *tre*, id. qd. *tra*, over, and *môr*, the sea. W. *tramor*.

TREMYN, s. m. A passage. *Pryce*. Arm. *tremen*.

TREMYN, s. m. Sight, look, aspect. *Benen, na gows muscogneth, râk an kêth dên-ma bythqueth nyn servyes, war ow ené; na rum fay my ny'n guylys may wodhfen tremyn yn beys yntredho ha'y gowethé*, woman, do not talk folly, for this same man never did I serve, on my soul; nor by my faith have I seen him, that I should know the look in the world between him and his companions. P.C. 1287. W. *tremyn*.

TRENC, adj. Sour. *Llwyd*, 5. W. *trwnc*. Arm. *trenk*.

TRENGES, s. f. Trinity. *Mêr woordhyans dhe'n Drenges, Tâs, ow grountya dhymo sylwans, wosé henna, ken 'dhew pell*, much worship to the Trinity, Father, in granting to me salvation hereafter, though it is long. C.W. 140. (See *Drenges*.) Written also *trengys*. *Râg henna gwrâf commena dhe leall Drengys ow ena*, therefore I do commend to the faithful Trinity my soul. C.W. 146. *An Drengys es a wartha*, the Trinity (that) is above. C.W. 162. A later form of *trenses*, with *g* soft, as that is of *trindas*, qd. v.

TRENNA, v. n. To thunder. ‡ *Patl yzhi a cylywi ha trenna*, how it lightens and thunders. *Llwyd*, 248. Derived from *taran*, qd. v. W. *taranu*.

TRENSA, adv. The day after to-morrow; two days hence. Written by Llwyd, 249, and Pryce, *trenzha*. W. *trenydh*.

TRENSES, s. f. Trinity. In construction *drenses*, qd. v. Another form of *trindas*, qd. v.

TRENYGE, v. a. To fly over. *Na nŷl oges nag yn pel ny's guelaf ow trenygé; hy re gafes dyhogel dôr dysechys yn nép le*, neither near nor far, I see her not flying over; she has certainly found earth dried in some place. O.M. 1142. Comp. of *tre*, id. qd. *tra*, over, and *nygé*, id. qd. *nija*, to fly. Written by Llwyd, 250, *trenydzha*.

TRES, adj. Adverse, cross, froward. *A na wylta ol mŷns es orth dhe viamyé yn soweth, hag ow ry dhys boxow tres, betegyns te ny sconyth*, seest thou not all the multitude that is blaming thee unhappily, and giving thee froward blows? nevertheless thou dost not refuse. M.C. 120. W. *traws*, † *trws*.

TRES, pron. prep. Between your. *Llwyd*, 244. A late abbreviated form of *yntré agas*.

TRESHEYS, s. m. A foot-length, a foot in measure. *Dhe'n leyff arall pan dothyans worth an grows râg y fasté; y fylly moy ys tresheys, dhe'n tol guris hy na hedhé*, to the other hand when they came on the cross to fasten it; it wanted more than a foot-length, to the hole made that it would not reach. M.C. 180. Written also *troisheys*, qd. v.

TRESSA, adj. Third. Written as commonly *tressé*. *Yn tressé dŷdh dybarth gwrâf yntré an môr ha'n tyryow*, on the third day I will make a separation between the sea and the lands. O.M. 25. *Ke wôth tressé treveth dhy, ha mŷr greel orth an wedhen*, go yet the third time to it, and look better at the tree. O.M. 790. *Onan yw an Tâs a néff, arall Crist y un vaw eff, a vŷdh a wyrchas genys, ha'n Sperys Sans yw tressa*, one is the Father of heaven, another, Christ his one Son, (that) shall be born of a Virgin, and the Holy Ghost is the third. O.M. 2664. *Y leverys ef yn wédh datherchy an tressa dédh y wre pûr wŷr hep fyllel*, he said likewise, that he would rise the third day very truly without failing. R.D. 5. Written also *tryssé*, qd. v. W. *trydydh*, † *tritit*, † *trydé*. Arm. *tredé*. Ir. *treas*, † *trede*. Gael. *treas*, *triteamh*. Manx, *trass*. Gr. τρίτον. Sansc. *tritiya*. Ang. Sax. *thridda*, *thridde*.

TREST, adj. Sad, sorrowful. *Na porth own vŷth, na védh trest, râg me a vŷdh genes prest orth dhe weres yn pûp le*, bear no fear ever, nor be sad, for I will be with thee, ready to help thee in every place. O.M. 1467. *Warlerch Cryst nar asos trest, lemmyn pûr lowenek fést bôs ty a ŷl*, after Christ if thou art sad, now very joyful indeed thou mayest be. R.D. 1417. *Me a'th cusyl dysempys blŷth na vy trest*, I advise thee immediately, never be sad. R.D. 2230. Another form of *trist*, qd. v.

TRESTERS, s. m. Beams. *War tu dylarch daras yn ty a wra yw port hynwes; tresters dredho ty a pyn a drus rag na vo degees*, on the hinder part a door in thou shalt nail across, that it may not be shut. O.M. 963. The plural of *troster*, qd. v.

TRETH, s. m. A sandy beach. See *Traith*.

TRETHON, pron. prep. Between us. *Llwyd*, 244. A late abbreviated form of *yntrethon*, qd. v.

TRETHYNS, pron. prep. Between them. *Llwyd*, 244. A late abbreviated form of *yntrethyns*, qd. v., which is another form of *yntrethé*, qd. v.

TREV, s. f. A dwelling place, a homestead, a home, a town. Pl. *trevow*, *trevon*, *treven*. *Ow lays ha'w lavarow suel a vynna y clewas, yn le may 'th én, yn trevow yn splan me a's derevas*, my laws and my words, whosoever would hear them; in the place that I was, in towns clearly I declared them. M.C. 79. *Mŷr lowené ol an bŷs, cytes rych, trevow a brys, castilly brâs hag huhel*, see the joy of all the world, cities rich, towns of price, castles large and high. P.C. 132. In the singular the abbreviated form *tré* was generally used, qd. v. ‡ *Na dâl dén gwil treven war an treath*, a man ought not to make houses on the sand. *Pryce.* *Treven* was used for the plural of *ty,* a house. *Llwyd,* 55. It is in frequent use in the names of places in Cornwall, Wales, and Brittany. C. *Tremain, Tregear, Trewen, &c.* W. *Trecastell, Trefynnon, Trewen, &c.* Arm. *Treger.* The Welsh also generally drops the final *v* before a consonant, in composition, though not always, *Trevdraeth, Trevlech,* being exceptions, but preserves it before a vowel, as *Trevonnen, Trevarclawdh, &c.* W. *trêv, trê,* †*treb.* Arm. *trev, tre,* †*treb.* Ir. *treabh,* †*treb.* Gael. *treubh,* (pronounced *trev.*) Lat. *tribus.* Germ. *thorp.*

TREVAS, s. m. Tillage. *Adam, a ol dhe drevas an dyves ran dhymmo gûs whêth in atal dhe kesky,* Adam, of all thy tillage, leave the tenth part to me, still to remain waste. O.M. 425. *Trevas* is probably a plural form, the singular of which would agree with W. *treva;* as *treva o ŷd,* a thrave of corn. Eng. *thrave.*

TREVEDIC, s. m. One from a country village, a country man, a rustic. Corn. Voc. *rusticus, colonus. Trevedic doer,* incola, lit. an inhabitant of the land. W. *trevedig.*

TREVETH, s. m. A time, or occasion. Written also *trevyth. Ke wêth tressê treveth dhy, ha mŷr gwel orth an wedhen,* go thou yet the third time to it, and look better at the tree. O.M. 799. *Y vôs êf re leverys, lyes trevêth y'n clewys, ma na ŷl y dhynachê,* that he is (so) he has said; many a time I heard him, that he cannot deny it. P.C. 1724.

TREVYTH, s. m. Any thing. *Râg gwander y a godhas, yn trevyth y nyng êns gynw dhe vethyll dris y vynnas,* for weakness they fell, in nothing were they fit to do beyond his will. M.C. 68. *Herodes a wovynnys orth Ihesus Crist lous tra, ha trevyth ny worthelys ma'n gevê marth a henna,* Herod asked many a thing of Jesus Christ, and He answered nothing, so that he had wonder thereof. M.C. 111. Comp. of *tra,* a thing, and *bŷth,* ever. Written also *travyth,* qd. v.

TREW, interj. Alas! sad! *Ha'n maystri brâs ol n'm bo, my re'n collas quyt drodho, may canaf trew,* and all the great power (that) I had, I have lost it quite through him, that I may sing 'alas.' P.C. 150. *Och, och, trew, uy re behas, ha re dorras an deffen,* Oh! Oh! sad I we have sinned, and have broken the prohibition. C.W. 62. *A trew, aylas, re'm ladhas, Caym, ow brodar,* Ah, sad, alas, thou hast killed me my brother. C.W. 82. Written also *tru,* qd. v.

TREWESY, adj. Sad, mournful, doleful. *En debell wrêk casadow gans mûr a dôth êth yn chy war hast dhe weithyll kentrow may fêns crêff ha trewesy,* the wicked hateful woman with much haste went into the house, in haste to make nails, that they might be strong and doleful. M.C. 150. *Ha'y veynys mar drewesy a's kemar, ha kymmys cueth,* and her pains so mournful seized her, and so much grief. M.C. 225. Written in the Dramas *trewysy. A Dâs Dew, Arluth huhel, my a'th wordh gans ol ow nel y'm colon pûr trewysy,* O Father God, high Lord, I worship thee with all my strength, in my heart very seriously. O.M. 511. *Râk ty dh'y gam worthyby, ty a vŷdh bos trewysy,* because thou answeredst him wrongly, thou shalt have a sad blow. P.C. 1209.

TREWETH, s. m. Pity, compassion. *Henna ydhyno trew-* *ath brâs,* that is a great pity. C.W. 74. Another form of *trueth,* qd. v.

TREWY, v. n. To spit. Written also *trewê. Ena mûr a vylyny Pedyr dhe Gryst a welas, y scornyê ha'y voxscusy, trewê yn y dhewlagas,* there much of villainy Peter saw (done) to Christ; mocking him and buffeting him, spitting in his eyes. M.C. 83. *Gans mowys y a'n scornyas, yn y fâs y a drewys,* with mowes they scorned him, they spat in his face. M.C. 95. *Hag ef moycha yn y beyn, yn y fâs y a drewê,* and he most greatly in his pain, they spat in his face. M.C. 196. Written in the Dramas *truê,* qd. v. In W. *trewi* is to sneeze, and *poeri,* to spit.

TREWYTH, adj. Pitiable, lamentable, wretched. *Y won dhe wŷr, Dew an Tâs re sorras drewyth benen,* I know truly, God the Father (that) a wretched woman has angered. O.M. 256. Written later *trewath. Henna ydhew trewath tra,* that is a lamentable thing. C.W. 62.

TREYHANS, card. num. Three hundred. *Whethouch menstrels ha tabours; treyhans harpes ha trompours, cythol, crowd, fylh, ha sawtry,* blow ye minstrels and tabours; three hundred harps and trumpets, dulcimer, fiddle, viol, and psaltery. O.M. 1996. Comp. of *trey,* id. qd. *tri,* three, and *cans,* a hundred; the initial is regularly changed after *tri* into the aspirate form of *ch,* here represented by *h.* So W. *trichant.* Arm. *trichant.*

TREYLE, v. a. To turn. 2 pers. s. imp., and 3 pers. s. fut. *treyl.* Part. pass. *treylys. May ma lyes gwrêk ha gour ow treylê dhodho toulh-da,* that there are many a woman and man turning to him speedily. P.C. 558. *A Peder, treyl dhe clethê, gorrê yn y wôn artê,* Ah Peter, turn thy sword, put it into its sheath again. P.C. 1155. *Yma ow treylê deffry ol an wlascor a iudi,* he is turning really all the kingdom of Judah. P.C. 1593. *Dhe'n dôr ty a dreyl artê,* to the earth thou shalt turn again. O.M. 64. (See *Dreyl.*) *Sâf yn ban yn clor, ha treyl dhe gŷk ha dhe woys,* stand thou up in glory, and turn to flesh and to blood. O.M. 66. *An welen-ma yn hy kunda treylys artê,* this rod into its natural form turned again. O.M. 1460. Written also *treylyê. Me re'n caffus ow treylyê agan tûs yn lyes lę, yn mês a grygyans pûp prŷs,* I have found him turning our people in many a place from their belief always. P.C. 1570. *Ow Tâs, mu ny ŷl lones may treylyo mernens dhe vês, saw y wodhuf dhym a reys, dhe volnegeth re bo gurês,* my Father, if it cannot be that death may turn away, but that I must needs suffer it, thy will be done. P.C. 1070. W. *treillio, treiglo.*

TREYNYE, v. a. To render miserable; to become miserable; to grieve. *Yn pryson môs ny treynyn agan bew kyn kentreynnyn ol agan kŷc, râk Ihesu, luen a versy, agan gor sur dhe'n kêth ioy, bŷth na dhyfye,* to go into prison we will not render our lives miserable, though we should rot all our flesh; for Jesus full of mercy will place us surely in that same joy, (that) will never fail. R.D. 73. Written also *trynyê. Genouch why môs ny drynyaf; dhum arludh lowen ydh âf,* to go with you I will not grieve; to my lord I will go gladly. R.D. 1797. W. *trueinio,* fr. *truan,* miserable. Arm. *truanti.*

TREYS, s. m. Feet. Plural of *troys,* qd. v. *Me a ryn môs dhe wrê ow Arluth, treys ha dewlê, gans onement kêr,*

TRIFIAS   345   **TRINSYS**

I will go to anoint my Lord, feet and hands, with precious ointment. P.C. 474. *Whyp an tŷn, kymer an pen, er an treys me a'n kylden aberth yn beydh,* Breech-whip, take thou the head, by the feet I will let him down within the grave. R.D. 2083. *Pyw a dhueth a'n beys yn rûdh, avel gôs, pen ha duscoudh, garrow ha treys,* who is it (that) is come from the world in red, like blood, head and shoulders, legs and feet? R.D. 2501. *Worth y dreys ha worth y ben,* by his feet and by his head. M.C. 236. (See also *Dreys.*) W. *traed.* Arm. *treid.*

TRI, card. num. Three. Used with nouns masculine as *teir* was with feminines. *Tri ugans,* three score, sixty. *Trihans,* three hundred. *Hag cf dhyn re leverys, kyn fe an temple dysercjs, yn tri dŷdh y'n dreafsé,* and he has said to us, though the temple were destroyed, in three days (that) he would rebuild it. P.C. 366. *Kyn fe dysercjs an temple yn tri dŷdh y'n drehafsé, bythqueth whet na fevé guel,* though the temple were destroyed, in three days (that) he would rebuild it, that never yet it was better. P.C. 383. *Onan ha try ôn yn gwŷr, en Tâs, ha'n Mâp, ha'n Spyrys,* one and three we are in truth, the Father, and the Son, and the Spirit. O.M. 3. *Agas try, deuch why genef,* ye three, come with me. P.C. 1021. *Aban yw henna laha, dhe'n mernans ol an try â,* since that is law, to death all the three shall go. P.C. 2400. *Tri* in Welsh and Armoric aspirates the initial following, which was also once the rule in Cornish, as is proved by *trihans,* three hundred. Generally however the rule was not followed. *Ef a galsé bôs guyrthys a try cans dyner ha moy,* it might have been sold for three hundred pence and more. P.C. 536. *Tri* in Cornish must be read *trei* or *trey*: (Llwyd, 230,) that is with the sound of the English word *try.* W. *tri.* Arm. *tri.* Ir. *tri.* Gael. *tri.* Manx, *three.* Sanse. *tri, trayas.* Gr. τρεῖς. Lat. *tres.* Fr. *trois.* Germ. *drei.* Aug. Sax. *threo, thry.* Eng. *three.*

TRIBET, s. m. That which has three feet, an andiron. Corn. Voc. *andena.* The late form was *trebath,* qd. v. Derived from the Lat. *tripes, tripete.* So also W. *tribedh.* Arm. *trebez.* Eng. *tripod, trivet.*

TRICCES, v. a. Thou hadst dwelt. 2 pers. s. pluperf. of *trigé,* qd. v.

TRICCIAR, s. m. A fuller, a tucker. *Trikkiar,* Llwyd, 34. See *Trycciar.*

TRIDDYDH, s. m. The space of three days. (*Tri-dŷdh.*) *Hag yn triddydd dyowgel cf a wra y trehevel,* and in three days undoubtedly he will build it up. P.C. 352. *Râg uy vew moy es tryddydh war lyrch dhe vones dhe dré,* for he will not live more than three days, after thou goest home. O.M. 820. *Hag arté y dhrehevel yn trydydh na vyé guel,* and again build it in three days, that it could not be better. P.C. 1311. *Y'n clewys ow leverel, treydydh wosé y terry, y wrefé y dhrehevel,* I heard him say, three days after destroying it, that he would rebuild it. P.C. 1315. W. *tridiau.*

TRIDZHA, adj. Third. Llwyd's orthography, 243, of *trygé,* qd. v. Written also in late Cornish, *tridga.* ‡ *Ha gothuar ha metten o an tridga journa,* and the evening and the morning were the third day. C.W. p. 190. ‡ *An tridga ha padgwerra henath,* the third and fourth generation. *Prycc.*

TRIFIAS, s. m. Spittle, saliva. Llwyd, 143. Derived from *treffia,* qd. v.

3 A

TRIG, s. m. The ebbing, or reflux of the sea. Llwyd, 136. *Môr lenol ha thrig,* the flow and ebb of the sea. 42. ‡ *Sâv a man, kcbmer dha li, ha ker dha'n hâl; môr-trig a metten travyth ne dâl,* get thou up, take thy breakfast, and go to the moor; the ebb in the morning is nothing worth. ‡ *Vedo why môs dho trig,* will ye go to the ebb? *Pryce.* W. *trai.* Arm. *treach, trech, tré.* Ir. *traigh.* Gael. *traigh.* Manx, *traie.*

TRIGE, v. n. To dwell, to inhabit, to abide, to stay, to tarry. Written also *triga.* 2 pers. s. imp. and 3 pers. s. fut. *tric, trig.* Part. *trygys. Omma ny wreuch why trygé, euch yn mês a dhysympys,* here ye shall not remain, go out immediately. O.M. 317. *Mar kŷf carynnyas, warnedhé y trŷg pûp preys,* if it shall find carrion, it will always stay upon it. O.M. 1104. *Ha lavar my dh'y warnyé vŷth na werella compressa ow tûs ûs tryggys ena,* and say thou that I warn him that he never oppress my people (that) are dwelling there. O.M. 1425. *Scon yn mês quyk a'm golok, na trŷk y'm cûr,* immediately out of my sight, quickly; stay not in my court. O.M. 1532. *An venenes ha'n flechys vedhens yn mês exilyys, na dheffo onan yn beys dhe trygé omma neffré,* let the women and children be exiled out, that not one in the world come to dwell here ever. O.M. 1578. *Ny vynnyth dhe pobel Duw gasé crês dhyn yn nép tu awos tryga yn pow-ma,* thou wilt not to the people of God allow peace to us on any side, for the purpose of dwelling in this country. O.M. 1599. *Ha why gynef re drygas yn temptacyon yn pûp le,* and ye have dwelt with me in temptation in every place. P.C. 805. *Ellas, ny won py tyller, bŷth moy py le y trygaf,* alas, I know not (in) what place, ever more where I shall dwell. P.C. 2598. *Ha nép na'n grûk war nép tro, yn peynys trygens eno,* and he that has not done it on any occasion, in pains let him dwell there. R.D. 159. *Ytho gyneuch me a trŷk,* now with you I will stay. R.D. 1308. *Hydhew a tryckes yn tré,* to-day if thou hadst staid at home. R.D. 1381. (See also *Drie.*) Llwyd, 40, writes the infinitive *trigia, dho trigia.* ‡ *Terra trigas dên ha bennen,* there lived a man and woman. 251. W. *trigo.* Ir. *aitrigh.* Gael. *aitrich.*

TRIGVA, s. f. A dwelling place, a habitation. *Râg henna fystyn, ke, gura gorhel a blankos playnyys, hag ynno lues trygva,* therefore hasten thou, go make a ship of planks planed, and in it many a dwelling. O.M. 951. *Arluth, ple 'dh ên alemma dhyn dhe gemeres trygafa, na dheffo dên vŷth gynen,* Lord, where shall we go from hence for us to take a dwelling, that not any man may come with us? R.D. 2392. Comp. of *trigé,* and *ma,* a place. W. *trigva.*

TRIHANS, card. num. Three hundred. *Ha tryhans kevelyn da an lester a vŷdh a hŷs,* and three hundred cubits good, the ship shall be in length. O.M. 955. Written also *Trehans. Trehans dynar a voné,* three hundred pence of money. M.C. 36. See *Treyhans.*

TRINDAS, s. f. Trinity. *An drindas,* the Trinity. Llwyd, 116. Written also *trinsys,* and *trenses,* in construction *drenses,* qd. v. W. *trindawd, y drindawd; trindod, y drindod.* Arm. *trinded,* † *trindet.* Ir. *trionaid,* † *triodatu.* Gael. *trionnid, trianaid.* Manx, *trinaid.* All from the Lat. *trinitus, trinitate.*

TRINSYS, s. f. Trinity. *My a wêl tyyr guelen gay, ny*

welys tekké rum fay bythqueth aban véf genys ; yn guyrder an thŷr guelen yw dysquythyans ha token a'n try person yn Drynsys, I see three gay rods, I have not seen fairer, by my faith, ever since I was born ; in truth the three rods are a declaration and token of the three persons in Trinity. O.M. 1734.

TRIST, adj. Sad, mournful, sorrowful. Corn. Voc. *tristis.* Written also *trest*, qd. v. W. *trist.* Ir. † *trist.* Gael.† *trist.* Lat. *tristis.*

TRISTANS, s. m. Sadness, sorrow. *Ha'y holon whêk a runné, me a lever, râg trystans, râg an grayth yn hy esé na's gwethé an Spyrys Sans*, and her sweet heart would have parted, I say, for sorrow, had not the Holy Ghost protected her for the grace that was in her. M.C. 222. Written also *tristyns. Hedré vy yn beys gynen, neffré trystyns ny 'gen býdh*, whilst thou art in the world with us, never is sorrow with us. P.C. 731. *Râk yma yn ow enef trystyns fast býs yn ancow*, for there is in my soul great sadness, even unto death. P.C. 1023. *Saw bones mûr ow thrystynys*, except that my sadness is great. R.D. 1588.

TRISTYS, s. m. Sadness, sorrow. *Gwyn y vŷs a vo trigys yn dhe servys, râg tristys nyn d'y gemmer vynytha*, happy his lot that may be dwelling in thy service, for sorrow will not seize him for ever. P.C. 123. *Ellas, pendra wrêth yn býs, cna anken ha trystys prest ow bones*, alas, what wilt thou do in the world ? there grief and sorrow always being. R.D. 204. Written also *tristyys. Na wrello y vôdh, gorf, y'n gefyth mûr a trystyys*, woe is he that doeth not his will ; he shall have much sorrow. O.M. 2094. W. *tristyd*, † *tristid.* Lat. *tristitia.*

TRIUGANS, card. num. Three score, sixty. (*Triugans.*) *Pymp mŷl strekis del iové, ha pedergwyth cans goly, ha tryugans moy gansé, ha pymthek pâr wŷr ês y*, five thousand strokes as there were, and four times a hundred wounds, and three score more with them, and fifteen, very truly were they. M.C. 227. W. *tri-ugain*, † *triuceint.* Arm. *tri-ugent.* Ir. *tri fichid.* Gael. *tri fichead.* Manx, *three feed.*

TRIVORU, adj. Three pronged. (*Tri—forh.*) *Forh trivorh*, a three pronged fork. Llwyd, 160. W. *tri-forch.*

TRIWADHEC, adj. Pitiful, courteous, mild, gentle. *Llwyd*, 48. Arm. *truezek.*

TRIWATH, s. m. Pity, compassion. *Nag es triueath vêth dho vi*, I do not at all pity ; lit. there is not any pity to me. Llwyd, 244. Another form of *trueth*, qd. v.

TRO, s. m. A turn, circuit, occasion, manner, sort. *A gadling, ty re wordhyas war nêp tro an fals losel*, O idle fellow, thou hast worshipped, on some occasion, the false knave. P.C. 2694. *Ef a wra dhynny drôk tro*, he will do to us an evil turn. P.C. 3066. *Ha nêp na'n grûk war nêp tro, yn peynys trygens eno*, and he who has not done it on any occasion, in pains let him dwell there. R.D. 158. *Quêth esa a dro dhodho ; prest an Edhewon debel dhe Ihesus esens a dro*, a cloth was about him ; readily the evil Jews were about Jesus. M.C. 140. See *Dro*, and *Adro.* W. *tro.* Arm. *tro.*

TRO, conj. That, as, so, that, than. *Llwyd*, 134, 232, 248, 249. *Ha Dew gwelas an golow tro va da*, and God saw the light that it was good. C.W. p. 189. Written also *tra*, and *try*, qd. v.

TROC, s. m. A trunk. *Arluth, yn trok a hôrn crêf yn dour Tyber ef a séf er y anfcus*, Lord, in a box of strong iron, in the water of Tiber he shall stay for his wickedness. R.D. 2135.

TROC, adj. Wretched. Corn. Voc. *miser.* Another form of *tru.* W. *tru.* Ir. † *trog*, † *truag.* Cf. *Trogus Pompeius*, a Gaul ; and *Trogmi.*

TROC, s. m. Evil, harm. *Mŷr worto, hag a ver spys a'th trôk ty a vŷdh yaoheys*, look thou at it, and in a short time thou shalt be cured from thy evil. R.D. 1730. An irregular mutation of *drôc*, qd. v.

TROCH, adj. Cut, broken. *May mohchaho hy hûth hy, dre will ow gorhemmyn trôch*, that her affliction may be increased, through making my commandment broken. O.M. 298. *Nyns ûs warnedhé crochen, nag yw trôch ha dyrushys*, there is no skin upon them (that) is not broken and peeled. P.C. 2686. *Namnag yw ow colon trôch râk galarow ha prynys*, my heart is almost broken for sorrows and pains. P.C. 3185. W. *trwch.* Arm. *trouch*, *troch.* Ir. † *truth.* Sanse. *trut*, to cut.

TROCHA, prep. Towards. *Stôp an wedhen trocha'n dôr, may hyllyf aga hedhes*, bend thou the tree towards the ground, that I may reach them. O.M. 201. *Cherubyn, kemmer cledhé, fystyn trocha parathys*, Cherub, take thou a sword, hasten towards Paradise. O.M. 332. The guttural was often softened into *h.* See *Troha.*

TROCHY, v. a. To cut, to break. 3 pers. s. imp. *trôch. Mar pué drôk a oberys, trôch y hy gans dhe gledhé*, if it was evil that she did, cut her with thy sword. O.M. 292. W. *trychu.* Arm. *troucha.*

TRODEN, s. f. A starling. Llwyd gives as the late form, *trodzhan*, pl. *edhnow trodzhan*, 10, 156, 140. W. *drudwen, drudwy*, pl. *drudwes.* Arm. *tred, dred.* Ir. *druid.* Gael. *druid.*

TROET, s. m. A turtle-dove. Corn. Voc. *turtur.* Called also *turen*, qd. v. W. *turtur*, from the Latin. Arm. *turzunel.*

TROHA, prep. Towards. *Adam, ke yn mês a'n wlâs, troha ken pow dhe wewé*, Adam, go out of the country towards another land to live. O.M. 344. *Fystynyueh troha'n daras, râg umma ny wreuch trygé*, hasten ye towards the door, for here ye shall not stay. O.M. 349. A softened form of *trocha*, qd. v.

TROHER, s. m. A cutter, the coulter of a plough. *Gora an sôch ha'n troher dha'n gôv*, put the share and the coulter to the smith. Pryce. W. *trychwr.* Arm. *troucher.*

TROHY, v. a. To cut, to break. 2 pers. s. imp. *trôh. Ny ŷl an gŷst yn y blâs, rehŷr ew a gevelyn, yn ewn greys an scarf trôh e*, the beam will not go into its place, too long it is of a cubit ; in the just middle of the joint cut thou it. O.M. 2530. *Pedyr a'n neyl tenewen yn mês a dennas cledhé, hag a drohas ryb an pen scovern onan anedhé*, Peter, from the one side drew out a sword, and cut beside the head the ear of one of them. M.C. 71. ‡ *Ha gen hedna, Dzhuan genz e gothan, trohaz (der an tol) mez a kein gûn an manah pîs pŷr round*, and with that, John with his knife cut (through the hole) out of the back of the monk's gown a piece very round. Llwyd, 252. A softened form of *trochy*, qd. v.

TROILLIA, v. a. To turn, to whirl. *Pollan troillia*, a whirlpool. Llwyd, 61. W. *troelli.* Arm. *troidella.*

TROIS, s. m. A foot. Pl. *treys*, qd. v. Dual, *dew-drois.*

Gans nader ydhof guanheys, hag ol warbarth vynymmeys, a fyne trois dhe'n golon, by a snake I am stung, and poisoned, from the end of the foot to the heart. O.M. 1758. *Preder my dhe'th whûl a dôr, haval dheym a'n pen dhe'n troys*, think that I have wrought thee of earth, like to me from the head to the foot. O.M. 68. *Yn mêdh Pedyr, dhym na ûs troys na leyff na vo golhys*, says Peter, leave thou not to me foot nor hand (that) it be not washed. M.C. 46. *Dew-droys Ihesus caradow, ha'y dhew-leyff y a delly*, the feet of Jesus the beloved, and his hands they bored. M.C. 159. *Trois* was often contracted into *trôs*, qd. v. The oldest form was *truit*, qd. v.

TROISHYS, s. m. A foot length, a foot in measure. (*Trois—hŷs.*) *Na wra wear trois-hys, me a wor guŷr*, it will not by a foot length, I know truly. P.C. 2757. Called in W. *troedvedh, (troed,* a foot, and *médh,* measure.) Arm. *troulad*.

TROM, adj. Heavy, weighty, sad. *Noe, râg kerengé orthys, ny ny gemeré neffré trom dyal war ol an veys, na dre dhyal pŷp ladhé*, Noah, for love to thee, I will never take heavy vengeance on all the world, nor destroy all by flood. O.M. 1200. *Dre trom dhyal war an veys, ty a wra pŷp ol marow*, by heavy vengeance on the world, thou wilt make every one dead. O.M. 1227. W. *trwm*, m. *trom*, f. Ir. *trom*. Gael. *trom*. Manx, *trome*.

TRON, s. m. What projects, a nose, a promontory, or headland. *Pryce*. Preserved in the names of places, as *Troan, Troon, Antron, &c.* The oldest form was *trein*, qd. v. Fr. *trogne*.

TRON, s. f. A throne. *Dûn dhe gyrhas Salamon, ha goryn cf yn y drôn avel mychtern yn y sé*, let us come to fetch Solomon, and let us place him in his throne, like a king in his seat. O.M. 2372. *Lowené dhys, Salamon, dûs genen ny quyc dhe trôn dhe dâs David, râg dewesnys ôs mychtern dhyn, ha kerenys a ver dermyn ty a vŷdh*, hail to thee, Solomon, come with us quick to the throne of thy father David; for chosen thou art a king to us, and crowned in a short time thou shalt be. O.M. 2378. *Scon y fŷdh gwrŷs, der ow rûs, nêv plâs ryall dhom trigva, ha'w thrôn sedha ow bôdh ew may fo henna*, immediately shall be made by my grace heaven, a royal place for my dwelling, and my throne of residence my will is that it to be that. C.W. 1. *Dha vôs yn trôn ysedhys*, to be seated in the throne. C.W. 14. W. *trôn*. Arm. *tron*. Ir. *tron*. Gr. Θρόνος. Lat. *thronus*. Eng. throne. Fr. *trône*.

TROPLESY, v. a. To vex, to grieve. *Pryce*. Probably from Eng. *trouble*.

TROS, s. m. A noise, a great noise, shouting, clamour. *Deuch geneff ha holyouch ve, gothvedhouch na rellouch trôs*, come ye with me, know yo that ye make not a noise. M.C. 63. *Yma ow cûl sacryfys, ha'y pobel cf kekeffrys, dhe'n kêth Dew-na gans mûr trôs*, he is making a sacrifice, and his people also, to that same God, with great noise. O.M. 1558. *Avos agas fas ha trôs, ny wra bom y worlené*, notwithstanding your bragging and noise, a blow will not quell him. P.C. 2110. W. *trwst*. Arm. *trouz*.

TROS, s. m. A foot. *Pyw a dhysquedhes dhyso dhe vôs noeth corf trôs ha brêch*, who disclosed to thee that thou wast naked as to body, foot and arm ? O.M. 262. *Râg ow dhe vôs descsys dhe trûs worth mên py stigé*, for fear of thy being hurt as to thy foot against stone or sticks. P.C. 98. *Me a's ten a dhysempys, an dhyw yn mês a'y dhywlé hag a'y dhew trôs kekyffrys*, I will draw them immediately, the two out of his hands, and from his two feet also. P.C. 3154. A contracted form of *trois*, qd. v.

TROSTER, s. m. A beam, a rafter. Corn. Voc. *trabes*. Plur. *tresters*, qd. v. W *trawst, trostyr*. Arm. *treûst, treustier*. Ir. † *trost*.

TROTH, adj. Poor, wretched. *Lhuyd*, 91. "We still say *an old trot*, speaking of an old miser, or covetous woman." *Pryce*.

TROVIA, v. a. To find. Pret. *trovias*, found. *Pryce*. Fr. *trouver*. Eng. *trover, trove*.

TRU, interj. Alas! pity I sad ! woe. *Tru, gocy, ellas, ellas bôs marow Adam ow thûs*, sad, woe is me, alas! alas ! that Adam my father is dead. O.M. 861. *Ellas, och, tru, tru, shyndŷys ôf gans cronck du*, alas, Oh, sad, sad, hurt I am by a black toad. O.M. 1777. *Mar ny dhue dhum confortyé, ow mornyngh vŷdh och ha tru*, if he comes not to comfort me, my mourning will be "oh" and "alas". R.D. 438. *Râg na'n guela dhym a nêp tu, kueth a portha, ny gansen tru*, for that I see him not, to me on any side, I feel sorrow; should I not sing "alas!" R.D. 866. W. *tru*.

TRUD, s. m. A trout. Corn. Voc. *tructa*. Not Celtic, being borrowed from the Lat. *trutta*, or Eng. *trout*. Fr. *truite*. Called in W. *brithyll*.

TRUE, v. a. To spit, to spit on. *Me a vyn y dhyscudhé, hag yn spyt dhodho trué war y fas ha'y dew lagas*, I will uncover him, and in spite spit at him on his face and eyes. P.C. 1304. *Me a tru un clotte bras waré yn y dhewlagas may cudho hanter y fâth*, I will spit a great clot soon in his eyes, that it may cover half of his face. P.C. 1390. Written also *trewy*, qd. v.

TRUETH, s. m. Pity, compassion. *Trueth vyé dên yw gulân falslych y vones dyswrŷs*, it would be a pity that a man (who) is pure should be falsely destroyed. P.C. 2437. *Yssyno hemma trueth brâs, bôs dhe corf kêr golnys gans tewel popel*, this is a great sorrow, that thy dear body is watched by wicked people. P.C. 3162. *Worto y keusys yn wêdh, y vyrys y wolyon;* aga guelas *o trueth*, I spoke to him also, I looked on his wounds; it was a pity to see them. R.D. 898. W. *truedh*. Arm. *truez*. Ir. *truagh*. Gael. *truaighe, truas*.

TRUIT, s. m. A foot. Corn. Voc. *pes*. *Goden truit, planta*, the sole of the foot. *Ibid*. The later forms were *trois* and *trôs*; pl. *treys, tryys*, qd. v. W. *troed*, pl. *traed*. Arm. *troed, troad*, pl. *treid*. Ir. *troidh, troigh*, † *traig*. Gael. *troidh*. Manx, *trie*. Sansc. *trad*, to press. Eng. *tread*.

TRULERCH, s. m. A foot path. Corn. Vocab. *semita*. Comp. of *tru*, for *truit*, a foot, and *lerch*, trace or footstep.

TRUMETH, s. m. Mercy. *Vŷth ny yllyn tremené an môr-ma, war ow ené, nyns ûs trumeth vŷth dhynny*, we shall never be able to cross this sea, upon my soul ; there is not any mercy for us. O.M. 1650.

TRUS, adj. Cross, thwart, transverse. *Otté an pren omma, nyns ûs tecka yn wlâs-ma, gurên crows annodho warnot. Yntré dew gurên y trehy, râk cafus trûs-pren dedhy, ha'y fastié gans ebyl pren*, behold the tree here, there is not a fairer in this country; let us make a cross of it speedily. In two let us cut it, for to get a cross piece of wood for it, and fasten it with wooden pegs. P.C. 2563, *A drús musury trylles*, athwart thou shalt measure three breadths. O.M. 393. *Me re peches marthys trús*, I have sinned wondrous perversely. P.C. 1505. W. *traws*, †*trus*. Arm. *treuz*. Ir. *trasd*. Gael. *trasd*. Lat. *trans*, (participle.) Sansc. *tar*, to cross.

TRUSSE, v. a. To cross, to go across. *An bewnans ny re gollas hag yn wêdh agan flechys ; omdhychtyn, trussen an wlâs ; fyan na veny kefys*, we have lost our life, and also our children ; let us dight ourselves, let us cross the country ; let us flee that we be not taken. M.C. 246. W. *trawsu*. Arm. *treuzi*.

TRUSU, s. m. Threshold. ‡ *Trúzú an daras*, the threshold of the door. *Llwyd*, 34. W. *trothwy*. Arm. *treuzou*. Ir. *tairseach*. Gael. *stairsneach*.

TRUZ, s. m. A foot. Pl. *treiz*. Llwyd, 119. *A drúz*, on foot. 115. *Golaz trúz*, the sole of the foot. *Trúz-blat (trúz—splat)* splay-footed. 121. *Trúz cbal*, the herb colt's foot. 108. *A ben hag a thrús*, of head and foot. 242. The late form of *trois*, qd. v.

TRY, adv. Whilst, whilst that, as long as, so that. Llwyd, 55, 56, 232, 249. Written also *tro*, and *tra*, qd. v. "It loses its vowel when annexed with a word beginning with one; as *maga liaz tres faut dhyuch*, as many as you have occasion for ; for *maga liaz try cz faut dhiuh*." Llwyd, 232. W. *tra*. Arm. *an dra*. Ir. *trath*. Gael. *trath*.

TRYBO, adv. As far as. Llwyd, 178. Written also *trebé*, qd. v.

TRYCCIAR, s. m. A fuller. Llwyd, 62, 240.

TRYDDYDH, s. m. The space of three days. See *Triddydh*.

TRYGE, adj. Third. *Del dhedhyesys dhymmo vy, y wrês yn ban dasfiwé dhe'n trygé dêdh yredy*, as thou p:omisedst to me, that thou wouldst revive up on the third day really. R.D. 452. *An trygé dêdh yn hydhew dhyworthyf aban êth e*, the third day is to-day, since he went from me. R.D. 465. *An trygé dêdh hep gow y wrûk dasserchy arté*, the third day without a lie, I did rise again. R.D. 2606. Another form of *tressa*, qd. v.

TRYHANS, card. num. Three hundred. See *Trihans*.

TRYHER, adj. Mighty. *Ambosow orth tryher gureys, annedhé nyua ês laha ; dre sor kyn fêns y werrys, dhe sconya my ny alla*, promises made by the mighty, of them there is not law ; though they be broken in anger, I am unable to resist. P.C. 1235.

TRYLLES, s. m. Three breadths. *Cafes moy dhys aban rês, try hrys dhe bâl kemery ; a drús musury trylles, ha givet na wra falsury*, since it is necessary for thee to have more, thou shalt take three lengths of thy spade ; across thou shalt measure three breadths, and take care that thou doest not falsehood. O.M. 393. Comp. of *try*, three, and *lês*, breadth.

TRYLYE, v. a. To turn, to change, to convert. Written also *trylé*. Part. pass. *trylys*. *Yma un guâs marthys prout ol an cyté ow trylyé*, there is a fellow wondrous proud, turning all the city. P.C. 578. *Re jovyn, drôk yw gyné na venta kammen trylé yn maner têk*, by Jove, I am sorry, that thou wilt not turn at all into a fair manner. P.C. 1293. *Ef re trylyas lyes cans yn mês a'n fey*, he has turned many hundreds out of the faith. P.C. 1995. *Manna allo an tebell ogus dhys bonas trylys*, that the evil one may not be turned near to thee. M.C. 19. *Un quêth têk hy a drylyas adro dhodho denympys*, a fair cloth she wrapped about him immediately. M.C. 177. The same word as *treylé*, qd. v.

TRYSSE, adj. Third. *Ow mebyon, my a gy peys, yn mês whêth dylleuch trysé*, my sons, I pray you, send outside yet a third. O.M. 1130. Another form of *tressa*, qd. v.

TRYYS, s. m. Feet. Pl. of *trois*, qd. v. *Sew olow ow thryys lyskys*, follow thou the burnt prints of my feet. O.M. 711. *Yn dan dryys may fo pottyys*, that it may be placed under feet. 2607. Written also contractedly *trýs*. *Arluth, yma dour tommys lour, may hallons bôs golhys aga trýs yn kettep pol*, Lord, there is water warmed enough, that may be washed their feet every one. P.C. 841. *Yma ow thrýs hn'm dulé dhyworthef ow teglené*, my feet and hands are loosening from me. P.C. 1216.

TSCECCE, s. m. A titmouse. Llwyd, 113, so calls *tskekké'r eithin*, which must rather mean the *whinchat*, or *furze chatterer* ; called in Welsh, *clochdar yr eithin*.

TSHAUHA, s. m. A chough, or red logged crow. *Pryce*. So called from its note. In W. *brân pig côch*, the redbilled crow.

TSHAWC, s. m. A jackdaw. Llwyd, 34, who also writes it *tshawcka*, 93. So called from its note.

TSHEI, s. m. A house. Llwyd, 232, thus writes *ty*, to give the sound of *chy*, qd. v. He also writes it *tshyi*. *Tshyi pobaz, tshyi vorn*, a bake house. 121. *Tshyi côg*, a cook shop. 123. *Ol mein y dshyi*, all in the house. 231.

TSHOWNLER, s. m. A candlestick. Llwyd, 46.

TSHICUC, s. m. A swallow. Llwyd, 65. Lit. a house cuckoo.

TSHYMMA, s. m. This house. *Aberth yn tshymma*, within this house. Llwyd, 240. The same as *chymma*, qd. v.

TU, s. m. A side, part, region. *Dew lader drews o danynys a ve dydhgtis gans Jhesu, ganso gf may fêns eregis, onon dhodho a bub tu*, two froward robbers that were condemned, were dighted with Jesus, that they might be hung with him, one on each side to him. M.C. 163. *Judas êth a neyl tu dhe omgrcgy*, Judas went one side to hang himself. M.C. 105. *War tu dylarch daras yn ty a wra*, on the hinder part a door in it thou shalt make. O.M. 961. *Ha war tu tré fystenens kefrys marrek ha squyer*, and let knight and squire likewise hasten towards home. O.M. 2003. W. *tu*. Arm. *tu*. Ir. *taobh*. †*toib*. Gael. *taobh*. 'Manx, *cheu*.

TUBAN, s. f. A dam, bank, rampart. Llwyd, 42.

TUBBY, s. m. Thomas. Llwyd, 10. A further corruption of *tubmy*, as that is of *tummy*.

TUBM, adj. Hot, burning. Llwyd, 45, 50. *Mar dubm*, so hot. 231. A late corruption of *tum*, id. qd. *toim*, qd. v.

TUBMA, v. a. To make hot, to heat, to warm. Llwyd, 45. *Dho tubma*. ‡ *Ha hedna vedna gus tubma a dhella e a rág*, and that will warm you behind and before. *Pryce*. A late corruption of *tumma*, id. qd. *tomna*, qd. v.

TUCH, s. m. A short space of time, a moment. *Na wreuch un tûch vŷth letyé*, do ye not any one moment delay. P.C. 1714. *Prâg y'm gyssys tuch dheworthys*, why hast thou left me a moment from thee ? P.C. 2937.

Yn dan dôr un tuch ny séf, under ground a moment be will not stay. R.D. 2112. Eng. *touch*.

TUE, v. n. He will come. The asp. mutation of *due*, qd. v. *Râg y tue lŷf war an beys*, for a flood will come on the earth. O.M. 1042. *Mar tue nêp guâs ha laddré rn gueel dheworthyn*, if any fellow comes and steals the rods from us. O.M. 2063. *Râg mar a tuefé yn chy, ef a's gor dheworthyn ny*, for if he comes into the house, he will take them from us. P.C. 3052. *Mar tufé ha datherchy*, if he comes and rises. R.D. 7.

TUEN, s. m. A strand. *Pryce*. The same as *Towan*, qd. v.

TUES, s. f. A people. *Dhe wûl defens a râk tues*, to make a defence against people. P.C. 2306. Generally written *tûs*, qd. v.

TUETH, v. n. He came. The asp. mutation of *dueth*, 3 pers. s. preter. of irr. v. *dôs*. *Mones dhe vyras deffry, mar a tueth ha dasserhy*, go to see indeed if he is come and risen. R.D. 683. *Yn beydh pau y'n gorsyn ny, wharré y tueth deulugy, warnan codhas*, when we put him in the grave, soon there came devils, they fell upon us. R.D. 2124.

TUHE, prep. Towards. *Ens pôp ol war tuhé tré, an guary yw dywydhys*, let every one go towards home, the play is ended. P.C. 3237. Written by Llwyd, *tyha*, qd. v. W. *tua*.

TULDER, s. m. Darkness. *Ha Dew deberhas an golow dhort an tulder*, and God separated the light from the darkness. M.C. p. 93.

TULGU, s. m. Darkness, obscurity. *Llwyd*, 162, 242. A contracted form of *tewolgow*, qd. v.

TULL, s. m. Deceit, fraud. *Dewdhec warnugans a virhas my a'm be, heb tull na gýll, a dhallathfas an bŷs-ma*, two and thirty daughters I have, without deceit or guile, from the beginning of this world. C.W. 144. *Kyn 'dhota' skymys yn wharth, yn dewedh, heb tull na gŷll*, why a *wêl deall uskys*, although thou art fallen into laughter, in the end without fraud or guile, you shall see a deluge immediately. C.W. 168. W. *tŵyll*. Arm. † *touell*. Ir. † *tul*.

TULLA, v. a. To hole, to perforate, to bore through. *Llwyd*, 117. From *tull*, id. qd. v. *toll*, a hole. Another form of *telly* and *tolly*, qd. v.

TULLE, v. a. To deceive. Part. *tullys*. *A debel venyn hep rûs, ty rum tullas hep kên, O* wicked graceless woman, thou hast deceived me without pity. O.M. 252. *Eva, prâg y whrusté sy tullé dhe bryes hep kên, an aval worth y derry, wosé my dhys dh'y dhefen*, Eve, why didst thou deceive thy husband without pity, by plucking the apple after I had forbidden it to thee? O.M. 278. *Tru, A Dhu, elhas, elhas, gans un huyn re bên tullys*, sad, O God, alas, alas, by a sleep we have been deceived. M.C. 246. Another form is *tolla*, qd. v. W. *twyllo*. Arm. *toucla, toella*.

TULLOR, s. m. A deceiver. Corn. Voc. *fallax*. W. *twyllwr*. Arm. *touellcr*.

TUM, adj. Hot, warm, heated. Corrupted in late Cornish into *tubm*. The early form was *toim*, qd. v.

TUMDER, s. m. Heat. Corn. Vocab. *calor*. Another form is *toimder*, qd. v. W. *twymder*. Arm. *tomder, tuemder*.

TUMMA, v. a. To heat, to make hot, to warm. *Pryce*. Another form is *tomma*, qd. v.

TUMMAS, s. m. A thump, a blow. Pl. *tummasow*. *Buxow leas heb kên ha tummasow kekyffris dhe Grist adro dhe dhewen gans nerth brûs a ve syttis*, buffets many without pity, and thumps likewise to Christ about his jaws with great force were set. M.C. 138.

TUN, v. a. To bear, to carry. *Ow tûn*, carrying. Llwyd, 248. The asp. mutation of *dûn*, more generally written *dôn*, qd. v.

TUOGU, s. m. The rabble. *Pobel tuogu*. Llwyd, 178. See *Tiogou*.

TUR, s. m. A tower. Corn. Voc. *turris*. Generally written in the Dramas *tour*, qd. v.

TUREN, s. f. A turtle dove. Corn. Voc. *turtur*. Another form was *troel*, qd. v. Arm. *turzunel*.

TURMA, s. m. A tower. Llwyd, 168.

TUS, s. f. A nation, a people; people, men. *Tús vyan ha tús vrâs*, people small and great. O.M. 1438. *Gans lŷf ny wrâf bynytha ladhé an dús gwyls na dôf*, by flood I will not ever destroy mankind wild nor tame. O.M. 1254. *An dús vâs u dheserya dhedhé gulâs nêf o kyllys*, the good folk desired for themselves the country of heaven (that) was lost. M.C. 4. *Yn médh Ihesus, nyng-ugy ow mychternes yn bŷs ma, hag a pe, ow thús dhe wy ny'm delyrfsens yn delma*, says Jesus, my kingdom is not in this world, and if it were, my people would not have given me up to you thus. M.C. 102. It was used in Cornish for the plural of *dên*, in the same manner as *gens* is used in French for the plural of *homme*. The *u* had the same sound as the Welsh *u*, being pronounced *tis*, or *tees*, as it was written in late times. (*Llwyd*, 229.) W. *tûd*, † *tut*. Arm. *tud*, † *tut*. Ir. *tuath*, † *tuad*. Gael. *tuath*. Oscan, *tuvtu*. Umbr. *tuta, tota*. Lith. *tauta*. Goth. *thiuda*. O. H. G. *diota*.

TUSHOC, adj. Tufted, spiked. *Les dushoc*, betonica, betony; lit. the tufted herb. Corn. Voc. W. *twysoc*, from *twys*, a tuft ; *twys ŷd*, ear of corn.

TUSTUN, s.m. A witness. It generally occurs in Cornish with the initial in the secondary form. (See *Dustun*.) W. *testun*, a theme.

TUSTUNE, v. a. To bear witness, to testify. (See *Dustuné*.) Arm. *testenia*. W. *testunio*, to set a theme.

TUSTUNY, s. m. A witnessing, testimony. (See *Dustuny*.) Arm. *testeni*.

TUTH, v. n. He came. The asp. mutation of *dûth*, qd. v. 3 pers. s. preter. of *dôs*.

TUTH, v. n. Thou wilt come. The asp. mutation of *dûth*, qd. v. 2 pers. s. fut. of *dôs*.

TUYLDER, s. m. Darkness, obscurity. Llwyd, 162. Written also *tulder*, and *tewlder*, qd. v.

TUYN, s. m. A sandy shore bank. *Pryce*. Another form of *towan*, qd. v.

TUYN, s. m. A hillock. *Pryce*. W. *twyn*. Arm. *tûn*. Ir. *tonnach*. Sansc. *tunga*. Fr. *dune*.

TUYTH, v. n. I came. The asp. mutation of *duyth*, qd. v. 1 pers. s. preter. of *dôs*.

TY, s. m. A house. Written in the Cornish Vocabulary *ti*, qd. v.

TY, s. m. An oath, an imprecation. *Ef a doys a dhesympys maga town ty del wodhyé gans Crist na vyé tregis, na bythqueth ef na'n quelsé*, he swore forthwith as deep an oath as he knew, that he had not been staying with Christ, nor had ever seen him. M.C. 85. W. *twng*, † *tug*. Ir. *tuinge*, † *tig*. Gael. *tuinge*.

TY, pron. Thou, thee. See *Ti*.

TY, pron. prep. To it. *My a vyn a dhysempys marogeth bŷs ty*, I will immediately ride presently even to it. O.M. 1971. Another form of *dy*, qd. v.

TY, v. a. To cover over, to cover, to roof, to thatch. 3 pers. s. fut. *ty*. *Yn hanow Dew, tyy py ny agan bêdh miêdh*, in the name of God cover it, or we shall have shame. O.M. 1078. *Cowyth profynyn an styllyow mars êns compes dhe'n fosow, may haller aga lathyé gans corbles lasys tennow, hag a's ty gans plynkennow*, comrade, let us try the rafters, if they are straight to the walls, that one may lay them with joists, laths, beams, and cover them with planks. O.M. 2474. *Tyorryon yn ketep chet, tycuch an temple hep let, na dheffo glaw dhe'n styllyow*, tilers, every fellow, cover ye the temple without delay, that rain come not to the rafters. O.M. 2487. *Gonesugy ken agesouch why ny's ty, râg sotel ouch yn pûp crêft*, workmen others than ye shall not cover it, for subtle ye are in every craft. O.M. 2490. W. *toi*. Arm. *tei, toi*. Lat. *tego*.

TYAC, s. m. A husbandman. See *Tioc*.

TYBELES, s. m. Wicked ones. *Mar ethuk yw dhe weles, may tyglyn an tybeles, pan y'n guellons, kettep pen*, so terrible it is to see, that the devils will wince when they see it, every head. P.C. 3047. More generally written *tebeles*, pl. of *tebel*, qd. v.

TYBM, adj. Warm. *Lhwyd*, 9. The same as *tubm*, qd. v.

TYBRY, v. a. To eat. The asp. mutation of *dybry*, qd. v. *Yma war garynnyas brâs ow tybry fest dybyté*, it is upon great carrion eating fast without pity. O.M. 1108.

TYBRYTH, v. a. Thou wilt eat. The asp. mutation of *dybryth*, 2 pers. s. fut. of *dybry*, qd. v. *Mar a tybryth a henna yw hynwyn pren a skyens*, if thou wilt eat of that (which) is called the tree of knowledge. O.M. 81.

TYBYANS, s. m. Thought, opinion. *Dhum tybyans whêth ef vy grŷs bôs Ihesu Cryst dasserchys dre y mûr râs*, to my thinking he does not yet believe that Jesus Christ is risen through his great grace. R.D. 1213. W. *tybiant*.

TYBYAS, v. a. To think, to suppose. *Taw, sedhé vyn ty Phelip, râk pûr wŷr ty a gam dip warnodho of*, be silent, sit wilt thou Philip, for very truly thou thinkest wrongly concerning him. R.D. 999. *Râk me a dyp bôs henna an kêth mâp êth alemma, yw mychtern lowené*, for I think that this one is the same son (that) went hence, (who) is the king of joy. R.D. 2508. W. *tybied*.

TYDH, s. m. A day. *Benyges re by pûp tŷdh*, blessed be thou every day. O.M. 831. The asp. mutation of *dŷdh*, qd. v.

TYE, v. a. To take an oath, to swear. *Me a levar, heb y dyé, genef Dew a wrûg serry, ha'y vollath yn pûr dheffry dhym a rôs*, I say, without swearing it, with me God was angry, and his curse in very earnest to me he gave. C.W. 118. Written also *toy*, qd. v.

TYEN, adj. Whole, entire, perfect. The asp. mutation of *dyen*, qd. v. *Toul an welen ol yn tyen dhe'n dôr uskys*, cast thou the rod all entirely to the grouud quickly. O.M. 1447. *Y vennath dheuch yn tyen, keffrys gorryth ha benen*, his blessing to you wholly, as well male as female. O.M. 2836.

TYENE, v. n. To pant, to faint. The asp. mutation of *dyené*, qd. v.

TYFFEN, v. a. To forbid. The asp. mut. of *dyffen*, qd. v.

TYFFONS, v. n. They may come. The asp. mut. of *dyffons*. 3 pers. pl. subj. of irr. v. *dôs*. *Ke gorhemmyn ol dhe'n masons yn cyté may tyffons umma myttyn war beyn cregy ha tenné*, go thou, command all the masons in the city that they come here to-morrow, on pain of hanging and drawing. O.M. 2279.

TYFFOUCH, v. n. Ye may come. The asp. mutation of *dyffouch*. 2 pers. pl. subj. of irr. v. *dôs*. *May tyffouch ol dhe sylwyans, sevouch yn agys cryggyans, râk dhum Tâs me â dhe'n nêf*, that ye may all come to salvation, stand in your belief, for I will go to my Father to heaven. R.D. 2388.

TYGLYN, v. a. He will wince. The asp. mutation of *dyglyn*, 3 pers. s. fut. of *dyglené*, qd. v.

TYHA, prep. Towards. *Tyha'n tempel*, towards the temple; *war tyha trê*, towards home. *Lhwyd*, 249. Written also *tuhé*, qd. v. *(tu—a.)* W. *tua*.

TYLDYE, v. a. To cover. *My a vyn lemyn tyldyé guartha an gorhyl gans quêth, ha henna a ra guyihé na dheffo glaw aberwedh*, I will now cover the top of the ark with a cloth, and that will keep that the rain may not come in. O.M. 1073.

TYLLER, s. m. A place. Pl. *tylleryow*. *Pan dothyans bŷs yn tyller, may 'thesé Crist ow pesy*, when they came even to the place, where Christ was praying. M.C. 65. *Dreuch bŷs omma dhum tyller*, bring ye even here to my place. P.C. 980. *Dh'y thyller arté glenes, kepar del ve*, to its place again let it stick, like as it was. P.C. 1153. *Ellas, ny won py tyller bŷth moy py le y trygaf*, alas! I know not (in) what place, ever more where I shall dwell. P.C. 2507. Written also *teller*, qd. v.

TYLLY, v. a. To bore a hole, to pierce. *Ha'n anken mûr a's grevyé, pan vyré worth y woly, yn tencwen ydh caé, dre an golon a's tylly*, and the great sorrow that grieved her, when she looked on his wound, in the side it was, through the heart pierced her. M.C. 231. Another form of *telly*, qd. v.

TYLYS, part. Paid, requited. *Y dhadder yw drôk tylys, pan y'n ladhsons dybyté*, his goodness is ill requited, when they killed him without pity. P.C. 3097. Part. pass. of *taly*, qd. v.

TYMARRHAR, s. m. A wooer or suitor. *Lhwyd*, 129.

TYMDER, s. m. Heat, warmth. *Lhwyd*, 240. The same as *tumder*, qd. v.

TYMMYN, s. m. Fragments, pieces. *Ow holan ol dhe dymmyn râg moreth a wra terry*, my heart all to pieces for grief will break. O.M. 357. Plural of *tam*, qd. v.

TYN, s. m. A draught, a pull, a pluck. *Pryce*. Another form of *ten*, qd. v.

TYN, adj. Tight, strait, sharp, keen, painful. *I beyn o mar grêff ha tyn caman na ylly bevé*, his pain was so strong and keen that he could not live any way. M.C. 204. *Ha'n wlos a's kemeras mar dyn may clandems hy arté*, and the sight took her so sharply that she swooned again. M.C. 171. *Yn ûr-na râg pûr dhwan, daggrow tyn gwrâf dyceré*, at that time for sorrow, bitter tears I shall shed. O.M. 402. *Pan cleefyf vy an tân tyn, parhap y wrussen fyé*, when I should feel the sharp fire, perhaps I should flee. O.M. 1351. *Gueyt y wrennyé prest yn tyn bŷth na scapyé*, take thou care to iron him very tightly, that he may never escape. P.C. 1887.

Cryst agan prennas yn tyn, Christ redeemed us painfully. R.D. 1204. W. *tyn.* Arm. *ten.* Ir. *teann,* † *teud.* Gael. *teann.* Manx, *chionn.* Lat. *tentus.* Gr. τατοs. Sansc. *tatas.*

TYNNE, v. a. To draw, to drag, to pull. *Euch, tynneuch an gaszdow usy ow cúl fals devcow yn més ngan temple ny,* go ye, drag the wretched woman, (that) is making false gods out of our temple. O.M. 2691. *Tynnouch ol gans mûr a grŷs,* drag ye all, with much of force. P.C. 2136. *Y'n ban tynnyn ef a'n dour,* up let us draw him from the water. R.D. 2265. *Tynnyn ef yn ban war ton,* let us draw him up on the wave. R.D. 2281. *Ha ty corf brâs mylyges dhe yfarn gans dhe enef gynen y fydhyth tynnes,* and thou, great cursed body, to hell with thy soul by us shalt be dragged. R.D. 2349. Written also *tenna,* qd. v. W. *tynnu,* † *tennu.* Arm. *tennn.* Ir. *teann.* Gael. *teann.* Manx, *chionn.*

TYNWENNOW, s. m. Sides. One of the plurals of *tenewen,* qd. v.

TYOR, s. m. One who covers, a thatcher, a slater, a tiler. Pl. *tyoryon. Ke gorhemmyn dhe'n cyté may teff-ons omma wharé war beyn aga bôs dysworga; masons ha karpentorryon, trehery-meyn, tyorryon, au temple may fe coul wreys,* go thou, command the city that they come here soon, on pain of their being destroyed; masons and carpenters, stone-cutters, tilers, that the temple may be fully made. O.M. 2411. *Dhe ol an karpentoryon, masons, yn wêdh tyorryon,* to all the carpenters, masons, also tilers. O.M. 2423. *Tyorryon yn ketep chet, tycuch an temple hep let, na dheffo glaw dhe'n styllyow,* tilers, every fellow, cover the temple, without delay, that the rain come not to the rafters. O.M. 2486. W. *toer.* Arm. *toer.*

TYOWGEL, adj. Certain, sure. The asp. mutation of *dyowgel,* qd. v. *Na corf dasserhy dhe vew, na dôr grŷs yn tyowgel,* nor a body rise again to life, nor the earth quake really. P.C. 3086.

TYR, s. m. Earth, land. See *Tir.*

TYR, card. num. Three. A contracted form of *tyyr, teir* or *teir,* qd. v., used with nouns feminine. *Pan o an tŷr Marya ogas dhe'n bêdh devethys, an meyn csa a wartha, y a'n guelas drehevys; en benenas yn delma yntredhé a leverys, dheworth an bédh an meyn-ma dhynny pu a'n ommelys,* when the three Maries were come nigh the grave stones (that) were above, they saw them raised; the women they said among themselves, these stones from the grave, who has turned them aside for us! M C. 253. *Dôg alena tŷr guelen a wrûk Moyses dhe plansé,* bring thou thence three rods (which) Moses did plant. O.M. 1045. *Hedré vyyu ow predery, yn glassygyon gesouch y aga thŷr dhe wrowedhé,* while I am considering, leave ye them on a green plot, the three (there) to lie. O.M. 2037. *Yn dôr ymons ol gurydhyys, ha'n thŷr dhe onan yw unys,* in the earth they are all rooted, and the three to one are joined. O.M. 2085.

TYRETH, s. m. Land, earth, country. See *Tireth.*

TYRNEWAN, s. m. A side. ‡ *Tyrnewan liear,* the page of a book. Llwyd, 111. A late corruption of *tenewen,* qd. v.

TYRRY, v. a. To break. *Lavar dhymmo, ty venen, an frût ple russys tyrry,* tell me, thou woman, where didst thou break off the fruit? O.M. 210. *Prâg y toîsté sy hep kén, worth hy thempté dhe dyrry an frût erbyn ow

dysen, why didst thou deceive her without pity, by tempting her to pluck off the fruit against my prohibition? O.M. 303. Another form of *terry* or *torry,* qd. v.

TYSCY, v. a. To teach, to learn. The asp. mutation of *dysey,* qd. v. *Prest ow tysky ynno pûp dén ol erygy,* always teaching every man to believe in him. P.C. 1596.

TYSHATAS, adv. Leisurely, by stroke and stroke. Pryce. *May haller ry yfle grâs, ha knoukyé prest tysha-tas,* that evil dole may be given; and to strike always tick and tack. P.C. 2077. *Gans ow scorge tysha-tas me a'th wŷsk, may fo drôk pŷn,* with my scourge, tick and tack, I will strike thee, that there may be a bad pain. P.C. 2107. *Powes lemmyn, losel vâs, ha knouk an hôrn tys-ha-tas,* stop now, idle fellow, and strike the iron tick-a-tack. P.C. 2719.

TYSQUEDHAS, v. a. He shewed. The asp. mutation of *dysquedhas,* qd. v. *Dhe vâp dén y tysquedhas pûr wûr mûr a kerengé,* to the sons of men he shewed, very truly, much love. R.D. 2637.

TYSTREWYS, v. a. Thou wouldst destroy. The asp. mutation of *dystrewys,* 2 pers. s. subj. of *dystrewy,* qd. v. *Fy dhyso, pan leversys temple Dew y'n tystrewys hag arté kyn pen try dŷdh guel ys kyns y'n drehevys, fy on thee!* when thou saidst the temple of God that thou wouldst destroy it, and again before the end of three days, better than before, wouldst rebuild it. P.C. 2660.

TYSTRYWY, v. a. To destroy. The asp. mutation of *dystrywy,* or *dystrewy,* qd. v. *Ow scollyé agan guara ha'n fêr orth y tystrywy,* scattering our wares, and destroying the fair. P.C. 342.

TYTHY, adv. Quickly. *An ioul a trylyas sperys, hag éth dh'y tyller tythy,* the devil turned spirit, and went to his place quickly. M.C. 18. From *tôth,* haste.

TYULDAR, s. m. Darkness. Llwyd, 13. Another form of *tulder,* or *tewlder,* qd. v.

TYVY, v. a. To grow. Part. pass. *tyvys.* 3 pers. s. fut. *tŷf. Ny dŷf guéls na flour yn bŷs yn kéth fordh-na may kyrdhys,* grass nor flower in the world will grow in that same road that I walked. O.M. 712. *My a welas hy gurydhyow bŷs yn yffarn dywenys, ha'y branchys yn van tyvys bŷs yn néf uhel golow,* I saw its branches even into hell descending, and its branches grown up, even to heaven high in light. O.M. 785. *Yn gordhyans dhe'n Tâs a néf, my a wra agas plansé; ha tregouch dh'y ordenanns ef, gurydhyouch ha tyvouch arté,* in glory to the Father of heaven I will plant ye; and dwell ye in his ordinance; take root and grow again. O.M. 1894. The same word as *tevy.* qd. v.

TYWEDH, s. m. End, conclusion. *A gasé y wokyneth, ha treylé dhe skentuleth, ow tywedh na ganno tru,* to leave his folly, and turn to wisdom, at last that he may not sing "alas." P.C. 1810. *A vŷl gadling, dues yn râg, wor tywedh whet crôk a'th tâg,* O vile vagabond, come thou forth, at last hanging yet will choak thee. P.C. 1818. The asp. mutation of *dywedh,* or *diwedh,* qd. v.

TYWLEL, v. a. To throw, to cast. *Me a vyn yn della dysky ow dyllas guella, ha tywlel a dhyragtho,* I will in that manner take off my best clothes, and cast before him. P.C. 257. Another form of *tewlel,* qd. v.

TYWYN, v. n. We will be silent. 1 pers. pl. fut. of

tewel, qd. v. *Ioy del ği ow dydhané, ny ny tywyn ow cané Gloria in excelsis Deo*, as joy may comfort me, we will not be silent, singing Glory to God in the highest. R.D. 2527.

TYYR, card. num. Three. Used with nouns feminine. *My a wél tyyr guelen gay*, I see three gay rods. O.M. 1729. *Na nahaf epscop goky, rág an thyyr guelen defry a ve gans Davyd plynsys*, I will not recant, foolish bishop, for the three rods really were by David planted. O.M. 2656. Written also *teyr* or *teir*, and contractedly *týr*, qd. v.

U.

This letter in Cornish had four sounds. 1. That of the Italian *u*, or English *oo*, as *gûr*, a man; *túr*, a tower; which are also written in Cornish *gour*, *tour*. This sound is now always represented in Welsh by *w*, as *gŵr*, *tŵr*, and in old manuscripts by *u*; and in Armoric by *ou*, as *gour*, *tour*. 2. That of *u*, in the English words *burn*, *turn*, &c., as C. *umma*, here; *unna*, there; represented in Welsh by *y*, as *yma*, *yna*. 3. That of the Welsh *u*, which is the same as that of *y*, in the English words *hungry*, *sundry*. Thus C. *tûs*, (written in later times *tees*,) a people; *rûdh*, crimson; *ugans*, (*iguns*,) twenty; W. *tûd*, *rhûdh*, *ugain*. 4. The diphthongal sound represented by *ew*, in the English words *few*, *new*. Thus C. *pu*, who; *Du*, God; *tu*, a side; which are also written in Cornish *pew*, *Dew*, *tew*.

UBBA, adv. In this place, here. Written also *uppa*. ‡ *Peswarra bledhan, mollath Dew war ef reeg dry hy uppa*, the fourth year, the curse of God on him that brought her here. Pryce. Both further corruptions of *ubma*, as that is of *umma*, qd. v.

UCCY, adj. Foolish, silly. *Taw, taw, na vŷdh dhymo mar ucky*, be silent, be not so foolish to me. C.W. 60. *Marth ew genaf a un dra, y vosta mar ucky*, I am surprised at one thing, that thou art so foolish. C.W. 166. A late form of *wocy*, a mutation of *gocy*, qd. v.

UCH, prep. Above, over. In Cornish and Armoric it always prefixes *a*. *A uch eglos têk yn wlás an yscdhva ydhesa*, above a fair church in the country the seat was. M.C. 13. *Ha'n Edhewon a worras a uch Ihesus Crist un mén*, and the Jews placed above Jesus Christ a stone. M.C. 237. *Drou' e dhymmo dhe tackyé a uch y pen*, bring ye it to me to fasten above his head. P.C. 2808. Another form was *us*, or *yus*, qd. v. W. *uch*. Arm. *uch, us*. Ir. *os, uas, suas,* †*soos*. Gael. *os, suas,* †*uchd*. Manx, *heose, scosé*. Germ. *hoch*. Eng. *high*. Sansc. *ut*.

UCHAF, adj. Upmost, uppermost, highest. Superl. of *uch*, high. *My pan esen ow quandré, clewys an ngl tenewen un êl ow talleth cané a uchaf war an wrdhen*, when I was walking about, I heard on one side an angel beginning to sing very high up on the tree. O.M. 216. W. *uchav*.

UCHEL, adj. High, lofty, towering. Comp. *uchellah*. Superl. *uchella*. *Alena y'n hombronkyas uchel war bun un menedh*, thence he led him high on top of a mountain. M.C. 16. *A vês dhe'n drê ydhesé menedh uchel yredy*, outside the town, there was a high mountain indeed. M.C. 162. *En Edhewon ny wynné bôs an laddron ow cregy ternos, rág pasch o dhedhé, dŷdh uchel y a sensy*, the Jews would not that the robbers should be hanging the day after, for it was Easter to them; a high day they held it. M.C. 229. *Cherubyn, an uchella ty a vŷdh, dês a rág uskys*, Cherubyn, the highest thou shalt be, come forth quickly. C.W. 4. It was also softened into *uhel*, and *huhel*, qd. v. W. *uchel*. Arm. *uchel, huel*. Ir. *uasal*. Gael. *uasal*, †*uchdall*. Manx, *ooasle*. Old Gaulish, *uxello*, in *Uxello-dunon, &c*. Sansc. *uk'ala*.

UCHELDER, s. m. Height, highness, loftiness. *Ihesu Crist múr gerensé dhe váb dén a dhysweedhas, a'n uchelder may 'thesé dhe'n bŷs pan deyskynnas pchadoryon rág perna, o desevijs dre Satnas*, Jesus Christ shewed much love to the son of man, when he descended from the height that he was, to redeem sinners that were felled by Satan. M.C. 5. The softened form is *uhelder*. W. *uchelder*. Arm. *uchelded*.—W. *uchder*. Ir. *uachdar*, †*ochtar*. Gael. *uachtar*. Manx, *eachtar, uchtagh*.

UCHELLE, v. a. To make high, to exalt; to hallow, to sanctify. Part. *uchelles*. *An Tás ny es yn néf, bedhens dhe hanow uchelles*, our Father which art in heaven, hallowed be 'thy name. Pryce. *Rág yn whêh dydhyow Dew a wrás an néf ha'n 'oar, ha'n môr, ha mŷns es ythens y, ha powesas an scythvas dŷdh, hag a'n uchellas*, for in six days God made heaven and earth, and the sea, and all that in them is, and rested the seventh day, and hallowed it. *Ibid*. W. *uchelu*. Arm. *uchelaat*.

UCHON, adv. On high, above. *Pan yllyn ny yntrethon drey dour a'n meen flynt garow, dre grás an Tás a uchon, guîr Dew yn y oberow*, when we can between ourselves bring water from the sharp flint stone, through the grace of the Father on high, true God in his works. O.M. 1861. *Henna ydhew convethys, der an diskans es dhymmo reis gans an Tás es a uchan*, that is understood through the science to me given by the Father that is on high. C.W. 156. W. *ucho, uchod*.

UDN, card. num. One. ‡ *Ankow ydhew devethys, ny vyn omma ow gasa dhe vewa udn spyes*, death is come, he will not here leave me to live here one space. C.W. 142. A late corruption of *un*, qd. v.

UDZHE, prep. After, posterior to. ‡ *Udzhé henna, udzhena, udzhé hedda*, afterwards; *udzhé hemma, udzhema*, hereafter. Lhuyd, 54, 124, 249. A late corruption of *wosé*, qd. v.

UDZHEON, s. m. An ox. ‡ *Na ra chee gavas whans warlyrch chy de contrevak, na e udzheon, na e rounzan, na traveth pêth yw e*, thou shalt not covet thy neighbour's house, nor his ox, nor his ass, nor any thing that is his. Pryce. A late corruption of *odion*, qd. v.

UFERETH, s. m. Vanity, idleness, frivolity. *Uferéth fól yw na'n gás, lemmyn môs dhe dharywas tra na wra lês*, foolish idleness it is that he does not leave it, but to go to assert a thing that will not do good. R.D. 950. *A nyns osé pryeryn, uferéth yw dhys govyn pŷth yw an marth a wharfé*, if thou art not a stranger, it is idleness for thee to ask what is the wonder that hath happened. R.D. 1262. Written also *evereth*, qd. v. W. *overedh*, fr. *over*, vain.

UHEL 353 UN

UFFYA, v. a. To know, to understand. *Me a levar dhys, Eva, ha cool orthaf, maga für te a vea avel Dew es awartha, hag a uffyn pûb tra*, I will tell thee, Eve, and listen thou to me, as wise thou wouldst be as God that is above, and know every thing. C.W. 44. A corrupted form of *wodhfyé*, qd. v.

UGANS, card. num. Twenty, a score. *Dêk warn-ugans*, thirty. *Dew ugans*, forty, two score. *Ha hanter cans kevelyn yn-wêdh ty a wra y lês ; yn uhelder my a vyn dêk warn-ugans y vôs gurés*, and half a hundred cubits also thou shalt make its width; in height I wish it to be made thirty (cubits.) O.M. 960. *Henna yw pûr scorn ha geys, râg y fué kyns y vôs gurés, dew ugens blydhen ha vché*, that is a very sneer and jest, for there were, before it was done, forty years and six. P.C. 351.. *Sŷth mŷl, ha sŷth cans blydhen, un dên kyn fo ow kerdhes, ow tôs kyn spedyé yn geydh dew ugans myldyr perfeyth omma ny alsé bones*, seven thousand and seven hundred years if a man should be travelling, and though he sped coming in a day forty miles complete, here he could not be. R.D. 2407. *Yn wêdh dewdhek warnugans a virhas my a'm be*, also a score and twelve daughters I have. C.W. 144. *Yn oys me yw yn ûr-ma try cans try ugans ha whôth pymp moy, yn gêdh hydhew*, in age I am now three hundred, three score, and yet five more on this very day. C.W. 152. W. *ugain, ugaint*, † *ugeint*. Arm. *ugent*. Ir. *fichid*, † *fichet*. Gael. *fichead*. Manx, *feed*. Gr. εἴκοσι. Lat. *viginti*. Sansc. *vinsati*.

UGORY, v. a. To open, to disclose. Part. *ugorys*. 2 pers. s. imp., and 3 pers. s. fut. *ugor*, written also *uger*. *Ugor daras dhe pryson, ha gor Ihesu ynno scon pols dhe powes*, open thou the door of thy prison, and put Jesus in it at once a while to rest. P.C. 1871. *Dew a erchys dhys, Moyses, dhe welen y kemeres, ha gwyskel an môr gynsy ; an dour a uger a lês, may hylly yn ta kerdhes ty ha'th pobel ol drydhy*, God has commanded thee, Moses, to take thy rod and smite the sea with it; the water will open wide, that thou mayst go well, thou and all thy people, through it. O.M. 1666. *Yn hanow Dew, ty môr glân, me a'th wŷsk gans ow guelen, uger a lês fordh dhynny*, in the name of God, thou fair sea, I strike thee with my rod ; open wide a road for us. O.M. 1677. Written also *agery, egery*, and *ygery*, qd. v.

UGY, v. subs. Is. *Y a tremyn hep dhanger, ugy Dew kêr ow cordhyé*, they shall pass without delay, (who) are worshipping the dear God. O.M. 1616. *Euch alemma gans Iudas dhe gerhas an guâs muscok ugy ow ymweryl mâp Dew*, go ye hence with Judas to fetch the crazed fellow (who) is making himself the Son of God. P.C. 962. *Yn mêdh Ihesus nyng-ugy ow mychternes yn bŷsma*, says Jesus, my kingdom is not in this world. M.C. 102. A corrupted form of *usy*, qd. v.

UHEL, adj. High, lofty, elevated. Comp. *uhellah*. Super. *uhella*. *My a'd peys, Arluth uhel*, I beseech thee, high Lord. O.M. 375. *Yn hanow an Tâs uhel, an gorhel gurên dyscudhé*, in the name of the high Father, let us uncover the ark. O.M. 1145. *Warnedhy yma gwedhen, uhel gans lues scoren*, on it there is a tree, high with many a bough. O.M. 776. *Kepar del ouch tûs uhel*, as ye are elevated men. P.C. 1716. *Gallos warnaf ny fyes, na fe y vôs grantys dhys dyworth uhella Arloth*, power over me thou wouldst not have, were it not that it was granted to thee from the most high Lord. P.C. 2189. Written also *huhel*, both being softened forms of *uchel*, qd. v.

UHELDER, s. m. Height, highness. *A Dâs Dew yn uhelder, bynyges re by neffré*, O Father God in height, blessed be thou ever. O.M. 937. *Ha hanter cans kevelyn yn-wêdh ty a wra y lês ; yn uhelder my a vyn dêk warn-ugans y vôs gurés*, and half a hundred cubits also thou shalt make its width; in height I wish it to be made thirty (cubits.) O.M. 959. A softened form of *uchelder*, qd. v.

UHELLE, v. a. To raise up on high, to exalt. Pryce. A softened form of *uchellé*, qd. v.

UIBREN, s. f. A cloud. Lhwyd, 100, thus writes *huibren*, qd. v. in the Cornish Vocabulary.

ULA, s. f. An owl. Lhwyd, 45, 99, 241. The late form of *hulé*, qd. v.

ULA, s. f. An elm. Pryce. Pl. *ulow*. Preserved in the local name *Killisullow*, a grove of elms, in St. Probus.

ULAIR, s. m. A cloak, a woman's mantle. Corn. Voc. *peplum*.

ULLIA, v. n. To howl, bark, or cry. Lhwyd, 176. Ir. *uallam, ualmhaighim*.

UM, a prefix used in composition, which reflects the action on the agent. Written also *em* and *om*, qd. v.

UMHELY, v. a. To throw one's self down, to overturn, to overthrow. Part. pass. *umhelys*. *Pan o pûr holerch an gŷdh, y tefnas un marrek del dêth an nêf war y fŷth, ef a welas golow têk, ha'n meyn umhelys yn wêdh esé a uch Ihesus whêk*, when the day was very well advanced, a soldier awoke as the sky came on his face; he saw a fair light, and the stones overthrown (that) were over Jesus sweet. M.C. 244. Written also *ommelys*, qd. v. *Râg cuvow sevel om sâf; war doer lemyn umhelaf*, for sorrow I stand upright; on the ground now I will cast myself. C.W. 88. W. *ymchwelyd*, † *ymchoelyd*.

UMMA, adv. In this place, here. *Vynytha hedré vynvy, umma nŷm gwelyth arté*, ever whilst thou livest, here thou shalt not see me again. O.M. 244. *Awos ol roweth Adam bŷs dhyn umma yn un lam ef a vŷdh kyrhys*, notwithstanding all the bounty of Adam, to us here in a trice he shall be brought. O.M. 885. Written also *omma*, qd. v.

UN, card. num. One, individual. It softens the initials of feminine nouns following, as in Welsh, and Armoric. *Yn ketella ty re wrûk, ha dheworth Urry re dhûk y un wrêk ef*, in that way thou hast acted, and from Uriah hast taken his one wife. O.M. 2245. *Onan* is also used substantively in Cornish to express the number one. *Onan yw an Tâs a nêff, arall Crist y un vaaw eff, a vŷdh a wyrchas genys, ha'n Sperys Sans yw tressa, try hag onan ow trega yn un dewsys, me a grŷs*, oue is the Father of Heaven, another Christ his one Son, (that) shall be born of a virgin ; and the Holy Ghost is the third ; three and one dwelling in one Godhead, I believe. O.M. 2662. *Kyns bôs un nôs tremenys, why a vŷdh pûr wŷr selandrys ahanaf ketep' mâp bron*, before one night be passed, ye shall be very truly offended for me, every son of the breast. P.C. 890. *Un wŷdh mar pŷdh dên marow, y spyrys, hep gow, bŷth ny dhue yn y vody*, once if man is dead, his spirit ever, without a lie, never will come into his body. P.C. 1748. *Un* is in constant

UNSEL 354 UR

use in Cornish, as in Armoric and French, for the indefinite article. *Alena y'n hombronkyas uchel war ben un menedh*, thence he led him high on top of a mountain. M.C. 16. *Clewys a'n ngl tencwen un êl ow talleth cané*, I heard on the one side an angel beginning to sing. O.M. 215. *Un sarf yn guedhen yma*, there is a serpent in the tree. O.M. 707. *My a welas yn paradys fenten râs*, ha warnydhy un wedhen, I saw in Paradise a fountain of grace, and by it a tree. O.M. 837. W. *un*. Arm. *unn, cunn, unan*. Ir. *aon, ean,* †*oen,* †*oin*. Gael. *aon*. Manx, *un, unnané*. Gr. *ἕν*. Lat. *unus*. Goth. *ains*. Sansc. *ún*.

UNCORN, s. m. An unicorn. Corn. Vocab. *unicornis*. Comp. of *un*, one, and *corn*, a horn. W. *ungorn*.

UNCOUTII, adj. Unknown, strange. *Dén uncouth*, written in the Cornish Vocabulary *den unclud*, advena, a stranger. *Yn dýdh-na te nyn wra ehan a whêl, te nyn dhy vâb, nyn dhy merch, nyn dhy dén whêl, nyn dhy môs whêl, nyn dhy lodnow, nyn dhy dén uncouth, nyn truvyth ês yn barth chy dhy darasow*, on that day thou shalt do no manner of work, thou, nor thy son, nor thy daughter, nor thy manservant, nor thy maidservant, nor thy cattle, nor thy stranger, nor any thing (that) is within thy house. *Pryce.* Ang. Sax. *uncuth*. Eng. *uncouth*.

UNDAMSI, s. m. A client, a dependent. Corn. Voc. *cliens* vel *clientulus*. This word is probably corrupt, but possibly connected with *yn dan*, under.

UNLIU, adj. Of one colour. Corn. Voc. *unus color*. Comp. of *un*, one, and *liu*, a colour. W. *unlliw*.

UNNA, adv. There, in that place. *Pryce.* Generally written *ena*, qd. v.

UNNA, pron. prep. In it. *Pryce.* Another form of *ynno*, qd. v.

UNNEC, card. num. Eleven. *Ariuth, ple 'dh ên alemma, dhyn dhe gemeres trygfa, na dheffo dén vyth gynen; ha pygyn Dew gallosek, del esen agan unnek, ha na moy gôr na benen*, Lord, where shall we go from hence, for us to take a dwelling, that not any man may come with us; and let us pray to mighty God, as we were eleven of us, and no more, man nor woman. R.D. 2395. W. *un-ardhêg*, †*undeg*. Arm. *unnek*. Ir. *aon deng*. Gael. *aon deug*. Manx, *unnaneig*. Gr. *ἕνδεκα*. Lat. *undecim*.

UNNECVES, adj. Eleventh. *Lhuyd*, 176, gives *ydnacvns*, as the latest form.

UNNIENT, s. m. An unguent, ointment. *Dworennus yn pûr brena ef êth dhe'n corf o marow gans unnient dhodho esa, ha spycis a vûr rasow*, by night in pure affection he went to the body (that) was dead, with ointment (that) he had, and spices of great virtues. M.C. 234. *Onement* and *oynment* were also used, qd. v. W. *ennaint*. Arm. *oignament*. Ir. *uinnemieint*. Lat. *unguentum*. Fr. *onguent*.

UNSEL, adj. Only, alone. Written also *unsol*. *Aban vynnyth pûp huny ladhé ol an nôr vys-ma, saw unsel ow tûs hammy, lâdh ny gansé magé ta*, since thou wilt kill every one (that is ou) the earth of this world, save only my people and me, kill us with them as well. O.M. 971. *Kynyver dên ês yn wlâs, na tra yn bŷs ow pewé, saw unsol ty ha'th flchas, gans lŷf a wrâf dhe ladhé*, as many as are in the land, or thing in the world living, save thee alone, and thy children, with a flood I will kill. O.M. 1031.

UNTYE, v. a. To anoint. *Benyn dyr vûr cheryté y box ryché, leun a yly, a uch Crist râg y untyé hy a vynnas y derry*, a woman through much charity her box rich, full of salve, over Christ to anoint him she wished to break it. M.C. 35. W. *eneinnio*.

UNVER, adj. Of one mind, unanimous, agreed. *Ef a leveris dhedhé; pÿth a vynnouch why dhe ry? ha me a ra dheuch spedyé, ow cafos Crist yredy; y fûns unver yntredhé kepar ha del wovyny*, he said to them, what are ye willing to give? and I will speed you, taking Christ forthwith; they were agreed among them, even as he asked. M.C. 39. W. *unvryd*. Arm. *unvan*.

UNYA, v. a. To make one, to unite, to join. Part. *unyys*. *Ariuth kêr, guella dhe vreys; yma tra varth wharvedhys haneth; an kêth guêl-ma yn dûr ymôns ol gurydhyys, ha'n thŷr dhe onan yw unyys, aban cthruch a le-ma*, dear lord, very good is thy judgment; a wondrous thing has happened this night; these same rods in the earth they are all rooted, and the three into one are joined, since you went from hence. O.M. 2085. W. *uno*. Arm. *unia, unani*. Gael. *aonaich*. Manx, *unnaneysey*.

UNYN, card. num. One, individual. *Del ony unyn ha try, Tâs, ha Mâb, yn Trinity*, as we are three, Father, Son, in Trinity. C.W. 26. *Me a gâth yn pûr dhefry, gordhya Dew, an lêl Drenges, ha'n Mâb gwella, ha'n Spyrys Sans, aga thry, del ŷns unyn, mc a grŷs*, I ought in very deed to worship God, the faithful Trinity, and the Son most good, and the Holy Ghost, them three, as they are one, I believe. C.W. 142. Another form is *onan*, qd. v. Arm. *unan*.

UNWYTII, adv. Once. *A Dew kêr, assoma squyth, wyn vcys a quellen unwyth an termyn dhe dhewedhé*, O dear God, I am weary, gladly would I see once the time to end. O.M. 685. *Y a wyth y vody na potré bys vynary, kyn fe yn bêdh mŷl vlydhen, na y grochen unwyth terry*, they will preserve his body, that it never decay, though it be in the grave a thousand years, nor shall his skin become broken. P.C. 3202. *Na ny vêth ôf dhe'n tâs unwyth dhe whelas govyans*, nor will I go the father once to seek forgiveness. C.W. 100. Comp. of *un*, one, and *gwŷth*, a time. W. *unwaith*.

UORDYN, s. f. Ireland. *Pryce.* W. *ywerdhon,* †*iwerdon*, the green isle. Arm. *iverdon,* †*yuerdon*. Ir. *cirin, erin*. Gael. *eircan*. Manx, *irin*. Gr. *οὐερνία, ιερνή*. Lat. *hybernia*.

UR, s. f. An hour. Pl. *urow*. *Yn ûr-ma*, at this hour, now. *Yn ûr-na*, at that hour, then. *Scon a onan a'th asow my a wra dhyso parow pûp ûr ol râg dhe weres*, forthwith from one of thy ribs, I will make to thee a mate, every hour to help thee. O.M. 101. *Râg bôs dhedhé ioy mar vrâs, ha my pûp ûr ow lesky*, for that there is to them great joy, and I always burning. O.M. 307. *Py ûr fûf vy y wythes*, what time was I his keeper? O.M. 576. *Lavar an ûr may tûth a'n nêf arté dhe'n lîr*, say the hour that thou wilt come from heaven again to the earth. R.D. 881. *Mâb Marya mûr a beyn a wodhevy yn ûr-na*, the Son of Mary much pain suffered then. M.C. 54. *Bet an ûr-ma*, (Arm. *bete an urcman,*) to this time. *Lhuyd*, 64. *Ar urow*, sometimes. 72. *Hunter ûr*, half an hour. 148. W. *awr*, pl. *oriau*. Arm. *eur*. Ir. *uair,* †*huair*. Gael. *uair*. Manx, *oor*. Gr. *ὥρα*.

Lat. *horn.* Fr. *heure.* Germ. *uhr.* Du. *uur.* Eng. *hour.* Scotch, *hoor.*

UR, v. n. He knows. *Ev a ûr,* he knoweth. *Llwyd,* 247. A late form of *wôr,* qd. v.

URAT, s. m. Ointment, salve. Corn. Voc. *unguentum.* W. *iraid.*

URE, v. a. To cover with any unctuous substance, to anoint, to embalm. Part. *urys. Me a vyn môs dhe uré ow arluth, treys ha dewlé, gans onement kêr,* I will go to anoint my Lord, feet and hands with precious ointment. P.C. 473. *Ha'm pen ol hy rum uras,* and all my head she has anointed. P.C. 526. *Na dhegouth sor yn colon worth nêb a ura ow uré,* do ye not bear anger in heart against (her) who has anointed me. P.C. 540. *Urys du yw yredy,* well embalmed he is indeed. P.C. 3203. *Nycodemus a uras corf Ihesus ha'y esely, oynment o a gymmys rôs may wethé corf heb pedry; nag onan ef ny asns heb uré a'y esely,* Nichodemus anointed the body and limbs of Jesus, the ointment was of so much virtue that it kept a corpse without putrefying; not one of his limbs he left without anointing. M.C. 235. W. *iro.*

URRIA, v. a. To worship. *Dho urria,* Llwyd, 171. A later corruption of *worria,* as that is of *wordhyé,* a mutation of *gordhyé,* qd. v.

URRIAN, s. m. The border, boundary, or limit of a country. *Pryce.* W. *or, gor-or.* Lat. *ora.* Gr. ὅρος.

US, s. m. The husk of corn, chaff. Pl. *usion.* Corn. Voc. *palea.* W. *us,* pl. *usion; eisin.* Arm. *usien.* Fr. *son,* bran.

US, v. n. Is, that is. *Kemys drûk ûs ow codhé, ha dewedhes hag avar,* so much evil is falling both late and early. O.M. 628. *Mŷns ûs yn tŷr hag yn môr, warnedhé kemer galloys,* all that is in land and in sea, over them take thou power. O.M. 69. *Pan ûs gweydh ow tesehé,* when the trees are drying. O.M. 1128. *Ens dew a'm dyscyblyon dhe'n castel ûs a ragon,* let two of my disciples go to the village that is before us. P.C. 174. *Pendra leverta a'n flechys ûs ow cané,* what sayest thou of the children that are singing ? P.C. 432. *Nêb ûs gynef ow tybry,* who is eating with me. P.C. 738. *Nag ûs fordh dhymmo, ellas, dhe vôs sylwys,* there is not a way for me, alas, to be saved. P.C. 1523. *Iosep, ûs dhyso cummyas an corf kêr dhe ancledhyas,* Joseph, is there permission to thee to bury the dear body ? P.C. 3139. *Kueth ûs y'm colon, eyhen,* sorrow is in my heart, alas. R.D. 700. *W. ys.—Ystavell Cyndhylan ys tywyll heno,* the hall of Cyndhylan is gloomy to-night. *Llywarch Hên.*

US, adv. Above. *Un Edhow a brederys, hag a leverys dhedhé, bonas pren yn dour lewlys, a us yn houl na vyé,* a Jew bethought and said to them, that there was a tree cast in the ground, that was not above in the sun. M.C. 152. *Te a'n gwêl yn corn ow thâl; gans dên pan vo convethys, worthnf ve ny dâl bôs mellyes a us nêb tra,* thou seest it in the horn of my forehead; by man when it is discovered, I must not be meddled with above anything. C.W. 118. (See also *uch.*) W. *udh.* Arm. *us.* Ir. *os, uas, †suas.* Gael. *os, suas.* Manx, *hçose, seose.* Sausc. *ut.*

USCYS, adv. Immediately, quickly, soon. *Dhe Egipt ydh ôf uskys, râk colenwel bôdh dhe vrŷs,* to Egypt I will go immediately to fulfil the will of thy mind. O.M. 1473. *My re bue ordh emlodh may 'th ên pûr sywyth; uskys na yllyn ponyé,* I have been wrestling till I was very tired, that I could not run quickly. P.C. 2510. *Marth dhym a'n deusys yma, mar uskys del dhueth omma,* there is to me a wonder of the Godhead, so swiftly as he came here. R.D. 2503. W. *csgud.* Arm. *cscuid.* Ir. *csgaidh.* Gael. *casgaidh.*

USY, v. irr. That is. *Euch, tynneuch an gasadow, usy ow cûl fals dewow, yn môs agan temple ny,* go ye drag the wretched woman, that is making falso gods, out of our temple. O.M. 2692. W. *y-sy.*

UTH, s. m. Horror, fright, terror, awfulness. *Agas clewas o pûr uth, cryé mar brâs,* to hear you was very horror, crying so greatly. R.D. 1768. *Pûr uth o clewas an cry genef orth agas gylwel,* very horror it was to hear the cry from me calling you. R.D. 2244. *Ha mŷl dén ef a wrûk dué yn dour-na rûk uth hng own,* and a thousand men he did end in that water for horror and fear. R.D. 2322. *Dhe vŷl deaul mar ny wrûk uth, marth yw gyné,* to a thousand devils if he hath not caused terror, I wonder. R.D. 2506. Written also *cuth,* qd. v. W. *uth.* Arm. *eus.* Ir. *uath.* Gael. *uamhas, † uath.*

UTHEC, adj. Horrible, frightful, terrible, awful. Written also *uthyc. Un sarf yn gwedhen yma, bêst uthek hep falladow,* there is a serpent in the tree, a horrible beast without failings. O.M. 798. *Heyl, volawch, volawcth, uthyk mûr yw dhe areth, leman worth agan gylwel,* hail, high priest, high priest, very awful is thy speech, now calling us. P.C. 954. *Ha yarow hag uthyk brâs, yn kerth gallas mês a'n bêdh,* and fierce and terribly huge, forth he went from the tomb. R.D. 531. *Uthyk yw clewas y lêf,* it is terrible to hear his voice. R.D. 2340. W. *uthyr.* Arm. *euzik.* Ir. *uathmhar.* Gael. *uamharr.*

UTHECTER, s. m. Horror, frightfulness. *Yn ûr-na whreuch pyjadow, may codhdho an mynydhyow warnouch râg cwn uthekter,* in that hour ye will make prayers that the mountains may fall on you for very horror. P.C. 2653.

UY, s. m. An egg. Corn. Voc. *ovum.* Written also *oy,* pl. *oyow,* qd. v. W. *ŵy,* pl. *wyau.* Arm. *vi, ui,* pl. *viou, uieu.* Ir. *ugh, † og.* Gael. *ubh.* Manx, *oo, ooh.* Gr. ὠόν. Lat. *ovum.* Fr. *oeuf.* Germ. *ey.* Eng. *egg.*

UYNNAS, v. a. Straightened. *Iosep dhe Gryst a uynnas y arrow ha'y dheffrech whêk, yn vaner del yn whâs, hag a's ystynnas pûr dêk,* Joseph for Christ straightened his legs and his sweet arms, in manner as usual, and stretched them out full gently. M.C. 232. This word may be read either as a variation of *ewnas,* preterite of *ewné,* qd. v., or *wynnas,* a mutation of *gwynnas,* preterite of *gwynné,* to whiten.

UYNYN, adj. One, alone. *Llwyd,* 244. Another form of *unyn,* qd. v.

UZ, s. m. Age. Pl. *uzow. Pryce. ‡Et e ûz côth,* in his old age. *Llwyd,* 244. A late form of *oys,* qd. v.

V.

This letter, sounded as in English, is a secondary in all the Celtic dialects. It represents two characters, viz.

bh, the soft mutation of *b;* and *mh*, the soft mutation of *m*. Thus C. *bara*, bread; *y vara*, his bread. W. *bara, ei vara*. Arm. *bara, he vara*. C. *mam*, a mother; *y vam*, his mother. W. *mam, ei vam*. Arm. *mamm, he vamm*. (In late Cornish it was used as in Manx, as the secondary mutation of *f;* as *fordh*, a way ; *an vordh*, the way.) In Irish and Gaelic, *bh* and *mh*, are always used as the secondary mutations of *b*, and *m;* both letters however having the sound of *v*. Thus *bean*, a woman, *bhean, (vean,)* O woman. *Muir*, sea ; *mór*, great ; *a mhuir mhor (a vuir vôr,)* the great sea. In Manx *v* is used as in Cornish, Welsh, and Armoric. Thus *bea*, life ; *e vea*, his life. *Moyrn*, pride ; *e voyrn*, his pride. *Foays*, advantage ; *nyn voays*, their advantage.

VA, s. f. A place. A mutation of *ma*, qd. v., as in *morva*, &c.

VA, pron. s. He, him. A late form of *ve*, qd. v.

VAB, s. m. A son. A mutation of *máb*, qd. v. *A váp whêk, ydhof euthys*, O sweet son, I am grieved. O.M. 1336. *Bodh dhe váp yn yn della*, the will of thy son is so. P.C. 2052.

VABM, s. f. The spleen. *Y vabm*, Llwyd, 79. A corrupted form of *vam*, a mutation of *mam*, qd. v.

VACHTETH, s. f. A virgin. A mutation of *machteth*, qd. v.

VADNA, v. n. I will. *Na vadna*, will not. Llwyd, 252. A late corruption of *vennaf*, 1 pers. s. fut. of *menny*, qd. v.

VADNA, adv. Up, above. *A vadna*. C.W. 130. A late corruption of *a van*, qd. v.

VAEZ, s. m. A boar. Pryce. A mutation of *baez*, id. qd. *buedh*, qd. v.

VAI, adj. Equal to, alike. A mutation of *mal*, qd. v.

VALLIC, adj. Fenced, walled. Pryce. *Tre-vallic ('Tre-vallack,)* the fenced town, in St. Kevern. More correctly *wallic*, being a mutation of *gwallic*, from *gwal*, a wall.

VALLOC, s. m. A flap, a valve ; the flap of the breeches. *Na lader, by my vallok, kyn fe vyth mar vrás quallok*, he shall not steal, by my flap, though he be ever so great a braggart. O.M. 2067. A mutation of *balloc*. W. *balog*. Arm. *balec*.

VALSA, v. n. It seems. *Me a wêl un gwedhan, marow sêch hy a valsa*, I see a tree, dead withered it seems to be. C.W. 130. Another form of *fulsé*, qd. v.

VAM, s. f. A mother. A mutation of *mam*, qd. v.

VAN, adj. That which is highest, foremost. A mutation of *ban*, qd. v. *My a welas hy gurydhyow bys yn yffarn dywenys, yn mysk múr a tewolgow ; ha'y branchys yn van tyeys bys yn nef uhel golow*, I saw its roots even into hell descending, in midst of great darkness, and its branches growing up even to heaven high in light. O.M. 785. *An Tás Dew, Arluth a van, re'm gorré dhe gosoleth*, the Father God, Lord above, may he put me to rest. O.M. 857. *Me u'n dreha arté, kyns pen trydydh, tcké ages kyns y van*, I will build it again, before the end of three days, fairer up than before. P.C. 348. "To make a *Van*, is to take a handful of the ore or tinstuff, and bruise, wash, and cleanse it on a shovel ; then by a peculiar motion of the shovel, to shake and throw forth upon the point of it almost all the ore that is freed from waste. This operation being repeated, the ore is collected and reserved ; and thence they form an estimate how many tons of copper ore, or how many hundred weight of block tin, may be produced out of one hundred sacks of that work or stuff of which the *Van* is made." Polwhele. Cf. Fr. *avant*.

VANAH, s. m. A monk. A mutation of *manah*, id. qd. *manach*, qd. v.

VANER, s. m. A banner. A mutation of *baner*, qd. v.

VANNAF, v. n. I will. *Ny vannaf aga guthyll, war ow fydh*, I will not make them, on my faith. M.C. 155. More correctly *vennaf*, being a mutation of *mennaf*, 1 pers. s. fut. of *menny*, qd. v.

VANNETH, s. f. A blessing. A mutation of *banneth*, qd. v.

VARA, s. m. Bread. *Me a ter torth a vara*, I will break a loaf of bread. R.D. 1314. A mutation of *bara*, qd. v.

VARCHVRAN, s. f. A raven. A mutation of *marchvran*, qd. v.

VAREN, s. f. A branch. A mutation of *baren*, qd. v.

VARHA, s. f. A market. ‡ *Varha Dzhou*, Market Jew. Llwyd, 252. A corruption of *varhas*, a mutation of *marhas*, qd. v.

VAROGETH, v. a. To ride. A mutation of *marogeth*, qd. v.

VAROGYON, s. m. Horsemen, soldiers. *En varogyon, pan glewas Pylat ow cows yn della*, the soldiers, when they heard Pilate speak so. M.C. 251. A mutation of *marogyon*, id. qd. *marogyon*, pl. of *marreg*, or *marheg*, qd. v.

VAROW, adj. Dead. *Cryst a fue dre galarow yn grows pren gurys púr varow*, Christ was through pains on the cross tree made very dead. R.D. 963. A mutation of *marow*, qd. v.

VARTH, s. m. A wonder. *Múr varth anibus dyogel*, a great wonder is surely to me. O.M. 371. *Henna múr varth vyé*, that would be a great wonder. P.C. 1728. A mutation of *marth*, qd. v.

VARTHEGYON, s. m. Wonders. *A Arluth kêr bynygos, yma dhum múr varthegyon*, O dear blessed Lord, there are to me many wonders. P.C. 770. Written also *varthogyon*. *Ow arluth mychtern Salmon, yma múr a varthogyon a'n kêth gyst-ma warvedhys*, my lord king Solomon, there are much of wonders by this same beam wrolight. O.M. 2546. A mutation of *marthegyon*, one of the plurals of *marthus*, qd. v.

VARTHUSEC, adj. Wonderful. A mutation of *marthusec*, qd. v.

VARWEN, v. n. I did die, I should die. A mutation of *marwen*, 1 pers. s. imperf. of *marwel*, qd. v.

VARWO, v. n. He shall have died. *Neffré yn dour hedré bo, uy dhue dresto na varwo gour, grueh, na bêst*, over in the water while he is, there will not come over it that dies not, man, woman, or beast. R.D. 2226. A mutation of *marwo*, 3 pers. s. 2 fut. of *marwel*, qd. v.

VAS, adj. Good. *Ol an dús vás*, all the good people. O.M. 814. A mutation of *más*, qd. v. The oldest form was *vat*, as *bennen vat*, in Corn. Voc. *matrona*, lit. a good woman.

VAW, s. m. A son, a boy. *Ty ha'th vavo, na strech lemmyn*, thou and thy boy, stay not now. R.D. 1992. A mutation of *maw*, qd. v.

VAY, s. m. A kiss. A mutation of *bay*, qd. v.

VAYLE, v. a. To wrap, to swathe. A mutation of *maylé*, qd. v.

VE, s. m. A burden, a load. *Kymer dhymmo vê kunys, gans lowan bedhens strothys, ha war dhe keyn doga ef,* take thou for me a load of fuel, with rope let it be bound, and on thy back carry it. O.M. 1296. *Otté omma vê kunys, ha fast ef gynef kelmys,* behold here a load of fuel, and it fast bound by me. O.M. 1299. A mutation of *bê,* qd. v.

VE, pron. s. I, me. *Tan, resyf dheworthyf ve ow degé, ha'm offryn gulán,* take, receive thou from me my tithe, and my clean offering. O.M. 503. *Kepar ha del veua ve an pwra lader yn pow,* as if I were the veriest thief in the country. M.C. 74. A mutation of *me,* qd. v.

VE, pron. subs. He, him, it. *Dro ve dhymmo dysempys, ha my a ra y dybry,* bring thou it to me immediately, and I will eat it. O.M. 247. *Kepar del fuvé dremmas,* like as he was a very good man. O.M. 864. *Otté ve musurys da, dên yn bês ny'n musyr guel,* behold it well measured ; no man in the world will measure it better. O.M. 2513. *Pysouch may fe ve evys,* pray ye that it may be drunk. P.C. 828. Another form of *e, ef,* generally used after the verb, and pronominal prepositions. W. *ve.*

VE, v. s. He was. A mutation of *be,* qd. v. 3 pers. s. pret. of *bós.*

VE, v. He may be. *El a'n nef ûf, danfenys rág guythé na ve ledhys dhe váp Ysac,* an angel from heaven I am, sent to preserve that be not killed thy son Isaac. O.M. 1373. *Dhodho ny ylleuch gûl drók, hedré ve y gys golok,* ye will not be able to do harm to him, while he is in your sight. R.D. 1915. A mutation of *be,* qd. v. 3 pers. s. subj. of *bós.* W. *vai,* † *vei.* Arm. *ve. Guell ve dif meruell,* it would be better for me to die. Buh. Noun, 40, 7.

VEA, v. subs. He would be. A mutation of *bea,* qd. v.

VEADZHEN, v. subs. I had been. ‡ *Me veadzhen,* Llwyd, 243. A corrupt form of *veasen,* a mutation of *beasen,* 1 pers. s. plup. of *bós.*

VEAN, v. subs. I should be. A mutation of *bean,* qd. v.

VEAN, adj. Little. *Pryce.* *Tre-vean,* the little town, in St. Kevern. Written also *vyan,* qd. v.

VEDN, v. n. He will. ‡ *Me vedn cens,* I would rather. Llwyd, 84. ‡ *Na vedn e nevra,* he never will. 101. ‡ *E vedn gys gil saw,* it will cure you. 244. A corrupt form of *ven,* a mutation of *men,* 3 pers. s. fut. of *menny.*

VEDO, v. n. Ye will. ‡ *Dry vedo hwi gil,* what will ye do ? Llwyd, 244. A later corruption of *vedno,* as that is of *vennouch,* a mutation of *mennouch,* 2 pers. pl. fut. of *menny.*

VEDH, s. m. A grave. *Dún, goryn y gorf yn vêdh,* let us come, let us put his body in (the) grave. O.M. 2367. A mutation of *bêdh,* qd. v.

VEDHI, v. subs. Be thou. *Na porth own vŷth, na vêdh trest, rág me a vŷdh genes prest, orth dhe weres yn púp le,* bear not fear ever, be not sad, for I will be with thee ready, helping thee in every place. O.M. 1467. A mutation of *bêdh,* 2 pers. s. imp. of *bós.* Written also *bŷdh, vŷdh.*

VEDHI, v. subs. He shall be. *Del y's brewaf yn dan gên, kekyfrys kŷc ha crohen, del vêdh luen a bodredhes,* as I shall strike her under the chin, flesh and skin also, as it shall be full of bruises. O.M. 2714. A mutation of *bêdh,* qd. v. 3 pers. s. fut. of *bós.*

VEDHAF, v. subs. I shall or will be. *My ny won leverel prák gans púp na vedhaf ledhys,* I know not how to tell why by every one I shall not be slain. O.M. 806. *Yn púp teller, dhym may fo rês, prest hep danger, vedhaf parys,* in every place, that there may be need for me, soon, without delay, I shall be ready. O.M. 1910. A mutation of *bedhaf,* qd. v.

VEDHE, v. subs. He would be. *Na fyllys, a Arluth da, na fout bythqueth ny gen lue ; yn agan ethom púp tra púp ûr parys dhyn vedhé,* it was not wanting, O good Lord, there never was default to us ; in our need every thing always would be ready for us. P.C. 918. Written also *vedha. Moycha dhodho dhók a wre, henna vedha an guella gués,* whoso did most evil to him, that one would be the best fellow. M.C. 112. A mutation of *bedha,* qd. v.

VEDHEN, v. s. I should be. *Ef a yrhys dhym kyrhas a mount Tabor gueel a rás, ma'm vedhen dredhé sylwans,* he ordered me to fetch from Mount Tabor rods of grace, that I might have salvation through them. O.M. 1958. A mutation of *bedhen,* id. qd. *bedhan,* qd. v.

VEDHENS, v. subs. They shall be. *Del lavaraf dhys, Moyses, war dhe lerch vedhens rewlys,* as I say to thee, Moses, after thee they shall be ruled. O.M. 1434. Written also *vedhons. Tús, venvnes, ha flechys, omma ny vedhons gesys,* men, women, and children, here shall not be left. O.M. 1589. *Marow vedhons kyns vytyn,* they shall be dead before morning. O.M. 1644. A mutation of *bedhens,* 3 pers. pl. fut. of *bós,* qd. v.

VEDHO, adj. Drunken. A mutation of *medho,* qd. v.

VEDHO, v. subs. He shall be. *An haccré mernans a vo, war ow fuy, ty a vedho,* the most horrid death that may be, on my faith, thou shalt have. R.D. 2034. ‡ *Rág dowt na vedho,* lost there be. Llwyd, 250. A mutation of *bedho,* 3 pers. s. 2 fut. of *bós.*

VEDHOUCH, v. subs. Be ye. A mutation of *bedhouch,* 2 pers. pl. imp. of *bós,* qd. v.

VEDHY, v. a. To drown. A mutation of *bedhy,* qd. v.

VEDHYN, v. subs. We shall be. *Ellas, lemyn pendra wrên ? marow vedhyn kettep pen,* alas, now what shall we do ? dead we shall be every head. O.M. 1655. A mutation of *bedhyn,* qd. v.

VEDHYTH, v. subs. Thou shalt be. A mutation of *bedhyth,* qd. v.

VEEN, s. m. Edge, point. *Ha'y veen mon, ha'y scorennow my a vyn trehy tennow,* and out of its slender top, and its branches I will cut beams. O.M. 2444. A mutation of *meen,* id. qd. *mîn,* qd. v.

VEF, v. subs. I was. *Na vythqueth pan vêf formys,* nor ever when I was formed. O.M. 616. *Ny welys tekké bythqueth aban vêf genys,* I have not seen fairer ever since I was born. O.M. 1731. A mutation of *bêf,* written also *buf, luef,* 1 pers. s. preterite of *bós.*

VEF, v. subs. I should be. *Ellas, a váp, mychtern y'th trón, ellas guelas tol y'th colon, marow na vêf,* alas ! O son ! King on thy throne ! alas ! to see a hole in thy heart ! that I should not be dead. P.C. 3171. A mutation of *bêf,* qd. v.

VEFE, v. subs. He was. *Lavar dhym, del y'm kerry, pa'n vernans a'n gevé ef, ha fetel vefé ledhys,* tell me, as thou lovest me, what death had he, and now was he killed ? O.M. 2220. Comp. of *ve,* was, and *fe,* id. qd. *ve,* he.

VEISDER, s. f. A window. A mutation of *beisder*, qd. v.

VEL, adv. Like, as, than. ‡ *Cy guêr vel an guelz*, as green as grass. *Kens vel*, rather than. *Moy vel*, more than. Llwyd, 248. A mutation of *mel*, or as always written *mal*, qd. v. W. *vel*. Arm. *evel*.

VELEN, adj. Yellow. Llwyd, 143. A mutation of *melen*, qd. v.

VELEN, adj. Brutal, cruel. A mutation of *melen*, qd. v.

VELHA, adv. Further. ‡ *Na velha*, no further. Llwyd, 251. A corrupted form of *fella*, the aspirate mutation of *pella*, qd. v.

VELLIN, s. f. A mill. A mutation of *melin*, qd. v.

VELLOW, s. m. Joints. A mutation of *mellow*, plural of *mâl*, qd. v.

VEMA, v. subs. I was. *Pardell vema ungrassyes, lemyn ydhoma plagys*, as I was ungracious, now I am plagued. C.W. 114. Comp. of *ve*, was, and *ma* for *me*, I.

VEN, s. m. A stone. *A fue ancledhyys, hag yn bêdh a vên gorrys*, who was buried, and placed in a tomb of stone. R.D. 2. A mutation of *mên*, qd. v.

VEN, adj. Strong. A mutation of *men*, qd. v.

VEN, s. f. A woman. *Pûr luen yma dhym ow whans, a'n ven cowethes ordnys*, very full there is to me my desire, of the woman ordained a help-mate. O.M. 92. A mutation of *ben*, id. qd. *benen*, qd. v.

VEN, v. subs. I may be. *Neffré ef dhe dhasserchy me ny fynnaf y grygy, bew hedré vên*, that he ever rose again I will not believe it, as long as I may be alive. R.D. 1046. A mutation of *bên*, 1 pers. s. subj. of *bôs*. Arm. *bén*, *vén*. *Gant oun ha poan na vên daffnct*, with fear and pain that I may not be condemned. Buh. Nom. 162, 6.

VEN, v. subs. We may be. *A Ihesu Cryst mychtern nêf, me a'th pŷs, clew agan léf, gans drôk tra na vên temptys*, O Jesus Christ, king of heaven, I pray thee, hear our voice, with evil thing that we may not be tempted. R.D. 2423. A mutation of *bên*, qd. v.

VEN, v. n. He will. *Me a ven*, I will. *Mi ven môs*, I will go. *E ven môs*, he will go. *Mi ven gavas*, I will have. Llwyd, 246, 247. A mutation of *men*, 3 pers. s. fut. of *menny*.

VENARY, adj. Continually, for ever. *Awos ol dhe fâth ha'th sôn, genen ny y fŷdh dhe thrôn yn ponvotter venary*, notwithstanding all thy faith and noise, with us shall be thy throne in trouble for ever. O.M. 898. *Drefen luen ty dhum servyé, ow crês a fit venary*, because thou hast served me fully, my peace thou shalt have for ever. O.M. 1020. *Mar ny voráf vy nag Aron aga ledya venary*, if I nor Aaron shall not lead them ever. O.M. 1876. A mutation of *benary*, qd. v.

VENDZHA, v. n. He had rather. ‡ *Me vendzha kens*, I had rather. Llwyd, 127. ‡ *Lebmen Dzhuan e na vendzha servia na velha, bez e vendzha moz teua dha e urêg*, now John would not serve any longer, but would go towards his wife. 251. A mutation of *mendzha*, a corrupt form of *mensé*, 3 pers. s. plup. of *menny*.

VENEDH, s. m. A mountain. *Dhe vâp Ysac a geryth, y offrynné reys yw dhys war venedh a dhysquedhaf dhyso gy*, thy son Isaac, (whom) thou lovest, it is necessary for thee to offer him upon a mountain (which) I will shew to thee. O.M. 1281. A mutation of *menedh*, qd. v.

VENEGES, adj. Blessed, holy. *Dŷsk dhe 'skyggyow quyk dhe vês, sevel war tŷr veneges a wrêth, del lavaraf dhys*, take off thy shoes quickly; stand on holy ground thou dost, as I tell thee. O.M. 1407. *A Dâs, veneges re by*, O Father, blessed be thou. O.M. 2023. A mutation of *beneges*, qd. v.

VENEN, s. f. A female, a woman. *Râg colé orth un venen gulân ef re gollas an plâs*, for listening to a woman he has clean lost the place. O.M. 919. *Bynyges re bo an prŷs may fe a venen genys*, blessed be the time that he was born of woman. R.D. 153. A mutation of *benen*, qd. v.

VENENES, s. f. Women. *An venenes ha'n flechys vedhens yn mês exilyys*, the women and the children shall be banished out. O.M. 1575. *Tûs, venenes, ha flechys, ymôns omma dynythys*, men, women, and children, they are come here. O.M. 1611. A mutation of *benenes*, pl. of *benen*, qd. v.

VENNAF, v. n. I will. *Me ny vennaf cafus lé yn guyryoneth*, I will not take less in truth. P.C. 594. A mutation of *mennaf*, 1 pers. s. fut. of *menny*, qd. v.

VENNAS, v. n. To will. *Ty a aswon an scryptor, ty dhe vennas sowthanas lemmyn yn mês a pûp for*, thou knowest the Scripture, that thou shouldst wish Satan now out of every path. P.C. 2417. A mutation of *mennas*, id. qd. *menny*, qd. v.

VENNATH, s. f. A blessing. *Y vennath dheuch yn tyen, keffrys gorryth ha benen*, his blessing to you wholly, men and women likewise. O.M. 2836. A mutation of *bennath*, qd. v.

VENNI, v. n. Thou wilt. *Ti a venni*, Llwyd, 246. A mutation of *menni*, 2 pers. s. fut. of *menny*, qd. v.

VENNO, v. n. Ye will. ‡ *Po na venno hui gil an dellana moi*, if ye will do so no more. Llwyd, 249. A mutation of *menno*, a late form of *mennouch*, 2 pers. pl. fut. of *menny*, qd. v.

VENNYN, v. n. We will. *Na ken mychtern ny vennyn ys Cesar caffos neffré*, no other king than Cæsar we will not have ever. M.C. 148. A mutation of *mennyn*, 1 pers. pl. fut. of *menny*, qd. v.

VENOUCH, adj. Frequent. *En venouch*, often. Llwyd, 249. A mutation of *menouch*, qd. v.

VENS, v. subs. They should be. A mutation of *bêns*, qd. v.

VENSEN, v. n. I would. *Ellas, râk y gallarow, vensen ow bones marow yn della y vôdh a pe*, alas, for his sorrows! I would that I had died, if so it were his will. P.C. 3167. A mutation of *mensen*, 1 pers. s. plup. of *menny*, qd. v.

VENTA, v. n. Thou wilt. *Drôk yw gyné, na venta kammen trylé yn maner têk*, I am sorry, that thou wilt not turn at all into a fair manner. P.C. 1293. *Pendra ny venté keusel*, why wilt thou not speak? P.C. 1775. A mutation of *menta*, qd. v.

VENTON, s. f. A well. Pryce. *Venton-vez*, the outer well, in St. Peran Sabulo. A mutation of *fenton*, qd. v.

VENY, v. subs. We may be. *Lavar dhymmo, cowyth mâs, py ûr â tûs dh'y gerchas, ha guet na veny tollys*, tell me, good fellow, what hour shall men go to fetch him, and take care that we be not deceived. P.C. 604. *A Dhew a néf dhe pysy a luen colon, guerres ny, rag y'n veny vylyny gans Pharow, yw mylyges*, O God of heaven, I pray thee with full heart, help us, that we may not have villainy from Pharaoh, (that) is accursed. O.M. 1609. *Lemman na veny ledhys nyng-es fordh dhe om-*

tecthé, now that we may not be killed there is not a way to keep ourselves. M.C. 245. Comp. of *vén*, a mutation of *bén*, 1 pers. pl. subj. of *bós*, and *ny*, we.

VENYS, adj. Small, little. A mutation of *menys*, qd. v.

VENYTHA, adv. Ever, for ever. *Arloth, Dew a'n nêf, an Tâs, kepar del ôs luen a râs, venytha gordhyys re by*, Lord, God of heaven, the Father, as thou art full of grace, for ever be thou worshipped. O.M. 107. *Banneth an Tâs ragas bo, hag ef prest ragas gwytho venytha yn cosoleth*, the blessing of the Father be on thee, and may it always preserve thee for ever in rest. O.M. 1725. A mutation of *benytha*, qd. v.

VER, adj. Short. *Me a wra y ascusié mar ver del alla dên vŷth*, I will excuse him as soon as any man can. P.C. 2212. *Gura gueres dhym a ver spys, del ôs sylwyas*, do help to me in a short space, as thou art Saviour. R.D. 1719. A mutation of *ber*, qd. v.

VER, adj. Great, big, large. *Squyth ôf dre vêr lafuryé*, tired I am through great labouring. O.M. 2040. *Ny vew dre vêr lavarow*, he will not live through great words. R.D. 986. *Porth yfarn me a torras, hag a dhrôs lyes enef a vêr dhrôk, tervyns, ha câs*, the gate of hell I have broken, and have brought many souls from great evil, tempest, and torment. R.D. 2576. A mutation of *mêr*, qd. v.

VERAS, v. a. To see, to behold. *Dûn ny dhe veras soon war an wonesugy*, let us come to look immediately on the workmen. O.M. 2326. A mutation of *meras*, qd. v.

VERH, s. m. A horse. *Rên verh*, horse mane. *Buzl verh*, horse dung. Llwyd, 242. A mutation of *merh*, qd. v.

VERN, s. m. Concern, sorrow, grief, regret. *Râg dhe salugy ny vern*, for to salute is no harm. P.C. 2126. *Ha'y lathé travyth ny vern*, and to kill him there is no regret. P.C. 2224. A mutation of *bern*, qd. v.

VERNANS, s. m. Death. *Lavar dhym, del y'm kerry, pa'n vernans a'n gevé ef*, tell me, as thou lovest me, what death did he meet with. O.M. 2219. A mutation of *mernans*, qd. v.

VEROW, v. n. He shall or will die. *Ty a verow cowal, awos dhe dhew, na'y vestry*, thou shalt die entirely, notwithstanding thy God or his power. O.M. 2737. A mutation of *merow*, 3 pers. s. fut. of *merwel*, qd. v.

VERTHURYE, v. a. To martyr. A mutation of *merthuryé*, qd. v.

VERWEL, v. n. To die. A mutation of *merwel*, qd. v.

VERWYS, v. n. He died. *An profus Ihesus dampnyas dhe vês gorrys yn grous pren; hag yn by ef a verwys*, the prophet Jesus he condemned to be put on the crosstree; and upon it he died. R.D. 1807. A mutation of *merwys*, 3 pers. s. preter. of *merwel*, qd. v.

VERYS, v. n. I saw. *Hag yn templis pan verys, y lyskys dhum dyscyblon*, and in temples when I saw, I taught my disciples. P.C. 1257. A mutation of *merys*, 1 pers. s. preter. of *meras*, qd. v.

VES, s. m. A field. *A vês*, without. *Dhe vês*, away. *A vês hag agy yn ta gans pêk bedhens stanchurys*, without and within well with pitch let them be staunched. O.M. 953. *Gallas an glaw dhe vês gulân*, the rain is clean gone away. O.M. 1097. *Dŷsk dhe 'skyggyow quyk dhe vês*, take off thy shoes quickly. O.M. 1406. A mutation of *mês*, qd. v.

VES, v. subs. Thou wast. *Te a wodhyé dhe honon, pe dre gen ré vês guarnys*, didst thou know it of thyself, or by others wast thou warned? M.C. 101. *Yn medh an lader arall, drôk dhên ôs, kepar del vês*, said the other thief, thou art a bad man, as thou hast been. M.C. 192. *Yn pûb otham a vês-ta, ef a wra dha succra*, in every necessity thou mayest be in, he will help thee. C.W. 140. *Ty a vesté*, thou hast been. Llwyd, 245. A mutation of *bês*, qd. v.

VESGA, adv. Ever. ‡ *Ni vesga*, never. Llwyd, 240. A mutation of *besga*, qd. v.

VESTER, s. m. A master. A mutation of *mester*, qd. v.

VESTRY, s. m. Power. A mutation of *mestry*, qd. v.

VETTYN, s. m. Morning. *Kyns vettyn*, before day. Llwyd. 230. A mutation of *mettyn*, or *metin*, qd. v.

VETH, adv. Ever. *Ni ôr dên vêth*, no man at all knows. Llwyd, 244. A mutation of *bêth*, qd. v.

VEVA, v. subs. He was. *Gwêf vŷth pan veva genys a dor y vam dhe'n bŷs-ma*, woe to him when he was born from his mother's womb to this world. M.C. 43. Comp. of *ve*, a mutation of *be*, was, and *ve*, he.

VEUCH, v. subs. Ye may be. *Pan veuch agey dhe'n cyté, why a dhyerlyn vcharré dên ow tôn pycher dour glân*, when ye are within the city, ye will meet soon a man bearing a pitcher of clean water. P.C. 627. *Ila gynef y tanfonas y te dheuch pare veuch vodr*, and by me he sent that he would come to you, as ye may be aware. R.D. 914. *Euch, whyleuch dhymmo Pilat; godhfydhcuch ma na veuch bad; tûs ôch a brŷs*, go seek for me Pilate; see that ye be not mad; ye are men of account. R.D. 1774. A mutation of *beuch*, 2 pers. pl. subj. of *bôs*.

VEUCHE, v. n. He may live. *Gor dhe gledhé yn y goyn, dhe Pedyr Crist a yrchys, râg dre gledhé a veuché, dre gledhé y fŷdh ledhys*, put thy sword into its sheath, Christ commanded Peter, for (he that) lives by sword, by sword shall be slain. M.C. 72. A mutation of *beuché*, 3 pers. s. subj. of a verb, whose root would agree with W. *buch, buchedh*. Arm. *buhez, buez*.

VEUR, adj. Great. A mutation of *meur*, qd. v.

VEVE, v. subs. I was. *Why re dhueth dhym gans arvow, gans fustow, ha clydhydhyow, kepar ha pan vevé vy an purê lader yn pow*, ye have come to me with arms, with staves and swords, as if I were the veriest thief in the land. P.C. 1773.

VEW, adj. Living, alive. *Nyns-ûs yn guêl nag yn prâs tûs vew saw ny, my a greys*, there are not in field nor in meadow men living, except us, I believe. O.M. 1152. *Yn vew*, alive. Llwyd, 230. A mutation of *bew*, qd. v.

VEW, v. n. He will live. *Ny vew dre vêr lavarow*, he will not live through many words. R.D. 986. *Saw ef ny vew, gâs dhe sôn*, but he is not alive, leave off thy noise. R.D. 1010. A mutation of *bew*, 3 pers. s. fut. of *bewé*, qd. v.

VEWAS, v. n. He has lived. *My re vewas termyn hŷr*, I have lived a long time. O.M. 2345. A mutation of *bewas*, 3 pers. s. preter. of *bewé*, qd. v.

VEWE, v. n. To live. *Adam, ke yn mês a'n wlâs, troha ken pow dhe vewé*, Adam, go out of the country, towards another land to live. O.M. 344. A mutation of *bewé*, qd. v.

VEWHE, v. n. He may live. *Sawyé pûp echen clefyon a veuché yn bewnans da*, he cured every sort of sick persons, (that) live in good life. P.C. 3110. A softened form of *veuché*, qd. v.

VEWNANS, s. m. Life. *Dour, may fêns y dysehys, a vewnans ry dedhé gura,* that they may be refreshed, the water of life do thou give to them. O.M. 1834. *Ef a leverys yn wêdh, try dêdh wogé môs yn bêdh, dhe vewnans y tasserhy,* he said also, three days after going into the grave, to life he would rise again. P.C. 1747. A mutation of *bewnans,* qd. v.

VEWO, v. n. He shall have lived. *Yn levyr yma scrifys, dre cledhé nêp a vewo, ef a vyru dredho,* in a book it is written (he that) shall have lived by the sword, he shall die by it. P.C. 1158. A mutation of *bewo,* 3 pers. s. 2 fut. of *bewé,* qd. v.

VEWSE, v. n. He had lived. *I beyn o mar grêff ha tyn caman na ylly bewé heb dascor y eneff gwyn; bythqueth yn lán re vewsé,* his pain was so strong and keen that he could not live any way without parting with his pure soul; ever clean he had lived. M.C. 204. A mutation of *bewsé,* 3 pers. s. pluperf. of *bewé,* qd. v.

VEYDII, v. subs. He shall or will be. *Râg orty ty dhe golé, mgl vâp mam a veydh damneys,* because thou hearkenedst to her, a thousand mother's sons shall be damned. O.M. 324. *A vâp ny dâl keles man; an pyth a dhue gwelis veydh,* O son, concealment avails nought; the thing (that) is coming will be seen. O.M. 854. A mutation of *beydh,* id. qd. *bydh,* 3 pers. s. fut. of *bôs.*

VEYF, v. subs. I may be. *Arluth, golhy mara qurêth ow treys, dhym y flyé mêth hedré veyf byw,* Lord, if thou wilt wash my feet, to me it would be a shame as long as I may be alive. P.C. 847. *Me a wra prest hep ynny, hedré veyf bew yn bys-ma,* I will do ever without denial, as long as I may be alive in this world. P.C. 1020. A mutation of *beyf,* 1 pers. s. subj. of *bôs.*

VEYN, s. m. Stones. *Ena yn wêdh y torras en wcyn o crêff ha culys,* there also the stones broke (that) were strong and hard. M.C. 209. A mutation of *meyn,* plur. of *maen,* qd. v.

VEYN, v. subs. We may be. *Ol del vynny, Arluth kêr, my a wra yn pûp tyller, hedré veyn bew yn bys-ma,* all as thou wishest, dear Lord, I will do in every place, as long as we may be alive in this world. P.C. 115. A mutation of *beyn,* 1 pers. pl. subj. of *bôs.*

VEYN, v. subs. We were. *Marrak arall a gowsas, govy vyth pan veyn genys, tru, a Dhu, elhas, elhas, guns un huyn re bên tullys,* another soldier said, woe is me, when we were born! Sad, O God, alas, alas, by a sleep we have been deceived. M.C. 246. A mutation of *beyn,* id. qd. *buen,* 1 pers. pl. preter. of *bôs.*

VEYS, s. m. The world. *Râk synsy glaw a wartha, dhe'n nôr veys may fe dyllys,* to hold the rain above, that it may be dropped to the earth of the world. O.M. 24. *Guyn veys a quellen an gydh,* happy should I see the day. O.M. 1012. *Hag a formyas nêf ha'n veys,* and made heaven and the earth. O.M. 1507. A mutation of *beys,* qd. v.

VEYS, v. subs. He shall or will be. *My ny dorraf bys vycken an acord ûs lemyn gureys yntré my ha lynneth dên; bys vynytha ef a veys,* I will not break for ever the agreement (that) is now made between me and the race of man; for ever it shall be. O.M. 1242. *Ty a dhebbar en dha whrys dhêth vara, pûr wŷr nefra, erna veys arta treyles a'n kêth doer, kyns a wrugnf,* thou shalt in thy sweat eat thy bread, very truly ever, until thou shalt be turned again to the same earth, I first made thee. C.W. 70. Another form of *veydh,* qd. v.

VI, pron. s. I, me. *Ma ko dho vi,* I remember. Lhwyd, 138. *Dho vi, dhymmo vi,* to me; *gen y vi,* with me. 244. A mutation of *mi,* qd. v.

VIA, v. subs. He should be. ‡ *Na vía ragoh huei, nei a vía tiz oll dizurêyz,* were it not for you, we should be all lost people. Lhwyd, 252. A mutation of *bia,* id. qd. *byé,* 3 pers. s. subj. of *bôs.*

VICCEN, adv. Ever, for ever. *My ny dorraf bys vycken an acord ûs lemyn gureys yntré my ha lynneth dên,* I will not break for ever the agreement (that) is now made between me and the race of man. O.M. 1239. *Nynsus gorryth na benen byth wel curyl bys vycken a lavarré,* there is not a male or female any better advice, to eternity, (who) can speak. R.D. 421. *Hag yn ngl bys vicken an record a vydh heb fall pûr wŷr kevys,* and in one (side) for ever the record will be without fail very truly found. C.W. 160.

VIL, card. num. A thousand. *Dhynny gueres ny dâl man; mgl vŷl dyaul a vyé guan er-y-byn ef,* nothing avails to help us; a million devils would be weak against him. R.D. 132. *Dhe vŷl draul mar ny wrûk uth, marth yw gyné,* to a thousand devils if he caused not terror, I am surprised. R.D. 2506. A mutation of *mil,* qd. v.

VIR, v. a. He shall or will see. A mutation of *mir,* 3 pers. s. fut. of *weres,* qd. v.

VIRAS, v. a. To see. *Corf Cryst dasserhys mars yw, môs dhe vyras,* the body of Christ if it is risen, go to see. R.D. 603. *Do viras,* to behold. Lhwyd, 230. A mutation of *miras,* qd. v.

VIS, s. m. A month. A mutation of *mís,* qd. v.

VLEDHEN, s. f. A year. *Mara pedhaf bew vledhen, my a'n talvyth dhywch,* if I shall be alive a year, I will pay it to you. O.M. 2386. ‡ *Trei pens a vledhan,* three pounds a year. Lhwyd, 251. A mutation of *bledhen,* qd. v.

VLEDHYNNOW, s. m. Years. A mutation of *bledhynnow,* plural of *bledhen,* qd. v.

VLEWENNOW, s. m. Hair. A mutation of *blewennow,* pl. of *blewen,* qd. v.

VLONOGETH, s. m. The will. *Dha vlonogeth rebo gwrys,* thy will be done. C.W. 154. A later form of *volnogeth,* qd. v.

VLYDHEN, s. f. A year. *Bys pen vlydhen,* till the end of a year. R.D. 72. *Kyn fe yn bêdh mgl vlydhen,* though it may be in the grave a thousand years. P.C. 3201. A mutation of *blydhen,* id. qd. *bledhen,* qd. v.

VO, v. subs. He may be. *Hen yw dŷdh a bowesva dhe pûp dên a vo sylwys,* this is a day of rest to every man (that) may be saved. O.M. 146. *Pan vo termyn dynythys,* when the time is come. O.M. 813. *Me a'n gura, pepenak vo,* I will do it, whatever it be. P.C. 1356. A mutation of *bo,* qd. v.

VOCH, s. m. The cheek. A mutation of *bôch,* qd. v.

VOCHESEGION, adj. Poor. A mutation of *bochesegion,* pl. of *bochesog,* qd. v.

VODH, s. m. The will. A mutation of *bôdh,* qd. v.

VOH, s. f. The cheek. A mutation of *bôh,* qd. v.

VOHODZHAC, adj. Poor. ‡ *An bohyl vohodzhak,* the poor people. Lhwyd, 230. A mutation of *bohodzhac,* a late corruption of *bohosog.*

VOHOSUGION, adj. Poor. *Gwragedh vohosugion,* poor

women. *Llwyd*, 243. A mutation of *bohosugion*, pl. of *bohosog*, qd. v.

VOLAVETH, s. m. High priest. *Heyl volaveth, volaveth, uthyk mûr yw dhe areth, leman worth agan gylwel*, hail, high priest, high priest, very terrible is thy speech, now calling us. P.C. 953. *Volaveth, we buth y com*, high priest, we be come. P.C. 1351. *Heil volaveth syr iustis, a wetta ny devethys warbarth ha'n kensa galow*, hail, high priest, sir magistrate, behold us come together with the first call. P.C. 2040.

VOLDER, s. m. An order, command. *Ihesus a ve hombronkis, ha war y lyrch mûr a lu dre volder tebel Iustis, râg y chanyé kyn 'dho Du*, Jesus was conducted, and much crowd after him by order of an evil Justice, to chase him though he was God. M.C. 163.

VOLNOGETH, s. m. The will. *Râg Dew a'n dysguedhas dheuch, ha'y volnogeth yw henna*, for God has declared him to you, and his will is that. O.M. 2352. Written also *volnegeth*. *Lavar dhymmo pendra yw dhe volnegeth*, tell me what is thy will. P.C. 957. *Dhe volnegeth re bo gurês*, thy will be done. P.C. 1072. A mutation of *bolnogeth* or *bolnegeth*, another form of *bolungeth*, qd. v.

VOLUNGETH, s. m. The will. *Herwydh y volungeth ef y fýdh gurfs*, according to his will it shall be done. O.M. 1320. *Yn pûr wŷr, Dew a uswon volungeth ol dhe colon*, very truly, God knows all the wish of thy heart. O.M. 1376. A mutation of *bolungeth*, qd. v.

VOMMENNOW, s. m. Blows. *Mar ny fystyn pûp huny, why a's bŷdh drôg vommennow*, if every one makes not haste, ye shall have bad blows. O.M. 2324. A mutation of *bomnennow*, pl. of *bommen*, qd. v.

VONES, v. subs. To be. *Ny gafaf vy kên ynno na blam dhe vones ledhys*, I find no cause in him or blame, that he should be slain. P.C. 2158. A mutation of *bones*, qd. v.

VONS, v. subs. They may or should be. *Mês pan vôns dyschys gulân, y a dynach agas duow myleges*, but when they are quite refreshed, they will reject their cursed gods. O.M. 1838. *Tarosfan a dhue deffry war lûs vâs pan vôns yn chy*, phantoms come indeed upon good people when they are in the house. R.D. 1451. A mutation of *bôns*, qd. v.

VOOG, s. m. Smoke. *Pryce*. A mutation of *moog*, id. qd. *môg*, qd. v.

VOOGA, s. f. A cavern. "We also call a hollow cavern in the earth, or mines, and made by the fretting of the sea, a *vooga* ; which Norden, in his description of Cornwall, calls a *googoo*, and the Welsh *ogo* ; but Llwyd (Arch. 47.) *ogov*, a den, a cave." *Pryce*.

VOR, s. f. A way. *An vor gôth*, the old way. *Llwyd*, 251. A late mutation of *for*, qd. v.

VORDH, s. f. A way. *An vordh*, the way ; *'gys vordh*, your way. *Llwyd*, 230, 241. A late mutation of *fordh*, qd. v.

VOREN, s. f. A maid, a jade. A mutation of *moren*, qd. v.

VORETHEC, adj. Grieved, sorrowful. A mutation of *morethec*, qd. v.

VORH, s. f. A fork. A late mutation of *forh*, qd. v.

VORN, s. m. An oven, a furnace. A late mutation of *forn*, qd. v.

VORVOREN, s. f. A mermaid. A mutation of *morvoren*, qd. v.

3 c

VOS, v. subs. To be. *Mâp dên a bry yn perfyth me a vyn y vôs formyys*, the son of man of clay perfectly I will that he be created. O.M. 56. *Lemyn gwyn ow beys, ow vôs sonys hep whethlow*, now happy my lot, that I am blessed without stories. O.M. 466. *Ow paynys a vŷdh garow, kyn vôs leskys dhe lusow*, my pains will be severe, before being burned to ashes. O.M. 1355. A mutation of *bôs*, qd. v.

VOS, v. u. To go. *Do vôs dhu'n drê*, to go to towu. *Llwyd*, 230. A mutation of *môs*, qd. v.

VOS, s. f. A maid. *Yw an vôs-na 'gys hôr*, is that maid your sister ? *Llwyd*, 240. A mutation of *môs*, qd. v.

VOSÊ, v. a. To drive away. A mutation of *mosê*, qd. v.

VOSSAW, v. a. I will send away. A mutation of *mossaf*, 1 pers. s. fut. of *mosê*, qd. v.

VOSTERYON, s. m. Braggarts, boasters. *Fy dheuch, a vosteryon plôs, awos agas fâs ha trôs ny wra bom y worlené*, fy on ye, O dirty boasters ; notwithstanding your bragging and noise, a blow will not quell him. P.C. 2100. A mutation of *bosteryon*, pl. of *boster*, from the English *boaster*.

VOSTETHES, s. m. Filth, dirt. A mutation of *mostethes*, qd. v.

VOSTYYS, adj. Defiled, filthy. A mutation of *mostyys*, id. qd. *mostys*, qd. v.

VOUNDER, s. m. A lane. *Pryce*. A mutation of *bounder*, qd. v.

VOWLZ, s. f. A reaping hook. *Llwyd*, 38, 241. A late mutation of *fowls*, qd. v.

VOY, adj. Greater, more. *An gweel gueres mar a'm vêdh, dhe Dew dhe voy y whon grâs*, if the rods shall be help to me, I give the more thanks to God. O.M. 2016. *Râk henna nêb a'm guerthas, mûr dhe voy ef re pechas*, therefore he that sold me, much the more he hath sinned. P.C. 2191. A mutation of *moy*, qd. v.

VRAMME, v. a. To fart. A mutation of *brammê*, qd. v.

VRAN, s. f. A crow. *An vrân vrâs, march-vrân*, the raven. A mutation of *brân*, qd. v.

VRAS, adj. Great, big. *Saw an wedhen dhym yma hy bôs sychys marthys vrâs*, but the tree, it is to me a great wonder that it is dried. O.M. 756. *Tûs vyan, ha tûs vrâs*, people small, and people great. O.M. 1438. A mutation of *brâs*, qd. v.

VRE, s. f. A mountain, a hill. *Moel-vrê*, the bare hill. A mutation of *bre*, qd. v.

VRECH, s. f. An arm. *Dyw vrêch*, the two arms, the arms. *Ystyn dhe vrêch war an pren*, stretch out thy arm on the tree. P.C. 2753. A mutation of *brêch*, qd. v.

VREDAR, s. m. A brother. A mutation of *bredar*, qd. v.

VREDER, s. m. Brothers, brethren. A mutation of *breder*, qd. v.

VREDER, s. m. Shortness. *A vreder*, shortly. A mutation of *breder*, qd. v.

VREH, s. f. An arm. A mutation of *brêh*, qd. v.

VRES, s. m. Understanding, judgment. *Guŷr vrês yw honna*, that is a true decision. P.C. 515. A mutation of *brês*, qd. v.

VRESYL, s. m. Judgment. *Aron whêk, pŷth a cusyl a rêth dhym orth am vresyl, a sôn an debel bobel*, sweet Aaron, what counsel givest thou to me for my judgment, at the noise of the wicked people. O.M. 1814.

A mutation of *bresyl*, or *bresel*; qd. v.

VREW, adj. Bruised, broken. A mutation of *brew*, qd. v.

VREWYON, s. m. Bruises. A mutation of *brewyon*, pl. of *brew*, qd. v.

VREYS, s. m. The will, mind. *Arluth kêr, an sacryfys a vŷdh gurŷs orth bôdh dhe vreys*, dear Lord, the sacrifice shall be done according to the wish of thy mind. O.M. 1266. Written also *vreus*. *Kepar hag ef ôn crousys, ha dre wŷr vreus quyt ingŷys râk agan drôk ober kens*, like as he we are crucified, and by quite true judgment sentenced for our evil deed before. P.C. 2901. A mutation of *breys*, or *breus*, qd. v.

VRINC, s. f. France. *Pryce*. A late mutation of *Frinc*, qd. v.

VRINCAO, s. f. The French language. *Lhwyd*, 62. A late mutation of *Frincae*, qd. v.

VRO, s. f. A country, region. A mutation of *bro*, qd. v.

VRODER, s. m. A brother. *Lavar ple ma dhe vroder*, tell where is thy brother. O.M. 572. *A vroder, ow banneth dhys*, O brother, my blessing to thee. O.M. 1327. *Moyses, kemer dhe welen, ha ty ha'th vroder Aren*, Moses, take thy rod, and thou and thy brother Aaron. O.M. 1842. A mutation of *broder*, qd. v.

VRUS, s. m. Judgment. *Dre guŷr vrûs y cothé dodho godhaf bôs ledhys*, by true judgment it is right for him to suffer being killed. O.M. 2237. *Godhaf dhe vrûs dhe honan*, suffer thine own judgment. O.M. 2248. A mutation of *brûs*, qd. v.

VRUSY, v. a. To judge. A mutation of *brusy*, qd. v.

VRY, s. m. Account, value. A mutation of *bry*, qd. v.

VRYES, s. m. A spouse, husband, or wife. *A vryes, hep falladow, mebyon ha myrhes kefrys*, O spouse, without fail, sons and daughters likewise. O.M. 1037. An irregular mutation of *pryes*, qd. v., the secondary form *bryes* being here made primary.

VRYONGEN, s. f. The throat. A mutation of *bryongen*, qd. v.

VRYS, s. m. Judgment. A mutation of *brŷs*, qd. v.

VUDHYS, part. Drowned. A mutation of *budhys*, qd. v.

VUEL, adj. Humble, obedicut. *Besy yw dhys bôs vuell; ha spernabyll y'th servys, manno allo an tebell oyns dhys bonas trylys*, it is needful for thee to be humble and submitting to thy service, that the evil one may not be turned near to thee. M.C. 19. Arm. *vuel*. By metathesis for *uvel*. W. *hwyll, uvell*. Ir. *umhail*. Gael. *umhal*. All from the Lat. *humilis*.

VUR, adj. Great, much. *Ty re gam wrûk eredy, ha re'n drôs dhe vûr anken*, thou hast done wrong verily, and hast brought him to much sorrow. O.M. 282. *My a grŷs yn pyrfeth aga bôs gurel a vûr râs*, I believe perfectly that they are rods of great virtue. O.M. 2012. *Mar vûr me re pechas*, so greatly I have sinned. P.C. 1510. A mutation of *mûr*, qd. v.

VURU, adv. Morrow. ‡ *Y vuru*, to-morrow. *Lhwyd*, 52. A late form of *avorow*, qd. v.

VURU, s. m. Ways, roads. *Pryce*. A late mutation of *furu*, qd. v.

VUSURE, v. a. To measure. A mutation of *musuré*, qd. v.

VY, pron. subs. I, me. *Lavar dhymmo vy wharé*, tell thou to me directly. O.M. 158. *Tan henna dheworthef ty*, take thou that from me. O.M. 206. *Colom genef vy yma*, a dove with me there is. O.M. 1189. *Arluth porth cûf yn drydh dywedh a'm encf vy*, Lord, bear remembrance on the last day of my soul. O.M. 1273. *Ow tâs a vy, marth yn teffry ûs dhym lemmyn*, my father of me, a wonder truly is to me now. O.M. 1309. *Arluth Dew kêr, klew ow lêf, ha gor vy dhe lowené*, dear Lord God, hear my voice, and bring me to bliss. O.M. 1896. *Ow nygys vy spedyé a vera*, my errand I will expedite. P.C. 1934. A mutation of *my*, or *mi*, qd. v.

VY, v. subs. Thou mayest be. *Eva kyns del vy serrys, my a wra ol del vynny*, Eve, rather than thou be angry, I will do all as thou wishest. O.M. 246. *Spern ha spedhes ow tevy, hedré vy may fo anken*, thorns and briars growing, that there may be trouble as long as thou mayest exist. O.M. 276. *Ymsaw scon yn nêp maner na vy marow*, save thyself immediately in some way, that thou mayest not be dead. P.C. 2893. *Me re dhûth dhe'th confortyé, nac na vy gy yn a wher*, I have come to comfort thee, that thou be not in sorrow. R.D. 474. *Me a'th cusyl dysempys bŷth na vy trest*, I advise thee immediately that thou be never sad. R.D. 2230. A mutation of *by*, 2 pers. s. subj. of *bôs*.

VYA, v. subs. He would be. *En box oll bedhens gwerthys, a vôs den râg y ranné dhe vohosogyon yn bŷs; gwel vya ys y scolyé*, let the box all be sold, and be for us to share it to the poor in the world; it would be better than spilling it. M.C. 36. More generally written *vyé*, qd. v.

VYAN, v. subs. We were. *Ni vyan*, we have been. *Lhwyd* 246. A mutation of *byan*, a late form of *buen*, qd. v.

VYAN, adj. Little, small. *Tûs vyan ha tûs vrâs*, people small and people great. O.M. 1438. *Saw warnouch agas honan, ha war 'gas flehes vyan kên dhe olé why a's bŷdh*, but on ye yourselves, and on your little children, cause to weep ye shall have. P.C. 2643. A mutation of *byan*, qd. v.

VYCHAN, adj. Little, small. *Pryce*. A mutation of *bychan*, id. qd. *bechan*, qd. v.

VYCHTERN, s. m. A king. *Me a ordyn y wyské yn purpyr rych kepar del gôth dhe vychtern*, I order to clothe him in rich purple, like as is becoming to a king. P.C. 2123. A mutation of *mychtern*, qd. v.

VYCHTERNETH, s. m. Royalty, sovereignty. *Arluth, fattel bŷdh haneth, mar ny wodhefaf ple 'dh êth pen vyehterneth*, Lord, how will it be to-night, if I know not where is gone the head of royalty? R.D. 720. A mutation of *mychterneth*, qd. v.

VYDH, v. s. He shall or will be. *Mar myn Dew, râg an gwella, del fydhyaf, ef a vŷdh gurŷs*, if God wills, for the best, as I trust, it will be done. O.M. 651. *Ty a vŷdh mernans calas*, thou shalt have a hard death. R.D. 2024. *Ple ma an offryn, a dds, a vŷdh leskys dhe Dhew râs râg y wordhyé*, where is the offering, O father, (that) shall be burnt to the God of grace, for worshipping him? O.M. 1317. A mutation of *bŷdh*, qd. v.

VYDH, v. subs. Be thou. *Ow arluth kêr, na vŷdh serrys, kettoth an gêr my a dhue dhys*, my dear lord, be not angry, as soon as the word I will come to thee. O.M. 1907. A mutation of *bŷdh*, qd. v.

VYDHONS, v. subs. They shall be. *Saw kyn fêns y morthelek, dhe wêth vydhons dhe'n cronek, ha garow yn y dhulé*, but though they be hammered, worse they shall be for the toad, and rough in his hands. P.C. 2732.

A mutation of *bydhons*, qd. v.

VYDHYTH, v. subs. Thou shalt be. *Mar nyth wolhaf, dre ow râs, yn nêff ny vydhyth tryggys*, if I wash thee not, by my grace, in heaven thou shalt not be dwelling. P.C. 858. A mutation of *bydhyth*, qd, v.

VYE, v. subs. He would be. *Yn crês an chy, rês vyé kafus gyst crêf na vo guan*, in the middle of the house, it would be necessary to have a strong beam, that it be not weak. O.M. 2481. *Mûr a gâs vyé gené trehy henna*, much dislike there would be with me to cut that. O.M. 2501. *Râk pûr vêjr gynen mar pês, ny a vyé pûr aties, ha lowen mûr*, for very truly if thou wert with us, we should be very much at ease, and very glad. R.D. 2443. A mutation of *byé*, qd. v.

VYEN, v. subs. I should be. *Arluth ny vyen lowen, mar fur torment a codhfen y bones dhys*, Lord, I should not be joyful, if I knew the fierce torment there was to thee. R.D. 2541. A mutation of *byen*, qd. v.

VYES, v. subs. Thou wouldst be. A mutation of *byes*, qd. v.

VYF, v. subs. I may be. *Me a'th pŷs, scrîf ow ené, pan vŷf marow, yn dhe rol*, I pray thee, write my soul, when I am dead, in thy roll. P.C. 422. *Mar callé bôs yn della, gorré an kêth mernans-ma dhyworthyf na vŷf ledhys*, if it can be so, put this same death from me, that I be not slain. P.C. 1036. A mutation of *bŷf*, qd. v.

VYGYDHYS, part. Baptized. A mutation of *bygydhys*, qd. v.

VYGYENS, s. m. Victuals, food. *Lemyn hanwaf goydh ha yâr, a sensaf edhyn hep pâr dhe vygyens dên war an beys*, now I name goose and hen, (which) I hold birds without equal for food of man in the world. O.M. 131. Perhaps a mutation of *bygyens*, derived from *boys*, meat. So W. *bwytal*, victuals, from *bŵyd*.

VYIN, s. m. Stones. *Fôs a vyin*, a stone wall. *Llwyd*, 230. A mutation of *myin*, id. qd. *meyn*, pl. of *maen*, qd. v.

VYL, card. num. A thousand. See *Vil*.

VYLEN, adj. Brutish. A mutation of *mylen*, or *milen*, qd. v.

VYLGY, s. m. The sea. "Mr. Gwavas doth from hence (and I think not improperly) derive the name of Trevylian, *the dwelling of seamen*; according to the old tradition and arms of the family of Sir John Trevylian." *Pryce*. W. *gwcilgi*, *y weilgi*. Ir. *fuirge*. Gael. *fairge*. Manx, *faarkey*.

VYLLYC, v. a. He will curse. A mutation of *myllyc*, 3 pers. s. fnt. of *mylygé*, qd. v.

VYLYGES, part. Accursed, wicked. *Ha Cryst mylyges, yn teêdh dew vylyges, y telleth warbarth aga bôs garris*, and Christ wicked, also two wicked men, it is incumbent that they be put together. P.C. 2533. A mutation of *mylyges*, part. pass. of *mylygé*, qd. v.

VYMA, comp. verb. I may be. *Ow dyskyblon, ysedhouch, hag omma pols powesouch, hedré vymu ow pygy*, my disciples, sit ye and rest here a while, whilst I am praying. P.C. 1013. A mutation of *byma*, comp. of *bŷf*, 1 pers. s. subj. of *bôs*, and *me*, I.

VYN, v. a. He will. *Pan vyn an Tâs yn della*, when the Father so wills. O.M. 648. *My a vyn môs dhyworthys*, I will go from thee. O.M. 822. *Ny a vyn formyé an bŷs*, we will create the earth. O.M. 11. A mutation of *myn*, 3 pers. s. fut. of *mynny*, qd. v.

VYN, s. m. Stones. *Pryce*. A contracted form of *vyin*, qd. v.

VYNARY, adv. Continually, ever. *Hag y a wŷth y vody, na potré bŷs vynary*, and they will keep his body, that it decay not for ever. P.C. 3200. *Dyscow y dhewortho, py ken ny wreuch drôk dhodho bŷs vynary*, strip it from him, or else yo will not do harm to him for over. R.D. 1872. A mutation of *bynary*, or *benary*, qd. v.

VYNC, s. f. A bench, a post. *Maras osé mâp Dew mûr, dyrskyn a'n vŷnk dhe'n lûr, ha dysué ran a'th veystry*, if thou art the Son of the great God, descend from the post to the ground, and shew a portion of thy power. P.C. 2868. A mutation of *bÿnc*, id. qd. *benc*, qd. v.

VYNE, s. m. The edge. To be read *vîn*, a mutation of *mîn*, qd. v.

VYNER, adv. Ever, always. *Saw vyner re dhewhylly genes my a wra pysy*, but always that thou mayest return with thee I will pray. O.M. 2196. A mutation of *byner*, qd. v.

VYNNA, v. a. He would. A mutation of *mynna*, 3 pers. s. imperf. of *mynnes*, qd. v.

VYNNA, v. a. I will. *Y offendyé ny vynna, kyn fên marow yn torma*, I will not offend him, though I should be dead at this time. O.M. 1330. *Ny vynna strecha pella*, I will not delay longer. O.M. 2288. An abbreviated form of *vynnaf*.

VYNNAF, v. a. *Mêsk ow pobel ny vynnaf na fella ugas godhaf*, among my people I will no longer endure you. O.M. 1594. A mutation of *mynnaf*, 1 pers. s. fut. of *mynnes*, qd. v.

VYNNAN, v. a. I would. *A Dhew yssé, fucf goky, pana vynnan vy crygy a'n bêdh y vôs dasserchys*, O God in thy seat, I was foolish, when I would not believe that he was risen from the grave. R.D. 1566. A mutation of *mynnan*, 1 pers. s. subj. of *mynnes*, qd. v.

VYNNAS, v. a. He would. A mutation of *mynnas*, 3 pers. s. preter. of *mynnes*, qd. v.

VYNNAS, s. m. Will, purpose. A mutation of *mynnas*, qd. v.

VYNNE, v. a. He would. *Otté ha coynt o an guâs, pana vynné gorthyby a dhyrak an arlythy dhe resons an doctors brâs*, see how cunning the fellow was, when he would not answer, before the lords, the arguments of the great doctors. P.C. 1820. A mutation of *mynné*, 3 pers. s. imperf. of *mynnes*, qd. v.

VYNNES, v. a. To will. *Dhe'n .Tâs huhel yn y trôn y grassaf lemmyn un câs, ty dhe vynnes dhym danfon, dhum confortyé, dhe vâp râs*, to the Father high on his throne, I give thanks now in the case, that thou art willing to send to me, to comfort me, thy Son of grace. R.D. 509. *A Arloth, ydhof lowen, ty dhe vynnes dôs gynen omma dh'agan lowenhé*, O Lord, I am glad, that thou wouldst come with us here to gladden us. R.D. 1166. A mutation of *mynnes*, qd. v.

VYNNO, v. a. He may wish. A mutation of *mynno*, 3 pers. s. subj. of *mynnes*, qd. v.

VYNNONS, v. a. They will wish. *Arluth, ny vynnons crysy, na clewas ow voys a vy, awos me dhe gows dhedhé*, Lord, they will not believe, nor hear my voice of me, notwithstanding that I speak to them. O.M. 1435. A mutation of *mynnons*, 3 pers. pl. fut. of *mynnes*, qd. v.

VYNNOUCH, v. a. Ye will wish. *Pahan cheyson a's bues why erbyn Ihesu Nazaré, pan vynnouch y dhystrewy*, what accusation have ye against Jesus of Nazareth, when ye wish to destroy him? P.C. 1972. A mutation of *mynnouch*, 2 pers. pl. fut. of *mynnes*, qd. v.

VYNNY, v. a. Thou wilt. *My a wra ol del vynny*, I will do all as thou wishest. O.M. 246. *Kee, kymmer myns a vynny*, go, take all that thou wilt. O.M. 403. *Arluth, pan vynny, yskyn*, Lord, when thou wilt, mount. O.M. 1968. *Ahanaf pendra vynny, lavar dhymmo vy deffry, a dhesempys*, what wilt thou of me, tell me really, immediately. R.D. 1614. A mutation of *mynny*, 2 pers. s. subj. of *mynnes*, qd. v.

VYNNYN, v. a. We will. *A vynneuch ol assentyé, râk pask my dhylyfryé Ihesu mychtern Yedhewon? A na vynnyn, sir iustys, saw Barabas ny a pýs ugy yn colm yn pryson*, will ye all agree, for passover that I should liberate Jesus, King of the Jews? Oh we will not, sir Justice, but Barabbas we pray, that is in bond in prison. P.C. 2040. A mutation of *mynnyn*, 1 pers. pl. fut. of *mynnes*, qd. v.

VYNNYTH, v. a. Thou wilt. *Ny vynnyth clewas Dew kêr, temyn môs dhe'n calctter*, thou wilt not hear the dear God, but go to hardness. O.M. 1523. *Govyn worthyn hep lettyé, py suel a vynnyth deffry*, ask of us, without hesitating, whatever thou wilt truly. P.C. 592. A mutation of *mynnyth*, 2 pers. s. fut. of *mynnes*, qd. v.

VYNS, v. subs. They may be. *Y a výdh guythys calas, hedré výns y yn ow gulâs*, they shall be worked hard, as long as they may be in my country. O.M. 1503. A mutation of *býns*, id. qd. *béns*, 3 pers. pl. subj. of *bôs*.

VYNSE, v. a. He would. *Me a vynsé y wythé, ha ny yllyn cammen výth*, I would have preserved him, and I could not any way. P.C. 3125. *Ow mâp whêk, me a vynsé a luen golon dhe pyyy*, my sweet son I would wish with full heart to pray to thee. R.D. 447. A mutation of *mynsé*, 3 pers. s. pluperf. of *mynnes*, qd. v.

VYNSYN, v. a. We would. *Pûr ryel, yn sûr certan, an re-ma yw obrrys, del vynsyn agan honan*, very royal, in sure certainty, these are wrought, as we would ourselves. O.M. 16. A mutation of *mynsyn*, 1 pers. pl. preter. of *mynnes*, qd. v.

VYNSYS, v. a. Thou wouldest. *Pendra yw henna dhynny, aban vymsys y werthé*, what is that to us, since thou wouldst sell him? P.C. 1510. A mutation of *mynsys*, 2 pers. s. preter. of *mynnes*, qd. v.

VYNTA, v. a. Thou wilt. *Aban na vynta cresy, ty a kyl ow herensé*, since thou wilt not believe, thou shalt lose my love. O.M. 241. *Ow mâp kerra, pendra vynta orthyf govyn*, my dearest son, what wilt thou ask of me? O.M. 1311. A mutation of *mynta*, comp. of *myn*, 3 pers. s. fut. of *mynnes*, and *te*, thou.

VYNYN, s. f. A female, a woman. *A vynyn ryth, ple ydh êth*, O woeful woman, where goest thou? R.D. 851. *A vynyn ryth, na tuche vy nés*, O woeful woman, touch me not nearer. R.D. 875. A mutation of *bynyn*, another form of *benen*, qd. v.

VYNYNES, s. f. Females, women. *My onan a'y vynynes, hag ê dhe'n emprour gynes*, I (am) one of his women, and will go to the emperor with thee. R.D. 1667. A mutation of *bynynes*, pl. of *bynyn*, id. qd. *benen*, qd. v.

VYNYTHA, adv. Ever. *Beys vynytha y wharthes, râg lowené*, for ever thou wouldst laugh for joy. O.M. 153. *Vynytha, hedré vynoy, umma ny'm gwelyth arté*, ever whilst thou mayest live, here thou shalt not see me again. O.M. 243. *Luen dyal war ol an veys ny gcmeraf vynytha*, full vengeance on all the world I will not take ever. O.M. 1234. *Vynytha syngys ôf dhys*, ever bound I am to thee. R.D. 96. A mutation of *bynytha*, qd. v.

VYOH, v. subs. Ye have been. ‡ *Hwei a výoh*, Llwyd, 245. A mutation of *byoh*, a late form of *beuch*, 2 pers. pl. preter. of *bôs*.

VYRAS, v. a. To see. See *Viras*.

VYRCH, s. f. A daughter. *Arlothes kêr, my a wra agas nygys fystyné, dyspyt dhe vyrch Thedama*, dear lady, I will hasten your errand, in spite of thy daughter Thedama. P.C. 1967. A mutation of *myrch*, qd. v.

VYRII, s. f. A daughter. A late form of *vyrch*. Llwyd, 242. makes *myrh*, an inflected genitive of *merh*, as *an vyrh*, of the daughter.

VYRU, v. n. He shall die. *Dre cledhé nêp a vewo, ef a vyrn drcdho*, whoever lives by the sword, he shall die by it. P.C.1157. A mutation of *myru*, 3 pers. s. fut. of *myrwel*, qd. v,

VYRWYF, v. n. I may die. *Ow tâs ymny wolowys, re bo gueres dheuch pûp prjs worth temptacyon an tebel, ma 'gas bo lowyné néf, pan vyrwyf dh'agus enef*, my Father in his lights, may he be a help to you always against the temptation of the evil one; that you may have the joy of heaven, when I die, to your souls. P.C. 227. A mutation of *myrwyf*, 1 pers. s. subj. of *myrwel*, qd. v.

VYRWYN, v. n. We shall die. *Râg fout guese ha goscotter namna vyrwyn râg anwos*, for want of raiment and shelter, we are well nigh dying from cold. O.M. 362. A mutation of *myrwyn*, 1 pers. pl. fut. of *myrwel*, qd. v.

VYS, s. m. The world. *Gwyn výs ynno nêb a grýs*, happy be that believes in him. P.C. 2706. A mutation of *býs*, qd. v.

VYSE, v. subs. Thou mayest be. *Arluth Cryst, me a'th pyssé a prydiry uhané, pan vysé yn dhe wlascor*, Lord Christ, I would pray thee to think of me, when thou art in thy kingdom. P.C. 2908. A mutation of *bysé*, comp. of *by*, 2 pers. s. subj. of *bôs*, and *se*, for *te*, thou.

VYSHEW, s. m. Misery. *Towles yw dhe ryshew brâs*, he is thrown into great misery. C.W. 108. A mutation of *myshew*; a late word, probably borrowed from Eng. *mischief*.

VYSMER, s. m. Contumely. A mutation of *bysmer*, qd. v.

VYST, s. f. A flail. Llwyd, 60, 166. A late form of *fýst*, qd. v.

VYSTERDEN, s. m. An architect. A mutation of *bysterden*, qd. v.

VYSY, adj. Diligent, important, grievous. *Pûr vysy a veydh dhedhé*, very grievous it shall be for them. O.M. 335. *Hag ordeyneuch guythysy dh'aga aspyé vysy, war peyn brâs, d'aga gwythé*, and appoint ye guards to watch them diligently, on great penalty, to keep them. O.M. 2030. A mutation of *lysy*, qd. v.

VYTTYN, s. m. The morning. *Mar a'th caffaf, re iowyn, y'ih ladhaf kyns ys vyttyn a'm dew luef*, if I find thee, by Jove, I will kill thee before morning with my hands. O.M. 1533. *Marow vedhons kyns vyttyn*, they shall be dead before morning. O.M. 1644. A mutation of *myttyn*, qd. v.

VYTH, adv. Ever, for ever, always. *Výth ny vyn an kéth dên-ma treylé dhe Dew awartha awos lavar leverys*, never will this same man turn to God above, because of word said. O.M. 1535. *Ha lavar my dh'y warnyé vŷth na wrella compressa ow tús ús trygys ena*, and say that I warn him that he never oppress my people that are dwelling there. O.M. 1424. *Awos tra vŷth a warfo*, notwithstanding any thing (that) may happen. O.M. 2355. A mutation of *bŷth*, qd. v.

VYTHETH, adv. Ever, at any time. *A Dew kér, assoma squyth, prynnyer derow ow trehy; vytheth powes my ny'm bŷdh, mar vrew ew ow yssyly*, O dear God, I am weary, cutting oak sticks; I shall never have rest, so bruised are my limbs. O.M. 1011. *Rág gwel dewes vytheth wŷn, wyns á yn agas ganow*, for any better drink of wine, will not go into your mouth. O.M. 1012. A mutation of *bytheth*, from *bŷth*, ever.

VYTHIOL, adj. Constant, continual. A mutation of *bythol*, qd. v.

VYTHQUETH, adv. Ever, always. *Ellas, vŷth, pan yw kyllys Abel whék, ow máp kerra, na vythqueth pan véf formys*, alas, ever, when is lost sweet Abel, my dearest son, nor ever that I was formed. O.M. 616. *Rág ny glewesyuch yn nép plás, sawor a'n par-ma vythqueth*, for ye have not smelt in any place savour of this sort ever. O.M. 1991. *Apert vythqueth y tyskys ow dyskes dhe'n Yedhewon*, openly always I taught my doctrine to the Jews. P.C. 1251. A mutation of *bythqueth*, qd. v.

VYUCH, v. subs. Ye may be. *H'agas mychtern ef synseuch, hedré vyuch byw yn bŷs-ma*, and consider him your king, while ye may be living in this world. O.M. 2349. *Rák hedré vyuch ow pleghyé, dhywhy bŷth ny's dŷsk neffré*, for as long as ye are yielding, he will never take it off for you. R.D. 1950. A mutation of *byuch*, written also *beuch*, 2 pers. pl. subj. of *bós*.

VYWY, v. n. Thou mayest live. *Vynytha hedré vywy, umma ny'm gwelyth arté*, ever as long as thou mayest live, here thou shalt not see me again. O.M. 243. Written also *vywhy*. *Iowan, otté dhe vam; yn della syns y, hep nam, hedré vywhy*, John, behold thy mother; so esteem her, without denial, as long as thou mayest live. P.C. 2930. A mutation of *bywy*, 2 pers. s. subj. of *bywé*, or *bewé*, qd. v.

VYYN, s. m. Stones. *Ke gorhemmyn ol dhe'n masons yn cyté may tyffons umma mytlyn, war beyn cregy ha tenné, dhe woil fos a vyyn bryntyn, hag a lŷm yn creys an dré*, go thou, command all the masons in the city, that they come here to-morrow, on pain of hanging and drawing, to make a wall of noble stones, and of lime in the middle of the town. O.M. 2281. A mutation of *myyn*, qd. v.

VYYN, v. subs. We may be. *Hedré vyyn ow predery yn glassygyon gesouch y, aga thŷr, dhe wroucedhé*, while we are considering, leave ye them, on a green plot, the three, to lie. O.M. 2035. A mutation of *byyn*, written also *bén*, *been*, *beyn*, 1 pers. pl. subj. of *bós*.

VYVYAN, v. n. To flee, to escape. *Pryce.* W. *chwyvan*.

W.

This letter is always a consonant in Cornish, as it is also in Armoric and Manx. In Welsh it is both a consonant and a vowel; and in the latter case it represents the Italian *u*, or English *oo*; which sound is represented in Cornish and Armoric by *ou*. Thus W. *gŵr*, a man; Corn. and Arm. *gour*. W. *dŵr*, water; Corn. and Arm. *dour*. In Cornish *w* is a primary and a secondary letter; when primary it is immutable; and when secondary it is a mutation of *g*, as *goloc*, sight; *an woloc*, the sight; *goys*, blood; *y woys*, his blood. *Govyn, dhe wovyn*, to ask. After certain words preceding this mutation is further made into an aspirate, *wh*. Thus *godhevys*, suffered; *ef a wodhevys*, he suffered. *War y gorf y whodhevys mûr a beynys*, on his body he suffered much pain. *Godhfouch*, ye may know; *na wodhfouch*, ye may not know; *may whodhfouch*, that ye may know. *Wh* is also found as an aspirate mutation of *c* in Cornish, as *colon*, a heart; *war ow wholon*, on my heart. *W* has no place in the Irish and Gaelic alphabets.

WAD, s. m. A forefather. Plur. *wadow*. *Dûn alemma dhe'n môr ruydh, tûs, venenes, ha flehys, dhe'n tyreth a dhy'th wadow yw reys gans Dew caradow dhyn, ena rág vôs trygys*, let us come hence to the Red Sea, men, women, and children, to the land (to which) thy ancestors went, (that) is given by the beloved God to us, there to be inhabited. O.M. 1624. *Rág na worsys ow hanow, rág an flehysygow a Israel, dyscryggyon, ny's goryth, hep falladow, dhe'n tŷr a dhy dhe wadow, ty na dhe vroder Aaron*, because thou honouredst not my name, and for the children of Israel, unbelievers, thou shalt not bring them, certainly, to the land where thy forefathers went; thou, nor thy brother Aaron. O.M. 1871.

‡ WALTOWAT, s. m. Fertility. Corn. Vocab. *fertilitas*. W. *gwalloviad, gwallmvind*.

WAN, v. a. He will pierce. *Rák ow colon ow honan gans ow hollan me a wán*, for my own heart with my knife I will pierce. R.D. 2043. A mutation of *gwán*, 3 pers. s. fut. of *gwané*, qd. v.

WANÉ, v. a. To pierce. *Kerchyn Longys, an guûs dal, gans guw dhe wané an gal yn y golon*, let us fetch Longius, the blind fellow, to pierce the villain with a spear in his heart. P.C. 2917. *Pan wylys vy y wané dre an golon gans an guw*, when I saw his being pierced through the heart with the spear. R.D. 431. A mutation of *gwané*, qd. v.

WAR, prep. On, upon. *Clewys a'n ûgl tenewen un íl ow talleth cané a uchaf war an wedhen*, I heard on one side an angel beginning to sing above on the tree. O.M. 216. *Dhe váp Ysac a geryth, y offrynné reys yw dhys war venedh a dhysquedhaf dhyso gy*, thy son Isaac (whom) thou lovest, it is necessary for thee to offer him on a mountain (that) I shall shew to thee. O.M. 1281. *May tyffons umma myttyn, war beyn cregy ha tenné*, that they come here in the morning, on pain of hanging and drawing. O.M. 2280. *Ol ny a bŷs, yowynk ha hên, war Dhu páp prŷs*, all we pray, young and old, to God always. P.C. 40. *Ha war woles pan vyrys, my a welas hy gurydhyow*, and when I looked on the bottom I saw its roots. O.M. 781. *Ha whâth gwêth war a'n gorré*, and yet worse did the tree, if he put it backward. M.C. 205. ‡ *War dhelhar*, backward. ‡ *War tya tré*, towards home. *Llwyd*, 137, 249. *War* is a mutation of W. *gwar*, which is over or upon. It enters into composition with the personal pronouns, and inserts an additional *n*, as in Welsh. (See *Warnaf*,

Warnas, &c.) W. *ar.* Arm. *war,* †*gwar,* †*voar.* Ir. *ar, air.* Gael. *air.* Manx, *er.* Anc. Gaul. *are.* Gr. ὑπέρ. Lat. *super.* Germ. *uber.* Eng. *over.*

WAR, adj. Gentle. *An guary yw dyscydhys, ha deuch avar avorow, my agas pŷs, dhe welas fetel sevys Cryst mês a'n bêdh, clêr ha wâr,* the Play is ended, and come ye early to-morrow, I pray you, to see how Christ rose out of the tomb, bright and gentle. P.C. 3242. Written also *whâr.* *In kêth gydh-na pûr avar, ha'n houl nowydh drehevys; tŷr Marea, cleyr ha whâr, a dhêth dhe'n bêdh leverys,* on that same day, very early, and the sun newly risen ; the three Maries, clear and gentle, came to the said tomb. M.C. 252. W. *gwâr, wâr ; gwarog.* Ir. †*fuarroch.*

WARAF, pron. prep. Upon me, over me. *Yn mêdh Ihesus yn ûr-na, mestry vŷth te ny vea waraff, drôk vŷth na da, ken onan dhys na'n rolla,* says Jesus then ; no power at all wouldst thou have over me, bad nor good, unless some one else had given it to thee. M.C. 145. An uncommon form of *warnaf,* qd. v.

WARBARTH, adv. Together. *Kelmeuch warbarth y dhywvreeh na allo dyank drewal,* bind ye together his arms, that he may not escape away. P.C. 1179. *May fo pûp dên ol ynno, ha pûp bêst warbarth budhys,* that in it every man may be, and every beast together drowned. O.M. 1044. *Ol warbarth y a'n nachas, hag a yrchys y ladhé,* all together they denied him, and bade to slay him. M.C. 147. Comp. of *war,* on, and *parth,* a side. In late Cornish it was corrupted into *warbarh.* Llwyd, 252.

WARBYN, prep. Against. *I vam whêk, Marya wyn, pûb ûr fystené a wre, may hallé doys war y byn, y mâb kemmys a garé,* his sweet mother, Mary blessed, always made haste that she might come to meet him, her son so much she loved. M.C. 171. *Rág henna warbyn cunda ydh o dhys môs dh'y ladha,* therefore against nature it was for thee to go to kill him. C.W. 94. *Warbyn* is another form of *erbyn,* qd. v. This was generally used in late Cornish, being corrupted into *warbidn.* ‡ *Na raz tiah gow warbidn de contrevak,* thou shalt not swear falsely against thy neighbour. Pryce. *Warbidn ; war aga phidn,* against them. Llwyd, 249, 252.

WARDHELHAR, adv. Backwards. Llwyd, 248. A late form of *war dhellurch.*

WARE, adv. At once, soon. *Me a vyn dyeskenné, ha môs yn tempil waré, dhe weles ol an fêr-na,* I will dismount, and go into the temple at once, to see all that fair. P.C. 314. *Me a lover dheuch waré,* I will tell you at once. P.C. 1450. Written also *wharré,* qd. v.

WARFO, v. n. It may happen. *Arluth, dhe vôdh my a wra, del degoyth dhym yn pûp tra, awos tra vŷth a warfo,* Lord, thy wish I will do, as it behoves me in all things, notwithstanding any thing that may happen. C.M. 2355. A mutation of *wharfo,* 3 pers. s. subj. of *wharfos,* qd. v.

WARLERCH, comp. prep. After. Written equally common *warlyrch. Rág ny vew moy es tryddydh warlyrch dhe vones dhe drê,* for he will not live more than three days, after that thou hast gone home. O.M. 830. *Del lavaraf dhys, Moyses, war dhe lerch vedhens revelys,* as I tell thee Moses, after thee they shall be ruled. O.M. 1434. *Rág henna, hep falladow, ol warlerch dhe gussullyow bŷs vyn-*

ytha my a wra, therefore, without fail, all after thy counsels for ever I will do. O.M. 2269. *Ihesus a ve hombronkis, ha war y lyrch mûr a lu,* Jesus was led on, and a great multitude after him. M.C. 163. Comp. of *war,* upon, and *lerch,* a footstep. *Ar ol,* is similarly used in Welsh. In late Cornish *warlerch* was softened into *warler.* Llwyd, 249.

WARNAF, pron. prep. Upon me. (*War—my.*) *Otté voys mernans Abel, dhe vroder, prest ow kelwel a'n dôr warnaf pûp teller,* behold the blood of the death of Abel, thy brother, now calling from the ground on me every where. O.M. 579. *Gallos warnaf ny fyes, na fe.y vôs grantys dhys dyscorth whella arloth,* power over me thou wouldst not have, were it not that it was granted to thee from the most high Lord. P.C. 2187. W. *arnav.* Arm. *warnoun.* Ir. *orm,* †*airium,* †*form.* Gael. *orm.* Manx, *orrym.*

WARNAN, pron. prep. Upon us. (*War—ny.*) *Govy ellas, ellas, codhys warnan an môr brâs, ny a vŷdh cowal vudhys,* woe is me, alas, alas, the great sea (is) fallen upon us, we shall be quite drowned. O.M. 1700. *Mar tue veninns vŷth ragtho, warnan ny ef re godho, ha war ol agan flechas,* if vengeance shall ever come for him, upon us may it fall, and upon all our children. P.C. 2502. W. *arnom, arnam.* Arm. *warnomp.* Irish, *orrainn,* †*forrainn.* Gael. *oirun.* Manx, *orrin.*

WARNAS, pron. prep. Upon thee. *Un quêth têk hy a drylyas adro dhedho desympys, ha warnans hy a'u quudhas rág gwythé na ve storys,* a fair cloth she wrapped around him immediately, and upon them she covered him to keep him from being starved (with cold.) M.C. 177. *Rág gwan spyr, hag ef yn ten, caman na ylly gwythé war nans un bossé y ben, rág an arlont a usyé,* for he breathed weakly, and he being tight that he could not keep any way, on them that he should not lean his head, for the garland that he wore. M.C. 205. The more general form is *warnedhé,* qd. v.

WARNAS, pron. prep. Upon thee. (*War—ty.*) *Arluth, warnas tregeryth,* Lord, upon thee (be) love. O.M. 1015. *Na allons cafflus cheson dhe wruthyl crothval na sôn warnas, a dâs veneges,* let them not be able to find cause to make a complaint, nor a sound against thee, O blessed Father. O.M. 1837. Written also *warnes,* and *warnos.* *A out warnes, drôk vewen,* O out upon thee, wicked woman. O.M. 221. *Râk ty yw dew gallogek dhe pûp a vo othommek, warnos a pyssé mercy,* for thou art a mighty God, to all that are needy, on thee that pray for mercy. R.D. 2378. W. *arnat.* Arm. *warnoud.* Ir. *ort,* †*fort.* Gael. *ort.* Manx, *ort.*

WARNEDHE, pron. prep. Upon them. (*War—y.*) *Mŷns ûs yn tŷr hag yn mûr, warnedhé kemer galloys,* all that is in land and in sea, over them take thou power. O.M. 70. *Fossow da gans lŷm ha pry ha pen crêf warnedhé y gureuch drehevel,* good walls with lime and clay, and a strong top upon them, do ye erect. O.M. 2451. W. *arnynt, arnadhynt,* †*arnadunt.* Arm. *warnezo.* Irish, *orra, ortha,* †*airiu,* †*forru.* Gael. *orra.* Manx, *orroo.*

WARNEDHIY, pron. prep. Upon her, or it. (*War—hy.*) *Warnedhy yma gwedhen, uhel gans lues scoren,* on it there is a tree, high with many boughs. O.M. 775. *Yn dewellens prehadow, gûl alter da eyé, ha dhodho agan lothnow warnedhy sacryfyé,* in atonement of sins, to make an altar would be good, and to him our bullock upon it to sacrifice. O.M. 1176. Written also *warnydhy*. *A dâs kêr, my a welas yn paradys fenten râs, ha warnydhy un wedhen*, O father dear, I saw in Paradise a fountain of grace, and upon it a tree. O.M. 837. *Degé ol agan edhyn, bestes yn wêdh maga ta, warnydhy my a offryn yn gordhyans dhe'n tâs guella*, tithe of all our birds, beasts also as well, I will offer upon it, in worship to the best Father. O.M. 1183. W. *arni*, †*arnry*, †*arnci*, †*erni*. Arm. *warnezhi*. Ir. *uirre, uirri*, †*fuirri*. Gael. *oirre, uirre, orra*. Manx, *urree*.

WARNODHANS, pron. prep. Upon them. *Mŷns és yn tŷr hag yn nôr, warnodhans kymar gallus*, all that is in land and in sea, over them take thou power. C.W. 28. A late form of *warnedhé*, and written by Llwyd, 244, *warnydhans*. This form agrees nearer with W. *arnadhynt*, †*arnadunt*; (*ar—hwynt.*)

WARNODHIO, pron. prep. Upon him or it. (*War—o.*) *Ny yllen travyth dhodho ; myshyf a gôdh warnodho, hag a ver spys*, we cannot (do) any thing to this man; harm will fall upon him, and in a short time. O.M. 1530. *Lemyn gorryn ef yn bedh, ewnyn an mên warnodho*, now let us put him in the grave ; let us adjust the stone upon it. P.C. 2207. *Me a gryes warnodho*, I believe in him. R.D. 263. W. *arno*, †*arnaw*. Arm. *warnhan, warnezhan*. Irish, *air*, †*airi*, †*fair*. Gael. *air*. Manx, *er*.

WARNOT, adv. On the instant, immediately. *Dûn ganso dhe drê warnot, dh'agan arluth*, let us bring him home immediately to our lord. O.M. 559. *How, otté an pren omma, nŷns ûs tecka yn wlâs-ma, gurên crous annodho warnot*, lo, behold the tree here, there is not a fairer in this country; let us make a cross of it immediately. P.C. 2560.

WARNOUCH, pron. prep. (*War—chowi.*) *Me a pŷs an tâs a nêf, re dhanfono vengeans crêf warnouch ol kyngys dybry*, I pray the Father of heaven, that he send heavy vengeance on ye all before eating. P.C. 2632. *Myrches a Ierusalem, na olouch na na wreuch drem warnaf vy, nag onan vŷth, saw warnouch agas honan, ha war 'gas flehes vyan, kên dhe olé why a's bŷdh*, daughters of Jerusalem, weep not, nor make lament on me, not any one, but on ye yourselves, and on your little children, cause to weep ye shall have. P.C. 2642. Written also *warnoch*. *Why a gvf bohosugyon pûp ûr warnoch ow karmé*, ye shall have the poor always calling upon you. P.C. 544. W. *arnoch*, †*arnawch*. Arm. *warnhoch*. Ir. *orraibh*, †*foraibh*, †*fuirib*. Gael. *oirbh*. Manx, *erriu*.

WARNYDHY, pron. prep. Upon her, or it. Written also *warnedhy*, qd. v.

WAROE, s. m. Merchandize. Corn. Voc. *merz*. From the English *ware*.

WARRAH, adj. Highest, chief, supreme. Llwyd, 159. A late form of *wartha*.

WARRE, adv. At once, soon. *Me a lever dheuch warré*, I tell you at once. P.C. 445. Another form of *waré*, or *wharré*, qd. v.

WARTHA, adv. Above. *Bedhens cbron dreys pûp tra râk kudhé mŷns ûs formyys, râk synzy glaw a wartha, dhe'n nôr reys may fe dyllys*, let the sky be above all things, to cover all (that) is created, to keep the rain above, to the earth of the world that it be sent forth. O.M. 23. (See *Awartha*.) A mutation of *gwartha*, id. qd. Welsh *gwarthav*, a summit.

WARWOLES, adv. Below. Llwyd, 248. See *War*, and *Woles*.

WARY, s. m. A state of freedom, liberty, licentiousness. Llwyd, 79. *Pan ethons oll dhe wary, ancombrys y rebon*, when they were all gone out, they were not of one mind. M.C. 34. *Mar mynnouch, me a'n chasty ol warbarth yn y cyté hag a'n delyrf dhe wary*, if ye will, I will chastise him once for all in his city, and let him go free. M.C. 127. *A ny worthas ow mestry, bôs dhymmo may fês ledhys, bo delyffris dhe wary*, knowest thou not my power, that it rests with me that thou shouldst be killed or let forth to liberty ? M.C. 144.

WAS, s. m. A servant, a fellow. *An côth wâs gôf*, the old smith follow. P.C. 1695. *Ty a'n gujsk avel cauch wâs*, thou strikest like a coward. P.C. 2103. *Ty wâs, dûs gynen yn mês a dhescmpys*, thou fellow, come with us out immediately. R.D. 1827. A mutation of *gwâs*, qd. v.

WASCAF, v. a. I will strike. *Del waskaf y peydrennow*, as I shall strike his buttocks. P.C. 2094. A mutation of *gwascaf*, 1 pers. s. fut. of *gwascel*, qd. v.

WASCO, v. a. He may strike. *Nynsus mâb gôf yn wlâsma, a wasko mar dhû, ha henna pûp ol a wôr*, there is not a smith's son in this country (that) can strike so well, and that every body knows. P.C. 2725. A mutation of *gwasco*, 3 pers. s. subj. of *gwascel*, qd. v.

WAST, adj. Idle. *Levereuch dhynny an kên agas bûs dhe wyl genen, nyns ôn tûs wast*, tell us the cause that ye have to do with us, we are not idle men. R.D. 2155.

WAT, s. m. A smart blow, a stroke. *Dysmyg lemmyn, ty guña smat, pyw a rôs dhyso an wat*, declare now, thou brave fellow, who gave thee the blow. P.C. 1384. Written also *what*, qd. v. W. *fat*.

WAYL, s. m. A work, an action. Pryce. A late form of *whél*, qd. v.

WAYLER, s. m. A workman. Pryce.

WEC, adj. Sweet. *A Dâs, Mâp, ha Spyrys Sans, gordhyans dhe'th corf wêk pûp prŷs*, O Father, Son, and Holy Ghost, glory to thy sweet body always. O.M. 86. More correctly written *whêc*, qd. v.

WECOR, s. m. A trader, a merchant. *Arté Iudas ow trylé ; gwan wecor nyn gové pâr, ny gl dén vŷth amontyé mŷns a gollas yn chyffar*, again Judas turning ; a weak trader, he found not an equivalent ; no man can compute how much he lost in the bargain. M.C. 40. A mutation of *gwecor*, another form of *gwiccur*, qd. v.

WEDRESIF, s. f. A lizard. Corn. Vocab. *lacerta*. W. *gwedresi*.

WEDH, s. f. Figure, form. *Yn wêdh* (W. *un wêdh*,) one form, likewise. *A wêdh*, also. Llwyd, 135. *Degé ol agan edhyn, bestes yn wêdh maga ta*, tithe of all our birds, beasts also as well. O.M. 1182. (See *Ynwêdh*.) A mutation of *gwêdh*, qd. v.

WEDHEN, s. f. A tree. *Fruit an wedhen a skyans dybbry bŷth na borth danger*, the fruit of the tree of knowledge to eat never make thou a delay. O.M. 167. *Cherubyn, êl Dew a râs yn wedhen me a welas*, a cherub angel of the God of grace, in the tree I saw. O.M. 804. A mutation of *gwedhen*, qd. v.

WEDHOH, v. n. Ye know. ‡ *Hwi a wedhoh*, ye know. Llwyd, 247. A mutation of *gwedhoh*, a late form of *gwedhouch*, 2 pers. pl. pres. of irr. v. *gon*, qd. v.

WEDHU, adj. Widowed. *Gwrêg wedhu*, a widow. *Ll.* 174. A mutation of *gwedhu*, qd. v.

WEDHYN, v. n. We knew. *Ni a wedhyn*, Llwyd, 247. A mutation of *gwedhyn*, 1 pers. pl. imperf. of irr. v. *gon*, qd. v.

WEGE, prep. After. *Wegé henna y fynnas Adam Eva dre y râs*, after that he would (create) Adam (and) Eve through his grace. O.M. 2828. More generally written *wogé*, qd. v. W. *wedi*.

WEIDWUR, s. m. A workman. *Weidwur ti*, architectus, an architect. Corn. Voc. A mutation of *gweidwur*, qd. v.

WEL, s. m. A sight. *Me a wolch scon ow dulé a wêl dheuch kettep onan*, I will wash immediately my hands in the sight of every one of you. P.C. 2500. *Dhynmo vy mar ny gresouch, ottengy a wêl ol dheuch, kepar ha del leverys*, if ye will not believe me, behold them in the sight of you all, as I said. P.C. 2689. *Ol ow ysyly yn ten, hag a wêl dhe lyes plu*, all my limbs tight, and in the sight of many a parish. R.D. 2584. A mutation of *gwêl*, qd. v.

WEL, v. n. He shall see. *My a wêl tyyr gwelen*, I see three rods. O.M. 1729. *Ty a wêl Mâp Dew owth esedhé*, thou shalt see the son of God sitting. P.C. 1328. *Wogé henma why a wêl Mâp Dew ow ysedhé*, after this ye shall see the son of God sitting. P.C. 1486. A mutation of *gwêl*, 3 pers. s. fut. of *gweles*, qd. v.

WEL, adj. Better. *Râg bythqueth my ny welys benen dhym a wel plekyé whêth yn nêp le*, for never have I seen a woman (that) pleases me better yet in any place. O.M. 2108. *Mŷl wel vyé yn bŷs-ma genys na ve*, a thousand (times) better it would be, that he had never been born into this world. P.C. 751. A mutation of *gwell*, qd. v.

WELAF, v. a. I shall see. *Yn tormont mar a'th welaf, gynes me a vŷdh marow*, in torment if I shall see thee, with thee I will die. P.C. 1029. A mutation of *gwelaf*, 1 pers. s. fut. of *gweles*, qd. v.

WELAS, v. a. He saw. *El Dew a râs yn wedhen me a welas*, an angel of the God of grace in a tree I saw. O.M. 804. *Fatel fue Cryst mertheryys râk kerengé tis an beys, why a welas yn tyen*, how Christ was martyred for love of the people of the world, ye have seen entirely. P.C. 3222. A mutation of *gweles*, 3 pers. s. pret. of *gweles*, qd. v.

WELAS, v. a. To seek, to look for. *My a'd peys, arluth uhel, dhe'u tŷr ty a ry cummyas, ma'm gasso kyns ys myrwel ynno bôs dhym dhe welas*, I pray to thee, high Lord, that thou wilt give leave to the earth, that it allow me before dying, iu it to seek food for myself. O.M. 378. Another form of *whelas*, qd. v.

WELEN, s. f. A rod. *Toul an welen ol yn tyen dhe'n dôr uskys*, throw thou the rod all entirely on the ground quickly. O.M. 1447. *An welen-ma yn hy kunda treylys arté*, this rod into its natural form (is) turned again. O.M. 1459. A mutation of *gwelen*, qd. v.

WELES, v. a. To see. *Dysqua lemman marthusow, may allyf vy y weles*, shew thou now miracles, that I may see them. P.C. 83. *Râk na yllyn dhe weles, cuth ny 'gen gâs*, for that we shall not see thee, sorrow will not leave us. P.C. 2455. Written also *welas*. *Avorow me agas pŷs dhe welas fetel sevys Cryst mês a'n bêdh, clêr ha wâr*, to-morrow I pray ye to see how Christ rose out of the tomb, bright and gentle. P.C. 3241. A mutation of *gweles*, qd. v.

WELEUCH, v. a. Ye shall see. *Guyn yw prest servyé yn ta pûr wŷr epscop a'n pâr-ma ; râg gentel yw, del weleuch*, it is always worth while to serve well very truly a bishop of this kind ; for gentle he is, as ye see. O.M. 2778. A mutation of *gweleuch*, 2 pers. pl. fut. of *gweles*, qd. v.

WELFYTH, v. a. Thou shalt see. *Whêth mŷr arté abervedh, hag ol ken ty a welfyth kyns ys dones a le-na*, look yet again within, and all else thou shalt see before coming from thence. O.M. 790. A mutation of *gwelfyth*, 2 pers. s. fut. of *gweles*, qd. v.

WELLA, adj. Best. *Ow mâp-lyen, kerch Annas, may hyllyf clewas pŷth yw an gusyl wella*, my clerk fetch Annas, that I may hear what is the best counsel. P.C. 555. A mutation of *gwella*, qd. v.

WELLA, v. a. He may see. *An kêth guâs-ma gorreuch why yn drôk pryson dhe peddry, golow na wella de̸ ffry*, this same fellow put ye in a bad prison to rot, that he may not see light really. R.D. 2003. A mutation of *gwella*, id. qd. *gwelo*, 3 pers. s. subj. of *gweles*, qd. v.

WELLA, v. a. He may better. *Yn della dhymmo y whêr; Arluth re wella ow cher war y lerch ef*, so to me there is sorrow ; may the Lord better my state after him. R.D. 710. A mutation of *gwella*, id. qd. *gwello*, 3 pers. s. subj. of *gwella*, qd. v.

WELOH, v. a. Ye shall see. ‡ *Hwi weloh*, ye see. Llwyd, 246. A late form of *welouch*, qd. v.

WELON, v. a. We shall see. ‡ *Ni a welon*, Llwyd, 246. A late form of *welyn*, a mutation of *gwelyn*, 1 pers. pl. fut. of *gweles*, qd. v.

WELOUCH, v. a. Ye shall see. *Teweuch râk mêdh, dew adla ; ymdhysquelhas ny tynna dhe plussyon, a welouch why*, be silent for shame, ye two knaves ; he would not have discovered himself to dirty fellows, do ye see. R.D. 1497. A mutation of *gwelouch*, 2 pers. pl. fut. of *gweles*, qd. v.

WELSEN, v. a. I had seen. *Mi a welsen*, Llwyd, 246. A mutation of *gwelsen*, 1 pers. s. plup. of *gweles*, qd. v.

WELTE, v. a. Thou shalt see. *Benen, a welté dhe flôch*, woman, seest thou thy son ? P.C. 2925. Written also *welta*. *Lemyn, lavar dhymo, abervedh pandra welta*, now tell me, what seest thou within. C.W. 130. *Lavar pandra welta moy*, tell what seest thou more. C.W. 132. Comp. of *wêl*, a mutation of *gwêl*, 3 pers. s. fut. of *gweles*, and *te*, thou.

WELYS, v. a. I saw. *Govy pan welys Eva*, woe is me, when I saw Eve ! O.M. 621. *My a wêl tyyr gwelen gay ; ny welys tekké, rum fay, bythqueth aban vêf genys*, I see three gay rods ; I have not seen fairer, on my faith, ever since I was born. O.M. 1730. A mutation of *gwelys*, 1 pers. s. preter. of *gweles*, qd. v.

WEN, adj. White. A mutation of *gwen*, which is properly the feminine form of *gwyn*, as in Welsh. The rule is not observed generally in Cornish, but is preserved in the local name *Treven*, the white town.

WERCHES, s. f. A virgin. *Ha venytha me a grŷs dhe vôs a werches genys, Mâp Dew, agan dysprynnyas*, and ever I will believe that thou art born of a virgin, Son of God, our Redeemer. P.C. 403. A mutation of *gwerches*, qd. v.

WERES, s. m. Help, aid, assistance. *Râg pûp tra ol a*

fýdh da, dre weres agan Dew ny, for all things will be good, by the help of our God. O.M. 535. *Guyn výs ynno uép a grýs ; rák dhe weres yn parys dhe'th servygy yn býs-ma*, happy is he that believes on him; for thy help is prepared for thy servants in this world. P.C. 2707. *A Tás, dre dhe luen weres dhe pygy menscn*, O Father, through thy full help I would pray thee. R.D. 443. A mutation of *gweres*, qd. v.

WERES, v. a. To help. A mutation of *gweres*, qd. v. *Scon a onan a'th asow my a wra dhyso parow púp úr ol rág dhe weres*, forthwith from one of thy ribs, I will make to thee an equal, always to help thee. O.M. 101. *Na porth own výdh, na védh trést, rág me a výdh prest orth dhe weres yn púp le*, bear no fear ever, nor be sad, for I will be with thee ready helping thee in every place. O.M. 1409. It is also the 3 pers. s. fut. *A ow máp kér, na porth a whér, Dew a'th weres*, O my dear son, do not complain, God will help thee. O.M. 1358. *Mars Cryst a weres deffry, ef a ládh gans fleyryngy ol ow glascor*, unless Christ will help indeed, he will kill with the stink all my kingdom. R.D. 2132.

WERESES, v. a. Let him help. *Dús a te-na, ty Gebal, gor an pren yn més gans mal, ha'th wereses Amalck*, come away, thou Gebal, carry the tree outside with a will, and let Amalek help thee. O.M. 2781. A mutation of *gwereses*, 3 pers. s. imp. of *gweres*.

WERN, s. f. An alder tree, the mast of a ship. A mutation of *gwern*, qd. v.

WERTHAS, v. a. He sold. *Oma vy nép a'th werthas dhe'n Hudhewon dhe ladhé*, am I he that sold thee to the Jews to kill thee? P.C. 756. A mutation of *gwerthas*, 3 pers. s. preter. of *gwerthé*, qd. v.

WERTHE, v. a. To sell. *Pendra yw henna dhynny, aban vynsys y werthé*, what is that to us, since thou wouldst sell him? P.C. 1510. A mutation of *gwerthé*, qd. v.

WERTHYS, v. a. I sold. *Dremas yw ef, leun a rás, nél re werthes, yn médh e*, he is a good man, full of grace, whom I have sold, said he. M.C. 103. A mutation of *gwerthys*, 1 pers. s. preter. of *gwerthé*, qd. v.

WERYSON, s. m. Guerdon. *Mar a kýll bones yacheys, ty a fýdh dhe lyfreson hag an our dhe weryson*, if he can be healed, thou shalt have thy liberty, and the gold thy guerdon. R.D. 1077. A mutation of *gweryson*, formed from the Fr. *guerdon*, or *guérison*, a cure.

WESY, v. a. To sweat, to perspire. *Máb Du o kymmys grevyys, rág tomder ef a wesé, dowr ha goys yn kemeskis weys Crist rág dhe gerensé*, the Son of God was so much grieved, from heat he sweated, water and blood mingled does Christ sweat for love to thee. M.C. 58. The substantive is generally written with an aspirate initial. (See *Whrys*, and *Whýs*.) W. *chwysu*. Arm. *chouezi*.

WESYON, s. m. Servants, fellows. *Me a wór ple móns purys, rág an wesyon ordenys*, I know where they are ready, for the fellows ordained. P.C. 2580. *Och, govy, ellas, guelas ow máp mar dyflas gans tebel wesion dychtys*, oh, woe is me, alas, to see my son, so shamefully by wicked fellows treated. P.C. 2605. A mutation of *gwesion*, plur. of *gwás*, qd. v.

WETRAS, v. n. He looked at. *Gans henna ef a clewas en colyck scon ow cané, ha Crist worto a wetras, a'n peynys brás may'th esé*, with that he heard the cock soon crowing, and Christ looked at him, from the great pains in which he was. M.C. 86. Another form of *whythras*, 3 pers. s. preter. of *whythré*, qd. v.

WETTE, adv. Behold. *A wetté vy lygth of foud, dheuch dynythys ; ahanaf pendra vynny*, behold me, light of foot, come to you ; of me what wilt thou? R.D. 1612. See *Awatta*.

WETH, s. f. A time, a turn. *A Ihesu, mychtern a rás, ioy dhym un wéth dhe welas*, O Jesus, king of grace, joy to me once to see thee. R.D. 815. A mutation of *gwéth*, qd. v.

WETH, s. f. A figure, form. *Dre múr hyreth ydhof púr squyth, ha'm corf dhe wéth, yscarn ha lýth*, through great longing, I am quite weary, and my body also, bones and back. R.D. 848. More correctly *wédh*, being a mutation of *gwédh*, qd. v.

WETH, adj. Worse. *Saw kyn féns y morthelek dhe wéth vydhons dhe'n cronek, ha garow yn y dhulé*, but though they be hammered, they shall be worse for the toad, and rough in his hands. P.C. 2732. *Yn della mar a whyrfýth, mýl wéth a výdh an dywedh*, if it happen so, a thousand (times) worse the end will be. R.D. 348. A mutation of *gwéth*, qd. v.

WETH, adv. Yet. *Ke wéth tressé treveth dhy, ha mýr gwel orth an wedhen*, go thou yet a third time to it, and look better at the tree. O.M. 799. More generally written *whéth*, qd. v.

WETHE, v. a. To keep, to preserve. *Pylat a yrchys dhedhé war beyn kylly an bewnans monas dhe'n corf dh' y wedhé, na'n kemerré y yskerans*, Pilate commanded them, on pain of losing their life, to go to the body to keep it, that his enemies might not take it. M.C. 241. A mutation of *gwethé*, id. qd. *gwythé*, qd. v. It is also the 3 pers. s. imperf. *Oynment o a gymmys rás, may wethé corf heb pedry*, the ointment was of so much virtue, that it kept a body without rotting. M.C. 235.

WETHYL, v. a. To make. *En debell wrék casadow gans múr a dóth éth yn chy, war hast dhe wethyll kentrow*, the wicked hateful woman with much of haste went into the house, in haste to make nails. M.C. 159. A mutation of *gwethyl*, qd. v.

WEW, s. m. Grief, woe. *My a'n kwouk ef er y wew; otté mellow y geyn brew*, I will beat him, to his grief ; behold the joints of his back broken. P.C. 2085. A mutation of *gew*, qd. v.

WEYDH, s. f. Figure, form. *Dew ha dén kepar del óf, an Tás yma ynnof, hag yn weydh my ynno ef*, like as I am God and man, the Father is in me, and likewise I in him. R.D. 2387. The same as *wédh*, qd. v., being thus written to show the long *e*.

WEYL, s. m. Sight. *A weyl ol dhe'n arlythy, me a's pe dhyso wharé*, in sight of all the lords, I will pay it to thee forthwith. P.C. 1558. A mutation of *gweyl*, id. qd. *gwél*, qd. v.

WEYL, v. a. He shall see. *Yn úr-na me a weyl mar a pedhyn ny abel dhe wúl defens a rák twes*, then I shall see if we shall be able to make a defence against people. P.C. 2304. The same as *wél*, qd. v.

WEYTH, s. m. A work. *Lavar dhyn mars 6s huder, drók na ýl dén výdh dhe wúl, na nýl dhé weyth, na dhé súl*, tell us if thou art a sorcerer, that no man ever is able to do harm to thee, neither work day, nor sunday. R.D. 1833. A mutation of *gweyth*, qd. v.

WEYTH, adv. Also, likewise. See *Weydh*.

WHAF, s. m. A blow. Pl. *whaffys*. *My a's guysk guns un blogon, vythqueth na ve bom a wen a rollo whuf war qales*, I will smite her with a bludgeon, that there never was a stroke I know that would give a blow so hard. O.M. 2711. *Nefré kyns môs alemma, ry whaf dhedhy my a wru gans myyn grow yn brâs garow*, ever before going hence give a blow to her I will, with gravel stones very sharply. O.M. 2775. *Powesouch, aflythygyon, râg marow yw an voron gans ow whaffys sed a breys*, rest ye, wretches, for dead is the jade by my blows a long time past. O.M. 2747. W. *chwaf*, a strong gust; *puf*, a blow.

WHANE, v. a. He should pierce. *Longis a'n barth dychow dhe grous Ihesus ydh esé, dhe'n marreg worth y hanow y a yrhys may whané*, Longius was on the right side of the cross of Jesus; to the soldier by his name they bade that he should pierce. M.C. 218. A mutation of *gwané*, 3 pers. s. subj. of *gwané*, qd. v.

WHANS, s. m. Desire, longing, appetite, lust. *Pûr luen yma dhym ow whans a'n ven cowethes ordnys*, very full is my desire to me of the woman ordained for a helpmate. O.M. 91. *A'y frût dybry ny'm bes whans dres dyfen ow arluth kêr*, of its fruit to eat I have not a desire against the prohibition of my dear Lord. O.M. 171. *An Tâs a'n nêf, dre y grâs, a danvou dheuch agas whans*, the Father of heaven, through his grace, will send to you your desire. O.M. 1806. *Yn top an wedhen dêk, ydh esa un virgin whêk, ha'y flôch pûr sevely waylyes yn y defran wondrys whans*, in the top of the fair tree there was a sweet virgin, and her child very seemly swaddled in her bosom wondrous desirably. C.W. 138. W. *chwant*, †*couuant*. Arm. *choant*, †*hoant*. Ir. *saint*, †*sant*. Gael. *sannt*. Maux, *saynt*. Sansc. *sansa*. Goth. *wan*. Eng. *want*.

WHANSEC, adj. Desirous. *A mester whêk, gordhys re by, pan wrêth mar têk agan dysky; asson whansek ol dhe pysy, lettrys ha lêk, war Dhu mercy*, O sweet Master, be thou worshipped, when thou dost so sweetly teach us; we are desirous all to pray, lettered and lay, to God for mercy. P.C. 37. *Y drobell ydhew kemys, whansek nyngew a drevyth*, his trouble is so much, he is not desirous of any thing. C.W. 130. W. *chwannog*. Arm. *choantec*.

WHAR, adj. Gentle. Written also *wâr*, qd. v. *Whâr* is also the regular mutation of *wâr*, after the adverbial particle *yn*. *Benegas yw nêb a gâr Du dris pûp tra ûs yn bŷs, hag a wodhaflo yn whâr dhodho ûs ordnys*, blessed is he that loves God beyond every thing that is in the world, and that suffers gently as much as is ordained to him. M.C. 24. *Yn hanow Du, te lavar, mars ôs Du, del omwressys; me yn, yn mêdh Crist yn whâr*, in God's name, say thou if thou art God as thou hast made thyself; I am, says Christ gently. M.C. 93.

WHARE, adv. Anon, presently, quickly, soon, at once. Written also *wharré*, *warré*, and *waré*. *Wharé yn mês y trylyas, ha'y golen namna dorré*, anon out he turned, and his heart all but broke. M.C. 87. *Yu nûes a'n gorhel wharré my ha'm gurêk ha'm flehas â*, out of the ark soon, I and my wife, and my children will go. O.M. 1167. *My a worthyp dhys warré*, I will answer thee presently. P.C. 1973. *Ha mar a lever dên vŷth er agas pyn why travyth, waré gurêch y gorthyby*, and if any man say anything against you, soon do ye answer him. P.C. 181.

WHARFOS, v. n. To happen, to occur, to fall out. Preterite *whyrfys*. Part. pass. *wharfedhys*, *wharvedhys*. *Ny won fatel fyl wharfos, ty, a dhên, omma dhe vôs, dynythys yn kŷc yn kuus*, I know not how it can happen, that thou, O man, shouldst be here, come in flesh and in blood. R.D. 229. *Arluth, mar callé wharfos gynen ty dhe vynnes bôs omma pûp ûr*, Lord, if it could happen, with us that thou wouldst be here always. R.D. 2439. *Yn della dhyn re wharfo*, so may it happen to us. O.M. 667. *My a vyn aga threhy, pepynng ol a wharfo*, I will cut them, whatever may happen. O.M. 1736. *A nyns osé pryeryn, uferêth yw dhys gowyn pŷth yw an marth a wharfé*, if thou art not a stranger, it is idleness for thee to ask what is the wonder (that) has occurred. R.D. 1263. *Ellas bôs wharfedhys yn ow gulâs myshyf a'n pâr-ma codhys*, alas to have happened in my country harm of this sort fallen. O.M. 1548. *Yma tra varth wharvedhys*, there is a wondrous thing happened. O.M. 2082. *Ha whâth moy wy a glewyth a dormont Crist del wharsé*, and yet more shall ye hear of Christ's torment how it happened. M.C. 132. W. *cyvarvod*. Arm. *choarvout*, *choarvezout*. See also *Whyrfys*, *Whyrfyth*, *Whyrys*.

WHARTH, s. m. Laughter. *Ow hothman, na gymer marth, ty a'n ool, ha lyas mŷl, kyn'dhota 'skynnys yn wharth, yn dywedh, heb tûll na gŷl, why a vêl deall uskys*, my friend, take thou not wonder, thou shalt weep, and many thousands, although thou art fallen into laughter; in the end without fraud or guile, ye shall see a deluge quickly. C.W. 168. W. *chwarth*. Arm. *choarz*. Ir. *gaire*. Gael. *gaire*.

WHARTHE, v. n. To laugh. 3 pers. s. future *wharth*. *Un dra a won, a'n godhfês, a russé dhe dhydhané; beys vynytha y wharthes râg lowené*, one thing I know, if thou knewest it (that) would amuse thee; for ever thou wouldst laugh for joy. O.M. 153. *A enefow, ol warbarth, deuch gynef; ol why a wharth, kemmys re wrûk bôdh ow thâs*, O souls, altogether, come with me; all ye shall laugh, as many as have done the will of my Father. R.D. 156. Another form is *wherthyn*, qd. v. W. *chwardhu*. Arm. *choarzi*. Ir. *gair*. Gael. *gair*. Manx, *gair*. Sansc. *hars*.

WHAS, adj. Good. *Iosep dhe Gryst a vynnas y arrow ha'y dhuffrech whêk yn vaner del (ve) yn whas, hag a's ystynnas pûr dêk*, Joseph for Christ made white his legs and sweet arms, in manner as was well, and stretched them out full gently. M.C. 232. An irregular aspirate mutation of *mâs*, the regular form being *yn fâs*. Cf. *what*, with W. *fat*; and *whâth* yet, with Ir. *fós*, and Gael. *fuathas*; and *whib*, *wib*, W. *chwiban*, with Ir. and Gael. *feudan*. Manx, *feddan*.

WHAT, s. m. A blow. *Desefsen dodho ry what*, we wished to give him a blow. R.D. 604. Written also *wat*, qd. v. W. *fat*.

WHATH, adv. Yet, still, again, over and above. *Whâth kentrow dhedhé nyngo Ihesus yn crows râg synsy*, still there were not nails to them to hold Jesus on the cross. M.C. 154. *Lucyfer kelmys yw whâth pûr fast yn y golmennow*, Lucifer is still bound very fast in his bonds. M.C. 212. *Yma Dew whâth ow percé, nêb ew arluth drys pûp tra*, there is a God yet living, who is Lord above every thing. O.M. 622. *Ny gresaf, awos an beys, bôs an horé whâth marow*, I will not believe for the world,

WHEL 271 WHETH

that the strumpet is yet dead. O.M. 2753. Written also *whîth*, qd. v. W. *chwaith*. Arm. *choaz*. Ir. *fós*. Gael. *feathast*. Manx, *foast*.

WHEAL, s. f. A work, a mine work. *Wheal stean*, a tin work. *Wheal cober*, a copper work. *Wheal glou*, a coal work. This word is still in common use in Cornwall, to denote a mine work, as *Wheal Basset*, *Wheal Seton*, *Wheal Tolgus*, &c. Written in the Ordinalia *wheyl*, and contractedly *whêl*, qd. v.

WHEC, adj. Sweet, pleasant, dear. Written indiscriminately *whêg*. Comp. *wheccah*. Sup. *whecca*, *wheccé*. *Ow broder whêc*, *dûn dhe dré*, my sweet brother, let us come home. O.M. 525. *Wy yn glân a bûb fyltê*, *mas nynjouch ol da na whêk*, ye are clean from every foulness, but ye are not all good nor sweet. M.C. 47. *An luef a'm grûk me a wêl, ha'y odor whekké ys mêl ow tôs warnaf*, I see the hand that made me, and his odour sweeter than honey, coming upon me. R.D. 144. W. *chwég*. Arm. *chouec*, + *huec*.

WHECTER, s. m. Sweetness, suavity, delight. *Yn mês a'm joy, ha'm whekter*, *rês yw keskar dre terros*, away from my joy and my delight, I must wander through lands. O.M. 359. Arm. *chouekder*.

WHEDDYDH, s. m. The space of six days. *Râg bones ol têk ha da yn wheddydh mŷns yw formyys*, *aga sona ny a wra*, for that all is fair and good, in six days all that is created, bless them we will. O.M. 142. Comp. of *whêh*, six, and *dŷdh*, a day.

WHEFFES, adj. Sixth. *Hedhyw yw an wheffes dŷdh aban dallethrys gonys*, *may râg nêf*, *môr*, *tŷr*, *ha gweeydh*, *bestes*, *puskes*, *golowys*, to-day is the sixth day since I began to work, that I made heaven, sea, land, and trees, beasts, fishes, lights. O.M. 49. ‡ *Ha godhihuar ha metten o an wheffas deydh*, and the evening and the morning were the sixth day. C.W. p. 195. Comp. of *whêh*, six, and *mes*, id. qd. W. *mêd*, a measure. W. *chweched*, + *chwechet*. Arm. *chouechved*. Ir. *seismheadh*, *scamhadh*, + *seised*. Gael. *seathadh*. Manx, *sheyoo*. Gr. ἕκτος. Lat. *sextus*.

WHEGOL, adj. Sweet, all sweet. *I vam whegol a welas del exons worth y dhygtyé*, his sweet mother saw how they were treating him. M.C. 164. *Ow arluth whêk-ol lâdh e*, *ken ef a wra ow shyndyé*, *war clew vŷth agan guary*, my all sweet lord, kill him, otherwise he will injure me, if he shall ever hear of our sport. O.M. 2132. W. *chwegol*.

WHEH, card. num. Six. *Henna yw pûr scorn ha geys*, *râg y fue kyns y vôs gurŷs dew ugens blydhen ha whê*, that is a very sneer, and jest, for there were before it was done, forty years and six. P.C. 351. *Whêh dydhyow te wra whêl*, *hag a wra mŷns ês dhys dhe wûl*, six days shalt thou work, and do all that thou hast to do. *Râg yn whêh dydhyow Dew a wrûs an nêf ha'n 'oar*, *an môr*, *ha mŷns ês ythens y*, for in six days the Lord made heaven and earth, the sea and all that is in them. Pryce. W. *chwêch*, *hwêch*. Arm. *chouech*. Irish, *se*. Gael. *se*. Manx, *shey*. Sansc. *shash*. Zend, *csas*. Gr. ἕξ. Lat *sex*. Mæso-Goth. *saihs*.

WHEHDEGVAS, adj. Sixteenth. Pryce. Comp. of *whehdeg*, sixteen, and *mês*, a measure.

WHEL, s. f. A work. *An sythvas dŷdh yw an Sabbath an Arluth dhe Dew*, *yn dŷdh-na te nyn wra ehan a whêl ; te nyn dhe vûb, nyn dhe verch, nyn dhe dén whêl, nyn dhe môs whêl*, the seventh day is the Sabbath of the Lord thy God ; in that day thou shalt do no manner of work ; thou nor thy son, nor thy daughter, nor thy workman, nor thy workwoman. Pryce. Written also *wheyl*, qd. v.

WHELAF, v. a. I shall see. *Och, gory, râk ow mâp kêr, dhe weles yn kêth waner may whelaf lemmyn dychtys*, Oh, woe is me, for seeing my dear son in such a manner that I see him now treated. P.C. 2945. The aspirate mutation of *gwelaf*, 1 pers. s. fut. of *gweles*, qd. v.

WHELAS, v. a. He saw. *Dre rûs an goys y whelas Ihesus Crist del o dythgtis*, through the virtue of the blood he saw how Jesus Christ was treated. M.C. 219. The asp. mutation of *gwelas*, 1 pers. s. fut. of *gweles*, qd. v.

WHELAS, v. a. To seek, to search for. Written also *whelé*. *Gustr dhym ty a dharyvas an warchvran-na dh'y whelé*, truly thou hast told me, to seek for that raven. O.M. 1106. *Yno gwell in-ta whelas bôs dhe'th ly ha dhe'th kynyow*, in it take care well to seek food for thy breakfast, and for thy dinner. O.M. 1139. *Nêb a wheleuch why me yw*, whom ye seek I am (lie.) M.C. 68. *En Edhewon yutrethé a whelas dustuncow*, the Jews among them sought witnesses. M.C. 90. *Na bŷth moy ken mam nefrê es hyhy te na whela*, seek thou not evermore any other mother than her. M.C. 198. *An pesworé a gewsys, na whelyn gwevyê an pow*, the fourth said, let us not seek to flee the country. M.C. 247. *Gans henna y a drylyas, hag êth tûs Crist râg whelas*, with that they returned, and went to seek for the people of Christ. M.C. 257. Written also *whylas*, qd. v. W. *chwilio*. Arm. *chouilia*. Manx, *shalee*.

WHELLO, v. a. He may see. *Guask gynsy dyncyth an mên ; may whello an debeles ow gueres menouch dhedhé*, strike with it twice the stone ; that the wicked may see my frequent help to them. O.M. 1849. The aspirate mutation of *gwelo*, 3 pers. s. subj. of *gweles*, qd. v.

WHELTH, s. m. A tale, a story. *Ef a garâ Crist gwelas, râg gymmys ydho praysys, ganso mar callo clewas whelth noreydh a o coynitys*, he loved to see Christ, for that he was so much praised, that he might be able to hear the new story that was recounted. M.C. 109. See *Whethl*.

WHER, s. m. A complaint, sorrow, ailment. *A ow mâp kêr, na portha whêr, Dew a'th weres*, O my dear son, do not complain ; God will help thee. O.M. 1357. *A vam whêk, na portha wêr, râk nesfrê yn pûp maner, me a vŷdh prest parys dhys*, O sweet mother, do not bear sorrow, for always in every manner I will be well prepared for thee. P.C. 2949. *Adam, pandra whêr dhe why, yn delma honas serrys*, Adam, what ails thee, in this manner to be troubled ? C.W. 88. *Yn della dhymmo y whêr*, so to me is sorrow. R.D. 709. *Bôs trest dhywhy pendra whêr*, what is your grief that ye are sad ? R.D. 1255. Written also *awher*, qd. v.

WHEROW, adj. Bitter. *Wogé ow da oberow, dywes a yrhys dedhé, dhym rosons lystyl wherow ; bŷth ny fynnys y evé*, after my good works, I asked drink of them ; they gave me bitter gall ; never would I drink it. R.D. 2001. Written by Pryce, *chwero*, qd. v.

WHETTAC, card. num. Sixteen. Pryce. More correctly *whedhec*. Arm. *chouezec*. Irish, *sedeag*. Gael. *se-deug*. Manx, *shey jeig*. Lat. *sedecim*. See *Hwetlag*.

WHETH, adv. Yet, again, ever, quite. *Whêth mŷr arté aberveth*, yet look thou again within. O.M. 780. *Whêth ol bywé y a wra*, all those are yet living. O.M. 1877,

Kyn fe dysyerys an temple, yn tri dydh y'n drehafsé bythqueth whêth na fe ve guel, though the temple were destroy in three days he would re-build it, that never yet it was better. P.C. 384. The same as *whêth*, qd. v.

WHETHE, v. a. To blow. 2 pers. s. imp. and 3 pers. s. fut. *whêth*. Part. pass. *whethys*. *Dyson hep whethé dhe gorn, dysempys gwra y dhybry*, quietly without blowing thy horn, do thou eat it immediately. O.M. 207. *Och, tru, tru, shyndyys bf gans cronek du, ha whethys gans y venym*, Oh, sad, hurt I am by a black toad, and blown by his venom. O.M. 1779. *Whethouch menstrels ha tabours*, blow ye minstrels and tabours. O.M. 1995. *Hep whethé corn na gûl sôn*, without blowing horn, or making a noise. P.C. 1358. *Me a wra ge dên a bry, haval dh'agan face wharé, hag a whêth yn y vody sperys, may hallas bewa*, I will make thee man of clay, like to our face anon, and will blow in thy body a spirit that thou mayst live. C.W. 28. Written also *whythé*, qd. v.

WHETHL, s. m. A tale, a story. Pl. *whethlow*. *Ef a'n pren, re synt iowyn, mar ny dhynach y whethlow*, he shall catch it, by Saint Jove, if he retracts not his tales. P.C. 360. *Pyth yw an whethlow, ha'n sôn a glevaf aberth yn pow*, what are the tales, and the report (that) I hear in the land? R.D. 609. *Taw ty wrêk gans dhe whethlow, ha cows gufr, del y'th pysaf*, be silent, thou woman, with thy stories, and speak truth as I pray thee. R.D. 901. The sing. is wrongly spelt *whelth*, in M.C. 109, qd. v. W. *chwedl*. Arm. *keel, kehezl*. Irish, *sgeal*, + *keadal*. Gael. *sgeul*. Manx, *skeeal*.

WHEYL, s. f. A work. *Pan vo ol dhyn lafurryys, agan wheyl a vêdh mothow*, when all is laboured by us, our work will be falling. O.M. 1216. *Ty vaow, darbar lym ha pry, meyn wheyl, slodyys, ha genow*, thou boy, prepare lime and clay, building stones, trucks, and wedges. O.M. 2318. *Rág ef a vyn hep lettyé wheyl y dás y golennel*, for he will, without stopping, fulfil the work of his Father. O.M. 2428. *My re wrûk y vusuré rág an kêth wheil-ma dewyth*, I have measured it for this work twice. O.M. 2560. Written in late Cornish *wheal*, and contractedly *whêl*. W. *chwgl*. Arm. *kouls*. Manx, *queryl*. Eng. *wheel, while*.

WHEYS, v. u. To sweat. *Wheys yw ow thâl dhyso gy ow fystené*, my forehead is sweating to you hastening. O.M. 2686. Written also *wesy*, qd. v.

WHODHEFYS, v. a. He suffered. *War y corf y whodhefys mûr a peynys râk sawyé lynnycth môp dên*, on his body he suffered many pains to save the race of mankind. R.D. 1808. The aspirate mutation of *godhefys*, 3 pers. s. preterite of *godhevel*, qd. v.

WHODHFOUCH, v. a. Ye may know. *A wotté ve ef gené, may whodhfouch yn pûr deffiry; ny gafaf vy kên ynno*, behold him with me, that he may know in very earnest, I find not cause in him. P.C. 2157. The aspirate mutation of *godhfouch*, 2 pers. pl. subj. of *godhfos*, qd. v.

WHOLHAS, v. a. He washed. *Y wholhas y dhewlagas gans y eyll leyfo gosys*, he washed his eyes with his one hand (that) was bloodied. M.C. 219. The aspirate mutation of *golhas*, 3 pers. s. preter. of *golhy*, qd. v.

WHOLON, s. f. The heart. *Ow broder whêk, dûn dhe dré ; yma un posygyon brûs tcur ow wholon ow codhé, pynag vo ve*, my sweet brother, let us come home, there is a great heaviness falling on my heart, whatever it may be. O.M. 527. An irregular aspirate mutation of *colon* ; the regular form being *ow holon*.

WHON, v. n. I acknowledge. *A'n gueel gweres mar a'm vêdh, dhe Dew dhe voy y whon grás*, from the rods if I shall have help, to God the more I give thanks. O.M. 2016. *Dhys y whon grás, rák dhe dhesyr, ioy yn ow yulds y fydh pûr wêr*, to thee I acknowledge thanks, for thy desire, joy in my land shall be very truly. R.D. 870. *Y whon guêfr Dew agen Tás y sor dhyn y teig pûr vrás*, I know truly God our Father his anger to us that he will bear very great. C.W. 62. The aspirate mutation of *gon*, qd. v.

WHRETH, v. a. Thou wilt do. *Prág y whrêth genaf flattra*, why dost thou flatter with me? C.W. 48. The asp. mutation of *gwrêth*, 2 pers. s. fut. of *gwrey*, qd. v.

WHREUCH, v. n. Ye will do. *Yn ûr-na whreuch pyjadow, may codhdho an mynydhyow warnouch rág ewn uthekter*, in that hour ye shall make prayers, that the mountains may fall upon you, for very horror. P.C. 2651. The aspirate mutation (after *y* understood) of *gwreuch*, 2 pers. plur. fut. of *gwrey*, qd. v.

WHRUSSONS, v. a. They did. *May whrussons cam dremené y vyllyk an prýs*, that they did the evil transgression they will curse the time. O.M. 337. The asp. mutation of *grussons*, 3 pers. pl. preter. of *gwrey*, qd. v.

WHRUSTE, v. a. Thou didst. *Eva prág y whrusté sy tullé dhe bryes hep kên, an aval worth y derry, wosé my dhys dh'y dhefen*, Eve, why didst thou deceive thy husband without pity, by plucking the apple, after I had forbidden it to thee ? O.M. 277. The asp. mutation of *grusté*, comp. of *gwrus*, id. qd. *gwres*, 2 pers. s. imperf. of *gwrey*, and *te*, thou.

WHRYLLY, v. a. Thou mayst do. *Kyn whrylly flattré mar mûr ahanas tra vgth ny'm dûr, kyn dhós bysy*, though thou mayst chatter so much, from thee nothing concerns me, though thou be busy. R.D. 1058. *Ty Pilat dhum artuth dues ; kyn whrylly vgth cows a drues dhynny lemmyn, genen ny ty á*, thou Pilate come to my lord ; though thou mayst speak ever against it to us now, with us thou shalt go. R.D. 1792. The asp. mutation of *guerylly*, 2 pers. s. subj. of irr. v. *gwrey*, qd. v.

WHUL, v. a. To do or make. *Adam, sáf yn ban yn clor, ha treyl dhe gk̂k, ha dhe weys ; preder my dhe'th whûl a dôr, huval dhymo a'n pen dhe'n troys*, Adam, stand up on the ground, and turn to flesh and to blood ; consider me to have wrought thee of earth, like to me from the head to the foot. O.M. 67. The asp. mutation of *gûl*, qd. v.

WHY, pron. subs. Ye or you. *Omma ny wrcuch why trygé ; euch yn més a dhysympys : why a geyl ow lowené a rýs dhyuch yn parathys*, here ye shall not stay, go out immediately ; ye will lose my joy, that I gave to you in Paradise. O.M. 317. *Botler, my a worhemmyn ha'th cowyth, guytheuch why y*, butler, I command (thee) and thy companion, guard ye them. O.M. 2043. *My a lever dheucheuhy why*, I say to you. O.M. 2209. *Why re leverys ow bós, ha pûr wêr yn della bf ; why a wra y aswonvos dêdh brûs, hag a'n k̂sf yn prôf*, ye have said that I am, and very truly so I am ; ye will acknowledge it on the day of judgment, and will have it in proof. P.C. 1493. This is the common form in the Ordinalia of *chui*, qd. v.

WHYFLYN, adj. Hissing. *Yn tân whyflyn ef a séf, ha paynys neffré a pŷs; ha'y gân a vŷdh och, goef dhe'n bŷs-ma pan fue genys*, in hissing fire he shall stay, and tormented ever shall pray; and his song shall be, Oh, woe is me, to this world when I was born. R.D. 2311. W. *chwifiawl*.

WHYL, s. f. A work. *Popel Ysral ny assaf, na's gorren y dhy whŷl créf*, the people of Israel I will not leave, that I put them not to hard work. O.M. 1490. A contracted form of *wheyl*, qd. v.

WHYLAS, v. a. To seek for, to search for. *Dhyn levereuch, pyw a whyleuch, A Yedhewon*, tell me whom ye seek, O Jews. P.C. 1109. *Iosep whyla corf mâb Maria dheworth Pylat*, Joseph, seek the body of the Son of Mary from Pilate. P.C. 3100. *Y laddré mar whylé dèn*, if a man seek to steal it. R.D. 370. *A dhysempys whylewhé (whyleuch why) maras ethé dhe cudhé*, immediately seek ye, if he is gone to hide. R.D. 537. *Tra vŷth ny amont dhynny y whylas ef na moy*, it avails us nothing to seek him any more. R.D. 560. *Nép a whyleth, nychsys y treys gans dhe dhyw pléth*, whom thou seekest, thou driedst his feet with thy two plaits. R.D. 853. *Me a'th pŷs, pyw a whylyth*, I pray thee, whom seekest thou? R.D. 1640. *An emprour reu danfonas a whylas yn pow gueras*, the emperor has sent me to seek help in the country. R.D. 1645. *An kéth profus a whylyes gurŷs yw marow*, the same prophet (that) thou wert seeking is killed. R.D. 1680. *Euch, whyleuch dhymmo Pilat*, go ye, seek Pilate for me. R.D. 1773. *Dûn ahanan, ha touth da dhe whyles an kéth guâs-na*, let us come hence, and with good haste to seek that same fellow. R.D. 1780. *Gans y gollan marthys soon ydh emwyskys yn golon; hager vernans a whylas*, with his knife wondrous soon he smote himself in the heart; a cruel death he sought. R.D. 2068. Written also *whelas*, qd. v. W. *chwilio*. Arm. *chouilia*. Manx, *shalee*.

WHYLFYTH, v. a. He shall see. *Yw syré, war ow ené, ha henna why a whylfyth*, it is sir, on my soul, and that you shall see. P.C. 2208. The asp. mutation of *gwylfyth*, 3 pers. s. fut. of *gweles*, qd. v.

WHYLLY, v. a. Thou mayest see. *Me a'th whyp war an wolok, may whylly gurychon ha môk dhe dhew-lagas a dre dro*, I will whip thee on the face that thou mayest see sparks and smoke round about thy eyes. P.C. 2101. The asp. mutation of *gwyly*, 2 pers. s. subj. of *gweles*, qd. v.

WHYLLYN, v. a. We shall see. *Amen may whyllyn Cryst agan prennas yn tyn*, Amen that we may see Christ (that) bought us painfully. R.D. 829. *Vynytha erna whyllyn, a travyth ny gemeryn nép lowené*, ever until we shall see (thee), from any thing we shall not receive pleasure. R.D. 2364. The asp. mutation of *gwyllyn*, 1 pers. pl. fut. and subj. of *gweles*, qd. v.

WHYLSYN, v. a. We saw. *Y whylsyn y verthuryé, hag yn grous pren y squerdyé*, we saw his being martyred, and torn on the cross-tree. R.D. 1282. *My ny wodhyen a'th vernans, na vŷth moy a'th daserchyans, pan y'th whylsyn dewedhys*, I knew not of thy death, nor any more of thy resurrection, when we saw thee come. R.D. 2546. The asp. mutation of *gwylsyn*, 1 pers. pl. preterite of *gweles*, qd. v.

WHYN, adj. White. *Maga whyn avel an léth*, as white as the milk. P.C. 3138. The asp. mutation of *gwyn*, qd. v.

WHYRFYS, v. n. Happened. *Yn Egip whyrfys yw câs; ow popel vy grevvys brâs gans Pharow yw mylyges*, in Egypt trouble has happened, my people, greatly aggrieved by Pharoah, (that) is accursed. O.M. 1415. Part. of *wharfos*, qd. v.

WHYRFYTH, v. n. He will happen. *Rág y whyrfyth an tyrmyn, dredhé may fether dhe wel*, for the time will happen, that they shall be improved by them. O.M. 45. *Yn della mar a whyrfeth, mŷl wéth a vŷdh an dywedh*, if it shall happen so, a thousand (times) worse the end will be. R.D. 347. 3 pers. s. fut. of *wharfos*, qd. v.

WHYRYS, v. n. It happened. *Dhyn kyns ef a leverys, ol annodho del whyrys yn nôr bŷs-ma*, to us before he told, all as it happened relating to him in the earth of this world. R.D. 1190. An abbreviated form of *whyrfys*, qd. v.

WHYS, s. m. Sweat, perspiration. *Y'th whŷs lavur dhe dhybry ty a wra, bŷs y'th worfen*, in thy sweat labour to eat thou shalt, even to thy end. O.M. 273. *An heys yw cales kylden, yn lafur, whŷs, hag anken, ha deydh ha nôs*, the world is a hard lodging, in labour, sweat, and sorrow, both day and night. R.D. 245. *Ow hanow yw Vernona; fûs Ihesu gynef yma, yn hyvelep gurŷs a'y whŷs*, my name is Veronica; I have the face of Jesus, in a likeness made by his sweat. R.D. 1705. Written by Llwyd, 157, *huês*. W. *chwŷs*. Arm. *choues*. Gr. ἶδος. Lat. *sudor*. Eng. *sweat*. Sansc. *svéda*.

WHYTHE, v. a. To blow. 3 pers. s. fut. *whŷth*. *Tân yn kunys gorraf uskys, whythé a wrâf*, fire in the fuel I will immediately put, I will blow. O.M. 1388. *Ny a whŷth yn dhe vody sperys may hylly bewé*, we will breathe into thy body a spirit that thou mayst live. O.M. 61. *Otté lour kunys gyné, whythyns lemmyn pûp yn fréth; nêb na whytho gréns fannyé gans y lappa worth an eth*, behold fuel enough with me; let all blow now vigorously; he that does not blow, let him fan with his lap to the blast. P.C. 1244. *Cowethé, hedhench kunys, ha my a whŷth gans mûr greys may lewé an tân wharré*, comrades, reach wood, and I will blow with much force, that the fire may kindle soon. P.C. 1220. Written also *whethé*, qd. v. W. *chwythu*. Arm. *choueza*. Ir. *seid*. Gael. *seid*. Manx, *sheid*. Germ. *wehe*. Sansc. *svas*.

WHYTHRE, v. a. To look at, to look for, to seek, to search for. 3 pers. s. fut. *whythyr*. *Ha mŷr a pûp tenewen; aspy yn ta pûp celwn; whythyr pûp tra ol bysy*, and look thou on every side; examine well every particular; search out every thing diligently. O.M. 748. *Ny allaf myres y'th fath râk golowder; nymbus grath a whythré warnas un prŷs*, I cannot look in thy face for the light; there is not grace to me to look on thee a while. O.M. 1414. *Whythrouch hedheu worthyf wharré; me yw Ihesu an Nazaré; lywyreuch whéth, pan'dh euch mar fréth, pyw a whyleuch*, look ye to-day at me presently; I am Jesus of Nazareth; say again, when ye are so bold, whom seek yo. P.C. 1113.

WHYTHRES, s. f. A deed, work. *Aban golsté worty hy, ha gruthyl dres ow defen; mylygé a wrâf defry an nôr y'th whythres hogen*, since thou hearkenedst to her, and actedst beyond my prohibition, I will assuredly curse the earth in thy evil deed. O.M. 272. *A Dâs Dew y'th wolowys, grannt dhe'th whythres, my a'd peys, nép péth a oel a vercy*, O God the Father in thy lights, grant to thy work, I pray thee some of the oil of mercy. O.M. 326. The asp. mutation of *gwythres*, qd. v.

WIB, s. f. A pipe. Corn. Voc. *musa.* W. *chwîb,* a pipe, whence *chwiban,* a whistle. Arm. *chouiban.* Ir. *feadan.* Gael. *feadan.* Manx, *feddan.*

WIBANOR, s. m. A sock or slipper. Corn. Voc. *sublularis.* W. *chwibanor,* what hisses or creaks, from the noise made by a sock or slipper.

WIBONOUL, s. m. A pipe or flute. Corn. Voc. *fistula.* Derived from *wiban,* a whistle, whence also *wibanor,* qd. v. W. *chwibanogyl.*

WIC, s. f. A village. *Pryce.* A mutation of *gwic,* qd. v.

WICCET, s. m. A little village. A mutation of *gwiccet,* dim. of *gwic.* It is preserved in the local name *Wickel,* in St. Agnes.

WIHITH, s. m. Care, caution. ‡ *Dho cymeras wihith,* to beware; lit. to take care. Llwyd, 47. A late form of *gwith,* qd. v.

WILECUR, s. m. A parasite. Corn. Voc. *parasitus.* It is possibly a corrupt reading of *wiledur,* which would be W. *gwledhwr,* a banqueter, from *gwlêdh.* Ir. *flendh,* † *fled.* Gael. *fleadh,* a feast.

WILI, s. m. A bed. ‡ *Môs dho wili,* to go to bed. Llwyd, 231. A mutation of *gwili,* id. qd. *gwely,* qd. v.

WIN, s. m. Wine. Corn. Voc. *vinum. Gwedran a win,* a glass of wine. Llwyd, 242. A mutation of *gwin,* qd. v.

WINAS, s. m. Nails. Llwyd, 28. An abbreviated form of *ewinnas,* pl. of *ewin,* qd. v.

WINDRAW, s. m. Numbness in the fingers from extreme cold. Llwyd, 165. A late corruption of *ewinrew,* qd. v.

WINNIC, adj. Marshy, fenny, moorish. *Pryce.* Preserved in the names of places, as *Trewinnick,* the marshy town, in St. Ervan, and Gwennap. *Arwenak,* on the marsh, near Falmouth. *Penwinnick,* the head of the marsh, in St. Agnes. *Winnic* is a mutation of *gwinic,* the adj. of *guen,* qd. v.

WINNOW, s. m. Moors. *Pryce. Trewinnow,* the town of moors, in Creed, and Davidstow. A mutation of *gwinnow,* pl. of *guen,* qd. v.

WIPHT, s. m. A piper. Corn. Voc. *tibicen.* Comp. of *wib,* a pipe, and *it,* which denotes the agent. W. *chwifiwr.*

WIR, adj. True. *En wir,* truly, indeed. Llwyd, 134. A mutation of *gwir,* qd. v.

WIRIONETH, s. m. Truth. *Pûr wyryoneth re geusys ahanaf,* very truth hast thou spoken of me. P.C. 1587. A mutation of *gwirioneth,* qd. v.

WISCY, v. a. To dress, to clothe. *Pryce.* A mutation of *gwiscy,* id. qd. *gwesca,* qd. v.

WITH, s. m. Care. *Cemer with,* take care. Llwyd, 251. A mutation of *gwith,* qd. v.

WITHEN, s. f. A tree. *Pryce.* More correctly *wydhen,* a mutation of *gwydhen,* qd. v.

WITHENIC, adj. Woody, full of wood. *Pryce.* More correctly written *wydhenic,* a mutation of *gwydhenic.*

WL, s. m. Will, desire. *Mara ieves wl dybôry, me a wor gwŷr yredy nag yw e Dew,* if he has a desire of eating, I know true clearly that he is not a God. P.C. 47. W. *ewyll, ewyllys.* Arm. *ioul,* † *youl.* Eng. *will.* Sansc. *val, vli,* to wish. Lat. *volo.*

WLAN, adj. Clean, clear, *Y vôs Dew ha dên yn wlân, dhe'n kêth tra-na crygyans rên,* that he is God and man clearly, to that same thing we give belief. P.C. 2405. A mutation of *glân,* qd. v.

WLAS, s. f. A country. *Ke yn mês a'n wlâs troha ken pow dhe vewê,* go thou out of the country, towards another land to live. O.M. 343. *Gorf a gullas an wlâs,* woe is he that has lost the country. O.M. 754. A mutation of *gwlâs,* qd. v.

WLASCOR, s. f. A kingdom. A mutation of *gwlascor,* qd. v.

WLETH, s. f. A kingdom. *Ha pesyn râg y cnê, may fo Dew luen a bytê, ra'n kyrho dhodho dh'y wleth,* and let us pray for his soul, that God may be full of pity, that he may fetch him to him to his kingdom. O.M. 2370. A mutation of *gwleth,* id. qd. *gwlâs,* qd. v.

WLOS, s. f. A sight. *Râg gwander war ben dowlyn hy a'n guelas ow codhê, ha'n wlos a's kemeras mar dyn may clamderas hy artê,* for weakness on his knees she saw him falling, and the sight took her so sharply that she swooned again. M.C. 171. More correctly *wolos.* A mutation of *golos,* id. qd. *goloc,* qd. v.

WOCY, adj. Foolish. *Thomas, ydhos pûr woky, dref'en na fynnyth cregy,* Thomas, thou art very foolish, because that thou wilt not believe. R.D. 1105. A mutation of *gocy,* qd. v.

WOCYNETH, s. m. Foolishness, folly. *Rum fey, mûr a wokyneth yw mones dhe lesky peyth a gl dên orto bewê,* by my faith, much of folly it is to burn a thing (that) a man can live upon. O.M. 473. A mutation of *gocyneth,* qd. v.

WODHAF, v. a. To bear, to suffer. *Ow Tâs, ma ny gl bones may treylyo mernens dhe vês, saw y wodhaf dhym a reys, dhe volneyeth re bo gurês,* my Father, if it cannot be that death be turned away, but I must suffer it, thy will be done. P.C. 1071. *A harlot ymskemunys, worth pôst ly a vûdh kelmys, dhe wodhaf an strewsow,* O knave accursed, to a post thou shalt be bound to suffer the blows. P.C. 2072. A mutation of *godhaf,* qd. v.

WODHAFFO, v. a. He may suffer. *Benegys yw nêb a gâr Du dris pûp tra ûs yu bŷs, hag a wodhaffo yn whâr dhodho kynwys ûs ordrnys,* blessed is he that loves God beyond everything that is in the world, and that suffers gently as much as is ordained to him. M.C. 24. A mutation of *godhaffo,* 3 pers. s. subj. of *godhevel,* qd. v.

WODHAN, v. a. We know. *An dên-ma re drehevys, gallas ny wodhan pelê,* this man has arisen, he has gone we know not where. M.C. 245. Written by Llwyd, 247, *wodhen; ni a wodhen,* we know. A mutation of *godhan,* 1 pers. pl. pres. of irr. v. *godhfos,* qd. v.

WODHAS, v. a. Thou knowest. *Ny geusyth, râk ny wodhas bôs grantys dhym gallos brâs hedhew may hallaf dyirys,* thou speakest not, for thou knowest not that there is granted to me great power, to-day that I may choose. P.C. 2181. *Taw Peder, ty ny wodhas lewyn pendra wrama dhys,* be silent Peter, for thou knowest not what I do to thee. P.C. 855. Written also *wodhes. Pendra wrâf, ny wodhes whêth; ty a'n godhvyth yu dyreedh wogê me môs ahanan,* what I shall do thou knowest not yet; thou shalt know it in the end, after my going hence. P.C. 848. A mutation of *godhas,* 2 pers. s. pres. of irr. v. *godhfus,* qd. v.

WODHEN, v. a. We know. *Râg fowt gwesc ha goscotter, namna vyrwyn râg anvos; ny wodhen râg ponvotter py'dh een yu gweel py yn côs,* for want of clothes and shelter, we are almost dying for cold; we know not for trouble whether we shall go into field or into wood.

O.M. 363. Llwyd, 247, gives *ni a wodhen*, and *wydhen*, we know. A mutation of *godhen*, 1 pers. pl. pres. of irr. v. *godhfos*, qd. v.

WODHER, v. pass. It is known. *Syr, arluth whêk, mâr y rás, yma ow conys dhyuwhy chyf guythoryon ol an gulás, a wodher dhe dysmeay,* Sire, sweet Lord, great his grace, there are working for you all the chief workmen of the land, (that) can be mentioned. O.M. 2332. A mutation of *godher*, 3 pers. pass. of *godhfos*, qd. v.

WODHEFAF, v. a. I shall know. *Arluth, fatlel bydh haneth, mar ny wodhefaf ple'dh êth pen vychterneth*, Lord, how will it be to-night, if I shall not know where is gone the head of royalty? R.D. 710. A mutation of *godhefaf*, 1 pers. s. fut. of irr. v. *godhfos*, qd. v.

WODHEFYS, v. a. He suffered. *Mûr a peyn a wodhefsya rûk kerengé tîs an bŷs, del yw mychtern a gallos,* much pain he suffered, for the love of the people of the world, as he is the king of power. R.D. 832. Written also *wodhevys*. *Ol pêch Adam pan prennas, pûr mŷr mûr a torment brâs hep dout a wodhevys cf*, when he redeemed all the sin of Adam, very truly much of great torment without doubt he endured. R.D. 2504. A mutation of *godhefys*, 3 pers. s. preter. of *godhaf*, or *godhevel*, qd. v.

WODHEVYTH, v. a. Thou shalt suffer. *In mêdh Pylat, marth a'm bês, kymmes drôk a wodhevyth, ha te rcson vŷth a drês, er aga fyn na gewsyth,* says Pilate, it is a marvel to me, how much evil thou endurest, and any reason against them thou sayest not. M.C. 120. A mutation of *godhevyth*, 2 pers. s. fut. of *godhevel*, qd. v.

WODHFEN, v. a. I should know. *Benen, na gows muscochneth, rûk an kêth dên-ma bythqueth nyn servys war ow ené, na rum fay my ny'n guelys, may wodhfen tremyn yn beys yntredho ha'y gowethé,* woman, speak not folly, for this same man I never served, ou my soul; nor by my faith, have I seen him, that I should know any difference in the world between him and his companions. P.C. 1287. A mutation of *godhfen*, 1 pers. s. subj. of *godhfos*, qd. v.

WODHFO, v. a. He will know. *Tra ny vŷdh yn pow adro na wodhfo dhe dharryvas,* there will not be a thing in the country, (that) he will not know how to declare. O.M. 100. *Me a'n conclud yredy, ma na wodhfo gorthyby un reson dhum argument,* I will silence him clearly, that he shall not know how to return one reason to my argument. P.C. 1600. A mutation of *godhfo*, 3 pers. s. 2 fut. of *godhfos*, qd. v.

WODHFOS, v. a. To know. *Guyn ow bŷs kafus cummyas dhe wodhfos pŷth vo ena,* happy my lot to have permission to know the thing (that) is there. O.M. 751. *Yma dhymmo mûr dysyr a wodhfes orthcuch an guŷr,* there is to me a great desire to know of you the truth. R.D. 195. A mutation of *godhfos*, qd. v.

WODHFYE, v. a. He would have known. *A pe profus bynyges, ef a wodhfyé y bâs hy pechadures, ny's gassé dh'y ylyé,* if he were a blessed prophet, he would have known that she is a sinner; he would not have permitted her to anoint him. P.C. 490. A mutation of *godhfyé*, 3 pers. s. subj. of *godhfus*, qd. v.

WODHFYTH, v. a. He shall know. *Me a vyn môs dhe vyras, hag a wodhfyth kyns denas a dhyscorio ol an câs,* I will go to see, and shall know, before withdrawing from it all the case. O.M. 1400. Written also *wodhvyth*. *Me a wodhvyth yn ûr-na pŷth yw dhe gallos,* I shall know then what is thy power. P.C. 63. A mutation of *godhfyth*, 3 pers. s. fut. of *godhfos*, qd. v.

WODHONS, v. a. They know. *A Tás whêk, gáf dhedhé y, râg ny wodhons yn teffry, py nŷl a wrôus drôk py da,* O sweet Father, forgive them, for they know not really whether they do evil or good. P.C. 2774. A mutation of *godhons*, 3 pers. pl. pres. of irr. v. *godhfos*, qd. v.

WODHOUCH, v. a. Ye know. *Mar a cofynnaf travyth, ny wodhouch ow gorthyby,* if I shall ask any thing, yo know not how to answer me. P.C. 1484. *A ny wodhouch why un dra,* know yo not one thing? R.D. 2445. Written also *wodhoch*. *Ny wodhoch pendra gewseuch,* ye know not what ye say. P.C. 443. A mutation of *godhouch*, 2 pers. pl. pres. of irr. v. *godhfos*, qd. v.

WODHYE, v. a. He knew. *Ihesus Crist a worthebys; y gowesys ef a wodhyé,* Jesus Christ answered; his speech he knew. M.C. 36. *Ef a doys a dheeympsys maga town ty del wodhyé,* he swore furthwith as deep an oath as he knew. M.C. 85. A mutation of *godhyé*, 3 pers. s. imperf. of irr. v. *godhfos*, qd. v.

WODHYEN, v. a. I knew. *Arluth, ny vyen lowen, mar fûr torment a codhfen y bones dhys; my ny wodhyen a'th vernans, na vŷth moy a'th daserchyans pan y'th whylsyn devethys,* Lord, I should not have been joyful, if I had known the fierce torment that was to thee, I knew not of thy death, nor any more of thy resurrection, when I saw thee come. R.D. 2544. *A Jhesu Cryst, lun a rás, my ny wodhyan dhe vonas alemma gyllys dhe'n boys,* O Jesus Christ, full of grace, I knew not that thou wert hence gone to the world. R.D. 2614. *Arluth, dhym gâf, del y'th pysaf war pen dewlyn an pŷth a wrên ; my ny wodhyen, rág ny wylyn, hag a quellen my ny'n grussen, kyn fen ledhys,* Lord, forgive me, as I pray thee on my knees what I did; I knew not, for I did not see; and if I had seen, I would not have done it, though I had been killed. P.C. 3021. A mutation of *godhyen*, 1 pers. s. imperf. of irr. v. *godhfos*, qd. v.

WODHYENS, v. a. They knew. *Un flouch yonk, gwyn y dhyllas, cyll o, ha y ny wodhyens ; scruith own mûr a's kemeras, rág an marthus re welscns,* a young child, white his raiment, an augel it was, and they knew it not ; a shiver of great fear seized them at the marvel they saw. M.C. 254. A mutation of *godhyens*, 3 pers. pl. imperf. of irr. v. *godhfos*, qd. v.

WOFFAS, v. a. Thou mayest know. *Adan, py'dhesta, golsow dhymmo, ha dês nês; yma genaf dhe'th pleysya; na barth dowt a'n bratt ês gwryes, may woffas dhym grussow,* Adam, where art thou? hearken to me, and come nearer ; I have (something) to please thee; bear no doubt of the deed (that) is done, that thou mayest acknowledge thanks to me. C.W. 54. A contracted form of *wodhfes*, a mutation of *godhfes*, 2 pers. s. subj. of irr. v. *godhfos*, qd. v.

WOFFE, v. a. He may know. *An Tás a wrûk ow formyé, a'm offryn re woffé grás, ha pan wryllyf tremené a'n bŷs, rum gorré dh'y wlás,* the Father who created me, to my offering may he acknowledge favour ; and when I shall pass away from the world, may he bring me to his land. O.M. 530. A contracted form of *wodhfé*, a mutation of *godhfé*, 3 pers. s. subj. of irr. v. *godhfos*, qd. v.

WOGE, prep. After. *Ty a wra wogé hemma gorré an' tús a le-na*, thou shalt after this bring the people thence. O.M. 1427. *Ef a leverys yn wêdh, try dêdh wogé môs yn bêdh dhe wewnans y lasserhy*, he said also, three days after going into (the) grave, to life that he would rise again. P.C. 1746. A corrupted form of *wosé*, qd. v. It was lastly corrupted into *udzhé*, qd. v.

WOLCH, v. a. He will wash. *Saw yn tokyn ow bôs gulán a gous Ihesu Nazaré, me a wolch scon ow dulé a wêl dheuch kettep onun*, but in token that I am clean of the blood of Jesus of Nazareth, I will wash immediately my hands, in the sight of every one of you. P.C. 2499. A mutation of *golch*, 3 pers. s. fut. of *golchy*, qd. v.

WOLE, v. a. To weep, to wail, to lament, to cry. *Fest yn lyn hy a wolé, dhe wherthyn nysteva vohans*, very bitterly she wept, to laugh she had not a desire. M.C. 222. *Ha hy a wolas kymmys, gans mar vêr nerth ha galloys, a'n fynten may trehevys ran yn ban du droka loys*, and she wept so much, with so great strength and power, that from the fountain a part was raised upwards, worst pang. M.C. 224. *A wola*, weeping. Lhwyd, 75, 248. Written also *olé*, qd. v. W. *wylo, gwylo*.

WOLES, s. m. The bottom. A mutation of *goles*, qd. v.

WOLHY, v. a. To wash. *Môs dhe wolhy ow dulé a dhesempes me a vyn omma yn dour*, go to wash my hands immediately I will here in water. R.D. 2202. Written by Llwyd, 77, *dho wolhya*. A mutation of *golhy*, qd. v.

WOLI, s. m. A province. Corn. Voc. *provincia*. W. *gwely, wely*, a bed, family, tribe.

WOLLAS, s. m. The bottom. *A wollas*, at the bottom, below. *Ha'n noor yn wêdh a wollas scon worth compas a vŷdh gwrys*, and the earth likewise below immediately by compass shall be made. C.W. 2. *An plâs yw ornys raetha, yn efarn barth a wollas*, the place is ordained for him, in hell on the lower side. C.W. 148. A later form of *woles*, qd. v.

WOLOC, s. m. The sight. *Me a wra dhys mûr a dhrôk, hag a'th whyp war an wolok, may whylly gurychon ha môk dhe dhewlagas a dre dro*, I will do to thee much evil, and whip thee on the sight, that thou mayst see sparks and smoke round about thy eyes. P.C. 2100. A mutation of *goloc*, qd. v.

WOLOW, s. m. Light. *Venytha nan geffo tam a wolow têk*, that he may never have a bit of fair light. O.M. 552. *Y wolow o mûr a splan*, his light was very brilliant. R.D. 535. Also the adj. *Gallas ef dhe nêf wolow gans eledh gwyn*, he is gone to bright heaven with angels white. R.D. 587. A mutation of *golow*, qd. v.

WOLOWYS, s. m. Lights. *Kyn wylly mûr wolowys, na dhout ny fydh ken ys da*, though thou shouldst see many lights, fear not, it will not be other than good. O.M. 717. *Ow Tâs, ynny wolowys, re bo gueres dheuch pûp prŷs*, my Father, in his lights, may he be a help to you always. P.C. 223. A mutation of *golowys*, pl. of *golow*, qd. v.

WOLSOWAS, v. a. To hear. A mutation of *golsowas*, qd. v.

WOLSYS, v. a. Thou watchedst. *Peder, ny wolsys y fâs, un prygwyth gynef golyas, kyns ys dôs ow torment tyn*, Peter, thou watchedst not well; a little while (thou shouldst) watch with me, before my sharp torment comes. P.C. 1054. A mutation of *golsys*, 2 pers. s. preter. of *golyas*, qd. v.

WOLY, s. m. A wound. *Maria, mŷr ow pym woly; crŷs ny dhe wŷr dhe dhasserchy*, Mary, see my five wounds; believe me truly to have risen. R.D. 867. *Neffré ny fynnaf crygy, er na hyndlyf y golon gans ow luef dre y woly*, I will not ever believe, until I touch his heart with my hand through his wound. R.D. 1532. A mutation of *goly*, qd. v.

WOLYOW, s. m. Wounds. *Ny leverys un gêr gow, râk dhym ol y wolyow a dhyswedhas*, I said not an untrue word, for to me all his wounds he showed. R.D. 1050. A mutation of *golyow*, pl. of *goly*, qd. v.

WON, v. irr. *Un dra a won*, I know one thing. O.M. 151. *My ny won leverel prâk gans pûp na vedhaf ledhys*, I know not how to tell why by every one I shall not be slain. O.M. 595. *Ny dhe gamwul y won gwŷr*, that we transgress, I know truly. P.C. 1066. A mutation of *gon*, qd. v. W. *gwn, ni wn, a wn*.

WON, s. f. A sheath. A mutation of *gôn*, qd. v.

WON, s. f. A level plain, a down. A mutation of *gôn*, qd. v.

WONEDHONS, v. a. They will work. *Mar ny wonedhons yn fâs, y a's tevyt anfugy*, if they will not work well, they shall have punishment. O.M. 2327. A mutation of *gonedhons*, 3 pers. pl. fut. of *gonedhy*, qd. v.

WONES, v. a. He will work. *Ha me yn wêdh, Arluth nêf, a'th leal wones del vo reys*, and I also, Lord of heaven, will faithfully serve thee as may be necessary. C.W. 102. A mutation of *gones*, qd. v.

WONESUGY, s. m. Workmen. *Conseler, dûn ny dhe veras scon war an wonesugy, counsellor*, let us come to look immediately over the workmen. O.M. 2326. A mutation of *gonesugy*, pl. of *gonesec*, qd. v.

WONAN, card. num. One. *Cyniver wonan*, every one. Lhwyd, 135, 176. *Wonnan warn igans*, one and twenty. Pryce. A late form of *onan*, qd. v. Written also *wonyn*. *Skon a wonyn dhe asow me a wra dhedha parow, pûb owr râg dhe weras*, immediately from one of thy ribs I will make to thee a help-mate, every hour to help thee. C.W. 30.

WONYS, v. a. To work, to cultivate, to till. *Dhe bales ha dhe wonys*, to dig and to till. O.M. 414. *Môs dhe wonys me a wra*, I will go to till. O.M. 1257. A mutation of *gonys*, qd. v.

WOR, v. irr. He knows. Used with all persons. *My a wôr prâg o ganso*, I know how it was with him. O.M. 165. *Ty a wôr gwŷr yredy*, thou knowest very truly. P.C. 1511. *Ef a wôr lyes cast râk dhe tollé*, he knows many a trick to deceive thee. P.C. 1884. *Lemyn ny a wôr yn ta*, now we know well. P.C. 1912. *Why wôr pyth yw guella dheuch dhe wruthyl*, ye know what is best for you to do. P.C. 468. *Râk y a wôr leverel kemmys dhedhé re gewsys*, for they know how to say as much as I have said to them. P.C. 1261. *Dew a wôr*, (W. *Duw a dŷr*,) God knows. O.M. 2509. A mutation of *gôr*, qd. v.

WOR, v. a. He will put. *Dhe'n Tâs Dew yn mûr enor war y alter my a wor grugyer têk hag achesyth*, to the Father God in great honour upon his altar I will put a partridge fair and tender. O.M. 1202. *My a'd wor scon bŷs dhedhy*, I will soon bring thee to her. O.M. 2072. A mutation of *gor*, 3 pers. s. fut. of *gora*, qd. v.

WORDH, v. a. He will worship. *A Dâs Dew arluth huhel, my a'th wordh gans ol ow nel y'm colon pûr treweyy, O Father God, high Lord, I will worship thee with all my strength, in my heart very seriously.* O.M. 510. *Rág dewes mar uys tewyth, y a dreyl-fyth, hag a wordh dewow tebel,* for if they get not drink, they will turn, and worship evil gods. O.M. 1818. A mutation of *gordh*, 3 pers. s. fut. of *gordhy*.

WORDHYANS, s. m. Worship, honour, glory. *Arluth kér, dhys mûr wordhyans; râg hŷr lour ew ow bewnans, kymmer dyso ow enef,* dear Lord, much worship to thee; for long enough is my life; take my soul to thee. O.M. 847. A mutation of *gordhyans*, qd. v.

WORDHYAS, v. a. He worshipped. *Ty re wordhyas, war urp tro, an fuls losel,* thou worshippedst, on some occasion, the false knave. P.C. 2002. A mutation of *gordhyas*, 3 pers. s. preter. of *gordhyé*.

WORDHYE, v. a. To worship. *Abel whék, dûn alemma dhe wordhyé an arluth gwella, del yrchys agan tâs dhyn,* sweet Abel, let us come hence to worship the best Lord, as our father commanded us. O.M. 447. A mutation of *gordhyé*, qd. v.

WORDHIYO, v. a. He may worship. *Râk ef a gerch dhyworthyn kemmys na wordhyo Iovyn,* for he will carry from us as many as worship not Jove. P.C. 1917. A mutation of *gordhyo*, 3 pers. s. subj. of *gordhyé*.

WORFEN, s. m. An end. *Prederys pêb a'y worfen, fettyl allo gurfennè,* let every one think of his end, how it may end. O.M. 225. *Na dybreuch, my a yrvyr, kŷc gans gôs bŷs worfen vrys,* eat ye not, as I enjoin, flesh with blood even to the end of the world. O.M. 1220. *Trank hep worfen,* time without end. P.C. 1562. A mutation of *gorfen*, qd. v.

WORHEL, s. m. A vessel, a ship, an ark. *A bûp kyndè edhen vâs, y'th worhel guet dew gorré,* of every kind of good birds, in thy ark take care two to put. O.M. 980. *Aga gora ty a wra yn dhe worhel abervedh,* thou shalt put them in thy ark within. O.M. 902. A mutation of *gorhel*, qd. v.

WORHEMMYN, s. m. A command. *Y a dhue dhe'th worhemmyn,* they will come to thy command. O.M. 121. *Fûr parys dh'y worhemmyn ny á dhy a ver termyn,* very readily to his commands we will go there in a short time. P.C. 1653. *Dre worhemmyn an Iustys,* by order of the magistrate. P.C. 3005. A mutation of *gorhemmyn*, qd. v.

WORHEMMYN, v. a. He will command. *My a worhemmyn wharé dhe'n glaw na moy na wrello,* I will soon command to the rain that it do no more. O.M. 1091. A mut. of *gorhemmyn*, 3 pers. s. fut. of *gorhemmyna*, qd. v.

WORHEMMYNADOW, s. m. Commands. A mutation of *gorhemmynadow*, pl. of *gorhemmynad*, qd. v.

WORLENE, v. a. To quell, to quiet. A mutation of *gorlené*, qd. v.

WORRE, v. a. To put, to place. *Yn pren crous grugh y worré,* on the cross tree do ye put him. P.C. 2357. *Awos trawyth nyns o reys môs dhe worré dhe'n mernans mâp Dew a'n nêf,* because of any thing it was not necessary to go to put to death the Son of the God of heaven. R.D. 1253. A mutation of *gorré*, or *gora*, qd. v.

WORSEUCH, v. a. Ye have placed. *Corf yn bêdh a worseuch why, a wre bôst a dhasserchy dhe pen try drydh,* the body (that) ye put in the grave, he boasted that it would rise again at the end of three days. R.D. 43. A mutation of *gorseuch*, 2 pers. plur. preter. of *gora*, qd. v.

WORSYN, v. a. We have placed. *An corf a worsyn yn bêdh,* the body wo have placed in the grave. R.D. 49. *Aberth yn bêdh del re'th worsyn, pen vychterneth, dre dhe cledh bŷdh socur dhyn,* within the grave as we have placed thee, head of royalty, by thy angels be thou a succour to us. R.D. 312. A mutation of *gorsyn*, 1 pers. pl. preterite of *gora*, qd. v.

WORSYS, v. a. Thou honouredst. *Rág na worsys ow hanow a rág an flehysygnw a Israel dyscryggyon, ny's goryth hep falladow dhe'n tŷr a dhy dhe wadow, ty na dhe vroder Aaron,* because thou honouredst not my name before the children of Israel unbelievers, thou shalt not place them, certainly, in the land where thy forefathers went, thou nor thy brother Aaron. O.M. 1807. A mutation of *gorsys*, a contracted form of *gordhsys*, 2 pers. s. preter. of *gordhy*, qd. v.

WORTE, pron. prep. To, from, at, by them. *(Worth—y.) Krêf yw gwrydhyow an spedhes, may 'thyne ow dywvrech terrys worté menouch ow guethé,* stroug are the roots of the briars, that my arms are broken, working often at them. O.M. 689. *Ha pedyr streyth vrâs defry ow resek a dywvorty; worté myres may 'tho whans,* and four great streams indeed flowing from it, that there was a desire to look at them. O.M. 774. Written also *orté*, qd. v.

WORTO, pron. prep. To, from, at, by him or it. *(Worth—o.) A out warnes, drôk venen, worto pan werussys colé,* Oh, out upon thee, wicked woman, when thou didst listen to him. O.M. 222. *Arluth, gallosek ha erêf, worto an porthow ny sêf,* Lord, powerful and strong, against him the gates will not stand. R.D. 119. *Worto y keusys yn wêdh,* I spoke to him also. R.D. 897. *Mŷr worto,* look at it. R.D. 1720. *Ydh o ow fous ha'm brustplat, purpur garow dhum strothé; dre an gôs a râk Pilat worto an kŷc a glenè,* my robe and my breastplate were hard purple to wring me, through the blood before Pilate the flesh stuck to it. R.D. 2594. *Ha pûr hardh a wovynnys corf Ihesus worto yn ro,* and begged very hard the body of Jesus from him as a gift. M.C. 215. Written also *orto*, qd. v.

WORTO, v. a. He will stay. *Yn plâs-ma me a worto anteeryst bŷs may teffo,* in this place I will wait until antichrist comes. R.D. 238. A mutation of *gorto*, 3 pers. s. fut. of *gortos*, qd. v.

WORTOS, v. a. To stay, to wait. *I wortos hy a vynnas, guelas Ihesus a garè,* she wished to wait for him, to see Jesus (whom) she loved. M.C. 163. A mutation of *gortos*, qd. v.

WORTY, s. m. A husband. *Attebres ty ha'th worty, a'n wedhen ha'y avalow,* if thou atest, thou and thy husband, of the tree and its fruits. O.M. 175. A mutation of *gorty*, qd. v.

WORTY, pron. prep. To, from, at, by her or it. *(Worth—hy.) Aban golstè worty hy, ha gruthyl dres ow defen,* because thou hearkenedst to her, and actedst beyond my prohibition. O.M. 260. *Rág ty dhe gola worty, ha tollé dhe bryes lên,* because thou didst hearken to her, and deceive thy faithful spouse. O.M. 293. *Sylteuch gystys worth an yet, agas dyscodh kettep chet, hertheuch worty hy yn wêdh,* put ye beams against the gate, your shoulders, every fellow, thrust ye against it also. P.C. 3069. Written also *orty,* qd. v.

WORTH, prep. At, by, to, for, with, from, against. *Crist worth an goyn a warnyas,* Christ at the supper gave warning. M.C. 42. *Pu a woras y'th colon cows yn delma worth iustis,* who put it in thy heart to speak thus to a justice? M.C. 81. *Dhe veras worth Crist y êth, hag ef yn crous ow cregy,* to look on Christ they went, while he was hanging on the cross. M.C. 216. *Dhe Herodes ydh esa pûr wôr worth Pylat sor brâs,* to Herod there was very truly against Pilate great anger. M.C. 110. *Ow Tâs, ynny wolowys, re bo gueres dheuch pûp prŷs worth tempacyon an tebel,* my Father, in his lights, be a help to you always against the temptation of the evil one. P.C. 225. *Worth hemma pŷth yw cusul,* for this what is advisable? P.C. 1915. *Gans kentrow worth an plynken bedhens tackys,* with nails to the planks let them be fastened. P.C. 2517. *An êl dhyn a leverys worth an bêdh y vôs yn ban dasserchys,* the angel said to us by the grave that he was risen up. R.D. 1063. *Worth henna whet me a wŷth,* from that I will yet preserve (myself.) R.D. 2035. *Worth* is used with the infinitives of verbs to form participles when pronouns are joined, and these are inserted in their possessive form. *Prâg y tolstê sy hep kên, worth hy themptê dhe dyrry an frût erbyn ow dyfen,* why didst thou deceive her without pity, by tempting her to break off the fruit against my prohibition? O.M. 303. *Hag y worth y dormontyê y cudhens y ben gans quêth,* and they tormenting him, covered his head with a cloth. M.C. 97. *Râg y hyller ervyrê ha'y welas yu suredy, y vôs prêst worth dhe vetyê dhe wêdh dhys ha belyny,* for it is possible to observe, and to see him surely, that he is ready to meet thee for shame to thee and villainy. M.C. 20. *Kyn fen neffrê ow ponyê yn pûp tol worth y whylas,* though we be ever runuing in every hole to seek him. R.D. 551. *Ages bones ol warbarth porrys worth ow duwenê,* all of you together being willed to grieve me. R.D. 1413. (This idiom obtains also in Welsh.) *Worth* enters into composition with the personal pronouns, as *worthyf, worthys, &c.* qd. v. *Worth* is written also *orth,* qd. v.

WORTH, adj. Opposite, contrary. *Ty a alsê crygy dhe'n abosteledh deffry, galsos pûr worth,* thou mightest believe the apostles really; thou art become very contrary. R.D. 1470. W. *gwrth, gorth, wrth,* † *gurt.* Ir. *frith, fri.* Gael. *frith.* Goth. *vithra.*

WORTHEB, s. m. An answer. A mutation of *gortheb,* qd. v.

WORTHEBY, v. a. To answer. *Ol Ihesus a'n godhevys, ha'y wortheby ny vynnas,* Jesus endured it all, and he would not answer him. M.C. 92. A mutation of *gortheby,* qd. v.

WORTHEBYS, v. a. He answered. A mutation of *gorthebys,* 3 pers. s. preter. of *gortheby,* qd. v.

WORTHEBYTH, v. a. Thou shalt answer. *Prâk na worthebyth,* why wilt thou not answer? P.C. 1757. A mutation of *gorthebyth,* 2 pers. s. fut. of *gortheby,* qd. v.

WORTHEUCH, pron. prep. To you. (*Worth—chui.*) *A arluth, dhychy mûr grâs; wortheuch why daryvas mûr me a câr,* O lord, great thanks to you; to you to show I shall greatly love. R.D. 1818.

WORTHYBY, v. a. To answer. *Geseuch vy dhe worthyby,* allow me to answer. P.C. 2493. A mutation of *gorthyby,* qd. v.

WORTHYBYS, v. a. He answered. *Yn ta ef re'n dyndylas, pan cam worthybys Cayfus, cafus drôk grûth,* well he has deserved it, when he rudely answered Caiaphas, to have bad dole. P.C. 1403. A mutation of *gorthybys,* 3 pers. s. preter. of *gorthyby,* qd. v.

WORTHYF, pron. prep. To me. (*Worth—mi.*) *Fystyn alemma duwhaus; worthyf na gous na moy gêr,* hasten thou hence quickly; speak not another word to me. O.M. 170. *Ol an bŷs-ma ty a fŷdh, colê worthyf mar mynnyth,* all this world thou shalt have, if thou wilt hearken to me. P.C. 129. Written also *orthyf,* qd. v.

WORTHYN, pron. prep. To us. (*Worth—ni.*) *Mysshyf lemmyn codhys worthyn nynsus bewê,* evil now has fallen upon us, there is no living. O.M. 1707. *Warbarth ol del y'n gurleyn, dhyragon ow cous worthyn,* all together as we have seen him, before us speaking to us. R.D. 1211. Written also *orthyn,* qd. v.

WORTHYP, s. m. An answer. *Yn y worthyp ny gufyn kên dh'y ladhê,* in his answer I found not cause to kill him. R.D. 1850. A mutation of *gorthyp,* qd. v.

WORTHYP, v. a. He will answer. *Me a worthyp dhyso lêl,* I will answer thee faithfully. P.C. 1751. A mutation of *gorthyp,* 3 pers. s. fut. of *gorthyby,* qd. v.

WORTHYS, pron. prep. To thee. (*Worth—ti.*) *Worthys me a wra govyn,* of thee I will ask. P.C. 1236. *Ellas, na allaf yn scon keusel worthys,* alas, that I cannot speak at once to thee. R.D. 762. *Yn y golon fast regeth mûr a garensê worthys,* into his heart there hath quite gone much of love towards thee. M.C. 115. Written also *orthys,* qd. v.

WOS, s. m. Blood. *Myschef a gôdh tyn ha crêf râk y wôs a vŷdh scollys,* mischief will fall sharp and strong, for his blood that shall be shed. P.C. 2460. A mutation of *gôs,* qd. v.

WOSE, prep. After. *Râg sythyn wosê hemma dew ugens dŷdh my a ôs glaw dhe godhê awartha,* for a week after this, forty days I will allow rain to fall from above. O.M. 1026. *Ha wosê henna ewyn, pûp ol adro, dracht a wfyn,* and after that let us drink, every one, all round, a draught of wine. O.M. 2626. *Wosê try dcydh ha hanter,* after three days and a half. R.D. 226. *Bŷth ny gîl, awos an bŷs, dên vŷth bones dasserchys wosê merwel,* never can, for the world, any man be raised after dying. R.D. 940. W. *gwedi, wedi,* † *guetig,* † *gueti.* Arm. † *goudé.* Ir. *feasad.* Gael. *feasd.*

WOSLEWYS, v. a. Let him hear. *Me a cache an casadow, pûp ny du yn lavarow; wortê dên na woslewys,* I will catch the villain, on all sides in words; to them let not a man listen. P.C. 454. A mutation of *goslewys,* 3 pers. s. imp. of *goslowas,* or *golsowas,* qd. v.

WOSTALLETH, adv. At first. *Awos godheval ancow, ny nahas hy lavarow, wostalleth na wostewedh,* notwithstanding suffering death, she retracted not her words, at first nor at last. O.M. 2762. Comp. of *wos* for *war,* on, and *talleth,* a beginning.

WOSTEWEDH, adv. At last finally. O.M. 2762. Written also *wotewedh. Ha wotewedh râg dennys ef a'n gevê awell boys,* and at last from manhood he had a desire of food. M.C. 10. *Ef o harlot tebel wâs, wotewedh lader vyê,* he was a scoundrel, an evil fellow, at last he was a thief. M.C. 38. Comp. of *wos* for *war*, on, and *diwedh*, an end. W. o'r *diwedh*. Ir. ✝ *fo-diud*.

WOTTA, adv. Lo, behold. *A wotta omma nêb gill tempell Du dowstoll squardyê, ha dh'y vâdh y dhrehevel*, behold here one who can tear to pieces the temple of God, and raise it at his will. M.C. 195. *Sevys, gallas dhe gen le, dên apert ha mûr y breys, a wotta an le may 'these, umma nyngew of tregis*, he is risen, he is gone to another place, a man clearly and much his worth, behold the place where he was; here he is not dwelling. M.C. 255. Written also *awatta*, qd. v.

WOTTEVE, comp. adv. Behold him. *(Wotta—ve.) Syrys, dhyrchy lowené, a wottevé ef gené, may whodhfouch yn pûr deffry*, sirs, joy to ye, behold him with me, that ye may know in very earnest. P.C. 2155.

WOTTENSE, adv. Behold it. *Eiené an nên me a wra; a wottensé ewnys da; dûn ny lemmyn war tu trê*, I will adjust the stone; behold it well adjusted; let us come now towards home. P.C. 3212.

WOTH, adj. Fierce. *My a worhemnyn wharé dhe'n glaw na moy na wrello; an lif woth gurêns yndenné*, I will soon command to the rain that it do no more; let the fierce flood withdraw. O.M. 1093. W. *gŵyth*, ✝ *gwith*.

WOULCH, v. a. He will wash. *Tommans onan dour war tân, râg wogé soper my a woulch ol agas trŷs*, let one warm water on the fire, for after supper I will wash all your feet. P.C. 835. The same as *wolch*, qd. v.

WOUR, s. m. A husband. *Rôf dhys ow thour; vedhaf dhe wour; warbarth ny a drŷg nefré*, I will give thee my palace; I will be thy husband; together we will live always. O.M. 2111. A mutation of *gour*, qd. v.

WOW, s. m. A lie, falsehood. *My yw Dew dhe tassow, Abram, Ysac, hep wow, ha Iacob yn wêdh keffrys*, I am the God of thy fathers, Abraham, Isaac, without a lie, and Jacob likewise. O.M. 1410. A mutatiou of *gow*, qd. v.

WOWHELES, v. a. To deceive. A mutation of *gowheles*, qd. v.

WOYS, s. m. Blood. *Treyl dhe gŷk ha dhe woys*, turn thou to flesh and to blood. O.M. 66. A mutation of *goys*, qd. v.

WRA, v. a. He will do. Used with all persons. *My a wra dhyso parow pûp ûr ol râg dhe weres*, I will make to thee an equal always to help thee. O.M. 100. *Y'th whŷs lavur dhe dhybry ty a wra, bŷs y'th worfen*, in thy sweat thou shalt labour to eat, even to thy end. O.M. 274. *Ef a wra dynythy un mâp da hep fulladow*, he shall beget a good son without fail. O.M. 638. *Aga sona ny a wra*, we will bless them. O.M. 143. A mutation of *gwra*, 3 pers. s. fut. and 2 pers. imp. of *gwrey*, qd. v. *Na wra kelas un dra*, do not conceal any thing. C.W. 130.

WRAF, v. a. I will do. *Mylygé a wráf defry an nôr y'th whythres hogen*, I will assuredly curse the earth in thy evil deed. O.M. 271. *Pandra wrôf, may te sorré, a Dâs whêk*, what shall I do, that I have angered thee, O sweet Father? O.M. 2257. A mutation of *gwráf*, 1 pers. s. fut. of *gwrey*. qd. v.

WRAMA, v. a. I shall do. *Taw, Peder, ty ny wodhas lemyn pedra wrama dhys*, be silent, Peter, thou knowest not what I shall do to thee. P.C. 856. *Pendra wrama, marnes dredhos, ny'm bŷdh guerês*, what shall I do? unless through thee, there will be no help to me. R.D. 2219. A contingent form of *wráf*.

WRE, v. a. He was doing, or would do. *Kyns ty a wre meystry dhyn*, rather thou shouldst do a wonder for us. P.C. 2982. *Me a'n glewas dyougel lyes gyŷth ow leverel an temple y wre terry, hag arté y dhrehevel yn try-dydh na vyé guel*, I heard him plainly several times saying that he would destroy the temple, and again raise it in three days, that it could not be better. P.C. 1309. *Govy y vones ledhys, kemmys dader prest a wre*, woe is me his being killed; so much good he always did. P.C. 3096. A mutation of *gwre*, 3 pers. s. imperf. of *gwrey*, qd. v.

WREANS, s. m. Creation, workmanship. A mutation of *gwreans*, qd. v.

WREAR, s. m. A maker, a creator. A mutation of *gwrear*, qd. v.

WREC, s. f. A wife, a woman. *Re'th ordené ty ha'th wrêk, pan vy marow, yn y cuer*, may he ordain thee and thy wife, when ye are dead, into his court. P.C. 685. *Noe ha'y wrêk ha'y flehes kefrys*, Noah and his wife and his children also. O.M. 932. A mutation of *gwrêc*, qd. v. Written by Llwyd, 243, *wrêg*. *Prederys yw an wrêg-na*, that wife is diligent.

WREFE, comp. v. He did, or would do. *(Wre—fe.) Ha me a dhêk dustymy y'n clewys ow leverel, trey-dydh wosé y terry y wrefé y dhrehevel*, and I bear witness, I heard him saying, in three days after destroying it that he would rebuild it. P.C. 1316. Written also *wrefa*. *Ha nêp na wynno crygy ny gl bôs a'm servusy; ma ny wrefa ow desyr y fydh dampnys dhe peynys*, and he that will not believe, cannot be of my servants; if he has not done my desire, he shall be condemned to pains. R.D. 2473.

WREGTY, s. f. The woman of the house, a housewife, a wife. *Adam, yn dywedh a'n beys, my a wronnt oel mercy dheys, ha dhe Eva dhe weregty*, Adam, in the end of the world, I will grant the oil of mercy to thee, and to Eve thy wife. O.M. 330. *Whêth gans Eva y wregty*, again with Eve his wife. O.M. 637. A mutation of *gwrêcty*, comp. of *gwrêc*, a woman, and *ty*, a house.

WREHA, v. a. To sow. Llwyd, 149. *Pandra ny vyn Dew gûl vry ahanaf, na sowyny an peŷth a wrehaf ny wra, ha pûp ûr chatel Abel y a sowyn mŷl blêk guel*, why will not God make account of me, nor thrive the thing that I sow will not, and Abel's chattels always thrive a thousand times better. O.M. 521.

WREITHON, v. a. We have done. *Ni a wreithon*, Llwyd, 246. A mutation of *gwreithon*, 1 pers. pl. preter. of *gwrey*.

WRELLEN, v. a. We may or should do. *Dûn ol dhe'n gorhyl tôth da, gans lif na wrellen budhy*, let us come to the ark quickly, that we be not drowned by the flood. O.M. 1048. *Ef a rûk agan dyfen, aval na wrellen dybbry*, he did forbid us, that we should not eat the apple. O.M. 183. A mutation of *gwrellen*, 1 pers. pl. subj. of *gwrey*, qd. v. Another form is *wryllyn*, qd. v.

WRELLES, v. a. Thou wouldst do. *A Tâs, dre dhe luen weres, dhe pygy mensen taryé lemmyn na wrelles, rûk yma dhymmo vy kên*, O Father, through thy full help, I would pray thee, that thou wouldst not tarry now, for there is anguish to me. R.D. 445. A mutation of *gwrelles*, 2 pers. s. subj. of *gwrey*, qd. v.

WRELLO, v. a. He should do. *Na wrello y vôdh, goef;*

y'n gryfyth mûr a trustyys, woe is he that doeth not his will; he shall have much of sorrow. O.M. 2093. Written also *wrella*. *Leverel dhum arluth gura, Ihesu na wrella dampnyé*, do thou say to my lord, that he do not condemn Jesus. P.C. 1958. A mutation of *gwrello*, 3 pers. s. subj. of *gwrey*, qd. v.

WRELLOUCH, v. a. Yo may do. *Ow arlothes gyné dre dhynnareh agas pygys na wrellouch cammen ladhé an profus a Nazaré*, my lady by me, through greeting, prayed you, that ye do not unjustly slay the prophet of Nazareth. P.C. 2196. A mutation of *gwrellouch*, 2 pers. pl. subj. of *gwrey*, qd. v.

WRELLYN, v. a. I may do. *A dâs cûf kêr, my a wra ; Arluth nêf roy dhym gûl da yn pûp ober a wrellyn*, O dearly beloved father, I will (go); may the Lord of heaven grant me to do well in every work that I may do. O.M. 445. A mutation of *gwrellyn*, 1 pers. s. subj. of *gwrey*, qd. v.

WREN, v. a. We shall do. *Pûp ober ol yn bŷs-ma a wrên, re bo plygadow*, every work in this world (that) we shall do, may it be agreeable. O.M. 1088. *Ellas, lemyn pandra wrên*, alas, now what shall we do ? O.M. 1654. A mutation of *gwrên*, 1 pers. pl. fut. of *gwrey*, qd. v.

WRENNYE, v. a. To iron, to fasten with iron. *Dên fel mûr yw, hag yngyn ; gwcyt y wrennyé prest yn tyn bŷth na scapyé*, a very cunning man he is, and ingenious; take thou care to iron him very tightly that he may never escape. P.C. 1887. Another form of *hernia*, qd. v.

WRENS, v. a. They did. *Ny wrêns y na hen scyle, lymyn syncyé aga bôdh*, they did no other ground, but followed their will. M.C. 175. *Gonys oll a wrêns yn fast, râg nag o Crist attendijs*, all did work quickly, for Christ was not attended. M.C. 202. A mutation of *gwrêns*, 3 pers. pl. imperf. of *gwrey*, qd. v.

WRÊR, v. pass. It shall be done. *Hag annedhé crous y wrêr, râg crousé Cryst ow mâp kêr*, and of them a cross shall be made, to crucify Christ my dear son.* O.M. 1936. *Ha mar ny wrêr y wythé, y dhyskyblon yn pryvé a'n lader yn mês a'n beydh*, and if it be not guarded, his disciples privily will steal him out of the grave. R.D. 341. A mutation of *gwrêr*, 3 pers. s. fut. pass. of *gwrey*, qd. v.

WRES, v. a. Thou wouldst do. *Del dhedhywsys dhymmo vy, y wrês yn ban dasfewé dhe'n trygé dêdh yrcdy*, as thou promisedst to me that thou wouldst revive up on the third day really. R.D. 451. A mutation of *gwrés*, 2 pers. s. imperf. of *gwrey*, qd. v.

WRETA, comp. v. Thou wilt do. (*Wrêth—te.*) *Ydh heurl bôs fulsury gynes, pan wreta tewel*, there seems to be falsehood with thee, when thou wilt be silent. P.C. 1320. *A gothman da, prâk y wretu dhymmo ammé*, O good fellow, why dost thou kiss me ? P.C. 1105. *Mar ny wreta y crygy, bŷth ny dhueth neffré dhe'n ioy ûs yn nêf*, if thou wilt not believe it, thou shalt never come to the joy that is in heaven. R.D. 1088.

WRETH, v. a. Thou shalt or wilt do. Used also as a present. *Adam, pandra wrêth, prâg na dhêth dhum wolcummé*, Adam, what art thou doing ? why camest thou not to welcome me ? O.M. 257. *Mar ny wrêth del lavaraf, ty a fŷdh pûr tormont sad*, if thou wilt not do as I say, thou shalt have very sad torment. O.M. 400. *David, ny wrêth dhymo chy bŷs venary*, David, thou shalt never make a house for me. O.M. 2333. A mutation of *gwrêth*, 2 pers. s. fut. of *gwrey*, qd. v.

WREUCII, v. a. Ye shall or will do. *Omma ny wreuch why trygé*, here ye shall not remain. O.M. 317. *Gonys a wreuch pûr vysy dhym del hevel*, ye work very diligently as it seems to me. O.M. 2448. *Na wreuch un luch vŷth letyé*, do not any one moment delay. P.C. 1714. *Myrehs a Ierusalem, na olouch na na wreuch drem warnaf vy nag onan vŷth*, daughters of Jerusalem, weep not, nor make lament on me, not any one. P.C. 2640. A mutation of *gwreuch*, 2 pers. plur. fut. and imp. of *gwrey*, qd. v.

WREYS, part. Made. *An temple may fe coul wreys*, that the temple may be fully made. O.M. 2412. A mutation of *gwrcys*, part. pass. of *gwrey*, qd. v.

WRONS, v. a. They shall or will do. *Mar tue moy nys tevyth man, rág noicn y wrôns clamderé*, if more come, it will not be enough, from hunger they will faint. O.M. 400. *A Tâs whêk, gâf dheudhé y, râg ny wodhons yn teffry py nŷl a wrôns drôk py da*, O sweet Father, forgive them, for they know not really whether they do evil or good. P.C. 2775. A mutation of *gwrôns*, 3 pers. pl. fut. of *gwrey*, qd. v.

WRONT, v. a. He will give. *Yn dywedh an bys my a weront oel mercy dheys*, at the end of the world I will grant the oil of mercy to thee. O.M. 320. A mutation of *gront*, 3 pers. s. fut. of *gronté*, id. qd. *grontyé*, qd. v.

WRONTE, v. a. He may grant. *Tays ha Mâb ha'n Speris Sans, wy a bŷs a leun golon, re wronté dheuch grûs ha whans dhe wolsowas y basconn*, Father, Son, and the Holy Ghost, ye shall beseech with a full heart, that he grant to you grace and desire to hear his Passion. M.C. 1. A mutation of *gronté*, 3 pers. s. subj. of *gronté*.

WRONTYAF, v. a. I will grant. *Bôs gwythyas a wrontyaf dhys*, to be a keeper I will grant to thee. O.M. 74. A mutation of *grontyaf*, 1 pers. s. fut. of *grontyé*.

WRONTYO, v. a. He may grant. *Y grâs dheuchwchy re wronntyo*, may he grant his grace to you. O.M. 1726. A mutation of *grontyo*, 3 pers. s. subj. of *grontyé*.

WROWEDIIE, v. a. To lie down. *Ny a'th dêg bŷs gorfen vŷs yn ponow dhe wrowedhé*, we will carry thee, till the end of the world in pains to lie. O.M. 904. A mutation of *growedhé*, qd. v.

WRUC, v. a. He did, or made. *Ef a wrûk ow husullyé*, he did advise me. O.M. 217. *An Tâs Dew a wrûk pûp tra*, God the Father made every thing. O.M. 1188. A mutation of *grûk*, qd. v. Written also *wrûg*. *Bynygys re bo an prŷs, may wrûg an êl ow guarnyé*, blessed be the time, when the angel warned me. O.M. 1980.

WRUGE, v. a. He did. *Pan wrugé dres ow dyfen, fest yn tyn cf rum sorras*, when he acted against my prohibition, very grievously he provoked me. O.M. 423. *Pan wrugé dres ow defen, mês a Parathys lowen an êl wharé a'n goras*, when he acted against my prohibition, out of happy Paradise the angel soon put him. O.M. 922. *Arluth, genyans dhum ené, govy pan wrugé pehé gans corf an debel venen*, Lord, pardon to my soul, woe is me when I did sin with the body of the wicked woman. O.M. 2250. A mutation of *grûg*, 3 pers. s. pretor. of irr. v. *gwrey*, *e* being added in a subjuuctive construction.

WRUSSEN, v. a. I had done, or would do. *Awos travyth ny wrussen venytha dhe guhudhas*, because of any thing

I would not ever accuse thee. O.M. 163. *Rág coln worth un venen, gwlân ef re gollas an plâs, a'm lêf dhychyove a wrussen*, for listening to a woman he has quite lost the place, (that) with my right hand I had made. O.M. 421, 921. *Pan clewfyf vy an tân, parhap y wrussen fyê*, when I should feel the fire, perhaps I should flee. O.M. 1352. A mutation of *gwrussen*, 1 pers. s. pluperf. of *gwrey*, qd. v.

WRUSSENS, v. a. They had done, or would do. *En Edhewon betcgyns gûl tol arall ny vynné, lemyn an tol re wrussens, y a vynné dhe scrwyê*, the Jews nevertheless would not make another hole, but the hole they had made, they would that it should serve. M.C. 180. *Hag a codhfons yredy, ny wrussens ow dystrewy*, and if they knew in truth, they would not destroy me. P.C. 2777. A mutation of *gwrussens*, 3 pers. pl. pluperf. of *gwrey*.

WRUSSOUCH, v. a. Ye did, or have done. *A's wrussouch cam tremené; cûth gucles y dhewedh fé, namna'n dallas*, what ye have done was a wrong ending; a grief it was to see his end, it almost blinded us. R.D. 40. *Why a vŷdh aquyttys da râk an onor yn torma a wrussouch dhymmo pûr wêr*, ye shall be repaid well for the honour in this time that ye have done to me very truly. P.C. 312. Written also *wrussyuch*. *Arluth whêk, ny amount man an pyt a wrussynch, lemyn moy dysenour dhys*, sweet Lord, nothing avails the pit (that) thou hast made, but more dishonour to thee. O.M. 2792. A mutation of *gwrussouch*, 2 pers. pl. preter. of *gwrey*, qd. v.

WRUSSYN, v. a. We did, or made. *Máp dên my re wrûk prenné, gans gôs ow colon na fé nêp a wrussyn ny kyllys*, mankind I have redeemed with the blood of my heart, that no one (whom) we have made should be lost. R.D. 2624. *Ny a fyn leverel ol, fatel wrussym ny keusel orth an Arluth kêr Ihesu*, we will tell all, how we did speak to the dear Lord Jesus. R.D. 1341. A mutation of *gwrussyn*, 1 pers. pl. preter. of *gwrey*.

WRUSSYS, v. a. Thou didst, hast done, or wouldst do. *Out warnes, drôk venen, worto pan wrussys colé*, out upon thee, wicked woman, when thou didst listen to him. O.M. 222. *Lavar dhym awos travyth, mara crusté leverel, ken fé an temple dyswrĝs, kyn pen try dydh y wrussys guel ys kyns y dhrehevel*, tell me, notwithstanding anything, whether thou didst say, though the temple were destroyed, before the end of three days thou wouldst raise it better than before. P.C. 1760. *Kepar del wrussys pûp tra, nag ês ken Dew agesos*, like as thou hast done everything, there is not another God than thou. R.D. 2476. A mutation of *gwrussys*, 2 pers. s. preter. of *gwrey*.

WRUSTA, v. a. Thou hast done. *Pan drôk-knleth a wrusta? gorthyp vy na vŷf tollys*, what evil deed hast thou done? answer me, that I be not deceived. P.C. 2007. A mutation of *gwrusta*, comp. of *gwrus*, id. qd. *gwres*, 2 pers. s. imperf. of *gwrey*, and *te*, thou. Used in questions.

WRUTHYL, v. a. To do or make. *A meys ôf ow predyry pandra allaf dhe wruthyl*, I am puzzled thinking what I can do. O.M. 194. *Arluth cûf, dhe archadow y wruthyl rês ew dhymmo*, dear Lord, thy commands need is to do them. 998. A mutation of *gruthyl*, qd. v.

WRYLLEUCH, v. a. Ye may do. *Ha dhywhy me re ordynas glûs nêf ynny râk trygé, kepar del ordenas an Tâs dymmo vy yn lowené; may wrylleuch yn lowené kefyrs dybry hag evé war ow bôs yn uhelder*, and for you I have ordained the kingdom of heaven, to dwell in it, like as my Father ordained for me in joy; that ye may eat and drink of my food on high. P.C. 811. A mutation of *gwrylleuch*, 2 pers. pl. subj. of *gwrey*.

WRYLLY, v. a. Thou mayst do. *Saw guel may wrylly cresy*, but take care that thou do believe. O.M. 1784. *Dhe pygy me a vynsé, na wrylly y dysyryê yn torma dhyworthyf vy*, I would pray thee, that thou wouldst not desire it at this time from me. R.D. 1933. A mutation of *gwrylly*, 2 pers. s. subj. of *gwrey*.

WRYLLYF, v. a. I may do. *An Tâs a wrûk ow formyê, a'm offryn re woffé grûs; ha pan wryllyf tremené a'n bŷs, rum gorré dh' y wlâs*, the Father (who) created me, to my offering may he acknowledge favour; and when I shall pass away from the world, may he bring me to his land. O.M. 531. *Penag a wryllyf ammé, henna yw ef rum lauté*, whomsoever I may kiss, that is he, by my truth. P.C. 1085. A mutation of *gwryllyf*, 1 pers. s. subj. of *gwrey*.

WRYLLYN, v. a. We may do. *Bŷs yn epscop fystynyn; warfor strechê na wryllyn, dûn scon ganso*, to the bishop let us hasten; wherefore that we may not delay, let us come with him soon. P.C. 1135. A mutation of *gwryllyn*, 1 pers. pl. subj. of *gwrey*. *Wrellen* is another form, qd. v.

WRYNCH, s. m. A trick. *Bysy yw dheuch bones wâr; coynt mûr yw an gulas hep mar, hag a aswon lyes wrynch*, it is good for you to be cautious; the fellow is very sharp without doubt, and knows many a trick. P.C. 1001. From the Ang. Sax. *wrence*, doceit. Scott. *wrink*, *wrynk*.

WRYS, part. Made, done. *Dûn dhe leverel yn scon d'agan arluth Salamon bones an temple coul wrŷs*, let us come to say forthwith to our lord Solomon, that the temple is quite done. O.M. 2581. A mutation of *gwrŷs*, part. pass. of *gwrey*.

WRYTH, s. m. Sorrow. *Ple ma haueth a wôr dên vŷth may caffen whêth Cryst lên a wryth*, where is there tonight any man (that) knows where I may find yet Christ full of sorrow? R.D. 850.

WUIR, s. f. A sister. Corn. Voc. *soror*. It is doubtful whether this word is to be read *wuir*, or *huir*, qd. v.

WUL, v. a. To do or make. *Ny sconnyyf yn nêp maner a wûl ol dhe voluneth*, I will not refuse in any manner to do all thy will. O.M. 1292. *Otté omma prynner genef dhe wûl tân, degys a drê*, behold here wood with me to make a fire, brought from home. O.M. 1314. A mutation of *gûl*, qd. v.

WULUDOC, adj. Rich. Corn. Voc. *dives*. W. *goludog*, fr. *golud*, wealth. Arm. *glad*.

WUTHYL, v. a. To do or make. *An Edhewon ny wodhyê an prennyer py fêns kefis dhe wuthyl crous anedhé*, the Jews knew not where the timbers should be found to make a cross of them. M.C. 151. *Fysteneuch ow leverel pendra reys dhyn dhe wuthul*, hasten ye to say what is needful for us to do. R.D. 2252. A mutation of *guthyl*, qd. v.

WY, pron. subs. Ye or you. *Tays hu Mâb ha'n Speris Sans wy a bŷs a leun golon*, Father, and Son, and the Holy Ghost ye shall beseech with a full heart. M.C. 1. *Euch yn fen dh'y dhyscyblon, ha leverouch wy dhedhé, ha dhe Pedyr, dôs yn scon erybyn dhe Alyté; ena Crist, an kûf colon, wy a'n kŷff yn lowené*, go ye quite to his disciples, and tell ye to them, and to Peter, to go forthwith to meet him to Galilee; there Christ, the loving heart, ye shall find in joy. M.C. 256. A softened form of *why*, qd. v.

WY, s. m. Water. *Pryce*. The general form used in forming local names in Cornwall is *gy*, qd. v. W. *gwy*, *wy*.

WYAN, s. m. Bream fish. *Pryce*. *I rôf henwyn dhe'n puskas dhe wyan, pengarnas, selyas, me a's recken oll dybblans*, I give names to the fishes, to breams, gurnards, congers, I will reckon them all distinctly. C.W. 32.

WYDHEN, v. a. We know. *Ellas, bythqueth kyns lemmen y vôs gwŷr Dew ny wydhen*, alas, ever before now, we did not know that he was true God. P.C. 1914. *Ni a wydhen*, we know; *ti a wydhy*, thou shalt know; *ti a wydhys*, thou didst know; *hwi a wydh*, ye did know. *Lhwyd*, 247. Another form of *wodhen, &c.* qd. v.

WYL, v. a. He shall see. *Ti a wŷl*, thou shalt see. *Lhwyd*, 246. Another form of *wêl*, a mutation of *gwêl*, 3 pers. s. fut. of *gweles*.

WYLA, v. a. Seek thou. *En kêth guñs-ma ydhesé gans Ihesu worth y servyé, ha'y naché bŷth ny wyla, râk dhe gous a brêf neffré dhe vôs dên a Galilé apert dhe pôp ús omma*, this same fellow was staying with Jesus serving him, and never seek thou to deny it, for thy speech proves ever that thou art a man of Galilee clearly to every man (that) is here. P.C. 1407. 2 pers. s. imp. of *whylas*, qd. v.

WYLFYTH, v. a. He shall see. *Ty a wylfyth an toknys; kyn wylly mûr wolowys, na dhout ny fŷdh ken ys da*, thou shalt see the tokens; though thou mayst see much light, fear not that it will be other than good. O.M. 716. *Me a lever dheuch deffry, pyw penag a'm gwellha vy ef a wylfyth ow Thás*, I say to you seriously, whoever hath seen me shall see my Father. R.D. 2384. A mutation of *gwylfyth*, 3 pers. s. fut. of *gweles*.

WYLLY, v. a. Thou mayst see. *Mŷr gwel orth an wedhen; mŷr pandra wylly ynny*, look better at the tree; look what thou canst see in it. O.M. 801. *Ty a vêdh prysonys, na wylly yolow yn bŷs, bŷs pen vlydhen*, thou shalt be imprisoned, that thou mayst not see light in the world, till the end of a year. R.D. 71. A mutation of *gwylly*, 2 pers. s. subj. of *gweles*.

WYLSTA, v. a. Thou hast seen. *A Seth, osa dynythys agy dhe yêt Paradys, lavar dhym pandra wylsta*, O Seth, thou art come within the gate of Paradise, tell me what thou hast seen. O.M. 765. *A wylsta ken yn torma ys del egé agensow*, hast thou seen different now than as it was just now? O.M. 795. A mutation of *gwylsta*, a compound form of *gwylsys*, 2 pers. s. preter. of *gweles*, and *te*, thou.

WYLSYN, v. a. We have seen. *Y vernans ef pan wylsyn, ellas*, when we saw his death, alas. R.D. 689. *Alemma dûn ny dhe trê, ha leveryn yn pûp le, del wylsyn ny*, hence let us go home, and let us say in every place as we have seen. R.D. 807. A mutation of *gwylsyn*, id. qd. *gwelsyn*, 1 pers. pl. preter. of *gweles*.

WYLSYS, v. a. Thou hast seen. *Mâb Dew o nêb a wylsys, avel flôch byhan maylys; ef a bren Adam dhe dâs*, the Son of God it was thou sawest, like a little child swathed; he will redeem Adam, thy father. O.M. 809. A mutation of *gwylsys*, id. qd. *gwelsys*, 2 pers. s. preter. of *gweles*.

WYLYN, v. a. I did see. *An pŷth a wrên my ny wodhyen, rág ny wylyn; hag a quellen, my ny'n grussen, kyn fên ledhys*, the thing I did I knew not, for I did not see; and if I had seen, I would not have done it, though I were killed. P.C. 3022. *Bŷth ny wylyn yn nêp tu*, I saw nothing on any side. R.D. 434. A mutation of *gwylyn*, id. qd. *gwelyn*, 1 pers. s. imperf. of *gweles*.

WYLYS, v. a. I have seen. *Ol an tekter a wylys, ny gîl taves dên yn bŷs y leverel bynytha*, all the beauty (that) I saw, the tongue of no man in the world can tell it ever. O.M. 766. *Ny fûf dên dhodho bythqueth, na ny wylys kyns lymman y lyw na'y fêth*, I have never been a man of his, nor have I seen his form nor his face before now. P.C. 1239. A mutation of *gwylys*, id. qd. *gwelys*, 1 pers. s. preter. of *gweles*.

WYN, adj. White, blessed. *I vam whêk, Marya wyn, pûb ûr fystené a wre, may hallé doys war y byn, y mâb kemmys a garé*, his sweet mother, blessed Mary, always made haste that she might come to meet him, her son so much she loved. M.C. 171. A mutation of *gwyn*, qd. v.

WYNYN, card. num. One. *Lhwyd*, 176. Another late form of *onan*, qd. v.

WYR, adj. True. See *Wir*.

WYR, v. irr. He knows. *Dew e wŷr*, God knows; *ev a wŷr*, he knoweth, or will know. *Lhwyd*, 232, 247. Another form of *teôr*, qd. v.

WYRAS, s. m. Liquor, drink. A mutation of *gwiras*, qd. v.

WYRCHAS, s. f. A virgin. *Onan yw an Tâs a nêf, arall Crist y un vaaw ef, a vŷdh a wyrchas genys*, one is the Father of heaven, another Christ, his one Son, (that) shall be of a virgin born. O.M. 2663. A mutation of *gwyrchas*, id. qd. *gwerches*, qd. v.

WYRHES, s. f. A virgin. *Bynyges re bo an prŷs, may fe a venen genys, an wyrhes kêr Maria*, blessed be the time that he was born of woman, the dear Virgin Mary. R.D. 154. A mutation of *gwyrhes*, qd. v.

WYRTHEWYS, v. irr. He knew. ‡ *Ev a wyrthewys*, he did know. *Lhwyd*, 247. A late corruption of *wodhvedhys*. A mutation of *godhvedhys*, 3 pers. s. preter. of *godhvos*, qd. v.

WYSC, v. a. He will strike. *Me a'th wysk gans ow gwelan*, I will strike thee with my rod. P.C. 2734. A mutation of *gwysc*, 3 pers. s. fut. of *gwyscel*, qd. v.

WYSCE, v. a. To clothe. *Me a ordyn y wyské yn purpyr rych, kepar del goth dhe vychtern*, I order that he be clothed in rich purple, like as is becoming to a king. P.C. 2121. A mutation of *gwyscé*, qd. v.

WYSCEL, v. a. To strike. *Arluth, lavar dyssempys dhynny, mars yw bôdh dhe vreys, ha bolen-goth an Tâs my dhe wyskel nêp ês worth dhe dalhenné*, Lord, say immediately to us, if it is the will of thy mind, and the wish of the Father, that I should strike with the sword him that is holding thee. P.C. 1140. A mutation of *gwyscel*, qd. v.

WYSKENS, v. a. They struck. *Gans pûb colmen may'th ellé, pan wyskens, yn mês an crow*, that with every knot the blood might come forth when they struck. M.C. 131. A mutation of *gwyscens*, 3 pers. pl. imperf. of *gwyscel*, qd. v.

WYSTRE, v. a. To whisper. *Apert vythqueth y tyskys ow dyskes dhe'n Yedhewon; worth golow uôs ny geusys, na ny wystrys yn scoforn*, openly always I have taught my doctrine to the Jews; by the light of night I have not spoken nor whispered in the ear. P.C. 1254. (W. *sibrwd, sisial.* Lat. *susurro.*)

WYTH, s. m. Care, guarding. *Ha'y Spyrys re worro wÿth a'm ené*, and may his Spirit set a guard over my soul. O.M. 1978. A mutation of *gwíth*, qd. v.

WYTH, s. m. A work, deed. *War agan keyn ef a dhue dhé dré, dh'y scityé dh'y le, râg pûr dha ew rág an wÿth*, on our back it will come home to put it in its place; for very good it is for the work. O.M. 2572. *Pûp dén yn bÿs-ma a wôr, dén vythol na'n drehafsé yn try dÿdh wÿth war nép cor*, every one in this world knows, that no man whatever would build it in three days' work, in any way. P.C. 388. *My ny garaf streché pel, na nÿl dhé wÿth na dhé súl*, I do not like to stay long neither work day nor sunday. R.D. 2250. A mutation of *gwÿth*, qd. v.

WYTH, s. f. A time, a course. *Drefen un wÿth dhe henwel, lydhys ôf pûr dhyogel*, because of naming thee once, I am killed very certainly. O.M. 2724. *Aban rés au brús un-wÿth, ny fynnaf y ry dywyth*, since I have given the judgment once, I will not give it twice. P.C. 2496. *Me re'n cusullyes mÿl wÿth*, I have advised him a thousand times. P.C. 1811. A mutation of *gwÿth*, qd. v.

WYTH, v. a. He will take care. *Ty â yn pryson na wylly deydh, ha me a wÿth na'n lyttry*, thou shalt go to prison, that thou see not day, and I will take care that thou steal him not. R.D. 58. A mutation of *gwíth*, 3 pers. s. fut. of *gwíthé*, qd. v.

WYTHE, v. a. To take care of, to keep. *My re bredyrys gûl prat, rág y wythé erbyn hâf*, I have thought of doing a thing, to keep it against summer. O.M. 488. A mutation of *gwíthé*, qd. v.

WYTHES, s. m. A keeper. *Nép ma'n ressys dhe wethé, dheworth henna goxynné; py ûr fúf vy y wythes*, he to whom thou gavest him to keep, demand him of that one; when was I his keeper? O.M. 576. A mutation of *gwythes*, qd. v.

WYTHRES, s. f. A work, deed. *A Dâs, del ôn dhe wythres, a bol hag a lyys formys*, O Father, as we are thy work, of clay and mire created. O.M. 1069. *Me a wrûk trespastyé créf, pan y'n nechys Dew a néf, hag ol y wythres kffrys*, I did trespass strongly, when I denied him the God of heaven, and all his work also. P.C. 1443. A mutation of *gwythres*, qd. v.

WYTHYES, s. m. A keeper. *Anodho mâr 'thes preder, worth y wythyes gowynné*, for him if there is anxiety, from his keeper ask him. O.M. 609. A mutation of *gwythyes*, qd. v.

Y.

This letter is chiefly used as in Welsh, and many words are spelt exactly the same in both languages, as *býth*, ever; *dÿdh*, a day; *ymma*, here; *yn*, in; &c. It is also used to express the diphthongal sound of *i*, as in the English words *wine*, *fine*, &c., which is always written in Welsh, *ei*; thus C. *y*; W. *ci*, his, her, its. It is also constantly used in the Ordinalia for *i*; thus we find *gwyn, gwyr, gwyryoneth*, for *gwin, gwir, gwirionedh*, &c. Y is the only letter in Welsh which has two distinct sounds. In monosyllables that of *u* in the English words *turn, burn*, &c. The following monosyllables are exceptions, and have the penultimate sound, viz. *y, ydh, ym, yn, yr, ys, vy, dy, myn*. Both sounds are expressed in the English word *sundry*. It is singular that the same rule obtains in Manx. "*Y* in the penultima, antepenultima, &c. is pronounced as *u* in the English turn, hunt, further, sturdy; or as *i* in bird, third; as *spyrryd, ymmyrchagh*. In the ultima or monosyllables, as *i* in tin, skin, thin, trim, except these monosyllables *y, ym, yn, gys, ayn, myn*, which sound *y* as in the penultima. The constant sound of *y* in the penultima, and its ordinary sound in the ultima, are both exemplified in the single word *sundry*." *Kelly's Manx Grammar*. This letter has no place in the Armoric, Irish, and Gaelic alphabet.

Y, pron. s. They, them. *Ro dhedhé aga hynwyn, y a dhue dhe'th worhemmyn*, give to them their names, they will come at thy command. O.M. 121. *Dew dhén a gefyth ena; gor y yn més descampys, pûr vyxy a veydh dhedhé*, two men thou shalt find there; put them outside immediately, very hard it shall be for them. O.M. 334. *Aga hynwyn y a vÿdh an houl, ha'n lôr, ha'n stergan*, their names shall be the sun, and the moon, and the stars. O.M. 35. *My a worhemmyn, guytheuch wchy y*, I command, watch ye them. O.M. 2042. *Guthyl crous annedhé y*, to make a cross out of them. O.M. 1952. W. *hwy, hwynt*, †*wy*, †*wynt*. Arm. *hi*, †*y*. Ir. *siad, iad*, †*é*. Gael. *iad*. Manx, *ad*. Gr. οἱ. Lat. *ii, eæ, ea*.

Y, pron. adj. His, her, its. The genders are determined by the initials following. After the pronoun masculine the initial assumes the soft form as *tâs*, a father; *y dâs*, his father. When feminine the initial is aspirated. The same rule is observed in Welsh and Armoric. *Iowan y vam a sensy Marya, Crist del arsé; yn pûb manner may hylly, y vam prest a's onoré; yn delma comfort dhydhy y mâb a wynnas dyglyé*, John esteemed Mary as his mother, as Christ had commanded; in every way that he could, as his mother he readily honoured her; thus her son would provide comfort for her. M.C. 199. *Rág porrys rÿs o dhodho gasé y ben dhe gregy, rág galsé glân dheworto y woys*, for it was very needful to him to leave his head to hang, for clean from him his blood had gone. M.C. 207. *War y holon may crunys dre nerth an bum fynten woys*, so that on her heart gathered through force of the blow a fountain of blood. M.C. 224. *Gans y gÿk ha'y woys*, with his flesh and his blood. O.M. 812. *Dre y vernans yredy ol an bÿs a vÿdh sylwys*, through his death clearly all the world will be saved. O.M. 817. *Pan varwo, gorry yntré y dhÿns ha'y davas*, when he dies, put them between his teeth and his tongue. O.M. 826. *Y wordhyé y wleth dhrys*, to worship him is incumbent on thee. O.M. 1775. *Lemmyn ny a gyll gwelas lavar Du maga del wra néb a vynno y glewas*, now we may see how the word of God will feed whosoever will hear it. M.C. 12. (*An temple*, fem.) *yn triddydh dyowgel ef a wra y trehevel*, (the temple) in three days easily he will raise it. P.C. 353. *Rák henna warbarth ol y fechas gulán dedhy hy y feydh gufys*, for that together all her sin to her shall be clean forgiven. P.C. 528. W. *ei*, †*e*, †*i*. Arm. *e*, *he*. Ir. *a*. Gael. *a*. Manx, *e*.

Y, a verbal particle used before a verb in affirmative sentences, when the nominative follows, or is omitted. *A* being used when the nominative precedes, as *ni a wra*, we will do. It aspirates the initials of words following, and requires *h* before vowels. *Avel Du y fedhyth guris*, like God thou shalt be made. M.C. 6. *Dheworté un lam bechan ydh êth pesy may hallé*, he went from them a little distance that he might pray. M.C. 53. *Y wholthas y dhewlagas gans y eyll leuff o gosys, dre rás an goys y whelas Ihesus Crist del o dydhgtis*, he washed his eyes with his one hand (that) was bloodied, through the grace of the blood he saw how Jesus Christ was treated. M.C. 219. *Rág henna y tanvonns Crist dhodho ef may 'n dampné*, therefore he sent Christ to him that he might condemn him. M.C. 108. Before vowels *ydh* is used qd. v. W. *y, ydh, yr*.

Y, prep. In. An abbreviated form of *yn*, qd. v. *Kyns y un teller yn beys dew kendoner ydh egé*, formerly in a place in the world, there were two debtors. P.C. 501. *Pûr wyr ef a fue genys y Bethlem Iudi*, very truly he was born in Bethlehem Juda. P.C. 1007. *Ken teffo y ges golok*, should he come into your sight. R.D. 1861. *Ena ny a réd y gen lyfryow*, there we will read in our books. R.D. 2411. The adverbial particle *yn* is similarly abbreviated. *A aleesta y aswonfos? Galsen y ta, dhe'n kensa fu*, couldst thou know him? I could well, at the first sight. R.D. 863.

YA, adv. Yea, yes. *Pryce*. Written also *ia*, qd. v.

YACH, adj. Sound, healthy. See *Iách*.

YACHE, v. a. To made sound, to heal. See *Inché*.

YACHES, s. m. Health. See *Iaches*.

YAR, s. f. A hen. Corn. Voc. *gallina*. See *Iár*.

YBBA, adv. In this place, here. *Lhwyd*, 65. A further corruption of *ybma*, as that is of *ymma*, qd. v.

YBBERN, s. m. The sky. *Yn ybbern y fydh gwelys*, in the sky it shall be seen. C.W. 180. Written also *ybron*. *Yn ybron ês awartha*, in the sky (that) is above. C.W. 6. Both later forms of *ibron*, qd. v.

YBEN, pron. subs. The other. *Gebal, a dystouch mars ty a dhég a neyl pen dhe dour Cedron, cachaf yben pûr anrhek*, Gebal, immediately if thou wilt carry the one end to the water of Cedron, I will seize the other very sharp. O.M. 2816. *Heys Crist y a gemeras a'n neyll léf bys yn yben*, the length of Christ they took from the one hand even to the other. M.C. 178. *Me ha'm cowyth a drcha dismas yn ban; gueres lemmyn me a'th pŷs, ha why drehevouch ybeyn, may farwé an dhew vylen*, I and my comrade will raise Dismas up; help now I pray thee; and do ye raise the other, that the two villains may die. P.C. 2826. Written also *hyben*, qd. v. This pronoun is peculiar to Cornish and Armoric, and is not found in Welsh, where *Hall* is the equivalent. In Armoric, *eben* is used for "the other," when feminine only. In Cornish it is used when masculine as well.

YBMA, adv. In this place, here. ‡ *Mîr Dzhûan, médh e vester; ybman dha guber*, see John, says his master, here are thy wages. *Lhwyd*, 251. A late corruption of *ymma*, qd. v.

YC, adv. Also. *Lhwyd*, 240. Eng. *eke*.

YD, s. m. Corn, standing corn. Corn. Voc. *seges*. Where it is also written *hit*, qd. v. The later form was *ys*, qd. v. W. *yd*, †*ith*, †*it*, (hence *gwenith*, wheat, lit. white corn.) Arm. *id, ed*, †*yd*. †*ith*, †*ioth*. Gael. †*ith*, †*ioth*. Gr. σῖτος. O.N. *arti*. Sanse. *utta*, oaten; *ad*, to eat.

YCHELLAS, v. a. To ascend. *Lhwyd*, 245. See *Uchellas*.

YDDRAC, s. m. Sorrow, grief. *Nymbes yddrac vŷth yn bŷs*, I have not any sorrow in the world. C.W. 110. The same as *edrec*, qd. v.

YDN, card. num. One. ‡ *Ydn marh*, one horse. ‡ *Ydn lygadzhac*, one-eyed. ‡ *Re a ydn dra*, too much of one thing. *Lhwyd*, 82, 231, 244. A late corruption of *un*, qd. v.

YDNAC, card. num. Eleven. *Lhwyd*, 176. A late corruption of *unnec*, qd. v.

YDNACAS, adj. Eleventh. *Lhwyd*, 176. A late corruption of *unneeves*.

YDNIC, s. m. A chick, or young bird. Corn. Voc. *pullus*. Diminutive of *edhen*, qd. v. (W. *ednan*. Arm. *evnik*.) *Lhwyd*, 132, gives *ydnunge* as a late form.

YDZHI, v. subs. He is. ‡ *Ydzhi gys tîs bew*, is your father alive? *Lhwyd*, 245, 246. Though a late form, it agrees closely with W. *ydi*.

YDZHENS, v. subs. They are. *Lhwyd*, 246. W. *ydynt*.

YDH, a particle used in composition before verbs when beginning with vowels, as *a* is before consonants. *Dhys ydh archaf, a dyreyth*, I command thee, O earth. O.M. 381. *Y honan ydh ymwanas*, himself he has stabbed. R.D. 2065. *Ydh ennoyskys yn golon*, he smote himself in the heart. R.D. 2067. *Dhe'n kéth plás-na dhyuch ydh áf*, to that same place to you I will go. R.D. 2400. W. *ydh*.

YDHAMA, v. subs. I am. *Why a'm gwél, overdevys ydhama warbarth gans blew*, ye see me, overgrown I am with hair. C.W. 110. A reduplicate form of *omu*, qd. v.

YDHANWAF, v. a. I name. *Ydhanwaf buch ha tarow*, I name cow and bull. O.M. 123. A contracted form of *ydh* and *hanwaf*, 1 pers. s. fut. of *hemvel*, qd. v.

YDHAPYAS, v. a. It happened. *Ydhapyas dhym gûl foly, trystya a wrêff y'th vercy*, it happened to me to do folly, trust I will in thy mercy. P.C. 1438. Comp. of *ydh*, and *hapyas*, 3 pers. s. pretor. of *hapya*, formed from Eng. *hap*.

YDHE, v. subs. He was. *Ihesu Crist yn pow may 'dhe, ef a sawyé an glevyon*, Jesus Christ in the country, where he was, he healed the sick. M.C. 25. A redupl. form of *e*, 3 pers. s. imperf. of *bôs*.

YDIEGE, v. subs. He was. *Kyns y un teller yn beys dew kendoner ydhegé dhe un dettor*, once in a place in the world there were two debtors to one creditor. P.C. 502. A redupl. form of *egé*, qd. v.

YDHEN, v. subs. I was. *Yn le may 'dhén, yn trevow yn splan me a's derevas*, in the place where I was, in towns clearly I declared them. M.C. 70. A redupl. form of *ên*, qd. v.

YDHENS, v. subs. They were. *Reson y a rey ragthé, mes war fals ydhens groundys*, reasons they gave for them, but on falsehood were they grounded. M.C. 118. A redupl. form of *êns*, qd. v.

YDHESAF, v. subs. I am. *Râk ewen anveous ny glewaf yender dhum troys; ydhesaf ow clamderé*, for very chilliness I feel not the cold to my feet; I am fainting.

P.C. 1234. A double reduplicate form of *ôf*, qd. v.

YDHESAS, v. subs. Thou art. *A Thomas, nynsyw goky; ydhesas ow nuwkegy, yn mês a furdh*, O Thomas, he is not foolish; thou art raving, out of the way. R.D. 1466. A double reduplicate of *ôs*.

YDHESE, v. subs. He was. M.C. 162. Read *ydh* and *esé*, qd. v.

YDHESES, v. subs. Thou wast. P.C. 2259. Read *ydh* and *eses*, qd. v.

YDHESOUCH, v. subs. Ye were. P.C. 332. Read *ydh* and *esouch*, qd. v.

YDHETA, v. n. Thou wilt go. *Prâg ydheta er y pyn, râk Cryst a brennas yn tyn omma a'th drôs*, why wilt thou go against him? for Christ, who painfully redeemed, brought thee here. R.D. 241. To be read *ydh*, and *eta*, poetic form of *êth*, qd. v.

YDHO, v. subs. He was. *A Bertyl, asogé mûs ha goky, dres ol an dûs py ydho fôl*, O Bartholomew, thou art mad and stupid, beyond all the people that were foolish. R.D. 973. A reduplicate form of *o*, qd. v.

YDHOF, v. subs. I am. *A vâp whêk, ydhof cuthys*, O sweet son, I am grieved. O.M. 1236. *Gans moreth ydhof lywnys*, with sorrow I am filled. O.M. 2104. A reduplicate form of *ôf*, qd. v.

YDHOMA, v. subs. I am. *Lemyn ydhoma plagys, del welouch why oll an prôf*, now I am troubled, as ye all see the proof. C.W. 114. A redupl. form of *oma*, qd. v.

YDHON, v. subs. We are. *Nynsus bewé na fella, ydhon warbarth myshevyys*, there is no living any longer, we are altogether destroyed. O.M. 1704. A reduplicate form of *ôn*, qd. v.

YDHOS, v. subs. Thou art. *Huhel ydhos ysedhys, ha dyantel, rom lautê*, high thou art seated, and dangerously, by my truth. P.C. 93. *Ydhos*, Llwyd, 245. A redupl. form of *ôs*, qd. v.

YDHOSE, v. subs. Thou art. *Prâg ydhosé mar wokky*, why art thou so foolish? P.C. 1290. A redupl. form of *osé*, qd. v.

YDHOSTA, v. subs. Thou art. *Me a vyn mûs alemma, râg ydhostu drôg ebal*, I will go from hence, for thou art a wicked colt. C.W. 174. A redupl. form of *osta*, qd. v.

YDHOUCH, v. subs. Ye are. *Dhe Arluth nêf ydhouch druyth*, to the Lord of heaven ye are brought. O.M. 1621. A redupl. form of *ouch*, qd. v.

YDHYN, s. m. Birds. *Adam, otté an puskes, ydhyn an nêf, ha'n bestes, kefrys yn tŷr hag yn môr*, Adam, see the fishes, the birds of heaven, and the beasts, equally in land and in sea. O.M. 118. Plur. of *edhen*, qd. v.

YDHYNS, v. sub. They are. *Dew vâb yma dhym genys, ha tewys ydhyns dha dens, why oll a's gwêl*, two sons are to me born, and grown they are to manhood, ye all see them. C.W. 78. A reduplicative form of *ŷns*, qd. v.

YDHYW, v. subs. He is. *Cryst, a fue yn grous gorrys, yn mês a'n bêdh dasserchys ydhyw*, Christ, (that) was put on the cross, out of the grave is risen. R.D. 1236. *Prâg ydh-yw rûdh dhe dhyllas*, why is thy raiment red? R.D. 2529. A redupl. form of *yw*, qd. v.

YECH, interj. Oh. *O yêch*, an outcry. Llwyd, 249.

YECHES, s. m. Health. See *Ieches*.

YEDHOW, s. m. A Jew. Pl. *Yedhewon*. *Lavar mars ôf vy Yedhow*, say thou if I am a Jew. P.C. 2003. *Pepenag wo a'n parth wêr a cleufyth ow voys yn tŷr,*

Sarsyn py Yedhow kyn fo, whoever is of the true part, shall hear my voice in the land, though he be a Saracen or Jew. P.C. 2027. *Lavar dhymo vy yn scon, yw ty mychtern Yedhewon, kepar del fûs acusyys*, tell me directly, art thou king of the Jews, like as thou hast been accused? P.C. 1998. Another form of *Edhow*, qd. v.

YEIN, adj. Cold, frigid. See *Iein*.

YEINDER, s. m. Cold, extreme cold. Llwyd, 141. Written also *yender*, or *iender*, qd. v.

YER, s. m. Air, sky. *Ha deydh brues dheuch of a dhue ha why a'n guylwyth yn yer, worth agas yuggé ol tûs an boys, crêf ha guan*, and the day of judgment he will come to you, and ye shall see him in the sky, judging you, all the men of the world, strong and weak. P.C. 1333. Another form of *ayr*, qd. v.

YER, s. m. Hens. Plur. of *yâr*, or *iâr*, qd. v.

YERL, s. m. An earl. *Goon Yerl*, the earl's down. Pryce. W. *iarll*. Arm. †*iarl*. Ir. *iarla*. Gael. *iarla*. Ang. Sax. *corl*.

YET, s. m. A gate. Pl. *yettys*. *Agy dhe'n yet gor dhe ben*, within the gate put thy head. O.M. 743. *A Seth, osa dynythys agy dhe yet paradys*, O Seth, thou art come within the gate of Paradise. O.M. 764. *Dûn tôth brâs dhe prennê agan yettys*, let us come in great haste to bar our gates. P.C. 3039. Prov. Eng. *yate*.

YEUES, v. a. A desire, wish. *A Dâs, del ôs bynyges, môs dhodho yw ow yeues, del yw e ow Arluth kêr*, O Father, as thou art blessed, it is my desire to go to him, as he is my dear Lord. P.C. 1046. *Râg ol ow yeues pûp prŷs ty a vŷdh pûr wêyr nefré*, for all my love always thou shalt very truly ever have. O.M. 2125.

YEUGEN, s. f. A ferret. Corn. Vocab. *feruncus*. W. *iewgen*.

YEUNY, v. a. To desire, to wish. *Mars yw hemma an Ihesu, wolcom yw re'u Arluth Dew; y wôles my re yeunys*, if this be the Jesus, he is welcome, by the Lord God; to see him I have wished. P.C. 1701.

YF, v. a. Drink thou. *Yn pow-ma nynsus guel gwŷn, râg hemma yw pyment fyn ; yyf ow Arluth hep parow*, in this country there is not better wine, for this is fine liquor ; drink it, my lord without equal. O.M. 1916. 2 pers. s. imp. of *evé*, qd. v. W. *ŷv*. Arm. *ef, iv*.

YFARN, s. m. Hell. See *Ifarn*.

YG, s. m. A hook. *Yg hôrn*, an iron hook. Llwyd, 242. Written also *îg*, qd. v.

YGE, v. subs. Is. *Dhe dhyskyblon yw serrys mûr, ha'n Yedhewon gans nerth pûp ûr ygé kerhyn*, thy disciples are very sad, and the Jews with great strength always are round about them. R.D. 886. A corrupted form of *usy*, qd. v.

YGERY, v. a. To open. Part. *ygerys*. Some of the tenses are formed from *ygory*. 2 pers. s. imp. and 3 pers. s. fut. *ygor*. 3 pers. s. preter. *ygoras*. *Râk an porthow hep dyecedh a vŷdh ygerys yn wêdh, may'th ello abervedh an mychtern a lowené*, for the everlasting gates shall be opened also, that may enter in the king of joy. R.D. 102. *Euch, ow dew êl, dhum servons lêl, yn pryson êns; hep ygery, na fûs terry, drew hy yn mês*, go my two angels, to my faithful servants, (that) are in prison; without opening or breaking wall, bring them out. R.D. 317. *Ty wâs geyler kesudow, ygor scon an darasow, ha hêdh an prysnes yn mês*, thou jailer, detestable fellow, open directly the doors, and haul the prisoners out. R.D. 632. *Me a's ygor wharré, an darasow agan naw,* I will open them soon, our nine doors. R.D. 638. *'An carna a ygoras, del o destrys dhodho ef,* that rock opened, as it was fated for him. R.D. 2335. *Ygor an daras,* open thou the door. P.C. 1985. Written also *egery,* qd. v.

YL, v. n. He will go. *Ny ĝl an ĝĝst yn y blâs ; re hĝr ew a gevelyn,* the beam will not go into its place; too long it is by a cubit. O.M. 2528. 3 pers. s. fut. of irr. v. *mones.* W. *êl.*

YLL, pron. adj. The one, one of two. *Gansé Crist a ve tewlys war an grous dhe wrowedhé, ha'y ĝll lêff a ve tackis orth en grous fast may 'thesé, ha'y ĝll troys a ve gorris poran war ben y golé,* by them was Christ thrown on the cross to lie, and one of his hands was nailed on the cross, so that it was fast, and one of his feet was put right over the other. M.C. 179. Another form of *eyl,* qd. v.

YLL, v. n. He shall or will be able. *Ganso kyn fi's tewlys, te a ĝll sevel arté,* though thou wert thrown down by him, thou wilt be able to rise again. M.C. 22. *Rĝg ny a ĝl ĝîl scovva,* for we may make a tent. O.M. 1717. *Pyw a ĝl henna bones,* who can that be? P.C. 771. *Synt Iowyn whêk re'n carro, ha dres pûp ol re'n gordhyo, kepar del ĝll e yn ta,* may sweet Jove love him, and honour him above every body, like as he can well. P.C. 1840. *Y a ĝl bones kechys gans tûs war fordh dhecorthyn,* they may be taken by people on the way from us. P.C. 2293. *Me a ĝl bûs morethek,* I may be mournful. P.C. 3187. *Ny won fatel ĝl wharfos,* I know not how it can happen. R.D. 229. *Pandra ĝl henna bones,* what can that be? O.M. 157. A mutation of *gĝll,* 3 pers. s. fut. of *gally,* qd. v.

YLLENS, v. n. They were able. *Ha dhodho a leverys, re saffé Crist heb strevyé ol dh'y vôdh gans golonvys, ha na yllens y gwythé, y vôdh na ve colenvys,* and (they) said to him, that Christ had risen incontestably, all to his will with lights, and they were not able to keep him, that his will should not be fulfilled. M.C. 248. A mutation of *gyllens,* 3 pers. pl. imperf. of *gally,* qd. v.

YLLONS, v. n. They shall or will be able. *Rĝg an lafur ûs dhedhé, vĝth ny yllons ymweres,* for the labour that is to them, they will never be able to help themselves. O.M. 1420. *Ny yllons bôs nyfyrys, an tûs ye marow,* they cannot be numbered, the people (that) are dead. O.M. 1544. A mutation of *gyllons,* 3 pers. pl. fut. of *gally,* qd. v.

YLLOUCH, v. n. Ye shall or will be able. *Ken teffo y ges golok, dhodho ny yllouch ĝîl drôk, me a grĝs,* though he should come into your sight, to him ye will not be able to do harm, I believe. R.D. 1862. *Un pols golyas ny yllouch dhum comfortyé,* one moment can ye not watch to comfort me? M.C. 55. A mutation of *gyllouch,* 2 pers. pl. fut. of *gally,* qd. v.

YLLY, v. n. He was able. *Camen Pylat pan wclas na ylly Crist delyffré,* when Pilate saw that he was not able any way to deliver Christ. M.C. 150. *Rĝg gwan spyr heg ef yn ten, camen na ylly gwythé,* from weak spirit, and he constrained, that he could not keep any way. M.C. 205. *Pan omseltyas dhe demptyé, guthyll pêch ni'b na ylly,* when he set himself to tempt him, who could

not commit sin. M.C. 20. A mutation of *gylly,* 3 pers. s. imperf. of *gally,* qd. v.

YLLY, v. n. Thou shalt have gone. *Arluth, pandra wrêf lemmen, pan ylly gy ahanan dhe'n nêf dhe'n Tâs,* Lord, what shall I do now, when thou shall have gone from us to heaven to the Father? R.D. 2452. 2 pers. s. 2 fut. of irr. v. *mones.* W. *eli.*

YLLYF, v. n. I may go. *Kymerouch, eveuch an guĝn, rĝg ny evnf bĝs dêdh fĝn genouch annodho na moy, bĝs may 'th yllyf yn ow gwlâs,* take, drink ye the wine, for I will not drink till the last day with you of it any more, until that I go into my kingdom. P.C. 726. 1 pers. s. subj. of irr. v. *mones.* W. *elwyc.*

YLLYN, v. n. We may go. *Yn ewn fordh dh'y may 'th yllyn, may feen hembrynkys, pesyn en Tâs Dew leun a vercy,* in the right road to it, that we may go, that we may be conducted, let us pray the Father God, full of mercy. O.M. 1972. *Yw ôn pâsk dhynny parys, ma yllyn môs dhe soper,* is the paschal lamb ready for us, that we may go to supper? P.C. 708. *Henna ny a vyn notyé le may 'th yllyn yn pûp le, y vôs dasserhys,* that we will make known, where we may go in every place, that he is risen again. R.D. 664. 1 pers. pl. subj. of irr. v. *mones.*

YLLYN, v. n. We shall or will be able. *Lavar, cowyth da del ôs, fatel yllyn aswonvos en harlot yn mĝsk y lûs,* say, good fellow as thou art, how shall we be able to know the knave among his people. P.C. 966. *Arluth, ny â dhy wharé, râk ny yllyn yn nêp trê trygé dres nôs,* Lord, we will go to it directly, for we shall not be able in any town to dwell over night. R.D. 2404. *Gynen bydhyth yn dewses, râk na yllyn dhe weles, cûth ny gen gâs,* with us thou shalt be in Godhead, because that we shall not be able to see thee, sorrow will not leave us. R.D. 2455. *Ni a yllin,* we can. Llwyd, 247. A mutation of *gyllyn,* 1 pers. pl. fut. of *gally,* qd. v.

YLLYN, v. n. I was able. *Me a vynsé y wythé, ha ny yllyn cammen vĝth ; pûp ol csé ow cryé y ladhé awos travyth,* I would have preserved him, and I could not in any way ; every one was crying to kill him notwithstanding anything. P.C. 3126. *Gans ow dew lagas ow sywel me a'n gwelas, ha garow hag uthyk brâs yn kerdh gallas môs a'n bêdh ; ny yllyn sywel yn ban râk own awodho,* with my eyes I saw him standing ; and fierce and terribly great, forth he went out of the tomb ; I could not stand upright for fear of him. R.D. 533. A mutation of *gyllyn,* 1 pers. s. imperf. of *gally,* qd. v.

YLLYR, v. pass. It is possible. *A Dâs Dew kêr venges, ny yllyr re dhe wordhé ; rĝg pûp ûr ol dhe wythres yw da, ha mûr dhe byté,* O Father, dear blessed God, it is not possible too much to worship thee ; for always thy work is good, and great thy compassion. O.M. 1852. A mutation of *gyllyr,* id. qd. *galler,* qd. v. See also *Hyller.*

YLLYTH, v. n. Thou shalt or wilt be able. *Yma dhys colon galas na le ys ty dhe vynnas gasé dhe vês an er brâs ; ken ny yllyth bôs sylwys,* thou hast a hard heart, that thou hast not lessened thy will, to leave off the great defiance (1 air,) else thou wilt not be able to be saved. R.D. 1526. *Pandra yw henna dhyso, guelhé ny yllyth dhymmo, pûr wĝr hep nuer,* what is that to thee ? thou wilt not be able to benefit me, very truly without doubt. R.D. 1643. A mutation of *gyllyth*, 2 pers. s. fut. of *gally*, qd. v.

YLSYN, v. n. We were able. *Lowené dhys Syr Pilat; awos bûs ny peswar smat, guythé an bêdh ny ylsyn,* joy to thee Sir Pilate, notwithstanding our being four fellows, we were not able to keep the tomb. R.D. 603. A mutation of *gylsyn*, 1 pers. pl. preter. of *gally*, qd. v.

YLTA, v. n. Canst thou. *(Yl—te.) Pyw a ylta gy bones, pan yw mar rûdh dhe dhylles, yn gulascor nêf,* who canst thou be, when thy clothing is so red, in the kingdom of heaven ? R.D. 2511.

YLWYS, adj. Successful. *Hag a'n grous, del o prŷs, corf Ihesus a gemeras; tŷr Marya, me a gris, pûr ylwys a'n gweresas,* and from the cross, as was time, the body of Jesus he took, the three Maries, I believe, very successfully helped him. M.C. 230. I connect this word with W. *hylwydh*.

YLWYS, v. n. He cried out. *Pûb onan ol a ylwys, Arluth Du, yw me hena,* every one exclaimed, Lord God, am I that one ? M.C. 43. *Pan y'n caffsons yntredhé, ol warbarth y a ylwys,* when they got him among them, they all cried out together. M.C. 142. A mutation of *gylwys*, 3 pers. s. preter. of *gylwel*, qd. v.

YLY, s. m. Ointment, salve, cure, remedy. Pl. *ylyow. Benyn dyr vûr cheryté y box ryche leun a yly a uch Crist rág y unlyé, hy a vynnas y derry,* a woman through much charity her box rich full of salve, over Christ to anoint him she wished to break it. M.C. 35. *Ha mar scon del y'n guylly, ef a'th saw hep ken yly ol a'th cleves yn tyrn,* and as soon as thou seest him, he will heal thee, without other remedy, of all thy malady entirely. R.D. 1695. *Y vyrys y wolyow, aga gwlas o trueth, dhe'n bŷs kyns êns ylyow,* I looked on his wounds, it was pitiful to see them; to the world rather they are healings. R.D. 900. *A Arluth pen ylyow, me a wêl dhe wolyow warbarth a lês,* O Lord, head of healings, I see thy wounds altogether disclosed. R.D. 1315. W. *eli, olew.* Arm. *oleou, eôl,* †*oleo.* Ir. *ola.* Gael. *ola, uillidh.* Manx, *ooil.* Gr. ἔλαιον. Lat. *oleum.* Goth. *alēv.*

YLYE, v. a. To anoint. *My a vyn môs dhe uré ow Arluth, treys ha dewlé, gans onemeni kêr, ha war y pen y scullyé, a pûp squythens y sawyé, hag ylyé y vrenyon,* I will go to anoint my Lord, feet and hands with precious ointment, and shed it upon his head; from all weariness to cure him, and anoint his bruises. P.C. 478. *A pe profus lynyges ef a wodhfyé y bûs hy pechadures, ny's gassé dh'y ylyé,* if he were a blessed prophet, he would know that she is a sinner; he would not permit her to anoint him. P.C. 492. W. *elio.* Arm. *eôli.*

YLYN, adj. Clean, fair. *Dywerto ma'm boma grâs, môs dhe blansé my a vyn en gweel gans reonté vrâs yn nêp plath têk hag ylyn,* from him that I may have grace, I will go to plant the rods with great care, in some fair and clean place. O.M. 2080. Written also *elyn*, qd. v.

YM, comp. pron. Used when the first person sing. is the object of a verb in the indicative or subjunctive mood. *Y'm* is compounded of the verbal particle *y*, and *am*, my. *En Tôs a nêf y'm gylwyr,* the Father of Heaven I am called. O.M. 1. *Lawar dhymmo dyowgel, del y'm kerry,* speak to me clearly, as thou lovest me. O.M. 1370. *A Dew, lemyn guyn ow beys, aban y'm sawyas ef,* O God, now I am happy, since he hath healed me. O.M. 1774. *Mars dhe wel y'm gorthebeuch, fast prysonys why a vŷdh* unless ye answer me for the better, fast imprisoned ye shall be. R.D. 47. W. *ym, y'm.*

YM, comp. prep. In my. *My re weles y'm hunrus a dhyragof êl dyblans.* I have seen in my dream a bright angel. O.M. 1934. *Ha Pylat râk y dhanfon me a'n carvyth y'm colon alemma bŷs gorfên beys,* and Pilate for sending him, I will love him in my heart henceforth to the end of the world. P.C. 1703. *Heys ol ow crochen scorgyys, down y'm kîc may'th o tellys lyes mîl tol,* all the length of my skin scourged, so that deep in my flesh were pierced many thousand holes. R.D. 2539. Comp. of the preposition *y*, for *yn*, and *am*, my. The same contraction occurs in Welsh. *I'm hing y gelwais ar v' Arglwydh,* in my distress I cried on my Lord. (Prys's Metrical Version of the 120th Psalm.) Arm. *em.*

YM, a particle prefixed to verbs, which reflects the action on the agent. Thus *gweres*, to help; *ymweres*, to help one's self. *Cregy*, to hang; *ymgregy*, to hang one's self. Written also *em*, and *om*, qd. v.

YMA, v. imp. There is, it is. *Pûr luen yma dhym ow whans,* very fully there is to me my desire. O.M. 91. *Yma Dew yn tyller-ma,* God is in this place. O.M. 1992. *Why â scon ahanan dhe Pilat, râk yma owdh ysedhé,* ye shall go immediately from us to Pilate, for he is sitting. P.C. 2342. Written as commonly separately *y ma.* See *Ma.*

YMA, adv. In this place, here. *Pŷth yw an gusyl wella dhe wruthil worth an treytor, ma yma lyes gwrêk ha gour ow treylé dhodho touth-da,* what is the best counsel to do with the traitor ? there is many a woman and many a man turning to him with great haste. P.C. 557. Variously written *umma, omma,* and by Llwyd, 222, *ymma.* See *Ma,* and *Omma.*

YMAMENDYE, v. a. To mend one's self. *Mar ny wrêth ymamendyé, ef a wra tyn dhe punssyé, may lewerry och ellas,* if thou wilt not mend thyself, he will severely punish thee, that thou wilt say, Oh, alas! O.M. 1526. Comp. of refl. part. *ym,* and *amendyé,* borrowed from English.

YMBITHIONEN, s. f. A sheet of paper, a schedule. Corn. Voc. *seeda* vel *scedula.* W. *peithinen.*

YMBREYSE, v. a. To judge one's self. *Ny vennaf pel ymbreysé, rág nyns yw an vanor vâs; dhe voy dên vŷth ny'm gorsé, kyn facyen mûr,* I will not longer judge, for the custom is not good; no man any more would place me, though we may pretend much. P.C. 1677. Comp. of reflect. part. *ym,* and *breysé,* id. qd. *brusy,* qd. v.

YMCENER, v. pass. Let it be sung to each other. *My a gân an conternot, ha ty, dyscant ymkener,* I will sing the counter note, and thou, let a descant be sung to each other. O.M. 562. 3 pers. s. imp. pass. of *ymcana,* comp. of refl. part. *ym,* and *cané,* to sing. W. *ymganu.*

YMCNOUCE, v. a. To beat each other. *Yma dheuch mûr a dhylyt a ymknouké,* there is to you much delight to beat each other. P.C. 2323. Comp. of refl. part. *ym,* and *cnoucé,* id. qd. *cnoucyé,* qd. v.

YMCUSYLLE, v. a. To consult one another. *Tra vŷth ny amont dhynny y whylas ef na moy; ymcusyllé gureny ny pŷth yw guella dhe bôs giorŷs,* it avails us nothing to seek him any more; let us consult together what is best to be done. R.D. 561. Comp. of refl. part. *ym,* and *cusyllé,* id. qd. *cusylyé,* qd. v.

YMDENNE, v. a. To draw one's self, to withdraw, to refrain. 2 pers. s. imp., and 3 pers. s. fut. *ymden.* (*Ym—tenné.*) *Ef o tebel edhen, néb a glewsys ow cuné, hag a'n doro dhe anken, mars ny a wra ymdenné,* he was an evil bird, whom thou heardest singing, and will bring us to sorrow, unless we do refrain. O.M. 226. *My a worhemmyn wharé dhe'n glaw na moy na wrello; an lyf woth gwréns ymdenné,* I will soon command the rain that it do no more; let the fierce flood withdraw. O.M. 1093. *Yn pûr wŷr Dew a aswon volungeth ol dhe colon, rág henna ymden yn scon a dhyworto ef deffry,* very truly God knows all the wish of thy heart; therefore withdraw thou immediately from him in earnest. O.M. 1377. *Mar asos fûr, ty a tew, hag a ymden,* if thou art wise thou wilt be silent, and wilt withdraw. R.D. 985.

YMDOWLA, v. a. To throw one another, to wrestle. (*Ym—towla.*) *Dho ymdowla,* Llwyd, 81. W. *ymdavlu.*

YMDOWLUR, s. m. A wrestler, a champion. *Llwyd,* 44, 81, 240. W. *ymdavlwr.*

YMDHREHEVEL, v. a. To raise one's self. (*Ym—drehevel.*) *Dên alemma cowethé; y wèles me a garsé owdh astel ymdhrehevel,* let us come hence comrades; I would have liked to have seen him endeavouring to raise himself. R.D. 395. W. *ymdhyrchavael.*

YMDHYSQUEDHAS, v. n. To shew one's self. (*Ym—dysquedhas.*) *Teweuch rák medh, dew adla, ymdhysquedhas ny rynna dhe plussyon, a wrlouch why,* be silent for shame, (ye) two knaves, he would not shew himself to wretches, do ye see. R.D. 1499. W. *ymdhadgwdhio.*

YMGREGY, v. n. To hang one's self. (*Ym—cregy.*) *Aban nag ûs ken maner, an arhans, kettep dyner, me a's deghes war an lwer, hag a ryn scon ymgregy,* since there is no other way, the silver, every penny, I brought upon the floor, and will forthwith hang myself. P.C. 1516. W. *ymgrogi.*

YMGUEN, v. a. To move one's self. *A'n bêdh pan dhueth, ha lammé, y fyys yn un vrammé, own keinerys, del levaraf, pen bronnen; rák ny alsé ymguen, del ol degys,* from the grave when he came, and leapt, I fled in a tremor, seized by fear, as I say, rush-head; for he could not move himself, as he was entirely shut up. R.D. 2097. W. *ymwringo.* Arm. *emcinca.*

YMMY, v. a. Thou shalt kiss. *Ty a saw a'n trôs dhe'n pen, dre vertu an thŷr guelen, may scon dhedhé del ymmy,* thou shalt be healed from the foot to the head, by virtue of the three rods, as soon as thou shalt kiss them. O.M. 1764. *Mar scon dhodho del ymmy kychouch ef yn vryougen,* as soon as thou kissest him, catch him in the throat. P.C. 1006. 2 pers. s. subj. of *ammé,* qd. v.

YMONS, v. imp. They are. Used with nouns plural, as *yma* is with nouns singular. *Ow popel ty grevyys brás gans Pharow, yw mylyges, ymôns dhymo ow cryé,* my people greatly aggrieved by Pharoah, (that) is accursed, they are crying to me. O.M. 1418. *Tûs revenes, ha flechys, ymôns oumu dynythys, ha'ga pŷth degys gansé,* men, women, and children, they are come here, and their things carried with them. O.M. 1612. *An kêth guél-ma, yn dôr ymôns ol gurydhyys,* these same rods, in the earth they are all rooted. O.M. 2064. Written often separately *y môns,* qd. v.

YMPYNYON, s. m. The brains. See *Impinion.*

YMSAWYE, v. a. To save one's self. (*Ym—sawyé.*) 2

pers. s. imp. *ymsaw.* *Mars ós máp Dew a vér brŷs, ymsaw scon a dhrokeleth,* if thou art the Son of God of great price, save thyself immediately from ill usage. P.C. 2866. *Ef a allas dywogel, del glowys y lewerel yn lyes le, sawyé brenens tûs erel; lemmyn y honan ny ýl ymsawyé,* he could indeed, as I heard it said in many places, save the life of other men; now himself he cannot save himself. P.C. 2878.

YMSCEMUNYS, part. pass. Accursed. *A dhyragouch me a pŷs ow lones ymskemunys, me mar a'n sewys bythqueth,* before you I pray that I may be cursed, if I have ever followed him. P.C. 1415. *Hemma yw deaul ymskemunys,* this is a devil accursed. R.D. 2089. Written also *ymskemenys.* *Ke dhe vês ymskemenys yn defŷth yn tewolgow,* go thou out, accursed, into desert into darkness. P.C. 141. The same as *emscumunys,* qd. v. Comp. of refl. part. *ym,* and *scumunys,* part. of *scumuna,* or *scemyna,* to curse.

YMSENSY, v. a. To feel one's self. (*Ym—senny.*) *Lawar dhym, del y'm kerry; pan vernans a'n gevé ef, ha fatel ve fe lwdhys, rág ef o stout ha gothys, hug a ymsensy dên crêf,* tell me, as thou lovest me, what death did he have, and how was he killed; for he was stout and proud, and felt himself a strong man. O.M. 2222.

YMSYWE, v. a. To follow each other. (*Ym—sywé.*) *Guyrgoneth a reys bôs dreys aberwdh yn mater-ma, ha lendury kekeffrys, rág ymisywé y a wra,* need is that truth be brought within this affair, and good faith also, for they do follow each other. P.C. 2450.

YMWANE, v. a. To stab one's self. (*Ym—gwané.*) *Arluth, Pylat yw marow, dre payn ha dre galarow; y honan ydh ymwenas,* Lord, Pilate is dead, through pain and through sorrows; himself he hath stabbed. R.D. 2065. W. *ymwanu.*

YMWEDHE, v. a. To pine. *A Arluth, ydhof lowen ty dhe wynnes dôs gynen omma dh'agan lowenhé; henna me a lever whêth, ydhesen dre pûr hyreth war dhe lerch owdh ymwedhé,* O Lord, I am glad that thou wouldest come with us hither to gladden us; that I will say likewise, I was, through great longing, after thee pining. R.D. 1170. W. *ymhiveth,* to beseech earnestly.

YMWERES, v. n. To help one's self. (*Ym—gweres.*) *Ydhunwnf bûch ha tarow, ha march, yw bêst hep parow dhe vâp dên rág ymweres,* I name cow, and bull, and horse, (that) is a beast without equals, for the son of man to help himself. O.M. 125. *Ymôns dhyno ow cryé, rág an lafur ûs dhedhé, vŷth ny yllons ymweres,* they are to me crying, for the labour that is to them, they can never help themselves. O.M. 1420. W. *ymwared.*

YMWRYL, v. a. To make one's self, to pretend. 3 pers. s. fut. *ymwra.* *Euch alemma gans Iudas dhe gerhas an guâs muscok ugy ow ymwryl Máp Dew,* go ye hence with Judas to fetch the crazed fellow (who) is making himself Son of God. P.C. 962. *Rág mychtern nép a ymwra, erbyn Cesur cous yma, hu'y ladhé travyth ny vern,* for he who makes himself a king, is speaking against Cæsar, and to kill him it matters not. P.C. 2222. *Ydh ymwruk pûr wŷr hep fal dew ha dên gans whethlow gow,* he hath made himself, without doubt, God and man with lying tales. P.C. 2395. Comp. of refl. part. *ym,* and *gwryl,* a contracted form of *gwrythyl,* to make. W. *ymwneud, ymwneuthur.*

YMWYTHE, v. a. To keep one's self. (*Ym—gwythé.*)

YN 389 YNNY

2 pers. s. imp. *ynncyth*. *Heil mychtern an Yedhewon, ynneyth lemman râg an kên*, hail, king of the Jews, preserve thyself from the torture. P.C. 2144.

YMWHELES, v. a. To throw one's self. *Ellas, a Cryst, ow mâp kêr, yn mûr payn pan y'th welaf, ellas dre kueth yn clamder dhe'n dôr prâg na ymwhelaf*, alas, O Christ, my dear son, in much pain when I see thee; alas, through shame in a faint to the earth why shall I not throw myself? P.C. 2594. Comp. of refl. part. *ym*, and *wheles*, to turn, (W. *chwelyd*,) whence *dewheles*, to return. W. *ymchwelyd, tymchoelyd*.

YN, prep. In, within, on, into, to. *Yn grows gans kentrow fastys*, on a cross with nails fastened. M.C. 2. *I êth ha Ihesus gansé bŷs yn Pylat o Iustis*, they went, and Jesus with them, unto Pilate (that) was Justice. M.C. 98. *A ryne gwarthé y ben war y gorff bŷs yn y droys; squardijs oll o y grohen, hag ef cudhys yn y woys*, from the very top of his head on his body to his feet; all his skin was torn, and he hidden in his blood. M.C. 135. *Pylat êth yn mês a'y hell, yn un lowarth a'n gevé*, Pilate went out of his hall into a garden (that) he had. M.C. 140. *En debell wrêk casadow gans mûr a dôth êth yn chy*, the wicked hateful woman with much of haste went into (the) house. M.C. 150. *Lucyfer kelmys yw whâth pûr fast yn y golmennow, hag ef a drŷk heb fyn-weth yn uffarn yn tewolgow*, Lucifer is still bound very fast in his bonds, and he shall dwell without end in hell in darkness. M.C. 212. *Yn* was abbreviated into *y*, qd. v. *Yn* enters into composition with pronouns, as *ynnof*, in me; &c. qd. v. W. *yn, y, †en, †in, †hin, †i*. Arm. *enn, e*. Irish, *ann, †in, †i, †hi*. Gael. *ann, anns*. Manx, *ayns*. Gr. *èv*. Lat. *in*.

YN, a particle, which placed before adjectives forms them into adverbs. It aspirates the mutable initials. Thus *da*, good; *yn ta*, well. *Brâs*, great; *yn frâs*, greatly. *Garow*, rough; *yn harow*, roughly. *Mâs*, good; *yn fâs*, well. *Yn dan*, beneath; *yn râg*, forward; *yn scon*, immediately; *yn tyn*, sharply. Instances are found where it softens the initial following, which is the rule in Welsh. *Glân*, clean; *yn lân*, cleanly. (W. *glân, yn lân*.) *I beyn o mar grêff ha tyn, caman na ylly bewé, heb daseor y cneff gwyn; bytliqueth yn lân rewewsé*, his pain was so strong and keen that he could not live any way without parting with his blessed soul; ever purely he had lived. M.C. 204.

YN, comp. pron. Him, it. Used when the personal pronoun is the object of the verb in the indicative or subjunctive mood, and is placed before it, when it is affixed to the verbal particle. *Y'n gurâf ytho scon yn torma*, I will do it now immediately in this time. O.M. 1275. *Hag ef dhyn re leverys, kyn fe an temple dymerŷs, yn tri dŷdh y'n dreafsé*, and he hath said to us, though the temple were destroyed, in three days he would rebuild it. P.C. 366. *Pan fue genouch acusyys, ef uy gufas fout yn bŷs, pan y'n danfonns of dhyn*, when he was accused by you, he found no fault in the world, when he sent him to us. P.C. 1861. *Ha dew a dhûk dustuny, y'n clewsons ow leverel*, and two bare witness (that) they heard him saying. M.C. 91.

YN, comp. pron. Us. Used with the first person plural, as in the preceding article. *A Dhew a nêf, dhe pysy a luen colon gurres ny, nag y'n veuy velyny gans Pharow yw mylyges*, O God of heaven, I pray thee with full heart,

help us that no villainy may be to us by Pharaoh, (that) is accursed. O.M. 1609. *Yn* is similarly used in Welsh, as *pan y'n gwelodh*, when he saw us.

YNA, adv. In that place, there. Lhwyd, 248. Generally written *ena*, qd. v.

YNAN, pron. subs. Self. *Da ynan*, thyself. Lhwyd, 167. A late form of *honan*, qd. v.

YNDAN, prep. Under. Arm. *indan*. See *Dun*.

YNDANNO, pron. prep. Under him. *(Yndan—o.) Me a vyn yn della dysky ow dyllas guella, ha tywlel a dhyragtho; yma gynef flowrys tèk yn onor dhum arluth whêk, aga skulyé yndanno*, I will also take off my best clothes, and cast before him; I have fair flowers in honour to my sweet Lord to scatter before him. P.C. 260. W. *dano*.

YNNE, pron. prep. In them. *(Yn—y.) Gostryth dhymo y a vŷdh, kekemys ûs ynné gwreys*, obedient to me they shall be, as much as is in them made. O.M. 54. *Otté spern grisyl gyné, ha dreyn lym ha scharp ynné a grup bŷs yn empynyon*, see sharp thorns with me, and spines rough and sharp in them, (that) will pierce even to the brains. P.C. 2116. W. *yndhynt, †endunt*. Arm. *ennhô*. Ir. *ionnta, †indib, †andsom*. Gael. *annta*. Manx, *ayndoo*.

YNNO, pron. prep. In him or it. *(Yn—o.) A wottevé ef gené, may whodhfouch yn pûr deffry, ny gafaf vy kên ynno dhe vones ledhys*, behold him with me, that ye may know in very earnest, I do not find cause in him to be slain. P.C. 2157. *Kepar del fuvé dremmas, yn dôr my a vyn palas tol may fo ynno cudhys*, like as he was a just man, in the earth I will dig a hole, that he may be covered in it. O.M. 866. W. *yndho, †endau, †yndaw*. Arm. *enn-han, †enhof, †enhaf, †ennaff*. Ir. *ann, ann-san, †indid*. Gael. *ann*. Manx, *aynsyn*.

YNNOF, pron. prep. In me. *(Yn—mi.) Mar ny fyn, dre y rusow, ow gueres a termyn ver, ow colon ynnof a ter pûr own dre fyannasow*, if he will not, through his graces, help me in a short time, my heart in me will break very really through troubles. R.D. 707. *Dew ha dên kepar del ôf, an ûs yma ynnof, hag yn wreydh my ynno ef*, like as I am God and man, the Father is in me, and likewise I in him. R.D. 2366. W. *ynov*. Arm. *eunoun*. Ir. *ionnum, †indiumm*. Gael. *annam*. Manx, *aynym*.

YNNON, pron. prep. In us. *(Yn—ni.) A nyns esé ynnon ny agan colon ow lesky, pan wrûk an bara terry, ha'n scryptor y egyry*, ah, was not within us our heart burning? when he did break the bread, and open the scripture. R.D. 1321. W. *ynom*. Arm. *ennomp*. Ir. *ionainn, †indiunn*. Gael. *annainn*. Manx, *ayadooin*.

YNNOS, pron. prep. In thee. *(Yn—ti.) Râg eannas ôs, hep danger, nyns ûs fout ynnos guelys*, for thou art a messenger, without delay, there is not a fault in thee seen. O.M. 2291. *Ihesus Cryst, arluth a nêf, a clow lemmyn agan lîf; nêp wa grŷs ynnos, gosf ny fŷth syltwys*, Jesus Christ, Lord of heaven, O now hear our voice who believes not in thee, miserable he; he will not be saved. R.D. 757. W. *ynnot*. Arm. *ennod*. Ir. *ionnad, ionnat, †indtt*. Gael. *annad*. Manx, *aynyd*.

YNNOUCH, pron. prep. In you. *(Yn—chui.)* W. *ynnoch*. Arm. *ennhôch*. Irish, *ionaibh, †indiib*. Gael. *annaibh*. Manx, *ayndiu*.

YNNY, pron. prep. In her or it. *(Yn—hy.) Ha dhywhy me re ordynas glâs nêf ynny râk trygé*, and to you I have ordained the kingdom of heaven, in it to dwell.

P.C. 808. *Gorré dhe'n mcrnans, gorré yn pren crous a dhysempis, ha kelmys treys ha dulé, ynny hy bedhens tackys,* put him to death, put him on the cross-tree forthwith; and bound feet and hands, on it let him be fastened. P.C. 2164. *Ha'y holon whêk a rauné, me'a lever, râg trystans, râg an grayth ynhy esé na's gwethé an Spyrys Sans,* and her sweet heart would have parted, I say, for sorrow, had not the Holy Ghost preserved her for the grace that was in her. M.C. 222. W. *yndhi,* †*yndi,* †*endi.* Arm. *enn-hi,* †*enhy.* Ir. *inte, innti,* †*inti,* †*indi.* Gael. *innte.* Manx, *aynjee.*

YNNY, s. m. A denial, refusal. *A Dâs, del ôs luen a râs, my a wra oi dd vynny; dhe worhemmyn yn pûp plâs del degoth dhyn hep ynny,* O Father, as thou art full of grace, I will do as thou wishest; thy command in every place, as it becomes me without denial. O.M. 1042. *Syr Arluth kêr, del vynny, my a wra prest hep ynny ol dhum gallus vynytha,* dear Sir Lord, as thou wishest, I will do at once, without refusal, all in my power ever. O.M. 2148.

YNNYA, v. a. To deny, to refuse. *Pryce.*

YNNYA, v. a. To press on, to urge. *Un veuyn hardh a ynnyas war Pedyr y vôs tregis gans Ihesus; ef a nachas y Arluth a dhesympys,* a bold woman urged on Peter that he was staying with Jesus: he denied his Lord forthwith. M.C. 84. *Mas rê war Gryst a ynnyas, ydh o dewas a yrchy,* but some urged on Christ, that it was drink (that) he asked. M.C. 201. *Yn mêdh Pylat pan a dra a ynnyouch vy warnodho,* says Pilate, what matter do ye urge against him? M.C. 90. W. *ynnio.*

YNNYAS, s. m. A repulse, a denial. Plur. *ynnyadow.* *Pryce.* Written by Llwyd, 242, *inniadow. Arluth cûf, dhe archadow, y wruthyl rês ew dhymmo; ydh âf hep ynnyadow dhe wonys a dro dhodho,* dear Lord, thy commands, used is to me to do them; I will go, without denials, to work about it. O.M. 999.

YNS, v. subs. They are. 3 pers. pl. pres. of *bôs. Avel olow aga threys, sŷch ŷns ol kepar ha lcys,* like the prints of their feet, they are all dry, like herbs. O.M. 761. *Yn plath may môns y a sêf, dredho ef pan ŷns plansys,* in the place where they are, they shall stand, through him when they are planted. O.M. 2092. *Dhe resous ŷns da ha fŷn,* thy reasons are good and fine. P.C. 822. *War an brys ny ŷns parow,* on the earth they are not equals. R.D. 1820. Written also *êns,* qd. v. W. *ŷnt.* Arm. *int.* Ir. *it.* Sansc. *anti.*

YNTA, adv. Well. Llwyd, 249, *yntd.* See *Yn* and *Ta.*

YNTER, prep. Between, among. *Ena hy a ve sevys yn ban ynter bennens,* there she was raised up again among the women. M.C. 172. More generally written *yntré. Par del won, lavaraf dhys yntré Du ha pehadur acordh del ve kemerys,* even as I know I will tell to thee between God and sinner how accord was taken. M.C. 8. *Pan varwo gorry, hep fal, yntré y dhŷns ha'y davas,* when he dies put them, without fail, between his teeth and his tongue. O.M. 826. *A Dâs yntré dhe dhewlé my a gymmyn ow ené,* O Father, into thy hands I bequeath my soul. O.M. 2362. It enters into composition with the pronouns, as *yntredho,* between him, &c. (Unknown to Welsh, where *rhwng* is used.) Arm. *entre, etre.* Ir. *idir, eadar,* †*indir,* †*etar.* Gael. *eadar.* Manx, *eddyr.* Lat. *inter.* Fr. *entre.* Sansc. *antar.*

YNTERDHOCH, pron. prep. Between ye. *A dhew har-lot, yma dheuch mûr a dhylyt a ymknouké; me a dhybarth ynterdhoch, hag a wra dheuch peunow couch,* O two knaves, there is much delight to you to beat each other; I will divide between you, and will make to you red heads. P.C. 2325. Another form of *yntredhouch,* qd. v.

YNTREDHE, pron. prep. Between them. (*Yntré—y.*) *Wharé y a'n kemeres, hag a'n sensys yntredhé,* anon they took him, and held him among them. M.C. 70. *En Edhewon yntredhé a whelas dustuneow,* the Jews among them sought witnesses. M.C. 90. *Par del won lavaraf dhys yntré Du ha pehadur acordh del ve kemerys, râg bonus 'gan pêch mar vûr, mayn yntredhé a ve gurŷs,* even as I know I will tell to thee between God and sinner how accord was taken; because our sin was so great, a mean was made between them. M.C. 8. (W. *rhyngdhynt.*) Arm. *entrezhô.* Ir. *catorra,* †*etorru,* †*eturtu.* Gael. *eutorra.* (Maux, *mastoc.*)

YNTREDHO, pron. prep. Between him. (*Yntré—o.*) *Benen na cows muscochneth, râk an kêth dén-ma bythqueth ny'n servyes, war ow ené, na rum fay my ny'n guylys may wodhfen tremyn yn beys yntredho hn'y gowethé,* woman, speak not folly, for this same man never did I serve, on my soul; nor by my faith have I seen him, that I should know the look in the world between him and his companions. P.C. 1298. (W. *rhyngdho.*)

YNTREDHON, pron. prep. Between us. (*Yntré—ui.*) *Dûs gené pols dhe wandré, ha dyso my a lever yntredhon tarlow pryeé,* come to walk with me a while, and I will tell thee between ourselves things private. O.M. 936. *Pan yllyn ny yntredhon drey dour a'n meen flynt garow,* when we can between ourselves bring water from the sharp flint stone. O.M. 1850. *Me a vyn lemmyn rauné yutredhon ol y dhyllas,* I will now divide between us all his clothes. P.C. 2842. (W. *rhyngom.*) W. *entrecomp,* †*entromp.* Ir. *eadrainn,* †*etronn.* Gael. *eadrainn.* (Manx, *mastain.*)

YNTREDHOUCH, pron. prep. Between ye. (*Yntré—chui.*) *Lemmyn ol crês yntredhouch, omma kepar del esouch worth ow gortos,* now all peace among you, here like as ye are waiting for me. R.D. 2433. Written also *ynterdhoch,* qd. v. (W. *rhyngoch.*) Arm. *entrezhoch,* †*eutroch.* Ir. *eadraibh,* †*eitraib,* †*etruib.* Gael. *eadraibh, eadruibh.* (Manx, *masteu.*)

YNWEDH, adv. Also, likewise. *Ha hanter cans kevelyn ynwedh ty a wra y lês,* and half a hundred cubits also thou shalt make its width. O.M. 958. *A bûb echen a kunda, gorow ha benow ynwedh, aga gora ty a wra yn dhe worhel ubervedh,* of all sorts of species, male and female also, thou shalt put them in thy ark within. O.M. 990. Comp. of *yn,* id. qd. *un,* one ; and *gwêdh,* form. W. *un wêdh.*

YNWYTH, adv. Once. Llwyd, 248. Id. qd. *unwyth,* qd. v.

YOLACIT, s. m. A bird. *Pryce.* A strange word, unknown elsewhere, and evidently a wrong reading of *volatil.* See Norris's Cornish Drama, ij. 435.

YONC, adj. Young, youthful, juvenile. Super. *yonka. Pûb lé dhe dhên gwra lewté, beva dên yonk bo dên côth,* always do thou loyalty to man, be he a young man or a old man. M.C. 175. *Worth an pen y a weles dhe'n bêdh, yw leveris kens, un flouch yonk gwyn y dhyllas, eyll o ha y ny wodhyens,* they saw at the head of the grave, (that) is mentioned before, a young child, white his raiment; an angel it was, and they knew it not. M.C. 254. *Scullyas y tcôs râk yonk ha lôs,* he shed his blood for young and grayheaded. R.D. 333. *Cayn ydhew ow mâb cotha, hag Abel ew ow mâb yonka,* Cain is my eldest son, and Abel is my youngest son. C.W. 78. Written in the Cornish Vocabulary, *iouenc, youonc.* W. *ieuanc,* † *iouenc.* Arm. *iaouanc.* Lat. *juvenis.* Sansc. *yuvan.*

YORCH, s. m. A roe. Corn. Voc. *caprea.* See *Iorch.*

YOW, s. m. Jupiter, Jove. *Du Yow,* Dies Jovis, Thursday. Llwyd, 232. See *Iow.*

YOWYNC, adj. Young, youthful. Pl. *yowynces,* used as a substantive, youth, young people. *Yowynk ha lous, kyn fo tollys dre y deunos, mercy gylwys,* let young and grey, though they be deceived by his subtilty, call for mercy. P.C. 19. *Ol ny a prŷs, yowynk ha hên, war Dhu pûp prŷs mercy gan kên,* all we pray, young and old, to God always mercy with pity. P.C. 39. *Thesu pendra leverta a'n flechys ûs ow cané; yowynkes menoch a wra yn yowynkneth mûr notyé,* Jesus, what sayest thou of the children (that) are singing? Young people often in youth do much to be noted. P.C. 433. Another form of *younc,* qd. v.

YOWYNCNETH, s. m. The state of youth, youth, youthfulness. See the authority in the preceding article. W. *ieuenctyd,* † *yewenctyt.* Arm. *iaouankiz, iaouanktiz, iouankted.*

YRCHSYS, v. a. Thou hast commanded. *Arluth kêr, dhe arhadow my a'n gura hep falladow, kepar del yrchsys dhynny,* dear Lord, thy commands I will do them, without fail, as thou hast commanded us. P.C. 187. *Arluth cuf kêr, ny a wra kepar del yrchsys dhynny,* dearly beloved Lord, we will do as thou hast commanded us. P.C. 642. 2 pers. s. preterite of *archa,* qd. v.

YRCHY, v. a. He asked for. *Mas rê war Gryst a ynnyas ydh o dewas a yrchy,* but some urged on Christ that it was drink (that) he asked for. M.C. 201. 3 pers. s. imperf. of *archa,* qd. v.

YRCHYS, v. a. He charged, commanded. *Gor dhe gledhé yn y goyn, dhe Pedyr Crist a yrchys,* put thy sword in its sheath, Christ commanded Peter. M.C. 72. *Ha dhyso Dew a yrchys,* and God has commanded thee. O.M. 1491. 3 pers. s. preterite of *archa,* qd. v.

YREDY, adv. Surely, verily, indeed, readily. *Me ny'th dampnaf yredy, ha na wra na moy pecha,* I will not condemn thee indeed, and do thou sin no more. M.C. 34. *Y hwalsons ol adro, mar caffons gôff yredy,* they sought all about if they could find a smith readily. M.C. 154. *Godhfos guŷr ol yredy, my a vyn môs dhyworthys,* to know all the truth indeed, I will go from thee. O.M. 821. Written also *credy,* qd. v.

YRHAN, s. m. The edge or brink, a margin. Llwyd, 86. W. *or.* Ir. *or,* *ur.* Gael. † *or.* Manx, *oir.* Lat. *ora.*

YRHYS, v. a. I asked for. *Wogé ow da oberow, dyuues a yrhys dedhé; dhym rosons bystyl wherow, bŷth ny fynnys yevé,* after my good works, drink I asked for of them; they gave me bitter gall, I would never drink it. R.D. 2600. A softened form of *yrchys,* 1 pers. s. preter. of *archa.* It is also used for the 3 pers. *Ef a yrhys dhym kyrhas a mount Tabor guel a rás, ma'm vedhen dredhé sylwans,* he ordered me to bring from Mount Tabor rods of grace, that I may have salvation through them. O.M. 1956.

YRHYS, part. Commanded. *May hallo vôs kerenys kepar del fue dhyn yrhys gans y dâs kyns tremené,* that he may be crowned, like as it was to us commanded by his father before passing away. O.M. 2375. A softened form of *yrchys,* part. pass. of *urcha,* qd. v.

YRVYRE, v. a. To consider, to observe, to devise, to enjoin. 3 pers. s. fut. *yrvyr.* Part. pass. *yrvyrys. Na dybreuch, my a yrvyr, kŷe gans gôs bŷs worfen verys, eat ye not,* I command, flesh with blood to the end of the world. O.M. 1219. *Yrverys ew rum lewté sol-a-dhŷdh dhe avonsyé a'n kynsé benfys a'n been,* it is thought of, on my truth, for a long time, to advance thee to the first benefice I have. O.M. 2611. *Symon, del ôf yrvyrys, yma dhymmo rum lauté nebes dhe leverel dhys, gosleuw orthyf vy wharré,* Simon, as I am considering, I have, by my truth, something to say to thee; hearken to me presently. P.C. 493. *Ty ny's golhyth yn nép câs, war bryns ôs ôf yrvyrys,* thou shalt not wash them in any case, for all the penalty I can think of. P.C. 554. *Ha bedhouch wâr colonow, râk Satnas yw yrvyrys, avel ŷs, y nothlennow dh'agas kroddré,* and be of cautious hearts, for Satan is desirous, as corn in winnowing sheets to sift you. P.C. 880. Written also *ervyré,* qd. v.

YRVYS, part. Armed. *Y êth yn un fystené, peswar marrek yrvys êns,* they went in a hurry, four armed soldiers they were. M.C. 241. *Yrvys fast bŷs yn dhewen,* armed quite to the jaws. M.C. 242. *Gor ost genes yrvys da, dhe omladh, del y'm kerry,* take a host with thee well armed to fight, as thou lovest me. O.M. 2141. Written also *ervys.* Part. pass. of *arva,* to arm.

YS, conj. Than. *Gwel vya ys y scollyé,* it would be better than to spill it. M.C. 36. *Yn nôs haneth, kyns ys bôs colyek clewys, Pedyr, ty a'm nâch tergweth,* this very night before that a cock is heard, Peter, thou wilt deny me thrice. M.C. 49. *Moy pêch o pan dyspresyys ys del o pan y'n gwerthé,* greater sin it was when he misprized him than when he sold him. M.C. 104. *Bŷth moy ys Edhow yn ta a bechas orth ow thrayla,* ever more than a Jew well he has sinned, in betraying me. M.C. 145. *Kyn wylly mûr wolowys, na dhout, ny fŷdh ken ys da,* though thou see much light, fear not, it will not be other than good. O.M. 718. *Saw kyns ys yn tour mones levereuch dhym,* but before going to the palace speak ye to me. O.M. 2030. *An lueff a'm grûk me a wêl, ha'y odor whekké ys mêl ow tôs warnaf,* the hand that made me I see, and his odour sweeter than honey, coming upon me. R.D. 144. Written also *es,* qd. v.

YS, comp. pron. Her, it. Used when the 3 personal pronoun feminine is the object of a verb in the indicative or subjunctive mood, before which it is placed and affixed to the verbal particle. (Yn is similarly used with masculines.) *Dre dhe vôdh, lavar pyro ôs, dyllas rûdh yn a'n codhfos, prâk y's guyskyth,* by thy will, say who thou art, red raiment in our knowledge, why dost thou wear it? R.D. 2549. It is also used for the 2 and 3 persons plural. *Aban ôf sefys a'n bêdh, godhfedheuch y's bŷdh sylwans,* since I am risen from the tomb, know ye that salvation shall be to you. R.D. 1574. *Dh'y dhyscyplys y trylyas, y's cafas ol ow coské.* to his disciples he turned, he found them all sleeping. M.C. 55. *Kemmys a wrûk bôdh an Tâs, y's gorras dhe lowené*, as many as wrought the will of the Father, he placed them in bliss. R.D. 2636.

YS, pron. adj. Your. ‡ *Dho ys cridzhé*, to believe you ; ‡ *thera vi war ys pisi*, I desire you. Llwyd, 244, 250. A late abbreviated form of *agys*, qd. v.

YS, s. m. Corn. Pl. *ysow. Ys bara*, bread corn. *Ys sewel*, standing corn. *Pen ŷs*, a ear of corn. *Ha bedhouch wâr colonow, râk Satnas yn yrwyrys, acel ŷs y nothlannow dh'agas koddré*, and be of cautious hearts, for Satan is desirous, as corn in winnowing sheets, to sift you. P.C. 881. *Me a wrûg oblashion vrâs, hag a loskas lower a ŷs*, I have made a great oblation, and have burnt much corn. C.W. 86. *An gwês a vynsé lesky agan ysow yn tefry, ny yllan porthy henna*, the fellow would have burnt our corn indeed, I could not bear that. C.W. 82. A later form of *ŷd*, qd. v.

YSCARN, s. m. Bones. *Ellas, bones dhe treys squerdys ; ol dhe yscarn dyscavylsys, tel y'th dywluef*, alas, that thy feet are torn; all thy bones strained; holes in thy hands. P.C. 3173. *Myrez y gorf, del yw squerdys, yscarn mâp Dew dygyvelsys, ha Dew warbarth*, to see his body, as it is toru; all thy bones strained, and a God at the same time. P.C. 3170. *Dre mûr hyreth ydhof pûr squyth, ha'm corf dhe wêdh yscarn ha lŷth*, through great longing, I am quite weary, and my body also, bones and limb. R.D. 848. Pl. of *ascorn*, qd. v.

YSCERENS, s. m. Enemies. *Pylat a yrchys dhedhé, war beyn kylly an bewnans, monas dhe'n corf dh'y wethé, na'n kemerré y yskerans*, Pilate commanded them on pain of losing their life, to go to the body, to keep it, that his enemies might not take it. M.C. 241. *Me a lever guyroweth, onan ahanouch haneth rum guerthas dhom yskerens*, I tell the truth, one of you this night has sold me to my enemies. P.C. 737. Plural of *escar*, qd. v.

YSCRYBEL, s. m. A labouring beast, used in carriage or tillage. Llwyd, 74, *yscrybl*. W. *ysgrubyl*, *ysgrubll*.

YSCYNNE, v. a. To ascend. *Kepar yn beys ha dues, dhe'n nêf grusses yskynné*, as thou camest into the world, to heaven thou wouldst ascend. O.M. 156. *Lemyn pêp ol yskynnens*, now let every one mount. O.M. 2001. *Yskyn yn ban, mars yw prŷs*, mount thou up, if it is time. P.C. 222. *Râg pan yskynnyf dhe nêf, me a fyn cafus gynef kekeffrys cledh ha sŷns*, for when I ascend to heaven, I will take with me also angels and saints. R.D. 188. *Kepar del sevys a'n bêdh dhe'n uêf gans mûr a eledh, ny dh'y weles yskynnys*, like as he rose from the tomb to the heaven with many angels, that we saw him ascended. R.D. 668. *A le-na ydh yskynnyf yn ban bŷs yn glascor nêf*, from that place I will ascend up even to the kingdom of heaven. R.D. 2401. *Yn ban dhe'n nêf Ihesu a wrûk yskynnê*, up to heaven did Jesus ascend. R.D. 2640. Written also *ascenna*, and *escynnya*, qd. v.

YSCYS, adv. Soon, speedily. Llwyd, 249. See *Uscys*.

YSEDHE, v. a. To sit, to be seated. 2 pers. s. imp. *ysé*. Part. *ysedhys*. *Ke war pynakyl an temple, hag caa gura ysedhé*, go thou upon the pinnacle of the temple, and there do sit. P.C. 85. *Me a vyn môs ow honan war an pynakyl yn ban dhe ysedhé*, I will go myself up on the pinnacle to sit. P.C. 89. *Huhel ydhus ysedhys*, high thou art seated. P.C. 93. *Dues nês, hag ysé gené*, come thou nearer, and sit with me. P.C. 576. *Y'n creys me re ysedhas*, in the midst I have sat. P.C. 803. *Ysedh-*

ouch, syre iustis, sit you, sir justice. P.C. 2230. *Râk yma owdh ysedhé*, for he is sitting. P.C. 2342. *A dhyne barth dhe Dhu Tâs ydh ysedhaf*, at the right side of God the Father I shall sit. R.D. 1173. *Ysé dhymmo a dhyow*, sit on the right to me. R.D. 1627. *Uch pûb êl ty a ysé*, above every angel thou shalt sit. C.W. 4. *Ha warnodho a ysedh êl benegns lowenek*, and on it sat an angel blessed joyful. M.C. 244. Written also *esedhé*, qd. v.

YSEL, adj. Low. See *Isel*.

YSOUCH, v. subs. Ye are. *Ysouch goky ha fellyon, ha teul yn agas colon*, ye are foolish and silly, and deceit in your heart. R.D. 1273. A reduplicate form of *ouch*, qd. v. W. *ydych*.

YSSE, comp. n. In thy seat. *A Ddew yssé, fucf goky pa na cynnan vy crygy a'n bêdh y vôs dasserchys*, O God in thy seat, I was indeed foolish, when I would not believe that he was risen again from the tomb. R.D. 1565. A contraction of *yn-dhe-se*.

YSSOS, v. subs. Thou art. *Yssos goky*, thou art foolish. R.D. 1464. A reduplicate form of *ôs*, qd. v. W. *ydwyt*.

YSSYW, v. subs. He is. *Ysyw hemma trueth brâs, bôs dhe corf kêr golyys gans tebel popel*, this is a great sorsow, that thy body is watched by wicked people. P.C. 3182. A reduplicate form of *yu*, qd. v. W. *ydyw*.

YSTIFERION, s. m. An eavesdropper, a talebearer. Pryce.

YSTYNE, v. a. To extend, to stretch out, to reach. *Adam ystyn dhym dhe dhorn*, Adam, reach to me thy hand. O.M. 205. *Ty, losel, ystyn dhe vrêch war au pren*, thou knave, stretch out thy arm on the wood. P.C. 2753. *Iosep dhe Gryst a wynnus y arrow ha'y dhe firech whêk, hag a's ystynnas pûr dêg*, Joseph for Christ made white his legs, and sweet arms, and stretched them out very fairly. M.C. 232. *Me a ystyn an skorrn*, I will reach the bough. C.W. 50. W. *estynu, ystynu*. Arm. *astenn*. (Ir. †*eiscsin*, porrectio. Gael. *cite, cileadh*, a stretching.) From the Lat. *extendo*.

YSY, v. subs. That is. Llwyd, 245. The same as *usy*, qd. v.

YSYLY, s. m. Limbs. *Dên yw corf gans ysyly*, man is a body with limbs. P.C. 1733. *Ol ow ysyly yn ten*, all my limbs stretched. R.D. 2583. *Vythelh ponces my ny'm blŷth, mar vrew ew ow ysyly*, there is never rest to me, so bruised are my limbs. O.M. 1012. Written also *ysely*. *Goys a'y ben ha'y ysely a dhroppyé war y dhew ver*, blood from his head and his limbs dropped on his legs. M.C. 173. Llwyd, 242, has *ysilli*. Plural of *esel*, qd. v.

YT, pron. prep. In thy. *Pu a woras yt colon cows yn detma worth iustis*, who put it into thy heart to speak thus to a Justice ? M.C. 81. To be read *yth*, qd. v.

YTA, adv. Lo, behold. *Adam, yta au puskas, edhen yn ayr, ha bestas*, Adam, behold the fishes, birds in the air and beasts. C.W. 30. A later form of *ota*, qd. v.

YTA, v. subs. He is. *Ha meer, Cayn yta ena devedhys dha drê tothda*, and see thou, Cain is there returned home in great haste. C.W. 90. *Nyns yta au sêth tennys, ha'n bêst yma grweskys*, now is the arrow shot, and the beast is struck. C.W. 114. *Del o au kensa dên a ve gans an Tâs formys, yn bêdh yta of lemyn*, as he was the first man that was by the Father formed, in the grave he is now. C.W. 152. This form occurs only in late Cornish. Written by Llwyd, 245, *otté*. W. *ydi*. Ir. *ata, ta*. Gael. *ta, tha*. Manx, *ta*.

YTAMA, v. subs. I am. *Dhum shape ow honyn ytama, why a vêl omma, treylys*, to my own shape I am turned, ye see here. C.W. 68. A reduplicate form of *oma*, qd. v

YTOWNS, v. subs. They are. *Ages gwarack ha sethow, genaf ytowns y parys*, your bow and arrows, with me they are ready. C.W. 103. *An pillars ytowns parys, gorrouch ynna au lewerow*, the pillars are ready, put in them the books. C.W. 158. *Nynges bêst na preif yn beys, benow ha gorow omma genaff dhe why yma dreys, yn lester ytowns yna*, there is not a beast or reptile in the world, male and female by me to you are brought, in the vessel they are there. C.W. 176.

YTTASEFSONS, v. a. They desired. *Yttaseffsons oll yn wêdh dre an golon y delly*, they all desired also to pierce him through the heart. M.C. 216. Comp. of *y* and *tesefsons*, a mutation of *desefsons*, 3 pers. pl. preter. of *desef*, qd. v.

YTTEREVYS, v. a. He declared. *Ytterevys dre sor brâs, dusteneow drûk na da, ny reys dhynny dhe welas arcos dampuyé an dên-ma*, he declared in great warmth, witnesses good nor bad we need not seek on account of condemning this man. M.C. 94. Comp. of *y* and *terevys*, a mutation of *derevys*, 3 pers. s. preterite of *derevas*, qd. v.

YTTERN, s. m. Pity, compassion. Pryce. In one MS. written *ynten*. *Calmana, ow hoer ffynten; gâs uy dha vôs a le-ma, râg nangew hy prŷs yttern; ma 'thew rês yn ker vaggyn*, Calmana, my sister, make haste; let us go hence, for it is now time to retire; it is necessary for us to go away. C.W. 96.

YTU, v. n. He went. *Gory vŷth pan ŷth dhodho, pan ôf ŷthys tergwyth hydhew*, woe is me when I ever went to him, when I am vanquished by him three times to day. P.C. 145. *Drefen ow bôs noeth hep quêth, ragos ŷdh ŷth dhe gudhé*, because I was naked without a cloth from thee I went to hide. O.M. 260. Another form of *êth*, 3 pers. s. preter. of irr. v. *môs*.

YTU, pron. prep. In thy. (*Y—uth.*) It aspirates the mutable initial. *Mylygé a wrâf defry an môr y'th whythres hogen*, I will assuredly curse the earth in thy evil deed. O.M. 272. *A Dûs kûf y'th wholowys*, O wise Father in the lights. O.M. 285. *Pandra synsyth y'th luef tenyn*, what holdest thou in thy hand now? O.M. 1442. *A'n lôst kynmer dhédhy yn ban, y'th torn hep gêr sens dhe honan*, by the tail take it up, in thy hand, without a word, hold it thyself. O.M. 1455. *Ow bennath y'th chy re bo*, my blessing be in thy house. P.C. 1803. *Cafus an bows-na hep gory, ûs y'th kerchyn, nie a vyn*, have that robe without seam, that is about thee, I will. R.D. 1922. This form is also used in Welsh. *Y'th berson dy hunan*, in thy own person. (Mabinogion, iij. 262.) *Vy nagrau dôd i'th gostrel; onid yn pôb pêth i'th lyvrau di, a wneuthum i yn dhirgel*, put my tears in thy bottle; is not every thing in thy books, that I have done secretly? (*Prys's* Metr. Version of 56th Psalm.)

YTH, comp. pron. Thy. Used when the second person singular is the object of a verb in the indicative or subjunctive mood, and is placed before it, when it is affixed to the verbal particle. *A Dhew a'n nef, clew agan lêf, del y'th pysaf*, O God of heaven, hear our voice, as I pray thee. O.M. 1390. *Mar a'th caffaf, re iovyn, y'th ladhaf kyns ys vyttyn a'n dew luef*, If I shall find thee, by Jove, I will kill thee before morning with my hands. O.M. 1533. *My ny wodhyen a'th vernans, na vŷth moy a'th daserchyans, pan y'th whylsyn dewedhys*, I knew not of thy death, nor any more of thy resurrection, when I saw thee come. R.D. 2546. *Yth* is similarly used in Welsh, as *pan y'th welais*, when I saw thee.

YTH, a particle used in construction before verbs beginning with vowels, as *y* is before consonants. More correctly written *ydh*, qd. v.

YTHENS, pron. prep. In them. *Râg yn whêh dydhyow Dew a râs an nêf, ha'n 'oar, ha'n môr, ha mŷns ôs ythens y, ha powesas an scythvas dŷdh, hag a'n uchelhas*, for in six days God made heaven and earth, and the sea, and all that is in them, and rested the seventh day, and hallowed it. *Pryce.* This form, like *ettans*, qd. v. is found only in late Cornish, the classic form being *yunné*, qd. v. *Ythens* however cannot be of late formation, as it contains *ns*, the characteristic of the third person plural, and agrees closely with W. *ynddynt*.

YTHO, adv. Now, then. *Ytho bedhyth mylyges pûr wŷr drys ol an bestes a gerdho war an nôr veys*, now thou shalt be accursed very truly above all the beasts (that) walk on the earth of the world. O.M. 311. *Ytho kymmer hy dew hŷs, râg cafos dhys ha'th woregty*, then take two lengths of it, for thee and thy wife to have. O.M. 387. *Lavar dhymmo 'pandra woruma; y'n gurâf ytho scon yn torma*, tell me what I shall do; I will do it now immediately at this time. O.M. 1275. *Ow Arluth kêr cûf colon, pyno ytho a's hembronk dhy, mar ny wrâf vy nag Aron aga ledyn venary*, my beloved Lord dear heart, who then will conduct them to it, if I nor Aaron do not lead them ever? O.M. 1874.

YTHYS, v. n. Thou wentest. *Ow benneth geneuch yn wêdh, a Cryst del ythys yn bêdh, ioy dheuch guthyl da hedhew*, my blessing with you always, as thou wentest to the grave of Christ, joy to you to do well to-day. R.D. 824. 2 pers. s. preter. of irr. v. *môs*. Written also *ethys*, qd. v.

YTUYW, v. subs. He is. See *Ydhyw*.

YUDHOW, s. m. A Jew. Pl. *Yudhewon*. *Dreuch bŷs omma dhum tyller an harlot guâs a lever y vôs mychtern Yudhewon*, bring ye even here to my place the knave fellow (that) says he is king of the Jews. P.C. 982. Written also *Yedhow*, and *edhow*, qd. v.

YUH, prep. Above. ‡ *Yuh an môr*, above the sea. Llwyd, 249. A late form of *uch*, qd. v.

YUHAF, pron. prep. Above me. (*Yuh—mi.*) *A yuhaf.* Llwyd, 244. A late form of *uchaf*, qd. v.

YUHAL, adj. High, tall, lofty. Llwyd, 128. A late form of *uchel*, qd. v.

YUHELLAS, v. a. To ascend. Llwyd, 245. A late form of *uchellas*, qd. v.

YUNNYE, v. a. To become one, to be united, to unite. *An thyyr guelen defry a ve gans Davyd plynsys, hag a iunnyas dhe onan yn token da a'n try person yn drynsys*, the three rods (that) were by David planted, and united to one, are a good token of the three persons in the Trinity. O.M. 2651. W. *uno*.

YURL, s. m. An earl. Corn. Voc. *comes* vel *consul*. More correctly *yarl*. W. *iarll*. From the English.

YUS, prep. Over, above. *Mychterneth war aga tûs a fe arlythy a-y-yus kyns ys lemyn, ha nêp a's lefo gallos, a vfjdh gans yowynk ha, lós henwys tûs vrûs pûp termyn*, dominion over their people has been to the lords over them before now, and he (that) has power will be by young and gray called a great man always. P.C. 786. Another form of *uch*, qd. v.

YW, v. subs. He is. *Drók dhên ôs kepar del vês, ny dhowtyth Du; te yw dall, râg gemen cregis neb ês dên glân yw a bêch heb fall, ynno eff dufout nyng-es, agan eregy ny yw mall, râg ny rebé laddron dres*, thou art a bad man, as thou wert; thou fearest not God; thou art blind, for he (that) is hung with us is a man pure from sin, without fail, in him is no default; our hanging is not wrong; for we have been froward robbers. M.C. 192. *Agan traytour yw kefys; rjs yw dheso y dhamnyé dhe mernans a dhesempys*, our traitor is found; need is for thee to condemn him to death forthwith. M.C. 98. *Pandra yw dhe nygys*, what is thy business? O.M. 815. *Ef yw an oyl a versy*, he is the oil of mercy. O.M. 733. *Yw guyr dhym a leveryth*, is it true (which) thou sayest to me? P.C. 1941. *Yw war ow ené*, it is upon my soul. P.C. 2207. *Lavar dhymmo vy yn scon, yw ty mychtern Yedhewon*, tell me directly, art thou king of the Jews? P.C. 1998. Written also *ew*, qd. v. W. *yw*, †*eu*. Arm. *eo*.

YWEGES, s. m. A steer, a young bull, or ox. Pryce. *Gaver, yweges, carow, daves, war ve lavarow, hy hanow da kemeres*, goat, steer, deer, sheep, after my words let them take their names. O.M. 126. More likely *a hind*, the feminine of *ewic*, qd. v.

YYNC, adj. Young. ‡ *An dên yync-na*, that young man. *Lluyd*, 242. A late form of *yonc*, qd. v.

YZHI, v. subs. It is. ‡ *Patl yzhi a cylywi ha trenna*, how it lightens and thunders! *Lluyd*, 248. A late form of *ysy*, qd. v.

Z.

THIS letter has properly no place in the Cornish alphabet. It is only used in late Cornish to express a softened and corrupted sound of *s*.

ZAH, s. m. A sack. *Lhuyd*, 30. A late corruption of *sâch*, qd. v.

ZAH, adj. Dry. *Lhuyd*, 30. A late corruption of *sûch*, qd. v.

ZAHAS, s. m. Thirst. *Lhuyd*, 151. Written by Pryce, *zohas*. A late corruption of *sehes*, qd. v.

ZAL, adj. Salted, salt. *Pesk zâl*, salt fish. *Pryce*. See *Sâl*.

ZALLA, v. a. To salt. *Pryce*. See *Salla*.

ZANZ, s. m. A saint. Pl. *zanzow*. Pryce. See *Sans*.

ZANZ, adj. Holy. *Pryce*. Hence *Penzance*, i. e. holy head. See *Sans*.

ZAWZ, s. m. An Englishman. Pl. *zawzen*. Pryce. See *Saws*.

ZAWZNAK, s. f. The English language. *Pryce*. See *Sawsnec*.

ZEAG, s. m. Grains after brewing. *Pryce*. See *Scag*.

ZEH, adj. Dry. *Haffa zêh*, a dry summer. *Pryce*. A late form of *sêch*, qd. v.

ZEHAR, s. m. Dryness, drought. *Pryce*. A corrupted form of *sechter*, qd. v.

ZETHAN, s. f. An arrow. *Pryce*. See *Sethan*.

ZETHAR, s. m. A sea mew, cob, or gull. *Pryce*. A late corruption of *scithor*, qd. v.

ZIGYR, adj. Slow, sluggish. *Pryce*. See *Sigyr*.

ZILGWETH, s. m. Sunday tide. *Pryce*. See *Silgweth*.

ZILLI, s. f. An eel. *Zillidouryr*, a conger. *Pryce*. See *Silly*.

ZOH, s. f. A ploughshare. *Lluyd*. A late form of *sóch*, qd. v.

ZONA, v. a. To charm, to hallow. See *Sona*.

ZOUL, s. m. Stubble, halm, reed to thatch with. *Pryce*. See *Soul*.

ZOULZ, s. m. A shilling. See *Sowls*.

REFERENCES.

THE letters M.C. denote examples from Mount Calvary, a Cornish Poem, of the fourteenth century.
O.M. from Origo Mundi, or the Beginning of the World.
P.C. from Passio Christi, or the Passion of our Lord.
R.D. from Resurrectio Domini, or the Resurrection.

These three Dramas, of equal antiquity with Mount Calvary, were published from the Manuscript in the Bodleian Library, in two vols. 8vo. Oxford, 1859.
C.W. from the Creation of the World, by Jordan.

THE FIRST CHAPTER OF GENESIS.
THE TEN COMMANDMENTS.   THE CREED.
THE LORD'S PRAYER, &c.
IN THE ORTHOGRAPHY OF THE CORNISH DRAMAS.

AN CENSA CADYDUL A'N LYVYR AN GENESIS.

1 Yn dalleth Dew a wrûg nêf ha'n nôr.

2 Hag ydh esé an nôr heb composter ha gwâg; ha tewolgow esé war enep an downder, ha Spyrys Dew rûg gwaya war enep an dowrow.

3 Ha Dew a leverys, bydhens golow, hag ydh esé golow.

4 Ha Dew a welas an golow may fe da: ha Dew a dhyberthas an golow dheworth an tewolgow.

5 Ha Dew a henwys an golow dŷdh, ha'n tewolgow ef a henwys nôs: ha'n gorthuer ha'n myttyn o an censa dŷdh.

6 Ha Dew a leverys, bydhens ebren yn creys an dowrow, ha gwrêns e dhybarthy an dowrow dheworth an dowrow.

7 Ha Dew a wrûg an ebren, ha dyberthas an dowrow esé yn dan au ebren dheworth an dowrow esé a uch an ebren: hag yn delna ydh o.

8 Ha Dew a henwys an ebren nêf: ha'n gorthuer ha'n myttyn o an nessa dŷdh.

9 Ha Dew a leverys, bydhens an dowrow yu dan an nêf cuntullys warbarth dhe un tyller, ha bydhens an tŷr sŷch dyscudhys: hag yn delna ydh o.

10 Ha Dew a henwys an tŷr sŷch an nôr, ha cuntullyans warbarth an dowrow ef a henwys môr: ha Dew a welas may fe da.

11 Ha Dew a leverys, gwrûns an nôr dry râg gwels, ha losow ow tôn hâs, ha'n gwŷdh ow tôn avalow warlerch aga echen, nêb usy aga hâs ynné aga honan, war an nôr: hag yn delna ydh o.

12 Ha'n nôr a dhrôs râg gwels, an losow ow tôn hâs warlerch aga echen, ha'n gwŷdh ow tôn avalow, nêb usy aga hâs ynné aga honan warlerch aga echen; ha Dew a welas may fe da.

13 Ha'n gorthuer ha'n myttyn o an tressa dŷdh.

14 Ha Dew a leverys, bydhens golowys yn ebren nêf dho dhybarthy an dŷdh dheworth an nôs, ha bydhens y râg tavasow, ha râg termynyow, ha râg dydhyow, ha râg bledhynuow.

15 Ha bydhens y râg golowys yn ebren nêf dhe rey golow war an nôr: hag yn delna ydh o.

16 Ha Dew a wrûg dew golow brâs; an brassa golow dhe rewlyé an dŷdh, ha'n behanna golow dhe rewlyé an nôs; lu'n stêr ef a's gwrûg yn wêdh.

17 Ha Dew a's goras yn ebren nêf, dhe rey golow war an nôr.

18 Ha dhe rewlyé an dŷdh ha'n nôs, ha dhe dhybarthy an golow dheworth an tewolgow, ha Dew a welas may fo da.

19 Ha'n gorthuer ha'n myttyn o an peswercé dŷdh.

20 Ha Dew a leverys, gwrêns an dowrow dry râg pûr vêr an taclow ûs ow gwaya gans bewnans, hag edhyn dhe nygé dres an nôr a lês yn ebren nêf.

21 Ha Dew a wrûg an morvilow brâs, ha ceniver tra bew ûs ow gwaya, nêb a rûg an dowrow dry râg pûr vêr, warlerch aga echen, ha ceniver edhen gans ascal warlerch hy echen; ha Dew a welas may fo da.

22 Ha Dew a wrûg aga benygé y, ha leverys, bydhouch luen a hâs, ha drouch râg pûr vêr, ha lenouch an dowrow yn môr, ha gwrêns an edhyn dry râg pûr vêr yn nôr.

23 Ha'n gorthuer ha'n myttyn o an pempes dŷdh.

24 Ha Dew a leverys, gwrêns an nôr dry râg an taclow bew warlerch aga echen, an lodnow, ha'n taclow cramyas, ha bestes an nôr warlerch aga echen; hag yn delna ydh o.

25 Ha Dew a wrûg bestes an nôr warlerch aga echen, ha'n lodnow warlerch aga echen, ha ceniver tra ûs ow cramyas war an nôr, warlerch aga echen; ha Dew a welas may fo da.

26 Ha Dew a leverys, gwrên dên yn agan del ny, warlerch agan havalder; ha gwrêns y cemeres gallos dres an pusces an môr, ha dres an edhen an ebren, ha dres an inilyow, ha dres ol au nôr, ha dres ceniver tra cramyas ûs ow cramyas war an nôr.

27 Yn delna Dew a wrûg dên yn havalder y honan, yn havalder Dew ef a'n gwrûg; gorrow ha benow ef a's gwrûg.

28 Ha Dew a wrûg aga benygé, ha Dew a leverys dhedhé, bydhouch luen a hâs, ha drouch râg pûr vêr, ha lenouch an nôr, ha bydhouch dresto; ha cemerouch gallos dres pusces au môr, ha dres an edhyn yn ebren, ha dres ceniver tra vew ûs ow gwaya war an nôr.

29 Ha Dew a leverys, mirouch, yma reys genef vy dheuch ceniver losow ow tôn hâs, nêb ûs war ol an nôr, ha ceniver gwedhen, ûs an avalow an gwedhen ynny ow tôn hâs, dheuch y fŷdh râg boys.

30 Ha dhe ol an bestes an nôr, ha dhe geniver edhen an ebren, ha dhe geniver tra ûs ow cramyas war an nôr, ûs bewnans ynné, yma reys genef ceniver lusuan glâs râg boys, hag yn delna ydh o.

31 Ha Dew a welas ceniver tra esé gwreys ganso, ha mirouch, ydh o ve pûr dha; ha'n gorthuer ha'n myttyn o an wheffes dŷdh.

AN DEC ARHADOW: PO, AN DEC GORDEMMYNADOW DEW.

Dew a gewsys an gerryow-ma ha leverys; Mo yw an Arluth dhe Dhew, nêb a's drôs dhe vês a'n Týr Misraim, dhe vês a'n chy habadin, (al. gwasanaeth.)

1 Te ny's býdh Dewyow erell mês ve.

2 Na wra dhys honan nêp del gravys, na havalder tra výth ûs yn nêf awartha, po yn nôr a wòles, po yn dour yn dan an nôr. Na wra ty plegy dhe remma, na 'ga wordhyé; râg me an Arluth dhe Dhew yw Dew a sor, hag a vyn dry pechasow an tasow war an flechys bŷs an tressa ha'n pesweré denythyans a'n nêb na'm pertho ve; hag a vyn dyscudhé trueth dhe milyow a'n uêb ûs ow caré, hag ûs ow gwythé ow gorhemmynadow.

3 Na wra cemeres hanow an Arluth dhe Dhew dhe seul, (al. hep ethom,) râg an Arluth dhe Dhew ny vyn sensy e dipêh, nêb ûs cymeres y hanow ef dhe seul, (al. yn gwâg.)

4 Perth côf dhe gwythé sans an dýdh Sabboth; whêh dydhyow te wra whêl, hag a wra mýns ûs dhys dhe wûl, mês an sythves dýdh yw an Sabboth an Arluth dhe Dhew. Yn dýdh-na te nyn wra echen a whêl; te na dhe vâb, na dhe verch, na dhe dhên whêl, na dhe vôs whêl, na dhe lodnow, na'n dên uncouth ûs aberth dhe dharasow. Râg yn whêh dydhyow Dew a wrûg an nêf, ha'n môr, ha mýns ûs ynné y, ha powesas an sythves dýdh, hag a'n uchellas.

5 Gwra perthy dhe dâs ha'th vam; may fo dhe dhydhyow hŷr war an týr ûs reys dhys gans an Arluth dhe Dhew.

6 Na wra ladhé mâb dên.

7 Na wra growedhé gans gwrêc dên arall výth.

8 Na wra ladré.

9 Na wra tyé gow erbyn dhe gontrevec.

10 Na cemer whans warlyrch ty dhe gontrevec, na cemer whans warlyrch gwrêc dhe gontrevec, na'y dhên whêl, na'y vôs whêl, ua'y odion, na'y ason, na tra výth a'n pew ef.

Arluth, cemer trueth ahanan, ha scrýf oll remma dhe arhadow aberth agan colouow, ny a'th pŷs.

CREGYANS A'N CANNASOW CRYST: PO, AN CREGYANS A'N ABESTELEDH.

Cresaf yn Dew an Tâs Olgallosec, gwrear a'n nef, ha'n nôr: Hag yn Ihesu Gryst y un mâb ef, agan Arluth ny: nêb a ve denythys dre an Spyrys Sans, genys a'n Werches Vary, a wodhevys yn dan Pontius Pilat, a ve crowsys, marow, hag ancledhys; Ef a dhyescynnas dhe iffarn; an tressa dýdh ef a dhedhoras dheworth an marow; hag a escynnas dhe'n nêf; hag yma ow sedhé war deru dyghow an Tâs Olgallosec; alena ef a dhue dhe crusy bew ha marow. Cresaf yn Spyrys Sans; an Eglos Sans dres an bŷs; cowethyans an Sansow; dewyllyans pechasow; dedhoryans an corf; ha'n bewnans hep dywedh.

PESAD AN ARLUTH; PO, PADER AN ARLUTH.

Agan Tâs, nêb ûs yn nêf, bydhens uchellys dhe hanow, dêns dhe wlascor, dhe vôdh re bo gwreys yn nôr cepar hag yn nêf. Ro dhynny hydhew agan pûb dýdh bara. Ha gâf dhynny agan cammow, kepar del gevyn ny uêb ûs ow cammé er agan pyn ny. Ha na dôg ny yn antel, mês gwýth ny dheworth drôc; râg genes yw an mychternoth, an crevder, ha'n wordhyans, râg bysqueth ha bysqueth.

Gordhyans dhe'n Tâs, ha dhe'n Mâb, ha dhe'n Spyrys Sans.

Cepar del ve yn dalleth, yma yn ûr-ma, hag y fŷdh bŷth trano hep worfen.

Grâs agan Arluth Ihesu Grist, ha cerensé Dew, ha cowethyans an Spyrys Sans, re bo genen ny oll bŷs venytha. Amen. Yn delna re bo.

ADDITIONS AND CORRECTIONS.

A, def. art. The. *Fystyn duwhans, gucres vy, ow tón a plos casadow,* hasten thou quickly, help me, bringing the foul villain. O.M. 892. *Râk dysrcythyl an bylen, mar kews erbyn a laha,* to destroy the villain, if he speaks against the law. P.C. 572. *Pan éth dreyn yn empynyon a púp parth dre a grogen,* when the thorns went into the brain from every part through the skin. R.D. 2558. An abbreviated form of *an,* qd. v. In modern Welsh *yr* is similarly abbreviated into *y,* which is generally used before consonants.

ABEM, s. m. A kiss. *Pryce.* A late corruption of *am,* by the common placing of *b* before *m.* . See *Ammé.*

ADRYFF, adv. Behind. *Y'n splan me a's derevas, ny gowsyn yn tewolgow, adryff tûs yn un hanas,* clearly I declared them, I spoke not in darkness behind people in a whisper. M.C. 79. Arm. *adreff.*

ANCOMBRYS, adj. Not of one mind. *Pan ethons oll dhe wary, ancombrys y rebea,* when they were all gone ont, they were not of one mind. M.C. 34. Comp. of *an,* neg. com, with, and *brŷs,* mind.

ARTHELATH, s. m. Lordship. *Pryce.* This is a wrong reading of the manuscript, where it is correctly *archelath,* or *archeledh,* archangels, being the plural of *archel,* id. qd. *archail,* qd. v.

ASEDHE, v. a. To sit down. *Ené ydh esé sedhek ; orto ef y asedhas, may clewo léff Ihesus whék,* there was a seat there; he sat down upon it, that he might hear the voice of sweet Jesus. M.C. 77. Written also *esedhé,* and *ysedhé,* qd. v. Arm. *azeza. Hag a azezas enô,* and sat there. Bub. Nonn. v. 1. *Hag azez aman,* and sit thou here.

AWAYL, s. m. Gospel. Wrongly rendered by Pryce a *tragedy. Puppenak may fo redys an awayl-ma, tavethlys hy a vŷdh púr wŷr neffré,* wherever may be read this Gospel, spoken of she shall be very truly ever. P.C. 550. *Reys yw vôs guŷr an awayl,* need is that the Gospel be true. P.C. 924. *Hag yn wédh why dew ha dew a pregoth yn aweyl grew yn ol an boys,* and also ye, two and two, do preach the Gospel in all the world. R.D. 2464. See *Geaweil.*

AWEL, s. m. A strong desire, eagerness. *Dewogans dŷdh ow penys y speynas y gŷk ha'y woys ; ha wot wedh rág densys ef a'n gevé awell boys,* two score days in doing penance, he spent his flesh and blood; and at last through manhood, he had a strong desire for food. M.C. 10. W. *awydh.*

AWHER, s. m. Sorrow, grief, sadness. W. *avar.*

BALLOC, s. m. A flap, a valve. See *Valloc.*

BARLYS, s. m. Barley. In South Wales *barlys* is the common name, and *haidh* in North Wales.

BEN, s. f. A woman. In construction *ven,* qd. v.

BEN, v. snbs. We have been. *Tru, a Dhu, elhas, gans un huyn re bén tullys,* sad, O God, alas, by a sleep wo have been deceived. M.C. 246. 1 pers. pl. preter. of *bôs ;* written also *buen,* qd. v.

BER, s. m. A shank, a leg. *Goys a'y ben ha'y ysely a dhroppyé war y dhew ver, rág dodho ef na yily dôn an grows rág gwander,* blood from his head and his lips dropped on his two legs, for on him he could not bear the cross for weakness. M.C. 173. W. *ber.*

BESY, adj. Important, needful. *Besy yw dhys bós vuell, ha spernabyll y'th servys, manno allo an tebell ogas dhys bonas trylys,* it is needful for thee to be humble and willing to be despised in thy service, that the evil one may not be turned near thee. M.C. 19. Written also *bysy,* qd. v.

BEWE, v. n. To live, to exist. 3 pers. s. fut. *bew.*

BEWHY, v. a. Thou mayst possess. *Oll an tŷr a bewhy ew malegas y'th ober,* all the land (that) thou possessest is cursed in thy deed. C.W. 84. A mut. of *pewy,* 2 pers. s. subj. of *pew,* qd. v.

BLYN, s. m. A point. W. *blaen.* Arm. *blîn.*

BOMMEN, s f. A blow. Pl. *bommennow.* See *Vommennow.*

BOXSCUSY, v. a. To strike a blow, to buffet. *Ena mûr a vylyny Pedyr dhe Gryst a welas, y scornyé hay corscusy,* there much of villainy Peter saw (done) to Christ, mocking him and buffeting him. M.C. 83. From *boxes,* a blow.

BREILU, s. m. A rose. Dr. Owen Pughe is quite correct in inserting this word in his Dictionary. It is a genuine Welsh word, and *breila,* and *breilwy,* are also frequently used, especially in poetry.

BRYS, s. m. The womb, the matrix. Compare Gr. ἐμβρυον.

BY, v. subs. Thou mayest be. *Kepar del ôs luen a rás, venytha gordhyys re by,* as thou art full of grace, for ever mayest thou be worshipped. O.M. 107. *Mylleges nefré re by,* cursed ever mayest thou be. O.M. 580. 2 pers. s. subj. of *bôs.* In construction it changes into *vy,* and *fy,* qd. v.

BYGYENS, s. m. Victuals, food. In construction *vygyens,* qd. v.

BYNS, f. subs. They may be. In construction *vŷns,* qd. v. 3 pers. pl. subj. of *bôs.* Written also *béns* and *bôns,* qd. v.

BYNYN, s. f. A female, a woman. In construction *vynyn,* qd. v. Written also *bynen,* and *benen,* qd. v.

BYYN, v. subs. We may be. In construction *vyyn,* and *fyyn,* qd. v. 1 pers. pl. subj. of *bôs.* Written also *bên, bern, beyn,* qd. v.

CABYDUL, s. m. A chapter. *An kensa Cabydul a'n lyvyr an Genesis,* the first chapter of the Book of Genesis. *Keigwin.* Ir. *caibidil.* Gael. *caibideal.* From the Lat. *capitulum.*

CEF, v. a. He shall have. 3 pers. s. fut. of irr. v. *cafos,* qd. v. In construction *géf,* qd. v.

CEFE, v. a. He did have. 3 pers. s. imperf. of irr. v. *cafos,* qd. v. In construction *gcfé,* qd. v.

CEFES, v. a. I found. 1 pers. s. preter. of irr. v. *cafos,* qd. v. In construction *gefes,* qd. v.

CEFO, v. a. He should have. 3 pers. s. subj. of irr. v. *cafos,* qd. v. In construction *geffo,* qd. v.

CLOR, s. m. The face of the earth. *Adam, sîf yn ban yn clôr, ha treyl dhe gŷk ha dhe woys,* Adam, stand up on the face of the earth, and turn to flesh and blood. O.M. 65. W. *clawr.*

COLON, s. f. A heart. Under this word read, *A vâp whék ydhof euthys, ow colon yw marthys cláf,* O sweet son, I am grieved, my heart is wondrous sick. O.M. 1337.

CROHEN, s. m. A skin. Pl. *crehen.*

CUSTA, v. n. Thou knowest. *A vyn Dew budhy an bŷs? Mara custa, lavar dhym, me a'th pŷs*, will God drown the world? If thou knowest, tell me I pray thee. C.W. 170. A mut. of *gusta*, an abbreviated form of *godhes-tc*.

CY, conj. Though. *Me a vyn môs dhe gudhu yn nêb bush, ky 'dh ew dhym greyf*, I will go to hide in some bush, though it is a grief to me. C.W. 112. An abbreviated form of *cyn*, qd. v.

DEGEN, v. a. Let us carry. *Degen genan agan pegans*, let us carry with us our necessaries. C.W. 96. 1 pers. pl. imp. of *degy*, qd. v.

DEGEVY, v. a. To tithe, to give tithe. *Ha penvo reys degevy, gorouch y dha'n mount Tabor, hag ena gworcwh aga lysky*, and when there is need to give tithe, put them to the Mount Tabor, and there do ye burn them. C.W. 78. W. *degymu*. Arm. *dcogi*. Ir. *deachmhuigh*. Gael. *deachamhaich, deichmhich*. Lat. *decimo*.

DELYOW, s. m. Leaves. One of the plurals of *delen*, qd. v.

DEN, v. n. Let us come. *Rág mêdh dên ny a lemma, dhe gudha yn tellar clôs*, for shame let us come from hence, to hide in a close place. C.W. 2. 1 pers. pl. imp. of irr. v. *dôs*. Written also *dûn*, qd. v.

DEWSCOL, adv. All abroad, all to pieces. Pryce. This is a wrong reading, and is correctly given from the manuscript by Mr. Stokes, *dowstoll*. It means *all to dust*. *Dowst* is now commonly used in Cornwall for Eng. *dust*.

DUETH, v. n. He came. 3 pers. s. preterite of *dós*, qd. v.

DUI, card. num. Two. Used with substantives feminine.

DY, pron. prep. To her, or it. *(Do—hy.) Un sarf yn guedhen yma, bêst uthek hep falladow: ke wêth tressé trewth dhy, ha mŷr gwel orth an wedhen*, the third is a serpent in the tree, an ugly beast without fail: go yet the third time to it, and look better at the tree. O.M. 799.

DYDHY, pron. prep. To her, or it. *(Do—hy.) Yn pûb maner may hylly, y vam prest asonoré: yn delma comfort dhydhy y máp a vynnas dygtyé*, in every way that he could, his mother he readily honoured: thus her Son would provide comfort for her. M.C. 199. *Pilat, gymef nynsynv mêdh, awos guyské an quêth, a fue yn kerchyn Ihesu, rák dhydhy yma dhym whans; dŷsk y dywhans*, Pilate, with me there is not shame because of wearing the cloth, (that) was about Jesus, for there is to me a desire of it; take it off quickly. R.D. 1938. Written also *dedhy*, qd. v.

DYFFONS, v. n. They may come. In construction *tyffons*, qd. v.

DYFFOUCH, v. n. Ye may come. In construction *tyffouch*, qd. v.

DYR, prep. Through. *Benyn dyr vûr cheryté y box rych, leun a yly, a uch Crist rág y untyé hy a vynnas y derry*, a woman through much charity her box rich, full of salve, over Christ to anoint him she wished to break it. M.C. 35. Another form of *dre*, qd. v. In late Cornish, *der*, qd. v.

DYR, card. num. Three. *Môs dhe blansé my a vyn yn dôr an dŷr guelen-ma*, I will go to plant these three rods in the ground. O.M. 1888. A mutation of *tŷr*, qd. v.

DYSOSY, adj. Bound, obliged. Pryce. *Pûr wŷr mar lyha ow grêf, my a'n a fŷdh dysosy; ken arluth agesov*

ef ny'n gordhyaf bŷs vynary, very truly, if he will lessen my pain, I shall be bound to him; other Lord than him I will not worship for ever. O.M. 1788.

EGA, v. n. To groan, to moan. *Ow fryns, gwella dha gear, gás dhe ola ha'th ega*, my spouse, make better thy word, leave off thy weeping and thy groaning. C.W. 94. W. *ochi*.

ELYN, adj. Clean, fair. Written also *ylyn*, qd. v.

EN, pron. adj. Our. *Ha dhe'n Tás gwrên oll pegy, na skydnya an kêth vengeans yn nêb termyn warnan ny, nag en flehys*, and to the Father let us all pray, that the same vengeance may not fall at any time on us, nor our children. C.W. 160. Another form of *an*, qd. v.

ENCOIS, s. m. Frankincense. Corn. Voc. *thus*. Regularly formed from the Lat. *incensum*, *n* before *s* being omitted, as in Corn. *moys, muis*; W. *mwys, †muis*; a table, from Lat. *mensa*. Corn. and W. *mis*, a month, from Lat. *mensis*.

ENEP, s. m. A face. In modern Welsh *wyneb* is the form; *wy*, as in numerous other instances, being substituted for *e*, but in the Oxford Glosses, (*Vocabula in Pensum Discipuli*. Bodl. 572,) the early Welsh form is found, and the manuscript is not later than the eighth century; et totam faciem meam, is there glossed by *ham oll enep*. In this sentence there is not the difference of a single letter between Cornish and Welsh.

ESCAR, s. m. An enemy. Pl. *yscerens*. W. *ysgar*, pl. *ysgoraint*.

ETTEN, pron. prep. In it.

ETH, v. n. He went. Written also *ŷth*, qd. v.

ETHYS, v. n. Thou wentest. Written also *ythys*, qd. v.

FEYNYS, s. m. Pains. A mutation of *peynys*, pl. of *peyn*, qd. v.

GWEVYE, v. a. To flee. *An pemoré a gewsys, na whelyn gwevyé an pow, kepar del ve dhe'n Iustis, dûn, leveryn war anow*, the fourth said, let us not seek to flee the country; let us come, let us say to the Justice by mouth how it was. M.C. 247. W. *chwiwio*.

GYSSEUCH, v. a. Ye left. 2 pers. pl. preter. of *gasé*. See under *Gyssy*.

GYSSYS, v. a. Thou leftest. 2 pers. s. preterite of *gasé*. See under *Gyssy*.

HANAS, s. m. A low sound, a whisper. *Púr apert hag yn golow y leveris ow dyskas; ow lahys ha'w lavarow, suel a cynna y clewas; yn le may'th ên yn trevow yn splan me a's derevas; ny gewsyn yn tewolgow a dryff lûs yn un hanas*, very openly and in light I spake my doctrine; my laws and my words, whoever would heard them: in the places where I was, in towns clearly I declared them; I spoke not in darkness behind people in a whisper. M.C. 79. Ir. *sanas*. Gael. *sanas*.

HAVALLA, adj. More like. *Ty a vŷdh máb denethys a dhe gorf, na wra dowtya; henna a vŷdh haval dheis, na fill dên bôs havalla, ha genaf y fŷdh kerrys*, thou shalt have a son begotten of thy body, do not doubt; he shall be like to thee, so that man cannot be more like, and by me he shall be loved. C.W. 96. Comparative of *haval*, qd. v.

UCHAF, pron. prep. Above me. *(Uch—mi.) My pan esen ow quandré, clewys a'n nêl wnewen un êl ow talleth cané a uchaf war an wedhen*, when I was walking about, I heard on the one side an angel beginning to sing above me on the tree. O.M. 216. The late form *a yuhaf* is given by Llwyd, 244.

AN DIWEDH. THE END.

SUBSCRIBERS' NAMES.

His Highness Prince Louis-Lucien Bonaparte 2 Copies.
The Right Hon. The Earl of Cawdor
The Right Hon. The Earl of St. Germans
The Right Hon. The Earl of Ilchester
The Right Hon. The Earl of Powis
The Right Hon. The Countess of Falmouth
The Right Hon. Viscount Falmouth 2 Copies.
The Right Hon. Viscount Feilding, Downing
The Right Rev. The Lord Bishop of St. Asaph 2 Copies.
The Right Rev. The Lord Bishop of St. David's
The Right Rev. The Lord Bishop of Exeter
The Right Hon. Lady Llanover
The Right Hon. Lord Talbot de Malahide
The Right Hon. Lord Vivian
Lady Charlotte Schreiber, Wimborne
Sir Rich. Vyvyan, Bart. Trelowarran
Rev. Sir Erasmus Williams, Bart. Chancellor of St. David's
Sir Henry Dryden, Bart. Canons Ashby 6 Copies.
Sir Stephen R. Glynne, Bart. Hawarden
Sir Charles Lemon, Bart. Carclew
Sir George Cornewall Lewis, Bart. M.P.
Sir Pyers Mostyn, Bart. Talacre
Sir Thomas Phillips, Bart. Middle Hill
Sir J. Gardner Wilkinson, F.R.S.
Colonel Sir Henry James, R.E. F.R.S.
Colonel T. P. Williams, M.P. Craig y Don 2 Copies.
Abergavenny Cymreigyddion Society
The Society of Antiquaries of Scotland
Cambridge University Library
The Cornwall Library, Truro
Exeter College Library, Oxford
The London Philological Society
The Penzance Library
Jesus College Library, Oxford

Anwyl, T. Lloyd, Esq. Vrondderw, Bala
Asher, Messrs. London and Berlin 6 Copies.
Babington, C. C. Esq. St. John's College, Cambridge
Banks, W. L. Esq. F.S.A. Brecon
Bannister, Rev. J. St. Day, Cornwall
Basset, J. F. Esq. Tehidy, Cornwall
Beale, W. P. Esq. Rotherham
Bennion, E. D. Esq. Oswestry
Bickford, J. S. Esq. Tuckingmill, Cornwall 3 Copies.
Blois, Count Aymar de, Quimper, Brittany
Bodmin Literary Institution
Boger, Deeble, Esq. Wolsdon, Devonport
Bolitho, T. S. Esq. Penzance
Bolitho, T. B. Esq. Trewidden, Do.
Bolitho, W. Esq. Alverne Hill, Do.
Bolitho, William, Jun. Esq. Do.
Bonnor, Very Rev. R. M., M.A., Dean of St. Asaph
Borlase, John, Esq. Marazion, Cornwall
Borlase, Capt. John, R.N. C.B.
Borlase, Sam. Esq. Castle Horneck, Penzance 2 Copies.
Borlase, Rev. William, V. Zennor, St. Ives
Bosworth, Rev. Professor, D.D. F.R.S. Oxford

Brereton, Andrew Jones, Esq. Mold
Briscoe, Rev. W. Fellow of Jesus College, Oxford
Callender, Rev. W., V. Blackmore, Essex
Carew, W. H. Pole, Esq. Antony
Carne, Rev. John, M.A. Eglos Merther
Carne, Miss, Penzance
Charles, Rev. David, B.A. Abercarn
Chevallier, Rev. Temple, B.D. Durham
Clark, G. T. Esq. Dowlais House, Merthyr
Clarke, D. Esq. London
Clough, Rev. A. B., B.D., R. Braunston
Courtney, L. H. Esq. Lincoln's Inn
Cunliffe, Rev. George, M.A., V. Wrexham
Dubb, F. W. Esq. Redruth
Davies, David, Esq. 2, Queen's Square, Bristol
Davies, Henry, Esq. Cheltenham
Davies, James, Esq. Hereford
Davies, Rev. John, M.A., R. Walsoken, Norfolk
Davies, Miss, Penmaen Dovey
Davies, Samuel, Esq. Cilvallen, Newcastle Emlyn
Davis, J. Barnard, Esq. F.S.A. Shelton, Staffordshire
Dykes, F. L. B. Esq. Cockermouth
Eddy, Walter, Esq. Vron, Llangollen
Edmunds, Rev. W. Lampeter
Edwards, Rev. John, M.A., R. Newtown
Edwards, Rev. R. Wynne, V. Meivod
Enys, J. S. Esq. Enys, Cornwall
Evans, Benjamin, Esq. Newcastle Emlyn
Evans, Rev. D. Silvan, R. Llanymowddwy
Evans, Rev. E., R. Llanvihangel yn Ngwynva
Evans, Rev. Edward, R. Halkin
Evans, Rev. Lewis, Ystrad Meurig
Evans, Ven. R. Wilson, B.D. Archdeacon of Westmoreland
Falconer, T. Esq., Judge of County Courts, Usk
Fenton, John, Esq. Glynymel
Ferguson, Robert, Esq. Morton, Carlisle
Foster, R. Esq. Castle, Lostwithiel
Foster, R. Jun. Esq. Do.
Garland, T. Esq. Redruth
Garrett, T. Esq. Douglas, Isle of Man
Gilbertson, I. Esq. Eryl Aran, Bala
Gilbertson, Rev. L. Fellow of Jesus College, Oxford
Glencross, Rev. J. Liskeard
Glynne, Rev. Henry, M.A., R. Hawarden
†Gore, W. Ormsby, Esq. Porkington
Gore, J. R. Ormsby, Esq. M.P.
Griffith, Rev. Thomas, M.A., V. Cwm, Flintshire
Griffiths, T. Taylor, Esq. Wrexham
Grylls, Henry, Esq., Redruth
Guest, Dr. Master of Caius College, Cambridge
Harries, Rev. Canon, Letterston
Hartshorne, Rev. C. H., M.A., R. Holdenby, Northampton
Harting, J. V. Esq. London
Heaton, Rev. C. Fellow of Jesus College, Oxford
Hotten, J. Camden, Esq. London
Howell, D. Esq. Dolguog, Machynlleth
Hughes, Hugh Robert, Esq. Kinmel

SUBSCRIBERS' NAMES.

Hughes, J. E. Esq. Tryeglwyn, Amlwch
Hughes, John, Esq. Lluest Gwilym, Aberystwyth
Hughes, Rev. Joseph, Meltham, Huddersfield
Hughes, Rev. Morgan, V. Corwen
James, Rev. Dr., Panteg
James, Rev. J. (Iago Emlyn), Clifton
James, Rev. T. Netherthong, Huddersfield
James, J. D. Esq. Prestatyn, Flintshire
Jesse, J. Esq. F.R.S. Llanbedr Hall, Ruthin
Johnes, A. J. Esq. Judge of County Courts, Garthmyl. 2 Cop.
Johnes, John, Esq. Dolaucothy
Jones, D. Esq. M.P. Pantglas
Jones, Rev. Edward, V. Nantglyn
Jones, Rev. J. Emlyn, M.A. Ebbw Vale
Jones, J. Daniel, Esq. Hawen, Newcastle Emlyn
Jones, J. M. Esq. Rhyd Lewis, do.
Jones, John, Esq. Vronheulog, Bala
Jones, Rev. J. Price, Newcastle Emlyn
Jones, Rev. J. Rhys, Kilsby, Rhaiadr
Jones, Mr. Owen, Rhippyn Llwyd, Cardigan
Jones, Rev. J. D., C. Brymbo
Jones, Rev. H. Longueville, M.A. H.M. Inspector of Schools
Jones, Rev. John, M.A., V. Llanarmon yn Iâl
Jones, Ven. J. Archdeacon of Anglesey
Jones, Rev. W. Basil, B.D. Prebendary of St. David's
Jones, Thomas, Esq. Chetham Library, Manchester
Joseph, Joseph, Esq. F.S.A. Brecon
Kerslake, Mr. Bristol 2 Copies.
Key, Professor, University College, London
Leighton, Stanley, Esq. Loton Park
Lethbridge. J. K. Esq. Tregeare
Lewis, D. J. Esq. Gilvach, Llandovery
Lewis, J. Prothero, Esq. Llandeilo Vawr
Lewis, Rev. T. W., M.A., R. Manavon
Lewis, Titus, Esq. Llanstephan
Lewis, Rev. W., R. Llanvihangel Glyn Myvyr
Llewellin, W. Esq. Glanwern, Pontypool
Llewelyn, Rev. R. Pendrill, V. Llangynwyd
Lloyd, Rev. H.R. M.A. V. St. Mark's Kennington
Lloyd, R. Howel, Esq. Rhagat
Lloyd, T. Lewis, Esq. Nantgwyllt
Lloyd, Rev. Rhys J., R. Troedyraur
Llwyd, Miss Angharad, Rhyl
Macadam, R., Esq. Belfast
Mackenzie, J. W. Esq. W. S. Edinburgh
Mainwaring, Townshend, Esq. M.P. Galltvaenan
Malan, Rev. S. G. M.A., V. Broadwinsor, Dorset
Manning, Mr. Serjeant, Hyde Park, London
Marrack, Philip, Esq. Penzance
Men, M Le. Quimper, Brittany
Morgan, Thomas O. Esq. Aberystwyth
Morris, T. Esq. Blaenywern, Newcastle Emlyn
Mould, J. A. Esq. Dartmouth
Mounsey, Capt. Carlisle
Nash, D. W. Esq. Cheltenham
Neaves, The Hon. Lord, Edinburgh
Noel, Rev. D. Llanvalon
Norris, Edwin, Esq. F.S.A. Foreign Office
Oldfield, Thomas, Esq. Bettws, Flintshire
Ormerod, George, Esq. D.C.L. F.R.S. Sedbury Park
Owen, Rev. H. Davies, D.D., R. Trevdraeth

Parry, T. L. D. Jones, Esq. F.S.A. Madryn, Pwllheli
Pedler, E. H. Esq. Liskeard
Phillips, F. Lloyd, Esq. Havod Neddyn
Phillips, Rev. Thomas, Hereford
Polwhele, General, Truro
Poste, Beale, Esq. Maidstone
Price, Rev. T. Rûg Chapel
Price, William, Esq. Glantwrch, Swansea
Price, J. Bruce. Esq. Duffryn
Pughe, J. Esq. F.R.S. Aberdovey
Quaritch, Mr. B. London 2 Copies.
Rashleigh, W. Esq. Menabilly, Cornwall
Reece, W. Esq. F.S.A. Birmingham
Rees, W. Esq. Tonn, Llandovery
Richards, John, Esq. Bron Menni
Richards. E. L. Esq. Judge of County Courts, Rhyl
Rogers, J. J. Esq. M.P. Penrose, Cornwall
Rogers, Rev. Thomas, Llangunllo
Rogers, Rev. William, R. Mawgan, Cornwall
Rodd, F. Esq. Trebartha Hall, Cornwall
Rowland, Rev. T., V. Pennant Melangell
Sandys, William, Esq. F.S.A. London
Scott, Rev. Dr. Master of Balliol College, Oxford
Selwyn, Rev. E. J., Lee Park, Blackheath, Kent
Skene, W. Esq. F.S.A. Edinburgh
Smirke, Edward, Esq. Vice-Warden of the Stannaries
Spurrell, Mr., Carmarthen
Stephens, Thomas, Esq. Merthyr Tydvil
Stokes, Whitley, Esq. Lincoln's Inn 2 Copies.
Symonds, Dr. Clifton
Thurnham, Dr. F.R.S. Devizes
Thomas, John, Esq. Nelson Square, London
Thomas, Rev. D. R., M.A. Cevn, St. Asaph
Todd, Rev. Dr. Trinity College, Dublin
Tregelles, Rev. Dr. Plymouth
Tremayne, J. Esq. Heligan, Cornwall
Tweedy, Robert, Esq. Tregolls, Truro
Tweedy, William, Esq. do. do.
Vivian, J. H. Esq. M.P. Swansea 2 Copies
Wakeman, T. F. Esq. Graig, Monmouth
Wallis, Rev. John, M.A., V. Bodmin
Way, Albert, Esq. Wonham Manor, Reigate
Wedgwood, H. Esq. London
Westlake, John, Esq. M.A., Lincoln's Inn, London
Williams, Rev. Canon, M.A., R. Nannerch
Williams, Rev. Dr. Principal of Jesus College, Oxford
Williams, Edward, Esq. Lloran House, Oswestry
Williams, Rev. Jer., V. Hope
Williams, Rev. J. H., R. Llangadwaladr, Anglesey
Williams, John, Esq. Treffos do.
Williams, Rev. Rowland, D.D., V. Broad Chalke, Salisbury
Williams, R. Lloyd, Esq. Denbigh
Williams, Rev. T., B.D., R. Llansantsior
Williams, Mr. Benjamin, (*Gwynionydd*,) Wenallt
Williams, W. Esq. Tregullow, Cornwall
Willyams, H. Esq. Carnanton, do.
Willis and Sotheran. Messrs. London 2 Copies.
Wordsworth, Rev. Dr., Canon of Westminster
Wynne, C. W. G. Esq. Voelas, Denbighshire
Wynne, Rev. J. H. G., M.A. St. Beuno's College, St. Asaph

www.ingramcontent.com/pod-product-compliance
Lightning Source LLC
Chambersburg PA
CBHW051243300426
44114CB00011B/873